Counseling and Psychotherapy: A Behavioral Approach *by E. Lakin Ph...*

Dimensions of Personality *edited by Harvey London and John E. Exner...*

The Mental Health Industry: A Cultural Phenomenon *by Peter A. M..., ... McDowell, and Ivan W. Miller III*

Nonverbal Communication: The State of the Art *by Robert G. Harper, Arthur N. Weins, and Joseph D. Matarazzo*

Alcoholism and Treatment *by David J. Armor, J. Michael Polich, and Harriet B. Stambul*

A Biodevelopmental Approach to Clinical Child Psychology: Cognitive Controls and Cognitive Control Theory *by Sebastiano Santostefano*

Handbook of Infant Development *edited by Joy D. Osofsky*

Understanding the Rape Victim: A Synthesis of Research Findings *by Sedelle Katz and Mary Ann Mazur*

Childhood Pathology and Later Adjustment: The Question of Prediction *by Loretta K. Cass and Carolyn B. Thomas*

Intelligent Testing with the WISC-R *by Alan S. Kaufman*

Adaptation in Schizophrenia: The Theory of Segmental Set *by David Shakow*

Psychotherapy: An Eclectic Approach *by Sol L. Garfield*

Handbook of Minimal Brain Dysfunctions *edited by Herbert E. Rie and Ellen D. Rie*

Handbook of Behavioral Interventions: A Clinical Guide *edited by Alan Goldstein and Edna B. Foa*

Art Psychotherapy *by Harriet Wadeson*

Handbook of Adolescent Psychology *edited by Joseph Adelson*

Psychotherapy Supervision: Theory, Research and Practice *edited by Allen K. Hess*

Psychology and Psychiatry in Courts and Corrections: Controversy and Change *by Ellsworth A. Fersch, Jr.*

Restricted Environmental Stimulation: Research and Clinical Applications *by Peter Suedfeld*

Personal Construct Psychology: Psychotherapy and Personality *edited by Alvin W. Landfield and Larry M. Leitner*

Mothers, Grandmothers, and Daughters: Personality and Child Care in Three-Generation Families *by Bertram J. Cohler and Henry U. Grunebaum*

Further Explorations in Personality *edited by A.I. Rabin, Joel Aronoff, Andrew M. Barclay, and Robert A. Zucker*

Hypnosis and Relaxation: Modern Verification of an Old Equation *by William E. Edmonston, Jr.*

Handbook of Clinical Behavior Therapy *edited by Samuel M. Turner, Karen S. Calhoun, and Henry E. Adams*

Handbook of Clinical Neuropsychology *edited by Susan B. Filskov and Thomas J. Boll*

The Course of Alcoholism: Four Years After Treatment *by J. Michael Polich, David J. Armor, and Harriet B. Braiker*

Handbook of Innovative Psychotherapies *edited by Raymond J. Corsini*

The Role of the Father in Child Development (Second Edition) *edited by Michael E. Lamb*

Behavioral Medicine: Clinical Applications *by Susan S. Pinkerton, Howard Hughes, and W.W. Wenrich*

Handbook for the Practice of Pediatric Psychology *edited by June M. Tuma*

Change Through Interaction: Social Psychological Processes of Counseling and Psychotherapy *by Stanley R. Strong and Charles D. Claiborn*

Drugs and Behavior (Second Edition) *by Fred Leavitt*

Handbook of Research Methods in Clinical Psychology *edited by Philip C. Kendall and James N. Butcher*

A Social Psychology of Developing Adults *by Thomas O. Blank*

(*continued on back*)

HANDBOOK OF
FORENSIC PSYCHOLOGY

Handbook of Forensic Psychology

Edited by

Irving B. Weiner
Fairleigh Dickinson University

Allen K. Hess
Auburn University

A Wiley-Interscience Publication

JOHN WILEY & SONS

New York • Chichester • Brisbane • Toronto • Singapore

This publication is designed to provide accurate and
authoritative information in regard to the subject
matter covered. It is sold with the understanding that
the publisher is not engaged in rendering legal, accounting,
or other professional service. If legal advice or other
expert assistance is required, the services of a competent
professional person should be sought. *From a Declaration
of Principles jointly adopted by a Committee of the
American Bar Association and a Committee of Publishers.*

Library of Congress Cataloging-in Publication Data:

Handbook of forensic psychology.

(Wiley series on personality processes)
"A Wiley-Interscience publication."
Bibliography: p.
Includes indexes.
1. Psychology, Forensic. I. Weiner, Irving B.
II. Hess, Allen K., 1945–   III. Series.

RA1148.H36 1987   614'.1   86-28992
ISBN 0-471-81735-X

Printed in the United States of America

10 9 8 7 6 5 4 3 2

*To those who have contributed
to the development of forensic
psychology and will be carrying it
forward in the future.*

I.B.W.

*To
—my father, a "mensch,"
—my mother, who lived with courage,
—my wife, for unflagging support, and
—Tanya, Clara, Joel, for the inspiration
and challenge they provide*

A.K.H.

Contributors

Anne M. Bartol, M.A.
Castleton State College
Castleton, Vermont

Curt R. Bartol, Ph.D.
Castleton State College
Castleton, Vermont

Paul Brinson, M.Ed.
Gifted Students Institute
Ft. Worth, Texas

James Neal Butcher, Ph.D.
University of Minnesota
Minneapolis, Minnesota

Charles R. Clark, Ph.D.
Center for Forensic Psychiatry
Ann Arbor, Michigan

Brian L. Cutler, M.A.
University of Wisconsin–Madison
Madison, Wisconsin

David F. Daniell, J.D.
Brown, Hudgens, Richardson,
    Whitfield S. Gillian, P.G.
Mobile, Alabama

Joseph H. Evans, Ph.D.
University of South Florida
Tampa, Florida

Stephen L. Golding, Ph.D.
University of Utah
Salt Lake City, Utah

Gail S. Goodman, Ph.D.
University of Denver
Denver, Colorado

Annette Hahn, M.A.
University of Denver
Denver, Colorado

Terri Cross Harlow, M.A.
University of Minnesota
Minneapolis, Minnesota

Allen K. Hess, Ph.D.
Auburn University
Auburn, Alabama

Kathryn D. Hess, M.S.
East Alabama Mental Health Center
Opeeika, Alabama

William G. Iacono, Ph.D.
University of Minnesota
Minneapolis, Minnesota

Nels Klyver, Ph.D.
Los Angeles Police Department
Los Angeles, California

Thomas R. Litwack, Ph.D., J.D.
John Jay College of Criminal Justice
New York, New York

Joan McCord, Ph.D.
Drexel University
Philadelphia, Pennsylvania

Gary B. Melton, Ph.D.
University of Nebraska–Lincoln
Lincoln, Nebraska

Michael A. Milan, Ph.D.
Georgia State University
Atlanta, Georgia

Max J. Mobley, Ph.D.
Arkansas Department of Corrections
Pine Bluff, Arkansas

Abraham Nievod, Ph.D.
Berkeley, California

Christopher J. Patrick
University of British Columbia
Vancouver, British Columbia

Steven D. Penrod, Ph.D.
University of Wisconsin–Madison
Madison, Wisconsin

Martin Reiser, Ed.D.
Los Angeles Police Department
Los Angeles, California

Daniel J. Reschly, Ph.D.
Iowa State University
Ames, Iowa

Ronald Roesch, Ph.D.
Simon Fraser University
Burnaby, British Columbia

Louis B. Schlesinger, Ph.D.
University of Medicine and Dentistry
of New Jersey
Newark, New Jersey

Margaret Thaler Singer, Ph.D.
University of California–
Berkeley
Berkeley, California

Ralph Slovenko, J.D.
Wayne State University
Detroit, Michigan

David Spiegel, M.D.
Stanford University Medical Center
Stanford, California

Herbert Spiegel, M.D.
College of Physicians and Surgeons
Columbia University
New York, New York

Barbara Stanley, Ph.D.
John Jay College of Criminal Justice
New York, New York

Harold J. Vetter, Ph.D.
University of South Florida
Tampa, Florida

Lenore E. Auerbach Walker, Ph.D.
Walker & Associates
Denver, Colorado

Irving B. Weiner, Ph.D.
Fairleigh Dickinson University
Rutherford, New Jersey

Series Preface

This series of books is addressed to behavioral scientists interested in the nature of human personality. Its scope should prove pertinent to personality theorists and researchers as well as to clinicians concerned with applying an understanding of personality processes to the amelioration of emotional difficulties in living. To this end, the series provides a scholarly integration of theoretical formulations, empirical data, and practical recommendations.

Six major aspects of studying and learning about human personality can be designated: personality theory, personality structure and dynamics, personality development, personality assessment, personality change, and personality adjustment. In exploring these aspects of personality, the books in the series discuss a number of distinct but related subject areas: the nature and implications of various theories of personality; personality characteristics that account for consistencies and variations in human behavior, the emergence of personality processes in children and adolescents; the use of interviewing and testing procedures to evaluate individual differences in personality; efforts to modify personality styles through psychotherapy, counseling, behavior, therapy, and other methods of influence; and patterns of abnormal personality functioning that impair individual competence.

IRVING B. WEINER

Fairleigh Dickinson University
Rutherford, New Jersey

Preface

Forensic psychology has become a rapidly emerging professional specialty. A growing number of clinicians are focusing their attention on matters of litigation and jurisprudence, and an increasing number of practitioners, whether sharing this interest or not, are being called upon for opinions concerning questions of child custody, competency, criminal responsibility, personal injury or handicap, suitability to work in law enforcement, and candidacy for probation or parole. In addition to this major new trend in clinical psychology over the last decade, developmental and experimental psychologists have come into demand for their expert opinions on such matters as the reliability of eyewitness testimony and lie detection.

Concurrently with the emergence of forensics as a new specialty within psychology, an expanding literature has addressed broad and diverse aspects of the interface between psychology and the law. These range from highly conceptual issues concerning the implications and intent of the law to very practical matters involving the evaluation and rehabilitation of those who break the law. Theorists and practitioners of many different persuasions have employed a variety of perspectives in proposing conclusions and recommendations on such matters.

The present book was developed to provide a comprehensive overview of the central topics in forensic psychology and detailed guidelines for the effective application of psycholegal knowledge in psychological practice. The contributors were chosen for their accomplishments both as scholars and practitioners, and they bring specialized knowledge and extensive experience to bear on the particular chapters they were asked to write. The individual chapters were formulated to meet the needs of psychologists who are currently or expect to become involved in some aspect of forensic theory, research, or practice. The text should accordingly serve both as a practice manual and as a reference guide to significant issues and relevant literature in the field.

The Handbook comprises six parts. The first part, on the Context of Forensic Psychology, provides a sense of the historical development, basic parameters, and recent innovations in forensic psychology. An introduction to the legal literature is included.

The second part, Areas of Application in Civil Proceedings, addresses the issues underlying the psychologist's standing in assessing personal injury and educational disability and the determination of civil competence.

The third part, Areas of Application in Criminal Justice, discusses the concepts involved in violence prediction and eyewitness testimony. Four chapters deal with recommending parole and probation, determining competence to stand trial, assessing insanity, and determining specific intent and diminished capacity. The three chapters concluding this part concern consulting with the police, issues involved in lie detection, and the use of forensic hypnosis.

Part four, Communicating Expert Opinions, concerns preparing written reports and the process of courtroom testimony.

The fifth part, Treatment, is devoted to intervention with incarcerated populations from both program planning perspectives and the perspective of the individual practitioner who treats offenders. A chapter deals directly with short-range treatment programs versus the more efficacious use of diversion programs. The concluding chapter addresses a frequently overlooked population, victims and survivors.

The sixth and final part, Professional Issues, concerns guiding principles such as ethics, credentials and standards of practice, and educational opportunities in forensic psychology on graduate, internship, and postgraduate levels.

The editors would like to express their appreciation to their colleagues whose cordiality, conscientiousness, and creative talents made the task of processing their contributed chapters a pleasurable labor. We are also grateful to Herb Reich, Wiley-Interscience editor, for the patient guidance and psychological sophistication with which he oversaw our work on this project. On a personal note, the support of Kathryn, Tanya, Clara, and Joel Hess, and the lessons in life they teach, are appreciated, and the assistance of Frances Weiner in the production process was invaluable.

IRVING B. WEINER
Rutherford, New Jersey
March 1987

ALLEN K. HESS
Auburn, Alabama
March 1987

Contents

PART ONE   BACKGROUND

1. History of Forensic Psychology   3
    Curt R. Bartol and Anne M. Bartol

2. Dimensions of Forensic Psychology   22
    Allen K. Hess

3. Accessing Legal Literatures   50
    David F. Daniell

PART TWO   AREAS OF APPLICATION ON CIVIL PROCEEDINGS

4. Informed Consent in Treatment and Research   63
    Barbara Stanley

5. Mediating Domestic Law Issues   86
    Paul Brinson and Kathryn D. Hess

6. Personality Assessment in Personal Injury Cases   128
    James Neal Butcher and Terri Cross Harlow

7. Assessing Educational Handicaps   155
    Daniel J. Reschly

8. Civil Competency   188
    Ralph Slovenko

PART THREE   AREAS OF APPLICATION IN CRIMINAL JUSTICE

9. Assessing and Predicting Violence: Research, Law, and
    Applications   205
    Thomas R. Litwack and Louis B. Schlesinger

10.   Evaluating Eyewitness Testimony   258
      Gail S. Goodman and Annette Hahn

11.   Assessing the Competence of Juries   293
      Steven D. Penrod and Brian L. Cutler

12.   Recommending Probation and Parole   319
      Harold J. Vetter

13.   Specific Intent and Diminished Capacity   352
      Charles R. Clark

14.   Defining and Assessing Competency to Stand Trial   378
      Ronald Roesch and Stephen L. Golding

15.   The Assessment of Criminal Responsibility: A Historical
      Approach to a Current Controversy   395
      Stephen L. Golding and Ronald Roesch

16.   Consulting with Police   437
      Martin Reiser and Nels Klyver

17.   What Psychologists Should Know About Lie Detection   460
      William G. Iacono and Christopher J. Patrick

18.   Forensic Uses of Hypnosis   490
      David Spiegel and Herbert Spiegel

PART FOUR   COMMUNICATING EXPERT OPINIONS

19.   Writing Forensic Reports   511
      Irving B. Weiner

20.   Consulting and Testifying in Court   529
      Margaret Thaler Singer and Abraham Nievod

PART FIVE   TREATMENT

21.   Intervention with Incarcerated Offenders   557
      Michael A. Milan and Joseph H. Evans

22.   Intervention as Prevention   584
      Joan McCord

23.   Psychotherapy with Criminal Offenders   602
        Max J. Mobley

24.   Intervention with Victim/Survivors   630
        Lenore E. Auerbach Walker

PART SIX   PROFESSIONAL ISSUES

25.   The Ethics of Forensic Psychology   653
        Allen K. Hess

26.   Training in Psychology and Law   681
        Gary B. Melton

Author Index   699

Subject Index   719

HANDBOOK OF
FORENSIC PSYCHOLOGY

PART ONE
Background

CHAPTER 1

History of Forensic Psychology

CURT R. BARTOL and ANNE M. BARTOL

Repeatedly we are told that psychologists do not care about the history of their profession. Instead, they are drawn to contemporary issues and theories and—yes—even fads. Classic research is musty and stale, attracting only the tenured academic types who absentmindedly haunt dimly lit library stacks. It is encouraging, then, that the editors of this volume allotted the first chapter to a historical perspective (although rumor has it that the pages will be perforated to allow readers to dispose of them without guilt).

The history of psychology reminds the profession of the need to understand whence it came and to continually assess where it is going. History—especially history corrected—offers perspective and adds to the understanding of any discipline. If more psychologists were to peruse the journals and books published at the turn of the century, they would be surprised to find many of the same issues, problems, and research findings that are reported and discussed today. Some researchers and scholars today are even "discovering" what was discovered decades ago and, in some cases, drawing less valid or enlightened conclusions.

In the following pages, we view forensic psychology broadly, as both (1) the *research endeavor* that examines aspects of human behavior directly related to the legal process (e.g., eyewitness memory and testimony, jury decision making, or criminal behavior), and (2) the *professional practice* of psychology within or in consultation with a legal system that embraces both criminal and civil law. On the criminal side, forensic psychology deals with such areas as corrections, law enforcement, issues of criminal responsibility, crime prevention, and treatment of criminal behavior. On the civil side, it has relevance for child custody and placement, questions of legal competence and liability for tortious conduct, involuntary civil commitment, hiring and retention policies, and educational practices, to name a few examples. Straddling both criminal and civil law is the troubling area of juvenile justice. With varying fervor and in different degrees, psychologists have appeared in virtually every one of these legal arenas.

We will focus, of course, on forensic *psychology* distinguished from forensic *psychiatry*, which has its own well-documented, rich history. It is time to disentangle the history of forensic psychology from psychiatric accounts and highlight its own distinct accomplishments. We will review the achievements of psychologists

3

from the end of the nineteenth century and extend our discussion to 1970, when forensic psychology came of age (Loh, 1981). In the early years, European psychologists dominated the field, and their work will be highlighted. Beginning with World War I, our review will focus exclusively on the forensic psychology discussed and practiced on this continent. The reader interested in more detail about the issues and individuals discussed might check landmark summaries of psychology and law published by Whipple (1909–1915, 1917), Hutchins and Slesinger (1929), Louisell (1955, 1957), Tapp (1976), Loh (1981), and Monahan and Loftus (1982).

IN THE BEGINNING

Do chestnut or oak trees lose their leaves earlier in autumn?

Do horses in the field stand with head or tail to the wind?

In what direction do the seeds of an apple point?

What was the weather one week ago today?

When J. McKeen Cattell posed these questions to 56 college students at Columbia University in March 1893, he was probably conducting one of the first experiments —albeit an informal one—on the psychology of testimony. The questions he asked his students were similar to those that "might naturally be asked in a court of justice" (Cattell, 1895, p. 761). His subjects were allowed 30 seconds to consider their answers, then told to write their responses. They were also asked to indicate their degree of confidence in each answer.

When Cattell conducted his experiment, it was reasonably well established that courtroom eyewitness testimony was unreliable and incomplete. Both French and German psychologists were familiar with the powerful influence of suggestion over sensation and perception. The specific conditions under which testimony was inaccurate were not known, however. Furthermore, as Cattell noted, "An unscrupulous attorney can discredit the statements of a truthful witness by cunningly selected questions. The jury, or at least the judge, should know how far errors in recollection are normal and how they vary under different conditions" (p. 761). But Cattell himself was surprised at both the degree of inaccuracy he uncovered and the wide range of individual differences in the levels of confidence expressed by the students. Answers to the weather question, for example, were "equally distributed over all kinds of weather which are possible at the beginning of March" (p. 761). Some subjects were nearly always sure they were correct, even when they were not, while others were consistently uncertain and hesitant in their answers, even when they were correct.

Cattell's experiment probably represents the beginning of modern forensic psychology because it sparked the interest of other researchers (mostly European) in the psychology of testimony. In America, Joseph Jastrow immediately replicated Cattell's procedure at the University of Wisconsin and obtained similar results (described by Bolton, 1896). Aside from this brief flirtation, however, American psychologists did not immediately embrace the study of legal issues.

Psychologists in Europe seemed more intrigued. First, Alfred Binet (1900) replicated the experiment in France. In addition, he summarized relevant experiments on the psychology of testimony that were being conducted in Europe and called for a "science psycho-judiciaire" (Binet, 1905; Binet & Clarparede, 1906). Most significant for the historical development of forensic psychology, however, was the apparent fascination Cattell's experiment and Binet's work held for (Louis) William Stern, who had received his Ph.D. in psychology at the University of Berlin under the tutelage of H. Ebbinghaus. In 1901 Stern collaborated with the criminologist F. V. Liszt in an attempt to lend realism to the Cattell design. Stern and Liszt conducted a "reality experiment" in a law class, staging a bogus quarrel between two students over a scientific controversy. The argument increased in vehemence until one student drew a revolver (Stern, 1939). At this point, the professor intervened and asked for written and oral reports from the class about aspects of the dispute. Although the witnesses were law students who, Stern asserted, should have known the pitfalls of testifying, none could give a faultless report. The number of errors per individual ranged from 4 to 12. Moreover, the researchers found that inaccuracies increased with respect to the second half of the scenario when excitement and tension were at their peak. They concluded—tentatively—that "emotions reduce accuracy of recall."

Stern became an active researcher in the psychology of testimony over the next few years (1906, 1910). He also helped establish the first journal on the psychology of testimony, *Betrage zur Psychologie der Aussage* (Contributions to the Psychology of Testimony), which he edited and which was published at Leipzig. The journal was superseded in 1908 by the much broader *Zeitschrift fur Angewande Psychologie*, the first journal of applied psychology. In his *Aussage* research Stern found, among other things, that "subjective sincerity" does not guarantee "objective truthfulness"; that leading and suggestive questions contaminate the accuracy of eyewitness accounts of critical events; that there are important differences between adult and child witnesses; that lineups are of limited value when the members are not matched for age and physical appearance; and that events between an occurrence and its recall can have drastic effects on memory. It can be concluded, therefore, that modern forensic psychology began with experimental research on the psychology of testimony.

As a parallel phenomenon, European—particularly German—psychologists at the turn of the century were beginning to be used as "expert witnesses" in criminal cases, often applying the knowledge gained from the newly established psychological laboratory. They testified both on matters of fact, such as reporting the results of a particular experiment, and on matters of opinion. Perhaps the earliest case was in 1896, when Albert von Schrenck-Notzing testified at the trial of a Munich man accused of murdering three women (Hale, 1980). There had been extensive and sensational press coverage of the murders in the months prior to the trial, and Schrenck-Notzing opined that this pretrial publicity, through a process of suggestion, probably led numerous witnesses to "retroactive memory-falsification" (Schrenck-

Notzing, 1897). That is, the witnesses could not distinguish between what they saw happen and what the press reported had happened. He supported his opinion with accounts of laboratory research on memory and suggestibility. Although the accused was convicted on the basis of solid evidence, Schrenck-Notzing's direct application of the psychology of suggestion to court processes helped stimulate the interest of both German jurists and psychologists (Hale, 1980).

EARLY AMERICAN FORENSIC PSYCHOLOGY: MUNSTERBERG

American psychologists at the turn of the century remained comparatively uninterested in applying research on topics related to law. First, they were just beginning to explore the wondrous psychological landscape and had little inclination to specialize in judicial or legal matters. A second factor that might account for their reticence was the probable influence of Wilhelm Wundt, who had trained many of the American pioneers in his Leipzig laboratory (Cattell being the first). Wundt was both a philosopher and an experimentalist, wary of applying psychology until sufficient research had been conducted. He believed that premature utilization of partial information could be disastrous. His students often took this caveat quite seriously, although some, like Cattell, eventually began to link the laboratory to the world outside.

One of Wundt's not-so-cautious students was the German psychologist Hugo Munsterberg, who arrived in the United States in 1892 at the invitation of William James, directed the psychology laboratory at Harvard University, and spent 24 years—until his sudden death in December 1916—trying to persuade the public that psychology had something to offer virtually every area of human endeavor. Munsterberg, now acknowledged as the father of applied psychology, believed psychological knowledge could be applied to education, industry, advertising, music, art, and, of course, to law. His claims were often exaggerated, however, and his proposals were rarely empirically based. He usually published in popular magazines rather than scholarly journals (some of his colleagues called his a "Sunday-supplement psychology"). He also incessantly promoted himself and his native Germany —a practice that alienated him increasingly from his colleagues and the public as World War I approached. Not surprisingly, the legal community vehemently resisted his intrusion into its territory (Hale, 1980). The great legal commentator Wigmore, who would eventually write, "Whenever the Psychologist is really ready for the Courts, the Courts are ready for him" (Wigmore, 1909) found it necessary to assail Munsterberg in a satirical and devastating law review article published in 1909.

Wigmore's attack was prompted by the publication of Munsterberg's controversial best-seller *On the Witness Stand* (1908), in which he asserted that the time was ripe to apply psychology to the practical needs of the legal system. Munsterberg had recently been a consultant in two murder cases. He had not testified directly in either one, probably because, as Moskowitz (1977) notes, the concept of expert witness had not yet been accepted in American courtroom procedure. In the first case,

Munsterberg sat in the courtroom, observed the behavior of the defendant, and interviewed him in private. In the second, he read a secondhand account of the courtroom testimony and expressed in a letter his certainty that the accused was innocent. The letter was leaked to the press, and Munsterberg was criticized for his interference with the judicial process (Moskowitz, 1977).

Munsterberg undoubtedly wrote *On the Witness Stand* partly to fuel the attention he was receiving. The book was directed more at the general public than at colleagues or those working within the legal system. Convinced that he had been correct in his assessments of previous cases, he asserted that psychologists, armed with their knowledge about perception and memory, could understand "the mind of the witness." Furthermore, this was only one of many areas in which psychology could benefit the law.

Nevertheless, in spite of his tendency toward self-promotion, Munsterberg had his cautious moments. For example, in discussing the emotional reactions of witnesses that might signal a dishonest answer, he noted that "a certain scepticism as to the practical application of [psychology's] methods is still in order . . . studies in this field of the bodily registration of emotions are still in their beginnings and so far many difficulties are not overcome; there are still contradictions in the results of various scholars" (1908, p. 131). On the whole, however, *On the Witness Stand* reflected little tolerance for lawyers (whom Munsterberg called "obdurate"), judges, or police officers, and it did not add to his credibility among professionals. If Munsterberg was hoping for a profitable, perhaps even symbiotic relationship between psychology and law, his tone belied it. Furthermore, Wigmore's review made such a relationship untenable, at least for the time being.

This did not deter Munsterberg from additional comments on courtroom behavior, witnesses, and juries, however. In 1914 he published a study of group decision making, using Harvard and Radcliffe students as subjects, which he titled "The Mind of the Juryman." He did not endear himself to women when he concluded that "the psychologist has every reason to be satisfied with the jury system as long as the women are kept out of it" (1914, p. 202, cited in Moskowitz, 1977). He based his conclusion on a finding that the female students in his study were less accurate in their final decisions than the male students.

Munsterberg has been accused of being more an opportunist than a trailblazer (Kuna, 1976, 1978), and it is tempting to blame his brashness for the tenuous and occasionally hostile initial relationship between psychology and law. Nonetheless, he undeniably pushed his reluctant American colleagues into the practical legal arena and made a seminal contribution to forensic psychology.

EARLY PSYCHOLOGISTS IN CRIMINAL JUSTICE

While Munsterberg was proselytizing, another American psychologist was quietly making inroads into a different forensic area. In 1909, clinical psychologist Grace M. Fernald worked with psychiatrist William Healy to establish the first clinic specifically designed for youthful offenders—the Juvenile Psychopathic Institute. It was initially developed to serve the newly established Juvenile Court of Chicago by offering clinical diagnoses of "problem" children. Fernald, who received her doctorate from the University of Chicago in 1907, was probably the first clinical psychologist to work under the supervision of a psychiatrist (Napoli, 1981), as well as one of the earliest psychologists to specialize in the diagnosis and treatment of juvenile delinquency. The Institute, which extended its services rapidly to include treatment and research as well as diagnoses, became a public agency in 1914, the Institute for Juvenile Research.

Healy and Fernald used the relatively new Stanford-Binet Intelligence Scale to test delinquents, but they soon realized the importance of obtaining "performance" measures as well. This prompted them to develop the Healy-Fernald series of 23 performance tests, which they began to use in 1911. The two eventually went their separate ways. Fernald became a specialist in mental deficiency and testing and taught psychology at UCLA for 27 years, until her retirement in 1948. Healy worked with and eventually married psychologist Augusta Bronner, an expert on female juvenile delinquency. Together they wrote *New Light on Delinquency and Its Treatment* (1936) and *The Value of Treatment and What Happened Afterward* (1939). Bronner remained active in her field, but she published very little with the exception of the two books with Healy.

Other psychologists at the beginning of the new century also seemed more comfortable with a peripheral involvement with the law, specifically by administering mental tests to criminals and delinquents at the requests of courts, corrections, and the fledgling juvenile justice system. Mental testing, as a matter of fact, became the mainstay of applied psychology in general from 1900 and continued to be its raison d'être until World War II. The two wars precipitated massive testing programs and saw the births of the Army Alpha and Army Beta.

Most psychologists employed by clinics that provided services to the legal system worked exclusively as psychometrists. The drudgery of day-to-day testing (often under the watchful eyes of a physician or psychiatrist) made applied psychology, as it was then known, less than appealing as a profession. Often, however, it was the place where female psychologists were most accepted. This trend continued through the first third of the twentieth century. During the 1930s, while men comprised over two-thirds of all American psychologists, over 60 percent of the applied psychologists were women (Napoli, 1981).

Lindner (1955) pinpoints 1913 as the first instance of psychological services being offered within a U.S. prison, specifically in a women's reformatory in New York State. The precise nature of the services and the identity of the psychologist who provided them is not known. In December 1916, a Psychopathic Laboratory was established at the New York City Police Department for the express purpose of examining certain prisoners (Keller, 1918). The staff included psychiatrists, neurologists, social workers, and psychologists, whose tasks were to conduct hasty pretrial evaluations. According to E. I. Keller, a consulting psychologist to the clinic, prisoners arrived for testing at 9 A.M. "The disadvantage is the lack of time, for all prisoners must be examined in time to get them to court by noon or earlier, and many courts are situated in distant parts of the city" (1918, p. 85). All of the professional staff members had to conduct the evaluation in less than three hours.

Louis Terman (1917) was the first American psychologist to use mental tests as screening devices in the selection of law enforcement personnel. On October 31, 1916, at the request of the city manager of San Jose, California, he administered an abbreviated form of the Stanford-Binet to 30 police and fire department applicants. They ranged in age from 21 to 38, with a median age of 30. Only four had attended high school, and none had gone beyond the sophomore year. Terman found that most of the applicants functioned near the dull-normal range of intelligence (68–84 on the Stanford Revision of the Binet-Simon Intelligence Scale); only three obtained an intelligence quotient over 100, the score considered average for the general population. Based on his experience with the intellectual capabilities of school-aged children, Terman suggested—somewhat arbitrarily—that applicants with intelligence quotients under 80 were not fit for police work or fire fighting. The city manager agreed, and 10 applicants were immediately excluded from further consideration.

A contemporary of Terman, psychologist Louis Thurstone, was also interested in the value of mental testing to police selection. Thurstone (1922) administered the newly developed Army Intelligence Examination (Army Alpha) to 358 members of the Detroit Police Department. Officers at all ranks scored below average; in fact, the more experienced the police officer, the lower was his intelligence. The average score for the 307 patrolmen was 71.44; the 34 sergeants averaged 54.71, and the 17 lieutenants 57.80 (Army Alpha mean 100, standard deviation 15). Thurstone concluded that law enforcement did not attract intelligent individuals. He also surmised that the more intelligent individuals who entered police service left for other occupations where their abilities and intelligence were presumably better recognized.

Police officers were vindicated somewhat, however, when Maude A. Merrill (1927) administered the Army Alpha to a group of officers and candidates. They scored at the average level (the sample's mean IQ was 104). The differences between her findings and those of Terman and Thurstone were probably due to department leadership factors, recruitment procedures, and selection ratios (Terrio, Swanson, & Chamelin, 1977).

While the aforementioned psychologists were among the first to study the cognitive capacities of police officers and candidates, there is no indication that they consistently participated in the screening of police personnel. At this point, we have no information about who might have been the first psychologist to assume this regular role. As late as 1939, Donald Paterson (1940) could only identify one professional psychologist—L. J. O'Rourke—who had actively investigated the validity of the civil service examination system, even though the Civil Service Commission had adopted routine competitive exams as far back as 1883.

In the early years of the twentieth century, psychologists also tentatively began to offer psychological perspectives on criminal behavior and to speculate about the causes of crime. Given the extensive early emphasis on testing, it is not surprising that the theories often centered on the measurable mental capacities of offenders.

Psychologists (the most notable was Henry H. Goddard (1914)) repeatedly found that most juvenile and adult offenders were mentally deficient, which led to the conclusion that a primary "cause" of crime was mental incompetence or deficiency. In large part, this belief reflected the pervasive influence of Darwinism, which contended that humans differ only in degree from their animal brethren (and that some humans were closer to their animal ancestry than others). The mentally deficient were considered both intellectually and emotionally less capable of adapting to modern society. Thus, they presumably resorted to more primitive ways of meeting their needs, such as crime.

In the history of psychology, few scholars have ventured to offer comprehensive theories on crime or delinquent behavior. Those who have (e.g., Eysenck, 1964) have often been strongly influenced by Darwinian thinking. Therefore, theoretical orientations focusing on mental deficiency or biological and constitutional dispositions have dominated psychological criminology. This perspective has dominated the psychiatric field even more, of course. Freud himself was strongly influenced by Darwin, and Freudian psychoanalytical theories on crime and delinquency are permeated with a strong Darwinian perspective.

EARLY PSYCHOLOGISTS IN THE COURTROOM

To continue our chronological account of forensic psychology, we pick up the historical thread in the decade preceding World War I when psychologists began to interact regularly with the legal system in areas other than mental measurement. However, although European psychologists during these years continued to testify in criminal courts, their American counterparts generally did not. In 1911, several psychologists testified at a Belgian murder trial in which a man was accused of raping and killing a nine-year-old girl. Two of the child's playmates had apparently seen the murderer but gave inconsistent and contradictory accounts. Among the psychologists retained by the defense was J. Varendonck, who designed a series of experiments based on the question format used at the preliminary hearing. He found that his subjects, children of approximately the same age as the two witnesses (ages 8 to 10), were inaccurate in their recall of important events. Despite protests from the prosecution, he was allowed to present the results of these experiments as well as the general research on the psychology of testimony that was available at that time. A jury found the accused not guilty.

Varendonck, it should be noted, was vehemently opposed to any use of child witnesses in the courtroom. In writing of his involvement with the murder case, he remarked, "Everyone accused of crime based on children's testimony does not encounter a psychologist to counter the indictment that lies heavily upon them. . . . When are we going to give up, in all civilized nations, listening to children in courts of law? . . . those who are in the habit of living with children do not attach the least value to their testimony because children cannot observe and because their suggestibility is inexhaustible" (cited in Goodman, 1984, p. 27). In contrast, both Binet (1900) and Stern (1939) believed that errors in recollection, whether by children or adults, were more a reflection of leading, suggestive courtroom questioning than of any "natural" tendency to distort reality.

Also in 1911, Karl Marbe, a psychology professor at the University of Wurzburg, became the first psychologist to testify at a civil trial, offering expert opinion on the psychological issue of reaction time as applied to a train wreck near Mullheim. Marbe was asked to testify as to the probable effect of alcohol on the mental status of the engineer as well as on the reaction time of the fireman and guard applying breaks. Based on reaction-time experiments, Marbe testified that the train could not have been stopped in time to avert disaster. During the same year, Marbe also testified in a criminal trial similar to the one in which Varendonck had challenged the credibility of child witnesses. Several German adolescent girls had accused their teacher of sexually molesting them. Marbe convinced the jury that the statements of the girls were unreliable, and the teacher was exonerated.

World War I placed in abeyance most of the exploration in applying psychology to law and shifted the attention of psychologists once again to the field of mental testing. Research on the psychology of evidence, a major interest of experimental psychologists, came to a standstill. Nevertheless, the war and early postwar years saw a few landmarks in American forensic psychology, including the gradual acceptance of psychologists as expert witnesses, particularly on matters of fact. The first psychologists were also appointed to law school faculties during these years.

It is generally believed that American psychologists have served as expert witnesses since the early 1920s (Comment, 1979), but pinpointing the exact date on which a psychologist first qualified as an expert in a court of law is an exercise in futility. According to Rogers (1910, 1918), the results of experimental research on visual perception were routinely accepted in trademark infringement cases, although not necessarily in the form of direct testimony. This was apparently considered a "safe" undertaking, since the psychologists were not infringing upon the territory of the "medical experts"—physicians and psychiatrists—who routinely testified on matters of criminal responsibility. As Louisell (1955) notes, however, since trial court records are generally unavailable and only appellate decisions are published, the testimony of psychologists, particularly in civil cases, may have been less rare than the paucity of documentation would indicate. We do know that psychological testimony was almost inevitably *rejected* in criminal cases involving the defendant's mental state. "As a general rule, only medical men—that is, persons licensed by law to practice the profession of medicine—can testify as experts on the question of insanity; and the propriety of this general limitation is too patent to permit discussion" (*Odom v. State*, 1911; cited in Comment, 1979, fn. 14).

The first published case in which an American psychologist qualified as an expert appears to be *State v. Driver* in 1921. The occasion was only a partial victory for forensic psychology, however. A West Virginia trial court accepted the chief psychologist of the state bureau of juvenile research as an expert on the matter of juvenile delinquency. However, it rejected his testimony, based on psychological test data, that a 12-year-old attempted-rape victim was a "moron" (a term coined by H. H. Goddard) and could not be presumptively believed. In agreeing with the trial court, the West Virginia Supreme Court noted, "It is yet to be demonstrated that psychological and medical tests are practical, and will detect the lie on the witness stand" (*State v. Driver*, 1921, p. 488). Although some commentators interpreted *Driver* as a major loss for psychologists wishing to achieve status as expert witnesses, Louisell (1955) noted that the decision was not a rejection of psychologists per se, only of the particular evidence offered by one psychologist. Nevertheless, it was not until much later, specifically the 1940s and 1950s, that psychologists testified in courts of law on a regular basis, at least in some jurisdictions.

PSYCHOLOGISTS AND LAW SCHOOLS

Another landmark for forensic psychology during these years was the 1922 appointment of the first American professor of legal psychology, William M. Marston at American University. Marston was perhaps the most influential U.S. psychologist associated with the legal system during this era, and in many respects he may be considered the father of American forensic psychology. He had received a law degree in 1918 and a Ph.D. in 1921, both from Harvard (he was a student of Munsterberg before the latter's death). His interests were multifaceted. (He was even the originator, cartoonist, and producer of the successful comic strip "Wonder Woman," under the pen name of Charles Moulton.) Although admitted to the Massachusetts bar, Marston soon gave up his law practice to concentrate on psychology.

As a laboratory assistant in psychology at Radcliffe College, Marston had discovered a significant positive correlation between systolic blood pressure and lying (Marston, 1917), which became the basis of the modern polygraph. One of his major contributions to the forensic area was his continuing work in lie detection (Marston, 1920, 1921, 1925). He frequently consulted with attorneys, police, and other criminal justice personnel, and his evidence was determinative in the acquittals of several defendants accused of murder. It is likely, therefore, that Marston— along with Terman and psychologists associated with the New York City Psychopathic Clinic—qualifies as one of the first psychological consultants to the criminal justice system, particularly to the police.

Marston also conducted the first serious research on the jury system (Winick, 1961). Using subjects in simulated jury conditions, he found in a series of studies (Marston, 1924) that written evidence was superior to oral evidence; that free narration—while less complete—was more accurate than cross examination or direct questioning; that a witness's caution in answering was a good indicator of accuracy; and that female jurors considered evidence more carefully than male jurors (compare with Munsterberg's conclusions about female jurors, mentioned earlier). Because of his legal background and his cautious style, Marston's ideas and research were more acceptable to the legal community than Munsterberg's had been, although there is little evidence that the legal system put his findings to extensive use.

Another psychologist, Donald Slesinger, a protégé of Robert M. Hutchins, also made his mark during the years immediately following World War I. Although he had no formal legal training, Slesinger was appointed by Acting Dean Hutchins as a one-year Sterling Fellow to the Yale Law School in 1927. The following year he became a research assistant. In 1929 he was appointed associate professor, teaching a course in the psychology of evidence, which appears to qualify him as the first psychologist granted faculty status in an American law school. Hutchins and Slesinger co-authored numerous summary articles on the status of legal psychology (1927, 1928a, 1928b, 1928c, 1929). Slesinger wrote another with Marion Pilpel in 1929, surveying 48 articles written by psychologists on issues relating to forensic psychology which had appeared in professional journals up to that time. Eleven were concerned with the psychology of testimony, 10 with deception, seven with intelligence and crime, and six with criminal behavior. The remainder focused on general topics such as the scientific method or legal research. Fifteen of the 48 articles had been written by German psychologists. In 1930, Slesinger followed Hutchins to the University of Chicago where he served as professor of law and, briefly, as dean of the law school.

THE QUIET PERIOD

Like applied psychology in general, forensic psychology experienced some remission between the two world wars and did not recoup its energy until the late 1940s and 1950s. In addition to Marston's work, the period did see scattered research by Weld (Weld & Roff, 1938; Weld & Danzig, 1940) on how juries formed opinions and verdicts, a master's thesis on the relationship between narrative and interrogative methods of questioning (Cady, 1924), another study on questioning and testimony (Snee & Lush, 1941), and a survey of legal and psychological opinions about the validity of some of Wigmore's rules of evidence (Britt, 1940).

Loh (1981) notes a revived interest in psychology and law during the late 1920s and the 1930s, but this interest was almost exclusively on the part of lawyers, who produced such books as *Legal Psychology* (Brown, 1926), *Psychology for the Lawyer* (McCarty, 1929), and *Law and the Social Sciences* (Cairns, 1935). Wigmore (1940), the foremost authority on rules of evidence, paved the way for the use of test data in the courtroom, noting that the psychometrist introducing test evidence would stand "on the same footing as the expert witness to insanity" (cited by McCary, 1956, p. 9). Nevertheless, Wigmore also required proof that such tests be recognized as valid and feasible by the general scientific community (Wigmore, 1909).

In 1931 Howard Burtt (who was also a former student of Munsterberg) wrote *Legal Psychology*—the first textbook in the area written by a psychologist. Burtt's primary interest was industrial psychology, however, and he himself did not conduct much research on legal issues. Although the book made a valuable contribution to the academic psychological literature, it had little discernible influence on the legal profession or on applied psychology in general. In 1935, Edward S. Robinson published *Law and the Lawyers*, which predicted that jurisprudence would become one of the family of social sciences and argued that all of its fundamental concepts must be brought into line with psychological knowledge. The book was lambasted by lawyers and essentially ignored by psychologists. In hindsight, contemporary scholars have found Robinson's ideas much more palatable (e.g., Loh, 1981; Horowitz & Willging, 1984).

Between the wars, psychologists also became more involved in the screening of law enforcement personnel and, perhaps, with the prison system. Wilmington, Delaware, and Toledo, Ohio, appear to share the distinction of being the first two cities to require ongoing psychological screening for use in police selection, in the form of mental and personality tests (Oglesby, 1957; Gottesman, 1975). The year was 1938. In the late 1930s, Darley and Berdie (1940) surveyed 13 federal and 123 state prisons and learned that they employed a total of 64 psychologists who called themselves "prison psychologists." Although all considered themselves clinical psychologists, only about half had Ph.D.'s in psychology. Later, Raymond Corsini (1945) expressed concern that there was as yet "no history of prison psychology." He estimated that during the 1940s there were approximately 200,000 individuals confined in U.S. correctional facilities who were served by a mere 80 psychologists. Their work consisted of (1) testing (personality, aptitude, and academic progress); (2) giving educational, vocational, and personal guidance (usually at the prisoner's request); and (3) maintaining working relationships with all members of the prison staff.

THE ERA OF CONFIDENCE

The 1940s, particularly after the war, and the 1950s are noteworthy as the time during which psychologists became more confident about their contributions to law. This was especially apparent in the growing acceptance of psychologists as expert witnesses, a phenomenon that Loh (1981) attributes to "increased professionalization . . . , the rapid growth of mental health professions during this period, and the formulation of legal doctrines of insanity consistent with modern psychiatry" (1981, p. 323). The legal literature attests to the profession's direct, increasing involvement with the courts. Psychologists offered opinions and presented data relevant to subjects as diverse as the influence of pretrial publicity on potential witnesses and juries, the effects of pornography on adolescents, the effect of certain educational practices on children, and the likely influence of advertisements on consumers (Louisell, 1955; Greenberg, 1956; Loh, 1981). This is not to say that there was widespread acceptance of the idea that psychologists deserved a niche in the courtroom. Resistance to the involvement of psychologists or, at best, a cautious approach consistently characterized much of the legal literature (Comment, 1979).

In the early 1940s and the postwar era, appellate courts began to support the use of qualified psychologists as expert witnesses on the issue of mental responsibility for criminal and tortious conduct. The first influential decision was *People v. Hawthorne*, a Michigan case. Hawthorne had been tried for the murder of his wife's lover and had pleaded not guilty by reason of insanity. The trial court refused to qualify as an expert witness a professor of psychology from Michigan State Normal College who had a Ph.D. and an impressive list of credentials. He had earned graduate credits from Harvard Medical School, had published extensively (including a textbook which was in its fifth edition), and had expertise in motivation, physiological psychology, and neurology (Louisell, 1955). In finding that the trial court had erred in not accepting the psychologist as an expert, the Michigan Supreme Court ruled that the standard for determining expert status was not a medical degree but the extent of the witness's knowledge. It advised trial courts to evaluate carefully the merits of a potential witness's claim to expertise, noting that a psychologist's ability to detect insanity could not be presumed inferior to that of a "medical man." The dissenters, however, believed that since insanity represented a disease, only a person with medical training should qualify as an expert.

Later, in *Hidden v. Mutual Life Insurance Co.* (1954), the 4th Circuit Court of Appeals allowed psychological expertise to be applied to a civil case. The insured claimed he had a "disabling nervous condition" that prevented him from engaging in any gainful occupation and was therefore a justification for disability benefits. A clinical psychologist with a doctoral degree testified on his behalf, after administering a battery of projective tests. When the lawyer for the insurance company objected, the trial judge instructed the jury to disregard the evidence on the grounds that the psychologist did not qualify as an expert. The circuit court ruled that this exclusion had been a mistake, specifying that the psychologist should have been qualified as an expert to express his opinion about the mental condition of the insured.

While some psychologists were struggling to be accepted as experts on questions of mental status, competence, and criminal responsibility, others during this era were joining the crucial legal battle against school segregation by testifying and consulting with attorneys in the numerous state cases that would ultimately culminate in the 1954 landmark ruling, *Brown v. Board of Education*. Richard Kluger (1975), in his informative and exhaustive case study, details the contributions of psychologists and other social scientists. David Krech, a social psychologist-author, along with Helen Trager, who had published articles on racial attitude tests, and Horace B. English, an expert on child psychology, testified at some of the school segregation trials. The most noteworthy contribution was that of Kenneth Clark who, with psychologist Mamie Clark, conducted the now-famous "doll research" to gauge the effects of segregation. Kenneth Clark then gave factual testimony reporting the results of this research (Kluger, 1975). When the NAACP appealed *Brown* and three other segregation cases to the U.S. Supreme Court, Clark coordinated the social science involvement in the brief-writing process, which culminated in the now-famous "Social Science Appendix."

The bitter debate over whether psychologists and other social scientists should have testified in the school segregation and other civil rights cases is well documented (e.g., Cahn, 1955; Greenberg, 1956; Kluger, 1975). There is far less disagreement over their participation in the brief-writing process. In *Brown*, the U.S. Supreme Court did not quote directly from the trial testimony of the many social scientists, leading some writers to speculate that these witnesses, who sometimes contradicted one another, had little influence on the final outcome of the case. However, when the Court concluded that separating children because of their race "affects their hearts and minds in a way unlikely to be undone," it noted that this conclusion was "amply supported" by modern authority. The modern authorities, including psychologists, were footnoted (the often-cited brief footnote 11).

Meanwhile, psychologists were continuing to make enough inroads testifying on the issue of criminal responsibility that psychiatrists felt the need to protect their turf. In 1954, the Council of the American Psychiatric Association, the Executive Council of the American Psychoanalytic Association, and the American Medical Association joined in a resolution stating that only physicians were legitimate experts in the field of mental illness for purposes of courtroom testimony. Other individuals could participate only if their testimony was coordinated by medical authority. The resolution greatly influenced trial courts (Miller, Lower, & Bleechmore, 1978), which became reluctant to accept independent psychological testimony.

Finally, in *Jenkins v. United States* (1962), the Court of Appeals for the District of Columbia gave its own direct, although conditional, support to the use of psychologists as experts on the issue of mental illness. Although the court was sharply divided, its decision remains the predominant authority for the use of psychologists in the area of criminal responsibility.

Jenkins raised an insanity defense to a variety of charges surrounding a housebreaking and assault. The trial judge had instructed the jury to disregard the testimony of three defense psychologists on the ground that they were not competent to give a medical opinion as to whether the accused suffered a "mental disease." The appeals court majority emphasized that a judge may not automatically disqualify a witness for lack of a medical degree. Like the earlier *Hawthorne* court, the D.C. Court of Appeals warned trial judges not to automatically exclude psychological testimony, but rather to look closely at the credentials of a proposed expert before ruling on his or her expert status. As Perlin (1977) notes, the *Jenkins* decision "opened the doors to the admission of psychological testimony in a multitude of legal areas." Since that time, qualified psychologists have continued to testify routinely in cases involving civil commitment, employment discrimination, eyewitness testimony, neurological injury, juvenile placements, and sentencing dispositions, to name a few, as well as the insanity defense.

During the late 1940s and 1950s, psychologists continued to consult with police departments. The psychological screening initiated by Wilmington and Toledo was adopted by other cities: Jacksonville in 1947, Berkeley in 1949, Oakland in 1950, New Orleans in 1952, and Pasadena, Philadelphia, Milwaukee, and Cleveland in 1953 (Oglesby, 1957; Gottesman, 1975). In June 1953, the Los Angeles Police Department began to administer a battery of psychological tests (MMPI, Rorschach, and a psychological interview) (Rankin, 1957, 1959). The 1957 Rankin article was the first to appear in the literature attesting to any ongoing program of psychological assessment for police applicants (Gottesman, 1975). Overall, the historical literature on psychological police screening and consulting is sparse.

PSYCHOLOGICAL CRIMINOLOGY EMERGES

In the early 1960s, psychological criminology began to show signs of life. Hans Toch (1961) edited one of the first books on that subject, *Legal and Criminal Psy-*

chology. Some may argue that Hans Gross published the first criminal psychology book in 1898 (*Kriminal psychologie*), the same year in which he was appointed Professor in Ordinary for Criminal Law and Justice Administration at the University of Czernowitz. However, Gross was a lawyer by training, in practice, and in spirit and eventually became a successful judge. His book details his observations of criminals, witnesses, jurors, and judges, but it relies very little on psychological research. This is not surprising, of course, because psychology in 1898 was far from being an integrated discipline with a rich body of knowledge. Nevertheless, it is significant that Toch's book, published over 60 years later, represents the earliest attempt to integrate, in an interdisciplinary fashion, the empirical research of psychologists relevant to criminal behavior and legal issues.

Hans J. Eysenck, in *Crime and Personality* (1964), formulated the first comprehensive theoretical statement on criminal behavior advanced by a psychologist. Shortly afterward, Edwin Megargee (1966) put forth his own heuristic statements regarding undercontrolled and overcontrolled personalities and their relationships to violence. Toch (1969) followed with *Violent Men*. The relationship between aggression and violence was studied seriously under the leadership of Leonard Berkowitz (1962), Albert Bandura (1959, 1973), and later Robert Baron (1977). The "psychopath" became the subject of vigorous theory building and research at the hands of Hare (1970) and others (e.g., Quay, 1965).

The 1970s saw a literature and research explosion in all areas of forensic psychology, which had, as Loh (1981) observes, "come of age." After an uncertain beginning and some stagnation during the postwar era, it was finally clear that this maturation was inevitable. In the following chapters, other contributors will assess forensic psychology's current status and the promise it holds for a future generation of psychologists, scholars, and legal practitioners. It is important, however, that today's researchers be continually mindful of the accomplishments and failures of the pioneers in their field.

One of the most sobering realities of the past has been the strained relationship between the legal profession and psychology. Law generally demands a conservative, skeptical perspective, but it often operates against a backdrop of social, political, and economic considerations. Psychology is a contemporary science that can go about its business more independently of these external forces. Furthermore, law seeks the absolute as it confronts the unique set of circumstances in each case it resolves. Psychology is more inclined to talk of group averages, to look for generalities and "laws" across time and situations, and to be tentative and cautious in its conclusions. Although these differences sometimes seem insurmountable, history reveals that progress in forensic psychology depends upon both psychology and law respecting and appreciating each other's perspective.

REFERENCES

Bandura, A. (1973). *Aggression: A social learning analysis.* Englewood Cliffs, NJ: Prentice-Hall.

Bandura, A., & Walters, R. H. (1959). *Adolescent aggression.* New York: Ronald Press.

Baron, R. A. (1977). *Human aggression*. New York: Plenum.

Berkowitz, L. (1962). *Aggression: A social-psychological analysis*. New York: McGraw-Hill.

Binet, A. (1900). *La suggestibilité*. Paris: Schleicher.

Binet, A. (1905). La science du termoignage. *L'Année Psychologique, 11*, 128–137.

Binet, A., & Clarparede, E. (1906). La psychologie judiciaire. *L'Année Psychologique, 12*, 274–302.

Bolton, F. E. (1896). The accuracy of recollection and observation. *Psychological Review, 3*, 286–295.

Britt, S. H. (1940). The rules of evidence—An empirical study in psychology and law. *Cornell Law Quarterly, 25*, 556–580.

Brown, M. (1926). *Legal psychology*. Indianapolis, IN: Bobbs-Merrill.

Brown v. Board of Education, 347 U.S. 483 (1954).

Burtt, H. E. (1931). *Legal psychology*. New York: Prentice-Hall.

Cahn, E. (1955). Jurisprudence. *New York University Law Review, 30*, 150–169.

Cairns, H. (1935). *Law and the social sciences*. New York: Harcourt, Brace.

Cattell, J. M. (1895). Measurements of the accuracy of recollection. *Science, 2*, 761–766.

Comment. (1979). The psychologist as expert witness: Science in the courtroom? *Maryland Law Review, 38*, 539–615.

Corsini, R. (1945). Functions of the prison psychologist. *Journal of Consulting Psychology, 9*, 101–104.

Darley, J. G., & Berdie, R. (1940). The fields of applied psychology. *Journal of Consulting Psychology, 4*, 41–52.

Eysenck, H. J. (1964). *Crime and personality*. London: Routledge & Kegan Paul.

Goddard, H. H. (1914). *Feeblemindedness: Its causes and consequences*. New York: Macmillan.

Goodman, S. A. (1984). Children's testimony in historical perspective. *Journal of Social Issues, 40*, 9–31.

Gottesman, J. (1975). *The utility of the MMPI in assessing the personality patterns of urban police applicants*. Hoboken, NJ: Stevens Institute of Technology.

Greenberg, J. (1956). Social scientists take the stand: A review and appraisal of their testimony in litigation. *Michigan Law Review, 54*, 953–970.

Hale, M. (1980). *Human science and social order: Hugo Munsterberg and origins of applied psychology*. Philadelphia: Temple University Press.

Hare, R. D. (1970). *Psychopathy: Theory and research*. New York: Wiley.

Healy, W., & Bronner, A. F. (1939). *Treatment and what happend after; a study from the Judge Baker Guidance Center*. Boston: Judge Baker Guidance Center.

Healy, W., & Bronner, A. F. (1936). *New light on delinquency and its treatment*. New Haven, CT: Yale Univ. Press.

Hidden v. Mutual Life Insurance Co., 217 F.2d 818 (4th Cir. 1954).

Horowitz, I. A., & Willging, T. E. (1984). *The psychology of law: Integration and applications*. Boston: Little, Brown.

Hutchins, R. M., & Slesinger, D. (1927). Some observations on the law of evidence—Consciousness of guilt. *University of Pennsylvania Law Review, 77*, 725–740.

Hutchins, R. M., & Slesinger, D. (1928a). Some observations on the law of evidence—The competency of witnesses. *Yale Law Journal, 37,* 1017–1028.

Hutchins, R. M., & Slesinger, D. (1928b). Some observations on the law of evidence—Spontaneous exclamations. *Columbia Law Review, 28,* 432–440.

Hutchins, R. M., & Slesinger, D. (1928c). Some observations on the law of evidence—Memory. *Harvard Law Review, 41,* 860–873.

Hutchins, R. M., & Slesinger, D. (1929). Legal psychology. *Psychological Review, 36,* 13–26.

Jenkins v. United States, 307 F.2d 637 (D.C. Cir. 1962) *en banc.*

Keller, E. I. (1918). Psychopathic laboratory at police headquarters, New York City. *Journal of Applied Psychology, 2,* 84–88.

Kluger, R. (1975). *Simple justice.* New York: Knopf.

Kuna, D. P. (1976). The psychology of advertising, 1896–1916. *Dissertation Abstracts International, 37,* 3048B. (University Microfilms No. 76–26, 875)

Kuna, D. P. (1978). One-sided portrayal of Munsterberg. *American Psychologist, 33,* 700.

Lindner, H. (1955). The work of court and prison psychologists. In G. J. Dudycha (Ed.), *Psychology for law enforcement officers.* Springfield, IL: C. C. Thomas.

Loh, W. D. (1981). Perspectives on psychology and law. *Journal of Applied Social Psychology, 11,* 314–355.

Louisell, D. W. (1955). The psychologist in today's legal world: Part I. *Minnesota Law Review, 39,* 235–260.

Louisell, D. W. (1957). The psychologist in today's legal world: Part II. *Minnesota Law Review, 41,* 731–750.

Marston, W. M. (1917). Systolic blood pressure changes in deception. *Journal of Experimental Psychology, 2,* 117–163.

Marston, W. M. (1920). Reaction-time symptoms of deception. *Journal of Experimental Psychology, 3,* 72–87.

Marston, W. M. (1921). Psychological possibilities in deception tests. *Journal of the American Institute of Criminal Law and Criminology, 11,* 551–570.

Marston, W. M. (1924). Studies in testimony. *Journal of Criminal Law and Criminology, 15,* 5–32.

Marston, W. M. (1925). Negative type reaction-time symptoms of deception. *Psychological Review, 32,* 241–247.

McCary, J. L. (1956). The psychologist as an expert witness in court. *American Psychologist, 11,* 8–13.

McCarty, D. G. (1929). *Psychology for the lawyer.* New York: Prentice-Hall.

McCary, J. L. (1956). The psychologist as an expert witness in court. *American Psychologist, 11,* 8–13.

Megargee, E. I. (1966). Undercontrolled and overcontrolled personality types in extreme antisocial aggression. *Psychological Monographs, 80* (No. 3).

Merrill, M. A. (1927). Intelligence of policemen. *Journal of Personnel Research, 5,* 511–515.

Miller, H. L., Lower, J. S., & Bleechmore, J. (1978). The clinical psychologist as an expert witness on questions of mental illness and competency. *Law and Psychology Review, 4,* 115–125.

Monahan, J., & Loftus, E. F. (1982). The psychology of law. *Annual Review of Psychology,* *33*, 441–475.

Moskowitz, M. J. (1977). Hugo Munsterberg: A study in the history of applied psychology. *American Psychologist, 32*, 824–842.

Munsterberg, H. (1908). *On the witness stand: Essays on psychology and crime.* New York: McClure.

Munsterberg, H. (1914). *Psychology and social sanity.* New York: Doubleday, Page.

Napoli, D. S. (1981). *Architects of adjustment.* Port Washington, NY: Kennikat.

Odom v. State, 174 Ala. 4, 7, 56 So. 913, 914 (1911).

Oglesby, T. W. (1957). Use of emotional screening in the selection of police applicants. *Public Personnel Review, 18*, 228–231, 235.

Paterson, D. G. (1940). Applied psychology comes of age. *Journal of Consulting Psychology, 4*, 1–9.

People v. Hawthorne, 293 Mich. 15, 291 N.W. 205 (1940).

Perlin, M. L. (1977). The legal status of the psychologist in the courtroom. *Journal of Psychiatry and Law, 5*, 41–54.

Quay, H. C. (1965). Psychopathic personality: Pathological stimulation-seeking. *American Journal of Psychiatry, 122*, 180–183.

Rankin, J. H. (1957). Preventive psychiatry in the Los Angeles Police Department. *Police, 2*, 24–29.

Rankin, J. H. (1959). Psychiatric screening of police recruits. *Public Personnel Review, 20*, 191–196.

Robinson, E. S. (1935). *Law and the lawyers.* New York: Macmillan.

Rogers, O. (1910). The unwary purchaser: A study in the psychology of trademark infringement. *Michigan Law Review, 8*, 613–644.

Rogers, O. (1918). An account of some psychological experiments on the subject of trademark infringements. *Michigan Law Review, 18*, 75–95.

Schrenck-Notzing, A. (1897). *Uber suggestion und erinnerungsfalschung im berchthold-process.* Leipzig: Johann Ambrosius Barth.

Slesinger, D., & Pilpel, M. E. (1929). Legal psychology: A bibliography and a suggestion. *Psychology Bulletin, 12*, 677–692.

Snee, T. J., & Lush, D. E. (1941). Interaction of the narrative and interrogatory methods of obtaining testimony. *Journal of Psychology, 11*, 225–236.

Snodgrass, J. (1984). William Healy (1869–1963): Pioneer child psychiatrist and criminologist. *Journal of the History of the Behavioral Sciences, 20*, 332–339.

State v. Driver, 88 W. Va. 479, 107 S.E. 189 (1921).

Stern, L. W. (1906). Zur psychologie der aussage. *Zeitschrift fur die gesamte Strafrechtswissenschaft, 23*, 56–66.

Stern, L. W. (1910). Abstracts of lectures on the psychology of testimony. *American Journal of Psychology, 21*, 273–282.

Stern, L. W. (1939). The psychology of testimony. *Journal of Abnormal and Social Psychology, 40*, 3–20.

Tapp, J. L. (1976). Psychology and the law: An overture. *Annual Review of Psychology, 27*, 359–404.

Terman, L. M. (1917). A trial of mental and pedagogical tests in a civil service examination for policemen and firemen. *Journal of Applied Psychology, 1*, 17–29.

Terrio, L., Swanson, C. R., Jr., & Chamelin, N. C. (1977). *The police personnel selection process*. Indianapolis, IN: Bobbs-Merrill.

Thurstone, L. L. (1922). The intelligence of policemen. *Journal of Personnel Research, 1*, 64–74.

Toch, H. (Ed.) (1961). *Legal and criminal psychology*. New York: Holt, Rinehart & Winston.

Toch, H. (1969). *Violent men: An inquiry into the psychology of violence*. Chicago: Aldine.

Weld, H. P., & Danzig, E. R. (1940). A study of the way in which a verdict is reached by a jury. *American Journal of Psychology, 53*, 518–536.

Weld, H. P., & Roff, M. (1938). A study in the formation of opinion based upon legal evidence. *American Journal of Psychology, 51*, 609–628.

Whipple, G. M. (1909). The observer as reporter: A survey of the "psychology of testimony." *Psychological Bulletin, 6*, 153–170.

Whipple, G. M. (1910). Recent literature on the psychology of testimony. *Psychological Bulletin, 7*, 365–368.

Whipple, G. M. (1911). Psychology of testimony. *Psychological Bulletin, 8*, 307–309.

Whipple, G. M. (1912). Psychology of testimony and report. *Psychological Bulletin, 9*, 264–269.

Whipple, G. M. (1913). Psychology of testimony and report. *Psychological Bulletin, 10*, 264–268.

Whipple, G. M. (1914). Psychology of testimony and report. *Psychological Bulletin, 11*, 245–250.

Whipple, G. M. (1915). Psychology of testimony. *Psychological Bulletin, 12*, 221–224.

Whipple, G. M. (1917). Psychology of testimony. *Psychological Bulletin, 14*, 234–236.

Wigmore, J. H. (1909). Professor Munsterberg and the psychology of testimony: Being a report of the case of *Cokestone v. Muensterberg*. *Illinois Law Review, 3*, 399–445.

Wigmore, J. H. (1940). *Evidence in trials at common law*. Boston: Little, Brown.

Winick, C. (1961). The psychology of juries. In H. Toch (Ed.), *Legal and criminal psychology*. New York: Holt, Rinehart & Winston.

CHAPTER 2

Dimensions of Forensic Psychology

ALLEN K. HESS

Civilization is nothing else but the attempt to reduce force to being the last resort.

ORTEGA Y. GASSET

This chapter is designed to describe the relationship between psychology and law, to develop the concept of discretion as a basis for the convergence of law and psychology, to suggest several ways forensic psychology can develop, and to consider areas of difference between philosophical assumptions of law and psychology.

The relationship between law and psychology is paradoxical. The argument is made that both fields concern the understanding and governing of human behavior. Examples of this convergence extend to antiquity. Yet forensic psychology with its long past has but a brief history. Some reasons for the recent development of forensic psychology are presented.

Discretion, the exercise of judgment, is central to various players in the criminal justice drama. Victims, offenders, police, prosecutors, judges and juries, and correctional personnel must make decisions that both affect and reflect facets of the criminal justice system. The state of the literature concerning the psychological processes of these decision makers is presented.

Areas of application of psychology to legal issues are further developed in the third section. These include questions of capacity and environment and perception.

Anyone working in forensic psychology needs to be aware of critical differences in the basic assumptions underlying legal and psychological practices. These assumptions and the examination of a solution proposed by some—the joint J.D.-Ph.D. degree—are presented.

A CONTEXT FOR FORENSIC PSYCHOLOGY

The first human act in the Bible is that of Eve, persuaded by the serpent, eating the forbidden fruit from the Tree of Knowledge. Adam follows suit. Thus Genesis be-

The author gratefully acknowledges the help of Herb Reich and Irving Weiner in improving the clarity of the chapter, and Kathryn, Tanya, Clara, and Joel Hess for their unflagging support.

gins with sin. When the Lord asks, "What is this you have done?" Eve projects blame, answering, "The serpent duped me, and I ate." The Lord punishes the serpent, ("On your belly shall you crawl"), Eve ("In pain shall you bear children"), and Adam ("By the sweat of your brow shall you get bread to eat") and casts them from the Garden of Eden, since "man has become like one of us, knowing good from evil," and might again eat from the tree and live forever. As if to make sure we do not miss the point, the second human act that is depicted in the Bible is a jealous Cain murdering Abel. Cain displays the psychological mechanisms of avoidance, guilt, and shame, and the Lord then forbids capital punishment ("If anyone kills Cain, sevenfold vengeance shall be taken on him") and marks Cain for all to see.

The Old Testament, the Code of Hammurabi, and the New Testament are replete not only with a catalog of perfidy but with the psychological sources as well (the jealousy of Saul, the lust of Samson perhaps fueled by the doting of his mother, the greed of Judas), processes concerning judgments (the Ninth Commandment not to bear false witness, the Solomonic decision to cut the disputed baby in two), selection of leaders (Saul from the small Tribe of Benjamin by Samuel so the large, fueding tribes knew King Saul would have no prejudice in favor of the others), administration of justice (the equity of the Code of Hammurabi wherein law, not a particular ruler's predilections, formed the basis for legal decisions), and even corporate crime (usurious money lenders in the Temple, and the political chicanery between the Saducees and the Pharisees). Of course the noblest of the human spirit is shown too (Jonathan and David's friendship, Jacob's love of justice, and Jesus' bountiful mercy), but critical to each deed or misdeed are the psychological threads woven through the characters and events.

It is surprising that, when we examine more contemporary times, we learn that psychology and law might as well have been alien disciplines, until the last two decades. This is most peculiar because when dealing with criminal responsibility issues, the Greeks and Romans emphasized the role of free will and hence capacity to harbor evil intent (mens rea) in determination of guilt, which are psychological questions. English common law resumed the Middle Age practice of finding technical guilt but granting pardons, until the frequency of such pardons established insanity as a recognized defense about the sixteenth century (Tancredi, Lieb, & Slaby, 1975). A century later, Hale distinguished total from partial insanity and cleared the way for Judge Tracy to articulate (in 1724, *Rex v. Arnold*) the "wild beast test," thought to have origins in the thirteenth or fourteenth century; to wit, a man must be so "deprived of understanding and memory and not know what he is doing, no more than an infant, than a brute, or a *wild beast*; such a one is never the object of punishment" (Tancredi et al., 1975, p. 4).

Among the reasons for the prime place of importance of the M'Naghten case (1843) is that it specified the mental components of the insanity defense ("laboring under a defective reason from disease of the mind as to not know the nature and quality of the act he was doing; or, if he did know it, that he did not know he was doing what was wrong"), and gave special status to the testimony of experts and physicians to aid in insanity determination. Consistent with general judicial practice, only isolated instances of attention to mental matters (New Hampshire Rule,

Toch, 1961, p. 154) and to the importance of "law in science and science in law" (cf. Oliver Wendell Holmes' incisive 1899 essay with the quoted phrase as its title) (Henson, 1960) mark the 1800s.

Psychological scholars (Levine & Howe, 1985) point to Judge Brandeis' use of social science data to fashion a "rational" not "arbitrary" decision regarding Oregon's ten-hour labor law for women (in *Muller v. Oregon*, 1908) as the first U.S. Supreme Court case to consider social facts. Ironically, the liberal Brandeis cited the "semi-pathological state of health of women," "female weakness," and "the particular construction of the knee and shallowness of the pelvis, and the delicate nature of the foot" making women less able than men to work long hours (Monahan & Loftus, 1982)—a line of reasoning which would vex contemporary feminists. Munsterberg's (1908) *On the witness stand* is widely cited, also, as a major psychological work influencing legal matters. However, Wigmore's (1909) derision of Munsterberg's efforts, as well as other forces, led to no significant rapprochment between psychology and law until five decades later.

The three confluent forces of the labor movement's growth and seeking of redress in the courts, the bureaucratization of our society, and the growth of the empirical and applied aspects of psychology contributed to the advent of social science in the courts. In terms of the latter, the use of Kenneth and Mamie Clark's research in *Brown v. Board of Education*, Topeka, Kansas, in 1954 heralded the court as an avenue for both the redress of civil rights violations and the legal standing of psychological facts. The Clarks studied the degree to which Northern and Southern black and white children ascribe qualities differentially to black and white dolls. On the heels of this decision (argued by Thurgood Marshall, later to become the first black U.S. Supreme Court justice), dismantling of racial segregation and correction of sundry civil rights violations occurred. In 1957, President Eisenhower mobilized the National Guard to integrate the Little Rock, Arkansas, school system in accord with judicial order, as President Kennedy was to do six years later at the University of Alabama. In effect our country experienced a revolution in social order with the process consisting of individuals nonviolently resisting injustice and placing the courts in the central position for providing justice for all races. The court's activism forced executive enforcement of the law.

Spasms of violence occurred, and, while the civil rights movement was met with brutality, the abhorrence that our citizenry felt about the violent reactions to civil rights demonstrations led to a peaceful revolution, later reinforced by civil rights legislation. The trials evolving from events in the 1960s led to social scientists' being used to help select jurors and to establish whether a jury panel was representative of the community. In fact, Bobby Seale in the Chicago Seven trial questioned whether any community in the United States could produce an appropriate peer panel to judge him at all.

In the same year as the *Brown* decision, Judge Bazelon brought M'Naghten issues into the twentieth century, expanding both the role and types of professionals in insanity determination. In the *Durham* decision, Bazelon said that insanity was to be considered as the "product" of "mental disease or defect." Emotional components, as they impaired intellectual functions, were accorded legal standing. Rather than quelling the concern about insanity tests, the 1954 Durham rule presaged the controversies later encountered on the Hinkley trial (Bower, 1984; Caplan, 1984; Taylor, 1982), which one might sardonically describe as having added a new set of emotional components, the public's, to the insanity controversy. Fueled by misunderstanding, the public was outraged by a Presidential assassin being adjudicated not guilty by reason of insanity when the typical citizen could watch the fact (*actus reus*) of the assassination attempt on the television news broadcasts and again on the weekend news summary programs.

Concurrent with the societal changes described here, psychology was changing. Its empirical base was firmly established, and social activism ("relevance versus vigor" was the label given to the curriculum debates at faculty meetings in the 1960s) carried students and faculty in its tide; in some cases these students and faculty led the way by riding the breakers of social change. The days of the trivial pursuits of Prisoner's Dilemma game paradigms gave way to a resurgence of Lewin's (1948) action research paradigm and the growth of community and preventive psychologies.

In concluding our list of influences, we must consider the complexity of society. The growth of the number of citizens in the United States eventually led to qualitative changes in and creation of social structures (Hess, 1985). Our society changed from town council meetings in the village squares of New England in the 1600s to an extensive, complex legal system mediating the conflicts among a quarter of a billion citizens. A litigious society is the term usually applied to the current lack of informal conflict resolution mechanisms.

Given the complexity of the legal system, it is difficult to begin to understand its parts as well as as how the parts interact. The next section is an introduction to the psychological aspects of the legal system.

DISCRETION AND FORENSIC PSYCHOLOGY

The undeservedly little-known article of Shaver, Gilbert, and Williams (1975) describes the concept of discretion. This is amplified in Konečni and Ebbesen's (1982) text. Essentially Shaver and colleagues review four junctures in the criminal justice system, at which critical decisions are made by individuals who operate on personal biases and predilections in making these judgments. These are the police, the prosecutor, the judge-jury, and the corrections official. Konečni and Ebbesen add the offender, victim, eye witness, and parole board to Shaver's list of subjective actors in the criminal justice system. The subjectivity of legal facts has been noted, too, as Goble (1955) describes the subjectivity of physical events: "But even facts are 'true' only as judged by a selected system of references." He proceeds to say that such a line of thought applies with greater force in the biological and social sciences, as opposed to the physical sciences. An overview of the criminal justice system, showing the different discretionary junctures, might be helpful. Figure 2.1 graphically depicts the flow of people in the criminal justice system. One can readily see at the left the large volume of crime that is undetected, unreported, unacknowledged, and

What is the sequence of events in the criminal justice system?

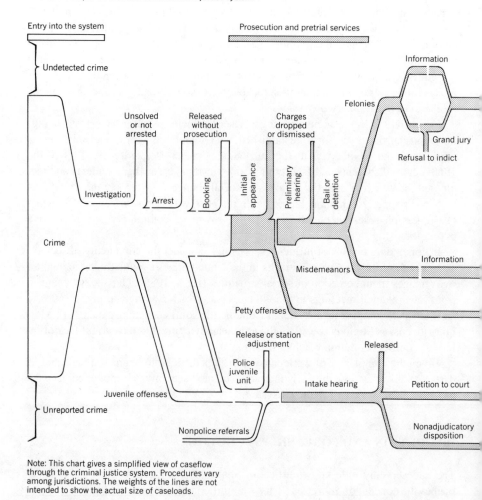

Note: This chart gives a simplified view of caseflow through the criminal justice system. Procedures vary among jurisdictions. The weights of the lines are not intended to show the actual size of caseloads.

FIGURE 2.1. Discretionary points in the criminal justice system (*Source*: From *Report to the Nation*

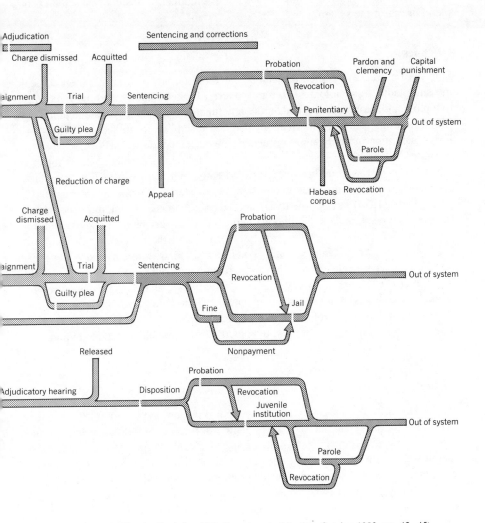

Adjudication

Sentencing and corrections

Charge dismissed   Acquitted

Probation   Pardon and   Capital
clemency   punishment

Revocation

aignment   Trial   Sentencing   Penitentiary   Out of system

Guilty plea   Parole

Reduction of charge   Habeas   Revocation
corpus

Charge   Appeal
dismissed   Acquitted   Probation

aignment   Trial   Sentencing   Revocation   Out of system

Guilty plea   Jail

Fine

Nonpayment

Released   Probation

Adjudicatory hearing   Disposition   Revocation   Out of system
Juvenile
institution

Parole

Revocation

and Justice, Bureau of Justice Statistics, U.S. Department of Justice, October 1983, pp. 42–45) simply eludes our grasp of study because of discretionary decisions that screen people in or out of the system.

Offender

Studies of correlates of offenders can be dated to Lombroso's careful phrenological measurements, to sociological factors (poverty, broken homes), and more recently to biological factors (cortical and autonomic functioning), and psychological factors (thrill seeking, delay of gratification, parental discipline techniques). Yet few efforts concerning more dynamic influences have been conducted. How does a mugger judge vulnerability in selecting victims, or a housebreaker judge which home to rob in terms of risk-benefit ratios? How do emotional factors influence a person's decision to partake in drugs or prostitution, or are economic concerns primary in the latter? Plate (1975) says crime really does pay and proceeds to itemize the hours, salaries, overhead, and the likelihood of conviction, of serving time and of the duration of the sentence for sundry perpetrators including the peep-show clerk, shoplifter, drug importer, securities thief, hotel night burglar, hit man, and tax evader. Sociologists have been schooled in ethnographic approaches of entering the world of street crime [Sutherland's (1937) *Professional thief*, Shaw's (1930) *Jack roller*] —an approach psychologists seem to have eschewed in favor of the contrasted groups (*t* test with a control and experimental group) method. There is every reason to use ethnographic approaches *and* to apply the experimental method to hypotheses discovered therein.

Victim

Before any criminal charges can be initiated by a person, the person must recognize that he or she has been harmed. Many factors influence an individual in reaching this threshold decision. For example, if an individual is ignorant of certain laws, then that person would not recognize that harm has taken place. Such a case can occur when a person was passed over for promotion or pay raises in a discriminatory fashion, or was subject to noxious work conditions, failing to know the conditions are in violation of statutes. Second, victims may be unaware of theft of property from their homes or of a hidden finance charge or of a poisoning of the food chain, as in the PBB (polybutylene biphenyl) disaster. Third, a victim may recognize an action and its illegality but decide not to pursue legal redress because of (1) lack of incontrovertible evidence, (2) a fear of recrimination, (3) a personal relationship with the perpetrator, (4) psychological costs such as exposure of one's own activities to police, prosecutors, and courts (as in the case of a "John" who is robbed by a prostitute or pimp), (5) time and monetary costs, or (6) lack of legal standing (a child cannot pursue legal actions as a practical matter of course).

We have scant empirical literature on the victim and the threshold factors leading to the recognition that a wrongful event occurred. Oliver Wendell Holmes' (1898–9) *Law in science and science in law* describes "the grounds upon which evidence of fresh complaint by a ravished woman is admitted as part of the government's case in an indictment of rape." He describes the prevailing assumption that the outrage is so great that a virtuous woman would disclose it at the first suitable opportunity. He contests this assumption, saying that it is about the last crime in which such a presumption could be made, instead saying a person with a picked pocket or assault upon himself would be more likely to reveal that victimization than a woman experiencing such a horror as rape. Ennis's (1967) household crime surveys confirm Holmes' thinking.

Police

The police are the only group of people to whom we give the discretionary power to take a citizen's life. Also, we cede to them the power to arrest citizens, or stop the citizens' abilities to govern their own actions. The most visible part of the criminal justice system, the police, are probably the most studied. Suffice it to say many factors influence police decision making. In the small college town in which I reside, most residents have color-coded parking stickers indicating whether the car can be parked in administrator-faculty (A), staff (B), or student (C and D) lots. Local rumor has it that A sticker cars are less prone to speeding tickets. Police discretion is crucial since police have major gatekeeping and evidence-gathering powers regarding who gets ensnared in the system and who is allowed a second chance. Among the sources for the interested reader to further explore police discretion are Bartol (1983), Broderick (1977), Niederhoffer and Blumberg (1973), Stotland and Berberich (1979), and Reiser and Klyver (Chapter 16).

Prosecutor

The prosecuting or district attorney of a municipality or county, and the parallel state office of the attorney general, is charged with the determination as to whether there is enough evidence gathered already or potentially available to sustain a charge at a particular level. A number of subjective factors may enter the district attorney's determination. The prosecutor, an elected official, sensing the public concern about an issue such as drunk driving (National Institute of Justice, 1985) and the court's propensity to treat the charge seriously, may conclude that it is worth investing the time and personnel in vigorously prosecuting such charges. A parallel example concerns domestic violence. All too often charges drawn in the conflict-filled/alcohol-fueled atmosphere of a Saturday night are dropped by spouses giving their remorse-filled, apologetic husbands "one more chance" on a peaceful Sunday morning. Frustrated prosecutors and police lobbied for and gained changes in the law in some jurisdictions. Denver (Colorado), for example, allows prosecutors to pursue assault charges in the absence of the wife's sustaining the charges.

On a more subtle level, prosecutors can decide how intensely they wish to prosecute charges, influenced in part by who the victim and the perpetrator happen to be. The public is most familiar with the aspect of this practice known as plea bargaining wherein a person who may know of some information gains an advantage of a lesser charge and lighter punishment being sought by the prosecutor in exchange for the information. Even more serious are the practices of "important" persons and their children escaping the same level of prosecution "ordinary" people might receive. The appearance of such incidents can concern the public, as happened in the Ted Kennedy–Mary Jo Kopechne tragedy or the Ferraros' son's alleged drug trafficking not being vigorously prosecuted. To be bipartisan, we must include the seemingly chronic nonprosecutorial stance of President Reagan's Department of Justice regarding labor racketeering or the bombings of abortion clinics, but the active prosecution by the Department of Justice of physicians in "Baby Jane Doe" cases involving failing to take heroic measures to continue terminally sick children's lives.

Such appearances of stratified justice, depending on socio-politico-economic levels, can erode public confidence quickly. Moreover, it can be used by convicted felons as handy rationalizations regarding their own punishment as being unjustified. I heard a litany of such comments when working as a prison psychologist during the period when Vice President Agnew pleaded nolo contendre to criminal charges. A person serving 2 years for a $700 theft is quick to point out that Agnew's alleged bribe-taking in his White House office netted him no time served at all.

With the exception of attempts to focus prosecutor task forces on targeted crimes (organized crime, prostitution, drugs), the prosecutor's decision-making and discretionary role has been the focus of almost no research (Shaver et al., 1975; Konečni & Ebbesen, 1982) concerning its crucial role in our justice system.

Judge–Jury

The very term *judge* indicates discretionary processes. Most people are surprised to learn that over 95 percent of criminal cases which go to trial are heard by judges alone, and not tried by juries. Why is there all the research and applied work on juror selection and jury dynamics, and the absence of social science research concerning judges? Probably the prime reason is the effect of trials on the psyche of our *polis* or political society. Trials generally, and jury trials specifically, serve us much as Greek tragedies and medieval "Everyman" plays served earlier societies. Even though the verdicts may be erroneous in the moment, influenced by public passions or political considerations, the lessons are vividly played out.

Consider the trial of Joseph Levy in 1905 in Atlanta. He was accused of raping a female. A mob, inflamed by anti-Semitic passions, hanged him after a hasty, error-filled trial. Bruno Hauptman, accused of the Lindbergh kidnapping and murder, was executed amid the anti-Teutonic feelings fueled by World War I and the subsequent decades. In 1919 Attorney General Palmer warned America of "60,000 dangerous alien radicals who, by virtue of bombings and assassinations, planned on transporting the virulent Bolshevik revolution to our shores." The next year Sacco and Vanzetti were indicted and tried for a payroll robbery and dual murder. After exhausting appeals, they were executed in 1927 with some scholars claiming the issues of guilt and of severity of sentencing being a function of the xenophobic fear of foreigners at that time (Weeks, 1958).

These trials captivate us because they encapsulate important moral issues for the public. The church council had to show that it was the church and not her own voices which Joan of Arc must heed. The fact that this hegemony went beyond the public sense of morality made the case famous. Levy was recently posthumously pardoned when, some 75 years later, another person admitted guilt. Doubts about the guilt of Hauptmann, Sacco and Vanzetti, and the Rosenbergs, accused of selling America's atomic secrets after World War II amid a growing McCarthyism, have been raised. These trials became notorious because the issues of fairness, due process, and legitimacy of the legal system mixed with the temper of the times. Shrewdly recognizing the need for legal justification or legitimization, Cromwell tried King Charles; Hitler tried those accused of burning the Reichstag; and the Soviets conducted sham trials of political dissidents with great ritualistic displays of due process (Koestler, 1968). Arnold (1965) cites the ex post facto Nuremberg trials as unfair since waging an aggressive war was not a criminal offense and since the tribunal was not impartial. But the Russians joined the tribunals which were to establish a moral principle of peaceful international relations. "They [trials] dramatically present the moral values of a community in a way that could not be done by logical formulation" (Arnold, 1965, p. 143). As an ironic aside, we note that participation in these morality plays is costly—Joan of Arc, Hauptman, Sacco and Vanzetti, Levy, and King Charles lost the trial and their lives. Scopes, Bobby Seale, Cosentino (prosecutor in the Ford Pinto case), Eldridge Cleaver, and Patty Hearst found that losing in contemporary times is less perilous to one's life span. Moreover, though in each case the trial was lost, the cause was won.

In recent times, and in civil cases too, the issues of consumer safety (the Pinto case in which the automotive company was alleged to have designed and produced a vehicle which carried the risk of immolating its passengers) and of homosexual couples' rights to adopt children play out the value problems of our society. The widow of a cigarette smoker and the mother of a deceased 18-year-old snuff user brought suits against tobacco companies for wrongful death by marketing a lethal product (in both cases the plaintiffs lost). Such trials are defining the current lines of responsibility between consumers and companies, from a former caveat emptor position where the consumer assumed much of the risk for products to a position in which the manufacturer must anticipate consequences of products (strict liability). Juries and judges will continue the moral education of the *polis* by defining values in the courtroom.

Cohen (1961), Cohn and Udolf (1979), Frankel (1973), Greenberg and Ruback (1982), Kerr (1982), Konečni and Ebbesen (1982), Saks and Hastie (1978), Winick (1961, 1979), and Winick, Gerver, and Blumberg (1961) have described the decision-making process, wide latitudes of discretion, and factors influencing these processes in juries. Judges' discretion has been less often the subject of research.

Corrections

By the end of 1984, 2.6 million Americans, or one in every 65, were in prison, on probation, or on parole (Harlow, 1986). Contrary to the image many law-and-order politicians convey, we lock up more of our citizens for longer periods of time than any other country except South Africa (the data on the Soviet Union are not conclusive). The typical state inmate has served 1½ years of an 8½-year maximum sentence (U.S. Department of Justice, 1982). This contrasts with Japan, for example, which has a typical sentence of several months to a year with the average maximum term of 3 years. The Japanese system is one of strict regimentation and a heavy moral resocialization program with tight schedules for each day. However, any correctional official abusing prisoners serves a term in that prison.

The U.S. system is replete with discretionary decisions. In jurisdictions with crowded state prisons, state inmates may remain in local jails serving time at the discretion of the local sheriff. It is not uncommon for such inmates to develop a relationship with the sheriff since this inmate may be in the jail for months while the typical jail inmate serves a mean of 17 days and a mode of 3 days. Thus the most logical trustee is the one who learns the jail routine; ironically a majority of jail inmates are not convicted of any crime but are being charged or awaiting trial, and they might be in the charge of a convicted felon. Who is remanded to state custody and who remains in jail is a local decision, typically the sheriff's in consultation with the district attorney and other local officials.

The classification of the prisoner and subsequent placement in various facilities with different types of programming is in the purview of the prison officials. In the film *Cool Hand Luke* the prison camp warden, played by Strother Martin, tells Luke, "Luke, you're mine." Times have changed in that many due process and other constitutional safeguards make incarceration more lawful, but corrections officials still have wide discretionary capacities. About 1983 a psychologist, faced with overcrowded prisons, placed a dangerous and habitual offender in the facility with the most difficult and long-term offenders. Within a month the prisoner was dead of stab wounds for being suspected as an informer. His family sued, claiming the psychologist should have believed the deceased person's claims of having enemies in the system. Different facilities provide vastly different kinds of time; though some are easier than others, none are "country clubs." Judging which kind of time a prisoner serves is at the discretion of correctional classification staff.

Within a facility a prisoner can be assigned field work in 100-degree temperatures or be a psychologist's clerk in air-conditioned offices, scoring other prisoners' intelligence and personality tests—quite different experiences. Prisons have courts within them to judge alleged infractions during the serving of the sentence. The time they mete out is just as real as that of the original court sentence.

The amount of time served (most often a third of the sentence or 6 years, 10 months) is determined by the parole board. For each person incarcerated, there are 3.8 persons on probation for an average of 3 years, 1 month, and for each person paroled, there are 1.7 persons in state prison (U.S. Department of Justice, 1985). Thus some 4.4 people are on community supervision for each person in custody. While studies by social scientists of correctional officers are not common, studies of parole and probation officers and their decision making are strikingly rare. This area is all the more critical when one considers that parole and probation sectors of corrections will continue to grow because of their cost effectiveness ($20,000 to incarcerate a felon versus a few hundred dollars for parole-probation per annum, and in some programs community-based felons pay the state, creating income for corrections), the burgeoning number of released offenders, and new developments such an electronically monitored home confinement (Ford & Schmidt, 1985). In summary, the people in various stages of the criminal justice system operate from psychologically determined frames of reference which merit further study.

FURTHER AREAS OF APPLICATION

Redmount (1965) described a number of ways lawyers can use psychologists. This section examines and extends his list and raises conceptual issues meriting exploration.

Capacity

A range of questions is subsumed by this concept. Essentially, to carry out a legal function, one must have the capacity to apprehend contemplated actions. For example, testamentary capacity (Spaulding, 1985) concerns the ability to make a valid will. Redmount suggests attorneys use psychological assessment at the time a will is drafted to support the will in the event that it is contested after the testator is deceased. Some attorneys have begun to use videotapes, some two decades after Redmount's advice, but considering the cost of a complete psychological test battery in contrast to the legal fees of a contested will litigation plus the possibility that a valid will (and the wishes of the decedent) may be denied, one can only wonder why such practices have not developed.

Capacity, of course, is important in many others areas. For example, a neurologist testified before a judicial tribunal concerning the fitness of an alcoholic judge who behaved erratically and likely suffered hemorrhagic brain dysfunction from substance abuse. Another hospital-based psychologist was called on to help determine which people could understand medical procedures so they could give valid consent, or when guardians or other family members needed to be consulted. In his practice this involved controversial sterilization procedures for indigent, unwed mothers raising many complex ethical issues. Among the factors he was asked to weigh was the mother's fitness to raise offspring should the mother not be sterilized and bear more children. Issues taught in graduate education seem neat and tidy and almost a polar opposite to the awesome and untidy decisions faced by psychologists in these examples.

Of course criminal lawyers have become accustomed to psychological testimony in terms of competency issues. Our adversarial system of justice is inherited from centuries past when good was pitted against evil in trials by combat. Sometimes the combat took malevolent turns such as when the Inquisition was used to excise the devil presumably inhabiting some individuals. Sometimes the excision was by fire, drawing and quartering and other torments of the flesh, much to the acute discomfort of the putative host. In more modern times it is required that when the State versus Jones, Jones be competent to assist his or her attorney in mounting the best possible defense. If Jones is incompetent to stand trial, as may be the case in a posttraumatic stress disorder victim (Daniels, 1984), then the fight, or trial, is unfair. These issues are ably enunciated in Slovenko (Chapter 8), and Roesch and Golding (Chapter 14).

Another capacity considered in criminal trials is whether the accused was sane at the time of the crime. Was the person capable of governing or "tokening" (Meehl, Livermore, & Malmquist, 1968) his or her behavior at the time of the crime? Tokening involves putting verbal, conceptual, and volutional "handles" on one's actions in a situation. Contrary to popular belief, insanity is a relatively uncommon defense and, when it succeeds, usually nets the defendant time in a prison unit of a state mental hospital or the hospital unit of a state prison (Pasewark & McGinley, 1985). Kaplan's (1977) article "The mad and the bad: An inquiry into the disposition of the criminally insane" perhaps says much in his title concerning the conceptual muddle we face after an insanity plea is sustained, despite attempts at semantic solutions such as guilty but mentally ill.

Insanity is a manifestation of a basic philosophical pillar of our justice system. This logic holds that people of reason will be governed by law. Law provides punishment severe enough that it should outweigh the hedonic gain of a crime, according to the philosophy of J. Bentham, J. Mill and J. S. Mill. Thus those incapable of reason or responsibility to make utilitarian , decisions cannot appreciate the nature of their actions, and thus cannot be criminally guilty. As Jones simply states, "Crime is *voluntary conduct that violates a public law and for which punishment may be imposed in the name of the state*" (1978, p. 3). Historically, those held to be incapable of voluntary, tokened conduct include animals, children, women, mentally impaired (retarded or abnormal), and blacks. While they could commit an *actus reus* or evil act, they were presumed to lack sufficient capacities to possess mens rea or the requisite evil mind. Before this turn of events, in Europe such specters could be seen as cows being hanged for falling on and killing a farmer. Eventually cows were ruled beyond the purview of the courts while the four other groups were attributed varying degrees of responsibility, ranging from a little (children) to complete legal capacity (women and blacks) although both of the latter groups may still face de facto limitations in courts and society.

Since these changes occurred, we have seen some exotic new defenses concerning capacity as in the "Twinkie" defense by Mike White in the killing of San Francisco Councilman Harvey Milk; the XYY defense (now largely discredited) (Owen, 1972); the premenstrual syndrome defense in which progesterone deficiency is said to trigger uncontrollable irritability in women; the "lawn fertilizer" defense in which a gardener pleaded that chemicals emitted from lawn fertilizer mentally affected him; and Zamora's "subliminal TV intoxication" defense where he claimed to have committed murder because of the hypnogogic influence of television on his ability to control himself. All such defenses, to date, have failed. More tragic is the woman who killed a five-year-old child in the belief that he was an attack rabbit poised to assault her. There is little question that insanity questions will continue to receive a disproportionate amount of attention relative to its use and effect in criminal trials. One hopes these tempests will occasion some empirical research on methods of defining insanity (Hans & Slater, 1984; Fingarette, 1985a, 1985b), on the dynamics and outcomes of such pleas, and on what happens to insanity defendants over time.

One rather curious procedure is the legal requirement that a person be certified as sane before he or she is executed (Slovenko, 1986). The law holds that the offender must appreciate or experience the punishment as fits the utilitarian position. If they cannot appreciate the punishment, there is no sense in administering it—an odd way to teach someone a lesson in the case of capital punishment.

One last general capacity bridges this section and the next. As we are exposed to more diverse information and more complex decisions, it seems that a shift in the burden of responsibility for products and services has occurred, as mentioned before, from a doctrine of caveat emptor or the buyer beware, to one of some burden residing in the producers. In part this is a recognition that consumers do not have the capacity to be able to make prudent decisions given the technical information involved in consuming certain products and services. Some advertising involves deception beyond the consumer's ability to decipher (Craswell, 1985). A related question arises because, in purchasing these goods and services, contracts are signed and warranties are assumed. Often these contracts and warranties are written in legalese. Consequently, there has been a brief and apparently ill-fated movement toward plain-talk contracts and product warranties so these documents can be understood by a generally educated consumer.

Environment and Perception

Living in the everyday world, we carry an unstated legal obligation to comport ourselves as would a "reasonable man." Yet what is reasonable for what sort of person under which circumstances is ill defined. Consider whether it might be reasonable for a young lady to punch a man in his jaw, breaking it and rendering him unconscious. Of course, if the woman were a flight attendant and if the fellow had screamed for no apparent reason that the airplane was going to crash because God told him so, with passengers growing increasingly upset and children beginning to weep, then the stewardess may be a heroine. Perhaps she even had a duty to perform in such a way, and lack of such actions would actually make her negligent. The standards of conduct we use in judging people's behavior are ill defined and dependent on various circumstances and capacities of the individual. Ironically, earning a diplomate in surgery or clinical psychology renders the practitioner legally liable for higher standards of performance or professional competence than the diplomate's nondiplomated colleagues. The point is that the reasonable man is a current pleasant fiction but that we may have the means, by gathering normative data, to make this fiction more factual for judicial and jury decision making.

Consider that tort law holds plaintiffs responsible for proving one of several degrees of foreseeability of harm by the defendant if the latter is to be judged guilty. If a person fails to exercise "ordinary care" in his or her actions, for example, leaving a loaded handgun around the house, or the car keys in the ignition, or allowing a party guest to drive from the party after heavy alcohol consumption, that person might be held negligent. If a person shows disregard for danger, say in letting a friend borrow a car knowing it has failing brakes, his or her actions might be judged reckless and wanton. If a person showed deliberate invasion of others' rights, as in writing a promotion or tenure letter about a colleague which knowingly contains falsehoods and costs the colleague tenure or promotion, or a young man refuses to let a woman leave his dwelling until she consents to a sexual act, he or she might be held to the degree of intentional harm. How are the degrees of intent and foreseeability of harm judged by people?

Johnson and Drobny (1985) consider the way a "causal unit" (Heider, 1944) or a psychological event may be construed by a jury. They show, in a series of experiments, that subjects allowed proximity to influence their determinations of liability, foreseeability, control and negligence—even though tort holds that physical remoteness (setting a bomb off at a distance), temporal remoteness (setting a time bomb), and mechanical remoteness (setting a "Rube Goldberg" causal chain in motion where device A triggers B which triggers C and so forth until the bomb is exploded)—are irrelevant as mitigations of guilt. Research in areas about how people construe liability, the degree to which psychologically based biasing factors affect decision making, and the mitigation of liability are fertile and unexplored areas for psycholegal and social psychology research.

Consider such problems as traffic signals and airport landing conditions. Cognitive and perceptual psychology has a direct contribution to make in terms of guiding traffic controllers to plan the optimum content, forms, and placement of traffic signals for people to perceive and process information. Concerning airports, the type of lighting, weather, and air traffic conditions are complex factors that the pilot and air controller consider in making critical decisions. Multimillion-dollar suits result each year from air disasters. While perceptual psychologists can serve as expert witnesses, it seems cost-efficient and humane to hire them in a preventive, planning role in designing airport control systems.

Each year about 300 people commit suicide in jail. Several multimillion-dollar suits for failure to provide care have resulted. Psychologists have been involved in jail design, jailer training, jail personnel and procedure policies, and in psychological autopsies.

Considering other aspects of our environment, psychologists have become central in debates on the effects of pornography and of viewing television violence and of the "mental control" of others on people's behavior. Perhaps the Zamora case is hyperbole, but the case of Patty Hearst's bank robbery and of Jim Jones' Guyanese "paradise," where he induced 900 suicide-murders, is less laughable. How do environmental factors fit into legal concepts of duress, of responsibility, and of diminished capacity?

Psychologists have become immersed in the study of eyewitness reliability (actually validity in terms of psychometric theory), but measurement of association is an area of cognitive psychology that has not received much attention. In trademark cases (e.g., *Coca-Cola Co. v. Chero-Cola Co.*) the central questions was, "Is the name, logo, or trademarked symbol of one company infringed upon by another due to the similarity of the symbols which the public might confuse." Thus a company which invested decades of time and millions of advertising dollars might have these investments "stolen" by a competitor. The National Broadcasting Company (NBC) began using a block letter "N" for its logo but discovered that this was the existing logo of the University of Nebraska. The two parties reached an out-of-court settlement.

The study of how noise, temperature, and crowding influence human and animal performance has had forensic impact. The first two factors have influenced conditions in some workplaces, while the latter contributed to court decisions on prison conditions. Sass (1986) asserts that workers have the right to know about hazardous work situations, to participate in discussion, and to refuse hazardous work.

A new set of terms denoting various disasters have occupied our thoughts: Love Canal, Chernobyl, Three Mile Island, Bhopal, AIDS, toxic shock syndrome, Dioxin, secondary smoking, acid rain, yellow rain, DDT, Agent Orange, cyanide laced Tylenol, asbestos fibers, red tide, vinyl chloride, PBBs, PCBs, red dye No. 2, and VDT. Psychologists have a role in assessing physical, psychomotor, neurophysical, cognitive, and emotional dysfunctions due to these toxic agents. Moreover, Foster (1986), a bioengineer, presented a sensitive psychological analysis of the data on video display terminals and their suspected link to birth defects and the way emotional factors played into creation of a debate. Specifically, he wrote that when the stakes are high and the data are ambiguous or complex, anxiety and miscommunication result. The question remains open as to whether external (VDT) rays, internal (anxiety, stress), or a commingling of factors account for maladies that may be technologically inspired.

Thus there are theoretically challenging and pragmatically important ways for psychologists to become involved in legal aspects of environmental issues. These include the study of fear (Janis, 1983) and stress (Lazarus, 1983), information diffusion, and rumor control. Psychologists can be involved in damage assessment and in consulting with companies on the amelioration of damage. This can occur by effective presentation of information and by prevention of damage. The disasters, from Love Canal to VDT, for the most part suggest unwitting or unintentional damage, hence no prevention efforts were made (if they were intentional, the clever schemer could hardly include prevention or intent could be inferred). Consider the possible role of the psychologist, skilled in ergonomics and motor functioning, in proactively helping to "harden" the targets of domestic terrorism. Can we design tamper-resistant packages which are still able to be opened by aged and arthritic consumers? We coped with airline hijacking. Can we do better in coping with assaults on our senses such as Custer's Revenge, a video game in which an animated Custer inflicts forced intercourse on an Indian maiden?

Mitroff and Kilmann (1984) cogently argue that business schools and their graduates are unschooled in social sciences to the point that their conceptual set does not include psychological factors. This failure to consider the range of constitutents in society results in vulnerability to moral indignity (Custer's Revenge), tort liability (Rely tampons), and criminal terrorism (cyanide lacing of Tylenol and Excedrin). They argue that we need to anticipate who are the shareholders and what are their stakes in order to prevent corporate tragedies. Thus, anticipating the 1984 Los Angeles Olympics as a terrorist theater, understanding terrorist motivation, and preempting it was a real success story. Understanding that the manufacturer of Custer's Revenge did not place a priority on customer relations or building his company's name but said, "We're in this business to make bank deposits" (Brown, 1982), allows us to know what effective sanctions to apply to him, and to propose such sanctions to prevent future egregious actions. There is much to be done in the converging areas of psychology, legal issues, and the environment.

Individual Differences

Measurement of individual differences is one of psychology's most heritable foundations. In addition to testing capacities for such qualities as competency and capacity, and for employee aptitudes, assessment for accident proneness and development of accident prevention programs have been conducted (DeBobes, 1986). Between 1980 and 1986 work stress claims increased from 4.7 percent to 11 percent of work-related disease claims, accounting for over $30 million of claims in 32 states surveyed (Goode, 1986). He says that the maladies our fathers shrugged off as a personal weakness such as admitting to mental stress, a new generation has no such qualms claiming. So far no one has screened stress-vulnerable people, and in fact the fabled type A workaholic seems to fit a favored stereotype, so employers have assumed the type A person was a desirable employee. Psychologists might find type A or B people to be differentially effective in different situations and be helpful in mitigating stress factors.

Police and corrections sectors of the criminal justice system employ psychologists for screening personnel. In fact not to do so and then have an employee misbehave for emotional reasons would leave the hiring agency legally vulnerable. Lie detection, too, has been explored by psychologists (Kleinmuntz, 1985) and merits more research (Iacono & Patrick, chapter 17).

Punishment is a major problem of the criminal justice system. It has been central to learning and motivation theories; yet punishment has not received any collaborative attention from law and psychology. Theories of psychopathy (Eysenck, 1976; Lykken, 1957; Quay, 1965) involve the concept of people who are differentially sensitive to stimuli. One of the avowed goals in sentencing felons is correcting or rehabilitating or at least deterring them in terms of future behavior. One of the biggest problems in prisons is idle time and lack of programming. Yet the major preoccupation of prisoners is passing time and of correctional psychologists is passing paperwork along or attending meetings (and passing time). Psychological reports are cosmetic with little differential treatment occurring consequent to classification. Despite the melodrama of Kubrick's movie *Clockwork Orange*, it seems that differential treatment has worked (Jesness, 1975) and should be extended to include more creative sentencing given a person's individual differences. As an example, if we know psychopaths tolerate boredom poorly, might psychopaths be responsive to solitary confinement and change their conduct to gain relief? Yet the gap between research on boredom susceptibility and therapeutic gain in the real world of the prison has not been bridged (Hess, 1973).

Bukstel and Kilmann (1980) reviewed 90 studies and found some individuals deteriorate in prison, some remain unchanged, and some improve on performance, personality, and attitude measures. They call for research on the complex interactions among crowding, solitary confinement, individual differences, institutional orientation, peer group affiliation, and determinate versus indeterminate sentencing. Since Clemmer's (1940) concept of "prisonization," the assumption of the taking on of folkways, mores, customs, and the culture of the penitentiary has been a truism. It is time the mores of the institution were prosocial and determined by responsible moral agents of our society. Psychologists should be centrally involved with such a movement.

Finally, research should include insightful analyses such as that of Perry (1984), who examined the motivations of Malcolm X and Jack Abbott, concluding they were anything but suited to live out of the prison by any measure of temperament or conduct or attitude at the time of their releases. The hidden dynamics of how Malcolm X, a streetwise criminal, pawned a stolen, inscribed ring for a dollar, leaving his name at the pawn shop, how his only parenting was by a caretaker "Ma" Swerlin in a detention home whereas his own parents nearly beat him to death, and how he felt protected from sinful distractions in prison, leads one to appreciate his personality dynamics. Abbott said there were fewer uncertainties in life in prison, that he did not recognize that he "turned the key on myself" spending almost all his years after age nine locked in a cell, and agitated, he called his literary agent because "he had no idea what kind of a store to go to buy toothpaste" (p. 225). Clearly, we have dual challenges of developing better theories and research on individual differences and system dynamics, and applying these in the real world.

PERSPECTIVES OF FORENSIC PSYCHOLOGY

How Psychology and Law Participate

Haney (1980) and Bartol (1983) describe three ways psychology and law relate or, to use the philosophical term, *participate* (i.e., help define the nature of each other). Psychology *in* the law refers to specific applications by psychologists such as testimony about insanity or about whether prison conditions in a specific setting are egregious to the point of violating the 5th and 14th amendments or whether one or another parent is more fit for child custody. Johnson & Johnson was in the news because of a contested will which divided over one-third of a billion dollars. Psychologists could be helpful "in the law" in such a case. Impact in a particular case can be potent, but unless a class action is involved (e.g., conditions of confinement), it is limited to the case at hand.

Psychology *and* the law studies facets of the legal system ranging from police discretion in wife abuse calls (Waaland & Keeley, 1985), eyewitness validity, decision strategies attorneys use on voir dire juror selections, the effects of qualitative versus quantitative standards of proof (Kagehiro & Stanton, 1985) on jury decisions, how the foremen of a jury is selected (Strodtbeck & Lipinski, 1985), what effect jury size has on the jury's decision, effects of using elderliness as a defense (Cohen, 1985), to how the victim–witness can be better treated so as to be spared further emotional trauma and to be able to render more telling testimony. Can we help define community standards on issues such as tolerance for pornography? A toy company was in the news for product safety issues where one of their products was found to be potentiallty injurious to infants and was recalled. Determination of danger and the effectiveness of various methods of alerting consumers about the recall would concern psychology and the law.

Psychology *of* the law involves such abstract issues as why some laws are obeyed and others flouted; how white-collar, corporate, and environmental pollution criminals rationalize their crimes; and what factors are involved in using female guards in male facilities in contrast to using male guards in female facilities (Crouch, 1985) —the former having encountered much more system resistance. How do citizens experience the stress of crime (Riger, 1985), and is the life-without-parole sentence a license to kill and, if so, from whose perspective (the inmate, his peers, the guards, the warden)? Is some of the public's sentiment for capital punishment merely the manifestation of lower Kohlbergian moral stages, or is there some innate emotional balance humans feel when they see young lives brutally snuffed out by a serial killer such as Bundy and they feel some measure of justice or balancing by taking his life? Johnson & Johnson has borne the brunt of the diabolical cyanide lacing of their Tylenol, a problem of psychology of the law. Notions of a "just world" (Lerner, 1975) and of how political ideas such as fairness and police power are formed in child and adolescence (Hess & Torney, 1967) are part of the psychology of the law.

Others

Some issues either fall outside this trichotomy of Haney and Bartol or overlap categories. For example, the social and legal implications of a child crisis telephone line (Ney, Johnston, & Herron, 1985) raise questions of liability for the individual allegedly mishandling a call, questions of making helpless and hapless children more proactive in that they can now report family problems, and questions about how communities now need to relate to children as other than a completely unempowered nonconstituency. Similarly, issues such as terrorism, elderly abuse, nicotine addiction, disposition of drunk driving, and forming neighborhood conflict resolution centers to relieve court calendars (National Institute of Justice, 1985) overlap the categories.

Some mention of the scope of legal fields will help the reader see that fields other than psychology are diverse. Law specialties include admiralty, administrative (Social Security, regulatory bodies), antitrust, banking/bankruptcy, business, civil rights, civil trial procedure, corporate, criminal, environmental, family, insurance, international, labor, military, real property, and tax law. Most of these law specialties also involve psycholegal issues.

Once one begins to understand psycholegal aspects of situations, it is hard not to see psycholegal dimensions. The July 1986 issue of the *Psychological Bulletin* contains seven review articles, four of which have direct impact on forensic psychology. The first concerns perceiving character in faces ("he just does not look like he would have molested that child"); the second is about sex differences in motor activity ("are women unsuited for some kinds of work"); the third concerns perception of force and weight (consider eyewitness perception of an accident or assault); and the fourth review concerns gaze and eye contact (consider judgments of whether a sexual or aggressive action was provoked). Yet we should examine whether there are some limits to psycholegal applications and how these disciplines intersect.

Caveat

One must wonder about the applicability of much social science research to individual legal cases. Monohan and Loftus (1982) discuss the issues of simulation studies. Sheehy (1985) raises four problems including failure to specify the precise function of simulation, failure to enumerate state variables which might obviate the findings, problems of generalization between simulation and referent systems (Hess, 1980), and problems with unreplicated simulations. Elliott (1985) wonders about the selective inclusion of research in an author's (or expert witness's) literature review, and the selective interpretation of reviewed research.

Advertisement for a recently published book presents a veiled threat to attorneys that if you use this book, "you'll have no excuse for neglecting the psychological injuries of your clients." No attorney wants the spectre of a suit from a client who claims that a case was not actively pursued. We face these crass marketplace pressures to skew data in order to win when forensic psychology is taken from the laboratory to the field.

Clearly we have entered a new era in which social science research may wind up in the courtroom. I have asked researchers about whether they thought of the forensic aspects of their work. Their reactions are most ironic. On one hand, they wish their work to have impact, yet when one asks them if they considered how their findings will look when quoted in court, they portray several reactions. First, they are puzzled, as if the questions were in need of translation, then various degrees of fear register. Finally, a few show mixtures of pleasure and solemnity, while most retreat from the question and the inquirer to go to class or the laboratory. Perhaps it is as it should be, with authors writing for journals, but a more realistic view holds that authors should weigh their words because their words are finding their way to the scales of justice.

We may have reached the stage of development in forensic psychology which calls for critique much as psychology per se has been criticized (cf. Gross's *The brain watchers*, 1962, and Packard's *The people shapers*, 1977). Levine and Howe (1985) fear the validity of scientific research may be decided in courts rather than in laboratories and in debates in colloquia and seminars. In the face of evidence that clinical judges were unreliable in predicting dangerousness, the U.S. Supreme Court, in *Barefoot v. Estelle* (1983) reasoned that the adversary process would protect against said unreliability in arriving at just decisions. Levine and Howe and the author are troubled by science, as in the Scopes case, being determined in courtrooms.

BASES OF PSYCHOLOGY AND LAW

We need to examine the bases on which law and psychology rest since anyone entering the convergent fields of psychology and law unmindful of these contrasting bases is headed for tragedy. Table 2.1 delineates prominent distinctions.

Knowledge

The type of knowledge differs between psychology and law in that the law deduces conclusions based on logic, precedent, and case law. Law tends to operate from general principles from which are drawn specific applications to the particularities of the case at hand. Social science, despite Kuhn's (1962) disclaimer, is cumulative or at least operates that way, attempting to develop parametric descriptions of natural laws. Data are generated in order to shape and sharpen scientific theories and general principles. Surely the data and methods are dependent on the prevailing theory, but the aim of science is for successive theory revision.

Methodology

Law uses cases, the $N = 1$ method in social science jargon, whereas psychology, in trying to develop generalizations, partials out variance and controls various factors experimentally, as typified by control group and contrasting group designs. In a word, ideographic methods are used more in law, while psychology is predominantly nomothetic.

Epistemology

Nature is potentially knowable for psychologists. Our quest is for an ever clearer view of reality. Lawyers predicate hypothetical situations and ask us, since the "truth" may be unknowable, to see their viewpoint and its ineluctable and inherent rightness. Yet they know the appearance of reality is all we can see, so they present an appearance that seems to fit the facts, and their clients interests, best.

Criterion

Psychologists must be conservative in accepting proof because a general law of nature is at stake which may require a retooling of the conceptual skills and procedures of a generation of practitioners. If, for example, Sternberg's (1985) triadic theory or Guilford's cube model or Cattell's two-factor theory of intelligence is "true," then the whole enterprise of intelligence (Matarazzo, 1972) testing must be changed in-

TABLE 2.1.   Contrasting Bases of Psychology and Law

	Psychology	*Law*
Knowledge	Empirical (based on research findings)	Rational (research consists of similar cases and logic or rationale binding to one's case)
Methodology	Experimental (control uses experimental or statistical methods such as control groups or regression analyses respectively)	Case Method (particularistic analyses of similarity or metaphor underlying the case with a precedent, or with logic compelling a new law)
Epistemology	Objectivity (presumes science sheds progressively more light on a hidden truth. Bias in a theory is assumed to be balanced by competing theories and through critical analysis and peer review)	Advocacy (truth is seen by a preeminent value held by one party who presumes to win since "good" is on his or her side)
Criterion	Conservative (a $p<0.05$ value is needed wherein a finding occurs less than once in 20 times if groups do not differ, so a hypothesis of difference is accepted)	Expedient (for many cases a preponderance or more than 50 percent will carry the the day: 51 percent will win. Sometimes "clear and convincing" [75 percent] or beyond a reasonable doubt [90 percent] is needed)
Nature of Law	Descriptive	Prescriptive
Principles	Exploratory (multiplicity of theories with new ones encouraged)	Conservative (the predominant theory prevails on the basis of stare decisis or a precedent decision)
Latitude of Courtroom Behavior	Limited (restricted to attorney's questions or amicus [friend of the court] briefs)	Broad (within rules of evidence, procedure and courtroom decorum can introduce theories and evidence in a desired sequence and style)

cluding test kits, test forms, student file forms, graduate courses, and graduate textbooks. On the other hand, the court needs to decide each individual case before it. Is this or that person right in this case? A decision must be made, often on a simple balance of the weight of the evidence at hand and not on the cumulative replication of studies.

Nature of Law

The term *law* for psychology is descriptive as Newton's or Einstein's laws by which nature is portrayed. "At what age do children make valid witnesses" is a *descriptive*, lawful question. The law is *prescriptive* in the legal arena. "Children below age seven cannot testify" is a prescription with no inherent root in nature other than accumulated observation distilled by rationale.

Principles

Dissertation committee members like to ask of degree candidates, "How else can you explain these data" (and there always seem to be more explanations than people in the room), illustrating the divergent and multiple theories in psychology. Lawyers prefer to have a judge convergently think, "By golly, there is only one way to see this evidence."

Latitude of Courtroom Behavior

The psychologist who forgets that the courtroom is the judge and attorney's province will soon learn a lesson in humility. The rules are drawn to satisfy legal needs, as described in Table 2.1. Even if the psychologist is also a trained attorney, he or she needs to decide which role to play. If they are a witness or consultant, they had best not try to serve in an attorney capacity as well. After thinking about these issues, one may feel the need for a dual education in law and psychology in order to practice forensic psychology. The next section considers the dual degree option.

THE JOINT J.D. - PH.D.

In the last decade about a half dozen universities offered programs leading to both law and psychology doctorates. One might think this is the wave of the future for forensic psychology. However, the movement toward J.D.-Ph.D. programs has remained static in the 1980s and is likely to remain so. Essentially a person can function as a psychologist or a lawyer but not both. It would be handy in special circumstances such as drawing up amicus curie briefs or writing law in areas such as domestic law and criminal law to have a background in law and psychology, but it is far better to have a preeminent psychologist review the literature on blended families and an expert lawyer draw up legally correct statutes than to expect both such levels of competence to reside in the same person. While a person may have dual doctoral degrees such as an M.D. and J.D., we find such a person practices usually one or the other profession (Schneller & Weiner, 1985). The person typically forms an occupational personality with accompanying values and identification with the first profession learned. One wonders what processes of identification or alienation are at work when the training is blended as in years one, three, and five being devoted to psychology training and years two, four, and six of graduate work being dedicated to law.

The lawyer can learn about psychology or the psychologist learn about law, even to the extent of earning joint degrees, but the most effective choice seems to involve devoting oneself to the area to which one feels most committed, be it by ability or by personal disposition.

CONCLUSION

Psychology and law share a problem in that they are "inherently 'relevant' and seemingly accessible. There is a sense in which everyone is a psychologist and there is no counterpart sense that everyone is a physicist or a chemist" (Elliott, 1985, p. 219). It is easy for people to play "pop psychologist," and I suspect some play "pop lawyer." True mastery of a field should be our goal.

I am reminded of the Chinese method of assessing acupuncture students' skills. At an exhibit, on top of the many-drawered medicine chest was a hollow metal human model with many pinholes. The teacher would dip the model in hot wax, and after the wax cooled and became opaque, would fill the model with water. The test of the student's skill would commence. If they placed the pin in the model and missed the hole, they would strike metal. If they correctly placed the pin, water would spurt out.

Our tests for competence are not as clear or sure, but just as necessary. We need to monitor carefully our own skills and observe those around us as to how well they "place their pins," whether the pins are excellence in research, excellence in theorizing, or excellence in practice.

REFERENCES

Arnold, T. (1965). The criminal trial as a symbol of public morality. In A. E. D. Howard (Ed.), *Criminal justice in our time*. Charlottesville, VA: The University Press of Virginia.

Barefoot v. Estelle, 51 L.W. 5189 (1983).

Bartol, C. R. (1983). *Psychology and American law*. Belmont, CA: Wadsworth.

Bower, B. (1984). Predicting dangerousness: Future imperfect. *Science News, 125*, 365, 367.

Broderick, J. J. (1977). *Police in a time of change*. Morristown, NJ: General Learning Press.

Brown, A. C. (1982, November). Cashing in on the cartridge trade. *Fortune*, 125–128.

Brown v. Board of Education, 347 U.S. 483 (1954) 74 S. Ct. 686, 98 L. Ed. 873.

Bukstel, L. H., & Kilmann, P. R. (1980). Psychological effects of inprisonment on confined individuals. *Psychological Bulletin, 88,* 469–493.

Caplan, L. (1984, July 2). Annals of Law: The insanity defense. *New Yorker,* pp. 45–78.

Coca-Cola Co. v. Chero-Cola Co., 273 Fed. 755 (D.C. Cir. 1921).

Clemmer, D. (1940). *The prison community.* New York: Holt, Rinehart and Winston.

Coca-Cola Co. v. Chero-Cola Co., 273 Fed. 755 (D.C. Cir. 1921).

Cohen, F. (1985). Old age as a criminal defense. *Criminal Law Bulletin, 21,* 5–36. *psychology.* New York: Holt, Rinehart & Winston.

Cohn, A., & Udolf, R. (1979). *The criminal justice system and its psychology.* New York: Van Nostrand Reinhold.

Craswell, R. (1985). Interpreting deceptive advertising. *Boston University Law Review, 65,* 657–732.

Crouch, B. M. (1985). Pandora's box: Women guards in men's prisons. *Journal of Criminal Justice, 13,* 535–548.

Daniels, N. (1984). Post-traumatic stress disorder and competence to stand trial. *Journal of Psychiatry and Law, 12,* 5–11.

DeBobes, L. (1986). The work environment: The psychological factors in accident prevention. *Personnel Journal, 65,* 34–36.

Elliott, R. (1985). On the reliability of *Eyewitness testimony*: A retrospective review. *Psychological Reports, 57,* 219–226.

Ennis, P. (1967). Criminal victimization in the United States: A report of national survey. Chicago: National Opinion Research Center.

Eysenck, H. J. (1976). The biology of morality. In T. Lickona (Ed.), *Moral development and behavior.* New York: Holt, Rinehart & Winston.

Fingarette, H. (1985a). The disability of mind doctrine. *Annals, AAPSS, 477,* 104–113.

Fingarette, H. (1985b). Losing touch: Criminal insanity. *Center Magazine, 18,* 51–58.

Ford, D., & Schmidt, A. K. (1985). Electronically monitored home confinement. National Institute of Justice Reports SNI 194, November 1985. Washington, DC: National Institute of Justice.

Foster, K. R. (1986). The VDT debate. *American Scientist, 74,* 163–166.

Frankel, M. E. (1973). *Criminal sentences: Law without order.* New York: Hill and Wang.

Goble, G. W. (1955). Nature, man and law. *American Bar Association Journal, 41,* 403 ff.

Goode, S. (1986, June 2). Payment for mental pressure. *I.S.I. Press Digest,* p. 9.

Greenberg, M. S., & Ruback, R. B. (1982). *Social psychology of the criminal justice system.* Belmont, CA: Brooks/Cole.

Gross, M. L. (1962). *The brain watchers.* New York: Random House.

Haney, C. (1980). Psychology and legal change: On the limits of a factual jurisprudence. *Law and Human Behavior, 4,* 147–200.

Hans, V. P., & Slater, D. (1984). "Plain Crazy": Lay definitions of legal insanity. *Journal of Psychiatry and Law, 7,* 105–114.

Harlow, C. W. (1986). Reporting crimes to the police. *Bulletin of the Criminal Justice Archive and Information Network (CJAIN).* Ann Arbor, MI: CJAIN.

Heider, F. (1944). Social perception and phenomenal causality. *Psychological Review, 51*, 358–374.

Henson, R. D. (1960). *Landmarks of law*. New York: Harper & Row.

Hess, A. K. (1973). Indoctrination of two types of criminal offenders as a function of altered arousal conditions. *Dissertation Abstracts International, 34*. (University Microfilms No. 74-9310)

Hess, A. K. (1980). Theories and models in clinical psychology. In A. K. Hess (Ed.), *Psychotherapy supervision*. New York: Wiley.

Hess, A. K. (1985). The psychologist as expert witness. *Clinical Psychologist, 38*, 75–76.

Hess, R., & Torney, J. V. (1967). *Development of political attitudes in children*. Chicago: Aldine.

Holmes, O. W. (1898-9). Law in science, science in law. *Harvard Law Review, 12*, 443–463.

Janis, I. L. (1983). The role of social support in adherence to stressful decisions. *American Psychologist, 38*, 143–160.

Jesness, C. F. (1975). Comparative effectiveness of behavior modification and transactional analysis programs for delinquents. *Journal of Consulting and Clinical Psychology, 43*, 758–779.

Johnson, J. T., & Drobny, J. (1985). Proximity biases in the attribution of civil liability. *Journal of Personality and Social Psychology, 48*, 283–296.

Jones, D. A. (1978). *Crime and criminal responsibility*. Chicago: Nelson Hall.

Kagehiro, D. K., & Stanton, W. C. (1985). Legal vs. qualified definitions of standards of proof. *Law and Human Behavior, 9*, 159–178.

Kaplan, L. V. (1977). The mad and the bad: An inquiry into the disposition of the criminally insane. *Journal of Medicine and Philosophy, 2*, 244–303.

Kerr, N. L. (1982). Trial participants behaviors and jury verdicts: An exploratory field study. In V. J. Konečni & E. B. Ebbesen (Eds.), *The criminal justice system: A social psychological analysis*. San Francisco: W. H. Freeman.

Kleinmuntz, B. (1985). Lie detectors fail the truth test. *Harvard Business Review, 63*, 36–43.

Koestler, A. (1968) *Darkness at noon*. New York: Bantam.

Konečni, V. J., & Ebbesen, E. B. (1982). *The criminal justice system: A social psychological analysis*. San Francisco: W. H. Freeman.

Kuhn, T. S. (1962). *The structure of scientific revolutions*. Chicago: University of Chicago Press.

Lazarus, R. S. (1983). The costs and benefits of denial. In M. S. Breznitz (Ed.), *The denial of stress*. New York: International Universities Press.

Lerner, M. J. (1975). The justice motive in social behavior. *Journal of Social Issues, 31*, 1–19.

Levine, M. (1984) The adversary process and social science in the courts: *Barefoot v. Estelle*. *Journal of Psychiatry and Law, 12*, 147–181.

Levine, M., & Howe, B. (1985). The penetration of social science into legal culture. *Law and Policy, 7*, 173–198.

Lewin, K. (1948). *Resolving social conflicts: Selected papers on group dynamics*. New York: Harper & Bros.

Lykken, D. J. (1957). A study of anxiety in the psychopathic personality. *Journal of Abnormal and Social Psychology, 55,* 6–10.

Matarrazo, J. D. (1972). *Wechsler's measurement and appraisal of adult intelligence* (5th ed.). Baltimore: Williams and Wilkins.

Meehl, P. E., Livermore, J. M., & Malmquist, C. P. (1968). On the justifications for civil commitment. *University of Pennsylvania Law Review, 117,* 75–96.

Mitroff, I. I., & Kilmann, R. H. (1984). *Corporate tragedies: Product tampering, sabotage, and the other catastrophes.* New York: Praeger.

M'Naghten Case (1843): House of Lords, 1843, 8 Eng. Rep. 718 (HL).

Monahan, J., & Loftus, E. F. (1982). Psychology of law. *Annual Review of Psychology, 33,* 441–475.

Muller v. Oregon, 208 U.S. 412 (1908) 28 S. Ct. 324, 52 L. Ed. 551.

Munsterberg, H. (1908). *On the witness stand.* New York: Doubleday.

National Institute of Justice. (1985). *Failing drunk drivers.* Washington, DC: U.S. Department of Justice.

Ney, P. G., Johnston, I. D., & Herron, J. L. (1985). Social and legal ramifications of a child crisis line. *Child Abuse and Neglect, 9,* 47–55.

Niederhoffer, A., & Blumberg, A. S. (1973). *The ambivalent force: Perspectives on the police.* San Francisco: Rinehart Press.

Owen, D. R. (1972). The 47, XYY Male: A review. *Psychological Bulletin, 78,* 209–233.

Packard, V. (1977). *People shapers.* Boston: Little, Brown.

Pasewark, R. A., & McGinley, H. (1985). Insanity plea: National survey of frequency and success. *Journal of Psychiatry and Law, 13,* 101–108.

Plate, T. (1975). *Crime pays.* New York: Simon & Schuster.

Perry, B. (1984). Escape from freedom, criminal style: The hidden advantages of being in jail. *Journal of Psychiatry and Law, 12,* 215–230.

Quay, H. C. (1965). Psychopathic personality as pathological stimulus seeking. *American Journal of Psychiatry, 122,* 180–183.

Redmount, R. S. (1965). The use of psychologists in legal practice. *The Practical Lawyer, 11,* 23–38.

Rex v. Arnold (1724) 16 How. St. Tr. 684.

Riger, S. (1985). Crime as an environmental stressor. *Journal of Community Psychology, 13,* 270–280.

Saks, M. J., & Hastie, R. (1978). *Social psychology in court.* New York: Van Nostrand Reinhold.

Sass, R. (1986). The worker's right to know, participate and refuse hazardous work: A manifesto. *Journal of Business Ethics, 5,* 129–136.

Schneller, E. S., & Weiner, T. S. (1985). The M.D.-J.D. revisited: A sociological analysis of cross educated professionals in the decade of the 1980's. *Journal of Legal Medicine, 6,* 337–372.

Shaver, K. G., Gilbert, M. A., & Williams, M. C. (1975). Social psychology, criminal justice, and the principle of discretion. A selective review. *Personality and Social Psychology Bulletin, 1,* 471–484.

Shaw, C. (1930). *The jack roller*. Chicago: University of Chicago Press.

Sheehy, N. P. (1985). Simulation approaches in forensic and legal psychology. *Irish Journal of Psychology, 7*, 1–7.

Slovenko, R. (1986, April 20). The execution of the death penalty: A Florida saga. *Tampa Tribune-Times*, p. 4-C.

Spaulding, W. J. (1985). Testamentary capacity. *Law and Human Behavior, 9*, 113–139.

Sternberg, R. J. (1985). *Beyond IQ*. New York: Cambridge University.

Stotland, E., & Berberich, J. (1979). The psychology of the police. In H. Toch (Ed.), *Psychology of crime and criminal justice*. New York: Holt, Rinehart & Winston.

Strodtbeck, F. L., & Lipinski, R. M. (1985). Becoming first among equals: Moral consideration in jury foreman selection. *Journal of Personality and Social Psychology, 49*, 927–936.

Sutherland, E. H. (1937). *The professional thief (by a professional thief)*. Chicago: University of Chicago Press.

Tancredi, L. R., Lieb, J., & Slaby, A. E. (1975). *Legal issues in psychiatric care*. Hagerstown, MD: Harper & Row.

Taylor, S. (1982, September). Too much justice. *Harper's Magazine*, pp. 56–66.

Toch, H. (Ed.). (1961). *Legal and criminal psychology*. New York: Holt, Rinehart & Winston.

U.S. Department of Justice. (1985). *Report to the nation on crime and justice*. Washington, DC: Bureau of Statistics.

Waaland, P., & Keeley, S. (1985). Police decision making in wife abuse: The impact of legal and extra legal factors. *Law and Human Behavior, 9*, 355–366.

Weeks, D. P. (Ed.). (1958). *Commonwealth vs. Sacco and Vanzetti*. Englewood Cliffs, NJ: Prentice Hall.

Wigmore, J. H. (1909). Professor Munsterberg and the psychology of testimony. *Illinois Law Review, 3*, 399–445.

Winick, C. (1961). The psychology of juries. In H. Toch (Ed.), *Legal and criminal psychology*. New York: Holt, Rinehart & Winston.

Winick, C. (1979). The psychology of the courtroom. In H. Toch (Ed.), *Psychology of crime and criminal justice*. New York: Holt, Rinehart & Winston.

Winick, C., Gerver, I., & Blumberg, A. (1961). The psychology of judges. In H. Toch (Ed.), *Legal and criminal psychology*. New York: Holt, Rinehart & Winston.

CHAPTER 3

Accessing Legal Literatures

DAVID F. DANIELL

With the growing intervention of government in every facet of American life, the increasingly important intermingling of psychology and law makes a working knowledge of the law upon which issues are decided, and access to legal resource materials, ever more important to the social scientist and practitioner. This chapter surveys the types of law and then looks at the use of the law library and the local resource material available.

TYPES OF LAW

The American legal system is derived from a common law tradition developed in England which is shared by most English speaking countries of the world.

There are basically five types of law: constitutional, legislative, executive, administrative, and judicial. As a general rule, most legal resource materials offer information on only one type of law from one particular source. Accordingly, a researcher needs to have a working knowledge of a variety of source materials so that research topics can be thoroughly reviewed.

Constitutional law is not limited to the U.S. Constitution which is, of course, the supreme law of the land. Each state is governed by a constitution that is supreme within its borders. The 10th amendment to the U.S. Constitution provides that all powers not delegated to the federal government and not specifically prohibited to the states are reserved to the states or to the people. In matters not preempted by the U.S. Constitution or federal law, state constitutional law is supreme.

Municipalities and counties are, in most cases, organized under charters. These charters are, in effect, constitutions for these political entities. The charter is superior to all ordinances enacted by these entities but is inferior to state and federal law.

Statutory law is derived from enactments by legislative bodies. Federal statutes are enacted by the U.S. Congress, state statutes by the legislatures of the various states, and ordinances by local governments.

Federal statutes are inferior only to the U.S. Constitution and are superior to all other laws. State statutes are enacted by legislatures and are binding within the state's borders if not in conflict with federal law or the state constitution. Executive

50

law is derived from proclamations issued by the chief executive officer of the executive branches of the federal and state governments.

Administrative law is created by state and/or federal agencies through the issuance of regulations or by decisions made by the administrative body to settle disputes in the subject area that it regulates. For example, the Internal Revenue Service issues not only tax regulations but also administrative rulings on disputed claims. Both are forms of administrative law that bind taxpayers. Where state and federal agencies share responsibilities for regulating certain activities, state administrative law is inferior to federal administrative law.

Judicial law or case law is the law developed through the history of the judicial system from the cases decided by the courts in the past. The courts generally operate on what is known as a common law system. The common law is the product of a history of court decisions. Each court—building on the decisions of prior courts—strives to treat similar cases in a consistent manner providing a base for common law. This principle of using prior decisions in deciding similar isues is called precedent or *stare decisis*. Because not all issues that may arise within our legal system are specifically covered by statute, judges frequently rely on precedent in making their decisions or rulings.

Each court within the U.S. judicial system has a defined jurisdiction. The jurisdiction is defined not only geographically but also by subject matter. Generally, state courts consider state law and issues arising within their geographical borders. Federal courts handle issues involving federal laws, constitutional issues, and controversies between citizens of different states.

Each state has its own common law history and its own case law, just as the federal court system has its own case law and common law history. Each court, whether state or federal, has a defined geographical district and handles only matters arising within that district.

The federal court system is divided into districts and circuits. The district courts are inferior to the circuit courts, which now number 13. The following breakdown illustrates the 13 circuits as they presently exist:

First Circuit	*Second Circuit*	*Third Circuit*
Maine	Vermont	Pennsylvania
New Hampshire	New York	New Jersey
Massachusetts	Connecticut	Delaware
Puerto Rico		
Fourth Circuit	*Fifth Circuit*	*Sixth Circuit*
West Virginia	Texas	Michigan
Virginia	Louisiana	Ohio
Maryland	Mississippi	Kentucky
North Carolina		Tennessee
South Carolina		
Seventh Circuit	*Eighth Circuit*	*Ninth Circuit*
Wisconsin	Arkansas	Montana

Seventh Circuit
Illinois
Indiana

Eighth Circuit
Missouri
Iowa
Minnesota
Nebraska
South Dakota
North Dakota

Ninth Circuit
Idaho
Washington
Oregon
Nevada
California
Arizona
Alaska
Hawaii
Northern Mariana
   Islands
Guam

Tenth Circuit
Wyoming
Utah
Colorado
Kansas
Oklahoma
New Mexico

Eleventh Circuit
Alabama
Georgia
Florida

D.C. Circuit
Washington, D.C.

Federal Circuit
Washington, D.C.

Prior to initiating research at the law library, a determination as to the jurisdiction involved must be made by the researcher. For example, a decision of the highest court of Florida will probably not be binding on the courts of Nebraska.

THE LAW LIBRARY

Law libraries can be found on law school campuses and in most larger municipalities. Generally, courthouses contain law libraries. Local public libraries may contain general introductory works and a few primary resources but will usually be inadequate for research.

Federal and state courthouse libraries are rarely officially open to the public but are often available with the consent of the librarian on duty. Most law school libraries are open to the public. These libraries are usually the best for general research in that they contain the widest variety of resource materials. In smaller communities, most law offices will have limited libraries. Access, of course, to these libraries must be obtained by permission.

It is important in legal research to define your problem by selecting the correct words to describe your particular area of research. All specialized fields have key words that are important in research. Law is certainly no exception. The first step for the researcher is to assemble all of the facts of the case. After this is done, a list of words that describe the particular situation should be compiled. This will aid the researcher in locating the resource materials.

The TARP system is a widely employed and useful tool in making such a list. After the researcher's facts are developed, key words should be segregated in the following categories:

> T—THING or subject matter
>
> A—cause of ACTION or ground of defense
>
> R—RELIEF sought
>
> P—persons or PARTIES involved

To illustrate the use of the TARP system, consider a situation where the researcher is researching a problem involving inadequate delivery of psychological services to a prisoner detained in a county jail. Using the TARP system, the researcher would break down the research by picking out words that describe the fact situation. The following words might be material:

Thing	Action	Relief	Parties
Jail	42 U.S.C. §1983	Damages	Municipalities
Prisoner	14th Amendment	Declaratory	Sheriff
Medicine	Equal Protection	Judgment	Counties
Psychology	Fifth Amendment	Immunities	Deputies
Psychiatry	Due Process		

An analysis of the facts through the use of the TARP system provides headings to be examined in an index of a publication, the descriptive word index of a digest, or a table of contents.

When the facts of the researcher's problem have been determined and a listing of subjects to be examined has been developed, the legal issues involved should then be ascertained. After determining the facts and isues in the case, the researcher is ready to research the applicable law. At this point, a decision must be made as to where to start the search. For example, in the previous problem involving inadequate delivery of psychological services to an inmate, probably the best place to begin would be with 42 U.S.C. §1983 (dealing with civil rights). Experience will give the researcher an edge in finding a starting point.

GENERAL REFERENCE SOURCES

If your topic or subject of research involves general legal principles, the researcher may want to begin with treatises or legal encyclopedias. Treatises are books written by experts in certain areas of the law and cover the entire subject such as criminal law, probate law, or civil rights. In a child custody case, for example, a review of a treatise on domestic law may be helpful. Treatises can explain the basic concepts of law. These texts can be located by looking in the card catalogue in the law library. Use it in the same manner as you would a card catalogue in a general library. At this point, the word list previously prepared becomes important. Each of the words should be looked up to find source materials related to the topic. In most law libraries, the publication date of each volume will be listed on the card found in the card catalogue. *Never rely on old material*. American law changes constantly, and it is always important that the most recent material be consulted.

Most law libraries will also contain one or more legal encyclopedias. Legal encyclopedias are arranged by subject providing statements as to general law supported by references to case authorities.

Corpus Juris Secundum (C.J.S.) is published by the West Publishing Company. Its intent is to set out American case law from the first reported cases to the present. This work supercedes *Corpus Juris (C.J.)*, an earlier edition, with references being made to the earlier edition for the earlier case law. This set, like most law books, is kept up-to-date by replacement volumes and annual pocket supplements which are inserted in the back covers of each volume. In using any legal encyclopedia, it is important to check the pocket supplements or the applicable replacement volumes to make sure the material reviewed is up-to-date. *C.J.S.* is arranged alphabetically. A list of topics is included in the beginning of the first volume of the general index and preceding the text of each volume.

American Jurisprudence (AmJur) is published by the Lawyers Cooperative Publishing Company and the Bancroft-Whitney Company. It began publication in 1936. Revised in 1962, *American Jurisprudence Second (AmJur2d)* was completed in 1976 superceding *AmJur*. *AmJur2d* contains an index volume arranged topically.

Other encyclopedias, notably, *AmJur Proof of Facts, AmJur Proof of Facts Second, American Jurisprudence Trials, AmJur Pleadings and Practice Forms, Annotated*, and *AmJur Legal Forms Second*, are available, but these are technical encyclopedias designed to assist in preparing a case for trial and will probably be of little benefit to the nonlawyer.

Some states have encyclopedias devoted to their own laws. California, Florida, New York, Ohio, and Texas have encyclopedias published by the Lawyers Cooperative Publishing Company and Bancroft-Whitney Company which follow the form of *AmJur2d*. Illinois, Maryland, and Michigan have encyclopedias published by West Publishing Company which are similar in form to *C.J.S.*

Legal periodicals provide additional resource material. There are three groups of legal periodicals: (1) law school publications, (2) bar association publications, and (3) special subject and interest periodicals. Law school reviews are distinctive in that their editorial management is controlled by student editors. These reviews will contain a number of selected articles dealing with various topics, primarily dealing with newly developing fields of law or changes in the law.

Bar association periodicals range from publications such as the *American Bar Association Journal* to some that are merely newsletters of local bar associations. Articles contained in the more familiar publications deal with subjects generally of current interest to the legal profession.

Subject and interest legal periodicals are journals devoted to one specific area of law. Generally published by private companies or law schools, they are aimed at practicing attorneys specializing in particular fields of law. The *Insurance Law*

Journal, the *Journal of Psychiatry and Law*, and the *Journal of Legal Medicine* are some of these titles. Most law libraries will not contain all of these publications. Smaller law libraries generally contain only locally or regionally published reviews or periodicals. The serious researcher who desires access to a wide range of legal periodicals should seek out a law school library. Often, law schools will provide a research service run by students who perform research for a modest fee. Such a service may be helpful to obtain copies of periodical articles if a large library is unavailable to the researcher locally.

Comprehensive periodical indexes are available to provide entry into legal periodicals. The *Index to Legal Periodicals* is the most comprehensive index available. Coverage is limited strictly to legal periodicals published in the United States, Great Britain, Canada, Australia, and New Zealand. The index is arranged alphabetically by both topic (civil rights, jails, mental health) and author. In using the *Index*, it is important to search for articles covering the same topic under two or more subjects because this index tends to contain inconsistent subject indexing. Although many other indexes or digests of periodicals are available, the *Index to Legal Periodicals* is the most comprehensive.

COURT REPORTS

Over 40,000 reports of court decisions are published in America each year. These reports are primarily decisions of federal and state appellate courts. Generally, decisions of trial courts are not published, with a few exceptions. Figure 3.1 illustrates the hierarchy of the federal court system.

Rarely will the social scientist deal with opinions of the court of claims, court of customs, and patent appeals. Most of the federal decisions that will have an impact on the research of the social scientist will be decisions of the district courts, the U.S. Courts of Appeals, or decisions of the U.S. Supreme Court. The district courts are the trial courts of the federal system. Many of the decisions of the U.S. District Courts are published in the *Federal Supplement (F. Supp.)* and *Federal Supplement Second (F. Supp. 2d)*, published by the West Publishing Company.

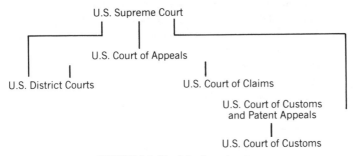

FIGURE 3.1 The federal court system.

The U.S. Courts of Appeals are composed of twelve circuits and the District of Columbia. The decisions of the U.S. Courts of Appeals are published by the West Publishing Company and consist of two series. The first series stopped with volume 300 and the second series started numbering at volume 1.

Until recently, almost all written opinions of the courts of appeals were published in the Federal Reporter System. However, each circuit has now adopted guidelines restricting the number of opinions actually published.

The opinions of the U.S. Supreme Court are presently published in five different publications:

1. *The United States Reports* (official edition)
2. *The United States Supreme Court Reports* (Lawyers' Cooperative Publishing Company)
3. *Supreme Court Reporter* (West Publishing Company)
4. *United States Law Week* (Bureau of National Affairs)
5. *Commerce Clearing House*, United States Court Bulletin

The official edition (U.S.) has been published since 1817. The Supreme Court generally has only one term of court each year beginning in October and ordinarily completed in June. This is known as the October Term. The opinions are initially issued separately as "slip" opinions immediately after being handed down to provide quick dissemination. They are subsequently published in "advance sheets" containing a compilation of the most recent decisions prior to binding. After the end of the October Term each year, the Advance Sheets are replaced by bound volumes.

The *United States Supreme Court Reports* (L.Ed.), privately published by the Lawyers' Cooperative Publishing Company and the Bancroft-Whitney Company, contains, in addition to the opinions of the Supreme Court, editorial treatments prepared by the publishers summarizing the cases in headnotes which precede the opinion. Summaries of the attorneys' briefs submitted to the Court are often included for selected important cases.

The *Supreme Court Reporter (S.Ct.)* published by West Publishing Company begins with opinions published in 1882 and contains a summary of each case and headnote preceding each of the opinions.

Since the decisions of the Supreme Court are immediately law of the land, their impact is paramount. State and federal courts must follow these decisions as precedent. Accordingly, it is important that lawyers and lay persons have immediate access to these opinions. The *United States Law Week (U.S.L.W.)* and *Commerce Clearing House Supreme Court Bulletin* are publications designed to disseminate these opinions as soon as they are handed down by the Court. Each of these publications receives the slip opinions on the day they are handed down and mails copies immediately to subscribers. The *United States Law Week* is a publication of two or more volumes by the Bureau of National Affairs in Washington. The publication contains Supreme Court opinions in their complete text in looseleaf form. In addition to current opinions, the volumes contain the minutes of all sessions of the Court held during the week, a listing of cases docketed or scheduled to be heard, a summary of cases recently filed, a summary of the oral arguments of the more important cases argued each week before the Court, and an index of cases pending.

The *Commerce Clearing House Supreme Court Bulletin* is also in a looseleaf form. In addition to photocopies of the current opinions, it includes an index to opinions and a status table of cases pending before the court.

State court decisions are generally published in official and unofficial reports. The most frequently consulted and generally most available are the publications of the National Reporter System. The National Reporter System is published by West Publishing Company and consists of two main divisions. The first is the opinions of the state appellate and trial courts, and the second is the opinions of the federal courts. The reporting of the federal court opinions has been previously addressed.

The opinions of the state appellate and trial courts are broken into seven regional reporters arranged by geographical divisions. Following is an outline of the system with its coverage:

Atlantic Reporter
Connecticut
Delaware
Maine
Maryland
New Hampshire
New Jersey
Pennsylvania
Rhode Island
Vermont
D.C. Municipal Court of Appeals

Northwestern Reporter
Iowa
Michigan
Minnesota
Nebraska
North Dakota
South Dakota
Wisconsin

Northeastern Reporter
Illinois
Indiana
Massachusetts
New York
Ohio

Pacific Reporter
Alaska
Arizona
California (to 1960)
Colorado
Hawaii
Idaho
Kansas
Montana
Nevada
New Mexico
Oklahoma
Oregon
Utah
Washington
Wyoming

Southeastern Reporter
Georgia
North Carolina
South Carolina
Virginia
West Virginia

Southwestern Reporter
Arkansas
Kentucky
Indian Territory
Missouri
Tennessee
Texas

Southern Reporter
Alabama
Florida
Louisiana
Mississippi

Supreme Court Reporter
U.S. Supreme Court

Federal Reporter
U.S. Circuit Courts
U.S. Courts of Appeals
U.S. Court of Customs and Patent Appeals
U.S. Court of Claims

Federal Supplement
U.S. District Courts

New York Supplement
New York

California Reporter
California (since 1959)

As you can see, in addition to the seven regional reporters, New York and California have their own individual reporters which are included in the National Reporter System.

Each bound volume contains two tables of cases: the first a single alphabetical list of all cases in the volume, and the second a separate alphabetical listing of all cases by states or courts.

To adequately treat the proper citation of court reports would require a rather lengthy volume. Accordingly, we will not attempt to go into this at length here. State decisions are generally cited with both the official and unofficial state report citations. For example:

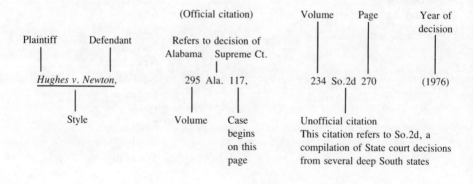

Many states have, in recent years, discontinued publication of official reporters. With regard to these more recent decisions, the citations will omit the official citation and appear as follows: *Jordan v. Miller*, 361 So.2d 1080 (Ala. 1978).

Federal decisions are cited in a similar fashion with the citation providing the volume, page, and year of decision.

STATUTES

Many legal questions involving social issues such as civil rights will involve either state or federal statutes. The techniques for using statute books vary little from state to state. Basically, a state's statutes will be codified in one of two ways. Some are organized by subject matter but most use a numbering system. To gain entry into the state statute codifications, the topical index should be consulted. This index is arranged alphabetically by subject matter. For example, if the researcher desires information concerning the involuntary commitment of mentally ill minors in Alabama, key words should be compiled using the TARP system. The initial compilation would probably include words such as "mentally ill" and "minors." Under "mentally ill" in the topical index of the *Code of Alabama* is found "See Juvenile Proceedings." Under "Juvenile Proceedings" the researcher will find the numbered reference to the particular statutes pertinent to the query.

Most of the codifications of state statutes are supplemented by pocket parts, which are periodic updates to the volume inserted in the back cover. A researcher must always remember to check the most updated pocket part to make sure that the statute reviewed is the most updated version.

A great number of legal issues are governed by federal statutes or by governmental regulations. The researcher should always check to see if federal statutes or regulations might apply to the researched topic. As with state statutes, the federal statutes are also codified. The official code published by the U.S. government is entitled *The United States Code (USC)*. Two unofficial annotated codes are the *United States Code Annotated (USCA)* and the *United States Code Service (USCS)*. Most law libraries will generally contain only one of these publications. These annotated codes are most helpful in that following each statute is an annotation containing summaries and citations of court decisions interpreting the statute.

There are several ways to locate a federal statute. If you were following a cite from another source, you should go directly to the most recent edition of the code and locate the volume containing the appropriate title and sections. For example, U.S.C., Title 42, made up of several volumes, contains all federal statutes dealing with "Public Health and Welfare." If you are interested in a particular act and know its name but not its location, you may travel four avenues. *Shepherds Acts and Cases by Popular Name* is a single volume edited to include only the names of acts and cases that the editors consider most important. It is organized alphabetically and updated by pocket parts which, as in most other legal publications, supplement the volume to provide the most recent information.

The USC has an "Acts Cited by Popular Name" table beginning on page one in a volume called "Popular Names and Tables," which will provide a citation to statute by its popular name. For example, Title 25, U.S.C.A. §§455–458e can be located in this table under its popular name, the "Indian Education Assistance Act." The USCA has a "Popular Name Acts" list at the beginning of each volume, but this list includes only the popular acts included in the title covered by that volume. The USCS has its complete popular name table in one of the "Tables" volumes which follow the general index volumes.

The key word to legal research is persistence and, above all, patience. Thorough knowledge of the facts behind the issue in question will greatly simplify the research.

PART TWO

Areas of Application on Civil Proceedings

CHAPTER 4

Informed Consent in Treatment and Research

BARBARA STANLEY

Over the past several decades the nature of the doctor-patient relationship (as well as that of the researcher and subject) has shifted dramatically. The quality of these relationships has moved from a paternalistic orientation on the part of the professionals to a more equal distribution of power between the professional and the consumer of the professional's services. The shift in the nature of the relationship appears to be the result, in part, of a heightened consumerism by the general public, abuses of patients particularly in the realm of human experimentation during World War II, and a series of legal cases that used lack of consent to a medical procedure as the basis for liability.

HISTORICAL PERSPECTIVES

Consent to Treatment

While the doctrine of informed consent as known to modern medicine has emerged only in the last three decades, the issue of patient consent has been present in legal doctrine for several centuries and has grown out of the common law that an unauthorized operation will subject the physician to liability in tort to the patient (Ludlum, 1972). Negligence was cited as the cause for action in the earliest cases. However, unlike contemporary cases, which have also cited negligence as the basis for a claim, the informed consent doctrine developed at the turn of the twentieth century from an assault and battery perspective (Rozovsky, 1984). Several cases are indicative of this approach to lack of patient consent: *Mohr v. Williams* (1905); *Pratt v. Davis* (1906); *Rolater v. Strain* (1913); and *Schloendorff v. Society of New York Hospitals* (1914).

In *Mohr v. Williams* the doctor performed a surgery on the patient's left ear but obtained permission only to perform the surgery on the right ear. Lack of patient consent, explicit or implicit, was held as "at least . . . a technical assault and battery" (Ludlum, 1972). In *Pratt v. Davis* and *Rolater v. Strain*, unauthorized removal of the uterus and ovaries in the former case and a bone from the foot in the latter constituted battery on the patient. In a landmark and well-known decision in *Schloendorff v. Society of New York Hospitals* (1914) the plaintiff had a fibroid tumor removed during a surgical procedure that was supposed to be for diagnostic purposes only. In this decision it was ruled that the surgeon had committed an assault. Particularly noteworthy is that the ruling included the statement, "Every human being of adult years and sound mind has a right to determine what shall be done with his own body." The ruling further stated that this held *regardless of the medical consequences* of such decisions. This emphasis on the right to self-determination departs strikingly from many earlier cases where it was seen as valid to perform an unauthorized procedure if it were for the patient's good.

A shift back to negligence as the basis for a case came in the 1950s. Ludlum (1972) cites three cases as important in this regard. In *Salgo v. Leland Stanford Jr. University Board of Trustees* (1957) the court held that "the physician subjects himself to liability if he withholds any facts which are necessary to form the basis of an intelligent consent by the patient to the proposed treatment." In *Natanson v. Kline* (1960) the plaintiff alleged negligence in the administration of cobalt radiation therapy which resulted in injuries to the patient. It was further alleged that the doctor failed to inform the patient of the possible risks of the treatment. The court ruled that the doctor was obliged to disclose to the patient the dangers of a proposed treatment. In another case (*Mitchell v. Robinson*, 1960) a similar ruling was made. In this case, the patient was administered insulin shock treatments. The patient reported that although convulsions resulting in bone fractures are hazards of this treatment, he was never informed of such hazards prior to treatment. The court ruled that the physician had the responsibility to inform the patient of the risks and that negligence was committed for failing to do so.

Leland (1972) states that on the basis of these cases the reasons for negligence as a cause for action can be separated from battery. Battery would be applied in cases where the treatment is against the patient's will or substantially different from that to which the patient consented. Negligence would be applied in cases where adequate disclosure of the possible risks and complications as well as the alternatives to the proposed treatment were not given to the patient.

Consent to Research

During the same time period that these negligence cases regarding treatment took place, some developments happened in the area of informed consent to experimentation. Unlike the development of informed consent in the treatment setting, which emanated from case law, in human experimentation very little exists in the form of case law. Instead, regulations and codes govern informed consent in research. Several states have written laws on research; federal regulations apply to much university-based research; and professional codes have been drafted with statements or sections on informed consent (cf. APA, 1982; DHHS, 1981).

The Nuremberg code (1949) which states a series of ethical principles in relation to human experimentation was developed following the research abuses of concentration camp prisoners during World War II. The Nuremberg code emphasized the importance of voluntary consent to any medical experimentation. The Declaration of Helsinki (1964) elaborated on the principles identified in the Nuremberg code. It placed substantial emphasis on the need for fully informing research participants of the "aims, methods, anticipated benefits and potential hazards of the study and the discomfort it may entail" (1964). Furthermore, the code emphasized the voluntary nature of research participation and the need for consent by an individual who is competent. A caution is also made to the researcher that requesting research participation may place subtle pressure on the patient when that individual is in some way dependent on the investigator, for example, when the researcher is also the patient's primary care physician.

Instances of abuses of participants in biomedical research led to the development of federal regulations protecting human research participants. (DHEW, 1973; DHHS, 1981). Some of the abuses stemmed from the fact that individuals were either unaware they were research subjects or were only partially informed about the experiment in which they were participating. The Jewish Chronic Disease Hospital and the Tuskegee Syphilis experiments (Levine, 1981) were two of the most publicized. In the Jewish Chronic Disease Hospital study, chronically ill patients were injected with live cancer cells without their permission. The Tuskegee Syphilis experiment which began in 1932 was designed to determine the natural course of syphilis. Over 400 men were recruited without their informed consent and were left untreated even after it became clear in the 1940s that penicillin was an effective treatment. It was not until 1972, when it became known to the public, that the study was halted (Brandt, 1978). (For a detailed review of these cases see Beecher, 1966; Katz, 1972; and Brandt, 1978.)

Not all cases with a lack of consent were biomedical studies. In the social sciences, abuses also came to light. Among the most well known of these is the Tearoom Trade studies. The purpose of these studies (Humphreys, 1970) was to develop a sociological description of homosexual practices in public restrooms. To accomplish this, the investigator either disguised or misrepresented himself at various points in the study. In addition to the lack of fully informed consent, these studies involved the use of deception.

During and following the period of these revelations, the federal government wrote a set of policies covering research with human beings (DHEW, 1973). In addition, professional organizations drafted ethical principles with special relevance to human experimentation. The American Psychological Association (1972) was a forerunner in this regard. Federal policies and ethical principles both emphasized the importance of informed consent. The federal policies were revised and became regulations in 1981. These regulations defined in precise detail what informed consent entailed.

WHAT IS INFORMED CONSENT?

While the informed consent doctrine has evolved over several decades and from a variety of sources, at this point there is general consensus on the three major elements of the doctrine: adequate disclosure of information, voluntariness, and competency (Meisel, Roth, & Lidz, 1977; Culver & Gert, 1982; Lynn, 1983). It is generally agreed that informed consent must be solicited whenever a procedure is intrusive, whenever there are significant risks, and whenever the purposes of the procedure are questionable (Beauchamp & Childress, 1983). Thus, surgery and most research procedures require informed consent. Further, it has been suggested that for some forms of pharmacologic treatment entailing high risk (e.g., use of neuroleptics which can have tardive dyskinesia as a side effect) informed consent should be obtained (Roth, 1983).

While a consent form can be the written documentation that an informed consent to the proposed procedure has taken place, a signed form is not all that is involved in obtaining consent. A process takes place during which the caregiver provides (usually verbally) the patient with the information relevant to the treatment decision at hand; the patient weighs that information and reaches a decision based on an adequate understanding of the information. The consent form, thus, ideally serves the function of documenting that this process has taken place.

Adequate information refers to the information needed by a patient that would affect the decision concerning which course of treatment would be chosen (Culver & Gert, 1982). The same principle applies to the decision to participate in research. There is some debate about exactly what is considered adequate in supplying patients with information. The federal regulations (DHEW, 1981) governing research with human subjects supply an extensive list of information: (1) the purposes, procedures, and duration of the research; (2) the risks and discomforts; (3) the benefits; (4) available alternatives; (5) the extent of confidentiality; (6) the voluntary nature of participants; (7) the extent of compensation and treatment for injuries; and (8) the name of appropriate contact person in case questions or problems arise. In the treatment setting, usually the first four items (i.e., risks, benefits, alternatives, and purposes and procedures) are thought to be the most important pieces of information. Integral to this element of informed consent is the notion that the information should be provided in a way that is understandable to the patient.

The second element of informed consent is voluntariness. This element refers to the requirement that the patient be free from coercive influences and undue pressure in reaching the treatment decision (Meisel et al., 1977; Culver & Gert, 1982). Coercion exists on a continuum from forced treatment and explicit threats if the patient does not comply with the proposed procedure to subtle pressure and manipulations of the individual. The use of pressure in psychiatry to obtain compliance is seen by some as greater than in other fields of medicine because the psychiatrist has the threat of involuntary hospitalization and treatment (Culver & Gert, 1982). Suggestions have been made about ways to minimize coercion in arriving at treatment decisions (President's Commission, 1982). These include allowing a certain amount of time to elapse between the doctor-patient discussion and the patient's actual decision; giving patients the opportunity to temporarily remove themselves from the environment which may be exerting influence on the individual; and for research, making available a professional not directly involved in the research project for patient consultation.

The third element of informed consent, competency, is the most problematic. It is often assumed that there is a consensually agreed upon or legally defined means for determining competency to give consent. However, this is a misconception. Several standards or definitions have been proposed, none of which has yet gained widespread acceptance. Since these standards vary in both the degree and the type of assessment performed, different decisions will be reached depending on the standard applied.

Proposed definitions of competency have arisen primarily from the legal and, to a lesser extent, psychiatric literature. It has been suggested that these standards which were proposed to assess competency to consent to or refuse treatment be adapted to the research setting (Stanley & Stanley, 1981). The tests are most clearly differentiated by the level of protection they provide to the patient and can be arranged in a hierarchical order. The protection inherent in each test is inversely related to the degree of independence granted to the research subject. In reviewing the standards, the level of protection that each test affords will be discussed.

Five basic functional tests of competency have been proposed: (1) evidencing a choice; (2) factual comprehension; (3) rational reasoning; (4) appreciation of the nature of the situation; and (5) reasonable outcome of choice (Sullivan, 1974; Friedman, 1975; Roth, Meisel & Lidz, 1977). Except for the last test, these tests are ordered according to the level of protection they provide, ranging from the lowest to the highest level. The reasonable outcome test does not fit comfortably at any one point in the hierarchy for reasons which will be explained later. Although these standards are presented separately here, they are not necessarily mutually exclusive, and two or more of the tests may be combined during a single assessment.

1. *Evidencing a choice.* This test focuses only on the presence or absence of a decision. If a person makes a decision, he or she is judged competent. This test is the least protective of the individual because assessment is minimal. Actually, this test is rarely used. It has been criticized on the grounds that the decision does not assure that the patient has a good understanding of the proposed treatment or experiment. However, in this regard, it has been argued that evaluation of the patient's rationality and ability to comprehend is inappropriate in a competency test because it is too paternalistic.

In testing competency according to this standard, the relevant information is simply presented to the prospective participant, and he or she either agrees or declines to become a subject. No effort is made to determine whether the information was understood or if rational reasoning was employed to reach the decision. The "yes" or "no" response by the individual is taken as enough to determine competency. Despite some arguments in favor of this test, it is generally agreed that the standard is too lenient.

2. *Factual comprehension.* This test requires that the patient understand the information relevant to the proposed treatment (e.g., the procedures, risks, benefits, and alternatives available). This standard does not take into account how reasonable the decision is or how rational the thought processes were in arriving at the decision. As a result, it is fairly respectful of the research subjects' sense of independence.

This probably is the most commonly used standard and is frequently thought to be the only way of assessing competency. In fact, almost all empirical studies of competency and informed consent employ this standard (Bergler, Pennington, Metcalfe, & Freis, 1980; Cassileth, Zupkis, Sutton-Smith, & March, 1980). Despite its widespread acceptance, it presents a major difficulty in that it relies heavily on individual's verbal skills, particularly verbal expression. As a result, there is a potential for a biasing of competency findings against the less verbally skilled. Some studies have shown that comprehension of consent information increases with the subjects' intelligence (Stanley & Stanley, 1981, in press). While this is not surprising, the policy implications are striking; individuals with lower IQs are less likely to be judged competent and, thereby, subject to exclusion from research.

Comprehension can be subdivided into understanding of the consent information at the moment of consent and retention of that information over a period of time. Retention, however, has been justifiably criticized as an invalid criterion (Stalney & Stanley, 1981). While it is important that a research subject remember that he or she can withdraw from an experiment, it may be completely unnecessary that he or she keep all the consent information in mind several weeks or months after the initial decision. The fact that an individual forgets information following a decision does not mean that he or she did not use it in decision making.

3. *Rational reasoning*. Under this standard, competency is defined as the capacity to understand the nature of the procedure, to weigh the risks and benefits, and to reach a decision for rational reasons (Friedman, 1975; Roth et al., 1977). This test focuses on the overall pattern of thought rather than on the particular result of the decision. It offers a high degree of protection to the subjects, but its application may express a bias toward a particular type of reasoning. In comparison with other competency tests, it is fairly paternalistic. While some authors have suggested that the rationality of the individual's entire reasoning processes be assessed under this standard (Appelbaum & Roth, 1982), others have recommended that assessment be tied more directly to the decision to participate in the research (Stanley & Stanley, 1981; Friedman, 1975). The former would be tested with a typical mental status examination designed to elicit severe impairment in judgment, thought disorder, hallucinations, and delusions. Actual judgment in daily life activities may also be assessed. The major problem with this sort of generalized testing is that we cannot be certain that when judgment is impaired in relation to some decisions it is also impaired with respect to decisions in an unrelated area of functioning.

This brings us to the second form of rationality assessment—rationality with respect to the decision. In this instance the patient's reasoning about his or her decision is directly elicited. The doctor must assess whether the patient's reasons make sense. The problem with this test is that the assessor's view of what is rational often becomes the standard rather than some objective determinant of rationality.

4. *Appreciation of the nature of the situation*. This standard of competency to give consent is closely aligned to the type of assessment that is performed when determining whether an individual was responsible for a criminal act. When applied to competency to give consent, subjects are tested to determine whether they appreciate their situation (Appelbaum & Roth, 1982). Do they understand the consequences of consenting or not consenting? Do they understand what information is relevant to the decision and what is not? Under this standard, comprehension of the

consent information is a prerequisite, with the additional requirement that the patient must be able to use that information in a rational manner. This test is highly protectionistic in that the demands placed on the subject are stringent. For example, it is not sufficient that a patient understand the risks, benefits, and alternatives to the research; he or she must also "appreciate" the implications of treatment acceptance or refusal. Even "nonvulnerable" populations have a difficult time appreciating that fact (McCullum & Schwartz, 1969).

5. *Reasonable outcome of choice*. This test evaluates the patient's capacity to reach a reasonable result. The person who fails to make a decision that is roughly congruent with the decision that a reasonable person would have made is viewed as incompetent (Friedman, 1975). This standard is applied quite frequently when non-investigational treatments are recommended and particularly when the patient's life is at stake. It has been highly criticized for its strong paternalistic orientation and, hence, lack of respect for the individual's rights. Any decision with which the competency reviewer disagreed might provide a basis for judging the individual incompetent. Its relevance to competency to consent to research can be problematic since research projects are, by their very nature, experimental. Thus, it is difficult to know what is reasonable.

There is, however, a clear advantage to this test in that it does not rely on the patient's verbal expression skills as does the comprehension standard, while at the same time it provides more of an assessment than the evidencing-a-choice criterion. Thus, the patient simply gives a yes-no response with some prior assessment about whether that is a reasonable response. It has been suggested that this standard could be adapted in such a way as to tap "capacity to reach reasonable decisions" about treatment, independent of the decision at hand (Stanley & Stanley, 1981).

INFORMED CONSENT, CONFIDENTIALITY, AND PSYCHOTHERAPY

While professional codes (e.g., Committee on Scientific and Professional Ethics and Conduct, 1984) stress the importance of informed consent with a clear delineation of the limits of confidentiality, it is unclear how often the doctrine of informed consent is followed in psychotherapeutic practice. Hare-Mustin, Maracek, Kaplan, and Liss-Levinson (1979), for example, point out that certain models of psychotherapy including psychoanalytic, behavioristic, and behavioral focus on how to produce change rather than on the rights of the individuals involved in the process. Consequently, "implications of certain procedures for the individual's welfare and dignity" can be overlooked (Hare-Mustin et al., 1979). Thus, the emphasis on achieving change can come at the expense of respecting an individual's autonomy and privacy needs.

Much of the discussion of informed consent to psychotherapy has centered on the bounds of confidentiality in therapy. This discussion arose in large part as the aftermath to the Tarasoff decision (Noll, 1976). In *Tarasoff v. Regents of University of California* (Noll, 1976), the court held that if a patient expresses a death threat toward a third party, it is the responsibility of the therapist to inform, in some way, that third party of the threat. Later cases have both modified and diverged from the Tarasoff decision. In *Thompson v. Alameda* (1980) it was decided that the need to notify held only when there was an identifiable victim. However, other cases have broadened the identifiable clause (*Davis v. Lhim*, 1983).

Whether Tarasoff is interpreted broadly or narrowly, it has made an impact on informed consent in psychotherapy. Noll (1976) has stated that the Tarasoff decision imposes a social control role on psychotherapists. In another article, he suggests that psychotherapists ought to disclose to prospective patients the "material risks" of psychotherapy (Noll, 1981). These risks include:

1.   Informing employers (present or potential) or insurers of psychiatric treatment may lead to a negative outcome such as loss of a job or denial of insurance.

2.   Using a third-party payer could lead to the information being recorded in a centralized computer bank (i.e., Medical Information Bureau) and thus become available to other insurers.

3.   Responding affirmatively to questions on insurance or application forms regarding previous psychotherapy can lead to further questioning by prospective employers or insurers.

4.   The information revealed by the patient may lead to his or her hospitalization (either voluntary or involuntary) or to the warning of potential victims of violence.

5.   Records maintained by the therapist may not be completely inaccessible to others. Access can be gained either by robbery or subpoena.

In addition to informing patients of the material risks posed by psychotherapy, it has been proposed by the American Psychological Association's ethics committee that the use of supervisors or consultants by a psychotherapist-in-training ought to be revealed to patients at the outset of therapy.

The issue of informed consent is particularly problematic in two settings: family therapy and the criminal justice system. In family therapy (Hines & Mare-Mustin, 1978) the bounds of confidentiality are unclear and thus make it difficult to obtain a fully informed consent at the beginning of treatment. If an individual family member reveals a confidence to the therapist, does the therapist share that confidence with other members of the family? To a certain extent, it depends on the therapist's model and the nature of the confidence.

In the forensic setting, the issue of informed consent has several dimensions. The first relates to treatment or rehabilitation refused. It has been argued that inmates ought to have the right to refuse rehabilitation but that they should be informed of the consequences of that refusal (Clingempeel, Mulvey & Reppucci, 1980). The second dimension of informed consent concerns the limits of confidentiality (Clingempeel et al., 1980) that may go beyond the usual limits in a therapist-patient relationship. For example, to what extent should patients be informed if the information obtained in therapy sessions is to be used in parole decisions, decisions about privileges, or the like? Monahan (1980) has framed this issue in terms of the mixed loyalties of the therapist and thus may not be amenable to simple solutions.

EMPIRICAL RESEARCH

Over the past 20 years, interest in informed consent in medical treatment and research has burgeoned. Evidence of this growing concern is the large number of published articles on consent in this 20-year span. Woodward (1979) reports that the number of articles about human experimentation and informed consent increased sixfold in the period following 1960 as contrasted with the 20-year period prior to 1960. Kaufmann (1983), in a review of articles relative to informed consent, found that medical journals published far more articles on informed consent than did either law or social science journals. In addition, she found that the social sciences lagged behind the other disciplines in both the point at which it began to study informed consent and the quantity of articles it produced.

A review of the published articles on the consent process shows that the majority of them have been opinion or position papers (Burra, Kimberley & Miura, 1980; Culver, Ferrell & Green, 1980; Loftus & Fries, 1979; Vaccarino, 1978). They serve to clarify the issues (Gray, 1978) involved in obtaining consent and aid in the development of a uniform doctrine. The opinions expressed in these articles run the gamut from the view that informed consent is the "absolute right" of the patient and is in no way detrimental to the goals of treatment and research (McLean, 1980; Park, Covi, & Uhlenhuth, 1967) to the opinion that informing the patient serves only to terrify him and cause undue anxiety, destroys the nature of the doctor-patient relationship, and may severely impede the progress of research (Coleman, 1974; Park & Slaughter 1966). Further, opinion also suggests on the one hand, that truly informed consent is a myth (Leeb, Bowers, & Lunch, 1976), a fiction, or an illusion (Goin, Burgoyne, & Goin, 1976; Hirsch, 1977; Laforet, 1976). On the other hand, it is believed that a reasonable consent can be obtained (Alfidi, 1971).

This diversity of opinion is also expressed with respect to obtaining consent from patients whose competence is suspect as in the case of severly disturbed psychiatric patients. Some view the presence of mental illness as limiting the possibility of obtaining a competent consent (Pryce, 1978). Others believe consent can be meaningfully obtained from many patients afflicted with psychiatric illness.

While opinion plays an important role of identifying and clarifying the issues, it is rather disappointing that many position papers which address ability to give consent do so without an empirical base substantiating their views. The questions surrounding informed consent are sorely in need of empirical investigation (Stanley & Stanley, 1981), and the social sciences could make contributions in this direction.

The available empirical research on consent falls into four major areas: (1) disclosure and comprehension of consent information, (2) patient's subjective reactions to consent information, (3) methods of decision making in the consent process, and (4) competence of the patient or research participant to give consent. Competence is closely related to comprehension but, for purposes of this review, studies that address populations of questionable competence will be reviewed separately. Furthermore, studies which investigate consent to treatment will be reviewed along with those that examine consent to research.

Comprehension and Disclosure

The first group of empirical data to be reviewed are studies that investigate comprehension of consent information by patients. The largest body of empirical research on the consent process falls into this category. Medical patients are the most frequently investigated. More than 20 studies have assessed understanding of consent information by patients (e.g., Bergler et al., 1980; Cassileth et al., 1980; Hasser & Weintraub, 1976; Kennedy & Lillehaugen, 1979; Marini, Sheard & Bridges, 1976; Penman, Bahna, Holland et al., 1980; Robinson & Merav, 1976; Schultz, Pardee, & Ensinck, 1975; Singer, 1978). The prototype of these studies is as follows. Patients are given a consent form for either a research protocol or standard treatment, and the form is usually read to them by a physician or investigator. Patients are then asked questions regarding their knowledge of the consent information. The point in time that they are asked these questions varies from immediately afterward to several months later. In the latter case, the study becomes one of testing recall instead of comprehension.

Although it is difficult to make comparisons across studies as a result of different methodologies, it is generally concluded that comprehension of consent information—irrespective of assessment time—is poor. Overall comprehension ranges from approximately 35 percent to 80 percent of the total information conveyed. Patients tend to be best informed about their diagnosis and the proposed treatment (for example, the name of the drug they were to take) and least knowledgeable about alternate treatments available and risks including side effects of drugs and possible complications of surgical procedures. In addition, some studies of research patients demonstrate that many were not aware or did not acknowledge that they were, in fact, participating in a research study (McCullum & Schwartz, 1969; Park et al., 1966).

While results of these studies are, at first glance, discouraging about the prospects of obtaining a fully informed consent, most of the studies have limitations which make it difficult to consider them conclusive (Meisel & Roth, 1981). First, in several studies we do not know exactly what information was conveyed to the patients (Cassileth et al., 1980; Goin et al., 1976; Priluck, Robertson & Buettner, 1979). Further, some studies gave patients the consent form to read and then tested knowledge of this form. It is not known whether all patients read the form (Olin & Olin, 1975). In this same vein, the amount of instruction given to patients varied from study to study. In some, instruction was minimal with no particular effort made to convey the consent information (Benson, Gordon, Mitchell & Place, 1977). In other studies, investigators went through a good deal of instruction with patients (Faden & Beauchamp, 1980).

Across studies, in general, greater instruction appears to be associated with greater understanding. This conclusion must be tentative, however, since most studies investigate only one level of instruction (i.e., consent form, videotape aids), and differences among sample characteristics and medical procedures for which consent was to be obtained vary greatly (Arluke, 1980; Muss, White, Michielutte et al., 1979; Stuart, 1978).

Another factor which makes it difficult to draw generalizable conclusions is that in many of the studies we do not know the level of complexity of the language of the consent form that was related in the consent session. Grundner (1980) and Morrow (1980) suggest that most consent forms are written in highly technical language. This may account for some of the poor comprehension attained in the empirical studies. However, this is a speculation because most studies do not report the readability of their consent material.

Epstein and Lasagna (1969) conducted one of the only studies that systematically varied complexity of consent material. They presented three different consent forms of varying length to normal volunteers. They found that comprehension was inversely related to the length of the consent form. Therefore, greater comprehension may be achieved by increasing instruction and decreasing the complexity of material. As simple a technique as giving the patient a consent form to take home with him prior to signing it increases knowledge (Morrow, Gootnick & Schmale, 1978). Also suggested are two-part or three-part consent forms, objective tests, videotape aids (Barbour & Blumenkrantz, 1978; Grabowski & Mintz, 1979; Schwartz, 1978; Silberstein, 1974; Stuart, 1978, Williams, Trenholme 1977).

Other studies have investigated the modality of disclosure (i.e., how the information is conveyed to the patient) to determine if comprehension systematically varies according to type of presentation—written information, videotape, discussion groups (Faden, 1977; Faden & Beauchamp, 1980). These initial studies show that modality does not seem to make a difference in level of comprehension. However, comparing innovative modalities of disclosure with the traditional one-to-one doctor-patient model is, as yet, untested. There is some suggestion (Muss et al., 1979) that instruction given by health professionals in addition to that given by the physician improves comprehension of consent information. But it is unclear whether this improvement is simply because of repeated exposure to the consent material or as a result of a qualitative difference.

Comparing studies of comprehension of consent information is further complicated when the methods for assessing comprehension are examined. Some investigators use multiple-choice or true-false tests as a means of assessment while others use open-ended questions with coded responses. Relevant literature on learning and psychological testing has shown that tests of recognition, such as multiple-choice tests, are easier than tests of recall using open-ended questions. Therefore, comparing results of studies which use open-ended questions with objective questions is problematic.

A further difficulty in comparing these studies lies in the fact that immediate understanding and recall at some later point in time are often treated interchangeably. However, results show, not surprisingly, that retention of information declines over time. The utility of assessing retention of all consent information must be questioned. Certainly it is important that a research subject remember that he has the freedom to withdraw from an experiment, but it may not be necessary that he keep all the consent information in mind several weeks or months after the initial decision. Further, the fact that an individual forgets information does not mean that it wasn't used at the time of the decision and then forgotten as part of the normal forgetting process.

It must be noted that in the studies reviewed here, there has been an assumption made by most of the investigators that knowledge of the consent information as measured by some form of objective test is equated with comprehension of that information. However, if an individual is able to repeat what he has been told, it does not necessarily mean he understands that information. In other words, knowledge is a necessary but not sufficient condition for understanding. A novel approach such as that taken by Mellinger, Huffine & Balter (1980) seems to be called for. They developed an assessment of comprehension that includes an objective test requiring subjects to make judgments about a series of statements in addition to a standard evaluation of comprehension. Illogical judgments indicate a lack of comprehension.

Lastly, the sample characteristics of the patients must be taken into account when we examine comprehension. Many of the studies have examined understanding of consent information by medical patients who have serious illnesses. Others have looked at the less seriously ill, and some have researched the normal volunteer (i.e., those without medical illness). Hospitalized and nonhospitalized patients have been studied. Comparability of these subject groups cannot be assumed. The ill patient is under more emotional stress than the healthy volunteer. This stress may interfere with comprehension of consent information. Further, differences may be found between the hospitalized and nonhospitalized patient. Some research suggests that hospitalization itself makes an individual feel more vulnerable, and this in turn may influence comprehension of consent information. Cassileth and associates (1980) found that ambulatory patients demonstrated greater comprehension of consent information for cancer treatment than those who were bedridden. Perhaps bedridden patients were preoccupied with more serious illness. Further, educational level and intelligence have shown some relationship with comprehension of consent information (Cassileth et al., 1980) although this is not a consistent finding.

Overall, the comprehension level of consent information is low. However, instructional aids seem to increase comprehension. In general, conclusions from these studies of comprehension must be drawn with caution because of their limitations.

Patient Reactions

In addition to studying the amount of consent information that patients understand, some investigators have conducted studies on how patients feel about being informed (Alfidi, 1971; Denney, Williamson, & Penn, 1975; Golden & Johnston, 1970; Lankton, Batchelder, & Ominslay, 1977). This area of investigation was popular a few years ago when the merits of informed consent doctrine were being hotly debated. This research typically was designed to assess whether informing the patient was harmful. To a large degree, this point is moot since consent is now required for most research projects and many standard treatments. Not informing the subject is no longer a possibility. Initial efforts are being made to redirect this research toward determining the least anxiety-producing manner for informing the patient (Faden, 1977; Faden & Beauchamp, 1980).

Patient reaction to consent information is typically assessed by asking patients whether the information disclosed in the consent session made them upset or anxious. While there are anecdotal reports that the disclosure made patients anxious or fearful, statistical studies find no differences in anxiety levels, either self-reported or by physician observers, between informed and uninformed patients (Denney et al., 1975; Lankton et al., 1977; Houts & Leaman, 1980). While two studies without uninformed controls (Alfidi, 1971; Houts & Leaman, 1980) found that consent information disturbed about 40 percent of the patients, only 1 percent decided not to go ahead with the recommended procedure, and 97 percent of the people regarded the information as useful. It is interesting to note that one study (Denney et al., 1975) found that anxiety levels postoperatively were lower in informed rather than uninformed patients. This finding suggests that knowledge of expected results makes the actual results more emotionally tolerable and less frightening. In fact, this notion serves as the basis for presurgical counseling which prepares patients through support and information.

In a study of family-planning-clinic patients, different methods of disclosing information to the patients did not have an impact on patients' level of anxiety (Faden, 1977). About 25 percent of the patients reported feeling more anxious than usual following the disclosure of information. However, the same percentage of patients who were faced with making the decision about contraception also reported more anxiety than usual despite the fact that they had not received the detailed information.

Thus, when conducting studies in this area, it is important to attempt to separate out normal anxiety induced by making a decision about a medical problem from anxiety induced by detailed information about the procedure. Further, it would be useful to conduct similar studies with medically ill patients to determine whether they respond differently than patients who are healthy (Golden & Johnston, 1970). A study that did examine chronically ill patients found that physicians who sounded angry and anxious but whose speech content was sympathetic had patients who were more content. This suggests that a very complicated set of factors is involved in patients' reactions in a medical setting (Hall, Roter & Rand, 1980).

Overall, this area of investigation would seem to be most fruitful if efforts were placed not in looking at whether consent information makes people upset or anxious, but instead toward finding the least anxiety-provoking manner in which to disclose information.

Decision Making

A small number of studies have investigated factors which influence patient decision making in the consent process. Some studies have shown that people feel that they have no choice and must participate (McCullum & Schwartz, 1969). Other studies do not find this, and the primary focus of them has been to determine whether disclosure of risks discourages patients or research subjects from giving consent (Alfidi, 1971; Lankton et al., 1977).

In a study of risk disclosure for anesthesia, patients did not refuse the procedure following detailed information about the risks (Lankton et al., 1977). Similarly, in two studies only a few patients refused angiography following a detailed risk disclosure (Alfidi, 1971). Perhaps the best-known study in this area was conducted on kidney donors (Fellner & Marshall, 1970). This study was designed to determine whether kidney donors utilized risk information in their decision to donate a kidney. It was found that decisions were made long before any detailed risk disclosure was made and further that disclosure had little impact on the donors. However, more recent research (Stanley, Stanley, Schwartz, Lautin & Kane, 1980; Stanley et al., 1981) has shown that participation in hypothetical research projects varies according to the risk of the project.

A few studies have attempted to relate comprehension of consent information to decision making (Epstein & Lasagna, 1969; Stuart, 1978). Findings seem to indicate that higher levels of comprehension are associated with a higher rate of agreement to the proposed procedure by the patient. However, interpretation of these findings is problematic because the risk-benefit ratios of the procedures must be known in order to determine whether the patients' affirmative decisions were sensible.

As an outgrowth of the studies which showed that risk disclosure does not seem to influence decision making with regard to medical procedures, some investigators have begun to identify factors that do influence decisions. In a study of participation in psychology experiments (Geller & Faden, 1979), the relative influence of standard consent information and personal testimony of one individual was examined. While recall of consent information was affected by testimony which contradicted it, the decision to participate was not affected. In another study, subjects reported that disclosed information was not the primary determinant in decisions regarding contraception. Instead, personal feelings were reported to have a greater influence on the decision (Faden & Beauchamp, 1980).

As an extension of this work, it seems worthwhile to adapt some of the techniques developed by investigators who research decision making and information processing (Janis & Mann, 1977; Jungerman, 1980). For example, it seems worthwhile to try to adapt the technique of "policy capturing" from the social sciences (Zedeck & Blood, 1974) to research on informed consent. In addition to asking subjects what influenced them, subjects could be placed in a variety of hypothetical situations and asked to make a decision about participation. In this way, the patient's ability to report influences—an ability which is not completely reliable—would not be so heavily depended upon. This hypothetical approach with its pitfalls can be balanced with the patient self-reports for a fuller picture of the decision-making process.

Competency

Competency to engage in the consent process has received attention only recently in the informed consent literature. A major difficulty with conducting research on competency lies in the fact that there is no standard definition of competence (Meisel et al., 1977; Roth et al., 1977), no accepted test of competency (Appelbaum, Mirkin, & Bateman, 1981; Appelbaum & Bateman, 1981; Dabrowski, Gerald, Walczak, Wororiowicz, & Zakowska-Dabrowski, 1978), and no clear agreement on the appropriate dividing line between competence and incompetence. In studies of comprehension, what one investigator believes as signifying competence (Woodward, 1979), another believes indicates incompetence (Bergler et al., 1980). Further, agreement is lacking on which groups of patients should be suspect as having "uncertain competence." Mentally ill patients have been identified as one such group and the few empirical studies on competency have focused on the mentally ill. However, other populations may also fall into this category of "questionable competence." These groups are the elderly, children, the mentally retarded, and those patients suffering from organic brain syndrome. Empirical investigation of these individuals is lacking.

The empirical evidence that is available with respect to the mentally ill presents a somewhat mixed picture. Under the rubric of mentally ill are primarily schizophrenic and psychotically depressed patients. One conclusion that can be safely drawn with respect to the mentally ill is that they certainly do no better than medical patients in the consent process. The evidence that they are less able to give consent is somewhat equivocal and to a certain extent depends on the definition of competency that is used.

With respect to comprehension of consent information, a few studies have assessed psychiatric patients' ability to understand consent information (Appelbaum et al., 1981; Grossman & Summers, 1980; Soskis & Jaffe, 1979; Roth et al., 1982). In general, patients do not have a very high level of understanding of consent information. However, when comparing studies of medical patients' comprehension with studies of psychiatric patients, understanding in both groups seems to be fairly equal (Grossman & Summers, 1980; Soskis & Jaffe, 1979). An example of this is seen in one study which found that schizophrenic patients understood about 50 percent of the material on a consent form which was read to them (Grossman & Summers, 1980). In a direct comparison of psychiatric and medical patients, it was found that schizophrenic patients were more aware of the risks and side effects of their medication than were medical patients (Soskis, 1978). On the other hand, medical patients were better informed about the name and dose of their medication as well as their diagnosis. The poor knowledge of diagnosis by psychiatric patients may be partly the result of a general reluctance by hospital staff to tell patients that they have schizophrenia.

Related to the comprehension level of psychiatric patients are studies that have examined the literacy skills of these patients. Despite the fact that psychiatric patients' comprehension of consent information seems to be equal to that of medical patients, research indicates that their reading comprehension scores were only at the fifth-grade level (Berg & Hammit, 1980; Coles, Roth, & Pollack, 1978). As a result, a suggestion is made that hospital documents be simplified for psychiatric patients (Berg & Hammit, 1980), as some have suggested for medical patients.

In studies of psychiatric patients' ability to consent to hospitalization, the results indicate that level of knowledge of patient rights is relatively poor (Applebaum et al., 1981; Palmer & Wohl, 1972). However, it is important to know whether medical patients would score higher than psychiatric patients, and also it is important to separate patients' inabilities from deficient information-giving on the part of the hospital admissions servite. In contrast to the studies which say that psychiatric patients may not be competent to give consent, one study concludes that 93 percent of the patients give a valid consent (Dabrowski et al., 1978). However, the standard for competency was set much lower than the standard in other studies described here.

In a study of consent to electroconvulsive therapy (Roth et al., 1982), about 25 percent of the patients were found to be incompetent based on their understanding of consent information and independent judges' opinions about their comprehension. This study is the first to take a comprehensive approach by coordinating objective information (i.e., patient comprehension) with legal judgments and psychiatric opinions and seems to be a fruitful direction for further research.

A few studies of psychiatric patients have examined the relationship between understanding and the decision to consent to or refuse the proposed procedure (Grossman & Summers, 1980; Roth et al., 1982). They found that, like medical patients, psychiatric patients who understood more of the consent information tended to agree to the procedure more often.

With respect to patients' rationale for deciding to agree to a treatment or research protocol, results are not clear-cut. One study found that the risks of psychotropic medication did not play a role in patients' decisions to refuse medication (Appelbaum & Gutheil, 1980). Psychological factors were cited as primary reasons. It is difficult to compare these results with those from medical patients because no medical study to date has attempted to delineate the psychological factors examined in the psychiatric study. In a study (Stanley et al., 1980; Stanley et al., 1981) which examined psychiatric and medical patients' willingness to participate in a series of hypothetical studies, no differences were found between the two patient groups. Both psychiatric and medical patients agreed to participate in the studies in a manner which was consistent with the level of risk attendant to the study protocol. It is important to conduct a parallel study which investigates participation rate in actual projects.

Overall, the empirical research on informed consent shows that psychiatric patients do have some impairment in their abilities. However, research also shows that in some respects they do not differ from medical patients. As a result, further studies involving comparison groups, particularly medical patients, are vital if conclusions are to be drawn about any one group of patients. In addition, it is also important to state precisely the standards used for determining competency so that comparisons can be more readily made from study to study. Conclusions, such as only a "quarter of the patients could give true consent" (Pryce, 1978), are helpful only if the criteria for true consent are disclosed.

In addition to psychiatric patients, two other groups of individuals—the elderly and children—have been identified as "vulnerable" populations and thus may have compromised competency to consent. With respect to the elderly, studies have shown some impairment in their ability to comprehend consent information (Stanley, Guido, Stanley & Shortell, 1984). Impaired recall of consent information has been noted in the elderly who have poorer verbal skills. It appears that although comprehension and recall may be affected by age, the overall quality of decision making is not (Stanley et al., 1984). In other words, the elderly typically reach similar decisions regarding agreement to proposed procedures in the same manner as their younger counterparts.

With respect to children, the picture seems to be somewhat comparable to the elderly. Children as young as nine years old reached treatment decisions the same way adults do (Weithorn & Campbell, 1982) although they did not understand consent information as well as adults. By the age of fourteen, children do not appear to differ in competency from the adult population (Weithorn & Campbell, 1982). In a conceptual analysis of adolescents' competency to make informed birth control and pregnancy decisions, Carter and Lawrence (1985) suggest that adolescents generally have the cognitive capacities necessary to make competent decisions.

CONCLUSION

This chapter has reviewed the historical and empirical literature on informed consent in the treatment and research settings. The doctrine of informed consent with its three elements of information disclosure, voluntariness, and competency has emerged from a series of lawsuits against practitioners and in response to abuses in the research setting. While the legal literature has defined what it considers to be the ideal in doctor-patient communication, the empirical literature shows that this ideal is not often achieved (in fact, comprehension of consent information is poor) nor are certain assumptions (for example, that children are incapable of giving a competent consent), which are embodied in the doctrine, borne out by empirical research.

REFERENCES

Alfidi, R. J. (1971). Informed consent: A study of patient reaction. *Journal of the American Medical Association, 216,* 1325–1329.

American Psychological Association. (1972). *Ethical principles in the conduct of research with human participants.* APA: Washington, D.C.

American Psychological Association. (1982). *Ethical principles in the conduct of research with human participants.* APA: Washington, D.C.

Appelbaum, P. S., & Gutheil, T. G. (1980). Drug refusal: A study of psychiatric inpatients. *American Journal of Psychiatry, 137,* 340–346.

Appelbaum, P. S., Mirkin, S., & Bateman, A. (1981). Competency to consent to psychiatric hospitalization: An empirical assessment. *American Journal of Psychiatry, 138,* 170–176.

Appelbaum, P. S., & Bateman, A. (1979). Competency to consent to voluntary psychiatric hospitalization: A theoretical approach. *Bulletin of the American Academy of Psychiatry and the Law, 7,* 390–399.

Appelbaum, P., & Roth, L. (1982). Competency to consent to research: A psychiatric overview. *Archives of General Psychiatry, 39*, 951–958.

Arluke, A. (1980). Judging drugs: Patients' conceptions of therapeutic efficacy in the treatment of arthritis. *Human Organization, 39*(1), 84–88.

Barbour, G. L., & Blumenkrantz, M. J. (1978). Videotape aids informed consent decisions. *Journal of the American Medical Association, 240*, 2741–2742.

Beauchamp, T. L., & Childress, J. F. (1983). *Principles of biomedical ethics* (2nd ed.). New York: Oxford Press.

Beecher, H. K. (1966). Ethics and clinical research. *New England Journal of Medicine, 274*, 1354–1360.

Benson, H., Gordon, L., Mitchell, C., & Place, V. (1977). Patient education and intrauterine conception: A study of two package inserts. *American Journal of Public Health, 67*, 446–449.

Berg, A., & Hammit, K. B. (1980). Assessing the psychiatric patient's ability to meet the literacy demands of hospitalization. *Hospital and Community Psychiatry, 31*(4), 266–268.

Bergler, J., Pennington, C., Metcalfe, M., & Freis, E. (1980). Informed consent: How much does the patient understand? *Clinical Pharmacology and Therapeutics, 27*, 435–439.

Brandt, A. M. (1978). Racism and research: The case of the Tuskegee syphilis study. *Hastings Center Report, 8*(6), 21–29.

Burra, P., Kimberley, R., & Miura, C. (1980). Mental competence and consent to treatment. *Canadian Journal of Psychiatry, 25*, 251–253.

Carter, P., & St. Lawrence, J. (1985). Adolescents' competency to make informed birth control and pregnancy decisions: An interface for psychology and the law. *Behavioral Sciences and the Law, 3*, 309–319.

Cassileth, B. R., Zupkis, R. B., Sutton-Smith, K., & March, V. (1980). Informed consent—Why are its goals imperfectly realized? *New England Journal of Medicine, 302*(16), 896–900.

Clingempell, W., Mulvey, E., & Reppucci, N. (1980). A national study of ethical dilemmas of psychologists in the criminal justice system. In J. Monahan (Ed.), *Who is the client?* Washington, DC: American Psychological Association.

Coleman, L. (1974). The patient–physician relationship: Terrified consent. *Physician's World, 607.*

Coles, G., Roth, L., & Pollack, I. (1978). Literacy skills of long-term hospitalized mental patients. *Hospital and Community Psychiatry, 29*, 512–516.

Committee on Scientific and Professional Ethics and Conduct. (1984). Policy statement on informed consent and supervision. *The Clinical Psychologist*, Spring, 67.

Culver, C. M., Ferrell, R. B., & Green, R. M. (1980). ECT and special problems of informed consent. *American Journal of Psychiatry, 137*, 5.

Culver, C. M., & Gert, B. (1982). *Philosophy in medicine: Conceptual and ethical issues in medicine and psychiatry.* New York: Oxford Press.

Dabrowski, S., Gerald, K., Walczak, S., Woronowicz, B., & Zakowska-Dabrowski, T. (1978). Inability of patients to give valid consent to psychiatric hospitalization. *International Journal of Law and Psychiatry, 1*(4), 437–443.

Davis v. Lhim, 335 N.W. 2d 481 (Michigan Ct. App. 1983).

Declaration of Helsinki: Recommendations guiding medical doctors in biomedical research involving human subjects. Adopted by the 18th World Medical Assembly, Helsinki, Finland, 1964, and as revised by the 29th World Medical Assembly, Tokyo, 1975.

Denney, M., Williamson, D., & Penn, R. (1975). Informed consent: Emotional responses of patients. *Postgraduate Medicine, 60,* 205–209.

Department of Health and Human Services. (1981, January). Federal Register, *46*(16), 8366–8391.

Department of Health, Education, and Welfare. (1973). National Institute of Health. Protection of human subjects: Policies and procedures. 38(221), November 16, 1973, *31,* 738–741, 749.

Epstein, L., & Lasagna, L. (1969). Obtaining informed consent: Form or substance. *Archives of Internal Medicine, 123,* 682–685.

Faden, R. (1977). Disclosure and informed-consent: Does it matter how we tell it? *Health Education Monographs, 5,* 198–214.

Faden, R., & Beauchamp, T. (1980). Decision-making and informed consent: A study of the impact of disclosed information. *Social Indicators Research, 7,* 13–36.

Fellner, C., & Marshall, J. (1970). Kidney donors—The myth of informed consent. *American Journal of Psychiatry, 126,* 1245–1251.

Friedman, P. (1975). Legal regulation of applied behavior analysis in mental institutions and prisons. *Arizona Law Review, 17,* 39–104.

Geller, D., & Faden, R. (1979). *Decision-making in informed consent: Base rate and individuating information.* Paper presented at the annual meeting of the American Psychological Association.

Goin, M., Burgoyne, R., & Goin, J. (1976). Facelift operation: The patient's secret motivations and reactions to "informed consent." *Plastic and Reconstructive Surgery, 58,* 273–279.

Golden, J., & Johnston, G. (1970). Problems of distortion in doctor-patient communication. *Psychiatry Medicine, 1,* 127–148.

Grabowski, J., & Mintz, J. (1979). Increasing the likelihood that consent is informed. (Communication). *Journal of Applied Behavior Analysis, 12,* 283–284.

Gray, B. (1978). Complexities of informed consent. *Annals of the American Academy of Political and Social Sciences, 437,* 37–48.

Grossman, L., & Summers, F. (1980). A study of the capacity of schizophrenic patients to give informed consent. *Hospital and Community Psychiatry, 31*(3), 205–207.

Grundner, T. M. (1980). On the readability of surgical consent forms. *New England Journal of Medicine, 302,* 900–902.

Hall, J., Roter, D., & Rand, C. (1980). *Communication of affect between patient and physician.* Paper presented at the annual meeting of the American Psychological Association.

Hare-Mustin, R., Maracek, J., Kaplan, A., & Liss-Levinson, N. (1979). Rights of clients, responsibilities of therapists. *American Psychologist, 34,* 3–16.

Hassar, M., & Weintraub, M. (1976). "Uninformed" consent and the wealthy volunteer: An analysis of patient volunteers in a clinical trial of a new anti-inflammatory drug. *Clinical Pharmacology and Therapeutics, 20,* 379–386.

Hines, P., & Hare-Muston, R. (1978). Ethical concerns in family therapy. *Professional Psychology, 9,* 165–171.

Hirsch, H. R. (1977). Informed consent: Fact or fiction. *J. Legal Med, 5*, 25.

Houts, P., & Leaman, D. (1980). *Patient response to information about possible complications of medical procedures.* Paper presented at the annual meeting of the American Psychological Association.

Humphreys, L. (1970). *Tearoom trade: Impersonal sex in public places.* Chicago: Aldine Publishing.

Janis, I., & Mann, L. (1977). *Decision-making: A psychological analysis of conflict choice & commitment.* New York: Free Press.

Jungerman, H. (1980). Speculations about decision-theoretic aids for personal decision making. *Acta Psychologica, 45*, 7–34.

Katz, J. (1972). *Experimentation with human beings.* New York: Russell Sage Foundation.

Kaufmann, C. L. (1983). Informed consent and patient decision making: Two decades of research. *Social Science Medicine, 17*(21), 1657–1664.

Kaufmann, D., Roth, L., Lidz, C., & Meisel, A. (1981). Informed consent and patient decision making: The reasoning of law and psychiatry. *International Journal of Law and Psychology, 4*, 345–361.

Kennedy, B. J., & Lillenhaugen, A. (1979). Patient recall of informed consent. *Medical and Pediatric Oncology, 7*(2), 173–178.

Laforet, E. G. (1976). The fiction of informed consent. *Journal of the American Medical Association, 235*, 1579–1585.

Lankton, J., Batchelder, B., & Ominslay, A. (1977). Emotional responses to detailed risk disclosure for anesthesia. *Anesthesiology, 46*, 294–296.

Leeb, D., Bowers, D. G., Jr., & Lynch, J. B. (1976). Observation on the myth of "informed consent." *Plastic and Reconstructive Surgery, 58*, 280–282.

Levine, R. J. (1981). *Ethics and regulation of clinical research.* Baltimore: Urban & Schwarzenberg.

Loftus, E. G., & Fries, J. F. (1979). Informed consent may be hazardous to health. (Editorial.) *Science, 204*, 4388.

Ludlum, J. (1972). *Informed consent.* Chicago: American Hospital Association.

Lynn, J. (1983). Informed consent: An overview. *Behavioral Sciences and the Law, 1*(4), 29–45.

Marini, J. L., Sheard, M. H., & Bridges, C. I. (1976). An evaluation of "informed consent" with volunteer prisoner subjects. *Yale Journal of Biology and Medicine, 49*, 427–437.

McCullum, A., & Schwartz, A. (1969). Pediatric research hospitalization: Its meaning to parents. *Pediatric Research, 3*, 199–204.

McLean, P. D. (1980). The effect of informed consent on the acceptance of random treatment assignment in a clinical population. *Behavior Research and Therapy, 11*, 129–133.

Meisel, A., & Roth, L. (1981). What we do and do not know about informed consent. *Journal of the American Medical Association, 246*(21), 2473–2477.

Meisel, A., Roth, L., & Lidz, C. (1977). Towards a model of the legal doctrine of informed consent. *American Journal of Psychiatry, 134*(3), 285–289.

Mellinger, G. D., Huffine, C. L., & Balter, M. B. (1980). Assessing comprehension in a survey of public reactions to complex issues. Institute for Research in Social Behavior.

Mitchell v. Robinson, 334 S.W. 2d 11 (Mo. 1960).

Mohr v. Williams, 95 Minn. 261, 104 N.W. 12 (1905).

Monahan, J. (Ed.). (1980). *Who is the client?* Washington, DC: American Psychological Association.

Morrow, G. (1980). How readable are subject consent forms? *Journal of the American Medical Association, 244*, 56–58.

Morrow, G., Gootnick, J., & Schmale, A. (1978). A simple technique for increasing cancer patients' knowledge of informed consent to treatment. *Cancer, 42*, 793–799.

Muss, H. B., White, D. R., Michielutte, R., Richards, F., II, Cooper, M. R., Williams, S., Stuart, J. J., & Spurr, C. (1979). Written informed consent in patients with breast cancer. *Cancer, 43*, 1549–1556.

Natanson v. Kline, 186 Kan. 393, 350 p.2d 1093 (1960).

Noll, J. (1976). The psychotherapist and informed consent. *American Journal of Psychiatry, 33*, 1451–1453.

Noll, J. (1981). Material risks and informed consent to psychotherapy. *American Psychologist, 36*, 915–916.

Nuremberg Code. (1949). From trials of war criminals before the Nuremberg military tribunals under control council law no. 10, *2*, 181–182.

Olin, G. B., & Olin, H. S. (1975). Informed consent in voluntary mental hospital admissions. *American Journal of Psychiatry, 132*, 938–941.

Palmer, A., & Wohl, J. (1972). Voluntary admission forms: Does the patient know what he's signing? *Hospital and Community Psychiatry, 23*, 250–252.

Park, L., Covi, L., & Uhlenhuth, E. (1967). Effects of informed consent on research patients and study results. *Journal of Nervous and Mental Disease, 145*, 349–357.

Park, L., Slaughter, R., Cori, L., & Kniffin, H. G. (1966). The subjective experience of the research patient. *Journal of Nervous and Mental Disease, 143*, 199–206.

Penman, D., Bahna, G., Holland, J., Morrow, G., Morse, I., Schmale, A., Long, C., Derogatis, L., & Mellis, N. (1980). *Patients' perceptions of giving informed consent for investigational chemotherapy.* Paper presented at the annual meeting of the American Psychological Association.

Pratt v. Davis, 224 Ill. 300, 79 N.E. 562 (1906).

President's Commission for the Study of Ethical Problems in Medicine and Biomedical and Behavioral Research. (1982). *Making health care decisions.* Washington, DC: U.S. Government Printing Office.

Priluck, I. A., Robertson, D. M., & Buettner, H. (1979). What patients recall of the preoperative discussion after retinal detachment surgery. *American Journal of Ophthalmology, 87*, 620–623.

Pryce, I. G. (1978). Clinical research upon mentally ill subjects who cannot give informed consent. *British Journal of Psychiatry, 22*, 209.

Robinson, G., & Merav, A. (1976). Informed consent: Recall by patients tested post-operatively. *Annals of Thoracic Surgery, 22*, 209.

Rolater v. Strain, 39 Okla. 1572, 137 p. 96 (1913).

Roth, L. H. (1983). Is it best to obtain informed consent from schizophrenic patients about the possible risk of drug treatment, for example, tardive dyskinesia, before initiating treatment or at a later date? *Journal of Clinical Psychopharmacology, 3*, 207–208.

Roth, L., Lidz, C., Meisel, A., Soloff, P., Kaufman, K., Spiker, D., & Foster, F. (1982). Competency to decide about treatment or research. *International Journal of Law and Psychiatry, 5*, 29–50.

Roth, L. H., Meisel, A., & Lidz, C. W. (1977). Tests of competency to consent to treatment. *American Journal of Psychiatry, 134*(3), 279–284.

Rozovsky, F. (1984). *Consent to treatment: A practical guide.* Boston: Little, Brown & Co.

Salgo v. Leland Stanford Jr. University Board of Trustees, 154 Cal. App. 2d 560, 578, 317 p.2d 170, 181 (1957).

Schloendorff v. Society of New York Hospitals, 211 N.Y. 125, 129-130, 105 N.E. 92, 93 (1914).

Schultz, A. L., Pardee, G. P., & Ensinck, J. W. (1975). Are research subjects really informed? *Western Journal of Medicine, 123*, 76–80.

Schwartz, E. (1978). The use of a checklist in obtaining informed consent for treatment with medication. *Hospital and Community Psychiatry, 29*, 97, 100.

Silberstein, E. (1974). Extension of two part consent form. *New England Journal of Medicine, 291*, 155–156.

Singer, E. (1978). The effects of informed consent procedures on respondents' reactions to surveys. *J. Consumer Res, 5*(1), 49–57.

Soskis, D. A. (1978). Schizophrenic and medical inpatients as informed drug consumers. *Archives of General Psychiatry, 35*, 645–647.

Soskis, D. A., & Jaffe, R. L. (1979). Communicating with patients about antipsychotic drugs. *Comprehensive Psychiatry, 20*, 126–131.

Stanley, B., Guido, J., Stanley, M., & Shortell, D. (1984). The elderly patient and informed consent. *Journal of the American Medical Association, 252*, 1302–1306.

Stanley, B., & Stanley, M. (1981). Psychiatric patients and research: Protecting their autonomy. *Comprehensive Psychiatry, 22*, 4, 420–427.

Stanley, B., & Stanley, M. (in press). Informed consent and competency in psychiatric research. *Archives of General Psychiatry.*

Stanley, B., Stanley, M., Lautin, A., Kane, J., & Schwartz, N. (1981). Preliminary findings on psychiatric patients as research participants: A population at risk? *American Journal of Psychiatry, 138*, 5, 669–671.

Stanley, B., Stanley, M., Schwartz, N., Lautin, A., & Kane, J. (1980). The ability of the mentally ill to evaluate research risks. *IRCS Medical Science: Clinical Pharmacology and Therapeutics; Psychology and Psychiatry; Surgery and Transplantation, 8*, 657–658.

Stuart, R. B. (1978). Protection of the right to informed consent to participate in research. *Behaviour Research and Therapy, 9*(1), 73–82.

Sullivan, T. M. (1974). The involuntarily confined mental patient and informed consent to psychiatric treatment. *Loyola University Law Journal, 5*, 578–609.

Taub, H., Kline, G., & Baker, M. (1981). The elderly and informed consent: Effects of vocabulary level and corrected feedback. *Experimental Aging Research, 7*, 137–146.

Thompson v. County of Alameda, 614 P.2d 728 (California 1980).

Vaccarino, J. M. (1978). Consent, informed consent and the consent form. (Editorial.) *N.E.J. Med, 298*(8), 455.

Weithorn, L., & Campbell, S. (1982). The competency of children and adolescents to make informed treatment decisions. *Child Development, 53*, 1589–1598.

Williams, R., & Trenholme, G. et al. (1977). The use of a test to determine that consent is informed. *Military Medicine, 142*, 542–545.

Woodward, W. E. (1979). Informed consent of volunteers: A direct measurement of comprehension and retention of information. *Clin. Res., 27*, 248–252.

Zedeck, S., & Blood, M. R. (1974). *Foundations of behavioral science in organizations.* Monterey: Brooks/Cole Publishing.

CHAPTER 5

Mediating Domestic Law Issues

PAUL BRINSON and KATHRYN D. HESS

Domestic law represents the sum total of society's conception of what a family ought to be; including the prejudices, conventions, and ideals which have grown up over time regarding the family.

This chapter intends to provide a general working knowledge of domestic and juvenile laws, practices, limits, trends, and an understanding of the issues and values around which these laws and procedures evolved. We shall focus on specific issues of interest to the clinician in dealing with marriage, divorce, child custody, differences in adult and juvenile court systems and domestic violence. This chapter intends to provide a practical framework upon which a clinician can develop an evaluation and a treatment plan or testimony, and to assist the clinician in the development of domestic and family policy.

OVERVIEW OF THE DOMESTIC COURT'S POSITION

To an unprecedented degree, the architects of our most intimate family life are no longer family and kinship ties but rather legislative statutes and the domestic courts. Through their judgments, domestic courts often define what parents a child has and knows, as well as the most intimate social context and value system in which a child is to develop. Parental or custodial rights may be terminated and family relationships extensively restructured on the premise that the judge or various experts know best how a family should function, although in many cases, experience has amply demonstrated that satisfactory family functioning cannot be dictated. In recognition of the fallacy of expert omniscience, domestic courts have become increasingly reluctant to intervene in ongoing family relationships any more than necessary to resolve the issues at hand; rather, the courts are encouraging families to reorganize themselves. Acknowledging the domestic court's conservative view toward intervention in domestic matters, it is incumbent on the clinician to formulate opinions and responses in conservative terms, sensitive to his or her personal biases and recognizing the family's essential right to self-determination.

The state's relationship with the family is typically supportive and unobtrusive.

In addition, the courts have interpreted the constitutional provisions for liberty to mean that the family is entitled to privacy and that parents generally have the right to raise their children as they see fit (*Bellotti v. Baird,* 1979; *Meyer v. Nebraska,* 1923; *Parham v. J.R.,* 1979; *Pierce v. Society of Sisters,* 1925; *Planned Parenthood v. Danforth,* 1976; *Wisconsin v. Yoder,* 1972).

While society generally recognizes the family's right to self-determination, a breakdown in the family structure or function triggers court involvement. In the event that the requisite threshold of disruption occurs, the courts will intervene to mediate the family's difficulties. In these cases the court's intervention is usually intended to minimize the disruption of the ongoing functions of the family, and the court is generally willing to allow families the opportunity to resolve their differences through negotiation and on their own terms. In the event that family members are unable or unwilling to negotiate an agreement, the court will provide a final decision which is presumably consistent with the values of the broader community. The goals of domestic jurisprudence are to achieve efficiency, harmony, and balance in the family order.

Mermin (1982) suggests a number of important services offered to society and the family by domestic jurisprudence. These services include (1) the definition of a status in society including minority, marriage, legitimacy, domains of responsibility, or immunity from responsibility; (2) the settlement of domestic disputes through arbitration or negotiation and as a final authority in reaching a decision; (3) the maintenance of order through policing, protection, and definition of the relationships between family members; (4) the protection of the family against the exercise of excessive or unfair government power; and (5) assurances that family members enjoy the minimum decencies of life, such as economic protection, preservation of social status, and maintenance of the individual's physical and psychological well-being.

The domestic or Chancery court has protection as its central purpose (Paulsen, Wadlington, & Goebel, 1974). The court has traditionally executed its responsibility through a determination of fault or failure to fulfill contractual marital responsibilities, agreements for custody and visitation following the dissolution of a marriage, and provision for the support and maintenance of those deemed unable to support themselves. With the formation of the juvenile court system in the United States in the late nineteenth century, the state extended its responsibility to the actions of delinquent children and their subsequent rehabilitation. More recently, the domestic courts have begun to intervene in support of children's relationships with grandparents and other significant family members. Important progress has been made into the intervention and development of policy regarding abused and neglected children, the termination of parental rights, abortion, and foster or adoptive placement.

In their interpretation of the standards of the community as well as maintaining the continuity of family relationships, the courts are generally conservative in their application of testimony and subsequent judgments on behalf of the litigants. More recently, in domestic court actions, the balance has shifted toward making expeditious decisions on behalf of any minors involved rather than finding fault.

The court's attention has become increasingly directed toward remedies which provide an economic foundation for protecting children and others unable to provide for themselves (Mermin, 1982). Issues of child abuse and maltreatment are exceptions to this trend and indicate that psychological and sociological factors are frequent considerations in arriving at judgments also.

The domestic court arrives at its decisions through the adversarial process, formal procedures, and standards reflective of previous case law. The adversarial process is viewed as the best means of arriving at a just decision while allowing the opposing parties to present the elements they feel are most relevant to their own interests and the issue in dispute. The adherence to formal procedures ensures that the rights of the parties are protected from infringement by the state or others without due process of the law. The application of case law as a basis for judgments assures the continuity of traditional values, preservation of the public interest, as well as the consistent development of sociolegal thought. Finally, in the event that one or the other of the disputants is dissatisfied with the decision of the court, there is opportunity to appeal to a higher court for an examination of the lower court's decision.

To aid in arriving at a just decision, the domestic court typically reviews a variety of relevant issues such as the psychological interests of the individuals (e.g., competency, developmental issues) as well as points of a practical nature such as the division of property and the securing of adequate financial resources to maintain the spouse or children. Reflecting its unique role as tailor of the social fabric, the domestic court frequently employs broad doctrines as guides in arriving at decisions—doctrines that may be based on philosophical notions of the proper relationships among family members rather than on empirical evidence.

In recognition of the unique demands of domestic jurisprudence, the domestic court is permitted broad dispositional powers and procedural limitations, especially in regard to its treatment of juveniles. In fulfillment of his responsibility, the domestic court judge will frequently follow principles developed in law as well as enlist the advice of professionals from other disciplines to assist in the identification of problems, the recommendation of various courses of action, or interpretation of the facts presented to the court.

It is into this dynamic arena for the resolution of some of life's most intense problems that a psychologist may be asked to offer professional input.

CLINICAL INPUT INTO THE DOMESTIC COURT

The development of the family court and juvenile justice system over the past 150 years has in many ways paralleled the growth in influence of psychologists and the social sciences. Indeed, from its inception, the juvenile justice system—a program initiated through the cooperative efforts of social workers and the court system—has had as its primary purpose the rehabilitation of juvenile offenders and the identification of children in need of care. These tasks are heavily invested in psychological theory, particularly as it concerns etiology of the problems before the court. The effective clinician grasps the close ties between the development of the contemporary domestic court and psychological thought and strives to clarify the potential of the family to function in its own behalf and assists in the redeployment of family resources toward this end.

In the past, input from the social sciences to the domestic court has primarily been limited to clinical input (Goldzband, 1983), frequently reflecting the judgment and personal bias of the psychologist rather than scientific fact. Firmly held dogma is no substitute for scientific evidence; the clinician must go beyond opinion to demonstrate the reliability and efficacy of canonical knowledge. Too often, psychologists have stepped beyond the limits of their knowledge in assessing the relationships between parents and their children. As a consequence, judges and attorneys are skeptical of the input from psychologists, especially in custody and divorce proceedings.

On the other hand, the domestic courts have done little to solicit empirical input from psychologists on domestic issues. Melton (1984) pointed out that Chief Justice Burger has in the past cited "common sense and intuition" as his primary authority on domestic issues. The reliance of the court on common sense and intuition is not altogether surprising in light of the court's support for the "reasonable man hypothesis" and "rule of reason" concepts. Melton points out that the use of intuition and unsupportable clinical lore represent a major threat to the application of empirical information in the courtroom since the legal system traditionally relies on previous commentary as a basis for current decisions.

With these points in mind, the question then becomes: "Do psychologists have knowledge to offer domestic jurisprudence which goes beyond common sense and clinical lore?" The answer must be "maybe," depending on the question at hand (Melton, 1984) and the need for absolute truths. By the same token, the question should be asked as to whether the court is ready or willing to accept information which may be at variance with commonly or traditionally held beliefs. Again, the answer must be a conditioned "maybe" depending upon the circumstances. The domestic court seldom has the opportunity of deciding a clearly right or wrong issue. More often than not the domestic court is asked to rule on circumstances which are not clear-cut in their evolution or consequences. For example, the courts have historically perceived children as passive agents, corruptible but essentially unable to act for their own benefit. As a consequence, child-related legislation is generally directed toward protection, salvation, and reeducation. The view of children as active agents of self-determination, for example, in issues relating to children's rights, vastly complicates decisions for the court, drawing into question fundamental social constructs which the court may be unwilling to breach. Before the courts can implement the empirical evidence regarding children, the necessary shifts in legal thought regarding minority status and competency may have to follow, and perhaps rightly so, the education and reformation of general popular thought regarding the status of children or other presumed incompetents. In this case, changes in popular opinion must necessarily precede legal interpretation.

If the psychologist's influence is to be felt in the domestic courtroom, it is incumbent on him to have a clear understanding of the questions at hand and for him to formulate his responses with an eye to their social, legal, and scientific implications.

GUIDELINES FOR THE PSYCHOLOGIST IN DOMESTIC COURT

While there are few specific guidelines to aid in determining specific standards of practice for psychological services in the courtroom, an examination of the standards developed by the American Psychological Association regarding professional practice should serve to assist clinicians in their participation in domestic legal issues (Ethical Principles of Psychologists, APA, 1981; Specialty Guidelines for the Delivery of Services, APA, 1981; Standards for Educational and Psychological Testing, APA, 1985; Standards for Providers of Psychological Services, APA, 1977). Following these general guidelines, reports and testimony to the court should be conservative, comprehensive, concise, and demonstrate a sensitivity to the complex emotional, psychological, and personal rights of all individuals and family members involved. Clinicians need to remember that they are not called upon by the court to render a decision, but rather to offer an evaluation and interpretation of the psychological issues presented as relevant to the questions before the court.

The clinician should also refer to Chapter 20 in this volume by Singer and Nievod to obtain further references on conducting oneself in the courtroom and also to Chapter 19 by Weiner regarding the written reports. Also extremely useful are the works by Blau (1984a, 1984b, 1985), Hess (1985), Shapiro (1984), I. B. Weiner (1985), and Ziskin (1981).

TRADITIONAL AND CONSTITUTIONAL PRINCIPLES
RELATED TO DOMESTIC JURISPRUDENCE

Responsibility of the Court

Although the traditional goal of the domestic court has been to protect and support the integrity of the family unit, the role of the contemporary domestic court has shifted significantly in the past 150 years. Historically, domestic jurisprudence has relied on common law concepts of the family as the basis for decisions in domestic proceedings. More recently, drawing upon the philosophical precepts of John Locke and John Stuart Mill regarding the proper relationship of the government to the governed and the intrinsic nature of man, the courts have frequently taken the position of defining individual liberties and the proper responsibilities among family members.

Significant related contributions have developed from the redefinition of the roles of family members from economic to psychological terms. These major shifts can be traced to changes in philosophic thought about the nature of man in the mid to late nineteenth century, the industrial revolution, and changing concepts regarding the roles of women, children, and families in general. Particularly in the United States, efforts to establish a more pluralistic democracy emphasized the role of education, equal participation in social institutions, and a change in perspective from children under the sole dominion of their parents to the family's role as a socializing agent of the greater society. Parallel developments can be observed in the growth of institutions serving the deaf and blind, adoption, social service agencies, and the court in the late 1800s. This significant departure in thought has resulted in a decreased reliance on common law theory as the basis for domestic judgments and a consequent increase in statutory provisions as a basis for judgments.

Finally, the changing sociopolitical philosophy of civil rights as well as the significant role of the courts as architects of an integrated American society responsive to individual and group liberties have contributed greatly to centering the responsibility for social change within the courts. Landmark decisions such as *Brown v. The Board of Education* (1954), *Row v. Wade* (1973), and *In re Gault* (1967) are examples of the significant redefinition of the social fabric which has taken place over the past century.

For example, the decision in *Row v. Wade* has extended the privacy protections of the 1st and 14th amendments in such a manner so as to define some areas of family interaction as so intimate and private that the court and state have no basis to intercede except under the most extreme circumstances. Thus, the issue of family privacy, while not expressly defined in the Constitution, has been defined by court interpretation of the 1st and 14th amendments.

Principles Governing the Domestic Court

Broadly speaking, the principles and doctrines governing the domestic court fall under three areas: jurisdiction, procedures, and disposition. Issues of jurisdiction relate to the basis under which the court is empowered to act in a given circumstance. Procedures reflect the judicial processes, such as giving testimony, and serve as the vehicle for offering the protection of individual rights from undue state interference. The third area, disposition, refers to the range of alternatives the court has at its disposal to implement its decisions. Similarities and differences in domestic court and the juvenile justice system will be explored.

Several themes thread themselves throughout the operation of the courts. Several of these major themes include the doctrine of *parens patriae*; the natural right to marry; the civil, contractual nature of marriage; issues of minority, competency, and responsibility; the best interests of the child doctrine; and the tender years doctrine.

Jurisdiction

The domestic court system falls under the responsibility of the individual states since it is not expressly provided for in the Constitution. The existence of the domestic court is well rooted in the English common law and the doctrine of *parens patriae*. The contemporary domestic courts are the direct descendents of the English Chauncery Court or "Common Court" and have responsibility for the resolution of disputes rising out of a marriage or issues involving the care or behavior of minor children.

Although the federal courts have traditionally avoided becoming involved in domestic issues, recent decisions such as *In re Gault* (1967) and the adoption of proposals such as the Uniform Marriage and Divorce Act (UMDA) (1979), the Uniform Child Custody Jurisdiction Act (UCCJA) (1979), and the Parental Kidnapping Prevention Act (PKPA) (1980) suggest a growing federal role in domestic issues. The increased federal activity has primarily centered around constitutional issues of due process and rights to privacy. The UMDA, the UCCJA, and the PKPA are federal responses to the growing problems of interstate disputes regarding marriage, child custody, and the removal of children by noncustodial parents. These acts are essentially recommended statutory legislation which individual states are encouraged to enact in an effort to create a uniform set of laws regarding marriage, child custody, and the interstate transportation of children of disputed custody.

While many have argued for the removal of domestic issues from the court system in favor of less adversarial administrative processes such as arbitration or mediation, there has been little development toward the reassignment of the domestic court's jurisdictional rights. On the contrary, the courts have vigorously defended their jurisdiction as the final arbiter of domestic issues.

In contrast to the extensive common law basis for the jurisdiction of the domestic court, the juvenile justice system is a relatively novel judicial program. Although the juvenile justice system clearly falls under the precepts of the *parens patriae* concept, the system, as it operates in America today, developed out of attempts to wed social and psychological thought with the judicial process, and to operate in the interests of the children brought before the court.

Since the juvenile court system was conceived and developed under the *parens patriae* concept, issues involving juveniles are considered to be civil rather than criminal in nature. Consequently, the juvenile court is not bound by many of the due process issues, rules of evidence, and right to representation that govern adults in criminal courts. From its inception, the juvenile court was intended to be rehabilitative in purpose and to focus on correcting the circumstances antecedent to the child's appearance before the court.

The procedures in juvenile court are generally informal, closed to public observation, and the attending juvenile judge has broad discretionary powers at his disposal in arriving at a decision. Because this broad discretionary power has at times been abused, several recent rulings [e.g., *In re Gault* (1967) and *Kent* (1966)] have addressed the issue of potential abuse and lax procedural limits, thereby serving as key cases in extending the protection of important due process provisions of the Constitution to juveniles.

Procedures

Procedures within domestic jurisprudence, exclusive of the juvenile court, are similar to other jurisdictions (civil or criminal) in that the procedural structures are intended to facilitate the presentation and illustration of relevant facts while protecting the rights of the individuals from undue government intrusion. The domestic court follows such standard evidenciary rules in the presentation of testimony as due process procedures, rights of appeal, and other procedures protected by the Constitution or by precedent. To the uninitiated, procedural limits frequently appear arbitrary or intended to unnecessarily extend legal proceedings thereby raising monetary and emotional costs. However, specific procedures have evolved over the centuries as the primary vehicle for protecting the basic rights granted by the Constitution or legislation, allowing the court to function as fairly as possible. The execution of formal procedures is the essence of our judicial system. Foster (1964) points out that well-defined legal procedures represent the vanguard of protection for individual freedoms, defining in practice the rights of individuals while assuring the distillation and evaluation of facts relevant to interests of the opposing parties and society.

Since the juvenile court system attempts to provide guidance and rehabilitation for the child rather than to assess responsibility and punishment, state courts have often held that the procedural safeguards enjoyed by adults are unnecessary to protect the interests of the child. The reasoning is that under the *parens patriae* doctrine the court is charged with protecting the interests of the child; therefore, there is presumed to be no conflict of interest between the needs of the state and the needs of the minor in question.

Drawing upon the presumption of mutuality of interest, procedures in juvenile court are relatively unstructured, informal, and directed toward the clinical needs of the children it serves. The unstructured nature of the procedures of the juvenile court has been justified by the need to protect children from the stress of traditional court procedures as well as to insulate them from the errors of their past.

These claims to protection from the "forgotten past" may be more rhetoric than fact since the integrity and ultimate secrecy of the facts surrounding a juvenile case are typically left to the discretion of the presiding judge. It should also be noted that police jurisdictions, social welfare agencies, and other public agencies frequently maintain records regarding juveniles under their care—records that may be solicited by other governmental or social agencies at a later date.

Until the mid-1960s, the need for separate legal structures for children went unchallenged; however, with the civil rights movement and an increased focus on individual liberties, changing social views on the nature of children, and examples of the potential abuses of power, the procedural practices of the juvenile justice system have come under closer examination.

Disposition

The court is granted the authority to take whatever action is necessary to protect vulnerable family members and to place a child into circumstances that the court feels are most favorable for the well-being of the child, provided the child's due process rights are protected. In fulfillment of this role, the court assumes or assigns custody or guardianship of the children involved, establishes responsibilities, and makes judgments regarding financial arrangements for the interests of the children and other family members.

The court is further vested with the power to encourage parental participation with the child through the assignment of custody and visitation and in programs such as counseling or therapy which are intended to contribute positively to the overall well-being of the child in question. If necessary, the court also has the power to terminate parental rights if, in the court's opinion, the present living conditions are a threat to the life or well-being of the child. In the disposition of a case, the clinician can be of particular service to the court by evaluating workable possibilities and suggesting alternatives which foster the reorganization of the family.

Summary

In each of these areas—jurisdiction, procedures, and disposition—the court may call on the advice of expert witnesses such as social workers and psychologists. The psychologist may be asked to assess the present living conditions and emotional atmosphere within the home, the competency of a minor, the legitimate religious beliefs of a parent refusing medical treatment of a child's illness, the suitability of prospective parents or children for adoption or foster placement, grounds for termination of parental rights, determination for treatment as a juvenile or an adult in a criminal case, or the ability of parents to act in the best interest of their children.

THEMES IN FAMILY LAW

Several other themes in addition to the *parens patriae* concept weave themselves throughout family law. These themes include the natural, basic right of all people to marry (*Loving v. Virginia*, 1967), the contractual or partnership nature of marriage, competency or fitness as a parent, and the parallel concepts about the nature and competency of minor children, responsibility or dependency, the best interests of the child doctrine, and concepts regarding the natural relationship and obligations existing between parents and their children. Most of these legal concepts have their origins in Roman law, common law, or ecclesiastical doctrines regarding the nature and purpose of marriage and the proper relationship between husbands and wives or parents and their children. Collectively, these themes contribute to the normative model family, its character and the proper relationships among family members.

From another perspective, shifts in the legal considerations of recent domestic issues can be examined as being parallel to the development of the philosophical and psychological concepts of the individual, his individual rights, and the dual responsibility of government to protect individual rights while concurrently providing for the protection of social order. As Western society has grown from the view of man as property, controlled by the central ruling figure, to an individual for whom the government has responsibilities, the themes governing domestic law have shifted from the guardianship of property rights to the protection of individual liberties.

Historically, the church has provided the primary force regarding the nature of marriage and the responsibilities of family members beyond economic issues (Paulsen et al., 1974). With the demise of the preeminent position of the church as the spiritual and governing body on issues relating to the nature of marriage and family relationships, public and social policy has shifted from being governed primarily by a partnership of canonical and civil jurisprudence to include the social sciences. Presently, while the influence of the church is still felt in domestic law, it is the social scientist, clinician, and physician who have moved to the forefront in influencing the development of social and philosophical thought regarding marriage and family life. Psychologists and social scientists have become the modern pastoral influence in domestic relations.

Parens Patriae

The doctrine of *parens patriae* is the central principle around which a significant measure of domestic law has developed. This doctrine, passed down from Roman law and adopted into English common law in about the eleventh century, presumes the state as protector and trustee for those persons determined to be unable to act in their own behalf. Under the *parens patriae* doctrine, the state, represented by the courts, is responsible for securing the property rights of minor children and other classes presumed incompetent to administer their own affairs against possible loss through the incapacity of the child's natural parents or guardians to protect their interests (Mack, 1925). Under common law, this threshold is presumed to have been crossed when the family is presented to the court as disrupted and unable to continue as an intact unit.

A number of significant questions have developed regarding the plausibility of the state's ability, over the parents' ability, to act as a guardian of the child's interests. The court typically presumes that the natural parent–child bonds in an intact family are sufficiently strong to assure the protection of a minor's interest. The implicit shift in thought, that in a disrupted family the natural bonds between parent and child no longer exert sufficient force of responsibility to assure the protection of the child's interest, is presumptive at best. By the same token, one must question the court's ability to balance the demands of the general public against the needs of the child in question. These sets of needs are mutually exclusive and represent possible conflicts of interest. It stretches the limits of reason to assume that the interests of the larger society are synonymous with the interests of the individual, yet this is precisely the task before the juvenile judge. Some jurisdictions have addressed this problem by providing for a guardian *ad litem*. The court appoints a neutral party (e.g., an attorney or psychologist) to the *ad litem* role who is competent to pursue the minor's interests, thus freeing the court from a conflict of interest.

Implicit within the *parens patriae* doctrine is the assumption that in matters concerning children, the court is the guardian of the well-being of any minor children involved. In fulfilling this role, the court is presumed to act in the best interests of the child and as such cannot be in a conflict of interest with the child's interests. Since it is the presumption that the wishes of the court are for the child's best interest, there has been a reluctance on behalf of the domestic courts to delegate their jurisdiction in matters involving children. While the court is forbidden to delegate this responsibility to outside agencies, it can through its broad discretionary powers employ a wide range of means to achieve its goals including requesting the intervention and input from psychologists.

The Contractual Nature of Marriage

Marriage is recognized, under common law, as a contract or civil partnership in which each member of the marriage is granted certain rights and charged with responsibilities, either implied or stated. Since marriage, as the fundamental family unit, is of vital importance to society, the state takes an active and continuing role in defining the expectations and relationship between marital partners and family members. Consistent with its esteemed social status, marriage is protected and regulated by statutes in virtually all jurisdictions (Kuchler, 1978). Further, the marital contract differs significantly from other civil contracts in that the implicit relationships between the marital partners are defined by the state and usually cannot be modified by the marital partners.

As a contract, the marriage is unique, in that it not only defines a relationship between a man and a woman, it extends beyond to establish rights and obligations evolving from a person's status as a married man or woman.

> Marriage, while from its very nature a sacred obligation, is nevertheless, in most civilized nations, a civil contract, and usually regulated by law. Upon it, society may be said to be built and out of its fruits spring social relations and social obligations and duties, with which the government is necessarily required to deal. (*Reynolds v. United States*, 1878)

Several specific conditions have been presumed to be implicit within the marital contract. The court recognizes marriage as a singular relationship between a man and a woman, and while not all jurisdictions specifically limit marriage to heterosexual unions, all cases which have come before the court have restricted marriage to individuals of the opposite sex (Strickman, 1982). In all jurisdictions, the courts have defined marriage between men and women of certain blood relationships as incestuous and therefore prohibited. While statutes in all jurisdictions prohibit incestuous marriages, they may differ as to what degree of consanguinity constitutes incest.

As a contract, marriage is generally subject to limits similar to other contracts including age limits, the competency of the parties to enter into the contract, statutes relating to fraud and full disclosure, and the freedom of choice for individuals to enter into marriage. In the absence of satisfactory fulfillment of these provisions, the marriage is subject to being voided, annulled, or dissolved under existing divorce statutes. While in theory mental incompetents are not permitted to marry, competency requirements are more loosely interpreted in marital issues and frequently do not arise until sometime after a marriage has taken place. If, under certain circumstances, one or the other of the marital partners should fail to maintain the exclusiveness of the marital bond, the other partner may petition the court for a divorce and the dissolution of the marital contract. In a divorce, in recognition of the unique support provisions implicit in the nature of the marital contract, the aggrieved party may seek continued support from the former marital partner. While courts have explicitly identified a constitutional right to marital privacy, extending to consensual sexual activities, to the use of contraceptives and to certain other sexual activities when confined to the marital domicile and in the absence of onlookers, it is unclear as to whether these protections extend to the discussion, outside of the home, of sexual activities taking place within the marital bedroom. Thus, it is not clear as to whether discussion of marital matters with a clinician, who might not enjoy the protection of privileged communication, would be protected under the doctrines governing the rights to marital privacy.

Competency, Responsibility, Dependency, and the Best Interests of the Child Doctrine

The concepts of competency, responsibility, dependency, and the best interests of the child are related. Children have been viewed traditionally by the courts as dependent and incapable of making sound independent judgments. They are treated differently than adults in almost all cases, from statutory law to representation in court, from treatment in juvenile court to issues of parental responsibility for the child. The court recognizes the natural bond between the parent and child and in almost all but the most extreme circumstances strives to maintain and support the parent–child relationship. The fundamental conceptions associated with a dependency status logically lead to the application of the best interests of the child doctrine in arriving at a decision.

This doctrine implies that the responsibility of the court is first to protect the interests of the child. On the other hand, it is under this doctrine that some of the most serious travesties of responsibility have taken place regarding judicial exercise of policies relating to children. Just as there are possible conflicts of interest when considering the rights of parents and the rights of children, so too there are serious questions about whether or not the interests of the child are synonymous with the court's interest. Under the *parens patriae* concept, the court has been put into the final role of mediating the needs of the social order and the needs of the child. Clearly, these needs are not always the same.

Under English common law, children under the age of majority are considered incapable of sound independent judgment and therefore must look to their parents or guardian for direction and decision making. Thus the normative model presupposes "an intact family system, characterized by dependent children, who rely on their parents for support care, nurture and protection" (Weithorn, 1982, p. 86), as well as a relationship among family members which transcends individual needs and possible conflicts of interest. English common law presupposes that the interests of the children are consonant with the interests of their parents and that parents will execute their trust to the benefit of their children. This model of mutual responsibility and the inalienable right of parents to execute this responsibility has been repeatedly supported in court.

What exactly is the nature of the legal concept of minority and of competence and, logically, at what point does a child become competent to make his or her own decisions? While there are no simple answers to the latter portion of the question, the courts have laid down a fairly clear framework for determining competence. According to one court's reasoning, competence represents "the capacity for individual choice" (*Ginsberg v. N.Y.*, 1968). While this description may not appear to be particularly illuminating, implicit within it is the understanding that "individual choice" requires an understanding on the part of the individual of the possible consequences of various alternative choices.

In her investigation into children's decision-making competence, Weithorn (1982) defines competence as "an individual's skills, abilities, knowledge or experience or a capacity to perform in a certain manner" (p. 89). While we question the assumption that all persons under 18 years of age are incompetent to make decisions regarding their welfare, states have strongly supported parents' rights to provide consent or refusal for actions of their children (Weithorn, 1982). This right to privacy in decision making on behalf of children has repeatedly been supported through the decisions in the courts (*Parham v. J.L. & J.R.*, 1979; *Prince v. Massachusetts*, 1944; *Wisconsin v. Yoder*, 1972).

CONCEPTS REGARDING THE NATURAL RELATIONSHIPS AND OBLIGATIONS EXISTING BETWEEN PARENTS AND THEIR CHILDREN

Individual Rights, Family Rights, and the Professional Consultant

The lines of demarcation between minority individual rights, the rights and responsibilities of parents, and the responsibilities of the court are not easily drawn, for providing minors with independent due process and privacy rights clearly interferes with common law parental rights and the responsibility of the courts toward juveniles under the *parens patriae* concepts (Lindsey, 1977). Juvenile law is essentially governed by the philosophy of status or membership within a group defined by specific criteria. On the other hand, custodial law has shifted its focus toward the individual as embodied in the best interests of the child doctrine. In spite of the shift in focus in custodial law, the question remains as to whether the rights of the family or individual rights should reign preeminent.

The concepts of differential treatment of children as well as others of differing status is well rooted in the English common law and philosophy regarding the legal status of children and incompetents.

It seems that a fundamental question which must be addressed in any analysis of the appropriate role of the professional consultant to the legal system is whether or not the child (or any other person at risk) is a creature of the state under the proximal care of a parent or guardian, or whether the parent-child relationship is sacred and reflective of the state of nature and therefore in need of statutory protection against encroachment by outside influences such as the state or its agents.

Philosophers, theologians, psychologists, legal theorists, and the public at large have generally recognized the legitimacy of differing statuses for groups and their subsequent differential treatment rights, depending on their present status (e.g., married persons and single persons, adulthood or minority, prisoner or freeman, mentally competent or mentally incompetent). In the past, differing legal statuses were clearly defined through constitutional discriminations based on age, wealth, race, or condition of servitude.

Prior to the mid-nineteenth century, domestic decisions were generally based on civil precepts of property, with children as chattel and men as sole proprietors of the family's wealth and relationships. With the advent of the Civil War and the equality provisions of the 14th amendment, the issue of different treatment for individuals of differing status became a problem for the courts. Problems which have been manifest in recent legal and social history include broad issues such as civil rights, women's rights, and abortion. Contributing to the complexity of the problem has been the parallel development of individual psychology in the late nineteenth century. Drawing upon the perspective of the individual and his development, the courts have also begun to weigh issues of rights to custody, individual and children's rights, the natural bonds between family members, and the proper developmental environment for children. Domestic rulings involving individuals of differing status implicitly address questions regarding the competency of parents to act in the interests of their children or the child's ability to act in his or her own behalf (a presumption placing the child on an equal status with the parents).

The implicit position of the court in a divorce and custody suit is that the marital disruption places the child at risk, and the court must assure that the interests of children are carefully protected. Under the mantle of *parens patriae* and guided by the best interests of the child doctrine, the court acts to insure the interests of any children involved. In the past, this action has resulted in the court radically restructuring parent-child relationships through custody, visitation, and support. In apparent recognition of the court's inability to dictate family relationships in all cases, several alternative arrangements have been developed, such as joint custody and protection of rights to visitation for the noncustodial parent.

The questions raised in consideration of parent and children's rights are far more complex, and the courts have been ambivalent in their direction and development of precedents in this area.

Marriage

Marriage is a personal relationship between a man and a woman arising out of a civil contract to which the consent of the parties is essential. A marriage licensed, solemnized, and registered as provided in this act is valid in this state. A marriage may be contracted, maintained, invalidated, or dissolved only as provided by law. (Uniform Marriage and Divorce Act)

Marriage is a social institution, universally recognized across all cultures, although it may take various forms in different parts of the world. In Western cultures, marriage has been primarily governed by religious precepts.

The early church held that marriage was a sacrament, ordained by God and consummated by His hand. Ecclesiastical doctrine specified the nature and conditions necessary for the marital contract including who could marry, minimum ages for marriage, the need for mutual consent, the purpose for marriage (procreation), and the conditions under which a marriage could be voided. These early doctrines, specified in the *Casti Connubi* and other church proclamations, were adopted with some statutory modification into English common law and the Anglican church upon its formation by Henry VIII.

In England, the church maintained control over marriage until 1857 when jurisdiction was transferred to the statutory domestic courts. The transfer of jurisdiction from the ecclesiastical courts to domestic courts did not promote much change in the law regarding marriage. Indeed the legislation effecting the transfer of authority stipulated that the courts base their decisions on precedents formulated in the ecclesiastical courts. In continental Europe, the Protestant clergy rejected the concept of marriage as a religious sacrament, insisting that it be honored as a contract based on civil law.

In the United States, marriage has always been considered a civil contract with special statutory status, governed by the domestic courts. All jurisdictions in the United States accept marriages performed by recognized clergy, and some jurisdictions recognize common law marriages, although the latter are viewed with increasing skepticism. The civil foundation for marriage in the United States should not imply the absence of religious influences; on the contrary, the civil statutes governing marriage reflect the adoption of virtues originating in traditional religious thought, only adopted and administered by the civil courts.

In the United States, jurisdiction over marriage rests with the various states; consequently, a wide range of legislation has developed over the years governing marriage. These laws, particularly those concerning divorce and child custody, have frequently conflicted with one another, causing confusion of jurisdiction when decisions in one state's jurisdiction are argued in another state. In an effort to reduce the number of conflicting statutes, the federal government has proposed several comprehensive laws for implementation in the various states, including the aforementioned UMDA, UCCJA, and PKPA statutes.

While the Constitution does not specifically deal with marriage, the Supreme Court recognized in *Meyer v. Nebraska* (1923) that the right "to marry, establish a home and bring up children" was an essential part of the liberty guaranteed by the 14th amendment. This judgment was strengthened in the case of *Skinner v. State of Oklahoma* (1942) in which the Supreme Court extended its view on the right to marry saying, "Marriage is one of the 'basic rights of man,' fundamental to our very existence and survival, therefore the state cannot force sterilization since a basic premise of marriage is procreation."

Marriage has generally been viewed as a contract, relation, or condition existing between one man and one woman. In the case of *Reynolds v. United States* (1878) the court held that polygamy is not legal, although it may be permitted by religious institutions. While not all states specify that marriages must be between males and females, no case presented to the courts for homosexual marriage has been approved (see *Baker v. Nelson*, 1971). Marriage is a contract for life that may only be terminated by the court following a formal hearing of the facts presented for divorce (*Popham v. Duncan*, 1930). Consistent with this concept of marriage for life, marriage cannot be performed for a period of time or in degrees of involvement. Thus, all privileges accorded the marital status are enjoyed by marital couples.

While persons planning to marry may enter into antenuptial agreements regarding a broad range of property issues, the court retains the privilege of examination to verify that certain minimal provisions of disclosure, consideration, and support have been given. Individuals may not contract away the legitimate power of the court to rule in marital issues (*Popham v. Duncan*, 1930). Thus, it might be said that marriage is a partnership between a man, a woman, and the state, with the state being the senior partner in the contract.

The state, through its statutory provisions for marriage, stipulates the antecedent conditions necessary for a valid marriage to take place. These qualifications to marry generally include minimum ages, general physical and mental conditions, presence of voluntary consent, absence of a presently valid marriage, and limitations on consanguinity.

Marital and Family Privacy

Several landmark cases have served to define and support the concept of marital and family privacy and parents' rights to control over their children (e.g., *Pierce v. Society of Sisters*, 1925). English common law viewed husband and wife as "being of one body"; consequently, there developed presumptions regarding the sacredness of the marital unit and subsequent need for protection from undue public interference. In the case of *Griswold v. Connecticut* (1965), Justice Douglas drawing on specified provisions from the 14th amendment prohibiting undue governmental interference stated:

> specific guarantees in the Bill of Rights have penumbras, formed by emanations from those guarantees that give them life and substance. . . . Various guarantees create zones of privacy. . . . We deal with a right of privacy older than the Bill of Rights —older than our political parties, older than our school system. Marriage is a coming together for better or for worse, hopefully enduring, and intimate to the degree of being sacred. It is an association that promotes a way of life, not causes.

While the specifics of the *Griswold* case affirm the right for married couples to use contraceptives, its more important impact is to acknowledge realms of married life as being so sacred and private that the state may not intrude.

Children are generally protected under the same rights to privacy as adults, although in some cases the courts have gone further, finding that under certain circumstances, the child's right to privacy may be superior to the interests of their parents (*Planned Parenthood v. Danforth*, 1976). The support for children's rights to privacy has been particularly evident in cases where children have attempted to avail themselves of community resources such as contraception (*Carey v. Population Serv. Intn'l*, 1972), family planning (*Planned Parenthood v. Danforth*, 1976), and drug abuse programs and psychological testing (*Merriken v. Cressman*, 1973).

Stanton (1982) points out that when the question arises as to who controls the rights to privacy, the family or the children, the courts have generally supported a family-based theory of privacy and integrity over the individual and autonomous rights of children. Notable exceptions have occurred in situations where children, either by their actions or petition, demonstrate competency in making their own decisions (*Planned Parenthood v. Danforth*, 1976).

The courts have generally recognized a number of areas of family life as so intimate that they are protected by provisions of the Constitution and the Bill of Rights. Specifically, the courts have ruled in favor of marital privacy in areas including abortion (*Row v. Wade*, 1973), procreation (*Skinner v. State of Oklahoma*, 1942), the marital couple's right to use contraception (*Eisendtadt v. Baird*, 1967; *Griswold v. Connecticut*, 1965), and family relationships, rearing and educating children (*Pierce v. Society of Sisters*, 1925; *Whalen v. Row*, 1977).

Privileged Communication among Family Members

Privileged communication refers to the common law or statutory rights granted to specified individuals which preserve communications from being compelled in testimony. Privileged communication is permitted in specified circumstances because the disclosure of designated information would frustrate a relationship which society has determined to be worthy of fostering and preserving (Stanton, 1982). Communications between spouses enjoy the status of privileged communication, and, consequently, marital partners cannot be compelled to provide testimony regarding private communications between them. On the other hand, marital partners are not foreclosed from giving testimony if they should so elect. The pivotal issue regarding privileged communications within the family is the necessarily narrow conditions which define private communications.

Although the privacy of communications between parents and their children has generally been supported by the courts, there is no common law provision granting privileged communication to family members beyond the spouses. The defense of privacy of communication among family members has typically fallen under the scope of rights to privacy rather than of privileged communication (see *In re A & M*, 1978) (Stanton, 1982). This becomes relevant as in the case where a child, under no coercion, discloses a parent's drug abuse to the authorities.

For any communication to be recognized under the provisions of privileged communication, several criteria must be met (Wigmore, cited in Stanton, 1982). These criteria include the following:

1.   The communications must originate in confidence that they will not be disclosed.

2.   The element of confidentiality must be essential to the full and satisfactory maintenance of the relation between the parties.

3.   The relation must be one which in the opinion of society ought to be sedulously fostered.

4. The injury that would inure to the relationship by the disclosure of the communication must be greater than the benefit thereby gained for the correct disposal of litigation.

A significant issue facing the clinician arises out of the common law provisions necessary to assure the status of privileged communication. Under common law, for a communication to be considered private, it must occur only between parties involved. A third party such as a child or other family member being present or information relayed between parties such as a child-parent-therapist may invalidate the provisions necessary for privileged communication. Since the statutes regarding privileged communication are derived through the state legislatures, clinicians should become familiar with their local statutes in order to assure their clients the extent and nature of the protection available under the scope of privileged communication. In particular, some jurisdictions provide that all competent and relevant evidence, unless specifically excluded by privilege, may become compelled testimony.

Dissolution of Marriage

Marriages are considered either void, voidable, or valid and may be dissolved through annulment, divorce, or death of a spouse. Specific conditions necessary for each action to dissolve a marriage are generally specified in individual state codes regarding marriage and divorce.

Void and Voidable Marriages

A void marriage is one that is forbidden by common law or statute, or would have been forbidden had the facts been known at the time of the marriage. Some marriages are void from the outset and are never recognized. Other marriages may be voidable, but are not considered void until some protest is made regarding the validity of the marriage.

A marriage may be void for a number of reasons including presence of a currently valid marriage, consanguinity or other relationships specified by statute, and, more pertinent to clinicians, violations of the presumptions governing contracts such as competency, consent to the marriage under duress, or failure to provide full disclosure of relevant facts or medical condition prior to the marriage.

Voidable marriages generally require a petition to the court to effect an annulment. A marriage may be voidable for a number of reasons—usually reasons that violate conditions of status or the basic conditions necessary for a valid marital contract. Violations of the premises of a valid contract include incompetency or failure to understand the nature and implications of the marital contract, marriage below minimum age requirements, duress, failure to disclose material information that may be relevant to the basis or purpose of the marriage, presence of a medical or psychiatric condition such as venereal disease, impotency, or genetic disorders that would incapacitate the individual from fulfilling the implied obligations of the marital contract.

Physical or mental difficulties having an onset following the marriage are not considered a basis for annulment. Mental defectives may be permitted to marry provided they are competent to give consent to the marriage and the cause of their difficulties are unlikely to be genetically transmitted. The presence of a mental disorder (e.g., schizophrenia) is not a necessary condition for voiding a marriage. For example, the court found that while it was understood between the parties that the defendent had a history of mental illness, the disorder was in a state of remission at the time of entering into the marital agreement; therefore, the contract was valid (Krause, 1977, p. 321).

A number of other conditions have been found to be a satisfactory basis for nullifying a marriage. Impotency, regardless of cause, physical or psychological, is considered a basis for nullifying a marriage (Krause, 1977). In another case, intoxication was found as a basis for nullifying a marriage on the grounds of incapacity to consent to a binding agreement, thus illustrating the need for knowledgeable consent for a contract to be binding (*Parken v. Saileau*, 1968).

In specific regard to the medical or psychological bases for annulment, the courts have held that the condition in question must have existed prior to the marriage and been concealed from the marital spouse.

Annulment

Annulment is a legal process which terminates and invalidates a void or voidable marriage. The major difference between an annulment and a divorce is that an annulment is retroactive to the inception of the marriage, and a divorce is effective from the date of the decree foreward, a point laden with important implications for inheritance. Consequently, the partners or heirs in an annulled marriage may have substantially different rights than in a marriage ended by a divorce.

Generally, for an annulment to be granted, the contested circumstances must have existed at the initiation of the marriage and have been concealed from the spouse. Annulment usually does not provide for permanent alimony or support obligations, although temporary support provisions may be granted, depending on the local statutes. The grounds for an annulment are similar to grounds for a divorce and include impotency, fraud, dare or jest, prior existing marriage, mental incapacity, and duress. Defenses to an annulment include continuing to live with the person after learning of grounds for annulment, antenuptial knowledge of the contested condition, and *Res judicata* or expiration of the statute of limitations.

Divorce

Divorce is the most common form for dissolution of a marriage and represents "the legal termination of a valid marriage" (Strickman, 1982, p. 309). Divorce must be concluded under the auspices of the court following a formal hearing. This degree of formality is necessary since the state is presumed to have a vital interest in the marriage. Further, it is presumed that the material interests of the estranged couple and any children of the marriage are at risk (Strickman, 1982). Divorce stands in marked contrast to the relatively informal procedural requirements for initiating a marriage. The procedural differences in treatment of marriage and divorce arise out of differing perceptions regarding the interests of the parties involved. In the case of marriage, it is presumed that the parties define their interests as similar and not conflictual; while in the case of divorce, the parties implicitly define their interests as different and unresolvably in conflict with one another, thus a state of risk exists.

Under common law, prior to granting a divorce, some basis or fault would have to be demonstrated in justification of the divorce. These grounds were typically presented as breaches of the implicit provisions of the marital contract including adultery, desertion, mental cruelty or inhumane treatment, abuse, insanity, drug addiction, and gross neglect, all of which could call for psychological expertise in presenting to a court. However, with the recent shift in focus from fault finding to expeditious decisions regarding marital property, support, and custodial issues, most states have enacted no-fault divorce statutes which permit a divorce without proof of wrongdoing.

There are several important points to consider regarding no-fault divorce statutes. In particular, note the conditions necessary to justify the divorce action. These conditions include a determination of complete incompatibility of temperament, a determination of an irretrievable breakdown of the marriage, and an unwillingness to reconcile differences between the estranged spouses. Generally, the court will accept statements from the parties in testimony of the necessary conditions, and the divorce will be granted forthwith.

The courts have attempted to objectify the decision-making process in no-fault divorces by defining the phrases: incompatibility of temperament, irretrievable breakdown in the marriage, and failure to reconcile. For example, in *Phillips v. Phillips* (1973), the court stated that incompatibility refers to conflicts in personalities and disposition so deep as to be irreconcilable and render it impossible for the parties to continue a normal marital relationship with each other. And in the case of *Rikard v. Rikard* (1980), reconciliation is defined as a resumption of marital cohabitation in the fullest sense of living together as husband and wife, having sexual relations, and, where possible, joint domicile. The intentions of the parties must be to resume their married life entirely and not merely to enjoy each other's company temporarily, for limited purposes, or as a trial reconciliation. The length of their cohabitation is not material in determining whether there has been a reconciliation sufficient to deny the cause of action in the divorce.

In the event that the divorce is contested, a number of actions may invalidate claims of an irretrievable breakdown in the marriage. For example, should the spouses continue actions traditionally reserved for married couples, such as cohabitation or continued sexual relations, or like activities, the court may justifiably question the basis for granting a no-fault divorce. In some jurisdictions, the courts have reserved the option to recommend counseling or mediation in an attempt to clarify the present state and condition of the marriage prior to granting a no-fault divorce.

A number of writers have viewed divorce, the results of divorce, and the problems associated with family reorganization as symptomatic of individual and family psychopathology. While it is true that the divorce process is associated with high levels of stress in the family, it is not necessarily symptomatic of chronic disturbance. It may be more fruitful to examine the processes which maintain friction after the divorce for evidence of pathology. While divorce may carry a stigma of failure, it may represent a transitional phase. There are many unpleasant passings in life: the death of a parent, spouse, or child, the loss of a job or other valued position. We do not necessarily assume that because of the passage of events or the stress experienced with these transitions that pathology or risk to family members exists. Rather, pathology exists when an individual is unable to work through and transcend the passing in a satisfactory way. The psychologist evaluating families about custodial issues needs to be aware of his or her own personal biases regarding marriage and divorce so as not to impose idiosyncratic opinions on the proceedings (see Goldzband, 1983, p. 689).

Among such biases are the treating of children as prizes or weapons in a divorce contest and the view that without legal intervention, children would be neglected, ignored, or left to fend for themselves. Another set of societal values is the assumption that youth know themselves and their prospective spouses well enough to make sagacious choices, and they anticipate parenthood and its responsibilities. The idealized dad, mom, and two children, a remnant of more pastoral times, were supported by extended family and an integrated community. A person's ties were more vertical and deep within a set of community members; whereas current relationships are horizontal and stratified continentally as seen by ties to people within socioeconomic strata, professional groups, and far-away relatives connected by telephones and transcontinental flights with time-shared children. Awareness of various values and sensitivity to the particular values of the client-family is the order of the day for the clinician entering the domestic court.

By submitting itself to the jurisdiction of the court, for a determination of custody, the divorcing spouses implicitly state that they are unable to resolve their differences and therefore submit their problem to the court for a decision. On the other hand, does the fact that a family seeks a divorce necessarily imply that the conflicts are unresolvable? The court's general agreement to go along with negotiated agreements worked out between the divorce attorneys for the division of property, custody arrangements, and the provisions for support indicates that the courts recognize the right of the families to decide for themselves how to best carry their family forward following divorce. The court decides only when no agreement can be reached.

Mediation and Conciliation

Recent developments in the psychological and legal literature regarding divorce have promoted several novel approaches to negotiating divorce and conflict resolution. These approaches have been variously called conciliation, mediation, or arbitration depending on the specific goal and circumstances under which they are employed. The goal of these approaches to negotiation is to facilitate communication and increased understanding between the estranged parties. Negotiation is favored as an alternative because it is rooted in the concepts of individual choice and the family's right to effect their own resolution to their differences. Further, many advocates of these negotiating strategies suggest that negotiated settlements are likely to be less expensive, more permanent, and reduce the stress of divorce and family reorganization on all family members, particularly children. Whether these ideals are realizable remains to be seen.

In an effort to understand the possibilities and drawbacks of negotiated settlements, we must first specify the goals, procedures, and responsibilities of the various participants. Although conciliation and mediation are appropriate for couples both with and without children, this discussion will assume that children are likely to be present and a matter for consideration.

Conciliation

The goal of formal conciliation processes is the reorganization and preservation of the marital unit. Conciliation may be initiated at any point in the negotiating process from the first recognition of difficulty through the first several weeks following a divorce action by the court. In the event that a conciliation is brought about, the marriage is reaffirmed and the court ceases action in the matter, and in this sense, conciliation is similar to marital therapy in its goals and methods (Sprenkle & Storm, 1983).

As an aspect of the court's support for marriage, conciliation programs have been adopted by many jurisdictions as a prerequisite or adjunct process to petitions for a divorce. In these cases, the courts often employ staff clinicians and social workers to meet with the divorcing couple and assess the likelihood of a reconciliation.

Mediation

Divorce mediation is intended to be a nonadversarial means of conflict resolution in contested areas of the divorce action such as financial, property, and custodial issues. The goal of mediation is to forge an agreement that fairly meets needs of all of the parties thereby avoiding litigation. Mediation is an attempt to arrive at a mutually satisfactory agreement regarding property and custodial issues thereby encouraging a family to arrive at their own solution to the conflicting issues surrounding divorce. The assumption is that a settlement in which the parties have taken an active role is more likely to be successful in resolving differences and encourages the development of a successful foundation for the resolution of postdivorce differences.

A satisfactory divorce is the presumed outcome from the mediation process. In this point, mediation stands in marked contrast to the conciliation process where the goal is the reaffirmation of the marriage. In both conciliation and mediation the family members are encouraged to articulate their differences and reorganize their roles toward each other (Foster & Freed, 1983; Irving, 1980).

Arbitration

Arbitration is a negotiating strategy in which the parties agree to present their case to a neutral third party, who then renders a decision that is binding on both of the parties to implement. Arbitration is most closely aligned with traditional jurisprudence in which the neutral judge renders a binding verdict.

In all three approaches the divorcing couple is permitted the opportunity to appeal for a court judgment should they disagree with the negotiated settlement.

Problems Associated with Nonlegal Divorce Interventions—Ethical Issues

While the role of peacemaker is attractive, divorce mediation represents an area of intervention which fosters complex ethical questions. Contributing to this confusion is the espoused role of the mediator—a neutral third party with ambiguous purpose, methods, and ethical limits. A number of significant questions have been addressed by members of the psychological and legal community as well as by the consumers of mediation services—divorcing couples.

While space does not permit an exploration of these issues, a therapist who is or is considering engaging in mediation needs to consider the following issues and consult the appropriate references:

1. Does a nonlawyer mediator engage in an unauthorized practice of law (Girdner, 1985b, 1986; Hyde, 1984; Manocherian, 1985)?

2. Does a lawyer mediator operate in a conflict of interest situation (Hyde, 1984; Silberman, 1982)?

3. Whom does the mediator/conciliator represent: the husband, the wife, or the children (Girdner, 1985a; Manocherian, 1985)?

4. What are appropriate expectations for consumers of mediation services (Foster & Freed, 1983; *Lange v. Marshall*, 1981)?

5. What is fair and equitable for all parties in a mediation (Goldzband, 1982, 1983; Girdner, 1986).

In a review of divorce therapy outcome research, Sprenkle and Storm (1983) surveyed 22 studies covering the areas of mediation and conciliation divorce groups, separation techniques, and marriage counseling with divorce as an unintended outcome. They concluded that among couples who resolved their differences regarding child custody, mediation facilitated high rates of pretrial agreements, high levels of satisfaction with their mediated agreements as compared with resolutions imposed by courts, a reduction in the amount of litigation following final order, an increase in joint custody arrangement, and a decrease in expenses frequently associated with court resolutions of custodial differences (Sprenkle & Storm, 1983, p. 240). They found that conditions which favored the mediation efforts included a moderate level of conflict between divorcing parties and acceptance of both parties of the divorce, no third parties involving themselves in the dispute, both parties' willingness to communicate, money not being a major issue, and the opposing attorney's acceptance and support of the mediation process.

In discussing theories behind the divorce and the mediation process, Kaslow (1979–1980, 1983, 1984a, 1984b) suggests that both the family and the individuals be assessed on the following areas prior to a clinical intervention such as conciliation or mediation:

1. Individual development including cognitive, emotional, chronological, and economic issues,
2. Family development including duration of the marriage, developmental levels of the children in the family, the nature of the couple's relationship including conflict and adjustment in the family, and
3. Present status of the marriage and conflict resolution abilities including perceptions of the marriage, perceptions of divorce actions to date, perceptions of default and desires for reconciliation.

She feels that from these factors and the couple's specified goals regarding the marriage outcome, the counselor/mediator can determine how best to proceed with the couple in the conciliation/mediation efforts.

CUSTODY

A clinician may be asked to serve as a consultant to the court in two general types of custody disputes. The first is more of a private dispute between the parents or a parent or other family member or third party following a divorce. In these cases the court is involved because there had been a breakdown in the ability to solve the custody issue among themselves. In the other type of custody issue, the parties involve the parent and the state (usually Division of Child Welfare or Department of Human Resources) in cases where there has been an allegation of parental abuse or neglect and may involve the attenuation or termination of parental rights.

As of 1984 all but the state of Massachusetts has enacted the Uniform Child Custody Jurisdiction Act (UCCJA). The Massachusetts Supreme Court has adopted a substantial portion of the UCCJA in *Murphy v. Murphy* (1980). In addition, 42 states have adopted some version of the Parental Kidnapping Prevention Act (PKPA) making child abduction by a noncustodial parent a felony.

The UCCJA provides a uniform framework around which custodial issues may be developed, thereby encouraging consistency in rulings across jurisdictions. In establishing a criteria for determination of custody, the UCCJA suggests the application of the following: (1) the age and sex of the child; (2) the wishes of the child as to his custodian; (3) the interactions and interrelationships of the child with parents, siblings, and significant others; (4) the child's adjustment to home, school, and community; and (5) the mental and physical health of all parties involved. The clinician can provide valuable input to the court on a number of these issues. The American Psychiatric Association (1984, pp. 237–255) and Shapiro (1984, pp. 99–108) provide guidelines for conducting the evaluations and avoiding pitfalls when having only part of the family system available for assessment.

Standards for a Determination of Custody

While the specific standards for a determination of custody may differ from state to state and even across jurisdictions within the same state, several themes and issues are characteristic of most custodial determinations. Perhaps the most common characteristic of custody is the fact that in an overwhelming majority of cases the mother retains custody of the children. This circumstance can be traced to several causes, including the presumption that mothers are more able to provide the care and nurturing necessary for raising children, the feelings on the part of many fathers that they are ill equipped to raise a child, and, significantly, the prejudices and assumptions of the court and attorneys. Attorneys frequently encourage fathers to negotiate a settlement in which the mother retains custody of the children and the fathers are given visitation rights, since many attorneys feel that if the case goes before a judge, custody will be awarded to the mother. This assumption of inferior opportunity for custody by fathers may be unfounded in that of the 10 percent contested custody cases which do go before the court, fathers retain custody of their children in about half of the cases. While this is a relatively small percentage of the total custody awards, it suggests that a father seeking custody, with the proper preparation, will stand an equal chance of being awarded custody. This is particularly true when it involves children over five or six years old.

In divorces prior to the late 1800s, fathers almost always retained custody of their children; however, with the shift in family work patterns, mothers were presumed to be more satisfactory caretakers for young children, particularly children under the age of six or seven years. The presumption in favor of mothers retaining custody became formalized in the tender years doctrine. The tender years doctrine was supported by theories of personality development which discounted the influence of the father in favor of the child's relationship with the mother. The influence of these mother-centered theories is exemplified in the research of John Bowlby who as late as the 1950s made the statement that there was no point in investigating the father–child relationship since it was, in his opinion, of no consequence to the development of children (Bowlby, 1969). Indeed, typical studies of father–child interaction in the period prior to the late 1960s involved questionnaires given to mothers who were asked to describe the relationships between fathers and their children (Bowlby, 1969).

More recent research has indicated that fathers and mothers are equally capable of fulfilling the needs of their children. Changing attitudes about child rearing, coupled with the movement of women into the full-time work force outside of the home, have encouraged the development of custodial arrangements which support and encourage the child's contact with both parents. During the past five years, much has been written on the role of psychology in custody disputes and the assessment of parenting (Litwack, Gerber, & Fenster, 1980; Muench & Levy, 1979; Musetto, 1981, 1982; Noble, 1983; Pearson & Theonnes, 1984; Steinhauer, 1983; Zarski, Knight, & Zarski, 1985).

Currently custody arrangements tend to fall into one of four patterns: sole custody, divided custody, split custody, and joint custody. Sole custody is the most commonly approved form of custody upon dissolution of a marriage. In this form custody is awarded to one parent with visitation rights to the noncustodial parent. While the noncustodian may by informal agreement have authority over some decisions concerning the child, the ultimate control and legal responsibility remain with the custodial parent. While noncustodial parents often experience feelings of loss of their children similar to bereavement, the custodial parents often feel overwhelmed, overburdened, and trapped by the responsibility. Hyde (1984) points out that it is difficult for a mother (still the most likely sole custodian) to establish a career, to earn a living for her family, to become financially independent, and to establish a social life as well as provide the child care normally provided by two parents. Perhaps the most negative indictment of sole custody is that it tends to indicate to a child that one parent is right and one is wrong regarding divorce and custody.

Divided or alternating custody allows each parent to have the child for a part of the year exercising full control over the child while the child is in his or her custody and having visitation rights for the period of time. Critics of divided custody generally believe that it creates confusion for the child with regard to authority and that shifting the child from home to home results in an unstable environment with lack of permanent associations for the child.

Split custody occurs when custody of one or more of the children is awarded to one parent with the remaining children being awarded to the other. As this arrangement may tend to further disrupt the family unit, it is not generally approved at this time unless there are compelling circumstances to indicate that it would be in the best interest of the children.

The fourth type of custody is joint or shared custody which is defined as a sharing of legal or physical custody by both parents so as to assure the access of the child to both separated or divorced parents in a frequent and continuing manner. While this is a relatively new model, there seems to be increasing support for it in those cases where there is a willingness of both parties—both parents are able to work out the flexibility, maintain similar environments, and have financial means and geographical proximity to carry out such a plan. For further discussion of factors involved in joint custody, the clinician is referred to Hyde (1984), Volgy and Everett (1985), Nehls and Morgenbesser (1980), Bernstein (1982), Grote and Weinstein (1977), Miller (1979), and Robinson (1982–1983).

While there have been a number of arguments for and against joint custody, ranging from attempting to make Solomonic decisions, to the likelihood of continuing strife between the parents, to the opportunity of preserving the functional integrity of the various parent–child relationships, the issue at hand is not to arrive at one state of law applicable to everyone. Rather, the goal is to develop a repertoire of custodial arrangements which might be applied to foster the best interests of the children and to encourage continued relationships between the parents and child, as well as with the broader social support network of the child.

A large number of psychologists and practitioners in domestic legal issues encourage placement of a child with the parent who seems most likely to encourage and foster the continued contact between the child and the noncustodial parent. Indeed, the California statutes favoring joint custody also provide that in the event sole custody is determined to be in the child's best interest, that the placement be made with the parent who evidences a willingness to share residential time as well as decision making with the child (Foster & Freed, 1983).

In her overview of child custody laws, B. A. Weiner (1985) notes that in the past decade there have been numerous changes in family law in response to the changing role of women, increased interest in parenting on the part of fathers, and interest in the rights of the children caught as unwitting third parties in the conflict. She feels that the only certainty that exists for the future is that the divorce rates will remain high, profoundly affecting the children, and that issues such as custody, visitation, and child support will continue to be litigated.

EFFECTS OF DIVORCE ON CHILDREN

According to Atkeson, Forehand, and Richard (1982), three areas of research have contributed to the extant body of knowledge regarding the effects of divorce on children. These areas include the research on father absence, clinical studies of children from divorced homes presented for psychological treatment, and direct research into the effects of divorce on nonclinical populations.

Father absence research has examined topical areas such as sex-role development, cognitive development, achievement, and delinquency. Although the validity of much of the father absence research has been questioned on methodological grounds, the majority of studies suggest that a number of important variables obscure the relationship between postdivorce adjustment and father absence. These confounding factors include the child's age at the time of the divorce, the child's sex, the family's economic and social condition, and the previous and subsequent relationship between the child and parents as well as the root cause for the parent's absence, for example, divorce, death, or change in employment condition (Atkeson et al., 1982).

Research into the behavioral consequences of divorce has suggested that children from father absent homes are more likely to be impulsive, aggressive, delinquent, or depressed. In addition, other psychopathological behaviors exhibited include enuresis, disruptions of sex-role identification, and a decrease in moral and social controls including impulsive behavior, predelinquent and delinquent behavior, and sexual promiscuity.

The research into the effects of father absence on children who have been presented for treatment in a clinical setting suggests numerous adaptive difficulties including anxiety, aggression, fear, depression and guilt, poor social adaptation with peers and adults, disruption in self-esteem and sex-role identification, and predelinquent behavior. As in the father absence studies, researchers have found differential behaviors depending on sex, age, and cause of father absence (Atkeson et al., 1982). In particular, Atkeson et al. cited studies by Rutter (1971) and Westman, Cline, Swift, and Kramer (1970) which indicated that the level of family discord prior to the divorce and following the divorce was highly associated with adjustment difficulties and psychopathology.

Studies which have been directed toward divorced families reveal that a number of changes are generally common to these families. Typically, divorced families experience lowered economic stability, higher levels of interpersonal stress, loyalty conflicts, and an increased reliance on external support systems such as relatives and institutional and social service providers to aid in meeting familial needs. In addition, children frequently experience major shifts in the amount and quality of parental contact available to them from both the custodial and noncustodial parents. While the detrimental effects of these shifts in circumstances are often ameliorated by the second or third year following the divorce (Hetherington, 1979; Hetherington, Cox, & Cox, 1979), the family may develop chronically inadequate means of meeting their needs. Some of the research suggests that these adjustment problems decrease significantly with time and assistance from external sources.

Generally, the most pervasive changes in children from divorced families are evident in disruptions in their academic achievement and social relationships. Research indicates that while divorced families are generally stabilized by the second or third year following the divorce, children from divorced families continue to perform behind children from intact families (Lamb, 1977). Atkeson et al. further cite the parents' personal adjustment and the postdivorce relationship between parents and between parents and their children as material factors affecting the child's adjustment.

The most important factor promoting the success of the child's postdivorce adjustment is the quality of the relationship which develops between the child and the divorced parents. High levels of consistent, quality contact between children and their custodial and noncustodial parents promotes the children's postdivorce adjustment. The critical aspect of postdivorce adjustment seems to be the necessity of providing a situation which promotes the reduction of emotional distance between the noncustodial parent and the children.

Guidubaldi, Perry, and Cleminshaw (1984), in reviewing the impact of divorce on children's development and adjustment, indicate that children are at least initially negatively affected by the divorce and disruption to the family. The type and degree of disruption varies depending on the age, sex, and nature of familial interaction. The level of conflict between the spouses and the length of time necessary for the transition to a new, stable family structure are critical ingredients to the child's subsequent postdivorce adjustment.

By the third year following the divorce, most children will have made a satisfactory adjustment to the new family structure. Adjustment may be facilitated by the thoughtful construction of a family structure which encourages cooperation while limiting the likelihood of conflict between family members (Hetherington, Cox, & Cox, 1978).

A large body of research indicates that the circumstances which foster the most positive social, intellectual, and moral development are high levels of contact with both parents provided the parents are able to minimize their personal conflicts (Hess & Camara, 1979; Jacobson, 1978a, 1978b, 1978c; Kurdek & Berg, 1983; Kurdek, Blisk, & Siesky, 1981; Kurdek & Siesky, 1980a, 1980b; Magrab, 1978; Rosen, 1977; Wallerstein & Kelly, 1980). By the same token, no research supports the presumption that it is to the child's benefit to minimize contact with the noncustodial parent, except in cases where the family is continually disrupted by verbal and/or physical conflict. In these cases, exposure to continued conflict is detrimental to the child's well-being in both divorced and intact families.

Consequently, the clinician faced with a chronically hostile family situation would be advised to suggest a custodial arrangement which maximizes parental contact with the child but minimizes contact between the parents. An example might provide for an exchange on neutral territory such as picking the child up after school and dropping the child off again in the morning. In cases where a determination of custody points toward placement of the child with one parent or the other and there is no clear basis for preferring either parent, research suggests that consideration should be given placement with the parent of the same sex as the child and who is most likely to encourage liberal contact with the other parent (Santrock & Warshank, 1979; Warshank & Santrock, 1983).

Finally, parents should be supported in their efforts to initiate independent lifestyles which recognize their status as functional parents. The stabilization process may be expected to take from two to five years depending on the level of conflict, economic changes, and development of a viable social network outside of the marriage. It is unreasonable to assume that interruption of parental contact with the children of the marriage will encourage a reorganization and stabilization including the children. Both parents need the active support of the court and broader social system during the process of reorganization.

The courts, in recognition of the need for stability and contact with both parents, should discourage modifications of custodial arrangements that further limit contact with both parents without the demonstration of substantial cause.

STEPPARENTS AND STEPFAMILIES

In 1981, it was estimated that over 15 million children currently lived in a stepfamily and many more lived in blended families involving both stepchildren and children born to the extant marriage. With the continued high rate of divorce and remarriage, these figures should continue to grow presenting a significant psychological, moral, and legal problem for which there is little direction toward solution in common law and recent case law.

Under common law and current domestic law, stepparents do not enjoy the same privileges regarding stepchildren as do natural parents.

Typically, remarriage of a person paying child support or alimony does not change the individual's obligation for paying either child support or alimony. The court assumes that the person marries with a full understanding of these obligations. Further, child support and alimony may not be discharged under bankruptcy proceedings.

Alimony will customarily stop if the receiver should remarry. While women have typically been the recipients of alimony, recent court decisions have awarded men alimony. Other arrangements reflect a shift toward remedial alimony or alimony which continues for a period while the recipient is retrained for employment so that the recipient can support himself or herself in the interim. In the past, the marriage of the individual receiving alimony was the criterion under which alimony would stop, resulting in many women living with men outside of marriage so as not to terminate the alimony payments. Recent court decisions have changed the criteria for cessation of alimony payments somewhat by including the condition of residing with another man for a period as sufficient reason to stop payments.

Visitation is a right rather than an obligation and needs to be considered in remarriage. Many problems between divorced spouses do not arise until one or the other remarries. The unmarried former spouse may react with jealousy and anger and, if that person has custody, may prevent the other former spouse from seeing the children. By the same token, the new stepparent, confused about his or her role with the stepchildren or resentful of the continued influence of the former spouse, may agitate the status quo which had been achieved between the divorced couple. The noncustodial parent may react to the marriage of a former spouse by a cessation of visitation or support payments. The clinician should be aware of the potential problems with the advent of a marriage within the divorced family, be aware of the legal responsibilities associated with the children, and be prepared to counsel his clients accordingly in an effort to reestablish a balance within the new family structure.

The blended family may be thought of as a family involving children from prior marriages as well as from the current marriage and involving several sets of interacting parents. It is likely that custodial and support issues will be aggravated in blended families and make the successful reorganization of both families more difficult.

Premarital counseling to address the financial and emotional shifts resulting from blending families may be useful in avoiding some of the destructive stress associated with joining two and three families. It might be helpful for the clinician to work with all of the parties, former spouses and new family members, to facilitate the adjustment of all families concerned.

Treatment of Children in Blended Families

One important area for consideration in working with blended families is the issue of discipline and the rights of the stepparent with regard to his or her stepchildren. Typically, custodial and noncustodial parents have the right and responsibility to invoke appropriate disciplinary procedures when dealing with children and are protected from abuse or liability statutes so long as their behavior and discipline fall within the broad disciplinary mores of the greater community. In addition, natural parents have rights with regard to visitation and contact with their children that are substantially different from rights for stepparents and other persons significant to the child.

A stepparent has no disciplinary or visitation rights regarding a stepchild. Their status is essentially that of any other nonfamily member. The result of this condition is that should a stepparent threaten or harm a stepchild, a reasonable parental act may turn into an assault or battery, subjecting the stepparent to both civil and criminal liability. Likewise, a reasonable touching by a biological parent to medicate or inspect a tender area might, when done by a stepparent, be taken out of context and viewed as sexual assault or fondling (Bernstein & Haberman, 1981, pp. 213–214). On the other hand, a stepparent who has adopted a stepchild would be accorded the full rights of the natural parents.

Bonding in the Stepfamily

Stepparents' fears about establishing a sound "parental" relationship with their stepchildren may be complicated by their limited rights of access to that child in the event of a divorce. As the laws stand now, in the event of a subsequent divorce within a blended family, the stepparent or foster parent would enjoy no rights toward the former spouse's children. A petition to the court to continue contact with the child following the divorce would be unsupportable under extant law. This condition would also hold true in the event of the death of a spouse in that the children would likely be remanded to the surviving natural parent.

This issue becomes doubly complicated in the case of multiple sets of children (mine, yours, and ours). Since this issue of the rights of stepparents toward their stepchildren has become a significant litigation issue, there has been some movement recognizing the possible relationships between stepparents and children. "Psychological parentage" represents the pivotal issue promulgated by Goldstein, Freud, and Solnit (1979) and is a substantial factor in determining the best interests of the child. This is a highly relevant issue in blended families for if the families are to be successful and if the interests of the court are to support marriage as well as the interests of the child, clearly legal work needs to be implemented to support more fully the blended family. Goldzband (1983) cites several cases in which the courts have upheld the rights of "psychological parents" over the rights of purportive custodial parents.

Priorities in Working with Blended Families

What should the priorities be for the clinician working with blended families? The clinician should first focus on the relationships among the parents and other significant adults. A stable relationship between the adults is the soundest foundation upon which to base a family. The clinician should help the newly organized family members clarify their goals and perceived obligations toward their new and former families. In addition, new visitation schedules, intrafamilial relationships and the feelings about the loss of previous relationships, the possibilities for future reconciliation, particularly children's fantasies about reconciliation, and fulfillment of financial obligations from former families may strain the resources of newly blended families.

Finally, clinicians should work with family members to consider the legal relationships of family members in the event of the failure of the blended family. It is important to note that contracts between parents or parents and stepparents regarding the care and custody of children might well be held invalid as the parents may not contract away the right of the court to rule on a custodial issue.

DOMESTIC VIOLENCE

Family violence as discussed in this chapter will include spouse abuse, child abuse, and incestuous relationships. Although domestic violence seems to have been present in both Eastern and Western cultures since recorded time (Davidson, 1978), the amount of attention being paid to it in the last 10 to 15 years has dramatically increased. Similarly, the legal system, in recognizing the convergence of family problems and criminal behavior, is developing new strategies for coping with abuse. The Bureau of Justice Statistics reports that when family violence occurs, about 88 percent of the violent behaviors are assaults, 10 percent are robberies, and 2 percent are rapes. They report that more than half of all violent crimes committed by relatives involve spouses or ex-spouses and that three-fourths of the spousal attacks involve individuals who are divorced or separated. About a quarter of persons violently victimized by a spouse or ex-spouse report a series of similar victimizations within the previous six months—a higher rate of previous victimizations than any other class of victims of violent crimes. They report that about 6 million people or 3.2 percent of all Americans are victims of violent crimes each year. While they report that men are three times more likely than women to be victimized by violent strangers, women are three times more likely than men to be victimized by family members (U.S. Department of Justice, 1986, pp. 1–8).

Incidence of domestic violence tends to be cyclical. Goodwin (1985) discussed the intergenerational patterns and the variety of forms the abuses can take over the life cycle of the family. While this chapter separates the issues, spouse and child abuse are believed to be variations of family violence rather than individual entities.

Spouse Abuse

Over the past 10 years numerous books have been written on the etiology of spouse abuse. A representative sample includes Martin (1976), Roy (1977), Davidson (1978), Dobash and Dobash (1979), Moore (1979), Walker (1979), and Straus, Gelles, and Steinmetz (1980). Domestic violence has been explored from a variety of views such as psychoanalytic, sociological, economic, and spousal interactivity (Gelles & Cornell, 1983; Straus et al., 1980). While initial research had consisted of surveys to identify the prevalence, extent, and types of violence, more recent studies have focused on interpersonal variables—for example, women's new status at the societal level, marital inequality, violence (Yllo, 1984), and the effect of domestic violence legislation on police intervention disposition (Bell, 1985). Initially, there had been difficulty in obtaining accurate statistics on all areas of domestic violence due to both unreliable record keeping from many sources of statistics and differences in defining the issue. Martin (1976, p. 36) reports, for example, that the police define domestic violence by its effect, legal systems by degree of severity, and social science researchers by degree of acceptance within the community.

Treatment and Reduction of Domestic Violence

As the police are changing their role in investigation and disposition of family disputes, there is a need for consultation in areas such as diffusing violence, problem resolution, mediation and appropriate referral, as well as in basic in-service information regarding abuse and the characteristics of the abused and the abusers. Dutton (1984), Loving (1980), Bell (1984), and Brown (1984) describe current attempts by various communities to provide more appropriate police services.

A second avenue for input in the legal system is through the courts. Both judges and lawyers are becoming more aware of the issues involved in the battered wife syndrome (Frazier & Borgida, 1985; Walker, 1984) and are accepting exculpatory testimony of expert witnesses in cases where the battered wife victims have fought back incurring assault or homocide charges. Consultation to lawyers is important in helping them understand the apparent inconsistencies in abused women's behavior, such as the fear of filing for divorce from a battering spouse, or leaving and returning to an abusive situation several times, or returning to request alimony and/or child support. Recent changes in statutes encourage changes in police and court interventions. The Ohio Revised Domestic Dispute and Violence Program (1979) was intended to enable the police to arrest domestic perpetrators without having the victim initiate criminal complaints. Bell (1985) found after a year's experience with it that the legislation had not yet been implemented adequately to make changes in rates of arrests or in prosecution benefiting the victims.

Treatment of both the abused and the abuser often begins with legal interventions. In many families the first step to resolving the abuse is contacting a crisis hotline or shelter where information regarding local legal alternatives is provided. For the abuser, the first contact may follow as a result of a legal intervention or at the suggestion of a divorce judge or lawyer. Treatment approaches may include individual, group, or marital sessions. Walker (1979) discusses the use of individual sessions for both partners in an abusive situation. Neidig (1984), in working with military families, has developed a treatment program for couples. Bograd (1984) examined the biases that may arise from family systems approaches and the implications these biases have on joint treatment. Sonkin, Martin, and Walker (1985) discuss identification and treatment of abusers.

Child Abuse

In 1874, the Society for Prevention of Cruelty to Children (SPCC) was established as an appendage to the American Society for the Prevention of Cruelty to Animals and came to be a determining force in obtaining child protective laws. Presently, although there is no official definition of maltreatment, all of the states have child abuse and neglect protection laws (Paulsen, 1974), and the Juvenile Justice Standards Project (1981) is the first set of legal definitions which explicitly state that harm to a child, not the characteristics of the abuser (individuals having poor parenting skills) or the acts of mistreatment (physical force or neglect), should serve as the determining factor in defining child abuse and neglect.

Kempe's use of the battered child syndrome sparked the public's attention to the issue. Since that time considerable research on etiology, treatment, and prognosis has occurred (Kemp, Silverman, Steele, Droemueller, & Silverman, 1962). The clinician needs to be familiar with the work on the etiology and treatment (Kempe & Helfer, 1972, 1980; Starr, 1982; Justice & Justice, 1976).

While clinicians are often called on to testify as expert witnesses regarding child abuse and neglect, they have been called on as material witnesses concerning abuse or neglect by parents or others when their clients are involved in litigation. Barth and Sullivan (1985) provide information on obtaining evidence that is useful in court cases in those cases when one is called as a material rather than as an expert witness and thus needs to present observations rather than opinions which have been derived from their observations. Such a case may occur when the clinician (or teacher or physician or school bus driver) observes fresh welts or bruises, a child sent out in snowstorms inadequately clothed, or acts of violence.

Children are victims of abuse from a variety of sources. Physical abuse, neglect, and sexual abuse may occur as a direct action of parents, siblings, and extended family.

Institutional as well as intrafamilial abuse is too often the outcome for child victims who are removed from their families' neglect or abuse and are placed in a foster care system only to be further abused. Protracted stay in foster care per se can be considered an abuse (Davidson, 1983), so the Adoption Assistance and Child Welfare Act of 1980 was designed to provide funding for services that would facilitate a speedy return of children to their parents or to assist in the adoption of those who were not able to return to their family of origin.

Sexual Abuse Incest

The National Center on Child Abuse defined child sexual abuse as "contacts or interactions between a child and an adult in which the child is used for sexual stimulation of the perpetrator or other person" (HEW, 1980, p. vii). It defines as a perpetrator in intrafamily child abuse as anyone who victimizes a child and is a parental figure or significant other in the child's intrafamily life. Finkelhor (1979), studying incidence of incest and child abuse through a survey of students, reported findings that most sexual victimization of children was incestuous in nature. Although the states vary on legal definitions of incest, most researchers include as incest all forms of sexual contact, sexual exploitation, and sexual overtures initiated by an adult who is related to the child by family ties or surrogate family ties (Vander Mey & Neff, 1982). For present purposes, an individual under the age of 18 can also be the perpetrator if that person is significantly older than the victim or in a position of power or control over the child. Finklehor (1984), Justice and Justice (1979), Kempe and Kempe (1978, 1984), Mrazek and Kemp (1981), Burgess, Groth, Holstrom, and Sgroi (1978) are useful references in learning about the etiology, treatment, and legal resources for dealing with incest and sexual abuse.

Whitcomb (1986) and Davidson (1983) review recent approaches to prosecuting child sexual abuse cases. The reforms generally fall into two categories: (1) those seeking to alleviate the perceived trauma of giving live in-court testimony, and (2) those authorizing mechanical interventions to obtain the child's testimony (videotape, anatomically correct dolls, and closed circuit television). Although statutes and innovative procedures are increasingly available for obtaining testimony in abuse cases, National Institute of Justice (NIJ) researchers have found that these techniques are still very rarely used (Whitcomb, 1986). Mrazek and Mrazek (1981) have reviewed 60 studies of the effects of sexual abuse and incest and have summarized the short-term (childhood and adolescent) and long-term (adulthood) effects of incest (pp. 242, 243). They found problems in sexual adjustment, interpersonal problems, and other psychological symptoms such as loss of self-esteem, guilt, obesity, somatic symptoms, impulsive self-damaging behavior, depression, and suicidal ideation to be present in both long- and short-term follow-up.

As more is published about sexual abuse and incest, and as more adult survivors are willing to talk about their experiences, additional research will be forthcoming on longer term effects in adulthood. Also, the effects of treatment programs are being studied. Lindberg and Distad (1985), Ellenson (1986), and Faria and Belohlavek (1984) have followed up adult survivors of sexual abuse and incest. Comparisons between male and female victims (Pierce & Pierce, 1985), treatment of victims and perpetrators (Barth & Schleske, 1985), and differences between sexual offenses involving family or nonfamily members (Baumann, Kasper, & Alford, 1984) form the vanguard of research imperatives for the future.

SUMMARY

We have surveyed a number of issues involving current domestic law and have tried to provide references for further study. While much has been accomplished in improving the statutes ensuring the rights of individuals and families, it is apparent that the job has just begun. Two examples of impending changes are Davidson's (1983) call for changes in intrafamily immunity in cases of severe physical or intrafamily sexual abuse, and Muench and Levy's (1979) discussion of the additional work needed in the area of foster care and psychological parentage.

Psychological findings can assist in making the optimal changes in the laws and in implementing the changes. Psychological research on parenting, bonding, effects of various custodial arrangements, and violent behavior is relevant information for those whose task it is to change the statutes. Through the collaborative efforts of lawyers and psychologists, we can continue to make the greatest changes.

REFERENCES

Adoption Assistance and Child Welfare Act of 1980, P.L. 96-272.

American Psychiatric Association. (1984). *Issues in forensic psychiatry*. Washington, DC: Author.

American Psychological Association. (1977). *Standards for providers of psychological services* (revised). Washington, DC: Author.

American Psychological Association. (1981). Specialty guidelines for the delivery of services by counseling psychologists. *American Psychologist, 36*, 652–663.

American Psychological Association. (1981). Ethical principles of psychologists (revised). *American Psychologist, 36*, 633–638.

American Psychological Association, American Educational Research Association, & National Council on Measurement in Education. (1985). *Standards for educational and psychological testing*. Washington, DC: Author.

Atkeson, B. M., Forehand, R. L., & Richard, K. M. (1982). The effect of divorce on children. In B. B. Lahey & A. E. Kaldin (Eds.), *Advances in clinical child psychology* (Vol. 5). New York: Plenum.

Baker v. Nelson, 291 Minn. 310, 191 N.W.2d. 185 (1971).

Barth, R. P., & Schleske, D. (1985). Comprehensive sexual abuse treatment programs and reports of sexual abuse. *Children and Youth Services Review, 7*, 285–298.

Barth, R. P., & Sullivan, R. (1985). Competent evidence in behalf of children. *Social Work, 30*, 130–136.

Baumann, R. C., Kasper, C. J., & Alford, J. M. (1984). The child sexual abusers. *Corrective and Social Psychiatry, 30*, 76–81.

Bell, D. J. (1984). The police response to domestic violence: An exploratory study. *Police Studies: The International Review of Police Development, 7*, 23–30.

Bell, D. J. (1985). Domestic violence: Victimization, police intervention, and disposition. *Journal of Criminal Justice, 13*, 525–534.

Bellotti v. Baird, 433 U.S. 622, 635 (1979).

Bernstein, B. E. (1982). Understanding joint custody issues. *Journal of Contemporary Social Work, 63*, 179–181.

Bernstein, B. E., & Haberman, B. G. (1981). Lawyer and counselor as a team: Problem awareness in the blended family. *Child Welfare, 60*, 211–219.

Blau, T. H. (1984a). Expert testimony. In R. Corsini (Ed.), *Encyclopedia of psychology*. New York: Wiley.

Blau, T. H. (1984b). *The psychologist as expert witness*. New York: Wiley.

Blau, T. H. (1985). The psychologist as expert in the courts. *Clinical Psychologist, 38*, 76.

Bograd, M. (1984). Family systems approaches to wife batterings: A feminist critique. *American Journal of Orthopsychiatry, 54*, 558–568.

Bowlby, J. (1969). *Attachment*. New York: Basic Books.

Brown v. The Board of Education, 311 U.S. 693 (1954).

Brown, S. E. (1984). Police responses to wife beating: Neglect of a crime of violence. *Journal of Criminal Justice, 12*, 277–288.

Burgess, A. W., Groth, A. N. Holstrom, L. L., & Sgroi, S. M. (1978). *Sexual assault of children and adolescents*. Lexington, MA: Lexington.

Carey v. Population Services International, 438 U.S. 678 (1972).

Davidson, H. A. (1983, December). Children's rights: Emerging trends for the 1980s. *Trial*, pp. 44–48.

Davidson, T. (1978). *Conjugal crime: Understanding and changing the wifebeating pattern*. New York: Hawthorne.

Dobash, R. E., & Dobash, R. (1979). *Violence against wives*. New York: Free Press.

Dutton, D. C. (1984). Interventions into the problem of wife assault: Therapeutic policy and research implications. *Canadian Journal of Behavioral Science, 16*, 281–297.

Eisendtadt v. Baird, 405 U.S. 438, 453 (1967).

Ellenson, G. S. (1986). Disturbances of perception in adult female incest survivors *Social Casework: The Journal of Contemporary Social Work, 67*, 149–159.

Faria, G., & Belohlavek, N. (1984). Treating female adult survivors of childhood incest. *Social Casework: The Journal of Contemporary Social Work, 65*, 465–471.

Finkelhor, D. (1979). *Sexually victimized children*. New York: Free Press.

Finkelhor, D. (1984). *Child sexual abuse: New theory and research*. New York: Free Press.

Foster, H. H. (1964). Social work, the law, and social action. *Social Casework, 45*, 383–386.

Foster, H. H., & Freed, D. J. (1983). Child custody and the adversary process: Forum conveniens? *Family Law Quarterly, 17*, 133–150.

Frazier, P., & Borgida, E. (1985). Rape trauma syndrome evidence in court. *American Psychologist, 40*, 984–993.

Gelles, R. J., & Cornell, C. P. (1983). *International perspectives on family violence*. Lexington, MA: Lexington.

Ginsberg v. N.Y., 390 U.S. 629, 649-50 (1968).

Girdner, L. K. (1985a). Adjudication and mediation: A comparison of custody decision-making processes involving third parties. *Journal of Divorce, 8*, 33–47.

Girdner, L. K. (1985b). Strategies of conflict: Custody litigation in the United States. *Journal of Divorce, 9*, 1–15.

Girdner, L. K. (1986). Child custody determination. In E. Seidman, & J. Rappaport (Eds.), *Redefining social problems* (pp. 165–183). New York: Plenum.

Goldstein, J., Freud, A., & Solnit, A. J. (1979). *Beyond the best interest of the child*. New York: Free Press.

Goldzband, M. G. (1982). *Consulting in child custody: An introduction to the ugliest litigation for mental health professionals*. Lexington, MA: Lexington.

Goldzband, M. G. (1983). Current trends affecting family law and child custody. *Psychiatric Clinics of North America, 6*, 683–693.

Goodwin, J. (1985). Family violence: Principles of intervention and prevention. *Hospital and Community Psychiatry, 36*, 1074–1079.

Griswold v. State of Connecticut, 381 U.S. 479, 85 S. Ct. 1678, 14 L.Ed.2d 510 (1965).

Grote, D. F., & Weinstein, J. P. (1977). Joint custody: A viable and ideal alternative. *Journal of Divorce, 1*, 43–53.

Guidubaldi, J., Perry, J. D., & Cleminshaw, H. K. (1984). The legacy of parental divorce. In B. B. Lahey, & A. E. Kazdin (Eds.), *Advances in clinical child psychology* (pp. 109–147). New York: Plenum.

Health, Education and Welfare, Department of, Office of Human Development Services. (1980). *Grant announcement bulletin*. Washington, DC: Administration for Children, Youth and Families.

Hess, A. K. (1985). The psychologist as expert witness: A guide to the courtroom arena. *Clinical Psychologist, 38*, 75–76.

Hess, R. D., & Camara, K. A. (1979). Postdivorce family relationships as mediating factors in the consequences of divorce for children. *Journal of Social Issues, 35*, 79–96.

Hetherington, E. M. (1979). Divorce: A child's perspective. *American Psychologist, 34*, 851–852.

Hetherington, E. M., Cox, M., & Cox, R. (1978). The aftermath of divorce. In J. H. Stevens & M. M. Mathews (Eds.), *Mother-child, father-child relations*. Washington, DC: National Association for the Education of Young Children.

Hetherington, E. M., Cox, M., & Cox, R. (1979). Play and social interaction in children following divorce. *Journal of Social Issues, 35,* 26–49.

Hyde, L. M. (1984). Child custody in divorce. *Juvenile and Family Court Journal.* Reno, NV: National Council of Juvenile Family Court Judges.

In re A & M, No. 61 A.D. 2d 426, 403 (New York State, 2d. 375, 381, 1978).

In re Gault, 387 U.S. 1 (1967).

Irving, H. H. (1980). *Divorce mediation: A rational alternative to the adversary system.* New York: Universe.

Jacobson, D. S. (1978a). The impact of marital separation/divorce on children—I: Parent child separation and child adjustment. *Journal of Divorce, 1,* 341–360.

Jacobson, D. S. (1978b). The impact of marital separation/divorce on children—II: Interparent hostility and child adjustment. *Journal of Divorce, 2,* 3–19.

Jacobson, D. S. (1978c). The impact of marital separation/divorce on children—III: Parent-child communication and child adjustment, and regression analysis of findings from overall study. *Journal of Divorce, 2,* 175–194.

Justice, B., & Justice, R. (1976). *The abusing family.* New York: Human Sciences.

Justice, B., & Justice, R. (1979). *The broken taboo: Sex in the family.* New York: Human Sciences.

Juvenile Justice Standards Project, Institute of Judicial Administration, American Bar Association. (1981). *Standards relating to abuse and neglect.* Cambridge, MA: Ballinger.

Kaslow, F. W. (1979–1980). Stages of divorce: A psychological perspective. *Villanova Law Review, 25,* 718–751.

Kaslow, F. W. (1983). Stages and techniques of divorce therapy. In P. A. Keller & L. G. Ritt (Eds.), *Innovations in clinical practice: A sourcebook, II.* Sarasota, FL: Professional Resource Exchange.

Kaslow, F. W. (1984a). Divorce: An evolutionary process of change in the family system. *Journal of Divorce, 7,* 21–40.

Kaslow, F. W. (1984b). Divorce mediation and its emotional impact on the couple and their children. *The American Journal of Family Therapy, 12,* 58–64.

Kempe, C. H., & Helfer, R. E. (Eds.). (1972). *Helping the battered child and his family.* Philadelphia: Lippincott.

Kempe, C. H., & Helfer, R. E. (Eds.). (1980). *The battered child* (3rd ed.). Chicago: University of Chicago Press.

Kempe, R. S., & Kempe, C. H. (1978). *Child abuse.* London: Fontana/Open Books.

Kempe, R., & Kempe, C. (1984). *The common secret: Sexual abuse of children and adolescents.* New York: W. H. Freeman.

Kempe, C. H., Silverman, F., Steele, B., Droemueller, W., & Silverman, H. (1962). The battered child syndrome. *Journal of the American Medical Association, 181,* 17–24.

Kent v. United States, 383 U.S. 541, 556 (1966).

Krause, H. D. (1977). *Family law in a nutshell.* St. Paul, MN: West.

Kuchler, F. W. (1978). *Law of engagement and marriage.* Dobbs Ferry, NY: Oceana.

Kurdek, L. A., & Berg, B. (1983). Correlates of children's adjustments to their parents' divorces. In L. A. Kurdek (Ed.), *Children and divorce*. San Francisco: Jossey-Bass.

Kurdek, L. A., Blisk, D., & Siesky, A. E. (1981). Correlates of children's long-term adjustment to their parents' divorce. *Developmental Psychology, 17*, 565–579.

Kurdek, L. A., & Siesky, A. E. (1980a). Sex role self-concepts of single divorced parents and their children. *Journal of Divorce, 3*, 249–261.

Kurdek, L. A., & Siesky, A. E. (1980b). Children's perceptions of their parents' divorce. *Journal of Divorce, 3*, 339–378.

Lamb, M. E. (1977). The effects of divorce on children's personality development. *Journal of Divorce, 1*, 163–174.

Lange v. Marshall, Mo. Ct. App. (1981).

Lindberg, F. H., & Distad, L. J. (1985). Post-traumatic stress disorders in women who experienced childhood incest. *Child Abuse and Neglect, 9*, 329–334.

Lindsey, D. (1977). Children of the asylum. Oceanside, NY: Dabor Science. Cited by Morse (1983) in *The Professional Psychologist's Handbook*, B.D. Sales (Ed). New York: Plenum.

Litwack, T. R., Gerber, G. L., & Fenster, A. (1980). The proper role of psychology in child custody disputes. *Journal of Family Law, 18*, 269–301.

Loving, N. (1980). *Responding to spouse abuse and wife beating*. Washington, DC: Policy Executive Research Forum.

Loving v. Virginia, 388 U.S. 1 (1967).

Mack, J. W. (1925). The chauncery procedure in the juvenile court. In (J. Addams, C. J. Herrick, A. L. Jacoby and others). *The child, the clinic, and the court: A group of papers*. (pp. 310–319). New York: New Republic, Inc.

Magrab, P. R. (1978). For the sake of the children: A review of the psychological effects of divorce. *Journal of Divorce, 1*, 233–245.

Manocherian, J. (1985). Family mediation: A descriptive case study. *Journal of Divorce, 8*, 97–118.

Martin, D. (1976). *Battered wives*. San Francisco, CA: Glide.

Melton, G. B. (1984). Developmental psychology and the law: The state of the art. *Journal of Family Law, 22*, 445–482.

Mermin, S. (1982). *Law and the legal system*. Boston: Little, Brown.

Merriken v. Cressman, 354 F. Supp. 913 (E.D. Penn. 1973).

Meyer v. Nebraska, 262 U.S. 390 (1923).

Miller, D. J. (1979). Joint custody. *Family Law Quarterly, 13*, 345–413.

Missing Child Act, P.L. 97–292.

Moore, D. M. (1979). *Battered women*. Beverly Hills, CA: Sage.

Mrazek, P. B., & Kempe, C. H. (1981). *Sexually abused children and their families*. Great Britain: Pergamon.

Mrazek, P. B. & Mrazek, D. A. (1984). The effects of child sexual abuse: Methodological considerations. In P. B. Mrazek & C. H. Kempe (Eds.), *Sexually abused children and their families*. Oxford: Pergamon, pp. 235–245.

Muench, J. H., & Levy, M. R. (1979). Psychological parentage: A natural right. *Family Law Quarterly, 13*, 129–163.

Murphy v. Murphy, 404 N.E.2d 69 (1980).

Musetto, A. P. (1981). The role of the mental health professional in contested custody: Evaluator of competence or facilitator of change. *Journal of Divorce, 4*, 69–79.

Musetto, A. P. (1982). Standards for deciding contested child custody. *Journal of Clinical Child Psychology, 10*, 1.

Nehls, N., & Morgenbesser, M. (1980). Joint custody: An exploration of the issues. *Family Process, 19*, 117–125.

Neidig, P. H. (1984). *Spouse abuse: A treatment program for couples*. Champaign, IL: Research Press.

Noble, D. N. (1983, September). Custody contest: How to divide and reassemble a child. *Social Casework*, pp. 406–413.

Ohio Revised Code Domestic Dispute and Violence Program (Section 3113.32A).

Painter v. Bannister, 258 Iowa 1390, 140 N.W.2d. 152 (1966).

Parental Kidnapping Prevention Act of 1980, P.L. 611.

Parham v. J.R., 422 U.S. 584 (1979).

Parken v. Saileau, 213 So. 2d. 190 (1968).

Paulsen, M. G., Wadlington, W., & Goebel, J. (1974). *Cases and other material on domestic relations* (2nd ed.). Mineola, NY: The Foundation.

Paulsen, N. (1974). The law and abused children. In R. E. Helfer & C. H. Kempe (Eds.), *The battered child*. Chicago: University of Chicago Press.

Pearson, J., & Theonnes, N. (1984). Mediating and litigating custody disputes: A longitudinal evolution. *Family Law Quarterly, 17*, 497–523.

Phillips v. Phillips, 274 So. 2d. 71 (1973).

Pierce, R., & Pierce, L. H. (1985). The sexually abused child: A comparison of male and female victims. *Child Abuse and Neglect, 9*, 191–199.

Pierce v. Society of Sisters, 268 U.S. 510 (1925).

Planned Parenthood v. Danforth, 423 U.S. 52, 75 (1976).

Popham v. Duncan, 87 Colo. 149, 285 p. 757, 70 A.L.R. 824 (1930).

Prince v. Massachusetts, 321 U.S. 158 (1944).

Reynolds v. United States, 98 U.S. 145 (1878).

Rikard v. Rikard, 378 So. 2d (1980).

Robinson, H. L. (1982–1983). Joint custody: An idea whose time has come. *Journal of Family Law, 21*, 641–685.

Rosen, R. (1977). Children of divorce: What they feel about access and other aspects of the divorce experience. *Journal of Clinical Child Psychology, 6*, 24–27.

Row v. Wade, 409 U.S. 817 (1973).

Roy, M., (Ed.). (1977). *Battered women: A psychosociological study of domestic violence*. New York: Van Nostrand Reinhold.

Rutter, M. (1971). Parent-child separation: Psychological effects on the children. *Journal of Child Psychology and Psychiatry, 12*, 233–260.

Santrock, J. W., & Warshank, R. A. (1979). Father custody and social development in boys and girls. *Journal of Social Issues, 35*, 112–125.

Shapiro, D. L. (1984). *Psychological evaluation and expert testimony*. New York: Van Nostrand Reinhold.

Silberman, L. J. (1982). Professional responsibility problems of divorce mediation. *Family Law Quarterly, 16*, 107–145.

Skinner v. State of Oklahoma, 316 U.S. 535, 541, 62 S.Ct. 1100, 1113, 86 L.Ed. 1655 (1942).

Sonkin, D. J., Martin, D., & Walker, L. E. (1985). *The male batterer: A treatment approach.* New York: Springer.

Sprenkle, D. H., & Storm, C. L. (1983). Divorce therapy outcome research: A substantium and methodological review. *Journal of Marital and Family Therapy, 9*, 239–258.

Stanton, A. M. (1982). Child-parent privilege for confidential communications: An examination and proposal. *Family Law Quarterly, 16*, 1–67.

Starr, R. (1982). *Child abuse prediction: Policy implications.* Cambridge, MA: Ballinger.

Steinhauer, P. D. (1983). Assessing for parenting capacity. *American Journal of Orthopsychiatry, 53*, 435.

Straus, M. A., Gelles, R., & Steinmetz, S. K. (1980). *Behind closed doors: Violence in the American family.* Garden City, NY: Anchor.

Strickman, L. P. (1982). Marriage, divorce and the Constitution. *Family Law Quarterly, 15*, 259–348.

Uniform Child Custody Jurisdiction Act, 9 UCA III (1979).

Uniform Marriage and Divorce Act, 402, 9A UCA 197–198 (1979).

U.S. Department of Justice, Bureau of Justice Statistics. (1986). *Crime and justice facts.* Washington, DC: Author.

Vander Mey, B. J., & Neff, R. L. (1982). Adult child incest: A review of research and treatment. *Adolescence, 24*, 717–735.

Volgy, S. S., & Everett, C. A. (1985). Systemic assessment criteria for joint custody. *Journal of Divorce, 8*, 131–150.

Walker, L. E. (1979). *The battered woman.* New York: Harper & Row.

Walker, L. E. (1984). *The battered woman syndrome.* New York: Springer.

Wallerstein, J. S., & Kelly, J. B. (1980). *Surviving the breakup: How children and parents cope with divorce.* New York: Basic Books.

Warshank, R. A., & Santrock, J. W. (1983). The impact of divorce in father-custody and mother-custody homes: A child's perspective. In L. A. Kurdek (Ed.), *Children of divorce: New directions for child development.* San Francisco: Jossey-Bass, pp. 29–46.

Weiner, B. A. (1985). An overview of child custody laws. *Hospital and Community Psychiatry, 36*, 838–843.

Weiner, I. B. (1985). Preparing forensic reports and testimony. *The Clinical Psychologist, 38*, 78–80.

Weithorn, L. A. (1982). Developmental factors and competence to make informed treatment decisions. *Child and Youth Services, 4*, 85–100.

Westman, J. C., Cline, D. W., Swift, W. J., & Kramer, D. A. (1970). The role of child psychiatry in divorce. *Archives of General Psychiatry, 23*, 416–420.

Whalen v. Row, 429 U.S. 589, 599 (1977).

Whitcomb, D. (1986). Prosecuting child sexual abuse: New approaches. *National Institute of Justice Reports, 197*, 2–6.

Wisconsin v. Yoder, 406 U.S. (1972).

Yllo, K. (1984). The status of women, marital equality, and violence against wives. *Journal of Family Issues, 5*, 307–320.

Zarski, L. P, Knight, R., & Zarski, J. J. (1985). Child custody disputes: A review of legal and clinical resolution methods. *International Journal of Family Therapy, 7*, 96–106.

Ziskin, J. (1981). *Coping with psychiatric and psychological testimony* (2 vols., 3rd ed.). Marina Del Rey, CA: Law and Psychology.

CHAPTER 6

Personality Assessment in Personal Injury Cases

JAMES NEAL BUTCHER and TERRI CROSS HARLOW

The annual cost of work-related injury in the United States is extremely high. According to Social Security Administration statistics the annual cost of workers' compensation payments for disability increased from $13.4 billion in 1980 to $18.5 billion in 1983 for 3.8 million disabled workers (Price, 1983). In the month of July 1984 alone a total of over $1.3 billion was paid to workers disabled for a year or more or whose disabilities were expected to result in death (DHHS, 1984). The staggering costs of disability and the extensive number of workers who are presently absent from the workforce as a result of disability reflect a problem of great magnitude. Moreover, issues and problems surrounding work compensation or Social Security disability are complex and increasingly involve interaction among the legal, medical, and psychological professions in addition to the representatives from industry, trade unions, insurance companies, and government agencies.

Psychologists in clinical practice are becoming more involved in the arena of compensation determination. This chapter explores the role psychological factors may play in physical injury cases and in cases of alleged psychological disability as a result of trauma in which litigation, workers' compensation, or Social Security disability determination is involved. We will explore some of the issues surrounding disability determination and examine some of the factors influencing disability claims. Later in the chapter we will examine methods of evaluating individuals in workers' compensation or civil litigation cases and discuss the psychologist's role in serving as an expert witness on cases involving personal injury litigation or workers' compensation claims. We will be dealing with objective methods of personality evaluation using the Minnesota Multiphasic Personality Inventory (MMPI) since this is the most widely used clinical assessment instrument.

The authors wish to thank Alan Roberts for his constructive comments on an earlier version of this paper. We, of course, take full responsibility for the contents of the paper.

WHAT IS WORKERS' COMPENSATION AND HOW DOES IT WORK?

Workers' compensation programs are based on the idea that industry is responsible for the damages its employees incur (Taylor, 1939), and compensation for work-related injury should be regarded as part of production costs (Rayback, 1966). Further, workers' compensation programs are based on the idea that, in the end, the consumer should bear the expenses arising from production of the goods it purchases (Goldberg, 1968). Typically, workers' compensation programs are funded by employers who purchase insurance policies from private companies although in some states workers actually pay a portion of the costs (Paradis, 1972). Other sources of support for workers' compensation have recently emerged. In 1983, for example, Minnesota became the first state to establish a competitive nonprofit state compensation insurance fund (Tinsley, 1983).

Disability benefits either partially replace lost wages or provide allowances for partial disabilities such as loss of sight under mandated payment schedules (Price, 1983). Social Security disability is more comprehensive and may provide workers' benefits even if the disability is not job related or if the workers' benefits under workers' compensation have expired. At present there are over 79 million workers (88 percent of the work force) covered by workers' compensation programs. This protection covers the disabled worker if the injury or sickness is work related regardless of fault (White, 1983).

For the reader to appreciate both the value and the extent of the disability system in the United States, it is useful to highlight some of the historical landmarks that marked the evolution of the work compensation system.

Historical Landmarks in Workers' Compensation

Numerous individuals from different professions and diverse political and social systems have contributed to the present philosophy of compensation. Compulsory accident insurance to protect workers was initiated in Germany in 1885. The United States lagged somewhat in its development of labor protection programs, probably because of the spirit of American individualism (Taylor, 1938) with its exploitation of a cheap and abundant but powerless work force (Selleck & Whittaker, 1962) and the belief that employees were free to decline employment they deemed dangerous or distasteful (Prosser, 1971).

In the era before workers' compensation laws, injured workers were compensated only if they were able to obtain damages from their employers through the courts under common law by proving that their employers were negligent. Employers had several lines of defense under common law: (1) *contributory negligence* in which workers had to prove that they were in no way at fault; (2) the *fellow-servant doctrine* in which proof of a fellow worker's negligence absolved the employer of responsibility; and (3) *assumption of risks* in which the workers' prior knowledge of job-related hazards relieved the employer of responsibility (Martin, 1975; O'Brien, 1981). Available information on the outcomes of such litigation suggests that, prior to workers' compensation laws, fewer than 30 percent of the cases provided compensation for employees (Prosser, 1971).

Toward the latter part of the nineteenth century some states, beginning with Alabama, passed employers' liability laws providing more adequate protection for workers by making failure to follow government safety regulations a condition of negligence. Liability was, however, limited to cases in which fault was determined. An important federal statute was passed by Congress in 1908 providing some employees of the United States compensation for injuries sustained in the course of employment. This statute was surpassed in 1916 when the more comprehensive and less restrictive Federal Employees' Compensation Act covering all civilian government employees was passed. Many states followed suit and later passed workers' compensation laws, though it was not until 1949 that all of the contiguous 48 states had enacted no-fault work compensation laws.

Beginning in the mid-twentieth century, workers' compensation laws were further liberalized. In 1953, for example, the Minnesota state legislature revised its 1913 Workers' Compensation Act by eliminating its prior requirements that a workers' injury be "caused by accident" and altering the definition of accident. Since that time, an employer has been liable for compensation "in every case of personal injury or death of his employee arising out of and in the course of employment without regard to the question of negligence," and the definition of personal injury has been extended to include conditions caused by occupational disease (Minnesota Statute, 1980).

During the 1960s, disabling deaths and injuries in industry increased alarmingly. Between 1966 and 1970 more Americans were killed in their workplace than in Vietnam (White, 1983). Major changes in workers' compensation benefits came in 1970 with the establishment of the Occupational Safety and Health Administration Act (OSHA) designed to adopt and enforce federal safety and health policies in work places of industries concerned with interstate commerce. OSHA has had an enormous impact on industrial safety. By 1971 over 4,000 rules affecting over four million businesses had been adopted, and thousands more were adopted during the years that followed (Robertson, 1983). These employee protection programs have not been without controversy, however, Employers have fought to avoid OSHA fines and the often-expensive safety measures necessary for compliance with agency regulations.

Workers' Compensation Today

While states differ considerably in the details of compensation laws (e.g., on time limitations for filing claims, waiting period requirements, the number of occupational diseases covered, determination of who selects the initial physician involved, and provision of rehabilitation benefits) and disability payment rates, the general provisions of most state programs are similar. Forty-six states, Washington D.C., and Puerto Rico provide full medical coverage under their statutes, as do the U.S. Federal Employees Compensation Act (FECA) and the Longshoremen's and Harbor Worker's Compensation Act (LHWCA). Arkansas, Georgia, New Jersey, and Ohio have special restrictive provisions, with New Jersey's probably the most restrictive (employer liability ceases after $100 of medical care, and the employee must petition for additional treatment) (United States Department of Labor, 1984).

Characteristic of most workers' compensation statutes is the no-fault principle. Four classifications of disability are defined: temporary total disability, temporary partial disability, permanent partial disability, and permanent total disability. Although the no-fault concept was designed to eliminate the need for litigation, this has not proved to be the case in many situations. In state workers' compensation programs, features distinctive of a litigation system are present, with "plaintiffs" and "defendants" on opposing sides and appeals common. In contrast, Social Security Disability Insurance (SSDI), which requires only proof of inability to work, regardless of causation, is seldom a source of litigation (White, 1983). In most states appeals are first processed through adjudicators with the workers' compensation system. Later appeals then go to courts. Jury trials are eschewed in most states because of their prohibitive costs and delays. The current workers' compensation system "nurtures adversity" (Martin, 1975, p. 33) and creates a climate in which the injured worker must attempt to prove both that the injury sustained has resulted in a disability which either prohibits return to work or reduces the market value of his or her skills and that the injury is job related. Moreover, the injured worker finds that the greater the degree of disability, the greater the amount of financial compensation is likely to be (Vega, 1983).

The process of filing a workers' compensation claim is complex, and litigation may arise at a number of points. An injured worker initially notifies a company representative of the injury and seeks referral to a physician for medical treatment. The employer must then file an initial report to the insurer in most states, as must the physician. Most claims are resolved at this stage, with involvement limited to the employer, employee, and insurance carrier. Failure of the employer to file a report, however, is tantamount to denial of the claim and requires an appeal often necessitating legal counsel. Failure of the physician to file a prompt report to the insuring agency may lead to an ill-formed judgment from the insurer, thus instigating the appeals process by the employee. Moreover, disagreement between the parties concerning the degree of injury and thus the amount of monetary compensation may also motivate employees to appeal. When the parties retain legal counsel and file an appeal with the state appeals board, they formally become legal adversaries (Martin, 1975; Vega, 1983).

Particular difficulties in determining compensability arise "when the line of demarcation between occupational and non-occupational disability is obscured, as in heart disease, ulcer disease, or psychiatric disorder" (Parlour & Jones, 1980). As interpretation of workers' compensation laws has become increasingly liberal, the number of claims citing job stress and resulting psychiatric difficulties has skyrocketed (Lasky, 1980; Marcus, 1983). Lack of psychiatric agreement and diagnostic clarity have led to "almost any psychological aberration being considered by plaintiff's psychiatric consultant as mental illness caused by the work place" (Parlour & Jones, 1980, p. 445). Parlour and Jones pointed out that the Michigan Supreme Court ruling on *Carter v. General Motors* was precedent setting in psychiatric cases in many states. The Michigan Supreme Court upheld the benefits awarded to a machine operator who became psychotic allegedly as a result of work pressure, despite the absence of physical injury and the lack of a specific precipitating event.

The majority of courts have held that such injuries are compensable, although guidelines have varied. The Wisconsin Supreme Court, for example, has ruled that such injuries are compensable if the employee can prove exposure to stresses and strains "beyond the ordinary day-to-day stresses and strains to which all employees were exposed" (*Swiss Colony, Inc. v. Department of Industry, Labor, and Human Relations*, 1976). Massachusetts courts consider the duration of the precipitating incident in determining compensability. Specific, documented traumatic events at work preceding the symptoms are likely to lead to compensation, but prolonged stress gradually leading to the development of difficulties is not because of a weaker cause-effect link (Staten & Umbeck, 1983).

In a recent court decision in California (*Albertson's Inc. v. Workers Compensation Appeals Board of the State of California*, 1982) the court found in favor of an employee who claimed that comments by her supervisor caused her great embarrassment and required her to seek psychiatric treatment for psychological problems. The court concluded that perceived job harassment was a sufficient cause for compensation but required that the employment situation must be a direct causal factor influencing the psychological condition as determined by "reasonable medical probability" by expert psychiatric opinion.

In cases of psychological injury it is important to ascertain the existence of a credible, stressful situation that is sufficient to produce the trauma. Information about the trauma-inducing nature of the stressful situation in question and the possible impact the situation might have had on the patient is usually difficult to obtain. Evaluations of persons in cases involving psychic trauma are some of the most difficult to conduct as we shall see later in this chapter.

In cases of physical injury, disabled workers must prove that it is "medically probable" beyond a reasonable doubt that their disabilities would not have been sustained had they not been employed in the job they held at the time of the accident. Statutes pertaining to psychiatric disability are less clearly defined in most states and less consistent across states, no doubt because such cases have been relatively rare until recently. Psychiatric injuries are often ill defined, and standards for normality and abnormality vague. Standards for determining the existence of both disability and liability are typically insufficient, as are standards for measuring disability. Moreover, the tendency has been for lawyers and judges to defer to psychiatric opinion rather than to extend the fact-finding themselves to a level not found in medical litigation. Additionally, the underlying rationale is not specified as decreased competitive ability in the labor market, which is at the root of the workers' compensation system (Lasky, 1980).

Although many states have adopted liberal policies with regard to psychiatric disability, in keeping with current economic retrenchment, some states have opted for more conservative stances. The Minnesota Supreme Court, for example, in 1981 overturned a lower court's decision and ruled that mental illness by job-related stress in the absence of physical trauma was not compensable under the Workers'

Compensation Act because it was unclear that the state legislature intended the Workers' Compensation Act, instituted in 1953, when no such cases had yet arisen, to include mental injury, and the prohibitive cost reallocation necessary would be a major policy change (*Lockwood v. Independent School District,* 1981). A 1984 Minnesota Supreme Court ruling held that a policeman's alleged depression was noncompensable because mental injury is not compensable under the Minnesota Workers' Compensation Act. However, the court found that the stress of being a policeman contributed to the plaintiff's development of an ulcer because the policeman showed objective evidence of exposure to "extreme or beyond day to day stress and evidence of outward manifestations of distress either subsequent to or contemporaneously with the claimed stress" (*Egeland v. City of Minneapolis,* 1984). This was the first time that an ulcer was found to be compensable in Minnesota under workers' compensation.

In states with more liberal policies toward work-related psychiatric difficulties, concern about fraud and claims exaggerations is widespread (Lasky, 1980; Staten & Umbeck, 1983). When standards are vague and conditions difficult to verify and assess, incentives to falsify claims are present and the potential for abuse is great.

ROLE OF PSYCHOLOGICAL FACTORS IN THE MANIFESTATION OF PHYSICAL SYMPTOMS

A number of studies have reported that psychological factors play an important role in the manifestation of physical disabilities. Studies have shown that personality factors appear to be associated with disability as a result of physical injury among some patients (Fordyce, 1964), and psychological factors are "closely associated in patients with disease and disability" (Phillips, 1964). Flor and Turk (1984) recently noted that pain patients tend to have a great deal more measured psychopathology than has the general population.

Psychological factors have been found to play an important role in the manifestation of industrially injured patients with different types of injuries (Beals & Hickman, 1972). The percentage of workers' compensation claimants who are suffering from mental disorders is believed to be high. A recent empirical finding confirmed this belief. Leeper, Badger, and Milo (1985) interviewed physical disability determination cases prior to their physical examination. They employed the Diagnostic Interview Schedule developed by NIMH to obtain reliable and valid clinical diagnoses. They found that 56 percent of the claimants for physical disability had one or more current psychiatric diagnoses. Another empirical study (Rader, 1984) reported that 80.4 percent of work compensation cases studied responded to personality testing as if they were emotionally disturbed.

Prolonged psychological stress has been determined to be a major causal factor in low back pain (Caillet, 1968; Sainsbury & Gibson, 1954). Negative factors such as stress have been found to be related to physical symptom expression, but positive factors too, such as financial rewards, have been tied to increases in physical disability claims. Robertson (1983) reported that economic incentives in the form of more available workers' compensation benefits served to increase the number of days lost due to injury: "Apparently, the workers in the plants studied reacted to economic incentives, by demanding more time off for injury" (p. 203). In a recent comparison of reports of chronic low back pain over a 20-year period, Fordyce, Roberts, and Sternbach (1984) found incredibly high increases of alleged disability:

> The population in 1980 was 126% of that in 1960. Using the averages of the first three years of SSDI (1957–9) (of the Social Security Disability and the three most recent years for which data were available (1973, 1975–6), awards for all categories of disability were 309% in the 1970's of awards in the 1950's. The corresponding increase in back pain was 2680%. Surely, no one argues that that increase represents a corresponding increase in occurrence of demonstratable physical findings in the same period, or in diagnostic prowess. The increase must be due in significant part to the interaction of increasing numbers of persons seeking the financial haven of SSDI. (p. 20–21)

In order to describe personality factors among persons with physically disabling symptoms such as pain, it is important to determine whether the pain is acute versus chronic. Beals and Hickman (1972) found that patients who had chronic pain differed from those who were experiencing acute pain. More chronic pain patients had personality profiles that included depression (Sternbach, Wolf, Murphy and Akeson, 1973).

Psychological Factors in the Experience of Physical Disease

The specific psychological mechanisms or processes by which psychological factors produce physical distress is not well defined. Given the same amount of organ stress or tissue damage, individuals vary in their subjective experiences of pain. Some individuals may accomplish enormous physical feats such as playing a football game or completing a marathon run in states of relative oblivion to the body's pain messages while some individuals overreact to minor physical problems with incapacitation.

Premorbid personality factors are considered to be important in determining an individual's reaction to physical injury or trauma. Personality traits such as extreme dependency may influence an individual toward seeking compensation as a result of even minor physical injury. Potential secondary gain factors are important to consider in evaluating an individual's disability behavior (Foster, 1964).

Interpretation of Psychological or Emotional Symptoms of Anxiety as Physical Problems

It has been observed clinically that the experiential feelings accompanying autonomic activity in response to stressful or anxiety-arousing situations (particularly the heart palpitations, excessive sweating, and increased respiration) may be interpreted by the individual as physical distress (Wolff, 1968). These normal physiological states may be interpreted by the individual as "real" physical problems or even indicative of major physical disorders such as heart disease, or indicative of potentially dire consequences such as death or disability. Clinicians working in a medical setting frequently see patients who are reporting hypertension or other coronary symptoms but who have no physical basis for their concerns.

False or exaggerated responses to autonomic activity are not the only physical processes that are misinterpreted by the patient. Normal, nonpathological muscle activity may also be taken by the person to mean that more serious physical problems are occurring. There are apparently great individual differences in the amount of muscle tension or pain individuals can tolerate before they interpret the experience as indicative of more serious problems or pain.

Recent work by Pennybaker and his colleagues has added to our understanding of the mechanisms involved in the physical expression of emotional or psychological processes. A series of studies were conducted aimed at describing the psychological parameters of physical symptoms. Pennybaker, Burnam, Schaeffer, and Harper (1977) reported the results of a large-scale study to determine the amount and types of symptoms normal individuals reported. They found that in various testing situations 79.6 percent of normals reported experiencing some degree of at least one symptom. They also noted that persons reporting one symptom were likely to report others. They did not find clusters or groups of symptoms that consistently loaded on a particular factor. Pennybaker and Skelton (1978) noted that self-reported symptoms were moderately related to physiological changes. However, diverse physical symptoms "appear to be subject to common psychological processes." That is, symptom reports of physical disease appear to be influenced by the individual's *focus of attention*.

Low Back Injury and Pain: Extent, Chronicity, and Unverifiability

One of the most common physical complaints related to industrial injury and compensation claims is low back pain. Musculoskeletal problems are among the most prevalent industrial injuries and are perhaps some of the most intractable. Hult (1954) reported that about 80 percent of the industrial and forestry workers he examined had symptoms related to low back pain, and about 25 percent of the cases reported that they had been incapacitated for some time with back problems. In a study of industrial workers in the United States, Rowe (1969) reported that about 35 percent of sedentary workers and 45 percent of heavy handlers had visited a physician for back problems.

Robertson (1983), surveying the data on individual injuries in three factories in three different states from 1973 through 1980, found that annual variation in accident rates was strongly related to OSHA citations and increments in workers' compensation claims. Actual verifiable injuries were found to be reduced as a result of the attention paid to safety because of occupational health safety citations in the workplace. However, overall injury claims were not reduced. Instead, injury claims increased in relation to increases in workers' compensation, but these increases were confined to nonverifiable injuries such as back strain and pain.

Problems related to low back pain or injury appear to be chronic. McGill (1968) reported that employees who are absent from work for more than six months have about a 50 percent chance of ever returning to work again. If the employee remains out of work for a period of a year, the probability that he or she will return to work drops to about 25 percent. If the employee remains absent from work for two years, the chances of him or her ever returning to work appear to be negligible.

Psychological Factors in Physical Disability: Relationship of Disability Claim to Symptomatic Status

Disability claim status—whether Social Security disability, work compensation (state, federal, or private carrier), or pending civil litigation—may be related to the nature and extent of psychological factors involved in the case. A number of investigators have noted that litigation was an important factor in the level of reported symptoms among pain patients (Sternbach, Wolf, Murphy, & Akeson, 1973; Pollack & Grainey, 1984). The "intensity" level of patient symptoms may be influenced, in part, by the fact that a disability claim is pending or compensation is fantasized. The client's expectation of obtaining substantial monetary reward or a life pension may clearly, though perhaps unconsciously, influence his or her symptom expression. Clinicians have observed that physical symptoms or pain behavior are not likely to abate substantially as long as claims or litigation is pending (Brown, Nemiah, Barr, & Barry, 1954; Foster, 1964).

Adequate understanding of psychological factors in physical disability claims is often contingent upon the type of case and the patient's perception of the legal processes involved in his or her case. Likewise compensation claims or law suits are likely to involve varying levels of psychological intensity depending on the legal jurisdiction or the state in which the case is being heard. States differ in their interpretation of what conditions are compensable under workers' compensation laws and may vary considerably with regard to what is admissible as evidence in civil court proceedings and which professionals are included in the hearings as expert witnesses.*

Psychological Factors in Physical Injury Cases: Problems of Determining Malingering

As disability insurance programs were developing, so were medical and psychiatric theories pertaining to prolonged symptom distress following accidental injury. Debate on the origin and verity of posttraumatic symptoms, both physical and emotional, has been in progress for over a century. Early medical writings from 1776 to the mid-1800s indicated that seemingly minor injuries to the spinal cord and brain could result in undetectable lesions leading to later diffuse symptomatology including depression, irritability, numbness, weakness, and paralysis. In 1866 John Erich Erichsen, professor of surgery at the University College Hospital in London, published an influential series of lectures on "nervous shock and other obscure injuries"

---

*For example, psychologists are not admitted as expert witnesses on matters of disability determination in some states (see Pacht, Kuehn, Bassett, & Nash, 1973).

received during railway accidents and ascribed posttraumatic symptoms including "neurotic" symptoms to organic changes (Trimble, 1981).

By the late 1800s, however, an opposing viewpoint was emerging. In 1883 Herbert Page, surgeon to the London and North-West Railway, published a book refuting Erichsen's views and purporting that symptoms following minor spinal injuries were the result of nervous shock arising from the extreme fear surrounding railway accidents. Page introduced the concept of functional as opposed to structural disorders. Other writers of the time, including Charcot, suggested that some cases of "railway spine" were due to "hysteria," and thus the controversy over injury sequelae began. In 1895 Freud and Breuer noted that following railway accidents the psychical effects of the frightening incident are converted into somatic experiences. In the mid-twentieth century posttraumatic symptoms came to be viewed as adaptational difficulties. Research on posttraumatic neurosis during wartime led Kardiner (1941) to suggest that posttraumatic symptoms stemmed from inadequate ego resources in the face of environmental change.

Although references to malingering are found in pre–twentieth-century writings, focus on the problem for financial compensation became extensive only after railway accidents became prominent and the first workers' compensation acts had been passed (Trimble, 1981). Trimble pointed out that as early as 1917 Collie noted that the number of industrial accidents rose 44 percent in the first six years after the 1906 Workman's Compensation Act in England was passed in spite of the decline in the workforce. With some exceptions, most early writers tended to separate malingering from hysteria on the basis of deliberateness, assuming that malingering involved conscious deceit while hysteria resulted from unconscious processes. Malingerers were thought to be hostile, secretive, uncooperative, shifty-eyed, and able to recall explicitly the details surrounding their alleged injuries. Hysterics were thought to be more dependent, cooperative, attention-seeking, and less consistent in their stories as well as less concerned with their problems (Trimble, 1981).

Meanwhile, as literature on malingering and psychological bases of posttraumatic symptoms was accumulating, researchers were searching for the organic bases of symptoms following physical trauma, particularly head injuries. Numerous animal experiments showed nerve fiber degeneration on autopsy following head concussions. Moreover, microscopic brain lesions were found in humans who died following seemingly minor head blows (Oppenheimer, 1968). Numerous other experiments on human cadaver skulls indicated that even minor head injuries may lead to tissue damage which may have widespread clinical effects. Abnormal electroencephalograms and reduced cerebral blood flow were also noted following minor head injuries. Furthermore, psychologists found that patients with even minor head injuries may experience cognitive impairments and that such deficits tend to diminish as posttraumatic symptoms decrease. It has also been noted that headaches, dizziness, fatigue, nervousness, and prolongation of symptoms have been found to occur in many head injury patients, including children, for whom compensation issues are irrelevant (Trimble, 1981).

World Wars I and II stirred interest in the topics of posttraumatic neurotic symptoms among military personnel. Numerous researchers focused on the issue of neurotic predisposition and collected data suggesting a link between war neuroses and prior psychiatric difficulties or neurotic predisposition. Later, researchers found similar correlations between posttraumatic symptoms and personal or family histories of psychiatric difficulties in nonmilitary injury cases. However, recent researchers studying survivors of disasters have found that posttraumatic symptoms are uniformly similar in presentation and duration and not substantially correlated with prior psychiatric symptoms (Slaikeu, 1984).

Thus, more than a century after debate on the origin (organic or psychological) of symptom prolongation following head and spine injuries began, the experimental and theoretical literature is still contradictory and full of conjecture. This lack of clinical consensus and diagnostic clarity has fueled the medico-legal controversy of workers' compensation cases, rendering support for opposing sides of the issue.

Evaluating Psychological Factors in Personal Injury Cases with the MMPI

One frequent problem facing professionals working in forensic settings involves the determination of whether an individual, who claims to have difficulties as a result of an injury or stressful experience or exposure to toxic substances, is manifesting symptoms consistent with such injuries. In these situations the professional involved—physicians and psychologists—may be asked to render an opinion or evaluate:

1. Whether there is a possibility that the individual's physical complaints are due to actual organic changes
2. Whether the symptoms of disability result from psychological disorder such as traumatic reaction to stress or "traumatic neurosis"
3. Whether the pattern of symptoms may be neither physical nor "psychological," but are instead contrived in order to gain compensation or to obtain special services or considerations such as job transfer or reduced work load. It has been noted that malingering is difficult to determine without direct objective evidence (Marcus, 1983).

Ziskin (1984) has pointed out that when it comes to courts making a workers' compensation disability determination only two factors are relevant: (1) whether the person is disabled, and (2) whether that injury was work related. In this section we will discuss some of the issues concerned with conducting psychological evaluations occurring in disability determination cases. A number of referral problems or forensic cases may be found in such determinations:

1. Individuals who are experiencing psychological symptoms as a result of having had some physical injury—for example, a passenger on a bus which was involved in an accident and who alleged that he received physical injuries resulting in his becoming sexually impotent
2. Individuals who are presently viewing themselves as physically disabled but who do not have a detectable organic condition—for example, an industrial

employee who had worked around "toxic" substances for a period of time and alleged that he had become disabled with memory problems and behavior changes as a result of breathing paint fumes

3. Individuals who view themselves as having psychological problems as a result of stress or trauma—for example, seven female coal miners in West Virginia who claimed that they had developed severe psychological problems as a result of the company's failure to provide private showers. They claimed that the male miners watched them shower, producing a great deal of psychological stress.

4. Individuals who present as having chronic psychological problems (these are commonly found among Social Security disability claimants) as a result of stressful life events.

Psychological evaluation may prove valuable in appraising personality factors contributing to an individual's symptom pattern or appraising the dynamics of an individual's response to an acquired physical disability. However, psychological evaluations in disability determinations have some inherent limitations. It is not possible to determine, on the basis of the MMPI, or any psychological test for that matter, whether a claimant's injuries are *actually* based on organic conditions or derive from personality factors. It is also not possible, with confidence, to determine on the basis of a psychological test alone whether the patient is malingering. It is not possible to establish, with any degree of certainty, the nature of an individual's premorbid personality and its influence on current functioning unless psychological testing was conducted at an earlier point in time prior to the present disability. There are no foolproof ways of detecting premorbid personality or preinjury functioning with only present-time measurement.

Psychological testing can be of value in disability determinations in a number of ways. If the psychological tests provide, as the MMPI does, scales that measure response attitudes, the individual's cooperation with the assessment and "believability" of the results can be assessed. Psychological assessment instruments, if they are objectively derived and validated, can provide a comparison of the client's symptomatic status with that of numerous other cases. Psychological testing can also provide some indication of the severity and long-term stability of the individual's problems.

MMPI Profiles of Disabled Individuals without Claims Pending

As a baseline from which to judge personality test performances of disability claimants with cases pending it is valuable to know how actually verifiable disability cases have responded on the psychological measures. Research on personality characteristics of individuals who were actually disabled and were not awaiting a disability determination decision have been published. Wiener (1948) and Warren and Weiss (1969) have found that groups of individuals who were actually disabled tended to produce MMPI profiles with scale scores in the nonpathological range, below $T = 70$. When disabled patients were classified according to type of disability, there were no characteristic MMPI profiles found for the various disability groups.

MMPI Profiles of Individuals Receiving Workers' Compensation

When personality profiles of pending disability claimants are studied, however, the response pattern appears to be more exaggerated and generally more pathological (Sternbach et al., 1973; Pollack & Grainey, 1984). Whether these differences reflect an element of "acuteness" versus chronicity or a trend toward excessive symptom claiming to emphasize perceived disability is not known. Most of the MMPI research involving work compensation cases, however, reflects this increased level of psychological symptoms. Work compensation claimants have been studied descriptively by a number of authors. In cases where physical injury is believed to be involved, the MMPI profile of workers' compensation cases usually involves extreme scale elevations on *Hs, D,* and *Hy* (Shaffer, Nussbaum, & Little, 1972; Repko & Cooper, 1983).

Snibbe, Peterson, and Sosner (1980) found that workers' compensation applicants had generally similar and rather disturbed MMPI profiles (with high elevations on scales *F, Sc, D, Hs, Hy, Pd*) regardless of the reason for the claim—psychiatric, low back pain, or head injury.

Vega (1983), in a study comparing work compensation cases of Mexican-Americans with Anglo-Americans, found that both groups had similar profiles shapes with *Hs, D,* and *Hy,* as the highest clinical scores. In this study, unlike previous research with Hispanics (Repko & Cooper, 1983), Mexican-American disability claimants had profiles that were relatively lower in elevation than the Anglo-American disability claimants, suggesting that there might be less malingering among Mexican-American clients than among Anglos.

In a study to determine possible motivational differences between disability applicants, Pollack and Grainey (1984) compared groups of individuals who were applicants for disability. One group was applying for disability from private insurance carriers and was presently being paid for injuries; the second disability group was applying for disability from the state compensation program and was presently not being supported. The researchers found clear MMPI-measured personality differences between profiles of disability applicants from private insurance carriers versus those applying for state compensation. The applicants in the private insurance group tended to be higher on *Hs* and *Hy* while the applicants for benefits from the state were elevated on a number of scales measuring exaggerated responding (*F*) and confusion and severe emotional problems (*D, Pd, Pa, Pt, Sc,* and *Si*). The state applicants were motivated to "look worse" in order to receive financial benefits.

One recent study found that individuals who had MMPI *Pt* scale scores prominent in their profile code tended to report more "intense" pain (Parker, Doerfler, Tatten, & Hewett, 1983). Client motivation in rehabilitation efforts has been evaluated. Salomone (1972) found that the MMPI *Pd* score differentiated unmotivated clients from motivated in a rehabilitation program. Levenson, Hirschfeld, and Hirschfeld (1985) found that workers who had higher elevations on MMPI scales (particularly *Hs, D,* and *Hy*) had longer periods of disability than workers with lowering-ranging MMPI profiles.

MMPI Profiles of Psychiatric Disability Claimants

One of the most important aspects of an individual's psychological test performance in evaluations where possible financial claims are pending is the subject's attitudes toward taking the tests. Persons whose claims are pending may choose to present their problems in an exaggerated manner to get their complaints heard. Consequently, psychological tests like the MMPI, which have scales to measure response attitude, are particularly valuable in putting the level or quality of symptom endorsement in perspective. The conditions under which a person takes the MMPI are known to influence both the elevation of the scales and the shape of the profile in addition to elevating the MMPI validity indicators.

In an interesting study measuring the psychological effects of "exposure" to Agent Orange during the Vietnam War, Korgeski and Leon (1983) contrasted veterans on the basis of objective evidence of past exposure to Agent Orange and according to the belief that they had been exposed. There were *no* neurological or personality differences between the veterans with an objectively determined high possibility of exposure versus those veterans with a low probability of past exposure. However, veterans who *believed* themselves to have been exposed to Agent Orange reported more significant psychological disturbance than those who did not believe they had been exposed. In other words, simply belief that they had been exposed tended to produce the most pathological psychological picture.

Early studies of faking on the MMPI generally showed that individuals who take the test under directions to feign psychological disorder tend to produce a distorted MMPI profile with detectable scale elevations on scale *F* (Cofer, Chance, & Judson, 1949; Fairbank, McCaffrey, & Keane, 1985; Hunt, 1948). Although two studies have questioned whether the MMPI validity indicators are effective in detecting exaggerated or feigned responding (Kroeger & Turnbull, 1975; Wilcox & Dawson, 1977), other research has shown the MMPI validity indicators to be effective in detecting exaggerated responding. Anthony (1971) studied attempts of psychiatric patients to exaggerate their complaints and found that these subjects tended to produce more scale elevations of psychotic types. However, he found that MMPI indices of faking discriminated the exaggerated profiles.

In a study of MMPI profiles among work compensation cases, Repko and Cooper (1983) found that a relatively small number of invalid or exaggerated profiles. In general, they found that workers' compensation patients were seen as persons who attempted to give a true and accurate self-description of their condition. However, there were patients with dramatic patterns of exaggeration among the range of workers' compensation cases. It is not known if any of these cases had claims pending—a condition that tends to increase the range of validity scale scores as we explain shortly.

The previous studies show general response distortion among work compensation cases suggesting that some claimants exaggerate problems. However, a more recent field study that bears directly on the question was conducted by Gallucci (1984) to determine whether MMPI validity measures F and F-K would detect a response set to claim psychological symptoms. Gallucci compared groups of veterans who were applying for compensation benefits as a result of psychological disability and a group of veterans who were psychiatric patients in the VA but were not applying for compensation. He found that veterans who were applying for compensation produced more high F profiles and greater dissimulation on the MMPI as measured by the F-K index.

Studies aimed at detecting faking or symptom exaggeration on the MMPI need to take into consideration the nature of the claim and whether it is in the interest of the patient to "look psychologically healthy but physically sick" or "to appear psychologically disturbed and unable to deal with life effectively." Validity patterns on the MMPI, as well as profile elevation and shape, tend to reflect these differing response attitudes.

Future research on psychological factors in disability claiming would be improved if the samples involved were refined with closer attention to possible motivational factors influencing the test administration. Researchers might more consistently employ measures of test-taking attitudes such as "faking good" versus "faking bad" in case selection procedures.

DISTORTED PATTERNS ON THE MMPI VALIDITY INDICATORS: EXAGGERATING PHYSICAL DISABILITY.   Individuals who wish to create an impression of having serious physical problems tend to produce MMPI profiles that have some common features:

1.   They tend to produce validity scale patterns that suggest exaggerated claims of personal virtue and complete honesty along with a clinical scale pattern emphasizing exaggerated symptom endorsement. The individual may produce high elevations on the L or K scales (or both). This presentation of self as very virtuous is done in order to project an image of believability with regard to the physical problems being claimed.

2.   Several possible clinical profile patterns result from distorted claims of physical disability. One frequent pattern involves an extremely elevated score on Hs. Elevations greater than a $T = 70$ tend not to occur among actual physically disabled cases (except individuals who are symptomatic for multiple sclerosis) unless there is a psychological component to their symptoms. Patients who have high elevations on this scale "overrespond" to somatic items or endorse numerous items which do not usually go together in actual physical disease—for example, headache symptoms accompanying a sprained wrist.

3.   Other neurotic scale elevations may accompany Hs scale elevations in characterizing the somatic overresponder. The D scale and the Hy scale are particularly likely to be elevated, although the Pt scale may be elevated in patients with intense somatic distress or symptoms related to the heart.

4.   Another MMPI pattern which includes prominent Sc scale elevations is common among individuals claiming to have been affected by toxic exposure or poi-

soning. Such symptoms as confusion, memory lapses, or various sensory problems are reported. Such symptom complaints may produce an elevation on the Sc scale.

DISTORTED PATTERNS ON THE VALIDITY INDICATORS: EXAGGERATING PSYCHO-LOGICAL DISABILITY.   Like patients exaggerating or falsely claiming physically disabling problems, patients who are attempting to make themselves appear psychologically disturbed also exaggerate complaints. Falsely claiming mental illness on the MMPI results in the following types of patterns:

1.   In the case of individuals attempting to present themselves as having more psychological problems than they actually have, the performance is usually characterized by claiming excessive symptoms or endorsing a large number of complaints that do not "hang together" in a meaningful way. The patient's overresponding takes the form of exaggerating psychological symptoms resulting in an elevated F scale score. Schneider (1979) found that the F scale of the MMPI predicted the individuals who were presenting a great deal of psychopathology in connection with their disability determinations for a pension on grounds of having service-connected psychopathology. These findings are congruent with earlier findings of Keller, Wigdor, and Lundell (1973) who studied individuals seeking compensation on the basis of psychologically disabling symptoms. The patients in this study were individuals who were seeking compensation on grounds that they were not employable but who had no physical disability. These individuals were found to be identifiable with respect to MMPI-measured personality factors and lifestyle. Primarily, they produced elevated F scale scores indicating an exaggeration of symptoms.

2.   Schneider (1979) found that individuals applying for disability benefits as a result of psychopathology have elevated Pa and Sc scores reflecting an expression of severe and chronic disorder involving thought disturbance and personal deterioration. Similarly, in the study by Keller et al. (1973) these patients presented significantly more psychopathology than controls on the MMPI with scale elevations on $Hs, D, Hy, Pt,$ and $Sc.$ In addition, they were found to be considered low in self-esteem, dependent, depressed, and socially isolated.

Treatment Outcome and Disability Claiming

A question that typically emerges in cases of litigation involving personal injury — particularly when it comes to assigning a monetary value to the claim — is the extent of the individual's disability, whether the injuries are permanent, and if the person can be rehabilitated. Rehabilitation of industrially injured patients with chronic problems is frequently difficult. White (1966) found that about 10 percent of low back patients are disabled more than six weeks, and of these long-term patients about 60 percent do not respond to any of the treatment methods used at the treatment center. Predicting the outcome of a rehabilitation case or determining, in advance, which individuals are likely to respond to programs of rehabilitation is quite difficult. One major determiner to rehabilitation is, of course, the individual's motivation to succeed. Pending outcome of the compensation claim can influence the success of a treatment program.

In a study employing patient self-report of recovery as the outcome measure, Kubiszyn (1984) found that, consistent with clinicians' impressions, individuals who were on workers' compensation or those whose claims were under litigation showed poorer treatment outcomes than individuals where economic factors were not relevant. Cairns, Mooney, and Crane (1984), Roberts (in press b), and Roberts and Reinhardt (1980)—like many researchers working with chronic pain patients —recognize that pain behaviors are quite intractable as long as compensation claims or litigation is pending.

Apart from the confounding relationships between excessive symptoms, compensation hopes, and treatment outcome, the question of whether personality factors are involved in rehabilitation outcome is an important one. Can personality factors provide useful information to rehabilitation counselors attempting to make predictions about rehabilitation results with clients who have been injured? Research on personality and rehabilitation success has been somewhat ambiguous. However, several investigators have found that MMPI-measured personality characteristics are related to treatment or rehabilitation outcome. Ayer, Thoreson, and Butler (1966) found that several MMPI scores were related to rehabilitation outcome and suggested that test scores assist in the measurement of motivation and "energy" for success. Gilbert and Lester (1970) reported that patients with the 1-3 MMPI profile had poorer rehabilitation outcomes. Three more recent studies (Kuperman & Golden, 1979; Dzioba & Doxey, 1984; Kubiszyn, 1984) found that high elevations on the *Hs* scale were related to poor treatment outcome. Wiltse and Rocchio (1975) found that MMPI scales *Hs, D,* and *Hy,* among their measures studied, provided the most effective predictors of outcome in rehabilitation among disabled clients. The greater the elevations on these scales, the less likely the individual was to have a positive treatment outcome.

In the support of these findings other research has thrown light upon the effectiveness of the MMPI as a prognostic indicator: Drasgow and Dreher (1965) found that the MMPI added substantially to the determination of readiness for training and rehabilitation. Salomone (1972) found that clients who were unmotivated for rehabilitation after injury were significantly higher on the MMPI *Pd* scale than were motivated clients. Flynn and Salomone (1977) found that the MMPI was able to yield modest improvements in predicting rehabilitation outcome; and Cairns et al (1984) found that the MMPI aided in the prediction of the success for either inpatient or outpatient rehabilitation treatment. Studies by Heaton and his colleagues (Heaton, Chelune, & Lehman, 1978; Newnan, Heaton, & Lehman, 1978) found that psychological tests like the MMPI, Halstead Battery, and WAIS had clinical utility for assessing patient's employability and other aspects of the patient's postinjury functioning.

The importance of conducting a comprehensive psychological evaluation in providing a rehabilitation program for industrially injured employees has been highlighted by Beals and Hickman (1972). They underscore the importance of recognizing the associated psychological factors accompanying industrial injury and also the need to incorporate psychological evaluations in treatment and rehabilitation efforts. Roberts (in press a), recognizing the important role that psychological factors may play in the manifestation of physical illness, has suggested the concept of "excessive disability" to recognize the importance of both psychological overresponding and underlying physical problems in disability. In his work with chronic pain management, Roberts has been cognizant of the *almost* irrelevant distinction that is often made between "real" (organic) causes and psychological components in physically disabling pain. When it comes to modifying pain behavior with chronic pain patients, it is generally desirable to avoid making the distinction between organic versus psychological causes and treat all chronic patients with similar behavioral strategies by recognizing that many patients who are disabled have excessive somatic complaints.

Forensic Evaluations in Personal Injury and Worker's Compensation Cases

Psychological evaluations of individuals in personal injury or stress-alleged psychological injury cases for litigation are becoming an increasingly important part of many psychological practices. Psychologists involved in such evaluations need to be aware of various causal factors possibly operating in workers' compensation or personal injury litigation cases. Theories of psychiatric defense in personal injury cases, such as those described by Blau (1984), Parlour and Jones (1980, 1981) and Ziskin (1980), might be of value in preparing cases for court testimony. An understanding of and an awareness of the published literature relating to possible psychological factors in physical injury and potential psychological stress factors in response to injury or trauma is important.

Moreover, psychologists who are preparing psychological evaluations that might become part of a court case need to consider a number of factors about this form of evaluation which are different from reports written for routine clinical psychological practice. If the evaluation forms part of a forensic disposition, the following considerations may be of value (see also chapter 19).

Pacht and colleagues (1973) pointed out that the psychologist as expert witness draws inferences from data that an ordinary witness would not be allowed to do: "He can state an opinion based on data from an area in which he has a proven [demonstrable] expertise. The closer the psychologist bases his testimony on his data, the greater likelihood of its acceptance" (p. 412).

Pacht and others (1973) also suggested that it is important for the psychologist to remember that he or she is testifying as an advocate regardless of the source of the fee. He testifies "*about* the client, not for or against him." Mental health professionals testifying in a court case or giving a deposition have usually been trained or counseled to provide an impartial viewpoint. However, the atmosphere of impartiality is seldom attained because of the essentially adversarial context in which most forensic cases are settled. Parlour and Jones (1981) pointed out that given the impracticality of courts being able to obtain impartial opinion, the judges and lawyers actually desire quality advocacy from expert witnesses.

Whatever role the psychologist as expert witness assumes, it is perhaps wise to follow the advice of Morse (1978) who noted that much of the data sought from mental health professionals is socially and morally evaluative rather than scientific.

He pointed out that mental health professionals have only limited scientific data to help assess social and moral questions and should be appropriately modest in their roles as expert witnesses.

In preparing for court testimony, it is desirable, in most cases, for the clinician to see the patient in person and not simply to go on the basis of a blind interpretation of the test results alone. A distinction is made here between the primary clinician in the case and an expert witness who is simply testifying on whether a test measures what it was designed to measure. There is a place for blind interpretations or computerized interpretive reports of tests in court testimony when the objectivity of the instrument is being established by expert witness testimony. In most court evaluations, however, the clinician has been asked by the client's attorney or by an insurance company or employer's attorney to evaluate a client. In some cases, this evaluation has been done in an adversarial context, and there will be at least two sets of opinions about the test data and the client's condition. It is important for the clinician to see the patient in person and any relevant family members, noting the points in time that the individual was seen. Often in personal injury cases, the hearing or trial might be delayed for months or years, and an assessment of the individual's behavior at different points in time may be important to the progression of the case and to an evaluation of the outcome of the alleged injury or psychological breakdown.

The nature of the interviews conducted with clients in forensic evaluations may differ considerably depending on whether the evaluation is conducted at the request of the defense or the plaintiff. Parlour and Jones (1981) described the problems and strategies involved when the defense psychiatrist conducts interviews with plaintiff-patients. Such interviews may be conducted under high levels of tension, suspicion, and antagonism. It is fairly common for plaintiff-patients to miss appointments or to present a negative stance throughout the interview. One such plaintiff-patient informed the senior author, "I want it clearly registered in your report that I am here under protest!" His responses during the interview, therefore, reflected virtually a total absence of cooperation and personal information.

It is important for the clinician to keep accurate records, case notes, and test interpretation data for cases that will involve court hearings and to have as complete a file as possible because the file may become part of the evidence in the case. In general clinicial practice, before seeing a client it is usually valuable to determine whether a court hearing will be involved so that the most accurate records can be kept. In many cases, however, in actual clinical practice the patient may have originally been seen for a nonforensic matter and only later the case became involved in litigation. In such situations it may be necessary to refer to previous appointment books and notes to ascertain accurate dates, times of sessions, and other pertinent information relevant to the case.

In the selection of psychological tests for cases that go to litigation, it is important to choose test procedures that have the greatest relevance for the problem in question. For example, if the question involves the individual's loss of intellectual or cognitive functioning as a result of an alleged injury at work, then it is important for the psychologist to employ the most robust measures of cognitive abilities to fully explore the range of the individual's cognitive functioning with a neuropsychological battery and not just to rely on a brief intelligence measure or a Bender-Gestalt drawing. The relevance of the selected tests for the problem is an important consideration because choosing an inappropriate measure would leave the psychologist vulnerable to criticism by the opposing attorney. It is equally important for the psychologist to incorporate "objective evidence concerning working conditions and the work situation" into the evaluation (Marcus, 1983) rather than to rely on professional opinions based on the plaintiff's allegations.

As important as test relevance is in choosing the psychological tests for a court evaluation, the necessity of choosing measures with the greatest demonstrated validity and reliability is perhaps more important. The attorney(s) for the opposition may have been well counseled in the importance of test validity and test reliability and may ask pointed questions about these issues in cross-examination. Several excellent sources are available to help attorneys prepare their case dealing with psychological or psychiatric testimony (Ziskin, 1980, 1981). It is advisable for the psychologist to stand ready to answer questions related to the validity and reliability of the chosen tests.

Test objectivity is another characteristic of psychological tests that is important to consider in selecting measures for forensic evaluations. Ziskin (1980) has pointed out that the psychologist is well advised to employ measures that are objective and that require little personal opinion or judgment in their interpretation. Courts are particularly sensitive to issues of subjectivity in testimony. In recent times, with the greater availability of computer scoring and interpretation, some courts have admitted computer-scored and -interpreted tests as evidence because they are viewed as being less susceptible to human error or subjective biases.

SUMMARY

With increasing frequency, clinical psychologists are being asked to testify in court cases involving compensation for alleged physical or psychological disability stemming from injuries acquired in the workplace. Historically, workers' compensation cases required proof of employer negligence with legal determination required. Increasing liberalization of workers' compensation laws throughout this century and adoption of no-fault statutes have failed to eliminate litigation in compensation cases. On the contrary, as compensation disability laws have been liberalized, the number of compensation cases involving legal adjudication has risen dramatically.

Currently workers' compensation is a multibillion-dollar business involving legal, medical, psychological, industrial, union, insurance, and government personnel in increasingly heated opposition. Concern over fraud and claim exaggeration has increased as economic retrenchment and policy liberalization have increased incentives for claims falsification. Conditions that are difficult to verify, such as psychological and stress-induced disability, have become subjects for consideration in compensation cases. Psychological professionals are thus increasingly in demand in cases where psychological factors raise questions about exaggeration, malingering, or exacerbation of physical problems.

The psychologist faced with such evaluations may be asked to assess whether a plaintiff's complaints are possibly due to stress or malingering. Clearly no foolproof method of determining such distinctions is available at this time. However, by selecting tests appropriate to the complaints, conducting careful interviews where possible, choosing the most objective, valid, and reliable test instruments, and carefully recording case notes and test reports, clinicians can be helpful in clarifying the extent to which psychological factors may be involved in personal injury cases.

More than a century of research and debate on the origin—organic or psychological—of symptom distress following head and spine injuries has yielded only inconclusive and contradictory results. However, considerable research literature has accumulated in recent years which can be useful to psychologists involved in litigation. Numerous studies have found that psychological factors are often present in disability cases and that financial incentives are correlated with prolongation and exacerbation of physical symptoms. Claims for problems difficult to verify, such as back strain, have risen dramatically. Additionally, variations in reported symptom distress have been found to be influenced by the individual's focus of attention on the problem, which is clearly high when litigation is underway. Poor motivation for rehabilitation, and consequently poorer treatment outcome, have been found when economic factors are involved.

Furthermore, MMPI research has demonstrated that organically disabled patients who are not involved in litigation are likely to produce more normal range profiles, while those involved in the claims process often produce extremely elevated, more pathologically appearing profiles, which may reflect motivation to appear in considerable distress. When actual physical injury is suspected, some elevations on Hs, D, and Hy have been found. Individuals who may be exaggerating physical symptoms tend to produce MMPI profiles with one or more of the following features: extreme elevations on scales L and or K (higher than scale F) and in the defensive range; high elevations on Hs, D, Hy, and sometimes on Pt and Sc. Claimants who may be exaggerating psychological symptoms—for example, to appear psychologically disturbed for a Social Security disability determination claim—tend to produce MMPI profiles with extremely exaggerated features such as elevations on F, Sc, and Pa; and also Hs, D, Hy, and Pt. Lack of motivation for rehabilitation has been found to be reflected in extreme elevations on the Pd scale and elevations on Hs, D, and Hy.

Personality assessment in personal injury cases is a growing field calling for more basic research concerning psychological sequelae to injury, and for more practitioners skilled in clinically examining claimants and artfully applying basic research to clinical cases.

REFERENCES

Albertson's Inc. v. Workers' Compensation Appeals Board of the State of California, 131 Cal. App. 3d, 182 Cal. Reptr. 304, 1982.

Anthony, N. (1971). Comparison of client's standard, exaggerated, and matching MMPI profiles. *Journal of Consulting and Clinical Psychology, 36*, 100–103.

Ayer, J., Thoreson, R., & Butler, A. (1966). Predicting rehabilitation success with the MMPI and demographic data. *Personnel and Guidance Journal, 44,* 531–537.

Beals, R. K., & Hickman, N. (1972). Industrial injuries of the back and extremities. *Journal of Bone and Joint Surgery, 54,* 1593–1611.

Berkowitz, M. (1975). The older workers stake in worker's compensation. *Industrial Gerontology, 2,* 53–61.

Blau, T. H. (1984). *The psychologist as expert witness.* New York: Wiley.

Bradley, L., Prokop, C., Margolis, R., & Gentry, W. (1978). Multivariate analysis of the MMPI profiles of low back pain patients. *Journal of Behavioral Medicine, 1,* 253–272.

Brock, J. C. (1975). Psychology and medicine: Rehabilitation of the industrially injured. *Ontario Psychologist, 7*(3), 24–25.

Brown, T., Nemiah, J.C. Barr, J. S., & Barry, H., Jr. (1954). Psychologic factors in low back pain. *New England Journal of Medicine, 251*(4), 123–128.

Caillet, R. (1968). *Low back pain syndrome.* Philadelphia: F. A. Davis.

Cairns, D., Mooney, V., & Crane, P. (1984). Spinal pain rehabilitation: Inpatient and outpatient treatment results and development of predictors for outcome, *Spine, 9*(1), 91–95.

Chelius, J. R. (1977). *Workplace safety and health: The role of workers' compensation.* Washington, DC: American Enterprise Institute for Public Policy Research.

Cofer, C. N., Chance, J., & Judson, A. J. (1949). A study of malingering on the Minnesota Multiphasic Personality Inventory. *Journal of Psychology, 27,* 491–499.

Department of Health and Human Services, Social Security Administration, Office of Policy, Office of Research, Statistics, and International Policy (1984, July), *Monthly benefit statistics: Summary program data* (No. 7). Washington, DC: U.S. Government Printing Office.

Department of Labor, Employment Standards Administration, Office of State Liaison and Legislative Analysis, Division of State Workers' Compensation Programs (1984, January). *State workers' compensation laws.* Washington, DC: U.S. Government Printing Office.

Doney, H. (1976). Psychological sequelae of accidental injury: A medicolegal quagmire. *Canadian Medical Association Journal, 96,* 487.

Drasgow, J., & Dreher, R. (1965). Predicting client readiness for training and placement in vocational rehabilitation. *Rehabilitation Counseling Bulletin, 8,* 94–98.

Dzioba, R. B., & Doxey, N. C. (1984). A prospective investigation into the orthopaedic and psychologic predictors of outcome of first lumbar surgery following industrial injury, *Spine, 9,* 614–623.

Egeland v. City of Minneapolis, 344 N.W.2d 597 (1984).

Fairbank, J. A., McCaffrey, R. J., & Keane, T. M. (1985). Psychometric detection of fabricated symptoms of posttraumatic stress disorder. *American Journal of Psychiatry, 142*(4), 501–503.

Fellner, C. H. (1968). Post-traumatic neurosis: Theme and variations. *Industrial Medicine and Surgery, 37,* 347–350.

Flor, H., & Turk, D. C. (1984). Etiological theories and treatments for chronic back pain: I. Somatic factors and interventions. *Pain, 19,* 105-122.

Flynn, R., & Salomone, P. R. (1977). Performance of the MMPI in predicting rehabilitation outcome: A discriminant analysis, double cross validation assessment. *Rehabilitation Literature, 38,* 12–15.

Fordyce, W. E. (1964). Personality characteristics in men with spinal cord injury as related to manner of onset of disability. *Archives of Physical Medicine and Rehabilitation, 45,* 321–325.

Fordyce, W., Fowler, R., & Delateur, B. (1968). An application of behavior modification technique to a problem of chronic pain, *Behavioral Research and Therapy, 6,* 105–107.

Fordyce, W. W., Roberts, A. H., & Sternbach, R. A. (1984). *Behavioral management of chronic pain: A response to critics.* Unpublished manuscript.

Foster, M. W., Jr. (1964). Neurosis and trauma. *Clinical Orthopedics, 32,* 64–59.

Gallucci, N. T. (1984). Prediction of dissimulation on the MMPI in a clinical field setting. *Journal of Consulting and Clinical Psychology, 52*(5), 917–918.

Gentry, W. D., Shows, W. D., & Thomas, M. (1974). Chronic low back pain: A psychological profile. *Psychosomatics, 15,* 174–177.

Gilberstadt, H., & Jancis, M. (1967). "Organic" vs. "functional" diagnosis from 1–3 MMPI profiles. *Journal of Clinical Psychology, 23,* 480–483.

Gilbert, D. H., & Lester, J. T. (1970). *The relationship of certain personality and demographic variables to success in vocational rehabilitation.* Los Angeles: Orthopedic Hospital.

Goldberg, R. W. (1968). *Occupational diseases in relation to compensation and health insurance.* New York: AMS Press.

Gough, H. G. (1947). Simulated patterns on the Minnesota Multiphasic Personality Inventory. *Journal of Abnormal and Social Psychology, 42,* 215–225.

Harris, J. E. (1980). Psychological overly in workers' compensation. *The Arkansas Lawyer, 14*(1), 42–47.

Heaton, R. K., Chelune, G. J., & Lehman, R. A. W. (1978). Using neuropsychological and personality tests to assess the likelihood of patient employment. *Journal of Nervous and Mental Disease, 166,* 408–416.

Heaton, R. K., Smith, H. H., Lehman, R. A., & Bogt, A. T. (1978). Prospects for faking believable deficits on neuropsychological testing, *Journal of Consulting and Clinical Psychology, 46,* 892–900.

Hult, L. (1954). The Munkfors investigation. *Acta Orthopaedica Scandinavica* (Supplement), 16.

Hunt, J. F. (1948). The effect of deliberate deception on Minnesota Multiphasic Personality Inventory performance. *Journal of Consulting Psychology, 12,* 396–402.

Kardiner, A. (1941). *The traumatic neuroses of war.* New York: Paul H. Hoeber.

Keller, R. A., Wigdor, B. T., & Lundell, F. W. (1973). Adjustment of welfare recipients and applicants: Investigation of some relevant factors. *Canadian Psychiatric Association Journal, 18,* 511–517.

Korgeski, G. P., & Leon, G. R. (1983). Correlates of self-reported and objectively determined exposure to Agent Orange. *American Journal of Psychiatry, 140,* 1443–1449.

Kroger, R. O., & Turnbull, W. (1975). Invalidity of the validity scales: The case of the MMPI. *Journal of Consulting and Clinical Psychology, 43,* 48–55.

Krusen, E. M., & Ford, D. E. (1958). Compensation factors in low back injuries. *Journal of the American Medical Association, 166,* 1128–1133.

Kubiszyn, T. (1984). *The MMPI, litigation and back pain treatment: A curvilinear relationship.* Paper presented at the meeting of the American Psychological Association, Toronto.

Kunce, J. T., & Worley, B. H. (1966). Interest patterns, accidents, and disability. *Journal of Clinical Psychology, 22,* 105–107.

Kunce, J., & Worley, B. (1970). Simplified prediction of occupational adjustment of distressed clients. *Journal of Counseling Psychology, 17,* 326–329.

Kuperman, S. K., & Golden, C. J. (1979). Predicting pain treatment results by personality variables in organic and functional patients. *Journal of Clinical Psychology, 35*(4), 832–837.

Lasky, H. (1980). Psychiatry and California workers' compensation laws: A threat and a challenge. *California Western Law Review, 17*(1), 1–25.

Leeper, J. D., Badger, L. W., & Milo, T. (985). Mental disorders among physical disability determination patients. *American Journal of Public Health, 75*(1), 78–79.

Levenson, H., Hirschfeld, M. L., & Hirschfeld, A. H. (1985). *Duration of chronic pain and the MMPI: Profiles of industrially-injured workers.* Paper presented at the 20th Symposium on Recent Developments in the Use of the MMPI, Honolulu.

Lockwood v. Independent School District, 312 N.W.2d 924 (1981). Lowe, C. M. (1967). Prediction of post-hospital work adjustment by the use of psychological tests. *Journal of Counseling Psychology, 14,* 248–252.

Marcus, E. H. (1983, Spring). Causation in psychiatry: Realities and speculations. *Medical Trial Technical Quarterly, 29,* 424–433.

Martin, R. A. (1975). *Occupational disability: Causes, prediction, prevention.* Springfield, IL: Charles C. Thomas.

May, H. J. (1975). A study of pre-injury demographic life history items associated with delayed return to work following compensable industrial back injury. *Dissertation Abstracts, 35* (12-B PTI), 6156.

McGill, C. M. (1968). Industrial back problems, a control program. *Journal of Occupational Medicine, 10,* 174–178.

Minnesota Statute, #176.021 Subd. 1 (1980).

Morse, S. J. (1978, August). Law and mental health professionals: The limits of expertise. *Professional Psychology,* 389–399.

Naftulin, D. H. (1970). The psychological effects of litigation on the industrially injured patient. *Industrial Medicine, 39*(4), 26–29.

Nelkin, D., & Brown, M. S. (1984). *Workers at risk: Voices from the workplace.* Chicago: University of Chicago Press.

Newnan, O. S., Heaton, R. S., & Lehman, R. A. W. (1978). Neuropsychological and MMPI correlates of patient's future employment characteristics. *Perceptual and Motor Skills, 46,* 635–642.

O'Brien, D. W. (1981). *California employer-employee benefit handbook* (4th ed.). Los Angeles: Winter Brook Publishing.

Oppenheimer, D. R. (1986). Microscopic lesions in the brain following head injury. *Journal of Neurology, Neurosurgery and Psychiatry, 31,* 299.

Pacht, A. R., Kuehn, J. K., Bassett, H. T., & Nash, M. M. (1973, November). The current status of the psychologist as expert witness. *Professional Psychology,* 409–413.

Paradis, A. A. (1972). *The labor reference book.* Philadelphia: Chilton Book.

Parker, J. C., Doerfler, L. A., Tatten, H. A., & Hewett, J. E. (1983). Psychological factors that influence self-reported pain. *Journal of Clinical Psychology, 39,* 22–25.

Parlour, R. R., & Jones, L. R. (1980). Theories of psychiatric defense in workmens' compensation cases. *Bulletin of the American Academy of Psychiatry and the Law, 8* (4), 445–455.

Parlour, R. R., & Jones, L. R. (1981). The role of the defense psychiatrist in workmens' compensation cases. *Journal of Forensic Science, 26*(3), 535–542.

Pear, R. (1984, December 9). Mentally disabled would get benefits under plan. *Minneapolis Star and Tribune,* pp. 1–8.

Pennybaker, J. W., Burnam, M.A., Schaeffer, M.A., & Harper, D. C. (1977). Lack of control as a determinant of perceived physical symptoms. *Journal of Personality and Social Psychology, 35,* 167–174.

Pennybaker, J. W., & Skelton, J. A. (1978). Psychological parameters of physical symptoms. *Personality and Social Pyschology Bulletin, 4*(4), 524–530.

Phillips, E. L. (1964). Some psychological characteristics associated with orthopaedic complaints. *Current Practices in Orthopaedic Surgery, 2,* 165–176.

Pollack, D. R., & Grainey, T. F. (1984). A comparison of MMPI profiles for state and private disability insurance applicants. *Journal of Personality Assessment, 48*(2),121–125.

Price, D. N. (1983). Workers' compensation: coverage, benefits, and costs, 1980. *Social Security Bulletin, 46*(5), 14–19.

Prosser, W. L. (1971). *Handbook of law and torts* (4th ed.). St. Paul, MN: West Publishing.

Rader, C. M. (1984). A psychological profile of industrially injured workers, *Occupational Health Nursing, 32*(11), 577–580.

Rayback, J. T. (1966). *A history of American labor* (2nd ed.). New York: Free Press.

Repko, G. R., & Cooper, R. (1983). A study of the average worker's compensation case, *Journal of Clinical Psychology, 39,* 287–295.

Roberts, A. H. (in press a). Exercise for the elderly: The behavioral management of excess disability. In P. M. Lewinson & L. Teri (Eds.), *Clinical assessment and treatment of older adults.* New York: Springer.

Roberts, A. H. (in press b). The operant approach to the management of pain and excess disability. In A. D. Holzman & D. C. Turk (Eds.), *Pain management: A handbook of treatment approaches.* New York: Pergamon.

Roberts, A. H., & Reinhardt, L. (1980). The behavioral management of chronic pain: Long term follow-up with comparison groups. *Pain, 8,* 151–162.

Roberts, J. M. (1976). *OSHA compliance manual.* Reston, VA: Reston Publishing.

Robertson, L. S. (1983). *Injuries.* Lexington, MA: Lexington Books.

Rowe, M. L. (1969). Low back pain in industry: A position paper. *Journal of Occupational Medicine, 11,* 161–169.

Sainsbury, P., & Gibson, J. G. (1954). Symptoms of anxiety and tension and the accompanying physiological changes in the muscular system. *Journal of Neurology and Neurosurgery, 17,* 216–224.

Salomone, P. R. (1972). Client motivation and rehabilitation counseling outcome. *Rehabilitation Counseling Bulletin, 16,* 11–20.

Schneider, S. (1979). Disability payments for psychiatric patients: Is patient assessment affected? *Journal of Clinical Psychology, 35*(2), 259–264.

Schwitzgebel, R. L., & Schwitzgebel, R. K. (1980). *Law and psychological practice*. New York: Wiley.

Selleck, H. B., & Whittaker, A. H. (1962). *Occupational health in America*. Detroit: Wayne State University Press.

Shaffer, J. W., Nussbaum, K., & Little, J. M. (1972). MMPI profiles of disability insurance claimants. *American Journal of Psychiatry, 129*(4), 64–67.

Slaikeu, K. A. (1984). *Crisis intervention: A handbook for practice and research*. Boston: Allyn & Bacon.

Snibbe, J. R., Peterson, P. J., & Sosner, B. (1980). Study of psychological characteristics of a worker's compensation sample using the MMPI and Millon Clinical Multiaxial Inventory. *Psychological Reports, 47*, 959–966.

Stander, I. (1982). Current trends in workers' compensation. *Law, Medicine & Health Care, 10*(2), 67–71.

Staten, M., & Umbeck, J. (1983). Compensating stress-induced disability: Incentive Problems. In J. D. Worral (Ed.), *Safety and the work force: Incentives and disincentives in workers' compensation* (pp. 103–127). Cornell University: ILR Press.

Sternbach, R. A., Wolf, S. R., Murphy, R. W., & Akeson, W. H. (1973). Traits of pain patients: The low back "loser." *Psychosomatics, 14*, 226–229.

Swiss Colony, Inc. v. Department of Industry, Labor, and Human Relations, 72 Wis.2d 46, 240 N.W.2d 128 (1976).

Taylor, A. G. (1939). *Labor problems and labor law*. New York: Prentice-Hall.

Taylor, P. J., & Fairrie, A. J. (1968). Chronic disability in men of middle age. A study of 165 in a general practice and a refinery. *British Journal of Preventive Social Medicine, 22*, 183–192.

Thurlow, H. J. (1971). Illness in relation to life situation and sick role tendency. *Journal of Psychosomatic Research, 15*, 13–88.

Tinsley, L. C. (1983, January). Workers' compensation in 1982: Significant legislation enacted. *Monthly Labor Review, 106*(1), 57–63.

Tinsley, L. C. (1984, February). Workers' compensation: Significant enactments in 1983. *Monthly Labor Review, 107*(2), 55–61.

Trimble, M. R. (1981). *Post-traumatic neurosis: From railway spine to the whiplash*. New York: Wiley.

Vega, S. (1983). *The cultural effects upon MMPI responses of industrially injured Mexican and Anglo-American males*. Unpublished doctoral dissertation, University of Southern California.

Warren, L. W., & Weiss, D. J. (1969). Relationship between disability type and measured personality characteristics. *Proceedings of the 77th Annual Convention of the American Psychological Association*.

White, A. W. M. (1966). Low back pain in men receiving workmen's compensation. *Canadian Medical Association Journal, 95*, 50–56.

White, L. (1983). *Human debris: The injured worker in America*. New York: Seaview/Putnam.

Wiener, D. N. (1948). Personality characteristics of selected disability groups. In G. S. Welsh & W. G. Dahlstrom (Eds.), *Basic readings on the MMPI in psychology and medicine*. Minneapolis: University of Minnesota Press.

Wilcox, P., & Dawson, J. G. (1977). Role played and hypnotically induced simulation of psychopathology on the MMPI. *Journal of Clinical Psychology, 33,* 743–745.

Wiltse, L. L., & Rocchio, P. H. (1975). Pre-operative psychological tests as predictors of success of chemonucleolysis and treatment of low back pain syndrome. *Journal of Bone and Joint Surgery, 57,* 478–483.

Wolff, H. G. (1968). *Stress and disease* (2nd ed.). Springfield, IL: Thomas.

Ziskin, J. (1980). *Use of the MMPI in forensic settings* (Clinical notes on the MMPI). Minneapolis: National Computer Systems.

Ziskin, J. (1981). *Coping with psychiatric and psychological testimony* (3rd ed.). Marina del Rey, CA: Law and Psychology Press.

Ziskin, J. (1984). Workshop on *Clinical Applications of the MMPI,* Annaheim, California.

CHAPTER 7

Assessing Educational Handicaps

DANIEL J. RESCHLY

Assessment of educational handicaps has become a major, rapidly expanding, and highly controversial role of psychologists in the United States. Although many kinds of psychologists may be involved with the educationally handicapped, the approximately 18,000 to 20,000 school psychologists in the United States have psychoeducational assessment with this population as their primary activity. This chapter discusses the nature of assessment of educational handicaps with attention devoted to legal influences, procedures mandated by law as well as those suggested by best professional practices, and current problems and controversies.

Assessment of educational handicaps has been prominent in school psychology since the earliest days of this specialty of professional psychology. Arnold Gesell, often credited as being the first school psychologist, was hired by the Connecticut State Department of Education in 1913 to examine school-age children suspected of being mentally retarded (Fagan & Delugach, 1984; Tindall, 1979). Throughout this century, special education services for handicapped students expanded gradually, as did school psychological services.

By 1970, there were at least some school psychologists in every state, and a number of states had well-developed school psychological services with ratios as low as 4000 or 5000 students to each psychologist. Special education legislation was the key factor in establishing psychological services in schools. Some states did not provide school programs for the handicapped, and there were few psychologists in those states. Other states provided relatively high levels of funding to local districts for provision of services to the handicapped, which usually led to employment of school psychologists (Kicklighter, 1976); however, up to about 1975, the development of school psychology was gradual and uneven.

The need for assessment of educational handicaps has expanded dramatically since 1975 because of mandatory special education legislation established through court precedents, state legislation, and, finally, federal legislation. The establishment of mandatory special education provisions in all states has led to a rapid expansion of employment of school psychologists whose numbers doubled from 1975 to 1985. Assessment of educational handicaps now involves the expenditure of hundreds of millions of dollars each year for services to the 4.3 million school-age children classified as handicapped and in need of special education. Approximately 11 percent of all children and youth between the ages of five and 17 are classified as handicapped and, therefore, are involved directly with these services (Department of Education, 1984). In short, assessment of educational handicaps is an enormous enterprise.

DECISION MAKING AND HANDICAP CLASSIFICATION

Psychoeducational assessment with students suspected of or classified as handicapped occurs within the context of a complex classification system and is related to two fundamental kinds of decisions. The decisions to be made are quite similar to diagnostic decision making in other areas of psychology such as clinical or counseling psychology, but the classification system may or may not resemble other classification systems. This chapter clarifies the fundamental decisions to be made and the context within which those decisions are made.

Handicapped Classification

Handicapped classification is based on a combination of diagnostic constructs which have evolved throughout the past century. It is not a pure classification system in the sense of a set of consistent principles or uniform underlying bases (Hobbs, 1975). Mercer (1979) described two fundamentally different approaches to diagnosis of handicapping conditions: the medical model and a social system model.

Medical Model

The term medical model is perhaps unfortunate in that it suggests that the assumptions and approaches to problems are typical of how professionals in medicine solve problems. Kauffman and Hallahan (1974) pointed out large differences in the concept of medical model as used in the social sciences and the approach to solving problems actually used in medicine. Therefore, the model should be seen as a heuristic device and not taken literally as indicative of practices in medicine.

Characteristics of medical model as an approach to the development of assessment devices and as an approach to conceptualizing child deviance were discussed by Mercer and Ysseldyke (1977) and Mercer (1979). The most important characteristics of the medical model for the purposes of this chapter are that abnormal patterns of behavior or development are attributed to an identifiable underlying biological pathology. The etiology or the cause, direct or indirect, of deviant behavior is seen as stemming from biological anomalies. Other important characteristics of the medical model are that it is cross-cultural—that is, the same underlying biological abnormalities cause approximately the same deficits in behavior regardless of the social class or the cultural group that might be involved. The medical model is seen as a deficit model, and the underlying biological anomaly is seen as an inherent part of the individual.

The medical model as a basis for diagnostic constructs is particularly useful and applicable in understanding various handicapping conditions that are based on physical abnormalities. These handicapping conditions are also often described as having low incidence, meaning that relatively small percentages of the school-age population have handicapping conditions with an underlying biological basis. The typical medical model handicaps involve sensory impairments such as vision or hearing, neuromotor disabilities such as cerebral palsy, and the more severe levels of mental retardation. In all of these classifications is an underlying biological anomaly which is associated with and frequently is the direct cause of observed deficits in behavior.

Many of the problems to be described later concerning appropriate classification of students are not relevant to medical model handicaps. In most instances, with the handicapping conditions explained by a medical model, there is little or no doubt about the existence of a handicapping condition. There are controversial issues in this area which, indirectly, involve assessment activities. These controversies generally have to do with the appropriate programming for these students and the degree to which they should be integrated with regular education students rather than whether they ought to be classified as handicapped.

Social System Model

In contrast to the medical model, the social system model uses an ecological perspective (Mercer, 1979; Mercer & Ysseldyke, 1977). Deviant behavior or abnormal patterns of development are seen *not* as inherent characteristics of the individual, but rather as reflecting a discrepancy between what the individual has learned in a cultural context and the expectations for normal behavior in a specific social role and social setting. Classification of certain patterns of behavior as being handicapped involve application of social norms within a particular social setting to observed patterns of behavior. The norms or expectations for behavior are determined by the larger society. The social system model suggests a complex interaction among the individual's learned patterns of behavior, the social setting in which a specific behavior is judged, the social role in which the individual is engaged, and the expectations for the behavior. In this model, social and cultural factors are extremely important to determine (1) what the individual learns to be appropriate behavior; (2) expectations for behavior in a specific role or setting; and (3) evaluation of the behavior.

The vast majority of educational handicaps are best understood from a social system model. The mild handicaps which account for 70 percent or more of all the children diagnosed as educationally handicapped—for example, speech difficulties, learning disabilities, emotional disabilities, and mild mental retardation—all reflect deviations from expected patterns of behavior. Furthermore, the cause or etiology of these handicapping conditions is usually unknown and cannot be related to identifiable biological anomalies.

To illustrate the distinction between social system and medical model handicaps, it is useful to consider the following examples. Most children with learning disabilities have difficulties with reading. Often there is no evidence of other difficulties at school, in the home, or in the community. Would a youngster with that pattern of development be regarded as handicapped in a society that did not have compulsory school attendance and strong expectations for the acquisition of literacy skills between the ages of five and 17? On the other hand, a youngster with cerebral palsy, which usually involves easily observed muscular difficulties, would in all likelihood be regarded as handicapped regardless of time, place, or nature of society. In a real sense, social system model handicaps are created by the demands we place on children and youth in a complex, rapidly changing, technologically sophisticated society. To attribute the etiology of these handicaps to societal expectations does not, however, make them any less real or any less serious for individuals involved.

The primary legal issues with social system model handicaps are (1) whether or not the specific youngster *ought* to be classified as handicapped, (2) which of the mildly handicapping classifications is most appropriate, and (3) whether overrepresentation of minority students in particular mildly handicapping classifications such as mild mental retardation or emotional disturbance or behavior disorder constitutes discrimination (Reschly, in press). For both types, the assessment generally involves two kinds of decisions: classification-placement and program planning-intervention.

Classification-Placement

Classification-placement decisions address the question of eligibility. Can the student be classified as handicapped? And if so, is special education required? It is important to note that both questions must be answered affirmatively, in the order given (i.e., classification first), then determination of need for placement, before a student can be regarded as educationally handicapped and placed in special education programs. It is possible, although rare, for a student to meet the criteria as handicapped but not need special education or related services.

Classification-placement decisions generally involve comparing an individual's pattern of behavior with age or grade-level expectations and norms. Specific criteria from the handicapped classification system must be applied (see later section). The type of assessment used in these decisions is often called *norm-referenced*, since the individual's performance is compared with the typical performance of some group, usually a representative sample of other students of the same age or grade level. The key questions involve (1) general areas of concern, (2) level of performance, (3) pattern of performance, and (4) degree of difference in relation to age or grade-level expectations. Standardized tests are often used in these comparisons, but other assessment methods are also relevant, such as classroom norms with behavior assessment (Alessi & Kaye, 1983) or curriculum-based assessment (Ysseldyke, Thurlow, Graden, Wesson, Algozzine, & Deno, 1983).

Criteria to evaluate norm-referenced assessment procedures, often using standardized tests, are available in a variety of sources (Anastasi, 1982; Brown, 1983; Cronbach, 1984; Salvia & Ysseldyke, 1985; Taylor, 1984). Briefly, these criteria specify the following:

1.   Test items or observation events reflect the behavior of concern (content validity).

2. The items or observations must be representative of an appropriate domain of behavior.

3. The items or observations must be sufficient to infer level of competence.

4. A representative sample to develop good norms must be available.

5. Appropriate derived scores must be used.

6. Subtest or composite scores used in classification must be highly reliable.

7. If comparisons among scores are to be carried out, the scores must be on the same scale, with *relatively* equal units throughout the scale.

Several examples of violations of these criteria have been reported (Shepard, 1983; Ysseldyke et al., 1983)—a problem discussed later in this chapter.

Program Planning-Intervention

Program planning-intervention decisions involve consideration of specific information on what needs to be taught or treated, and how instruction or treatment will be carried out. For these decisions, specific information is needed on skills or competencies. Assessment to address these questions, often called *criterion-referenced*, is designed to pinpoint as precisely as possible what the child can and cannot do in some important domain of behavior. Criterion referenced assessment generally requires the following:

1. Instruments or observations which provide thorough coverage of important skills or competencies.

2. Items or observations should be clearly related to important objectives.

3. The objectives are organized into a meaningful hierarchy or developmental sequence.

Most currently available standardized or informal instruments do not meet the criteria for both norm-referenced and criterion-referenced assessment. Most instruments are useful for one or the other. Of course, some instruments do not meet the criteria for either. Many of the mistakes in assessment originate in failure to clarify whether the purpose is for classification-placement or program planning-intervention. Occasionally, there are attempts to use the same instrument for both purposes—an enterprise nearly always destined to failure and legal vulnerability.

Judgments of quality and appropriateness of test use through expert testimony or citing authoritative sources (e.g., the *Buros Mental Measurements Yearbooks*) must take purpose for assessment into account. A test may have excellent technical qualities in terms of reliability, validity, and norms but yield little if any useful information about what to teach or to treat. Other tests or observation methods may provide quite precise information on what skills or behaviors are possessed and exhibited by the student but provide no information about how the student compares with other students, or the degree of difference or deviance from grade- or age-level expectations. Both assessment methods are essential in determining educational handicaps.

LAYERS OF LEGAL INFLUENCE

Legal influences on assessment of educational handicaps emanate from several levels and a variety of sources. Litigation involving assessment questions has been highly influential on legislation which, in turn, has provided the basis for additional litigation. Through this dynamic process, a wide variety of requirements for assessment has gradually evolved (Bersoff, 1982a; Prasse, 1978; Reschly, 1983).

Litigation-Legislation-Litigation

Bersoff (1982a) pointed to the increasing legal regulation of school psychology and, more broadly, of all professions involved with assessment of educational handicaps. This legal regulation has evolved through a process of litigation, then legislation, then further litigation, which continues today and can be expected to continue into the future. The general sequence of events has been litigation in the federal courts, followed by legislation at the state and federal level, and then further litigation based on that legislation.

Pre-1975 Litigation

Although a number of court cases dealing with testing and educational assessment issues appeared before 1970 (see Bersoff, 1979) major cases dealing directly with individual assessment of the handicapped did not appear until the early 1970s. Two distinct types of cases had an enormous impact on subsequent developments.

Right to Education

Two cases in the federal district courts (*Mills v. Board of Education*, 1972; *PARC v. Commonwealth of Pennsylvania*, 1972) established the rights of handicapped students to educational services. Prior to these landmark cases, many handicapped students were either excluded entirely from the public schools by local, district, and state policies or were provided educational services which were not sufficient to meet their unique needs. The plaintiffs in these cases—advocacy groups usually formed by parents of students who had medical model handicaps—asked federal district courts to apply the 14th amendment concepts of equal protection and due process and to force the states to provide appropriate educational services to *all* students. The courts agreed with the parental claims, deciding that exclusion of handicapped students from public schools constituted a violation of the concept of equal protection of laws and the concept of due process. Further discussion of the legal bases can be found in Bersoff, 1982a; Reschly, 1983.

The major impact of these cases was the advancement of the rights of handicapped students to educational services and to due process protections in educational decisions made about them. These court precedents in 1972 were used by parent advocacy groups throughout the United States in efforts to convince state legislatures to pass mandatory special education legislation. In fact, virtually every state passed such mandates between about 1972 and 1975, largely in response to the court precedents. Thus, the litigation establishing the rights of handicapped students to appropriate educational services and guaranteeing due process protections in decision making were the crucial steps leading to the enormous expansion of services for the handicapped and the accompanying upsurge in demands for assessment services.

Placement Bias Cases

A second kind of case also applying the concepts of equal protection and due process, but advocating *less* rather than more special education services, appeared in the federal district courts at about the same time. Cases alleging discriminatory assessment practices and improper special education placement and programming were destined to have a profound influence on subsequent legislation and on assessment of the handicapped. Three cases (*Diana v. State Board of Education*, 1970; *Guadalupe Organization v. Tempe Elementary School District No. 3*, 1972; and *Larry P. v. Riles*, 1972; 1974) were filed on behalf of minority students placed in special class programs for the mildly retarded, a social system kind of handicap. In the three districts involved, Monterey County, California in *Diana*, Tempe, Arizona in *Guadalupe*, and San Francisco in *Larry P.*, minority students were placed in programs for the mildly retarded at about 1.5 to 3 times the rate of placement for nonminority students. Plaintiffs claimed this overrepresentation represented a denial of equal protection of the laws and that the procedures whereby students were referred, evaluated, and placed violated fundamental principles of due process.

The *Diana* and *Guadalupe* cases, involving bilingual Hispanic or Native American students, were settled by consent decrees which established a number of safeguards in the classification-placement process including determination of primary language, assessment instruments administered using procedures consistent with the student's primary language, reliance on performance rather than on verbal measures with language minority children, greater reliance on adaptive behavior measures, and due process protections. The outcomes of these cases were highly influential on state and federal legislation. Some of the phrases that appeared in the *Diana* or *Guadalupe* consent decrees appear verbatim in the rules and regulations accompanying state and federal legislation passed in the mid-1970s (Reschly, 1979).

The *Larry P.* case was somewhat different in that the primary language of the home was not a central issue. The plaintiffs were black students, and intelligence tests became the central issue in the case. *Larry P.* resulted in injunctions in 1972 and 1974, restraining, first, the San Francisco Unified School District and, later, the entire state of California, from using IQ tests with black students.

There is a clear irony in the pre-1975 litigation. In one type of case, school districts were cited by the federal courts for violation of equal protection and due process rights because special education services were *not* provided, and, in another type of case, the same constitutional principles were the basis for ruling that special education with minority students was used excessively. Different types of handicaps were involved—a critical feature often ignored in commentaries on the cases. Although the cases seem very different, the same general principles emerged from both types. Classification-placement decisions must be made using a process that ensures accountability and fairness, and different treatment (either placement or nonplacement) must be justified. These principles have had an enormous impact.

State and Federal Legislation

State legislatures passed mandatory special education bills in every state by the mid-1970s. This legislation was generally similar with regard to general provisions. Handicapped students had to be served by the public schools, and the educational programs had to meet certain standards. Generally, the legislation provided state monies for these programs, thus alleviating part of the burden incurred by local districts. Rather than attempting further discussion of state legislative mandates, the key principles in a subsequent federal law with which all states but one now comply will be discussed (Gerber, 1984). This federal law also incorporated the major principles from the pre-1975 litigation.

Public Law 94-142, the Education of All Handicapped Children Act of 1975, provides federal monies to assist state and local agencies in educating handicapped children. In order to qualify for this assistance, the educational services for handicapped students must meet certain requirements.

Free, Appropriate Education

The first and most important of the general principles was the right of handicapped students to free appropriate educational services. The effect of this principle was that more students were classified as handicapped and new populations of handicapped students previously excluded had to be provided appropriate educational services in school settings. The implications for assessment of the right to education were a greatly increased need for individual psychoeducational assessment services and the need for specialized skills not previously emphasized in school psychology graduate programs, particularly assessment of low incidence and more severely handicapped students (Gerken, 1979).

Least Restrictive Environment

A second important legislative principle is least restrictive environment (LRE). LRE had the effect of greater integration of handicapped students with regular education students. Handicapped students are to be served in as normal an environment as possible including regular classrooms with support services or part-time special education. The LRE effect on assessment services was to place more emphasis on assessment in the natural environment through behavioral methods, observation and interview, and the development and evaluation of interventions in the natural environment.

Individualized Education Program

Handicapped students were also guaranteed an individualized educational program (IEP) which was to be reviewed annually and modified as appropriate. The emphasis on greater individualization increased demands for criterion-referenced assessment leading to clear specification of strengths and weaknesses, and the development of assessment information useful in designing and evaluating instructional interventions or psychological treatments.

Due Process

The due process protections established in the courts, then mandated in state and federal legislation, have the effect of providing clients—in the case of minor children, their parents or guardians—with access to nearly everything a psychologist might do as part of assessment of educational handicaps. The due process protections provide the opportunity for greater scrutiny of the entire decision-making process including the assessment conducted by psychologists. The general principle concerning access to records is that any document which becomes part of the educational record or which is used as the basis for decision making can be examined by the client or the representative of the client. This means, for instance, that test protocols can be examined and challenged by parents. The overall effect of the due process principle is to place greater emphasis on communication with parents concerning the decisions to be made, the assessment devices and procedures to be used, the results of assessment activities, and the recommendations based on assessment data.

Note the enormous change with respect to parental access to records over the past decade. Prior to 1975, nearly all of the protocols and most of the reports developed by psychologists were regarded as confidential and the actual content not shared with clients or representatives of the client. The court interventions in the early 1970s, resulting in legislation in the mid-1970s, dramatically changed that relationship. Parents now have access to the process and procedures from which significant decisions are made.

Protection in Evaluation Procedures

The legal principles from litigation and legislation which have the greatest influence on assessment are frequently subsumed under the title of protection in evaluation procedures (PEP). The PEP section in the PL 94-142 legislation and accompanying rules and regulations (*Federal Register*, 1977a) is relatively brief. It is reprinted here as Table 7.1. The PEP requirements have been cited in major cases involving questions about assessment of the handicapped. The PEP provisions are about as close as we have to a uniform set of legal requirements concerning assessment.

Subsection 530, General, requires the State Department of Education to monitor implementation of the regulations that follow. This section also includes the highly significant provision forbidding racial or cultural discrimination in testing and evaluation materials and procedures used to evaluate and place students as handicapped. This sweeping generalization forbidding discrimination is difficult to implement because there is no definition of discrimination, nor criteria that might be applied to assessment processes, assessment procedures, or placement outcomes (Reschly, 1979; 1982). The meaning of the nondiscrimination clause is the subject of continuing litigation to be discussed in a subsequent section.

Subsection 531, Preplacement Evaluation, requires a thorough *individual* evalu-

TABLE 7.1   Protection in Evaluation Procedures Provisions of PL 94-142 Rules and Regulations

Protection in Evaluation Procedures

§ *121a.530 General*

  (a) Each State educational agency shall insure that each public agency establishes and implements procedures which meet the requirements of §§ 121.a-530-121a.534.

  (b) Testing and evaluation materials and procedures used for the purposes of evaluation and placement of handicapped children must be selected and administered so as not to be racially or culturally discriminatory.

(20 U.S.C. 1412(5)(C).)

§ *121a.531 Preplacement evaluation.*

  Before any action is taken with respect to the initial placement of a handicapped child in a special education program, a full and individual evaluation of the child's educational needs must be conducted in accordance with the requirements of § 121a.532.

(20 U.S.C. 1412(5)(C).)

§ *121a.532 Evaluation procedures.*

  State and local educational agencies shall insure, at a minimum, that:

  (a) Tests and other evaluation materials:

   (1) Are provided and administered in the child's native language or other mode of communication, unless it is clearly not feasible to do so;

   (2) Have been validated for the specific purpose for which they are used; and

   (3) Are administered by trained personnel in conformance with the instructions provided by their producer;

  (b) Tests and other evaluation materials include those tailored to assess specific areas of educational need and not merely those which are designed to provide a single intelligence quotient;

  (c) Tests are selected and administered so as best to ensure that when a test is administered to a child with impaired . . . sensory, manual, or speaking skills, the test results accurately reflect the child's aptitude or achievement level or whatever other factors the test purports to measure, rather than reflecting the child's impaired sensory, manual, or speaking skills (except where those skills are the factors which the test purports to measure);

  (d) No single procedure is used as the sole criterion for determining an appropriate educational program for a child; and

  (e) The evaluation is made by a multidisciplinary team or group of persons, including at least one teacher or other specialist with knowledge in the area of suspected disability.

  (f) The child is assessed in all areas related to the suspected disability, including, where appropriate, health, vision, hearing, social and emotional status, general intelligence, academic performance, communicative status, and motor abilities.

(20 U.S.C. 1412(5)(C).)

  Comment. Children who have a speech impairment as their primary handicap may not need a complete battery of assessments (e.g., psychological, physical, or adaptive behavior). However, a qualified speech-language pathologist would (1) evaluate each speech impaired child using procedures that are appropriate for the diagnosis and appraisal of speech and language disorders, and (2) where necessary, make referrals for additional assessments needed to make an appropriate placement decision.

§ *121a.533 Placement procedures*

  (a) In interpreting evaluation data and in making placement decisions, each agency shall:

   (1) Draw upon information from a variety of sources, including aptitude and achievement tests, teacher recommendation, physical condition, social or cultural background, and adaptive behavior;

   (2) Insure that information obtained from all of these sources is documented and carefully considered;

TABLE 7.1   *(Continued)*

(3) Insure that the placement decision is made by a group of persons, including persons knowledgeable about the child, the meaning of the evaluation data, and the placement options; and

(4) Insure that the placement decision is made in conformity with the least restrictive environment rules in §§ 121a.550–121a.554.

(b) If a determination is made that a child is handicapped and needs special education and related services, an individualized education program must be developed for the child in accordance with §§ 121a.340-121a.349 of Subpart C.

(20 U.S.C. 1412(5)(C); 1414)(a)(5).)

Comment: Paragraph (a)(1) includes a list of examples of sources that may be used by a public agency in making placement decisions. The agency would not have to use all the sources in every instance. The point of the requirement is to insure that more than one source is used in interpreting evaluation data and in making placement decisions. For example, while all of the named sources would have to be used for a child whose suspected disability is mental retardation, they would not be necessary for certain other handicapped children, such as a child who has a severe articulation disorder as his primary handicap. For such a child, the speech-language pathologist, in complying with the multisource requirement, might use (1) a standardized test of articulation, and (2) observation of the child's articulation behavior in conventional speech.

§ *121a.534 Reevaluation.*

Each State and local educational agency shall insure:

(a) That each handicapped child's individualized education program is reviewed in accordance with §§ 121a.340-121a.349 of Subpart C, and

(b) That an evaluation of the child, based on procedures which meet the requirements under § 121a.532, is conducted every three years or more frequently if conditions warrant or if the child's parents or teacher requests an evaluation.

(20 U.S.C. 1412(5)(C).)

---

ation of the child's educational needs prior to placement. The most important provisions here are the requirements that the evaluation be individual and that it focus on specific needs.

Subsection 532, Evaluation Procedures, contains a number of crucial, but somewhat ambiguous, requirements concerning assessment of the handicapped. Each of these requirements might be interpreted differently by various persons involved with assessment of the handicapped. For example, when is it clearly not feasible to administer an evaluation procedure in a child's native language? Does this mean that bilingual examiners have to be provided for all non–English-speaking students suspected of being handicapped? What alternatives should be applied if it is impossible to provide an examiner fluent in the child's language? Is interpretation of test items acceptable, despite the many problems cited by Sattler (1982a)? What does "validated for the specific purpose" mean with respect to educational and psychological tests? Is a predictive validity coefficient of .5 or .7 sufficient? Moreover, how stringently should specific purposes be interpreted?

Other provisions in this subsection that are particularly important in legal proceedings include the requirement of trained personnel, the concept of educational need rather than a single general intelligence quotient, test results accurately reflecting the child's aptitude or achievement rather than sensory impairment, the multidisciplinary team notion including at least one teacher, and the last paragraph often referred to as the requirement of multifactored assessment. It should be noted that the areas listed in the last section are to be assessed "where appropriate." This provision has sometimes been misinterpreted as indicating that all students must be assessed in all of the areas. This is clearly not the case since some of the areas stated may not be related to the suspected disability and would, therefore, not be a required part of the preplacement evaluation.

The placement procedures are discussed in *Subsection 533* with a number of requirements designed to insure that evaluation data are interpreted properly and considered carefully in the placement decisions. Here again there is emphasis on a variety of sources of information, including careful documentation and consideration, group decision making, and consideration of placement in a variety of educational programs.

Reevaluation of students classified as handicapped and placed in a special education program is required every three years according to *Subsection 534*. the issue of what constitutes an appropriate reevaluation is addressed in Section 532, Evaluation Procedures. Again, there is the recurring question of whether all areas mentioned in Subsection 532 must be assessed in the reevaluation. The obvious, but frequently overlooked, requirement is that all areas related to the suspected disability be assessed *as appropriate*. This does not mean, as it has sometimes been misinterpreted, that every area assessed in the original preplacement evaluaion has to be assessed in the reevaluation. The best professional practices in reevaluation, like all evaluation, require careful specification of decisions that need to be made—minimally, decisions about whether classification as handicapped is still appropriate, whether the current placement in special education continues to be appropriate, and the general goals and specific objectives for the special education program. The evaluation should be designed to address those questions rather than merely to repeat assessment of areas covered in the preplacement evaluation (Hartshorne & Hoyt, 1985; Ross-Reynolds, 1983).

A virtual revolution in assessment of the handicapped has occurred over the last decade or so. Numerous legal requirements have been established where relatively little legal influence existed previously. Many of these requirements, as noted before, are ambiguous and subject to different interpretations. The general effect, however, is clear. General principles are now firmly established governing assessment of the handicapped, and due process regulations accompany these provisions ensuring the rights of parents and others to carefully monitor and challenge the assessment services provided by psychologists and other professionals. The meaning of some of these provisions is now in the process of being clarified through further litigation.

Post-1975 Litigation

Over the past 10 years both of the types of litigation discussed earlier have continued at all levels in the state and federal judiciary. Since the enactment of Public Law 94-142, most of this litigation has cited one or more of the legislative principles just discussed as the basis for initiating court action. In many instances, Section 504 of the Rehabilitation Act of 1973 was also cited in this litigation, often because of technical matters related to possible recovery of attorneys' fees if the plaintiffs prevailed in court. However, the Supreme Court recently ruled that PL 94-142 was the "exclusive avenue" for adjudication of educational claims (*Smith v. Robinson*, 1984), which has the effect of denying recovery of attorneys' costs to parents even if they win in the court decision. Clearly, the provisions of Public Law 94-142 are the primary legal requirement for cases dealing with educational rights of the handicapped and assessment of handicapped persons.

Educational Rights Cases

Much of the litigation since 1975 can best be understood as efforts to clarify the meaning of the general principles in PL 94-142 through application to specific situations. Assessment of handicapped students is involved indirectly with various claims pertaining to the meaning of appropriate education, least restrictive or most normal environment, and individualized education program. For example, the Supreme Court ruled in *Board of Education v. Rowley* (1982) that "appropriateness" meant "reasonable educational benefit" rather than ideal, most effective, or best educational program. The assessment data—which indicated that the plaintiff, Amy Rowley, a deaf youngster of high school age, was achieving at or above grade level in all of her high school subjects—were a key factor in the court's determination that an "appropriate" education in this instance did not require the employment by the district of a sign language interpreter.

In another series of cases involving clarification of the meaning of "appropriate," several courts have now ruled that statutory limitations on the length of the school year violate the rights of severely handicapped students. According to claims advanced by their parents in court, severely and profoundly handicapped students require year-round educational services because of the large degree of skills regression experienced during academic recesses (*Education of the Handicapped Law Report*, 1984; *Yaris v. Special School District of St. Louis County*, 1983). The courts have not ruled that severely handicapped students must receive 12-month educational programs, rather that states cannot place absolute limits on the length of the school year. If needed, a year-round school program must be available. Herein lies a complicated assessment issue. Which handicapped students will experience a large loss of skills over a summer recess so as to render their academic-year special education program "not appropriate"? At this writing, state departments of education and school districts throughout the United States would greatly appreciate an assessment procedure that would predict skills regression over the summer so that summer programs can be restricted to those students who really need them. That procedure would certainly have to be reasonably reliable and valid in view of the important decisions being made as well as the inevitable court challenges that would result. In fact, such procedures are not well developed.

A final question concerning the general right to education is the degree to which severely handicapped—usually with physical handicaps and, sometimes, severe levels of retardation—should be educated with regular students in regular school attendance centers. Some interpretations of the LRE principle suggest that nearly all, if not all, children should be educated in the "mainstream," meaning that there should be opportunities for interaction with regular education students with programs in regular school attendance centers. This would mean eliminating many of the special education centers that exist in most large and many medium-sized districts throughout the United States. The question here is the benefits of mainstreaming to handicapped students as well as to regular education students.

The benefits of mainstreaming have recently been questioned for mildly handicapped students (Gresham, 1982), and these concerns are undoubtedly even more pertinent to the possible benefits of mainstreaming for more severely handicapped students. Again, the question involves assessment. Does increased contact with the mainstream lead to increased social interaction and educational benefit for handicapped students? These questions, now before the courts in various forms, create extraordinary challenges for professionals involved with assessment. Many of these questions, for which immediate answers are demanded, require basic and applied research that has only just begun as well as assessment technology which does not yet exist.

Placement Bias Cases

A second major kind of litigation, based primarily on PL 94-142 continues the placement bias cases in the pre-1975 era. The post-1975 cases deal with the same issues: overrepresentation of minority students in special classes for the mildly retarded as well as challenges to the appropriateness of traditional assessment devices. The cases have been filed and adjudicated primarily on the basis of Public Law 94-142, particularly the protection in evaluation procedures provisions discussed in the previous section. In contrast to earlier cases, several placement bias cases have been heard in lengthy trials and decided by opinions. However, refinement and clearer understanding of the meaning of these principles has not occurred to date because of contradictory court opinions on the fundamental questions.

The two most fundamental questions involved with the placement bias litigation have to do with the appropriateness of conventional measures of intelligence with black students and whether disproportionate placement of minority students in programs for the mildly retarded constitutes a violation of the nondiscrimination clause in Subsection 530 of PEP. Although other questions have been addressed by these court cases, these continue to be the most fundamental issues. In *Larry P. v. Riles* (1979), Judge Peckham ruled that IQ tests were biased against black students and that IQ test use was primarily responsible for the overrepresentation of black students in special classes for the mildly retarded which, in turn, was regarded by Judge Peckham as a violation of the nondiscrimination principle of the protection in evaluation procedures provisions. That decision was recently affirmed by the Ninth Circuit Court of Appeals (*Larry P.*, 1984) and may be appealed to the Supreme Court.

In a similar case dealing with the same issues and featuring much of the same expert witness testimony, Judge Grady in a federal district court in Illinois ruled that IQ test use was not biased, that IQ tests were not responsible for the overrepresentation of black students in special classes for the mildly retarded, and that overrepresentation in special classes for the mildly retarded was not discriminatory if the other protections in Public Law 94-142 were followed carefully (*PASE v. Hannon*, 1980). Finally, a federal district court in Savannah, Georgia (*Marshall v. Georgia*, 1984) ruled recently that overrepresentation of black students in programs for the mildly retarded and lower-ability tracks did not constitute discrimination as such. The defendants in *Marshall*, 10 local districts and the State of Georgia, were successful in arguing that the same process was used, the same evaluation procedures were applied, and the same decisions were made given equal results, *regardless of the race of the student.*

In essence, the defendants in *Marshall* met the criterion of equal treatment, an important conception of fairness (Lerner, 1981). Another concept of fairness or of nondiscrimination, termed "equal results," was severely criticized by Lerner. The equal results conception of fairness would require, in effect, the establishment of quotas for placement of students in different kinds of special and regular education programs.

We now have the rather unfortunate situation of three federal courts from three different parts of the country rendering entirely contradictory decisions on some basic questions dealing with assessment of handicapped students. If one applied the *Larry P.* decision, IQ tests would not be used with black students if a classification of mild mental retardation was being considered. It should be noted that the IQ test ban in *Larry P.* was rather narrow, applying only to black students and the special education classification of mild or educable mental retardation. However, that IQ test ban in *Larry P.* was accompanied by what amounted to a quota meaning that black students could not be overrepresented in programs for the mildly retarded. Following the *PASE* and *Marshall* decisions, however, assessment personnel would continue to use IQ tests but would be careful to ensure that other procedural protections were followed and that a wide variety of information, not just IQ, was developed and considered in classification and placement decisions.

A number of critiques of the *Larry P.* and *PASE* decisions have appeared in the literature in recent years (Bersoff, 1982b; Elliott, 1985; Reschly, 1980b, 1981; Prasse & Reschly, 1986). Both *PASE* and *Larry P.* have been severely criticized for failure to understand research evidence and for use of highly subjective procedures to resolve complicated issues like test-item bias. In addition, it is obvious that a number of implicit issues and underlying assumptions were crucial to plaintiffs' motives in pressing the cases (Elliott, 1985; Reschly, 1979, 1981). Plaintiffs were probably motivated to use the issue of overrepresentation to mount a court challenge which could be used in a broader social context to refute the hereditary-differences-among-races hypotheses of Jensen (1980) and others. Furthermore, plaintiffs assumed that special programs for the mildly retarded were ineffective, that intelligence tests were the primary determinant of placement, and that overrepresentation proved bias. Analyses of these claims is beyond the scope of this chapter, but the interested reader is referred to Elliott (1985) or Reschly (1981).

The future course of placement bias litigation is, of course, impossible to predict. If *Larry P.* is appealed to the Supreme Court and if that Court upholds the lower court decisions, one of the most frequently used assessment devices with handicapped students will be eliminated, at least with black students when the classification of mild mental retardation is being considered. The effects of the Supreme Court decision on *Larry P.*, though, are difficult to anticipate, because it is impossible at this point to determine whether upholding the original trial court decision would result in a highly selected ban as noted here or whether it would be regarded as a more general prohibition against the use of IQ tests with black students regardless of possible diagnosis—or even more broadly as a ban on the use of IQ tests with all minority students.

Summary on Litigation and Legislation

Although relatively little legislative activity in recent years has been related to assessment of educational handicaps, litigation has continued at a high rate. The litigation generally involves refinement of general principles embodied in state and federal legislation enacted in the mid-1970s. The decisions from this litigation continue to have indirect and direct influences on assessment. Continued influence in the future should be anticipated. Scholars and practitioners need to make every effort to be well informed about the evolution of legal influences on assessment. One of the best sources of information on legal influences, particularly regarding court cases, is the publication, *Education of the Handicapped Law Report*, which provides the most current information on litigation and other legal proceedings. The analyses are especially useful to persons concerned with legal trends.

Administrative Proceedings

In addition to state and federal courts, a complex set of provisions in state and federal legislation established administrative proceedings to resolve disputes between parents and local or state education agencies. These administrative proceedings are part of the due process regulations. The administrative procedures are used most often in disputes involving individual students rather than in class action cases on behalf of groups of handicapped students.

The due process regulations require parents or guardians to be given adequate notice prior to the initiation of the preplacement evaluation. If parents refuse consent, the school district may appeal the parental decision, which would then trigger the establishment of a due process hearing. Due process hearings are designed to resolve disputes between parents and local or state education agencies. Either the parent or the school agency may initiate an appeal, but it is the responsibility of the party that proposes to change the student's educational program to initiate the appeal. For example, if a parent refuses consent for preplacement evaluation, the school district would be required to file the appeal and then, in a due process hearing, demonstrate why the preplacement evaluation should be undertaken. The due process hearing may be conducted at either the state or local level, depending on state statute, by a qualified, impartial hearing officer. The hearing is a quasilegal proceeding in that (1) the hearing officer must be impartial, (2) both parties have the right to be represented by legal counsel, (3) both may present evidence and confront, cross-examine, and compel the attendance of witnesses, (4) both can obtain a written or recorded record of the hearing, and (5) both have the right to written findings of fact and the hearing officer's decision. The due process hearings are separate from state and federal courts. In most instances, the civil courts require that the administrative remedies be pursued prior to their consideration of cases filed either by parents or school districts (*Education of the Handicapped Law Report*, 1984).

The decisions of the hearing officer can be appealed to state or federal court, but if the decision is not appealed to court, the hearing officer's decision is final and must be implemented. The purpose of the hearings is to provide a relatively inexpensive and direct method to resolve disputes concerning education of handicapped students. It is important to note that relatively few hearings occur. Recall that 4.3 million students are classified as handicapped, and a due process hearing could be initiated for every one of them. In fact, far fewer than 1 percent of the potential cases are actually appealed to a due process hearing, and a much smaller percentage of those cases actually ends up in the state or federal courts.

The due process hearing does represent another source of influence on the assessment provided by professional personnel. Parents might appeal the classification recommended by a psychologist. This appeal would be heard by a hearing officer. Prior to the hearing, the parents have the right to obtain copies of all original records which, for all practical purposes, means virtually everything generated by a psychologist. The parents also have the right to obtain an independent evaluation which must be considered by the school district and, in any case, can be entered as evidence in the hearing. Furthermore, the parents either on their own behalf or through legal counsel can challenge the testimony of the psychologist through direct or cross-examination as well as through evidence from other sources, written or verbal. Clearly, the due process hearing subjects the assessment work of psychologists and other professionals to intense scrutiny. This scrutiny has provided further impetus to trends which are changing psychoeducational assessment practices.

DIAGNOSTIC CONSTRUCTS AND CLASSIFICATION CRITERIA

As noted in the previous section, most psychoeducational assessment with handicapped students has the purposes of classification-placement or program planning-intervention. To receive special education and related services, a student must be diagnosed as handicapped *and* in need of special education interventions. The diagnostic constructs—that is, the areas in which a student can be classified as handicapped—reflect a combination of medical and social system model principles. Handicapped child classification systems usually specify about 10 areas in which a student can be classified as handicapped.

It is important to distinguish between two somewhat separate aspects of the diagnostic construct: the conceptual definition and the classification criteria. The conceptual definition is usually a relatively brief statement describing the fundamental basis for the construct. In contrast, the classification criteria are usually far more detailed with specification of the domains of behavior to be assessed, assessment procedures, and decision rules. In some instances, the conceptual definition and classification criteria are not entirely consistent or well integrated.

Federal Definitions

Definitions of what is meant by "handicapped children" are provided in the PL 94-142 rules and regulations (*Federal Register*, 1977a, pp. 42478–42479). There are 11 areas specified in these federal rules and regulations: deaf, deaf-blind, hard of hearing, mentally retarded, multihandicapped, orthopedically impaired, other health impaired, seriously emotionally disturbed, specific learning disability, speech impaired, and visually handicapped. In all instances except one (seriously emotionally disturbed), a relatively brief paragraph is provided. For the area of emotionally disturbed, two subsections and five additional paragraphs describe the general domains of behavior and the characteristics of emotional disturbance.

The definition provided for "mentally retarded" is typical of the *Federal Register* definitions: "Mentally retarded means significantly subaverage general intellectual functioning existing concurrently with deficits in adaptive behavior and manifested during the developmental period, which adversely affects a child's educational performance" (*Federal Register*, 1977a, p. 42478). This conceptual definition suggests two major domains of behavior—intellectual functioning and adaptive behavior —which should be described further in classification criteria. The federal definition of mentally retarded is virtually identical to the recent American Association on Mental Deficiency definitions (Grossman, 1973; 1983). It should be noted, however, that the general conceptual definition for mentally retarded leaves a great deal undefined such as how *low* the intellectual functioning must be in order to meet the criterion of significantly subaverage and *what* deficits in adaptive behavior should be considered in the diagnosis. Answers to these questions are typically provided in classification criteria developed through state legislation and the state rule-making process. Except for learning disabilities, there are no classification criteria provided in federal legislation or federal rules and regulations.

Congress mandated the Federal Bureau of Education for the Handicapped, now called Office for Special Education Programs, to devise criteria to ensure appropriate classification in the area of learning disabilities which Congress feared, as it turns out quite rightly, would be used excessively by school personnel because of difficulties in precise definition and exact classification criteria. These additional regulations were provided later in 1977 (*Federal Register*, 1977b) but have not, apparently, been successful in limiting the number of students who might be classified as learning disabled (Gerber, 1984; Ysseldyke et al., 1983).

State Definitions and Classification Criteria

States have considerable freedom in formulating diagnostic constructs and classification criteria concerning educational handicaps. Terminology varies considerably among states and is frequently not like the federal definitions. For example, a wide variety of definitions and terminology for the area of mentally retarded were reported by Patrick and Reschly (1982). Some states did use the federal definition, but many other states used terminology such as "mentally disabled" or "mentally handicapped" and definitions which departed significantly from the federal definition. For example, some states did not specify adaptive behavior either in their definition or in their classification criteria. Similar variations exist for the other handicapping conditions.

In contrast to the federal definitions, the state definitions are almost always supported by specific classification criteria. For example, nearly all of the states provide IQ cutoff scores to guide diagnostic personnel in determining whether the intellectual functioning is sufficiently low to meet criteria for the classification "mentally retarded." However, these IQ cutoff scores vary among the states, with some as low as 69 or 70, others at 75, still others at IQ 79 or 80, and one state at 85 (Patrick & Reschly, 1982). Thus, it is entirely possible for a student to be classified as mildly mentally retarded in one state and either classified in a different handicapping area in another state or not classified at all. This is especially true in the mild levels of severity and in the social system model handicaps. In rare instances, there is even variation within states concerning classification criteria. For example, some states allow the local districts to set IQ cutoff scores for mental retardation. (I have personal knowledge of at least two states in which this practice is followed, and it leads to, not surprisingly, considerable variation in who might be classified as mentally retarded.)

The criteria must be studied carefully in determining whether a specific student can be classified as handicapped. These criteria are complicated. Moreover, there are numerous instances where the classification criteria do not cover all of the domains mentioned in the diagnostic construct (Patrick & Reschly, 1982), and in many other instances the criteria are imprecise. These imperfections in classification criteria generally reflect the gaps in knowledge about various handicapping conditions as well as the inadequacy of current technology regarding assessment of certain complex patterns of behavior. When knowledge and technology are inadequate, the ultimate decision is usually guided by general descriptions of the diagnostic construct, the domains and settings in which the behavior should be evaluated, and the professional judgment of the members of a multidisciplinary team. Certainly a great deal, if not all, of the diagnostic work with handicapped students resides at some level on professional judgment.

The state definitions and classification criteria are probably far more important than the federal definitions. In court proceedings, the discussion is nearly always around whether the state diagnostic construct and classification criteria were applied appropriately (*Larry P.*, 1979; *Marshall*, 1984; *PASE*, 1980). There are no instances of which I am aware in which federal definitions took precedence over the state definitions and classification criteria. These state definitions and classification criteria are available from the state departments of education, usually in the form of a manual with a title like, *Special Education Rules and Regulations*. Additional guidelines concerning assessment procedures are often developed by the state department or the professional associations like the state school psychology association or the state association of speech and hearing clinicians on the classification criteria and assessment procedures which provide further guidance to practitioners in classification-placement decision making. Further information on state rules and regulations as well as guidelines can usually be obtained from the division of special education of the state department of education.

ASSESSMENT PROCESS, SEQUENCE, AND CONTENT

Federal and state legal requirements as well as conceptions of best professional practices (Thomas & Grimes, 1985) have stressed the importance of decisions based on a comprehensive evaluation involving consideration of information from a variety of sources, systematic well-designed assessment procedures, and involvement of professionals with unique expertise in several areas. Assessment which meets these criteria is more likely to result in appropriate classification-placement decisions as well as to serve to protect the individual from misclassification or inappropriate educational placement. Misclassification or inappropriate placement could have disastrous effects on the individual's development (e.g., placement of a person with normal intelligence in a class for the mentally retarded at a very young age). An overview of the process, sequence, and content that should be used in the assessment of educational handicaps is provided in Table 7.2.

The outline of assessment process, sequence, and content in Table 7.2 is based on federal regulations and current thought about assessment with the handicapped (Reschly, 1980b; Tucker, 1977). The sequence of activities is important. The screening phase should occur prior to the initiation of the individual evaluation to ensure that the referral is appropriate, that other methods of coping with the learning or adjustment problem have been attempted, and that a significant deficit in expected level or pattern of performance probably exists. Preplacement evaluations to determine classification-placement should be initiated only after other methods of coping with the learning problem have been attempted unsuccessfully. The initial phase of the preplacement evaluation is to carry out the due process procedural safeguards. These procedural safeguards involve, among other things, obtaining informed consent from parents to conduct the evaluation. Bersoff (1978) provided an excellent discussion of different levels of implementation of due process procedures. Once informed consent is obtained, then a multidisciplinary team should be formed and the preplacement evaluation tailored to the individual. Much can be said about this multidisciplinary team. Two important points are that the different specializations on the team should be based on the nature of the individual's difficulties and that the preplacement evaluation should be tailored to the individual. This latter point is frequently a problem. There are many well-documented instances in which the same psychological assessment procedures are used regardless of the nature of the referral problem, the kind of decisions to be made, or the characteristics of the student (Batsche, 1985; Keogh, Kukic, Becker, McLaughlin, & Kukic, 1975; Salvia & Ysseldyke, 1985; Ysseldyke et al., 1983).

The next step is the low inference part of the preplacement evaluation. Level of inference can be viewed as the relationship between what is observed and the interpretation of that observation. Low inference procedures should be pursued prior to high inference procedures because they generally involve simpler solutions to complex problems; and the results from the low inference procedures often significantly influence selection, administration, and interpretation of the high inference procedures. For example, knowledge that the child had a mild to moderate hearing loss should influence the selection, administration, and interpretation of an individually administered intelligence test. If the low inference information, in this case, sensory screening, is not available, then an inappropriate instrument might be selected leading to an extremely unfortunate, potentially disastrous decision about ability. Similar reasoning applies to the importance of language dominance and educational evaluation. All of the low inference areas should be assessed thoroughly before the higher inference procedures are pursued.

The high inference phase of the preplacement evaluation generally involves efforts to assess underlying traits—presumably stable individual patterns of behavior. Since these traits can never be observed directly, some degree of inference is always involved. The four areas listed in the high inference part of the placement evaluation should be seen as optional. Depending on the nature of the referral problem and the individual's characteristics, one or more of these areas might be deleted from the preplacement evaluation.

The final phase is decision making, which should be guided by the considerations indicated in Table 7.2. Although some of these may seem trite, examples of students placed in special education without meeting the eligibility requirements are all too common (Shepard, 1983).

ASSESSMENT TRENDS AND IMPROVED EVIDENCE

Use of psychoeducational assessment in legal or quasilegal proceedings has usually been restricted to testimony of expert witnesses or examination of the results from standardized tests. Although this kind of information can be quite valuable, certain limitations are obvious. In most instances, at least one or more experts can be found to disagree with other expert testimony. Furthermore, the relevance of nationally standardized tests, particularly if other information is unavailable, is often criticized severely (Hilliard, 1980). A number of advances in assessment procedures—influenced by legal developments as well as trends in psychological theory and research (Reschly, 1980b)—can be used to improve significantly the quality and usefulness of psychoeducational assessment information as evidence in court.

Low Inference

Level of inference refers to the relationship between the behavior observed and the meaning attributed to that behavior. There is a long, and unfortunate, tradition in applied areas of psychology of highly inferential interpretations of rather simple behavior events (Rapaport, Gill, & Schafer, 1968). The Bender Motor Gestalt Test

TABLE 7.2   Considerations for Content, Process, and Sequence in Preplacement Evaluations

A. *SCREENING PHASE*
   1. *Referral.* Clarify referral through teacher interview, classroom observation, and examination of daily work.
   2. *Educational history.* Review current and previous educational records including special services involvement, classroom performance, standardized tests, etc. Consider use of regular education options and interventions.

IF THERE IS A SEVERE DISCREPANCY, OR IF THE DEFICIENCY IN PERFORMANCE IS COMPREHENSIVE AND LONG TERM, *AND* IF REGULAR EDUCATION OPTIONS HAVE BEEN ATTEMPTED UNSUCCESSFULLY, THEN (and only then) INITIATE THE PREPLACEMENT EVALUATION.

B. *PREPLACEMENT EVALUATION (Initial Phase)*
   3. *Due Process/Procedural Safeguards.* Follow procedural safeguards to meet legal requirements *and* to establish communication with home.
   4. *Multidisciplinary Team.* Form multidisciplinary team, develop hypotheses, tailor the preplacement evaluation to the individual, assign responsibilities and establish time lines.

C. *PREPLACEMENT EVALUATION (Low Inference Procedures)*
   5. *Sensory Screening, Health, Developmental.* Physical examination (if needed), health and developmental history, and sensory assessment by specialists.
   6. *Language Dominance.* Determine the child's primary language competence through formal measures and/or home interview.
   7. *Educational Evaluation.* Determine level, pattern, strengths and weaknesses in academic skills through formal and informal measures administered and interpreted by specialists.

D. *PREPLACEMENT EVALUATION (Optional High Inference Procedures)*
   8. *Perceptual-Motor/Psychological Process.* Where appropriate, determine if severe process deficits are related to learning problem through administration of formal instruments, observation, and interview.
   9. *Adaptive Behavior—Outside School.* Where appropriate, investigate social competence outside of school through structured and unstructured interview.
   10. *Social/Emotional.* Where appropriate, determine nature and extent of social/emotional involvement or behavior disorders through interviews, observations, checklist, etc.
   11. *Intelligence (Academic Aptitude).* Where appropriate, determine general level of expectations for academic achievement through administration of individual intelligence test.

E. *DECISION-MAKING CONSIDERATIONS*
   a) What evidence exists which documents the consideration of a broad variety of information, including both strengths and deficits, in determining educational needs and selection of placement options?
   b) Does the determination of educational needs and selection of placement option include the contributions of relevant professional personnel and parents?
   c) Are current educational status and educational needs stated precisely and supported by data?
   d) Are alternative options considered for meeting these needs including regular education with or without support services?
   e) Are special education eligibility recommendations made in conformance with the criteria for primary handicapping conditions as defined in the State Special Education Rules and Regulations?
   f) In making the special education eligibility recommendations, did the multidisciplinary team consider a broad variety of information?
   g) Are a variety of program options considered in view of the information from the multifactored assessment?
   h) What evidence supports the choice of program option as an appropriate alternative for meeting the child's needs?

(Bender, 1938) is one of the most frequently used psychological tests with children and with adults (Wade & Baker, 1977). The Bender, which involves a series of eight relatively simple geometric designs which the individual is to copy, has been interpreted as revealing information about level of intelligence, neurological dysfunction, and personality or emotional characteristics (Koppitz, 1975). Examples of good and poor reproductions of one of the Bender drawings is provided in Figure 7.1.

The very poor drawing noted as "Danny's Bender" might be interpreted as revealing poor copying skills or poor visual motor skills, both of which would be regarded as reflecting relatively low levels of inference. A higher level of inference would be involved with interpretation of Danny's Bender as indicating immaturity or development lag. Very high levels of inference are involved with interpretation of this drawing as indicative of neurological dysfunction or emotional-personality status.

Highly inferential interpretations are generally not in the student's best interests for a variety of reasons: (1) such interpretations are rarely supported by research data; (2) the variables identified in highly inferential interpretations are usually difficult if not impossible to influence therapeutically; (3) the highly inferential interpretations are rarely related to educational interventions or psychological treatment; and (4) the highly inferential interpretations, because they focus on deep underlying problems, frequently deflect interest from and effort toward practical treatment or

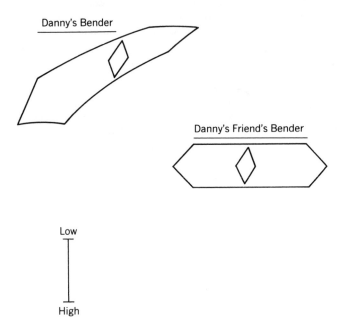

FIGURE 7.1. Danny's Bender. (1) Poor copying skills, (2) poor visual-motor skills, (3) developmental lag or immaturity, (4) neurological dysfunction, and (5) emotional symptoms, personality dynamics.

intervention. This latter point, although subtle, is extremely important. Problems described in terms of neurological dysfunction or deep underlying emotional conflict certainly do not seem to be amenable to instruction or treatment available in educational settings. On the other hand, straightforward and precise descriptions of the same behavior without the presumed underlying cause is much more likely to be regarded as amenable to instruction or treatment (Bergan & Kratochwill, 1985; Tombari & Bergan, 1978).

Highly inferential court testimony is also tenuous. Such testimony is likely to be refuted by other expert witnesses and is quite vulnerable to impeachment during cross-examination (Ziskin, 1981).

Behavioral Assessment

Systematic collection of data in natural settings to reflect precisely defined behavioral patterns or events has continued to be one of the fastest growing areas of psychoeducational assessment (Kratochwill, 1982). Behavioral assessment procedures are designed to provide very precise descriptions of the behavior as well as the antecedent, concurrent, and consequent events associated with behavior. Even more important is the use of behavioral assessment data to develop, monitor, and evaluate the outcomes of interventions. Behavioral assessment data possess numerous advantages for classification-placement, for program planning-intervention, and as evidence in court proceedings. Behavior assessment generally involves low levels of inference in that behavior and the conditions surrounding the behavior are precisely and objectively described. The behavior assessment data are often useful as adjuncts to and as further examples of the results of standardized tests.

Multiple Normative Comparisons

As noted previously, classification-placement decisions usually involve comparison of an individual to age or grade-level expectations. These expectations are normative comparisons, with the usual frame of reference being a national representative sample stratified by variables such as age, region, socioeconomic status, and race. The norms could also be based on a state-, district-, or classroom-referenced behavioral assessment described by Alessi (1980) and Alessi and Kaye (1983). The comparison of the individual's pattern of behavior or level of performance to other persons of the same age, and usually of the same sex, from the same district or even the same classroom is a valuable adjunct to the results from standardized tests. Standardized test results, typically interpreted using national norms, are often viewed as irrelevant to specific districts or classrooms (Hilliard, 1980). The nationally standardized tests also use standard score scales, which often are misinterpreted, as in the placement bias litigation (Reschly, 1982).

Comparison of a specific student to other students in the same class and of the same age and sex, provides an alternative way to estimate the degree of deviance from age or grade-level expectations. This approach which might be called norm-referenced behavioral assessment has been described well by Alessi (1980), Alessi and Kaye (1983), and Deno, Mirkin, and Chiang (1982). This method might also be used in instances where there are a relatively small number of a unique sociocultural group (e.g., the Hmong from Southeast Asia). Any comparison of recent immigrant Hmong students to national norms based on students in the United States would be questionable. However, comparison of a specific Hmong student with other Hmong students of the same age and sex could be used (cautiously) to determine whether or not a specific learning deficit or behavioral problem reflected a sociocultural difference or an individual handicap. Although such comparisons obviously need to be undertaken cautiously, they clearly have some advantages over use of national norms with persons who are different from the general population.

Alternative Evidence

Psychologists often experience frustration in attempting to explain complex patterns of behavior with imprecise but intricate diagnostic constructs and complicated classification criteria. Explanations of these matters in legal proceedings can be particularly trying when cross-examination may be devoted to undermining the salience and credibility of the testimony. Sattler's (1982b) account of his experiences in *Larry P.* is an excellent illustration of this problem. Although sound testimony from genuine experts is probably essential and irreplaceable, this testimony can be significantly enhanced if supported by a variety of evidence. In the *Marshall v. Georgia* (1984) trial, a videotape was shown in which black and white regular education students of approximately average ability were contrasted with black and white students classified as mildly retarded and placed in special education programs. The children were about 10 years old. Each child was shown in a brief interview and then asked to perform common, everyday cognitive skills like telling time, performing simple computations, and reading a brief passage. Differences among these students were not apparent in the interview or from casual observation. However, dramatic differences among the students on these relatively simple intellectual tasks were obvious to everyone in the court. The critical differences among handicapped and nonhandicapped were exemplified far better by the videotape than any expert witness using protocols from standardized tests, normal curve distributions, and deviation IQ scores could ever have shown. The videotape provided a means whereby far more tangible examples of the basic issue in the litigation could be presented. Similar uses of videotape would seem appropriate and desirable in due process hearings and civil court proceedings concerning handicapped students.

In addition to videotape, a variety of other kinds of evidence such as audiotape, samples of daily work, observation protocols, and interview schedules can be used to support expert testimony. A major problem with some of the previous placement bias cases—*Larry P.* and *PASE*—is the relatively sparse use of these alternative kinds of evidence which left federal district court judges with the unenviable tasks of determining item bias and whether certain students were truly retarded. There was relatively little examination of tangible evidence, other than test protocols, in those cases. The judges in *Larry P.* and *PASE* would have undoubtedly developed a more accurate perception of mild mental retardation if there had been additional evidence of this kind. Although the decisions may not have changed, the reasoning might have been improved. Greater attention to the development of a variety of evidence is a promising avenue for improving testimony and clarifying issues in litigation for all parties concerned.

CURRENT ISSUES AND PROBLEMS

A number of current issues and problems have been influential on litigation concerning assessment of educational handicaps. These issues and problems often represent long-standing concerns in psychology and education. Some of these concerns have been complicated by, as well as being complicating factors in, recent litigation.

Nondiscrimination

Nondiscrimination continues to be a serious concern in assessment of educational handicaps. As noted earlier, overrepresentation of minorities, allegedly due to biases in existing measures of ability and achievement, has been the central issue in numerous federal court cases over the past decade or so. A National Academy of Science panel, after thorough study, came to what was regarded by many as a surprising conclusion. They asked, "Why was overrepresentation in special education for the mildly retarded viewed as a problem?" (Heller, Holtzman, & Messick, 1982), when such classification leads to greater expenditures of monies, more resources, greater individualization and thorough evaluation of progress. Overrepresentation per se is not the problem since there is even greater overrepresentation in certain other special programs such as Chapter 1 and Head Start. Why indeed? As noted earlier, the placement bias litigation is understandable only if the implicit assumptions and underlying issues are considered (damaging effects of labels, poor educational programs, nature-nurture, and IQ test bias) (Reschly, 1979, 1982).

The National Academy Panel, although naive in certain respects (Reschly, 1984), focused on the most important issue, instructional validity, rather than on causes of overrepresentation. The ultimate criterion concerning overrepresentation should be outcomes for individuals (Reschly, 1979). First, special education should not be considered unless regular education alternatives have been exhausted. Collection and interpretation of data on the student's performance in regular education is a challenging part of the preplacement evaluation and an essential assessment activity. If special education is used, precise, criterion-referenced assessment should be developed to design, monitor, and evaluate instruction or treatment. Instructional and treatment validity are crucial to positive outcomes, and good assessment is an essential component.

Questions other than bias in tests, which has been found to be relatively rare (Jensen, 1980; Reynolds, 1982), need to be addressed in future work toward nondiscrimination. The most crucial issues are the degree to which regular education alternatives were attempted, implemented, and evaluated prior to referral, and the effectiveness of the special education program subsequent to classification and placement. This assumes, as has been the case in recent litigation, that the students classified and placed, minority and majority, did meet eligibility criteria. In the future, more attention also needs to be devoted to assessment of adaptive behavior, in school and out of school, as well as the development of functional academic skills (Edgerton, 1984; Reschly, 1985).

Overidentification of Learning Disabilities

Another controversial issue in assessment of the handicapped is overidentification of children as being learning disabled. The number of students classified as learning disabled has increased every year since 1976 when such statistics were first obtained in a uniform fashion (Gerber, 1984). There are difficulties with this diagnostic construct at all levels from basic conception of learning disabilities, classification criteria, assessment related to the classification criteria, and the educational programs provided for students classified as learning disabled (Coles, 1978; Gerber, 1984; Ysseldyke et al., 1983). The current trend is toward classification criteria using a severe discrepancy between ability and achievement based on regression analyses (Reynolds, 1984; Telzrow, 1985). Even if more objective methods of quantifying the severe discrepancy between ability and achievement are adopted widely, numerous additional problems will continue to complicate psychoeducational assessment in this area. Efforts to reduce numbers of students placed in learning disability programs because of burgeoning costs may provoke further litigation pressed by parents who want their children classified as learning disabled so they will receive remedial educational services. In view of the complicated issues in learning disabilities, that litigation will almost undoubtedly be difficult for the courts, for school districts and state departments, and for psychologists testifying for the different sides.

Classification System Reform

In view of these problems with learning disabilities, as well as concerns about discrimination with minority students in the area of mild mental retardation, considerable effort has been devoted in recent years to develop more functional classification-placement policies for handicapped students (Reynolds & Wang, 1983; Wang & Birch, 1984). These alternatives, reminiscent of the reforms suggested by Hobbs and his colleagues (Hobbs, 1975), would place far more emphasis on educational needs and far less emphasis on underlying traits like ability or emotional disturbance. These reforms may avoid many of the problems encountered in recent years with the mildly handicapping classifications of educable or mild mental retardation and learning disability. These reforms involve, among other things, far greater interaction of regular and special education with more emphasis placed on a variety of remedial or compensatory educational programming within the regular classroom. These reforms, although initially popular, may be undermined by the numerous vested interests of diverse groups including parent advocacy groups like the Association for Children and Adults with Learning Disabilities, special educators such as learning disabilities resource teachers, and related-services personnel such as school psychologists and social workers.

Although there is near unanimity in recognizing the need for classification system reform, I suspect there is at the same time virtual anarchy in thought about the kind and nature of reforms. Considerable resistance to substantial changes in the decision-making processes and mildly handicapping diagnostic constructs should be anticipated.

Professional Competence and Technical Adequacy

A continuing problem in assessing educational handicaps is the competence of professionals and the technical adequacy of the instruments and procedures chosen by these persons. Some recent research has yielded disturbing results (Bennett & Shepard, 1982; Ysseldyke et al., 1983). In a study of learning disabilities classification, Shepard (1983) reported that severe discrepancies between ability and achievement were sometimes based on comparisons of test results using different score scales. In numerous instances, ability scores around 90 or so were interpreted as "average ability" while percentile ranks at 25 or so on educational achievement measures were interpreted as well below grade level. In fact, an IQ score of 90 has a percentile rank of 25. In other research carried out under my direction (Skillings, 1981) a substantial number of students classified as learning disabled either had no discrepancy at all between ability and achievement or the discrepancy was in the wrong direction (i.e., achievement was higher than ability). These are two examples where serious questions have to be raised about the professional competence of individuals making decisions about handicapped students.

The technical adequacy of the instruments chosen by professionals is a source of further concern, which is not unique, however, to assessment of educational handicaps. Surveys of the most frequently used assessment instruments in clinical psychology indicate that instruments with questionable reliability and validity such as figure drawings and projectives are used frequently (Wade & Baker, 1977). Similar results have been obtained in studies of school psychologists and others responsible for psychoeducational assessment (Ysseldyke et al., 1983). A possible complicating factor in the Ysseldyke et al. research is that relatively few instruments were regarded by these investigators as "technically adequate." Once assessors in the simulation studies had exhausted the use of the achievement and ability instruments, use of less technically adequate instruments was virtually unavoidable. Part of the problem is that relatively few instruments—principally achievement and ability tests—meet stringent standards for technical adequacy, but, of course, decisions about other domains of behavior must be considered (e.g., adaptive behavior). In those situations, convergence among different sources of information concerning a particular domain of behavior or kind of classification criterion must be sought.

Status of Technology

The currently available assessment technology is inadequate for some of the difficult decisions that must be made in assessment of educational handicaps. Numerous problems with the severe medical model indirectly pose serious challenges to the adequacy of assessment services. Two of these problems—what constitutes an "appropriate" education as noted in the extended school year cases (*Yaris*, 1983) and the degree to which severely handicapped students should be integrated with regular education students and programs (*St. Louis Developmental Disabilities v. Mallory*, 1984)—are before the federal courts throughout the United States. Both of these issues must be resolved primarily through use of assessment data. In the extended school year case the question is degree of regression in skills over a two- or three-month summer recess, while the question with integration is benefits of mainstreaming. The present assessment technology provides relatively little guidance to resolution of these problems. However, the problems will not wait for assessment technology. Decisions will be made and some kind of assessment will be used. In addition to the usual call for more research is the clear need to apply the best assessment technology we have and then to interpret the results for the courts in light of various limitations. Carrying out this challenge, particularly in court settings, will constitute an enormous challenge to psychologists, attorneys, and judges.

CONCLUSIONS

Legal influences on school psychology and other professions associated with assessment of educational handicaps have expanded enormously over the past 15 years. Further influence through the gradual evolution of case law and the enactment of legislation should be anticipated in the future. The uneasy relationship between the courts and psychologists and the occasional misuse and distortion of psychological evidence by the courts requires substantial additional efforts toward mutual understanding. Greater appreciation on the part of psychologists for the essential role of the courts in determining educational rights of the handicapped is needed as well as greater understanding by the courts and officers of the courts of the strengths and limitations of psychoeducational assessment. Better assessment can produce better evidence which, in turn, will improve legal decisions that affect the lives of children and adults.

REFERENCES

Alessi, G. J. (1980). Behavioral observation for the school psychologist: Responsive-discrepancy model. *School Psychology Review, 9*, 31–45.

Alessi, G., & Kaye, J. (1983). *Behavioral assessment for school psychologists*. Washington, DC: National Association of School Psychologists.

Anastasi, A. (1982). *Psychological testing* (5th ed.). New York: MacMillan.

Batsche, G. (1985). *Referral oriented case consultation*. Washington, DC: National Association of School Psychologists.

Bender, L. A. (1938). A Visual Motor Gestalt Test and its clinical use. *Research Monographs of the American Psychiatric Association*, No. 3.

Bennett, R. E., & Shepard, M. J. (1982). Basic measurement proficiency of learning disability specialists. *Learning Disability Quarterly, 5*, 177–184.

Bergan, J., & Kratochwill, T. (1985). *Behavioral consultation*. New York: Plenum.

Bersoff, D. (1978). Procedural safeguards. In L. Morra (Ed.), *Due process: Developing criteria for evaluating the due process procedural safeguards provisions of Public Law 94-142*. Washington, DC: U. S. Office of Education, Bureau of Education for the Handicapped.

Bersoff, D. (1979). Regarding psychologists testily: Legal regulation of psychological assessment in the public schools. *Maryland Law Review, 39*, 27–120.

Bersoff, D. (1982a). The legal regulation of school psychology. In C. R. Reynolds & T. B. Gutkin (Eds.), *The handbook of school psychology*. New York: Wiley.

Bersoff, D. (1982b). *Larry P.* and *PASE*: Judicial report cards of the validity of individual intelligence tests. In T. Kratochwill (Ed.), *Advances in school psychology: Vol. 2*. Hillsdale, NJ: Erlbaum.

Board of Education v. Rowley, 102 S Ct 3034 (1982).

Brown, F. G. (1983). *Principles of educational and psychological testing* (3rd ed.). New York: Holt, Rinehart, & Winston.

Coles, G. S. (1978). The learning disabilities test battery: Empirical and social issues. *Howard Educational Review, 48*, 313–340.

Cronbach, L. J. (1984). *Essentials of psychological testing* (4th ed.). New York: Harper & Row.

Deno, S. L., Mirkin, P. K., & Chiang, B. (1982). Identifying valid measures of reading. *Exceptional Children, 49*, 36–45.

Department of Education (1984). *Executive Summary: Sixth Annual Report to Congress on the Implementation of Public Law 94-142: The Education for All Handicapped Children Act*. Reprinted in *Exceptional Children, 51*, 199–202.

Diana v. State Board of Education, C. A. No. C-70-37 (N. D. Cal., July 1970) (Consent decree).

Edgerton, R. B. (Ed.). (1984). *Lives in process: Mentally retarded adults in a large city*. Washington, DC: American Association on Mental Deficiency.

Education of the Handicapped Law Report. (1984). EHLR Analysis: Special Education and the Courts, 1983–84. Supplement 131, October 26, 1984. Alexandria, VA: CRR Publishing.

Elliott, R. (1985). *The banning of IQ tests in California*. Unpublished manuscript, Dartmouth College.

Fagan, T. K., & Delugach, F. J. (1984). Literary origins of the term, "school psychologist." *School Psychology Review, 13*, 216–220.

Federal Register. (1977a). Regulations implementing Education for All Handicapped Children Act of 1975 (Public Law 94-142). August 23, *42*(163), pp. 42474–42518.

Federal Register. (1977b). Procedures for evaluating specific learning disabilities. December 29, *42*(250), pp. 65082–65085.

Gerber, M. M. (1984). The Department of Education's Sixth Annual Report to Congress on PL 94-142: Is Congress getting the full story? *Exceptional Children, 51*, 209–224.

Gerken, K. C. (1979). Assessment of high-risk and preschoolers and children and adolescents with low-incidence handicapping conditions. In G. D. Phye & D. J. Reschly (Eds.), *School psychology: Perspectives and Issues*. New York: Academic Press.

Gresham, F. (1982). Misguided mainstreaming: The case for social skills training with handicapped children. *Exceptional Children, 48*, 422–433.

Grossman, H. J. (Ed.). (1973). *Manual on terminology and classification in mental retarda-tion*. Washington, DC: American Association on Mental Deficiency.

Grossman, H. J. (Ed.). (1983). *Classification in mental retardation*. Washington, DC: American Association on Mental Deficiency.

Guadalupe Organization v. Tempe Elementary School District No. 3, No. 71-435 (D. Ariz., January 24, 1972) (Consent decree).

Hartshorne, T. S., & Hoyt, E. B. (1985). Best practices in conducting re-evaluations. In A. Thomas & J. Grimes (Eds.), *Best practices in school psychology*. Kent, OH: National Association of School Psychologists.

Heller, K., Holtzman, W., & Messick, S. (Eds.). (1982). *Placing children in special education: A strategy for equity*. Washington, DC: National Academy Press.

Hilliard, A. (1980). Cultural diversity and special education. *Exceptional Children, 46*, 584–588.

Hobbs, N. (1975). *The futures of children*. San Francisco: Jossey-Bass.

Jensen, A. R. (1980). *Bias in mental testing*. New York: The Free Press.

Kauffman, J., & Hallahan, D. (1974). The medical model and the science of special education. *Exceptional Children, 41*, 97–102.

Keogh, B., Kukic, S., Becker, L., McLaughlin, R., & Kukic, M. (1975). School psychologists' services in special education programs. *Journal of School Psychology, 13*, 142–148.

Kicklighter, R. (1976). School psychology in the U. S.: A quantitative survey. *Journal of School Psychology, 14*, 151–156.

Koppitz, E. (1975). *The Bender Gestalt Test for young children: Vol. 2. Research and application, 1963–1973*. New York: Grune & Stratton.

Kratochwill, T. R. (1982). Advances in behavioral assessment. In C. R. Reynolds & T. B. Gutkin (Eds.), *The handbook of school psychology*. New York: Wiley.

Larry P. v. Riles, 343 F. Supp. 1306 (N. D. Cal. 1972) (preliminary injunction) aff'd 502 F. 2d 963 (9th Cir. 1974); 495 F. Supp. 926 (N. D. Cal. 1979) (decisions on merits) aff'd (9th Cir. No 80-427 Jan. 23, 1984).

Lerner, B. (1981). Equal opportunity versus equal results: Monsters, rightful causes, and perverse effects. In W. B. Schrader (Ed.), *Admissions testing and the public interest: New directions for testing and measurement, Number 9*. San Francisco, CA: Jossey-Bass.

Marshall v. Georgia, U. S. District Court for the Southern District of Georgia, CV482-233, June 28, 1984.

Mercer, J. (1979). *System of multicultural pluralistic assessment, technical manual*. New York: Psychological Corporation.

Mercer, J., & Ysseldyke, J. (1977). Designing diagnostic-intervention programs. In T. Oakland (Ed.), *Psychological and educational assessment of minority children*. New York: Brunner/Mazel.

Mills v. Board of Education, 348 F. Supp. 866 (D.D.C.1972). (PARC) Pennsylvania Association for Retarded Children v. Commonwealth of Pennsylvania, 343 F. Supp. 279 (E.D. Pa. 1972).

PASE (Parents in Action on Special Education v. Joseph P. Hannon. U. S. District Court, Northern District of Illinois, Eastern Division, No. 74 (3586), July, 1980.

Patrick, J., & Reschly, D. (1982). Relationship of state educational criteria and demographic variables to school-system prevalence of mental retardation. *American Journal of Mental Deficiency, 86,* 351–360.

Prasse, D. (1978). Federal legislation and school psychology: Impact and implication. *Professional Psychology, 9,* 592–601.

Prasse, D., & Reschly, D. (1986). *Larry P.*: A case of segregation, testing, or program efficiency? *Exceptional Children, 52,* 333–346.

Rapaport, D., Gill, M., & Schafer, R. (1968). *Diagnostic psychological testing* (rev. ed. by R. Holt). New York: International Universities Press.

Reschly, D. (1979). Nonbiased assessment. In G. Phye & D. Reschly (Eds.), *School psychology: Perspectives and Issues.* New York. Academic Press.

Reschly, D. (1980a). Psychological evidence in the *Larry P.* opinion: A case of right problem—wrong solution. *School Psychology Review, 9,* 123–135.

Reschly, D. (1980b). School psychologists and assessment in the future. *Professional Psychology, 11,* 841–848.

Reschly, D. (1981). Psychological testing in educational classification and placement. *American Psychologist, 36,* 1094–1102.

Reschly, D. (1982). Assessing mild mental retardation: The influence of adaptive behavior, sociocultural status and prospects for nonbiased assessment. In C. R. Reynolds & T. B. Gutkin (Eds.), *The handbook of school psychology.* New York: Wiley.

Reschly, D. (1983). Legal issues in psychoeducational assessment. In G. Hynd (Ed.), *The school psychologist: Contemporary perspectives.* Syracuse, NY. Syracuse University Press.

Reschly, D. (1984). Beyond IQ test bias: The national academy panel's analysis of minority EMR overrepresentation. *Educational Researcher, 13*(3), 15–19.

Reschly, D. (1985). Adaptive behavior. In A. Thomas & J. Grimes (Eds.), *Best practices in school psychology.* Kent, OH: National Association of School Psychologists.

Reschly, D. (in press). Economic and cultural factors in childhood exceptionality. In R. Brown & C. Reynolds (Eds.), *Psychological perspectives on childhood exceptionality.* New York: Wiley.

Reynolds, C. R. (1982). The problem of bias in psychological assessment. In C. R. Reynolds & T, B. Gutkin (Eds.), *The handbook of school psychology.* New York: Wiley.

Reynolds, C. R. (1984). Critical measurement issues in learning disabilities. *Journal of Special Education, 18*(4), 451–476.

Reynolds, M. C., & Wang, M. (1983). Restructuring "special" school programs: A position paper. *Policy Studies Review, 2* (Special No. 1), 189–212.

Ross-Reynolds, J. (1983). Three year re-evaluations: An alternative to the re-evaluation-means-re-test model. In J. Grimes (Ed.), *Communicating psychological information.* Des Moines, IA: Iowa Department of Public Instruction.

Salvia, J., & Ysseldyke, J. (1985). *Assessment in special and remedial education* (2nd ed.). Boston: Houghton-Mifflin.

Sattler, J. (1982a). *Assessment of children's intelligence and special abilities* (2nd ed.). Boston: Allyn & Bacon.

Sattler, J. (1982b). The psychologist in court: Personal reflections of one expert witness in the case of *Larry P. School Psychology Review, 11,* 306–319.

Shepard, L. A. (1983). The role of measurement in educational policy: Lessons from the identification of learning disabilities. *Educational Measurement: Issues and Practice, 2*, 4–8.

Skillings, L. S. (1981). *A comprehensive analysis of the statistical characteristics of a population of learning disabled children.* Unpublished specialist thesis, Iowa State University.

Smith v. Robinson, 468 U. S. 992; 52 LW 5179 (1984).

St. Louis Development Disabilities Treatment Center Parents Association v. Mallory. U. S. DC, Western District of Missouri, No. 80-4012-CV-C-H, August 8, 1984.

Taylor, R. L. (1984). *Assessment of exceptional students.* Englewood Cliffs, NJ: Prentice-Hall.

Telzrow, C. F. (1985). Best practices in reducing error in learning disability qualification. In A. Thomas & J. Grimes (Eds.), *Best practices in school psychology.* Kent, OH: National Association of School Psychologists.

Thomas, A., & Grimes, J. (Eds.). (1985). *Best practices in school psychology.* Kent, OH: National Association of School Psychologists.

Tindall, R. (1979). School psychology: The development of a profession. In G. Phye & D. Reschly (Eds.), *School psychology: Perspectives and issues.* New York: Academic Press.

Tombari, M., & Bergan, J. (1978). Consultant cues, teacher and teacher verbalizations, judgments, and expectancies for children's adjustment problems. *Journal of School Psychology, 16*, 212–219.

Tucker, J. (1977). Operationizing the diagnostic-intervention process. In T. Oakland (Ed.), *Psychological and educational assessment of minority children.* New York: Brunner/Mazel.

Wade, T. C., & Baker, T. B. (1977). Opinions and use of psychological tests: A survey of clinical psychologists. *American Psychologist, 32*, 874–882.

Wang, M. C., & Birch, J. W. (1984). Comparison of a full-time mainstreaming program and a resource room approach. *Exceptional Children, 51*, 33–40.

Yaris v. Special School District of St. Louis County, 558 F. Supp. 545 ED MO 1983.

Ysseldyke, J. E., Thurlow, M., Graden, J., Wesson, C., Algozzine, B., & Deno, S. (1983). Generalization from five years of research on assessment and decision making: The University of Minnesota Institute. *Exceptional Education Quarterly, 4*, 75–93.

Ziskin, J. (1981). *Coping with psychiatric and psychological testimony* (3rd ed.). Venice, CA: Law and Psychology Press. (Also, *1983 Supplement* to 3rd ed.)

CHAPTER 8

Civil Competency

RALPH SLOVENKO

Lawyers call doctors incompetent. Chief Justice Warren Burger calls lawyers incompetent. Everywhere there seems to be incompetency, even in the ranks of professionals, and the laws on licensing or certification are not assuring.

Laurence J. Peter of the now-famous "Peter principle," formulated in 1969, said that in a hierarchy every employee tends to rise to his or her level of incompetence. Peter observed that an employee starts off as competent, then rises, through promotion, to a position where he or she is not competent to perform the job. In other words, the cream rises to the top, until it sours. Peter, when he first wrote about the Peter principle (Peter & Hull, 1969), assumed it applied to all or at least most professions, but he was not certain. He confirms it in the sequel, *The Peter Prescription* (1972).

Societies or management have resorted to various techniques to protect competence. The kibbutzim in Israel rotate the jobs of their members every three or four years. General Motors for its new Saturn plant in Tennessee has announced a series of new work rules to enhance morale and productivity. Instead of performing a single tedious task, employees will work together in self-directing teams of six to 15 people. Each team will be responsible for large sections of the car, and its members will have the latitude to reach a consensus on how to divide and rotate job assignments. The workers will receive a salary instead of an hourly wage, with the pay directly tied to performance (Alexander, 1985).

From such verities derives the difficulty in knowing whether incompetence lies with the person, with others, or with the system. A legal standard of measuring incompetence is related to the vocational, social, educational and other circumstances of the day. If millions of people behave foolishly, it is still foolish, but we tend to approve it. Custom or state of the art is a measure of competency, or negligence. Thus, in *Stepakoff v. Kantar*, a suit against a psychiatrist, where it was alleged that the psychiatrist's negligence led to the patient's suicide, the court held that the psychiatrist was only required to exercise the care and skill customarily exercised by an average qualified psychiatrist. In a malpractice (professional negligence) action, the complainant is obliged as a matter of law to call as an expert witness a member of the profession (or one familiar with the profession) to testify as to the standard of care of the profession.

Webster defines competency as "the quality or state of being functionally adequate or of having sufficient knowledge, judgment, skill, or strength (as for a particular day or in a particular respect)." Competency depends on the activity or the task. In a dialogue in Richard Condon's *Prizzi's Honor*, a novel turned into a celebrated film, Charley (a mafia hit man) asks, wondering whether he can trust a woman he thinks he loves, "Do I ice her? Do I marry her?" Replies girlfriend Maerose, "Just because she's a thief and a hitter don't mean she ain't a good woman in all other departments."

COMPETENCY OF A PROFESSIONAL

Every professional organization, in one way or another, must face up to the incompetency of a member. The expulsion or discipline of a member may be based either on emotional instability or on professional misconduct. The degree of proof necessary to justify loss of membership or suspension varies from state to state, however. In some states professional misconduct must be shown by a preponderance of the evidence; in others, by clear and convincing evidence. Seldom does a malpractice suit trigger a hearing by a disciplinary board. Negligence as established in litigation is not equated with incompetency to practice, nor even with a presumption of incompetency. Seldom is mental or emotional instability a sufficient ground for disciplinary action. Generally, acts or omissions, which themselves would be ground for discipline, bring to light mental or emotional problems. Often, the issue of mental instability is raised in mitigation of the wrongful conduct. In a few cases, however, the petition for suspension is based on a rule that provides for the suspension of individuals who are mentally or emotionally unstable.*

In the case of lawyer competency in criminal cases, until the 1970s, the prevailing standard of "effective" assistance of counsel was the mockery-of-justice test under which representation was considered ineffective or incompetent only when it was so poor as to "reduce the trial to a farce" or render it a "mockery of justice." Under this test, lawyers could appear in court drunk or could fall asleep during trial and still not be found ineffective. (Disciplinary action, however, may be brought against an attorney for appearing in court intoxicated.) The test required "such a minimal level of performance from counsel" that it was called "a mockery of the Sixth Amendment" (Bazelon, 1973). Among the reasons underlying the reluctance to find ineffectiveness are that to honor such claims is to force the trial judge to intervene whenever possible error is being committed, to lead appellate courts to second-guess defense tactics with the benefit of hindsight, to make lawyers more reluctant to accept court assignments, and to encourage lawyers with desperate cases to commit errors deliberately. In the early 1970s, the Supreme Court approached the issue of ineffective counsel in terms of whether counsel fell "within the range of competence demanded of attorneys in criminal cases" (*McMann v. Richardson*,

---

*"Validity and Application of Regulation Requiring Suspension or Disbarment of Attorney Because of Mental or Emotional Illness," 50 A.L.R.3d 1259.

1970). In a recent decision, the Supreme Court ruled that reversal of a conviction will only be required when the defendant shows that the attorney acted improperly in a way which directly and adversely affected the result at trial.*

COMPETENCY OF A WITNESS

As a general rule, every witness is presumed competent to testify unless it can be shown that the witness does not have personal knowledge of the matters about which he is to testify, that he does not have the ability to recall the subject matter, or that he does not understand the duty to testify truthfully (Rule 601). Any objection to the competency of a witness must be raised at the time the party is presented as a witness; absent objection at that time, the claim of incompetency is waived.

Generally, the decision concerning whether or not to hold a competency hearing is a matter entirely within the discretion of the trial judge. A witness may be found competent despite the fact that in another case he may have been found criminally insane or incompetent to stand trial. In these or other cases, a psychiatrist or psychologist may be called to testify whether the witness has sufficient memory, understands the oath, and has the ability to communicate (*U.S. v. Odom*, 1984).

The rule that allows an individual to testify, though deemed insane, assumes that jurors are capable of evaluating a witness's testimony. "If a lunatic takes the stand and babbles gibberish, the jury will ignore it and the defendant will not be harmed," one court observed (*U.S. v. Gutman*, 1984). In that case, the witness had been hospitalized 13 months earlier and was described as "highly depressed" with "some psychiatric thought disorder in addition to the difficulty he has in organizing and being relevant." This witness, for the state, was again hospitalized some two months after testifying. The court noted several factors in deciding not to order an examination of the witness's ability to testify: (1) protection of the witness's privacy interests, (2) potential for harassment of witnesses, (3) the possibility that a mental exam will hamper law enforcement by deterring potential witnesses from coming forward, (4) whether the witness was a key to the case, and (5) whether there are substantial indications that the witness is suffering from a mental abnormality at the time of trial.

The issue of competency of a child witness to testify came before the U.S. Supreme Court in 1895 in *Wheeler v. U.S.* The question was whether a five-year-old son of a murder victim could testify. The homicide took place on June 12, 1894; the boy was five years old on the 5th of July following. The case was tried on December 21, at which time he was about five and a half years of age. (In those days trials took place soon after the event.) The boy, in reply to questions put to him on his voir dire, said among other things he knew the difference between the truth and a lie; that

---

*For a holding of ineffective assistance of counsel, under the test announced by the Supreme Court in *Strickland v. Washington*, "the professional conduct must be unreasonable under the circumstances and a reasonable probability that, but for the unchallenged conduct, the result of the particular proceedings could have been different."

if he told a lie the bad man would get him, and that he was going to tell the truth. When further asked what they would do with him in court if he told a lie, he replied that they would put him in jail. He also said that his mother had told him that morning to "tell no lie," and in response to a question as to what the clerk said to him, when he held up his hand, he answered, "Don't you tell no story." Other questions were asked as to his residence, his relationship to the deceased, and as to whether he had ever been to school, to which he responded in the negative. The Supreme Court said:

> That the boy was not by reason of his youth, as a matter of law, absolutely disqualified as a witness, is clear. While no one would think of calling as a witness an infant only two or three years old, there is no precise age which determines the question of competency. This depends on the capacity and intelligence of the child, his appreciation of the difference between truth and falsehood, as well as of his duty to tell the former. The decision of this question rests primarily with the trial judge, who sees the proposed witness, notices his manner, his apparent possession or lack of intelligence, and may resort to any examination which will tend to disclose his capacity and intelligence as well as his understanding of the obligations of an oath. As many of these matters cannot be photographed into the record, the decision of the trial judge will not be disturbed on review unless from that which is preserved it is clear that it was erroneous. . . . [T]he boy was intelligent, understood the difference between truth and falsehood, and the consequences of telling the latter, and also what was required by the oath which he had taken. At any rate, the contrary does not appear. Of course, care must be taken by the trial judge, especially where, as in this case, the question is one of life or death. On the other hand to exclude from the witness stand one who shows himself capable of understanding the difference between truth and falsehood, and who does not appear to have been simply taught to tell a story, would sometimes result in staying the hand of justice (*Wheeler v. U.S.*, 1895, pp. 524–525).

The legal standards for the competency of a child witness have slowly evolved away from religious concepts to attempts at assessment of moral and cognitive functions. In early law, a child or adult could be automatically barred from testifying because of insufficient religious training. Wigmore, the leading authority on evidence, in 1935 recommended that there be no requirement of competency of a child witness (Wigmore, 1979). He argued against the qualifying of witnesses by judges because of the judiciary's lack of expertise in this area. He argued for permitting children to testify and allowing the jury or judge to assess the overall credibility of the testimony. Although Wigmore's view has not been entirely adopted, numerous studies support the competency of child witnesses. Studies have found that, although older witnesses are better able to freely recall more information about a particular event, young witnesses were much more likely to correctly recall items they actually remembered (Marin, Holmes, Guth, & Kovac, 1979). Children are poorer at free recall than adults, but what they report is not necessarily less accurate. Existing data seem to show that the rate of loss of information in short-term memory is comparable across age levels, but there is more loss in long-term memory in children. In distinguishing the source of memory, both adults and children have a problem—they both confuse fantasy and reality. Furthermore, there seems to be little correlation between age and honesty (Lickona, 1976; Goleman, 1984).

At common law, it was presumed that a child under age 14 was not competent. At present there is no fixed age below which a witness is deemed incompetent, although children under age 10 or 14 are routinely examined by the court. (In dicta, in *Wheeler v. U.S.*, the Supreme Court commented that no one would think to call as a witness an infant only two or three years old.) As it is generally understood, the question in each case is whether the witness understands the obligations of the oath and has sufficient intelligence to give evidence. Age is considered along with the infant's understanding of all the facts and circumstances of the case. It is often essential that the child have an understanding of the obligation of an oath and the obligation to tell the truth. For these purposes, it is generally sufficient if the child knows it is wrong to lie and that if he does he will be punished. In this regard, it was significant in *State v. Green* that a child witness said he would be spanked if he lied.

The level of suggestibility of a witness is an important factor in determining competence. Of particular concern is the nature of certain kinds of evidence. For instance, the sex offense cases are particularly difficult when they involve children or mentally abnormal victims. In *Riggs v. State* (1956), the prosecutor asked the young girl whether she had had sexual intercourse with the defendant when no evidence was presented as to the girl's understanding of sexual intercourse. The Indiana Supreme Court held that the trial court had erred in not seeking validation of the child witness's comprehension of the meaning of sexual terms and behavior when she answered "yes" to the question. In one or two jurisdictions, corroboration of the minor's allegations is required in sex-offense cases as a matter of law (Melton, 1981; Margolick, 1984; see also Press, 1985; Renshaw, 1985).

The vast majority of the literature on suggestibility shows that young children (age seven) are very susceptible to an experimenter's suggestion and that resistance to suggestion increases with age (Yarmey, 1984). The courts under the law of evidence recognize that leading questions are undesirable, but they make an exception in the case of children. Yet it is the child witness who is probably most easily misled by a suggestive question. (If the suggestion is based on subtle use of language, the child may actually be less vulnerable.) Children are especially suggestible and compliant with parents and those adults whom they seek to please and protect. The issue of suggestibility, thus, very much depends on the examiner. On cross-examination, we know, attorneys ask questions that confuse the child; they confuse adults, too. Children tend to speak and think slowly, and the adult world gets impatient with them. They take longer to understand questions and to give answers. The adult tries to string the child into a story that makes sense from one point of view. Children may have only one word for an object. They do not know the meaning of grown-up words such as penis, vagina, or anus. They do not have the same sense as adults of time and chronology—thus confusing, for example, lunch and dinner.

By and large juries are biased against child witnesses. Over 60 percent of juries feel they are unreliable, and over 80 percent of health professionals do not feel they are reliable. Children fidget, their voices drop, they look down or away. This can be interpreted as not telling the truth or being less effective. For security, a child may hug a doll while testifying, and that may impugn credibility (see Goodman & Michelli, 1981).

COMPETENCY TO MAKE A WILL

A will or testament, by definition, is a legal document that describes the wishes of the person who dies regarding the disposition of his or her property. It is what might be called "a dead giveaway." At the time of the making of the will, the testator must have "testamentary capacity," which means the capacity to understand and remember the nature and extent of his property, the persons who are the natural objects of his bounty, and the disposition he is making of his property.

Making a will actually requires only minimal competency. It is an easy task. Moreover, while the terms of the disposition in the will are the testator's, the actual writing of the will is usually done by a lawyer. The formalities in making a will are simple, though estate planning is a complex subject. Even a considerable degree of eccentricity will not incapacitate a person in making a will. However, despite the language of courts upholding freedom of testation, the testamentary capacity concept has been used to undo the testamentary act in furthering society's interests. The interests of society in family maintenance are greater than its interests in the protection of one's freedom of testation. Generally speaking, a will is difficult to challenge, but where there's a will, there's a way.

Usually the only way a disappointed heir can contest a will is on the grounds of a lack of testamentary capacity at the time of the making of the will. The will may also be challenged on the grounds that the testator was susceptible, because of mental condition, to the undue influence of others in the making of the will. These challenges most frequently focus on some sort of bodily disease or infirmity, an alcohol or drug condition, or cerebral arteriosclerosis. To establish either capacity or incapacity, or undue influence, psychiatric testimony is usually presented.

A person who is addicted to drugs or liquor does not lack testamentary capacity if he is lucid or sober when the will is made. One who contests the will must establish that the influence of the drugs or liquor negated the "calm judgment" that the law requires. The burden of proof is on the contestant of the will to establish that the testator was not lucid at the time of the making of the will. It is a heavy and difficult burden. Proof of addiction alone, for example, is not sufficient to carry the burden. The contestant must affirmatively show that the testator was intoxicated, affecting lucidity, at the time the will was made (an early case illustrating this point is *Elkinton v. Brick*, 1888).

Proof that the testator suffered from an insane delusion when making the will may also be enough to render the act invalid. An insane delusion is defined as a belief in things which do not exist and which no rational mind would believe to exist. The subject matter of the delusion must have no foundation in fact, is unable to be dispelled by reason, and can only be accounted for as the product of mental disorder, or the product or offspring of a delusion. For an excellent discussion of deciding whether an act is or is not a product of mental illness, see Bursten, 1984; see also *Warn v. Whipple*, 1932. Delusional religious beliefs are a common source of litigation but do not generally affect capacity unless the mind of the believer assumes a chronic delusional state which controls and dictates the conduct of the testamentary act. A belief in witchcraft is not necessarily conclusive on the issue of insanity (*Rice v. Henderson*, 1954).

The effect of a lack of testamentary capacity is to invalidate the entire will. In general, one part of the will cannot be rejected for lack of capacity while another part, which is written at the same time, is acceptable as the decedent's will.* However, there is a growing trend in cases where a part of the will is affected by an insane delusion. Some courts will strike out that particular provision if in doing so there is no effect on the other parts of the will which are not a result of the delusion.

COMPETENCY TO CONTRACT

An individual is usually considered competent to contract if he understands the nature of the contract and its consequences. If the individual is actually incompetent at the time of entering into the contract, but has not been declared legally incompetent, the contract is usually considered voidable rather than void. That is, the impaired individual has the option of affirming the contract, and if he wishes to nullify it, he must seek court action. The interests of commerce dictate preserving the validity of contracts, but at the same time, society has a *parens patriae* interest in protecting the welfare of impaired individuals.

An individual who lacks the ability to know the extent of his property or to handle his affairs with some degree of prudence may be adjudicated incompetent. A guardian is thereupon appointed (usually a family member or an attorney) to handle his affairs. In some states the determination of incompetency is a "blanket" incompetency ruling, which deprives the individual of any contractual capacity, including even buying groceries. In other states a determination of incompetency may be limited, for example, to the managing of business affairs (Slovenko, 1973; Weihofen, 1966; Note, 1959). In the ordinary course of events, a merchant would find it awkward and time-consuming to go down to the courthouse to check on the legal status of every contracting party. People do not wear badges indicating competency, hence one contracts at a risk.

From time immemorial, there have been calls for simple language in commercial transactions as well as in the law generally. Napoleon simplified the civil code to make it understandable. However, the devotion to archaic language is rooted in a desire for well-settled meaning, and the use of seemingly redundant terms stems from a prudent effort to cover every contingency. The informed consent form used by physicians and hospitals in medical care likewise tends to be boilerplate. In recent years, there has been a crescendo of voices calling for plain and readable language. Some legislatures have enacted "plain English" laws calling for simple language in contractual forms in sales, mortgages and leases.

---

*"Partial Invalidity of a Will," 64 A.L.R.3d 261.

Why not instead, one law professor asks, plain Yiddish? One with a rudimentary knowledge of Yiddish will find it more expressive and informative. The use of plain Yiddish, the professor suggests, can vastly expand our communicative powers (Uelmen, 1985). Judge H. Sol Clark of the Georgia Court of Appeals was called on to decide an appeal by a man convicted of breaking into the sheriff's office in a county courthouse and stealing eight pistols and five shotguns. Judge Clark could not find a plain English word to describe appropriately the brazen gall that crime requires, but he found what he needed in the classic Yiddish expression, *chutzpah*.

Many researchers (Mariner & McArdle, 1985) have noted that the informed consent forms used by physicians in the care of patients are written at a level too difficult for most people to understand. In order to protect the patient's right to make a voluntary and knowledgeable (informed) decision about treatment, the law imposes a correlative duty on the part of the physician to disclose the relevant risks and benefits, which the patient might be expected not to know. Actually, the informed consent document is designed more to have evidence of the consent than it is to help a patient make a decision about treatment. In the ordinary course of medical practice, the physician discusses the illness and proposed treatment with the patient. The consent form is usually distributed by the nurse or administrator shortly before the procedure is to take place. In any event, the document as evidence may backfire under the theory that "if contracting parties write at all they must write it all because the law presumes they wrote it all if and when they write at all."

COMPETENCY REGARDING MEDICAL CARE

In general, the courts have upheld the ability of a competent adult to refuse medical treatment, even if that care is deemed necessary to save or sustain life. The New York Court of Appeals has upheld the termination of respiratory capabilities by a patient who had previously manifested, while competent, a desire not to be placed on a respirator. The rule is more sparingly applied in the case of incompetent patients, however. In a companion case, the court refused to terminate treatment of a patient who was never competent (*Storar*, 1981).

The doctrine of substituted judgment is often used as a method by which the court makes a decision for the incompetent person. Originally, in the appointment of a guardian, the doctrine was used as a method for authorizing the disposition of an incompetent's property. Then it came to be employed in deciding whether to authorize withholding medical treatment for incompetents. The doctrine has as its goal to make the decision that the incompetent person would make were he or she capable of deciding the issue. It is often put in language which emphasizes the "best interests" of the person affected. For instance, sterilization proceedings may be included under the broad equity powers of probate courts to act for incompetent persons. The rationale: All persons have a privacy right to choose to be sterilized, and incompetent persons must be afforded a means for making such a decision. In general, however, a guardian's decision as to what is in the person's best interests is granted only on a showing of clear and convincing evidence that he or she is competent to speak on behalf of the incompetent person.

Decisions concerning euthanasia or the termination of life-support systems raise even more serious questions about competency. Can one ever be competent to make a decision about death? The New York cases draw a distinction between competent and incompetent decisions about death, although it is difficult to explain the difference. Ernest Becker writes in his book *The Denial of Death* (1973) that "the idea of death, the fear of it, haunts the human animal like nothing else, it is a mainspring of human activity—activity designed largely to avoid the fatality of death, to overcome it by denying in some way that it is the final destiny of man" (see Haber, 1982). Becker's thesis is that under no condition can a person make a rational decision about his own death, but rather he is always *in extremis* hence *non compos mentis* on this matter. Notwithstanding such metaphysics, however, the courts continue to employ the doctrine of substituted judgment.

An individual engaging a physician or therapist is often *in extremis*—exceedingly vulnerable and dependent. Hence the informed consent document is regarded much like a contract of adhesion—one that is looked upon with a great deal of circumspection.*

COMPETENCY OF A MINOR TO CONSENT TO TREATMENT

Minors (typically one under age 18) are not legally competent to act on their own. The consent, express or implied, of a parent or guardian is necessary to authorize treatment or services for them. Absent that consent, treatment in law regardless of the outcome constitutes a battery or possibly negligence. To this general rule, however, there are a number of exceptions: (1) *parens patriae*, (2) emergencies, (3) emancipated minors, (4) mature minors, and (5) certain types of care.

1.   The state in its capacity as *parens patriae* (father of the people) may protect the best interests of a minor in the face of parental refusal to consent to treatment deemed necessary to preserve the life or health of the minor. Under this authority, for example, the state can compel vaccination or fluoridation. And the state may override parental consent. Even with parental consent, sterilization or transplantation involving a minor is a procedure fraught with legal hazard, so court authorization is warranted (as in *Hart v. Brown*, 1972). In the case of mental hospitalization, the responsibility for the care and treatment of the patient becomes invested in the hospital or court, so a parent has no right of access to the minor's records (In re *J.C.G.*, 1976).

2.   In an emergency where delay would produce serious risks for the minor, a physician may proceed with treatment without awaiting parental consent. Consent is implied from the emergency. An emergency is defined as "a situation wherein, in competent medical judgment, the proposed surgical or medical treatment or procedures are immediately or imminently necessary and any delay occasioned by an at-

---

*An "adhesion contract" is a contract so heavily restrictive of one party, while so non-restrictive of another, that doubts arise as to its representation as a voluntary and uncoerced agreement. It implies a grave inequality of bargaining power.

tempt to obtain a consent would reasonably jeopardize the life, health or limb of the person affected, or would reasonably result in disfigurement or impairment of faculties" (Mo. Ann. Stat.). When the question arises, the courts give a broad interpretation to emergency. Thus the treatment of a fracture has been deemed an emergency though it was not life-saving but done to stop pain and suffering (*Greenspan v. Slate*, 1953; *Sullivan v. Montgomery*, 1935).

3.   An emancipated minor—a minor who is free from the care, custody and control of his or her parents—may give a legally valid consent. By dint of certain legislation, pregnancy amounts to emancipation. Alabama's statute, for example, provides: "Any minor who is married, or having been married is divorced, or has borne a child may give effective consent to any legally authorized medical, dental, health or mental health services for himself, his child or for herself or her child" (Ala. Code).

4.   Under the mature minor doctrine, a minor is permitted to consent to medical treatment if he or she is sufficiently mature to understand the nature of the procedure and its consequences and the alternatives to that treatment. The usual standard is ease of application, but maturity is a matter of dispute. It is a behavioral test. One pediatrician has suggested that any child who could get to the doctor's Greenwich Village office by subway from the Bronx was, in her eyes, an adult. The mature minor doctrine has found application in cases where the minor is at least 15 years of age, the treatment is for the benefit of the minor, and the procedure is something less than major or serious in nature. There is apparently only one case (*Bonner v. Moran*, 1941) where liability has been imposed on a doctor for treating a minor without parental consent. The operation in this case, however, was not for the benefit of the minor, a 15-year-old, but rather was a transplant operation for the benefit of a cousin (consent was by an aunt), yet the case has been cited or relied upon in discussions as to the need for parental consent in every situation.

5.   In recent years ad hoc exceptions have been made to parents' authority to consent, usually to help deal with problems that have high social costs, such as venereal disease, drug or alcohol abuse, contraception, and pregnancy. Underlying psychodynamics may be identical among individuals showing different symptoms or behavior, but it is only the named symptom or behavior that opens the door to care or treatment without parental consent. Some states set a minimum age for consent in these treatments or procedures. Many people—for example, Eunice Kennedy Shriver (Sex Values, 1981), who suggests that programs involving parents in their children's lives are more worthy of support than those that isolate them—argue that such services should not be provided without parental consent, notice, or consultation. In any event, the majority of states have enacted statutes permitting minors to consent without parental notice or consultation to receive treatment for venereal disease and drug or alcohol abuse, and to seek and receive counseling on and devices for birth control or contraception. In *Carey v. Population Services* (1977) the Supreme Court has upheld the right of minors to obtain contraceptives without parental consent. In the wake of that decision the Sixth Circuit Court of Appeals in *Doe v. Irwin* (1980) ruled that contraceptives may be provided to minors without also the knowledge of their parents. A number of state statutes specifically

provide that records concerning the treatment of a minor for venereal disease or the performance of an abortion shall not be released or in any manner be made available to the parent.* However, in the event the minor is using a family insurance plan to pay for service, the parents may learn about it when they receive a benefit report from the insurer.

The Supreme Court in 1976 in *Planned Parenthood of Missouri v. Danforth* ruled that a parent may not veto a minor's decision to have an abortion, but the Court went on to say: "We emphasize that our holding . . . does not suggest every minor, regardless of age or maturity, may give effective consent for termination of her pregnancy." From this language it might be implied that nonmature or noncompetent minors would be required to have parental consent to abortion, even in the first trimester, as they would for any other procedure. That issue came to the Supreme Court in 1979 in *Bellotti v. Baird*. In that case the Court said that every minor has the right to go directly to a court without consulting her parents. Justice Powell said, "A pregnant minor is entitled in such a proceeding to show either: (1) that she is mature enough, well enough informed to make her abortion decision, in consultation with her physician, independently of her parents' wishes; or (2) that even if she is not able to make this decision independently, the desired abortion would be in her best interests."

The question has been raised whether a state may impose a requirement of parental notice (as opposed to consent or consultation) as a condition of a minor's receiving an abortion. Given notice, parents may be supportive and may dissuade their minor from having an abortion. Justice Stevens in the *Bellotti* case in 1979 remarked in a footnote: "[Our previous decisions do not determine] the constitutionality of a statute which does no more than require notice to the parents, without affording them or any other third party an absolute veto." In its 1981 decision in *H.L. v. Matheson* the Supreme Court by a 6-3 veto upheld a Utah parental notification law. The Court said: "A statute setting out a 'mere requirement of parental notice' does not violate the constitutional rights of an immature, dependent minor. The Utah statute gives neither parents nor judges a veto power over the minor's abortion decision." The Court's decision does not make parental notification mandatory nationwide but leaves it up to each state to decide whether to impose the requirement. There are more than 400,000 abortions a year performed on teenagers in the United States, and an estimated one-quarter of these girls do not tell their parents about the pregnancy (*New York Times*, 1981).

As a matter of practice, the procedure set out by the Court in the *Bellotti* case has been and continues to be ignored. Abortion clinics around the country are carrying out abortions on minors just as they are on adults. No path is beaten to the courthouse door for a determination of maturity or best interests. Should there be complications, however, the minor will usually find that a hospital will not admit her without parental consent. Emergency care in a clearly life-saving situation may be

*N.Y. Public Health Law Ch. 763 (McKinney 1977).

available, but even then the hospital (while administering such care) will as a matter of practice attempt to contact parent or guardian.

What actually is the hazard in treating a minor without parental consent? In general, physicians and other therapists appear to be overly fearful in the care and treatment of minors, leading quite often to tragic results. While the law defines an emergency broadly, many physicians and hospitals define it very narrowly. One recently publicized case (Ramos, 1981) involved a minor who split his lip and was spurting blood, but the doctor in the emergency room refused to suture it without parental consent. In actual fact, there is not a reported case in any state, apart from the aforementioned transplant case, in which a physician or health facility has been held liable for treating a minor over age 15 without parental consent (Pilpel, 1972). And consent is no insulation against liability.

Parental consent or no, there may be liability in the case of faulty treatment. Consent protects from a charge of battery, but not from negligence or malpractice. In the case where the treatment measures up to acceptable standards of care but there is no parental consent or applicable exception, the parents may claim that their expenses for the support and maintenance of their child were increased by an unfavorable result of the treatment, but that is not likely. Treatment of a minor without parental consent is technically a battery—but in these cases only for nominal damages—and the doctor is entitled to have the jury so instructed (*Lacey v. Laird*, 1956). More likely, the court would allow the doctor payment for his services.

CONCLUSION

Competency in law depends on the context. It is defined in relation to a particular act: whether one is competent to write a will, make a contract, or testify in court. Even then, it depends on the nature of the will or contract or type of case. Rarely is a person totally incompetent to carry out any type of act. Incompetency may be the symptom of an illness and, like other symptoms, may respond to treatment.

REFERENCES

Ala. Code title 22, § 104 (16) (Supp. 1973).

Alexander, C. P. (1985, August 5). GM Picks the Winner. *Time*, p. 42.

Bazelon, D. (1973). The defective assistance of counsel. *University of Cincinnati Law Review, 42*, 1.

Becker, E. (1973). *The denial of death*. New York: The Free Press.

Bellotti v. Baird, 428 U.S. 132 (1979).

Bonner v. Moran, 75 U.S. App. D.C. 156, 126 F.2d 121 (1941).

Bursten, B. (1984). *Beyond psychiatric expertise*. Springfield, IL: Thomas.

Carey v. Population Services International, 431 U.S. 678 (1977).

Doe v. Irwin, 615 F.2d 1162 (6th Cir. 1980).

Elinton v. Brick, 44 N.J. Eq. 154, 15 Atl. 391 (1888).

Goleman, D. (1984, November 6). Studies of children as witnesses find surprising accuracy. *New York Times*, p. 19.

Goodman, G. S., & Michelli, J. A. (1981, November). Would you believe a child witness? *Psychology Today*, p. 82.

Greenspan v. Slate, 12 N.J. 426, 97 A.2d 390 (1953).

Haber, H. G. (1982). In re *Storar*: Euthanasia for incompetent patients, a proposed model. *Pace Law Review, 3*, 351.

Hart v. Brown, 29 Conn. Sup. 368, 289 A.2d 386 (1972).

H.L. v. Matheson, 450 U.S. 398 (1981).

In re J.C.G., 144 N.J. Super. 579, 366 A.2d 733 (1976).

Lacey v. Laird, 166 Ohio St. 1219, 139 N.E.2d 25 (1956).

Lickona, T. (Ed.). (1976). *Moral development and behavior: Theory, research, and social issues*. New York: Holt, Rinehart & Winston.

Margolick, D. (1984, September 22). The corroboration requirement in prosecuting sexual abuse. *New York Times*, p. 13.

Marin, B., Holmes, D., Guth, M., & Kovac, P. (1979). The potential of children as witnesses. *Law and Human Behavior, 3*, 295.

Mariner, W. K., & McArdle, P. A. (1985). Consent forms, readability, and comprehension: The need for new assessment tools. *Law, Medicine and Health Care, 13*, 68.

McMann v. Richardson, 397 U.S. 759 (1970).

Matter of Storar, 52 N.Y.2d 363, 420 N.E.2d 64, 438 N.Y.S.2d 266 (1981).

Melton, G. B. (1981). Children's competency to testify. *Law and Human Behavior, 5*, 73.

New York Times. (1981, March 24), p. 1.

Note. (1959). Mental illness and the law of contracts. *Michigan Law Review, 57*, 1020.

Peter, L. J. (1972). *The Peter prescription*. New York: Morrow.

Peter, L. J., & Hull, R. (1969). *The Peter principle*. New York: Morrow.

Pilpel, H. (1972). Minor's rights to medical care. *Albany Law Review, 36*, 462.

Planned Parenthood of Missouri v. Danforth, 428 U.S. 52 (1976).

Press, A. (1985, February 18). The youngest witness: Is there a "witch hunt" mentality in sex-abuse cases? *Newsweek*, p. 72.

Ramos, S. (1981, January 22). Insuring medical aid if parents are away. *New York Times*, p. 15.

Renshaw, D. C. (1985, July). When sex abuse is falsely charged. *Medical Aspects of Human Sexuality*, p. 116.

Rice v. Henderson, 140 W. Va. 284, 83 S.E.2d 762 (1954).

Riggs v. State, 235 Ind. 499, 135 N.E.2d 247 (1956).

Rule 601, Federal Rules of Evidence.

Sex values for teens. (1981, March 1). *New York Times*, p. E-21.

Slovenko, R. (1973). *Psychiatry and Law*. Boston: Little, Brown.

State v. Green, 267 S.C. 599, 230 S.E.2d 618 (1976).

Stepakoff v. Kantar, 393 Mass. 836, 473 N.E.2d 1131 (1985).

Strickland v. Washington, 104 S. Ct. 2052 (1984).

Sullivan v. Montgomery, 155 Misc. 448, 279 N.Y.S. 575 (1935).

Uelman, G. F. (1985). Plain Yiddish for lawyers. *American Bar Association Journal, 71*, 78.

United States v. Gutman, 725 F.2d 417 at 420 (7th Cir. 1984).

United States v. Lightly, 677 F.2d 1027 (4th Cir. 1982).

United States v. Odom, 736 F.2d 104 (4th Cir. 1984).

Warm v. Whipple, 45 Ohio App. 285 (1932).

Weihofen, H. (1966). Mental incompetence to contract or convey. *Southern California Law Review, 39*, 211.

Wheeler v. United States, 159 U.S. 523 (1895).

Wigmore, J. (1979). *Evidence* (rev. ed.). Boston: Little, Brown.

Yarmey, A. D. (1984). Age as a factor in eyewitness memory. In G. L. Wells & E. F. Loftus (Eds.), *Eyewitness testimony/psychological perspectives* (p. 142). New York: Cambridge University Press.

PART THREE

Areas of Application in Criminal Justice

CHAPTER 9

Assessing and Predicting Violence: Research, Law, and Applications

THOMAS R. LITWACK and LOUIS B. SCHLESINGER

Our legal system frequently requires or allows decisions to be made that significantly affect the lives of many individuals based on assessments of their potential for violence (Shah, 1978a; Dix, 1980; *Jurek v. Texas*, 1976). Despite professional and judicial misgivings (American Psychological Association, 1978; American Psychiatric Association, 1974; *Barefoot v. Estelle*, 1983, dissenting opinion), mental health professionals are often called on to at least assist in making such decisions.

The purpose of this chapter, therefore, is to provide mental health professionals, other social scientists, and legal professionals with a framework for approaching the issue—and task—of predicting violence. More specifically, we hope to (1) clarify what conclusions regarding the ability or inability of mental health professionals to predict violence can and cannot legitimately be drawn from the relevant research; (2) analyze leading Supreme Court decisions and opinions on the subject in light of this research; and (3) suggest how mental health professionals can most usefully and legitimately serve in the future regarding the prediction of violence.

To begin with, however, we wish to acknowledge the work of John Monahan (1981, 1984) in this area. In this chapter we will take issue with some of Monahan's conclusions. Indeed, one of the purposes of this chapter is to correct some misconceptions we believe might result from Monahan's work. But Monahan's work forms a comprehensive and thoughtful survey of the issues and research concerning the prediction of violence, and this chapter, though also intended to stand alone, should be read in conjunction with Monahan's work (and with a more recent survey of the relevant literature by Wettstein, 1984). (See also the critical review of the literature by Dix (1980) which, in a law review article, arrived at many of the same reservations concerning this literature that we, independently, have arrived at here.) In addition, section III should be read in conjunction with Mulvey and Lidz's (1984) review of the literature. We will, however, focus on those issues and points which, in our view, Monahan's monograph (and Wettstein's review) did not adequately address.

Preliminary Statement

Critics of prediction of violence by mental health professionals often claim that (1) mental health professionals have no ability to predict violence (Ennis & Emery, 1978); or (2) even under the best of circumstances for prediction, predictions of violence by mental health professionals (or anyone else) are likely to be wrong in at least two out of three cases (*Barefoot v. Estelle*, 1983, dissenting opinion; Bottoms & Brownsword, 1983); or (c) in any event, mental health professionals have no *special* ability to predict violence (Steadman & Cocozza, 1978; Ennis & Litwack, 1974). Indeed, Megargee (1981) has written that "the identification of the potentially violent individual with sufficient accuracy to warrant preventative detention . . . is an *impossible quest*" (p. 181; emphasis added).

In fact, however, none of these statements has been established by the relevant research findings and, in all probability, they are simply wrong. As Monahan has observed, "A . . . judicious assessment of the research to date is that we know very little about how accurately violent behavior may be predicted in many circumstances" (1981, p. 37). He later said, "It may be possible to predict it accurately enough to be useful in some policy decisions" (1984, p. 11).

More specifically:

1. There is no research that contradicts the commonsense notion that when an individual has clearly exhibited a recent history of repeated violence, it is reasonable to assume that that individual is likely to act violently again in the foreseeable future unless there has been a significant change in the attitudes or circumstances that have repeatedly led to violence in the recent past.

2. There is no research that contradicts the notion that even when an individual's "history" of violence is a somewhat distant history of a single act of (serious) violence—which has led to a continuing confinement—it can reasonably be assumed that that individual will act violently again, if released from confinement, if it can be shown that he or she maintains the same complex of attitudes and personality traits (and physical abilities) that led to violence in the past and that, if released, the individual would confront the same circumstances that led to violence in the past.

3. There is no evidence regarding the validity of predictions of violence that are based upon threats, or statements of intention, to commit violence.

4. Even in the absence of a history or threats of violence, there may be occasions (e.g., when an individual is clearly on the brink of violence) when preventative action is justified based on a prediction of violence.

5. Although mental health professionals have yet to demonstrate any special ability, not shared equally by lay persons, to predict violence, they may well yet demonstrate such an ability—at least in certain circumstances—or, at least, they may well possess special techniques or understandings that can improve the accuracy of predictions of violence.

However, as we will also argue here at greater length, there is also good reason to believe that without a history of violence, evidence of intentions to commit violence, or other, clear evidence that an individual is on the brink of violence, violence can never be predicted with sufficient accuracy to justify an extended preventative detention on that ground. Even when an individual has a known history of recent violence, predictions of that individual's behavior in environments very different from that in which his or her violence occurred in the past are likely to be highly subject to error.

I.   THE RESEARCH

Predictions of Violence in the Community

Perhaps the most widely cited (and relied upon) study for the oft-stated proposition, recently asserted by three judges of the U.S. Supreme Court (*Barefoot v. Estelle*, 1983, Blackmum, J., dissenting), that predictions of violence are likely to be wrong in two out of three cases—even when based on a known history of violence—is a study by Kozol, Boucher, and Garafolo (1972). A close examination of this report, however, will illustrate how little, if anything, can legitimately be concluded from most studies of predictions of violence.

From clinical examinations, extensive life histories, and psychological tests, a team of mental health professionals evaluated 592 males convicted (in Massachusetts) of assaultive offenses (usually sexual in nature) and sentenced to a special facility for continued evaluation and treatment. Of these men, 386 were eventually diagnosed as *not* dangerous by the evaluating team and eventually released. In addition, 49 men diagnosed as still dangerous were released by judicial or parole authorities *against* the advice of the professional staff.

The released individuals were followed up in the community. At the end of the follow-up period 8 percent of the patients considered by the evaluating teams to be nondangerous, and 34.7 percent of the patients they viewed as still dangerous, were found to have committed a serious assaultive crime.

Kozol et al. (1972) viewed their study as demonstrating that "dangerousness *can* be reliably [i.e., validly] diagnosed" (p. 392; emphasis added) because the recidivism rate of offender patients released against the advice of the evaluating teams was much higher than the recidivism rate of patients viewed as nondangerous by the teams (Kozol, Boucher, & Garofalo, 1973). This conclusion has been challenged, however, not only because the authors themselves report a false-positive rate of 65 percent (Monahan, 1973) but also because, on the average, the relatively small number of patients predicted to be violent (but nevertheless released) were at large in the community—and, therefore, at risk for recidivism—far longer than those predicted to be nonviolent (Steadman, 1978, p. 127).

Our focus, however, is on any suggestion that this study established that even when predictions of violence are made regarding individuals with a proven history of violence, and based on clinical examinations, such predictions are likely to be wrong two-thirds of the time (see, e.g., Monahan, 1981, p. 77; Ennis & Litwack, 1974, n. 64; Megargee, 1981, p. 180).

To begin with, Kozol et al. reported subsequently (1973) that at least 14 of their 49 patients diagnosed as dangerous and yet released were patients who had been committed and studied during the early years of their program and who would not have been diagnosed as dangerous in the latter years of their study (when, presumably, their diagnostic techniques and judgments were more refined). Thus, Kozol et al. may eventually have developed a diagnostic system that was able to predict which of their sample of patients would be dangerous if released with at least 50 percent accuracy.

Second, the recidivism rate reported by Kozol for the patients predicted to be violent—be it 35 percent or 50 percent—may have been far less than the actual recidivism rate of those patients. Hall (1982) has pointed out that there is good reason to believe that only 20 percent of serious crimes lead to an arrest (see also Shah, 1981, pp. 162–163). Thus many seeming false-positives (especially among individuals with a history of serious violence) may, in fact, be undiscovered true-positives. Monahan (1981, pp. 82–85) has countered that since many (ultimately detected) offenders apparently commit many undetected crimes, most unsolved crimes are committed by individuals whose dangerousness is, eventually, discovered. Thus, Monahan has argued, most of the false-positives reported in the literature are probably indeed false-positives (though he recognizes that "obviously, some of the unreported and unsolved violence is committed by persons who [continue to escape] detection and are thus labeled as erroneous predictions" (p. 85)). But even if their violence would have been discovered eventually, the violence of serious offenders predicted to be violent in the future might not be discovered during the always somewhat limited follow-up period for testing the validity of those predictions. Since Kozol et al.'s subject population were all serious offenders (most of them seriously violent offenders), it is reasonable to suppose that a significant if indeterminable percentage of their seeming false-positives were, in fact, undetected true-positives. (Most—63 percent—of the 49 patients released against the evaluating teams' advice were released prior to entering the treatment program, which mitigates against any notion that these patients would have a lower recidivism rate than most offenders because they had received treatment.)

In any event, however—and most important—the 49 patients released despite predictions of violence were not a representative sample of the patients predicted to be violent in this study—much less of any other sample of supposedly dangerous individuals. Since these were individuals who were released by judicial or parole authorities despite professional predictions that they would be violent in freedom (and despite the fact that they all had a known history of violence), these patients were most likely "borderline" patients who gave much evidence of being no longer dangerous (as well as some evidence to the contrary). Why else would they have been released (unless their confinements were legally improper to begin with)? Presumably, therefore, if the far larger number of patients diagnosed as dangerous by the teams and not released *had been* released, the apparent accuracy of predictions of violence would have been far higher than for the borderline patients. Thus, the study of Kozol et al. in no way demonstrates (or even supports the notion) that predictions of violence are likely to be wrong two-thirds of the time even when based on a history of violence and extensive individualized evaluations—certainly not when legal authorities do not disagree with the predictions of violence made by mental health professionals.*

In particular, nothing in this study contradicts the possibility that predictions of violence based on careful and extensive evaluations by experienced and thoughtful mental health professionals of individuals who have acted violently in the past—or who are currently threatening violence—may be quite accurate. And predictions of violence based primarily on the occurrence of violent behavior in the somewhat distant past have little bearing on predictions of violence based primarily on very recent acts, or threats, of violence—such as the predictions of violence on which emergency civil commitments are typically based (cf. Monahan, 1981, pp. 90–92).

Other widely cited but equally inadequate studies on the prediction of violence, described by the authors as "a demonstration of the futility of such prediction," are those of Wenk, Robison, and Smith (1972, p. 402). In the first study, a violence prediction scale was developed which employed commitment offense, number of prior commitments, opiate use, age, and length of imprisonment to predict which parolees would violate their parole by a "violent or potentially violent" act. Yet, only 14 percent of those predicted to be violent by the instrument were in fact discovered to have thus violated their parole—compared with 5 percent of parolees in general.

In the second study, all parolees released to supervision were classified as to their dangerousness into one of six categories "according to past aggressive behavior" and "psychiatric reports assessing violence potential" (p. 395). Yet the rate of discovered violence during a one-year follow-up was only .31 percent (i.e., five) of the 1,630 parolees in the two most "potentially aggressive" categories (which was insignificantly higher than the discovered rate of violent crimes—.28 percent— among the supposedly less aggressive parolees).

In the third study, case histories, psychiatric diagnoses, the results of certain nonprojective psychological tests, and counselors' ratings of academic and vocational potential of 4,146 California Youth Authority (CYA) wards were analyzed retrospectively to see if it could be determined whether there was a classification scheme, based on these measures, which would have identified and distinguished the 104 wards who committed a known violent offense within 15 months after release. The effort proved futile.

However, the studies of Wenk et al. hardly demonstrate that predictions of violence are likely to have a high rate of error regardless of the bases for the predictions: All of these studies dealt with predictions of violence regarding individuals who most recently had been in confinement for some time. Thus, none dealt with

*A similar study concerning inmate-patients released from the Maryland Defective Delinquency program yielded results both alike and subject to like criticism as those of Kozol et al. See Steadman (1977); Gordon (1977); Dix (1980, pp. 539–542).

predictions based on a recent history of repeated violence without a subsequent confinement (cf. *Schall v. Martin*, 1984, discussed in section II). None dealt with predictions based on evidence of current intentions to commit violence, and none examined predictions based on careful clinical examinations.

The first and third study simply did not in any way involve clinical predictions (using individualized examinations) by anyone—much less by mental health professionals. Rather, those studies demonstrated, at most, only that "violence cannot be predicted by the violence prediction scale and other [actuarial] classification modalities" that were used (Kozol et al., 1973). And the great majority of the CYA subjects had no known history of violence (Wenk & Emrich, 1972; Dix, 1980, pp. 534–535).

As for the second study reported previously, although the authors stated that "the classification procedure involved both actual offender histories and psychiatric reports assessing violence potential," the authors also state that ratings of dangerousness were made "according to past aggressive behavior" (p. 395). Because no information is given regarding the nature of the psychiatric contributions to the ultimate predictions, no meaningful conclusions can be derived from this report regarding the ability of mental health professionals to predict violence. No data are furnished regarding the validity of any predictions that may have been made by psychiatrists or the nature of the data and examinations upon which the psychiatric reports were based. Certainly there is no indication that the psychiatric reports (or predictions, if there were any) were based on careful clinical examinations.

Moreover, Cohen, Groth, and Siegel (1978) have observed that the fact that the subjects studied by Wenk et al. were under parole supervision during the various follow-up periods may have hidden their actual potential for violence because there is evidence that "many parolees [do] not participate in crime while under parole supervision but get into difficulty when their parole period is ended" (Shapiro, Cohen, and Bugden, 1959). And the low recidivism rates discovered by Wenk et al. in their second study may also be attributable to the fact that these researchers used the fact of being convicted and returned to prison as their criteria for recidivism, which, as Monahan (1981, p. 101) has pointed out, may greatly underestimate actual violence. Thus, a study by the Michigan Department of Corrections (Murphy, 1980; reported by Monahan, 1981) using arrests for a violent crime as the index of violence, an actuarial prediction device focusing on the seriousness of the commitment offense and institutional misconduct, and the age of first offending was able to identify a very high-risk group of offenders who exhibited a 40 percent recidivism rate while on parole over 14 months. Since these offenders, too, were on parole during the follow-up period, the 40 percent recidivism rate probably seriously underestimated their actual or future dangerousness. And while some of the arrests were undoubtedly undeserved, given the relatively high rate of probable recidivism for these high-risk offenders, in all likelihood far more of them than the 40 percent who were arrested committed unsolved violent acts while on parole (cf. Monahan, 1981, pp. 82–87).

Finally, as noted earlier, none of these studies examined predictions based on a *recent* history of *repeated* violence (i.e., absent a subsequent confinement). Indeed, the report of these studies does not allow for any determination of the discovered accuracy of predictions based on a history of repeated violence, even if prior to confinement, as opposed to an isolated act of violence. Repetitive violence is more likely to stem from relatively enduring personality traits, rather than from unpredictable chance occurrences, or crises. And, most important, no data were presented regarding the accuracy of predictions based on a combination of a history of repeated violence and a current, individualized examination and evaluation of the violent offender. Such an examination would be necessary to determine the causes of the offender's previous violence and whether or not those causes were still active and likely to lead the offender to act violently again if released. (Such an exam would, or should, be required to justify a preventative detention—cf. *Schall v. Martin*, 1984.) Thus, the studies reported by Wenk et al. leave open many questions about the predictability of future violence and do not justify a conclusion that any and all attempts to predict, or schemes for predicting, future violence will necessarily result in an unacceptable number of false-positives (cf. *Schall v. Martin*, 1984, dissenting opinion).

Another quite different group of studies on the prediction of violence is exemplified by the well-known "Baxstrom" studies (Steadman & Cocozza, 1974) and the similar studies of Thornberry and Jacoby (1979). Briefly stated, these studies concerned hundreds of individuals confined, often for many years, in hospitals for the criminally insane because, supposedly, they were considered to be too dangerous to be released to civil mental hospitals, much less to the community. Yet, as a result of judicial decisions, these patients were nevertheless transferred to civil hospitals, and follow-up studies determined that only a small percentage of these supposedly dangerous individuals were violent in the civil hospitals to which they were transferred. Many were soon released to the community with, again, relatively few having to be returned to confinement because of violent behavior.

It is clear, however, that the determinations of dangerousness on which these patients' unnecessarily severe confinements were grounded were based *not* on careful, individualized clinical examinations (Steadman & Cocozza, 1980) but on what have been described as administrative decisions (*Baxstrom v. Herald*, 1966, n. 3), global assessments (Steadman & Cocozza, 1980, p. 212), and political predictions (Thornberry & Jacoby, 1979). Nor is there any evidence that the psychiatrists who made these decisions were anything like a representative sample of psychiatrists (or mental health professionals). Given the fact that many of these patients had become old, it is hard to believe that a representative sample of mental health professionals would have viewed so many of them as dangerous.

Monahan (1981) took note of but rejected this criticism as follows:

It is sometimes claimed regarding the Baxstrom and Dixon patients [the latter studied by Thornberry and Jacoby] that no one really believed that they would be violent if released—that the predictions were merely a bureaucratic ploy to keep "chronic" patients in the hospital. . . .

It is difficult to respond to the criticism that mental health professionals were not telling the truth when they predicted violence so that they could facilitate their bureaucratic hold on patients. . . .

Yet all research can do is take psychiatrists and psychologists at their word when they predict violence and assume the predictions are made in good faith. It is not an acceptable retort to the research for psychiatrists and psychologists to say, after the fact, that they did not *really* believe the patients to be violent. If bureaucratic pressure influences prediction, then that pressure is part of the social reality that should be empirically studied. And even in the case of the Baxstrom patients, *somebody* believed them to be violent, or else judo training would not have been given to the staff of the civil hospitals to which they were sent. (p. 81)

Indeed, Monahan (1984) maintained that these studies (and that of Kozol et al., 1972) "demonstrated that clinical predictions of violent behavior among institutionalized mentally disordered people are accurate at best one-third of the time" (p. 13). And he went on to argue that "more studies concluding that psychiatrists and psychologists are relatively inaccurate clinical predictors of whether mentally disordered offenders who have been institutionalized for lengthy periods of time will offend once more are not needed. There are so many nails now in that coffin that I propose we declare the issue officially dead" (p. 13).

Yet the limitations of the Baxstrom and Dixon studies cannot be so easily ignored. The fact remains that the predictions of violence that turned out to be so wrong in those studies were not based on individualized much less careful clinical examinations. Therefore, whether or not those predictions were believed—by the administrators making them or the people who were informed of them—the inaccuracy of those predictions is simply irrelevant to determining the accuracy of clinical predictions that *are* based on careful, individualized examinations. Accordingly, these studies do not demonstrate that "clinical predictions of whether mentally disordered offenders who have been institutionalized for lengthy periods of time will offend once more" are fated to be highly inaccurate (which would make it impossible to determine when, if ever, to release insanity defense acquittees).

In particular, nothing in the results of these studies contradicts our earlier suggestion: If it can be demonstrated that an individual with a history of violence still retains the same complex of attitudes and personality traits (and physical abilities) that led to violence in the past—and that, if released, the individual would again confront the same circumstances that led to violence in the past—then, even if that individual has been confined for some time, it can reasonably be assumed that, if released, that individual will act violently again. And, as Monahan himself has emphasized (1981, pp. 90–92; 1984) the Baxstrom and Dixon studies have no bearing on the potential accuracy of predictions of violence made in very different circumstances (e.g., when based upon a recent history of threats of violence).*

The Baxstrom and Dixon studies do demonstrate something of considerable importance: Just because a mental health professional deems an individual to be dangerous, that alone does not justify giving that conclusion any credence (Ennis &

---

*Contrary to Monahan's apparent fear that mental health professionals will use critiques of the Baxstrom and Dixon studies to claim more expertise than they have, professional organizations have been more likely to uncritically accept and even rely on the surface results of these studies (in amici curiae) to eschew any responsibility for erroneous predictions.

Litwack, 1974; *O'Connor v. Donaldson*, 1975). Rather, predictions of violence should be given credence, if at all, not because of the professional title (or hunches) of the predictor but only because there is substantial concrete evidence to support the prediction (*Addington v. Texas*, 1979; Litwack, Gerber, & Fenster, 1980; American Psychiatric Association, 1974, p. 33).

This is particularly so when one considers the many reasons why, generally, violence is extraordinarily difficult to predict—reasons that have been well canvassed by Megargee (1976) and which have been summarized by Mulvey and Lidz (1984) as follows:

> Two issues arise regularly in the theoretical literature related to the prediction and management of violent or dangerous behavior. First, it is a relative, context bound behavior with multiple definitions. Second, it is attributable to a complex interaction of individual pre-dispositional and situational factors. Given these two pervasive themes, the clinician, searching for a grasp of the current state of the art regarding these issues, is faced with a formidable task. (pp. 379–380)

These difficulties are reflected in other studies of the prediction of dangerousness— for example, studies of the accuracy of predictions of intra-institutional violence that were based on the patients' behavior prior to institutionalization.

Predictions of Intra-Institutional Violence

In the most prominent of these studies, Cocozza and Steadman (1978) observed the accuracy of assessments of dangerousness made by psychiatrists for the purpose of determining whether or not defendants found incompetent to stand trial should be remanded to secure facilities. Although 42 percent of the patients evaluated as dangerous did commit an assaultive act immediately following hospitalization, the authors report that "the patients evaluated as dangerous by the psychiatrists were not *more* dangerous than those evaluated as not dangerous" (p. 272; emphasis added). (In fact, the data supplied by the authors indicate only that roughly the same percentages of defendants diagnosed as dangerous and nondangerous acted assaultively during their hospitalization. No data were provided regarding the total number or seriousness of assaultive acts committed by each group.) Moreover, Cocozza and Steadman found that although the clinicians in their study downplayed the severity of the crime charged as a reason for a finding of dangerousness—claiming to focus on impaired and delusional thinking instead—in fact, 73 percent of the patients charged with a violent crime were determined to be dangerous, and the severity of the patient's current offense was the only factor that actually distinguished between those defendants labeled as dangerous and those labeled nondangerous.

Cocozza and Steadman took their findings to "clearly indicate that no [psychiatric] expertise [to predict dangerous behavior] exists and that the attempt to apply this supposed knowledge to predict who will be dangerous results in complete failure" (1978, p. 274). They earlier had said that "since a lay person provided with only the alleged offense could have made predictions very similar to those of the psychiatrists, the apparent importance of this factor [also] raises the question of the supposed special expertise brought to bear by psychiatrists in the prediction of dangerousness" (1976, p. 1096).

The findings of Cocozza and Steadman in this study question whether mental health professionals have any unique or very good ability to make the kinds of predictions that were asked of them here, at least in most instances. However, any notion that these results indicate that mental health professionals have no ability, or no special ability, to predict violence regardless of the circumstances, is unwarranted. To begin with, the clinicians in this study were asked to predict behavior in an environment (secure confinement) very different from the environment in which the behavior occurred that led to the patient's arrest. Thus, the performance of the clinicians in this study has no bearing on the validity of predictions made regarding behavior in conditions like those in which violence has occurred in the past. (The authors also found that there was no difference between the patients rated as dangerous and those rated as nondangerous regarding their likelihood of committing a violent act subsequent to their release. However, the patients were not being evaluated for their long-term potential for violence but, rather, solely for their likely dangerousness during their immediately-to-follow hospitalization.) It should not be surprising that predictions of violence concerning settings very different from those in which violence has occurred in the past will be highly subject to error (Monahan, 1981), especially when the setting within which violence is predicted is relatively restrictive. Even then, the predictions at issue here may not have been as poor as may appear at first glance. The predictions were almost certainly that those predicted to be violent would be so unless suitable precautions were taken—and, because of these predictions, such precautions may well have been taken (thus reducing the incidence of violence).

Cocozza and Steadman report that the two facilities to which dangerous and nondangerous patients were sent were, in fact; "practically identical" (1978, p. 272). But even if the two facilities did not differ in the treatment they offered, the staff at the facility for supposedly dangerous patients may well have been more on guard for possible outbreaks of violence and quicker to take action to prevent possible violence from occurring. Indeed, when the authors compared the assaultiveness of their subjects during subsequent as well as during their initial hospitalization —when special precautions would be less likely to be taken—they found that the patients predicted to be dangerous were indeed significantly more assaultive in a hospital setting than those evaluated as nondangerous (Steadman & Cocozza, 1978). And, as already noted, the overall magnitude of the violence exhibited by those patients predicted to be violent may well have been considerably greater than that of those patients evaluated as nondangerous.

Finally, despite Steadman and Cocozza's suggestion that their findings indicate that mental health professionals have no special abilities to predict violence, nothing in their findings contradicts the possibility that there may well be particular circumstances in which mental health professionals can make unique and valid contributions to the task of assessing the dangerousness of particular individuals. (See also the criticism leveled against this study by Dix, 1980, p. 544.)

Results similar to those just described were also obtained by Werner and his colleagues (Werner, Rose, & Yesavage, 1983; Werner, Rose, Yesavage, & Seeman, 1984). Fifteen psychiatrists and fifteen psychologists predicted whether or not 40 patients admitted to an intensive-care psychiatric unit would commit an assaultive act within one week after admission. The predictions were based on admission ratings on the 18 scales of the Brief Psychiatric Rating Scale (BPRS) and on an indicator of whether or not the patient had recently committed an assaultive act leading to hospitalization. Although evidence of hostility, excitement, uncooperativeness, grandiosity, conceptual disorganization, tension, suspiciousness, and "mannerisms and posturing" (on the BPRS)—and a recent assaultive act prior to admission—were significantly correlated with predicted violence, none of those BPRS variables significantly correlated with actual violence on the ward. Evidence of hallucinatory behavior and the absence of emotional withdrawal, and an assault leading to admission also correlated significantly but not highly with assaultive behavior following admission.

Thus, in this study, the correlation between actual violence and psychiatrists' and psychologists' predictions of violence was not significant. Again, however, predictions were made regarding future behavior in a context very different from that in which past violence (or threats of violence) had occurred. Indeed, the predictions concerned behavior in an environment specifically designed to forestall violence (an intensive-care psychiatric unit). And the predictions were not based on clinical evaluations.*

Rofman, Askinazi, and Fant (1980) also studied the in-hospital assaultiveness of 59 patients committed after an examination on the ground that they were mentally ill and physically dangerous to others. Forty-one percent of the patients engaged in an assaultive act or threat—compared to 8 percent of a control group of largely voluntary patients hospitalized without a specific finding of dangerousness.

Rofman et al. took their results to mean that "the clinical determination of dangerousness . . . for emergency psychiatric commitment predicts the patients at risk of in-hospital assaultive behavior to a statistically significant degree. . . . This finding supports the hypothesis that predictions of dangerous behavior have validity when the time of prediction and the time of validation are relatively close together" (p. 1063). It must be noted, however, that only a minority of the dangerous emergency committees threatened or committed violence during their hospitalization.

---

*Just as Cocozza and Steadman's (1978) report suggests that professional predictions of violence are often based on facts other than those acknowledged by the professionals themselves as being the bases for their judgments, the reports of Werner et al. (1984) suggest that "the small correlation between actual violence and psychiatric predictions may be the result of psychiatrists emphasizing cues other than those in fact most predictive of violence" (p. 265). As Werner et al. (1984) acknowledge, however, since ward staff follow a "judgment strategy" similar to that of the psychiatrists studied regarding which patients are targeted as dangerous (those who were hostile, agitated, and suspicious) the patients predicted to be violent on the ward may not have been so specifically because, as a result of those predictions, they received special attention. Indeed, the authors suggest that the "larger meaning" of their study may be that of identifying a potentially violent group of patients—those exhibiting "hypervigilence, engagement or attentiveness" and hallucinations—who "may not fit the usual model" of the potentially violent inpatient (p. 266).

Moreover, 31 percent of all the assaultive incidents noted were threats that led to no action; 27 percent were threats (only) that led to restraint; 17 percent were acts that required immediate intervention to prevent a battery; and only 25 percent were actual batteries. Thus, apparently, less than 20 percent of the dangerous patients committed violent acts during their hospitalization.

On the other hand, the prediction that led to these patients' confinements were predictions of how they would act *in the community* if not confined. And, as Rofman et al. point out, all of the assaults in their study "took place in a structured hospital setting where attempts to understand feelings, opportunities for ventilation, and the ability to control aggressive behavior were apparent. All patients . . . were receiving adequate doses of appropriate antipsychotic medication. It is likely, therefore, that the probability of the patients [committed as dangerous to others] (who would be unmedicated outside the hospital) committing assaults in the community would have far exceeded [their rate of violence in the hospital]" (p. 1063). In short, therefore, this study neither proves nor disproves that mental health professionals can validly predict violence in the community or in the hospital in the circumstances that were involved in these emergency civil commitments. Moreover, in the absence of information regarding the factors upon which the predictions of dangerousness were based, little can be derived from this report regarding what specific factors can reasonably lead to a prediction of violence.

Still another, rather elaborate study of the prediction of violence during (and after) institutionalization which, by the authors' own admission, also yielded equivocal results is that of Webster and his colleagues (1984). Two hundred and seventeen offenders remanded to a brief assessment unit were evaluated for "dangerousness to others in the future" on a seven-point scale by psychiatrists assisted by a team of mental health professionals. After a two-year follow-up, information was obtained on 158 of the former patients, and each was evaluated on an 11-point scale for discovered dangerousness. Predictions correlated with outcomes at the level of .19. The authors note many reasons why higher prediction-outcome correlations were not achieved: In particular, (1) the clinical examinations were brief; (2) predictions of violence may have led to incarceration or hospitalization—thus reducing the likelihood that violence would occur; (3) the clinicians in the study were obligated to make predictions in all cases regardless of their confidence in their ability to do so; and (4) the outcome measure underestimates the actual amount of violent behavior in the follow-up period. In addition, the predictions were based on recent offense histories ranging from failure to appear before the court to murder. Therefore, this report—like the others—has little if any bearing on the validity of predictions of violence in many other circumstances.

(In this and an earlier report (Sepejak et al., 1983), the authors found that predictive ability varied greatly—from prediction-outcome correlations of 0 to nearly .50—among the four psychiatrists who engaged in predictions. Moreover, in the earlier study psychiatrists and psychologists as a group were somewhat better predictors than nurses and social workers. But in the latter study the psychiatrists, as a group, did less well than two trained research assistants.)

The studies of clinical predictions of intra-institutional violence raise doubts about the ability of mental health professionals or anyone else to accurately predict intra-institutional violence from extra-institutional behavior or, in general, from clinical examinations (see section III; *Barefoot v. Estelle*, 1983, discussed in section II). And, in general, it is probably difficult to accurately predict violence in environments or circumstances quite different from those in which the subjects of the predictions have acted violently in the past. However, some studies have indicated that the use of psychological tests may allow for more accurate predictions of intra-institutional violence in certain circumstances.

Hooper and Evans (1984) found that, when applied to juvenile offenders with a high base rate of previous violence in the community, variable combinations of subtest scores from the Psychological Screening Inventory and Shipley-Hartford Scale could predict as high as 91 percent of the offenders who acted-out aggressively in a residential treatment facility, while correctly classifying 80 percent of those who did not. Similarly, in a postdictive study, Jones, Beidleman, and Fowler (1981) found that a discriminant function equation based on a discriminant analysis derived from 22 MMPI scales and four demographic variables (age, race, IQ, and a reading achievement test score) correctly classified 73 percent of violent prison inmates and 80 percent of nonviolent inmates. And Megargee (1981) has reported a thesis by McGuire (1976) which derived an equation combining psychological tests and case history variables that correctly identified 89 percent of violent inmates in a federal correctional institution—but with a false positive rate of 62 percent.*

Of course the high rates of identification of intra-institutional offenders obtained in these studies depended upon applying the psychological tests at issue to individuals with a recent (if extra-institutional) history of antisocial behavior. Nothing in our independent review of the literature, or that of Monahan (1981, p. 80) or Wettstein (1984), contradicts Megargee's conclusion in 1970 that "[t]hus far no structured or projective test scale has been derived which, *when used alone*, will predict violence in the individual case in a satisfactory manner" (p. 145; emphasis added). (See also Megargee, 1981; Mullen & Reinehr, 1982.) However, the studies cited here suggest that psychological tests—or, for that matter, clinical examinations (which are another way of obtaining the data often derived from psychological tests)—may ultimately prove useful in determining which individuals with a history of violence should receive special attention. (The potential utility of psychological tests—including projective tests—as adjunct devices in predicting violence will be discussed again in section III.)

---

*In a study that suggests another potentially fruitful means of predicting intra-institutional violence through psychological tests, Selby (1984) found that mean scale scores on the Novaco Anger Inventory (NAI), the Buss-Durkee Hostility Inventory, the MMPI Overt Hostility Scale, and the Marlow Crowne Social Desirability Scale significantly distinguished between violent and nonviolent criminals, and a discriminant analysis of the NAI yielded 25 items which distinguished between violent and nonviolent criminals with 90 percent accuracy. (The revised NAI consists of 80 items describing situations which provoke many people to anger. The respondent is asked to indicate, on a five-point scale, the degree to which each situation makes him or her angry (Novaco, 1975).) And Lothstein and Jones (1978) found that the Buss-Durkee Hostility Scale and certain MMPI scales significantly distinguished highly assaultive from low assaultive adolescent offenders.

Predictions of Violence by Paraprofessionals

Two other studies should be mentioned at this juncture. Levinson and Ramsay (1979) studied the accuracy of predictions of violence made by paraprofessional Mental Health Associates (MHAs) following home visits by the MHAs in response to requests for help with subjects "acting in a peculiar or disruptive fashion because of suspected mental disturbance" (p. 180). The authors expected that the MHAs would be "less hampered by structural and situational disadvantages than the hospital based psychiatrist in predicting dangerousness." In particular, the MHAs evaluated their patients in their home environment and were from socioeconomic backgrounds closer to those of their patients than are most mental health professionals. However, after a year-long follow-up period, the MHA predictions did not significantly differentiate between those manifesting dangerous behavior and those who did not; and their false-positive rate was 71 percent.

Here too, however, the meaning of these results is, at best, ambiguous. Since no information was provided by the authors regarding how the predictions of violence were made, one cannot conclude from this study that a high rate of false-positives will necessarily occur in all circumstances. Moreover, approximately half of the subjects examined by the MHAs were hospitalized or provided with counseling after the home visit, which, of course, may have substantially reduced the potential for violence originally observed by the MHAs. This is especially likely in light of Levinson and Ramsay's further finding that stress played a major role in causing the dangerous behavior that occurred among their subjects. Brief counseling or hospitalization is not likely to change personality structures but may help an individual to deal with (or escape from) stressful situations. Indeed, the supposedly dangerous subjects may have received more treatment, or other forms of assistance, than the seemingly nondangerous patients. Unfortunately, however, Levinson and Ramsay did not provide any information in this regard.

Mullen and Reinehr (1982) found that of patients judged as dangerous at some time during their hospitalization on a forensic unit by staff members who were "personally familiar" with the patients, only 11 percent were arrested for a violent act in the community within two years, on the average, of their release. But no definition of dangerousness was given to the staff members, and the assessments were not prerelease predictions.

Predictions Based on Threats of Violence

What about individuals who are actively threatening to commit violence? As has already been noted, few, if any, of the studies discussed so far bear on this question at all: Either the patients predicted to be dangerous (but not found to be dangerous) were clearly not threatening to commit violence (e.g., Kozol et al., 1972), or it is impossible to determine from the data presented to what extent threats of violence played a role in the predictions studied (e.g., Rofman, et al., 1980). By contrast, MacDonald (1963, 1967) directly studied the postrelease behavior of a cohort of patients hospitalized because they had made threats to kill. Of 77 (out of 100) such patients about whom follow-up information was obtainable, three had later taken the lives of others, and four had committed suicide. This might suggest that predictions of violence based on threat of violence have little validity. However, since all the patients in MacDonald's cohort were hospitalized, it is impossible to know how many would have acted violently without the intervention of hospitalization. And there is good reason to believe that, for these patients at least, hospitalization significantly reduced their inclinations toward violence. Mentally ill individuals threatening murder are likely to be reacting to acute environmental and internal stresses that may be significantly relieved by hospitalization. Indeed, the patients in MacDonald's cohort would not have been released, presumably, unless they apparently no longer had intentions to kill.

Similarly, in a study of the possible effects of the *Tarasoff* decision (1976) on therapeutic practice, Beck (1982) reported that of 39 cases studied in which psychiatrists seriously feared violence, based on patients' fantasies of committing violence, none resulted in imminent violence (though two resulted in serious later violence). However, in many of the cases, apparently, the therapists' fears were based on statements of fantasies rather than on clear statements of intentions to commit violence. Most if not all of the patients remained in treatment, and some were hospitalized. And some potential for violence was apparently defused by the provision of warnings to potential victims, usually with the patients' knowledge.*

Thus, there is no research (to our knowledge) that indicates how well, if at all, violence can be predicted regarding individuals who are clearly threatening or stating intentions to commit violence. Nor, in all likelihood, will there ever be such research for the simple reason that when individuals who are apparently mentally ill are stating intentions to commit violence they will, in all likelihood, be hospitalized if at all possible or other action will be taken to reduce the possibility of violence. Indeed, for mental health professionals not to take such action with such patients would make such professionals vulnerable to damage suits by any victims of the unrestrained patient's violence (*Tarasoff v. Regents*, 1976). In short, as Monahan (1981) has observed, "The ethical questions involved in doing randomized experiments with possibly violent persons make it doubtful whether definitive tests of predictive accuracy in many situations will ever be done" (p. 37).**

The Reliability of Predictions of Violence

Studies of the reliability of predictions (and means of predictions) of violence by mental health professionals (Harding & Adserballe, 1983; Honig, 1982; Menzies, 1982; Montandon & Harding, 1984; Pfohl, 1978; Quinsey & Ambtman, 1979; Webster et al., 1984; Werner et al., 1983, 1984) and other studies cited by Wettstein (1984, pp. 310–311) indicate that the reliability of such judgments tends to be

---

*Beck's (1982) report suggests that the provision of warning to potential victims of patients with violent ideation is more likely to help than harm the therapeutic relationship—as long as the warnings are provided with the patient's knowledge.

**Schlesinger, S.E. (1978) has detailed many of the serious practical difficulties involved in doing field research on the validity of predictions of dangerousness. See also Menzies, Webster, and Sepejak (1985, pp. 50–53).

low and that "it appears difficult to determine if clinical standards for the prediction of violent behavior exist in any mental health context" (Wettstein, 1984, p. 311). In other words, mental health professionals seem to often rely (or focus) on rather different techniques, considerations, and sources of information in evaluating and assessing dangerousness (Webster, Menzies, & Jackson, 1982, p. 177), and they require greatly varying lengths of examinations to be confident about their judgments (Menzies, Webster, & Butler, 1981).

These studies, then, mirror the results of the studies of the validity of predictions of violence by mental health professionals. They indicate that such predictions should not be viewed as objective (or scientific) judgments (in the absence of clear evidence of dangerousness). At least the professional credentials of a predictor of violence, alone, should not be taken as a guarantor of the predictor's expertise or objectivity (Diamond, 1959). But because the circumstances (or hypothesized circumstances) that yielded low predictive reliability in these studies were highly ambiguous, these studies have not demonstrated that predictions of violence will be unreliable regardless of the circumstances. That is, as with studies of the validity of predictions of violence, these studies do not exclude the possibility that clear evidence of dangerousness—and reliable judgments of dangerousness—may be obtainable in certain circumstances. What such circumstances might be will be discussed below.

Sources of Predictive Error

Studies of clinical strategies and assumptions regarding the prediction of violence can and do suggest possible sources of error in the making of such predictions, however. For example, based on his observations of the diagnostic procedures used by teams of mental health professionals in evaluating the dangerousness of inmates of a hospital for the criminally insane (which in fact housed defendants found incompetent to stand trial, mentally ill prisoners, sexual psychopaths, and violent civil committees as well as insanity defense acquittees), Pfohl (1978) believed he observed the following sources of diagnostic (and, presumably, predictive) error:

1. Preconceptions derived from the patient's (possibly inaccurate) record that biased subsequent interviews and, thus, evaluations
2. Selective questioning during interviews
3. Assuming explanations of patient's behavior and assessing the patient's insight by his or her agreement with preconceived evaluations
4. Selectively hearing patient's answers to questions—or mishearing answers—according to prior expectations
5. Focusing on facts that support preconceptions and conclusions and deemphasizing or ignoring those that do not
6. Discounting cultural, class, and political realities "in favor of a focus on the individual roots of violence" (p. 212)
7. Denying individual and collective doubts and presenting theories and hunches as findings

Indeed, Pfohl claims to have observed:

numerous cases in which retrospective and reconciliating influences and modifications in theorizing, due to a variety of social contingencies, are left out of the explicit frame of a final psychiatric decision. All of these things go into the framing of a particular decision, but are in the final product hidden by the frame itself. This is the essential thing to remember about this last step in the patient review process. It is a step which transforms loose indexical theorizing into tight, reflexively realized "fact." The interactionally determined basis for a conclusion is lost in the reading of the expertly stated conclusion itself. Ad hoc theories become objective findings. The many steps which generate a decision are disguised by the one step which announces that decision. (p. 213)

Moreover, Pfohl reports that the evaluating teams, while agreeing that predictions of dangerousness required a past history of violence and that dangerousness was revealed in the stress of interviewing, otherwise operated under varied assumptions:

One team appeared to place a greater emphasis on the past record. Another team focused more on a patient's ability to express insight into past deeds of violence. Another paid more attention to a patient's verbalization of his or her dreams and fantasies. Another believed the results or psychological testing were very helpful. . . . Still another team paid considerable attention of signs of dangerousness that it believed to be present in a patient's "repressed anger." (pp. 109–110)

Pfohl's observations can serve as useful reminders to mental health professionals regarding possible sources of bias or error pertaining to the task of predicting dangerousness. (Ennis and Litwack (1974, pp. 719–734) and Monahan (1981, pp. 57–65) have also elucidated various potential sources of diagnostic and predictive error.) However, since Pfohl furnished no data regarding the validity (or reliability) of the predictions he studied, his findings do not directly speak to the actual or potential ability of mental health professionals to predict dangerousness. Moreover, since he furnished no data regarding the frequency of alleged lapses in diagnostic objectivity, no conclusions can be drawn from this study regarding the likelihood of such lapses. Indeed, though he is highly critical of the diagnostic process, he provided no data regarding the validity of *any* of the judgments reached by the teams he studied (though, by taking diagnostic comments out of context, and by viewing the hypothesis testing and give-and-take process of coming to diagnostic agreement as evidence of diagnostic unreliability, Pfohl suggests that psychiatric judgments are highly unreliable). In particular, his conclusion that psychiatric diagnoses do not measure "what they say they measure—the psychiatric reality of patients" (p. 226) is wholly unsupported by any data. But Pfohl's report does attest to the wisdom of Mulvey and Lidz's observation that "a clinician can benefit from an ongoing self-consciousness regarding the factors that motivate his/her predictions. It is clear that a clinician must do a selective sorting and simplification of available information. Being aware that this process may be influenced by a variety of contextual and practical factors is a necessary first step in improving performance of this difficult task" (1984, p. 396).

The Base Rate Problem

A problem regarding the prediction of violence which we have yet to discuss is the problem of base rates. The problem has been well stated in an oft-cited example provided by Livermore, Malmquist, & Meehl (1968, p. 84):

> Assume that one person out of a thousand will kill. Assume also that an exceptionally accurate test is created which differentiates with 95 percent effectiveness those who will kill from those who will not. If 100,000 people were tested, out of the 100 who would kill, 95 would be isolated. Unfortunately, out of the 99,900 who would not kill, 4,995 people would also be isolated as potential killers. In these circumstances it is clear that we could not justify incarcerating all 5,090 people. If, in the criminal law, it is better that ten guilty men go free than that one innocent man suffer, how can we say in the civil commitment area that it is better that 54 harmless people be incarcerated lest one dangerous man be free?

Thus, Megargee (1981) has gone so far as to argue that "unless the rate of violence increases vastly within our society, the identification of the violent individual with any degree of precision appears to be an impossible task" (p. 191).

The base rate problem can be greatly exaggerated, however. When predictions of violence are limited to individuals belonging to groups which have a high base rate of violence, the number of false-positives will decrease dramatically.* And, as Shah (1981) has pointed out, "Much recent evidence points clearly to certain groups of delinquents and criminals who have high rates of committing serious and violent offenses" (p. 162; Moore, Estrich, McGillis, & Spelman, 1984).

More generally, common sense would dictate—and no research contradicts the conclusion—that individuals with a recent history of repeated violence have a high base rate of future violence, particularly if they remain in the same circumstances that led to violence in the past; and no intervening circumstances, or personality changes, tending to reduce their violent tendencies have occurred (Hall, 1984; Scott, 1977). And we simply do not know the base rate of violence for many types of individuals about whom predictions of violence are likely to be made (e.g., paranoid individuals who state intentions to commit violence and individuals who have committed serious violence in the past and who clearly retain the same attitudes and personality traits that led to violence in the past.** As we have noted repeatedly, studies demonstrating a low rate of accuracy for predictions of violence have *not*

---

*Vanderplas and Vanderplas (1979) have attempted to demonstrate, by using a mathematical model, that it is not necessarily the case that many false-positives will result when predictions are made regarding events that have a low base rate in the general population. At least in theory, they argue, "employment of multiple-index predictors . . . provide a means of removal of some or all of the false positive cases without necessarily sacrificing accuracy of prediction of true positive cases." The key is to rely on indexes which, taken together, separate what would otherwise be false-positives from true-positives. See also Quinsey (1980) but compare with Reinhardt (1979).

**At the beginning of the same article in which he states that "the identification of the violent individual with any degree of precision appears to be an impossible task," Megargee (1981) describes the following case:

been studies of predictions regarding individuals (i.e., cohorts of individuals) with a high base rate of violence. Thus, for example, to our knowledge there is no empirical study which in the slightest contradicts the following observation (Dembitz, 1978) by an experienced New York City family court judge:

> I disagree with the popular view that it is impossible to predict whether a criminal is dangerous. With some youthful criminals it is predictable that they will for the foreseeable future continue to commit crimes. It is predictable, for example, that a fourteen-year-old will commit another crime [if not confined] when he cuts a woman with a knife while robbing her in an elevator; has aided in a robbery at gun-point and committed a burglary during the preceding year; has been out of school for several years, his whereabouts unknown to his mother for weeks at a time; [and] has refused to attend community rehabilitative programs. It is predictable, in short, that a youth exposed to no other way of life than a criminal life will commit another crime [if not confined].

Moreover, even a somewhat high rate of false-positives may be tolerable depending on the consequences of a false prediction of dangerousness. As Megargee (1981) himself has observed: "If the only consequences of [falsely] being labelled potentially violent were perhaps being placed in a dormitory with greater staff coverage or being subjected to further evaluation, then the results would not be distressing" (p. 189).

Evidentiary Considerations

Megargee (1981) has also argued, however, that "the identification of the potentially violent individual with sufficient accuracy to warrant . . . preventative detention . . . is an impossible quest" (p. 181). But in neither law nor logic is that position tenable—unless one holds to the view that the possibility of any false-positive renders preventative detention unacceptable.

The Supreme Court has ruled that "clear and convincing evidence" of dangerous-

---

> I have been involved recently in a comprehensive psychological study of a rapist and multiple murderer [who confessed to two particularly brutal and lurid murders]. . . .
>
> After [he was convicted, this individual] took the stand in the penalty portion of [his] trial and told the jury that if released he would doubtlessly kill again. Moreover, he maintained that if sentenced to life in prison he would kill fellow inmates or be killed by them. . . .
>
> I interviewed and tested [this man] and . . . concurred with his self-diagnosis. If called on to testify, I, too, would have classified him as a dangerous individual and stated that in my expert opinion, at this time, he is likely to engage in further violence if given the opportunity. . . .
>
> Despite all these data, and despite my absolute certainty, shared by [the offender], that he has been and continues to be extremely dangerous, the research evidence indicates that the odds are 2 to 1 against my prediction being correct. (pp. 179–180)

Megargee's hesitancy is ill-founded. In fact, there are no studies regarding the validity of predictions of violence regarding individuals who brutally murder and state intentions to murder again. Nor will there ever be such studies because (as Megargee recognized) when individuals exhibit such characteristics, they will be confined if at all possible. For all we know, however, the base rate for violent behavior in the foreseeable future for such individuals (if allowed to remain at liberty) is 100 percent.

ness must exist to legitimize an extended civil commitment—or, presumably, any extended preventative detention (in the absence of a criminal conviction)—on the ground (*Addington v. Texas*, 1979). We suggest again that such clear and convincing evidence exists whenever any of the following indicia of future violence are evident: (1) a recent history of repeated violence (absent subsequent treatment or evidence of significant changes in the circumstances or attitudes that led to violence in the past (Hall, 1984)); (2) a more distant history of violence together with clear and convincing evidence that the complex of attitudes and personality traits (and physical abilities) that led to violence in the past still exist and that there is a likelihood that the circumstances (or like circumstances) that led to violence in the past will recur in the foreseeable future (or, in any event, before the individual's violence-tending attitudes are likely to change); (3) unequivocal threats or other like evidence of serious intentions to commit violence—especially when based on delusional thinking; and (4) other clear and convincing evidence that the individual whose violence is being predicted is on the brink of violence. One example of this latter criteria would be that of a man who sat incessantly at the edge of his bed with a loaded rifle vigilantly waiting, because of his paranoid delusions, for his home to be attacked.* Other examples would include individuals with a history of violence who express paniclike fears of losing control over violent impulses (Bach-y-Rita et al., 1971; Lion, Bach-y-Rita, & Ervin, 1969) or who feel driven toward violence (e.g., by command hallucinations) (Cox, 1982).

These criteria—and the problem of deriving clinical evidence to support these criteria—will be discussed at greater length in section III. For now, we note again that while research has yet to establish the predictive power of these indices—and because of the practical and ethical problems involved may never do so—neither (to our knowledge) is there any evidence that refutes the legitimacy of relying on these indices to establish "clear and convincing" evidence of "dangerousness" (cf. Monahan & Wexler, 1978).** On the other hand, we question, again, whether "clear

*Gunn (1982) has observed: "Two . . . important aspects of prediction that Monahan does not touch are declared intentions and continuous surveillance. An important clinical addition that one can make to the statistical analysis of a violent person is an accurate understanding of the person's wishes and intentions" (p. 146). However, while it is true that Monahan, in his monograph (1981), did not discuss the importance of intentions, significantly he ended his monograph with a hypothetical case study and "clinical report" that relied upon (hypothesized) barely veiled threats of violence to justify his conclusion that the (hypothetical) individual in issue was "more likely than not" to be violent in the near future (pp. 161–168).

**Cocozza and Steadman (1976) have claimed: "It . . . appears that psychiatrists cannot even predict accurately enough to be more often right than they are wrong. Thus, any attempt to commit an individual solely on the basis of dangerousness would be futile if psychiatric testimony were subjected to any of [the usual] standards of proof" (p. 1101). And Dix (1980) has argued that, while mental health professionals may be able to identify some individuals at risk for violence, "a mental health professional should be banned from expressing a predictive opinion more specific than that the subject poses a greater risk than the average person of engaging in future assaultive or otherwise criminal conduct" (p. 575). We suggest that evidence of the four indicia of dangerousness outlined here—or that an individual is a habitual offender (Moore et al., 1984)—allows for a far stronger statement than Cocozza and Steadman or Dix would allow (even stronger than a statement that the individual poses a "substantially" greater risk of assaultive conduct "than the risk posed by most persons") (Dix, 1983, p. 256). Certainly, there is no evidence that mental health professionals are wrong more often than they are right when they predict violence on the basis of these indicia (cf. Stone, 1975, p. 830).

and convincing" evidence of dangerousness can be had without any of these or similar indicia.

By focusing on overt indices of dangerousness, we do not mean to imply that psychodynamic factors should be ignored in predicting violence. Indeed, in section III we will discuss the importance of considering such factors in certain instances. But it is worth remembering Shah's (1978b) caution that "by focusing *primarily* on [a] person's mental condition and on vague and often very speculative psychodynamic factors mental health professionals may well tend to *decrease* their predictive validity" (p. 179).

Similarly, Monahan has suggested that "focusing on a limited number of *relevant* and *valid* predictor items . . . is more important than an exhaustive examination that yields much irrelevant and ultimately confusing information" (1981, p. 126).*

It is not for mental professionals but for courts and legislatures, subject to constitutional constraints, to determine what degree of proof (or what probability) of what degree of dangerousness justifies various kinds of governmental intervention into people's lives. It is worth noting, however, that less proof than "clear and convincing" evidence of dangerousness may be sufficient to justify certain kinds of governmental interventions designed to prevent violence (and a higher rate of false-positives). For example, in *Addington v. Texas* (1979) the Supreme Court limited to extended civil commitments its requirement of clear and convincing evidence of the need for involuntary confinement. Thus, presumably, the Court would consider confinements based on a lower standard of proof of dangerousness (and mental illness)—and more false-positives—to be constitutionally acceptable when the loss of liberty that would ensue would be relatively brief (and, presumably benign).

Consider, also, the following observation of the First Circuit Court of Appeals regarding the involuntary imposition of psychiatric medication to forestall violence: "[I]f the violence feared is potentially life-threatening, and the patient's prior experience with antipsychotics favorable, it would be patently unreasonable to require that [psychiatrists] determine that the probability of the feared violence occurring is greater than fifty percent before they can act" (*Rogers v. Okin*, 1980, p. 656). And warning potential victims about a patient's potential violence may be

---

*There is little doubt that actuarial predictions of future violence will, on the whole, be superior to clinical predictions in many circumstances (Monahan, 1981; Steadman, 1980). And Monahan (1981) has suggested that employing such correlates of violent behavior as age (young), sex (male), race (nonwhite) and socioeconomic status in the prediction of violent behavior will improve the accuracy of such predictions. However, while the employment of such predictors in a proper fashion will improve the overall accuracy of predictions, the important question is whether the use of such predictors will ever aid prediction enough to justify taking differential action—at least concerning commitment decisions—in individual cases. We believe the answer is no. In particular, if an individual exhibits any of the four indicia of "clear and convincing evidence" of dangerousness, we suggest, violence can reasonably be predicted *regardless of the individual's sex, race, age or socioeconomic status*. Conversely, if none of those indicia are present, then violence cannot be predicted with any certainty regardless of the individual's sex, age, race, socioeconomic status or like qualities. Thus, for individualized predictions, such variables are, or should be, meaningless. Indeed, just as a focus on psychodynamic factors can distract the clinician from focusing on the most important variables regarding the prediction of violence, and thus lower predictive validity, so can a focus on race and socioeconomic status (Ennis & Litwack, 1974, pp. 724–726).

ethically permissible (if not ethically, or legally, mandated) in circumstances that would not justify preventative detention (Wettstein, 1984, p. 309; Beck, 1982).

The Expertise of Mental Health Professionals

The question remains, however: Do mental health professionals have any special expertise, not shared equally by lay persons, to predict violence? This question will also be addressed in greater detail in section III. For now, however, two answers to the question, based on the results of the research we have canvassed, can be given: (1) mental health professionals have yet to demonstrate any special ability to predict violence (Steadman, 1980, pp. 95–96); and (2) there may well be certain circumstances in which mental health professionals can make unique and valid contributions to the assessment of the dangerousness of particular individuals. Just as "we know very little about how accurately violent behavior can be predicted in many circumstances" (Monahan, 1981, p. 37), we know little about how well mental health professionals can aid in the prediction of violence in many circumstances (Steadman, 1983, p. 389). At the least, however (as one of us has written elsewhere):

> Presumably—or, at least, arguably—mental health professionals have interviewing techniques not shared by most laypersons which make them better able than laypersons to get disturbed individuals to disclose violent intentions which they are *harboring* but not readily disclosing. Similarly, psychological test results may indicate that seemingly controlled or benign individuals are harboring violence laden emotions or fantasies to such an extent that further examination is warranted—and further examination, which might otherwise have been foregone, might well disclose that the individual is harboring violent intentions, or has recently acted violently as well. And mental health professionals may be better able than laypersons to determine if an individual with a history of violence still retains the attitudes and characteristics of personality that led to violence in the past. (Litwack, 1984, p. 19; cf. Ennis & Litwack, 1974, pp. 749–750; see also Dix, 1980, n. 167)

Indeed (as will be discussed further in section III), mental health professionals familiar with the relevant literature may be uniquely aware of certain behavioral and psychodynamic indices of dangerousness, and such knowledge may allow for "timely treatment of patients exhibiting symptoms which have . . . empirically been shown to correlate with violence" (Yesavage, 1983, p. 556; Werner, et al., 1983, 1984). Conversely, mental health professionals may be better able than laypersons to determine when the psychodynamics behind particular acts of violence make it unlikely that the aggressor will act violently again (or in different circumstances).

II.   PREDICTIONS OF VIOLENCE AND THE SUPREME COURT

Between 1983 and 1984, the Supreme Court of the United States decided two cases that required the Court to focus on the issue of the validity of predictions of violence by mental health professionals and which produced profoundly different opinions regarding that issue by different members of the Court.

Barefoot v. Estelle

In *Barefoot v. Estelle* (1983) the Court was faced with a constitutional challenge to a capital sentence that was apparently based, in part, on the testimony of two psychiatrists that the petitioner, Thomas Barefoot, would continue to act violently if not subjected to capital punishment. Barefoot argued that such testimony was inherently too unreliable to be admissible in capital sentencing proceedings especially when, as was the case here, the mental health professionals in issue did not examine the petitioner and based their conclusions on hypothetical questions.

Barefoot was convicted of intentionally murdering a police officer, apparently with premeditation. According to testimony at his trial, Barefoot "told others in advance that he planned to kill a . . . policeman" and later "boasted of his guilt to friends" (*Barefoot v. Estelle*, 1983). Moreover, apparently, he killed the officer shortly after he set fire to a building to create a diversion while he committed a robbery. It was established at his sentencing that Barefoot had two prior convictions for drug offenses and two prior convictions for unlawful possession of firearms. And evidence was presented at his trial that Barefoot had previously escaped from jail while being held on charges of statutory rape and "unlawful restraint of a minor child with intent to commit sexual penetration against the child's will," and that he had a "reputation for lawlessness" in the community.

Basing their opinions on this information, at his capital sentencing hearing the psychiatric witnesses for the prosecution testified that Barefoot was an untreatable "criminal sociopath" who would continue to commit criminal acts of violence even if incarcerated. Especially worth noting is the testimony of one of the two psychiatrists who testified against Barefoot:

"Doctor . . . do you have an opinion within reasonable psychiatric certainty whether or not there is a probability that the defendant . . . will commit criminal acts of violence that would constitute a continuing threat to society?"

"Yes, he most certainly would."

"Would you state whether or not that would be true regardless of where he is?"

"It wouldn't matter whether he was in the penitentiary or whether he was free. Wherever he is he's going to continue what he's already been doing."

"Would you state whether or not, Doctor, you have an opinion within reasonable psychiatric certainty as to the degree of that probability that you have just expressed to this jury?"

"Well, yes, sir, I would put it at one hundred percent and absolute." (*Texas v. Barefoot*, Record at 2131, quoted by Applebaum, 1984, at p. 169)

By a 6-3 margin, a majority of the Supreme Court upheld the constitutionality of Barefoot's sentence. Despite the claims of Barefoot and the dissenting Justices (and the American Psychiatric Association, in a friend-of-the-court brief) that psychiatric predictions of dangerousness were too subject to error yet too likely to be accepted uncritically by jurors to constitutionally support a death penalty, the majority concluded that they were "not persuaded that such testimony is almost entirely [i.e., always] unreliable [i.e., invalid] and that the factfinder and the adversary system will not be competent to uncover, recognize and take due account of its shortcomings" (77 L.Ed. 2d at 1108).

To this conclusion Justice Blackmun (joined by Justices Brennan and Marshall) issued a blistering dissenting opinion, which he briefly summarized as follows:

> The Court holds that psychiatric testimony about a defendant's future dangerousness is admissible, despite the fact that such testimony is wrong two times out of three. The Court reaches this result . . . because, it is said, the testimony is subject to cross-examination and impeachment. In the present state of psychiatric knowledge, this is too much for me (77 L.Ed. 2d at 1119).

It may be instructive, however, to quote Justice Blackmun's opinion at greater length:

> Neither the Court nor the State of Texas has cited a single reputable scientific source contradicting the unanimous conclusion of professionals in this field that psychiatric predictions of long-term future violence are wrong more often than they are right.
>
> The APA [American Psychiatric Association] also concludes . . . as do researchers that have studied the issue, that psychiatrists simply have no expertise in predicting long-term future dangerousness. A layman with access to relevant statistics can do at least as well and possibly better; psychiatric training is not relevant to the factors that validly can be employed to make such predictions, and psychiatrists consistently err on the side of overpredicting violence. Thus, while [the psychiatrists at issue] were presented by the State and by self-proclamation as experts at predicting future dangerousness, the scientific literature makes crystal clear that they had no expertise whatever. Despite their claims that they were able to predict Barefoot's future behavior "within reasonable psychiatric certainty," or to a "one hundred percent and absolute" certainty, there was in fact no more than a one in three chance that they were correct. (77 L.Ed.2d at 1122–1123)

It is beyond the scope of this chapter to consider at length — much less to attempt to adjudicate — all of the questions posed by *Barefoot v. Estelle* beyond noting those questions which we will not consider further here: (1) Does the opportunity for cross-examination and the presentation of rebuttal witnesses adequately protect against the possibility of undue jury reliance on (quite possibly erroneous) professional predictions of violence (especially when those predictions are made with great confidence)? (2) Is there any legitimate reason, in capital sentencing hearings, to allow arguments attesting to a defendant's dangerousness to be made by mental health professionals who have not examined the defendant, rather than by the prosecuting attorneys (even if relevant descriptions and analyses of a defendant's mental state and psychodynamics could and should be offered by mental health professionals when they have clinically examined the defendant)? That is, can it reasonably be supposed that mental health professionals have some special ability to predict violence in cases in which they have not examined the person(s) about whom their predictions are made?* (3) May a diagnosis of "untreatable sociopath" be legitimately made based on hypothesized facts without examining the subject of the diagnosis (Applebaum, 1984)? (4) Should psychiatric diagnoses be admissible under any circumstances in capital sentencing (or any other legal) proceedings—or are such diagnoses more likely to prejudice than to aid the fact-finding process (Ennis & Litwack, 1974)? (5) Why were no witnesses called to rebut the predictions of dangerousness that were made in Barefoot's case? Was it because Texas law provided for the payment of only $500 for "expenses" incurred for purposes of "investigation and expert testimony" in cases of indigency? Or was it because no credible witness could be found who was willing to state that Thomas Barefoot was not a dangerous psychopath?

In any event, with regard to their analyses of the basic issue in this case—Can capital sentences be legitimately based, at least in part, on predictions of violence?—both the majority and dissenting opinions in *Barefoot* leave much to be desired. As for the dissent, Justice Blackmun's repeated insistence that any predictions about Barefoot's long-term future dangerousness would be highly subject to error is, simply, unsupported by the research literature: There are no studies of the validity of predictions of future violence (long-term or short-term) regarding individuals with a history of antisocial and violent behavior and attitudes like that of Thomas Barefoot. And, as discussed in section I, the studies that are typically taken to prove that predictions of violence are more likely to be wrong than right, regardless of the circumstances (e.g., Kozol et al., 1972) do not, in fact, justify such a conclusion. Thus, while Justice Blackmun was surely right to question whether predictions of future dangerousness could ever be sufficiently accurate—especially regarding behavior in prison, and especially in the absence of a proven history of repetitive violence (dissenting opinion, n. 5)—to justify a death penalty, his suggestion that long-term predictions of violence are more likely to be wrong than right in all classes of cases, and regardless of the circumstances, was as "baseless" as he believed the testimony in issue to be (77 L.Ed. 2d at 1123).**

The majority's opinion was equally wanting in logical analysis, however. While correctly recognizing that the research literature left open the possibility that future violence could be predicted with considerable accuracy regarding certain types of individuals, in certain circumstances (within a certain length of time), the majority failed to directly address the key issue in this case—namely, could Barefoot's behavior in prison be predicted with sufficient accuracy to justify a capital sentence?

After all, whether or not there was a "reasonable certainty" that Barefoot would

---

*Defendants subject to capital sentencing hearings cannot be required to submit to psychiatric examination nor, under the fifth amendment, may their failure to do so be used as evidence against them.

**Even if all predictions of violence by mental health professionals, taken together, were inaccurate two-thirds of the time, that has no logical bearing on the accuracy of predictions made in circumstances that were clearly and logically distinguishable from the great mass of predictions. Were it otherwise, the "clear and convincing evidence" of dangerousness required for a civil commitment on that ground could never be had. Moreover, even if very long-term predictions of violence are highly subject to error, the more relevant issue in this case was whether Barefoot would commit other serious acts of violence *at sometime in the future* (even years later) if special steps were not taken.

act violently in the community if not executed or imprisoned was largely irrelevant to whether or not a capital sentence was justified, in his case, on the ground of future dangerousness, because Barefoot was not likely to be released from confinement in any case (at least until there was a manifest change for the better in his psychology). Thus, to the extent that his potential for future violence (if he was not executed) was relevant to the sentencing decision, the key issue was his potential for violence in prison (although the chances that a defendant could be rehabilitated might, arguably, also be relevant to a capital sentencing decision). And even if it could be determined with reasonable certainty that Barefoot would act violently again if at liberty (in the foreseeable future), could his known history reasonably justify a conclusion—with sufficient certainty to justify the death penalty—that he would also instigate violence in the unique environment of a prison?

In fact, as discussed previously, there is ambiguous evidence regarding the ability of mental health professionals or, presumably, anyone else, to predict intra-institutional violence from extra-institutional behavior. Moreover, the studies that have been conducted have involved relatively short-term predictions, rather than the mid- to long-term predictions, which would have a much greater period of time to prove accurate and that are most relevant to capital sentencing determinations. And an argument could be made that an individual with a history such as that of Thomas Barefoot would be particularly likely to engage in violence in an environment as conducive to violence as most prisons (especially most Texas prisons).

Nevertheless, given the relative paucity of a proven history of repetitive violence in Barefoot's case (dissenting opinion, n. 5) and the absence of any direct evidence —such as might be obtained from clinical interviews (if the defendant waived his fifth amendment privilege against self-incrimination)—that his attitudes toward violence (or his psychodynamics) would lead him to instigate serious violence in prison, was there sufficient evidence that Barefoot would be violent in prison to justify his capital sentence?* Indeed, given the general unpredictability of behavior across circumstances (Monahan, 1981, pp. 64–65), and the absence of any definitive evidence that predictions of intra-institutional violence can be made with a high degree of accuracy from extra-institutional behavior alone, should it not be the law that capital sentences have to be justified without resort to predictions of violence?**

---

*As long as defendants insist on maintaining their fifth amendment privilege not to be interviewed by mental health professionals regarding their potential dangerousness, in the absence of a history of truly pan-situational violence (or evidence that a defendant was indeed planning to commit violence in prison), it is difficult to see how it could be proven with reasonable certainty that an individual would instigate serious violence in prison. On the other hand, defendants in capital cases might wish to themselves enter testimony from mental health professionals to the effect that, despite their violent history, their psychodynamics were such that they would be highly *unlikely* to instigate violence in prison, and/or that they were rehabilitatable. Then, of course, they would have to submit themselves to examination by mental health professionals chosen by the prosecution—and the possibility that such professionals would come up with evidence and testimony to the contrary.

**In *Barefoot*, the majority stressed that it was "unconvinced, . . . *as of now*, that the adversary process cannot be trusted to sort out the reliable from the unreliable evidence and opinion about future dangerous-

Schall v. Martin

In *Schall v. Martin* (1984) the Supreme Court also considered the predictability of future violence. At issue was whether the accurate prediction of future criminal conduct was sufficiently possible to constitutionally justify the pretrial detention of juvenile arrestees on the ground that there was a "serious risk" that, if released, they would commit a crime prior to their next court appearance.

A majority of the Court said yes, stating that "from a legal point of view there is nothing inherently unattainable about a prediction of future criminal conduct." The majority went on to add that:

> Such a judgment forms an important element in many decisions, and we have specifically rejected the contention, based on . . . sociological data . . . , "that it is impossible to predict future violent behavior and that the question is so vague as to be meaningless." *Jurek v. Texas*, 428 U.S. 262, 274. . . .

> We have also recognized that a prediction of future criminal conduct is "an experienced prediction based on a host of variables" which cannot be readily codified.

In an opinion by Justice Marshall (joined by Justices Brennan and Stevens) the dissenters disagreed in the following language:

> Family Court judges are incapable of determining which of the juveniles who appear before them would commit offenses before their trials if left at large and which would not. . . . On the basis of evidence adduced at trial, supplemented by a thorough review of the secondary literature, the District Court found that "no diagnostic tools have as yet been devised which enable even the most highly trained criminologists to predict reliably which juveniles will engage in violent crime." The evidence supportive of this finding is overwhelming.

The overwhelming evidence cited by the dissent in support of this statement consisted of the empirical studies reported by Cocozza and Steadman (1976), Steadman and Cocozza (1978), and Wenk, et al. (1972); a review of the literature by Ennis and Litwack (1974) which focused on the Baxstrom studies and that of Kozol et al. (1972); and various position papers (e.g., American Psychiatric Association, 1974) which purported to analyze the relevant literature.

Once again, issue can be taken with both the majority and dissenting opinions. Contrary to the dissenters' conclusion, the evidence is not "overwhelming" that "Family Court judges are incapable of determining which of the juveniles who appear before them would commit offenses before their trial if left at large." It may be true that regarding most juvenile arrestees there is no way of determining, with reasonable accuracy, whether they would commit serious crimes in the foreseeable future if not detained. That is, for the bulk of juvenile arrestees, there may not be suf-

---

ness, particularly when the felon has the opportunity to present his own side of the case" (77 L.Ed. 2d at 1109; emphasis added). Thus, the Court may soon be willing to reconsider the difficult questions raised by *Barefoot*.

ficient information available to allow for a legitimate prediction of violence, or whether or not they would commit future violence may depend on the occurrence, or nonoccurrence, of chance circumstances, or crises (Wenk et al., 1972, p. 401), that are impossible to foresee. But, contrary to the dissenters' suggestion, that does not mean that predictions of violence have been proven to be highly inaccurate regardless of the criteria that might be used for predicting violence or that there is no identifiable subclass of juvenile arrestees about whom predictions can reasonably be made (i.e., without yielding an unacceptable number of false-positives).

Our review of the research literature indicates otherwise. There is no meaningful evidence regarding the accuracy of predictions of violence that are based on a well-documented history of recent and repeated violence (much less when predictions are based, in addition, on individualized examinations as well). Accordingly, and more specifically, there is, we believe, no substantial evidence that contradicts what we believe is a commonsense notion: A juvenile arrestee with a recent history of repeated serious criminal conduct may legitimately be considered to be likely to again commit a criminal act prior to trial, if not detained, unless there is evidence that his or her control over criminal tendencies, or the circumstances that led to criminal conduct in the past, or both, had changed, significantly, for the better.

Consider, for example, the stated facts concerning two or the plaintiffs in *Schall*:

[One] was charged with attempted first-degree robbery and second-degree assault for an incident in which he, with four others, allegedly tried to rob two men, putting a gun to the head of one of them and beating both about the head with sticks. . . . [He also] had another delinquency petition pending for knifing a student, and two prior petitions had been adjusted.

[Another] was charged with attempted robbery and attempted grand larceny for an incident in which he and another boy allegedly tried to steal money from a 14-year-old girl and her brother by threatening to blow their heads off and grabbing them to search their pockets. . . . He had been arrested four previous times, and his mother refused to come to court because he had been in trouble so often she did not want him home.

Assuming there was "clear and convincing evidence" that these individuals had indeed acted as was alleged, and absent evidence that their attitudes toward violence —or the circumstances that led to violence in the past—had changed for the better, nothing in the empirical (or theoretical) literature contradicts the reasonableness of a conclusion that there was a "serious risk" that they would commit additional crimes "before trial if left at large" for a substantial period of time.*

As suggested earlier, however, the Court's majority almost certainly overstated

---

*Whether or not "clear and convincing" evidence of past conduct and present mental state can be obtained by family court judges is another issue—and one that is beyond the scope of the chapter. The dissenters in *Schall* argued that "an independent impediment to identification of the defendants who would misbehave if released is the paucity of data available at an initial appearance." The majority suggested, however, that sufficient evidence could be obtained. We note only the obvious point that the less complete and the less trustworthy the information available to the court is, the less accurate—and the less justified—would be any predictions of violence on which it was based.

its case when it said that "there is nothing inherently unattainable about a prediction of future criminal conduct." To the extent that an offender's previous violence resulted from an unfortunate combination of circumstances, or crises, that are unlikely to reoccur—or, even more certainly, in the absence of a known history of violence or known current intentions to commit (or clear evidence that an individual is on the brink of violence)—an individual's future violence may indeed be inherently unpredictable. And it remains an open question whether family court (or other) judges can be relied upon to exercise the power of preventative detention in a judicious and, ultimately, valid manner.

III.   THE CLINICAL PREDICTION OF VIOLENT BEHAVIOR*

As noted in the first section of this chapter, a common belief persists that clinical predictions of violence are necessarily tenuous and unreliable, even though the relevant research when closely examined leaves open the possibility that under certain conditions psychologists and other mental health professionals can make such predictions with reasonable accuracy. Just as it is a mistake to assume that clinicians cannot predict violence with any reliability or validity, it is also a mistake to expect them to prophesize a definite future event, such as suicide or homicide, rather than to merely describe a behavioral tendency, propensity, or proclivity (Tanay, 1975, p. 23), or, perhaps in some cases, a probability or clear likelihood.

In any event, the question that needs to be asked when predictions of violence are at issue is not whether the predictions can be made with perfect accuracy but whether the prediction is likely to be sufficiently accurate to justify a certain type of preventative action. Thus, the issue is not simply whether mental health professionals can predict violence but, rather, what types of predictive statements can they offer, with what type of certainty, with what types of patients, under what types of circumstances.

If, as we have already suggested, mental health professionals can predict violence with reasonable accuracy (and may have some special ability to predict violence) in at least some circumstances, why does the assumption persist that they cannot? One reason, certainly, is that they do frequently overpredict violence, for reasons reviewed by Ennis and Litwack (1974) and Monahan (1981). In particular, overprediction may occur because mental health professionals are extremely fearful of the grave consequences of a false-negative prediction and are determined to be cautious. Mental health professionals—trained to focus on intra-psychic determinants of behavior—may give undue weight to situational determinants of violence. Because so many conditions (among them paranoid schizophrenia, intoxication, and cruelty to animals) have been associated with violence, a prediction of violence is usually readily at hand.

*As noted earlier, this section should be read in conjunction with Mulvey and Lidz's (1984) review article on the subject.

Moreover, psychologists are faced with such an enormous body of literature in the area of violence and aggression (Burquest (1981) has estimated over 350 books on the topic) that they may find it difficult to remember or understand the relevant facts and findings and apply them appropriately. Connections have been found, for example, between violence and (1) various organic pathologies (Mark & Ervin, 1970); (2) toxic states (Powers & Kutash, 1978); (3) such psychiatric disorders as paranoid schizophrenia (Swanson, Bohnert, & Smith, 1970), episodic dyscontrol (Monroe, 1970), and antisocial personality (Schlesinger, 1980); (4) stress (Steadman, 1982; Schlesinger & Revitch, 1980; Gelles, 1973; Schlesinger, Zornitzer, & Benson, 1982); (5) enuresis, fire setting, and animal cruelty (Hillman & Blackman, 1966); (6) absence of anxiety and presence of parental assaultiveness (Pfeffer et al., 1983); (7) preference for violent television shows (Lefkowitz, Eron, Walder, & Heusmann, 1977); and (8) self-mutiliation (Bach-y-Rita & Veno, 1974).

In contrast to this vast literature on the phenomenon of aggressive behavior, the information on just how a psychologist develops a clinical prediction is sparse. There have been many attempts to classify violent and antisocial offenders (for example, Clark, 1971; Brancale, 1955; Halleck, 1971; Megargee & Bohn, 1979; Tanay, 1969), but few of them focus on prognostication (Mulvey & Lidz, 1984). Miller and Looney (1974), in their study of adolescent homicide, drew important conclusions concerning prediction—namely, that an offender's capacity for violence can be determined by the degree of his tendency to dehumanize his victim. But their system is limited in application to their subject population (see also Hall, 1984). In contrast, the classification system discussed and illustrated in the following pages of this chapter was developed by Revitch and Schlesinger (1978, 1981) with the express purpose of aiding in the solution of prognostic and dispositional problems. Specifically, this system can help the clinician to make predictions under three different conditions: (1) where the offender has a history of violence, (2) where the offender has no history of violence but expresses an intention to behave violently, and (3) where there is neither a history of violence nor a clearly stated intention to commit violence.

Classification for Predictive Purposes: The Motivational Spectrum

In search of a common denominator to be used as a basis for classifying antisocial behavior, Revitch and Schlesinger (1978, 1981) arrived at the concept of a motivational spectrum, with primarily exogenous stimuli at one end of the scale and primarily endogenous at the other end. (Acts of violence that are a direct outgrowth of a primary psychiatric disorder, such as paranoid schizophrenia, or that stem from organic and toxic states are excluded from this spectrum but are part of the overall classification for predictive purposes.) Under this system, offenses (and offender) are divided into five categories: (1) environmental or sociogenic, (2) situational, (3) impulsive, (4) catathymic, and (5) compulsive. Exogenous factors play less and less of a role in causing violence as one approaches the end of the scale occupied by the compulsive offenders. Personality and psychodynamic variables (that is, endogenous factors) play a lesser role in the sociogenic offenses, where environmental influences dominate.*

Environmental offenses stem primarily from the offender's identification and participation with a social network that condones violence. The prototype of an individual who commits violence as a result of values obtained from a social network is the delinquent gang member. The second category, situational offenses, consists essentially of reactions to stressful situations. These offenses may be committed by individuals with little or no overt psychopathology; however, any type of personality may be involved. About 70 percent of all homicides are, in significant part, situational, usually stemming from domestic disputes or arguments (U.S. Dept. of Justice, 1978). The third category of offender, the impulsive, reacts to many situations in a diffuse, stimulus-response manner. This type of individual has a life pattern characterized by lack of direction and unpredictability; therefore he or she drifts in and out of difficulties.

In the fourth category, close to the endogenous end of the spectrum, is the catathymic offender. The concept of catathymic crisis was introduced into forensic science by Wertham (1937) and continued to be used by numerous investigators (Sedman, 1966; Gayral, Millet, Moron, & Turnin, 1956; Satten, Menninger, & Mayman, 1960) as a diagnostic entity, to explain various unprovoked episodes of severe violence without organic etiology. Revitch and Schlesinger (1978, 1981) updated Wertham's original concept and viewed catathymia not as a diagnostic entity but, rather, as a psychodynamic process, frequently accompanied by disorganization and characterized by an accumulation of psychic tension released through the violent act and followed, typically, by relief.

Two types of catathymic process, acute and chronic, have been defined. Their specific differentiating characteristics are listed in Table 9.1. The acute process is a sudden, unprovoked act of violence without apparent motive triggered by a sudden overwhelming affect, typically attached to ideas or what Wertham called "complexes of symbolic significance."** In the chronic process, depressed mood, loose schizophrenic-like thinking, and obsessive rumination lasting for weeks or even months may precede the violent act. The individual comes to believe that only

---

*This classification is not intended to be rigid, since borderline cases with characteristics belonging to adjoining areas are inevitable, and there will always be cases where one finds a mixture of traits, with one trait playing a dominant role. For instance, a person with an impulsive lifestyle may harbor a compulsive need to commit a specific act, such as murder or rape. This compulsion may also be found in individuals with an essentially stable life pattern. A chronic schizophrenic may commit a socially stimulated crime, where the mental illness plays only a secondary role, if any, with regard to prognostication. An individual with a compulsion to commit sadistic acts may act only under conditions of social instability or in an environment where such aggression can be released with some degree of social sanctions.

**For examples, see Satten et al. (1960); Revitch and Schlesinger (1978, pp. 155–157), Schlesinger and Revitch (1980, pp. 183–184). The acute catathymic process should be differentiated from situational murders and assaults committed in an explosion of anger, fear, or jealousy or under the influence of paranoid delusions, drugs, or alcohol. Deeper sources of emotional tension are tapped and release an overwhelming affect attached to "complexes of ideas" that are disturbed. In fact, the perpetrator of the acute catathymic assault cannot give a reasonable explanation for the act and in many cases can only partially recall the event.

TABLE 9.1   Differentiating Characteristics of Acute and Chronic Catathymic Process

	Activation of Process	Incubation Period	Feeling Following the Event	Victim	Memory of Event
Acute	Triggered by a sudden overwhelming affect attached to ideas of symbolic significance	Several seconds or longer	Usually a flattening of emotions	Usually a stranger	Usually poor
Chronic	Triggered by a buildup of tension, a feeling of frustration, depression, and helplessness	Days to a year	Usually relief	Usually with close relationships with family members	Usually preserved

through violence can he free himself from a source of threat to his psychic homeostasis (Menninger & Mayman, 1956). Indeed, after the violent act, relief is felt. In retrospect, however, the event itself often seems ego alien and has a dreamlike quality. The typical victim of the chronic catathymic process is a family member or a boyfriend or girlfriend; however, sometimes the rage is turned inward, and suicide or a murder-suicide results (Revitch & Schlesinger, 1978).

Compulsive offenders, at the extreme endogenous end of the motivational spectrum, are influenced almost entirely by inner psychogenic sources. Compulsive offenses may be committed in a specific, ritualistic manner, or they may be more diffuse (Revitch & Schlesinger, 1981). Fantasies of violence may precede the act by many years. Once the violence begins, however, repetition is usually frequent and at close intervals (although, in some cases, many years elapse between crimes). Schlesinger and Revitch (1983) report that most, but not all, of the compulsive acts of violence have an underlying basis of sexual conflicts. The sexual dynamics may be overt as in cases of rape or sex murder; or they may be covert as in some break and entries, muggings, or robberies, so that the sexual dynamics can be elicited only through careful clinical examination and with the aid of psychological tests (Schlesinger & Kutash, 1981) or narcoanalysis.

With this brief introduction in mind, we will now consider how the motivational spectrum may be of help in predicting future violence.

Prediction with a History of Violence

Whether or not there is a history of repeated violence or a recent or distant history of a single act of violence, the prognostic evaluation does not change substantially. The motivational stimuli for the violent act should always be evaluated within the context of the offender's ego organization, ethical standards, and capacity for empathy (Kozol et al., 1972). In general, the situational offender has the best, and the compulsive offender has the worst prognosis in terms of repetitiveness. The prognosis for the socially stimulated offender depends on the social network to which he

returns. The impulsive individual typically has a better future than the more disturbed catathymic case.

Environmentally Motivated Offenses

Prediction with environmentally influenced offenders will depend largely on an
evaluation of their value systems, their maturity, and the milieus and associations to
which they will return. The probability of future violence was great, for example, in
the case of a 17-year-old male who had been arrested 12 different times for separate
incidents of violence occurring in conjunction with his youth gang. He remained attached to his gang—indeed, dependent on his gang membership, and participation
in gang violence, for his sense of identity.

Situationally Motivated Offenses

Situational offenders should be least likely to behave violently again. Wolfgang
(1958), for example, found that homicides stemming from domestic disputes (basically situational violence) are unlikely to be repeated. Halleck (1978) believes that
such perpetrators of situational violence cease to be a threat the moment after the act
has occurred. The type and amount of stress present and contributing to the situational event must be carefully studied, however, since recurrence of the stressor
could possibly, but not necessarily, result in another episode of violence. A typical
case of a situational murder (with a unique set of stressful conditions) with a good
prognosis is the following:

CASE 1

A 53-year-old businessman was evaluated to help in the determination of sanity as
he stood charged with the murder of a customer at one of his stores. J.G. owned
about ten dry cleaning stores in a blighted, inner-city area which had deteriorated
markedly in the past 15 years. Crime in the neighborhood of his businesses became
so serious that, in order to get employees to work for him, he had to erect bullet-
proof glass separating the customers from the cashiers. One week prior to the murder, his wife had been the victim of an assault and attempted rape at one of his
stores; the rape attempt was foiled when an employee of the store came to her aid.
Also during the week preceding the murder, one particular customer had continually
appeared at several of the locations demanding refunds, complaining, and making
harsh accusations of improper treatment. On the day of the murder, J.G. was called
to settle an argument between that customer and a female cashier. The argument es-
calated, and the owner, wearing a licensed gun that was visible, could not calm the
irate customer. As tensions increased, the customer threw an adding machine at
J.G. and began to climb over the counter to jump at him. At this, J.G. drew his
gun, shot the man, and killed him. Another customer was injured as the bullet
ricocheted.

J.G. showed no evidence of significant psychopathology—either clinically, on
the psychological tests, or by history. He was a stable, middle-class individual who,

like other merchants in the area, carried a gun only because the police had recommended it. The background of tremendous stress, fear, and intimidation contributed to this situationally induced homicide. If it were not for the generalized stress of his business, the specific stress of the events of the week prior to the incident, and the immediate provocation, J.G. would probably never have acted violently.

Thus, in evaluating an offender's potential future dangerousness, it is obviously important to know the facts concerning the offender's current offense, past history of violence, relevant personal characteristics, and social circumstances. In this regard, the following observation by Scott (1977) is perhaps worth keeping in mind:

> Before [such] factors can be considered they must be gathered. It is patience, thoroughness and persistence in this process, rather than any diagnostic or interviewing brilliance, that produces results. In this sense the telephone, the written request for past records, and the checking of information against other informants are the important diagnostic devices. (p. 129)

Impulsive Offenders

The impulsive offenders differ from the situational ones by the multiplicity of their antisocial acts and by their poor impulse control. Their violence, however, is not necessarily severe or homicidal. Their offenses are diffuse, poorly structured, and unpremeditated or only partially premeditated. Psychological evaluation of these individuals typically reveals a striking lack of personality integration. However, they are not necessarily explosive or overreactive to external stimuli but, instead, are often passive, easily led (sometimes into crime) and influenced to a great extent by external circumstances (Meissner, Mack, & Semrad, 1975). Chronic feelings of anger and revenge, low self-esteem, and compensatory strivings for recognition frequently contribute to the impulsive antisocial act (Wishnie, 1977). Prediction is difficult with impulsive offenders since the likelihood and magnitude of future violence on their part depends so much on the occurrence (or nonoccurrence) of chance circumstances.

The conception of the impulsive offender offered here cuts across prior diagnostic groupings and emphasizes the distinct characteristics of randomness of behavior. For example, an impulsive offender who commits homicide is not driven by a compelling need to kill. Instead, the homicide is just one circumstantial incident among other incidents of his life. In the experience of one of us (L.B.S.), many impulsive offenders were raised in families and social networks that were disorganized, and a smaller group had signs of congenital dysfunctions that seemed to have interfered with proper socialization, self-esteem, and personality integration. The following case typifies the impulsive offender who will in all likelihood continue to be involved in minor problems. He may or may not commit serious violent acts, however, depending on the circumstances in which he finds himself.

CASE 2

A 25-year-old male (A.D.) stabbed two people, one of whom died as a result. On the day of the incident, there was an argument between A.D. and the owner of a tavern who allegedly threatened A.D. with a hammer. In anger, A.D. left the tavern and returned with a knife to show that "no one could just walk all over me." At his return, the argument resumed and resulted in the impulsive stabbings of the victims.

When interviewed, A.D. had a tendency to gloss over and minimize the various aggressive acts in his past, presenting them as purely incidental, unrelated, and of little importance. There was a history of fighting, gambling, arrests for arguments with police officers, and domestic disputes. The police were frequently called to his home to quell heated arguments precipitated by suspected infidelity on the part of his wife. Psychological tests found him to be of low average intelligence, while projective tests elicited suspiciousness, emotional instability, and very poor self-concept. He was a drifter with unskilled jobs, and his entire life was characterized by lack of direction.

Catathymic Offenses

Acute catathymic acts of violence are typically one-shot incidents (Weiss, Lamberti, & Blackman, 1960; Blackman et al. 1963; Satten et al., 1960) resulting from a brief failure of ego function in an individual who is relatively well adjusted both before and after the episode (Medlicott, 1966), although the prognosis is less hopeful for individuals who are very disturbed and poorly integrated. In any event, an injury to the pride system is probably instrumental in provoking extreme (rageful) acute catathymic episodes (Ruotulo, 1968).

Revitch and Schlesinger (1981) have reported that the catathymic crisis in its pure form occurs within the framework of an ego-threatening relationship, which may activate "(a) [a feeling of] sexual inadequacy or an intensification of unresolved incestuous and homosexual conflicts (b) a transfer of negative emotions to the victim from another subject, so that the victim has only a symbolic significance for the offender; and (c) a feeling of helplessness and confusion" (p. 128). Whatever the releasing mechanism, the conflict, once triggered, appears to lead to unbearable tension, which is released through the violent act (for an example, see case 4).

In contrast to acute catathymic acts of violence, the chronic catathymic process can be repeated even after long prison terms if the underlying dynamics that led to the violence have not been resolved. One such individual, after serving a 20-year term for the murder of his girlfriend, killed his new girlfriend in a similar catathymic manner and then killed himself. Chronic catathymic violence commonly occurs within a boyfriend-girlfriend relationship. It is the relationship itself—and not its breakup—that shatters the perpetrator's psychological homeostasis (Revitch, 1965). Psychotherapy with emphasis on resolving such conflicts can help to prevent a future occurrence. (For description of a successful case followed for about 20 years, see Revitch and Schlesinger, 1981.)

Compulsive Offenders*

Individuals who have a history of serious violence of a seemingly compulsive nature are obviously powerfully disposed to violence and may well act violently again even after lengthy prison terms or hospital stays. Indeed, there are numerous accounts of individuals who committed bizarre murders after having served lengthy prison sentences for similar homicides (e.g., Guttmacher, 1951, 1963; Kozol et al., 1966, 1972). The following case of compulsive fetishism resulting in murder, previously reported elsewhere (Schlesinger & Revitch, 1980), illustrates the strength of the compulsion that this type of offender is often unable to conquer:

CASE 3

In the early 1950s, A.A. was apprehended for bizarre solo break and entries that were apparently sexually motivated. While in psychotherapy with an experienced forensic psychiatrist, he was arrested after killing a woman by stabbing her repeatedly. Before he killed her, he had followed her in his car for 30 miles because he became sexually stimulated at the sight of her black leather gloves. A.A. was also under suspicion for several other murders at the time, but he never confessed to them and was not convicted of them. While in prison, he earned a master's degree and essentially became a model prisoner. He was released on parole in the 1970s to attend college.

During his first week out, he seriously assaulted seven women after becoming stimulated by their black leather apparel. After another imprisonment, and parole in 1981, he was again arrested for attempted murder of a woman wearing a black leather coat. When interviewed by one of us (L.B.S.) shortly after his second imprisonment, he stated that for years he had fantasized about "holding women who wore leather." He described headaches and tremendous frustration to the point of explosive angry episodes to relieve tension when the act could not be accomplished. While he was in the structured world of prison, he was able to control the compulsive urge to deal with the accompanying psychic tension. After he was released, however, his own controls were too fragile, and he acted out even though he stated that he absolutely did not want to do it.

Careful examination of the patient's fantasy life is thus particularly important when a compulsive process is suspected (whether or not the patient has yet acted violently). Especially in cases of gynocide and sexual assault there is frequently a history of sadistic fantasies. To elicit such dangerous fantasies, there is no substitute for a thorough, unhurried interview. Some projective psychological tests, most notably the thematic techniques, may also be helpful (Schlesinger & Kutash, 1981).

However, the patient often will not reveal such fantasies, even though he is har-

---

*Both obsessive-compulsive neurotics and compulsive offenders experience a compelling urge for some type of acting out, but the clinical features of the acting out and the underlying dynamics have nothing in common (Revitch & Schlesinger, 1981).

boring them. Moreover, compulsive offenders may sometimes evidence consider-able insight into their condition and yet retain their compulsive tendencies. Thus, compulsive offenders who have been in confinement for some period of time may evidence few signs of continued dangerousness, and their continued dangerousness may easily escape detection—especially if insufficient weight is given to the details of their compulsive history. But, given the severity of the compulsive disorder—es-pecially when there is a history of repeated violence or violence mixed with sexual impulses—extreme caution should be exercised before any presumption of non-dangerousness is arrived at in such cases. (The dynamics and evaluation of the com-pulsive offender will be discussed further.)

Prediction Based on a Nonrecent History of Violence

How can dangerousness be evaluated regarding individuals who have acted vio-lently in the (nonrecent) past but who have been in confinement, and peaceably so, for lengthy periods of time? We have already suggested that, in such instances, a simple, commonsense principle should guide efforts at prediction: If it can be dem-onstrated that the individual retains the same complex of attitudes and psychody-namics and, if released, is likely to confront the same sort of circumstances that led to violence in the past, it should be strongly suspected that, if released, the individ-ual will act violently again. Many obvious examples could be offered to illustrate this principle (e.g., career criminals who clearly retain their allegiance to their crim-inal subculture; paranoid individuals who clearly retain the delusions that led to vio-lence and who are likely (if released) to again be faced with the kind of situation(s) that led to violent action in the past).

But what of previously violent individuals who no longer clearly evidence the at-titudes or delusions or personality traits that led to violence in the past? How can it be determined if the individual still harbors the psychodynamics or intentions that led to violence in the past? And how can mental health professionals predict whether delusions in remission will reoccur if a previously delusional individual is released to the open community and its accompanying stresses?

Without suggesting that there are validated answers to these questions, on logical and experiential grounds the following hypotheses can be offered:

1.   As Kozol and associates (1972, p. 379) have observed, "The essence of dan-gerousness appears to be a paucity of feeling-concern for others. . . . The potential for injuring another is compounded when this lack of concern is coupled with an-ger." And as Scott (1977, p. 140) has observed: "Unless there is some recognizable sympathy for others, and revulsion at causing suffering, there is always a vulnera-bility to situational aggressive impulses which are bound to recur." Thus, a thor-ough evaluation of the patient's ability to empathize with the pain of others (and of the patient's feelings toward others like his or her previous victims) is crucial. In this regard, both stress interviews and psychological tests may be useful. In particu-lar, every effort should be made to have the interviewee vividly imagine—and in-deed "relive"—his or her past violent acts to determine if he or she truly experi-

ences revulsion at the thought of such violence, and if he or she can truly empathize with—indeed, vicariously experience—the pain of his or her victim. (Verbal expressions of guilt and remorse are perhaps more easily manufactured than emotional and behavioral expressions of empathy.) Efforts should also be made to have the interviewee vividly imagine in detail how he or she would now react to circumstances like those that triggered violence (or threats of violence) in the past. If the individual strenuously resists doing so, it would strongly suggest that he or she is still unable to deal with the affects that led to violence in the past.

1a.   Similarly, projective testing may be extremely useful in evaluating a patient's underlying sense of relatedness (or nonrelatedness) to, or dehumanization of, other human beings; the extent to which themes of violence continue to pervade his or her fantasy life; and whether primitive impulses remain prepotent (though otherwise well hidden) in the individual's psyche. (For a more detailed discussion of the use of psychological tests in evaluating dangerousness, see Revitch and Schlesinger, 1978, pp. 142–144; 1981, pp. 24–46.)

1b.   The starting point for evaluating the patient's dangerousness, however, should be a "meticulous description" and evaluation of the patient's past violence (Kozol et al., 1972, p. 384). Indeed, Kozol et al. have observed that their "most serious errors in diagnosis have been made when [they] ignored the details in the description of the assault."

2.   Group therapy may also be useful—if not indispensable—in determining whether a previously violent offender still lacks "genuine empathy" for others.

Evidence of this sort [may] be impossible to acquire in any other way. . . . The mercurial flashpoint(s) of a dynamic group [often provides for the] disclosure of the patient's inner world. . . . The dynamics of the situation are far removed from those of a formal assessment session, in which he may well be asking himself about the wisdom of making a particular reply to a question. . . . [And the] spontaneity [of the group] offers us an insight into the ways in which the patient deals with unknown situations. (Cox, 1982, p. 83)

Cox (1982) has also suggested that group therapy may be useful in ferreting out powerfully felt (but generally suppressed) drives toward violence.

[An] important theme [is] a patient's "sense of inevitability" about his history. . . . [This] refers not only to the psychotic patient's act of obedience to a divine injunction to kill. It also refers to a more pervasive, though difficult to define, awareness that a non-psychotic patient has of inevitability of his yet unexperienced future offense —. . ."these are the tracks and I'm on them." This [is] extremely sinister. . . .

The most sinister constellation of all is when a patient experiences a sense of inevitability about his history and, at the same time, has an awareness that a previous offense was only "partial" (albeit fatal to the victim), so that he has a sense of unfinished business. . . . [A] patient who is in a therapeutic group with its spontaneously evolving, unpredictable emotional life, tending to mobilize disclosure potential may, for the first time, declare within such a group that it is unfinished business which preoccupies him. (pp. 86–87)

3.   Determining the patient's level of insight regarding the genesis and dynamics of his or her previous violence (and violent intentions) can be crucial—especially when the individual is not psychopathic, denies violent (or paranoid) attitudes, and has been cooperative, friendly, and even helpful to others in the institution. To the extent that an individual's violence in the past stemmed from, and was a defense against, psychic pain, evidence that the individual understands and can nonviolently deal with his or her emotional difficulties and vulnerabilities is a positive prognostic sign. Some offenders, however, particularly psychopathic and compulsive offenders, may well be able to give the appearance of having considerable insight regarding the genesis of their past difficulties or, at least, of understanding how to deal with stress-provoking situations in a nonviolent way in the future while still retaining their most deep-seated, and most dangerous, pathology. However, if the patient cannot achieve a meaningful (i.e., seemingly accurate and affect-laden) understanding of the psychological forces, defects, and vulnerabilities that led to his or her previous violence, that would strongly suggest that the patient is still unable to deal with these forces. Therefore, if events again triggered off such forces and vulnerabilities, violence, as a means of psychic self-protection, would be likely to again ensue.*

4.   An even more important prognostic indicator than the patient's ability to understand the roots of his or her previous violence, however, may be the patient's level of self-esteem—and his or her ability to relate to other people well enough to maintain self-esteem. To the extent that a patient's previous violence stemmed from a blow (or blows) to his or her self-esteem, or a need to gain self-esteem, as is frequently the case (Cox, 1982, p. 82), indications that the patient remains highly susceptible to overwhelming feelings of worthlessness or emptiness (Wishnie, 1977) should be worrisome signs (even if the patient understands having these feelings and that they led to violence in the past—though, to be sure, insight is an important step toward controlling and overcoming such powerful and destructive feelings). Similarly, to the extent that a patient's lack of self-esteem—and resulting violence—has stemmed from perceived rejections from significant others (or symbolic representatives of significant others), a positive prognostic sign would be evidence that the patient has developed a sufficient ability to relate well to others (and sufficient confidence in that ability) to be able to avoid or withstand continuing rejections or loneliness. Conversely, the persistence of severe interpersonal difficulties suggests that the patient has yet to overcome his or her deepest psychological problems and that away from a protective environment the patient is likely to suffer, and suffer from, continued rejection.

---

*The use of stress interviews, observing the patient in intensive group interactions, and evaluating the patient's level of insight regarding previous violent tendencies may also help to determine if individuals who previously threatened violence are still harboring (though denying) violent intentions.

Dix (1975) found that criteria similar to those suggested here (namely, whether or not the patient accepted personal responsibility for his or her offenses and was able to articulate nonviolent resolutions of stress-producing situations;* the nature of the patient's fantasy life; the patient's behavior in the hospital; and the nature of the circumstances to which the patient was likely to return if released) were used to determine the current dangerousness of convicted and institutionalized "psychologically abnormal sex offenders" (cf. Cohen et. al., 1978). Dix objected to reliance on these criteria, however, because of the lack of "established and quantifiable relationships" (p. 340) between such criteria and actual dangerousness. However, as we suggested in section I, it is impossible to validate many assumed indices of dangerousness (such as these) without releasing into freedom precisely those individuals who are most certainly believed to be most seriously dangerous. Thus, mental health professionals and the legal system will have to continue to rely on clinical logic (and common sense) to justify many determinations of dangerousness.**

It might be useful, however, to retroactively examine release decisions by mental health professionals (or legal authorities) that went awry (i.e., that resulted in unjustified violence by the released patients) to determine if and when (and how) such errors could be avoided (without unduly increasing the incidence of false-positives). Similarly, a study involving (1) intensive clinical examinations and follow-ups of mentally disturbed (but not insane) convicted offenders soon to be released from confinement (such as reported by Kozol et al., 1972) *and* (2) a reexamination and retrospective analysis of those releasees who continued to offend (not reported by Kozol et al.) might also yield results that would be useful in making future release decisions (though, again, the problem of false-positives would have to be kept in mind and evaluated). To our knowledge, however, such studies have yet to be done (see also Mulvey & Lidz, 1985).

Prediction with the Paranoid, Organic, and Toxic Group

Predicting future violence by individuals who previously committed acts of violence as a result of paranoid delusions may be fairly simple in certain such cases. Swanson and colleagues (1970) have mentioned the high frequency of morbid jealousy and paranoid delusions as a cause of homicide and other aggressive acts. Lanzkron (1963) sampled 150 mental patients charged with murder and found that 37.3 percent had paranoid delusions and that 20 percent had pathological jealousy as the trigger for their crime. In numerous studies (see, for example, Inamdor, Lewis, Siomopoulos, Shanok, & Lamela, 1982; Phillips & Nasr, 1983), acute psychosis, particularly paranoid psychosis, has been statistically associated with violent behav-

---

*We suggest that a patient's level of self-esteem and his or her degree of insight regarding the psychogenesis of his or her previous violence are better (i.e., deeper and less easily manufactured) prognostic indicators than merely accepting personal responsibility for such violence or being able to articulate nonviolent ways of dealing with stress-producing situations in the future.

**Insanity defense acquittees may, constitutionally, be required to bear the burden of proving that they are no longer dangerous in order to gain their release from confinement (*Jones v. United States*, 1983).

ior among hospitalized patients. Obviously, if the individual's violence was a direct result of the paranoid illness, the likelihood of repetition depends on the degree to which the illness can be controlled (perhaps with medication or other forms of intervention). Some cases of chronic schizophrenia are intractable; therefore, the patient may remain highly dangerous despite years of hospitalization and treatment. Since there is a whole spectrum of paranoid conditions with various degrees of personality disorganization—ranging from paranoid personality, which often blends imperceptibly with normal behavior, through paranoia, to the more disorganized cases of schizophrenia—lack of florid symptoms and adequate hospital adjustment should not be the sole basis of prognostication. In addition, every effort should be made to determine whether persistent violence-laden delusions exist. Simple, direct questions are often very useful in this regard.

A similar approach can be taken with individuals whose past violence was a direct outgrowth of an organic disorder. Here, however, the connection between violence and brain injury is not as direct as in the paranoid cases. There is much more debate about the role of various organic pathologies in violence; therefore, arriving at a conclusion that the violence was solely a result of organicity is much more difficult; consequently, prediction in these areas is also more difficult (see, e.g., Lewis, 1975; Mark & Ervin, 1970; Leicester, 1982). For example, several curious cases reported in the literature indicate, that ictal manifestations cannot easily be distinguished from purely psychogenic manifestations, so that it often "becomes a matter of speculation whether the disturbance is physiogenic—epileptic; or psychogenic—neurotic" (Williams, 1956, p. 29).

If an individual has a history of repeated violence when under the influence of various intoxicants and is nonviolent when not under the influence, the prediction problem is obvious: The question becomes whether or not the individual is likely to be able to refrain from using intoxicants in the future—and how that can be determined. The most commonly used substance connected with violent and aggressive behavior is alcohol. In Wolfgang's (1958) classic study of homicides committed in Philadelphia, 54 percent of the offenders and 53 percent of the victims were under the influence of alcohol. Mayfield (1975, p. 290) concludes that most alcoholic murders are impulsive and unplanned, committed for frivolous reasons, and distinguished by "a mutual state of intoxication and a readily available and lethal weapon." Under the influence of alcohol, some premorbidly aggressive individuals become more aggressive; however, some seem to be relieved of their aggressive feelings while intoxicated. Moreover, some passive people may become extremely violent under the influence of alcohol, because their pent-up hostility is thereby released.

Of all the abused substances, phencyclidine (PCP or "angel dust") is most likely to cause extreme violence. Acute intoxication with PCP induces feelings of estrangement, expansion of time, poor muscular coordination, increased sense of strength, auditory and visual hallucinations, and anxiety with a sense of impending doom. PCP may cause an acute florid psychosis, which may not remit for several months. Patients are a danger to others "because of paranoia and strong tendencies towards violence" (Peterson & Stillman, 1979, p. 142). Amphetamine abuse frequently results in paranoid psychosis with excitement. Ellinwood (1971) has reported 13 cases of homicide by offenders under the influence of this drug. Other drugs reported as causes of severe violence are secobarbital (Tinkleberg, Murphy, Darley, Roth, & Kopell, 1974), lysergic acid diethylamide (Reich & Hepps, 1972), and to a lesser extent various inhalants (Cohen, 1975).

Prediction without a History of Violence but with Current Intentions

MacDonald (1963, 1967, 1968) was one of the first to stress the prognostic importance of homicidal threats: "Whether the threat is uttered briefly or bombastically, seriously or in jest, in anger or in deceptive calm, as an offhand comment or accompanied by assault, the outcome may be tragedy" (MacDonald, 1967, p. 149). As noted in section I, it is ethically impossible to carry out well-controlled studies to determine when threats of violence should or should not be taken seriously. MacDonald (1967) concluded, however, that prognostic factors associated with a threat to commit violence are (1) the absence of suicide attempts, (2) severe current stresses, (3) the presence of weapons, and (4) the presence of a potential victim who might provoke an attack.

Many chronic catathymic homicides and attacks could have been prevented if the perpetrator's intentions had been taken seriously. Wertham's (1978) five-stage description of the catathymic crisis can be simplified into just three stages: (1) incubation, (2) violent act, (3) relief. It is during the incubation stage that the offender becomes obsessively preoccupied with the prospective victim; struggles against a surging need to commit violence; and often informs friends, clergymen, or others of his intentions to explode. Indeed, such an individual often seeks the help of mental health professionals. Much of the time, however, his warning is minimized, misunderstood, or ignored.

As mentioned, the accumulated catathymic tension is typically released against some individual who is in close relationship with the offender. Yet sometimes the violence may be directed at a stranger or a group of strangers. A notorious case of mass murder preceded by statements of intentions to kill was that of Charles Whitman, who murdered 12 and wounded 31 individuals from a tower on the University of Texas campus. Whitman had told his psychiatrist of "overwhelming periods of hostility" and of his fantasy to commit mass murder (Nevins, 1966). As in many cases, the warning, a possible cry for help, was not taken seriously. The description of Whitman's behavior the night before the event suggests depression, preoccupation, and a decision to commit the act—all classic signs of the incubation phase of the chronic catathymic process. The following case of an individual whose warning of an intention to kill was also not taken seriously is illustrative:

CASE 4

A 29-year-old male (G.W.) and his 26-year-old wife began having marital problems shortly after their two-year union began. G.W. stated, "She always went back to her parents when we had an argument or a problem." After several brief separations, the wife decided to file for divorce and remained at her parents' home. G.W. became depressed and sought treatment at a local mental health center. His depression intensified as the holidays approached, and he toyed with suicide. Then his suicidal ideas transformed into a preoccupation with violence. He told his therapist that he intended to kill his wife, but the therapist did not take him seriously. G.W. then bought a gun and showed it to his wife "to try to get her to come back"; but this action, though related by the patient, still did not alert the treating psychiatrist. On Christmas Eve, G.W. followed his wife home from church and killed her with multiple shots to the head. After he shot her, he expressed his love for her and kissed her. In this case the incubation phase of the catathymic process was preceded by depression and suicidal preoccupation, later mixed with and finally diminished by homicidal drive. Unfortunately, the psychiatrist mistakenly believed that there was little danger "because G.W. expressed himself in therapy—he brought it up and didn't hide it."

The prognostic failure here was not due to the lack of any specific interviewing technique. Rather, it was due to the failure to recognize that the patient's preoccupation with violence was the outgrowth of a severe and building catathymic crisis. In other instances, however, a failure to take due account of a patient's violent ideation or intentions may be due to a failure to elicit sufficient information from the patient —perhaps because the clinician is uncomfortable with or frightened by violent ideation. As Kutzer and Lion (1984) have observed, "The biggest obstacle to assessment is the clinician's denial" (p. 71).

> Overt homicidal ideation and the availability of a victim . . . signal the need for limits . . . until the situation can be resolved. The clinician should inquire about the availability of weapons. He or she should also query the use of an automobile, which should also be considered a weapon. . . . Finally and most obviously, the clinician should ask the patient outright how violent he or she has ever been and what the most violent thing he or she has ever done is. (See also MacDonald, 1976.)

If the clinician is uncertain of his patient's intentions, further examination is necessary to help uncover an underlying delusion, a building catathymic process, or merely a serious ego-syntonic idea to commit violence. Certainly, if drugs or alcohol are involved, or if the individual is experiencing severe stress, the risk of violence is greater.

Prediction without a History of Violence or Specific Intentions

Compulsive offenders rarely reveal their intention to act violently. They are mostly introverted, isolated, schizoid individuals who harbor intense fantasies of a violent nature but do not share these fantasies with others. Fantasy may serve as a "substitute for action," but it also may "prepare the way" for action (Beres, 1961). At times the inner urge to act out is so strong that the attempt to resist it may bring on anxiety with somatic manifestations. William Heirens, famous for saying, "Catch me before I kill more, I can't help myself," reported tearing bed sheets, drawing up and destroying plans, and breaking into a sweat when he tried to contain the compulsion to kill women (Kennedy, Hoffman, & Haines, 1947). All this goes on within the individual, and even those close to him are frequently unaware of the pressure with which he secretly struggles.

In one case reported by Revitch and Schlesinger (1978) fantasies of attacking women went on for 30 years before the first episode of actual violence took place. Similarly, in the case of many compulsive offenders, sexual conflicts—including hostility to women, preoccupation with maternal sexual conduct, overt or covert incestuous preoccupations, guilt over and rejection of sex as impure, feelings of sexual inferiority, and, at times, a need to completely possess the victim or whatever she may represent—are present long before any act of violence emerges.*

Thus, while compulsive offenders may have little history of serious antisocial tendencies prior to committing their first violent (or criminal) act, many do have a history of contacts with mental health workers prior to acting out their compulsions or expressing directly any intention to do so. And clinical experiences suggest that the following signs are indicative of an underlying compulsive syndrome. Indeed, when seen in combination, they should alert the psychologist to the possibility of severe dangerousness, even if the individual is not psychotic, has no history of violence, and has not directly expressed an intent to commit violence:

1. A history of mistreatment of women or fantasies of assaulting women
2. Breaking and entering committed alone and under bizarre circumstances
3. Fetishism for female underclothing and destruction of female clothes
4. Expressions of hatred, contempt, or, more important, fear of women
6. Dislike for cats or actual violence against cats or other animals
6. Violent and primitive fantasy life
7. Confusion of sexual identity, as elicited on projective tests
8. Sexual inhibitions and moral preoccupation with sexual conduct
9. Feelings of isolation and blurring of reality boundaries

These clinical signs are of even greater prognostic importance in some cases than a history of a violent act. The most violent act, even murder, may be situational and may offer a good prognosis. Some nonviolent acts, such as stealing female undergarments and destroying them, may end with gynocide.

---

*Hostility to women is outstanding in adult cases; whereas adolescents are chiefly concerned with maternal sexual conduct and sexual morality (Revitch, 1965). In almost all compulsive cases, there is some unhealthy emotional involvement with the mother. The mother may be rejecting or punitive, or she may be seductive, overprotective, and infantilizing. In other cases there is sexual stimulation of the son, who may know about or witness the mother's sexual activities. In all these cases, repressed incestuous feelings may be the main dynamic leading to sexual violence. In other words, sexual-motivated gynocide is often a displaced matricide.

The following case describes a dangerous adolescent who, prior to the described act of violence, had no history of violence and had not revealed any intention to act violently. Yet he had many of the characteristics just described, which could have been easily elicited with proper questioning.

CASE 5

L.A. was a 16-year-old male referred for psychological evaluation after being apprehended for breaking and entering and assault. There were three break-ins. During the first, L.A. defecated on one of the beds and rummaged through drawers looking for female undergarments. During the second, he broke a bottle over the head of the 17-year-old female occupant and later made an obscene call to her where he stated: "Next time you'll be pregnant." When he attempted to break in a third time, he was apprehended by a neighbor.

Even prior to any evidence of acting-out of violence, when presented with a case of this type, mental health professionals should seriously consider taking preventative action to protect potential victims. Such action might include (1) immediate involvement of the patient in individual psychotherapy together with close monitoring of the patient's behavior by responsible family members; (2) encouraging the patient to accept voluntary hospitalization for more intensive evaluation and treatment; and (3) perhaps warning any individual whom the patient has identified as a potential victim (cf. *McIntosh v. Milano*, 1979; *Tarasoff v. Regents*, 1976; *Jablonski v. United States*, 1983; Shapiro, 1983; *Behavioral Sciences and the Law*, 1984).

CONCLUSION

We suggest that mental health professionals can play a legitimate—and even an indispensable—role in assessing the dangerousness of previously or potentially violent individuals. To be sure, predictions of violence should not be given credence merely because they are offered by a mental health professional. Rather, they should be given credence only when they are supported by concrete evidence and persuasive logic. But, like other professional investigators, mental health professionals, by using specialized assessment techniques, may be able to discover evidence relevant to assessments of dangerousness that is not readily ascertainable by lay persons. Like experts in other fields, they can help legal authorities to understand the meaning of the evidence that is before them when assessments of dangerousness are in issue. And just as the ability to recognize the import of particular patterns of phenomena is often the mark of expertise, at least in certain circumstances (and when knowledgeable about the predictive task at issue), mental health professionals may be uniquely aware of and able to perceive syndromes of attitudes, affects, and behavior that are indicative of potential violence.

REFERENCES

Addington v. Texas (1979). 441 U.S. 418.

American Psychiatric Association (1974). *Clinical Aspects of the Violent Individual.* Washington, D.C.: American Psychiatric Association.

American Psychological Association (1978). Report of the Task force on the Role of Psychology in the Criminal Justice System. *American Psychologist, 33,* 1099–1113.

Applebaum, P. S. (1984), Hypotheticals, psychiatric testimony, and the death sentence. *Bulletin of the American Academy of Psychiatry and the Law, 12,* 169–177.

Bach-y-Rita, G., Lion, J. R. Climent, C. E., and Ervin, F. R. (1971). Episodic dyscontrol: A study of 130 violent patients. *American Journal of Psychiatry, 127,* 1473–1478.

Bach-y-Rita, G., & Veno, A. (1974). Habitual violence: A profile of 62 men. *American Journal of Psychiatry, 131,* 154–217.

Barefoot v. Estelle (1983). 77 L. Ed. 2d 1090.

Baxtrom v. Herald (1966). 383 U.S. 107.

Beck, J. C. (1982). When the patient threatens violence: An empirical study of clinical practice after Tarasoff. *Bulletin of the American Academy of Psychiatry and the Law, 10,* 189–201.

Behavioral Sciences and the Law (1984). Duty to Warn Third Parties. *2,* 235–329.

Bennett v. Jeffries (1976). 10 N.Y. 2d 543, 356 N.E. 2d 277, 387 N.Y.S. 2d 821.

Blackman, N., Weiss, J. M. A, and Lamberti, J. W. (1963). The sudden murderer. *Archives of General Psychiatry, 8,* 289–294.

Bottoms, A. E., & Brownsword, R. (1983). Dangerousness and rights. In J. W. Hinton (Ed.), *Dangerousness: Problems of assessment and prediction,* (pp. 9–22). London: George Allen and Unwin.

Brancale, R. (1955). Problems of classification. *National Probation and Parol Association Journal, 1,* 118–125.

Burquest, B. (1981). The violent girl. *Adolescence, 16,* 749–764.

Clark, R. (1971). *Crime in America.* New York: Pocket Books.

Cohen, M. L., Groth, A. N., & Siegel, R. (1978). The clinical prediction of dangerousness. *Crime and Delinquency, 24,* 28–39.

Cohen, S. (1975, October). Inhalant abuse. *Drug and Alcoholism Newsletter.*

Cocozza, J. J., & Steadman, H. J. (1974). Some refinements in the measurement of dangerous behavior. *American Journal of Psychiatry, 131,* 1012–1014.

Cocozza, J. J., & Steadman, H. J. (1976). The failure of psychiatric predictions of dangerousness: Clear and convincing evidence. *Rutgers Law Review, 29,* 1084–1101.

Cocozza, J. J., & Steadman, H. J. (1978). Prediction in psychiatry: An example of misplaced confidence in experts. *Social Problems, 25,* 265–276.

Cox, M. (1982). The psychotherapist as assessor of dangerousness. In J. R. Hamilton & H. Freeman (Eds.), *Dangerousness: Psychiatric assessment and management,* (pp. 81–87). London: Gaskell.

Dembitz, N. (1978). New standards for juvenile justice. *New York Law Journal,* December 28, p. 26.

Diamond, B. L. (1959). The fallacy of the impartial expert. *Archives of Criminal Psychodynamics, 3*, 221–236.

Dix, G. E. (1975). Determining the continued dangerousness of psychologically abnormal sex offenders. *Journal of Psychiatry and the Law, 3*, 327–334.

Dix, G. E. (1980). Clinical evaluation of the "dangerousness" of "normal" criminal defendants. *Virginia Law Review, 66*, 523–581.

Dix, G. E. (1983). A legal perspective on dangerousness: Current status. *Psychiatric Annals, 13*, 243–256.

Ellinwood, E. H. (1971). Assault and homicide associated with amphetamine abuse. *American Journal of Psychiatry, 127*, 1170–1175.

Ennis, B. J., & Emery, R. (1978). *The rights of mental patients.* New York: Avon.

Ennis, B. J., & Litwack, T. R. (1974). Psychiatry and the presumption of expertise: Flipping coins in the courtroom. *California Law Review, 62*, 693–752.

Ervin, F., & Lion, J. (1969). Clinical evaluation of the violent patient. In D. Mulvihill & M. Tunin (Eds.), *Crimes of violence.* Washington, D.C.: U.S. Government Printing Office.

Gayral, L., Millet, G., Moron, P., & Turnin, J. (1956). Crises et paroxysmes catathymiques. *Annales Medico-Psychologiques, 114*, 25–50.

Gelles, R. J. (1973). Child abuse as psychopathology: A sociological critique and reformulation. *American Journal of Orthopsychiatry, 43*, 611–621.

Gordon, R. A. (1977). A critique of the evaluation of Patuxent institution with particular attention to the issues of dangerousness and recidivism. *Bulletin of the American Academy of Psychiatry and the Law, 5*, 210–255.

Gunn, J. (1982). An English psychiatrist looks at dangerousness. *Bulletin of the American Academy of Psychiatry and the Law, 10*, 143–152.

Guttmacher, M. (1951). *Sex offense: The problem, causes and prevention.* New York: Norton.

Guttmacher, M. (1963). Dangerous offenders. *Crime and delinquency, 9*, 381–390.

Hall, H. V. (1982). Dangerous predictions and the maligned forensic professional: Suggestions for detecting distortions of true basal violence. *Criminal Justice and Behavior, 9*, 3–12.

Hall, H. V. (1984). Predicting dangerousness for the court. *American Journal of Forensic Psychology, 2*, 5–25.

Halleck, S. (1971). *Psychiatry and the dilemmas of crime.* Los Angeles: University of California Press.

Halleck, S. (1978). Violence: Treatment versus correction. In I. L. Kutash, S. B. Kutash, & L. B. Schlesinger (Eds.), *Violence: Perspectives on murder and aggression.* San Francisco: Jossey-Bass.

Harding, T. W., & Adserballe, H. (1983). Assessments of dangerousness: Observation in six countries. *International Journal of Law and Psychiatry, 6*, 391–398.

Hillman, D. S., & Blackman N. (1966). Enuresis, firesetting and cruelty to animals: A triad predictive of adult crime. *American Journal of Psychiatry, 122*, 1431–1435.

Honig, A. L. (1982). *Assessing future dangerous behavior.* University Microfilms International.

Hooper, F. A., & Evans, R. G. (1984). Screening for disruptive behavior of institutionalized juvenile offenders. *Journal of Personality Assessment, 48*, 159–161.

Inamdar, S. C., Lewis, D. O., Siomopoulos, G., Shanok, S. S., & Lamela, M. (1982). Violent and suicidal behavior in psychotic adolescents. *American Journal of Psychiatry, 139*, 932–935.

Jablonski v. United States, 712 F. 2d 391 (9th Cir.) (1983).

Jones v. United States, 463 U.S. 354, 77 L. Ed. 2d 694, 103 S.Ct. 3043 (1983).

Jones, T., Beidleman, W. B., & Fowler, R. (1981). Differentiating violent and nonviolent prison inmates by use of selected MMPI scales. *Journal of Clinical Psychology, 37*, 673–678.

Jurek v. Texas, 428 U.S. 262, 49 L.Ed. 2d 929 (1976).

Kennedy, F., Hoffman, H. and Haines, W. (1947). A study of William Heirens. *American Journal of Psychiatry, 104*, 113–121.

Kozol, H. L., Boucher, R. J., & Garofalo, R. F. (1972). The diagnosis and treatment of dangerousness. *Crime and Delinquency, 19*, 371–392.

Kozol, H. L., Boucher, R. J., & Garofalo, R. F. (1973). Dangerousness: A reply to Monahan. *Crime and Delinquency, 19*, 554–555.

Kozol, H. L., Cohen, M. I., & Garofalo, R. F. (1966). The criminally dangerous sex offenders. *New England Journal of Medicine, 275*, 79–84.

Kutzer, D., & Lion, J. R. (1984). The violent patient: Assessment and intervention. In S. Saunders, A. M. Anderson, C. A. Hart, & G. M. Rubenstein (Eds.), *Violent individuals and families: A handbook for practitioners* (pp. 69–86). Springfield, IL: Charles C. Thomas.

Lanzkron, J. (1963). Murder and insanity. *American Journal of Psychiatry, 119*, 254–258.

Lefkowitz, M., Eron, L., Walder, L., & Heusmann, L. (1977). *Growing up to be violent.* New York: Pergamon Press.

Leicester, J. (1982). Temper tantrums, epilepsy and episodic dyscontrol. *British Journal of Psychiatry, 141*, 262–266.

Levinson, R. M., & Ramsay, G. (1979). Dangerousness, stress, and mental health evaluations. *Journal of Health and Social Behavior, 20*, 178–187.

Lewis, J. A. (1975). Violence and epilepsy. *Journal of the American Medical Association, 232*, 1165–1167.

Lion, J. R., Bach-y-Rita, G., & Ervin, F. R. (1969). Violent patients in the emergency room. *American Journal of Psychiatry, 125*, 1700–1711.

Litwack, T. R. (1984). The moral foundations of the insanity defense. *Criminal Justice Ethics, 3*, 12–19.

Litwack, T. R., Gerber, G. L., & Fenster, C. A. (1980). The proper role of psychology in child custody disputes. *Journal of Family Law, 18*, 269–300.

Livermore, J., Malmquist, C., & Meehl, P. (1968). On the justifications for civil commitment. *University of Pennsylvania Law Review, 117*, 75–96.

Lothstein, L. M., & Jones, P. (1978). Discriminating violent individuals by means of various psychological tests. *Journal of Personality Assessment, 42*, 237–243.

MacDonald, J. M. (1963). The threat to kill. *American Journal of Psychiatry, 120*, 125–130.

MacDonald, J. M. (1967). Homicidal threats. *American Journal of Psychiatry, 124*, 475–482.

MacDonald, J. M. (1968). Homicidal threats. Springfield, IL: Charles C. Thomas.

MacDonald, J. M. (1976). *Psychiatry and the criminal: A guide to psychiatric examination for the criminal courts (3rd ed.).* Springfield, IL: Charles C. Thomas.

Mark, V. M., & Ervin, F. R. (1970). *Violence and the brain.* New York: Harper & Row.

Mayfield, D. (1976). Alcoholism, alcohol intoxication and assaultive behavior. *Diseases of the Nervous System, 37*, 288–291.

McGuire, J. S. (1976). *Prediction of dangerous behavior in a federal correctional institution.* Unpublished doctoral dissertation, Tallahassee, Fl: Florida State University.

McIntosh v. Milano, 168 N.J. Super. 466, 403 A. 2d 500 (1979).

Medlicott, R. W. (1966). Brief psychotic episodes (temporary insanity). *New Zealand Medical Journal, 65*, 966–972.

Megargee, E. I. (1970). The prediction of violence with psychological tests. In C. Spielberger (Ed.), *Current topics in clinical and community psychology* (pp. 98–156). New York: Academic Press.

Megargee, E. I. (1976). The prediction of dangerous behavior. *Criminal Justice and Behavior, 3*, 3–22.

Megargee, E. I. (1981). Methodological problems in the prediction of violence. In J. R. Hays, T. K. Roberts, & K. S. Solway (Eds.), *Violence and the violent individual* (pp. 179–191). New York: Spectrum.

Megargee, E. I., & Bohn, M. J. (1979). *Classifying criminal offenders: A new system based on the MMPI.* Beverly Hills, CA: Sage.

Meissner, W. W., Mack, J. E., & Semrad, E. D. (1975). Themes of personality and psychopathology. In A. M. Freedman, H. I. Kaplan, & B. J. Sadock (Eds.), *Comprehensive textbook of psychiatry, Vol. 1.* Baltimore, MD: Williams and Wilkins.

Menninger, K. A., & Mayman, M. (1956). Episodic dyscontrol: A third order of stress adaptation. *Bulletin of the Menninger Clinic, 20*, 153–163.

Menzies, R. J. (1982). The parameters of psychiatric decision making: Clinical and legal determinants of forensic assessments. In C. D. Webster, R. J. Menzies, & M. A. Jackson (Eds.), *Clinical assessment before trial: Legal issues and mental disorder* (pp. 202–238). Toronto: Butterworths.

Menzies, R.J., Webster, C.D., & Butler, B.T. (1981). Perceptions of dangerousness among forensic psychiatrists. *Comprehensive Psychiatry, 22*, 387–396.

Menzies, R. J., Webster, C. D., & Sepejak, D. S. (1985). The dimensions of dangerousness: Evaluating the accuracy of psychometric predictions of violence among forensic patients. *Law and Human Behavior, 9*, 49–70.

Miller, D., & Looney, J. (1974). The prediction of adolescent homicide: Episodic dyscontrol and dehumanization. *American Journal of Psychoanalysis, 34*, 187–198.

Monahan, J. (1973). Dangerous offenders: A critique of Kozol et al. *Crime and Delinquency, 19*, 418–420.

Monahan, J. (1981). *Predicting violent behavior: An assessment of clinical techniques.* Beverly Hills, CA: Sage.

Monahan, J. (1984). The prediction of violent behavior: Toward a second generation of theory and policy. *American Journal of Psychiatry, 141*, 10–15.

Monahan, J., & Wexler, D. B. (1978). A definite maybe: Proof and probability in civil commitment. *Law and Human Behavior, 2*, 37–42.

Montandon, C., & Harding, T. (1984). The reliability of dangerousness assessments: A decision making exercise. *British Journal of Psychiatry, 144*, 149–155.

Monroe, R. R. (1970). *Episodic behavioral disorders*. Boston: Harvard University Press.

Moore, M. H., Estrich, S. R., McGillis, D., & Spelman, W. (1984). *Dangerous offenders: The elusive target of justice*. Cambridge, MA: Harvard University Press.

Mullen, J. M., & Reinehr, R. C. (1982). Predicting dangerousness of maximum security forensic mental patients. *Journal of Psychiatry and the Law, 10*, 223–231.

Mulvey, E. P., & Lidz, C. W. (1984). Clinical considerations in the prediction of dangerousness in mental patients. *Clinical Psychology Review, 4*, 379–401.

Mulvey, E. P., & Lidz, C. W. (1985). Back to basics: A critical analysis of dangerousness research in a new legal environment. *Law and Human Behavior, 9*, 209–219.

Murphy, T. (1980). *Michigan risk prediction: A replication study*. Lansing, MI: Department of Corrections Program Bureau.

Nevin, D. (1966). Charlie Whitman: The egale scout who grew up with a tortured mind. *Life, 11*, 28–31.

Novaco, R. (1975). *Anger Control: The Development and Evaluation of an Experimental Treatment*. Lexington, MA: D. C. Heath.

O'Connor v. Donaldson (1975). 422 U.S. 563.

Petersen, R. C., & Stillman, R. C. (1979). Phencyclidine: A review. *Journal of the Medical Society of New Jersey, 76*, 139–144.

Pfeffer, C., Plutchik, R., & Mizruchi, M. S. (1983). Prediction of assaultiveness in latency age children. *American Journal of Psychiatry, 140*, 31–35.

Pfohl, S. J. (1978). *Predicting dangerousness*. Lexington, MA: Lexington Books/D.C. Heath.

Phillips, P., & Nasr, S. J. (1983). Seclusion and restraint and prediction of violence. *American Journal of Psychiatry, 140*, 229–232.

Powers, R. J., & Kutash, I. L. (1978). Substance induced aggression. In I. L. Kutash, S. B. Kutash, & L. B. Schlesinger (Eds.), *Violence: Perspectives on Murder and Aggression*. San Francisco, Jossey-Bass.

Quinsey, V. L. (1980). The baserate problem and the predictions of dangerousness. *Journal of Psychiatry and Law, 8*, 329–340.

Quinsey, V. L., & Ambtman, R. (1979). Variables affecting psychiatrists' and teachers' assessments of the dangerousness of mentally ill offenders. *Journal of Consulting and Clinical Psychology, 47*, 353–362.

Rappeport, J. R. (1967). *The Clinical Evaluation of the Dangerousness of the Mentally Ill*. Springfield, IL: Charles C. Thomas.

Reich, P., & Hepps, R. B. (1972). Homicide during psychosis induced by LSD. *Journal of the American Medical Association, 219*, 869–871.

Reinhardt, H. E. (1979). Statistical theory and clinical practice in predicting rare phenomena. *Psychological Reports, 45*, 468–470.

Revitch, E. (1965). Sex murder and the potential sex murderer. *Diseases of the Nervous System, 20*, 640–648.

Revitch, E., & Schlesinger, L. B. (1978). Murder: Evaluation, Classification and Prediction. In I. L. Kutash, S. B. Kutash, & L. B. Schlesinger ((Eds.), *Violence: Perspectives on Murder and Aggression*, 138–164. San Francisco: Jossey-Bass.

Revitch, E., & Schlesinger, L. B. (1981). *Psychopathology of Homicide*. Springfield, IL: Charles C. Thomas.

Rofman, E. S., Askinazi, C., & Fant, E. (1980). The prediction of dangerous behavior in emergency civil commitment. *American Journal of Psychiatry, 137*, 1061–1064.

Rogers v. Okin, 634 F. 2d 650 (1st Cir.) (1980).

Ruotolo, A. (1968). Dynamics of sudden murder. *American Journal of Psychoanalysis, 28*, 162–176.

Satten, J., Menninger, K. A., & Mayman, M. (1960). Murder without apparent motive: A study in personality disorganization. *American Journal of Psychiatry, 117*, 48–53.

Schall v. Martin, 81 L. Ed. 2d 207. (1984).

Schlesinger, L. B. (1980). Distinctions between psychopathic, sociopathic and anti-social personality disorders. *Psychological Reports, 47*, 15–21.

Schlesinger, L. B., Benson, M. C., & Zornitzer, M. (1982). Classification of violent behavior for purposes of treatment planning: A three-pronged approach. In M. Roy (Ed.), *The abusive partner*. New York: Van Nostrand Rinehold.

Schlesinger, L. B., & Kutash, I. L. (1981). The criminal fantasy technique: A comparison of sex offenders and substance abusers. *Journal of Clinical Psychology, 37*, 210–218.

Schlesinger, L. B., & Revitch, E. (1980). Stress, violence and crime. In I. L. Kutash, S. B. Kutash, & L. B. Schlesinger (Eds.), *Handbook on stress and anxiety* (pp. 174–188). San Francisco: Jossey-Bass.

Schlesinger, L. B., & Revitch, E. (1983). Sexual dynamics in homicide and assault. In L. B. Schlesinger & E. Revitch (Eds.), *Sexual dynamics of anti-social behavior* (pp. 206–227). Springfield, IL: Charles C. Thomas.

Schlesinger, L. B., Zornitzer, M., & Benson, M. (1982). Classification of violence for purposes of treatment planning. In M. Roy (Ed.), *The Abusive Partner*, 148–169. New York: Van Nostrand Reinhold.

Schlesinger, S. E. (1978). The prediction of dangerousness in juveniles: A replication. *Crime and Delinquency, 24*, 40–48.

Scott, P. D. (1977). Assessing Dangerousness in Criminals. *British Journal of Psychiatry, 131*, 127–142.

Sedman, G. A. (1966). A comparative study of pseudohallucinations-imagery and hallucination. *British Journal of Psychiatry, 112*, 9–17.

Selby, M. J. (1984). Assessment of violence potential using measures of anger, hostility, and social desirability. *Journal of Personality Assessment, 48*, 531–544.

Sepejak, D., Menzies, R. J., Webster, C. D., & Jensen, F. A. S. (1983). Clinical predictions of dangerousness: Two-year follow-up of 408 pretrial forensic cases. *Bulletin of the American Academy of Psychiatry and the Law, 11*, 171–182.

Shah, S. A. (1978a). Dangerousness: A paradigm for exploring some issues in law and psychology. *American Psychologist, 33*, 224–238.

Shah, S. A. (1978b). Dangerousness and mental illness: Some conceptual, prediction, and policy dilemmas. In C. J. Frederick (Ed.), *Dangerous Behavior: A Problem in Law and Mental Health*, (DHEW Publication No. ADM 78-563), 153–191. Rockville, MD: National Institute of Mental Health.

Shah, S. A. (1981). Dangerousness: Conceptual, prediction, and public issues. In J. R. Hays, T. K. Roberts, & K. S. Solway (Eds.), *Violence and the Violent Individual*, 151–178. New York: Spectrum Publications.

Shapiro, (1983). The psychologist and the potentially violent patient: Guidelines in professional practice. *American Journal of Forensic Psychology, 1*, 13–27.

Shapiro, L., Cohen, M., & Bugden, W. (1959). Parole violation and the early development of internal controls: Preliminary report. *Archives of Criminal Psychodynamics, 3*, 254–259.

Steadman, H. J. (1977). A new look at recidivism among Patuxent inmates. *Bulletin of the American Academy of Psychiatry and the Law, 5*, 200–209.

Steadman, H. J. (1978). Employing psychiatric predictions of dangerous behavior: Policy vs. fact. In C. J. Frederick (Ed.), *Dangerous behavior: A problem in law and mental health*. DHEW Publication No. ADM 78-563, 123–136. Rockville, MD: National Institute of Mental Health.

Steadman, H. J. (1980). The right not to be a false positive: Problems in the application of the dangerousness standard. *Psychiatric Quarterly, 52*, 84–99.

Steadman, H. J. (1982). A situational approach to violence. *International Journal of Psychiatry and Law, 5*, 171–186.

Steadman, H. J. (1983). Predicting dangerousness among the mentally ill. Art, magic, and science. *International Journal of Law and Psychiatry, 6*, 381–390.

Steadman, H. J., & Cocozza, J. (1974). *Careers of the criminally insane*. Lexington, MA: D. C. Heath & Company.

Steadman, H. J., & Cocozza, J. (1978). Criminology: Psychiatry, dangerousness and the repetitively dangerous offender. *The Journal of Criminal Law and Criminology, 69*, 226–231.

Steadman, H. J. and Cocozza, J. (1980). The prediction of dangerousness—Baxtrom: A case study. In G. Cooke (Ed.), *The role of the forensic psychologist* (pp. 204–215). Springfield, IL: Charles C. Thomas.

Stone, A. A. (1975). Comment. *American Journal of Psychiatry, 132*, 829–831.

Swanson, D. W., Bohnert, P. J., & Smith, J. A. (1970). *The paranoid*. Boston: Little, Brown.

Tanay, E. (1969). Psychiatric study of homicide. *American Journal of Psychiatry, 125*, 1252–1258.

Tanay, E. (1975). Dangerousness and psychiatry. *Current Concepts in Psychiatry, 1*, 17–26.

Tarasoff v. Regents of the University of California, 17 Cal. 3d 425, 551 P. 2d 334, 131 Cal. Rptr. 14 (1976).

Thornberry, T. P., & Jacoby, J. E. (1979). *The criminally insane: A community follow-up of mentally ill offenders*. Chicago: University of Chicago Press.

Tinkleberg, J. R., Murphy, P. L., Darley, C. F., Roth, W. J., & Kopell, B. S. (1974). Drug involvement in criminal assaults by adolescents. *Archives of General Psychiatry, 30*, 685–689.

United States Dept. of Justice (1978). *Uniform Crime Reports*. Washington, DC: United States Government Printing Office.

Vanderplas, J. M., & Vanderplas, J. H. (1979). Multiple-versus single-index predictors of dangerousness, suicide, and other rare behaviors. *Psychological Reports, 45*, 343–349.

Webster, C. D., Menzies, R. J., & Jackson, M. A. (1982). *Clinical assessment before trial: Legal issues and mental disorder.* Toronto: Butterworths.

Webster, C. D., Sepejak, D. S., Menzies, R. J., Slomen, D. J., Jensen, F. A. S., & Butler, B. T. (1984). The reliability and validity of dangerous behavior predictions. *Bulletin of the American Academy of Psychiatry and the Law, 12*, 41–50.

Weiss, J. M. A., Lamberti, J. W., & Blackman, N. (1960) The sudden murderer. *Archives of General Psychiatry, 2*, 669–678.

Wenk,, E. A., & Emrich, R. L. (1972). Assaultive youth: An exploratory study of the assaultive experiences and assaultive potential of California Youth Authority wards. *Journal of Research in Crime and Delinquency, 9*, 171–196.

Wenk, E. A., Robison, J. O., & Smith, G. W. (1972). Can violence be predicted? *Crime and Delinquency, 18*, 393–402.

Werner, P. D., Rose, T. L., & Yesavage, J. A. (1983). Reliability, accuracy, and decision-making strategy in clinical predictions of imminent dangerousness. *Journal of Consulting and Clinical Psychology, 51*, 815–825.

Werner, P. D., Rose, T. L., Yesavage, J. A., & Seeman, K. (1984). Psychiatrists' judgments of dangerousness in patients on an acute care unit. *American Journal of Psychiatry, 141*, 263–266.

Wertham, F. (1937). The catathymic crisis: A clinical entity. *Archives of Neurology and Psychiatry, 37*, 974–977.

Wertham, F. (1978). The catathymic crisis. In I. L. Kutash, S. B. Kutash, & L. B. Schlesinger (Eds.), *Violence: Perspective on murder and aggression.* San Francisco: Jossey-Bass.

Wettstein, R. M. (1984). The prediction of violent behavior and the duty to protect third parties. *Behavioral Sciences and the Law, 2*, 291–317.

Williams, D. (1956). The structure of emotions reflected in epileptic experiences. *Brain, 79*, 29–67.

Wishnie, H. (1977). *The impulsive personality.* New York. Plenum.

Wolfgang, M. E. (1958). *Patterns of criminal homicide.* Philadelphia: University of Pennsylvania Press.

Yesavage, J. A. (1983). Bipolar illness: Correlates of dangerous inpatient behavior. *British Journal of Psychiatry, 143*, 554–557.

CHAPTER 10

Evaluating Eyewitness Testimony

GAIL S. GOODMAN and ANNETTE HAHN

The scientific study of eyewitness testimony has intensified dramatically in recent years. In fact, we are currently in the midst of an explosion of research aimed at specifying how well people remember real-life criminal events. Part of the fascination with this field derives from the willingness of many courts to permit psychologists to educate judges and jurors about eyewitness testimony. In educating the court, psychologists may testify as expert witnesses about relevant research findings or provide an evaluation of a specific witness. In either case, a firm grounding in current knowledge about eyewitness reports is essential.

We examine issues and research findings of importance to psychologists who serve as expert witnesses concerning eyewitness testimony. The literature in this field is extensive, so rather than reviewing it all, we focus on key issues. (For more in-depth coverage, several recent books and journals are available: see Goodman, 1984; Lloyd-Bostock & Clifford, 1983; Loftus, 1979a; Wells & Loftus, 1984; and Yarmey, 1979). Our goal is to present a more balanced view than is common in discussions of eyewitness testimony. Most research in this area and, consequently, most reviews focus on the inaccuracies of human memory. In contrast, we present evidence relevant to both accuracies and inaccuracies of eyewitness reports.

HUMAN MEMORY

The scientific study of eyewitness testimony capitalizes on a simple fact: An objective record of the original event is available against which to evaluate the witness's report. Without this, the validity of a witness's statements cannot be determined. For actual crimes, the availability of an objective record is extremely unlikely. There is usually no definitive way to know whether the witness's report—even a detailed one given with great confidence—is correct or not. Many clinical discussions of memory for traumatic events, while valuable as sources of anecdotal information, are seriously flawed because no objective record is available. In contrast, scientific studies of eyewitness testimony provide many replicable findings which can be used to evaluate a witness's report.

When a record of the original event is available, one finds that memory is not perfect. Eyewitness reports contain accuracies but inaccuracies as well. The presence of accuracies and inaccuracies is consistent with theories of memory that emphasize its reconstructive nature (e.g., Bartlett, 1932; Loftus, 1979a). A reconstructive approach proposes that memory is not like a videotape recorder which stores all information encountered. Instead, forgetting may occur, and human memory becomes an amalgamation of what actually happened (the source of accuracies) and what a person intuits, hears, or infers must have happened (sources of inaccuracies).

The reconstructive view of memory is generally accepted among psychologists who study human memory and eyewitness testimony, and it is the view taken here. But an important debate exists about whether memory for events can change irreversibly (as implied by the reconstructive view) or whether memories are more permanent (see Alba & Hasher, 1983; McCloskey & Egeth, 1983). Under the latter view, "forgetting" does not occur but retrieval failures do. That is, the original memory is retained but cannot be retrieved unless the right retrieval "cue" can be found. Without attempting to resolve this controversy here, we take the view that, for all practical purposes, memories may be permanently lost or changed because retrieval conditions may not be found—if indeed they exist—that can provide the cues needed to unleash the "true" memory.

According to a reconstructive approach, memory can be divided into three stages: acquisition, retention, and retrieval. Acquisition refers to the encoding of information into memory. Retention refers to the storage of information over time. Retrieval refers to the witness's ability to access what has been retained. Many factors—to be reviewed here—affect each of these stages and consequently affect witnesses' reports.

When a complex event such as a crime occurs (the *encoding* stage), it is impossible to attend to, mush less remember, every detail of the incident. Instead, people form a general interpretation of the event (e.g., "I'm being robbed") and encode what they can based on what seems most important, novel, and salient to them at the time (e.g., "He has a gun"). If a detail is only glimpsed but not throughly examined, a witness's expectations may distort what is seen—for example, a stick in an assailant's hand might be encoded as a gun. Thus, even at this early stage, a totally complete and accurate representation of the event is unlikely to be stored. During the *retention* stage, the interpretation of the event may be retained relatively well, but details may be readily forgotten or undergo further change and distortion. One source of memory change is misleading "postevent" information offered by other witnesses or interviewers. Finally, during the *retrieval* stage, when a witness tries to communicate his or her memory of what happened, the conditions of retrieval will have an important influence on what is remembered.

When psychologists testify in courts of law about eyewitness testimony, they often begin by explaining that memory can be divided into the three stages just described. We have therefore organized this chapter by first discussing factors that affect these three stages. Next we turn to issues specific to eyewitness identifications—that is, to people's ability to recognize culprits. Individual differences, such as intelligence, are then discussed. After examining these traditional topics, we explore what is known about the testimony of children and of crime victims—two important but often neglected classes of witnesses. Finally, we consider the impact of expert testimony on jurors' decisions and the ethical issues faced by experts who testify about eyewitness reports.

Acquisition

When a crime takes place, many factors affect how well a witness can encode the event. The crime (e.g., a mugging) may last only a few seconds, occur once, and be violent. On the other hand, the crime (e.g., incest) might last minutes or hours, take place repeatedly, and be committed with minimal force. Factors such as these will affect how well the witness can encode and later remember what happened.

Temporal Factors

A number of temporal factors influence a witness's ability to encode an event. One of the most significant is the length of time a witness has to view it. In general, the longer the exposure, the more accurate the witness's testimony (Clifford & Richards, 1977; Ellis, Davies, & Shepherd, 1977; Laughery, Alexander, & Lane, 1971). This principle is well known from the general field of memory research (see Klatsky, 1980; Loftus & Loftus, 1976).

While longer exposures lead to increased accuracy, the duration of an event must often be judged by the witness's report. This can be problematic since there is a pervasive human tendency to overestimate the duration of criminal events (Buckhout, 1974; Johnson & Scott, 1976; Marshall, 1966). Time markets may serve as aids for reporting durations, however. If the witness was watching a half-hour TV show during the time of a robbery, that show can be used to help gauge how long the event lasted or the approximate time that it occurred. Similarly, people also show a systematic error in underestimating how long ago events occurred, and landmarks (e.g., the witness's birthday, Presidential elections) can help date when an incident took place (Loftus & Marburger, 1983).

While exposure duration constrains encoding, the type of information processing a witness performs during the exposure period is also important. For example, given the same exposure period, subjects who engage in deeper processing (e.g., semantic judgments such as those about a person's personality) are later more likely to recognize the person's face than are subjects who engage in more shallow processing (e.g., structural judgments such as focusing on a specific facial feature) (Baddeley, 1979; Bower & Karlin, 1974; Winograd, 1981).

How frequently an event was experienced is another temporal factor likely to affect eyewitness reports. Traditional laboratory studies indicate that the more frequently an item is experienced, the better it is retained (e.g., Ebbinghaus, 1885/1964). But one difference between laboratory and real-life events is that, while the former can be repeated in an identical fashion, no two real-life events will be identical. Also, real-life events are more complicated and detailed than stimuli used in traditional laboratory studies. Children who are victims of incest or repeated sexual assault are not always able to remember the details of each incident or whether a certain act occurred during the first or fiftieth assault. Studies of repeated, realistic incidents indicate that as an event reoccurs, it may become difficult to remember exactly when a specific detail or act was experienced (Fivush, 1984; Fivush, Hudson, & Nelson, 1984; Nelson & Gruendel, 1981), even though what is recalled is quite accurate. Also, as one might expect, the more often a person is seen, the easier it is to identify him or her (Sanders & Warnick, 1979).

While some crimes do reoccur, many criminal events are novel, one-time incidents. For these kinds of events, memory—even children's memory—can be quite accurate and fairly detailed (Fivush, 1984; Linton, 1982).

The Core Event versus Peripheral Detail

Witnesses are most likely to encode and remember what is often called the core event—for example, that they experienced a robbery, a kidnapping, or a sexual assault. As part of the core event, actions are more likely to be encoded and retained than are peripheral detail or the culprit's physical features. Clifford and Scott (1978) report that adults who had just viewed a videotape of a violent incident (physical assault) or a nonviolent incident (verbal exchange) recalled more about the assailants' actions than about their physical appearance (see also Pear & Wyatt, 1914). However, recall of both actions and appearance were poorer for the violent as compared with the nonviolent incident. Thus, if a witness interprets an event correctly, and if the witness was not too terrified, he or she may be able to recall a great deal about the actions that took place.

Sometimes, however, a witness will misinterpret the core event or important parts of it. Not surprisingly, such witnesses are less likely to provide accurate reports. Buckhout's (1974) subjects, who viewed a videotape of a card game and a subsequent assault, were later asked to recall what happened. Witnesses who misinterpreted the attack recalled the events less accurately than those who interpreted it correctly.

In addition to remembering actions that occurred, witnesses may recall many other features of an event that are important to police investigation or courtroom testimony. For example, a license-plate number or what the culprit was wearing may be crucial bits of evidence. Because attention is selective, it may be impossible for the witness to encode all of the relevant information. The most salient details are likely to be best attended and retained (Marquis, Marshall, & Oskamp, 1972). A gun, for example, pointed at the witness is likely to be better attended than the color of the culprit's shirt. For some reason, the upper part of the face (e.g., eyes and nose) appears to be more salient than the lower part (e.g., mouth and chin; Laughery et al., 1971).

People often assume that someone who can provide testimony about peripheral detail must have been paying close attention to the central events as well or must have an exceptional memory. But a person's testimony can be accurate about central issues without including peripheral detail, and vice versa. Wells and Leippe (1981) reported a negative correlation between the ability to recognize a confederate and the ability to recall unimportant details. Subjects in the experiment watched a man steal a calculator. Those who attended to the culprit's face and later recognized him accurately were less likely to remember minor details about the room. Unfortunately, jurors are impressed by memory for peripheral detail and may be less willing to believe a witness who cannot remember such information.

Expectations

A person's expectations can either enhance or impede accurate perception and memory. When an event is predictable, expectations support rapid encoding and recall of it. A study by Zadny and Gerard (1974) exemplifies this point. They asked subjects to observe a skit involving a student registering for classes. Subjects were led to believe that the student was either a chemistry, psychology, or music major, and the student carried items relevant to all three of these fields. Those biased to believe that the student was a chemistry major recalled proportionally more chemistry-related items than those biased to believe the student was a psychology or music major. Subjects in the latter two groups recalled more psychology- and music-related items, respectively. The authors concluded that the biasing information affected the encoding stage because subjects who were biased *after* viewing the event recalled items relevant to all three majors.

Unfortunately, expectations can also lead to inaccuracies. Accurate recall of expected information is often accompanied by "recall" of expected information not actually encounter (Bartlett, 1932; Graesser, 1981). Expectations may be used to confirm the presence of expected information but at the same time to supersede detailed analysis, so that a person might remember seeing a car, for example, but be unable to say what it looked like (Friedman, 1979). Moreover, expectations may so bias an observer that he or she fails to notice detail that seems irrelevant or fails to match his or her encoding scheme, as when supporters of a football team see all the infractions made by the other side but not those made by their own team (Hastorf & Cantril, 1954).

Expectations are especially likely to lead to inaccuracies when an event is viewed under ambiguous, fast-moving circumstances. For example, hunting accidents often occur when a hunter's expectations lead to the misperception of a person as prey. The hunter hears rustling in the forest, glimpses part of an animal's torso, and then "sees" a deer or other animal—only to find after the shot is fired that it has killed a fellow hunter (Loftus, 1979a; Sommer, 1959). Laboratory studies also confirm the important role expectations play in biasing perceptions and memory when ambiguous information is quickly viewed. In a classic study, Bruner and Postman (1949) presented pictures of playing cards to subjects for very brief intervals. Most of the deck contained regular cards, but a few had been altered to depict, for example, a black ace of diamonds. Subjects either misperceived the altered cards according to their expectations (e.g., a red ace of diamonds) or formed "compromise memories" in which the cards were seen as purplish in color.

When longer processing time is possible, expectations can increase the attention paid to unexpected details. Expected information serves this function because it defines what is unexpected. In order to interpret the unexpected event, attention may quickly shift to detailed encoding of the novel event (Friedman, 1979; Loftus & Mackworth, 1978). As a consequence, unexpected information may later be recognized with heightened accuracy (Friedman, 1979; Graesser, 1981).

As many of these examples suggest, expectations can bias perception. When an event is not ambiguous or does not occur too rapidly, however, expectations typically support rather than hamper perception.

Violence and Stress

Many criminal events are violent in nature and therefore distressing or, because of their potential for violence, cause witnesses to feel anxious. Controversy exists over the effects of stress on memory. In particular, questions arise concerning how well laboratory researchers have been able to mimic the levels of stress induced by criminal events (Deffenbacher, 1983; Egeth & McCloskey, 1984).

Despite the controversy, psychologists generally accept the Yerkes-Dodson law as an accurate description of the relation between stress and memory (Yerkes & Dodson, 1908). This law states that, for complex tasks, performance peaks at moderate levels of stress or arousal but then declines as arousal becomes intense. For ethical reasons, tests of the law using human subjects are problematic, but some experiments, conducted before the activation of current ethical guidelines, exemplify the law quite well. For example, Baddeley (1972) described studies of soldiers' performance in mock-war situations. In these studies, soldiers, equipped with a radio, ventured out alone onto a "battleground." Half of the soldiers (the stressed group) were then falsely informed that they were in a highly radioactive area or that the ammunition being used was real rather than fake. The soldiers were requested to call headquarters on their radios so they could escape the dangerous situation. The remaining half (the control group) were not misled about danger but were merely told to call headquarters. Upon trying to call, both groups found their radios jammed. The stressed subjects took longer than control subjects to fix their radios (following instructions that had been provided to everyone), confirming part of the Yerkes-Dodson law. Thus, under conditions of high (life-threatening) arousal, performance declined.

One way to think about the Yerkes-Dodson law in relation to the effects of stress on memory has been offered by Easterbrook (1959). He proposed that arousal has the effect of limiting the range of attention and hence the number of cues that can be used in solving a task. Under moderate levels of stress, attention narrows to include only salient or immediately relevant cues. Peripheral or less important cues go unattended. Performance is usually heightened under such conditions because potentially distracting, irrelevant cues are ignored, and processing focuses only on relevant cues. Under very high levels of arousal, however, the range of attention is further narrowed so that even some relevant cues are ignored, causing performance to decline. While arousal may affect memory storage (Glickman, 1961) and retrieval (Warrington & Weiskrantz, 1970) as well as encoding, Easterbrook's proposal remains a popular general account of the effects of stress on memory.

Does research on eyewitness testimony confirm predictions based on the Yerkes-Dodson law? Deffenbacher (1983) recently reviewed the existing literature and found that about half of the studies did, whereas the other half did not. The studies varied considerably in the stress levels involved, however. For example, in one study (Loftus & Burns, 1982), subjects were asked to view a film depicting a bank robbery. At the end of the film, the robbers, chased by guards, turn and shoot. In the nonviolent version, no one is hit. In the violent version, a bullet hits a young boy in the face. The boy covers his face in pain as he falls to the ground bleeding. Subjects who viewed the violent version remembered less about the film than those who saw the nonviolent version.

Compare, however, the degree of stress likely to be involved in this study with that experienced in another. Leippe, Wells, and Ostrom (1978) exposed subjects to a staged theft of an unknown person's calculator (high serious theft) or cigarettes (low serious theft). When subjects knew the value of the items before the theft occurred, those in the high serious condition recognized the confederate with 56 percent accuracy, while those in the low serious condition recognized him with only 19 percent accuracy. These results might be taken to indicate that, in contrast to the Yerkes-Dodson law, high arousal improves rather than inhibits memory. It might be more reasonably argued, however, that subjects in the high serious condition of Leippe et al.'s study were moderately aroused and not as shocked as subjects in Loftus and Burns' high stress condition. When Deffenbacher divided the 21 studies into those likely to have produced high stress versus those unlikely to have done so, the Yerkes-Dodson law was upheld.

Deffenbacher's review has been criticized by Egeth and McCloskey (1984), who argue that one cannot legitimately divided the studies into two categories post hoc since independent ratings of subjects' stress were unavailable. It should be noted, too, that none of the studies reviewed by Deffenbacher involved traumatic events directly experienced by subjects. Such events would be more likely to induce high levels of arousal and might provide more definitive tests of whether stress interferes with memory. In two recent studies reported by Goodman, Aman, and Hirschman (in press) participants experienced events that more closely approximated a victimization experience. Children, 3 to 6 years of age, were videotaped in medical clinics while having their blood drawn or while being given shots. (The procedures were required for medical purposes and were not imposed by the researchers.) For some of the children, the procedures were quite stressful, requiring the children to be held down while they cried and fought to get away. The children were later interviewed about what happened. A significant relation between the children's stress and memory was not found.

Of course, even if the stress involved in many criminal events does inhibit memory, this does not mean that the witnesses to traumatic incidents will remember nothing or that what they do remember will be inaccurate. It may simply mean that their memories will be relatively limited. What they do remember might still be quite accurate.

Weapons are one source of stress in many criminal situations. It has been proposed that when a weapon is in view, attention becomes focused on it, resulting in less attention directed at the culprit's face. Evidence for such a "weapon focus" was found by Johnson and Scott (1976), in whose study subjects waited individually for their turn to participate in an experiment. While waiting, subjects in the high arousal condition overheard an argument followed by crashing chairs and bottles breaking. A confederate then entered the waiting room holding a bloodied letter opener, said a few words, and left. Subjects in the low arousal condition overheard an innocuous conversation, followed by the confederate entering the waiting room with a pen in his hand, uttering a few words, and then departing. Subjects were later asked to recall what had happened and to identify the confederate in a set of 50 photographs. In the high arousal condition, nearly every subject mentioned the letter opener; whereas very few in the low arousal condition mentioned the pen. Furthermore, when a weapon was not present, 49 percent of the subjects accurately recognized the confederate; whereas only 33 percent did when a weapon was in view. Apparently subjects focused their attention on the weapon at the expense of encoding the culprit's face. This study, while often cited, has never been published, perhaps because of methodological flaws.

Because attention is limited, people cannot encode everything about real-life events, particularly those as complex as most crimes. We have reviewed the ways in which temporal factors, such as exposure duration, affect encoding, and how attention is most likely to focus on central, salient information. Our expectations can distort what is encoded, though they usually do not, and violent events may lead to reduced, though still largely accurate, memory. These factors influence what is encoded, which in turn determines what can be stored and retained.

Retention

Retention is the second stage of memory. During the retention interval, encoded information may be affected by various factors. The length of time that passes between an event and its attempted report may lead to forgetting. In addition, information acquired during the retention interval can, under certain circumstances, distort the original memory (or at least the witness's report of it). We will examine some of the factors that can lead to such malleability of memory and also discuss conditions that make memory relatively resistant to change.

Delay

One of the most replicable findings of memory research is that forgetting increases with time. Ebbinghaus' (1885/1964) famous "forgetting curve" represented the fact that the rate of forgetting of nonsense syllables is steepest during the first few postexposure minutes and then levels off. Forgetting also occurs for real-life events, but the rate at which information is lost varies considerably (see Ellis, 1981, and Shepherd, 1983, for reviews). Memory for highly familiar information may decline quite slowly. For example, in a study by Bahrick, Bahrick, and Wittlinger (1975), recognition memory for pictures of high school classmates remained almost perfect after 35 years and was still quite accurate after an average delay of 45 years.

Even studies that involve recognition of strangers do not always find a decline in accuracy, at least over the delay intervals tested. In a review of seven roughly comparable eyewitness identification experiments which employed delays ranging from an immediate to a five-month interval, Shepherd (1983) found no clear relationship between delay and correct recognitions or incorrect choices. These findings led Shepherd to conclude that, at least for face recognition, other factors such as amount of attention received by the target during encoding may be more important than delay. This hypothesis receives some tentative support from a study by Shepherd and Ellis (1973) in which decline in recognition accuracy during an interval of six days or five weeks was observed only for faces previously rated as average in attractiveness. No decline occurred for high and low attractive faces, which probably received more attention during encoding.

However, with sufficiently long delays, people almost invariably forget some of what was originally encoded. While the gist of an event may be remembered indefinitely, more specific information (e.g., what the suspect looked like, exactly how the event unfolded) tends to become lost. Examples are not hard to find. When subjects were exposed to an irate stranger for 45 seconds, their ability to later pick him out of a video lineup dropped considerably over time from 65 percent of the subjects providing correct recognitions after a one-week delay to only 10 percent correct recognitions after an 11-month delay (Shepherd, 1983, Experiment 2). Even when the number of correct recognitions does not decline with time, the number of false recognitions of innocent people can increase dramatically. In Egan, Pittner, and Goldstein's (1977) experiment, subjects viewed two live "suspects" for 15 seconds. The rate of correct identifications of at least one of the suspects was 91 percent after a two-day delay, and it was not significantly lower after 21 or 56 days. The rate of incorrect identifications did vary, however, as a function of delay and was 48 percent after two days, 62 percent after 21 days, and 93 percent after 56 days. In the American justice system, false recognition of an innocent person is considered more grievous than failing to identify a true culprit, making false recognition an error of substantial import.

Faces represent a class of stimuli which are so overlearned that one might expect memory for them to be particularly resistant to forgetting. Yet forgetting clearly occurs; probably more rapidly the more unfamiliar the person, the briefer the exposure duration, and the more typical the face, for instance. A similar decline in memory occurs for other types of information. Lipton (1977) studied memory for the details of a staged murder presented on film. Accuracy of report significantly declined after a delay of only one week, as did the amount of information reported (see also Marshall, 1966). In a more recent study of memory for a novel, naturalistic event (e.g., children's sole visit to a special archeology museum), recall of the actions that took place remained stable after six weeks but declined after a year (Fivush et al., 1984). Interestingly, what the children did report after a year remained quite accurate. It seems, then, that forgetting of real-life events does not necessarily occur as rapidly as the typical Ebbinghaus forgetting curve for nonsense syllables might imply.

Malleability of Memory

In evaluating studies of eyewitness testimony, it is important to pay special attention to whether memory merely fades over time or whether inaccuracies begin to appear in subject's reports. One source of inaccuracies is misleading postevent information. This information can be introduced during the retention interval in various ways—through discussions held by witnesses after a criminal event, through questioning by police and attorneys, through exposure to newspaper articles and television news, and even through one's own thoughts and dreams. Loftus (1975, 1977, 1979a) has demonstrated that, through the use of misleading questioning, witnesses can be made to report such things as barns that were not seen (Loftus, 1975), an assailant with curly hair whose hair was in fact straight (Loftus & Greene, 1980), broken glass in car accidents which in reality involved no broken glass (Loftus & Palmer, 1974), incorrect colors of objects (Loftus, 1977), and changes in the frequency of one's own headache pain (Loftus, 1979a). Loftus has interpreted these results as indicating that a witness's memory can become distorted and, perhaps, irreversibly changed.

In a typical study, Loftus and her colleagues (Loftus, Miller, & Burns, 1978) asked subjects to view a car-pedestrian accident presented on slides. After a delay interval but before a memory test, misleading information was introduced via a questionnaire. The misleading questions falsely presupposed the existence of some item, for instance a stop sign: "Did another car pass the red Datsun while it was stopped at the stop sign?" Actually, half of the subjects had viewed a yield sign rather than a stop sign. Later, when faced with a recognition test between two slides containing the Datsun at a stop sign and at a yield sign, subjects who had been exposed to the misleading information falsely recognized the stop sign. Their performance (41 percent correct recognitions) represented significantly less than chance (50 percent) responding and was also significantly worse than the performance of subjects who had been exposed to correct information (74 percent correct recognitions). Lending support to Loftus' proposal that the misleading information actually changed subjects' memory for the original information, "demand characteristics" did not seem to explain the effects. That is, subsequent studies suggested that subjects did not merely indicate the stop sign on the recognition test because of subtle pressure from the experimenter (Weinberg, Wadsworth, & Baron, 1983).

Misleading questions are especially effective in altering eyewitness reports when the questions are complex and therefore direct subjects' attention away from the misleading detail. The relatively simple question, "Did you see the stop sign?" falsely presupposes information but directs subjects' attention to the presupposition, so fewer subjects are misled (Johnson, 1979, as cited in Loftus & Ketchum, 1983). Timing is also important in evaluating the effects of misleading questioning. The greatest distortion occurs when misleading information is introduced after a delay and just before the final memory test, instead of right after the initial event (Loftus, 1979a). Because of the delay, memory may fade to the point where witnesses do not notice that the misleading information is incorrect.

Another way to add postevent information to witnesses' reports is to use verbs of different strengths in asking questions. Loftus and Palmer (1974) found that subjects' estimates of the speed of cars seen in a film were higher when the question was, "About how fast were the two cars going when they *smashed* into each other?" than when the verb *hit* was used. Furthermore, on a later memory test subjects exposed to the stronger verbs were more likely to report the presence of broken glass at the accident scene even through none had been present. Since smashing and broken glass are both associated with severe accidents, subjects apparently inferred that broken glass must have been present and incorporated this inference into their reports (see also Christiaansen, Sweeney, & Ochalek, 1983). Even more subtle changes in the wording of a question can significantly change a witness's report. If a witness is asked, "Did you see *the* stop sign?" a "yes" response (even though a stop sign had not been seen) is more likely than if the witness is asked, "Did you see *a* stop sign?" (Loftus & Zanni, 1975).

Misleading information is most likely to be accepted if the source of the communication is of high status or appears to be unbiased (Bregman & McAllister, 1982; Ceci, Ross, & Toglia, in press; Dodd & Bradshaw, 1980; Loftus, 1980; see also Eagly, 1978). Thus, if a person involved in a car accident claimed that the accident occurred in front of a yield sign instead of a stop sign, witnesses would be less likely to change their reports than if a police officer made the same claim. The police officer would presumably be both high in status and unbiased.

While the effects of misleading information on eyewitness reports have been clearly established, it is important to note that virtually all these demonstrations involve peripheral detail (Yuille, 1980). It is much more difficult to change a witness's report about central information (Dritsas & Hamilton, as cited in Loftus, 1979a; see also Loftus, 1979b) or information with high memory strength (Marquis, Marshall, & Oskamp, 1972; Read & Bruce, 1984). However, if a person's memory is weak enough, for example, because of a long time interval between encoding and retrieval, it is possible that reports might even change for more central information.

Recent research has challenged the proposal that original memories are erased as a result of exposure to misleading questioning. McCloskey and Zargosa (1985) varied Loftus' procedure by including on the final memory test the item originally seen (e.g., a hammer) and an item neither seen nor suggested (e.g., a wrench). If the suggested item (e.g., a screwdriver) had erased the witnesses' original memory, then witnesses should only be able to guess when forced to make a choice between the original and a new item. Instead, witnesses exposed to misleading information remember the original item about as well as witnesses who were not exposed to misleading information. Thus, it appears that misleading questioning does not necessarily erase a witness's memory. If the right testing conditions can be found, the original memory can be recovered (but see Loftus, Schooler, & Wagenaar, 1985).

Resistance to Misleading Information

Are there ways to make reports more tamper-resistant? One might expect that warning people about the possible presence of misinformation would help ward off the ill effects, and it does. If a witness is told, for example, "Some of the questions you were asked may have contained incorrect information: Please answer the questions now only on the basis of what you actually experienced during the incident," and if the witness has been educated about the effects of leading questions, he or she may be able to edit from memory much of the incorrect information (Christiaansen & Ochalek, 1983; Read & Bruce, 1984; but see Greene, Flynn, & Loftus, 1982). It seems that the more explicit the warning, the better people can recover their original memories (e.g., Hasher, Attig, & Alba, 1981). It is also helpful to provide at least one of the warnings immediately before the witness's report. In this case, the warning can come as much as 45 minutes after the misleading information and still be effective (Christiaansen & Ochalek, 1983).

Because people are more resistant to blatant than to subtle misinformation, exposure to blatant misinformation can serve as a warning. If we suggested to a witness that a purple gorilla had been present at the crime scene, the witness would be unlikely to incorporate that information into his or her eyewitness report. Interestingly, blatantly misleading information has an alerting effect so that subjects reject more subtle misinformation as well (Loftus, 1979b). The beneficial effects are present, however, only when both kinds of misleading information are presented at the same time; not when the blatant misinformation is delayed.

Subjects' commitment to their initial report may also make memory more resistant to change, as shown by Bregman and McAllister (1982). They asked subjects to view a videotaped car accident and, afterward, to fill out a questionnaire concerning what had happened. Those in the commitment condition were requested to sign their name on the questionnaire before turning it in. After all subjects were subsequently exposed to misleading information, the "committed" ones were less likely to change their reports.

Finally, witnesses may be better able to overcome the effects of misleading information if the order of questioning matches the original input sequence. In Loftus' studies, subjects view a criminal incident, are subjected to misleading information, and then are questioned about what originally happened. If the final memory test consists of questions presented in random order, the predicted distortions emerge — many subjects incorporate misleading information into their reports. But if the questions on the memory test are given in an order that matches the original event sequence, the effect disappears (Bowers & Bekerian, 1983; but see Bekerian & Bowers, 1984). Unfortunately, in real criminal investigations the original order will often be unknown, making it difficult to decide how best to order the questions.

In sum, memory can suffer during the retention interval because of both forgetting and contamination by postevent information. This decline in quantity and accuracy of report is not inevitable, however. It depends on the kind of information encoded: Central, familiar, or well-encoded information is more resistant to forgetting and distortion than is more peripheral, less familiar, or poorly encoded information. It also depends on the credibility and status of the source of misinformation: High status and unbiased sources are more likely to produce change. It depends on whether warnings were given and whether subjects committed themselves to an earlier report. Finallly, it depends on the interviewing technique used.

Retrieval

During retrieval, the information that was encoded and then retained is brought back into the open. Typical retrieval situations for witnesses include reporting to the police, viewing lineups, recountings to friends and mental health professionals, and testifying in court. We will review the ways in which accuracy and quantity of testimony can depend on the interviewing techniques used and the retrieval environment. We will also examine the relationship between witnesses' confidence in their memory and the accuracy of their statements.

Interviewing Techniques

Ideally, testimony should be accurate and rich in detail. Unfortunately, there is often a trade-off between accuracy and completeness. Interviewing techniques that yield the highest accuracy also yield the least complete testimony; whereas techniques that yield more detailed reports also yield the most inaccuracies (Cady, 1924; Dent & Stephenson, 1979; Lipton, 1977; Marquis et al., 1972). For example, Marquis et al. presented a film showing a woman being knocked down by a car in a parking lot and an ensuing struggle between the woman's companion and the driver of the car. Afterward, the experimenters interviewed subject-witnesses using the following interview techniques: free recall, in which subjects were asked to report everything they could remember about the movie; open-ended questions that probed for general or specific information; multiple-choice questions that mentioned several alternative answers; and leading questions that suggested an answer (e.g., "There were cars in the area?" or "The events you saw took place in the street, didn't they?"). Marquis et al. found that for easy items (items that had been recalled with high probability in a pretest), type of question made little difference—accuracy and completeness were high regardless of question type. But for difficult items, question type did matter: Free recall yielded perfect accuracy but the least complete testimony; multiple-choice and leading questions produced the most complete but also the least accurate reports; and open-ended questions fell between these extremes.

Given these results, the best way to interview a witness would seem to be first to elicit free recall (e.g., "Tell me what happened"), followed by open-ended and then more specific questions. Multiple-choice and leading questions should be avoided. In this way, both accuracy and completeness can be encouraged (Snee & Lush, 1941).

The question often arises whether it is best to interview a witness immediately after a stressful event or wait until the stress subsides. Unfortunately, there is little scientific research on this important question. Several studies of recall of arousal-producing words indicate that memory improves over time (Butters, 1970; Kleinsmith & Kaplan, 1963), but the finding is not always replicated and, in any case, may not generalize to eyewitness tasks. When such "hypermnesia" is examined by asking for repeated recall of nonstressful criminal events, increases in the reporting of accurate information are accompanied by increases in the reporting of inaccuracies, nullifying the beneficial effect (Buckhout, 1974).

Intentionally or unintentionally, an interviewer can bias a witness's report. We have already discussed bias introduced by the use of certain wording (e.g., "Did you see *a* car?" versus "Did you see *the* car?") or presuppositions (e.g., "How fast was the car going when it passed the barn on the country road?" when a barn had not been seen), but there are other types of bias as well. For example, when a witness tries to identify a culprit, bias can be introduced by the composition of the lineup and by the social atmosphere surrounding the witness.

A "show-up," in which a single person is brought before the witness, is one of the most biased forms of identification. The suspect, who may be handcuffed and escorted by police, is obviously placed in an incriminating position. When a number of individuals are viewed, as in a more typical lineup, bias is introduced if only one person matches the description of the suspect or if a police officer implies that the suspect is present among the alternatives (Buckhout, 1974; Hosch, Leippe, Marchioni, & Cooper, 1984; Malpass & Devine, 1981a). In these situations, the number of incorrect identifications increases, particularly if the actual culprit is not among the alternatives. Biased instructions (e.g., "We have reason to suspect the culprit's picture is included here") may compound other biases present in the lineup—as when the alternatives differ in facial expression (one person is frowning while all others are smiling) or only one photograph is placed at an angle (Buckhout, 1974). In such cases, the person frowning or placed at an angle is more likely to be identified as the culprit. It is crucial that the initial identification be presented in an unbiased fashion. Once an incorrect identification is obtained, it may be difficult to obtain an accurate one even when the witness is faced with the actual culprit (Gorenstein & Ellsworth, 1980).

The retrieval atmosphere may also introduce bias. Whenever a witness is approached by the police, there may be subtle social pressure to identify someone or give a lengthy report. As Buckhout (1974) points out, the police would hardly bother to have a witness come in for an identification unless they have a suspect in mind. Also, high status interviewers tend to elicit longer reports from lower status individuals (Marquis et al., 1972).

When the retrieval atmosphere is intimidating, one might expect a drop in accuracy. The only study that has investigated hostile versus friendly interviewers surprisingly found no differences in accuracy or quantity of report (Marquis et al., 1972). However, in at least some situations an intimidated witness will be less accurate. When forced to identify an assailant by touching him or her (as was done in England), accuracy suffers (Dent, 1977).

Context Reinstatement

The extent to which the retrieval environment matches the encoding situation is an important determinant of a person's ability to provide accurate and complete eyewitness testimony (see Tulving, 1983, for a theoretical account). The more cues shared at acquisition and retrieval, the better retrieval will be. This fact has important implications for interviewers because it implies that testimony may be greatly enhanced as more and more retrieval cues can be found.

One way to provide additional cues is through the use of guided memory. Malpass and Devine (1981b) used this procedure to enhance the eyewitness identifications of subject-witnesses who had viewed a staged vandalism five months earlier. Subjects were helped to visualize the classroom where the incident took place, their position in it, the suspect, the vandalism itself, and their reaction to it. When then presented with a photo lineup that included the culprit, 60 percent of the subjects were correct in their identifications. In comparison, only 40 percent of the subjects who were not given the guided-memory task correctly identified him. The guided-memory procedure did not lead to more false identifications or false rejections of the culprit. These results are impressive, but some of the cues provided by the experimenter would probably be unavailable if a real crime had taken place.

Krafka and Penrod (1985) studied the effect of more realistic memory aids. Two or 24 hours after a confederate made a purchase at a store, clerks were asked to recall the transaction and visualize the customer's face. Physical cues were also used—a photocopy of the customer's credit card and one of his traveler's checks. Again context reinstatement led to more correct identifications (55 percent versus 29 percent for the control group) without increasing error rates.

Context reinstatement may also explain why it is easier to identify someone from a live lineup than from a photo lineup (Egan et al., 1977). Because witnesses view criminals in the flesh, it is easier for them to identify the person when he or she again stands before them. In fact, context reinstatement may be a problem for the "ecological validity" of eyewitness testimony research that presents "assailants" on slides or videotape and tests subjects' memory using the same medium. Because context reinstatement effects will be strong, the rate of correct identifications may be atypically high compared to real-life crime investigations where the assailant is first seen live and then identified via photographs (Maass & Brigham, 1982).

Confidence and Accuracy

At retrieval, some witnesses will seem quite confident of their statements, while others will not. Are confident witnesses necessarily more accurate? When Deffenbacher (1980) reviewed the extant literature, he found 22 independent experiments that indicated a significant positive correlation between confidence and accuracy. At the same time, 21 studies found nonsignificant or even negative correlations between confidence and accuracy. Deffenbacher attempted to resolve these contradictory results by examining the encoding, retention, and retrieval conditions witnesses experienced in each study. He found that when these conditions were "optimal," a positive correlation between confidence and accuracy typically emerged. When they were not, no relation or a negative relation existed. Given that confidence and accuracy are often uncorrelated, Deffenbacher concluded that "the judicial system should cease and desist from a reliance on eyewuitness confidence as an index of eyewitness accuracy" (p. 258).

Deffenbacher's optimality hypothesis has not gone unchallenged (Egeth & McCloskey, 1984; Stephenson, 1984; Wells & Murray, 1983). Nevertheless, eyewitness confidence seems to be modifiable, as a study by Wells, Ferguson, and Lindsay (1981) shows. They staged a calculator theft, had witnesses attempt to identify the thief, and then cross-examined the witnesses. Half of the subjects were briefed before cross-examination (e.g., by telling them "[the cross-examiner] will do her utmost to discredit your testimony in the eyes of the jury. . . . Rehearse how you will answer questions"). Wells and others found that, after cross-examination, briefed inaccurate witnesses were as confident as accurate witnesses and more confident than unbriefed inaccurate witnesses. Thus, briefing raised witness confidence even if he or she provided inaccurate testimony. Wells et al. videotaped the cross-examinations and then showed the recordings to mock jurors whose task was to rate the witnesss' confidence and accuracy. Briefed inaccurate witnesses were perceived as being more accurate than the truly accurate witnesses. Since confidence in an inaccurate identification can be enhanced by a simple briefing and has such dramatic effects on jurors, confidence (as Deffenbacher argued) seems to be a dubious criterion for judging the trustworthiness of a witness.

Face Recognition

The ability to recognize an unfamiliar face varies considerably depending on the conditions of encoding, retention, and retrieval. Under some conditions, recognition may approach 100 percent. In others it is only at chance (see Chance & Goldstein, 1984; Deffenbacher & Horney, 1981; Shepherd, 1983, for reviews). Although we have already examined many of the factors that affect eyewitness identifications (e.g., encoding opportunity, delay interval), it is worthwhile here to consider several topics specific to face recognition.

Cross-Racial Identification

The majority of studies to date indicate that cross-race identifications are more difficult than same-race identifications (Chance, Goldstein, & McBride, 1975; Feinman & Entwisle, 1976; Galper, 1973; Luce, 1974; Malpass & Kravitz, 1969; Malpass, Lavigueur, & Weldon, 1973; see Brigham & Malpass, 1985, for a review). More specifically, these studies show that it is more difficult for members of one race (e.g., Caucasians) to recognize someone from a different race (e.g., black) than someone of their own race (e.g., Caucasian). However, a recent review of the literature (Lindsay & Wells, 1983) did not lead to the conclusion that the accuracy of cross-racial identifications has to be inferior. The effect increases with age of the witness (Goldstein & Chance, 1980), however, and is likely to be at least partly a function of meaningful experience with members of different races (Brigham, Maass, Snyder, & Spaulding, 1982; Feinman & Entwisle, 1976).

Lineup Fairness

Imagine that you have witnessed a crime, and a week later the police ask you to view a photo lineup of three men. It turns out that two of them are suspects in the crime. If you were randomly guessing when attempting the identification, what would be the chances of selecting one of the two men? The chances are high (66 percent if you feel you must make a choice and 50 percent if you include "none" as an option). Most defense attorneys would claim that the lineup was unfair.

Psychologists have devised several ways to evaluate the fairness of a lineup (Doob & Kirshenbaum, 1973; Malpass, 1981a; Wells, Leippe, & Ostrom, 1979). It is generally acknowledged that a lineup consisting of, say, nine foils and one suspect (nominal size = 10) may in effect be much smaller. If the foils are so dissimilar from the suspect that even mock witnesses (people not present at the crime scene but who have read a description of the suspect) identify the suspect more often than would be expected by chance, the lineup is biased. Malpass (1981a) provides a detailed description of how to evaluate the fairness of a lineup (see Wells & Lindsay, 1980, for a discussion of the diagnosticity of nonidentifications).

Unconscious Transference

Sometimes we recognize a face but cannot recall the circumstances in which we have seen it before. A phenomenon called unconscious transference may result: A face in a lineup looks familiar to the witness, who then identifies the person as the culprit. But the reason for the recognition may be a previous encounter that had nothing to do with the crime, or the person may have been an innocent bystander at the crime scene. Unconscious transference has led to mistaken identifications in actual trials (Houts, 1956), and the effect has been demonstrated in the laboratory (Brown, Deffenbacher, & Sturgill, 1977; Buckhout, Figueroa, & Hoff, 1975; Loftus, 1976). Unconscious transference may also result from viewing mugshots, if an individual seen in the photographs is then presented in a live lineup (Brown et al., 1977).

Interference

Seeing other faces does not always result in unconscious transference but it may still affect retrieval. Searching through mugshots, for example, may make it harder to identify the face of a suspect because the intervening faces may interfere with memory (Laughery et al., 1971). Another possibility is that a negative set develops: After viewing hundreds of mugshots, witnesses may become less willing on a later identification test to claim that they have seen a particular person before, even though they have. Unlike an interference explanation, an explanation in terms of negative set does not imply that the original memory has been destroyed. Therefore, various techniques, such as telling subjects that the suspect was not among the mugshots searched, might undo the effects (Davies, Shepherd, & Ellis, 1979).

Disguises

Sometimes we fail to recognize a familiar person because he or she has lost weight, gotten a new hairstyle, or is now wearing glasses. Witnesses encounter this problem if the mugshot of a criminal looks very different from the criminal in person. Patterson and Baddeley (1977) showed that changes in pose and facial expression do not lead to decreased accuracy of identification (see also Laughery et al., 1971), but that changes in hairstyle, facial hair, or glasses significantly decrease identification accuracy. Since upper facial features seem to be more readily encoded, disguises that cover or distort them may be particularly effective (Ellis, 1984). Similarly, a disguised voice makes voice recognition more difficult (see Clifford, 1980, 1983).

Individual Differences

Can we predict who is likely to provide accurate testimony? The answer at this time appears to be "no," although a few individual difference measures seem to hold promise.

Intelligence and Cognitive Abilities

Are more intelligent witnesses more accurate witnesses? The relation between intelligence and eyewitness testimony has been examined in numerous studies employing a variety of intelligence measures—standardized intelligence tests, achievement tests, digit span, "social intelligence" tests, and verbal fluency (Chance & Goldstein, 1984; Feinman & Entwisle, 1976; Gilliland & Burke, 1926; Goetze, 1980; Goldstein & Chance, 1964; Howells, 1938; Kaess & Witryol, 1955;

King, 1984; Powers, Andriks, & Loftus, 1979). No consistent relation between intelligence and eyewitness accuracy has been found. The two tasks—eyewitness reports and intelligence tests—seem to tap quite different abilities.

One might expect, however, that as two tasks become more similar, a positive correlation would appear. Indeed there is research to suggest that this is so (Boice, Hanley, Shaughnessv, & Gansler, 1982), but it is insufficient to justify the use of general tests such as a general test for suggestibility or face recognition (Deffenbacher, Leu, & Brown, 1981).

Eidetic imagery and visual imagery are two other cognitive abilities that are sometimes mentioned as possibly related to eyewitness accuracy. There is little reason to believe that either of these can be used to predict accurate testimony (Chance & Goldstein, 1984; Clifford & Bull, 1978; Courtois & Mueller, 1981).

Cognitive Style, Personality Measures, and Attitudes

Inconsistent findings typically emerge when one attempts to predict the accuracy of a witness's report from measures of cognitive style or personality. For example, field dependence-independence has been found to correlate with eyewitness accuracy in some studies but not in others (Hoffman & Kagan, 1977; Lavrakas, Buri, & Mayzner, 1976; Marin, Holmes, Guth, & Kovac, 1979; Messick & Damarin, 1964; Witkin, Dyk, Faterson, Goodenough, & Karp, 1974; see Clifford & Bull, 1978, for a review). Measures of self-monitoring, extroversion-introversion, and reflection-impulsivity have met a similar fate (Hosch & Platz, 1984; Hosch et al. 1984; Hunt, 1928; King, 1984). For most of these measures and others (e.g., need for approval; Schill, 1966), little research has been conducted so firm conclusions are premature.

Studies investigating people's attitudes toward various groups or crimes (e.g., attitudes toward blacks, attitudes toward rape) and memory for faces or for criminal events have generally found no relation between attitudes and memory, produced inconsistent results, or suffered from such severe methodological flaws that conclusions based on them are questionable (Brigham & Barkowitz, 1978; Galper, 1973; Lavrakas et al., 1976; Seeleman, 1940; Yarmey & Jones, 1983; see Shepherd, 1981, for a review).

Sex

Do males or females make better witnesses? Given the available research, the best answer to this question is that males and females sometimes notice and remember different things, but one group is not better than the other. Powers et al. (1979) asked adult subjects to view a videotape showing a male and female who happen upon a confrontation in a parking lot. A day later, subjects were exposed to misleading information and then asked questions about the original event. Females were found to be more accurate and resistant to suggestion about female-oriented details, whereas men were more accurate and resistant to suggestion about male-oriented details. There may be two exceptions to the general similarity of male and female witnesses. First, many experiments investigating sex differences in face recognition have produced evidence favoring female superiority (see Shepherd, 1981, for a review). Most of these studies are traditional laboratory experiments, however, which differ in important ways from real-life criminal events, so it will be important to see if the female advantage generalizes to more ecologically valid research. Second, if an event is violent, female bystander witnesses may be at a slight disadvantage on eyewitness tasks (Clifford & Scott, 1978; Johnson & Scott, 1976).

Anxiety

Earlier we reviewed evidence relevant to the claim that memory is relatively poor for stressful events. In a similar vein, it has been proposed that people who are highly anxious may retain less than their calmer counterparts (Eysenck, 1979; Mandler, 1984), perhaps because anxious people are preoccupied with "task irrelevant processing" such as noticing their own feelings of nervousness. Siegel and Loftus (1978) measured subjects' anxiety levels and self-preoccupation. Subjects then viewed slides of a purse-snatching incident. Immediately after viewing the slides, subjects completed a questionnaire designed to determine eyewitness accuracy. The more anxious and self-preoccupied subjects performed more poorly on the questionnaire. Other studies, while not always as representative of eyewitness tasks, have produced somewhat more ambiguous but generally similar results (Buckhout, Alper, Chern, Silverberg, & Slomovits, 1974; Mueller, Bailis, & Goldstein, 1979; Nowicki, Winograd, & Millard, 1979; Zanni & Offermann, 1978).

Training

Obviously, it would be advantageous if people could be trained to become better witnesses. Training studies indicate that it is possible to improve adults' ability to recognize "other-race" faces through a variety of techniques (Elliott, Wills, & Goldstein, 1973; Lavrakas et al., 1976; Malpass et al., 1973), but it is more difficult to improve recognition of "same-race" faces. Sometimes training even decreases recognition accuracy (Woodhead, Baddeley, & Simmonds, 1979; see Ellis, 1984; and Malpass, 1981b, for reviews). Because recognition of other-race faces often falls behind recognition of same-race faces, there is greater room for improvement—making training effects more plausible. In any case, it is not clear how long the training effects last. Lavrakas et al. (1976) found immediate effects of other-race face recognition training, but the improvement did not last over a one-week period.

It is often claimed that police are trained to be accurate observers. Psychologists have investigated whether police are more accurate in recognition of culprits or in recalling events. Two findings emerge. One is that police officers are more likely than civilians to "see" criminal events in ambiguous circumstances (Tickner & Poulton, 1975; Verinis & Walker, 1970). The second is that police are generally no better than civilians in recognizing faces (Billig & Milner, 1976) but may remember more information about specific details, such as license-plate numbers, dress, and physical appearance, especially if given sufficient time to encode these features (Clifford & Richards, 1977). Thus, training can be helpful but not always as helpful as might be hoped.

THE CHILD AND THE ELDERLY WITNESS

Another individual difference variable is age. Because of the importance of this variable to the criminal justice system, we have dedicated a separate section to it.

The Child Witness

Children, like adults, witness and are victimized by crime. And, like adults, children may be interviewed by police and testify in courts of law. Children not infrequently become the key or sole witness to events as consequential as murder, domestic violence, and serious accidents. Moreover, crimes against children (e.g., sexual assault, incest, child abuse) are being reported with increasing frequency, bringing more and more children into contact with the legal system.

It has long been held that, because of heightened suggestibility, children make poor, if not dangerous, witnesses (Whipple, 1911). Several influential developmental theories (e.g., Piagetian, Freudian) also contributed to this view. But recent studies that specifically examine children's eyewitness testimony do not support the simplistic idea that children are necessarily worse witnesses than adults.

A fairly consistent set of findings is emerging from developmental research on eyewitness testimony and memory for naturalistic events. In these studies, children almost invariably recall less than adults do (Goodman & Reed, in press; King, 1984; Marin et al., 1979). But, while children recall less, they are also less likely to make "intrusion" errors—that is, to recall information that was not encountered but easily might have been (Goodman & Reed, in press). At least two studies have shown that five- and six-year-olds equal adults in correctly answering objective questions (e.g., "Did the man knock before he came in?") and in face recognition (Goodman & Reed, in press; Marin et al., 1979; but see King, 1984).

Children are, at least under some circumstances, more suggestible than adults, however (Cohen & Harnick, 1980; Goodman & Reed, in press; King, 1984). These circumstances seem to be the same as those that lead to heightened suggestibility in adults—a relatively weak memory and a relatively high-status interviewer (Ceci et al., in press; Goodman, 1984; Loftus, 1979a). When children's memory is equivalent in strength to adults', age differences in suggestibility are less likely to occur and may even be reversed (Duncan, Whitney, & Kunen, 1982).

Several qualifications of these statements are in order, however. One concerns the child's age. While few studies have included children as young as three years of age (see Goodman & Reed, in press, and Goodman et al., in press, for exceptions), it appears that three-year-olds provide less accurate testimony than older children on all four of the standard eyewitness testimony tasks (free recall, answers to objective and suggestive questions, and eyewitness identifications). In the Goodman and Reed (in press) study, subjects interacted with a confederate for five minutes and were then tested four to five days later. At testing, 74 percent of adults and 95 percent of six-year-olds recognized the confederate accurately from a photo lineup. In comparison, only 40 percent of the three-year-olds did. However, given sufficient exposure durations, short delays, and greater familiarity with the interviewer, even three-year-olds might be able to provide accurate, though limited, testimony.

Second, many factors in addition to age will affect the accuracy and detail of children's testimony—their understanding of the incident, the stress involved, the type of memory test used, and so forth. A study by Price and Goodman (1985) shows that the type of memory test is particularly important. Specifically, if young children are provided with props to aid their reports, their testimony can become more detailed and accurate.

If children are questioned properly, their errors are usually those of omission rather than commission—that is, children tend to omit details or refuse to answer but are unlikely to invent things that never happened. The one exception to this rule concerns children's suggestibility. Children, like adults, are sometimes led to report details that were not actually seen (Dale, Loftus, & Rathbun, 1978; Dent, 1982). To the extent that children are more suggestible than adults, it is essential that interviewers avoid asking leading questions of them. Even if the child does not accept the suggestion, attorneys can use the fact that suggestive questioning was employed to discredit perfectly accurate testimony. Jurors typically view children as highly suggestible (Goodman, Golding, & Haith, 1984; Yarmey & Jones, 1983), and in some jurisdictions jurors are read instructions by the judge explicitly stating that children are particularly suggestible.

In addition to the complex psychological issues surrounding the child witness, when a child takes the stand, he or she will be subject to somewhat different laws than adult witnesses. (See Bulkley, 1982, and Goodman, 1984, for in-depth discussions of the various laws concerning children's testimony.) Perhaps the most important is that children under age 14, 12, or 10 years (depending on the state) typically must pass a competence examination before being permitted to testify. This examination consists of a courtroom interview, usually conducted at a preliminary hearing by the judge and attorneys. The court may also seek the advice of a psychologist who has interviewed the child. But, in the end, the child's competence is officially determined by the judge. If he or she finds the child incompetent, the child will not be permitted to testify. While the requirement of competence examinations for children has been dropped in several states and in federal courts, attorneys still can (and typically do) challenge a child's competence, in which case a competence examination ensues anyway.

It appears that children are most likely to testify in trials concerning sexual molestation. These cases are difficult to prosecute because the molestation may not involve sexual penetration; therefore, corroborating medical evidence to support the child's statements is often unavailable. Thus, the case often revolves around the child's versus the defendant's statements. In evaluating a child's claims of sexual assault, several factors should be taken into consideration. First, if the child is too young to know about sexual matters yet can describe sexually explicit acts, it would seem to increase the likelihood that he or she was victimized. Second, children, especially those who have been victimized by family members, not uncommonly recant. These children report the abuse, but then out of guilt, pressure, or fear deny that the assault occurred (Avery, 1983). And third, in contrast to the conditions surrounding most laboratory studies, child abuse victims may have reason to hide what actually happened. These victims may have been threatened not to tell, may be embarrassed, may fear that they will go to jail or be taken from their homes, and so on. Thus, their initial reports may not be the most accurate.

Finally, children's suggestibility as evidenced in typical laboratory studies may not predict children's suggestibility in investigations of child abuse. Most studies suffer from a lack of ecological validity in that the questions do not mimic those asked in actual investigations of this type. In an attempt to overcome this problem, Rudy and Goodman (1986) interviewed 4- and 7-year-olds 11 days after the children had played games with a male confederate. During the games, half of the children at each age were dressed in a clown costume, which was placed over their clothes. At the interview, the children were asked a variety of suggestive and objective questions such as "How many times did he spank you?" "Did he kiss you?", and "He took your clothes off, didn't he?" In actuality, none of the suggested actions had occurred. The children, even the 4-year-olds, were quite accurate in responding to these queries. Thus, when the questions concerned salient actions involving the children's own bodies, the vast majority of the children were able to resist the suggestions.

The Elderly Witness

Relatively little research exists on the testimony of elderly witnesses, but several relevant studies have been conducted by Yarmey (Yarmey & Kent, 1980; Yarmey, Jones & Rashid, 1984; see Yarmey, 1984, for a review). Across several studies, Yarmey found that the elderly, compared to younger adults, recalled less about events. While the elderly did not differ from younger adults in the number of correct identifications of suspects, the older subjects produced a greater number of false identifications of innocent people such as bystanders (e.g., Yarmey & Kent, 1980). The elderly were also less confident of their memory, even when they were correct. However, not all elderly were poor witnesses—some performed as well as younger adults. More studies are needed before we will know whether conditions exist under which the elderly perform more comparably to other adult witnesses.

CRIME VICTIMS

For many criminal acts, the most important witness is the victim. For ethical reasons, it is difficult to study the testimony of victims in the laboratory—we cannot kidnap, assault, or rob subjects in our experiments (but see Hosch & Cooper, 1982; Hosch et al., 1984). Therefore, to say anything about the testimony of victims, it is necessary to abstract, cautiously, from the few relevant studies available—most of which either are not geared to eyewitness testimony or are of scientifically questionable quality. Thus this section of our chapter is somewhat speculative.

In the typical laboratory study of eyewitness testimony, such as most of those described in this chapter, bystander witnesses view a staged or videotaped event from a safe distance and are not personally involved. The event, and the witnesses' testimony, may have little significance for their lives or for the "assailant's." In contrast, crime victims—particularly those subjected to violent crime—will be psychologically and physically traumatized during the incident and, afterward, eager for the culprit to be apprehended, and cognizant of the possible consequences for the person accused. In cases of family violence or incest, this latter possibility sometimes produces considerable conflict for the victim since his or her testimony might result in a loved one going to jail, financial loss, or revenge.

Brown and Kulik (1977) proposed that events of personal significance or high consequentiality are remembered well, even many years later. In support of this idea, Brown and Kulik found that many people claim to remember with clarity the events surrounding the assassinations of John F. Kennedy or Martin Luther King. Unfortunately, an objective record that could verify these reports was unavailable. The recollections, in part or in whole, may have been unintentional fabrications. Thus, their proposal of highly accurate, "flash bulb" memories, while interesting, remains to be scientifically verified (see Neisser, 1982).

Other, more rigorous studies, however, support the notion that personally significant events are retained better than personally insignificant events. For example, Keenan, MacWhinney, and Mayhew (1977) found that statements with high interactional content (i.e., statements conveying information about the speaker-listener interaction) made by a colloquium speaker were remembered far better than other statements, even after a 30-hour delay. In a second study, the effect was replicated after a 72-hour delay (MacWhinney, Keenan, & Reinke, 1982). It was also found that subjects comparable to bystander witnesses in laboratory experiments of eyewitness testimony remembered much less than did subjects who were comparable to participant witnesses.

While the previously cited studies indicate that memory can at times be quite accurate, the situations examined did not involve stress, loss of property, or threat of bodily harm. The Yerkes-Dodson law, referred to earlier, would predict that the stress associated with a crime or accident would restrict attention and hinder memory. Most studies investigating victims' memory for stressful events take advantage of real-life traumas and do not have the advantage of a complete, objective record of what happened (but see Goodman et al., in press). For example, Kuehn (1974) examined police reports of crimes such as rape, assault, and homicide. In the latter case, reports were sometimes obtained from victims on the verge of death. He found that most victims were able to provide gross characteristics of the assailant (e.g., age, race, sex, and hair color). Unfortunately, it is impossible to tell from this study whether the reports were accurate.

In a few studies, an objective record of part of what happened was available. Dodge (1983) reviewed reports made by 20 survivors of a KLM and Pan Am airplane crash that occurred on the Canary Islands in 1977. At that time, the crash was the worst airplane disaster in history. Objective information was available about the time of the crash, the weather conditions, and the seating position of the passengers. According to the sketchy report provided by Dodge, respondents accurately remembered their seating positions, and many were able to give information about others seated near them, such as their names and seat numbers. (This information was probably gained well before the crash, however.) Only 20 percent accurately reported the time of the accident with 15 minutes, with some estimates being as much as an hour and a half off. Memory for weather conditions was somewhat variable as well. Surprisingly, most respondents reported feeling calm and/or confused rather than terrorized or panicked, suggesting that survivors who were most shaken by the incident did not fill out the questionnaire, thus limiting the generalizability of the results.

Terr (1979, 1983) also interviewed survivors of a real-life traumatic incident —the kidnapping of a school bus full of children in Chowchilla, California. Unlike the respondents in Dodge's study, the children were terrified, and virtually all of them showed signs of posttraumatic stress (e.g., nightmares, posttraumatic play) that have lasted for years (Terr, 1983). Terr (1979) reports that while the children evidenced time distortions, omen formation, and partial denial of the significance of the event, they were each able to give a detailed description of what happened. Unfortunately, Terr was not able to interview the children until almost a year after the incident. By then the children would have had ample opportunity to rehearse the events with each other and hear about the incident on television and radio, among other reminders of the event.

The studies by Kuehn, Dodge, and Terr underline the problems associated with examining memory for real-life traumatic events. Again we must retreat to the laboratory and, as a consequence, examine events that are less stressful. Hosch and his colleagues (Hosch & Cooper, 1982; Hosch et al., 1984) have examined the effects of victimization on eyewitness testimony. In their studies, subjects either witnessed a theft of someone else's calculator, witnessed the theft of their own wrist watches (the "victim" group), or did not witness a theft. Across the three groups, subjects did not differ in their ability to identify the culprit unless they were given biased instructions at test (Hosch et al., 1984). All subjects had been led to believe the theft was real and were questioned by campus police and then given a photo lineup. Half of the subjects in each group were told the culprit was probably in the lineup (biased instructions). The subject-victims given the biasing information were least accurate in their identifications. This result probably reflects the victims' greater motivation to find the culprit (and recover their watches) rather than a poorer memory caused by stress. In fact, stress ratings were not taken, so we do not know how stressful the event was for the victims.

In sum, little definitive evidence exists on which to build an understanding of memory for stressful and personally significant real-life events such as those experienced by victims of crime. Much more work needs to be done in this area.

ECOLOGICAL VALIDITY

One frequently asked question concerns ecological validity: How much do findings from the laboratory generalize to forenic situations? For example, how much do subjects who know that their testimony has no serious consequences act like real-life eyewitnesses? Some studies have tried to create conditions more similar to actual legal situations (Brigham et al., 1982; Malpass & Devine, 1981c; Murray & Wells, 1982) with some surprising results. For example, it might be argued that the rate of false identification in eyewitness research is often high because subjects know that their responses will not result in arrest. In real life, witnesses might be more cautious. Yet when a realistic vandalism was staged and subjects were led to believe that the suspect would go to jail, they attempted *more* identifications (83 percent) than did those who thought "he would get a good talking to" (26 percent), while the two groups did not differ overall in the number of errors committed (Malpass & Devine, 1981c). More realistic research of this type is needed. While it is likely that many of the general principles derived from memory research will extend to real-life criminal events, we may be able to learn more about accuracy levels reached by witnesses, about factors which affect memory that have not yet been explored, and about the interaction of variables such as age, stress, and expectancy.

THE PSYCHOLOGIST AS EXPERT WITNESS

Having completed our review of the literature, we would like to comment briefly on the role of the expert witness on eyewitness testimony. Expert testimony about eyewitness reports has been allowed in many states but not without controversy.

When psychologists testify about eyewitness testimony, they typically describe the findings of relevant studies, as we have done in this chapter. Depending upon the judge, the expert may also be permitted to express an opinion about the credibility of a specific witness. The latter is particularly likely if the psychologist has interviewed or tested the witness.

In order to testify, a psychologist must qualify as an expert by passing a competence examination conducted by the judge and attorneys. Criteria used in determining competency include the following: (1) the witness must be a qualified expert; (2) the testimony must concern a proper subject matter; (3) the testimony must be in accordance with a generally accepted explanatory theory; and (4) the probative value of the testimony must outweigh the prejudicial effects. As can be inferred from these rather vague criteria, the trial judge has broad discretion in qualifying an expert and admitting his or her testimony.

Both legal and psychological controversy surrounds the use of expert testimony. The legal controversy revolves around the fear that psychological experts' testimony will invade the province of the jury, have an undue influence on jurors, provide information already familiar to jurors, and waste time by possibly leading to a battle of the experts (Loftus, 1984). Thus some courts are not open to expert testimony on human memory. Other courts, however, feel that psychologists can aid the determination of fact by educating the courts about the accuracies and inaccuracies of eyewitness reports. Aside from knowing the predisposition of the judge and the legal history of his or her jurisdiction, it is difficult to say in advance whether expert testimony by a psychologist will be admitted.

The psychological controversy concerns the status of research on eyewitness testimony. Do psychologists possess a body of replicable, relevant, and valid facts that go beyond jurors' common knowledge? McCloskey and Egeth (1983) recently raised this question and suggested that psychologists are not yet in a position to educate the courts. Responses to their attack were immediate and vigorous (Loftus, 1983), but the controversy continues (Egeth & McCloskey, 1984; Loftus, 1984; Wells, 1984). It is currently a matter of personal judgment on the part of professionals whether and when they feel capable of presenting expert opinion in courts of law. We hope that the review presented in this chapter will help psychologists decide when to accept an offer to serve as an expert on eyewitness testimony.

Research on the psychology of testimony began almost 100 years ago, and research on human memory began even earlier. Looking at the many years of accumulated research, we know that eyewitness testimony can be far from perfect, and we have identified many of the factors that affect eyewitness reports. We still have more to learn about the accuracies and inaccuracies of human memory, however. In particular, more realistic research is needed, and research should explore age differences in eyewitness testimony, the testimony of crime victims, and techniques to improve the accuracy of testimony. Nevertheless, in some cases we can provide valuable information to the courts.

REFERENCES

Alba, J. W., & Hasher, L. (1983). Is memory schematic? *Psychological Bulletin, 93*, 203–231.

Avery, M. C. (1983). The child abuse witness: The potential for secondary victimization. *Criminal Justice Journal, 7*, 1–48.

Baddeley, A. D. (1972). Selective attention and performance in dangerous environments. *British Journal of Psychology, 10*, 293–301.

Baddeley, A. D. (1979). Applied cognitive and cognitive applied psychology: The case of face recognition. In L. G. Nilsson (Ed.), *Perspectives on memory research.* Hillsdale, NJ: Erlbaum.

Bahrick, H. P., Bahrick, P. O., & Wittlinger, R. P. (1975). Fifty years of memory for names and faces: A cross sectional approach. *Journal of Experimental Psychology: General, 104*, 54–75.

Bartlett, F. C. (1932). *Remembering.* Cambridge: Cambridge University Press.

Bekerian, D. A., & Bowers, J. M. (1983). Eyewitness testimony: Were we misled? *Journal of Experimental Psychology: Learning, Memory and Cognition, 9*, 139–145.

Billig, M., & Milner, D. (1976). A spade is a spade in the eyes of the law. *Psychology Today, 2*, 13–15, 62.

Boice, R., Hanley, C. P., Shaughnessy, P., & Gansler, D. (1982). Eyewitness accuracy: A general observational skill? *Bulletin of the Psychonomic Society, 20*, 193–195.

Bower, G. H., & Karlin, M. B., (1974). Depth of processing pictures of faces and recognition memory. *Journal of Experimental Psychology, 103*, 751–757.

Bowers, J. M., & Bekerian, D. A. (1984). When will postevent information distort eyewitness testimony? *Journal of Applied Psychology, 69*, 466–472.

Bregman, N. J., & McAllister, H. A. (1982). Eyewitness testimony: The role of commitment in increasing reliability. *Social Psychology Quarterly, 45*, 181–184.

Brigham, J. C., & Barkowitz, P. (1978). Do 'they all look alike'? The effect of race, sex, experience, and attitudes on the ability to recognize faces. *Journal of Applied Psychology, 8*, 306–318.

Brigham, J. C., & Malpass, R. S. (1985). The role of experience and contact in the recognition of faces in own- and other- race persons. *Journal of Social Issues, 41*, 139–156.

Brigham, J. C., Maass, A., Snyder, L. D., & Spaulding, K. (1982). Accuracy of eyewitness identifications in a field setting. *Journal of Personality and Social Psychology, 42*, 673–681.

Brown, E. L., Deffenbacher, K. A., & Sturgill, W. (1977). Memory for faces and the circumstances of encounter. *Journal of Applied Psychology, 62*, 311–318.

Brown, R., & Kulik, J. (1977). Flashbulb memories. *Cognition, 5*, 73–99.

Bruner, J. S., & Postman, L. (1949). Perception, cognition, and behavior. *Journal of Personality, 18*, 14–31.

Buckhout, R. (1974). Eyewitness testimony. *Scientific American, 231* (12), 23–31.

Buckhout, R., Alper, A., Chern, S., Silverberg, G., & Slomovits, M. (1974). Determinants of eyewitness performance on a lineup. *Bulletin of the Psychonomic Society, 4*, 191–192.

Buckhout, R., Figueroa, D., & Hoff, E. (1975). Eyewitness identification: Effects of suggestion and bias in identification from photographs. *Bulletin of the Psychonomic Society, 6*, 71–74.

Bulkley, J. (1982). *Intrafamily child sexual abuse cases.* Washington, DC: American Bar Association.

Butters, M. J. (1970). Differential recall of paired associates as a function of arousal and concreteness-imagery levels. *Journal of Experimental Psychology, 84*, 252–256.

Cady, H. M. (1924). On the psychology of testimony. *American Journal of Psychology, 35*, 110–112.

Ceci, S., Ross, D., & Toglia, M. P. (in press). Suggestibility of children's memory: Psycholegal implications. *Journal of Experimental Psychology: General.*

Chance, J., & Goldstein, A. G. (1984). Face-recognition memory: Implications for children's eyewitness testimony. *Journal of Social Issues, 40*(2), 69–86.

Chance, J., Goldstein, A. G., & McBride, L. (1975). Differential experience and recognition memory for faces. *Journal of Social Psychology, 97*, 243–253.

Christiaansen, R. E., & Ochalek, K. (1983). Editing misleading information from memory: Evidence for the coexistence of original and postevent information. *Memory & Cognition, 11*, 467–475.

Christiaansen, R. E., Sweeney, J. D., & Ochalek, K. (1983). Influencing eyewitness descriptions. *Law and Human Behavior, 7*, 59–65.

Clifford, B. R. (1980). Voice identification by human listeners: On earwitness reliability. *Law and Human Behavior, 4*, 373–394.

Clifford, B. R. (1983). Memory for voices: The feasibility and quality of earwitness evidence. In S. Lloyd-Bostock & B. R. Clifford (Eds.), *Evaluating witness evidence* (pp. 189–218). Chichester, U.K.: Wiley.

Clifford, B. R., & Bull, R. (1978). *The psychology of person identification*. London: Routledge & Kegan Paul.

Clifford, B. R., & Richards, V. J. (1977). Comparison of recall by policemen and civilians under conditions of long and short durations of exposure. *Perceptual and Motor Skills, 45*, 503–512.

Clifford, B. R., & Scott, J. (1978). Individual and situational factors in eyewitness testimony. *Journal of Applied Psychology, 63*, 352–359.

Cohen, R. L., & Harnick, M. A. (1980). The susceptibility of child witnesses to suggestion. *Law and Human Behavior, 4*, 201–210.

Courtois, M. R., & Mueller, J. H. (1981). Target and distractor typicality in facial recognition. *Journal of Applied Psychology, 66*, 639–645.

Dale, P. S., Loftus, E. F., & Rathbun, L. (1978). The influences of the form of the question on the eyewitness testimony of preschool children. *Journal of Psycholinguistic Research, 7*, 269–277.

Davies, G. M., Shepherd, J. W., & Ellis, H. D. (1979). Effects of interpolated mugshot exposure on accuracy of eyewitness identification. *Journal of Applied Psychology, 64*, 232–237.

Deffenbacher, K. (1980). Eyewitness accuracy and confidence: Can we infer anything about their relationship? *Law and Human Behavior, 4*, 243–260.

Deffenbacher, K. (1983). The influence of arousal on reliability of testimony. In S. Lloyd-Bostock & B. R. Clifford (Eds.), *Evaluating witness evidence* (pp. 235–254). Chichester, Great Britain: Wiley.

Deffenbacher, K., & Horney, J. (1981). Psycho-legal aspects of face identification. In G. Davies, H. Ellis, & J. Shepherd (Eds.), *Perceiving and remembering faces* (pp. 201–226). London: Academic Press.

Deffenbacher, K. A., Leu, J. R., & Brown, E. L. (1981). Memory for faces: Testing method, encoding strategy, and confidence. *America Journal of Psychology, 94*, 13–26.

Dent, H. (1977). Stress as a factor influencing person recognition in identification. *Bulletin of the British Psychological Society, 30*, 339–340.

Dent, H. (1982). The effects of interviewing strategies on the results of interviews with child witnesses. In A. Trankell (Ed.), *Reconstructing the Past*, pp. 279–298. Deventer, Netherlands: Kluwer.

Dent, H. R., & Stephenson, G. M. (1979). An experimental study of the effectiveness of different techniques of questioning child witnesses. *British Journal of Social and Clinical Psychology, 18*, 41–51.

Dodd, D. H., & Bradshaw, J. M. (1980). Leading questions and memory: Pragmatic constraints. *Journal of Verbal Learning and Verbal Behavior, 19*, 695–704.

Dodge, R. E. (1983). Aircraft accident survivors as witnesses. *Aviation, Space, and Environmental Medicine, 54*, 165–167.

Doob, A. N., & Kirshenbaum, H. (1973). Bias in police lineups—Partial remembering. *Journal of Police Science and Administration, 1*, 287–293.

Duncan, E. M., Whitney, P., & Kunen, S. (1982). Integration of visual and verbal information in children's memories. *Child Development, 53*, 1215–1223.

Eagly, A. H. (1978). Sex differences in influenceability. *Psychological Bulletin, 85*, 86–116.

Easterbrook, J. A. (1959). The effect of emotion on the utilization and organization of behavior. *Psychological Review, 66,* 183–201.

Ebbinghaus, H. E. (1885/1964). *Memory: A contribution to experimental psychology.* New York: Dover.

Egan, D., Pittner, M., & Goldstein, A. G. (1977). Eyewitness identification: Photographs vs. live models. *Law and Human Behavior, 1,* 199–206.

Egeth, H. E., & McCloskey, M. (1984). Expert testimony about eyewitness behavior: Is it safe and effective? In G. L. Wells & E. F. Loftus (Eds.), *Eyewitness testimony* (pp. 283–303). Cambridge: Cambridge University Press.

Elliott, E. S., Wills, E. J., & Goldstein, A. G. (1973). The effects of discrimination training on the recognition of white and oriental faces. *Bulletin of the Psychonomic Society, 2,* 71–73.

Ellis, H. D. (1981). Theoretical aspects of face recognition. In G. M. Davies, H. D. Ellis, & J. W. Shepherd (Eds.), *Perceiving and remembering faces* (pp. 171–197). London: Academic Press.

Ellis, H. D. (1984). Practical aspects of face memory. In G. L. Wells & E. F. Loftus (Eds.), *Eyewitness testimony* (pp. 12–37). Cambridge: Cambridge University Press.

Ellis, H. D., Davies, G. M., & Shepherd, J. W. (1977). Experimental studies of face identification. *National Journal of Criminal Defense, 3,* 219–234.

Eysenck, H. J. (1979). Anxiety, learning, and memory: A reconceptualization. *Jounal of Research in Personality, 13,* 363–385.

Feinman, S., & Entwisle, D. R. (1976). Children's ability to recognize other children's faces. *Child Development, 47,* 506–510.

Fivush, R. (1984). Learning about school: The development of kindergarteners' school scripts. *Child Development, 55,* 1697–1709.

Fivush, R., Hudson, J., & Nelson, K. (1984). Children's long-term memory for a novel event: An exploratory study. *The Merrill-Palmer Quarterly, 30,* 303–316.

Friedman, A. (1979). Framing pictures. The role of default knowledge in automized encoding and memory for gist. *Journal of Experimental Psychology: General, 108,* 315–355.

Galper, R. E. (1973). Functional race membership and recognition of faces. *Perceptual and Motor Skills, 37,* 455–462.

Gilliland, A., & Burke, R. (1926). A measure of sociability. *Journal of Applied Psychology, 10,* 315–326.

Glickman, S. E. (1961). Perseverative neural processes and consolidation of the memory trace. *Psychological Bulletin, 58,* 218–233.

Goetze, H. (1980). *The effect of age and method of interview on the accuracy and completeness of eyewitness accounts.* Unpublished dissertation, Hofstra University, New York.

Goldstein, A. G., & Chance, J. E. (1964). Recognition of children's faces. *Child Development, 35,* 129–136.

Goodman, G. S. (Ed.). (1984). The child witness. *Journal of Social Issues, 40(2).*

Goodmen, G. S., Aman, C., & Hirschman, J. (in press). Child sexual and physical abuse: Children's testimony. In S. Ceci, M. Toglia, & D. Ross (Eds.), *Children's eyewitness memory.* New York: Springer.

Goodman, G. S., Golding, J. M. & Haith, M. M. (1984). Jurors' reactions to child witnesses. *Journal of Social Issues, 40*(2), 139–156.

Goodman, G. S., & Reed, R. S. (in press). Age differences in eyewitness testimony. *Law and Human Behavior*.

Gorenstein, G. Y., & Ellsworth, P. C. (1980). Effect of choosing an incorrect photograph on a later identification by a witness. *Journal of Applied Psychology, 65*, 616–622.

Graesser, A. (1981). *Prose comprehension beyond the word*. New York: Springer.

Greene, E., Flynne, M. B., & Loftus, E. F. (1982). Inducing resistance to misleading information. *Journal of Verbal Learning and Verbal Behavior, 21*, 207–219.

Hasher, L., Attig, M. S., & Alba, J. W. (1981). I knew it all along: Or, did I? *Journal of Verbal Learning and Verbal Behavior, 20*, 86–96.

Hastorf, A. H., & Cantril, H. (1954). They saw a game: A case study. *Journal of Abnormal and Social Psychology, 49*, 129–234.

Hoffman, C., & Kagan, S. (1977). Field dependence and facial recognition. *Perceptual and Motor Skills, 44*, 119–124.

Hosch, H. M. & Cooper, D. S. (1982). Victimization as a determinant of eyewitness accuracy. *Journal of Applied Psychology, 67*, 649–652.

Hosch, H. M., Leippe, M. R., Marchioni, P. M., & Cooper, D. S. (1984). Victimization, self-monitoring, and eyewitness identification. *Journal of Applied Psychology, 69*, 280–288.

Hosch, H. M., & Platz, S. J. (1984). Self-monitoring and eyewitness accuracy. *Personality and Social Psychology Bulletin, 10*, 289–292.

Houts, M. (1956). *From proof to evidence*. Springfield, Ill.: Charles C. Thomas.

Howells, T. H. (1938). A study of ability to recognize faces. *Journal of Abnormal and Social Psychology, 33*, 124–127.

Hunt, T. (1928). The measurement of social intelligence. *Journal of Applied Psychology, 12*, 317–333.

Johnson, C., & Scott, B. (1976). *Eyewitness testimony and suspect identifications as a function of arousal, sex of witness and scheduling of interrogation*. Paper presented at the meeting of the American Psychological Association, Washington, DC.

Kaess, W. A., & Witryol, S. L. (1955). Memory for names and faces: A characteristic of social intelligence. *Journal of Applied Psychology, 39*, 457–462.

Keenan, J. M., MacWhinney, B., & Mayhew, D. (1977). Pragmatics in memory: A study in natural conversation. *Journal of Verbal Learning and Verbal Behavior, 16*, 549–560.

King, M. A. (1984). *An investigation of the eyewitness abilities of children*. Unpublished doctoral dissertation, University of British Columbia.

Klatzky, R. L. (1980). *Human memory* (2nd ed.). San Francisco: Freeman.

Kleinsmith, L. J., & Kaplan, S. (1963). Paired associated learning as a function of arousal and interpolated interval. *Journal of Experimental Psychology, 65*, 190–193.

Krafka, C., & Penrod, S. (1985). Reinstatement of context in a field experiment of eyewitness identification. *Journal of Personality and Social Psychology, 49*, 58–69.

Kuehn, L. L. (1974). Looking down a gun barrel: Person perception and violent crime. *Perceptual and Motor Skills, 39*, 1159–1164.

Laughery, K. R., Alexander, J. F., & Lane, A. B. (1971). Recognition of human faces: Effects of target exposure time, target position, pose position, and type of photograph. *Journal of Applied Psychology, 51*, 477–483.

Lavrakas, P., Buri, J., & Mayznere, M. (1976). A perspective on the recognition of other-race faces. *Perception and Psychophysics, 20,* 475–481.

Leippe, M. R., Wells, G. L., & Ostrom, T. M. (1978). Crime seriousness as a determinant of accuracy in eyewitness identification. *Journal of Applied Psychology, 63,* 345–351.

Lindsay, R. C. L., & Wells, G. L. (1980). What price justice? Exploring the relationship of lineup fairness to identification accuracy. *Law and Human Behavior, 4,* 303–314.

Lindsay, R. C. L., & Wells, G. L. (1983). What do we really know about cross-race eyewitness identification? In S. Lloyd-Bostock & B. R. Clifford (Eds.), *Evaluating witness evidence* (pp. 219–233). Chichester, Great Britain: Wiley.

Linton, M. (1982). Transformations of memory in everyday life. In U. Neisser (Ed.), *Memory observed* (pp. 77–91). San Francisco: Freeman.

Lipton, J. P. (1977). On the psychology of eyewitness testimony. *Journal of Applied Psychology, 62,* 90–95.

Lloyd-Bostock, S. M., & Clifford, B. R. (1983). *Evaluating witness evidence.* New York: Wiley.

Loftus, E. F. (1975). Leading questions and the eyewitness report. *Cognitive Psychology, 7,* 560–572.

Loftus, E. F. (1976). Unconscious transference in eyewitness identification. *Law and Psychology Review, 2,* 93–98.

Loftus, E. F. (1977). Shifting human color memory. *Memory and Cognition, 5,* 696–699.

Loftus, E. F. (1979a). *Eyewitness testimony.* Cambridge, MA: Harvard University Press.

Loftus, E. F. (1979b). Reactions to blantantly contradictory information. *Memory and Cognition, 7,* 368–374.

Loftus, E. F. (1980). Impact of expert psychological testimony on the unreliability of eyewitness identification. *Journal of Applied Psychology, 65,* 9–15.

Loftus, E. F. (1983). Silence is not golden. *American Psychologist, 38,* 564–572.

Loftus, E. F. (1984). Expert testimony on the eyewitness. In G. L. Wells & E. F. Loftus (Eds.), *Eyewitness testimony* (pp. 273–282). Cambridge: Cambridge University Press.

Loftus, E. F., & Burns, T. E. (1982). Mental shock can produce retrograde amnesia. *Memory and Cognition, 10,* 318–323.

Loftus, E. F., & Greene, E. (1980). Warning: Even memory for faces may be contagious. *Law and Human Behavior, 4,* 323–334.

Loftus, E. F., & Ketcham, K. E. (1983). The malleability of eyewitness accounts. In S. Lloyd-Bostock & B. R. Clifford (Eds.), *Evaluating witness evidence* (pp. 159–171). Chichester, Great Britain: Wiley.

Loftus, E. F., & Marburger, W. (1983). Since the eruption of Mt. St. Helens, has anyone beaten you up? Improving the accuracy of retrospective reports with landmark events. *Memory & Cognition, 11,* 114–120.

Loftus, E. F., Miller, D. G., & Burns, H. J. (1978). Semantic integrations of verbal information into a visual memory. *Journal of Experimental Psychology: Human Learning and Memory, 4,* 19–31.

Loftus, E. F., & Palmer, J. C. (1974). Reconstruction of automobile destruction: An example of the interaction between language and memory. *Journal of Verbal Learning and Verbal Behavior, 13,* 585–589.

Loftus, E. F., Schooler, J. W., & Wagenaar, W. A. (1985). The fate of memory: Comment on McCloskey and Zaragosa. *Journal of Experimental Psychology: General, 114* 375–380.

Loftus, E. F., & Zanni, G. (1975). Eyewitness testimony: The influence of the wording of a question. *Bulletin of the Psychonomic Society, 5*, 86–88.

Loftus, G. R., & Loftus, E. F. (1976). *Human memory: The processing of information.* Hillsdale, NJ: Erlbaum.

Loftus, G. R., & Mackworth, N. H. (1978). Cognitive determinants of fixation location during picture viewing. *Journal of Experimental Psychology: Human Perception and Performance, 4*, 565–572.

Luce, T. S. (1974). *The role of experience in inter-racial recognition.* Paper presented at the annual meeting of the American Psychological Association, New Orleans.

Maass, A., & Brigham, J. C. (1982). Eyewitness identification: The role of attention and encoding specificity. *Personality and Social Psychology Bulletin, 8*, 54–59.

MacWhinney, B., Keenan, J. M., & Reinke, P. (1982). The role of arousal in memory for conversation. *Memory & Cognition, 10*, 308–317.

Malpass, R. S. (1981a). Effective size and defendant bias in eyewitness identification lineups. *Law and Human Behavior, 5*, 299–309.

Malpass, R. S. (1981b). Training in face recognition. In G. M. Davies, H. D. Ellis, & J. W. Shepherd (Eds.), *Perceiving and remembering faces* (pp. 271–285). London: Academic Press.

Malpass, R. S., & Devine, P. G. (1981a). Eyewitness identification: Lineup instructions and the absence of the offender. *Journal of Applied Psychology, 66*, 482–489.

Malpass, R. S., & Devine, P. G. (1981b). Guided memory in eyewitness identification. *Journal of Applied Psychology, 66*, 343–350.

Malpass, R. S., & Devine, P. G. (1981c). Realism and eyewitness identification research. *Law and Human Behavior, 4*, 347–358.

Malpass, R. S., & Kravitz, J. (1969). Recognition for faces of own and other race. *Journal of Personality and Social Psychology, 13*, 330–334.

Malpass, R. S., Lavigueur, H., & Weldon, D. E. (1973). Verbal and visual training in face recognition. *Perception and Psychophysics, 14*, 285–292.

Mandler, G. (1984). *Mind and body: The psychology of emotions and stress.* New York: W. W. Norton.

Marin, B. V., Holmes, D. L., Guth, M., & Kovac, P. (1979). The potential of children as eyewitnesses: A comparison of children and adults on eyewitness tasks. *Law and Human Behavior, 3*, 295–305.

Marquis, K. H., Marshall, J., & Oskamp, S. (1972). Testimony validity as a function of question form, atmosphere, and item difficulty. *Journal of Applied Social Psychology, 2*, 167–186.

Marshall, J. (1966). *Law and psychology in conflict.* New York: Bobbs-Merrill.

McCloskey, M., & Egeth, H. E. (1983). What can a psychologist tell a jury? *American Psychologist, 38*, 550–563.

McCloskey, M., & Zaragosa, M. (1985). Misleading postevent information and memory for events: Arguments and evidence against memory impairment hypotheses. *Journal of Experimental Psychology: General, 114*, 1–16.

Messick, S., & Damarin, F. (1964). Cognitive styles and memory for faces. *Journal of Abnormal and Social Psychology, 69*, 313–318.

Mueller, J. H., Bailis, K. L., & Goldstein, A. G. (1979). Anxiety and orienting tasks in picture recognition. *Bulletin of the Psychonomic Society, 13*, 145–148.

Murray, D. M., & Wells, G. L. (1982). Does knowledge that a crime was staged affect eyewitness accuracy? *Journal of Applied Social Psychology, 12*, 42–53.

Neisser, U. (Ed.). (1982). *Memory observed: Remembering in natural contexts*. San Francisco: Freeman.

Nelson, K., & Gruendel, J. (1981). Generalized event representations: Basic building blocks of cognitive development. In A. Brown & M. Lamb (Eds.), *Advances in developmental psychology* (Vol. 1), Hillsdale, NJ: Erlbaum.

Nowicki, S., Winograd, E., & Millard, B. A. (1979). Memory for faces: A social learning analysis. *Journal of Research in Personality, 13*, 460–468.

Patterson, K. E., & Baddeley, A. D. (1977). When face recognition fails. *Journal of Experimental Psychology: Human Learning and Memory, 3*, 406–417.

Pear, T. H., & Wyatt, S. (1914). The testimony of normal and mentally defective children. *British Journal of Psychology, 3*, 388–419.

Powers, P. A., Andriks, J. L., & Loftus, E. F. (1979). Eyewitness accounts of females and males. *Journal of Applied Psychology, 64*, 339–347.

Price, D. W. W., & Goodman, G. S. (1985, April). *The development of children's comprehension of recurring episodes*. Paper presented at the meeting of the Society of Research in Child Development, Toronto.

Read, J. D., & Bruce, D. (1984). On the external validity of questioning effects in eyewitness testimony. *International Review of Applied Psychology, 33*, 33–49.

Rudy, L., & Goodman, G. S. (1986). *"Did he kiss you?": Children's testimony*. Unpublished manuscript, University of Denver, Denver, CO.

Sanders, G. S., & Warnick, D. (1979). Some conditions maximizing eyewitness accuracy: A learning/memory model. *Basic and Applied Social Psychology, 2*, 67–69.

Schill, T. (1966). Effects of approval motivation and varying conditions of verbal reinforcement on incidental memory for faces. *Psychological Reports, 19*, 55–60.

Seelman, V. (1940). The influence of attitude upon the remembering of pictorial material. *Archives of Psychology, 36*, 1–64.

Shepherd, J. W. (1981). Social factors in face recognition. In G. Davies, H. Ellis, & J. Shepherd (Eds.), *Perceiving and remembering faces* (pp. 55–79). London: Academic Press.

Shepherd, J. W. (1983). Identification after long delays. In S. Lloyd-Bostock & B. R. Clifford (Eds.), *Evaluating witness evidence* (pp. 173–187). Chichester, Great Britain: Wiley.

Shepherd, J. W., & Ellis, H. D. (1973). The effect of attractiveness on recognition memory for faces. *American Journal of Psychology, 86*, 627–633.

Siegel, J. M., & Loftus, E. F. (1978). Impact of anxiety and life stress upon eyewitness testimony. *Bulletin of the Psychonomic Society, 12*, 479–480.

Snee, T., & Lush, D. (1941). Interaction of the narrative and interrogatory methods of obtaining testimony. *Journal of Psychology, 11*, 229–230.

Sommer, R. (1959). The new look on the witness stand. *Canadian Psychologist, 8*, 94–99.

Stephenson, G. M. (1984). Accuracy and confidence in testimony: A critical review and some fresh evidence. In D. J. Mueller, D. E. Blackman, & A. J. Chapman (Eds.), *Psychology and law* (pp. 229–248). Chichester, Great Britain: Wiley.

Terr, L. (1979). Children of Chowchillla: Study of psychic trauma. *Psychoanalytic Study of the Child, 34*, 547–623.

Terr, L. (1983). Chowchilla revisited: The effects of psychic trauma four years after a school bus kidnapping. *American Journal of Psychiatry, 140*, 1543–1550.

Tickner, A., & Poulton, E. (1975). Watching for people and actions. *Ergonomics, 18*, 35–51.

Tulving, E. (1983). *Elements of episodic memory*. Oxford: Clarendon Press.

Verinis, J. S., & Walker, V. (1970). Policeman and the recall of criminal details. *Journal of Social Psychology, 81*, 217–221.

Warrington, E. K., & Weiskrantz, L. (1970). Amnesic syndrome: Consolidation or retrieval? *Nature, 228*, 628–630.

Weinberg, H. I., & Baron, R. S. (1982). The discredible eyewitness. *Personality and Social Psychology Bulletin, 8*, 60–67.

Weinberg, H. I., Wadsworth, J., & Baron, R. S. (1983). Demand and the impact of leading questions on eyewitness testimony. *Memory & Cognition, 11*, 101–104.

Wells, G. L. (1984). A reanalysis of the expert testimony issue. In G. L. Wells & E. F. Loftus (Eds.), *Eyewitness testimony* (pp. 304–314). Cambridge: Cambridge University Press.

Wells, G. L., Ferguson, T. J., & Lindsay, R. C. L. (1981). The tractability of eyewitness confidence and its implications for triers of fact. *Journal of Applied Psychology, 66*, 688–696.

Wells, G. L., & Leippe, M. R. (1981). How do triers of fact infer the accuracy of eyewitness identifications? Memory for peripheral detail can be misleading. *Journal of Applied Psychology, 66*, 682–687.

Wells, G. L., Leippe, M. R., & Ostrom, T. M. (1979). Guidelines for empirically assessing the fairness of a lineup. *Law and Human Behavior, 3*, 285–293.

Wells, G. L., & Lindsay, R. C. L. (1980). On estimating the diagnosticity of eyewitness nonidentifcations. *Psychological Bulletin, 88*, 776–784.

Wells, G. L., & Loftus, E. F. (Eds.). (1984). *Eyewitness testimony*. Cambridge: Cambridge University Press.

Wells, G. L., & Murray, D. M. (1983). What can psychology say about the *Neil v. Biggers* criteria for judging eyewitness accuracy? *Journal of Applied Psychology, 68*, 347–362.

Whipple, G. M. (1911). The psychology of testimony. *Psychological Bulletin, 8*, 307–309.

Winograd, E. (1981). Elaboration and distinctiveness in memory for faces. *Journal of Experimental Psychology: Human Learning and Memory, 7*, 181–190.

Witkin, H., Dyk, R., Faterson, H., Goodenough, D. & Karp, S. (1974). *Psychological differentiation: Studies in development*. Hillsdale, NJ: Erlbaum.

Woodhead, M. M., Baddeley, A. D., & Simmonds, D. C. V. (1979). On training people to recognize faces. *Ergonomics, 22*, 333–343.

Yarmey, A. D. (1979). *The psychology of eyewitness testimony*. New York: The Free Press.

Yarmey, A. D. (1984). Age as a factor in eyewitness memory. In G. L. Wells & E. F. Loftus (Eds.), *Eyewitness testimony* (pp. 142–154). Cambridge: Cambridge University Press.

Yarmey, A. D., & Jones, H. P. T. (1983). Is the psychology of eyewitness identification a matter of common sense? In S. Lloyd-Bostock & B. R. Clifford (Eds.), *Evaluating witness evidence* (pp. 13–40). Chichester, Great Britain: Wiley.

Yarmey, A. D., Jones, H. P. T., & Rashid, S. (1984). Eyewitness memory of elderly and young adults. In D. J. Muller, D. E. Blackman, & A. J. Chapman (Eds.), *Topics in psychology and law,* pp. 215–228. Chichester, Great Britain: Wiley.

Yarmey, A. D., & Kent, J. (1980). Eyewitness identification by elderly and young adults. *Law and Human Behavior, 4,* 123–137.

Yerkes, R. M., & Dodson, J. D. (1908). The relation of strength of stimulus to the rapidity of habit-formation. *Journal of Comparative and Neurological Psychology, 18,* 459–482.

Yuille, J. C. (1980). A critical examination of the psychological and practical implications of eyewitness research. *Law and Human Behavior, 4,* 335–345.

Zadny, J., & Gerard, H. B. (1974). Attribution intentions and information selectivity. *Journal of Experimental Social Psychology, 10,* 34–52.

Zanni, G. R., & Offerman, J. T. (1978). Eyewitness testimony: An exploration of question wording upon recall as a function of neuroticism. *Perceptual and Motor Skills, 46,* 163–166.

CHAPTER 11

Assessing the Competence of Juries

STEVEN D. PENROD and BRIAN L. CUTLER

Although social scientists have been studying the jury since at least the turn of the century (Munsterberg, 1909), the quality, volume, and scope of jury research has expanded dramatically in the past decade (Kerr & Bray, 1982; Horowitz & Will-ging, 1984; Konecni & Ebbeson, 1982; Hans Vidmar, 1986). Increasingly, social scientists are being called on to aid lawyers and judges in the application of their re-search findings.

In this chapter we will examine two different types of social science research on the jury. Indeed, we shall argue that empirical examinations of jury decision making and jury competence have followed two general paths. A considerable body of re-search has emerged concerning the relationship between individual juror character-istics such as demographic, attitudinal, and personality dimensions and jury deci-sion making. Such research has evolved into an interesting enterprise—that of social scientific jury selection—and we will examine the promise and perils of this method. Another body of literature is more recent in vintage and is growing at a rapid rate. This research examines both the soundness of legal assumptions about the nature and quality of jury decision making and the effects of typical legal proce-dures on jury behavior. A review of both these domains follows, and the role of the social scientists in each domain is discussed.

SCIENTIFIC JURY SELECTION

A novel controversy has recently overtaken the American jury system. The princi-pal issue can be summarized succinctly: Does the use of social scientific techniques in the selection of trial jurors (voir dire) threaten to undermine the objectives of fair-ness and impartiality on which the jury system is based? The controversy is particu-larly modern, for the use of social scientific methods in jury selection first occurred

Preparation of this chapter and portions of the research described herein were funded by the National Sci-ence Foundation grant SES-8411721 and National Institute of Justice grant 84-IJ-CX-0010 to the second author. The authors wish to thank James Coward for his assistance with the preparation of the manu-script.

293

in 1971 (Schulman, Shaver, Colman, Emrich, & Christie, 1973), and the potential implications of the methods have only acquired widespread recognition in the last 15 years (Etzioni, 1974; Hans & Vidmar, 1982; Loh, 1984; Tivnan, 1975; Saks, 1976; Herbsleb, Sales, & Berman, 1978).

Critics (e.g., Etzioni) assail the methods as "social science jury stacking"; adherents (e.g., Schulman) argue that the methods help to assure that the objectives of the jury system are realized. Less passionate observers (e.g., Herbsleb, Hans, & Vidmar, and Loh) raise questions about the discoverability of social science findings and the ethics of social scientist participation in the jury selection process. Others (e.g., Saks) observe that currently there is virtually no evidence that the method does or could consistently make a difference in trial outcomes.

Okun (1968), in a penetrating and prescient consideration of the possible role of social scientific methods in jury selection, was probably the first person to anticipate the manner in which psychologists and other social scientists would find their way into the selection process at the voir dire stage. Little more than three years later, a group of social scientists was actively accumulating and, with the use of computers, combining information for use in the selection of jurors in the Harrisburg Seven conspiracy case. The social scientists—supporters of the defendants (including most notably Philip Berrigan) and themselves antiwar activists—volunteered to assist the defense. A now oft-cited summary of their efforts was published a year after the defendants' acquittal (Schulman et al., 1973). As their first step, Schulman et al. conducted telephone interviews of a cross-section of 840 residences of the 11 counties from which jurors were to be drawn.

Using information such as this, Schulman and colleagues employed statistical methods to formulate "profiles" of desirable and undesirable jurors for use in exercising peremptory challenges. Judging from Schulman et al.'s description, the survey information played a significant role in guiding the evaluations of the jurors. Yet, despite the defendants' acquittal, the authors downplayed the importance of the survey.

Some writers (e.g., Saks, 1976) have credited sociologist Schulman and social psychologists Christie and Shaver with devising a very creative and possibly powerful method of introducing social scientific insights into jury selection. Of course, these individuals were not alone in their endeavors. Sage (1973) reports the efforts of a group of five psychologists to aid Angela Davis' defense attorneys in the selection of a jury for her 1972 murder, kidnapping, and conspiracy trial. Similarly, a group of psychologists aided the attorneys of Daniel Ellsberg and Anthony Russo in their trial (Ungar, 1972). Defendants of other political persuasions also learned to make use of social scientific methods. DiMona (1974) and Zeisel and Diamond (1976), for example, reported extensively on the jury selection in the Mitchell-Stans-Vesco conspiracy trial where a telephone poll was used to construct demographic profiles of favorable and unfavorable jurors.

The issue of social scientific jury selection—that is, selection of jurors on the basis of demographic or personality characteristics or group status based on "scientific findings"—must be framed within the context of the legal premise of the voir dire. There are two basic procedures for selecting and striking jurors, and the primary legal assumptions underlying the voir dire process are embodied within these procedures. First, to obtain a population of potential jurors from which to sample, potential candidates are generally selected from voter registration, phone directories, driver registration, tax roles, and other lists of community members. Prospective jurors may then be sent questionnaires in order to determine their qualifications to serve on a jury.

In most jurisdictions the juror must be at least 18 years of age, have residence in the jurisdiction for a specified period of time, must be capable of reading and writing English, and must not have a criminal record (Greenberg & Ruback, 1982). Members of the community who fulfill these qualifications remain in consideration for jury duty unless they demonstrate their incapability to serve (e.g., hardships or health problems). The resultant venire is generally presumed to be representative of the community at large. On a case-specific level, the remaining potential jurors are questioned individually by the prosecution and defense attorneys, by the judge, or by both; and on the basis of their responses, individuals who are presumed to be biased may be challenged and excused from jury duty.

Two basic challenges are available to the attorney: challenges for cause and peremptory challenge. Challenges for cause can be for either specific provable biases such as relational or economic ties to litigants, or for nonspecific biases, such as group membership, personality, or some other demographic characteristics. Attorneys are given no limit to the number of challenges for cause, but each challenge must be approved by the presiding judge. On the other hand, peremptory challenges, which may be exercised without providing a justification, are limited in number (although the specific number can vary across jurisdictions and types of cases). Peremptory challenges may but need not be based on specific biases. (See Penrod and Linz, 1986, for a review of the legal precedents for the exercise of peremptory challenges.)

The provision of peremptory challenges (which is most prevalent in the United States as compared with Canada and England) rests on several underlying and interrelated propositions: (1) that attorneys should be allowed to act on intuitions (and stereotypes) about the predilections of jurors; (2) that the specific intuitions and stereotypes held by attorneys are justifiable in that they reflect actual cognitive or behavioral predilections; and (3) that disqualification of potential jurors on the basis of intuitions and stereotypes enhances the quality of the deliberation and the final decisions. It is clear that the first proposition is predicated on the validity of the second and third, both of which may be untenable. The second and third propositions can be translated to the following empirical questions: Can jurors be reliably discriminated on the basis of attitudinal and demographic characteristics, and do the characteristics by which jurors are discriminated reliably correlate with prosecution- or defense-proneness, and ultimately with verdict preferences? In fact, the enterprise of scientific jury selection also rests on the previously stated propositions, and it is to those empirical questions that much research over the past two decades has attended.

In employing scientific methods of jury selection, surveys can be conducted to develop profiles of desirable jurors (e.g., Shulman et al., 1973). This method relies on the aforementioned proposition that verdict preferences reliably relate to dispositional characteristics—that form of constellation associated with "conviction-proneness" or "acquittal-proneness."

Description of the Survey Method of Scientific Jury Selection

Survey methods are fairly common and follow a general procedure. A random sample survey such as the one described in the Harrisburg Seven case provides the basic data for the development of juror profiles. Executing such a survey is a complicated task, the validity and results of which are highly dependent on several critical factors.

Representativeness

As Berman and Sales (1977) have noted, care must be taken to insure that the individuals sampled in the survey are representative of the population from which the venire is to be drawn. Thus, members of groups such as policemen, lawyers, and teachers, who may be excused from sitting on juries, should be excluded from the sample. Second, it may be difficult to determine the actual representativeness of the pool from which the venire is drawn, because, as mentioned, multiple lists are used to sample the population. Hence, it can be difficult to draw a sample that is representative of the venire. Any meaningful difference between the surveyed sample and the actual venire poses grave threats to the generalizability of the survey results. A third problem is that surveys typically employ volunteer interviewers, a group which is sometimes beset with a high attrition rate (Berman & Sales, 1977), and the results of the survey can be threatened by unreliable interviewers.

Questionnaires

A second critical consideration is the selection of questions for the survey. The questions are generally of three types: (1) questions tapping attitudes about the particular case and issues to be raised in the case; (2) questions about the respondents' knowledge of the case and of the defendants; and (3) background questions concerning demographic characteristics, personality attributes, and leisure activities. From this perspective, there are problems with selecting both the independent and dependent variables.

With respect to independent variables, the conclusions drawn from the survey data assume that individuals have been reliably classified into groups differing with respect to demographic, attitudinal, and traitlike attributes. With some demographic characteristics, the reliability issue (e.g., age, race, gender) may be moot (to the extent that survey participants are willing to reduce their anonymity). But reliability of attitude and trait measures, and hence the construct validity of the hypothetical dimensions purportedly assessed by these dimensions, have long been in question. These problems of reliability are exacerbated by the fact that sample items are often drawn from marginally reliable scales (and unreliable scales), and sometimes even single items are used to sample a constellation of attitudes.

Equally as troublesome is the choice of dependent variables. Ideally, the survey is designed to provide a set of juror attributes that will allow social scientists and defense attorneys to accurately predict how a juror with a particular profile will vote on the case at hand. However, no one interviewed in the survey will have heard the case evidence or been actually confronted with the task of deciding the defendant's guilt or innocence. Therefore, it is extremely difficult to specify precisely what type of questionnaire responses will serve as an adequate predictor of how an individual will vote on a given case. The problem is to find an adequate substitute dependent or criterion variable.

Data Analysis

Berk, Hennessy, and Swan (1977) have noted that the lack of a clear-cut criterion variable often promotes the use of factor analytic procedures for data reduction. Factors defined by combinations of items (if simple structure is obtained) often serve as dependent variables. Once a factor is designated as the dependent variable, several methods of analysis may be employed, such as Automatic Interaction Detector (AID; Sonquist, Baker, & Morgan, 1973) or multiple regression (Cohen & Cohen, 1975). Berk et al. note that regression models obtained from jury surveys typically account for about 25 percent of the variance in the criterion variable chosen by the researcher.

Evaluation of the Social Scientific Method of Jury Selection

In practice it is quite difficult to assess the relative effect of the jury selection strategy because of the other evidential issues involved. The practitioners of social science selection have been relatively circumspect in assessing their work, and most of the hyperbole has been generated by their critics. Unfortunately, no precise estimates of the method's efficacy have been reported. Kairys, Schulman, and Harring (1975) and Silver (1978) have claimed an accuracy rate of 70 percent, based on posttrial interviews with both selected and challenged jurors in a number of trials; however, they fail to provide either the size of the data base or, more important, the precise meaning of 70 percent accuracy.

One systematic approach to evaluating the social scientific method of jury selection is to examine the relation between juror dispositional characteristics and attitudes and juror behavior in controlled settings. Indeed, the basic foundation for the scientific method of jury selection rests on the assumption that dispositions and attitudes reliably correlate with juror behavior. A strong argument can be made that the mock trial paradigm affords the advantage of assessing actual verdict preference, controlling for evidence and procedural issues and using (somewhat) more reliable classification schemes (Hastie, Penrod, & Pennington, 1983). In the next section we examine in some detail both simulation research and research with actual jurors in an effort to assess the efficacy of scientific jury selection methods.

A typical approach to examining the relationships among attitudes, personality and demographic characteristics, and group membership to verdict preferences is to assess the mock jurors' characteristics of interest (usually by demographic, self-history, and personality questionnaires), to expose mock jurors to a criminal or civil case description, and finally, to have the mock jurors render verdicts or determine awards or penalties for parties involved in the case. Experiments differ widely in degree of realism or external and ecological validity. Some of the dimensions on which experiments differ are subject pool (college student sample, members of a community, experienced jurors), nature of case (civil or criminal, as well as specific type of case and charge), detail of case (ranging from short summary to unedited transcript), case presentation medium (written summary, audiotape, videotape), extent of voir dire (ranging from none to extensive), and deliberation (ranging from none to unlimited). All of these factors are likely to affect outcomes at some level, thus threatening the comparability of experimental findings.

Using this methodological approach, many investigators have examined the relationships between juror behavior and juror attitudes, personality, and demographic characteristics. Saks (1976) reviews a small portion of this research. Gerbasi, Zuckerman, and Reis (1977) go into slightly more detail (though their focus is not on verdict preferences), while Hans and Vidmar (1982) discuss the broadest range of studies. In general, the findings from these studies indicate that individual juror differences are not especially potent predictors of juror verdict preferences—though, of course, it can be argued quite persuasively that if individual differences *were* strong predictors, attorneys and judges would not require social science methods to establish such relationships.

In one such project, Simon (1967) examined the relationships between jurors' characteristics and their votes in two mock cases involving the insanity defense. She found no significant relationships for juror occupation, gender, income, religion, or age. Simon did find, however, a difference in verdict preferences attributable to race (blacks vs. others) and education for the two cases, but the variance accounted for by these predictor variables is small (less than 5 percent for the first case).

In Saks' dissertation research (1977), a total of 480 jurors viewed a videotaped burglary trial and deliberated in juries to a verdict. Saks assessed demographic and attitudinal characteristics and attempted to predict jurors' verdicts from this information. The single most powerful predictor (whether jurors believed crime was mainly the product of "bad people" or of "bad social conditions") accounted for 9 percent of the variance, and the four best predictors together accounted for slightly less than 13 percent.

Boehm (1968) developed a questionnaire to distinguish between biased and unbiased jurors (the Legal Attitudes Questionnaire; LAQ). Boehm based her research strategy on the hypothesis that authoritarian persons (conservative, rigid, conventional, superstitious, preoccupied with conformity and authority; Adorno, Frenkel-Brunswick, Levinson, & Sanford, 1950) would be conviction-prone. However, her results were only marginally significant, and she did not report a direct comparison between LAQ scores and verdict preferences.

Berg and Vidmar (1975) also tested Boehm's LAQ as a predictor of jurors' verdicts. In their study, 90 students completed the LAQ and rendered verdicts in two trials involving student misconduct. Although LAQ scores predicted recall and sentencing habits, they were not significantly related to perceptions of guilt. Buckhout and colleagues (1979) also failed to find a significant relationship between

LAQ scores and verdict preferences among students who viewed a videotaped murder trial.

Jurow (1971) administered the three LAQ scales and seven additional scales to a sample of 211 adults who rendered verdicts on a robbery case and a murder-rape case. Jurow's central focus was on jurors without and with scruples against the death penalty. Eight of the 10 scales correlated significantly with verdicts on the first case, but only 2 out of 10 correlated significantly with verdicts on the second case. The LAQ predicted verdicts on both cases; whereas the California F scale (the original measure of authoritarianism) proved to be a nonsignificant predictor of verdicts in both cases. Although Jurow found significant predictors, none accounted for an overwhelming proportion of variance.

Sosis (1974) pretested 70 high school students using another personality scale, the Rotter Internal-External Locus of Control (I-E), and asked the students to render verdicts in a case involving a drunk driver. Internals refer to people who tend to see themselves as responsible for their outcomes, or "masters of their own fate," whereas externals tend to attribute responsibility for outcomes to external, less controllable factors. Although there was no relationship between I-E score and perceived guilt (perhaps because of a ceiling effect on guilty scores due to overly compelling evidence), externals and moderate I-E scorers did differ from internals on recommended sentences. On the other hand, Kauffman and Ryckman (1979) found that locus of control did not predict ratings of the defendant's "criminal responsibility."

In one of the most ambitious studies of the links between personality characteristics and verdict preferences, Moran and Comfort (1982) surveyed by mail 319 jurors who had heard felony cases in Dade County, Florida. Although the study is marred by a low response rate (23 percent of the nearly 1400 jurors who received questionnaires responded), Moran and Comfort were able to establish links between personality and verdict preferences (between 6 percent and 11 percent of the variance accounted for). It can be argued that verdict (pre- and post-deliberation) is a gross measure of juror peformance, and with verdict as a dependent variable, it is difficult to detect the influence of dispositional factors. Factors such as age, race, and general heterogeneity of the jury may have effects on other aspects of the quality of deliberation. Moran and Comfort (1982) began to address this question by having their sample not only give their pre- and post-deliberation verdicts, but rate their degree of participation and perceived influence as well. Moran and Comfort found that age, membership in social organizations, and authoritarianism were predictors of self-reported participation among females (proportion of explained variance was .27). Females were more likely to participate if they were younger, involved in social organizations, and had lower rigidity scores. In comparison to jury verdict, measures of jury behavior might be more sensitive to person factors. Furthermore, use of jury behavior measures might help to explain process-oriented issues of social influence.

In a research effort similar to Boehm's (1968), Kassin and Wrightsman (1983) developed the Juror Bias Scale (JBS) that is intended to assess inherent conviction-proneness on an individual differences basis. Although Kassin and Wrightsman report some significant correlations between JBS scores and verdicts in mock trials, theoretical and methodological issues associated with scale construction and personality measurement raise some questions about the conclusions that are reached from their data. For example, the authors set out to measure two presumably orthogonal constructs, "probability of commission" (PC; the general belief that an individual who is brought to trial is likely to be guilty) and "reasonable doubt" (RD; the specific reasonable doubt standard employed by the juror). In constructing their scale, Kassin and Wrightsman included only those items that correlated significantly with the total scale—that is, with both subscales combined. It is not too surprising, therefore, that with the items retained, the two "theoretically unrelated" subscales, PC and RD, correlated .60! Thus, although statistically significant correlations were found between JBS scores and mock juror verdicts, it is not clear precisely what the JBS is measuring.

Although the use of personality characteristics as predictors of conviction- or acquittal-proneness shows some promise, some have argued that the use of attitudes toward crimes or toward particular crimes might be more predictive of verdict preference than personality characteristics. It is clear, however, from the social psychological literature that traditional approaches to attitude-behavior assessment have shown that attitudes are often weak predictors of behavior (Ajzen & Fishbein, 1980; Fishbein & Ajzen, 1975).

Field (1978) examined the relationships between background characteristics and attitudes on eight rape attitude factors. In general, the intercorrelations were quite low (60 percent of the 56 correlations were below .10). The highest correlation, .22, was between education and attitudes on punishment of rape. Jurors' gender yielded 6 of the 13 significant correlations with attitudes. Correlations between background and attitude variables and recommended sentences were also reported. The two highest correlations were for attitudes on punishment (-.42 for nonprecipitory rape and -.36 for precipitory rape). Field concludes that background characteristics are poor predictors of rape decisions, while attitudes are better predictors. However, the most troubling aspect of Field's findings is that his primary dependent variable is recommended punishment. This fact threatens the generalizability of the findings, as sentencing is not within the power of the juror, and deciding sentences is quite different from determining guilt or innocence on the basis of the evidence provided at trial.

Results of a study by Hastie et al. (1983) indicate that jurors' attitudes are not strongly related with their verdict preferences. In their study a sample of 828 subjects who were serving jury duty viewed a videotaped reenactment of an actual murder trial and deliberated to a verdict. At the conclusion of deliberation, the jurors completed an extensive questionnaire regarding demographic and other dispositional characteristics. Using predeliberation verdict as a dependent variable, the variables were examined in a stepwise regression analysis. Only four variables predicted predeliberation verdict, and, in total, only 3.2 percent of the variance in verdicts was accounted for by these four predictors. However, a subsample of 269 of the jurors completed a more extensive questionnaire which included attitudinal dimensions. Using these additional variables as predictors of predeliberation verdict in another regression analysis, five predictors were significant, accounting for a total of 10 percent of the variance in verdict preferences.

Like Moran and Comfort, Hastie et al. (1983) also discuss the role of jurors' dispositional factors in jury deliberation processes. With respect to demographic characteristics, it was found that socioeconomic status variables such as education, occupation, and income were predictive of recall of instructions and deliberation performance. These researchers found that persuasiveness of a juror (i.e., the extent to which other jurors reported being influenced by a juror) was related to amount of speaking. Four groups of persuasiveness were formed (ranging from low to high), and the mean number of statements made by each group were 42, 66, 94, and 151, respectively. Persuasive jurors not only spoke more than less-persuasive jurors, but used their speaking time differently. Content analysis revealed that persuasive jurors added diversity to facts, issues, and fact-issue relationships as compared with their less-persuasive counterparts. Thus, Hastie et al. conclude that persuasiveness, as an individual difference variable, is systematically related to the quality of the juror's contribution to the deliberation.

Open-mindedness, which correlated with persuasiveness, was also associated with volume of speech and was positively related to discussion of legal terms, fact-issue relationships, organizational directives, legal issues, and key facts, but not with verdict preferences. Open-minded jurors also perceived less pressure from other jurors and greater confidence in and agreement with jury verdict, as evidenced by postdeliberation ratings. Hastie et al. also examined the background of 120 "holdout" jurors—that is, jurors whose votes contradicted those of the majority at the end of the trial. These holdout jurors did not differ from the remaining sample on any demographic or behavioral dimensions. Although there were some differences between holdouts and the other jurors on trial perceptions, none of the dimensions on which the differences were obtained would allow preselection of jurors during voir dire that would increase the likelihood of a favorable outcome.

Penrod (1980) assessed attitudes and demographic characteristics of 367 actual jurors and had them give verdicts on four unrelated criminal cases of murder, rape, robbery, and negligence. Penrod regressed 21 attitudinal and demographic items over each of the verdicts separately and found that the overall variance in explained verdict was relatively modest (.141 for murder, .157 for rape, .049 for robbery, and .098 for negligence). Furthermore, there was little consistency in individual predictors of verdict; no single dimension was a significant predictor of the four verdicts or even any combination of three verdicts. The lack of consistency in attitude-verdict relationships was underscored by a second analysis. Penrod argued that irrespective of the dispositional measures, the stability of conviction- or acquittal-proneness should be evident in significant intercorrelations among verdicts for the four cases. The highest correlation between any two verdicts was only -.13 ($p < .02$), which was between the rape and murder verdicts. Thus, Penrod's results confirm that it is possible to detect modest relationships between attitudinal measures and verdict preferences but that the pattern of relationships may vary from case to case.

The conclusion we draw from existing research on juror verdict preferences and juror attitudes and personality variables is that no tremendously powerful relationships can be detected. There are probably modest relationships which will vary from case to case and even locality to locality. There are essentially no generalizations to be drawn, no magic questions to put to prospective jurors, not even a guarantee that a particular survey will detect useful attitude-behavior or personality-behavior relationships. Nonetheless, there is reason to think that surveys can offer marginal advantages to litigants who can afford to employ them.

The studies of the attitude-verdict relationship suggest that modest relationships can be detected on a case-by-case basis, with personality and attitudinal variables accounting for between 5 percent and 15 percent of the variance in juror verdicts. Although such relationships are modest in magnitude, they may be important and useful in particular cases. One way to view these relationships is in terms of the jury selection advantage they might provide. As Rosenthal and Rosnow (1984) point out, even ostensibly weak relationships can translate into significant real-world effects. Take an attorney operating without the benefit of this information who is essentially guessing which jurors might be favorably and unfavorably disposed to his case. If half the pool were favorable and half unfavorable, the attorney's guesswork would correctly classify half the jurors—chance level performance. However, if we consider a situation in which a jury survey detected a reliable relationship in which 5 percent of the variance in verdict preferences was accounted for by attitudinal and personality measures, successful use of that information would increase the attorney's performance significantly—61 percent of jurors could be correctly classified. With 15 percent of the variance accounted for, 69 percent of the jurors could be correctly classified. Thus, weak relationships can produce dramatic changes in jury selection performance.

Death-Qualified Juries

Before concluding this discussion of jury selection, we want to note one other attitudinal dimension—attitudes toward the death penalty. Death penalty attitudes have been studied intensively, and it has been shown that such attitudes are linked to a constellation of dispositions related to conviction-proneness. Traditionally, prospective jurors who have conscientious scruples against the death penalty were excused from sitting on capital juries (see *Witherspoon v. Illinois*, 1968). Beginning with *Witherspoon*, psychologists and legal scholars have studied both the process and outcome of selecting capital trials. While some research deals with the effects of the death qualification process itself (e.g., Haney, 1984a, 1984b), others (e.g., Cowan, Thompson, & Ellsworth, 1984; Moran & Comfort, 1986) have studied the dispositions and behavior of the resulting death-qualified jury and the *Witherspoon* excludables (those who would otherwise be capable of sitting on a jury but were challenged because they had conscientious scruples against the death penalty).

In Fitzgerald and Ellsworth's (1984) survey of 811 individuals who were eligible for jury service, it was found that 17 percent would be excludable under *Witherspoon*. Blacks and women were more likely to be excluded from sitting on capital cases, and the resulting jury pool tended to favor the prosecution. Cowan et al. (1984) found that death-qualified jurors were more likely to convict in a mock trial than were excludables.

Besides threatening the heterogeneity of capital juries by systematically excluding blacks and women, the resulting jury is also more likely to be relatively homogeneous with respect to attitudes. Several studies have found that attitudes toward the death penalty are correlated with antilibertarian attitudes (e.g., Bronson, 1980; Buckhout, Baker, Perlman, & Spiegel, 1977). In a more recent study, Moran and Comfort (1986) conducted two surveys (sample sizes of 282 and 346) of impaneled jurors in which they examined the interrelationships among demographic characteristics, personality characteristics, attitudes toward capital punishment, and juror experience. In both studies, attitudes toward the death penalty were uncorrelated with final verdict. In study 1, however, attitudes toward the death penalty were correlated with predeliberation verdict among females ($r = .21$) but not among males ($r = .05$). In study 2 this correlation was .11 (collapsed across gender). Results also indicated that Caucasian, male, wealthy, married, authoritarian, and conservative individuals were more likely to endorse favorable attitudes toward the death penalty. Although the relationship between attitudes toward the death penalty and predeliberation verdict is reliable, its magnitude is, once again, not large in traditional social scientific terms. Nonetheless, attitudes toward the death penalty, especially when used in the selection of capital trials, appear to pose a threat to the heterogeneity of the jury with respect to both demographic and personality characteristics. Of course, despite these findings, the Supreme Court in *Lockhart v. McCree* (1986) has ruled that the death qualification process is constitutional.

Although Justice Rehnquist, writing for the majority, criticized the social science research on the effects of the death-qualification process, he pointedly noted even if "the studies are both methodologically valid and adequate to establish that 'death qualification' in fact produces juries somewhat more 'conviction-prone' than 'non-death-qualified' juries . . . (w)e hold, nonetheless, that the Constitution does not prohibit the states from 'death qualifying' juries in capital cases" (*The New York Times*, May 6, 1986).

Finally, we should note that Penrod and Linz (1986) discuss some plausible alternatives for effective use of the voir dire. For example, Crump (1980) advises that the attorney could capitalize on voir dire to emphasize favorable law or facts; limit the effects of unfavorable law; obtain commitments from jurors; personalize the client; argue the case itself; condition the jurors to accept one's proof; build rapport with the client; downplay the adversary; minimize or accentuate the impact of concerns that are unrelated to the evidence; and set the norm for conduct of jurors during deliberation. Research by Elwork, Sales, and Alfini (1977, 1982) and Severance and Loftus (1981/1982) indicates that jurors have difficulty understanding some aspects of the case law to be applied while deliberating. Attorneys could use voir dire to highlight aspects of the case law that are crucial to the favorability of the outcome and maximize the likelihood that the case law will be applied appropriately.

ASSESSING JURY COMPETENCE

Juror Comprehension of Standard Instructions

The jurors' comprehension of legal instructions and terminology in cases has been the focus of considerable research. Within this domain psychologists and other scholars have studied juror performance in comprehension of judges' instructions (e.g., Charrow & Charrow, 1979); decision making in joined trials (e.g., Tanford & Penrod, 1982, 1984), in complex civil suits (Greene, Wilson & Loftus, 1986), in cases involving presumption instructions (Cutler, Penrod, & Schmolesky, 1985), in cases involving eyewitness testimony (Wells, Lindsay, & Ferguson, 1979); the use of mathematical, statistical, and probabilistic evidence (Thompson, 1986); and the effects of pretrial publicity (e.g., Constantini & King, 1980/1981). The majority of this research concerns the effects of instructions given to the jury by the judge and may be extremely useful to attorneys who are challenging the use of traditional instructions, formulating arguments about or drafting special instructions to jurors, or are confronted with procedural issues to which the research is relevant.

A substantial body of scientific research on juror comprehension of legal instructions raises serious doubts about the extent to which jurors comprehend and appropriately apply legal instructions. The problem with instructions is in their composition and structure. A number of psychologists and linguists have examined and evaluated the comprehensibility of the language used in typical jury instructions. This research has not only documented the fact that jurors have difficulty understanding and applying legal instructions, but the research has established the major sources of confusion and specified some of the possible remedies. As early as 1935, Hunter conducted a series of studies demonstrating the problems jurors have with legal language (see also the Report of the Cincinnati Conference on Trial by Jury, 1937). More recently, researchers have evaluated juror comprehension of standard instructions from Arizona (Sigwirth & Henze, 1973); California (Charrow & Charrow, 1979); Florida (Buchanan, Pryor, Taylor, & Strawn, 1978; Elwork et al., 1982); Michigan (Elwork et al., 1977); Nevada (Elwork et al., 1982); Wisconsin (Heuer & Penrod, 1986; Penrod, 1984); and Washington (Severance & Loftus, 1981/1982).

These researchers have employed a variety of methods to test juror comprehension of instructions, and the results of the studies are both surprisingly consistent and distressing. For example, in the Elwork et al. (1982) study, 39 percent of volunteer jurors who viewed a videotaped trial and received standard instructions rendered incorrect verdicts as opposed to 13 percent of jurors who received instructions specifically revised to improve comprehension. Charrow and Charrow (1979) had individuals who were called for jury duty listen to pattern jury instructions and then paraphrase what they had heard. Charrow and Charrow found that on the average, only 55 percent of important elements of the instruction were understood. In the Elwork and others (1982) study of a set of Nevada criminal instructions, the researchers found that viewers of videotaped instructions could answer only 15 percent of 89 questions posed to them about the instructions. Of course, since juries are composed of groups of individuals, one can ask how often a substantial portion of jurors will understand a critical point of law. If a substantial proportion of jurors on a jury understand the point of law, then perhaps discussion between jurors will clarify the point for all of the jurors. When the researchers set the following standards—(1) that 8 of 12 *jurors* in a jury and (2) 8 of 10 *juries* understand the law—they found that only one-sixth of the questions were adequately understood. After one rewrite of the instructions, performance improved to 66 percent, and after a second rewrite, performance improved to 80 percent.

Heuer and Penrod (1986) have investigated procedural alternatives designed to increase juror comprehension of instructions and other aspects of the trial. Their research examined the effects of several communication strategies on jury decision making and jurors' trial perceptions in a total of 96 jury trials conducted in Wisconsin between January of 1984 and April of 1985. Four jury communication techniques were independently manipulated within the trials using a factorial design. The four procedures manipulated were (1) jurors in some juries were allowed to pose questions to witnesses; (2) at the outset of the trial some juries were provided with a set of procedural instructions which included pattern instructions as well as any other instructions that were likely to be heard throughout the trial; (3) some juries were allowed to take notes during their trials; and (4) some juries were given written copies of the judge's instructions to refer to during the deliberations. Both civil suits and criminal cases were studied. All jurors completed extensive questionnaires about the trial proceedings.

Jurors allowed to ask questions were more satisfied with the information obtained from witnesses and were more satisfied that a responsible verdict had been reached. Providing jurors with preliminary instructions significantly increased juror satisfaction with the trial process, and judges reported significantly greater satisfaction with the verdicts reached by the juries in trials in which the juries received preliminary instructions. Two-thirds of the jurors that were allowed to take notes did so, and note-taking had little effect on the memory for the judge's instructions. Overall, providing the jurors with written instructions also yielded few benefits. However, most relevant to our discussion was the finding that juror comprehension of instructions given in civil cases averaged less than 50 percent, and comprehension of standard instructions given in criminal cases averaged only 71 percent (Heuer & Penrod, 1986). It should be emphasized that the jurors were tested on the most commonly administered instructions, and the questionnaire to which they responded was constructed in collaboration with four senior trial judges.

As another example, Hastie and colleagues (1983) studied the decision making of 828 actual jurors who, during the course of their jury service, sat as jurors in 69 separate juries. These jurors viewed a three-hour reenactment of an actual murder trial and deliberated together to reach a verdict. Deliberations were videotaped and later content analyzed to assess the quality of the jury deliberations. After deliberation was completed, the jurors were tested on their memory for the judge's instructions. It is important to emphasize that this was a short and simple trial that lasted less than three hours and contained only seven witnesses. Neither the trial nor the instructions were unusually demanding. Furthermore, the deliberations averaged

105 minutes, so the juries did have an extended opportunity to discuss and arrive at an understanding of the instructions.

Despite these considerations, the average juror correctly recalled only 44 percent of the judge's instructions on which they were tested. Even when one accounts for the fact that the "collective" memory of 12 jurors is better than the recall of any single juror (by assessing whether at least one of the jurors in a jury correctly recalled each item of the tested information), jury recall of judges' instructions averaged only 82 percent. However, the collective memory figures assume that each juror would actually communicate his or her memory to other jurors during the course of deliberation. Such an assumption is challenged by other findings from the study which indicated that the jury deliberations were not fully exhaustive. The average jury considered less than half of the different legal issues raised by the case.

The fundamental point is that jurors find it difficult to understand and to apply standard legal instructions. Indeed, one may go further: The research indicates that standard jury instructions which have been prepared without a systematic effort to assure their comprehensibility to lay persons are likely to be understood by only about half of the jurors called to jury duty. A cautious review of instruction comprehension should start with the presumption that jurors cannot understand traditional pattern instructions. It should be emphasized that these difficulties are not the product of juror inadequacies but are a product of the instructions themselves. Lind and Partridge (1982) reviewed the problems of standard instructions for a national committee formed to produce a set of federal criminal instructions. They identified a number of syntactical and grammatical features which make it difficult for jurors to comprehend and apply instructions.

Jurors' Application of Presumption Instructions

Given the apparent difficulty with which jurors comprehend standard judges' instructions, it seems unlikely that jurors will fare better in cases involving more complex and case-specific instructions. An example of a more complex instruction is the presumption instruction. A presumption instruction is a deductive device that allows the fact finder to assume the existence of one fact (the presumed fact) upon proof of another fact (the basic fact). It is sometimes used in cases in which an important element of a crime is difficult to prove beyond a reasonable doubt, such as, possession of a firearm (*County Court of Ulster County v. Allen*, 1979), the knowing importation of marijuana (*Leary v. the United States*, 1969) or of illegal narcotics (*Turner v. United States*, 1969), transportation of weapons in interstate commerce (*Tot v. United States*, 1943), operation of an illegal still (*United States v. Gainey*, 1965; *United States v. Romano*, 1965), or that an individual intended the consequences of his actions (*Sandstrom v. Montana*, 1979).

There is currently much debate in the legal literature regarding jurors' comprehension and application of presumption instructions, about which presumption instructions are constitutionally permissible, and about the standard of evaluation of presumption instructions (see Schmolesky, 1981, for an overview of the legal issues). Cutler, Penrod, and Schmolesky (1985) have conducted an experiment to examine mock jurors' understanding and application of three types of presumption instructions: conclusive, mandatory (both production and persuasion shifting), and permissive (see Cutler, et al., 1985, or Schmolesky, 1981, for a full discussion of presumptions). Mock jurors had considerable difficulty understanding the instructions, as evidenced by the breakdown of legally acceptable and unacceptable verdicts. In all, 8 percent of verdicts rendered were legally unacceptable convictions; whereas 18 percent were nullifications (acquittals in circumstances where a conviction was legally mandated). The effects of presumptions on verdicts were further qualified by presumption type (although there was an appreciable number of erroneous verdicts rendered under each type) and defendant culpability.

The problems with presumption instructions are further aggravated by the fact that many presumptions are not neatly classified as conclusive, mandatory, or permissive. In fact, the specific classification of the presumption is not nearly as important as the typical juror's interpretation of the meaning of the instruction. This point is exemplified in *Sandstrom v. Montana* (1979). In the case against David Sandstrom, who was accused of murder, the court instructed the jury that "the law presumes that a person intends the ordinary consequences of his voluntary acts" (p. 513). Although this presumption may have been intended to shift only the burden of production to the defendant, the Supreme Court surmised that a rational juror may have interpreted the presumption as shifting the burden of persuasion to the defendant, and the mere possibility of misinterpretation of the instruction was sufficient evidence for the lower court's conviction to be reversed.

Given the Supreme Court's reliance on the jurors' plausible interpretation of the presumption instruction, it is clear that format and wording of the specific instruction given to the jury should be of critical concern. Presumption instructions are considerably more complicated than standard legal instructions; but, if given clearly and concisely in terms with which the typical juror is familiar, fewer errors of interpretation and application are likely to occur (although this is another empirical issue that has yet to be addressed).

Jurors' Use of Statistical Information

Another area in which jurors have difficulty concerns the use of mathematical, probabilistic, and statistical evidence. It is common in criminal cases to attempt to match characteristics of a perpetrator or of the perpetrator's possession with key evidence in the case (Peterson, Mihajlovic, & Gilliland, 1984). Tests devised to aid in such comparisons include fingerprint and ballistic tests and comparisons of samples of hair, blood, paint, fibers, and other relevant substances. In cases in which a defendant's identity is in question, testimony about matches between these samples is common (Thompson, 1986). Accompanying the testimony are statistics relevant to incidence rate of a given characteristic on which there is a match and the reliability of the test performed. Thompson outlines two concerns regarding such testimony. First, there is the potential for such statistical information to be presented in a deceptive manner. Second, even if the information is presented impartially, the jury may misinterpret the statistical information or not weight it appropriately.

Thompson (1986) describes the types of errors that mock jurors have made in his experiments (Thompson, 1984; Thompson & Schumann, 1985). Fallacious use of incidence rates, or the "prosecutor's fallacy," refers to instances in which the juror infers the defendant's guilt by subtracting the incidence rate of a matching feature from one. For example, one may suppose the features of a defendant's automobile, which was implicated in a hit-and-run accident, were such that only one car out of 100 randomly chosen cars would meet the description. To assume that the probability that the defendant is guilty is therefore $1 - .01$ or $.99$ is to ignore the possibility that the defendant's car was not chosen randomly. Indeed, the defendant may have been confronted as a potential suspect precisely because his car matched a description given by a witness! In the Thompson and Schumann (1985) study, approximately 20 percent of the subjects made this type of error.

Conversely, about 50 percent of the subjects in the Thompson and Schumann study made what Thompson (1986) refers to as the "defense attorney's fallacy," which involves the mistaken assumption that incidence rates are irrelevant. Consider a case in which blood found on a beaten victim matches that of the suspect held in custody. Further suppose that together with this information, the jury is told that the incidence of this blood type is 5 percent. It could be reasoned that in a city of 500,000, therefore, there are roughly 2500 other individuals who have this blood type, and that hardly incriminates the defendant. The problem with this type of reasoning is that the overwhelming majority of the 2500 are not and probably could not reasonably be considered suspects in the crime. Given the difficulties associated with the use of such statistical information by jurors, attention must be given to techniques that may improve juror performance. For example, Thompson (1986) recommends a Bayesian analysis to determine appropriate probabilistic evidence when issues of identity are at stake.

Juror Decision Making in Joined Trials

A growing body of research indicates that a number of concerns expressed by defense attorneys—and sometimes by appellate courts—are grounded in reality. Studies show that factors such as the complexity of the trial, the length of the trial, the similarity of charges within a single trial, and the similarity of the evidence presented on multiple charges can operate together to foster an impression with the jurors that defendants in a case are "criminals." Such an inference of criminality will be aggravated by any evidence of prior criminal records on the part of any of the defendants. Although there are a number of studies of juror decision making in joined criminal trials (Bordens & Horowitz, 1983; Greene & Loftus, 1985; Horowitz, Bordens, & Feldman, 1980; Tanford & Penrod, 1982, 1984; Tanford, Penrod, & Collins, 1985), the most realistic and exhaustive of these studies is the one by Tanford and Penrod (1984). That study confirmed the findings of all previous studies of joinder—when a number of charges against a defendant are joined in a single trial, the probability the defendant will be convicted on any single charge is significantly higher than when the charge is tried alone. In the Tanford and Penrod (1984) study, the probability of conviction on a particular charge increased from .24 when tried alone to .39 when joined with two other charges.

More important, Tanford and Penrod were interested in why joinder increases the probability of conviction. One of the strongest effects they observed was that jurors in trials of joined charges were substantially more likely to make the inference that the defendant was "criminallike." When charges were joined, the jurors found the defendant less sincere, less believable, less honest, more immoral, more likely to commit a future crime, less likable, and more like a typical criminal. These negative impressions had two different effects on jurors. First, they directly influenced verdicts—as impressions of defendants grew more negative, defendants were more likely to be convicted. Second, these impressions also strongly influenced jurors' assessments of trial evidence, which in turn influenced verdicts. In particular, an inference of criminality made the prosecution evidence look more compelling. A virtually identical pattern of criminal inferences and changes in the weight of evidence have been observed in a second study by these authors (Tanford et al., 1985), and similar patterns of negative inferences about defendants are reported by Greene and Loftus (1985).

Another of the important findings to emerge from the joinder research is the observation of evidence cumulation in the judgments of jurors confronted with joined trials. In their study Tanford and Penrod asked jurors to make three separate ratings of the probative value of defense and prosecution evidence. Not too surprising, these ratings were related to the jurors' verdicts, and the strongest relationship was between ratings of the prosecution evidence and verdicts. The study further demonstrated that jurors' impressions that a defendant is like a criminal can actually change the jurors' perceptions of the weight of trial evidence. When a defendant seems more like a criminal (an impression strongly fostered by joinder), this makes the prosecution's evidence appear more compelling than the defendant's.

It is important to understand that this effect does not appear to arise simply because joinder directly changes the apparent weight of trial evidence. But jurors draw an inference of criminality, and, in light of this inference, the evidence looks more compelling. We know from the Tanford and Penrod study that joinder, by itself, produces small changes in the apparent probative value of evidence. Rather, joinder strongly affects the impression of the defendant; this impression, in turn, strongly affects evaluations of the trial evidence. The problem of "joinder leads to criminal inferences which leads to evidence cumulation" is not a problem of memory, it is a problem of impression formation and the influence of impressions on evaluations of evidence. Thus, even if jurors could properly collate evidence and defendants, impressions of criminality can strongly influence assessments of guilty by changing the apparent weight of the evidence.

Some appellate courts have been sensitive to the possibility of criminal inferences and cumulation of evidence and have, therefore, fashioned instructions to jurors that are designed to offset such untoward influences. To test the possibility that such instructions could undo or reverse the joinder-induced inference and cumulation effects, Tanford and Penrod had the judge in their videotaped trials present to half of the juries a set of very strong admonitions to avoid making such inferences and avoid cumulation of evidence. The instructions were patterned after those actually employed in the federal courts, but were stronger and more extensive. They were also totally ineffective in eliminating or even reducing the effects of joinder on experienced jurors' inferences of criminality and the consequent changes in juror's assessments of the trial evidence.

Juror Decision Making in Cases involving Eyewitness Memory

The unreliability of eyewitness identification and recall of details of criminal incidents has been amply documented (Loftus, 1979; Penrod, Loftus, & Winkler, 1982; Yarmey, 1979). Since eyewitness identifications from photos and lineups is often a major source of evidence in many cases, guidelines are needed by which to evaluate the reliability of identifications. Left to their intuitions, lay persons demonstrate fairly inadequate knowledge regarding memory processes and factors that influence memory (see Wells, 1984, for an overview of this literature). Psychologists, on the other hand, have rigorously studied memory since the late nineteenth century and have developed elaborate theories of underlying processes in memory. With respect to even the subarea of face recognition, hundreds of experiments have accumulated, and the body of research demonstrates some consistent influences on facial recognition abilities (Shapiro & Penrod, 1986).

Psychologists have recently become extensively involved in legal issues concerning eyewitness testimony, prompted in part by the relaxing of the traditional *Frye* criteria which required that scientific testimony be based on theories and methods with widespread acceptance within the relevant scientific community. Another impetus leading to psychologists' involvement was the finding, from a number of studies, that jurors are ill informed about memory processes and of the variables that affect identification accuracy and other types of eyewitness memory. Examples of commonly held misconceptions are that individuals are better able to recognize people if they were under a great deal of stress at the time; that cross-racial identifications are just as likely to be as correct as same-race identifications; and that confident eyewitnesses are much more likely to be correct than less confident witnesses (Wells, 1984). On the contrary, psychologists have found that cross-racial identifications are generally less accurate than same-race identifications (Shapiro & Penrod, 1986); that extreme stressfulness of a situation is inversely related to identification accuracy (see Deffenbacher, 1983, for a review); and that eyewitness confidence is at best a weak predictor of identification accuracy (Cutler & Penrod, 1985; Deffenbacher, 1980; Wells & Murray, 1983).

Studies of the jurors' use of eyewitness evidence document the overreliance of factors such as eyewitness confidence, which are not diagnostic of identification accuracy. Mock jurors are more likely to believe in and convict on the basis of testimony of confident witnesses and are likely to place less credibility on the testimony of less confident witnesses (Brigham & Bothwell, 1983; Cutler & Penrod, 1986; Wells, Lindsay, & Ferguson, 1979). A realistic jury simulation study by Cutler and Penrod (1986) exemplifies these findings.

Cutler and Penrod exposed mock jurors to a videotaped trial involving a liquor store robbery and had subjects complete a questionnaire concerning the trial. The questionnaire required subjects to render verdicts, to rate the probability that the identification was correct, and to recall the relevant details of the trial. Within the trial tapes, 10 variables were manipulated: disguise of robber; retention interval; stressfulness of robbery; exposure to mugshots prior to the lineup test; the visual presence of a weapon; the confidence of the witness in her identification of the robber; the size of the lineup; the instructions given to the witness before making a decision on the lineup test; the degree to which other lineup members resembled the target in physical description; and whether or not the witness was allowed to hear samples of the lineup members' voices. Virtually all of these variables have been shown to be predictive of identification accuracy except voice samples in the lineup (Cutler, Penrod, & Martens, 1986; Cutler, Penrod, O'Rourke, & Martens, in press; Shapiro & Penrod, 1986). The confidence of the witness, as previously mentioned, is a weak, though statistically significant, predictor of identification accuracy.

Cutler and Penrod (1986) found that only 1 of the 10 variables—the confidence of the witness—had a significant impact on jurors' verdicts and rated probability that the identification was correct. Mock jurors were insensitive to the impact of variables such as disguise, retention interval, and lineup instructions—all of which yield large effects on identification accuracy in our and others' eyewitness identification experiments. It is important to note that the mock jurors were clearly aware of the levels of these variables. Tests of mock jurors' memories for the levels of the variables that were manipulated (e.g., How much time elapsed between the robbery and the lineup test? How many suspects were in the lineup from which the suspect was identified?) and other manipulation checks were administered. Mock jurors correctly reported almost all of the items (often above 90 percent), and manipulation checks all indicated that our variables had an impact on subjects' general perceptions of the trial.

Why, then, do these factors have little effect on verdicts or perceptions of the reliability of the identification? The answer is there appears to be a general lack of knowledge of memory processes involved in identification and of the manner in which some factors affect eyewitness memory. A proposed solution to this problem is to allow psychologists or other experts to testify on memory processes that are relevant to the particular case. There is considerable evidence that expert testimony on eyewitness memory has a powerful impact on jurors' processing of eyewitness evidence and their subsequent verdicts (Hosch, Beck, & McIntyre, 1980; Loftus, 1980; Weinberg & Baron, 1982; Wells, Lindsay, & Tousignant, 1980).

Pretrial Publicity

Pretrial publicity can predispose jurors against a defendant, and these effects are aggravated if the pretrial publicity places a defendant in a bad light. These effects have been thoroughly documented both in studies of actual cases (e.g., Constantini & King, 1980/1981) and in experimental studies involving simulated trials (e.g., Padawer-Singer, Singer, & Singer, 1974; Sue, Smith, & Gilbert, 1974; Sue, Smith, & Pedroza, 1975). In a situation where most prospective jurors have exposure to a case as a result of pretrial publicity, it can be extremely difficult to assess—even through extensive voir dire—the depth and extent of the effects of the pretrial publicity on jurors' predispositions. Studies designed to test whether the effects of pretrial publicity can be reduced through voir dire show that the effects remained even after jurors who acknowledge a bias have been removed from the panel (Sue et al., 1975). Furthermore, in the Padawer-Singer and associates (1974) study, careful analysis of the jury results indicates that voir dire can actually increase conviction rates of jurors exposed to neutral pretrial publicity.

There are two primary reasons why pretrial publicity effects may be difficult to eliminate. First, jurors may have grave difficulty understanding the influence that pretrial publicity has had upon them. While jurors may recognize that they have read or heard about the case, it is extremely difficult—and often impossible—for jurors to introspectively assess the impact that the pretrial publicity has had upon their views of defendants and the case more generally. Second, the typical voir dire is conducted under circumstances in which jurors are implicitly encouraged and told that it is appropriate for them to simply state that their pretrial exposure will not affect their decision making (Haney, 1984a, 1984b). Unless pressed to consider the ways in which pretrial publicity has affected such things as their perceptions of defendants and the charges against the defendants and voir dired under conditions that allow them to acknowledge these influences, voir dire is unlikely to detect jurors whose views have been influenced by pretrial publicity. Thus, voir dire is unlikely to offset the effects of pretrial publicity unless counsel is given generous challenges for cause and peremptory challenges—and an opportunity for extensive individual voir dire of prospective jurors.

Perhaps the most troublesome aspect of pretrial publicity is that it can produce prejudicial effects even if jurors assiduously avoid discussion of information and impressions formed as a result of exposure to pretrial publicity. Research on curative and limiting instructions raises grave doubts about their efficacy. Kline and Jess (1966), Padawer-Singer and colleagues (1974), Sue and associates (1974), and Sue and others (1975) all found that judicial admonitions did not eliminate the prejudicial effects of pretrial publicity. Furthermore, in many instances the jurors discussed the pretrial publicity in direct defiance of the judicial instructions. The only certain safeguard against the effects of pretrial publicity is to impanel a jury which has not been exposed to pretrial publicity.

CONCLUSIONS

Psychologists and other social scientists are increasingly involved in the judicial process, and the issues psychologists are addressing are becoming increasingly diverse. This diversity has yielded some areas in which social scientific research has been particularly fruitful, and others that have yielded less success. Social scientific jury selection, though sometimes attacked as a perversion of justice, appears at present to be less powerful than critics fear. Research on jurors indicates that individuals' attitudes and dispositional characteristics are related to verdict preferences, but the relationships are typically not strong and probably depend on the particular case and location of the trial. Thus, although pretrial jury selection surveys probably can provide an edge in the jury selection process, that edge is not overwhelmingly strong. Additionally, research on the effects of juror disposition on various aspects of the deliberation process, such as participation habits and contribution, also reveals systematic relationships, though there is, as yet, no reliable method for translating these relationships into a sound jury selection strategy.

In other domains, social scientists have been particularly successful at identifying evidential issues that pose challenges to jurors' abilities to perform adequately. A substantial portion of this research has concerned the jurors' understanding of the judge's instructions, both with respect to standard instructions and instructions that are used in particular cases, such as the presumption instruction. It is appropriate to take the perspective that jurors are indeed capable of understanding what is required of them, if the instructions are put to them in language to which they are accustomed. Attempts to improve juror comprehension by reformatting and rewording the instructions have met with considerable success (e.g., Elwork et al., 1982) and provide some guidance for trial work.

Other evidential problems, however, may not be easy to correct through instructions. The deleterious effects of joined trials are difficult to remove even with extensive and strongly worded instructions. Likewise, pretrial publicity effects may be intractable to either voir dire or instructions, as individuals are relatively unaware of the extent to which they have been influenced by pretrial publicity.

In conclusion, it is clear that social scientists are playing an increasingly important role in the judicial process. Research on jury decision making has yielded important insights into the relationship between individual juror characteristics and juror decision making (relationships that can be employed in jury selection), into the practical problems jurors confront when evaluating trial evidence (e.g., using probabilistic information and eyewitness identifications), and into problems jurors confront when applying legal instructions (e.g., general comprehension, presumption instructions, and curative instructions). The research also identifies procedural domains in which legal assumptions about juror decision making can be seriously questioned (e.g., joinder effects and the effects of pretrial publicity). With the exception of the use of pretrial surveys in support of motions to change venue and select jurors, and a movement toward simplified jury instructions, little of the research has found its way into the courts. And, although the legal implications of the remaining research are not always clear, it is our conviction that with creative collaboration among social scientists and lawyers and judges, the recent research on juries can and will be put to use in the courtroom.

REFERENCES

Adorno, T., Frenkel-Brunswik, E., Levinson, D., & Sanford, N. (1950). *The authoritarian personality*. New York: Harper.

Ajzen, I., & Fishbein, M. (1980). *Understanding attitudes and predicting social behavior*. Englewood Cliffs, NJ: Prentice-Hall.

Berg, K., & Vidmar, N. (1975). Authoritarianism and recall of evidence about criminal behavior. *Journal of Research in Personality, 9*, 147–157.

Berk, R. A., Hennessy, M., & Swan, J. (1977). The vagaries and vulgarities of scientific jury selection: A methodological evaluation. *Evaluation Quarterly, 1*, 143–158.

Berman, J., & Sales, B. D. (1977). A critical evaluation of the systematic approach to jury selection. *Criminal Justice and Behavior, 4*, 219–240.

Boehm, V. (1968). Mr. Prejudice, Miss Sympathy and the authoritarian personality: An application of psychological measuring to the problem of jury bias. *Wisconsin Law Review*, 734–750.

Bordens, K. S., & Horowitz, I. A. (1983). Information processing in joined and severed trials. *Journal of Applied Social Psychology, 13*, 351–370.

Brigham, J. C., & Bothwell, R. K. (1983). The ability of prospective jurors to estimate the accuracy of eyewitness identifications. *Law and Human Behavior, 1*, 19–30.

Bronson, E. J. (1980). Does the exclusion of scrupled jurors in capital cases make the jury more likely to convict? Some evidence from California. *Woodrow Wilson Journal of Law, 3*, 11–34.

Buchanan, R. W., Pryor, B., Taylor, K. P., & Strawn, D. V. (1978). Legal communication: An investigation of juror comprehension of pattern jury instructions. *Communication Quarterly, 26*, 31–35.

Buckhout, R., Baker, E., Perlman, M., & Spiegel, R. (1977). Jury attitudes and the death penalty. *Social Action and the Law, 3*, 80–81.

Buckhout, R., Licker, J., Alexander, M., Gambardella, J., Eugenio, P., & Kakoullis, B. (1979). Discretion in jury selection. In L. E. Abt & I. R. Stuart (Eds.), *Social psychology and discretionary law* (pp. 176–196). New York: Van Nostrand Reinhold.

Charrow, R. P., & Charrow, V. R. (1979). Making legal language understandable: A psycholinguistic study of jury instructions. *Columbia Law Review, 79*, 1306–1374.

Cohen, J., & Cohen, P. (1975). *Applied multiple regression/correlation analysis for the behavioral sciences*. New York: John Wiley.

Constantini, E., & King, J. (1980/1981). The partial juror: Correlates and causes of prejudgment. *Law and Society Review 15*, 9–40.

Cowan, C. L., Thompson, W. C., & Ellsworth, P. C. (1984). The effects of death qualification on jurors' predisposition to convict and on the quality of deliberation. *Law and Human Behavior, 8*, 53–79.

Crump, D. (1980). Attorney's goals and tactics in voir dire examination. *Texas Bar Journal*, 244–247.

Cutler, B. L., & Penrod, S. D. (1985). *Calibrating confidence and accuracy: Recognizing faces*. Manuscript submitted for publication.

Cutler, B. L., & Penrod, S. D. (1986, June). *Jury decisionmaking in eyewitness identification cases*. Paper presented at the annual meeting of Law and Society, Chicago.

Cutler, B. L., Penrod, S. D., & Martens, T. K. (1986). *The reliability of eyewitness identification: The role of system and estimator variables*. Manuscript submitted for publication.

Cutler, B. L., Penrod, S. D., & O'Rourke, T. E., & Martens, T. K. (in press). Unconfounding the effects of contextual cues on eyewitness identification accuracy. *Social Behavior*.

Cutler, B. L., Penrod, S. D., & Schmolesky, J. N. (1985). *Presumption instructions and juror decisionmaking*. Manuscript submitted for publication.

Deffenbacher, K. (1980). Eyewitness accuracy and confidence: Can we infer anything about their relationship? *Law and Human Behavior, 4*, 243–260.

Deffenbacher, K. (1983). The influence of arousal on reliability of testimony. In S. Lloyd-Bostock & B. R. Clifford (Eds.), *Evaluating eyewitness evidence*. Chichester, Great Britain: Wiley.

DiMona, J. (1974, July 8). The real surprise of the Mitchell-Stans trial. *New York*, pp. 31–37.

Elwork, A., Sales, B. D., & Alfini, J. J. (1977). Juridic decisions: In ignorance of the law or in light of it? *Law and Human Behavior, 1*, 163–189.

Elwork, A., Sales, B. D., & Alfini, J. J. (1982). *Making jury instructions understandable*. Charlottesville, VA: The Michie Co.

Etzioni, A. (1974, May 26). Science: Threatening the jury trial. *Washington Post*, sec. C, p. 3.

Field, H. (1978). Juror background characteristics and attitudes toward rape. *Law and Human Behavior, 2*, 73–93.

Fishbein, M., & Ajzen, I. (1975). *Belief, attitude, intention and behavior: An introduction to theory and research*. Reading, MA: Addison-Wesley.

Fitzgerald, R., & Ellsworth, P. C. (1984). Due process vs. crime control. *Law and Human Behavior, 8*, 31–51.

Gerbasi, K. C., Zuckerman, M., & Reis, H. T. (1977). Justice needs a new blindfold: A review of mock jury research. *Psychological Bulletin, 84*, 323–345.

Greenberg, M. S., & Ruback, B. (1982). *Social psychology of the criminal justice system*. Reading, MA: Addison-Wesley.

Greene, E., & Loftus, E. F. (1985). When crimes are joined at trial. *Law and Human Behavior, 9*, 193–207.

Greene, E., Wilson, L., & Loftus, E. F. (1986, March). *Impact of hypnotic testimony on the jury*. Paper presented at the annual meeting of the American Psychology-Law Society, Tucson, AZ.

Haney, C. (1984a). On the selection of capital juries: The biasing effects of death qualification process. *Law and Human Behavior, 8*, 121–132.

Haney, C. (1984b). Examining death qualification. *Law and Human Behavior, 8*, 133–154.

Hans, V. T., & Vidmar, N. (1982). Jury selection. In N. L. Kerr & R. M. Bray (Eds.), *The psychology of the courtroom*. New York: Academic.

Hans, V. T., & Vidmar, N. (1986). *Judging the jury*. New York: Plenum.

Hastie, R., Penrod, S., & Pennington, N. (1983). *Inside the jury*. Cambridge, MA: Harvard University Press.

Herbsleb, J. D., Sales, B. D., & Berman, J. J. (1978). When psychologists aid in voir dire: Legal and ethical considerations. In L. E. Abt & I. Stuart, (Eds.), *The social psychology of discretionary law*. New York: Van Nostrand Reinhold.

Heuer, L. B., & Penrod, S. D. (1986). *A field experiment on jury decisionmaking*. Unpublished manuscript.

Horowitz, A., Bordens, K. S., & Feldman, M. S. (1980). A comparison of verdicts obtained in severed and joined criminal trials. *Journal of Applied Social Psychology, 10*, 444–456.

Horowitz, I. A., & Willging, T. E. (1984). *The psychology of law: Integrations and applications*. Boston: Little, Brown.

Hosch, H. M., Beck, E. L., & McIntyre, P. (1980). Influence of expert testimony regarding eyewitness accuracy on jury decisions. *Law and Human Behavior, 4*, 287–296.

Hunter, R. M (1935). Law in the jury room. *Ohio State Law Journal, 1*, 1–19.

Jurow, G. (1971). New data on the effect of a death qualified jury on the guilt determination process. *Harvard Law Review, 84*, 567–611.

Kairys, D., Schulman, J., & Harring, S. (1975). (Eds.). *The jury system: New methods for reducing prejudice*. Philadelphia: National Jury Project and National Lawyers Guild.

Kassin, S. M., & Wrightsman, L. S. (1983). The construction and validation of a juror bias scale. *Journal of Research in Personality, 17*, 423–442.

Kauffman, R. A., & Ryckman, R. M. (1979). Effects of locus-of-control, outcome severity, and attitudinal similarity of defendant on attributions of criminal responsibility. *Personality and Social Psychology Bulletin, 5*, 340–343.

Kerr, N. L., & Bray, R. M. (1982). *The psychology of the courtroom*. New York: Academic.

Kline, F. G., & Jess, P. H. (1966). Prejudicial publicity: Its effects on law school mock juries. *Journalism Quarterly, 43*, 113–120.

Konecni, V. J., & Ebbesen, E. B. (1982). The criminal justice system: A social psychological perspective. San Francisco: W. H. Freeman.

Leary v. United States, 395 U.S. 6 (1969).

Lind, E. A., & Partridge, A. (1982). Suggestions for improving juror understanding of instructions. In P. Marshall, T. Flannery, & P. E. Higginbotham, (Eds.), *Pattern criminal jury instructions*. Washington, DC: Federal Judicial Center.

Lockhart v. McCree, decided by Supreme Court on May 5, 1986.

Loftus, E. F. (1979). *Eyewitness testimony*. Cambridge, MA: Harvard University Press.

Loftus, E. L. (1980). Impact of expert psychological testimony on the unreliability of eyewitness identification. *Journal of Applied Psychology, 65*, 9–15.

Loh, W. D. (1984). *Social research in the judicial process: Cases, readings, and text*. New York: Sage.

Moran, G., & Comfort, J. C. (1982). Scientific juror selection: Sex as a moderator of demographic and personality predictors of impaneled felony juror behavior. *Journal of Personality and Social Psychology, 43*, 1052–1063.

Moran, G., & Comfort, J. C. (1986). Neither "tentative" nor "fragmentary": Verdict preference of impaneled felony jurors as a function of attitude toward capital punishment. *Journal of Applied Psychology, 71*, 146–155.

Munsterberg, H. (1909). *On the witness stand: Essays on psychology and crime*. Garden City, NY: Clark, Boardman.

Okun, J. (1968). Investigation of jurors by counsel: Its impact on the decisional process. *Georgetown Law Journal, 56*, 839–879.

Padawer-Singer, A. M., Singer, A. N., & Singer, R. L. (1974). Voir dire by two lawyers: An essential safeguard. *Judicature, 57*, 386–391.

Penrod, S. (1980). *Confidence, accuracy, and the eyewitness*. Unpublished manuscript, University of Wisconsin.

Penrod, S. (1984, October). *Conducting experimental research with real trials*. Paper presented at the meeting of the Society for Experimental Social Psychology, Salt Lake City, UT.

Penrod, S., & Linz, D. (1986). Voir dire: Uses and abuses. In M. Kaplan (Ed.), *The impact of social psychology on procedural justice* (pp. 135–166). Springfield, IL: Charles C. Thomas.

Penrod, S., Loftus, E., & Winkler, J. (1982). The reliability of eyewitness testimony: A psychological perspective. In N. L. Kerr & R. M. Bray (Eds.), *The psychology of the courtroom*. New York: Academic Press.

Peterson, J. L., Mihajlovic, S., & Gilliland, M. (1984). *Forensic evidence and the police: The effects of scientific evidence on criminal investigations.* Washington, DC: U.S. Department of Justice, National Institute of Justice.

Report of the Cincinnati Conference on Trial by Jury. (1937). *University of Cincinnati Law Review, 11,* 119–246.

Rosenthal, R., & Rosnow, R. L. (1984). *Essentials of behavioral research.* New York: McGraw-Hill.

Sage, N. (1973, January). Psychology and the Angela Davis jury. *Human Behavior*, pp. 58–61.

Saks, M. J. (1976). The limits of scientific jury selection. *Jurimetrics Journal, 17,* 3–22.

Saks, M. J. (1977). *Jury verdicts: The role of group size and social decision rule.* Lexington, MA: Lexington Books (D.C. Heath).

Sandstrom v. Montana, 442 U.S. 510 (1979).

Schmolesky, J. M. (1981). *County Court of Ulster County v. Allen* and *Sandstrom v. Montana*: The Supreme Court lends an ear but turns its face. *Rutgers Law Review, 33,* 261–316.

Schulman, J., Shaver, P., Colman, R., Emrich, B., & Christie, R. (1973, May). Recipe for a jury. *Psychology Today*, pp. 37–83.

Severance, L. J., & Loftus, E. F. (1981/1982). Improving the ability of jurors to comprehend and apply criminal jury instructions. *Law and Society Review, 17,* 153–197.

Shapiro, P., & Penrod, S. D. (1986). A meta-analysis of the facial recognition studies. *Psychological Bulletin, 100,* 139–156.

Sigwirth, H., & Henze, F. (1973). *Jurors' comprehension of jury instructions in southern Arizona.* Unpublished report prepared for the Committee on Uniform Instructions of the State of Arizona.

Silver, D. (1978). A case against the use of public opinion polls as an aid in jury selection. *Journal of Computers and Law, 6,* 177–195.

Simon, R. J. (1967). *The jury and the defense of insanity.* Boston: Little, Brown.

Sonquist, J. A., Baker, E., & Morgan, J. (1973). *Searching for structure.* Ann Arbor, MI: Institute for Social Research.

Sosis, R. (1974). Internal-external control and the perception of responsibility of another for an accident. *Journal of Personality and Social Psychology, 30,* 393–399.

Sue, S., Smith, R. E., & Gilbert, R. (1974). Biasing effect of pre-trial publicity on judicial decisions. *Journal of Criminal Justice, 2,* 163–171.

Sue, S., Smith, R. E., & Pedroza, G. (1975). Authoritarianism, pretrial publicity and awareness of bias in simulated jurors. *Psychological Reports, 37,* 1299–1302.

Tanford, S., & Penrod, S. (1982). Biases in trials involving defendants charged with multiple offenses. *Journal of Applied Social Psychology, 12,* 453–480.

Tanford, S., & Penrod, S. (1984). Social inference processes in juror judgments of multiple-offense trials. *Journal of Personality and Social Psychology, 47,* 749–765.

Tanford, S., Penrod, S., & Collins, R. (1985). Decisionmaking in joined criminal trials: The influence of charge similarity, evidence similarity, and limiting instructions. *Law and Human Behavior, 9*, 319–337.

Thompson, W. C. (1984, August). *Judgmental bias in reactions to mathematical evidence.* Paper presented at the meeting of the American Psychological Association, Toronto.

Thompson, W. C. (1986, March). *Mathematical evidence in criminal trials: Improving the probability of justice.* Paper presented at the midyear meeting of the American Psychology-Law Society, Tucson, AZ.

Thompson, W. C., & Schumann, E. L. (1985, August). *Fallacious interpretations of statistical evidence in criminal trials.* Paper presented at the meeting of the American Psychological Association, Los Angeles.

Tivnan, E. (1975). Jury by trial. *New York Times Magazine*, pp. 30–31.

Tot v. United States, 319 U.S. 463 (1943).

Turner v. United States, 396 U.S. 398 (1969).

Ungar, S. J. (1972, November). The Pentagon papers trial. *Atlantic Monthly*, pp. 22–23, 26–28, 30, 32, 34.

United States v. Gainey, 380 U.S. 63 (1965).

United States v. Romano, 382 U.S. 136 (1965).

Weinberg, H. I., & Baron, R. S. (1982). The discredible eyewitness. *Personality and Social Psychology Bulletin, 8*, 60–67.

Wells, G. L. (1984). How adequate is human intuition for judging eyewitness testimony? In G. L. Wells & E. F. Loftus (Eds.), *Eyewitness testimony: Psychological perspectives.* New York: Cambridge University Press.

Wells, G. L., Lindsay, R. C. L., & Ferguson, T. J. (1979). Accuracy, confidence, and juror perceptions in eyewitness identification. *Journal of Applied Psychology, 64*, 440–448.

Wells, G. L., Lindsay, R. C. L., & Tousignant, J. P. (1980). Effects of expert psychological advice on human performance in judging the validity of eyewitness testimony. *Law and Human Behavior, 4*, 275–285.

Wells, G. L., & Murray, D. M. (1983). What can psychology say about the *Neil v. Biggers* criteria for judging eyewitness accuracy? *Journal of Applied Psychology, 68*, 347–362.

Witherspoon v. Illinois, 88 U.S. 1770 (1968).

Yarmey, A. D. (1979). *The psychology of eyewitness testimony.* New York: Free Press.

Zeisel, H., & Diamond, S. (1976). The jury selection in the Mitchell-Stans conspiracy trial. *American Bar Foundation Research Journal, 1*, 151–174.

CHAPTER 12

Recommending Probation and Parole

HAROLD J. VETTER

Although the law requires that violators receive specific penalties, it also provides for the mitigation of severe sentences. Persons convicted of crimes may be placed on probation rather than being incarcerated, may be paroled from prison prior to the expiration of sentence, may have their prison terms or fines commuted to a lesser penalty, or may receive a full or conditional pardon (with a restoration of civil rights). Still another method of mitigating the full force of legal sanctions is called amnesty—a group pardon.

Offenders sent to prison return, sooner or later, to free society. Because so many freed criminals revert to crime, however, society has continually sought alternatives to confinement. The emphasis in recent years has been on involving offenders in programs and facilities within the community. Such programs allow society to provide offenders with only the amount of supervision they require. And because crime has its roots within the community, it is reasonable to expect the community to assume some responsibility for dealing with offenders. This approach also tends to minimize the problem of reintegration.

Probation and parole are the two methods most often used to replace imprisonment with community supervision. The U.S. Department of Justice *Report to the Nation on Crime and Justice* (1984, p. 73) indicated that state or local governments operate more than 2,000 probation agencies, which supervise more than 1.5 million adults and juveniles on probation. Probation is the most widely used form of correctional disposition in the United States. Despite widespread dissatisfaction with parole selection procedures and skepticism about the effectiveness of parole, "an examination of national parole population trends suggests that more and more offenders are being placed on parole every year" (McCarthy & McCarthy, 1984, p. 243).

During the past decade, the prison population in the United States has nearly doubled, and construction costs for new prisons have tripled or quadrupled. At present, a single prison cell in a maximum security institution equals or exceeds the cost of a single-family home. This situation has created extreme pressures on criminal justice authorities to find less expensive alternatives to institutionalization at a time when the public is demanding protection from violent offenders by means of lengthy terms of incarceration. In the crisis atmosphere generated by these demands, state and local officials have resorted to such expedients as early release, double- or even triple-bunking, and mass transfers to temporary, makeshift facilities.

Given the inadequacy of such expedients, we can anticipate the increasing use of diversion procedures which limit the penetration of offenders into the criminal justice system. Inevitably the burden of supervising these offenders will fall upon probation and parole services because they represent the largest available group of criminal justice practitioners with the requisite skills and organizational resources to deal with the influx of offenders. Probation and parole officers are the only community correctional resource with both the capacity and the formal authority to carry out the supervision mandated by the courts.

PROBATION, PAROLE, AND PSYCHOLOGY

Probation and parole officers act as both change agents for their clients and control agents for society. Many of the tasks they perform are accomplished through the process of case management, which involves the procurement of required or desired services from a variety of sources outside the probation or parole agency. Among these are psychological services of various kinds, ranging from testing and assessment to counseling and psychotherapy.

Providing psychological services for clients who are referred by agents of the criminal justice system presents certain issues and problems with which many psychologists may be unfamiliar. They may be inclined to adopt policies which effectively exclude such clients from access to psychological services because they lack familiarity. Both professional ethics and professional self-interest ought to encourage psychological service providers to take a closer look at this potentially large population of prospective clients. Indeed, encouragement of this sort is one of the objectives of this chapter.

Psychologists may contribute to probation and parole in a number of other ways. Psychology can provide a professional background and orientation for the training of probation and parole officers (POs) that helps sensitize officers to individual patterns of adjustments and various methods of attempting to cope with given situations which may aid in understanding and relating to clients. Such training may also help POs to recognize areas of dysfunctioning as a first step toward making appropriate referrals.

Perhaps the most substantial contribution that psychologists can make to probation and parole is in the application of highly developed research skills to a lengthy list of problems and issues which confront officers and administrators in their daily work. Indeed, one of the major objectives of the present chapter is to underscore the need for psychologists in growing numbers to take a more active role in community corrections research.

PROBATION

Probation has been called "the least visible, least studied, most diffuse and most underfunded part of the criminal processing apparatus" (Krajick, 1980, p. 7). Yet probation is the sanction that an American criminal court is most apt to impose on offenders. Between 60 and 80 percent of the sentences meted out by the courts involve probation. Probation services are spread among many agencies and facilities, from the municipal level to the federal level. Some jurisdictions practice "postcard probation," in which clients report their activities once or twice a month by sending in preaddressed postcards. This kind of probation comes to an end when clients misplace or lose their supply of cards.

Probation is intended as a combination of treatment and punishment. An offender serving time on probation is also supposed to be treated in the context of community-based supervision. Ideally, probationers receive counseling and guidance to aid them in adjusting to free society. But probation is also punitive, because restrictions are placed on the probationer. Many authorities deny the punitive aspects of probation and insist that their policies are entirely rehabilitative.

Both liberal and conservative critics of the criminal justice system agree that placing an offender on probation without making use of community resources and services is equal to doing nothing. Such actions are neither treatment nor punishment. As a criminal court judge observed: "The offender continues with his life style. . . . If he is a wealthy doctor, he continues with his practice; if he is an unemployed youth, he continues to be unemployed. Probation is a meaningless ritual; it is a sop to the conscience of the court" (Krajick, 1980, p. 7).

A major problem in probation is the built-in role conflict of probation officers. Are they police officers or counselors? Is their primary responsibility surveillance, or should they be agents of active social change? Many of the difficulties that plague probation—high staff turnover, low morale, burnout—stem from this basic conflict.

Suspended Sentence: Birthplace of Probation

Probation is derived from the suspended sentence, handed down indirectly from our judicial past (Gottfredson, 1983). A suspended sentence and probation are both forms of mitigating punishment through judicial procedure. Their earliest antecedent is the right of sanctuary, which is frequently cited in the Bible; holy places and certain cities were traditionally set aside as places of sanctuary.

The practice of right of sanctuary was written into Mosaic Law. To escape the blood vengeance of a victim's family, a killer could go to a certain place and find refuge. During the Middle Ages, many churches were able to offer sanctuary for those hiding from harsh secular laws. The practice of sanctuary disappeared in England during the seventeenth century and was replaced with "benefits of clergy." This practice, originally reserved for clerics, was eventually extended to those who could pass the "Psalms 51 Test," which required the ability of the offender to read the biblical verse beginning "Have mercy on me." The result was a form of suspended sentence which allowed the offender to move about in society without undue fear of retribution (Smykla, 1981).

The suspended sentence differs from probation even though the terms are sometimes used interchangeably. The suspended sentence does not require supervision and usually does not specify a particular set of goals for the offender. It is merely a form of quasifreedom which can be revoked and the sentence imposed at the discretion of the court. The practice of suspended sentence, like the right of sanctuary, outlived its usefulness and has generally been replaced by supervised probation in the United States (Henningsen, 1981).

John Augustus: Father of Probation

A nineteenth-century Boston shoemaker named John Augustus is regarded as the father of probation. Augustus spent a good deal of his leisure time in the courts and was distressed by the fact that common drunks were forced to remain in jail because they had no money to pay their fines (Augustus, 1852). A humane and sympathetic man, Augustus convinced the authorities to allow him to pay offenders' fines; after their release, he provided them with friendly counsel and supervision. Between 1841 and 1859, he bailed out more than 2,000 persons. He was sharply criticized for his "strange" ideas. Barnes and Teeters (1959) have described his approach:

> His method was to bail the offender after conviction, to utilize this favor as an entering wedge to the convict's confidence and friendship, and through such evidence of friendliness as helping the offender to obtain a job and aiding his family in various ways, to drive the wedge home. When the defendant was later brought into court for sentence, Augustus would report on his progress toward reformation, and the judge would usually fine the convict one cent and costs, instead of committing him to an institution. (p. 544)

John Augustus' efforts encouraged his home state of Massachusetts to pass the first probation statute in 1878. Five more states followed suit before the turn of the century. Probation was established as a legitimate alternative to penal confinement and was given great impetus by the creation of the first juvenile court in 1899. The need to provide supervision for youths in trouble and to keep them out of adult prisons provided strong motivation toward the development of probation in the United States.

Imposing Probation

Three methods of implementing probation are used: The law may allow the trial judge to suspend the execution of sentence and place the offender on conditional probation. A state statute may, on the other hand, require sentencing but permit the suspension of imposition. A third method leaves both alternatives to the discretion of the trial judge. In the case of the offender upon whom sentence has been imposed but not executed, violation of conditions of probation results in the judge ordering the execution of the original sentence. When the judge has suspended the imposition of sentencing, violation of probation might result in a stiffer sentence than would originally have been imposed (Killinger, Kerper, & Cromwell, 1976).

Probation without Adjudication

Once the court has determined that probation will be granted, the sentencing judge must make another decision as to whether the offender should be adjudicated guilty (and labeled a "convicted felon") or placed on probation without adjudication. The factors that bear on this decision have been outlined by Murchek (1973):

> Although adjudication of guilt may provide certain safeguards to society such as: requiring criminal registration, serving notice to prospective employers that the applicant has been convicted of a criminal offense, preventing the offender from voting, holding public office, serving on a jury and perhaps making it more difficult to obtain firearms, it appears to provide very little appreciable effect in providing protection to society. It does, in fact, seriously hamper the offender's chances of rehabilitation.

> The withholding of adjudication of guilt, on the other hand, is consistent with the philosophical concepts of probation which combine community-based treatment with the full utilization of available community resources as a viable alternative to imprisonment and the accompanying degradation and stigma associated with same. (p. 27)

Actually, probation without adjudication was the original practice at the time of John Augustus. Augustus convinced the judge to withhold sentencing on those released to him for a period of three weeks, after which the offender would return for sentencing. This procedure gave offenders a chance to prove themselves and usually resulted in a simple fine rather than imprisonment in the House of Corrections. This system of delayed sentence provided the advantage of keeping the offender in the community, under supervision, without a criminal record and its inherent handicaps. This ability to function in the community without the stigma of a criminal conviction has been viewed as a source of uplift for the offender, which may contribute toward the desire to seek self-improvement and reform (Dressler, 1969; Smith & Berlin, 1979).

Presentence Investigation and Report

Probation is a method of individualization and is predicated on the proper selection of offenders. To determine which offenders will make promising candidates for probation, sentencing judges rely heavily on thorough, carefully prepared presentence reports. According to Killinger et al. (1976), "The ultimate merit of probation as a correctional tool is dependent to a very large extent upon the nature and quality of the presentence report" (p. 68). Although the information secured for this report is primarily intended to aid in the assessment of factors that bear importantly on successful community adjustment in lieu of incarceration, the presentence investigation report (PSI) can be used at almost every stage in the criminal justice system and process: (1) by the courts in deciding the appropriate sentence; (2) by the prison classification team in assigning custody level and treatment; (3) by the parole board in determining when the offender is ready to be returned to the community; (4) by probation and parole officers as they aid the offender in readjusting to the demands of free society; and (5) by correctional researchers as they try to identify the characteristics that are most closely associated with success on probation (Carter & Wilkins, 1976).

There are wide variations in the scope and depth of information contained in the

PSI report. The probation officer who prepares the report has considerable latitude in what to include in the report, but certain facts that are pertinent to the case are usually covered: a description of the offense, including statements of co-defendants; the defendant's own version of the offense and prior criminal record; family and marital history; description of the neighborhood in which the defendant was reared; and facts regarding the defendant's education, religion, interests, mental and physical health records, employment history, and military service record. Officers may choose to include other optional data, such as "attitudes of defendant toward arresting officers" and amount of bond, if they feel that such information adds substantially to the report. Judges in many jurisdictions ask for recommendations from probation officers for sentencing alternatives or, if the defendant is placed on probation, recommendations concerning what kind of treatment plan should be instituted.

Conditions of Probation and Parole

Even though probation usually is managed by the courts and parole by an executive department of government, the general and specific conditions are similar for both. The conditions are customarily established jointly by the legislature, the court, and the probation and parole commission. Some regulations are fixed by statute and affect all persons on probation and parole (e.g., requirements to report regularly to one's probation or parole officer, to not leave the state without the court's permission, and to pay court costs). These general conditions make no allowance for discretion by the trial court or the probation and parole commission. Unique conditions may be imposed in certain individual cases. For example, probationers or parolees may be required to stay home or leave home, support their parents, get a steady job working days, make restitution to their crime victims, or attend church regularly.

Conditions of probation and parole have often been challenged because of their vagueness, overgenerality, interference with an individual's constitutional rights, or lack of relationship to the underlying offense. For instance, the condition that a probationer "live honorably" was found to be impermissibly vague in *Norris v. State* (1980). Conditions may be imposed which are impossible for performance: Ordering an alcoholic to stop drinking or a drug addict to refrain from the use of drugs constitutes the imposition of unlawful "impossible" conditions (*Sweeney v. United States*, 1965). On the other hand, requiring a person to obtain treatment or to submit to reasonable tests in order to determine progress would tend to be upheld by the courts.

Revocation of Probation and Parole

The term *revocation*, as Cohen (1983) points out, at times refers to the act of imprisonment or reimprisonment, and at other times to the process of establishing that a violation has occurred. Cohen suggests that revocation may be best viewed as a process resembling a "cameo trial at which facts are alleged and proven to show a violation; that is, that the supervisee was at 'fault' by committing a new crime or violating a condition of his release" (p. 1244).

The decision to grant probation or parole is highly discretionary; the probationer or parolee has relatively few legal rights. But once probation or parole is granted, the candidate receives a form of conditional liberty that bears important legal consequences with regard to both supervision within the community and any decision to revoke this conditional freedom. One of the most significant developments in this area is the constitutional basis for the revocation process, and in the section dealing with parole, we shall discuss several decisions of the Supreme Court and lower federal courts which have had an impact on the granting and revocation of probation and parole.

Role Conflict and the Probation Officer (PO)

Probation and parole both involve supervision of the offender within the community as a consequence of actions by the court or by parole authorities. In both instances, the offender is required to conform to certain conditions as a basis for securing an alternative to imprisonment. The PO is the person who is charged with the responsibility of seeing to it that the offender lives up to and carries out the terms imposed by these conditions. Thus, supervision of the offender within the community imposes the task of surveillance on the PO. Surveillance is difficult to regard as anything other than a police function.

On the other hand, the PO is also expected to provide, or make arrangements for the provision of, a variety of human services to the probationer or parolee—that is, the officer is expected to perform as a social caseworker. The influence of social work on the provision of services to the probationer has had a profound effect on the development of probation services. Earlier, an overemphasis on casework and the medical model, which conceived of the criminal offender as "sick," resulted in a narrow focus on the relationship between the probationer and the officer. This led, in turn, to a tendency to overlook the connection between crime and such contributing factors as poverty, racism, unemployment, poor health, substandard housing, and lack of education.

One inherent drawback in the casework model is the ease with which functions not related to probation may be assumed. Placement in foster homes, operation of shelters, alcoholism, drug addiction, and mental illness may be more properly handled by community mental health facilities or other appropriate agencies. One probation officer alone could not possess the background required to deal with all the problems of probationers. On the other hand, probation officers are expected to account for their probationers if they get into trouble again. One of the first questions asked by the court in this situation is usually, "When did you last see your client?" In a system which demands accountability of this kind, POs are usually led to overextend themselves in an effort to prevent or justify the failure of their clients.

A discussion of parole in a later section will briefly examine how the issue of whether POs are police officers or counselors has fared in California's approach to conditional release. For many POs, this conflict in roles constitutes the major source of stress in their daily work.

Success Rates in Probation

It is generally estimated that placing a person in prison costs about ten times as much as it costs to place someone on probation for a comparable period (Smykla, 1981). Granted that probation is more economical than incarceration as a method of responding to offenders, is it successful in rehabilitating the offender? How do we measure "success" in probation? How do we gauge whether probation has been a failure?

Allen, Carlson, and Parks (1979) pointed out that surprisingly few studies have attempted to compare the effectiveness of probation with that of other sentencing alternatives. Available research could be divided into three categories:

1. Studies that compare the performance of probationers with the performance of offenders receiving alternative dispositions
2. Studies that measure probation outcomes without comparison with any other form of sanction
3. Studies that measure probation outcome and attempt to isolate characteristics which tend to discriminate between success and failure.

The results of 10 of these studies are summarized in Table 12.1. As a rule of thumb, if the failure rate in the particular study was 30 percent or below, probation was considered effective; if the failure rate exceeded 30 percent, probation was judged to have been of limited success or ineffective.

Allen and his colleagues noted that "it is nearly impossible, not to mention inappropriate, to draw any conclusions from these studies about the effectiveness of probation compared to other alternative dispositions" (p. 33), as a consequence of wide disparities in methods and approaches. In particular, there are basic discrepancies in the way recidivism—the crucial factor in the determination of success or failure of probation—is defined from one study to another. Given these differences in defining success or failure and variations in the follow-up period employed in the various studies, the one characteristic that seemed to be most consistently associated with failure was the probationer's previous criminal history. Individuals with a background of persistent law violation, regardless of type, appear to make poor probation risks. Probation is most likely to have a significant impact on first offenders. In addition, the studies tend to indicate that severity of violation increases with severity of disposition.

Women on Probation

Norland and Mann (1984) have reported the results of exploratory research directed toward sex differences in reported violations of community supervision among female and male probationers and parolees for the period from 1975 to 1977. They discerned two patterns in the violation reports: (1) women are less likely than men to be charged with violations; and (2) violation reports against women are more likely to be based on technical charges than are those for men, whose reports tend to be grounded on the commission of felonies.

TABLE 12.1 Studies Reporting Recidivism Rates for Probationers

Study	Instant Offenses	Failure	Follow-up	Failure Rate
Caldwell 1951	Internal Revenue Laws (72%)	Convictions	Post-probation: 5½–11½ years	16.4
England 1955	Bootlegging (48%); forgery and counterfeiting (9%)	Convictions	Postprobation: 6–12 years	17.7
Davis 1955	Burglary; forgery and checks	2 or more violations and revocation (technical and new offenses)	To termination; 4–7 years	30.2
Frease 1964		Inactive letter, bench warrant, and revocation	On probation: 18–30 months	20.0
Landis 1969	Auto theft, forgery and checks	Revocation (technical and new offenses)	To termination	52.2
Irish 1972	Larceny and burglary	Arrests or convictions	Postprobation: Minimum of 4 yrs.	41.5
Missouri Division of Probation and Parole 1976	Burglary, larceny and vehicle theft	Arrests and convictions	Postprobation: 6 months–7 years	30.0
Kusuda 1976	Property	Revocation	To termination: 1–2 years	18.3
Comptroller General 1976		Revocation and postrelease conviction	Postprobation: 20 month average	55.0
Irish 1977	Property	Arrests	Postprobation: 3–4 years	29.6

The authors note that several factors operate to lower the number of violation reports against women. Overcrowding of institutional facilities for both male and female offenders discourages probation and parole officers from reporting violations by any but the most troublesome offenders of either sex. Also, probation and parole officers are reluctant to report violations by women because of their paternalistic beliefs that familial obligations and responsibilities are heavier for women than for men. These factors combine with a low level of female involvement in felony offenses to produce a low level of reported violations for women under community supervision.

Norland and Mann state that probation and parole officers tend to view women as troublesome clients because they threaten routine patterns of interaction between POs and clients. They take up too much time with what officers perceive as minor problems and tend to develop dependency relationships rather than the typical pattern of amiably superficial contacts that characterize relationships with male supervisees. In addition, women may be seen as more troublesome because their focus on such factors as family, children, and welfare is perceived to be outside the scope of the PO's competence.

Intensive Supervision

Gettinger (1985) defines intensive supervision as the "strictest form of probation for adults in the United States. . . . With heavy surveillance and other features [community service, restitution, fines, and community sponsors] the intensive program adds up to a substantial penalty" (p. 220). Intensive supervision programs have been developed as an alternative or supplement to traditional probation. They are primarily intended to relieve prison overcrowding at an acceptable cost, but other purposes are served as well. As Irwin (1985) notes with regard to Georgia's intensive supervision probation program, "Its main intention was to demonstrate that serious offenders could be supervised effectively in the community" (p. 27); therefore the state could be spared the expense of building additional prisons to handle an increased load of offenders.

An example of extensive supervised custody in the community is Florida's community control program, which opened on October 1, 1983, as a result of the passage of the Correctional Reform Act of 1983 by the Florida state legislature. Its objectives were to (1) help reduce prison overcrowding; (2) provide safe punishment-oriented community alternatives to imprisonment; (3) divert offenders from prisons and jails; (4) provide weekend, as well as weekday, surveillance and supervision; (5) provide public work programs for community controlees; (6) limit community control caseloads to 20 cases per officer; and (7) impose and enforce noninstitutional sanctions and house arrest.

Under the community control program, more than 5,000 offenders have become "outmates," who live in their own neighborhoods, in their own houses or apartments, with their own families. Outmates can expect at least 28 unexpected visits per month from the community control (CC) officers. A daily log listing activities, hour by hour, must be filled out by the offender. Community service work is required, and prisoners must often make financial restitution to their crime victims. They are also expected to pay up to $50 per month to the Department of Corrections for their supervision. At the direction of CC officers, outmates must participate in self-help programs, ranging from Alcoholics Anonymous to psychological counseling. On demand, they must submit to breathalyzer, urinalysis, and blood tests. CC officers are responsible for knowing what their charges are doing at all times.

From the outset, representatives from probation and parole, the police, the courts, and the general public have been receptive to community control because the program emphasizes punitive sanctions, accountability and responsibility, and small caseloads to insure credibility and public safety. Since much of community control work has been a pioneering effort, a wide range of techniques and procedures has evolved. Only experienced probation and parole officers have been used as staff, and they have been given opportunities for extensive training. Additional pay incentives are needed, however, to continue to attract experienced professionals of high caliber who are vital to the success of the program.

In a review of evaluations of intensive supervision programs in the United States, Travis (1984) found that the failure rates of regular and intensive supervision programs were similar. He noted, however, that new offenses and technical violations—which are more likely to be detected under the increased scrutiny of intensive supervision programs—might mask the success of intensive supervision programs in reducing new offense behavior. It should be emphasized that comparable or slightly higher violation rates can be considered a success in situations where intensive supervision programs serve a higher-risk population than is handled in a traditional probation program.

Electronic Monitoring

Computerization and electronic monitoring have provided tools or instruments which have been proposed as the means for reducing prison overcrowding, increasing probation effectiveness, and improving community protection. Probationers are equipped with an anklet or bracelet that emits a constant signal which is transmitted to the PO's office. Once an offender violates his or her space, the circuit is broken and an alarm is sounded at the sheriff's office or police headquarters. A computer can also be programmed to contact the offender's residence at intervals, and the offender's presence or absence is recorded at the central office.

As of 1984, Pride, Incorporated (Palm Beach, Florida) has operated a system of electronic monitoring. Originally developed in Albuquerque, New Mexico, by Michael Goss, the system consists of three components: (1) a miniaturized transmitter worn by the offender as an anklet or wristlet; (2) a receiver-dialer in the offender's residence; and (3) a central computer-probation officer monitor/alert system (National Institute of Justice, 1986, p. 2). A computer tape of random curfew checks is verified against each offender's schedule for violations. If necessary, the offender is returned to court and probable incarceration. Kentucky, Oregon, Michigan, Utah, and New Mexico have implemented or expanded this program for both felons and misdemeanants; and the state of Florida is currently considering grants for a statewide extension of the program.

Probation in Retrospect

Probation has traditionally been imposed as a disposition in cases involving juveniles, youthful offenders, first offenders, and minor property offenders. For more than a century, probation services were dominated by the precedents established by John Augustus. Probation officers acted primarily as counselors rather than surveillance officers and performed the functions of community resource broker and social change agent. In the dichotomy between rehabilitation of the offender and protection of society which lies at the base of probation as a court-imposed criminal sanction, rehabilitation was rarely perceived as being in conflict with community safety.

During the past two decades, however, probation has come to be viewed as an unacceptable exercise in leniency on the part of the courts. Petersilia, Turner, Kahan, & Patterson (1985) assert that "California's probation population is posing an increasingly serious threat to public safety" (p. 4). Barkdull (1976) states that probation, "as it is understood by the public, does not seem to do anything to the offender or for the public. It does not even serve a positive symbolic function" (p. 4). Conrad (1985) claims that public support for probation has dwindled to the vanishing point.

There is little doubt that conventional approaches to probation are not equipped to handle what McCleary (1978) called "dangerous men." For these individuals who cannot be controlled in open society, there is the prison alternative of incapacitation. On the other end of the spectrum are the youthful offenders and minor property criminals for whom traditional probation continues to be an appropriate sentencing alternative. Between these extremes lie the offenders who need closer supervision than is provided by traditional probation but do not require the close custody of prison. Proponents of intensive supervision or community control have argued that the combination of house arrest, community service, restitution, and supervision fees is an approach to dealing with the mid-range offender who represents a more suitable sentencing alternative than either traditional probation or incarceration. In addition, it is claimed that revamping probation to meet the changing needs of community protection makes more sense in terms of cost-effectiveness than building new prisons—which the public does not want to pay for in the first place.

Petersilia et al. (1985) say, "We believe that intensive surveillance/supervision programs will be the most significant experiment made by the criminal justice system in the next decade" (p. 91). John Conrad (1985) cautions, "We'll see" (p. 417). Regardless of what happens with intensive supervision programs, probation services need major improvements in organization, staffing, and funding. Also needed is the development of a more effective system for the selection of probationers. Since 1972, the U.S. Parole Commission has used an actuarial instrument as an aid in assessing parole diagnosis in conjunction with explicit decision guidelines (Hoffman, 1983). These guidelines use a two-dimensional matrix to establish a range of time to be served (in months) for various combinations of offenses, ranked in order of severity, and offender characteristics. I examine this instrument in a discussion of parole prognosis in a later section. Corresponding applications of prediction methods in probation are currently within reach and await only testing and large-scale research (Albanese, Fiore, Powell, & Storti, 1981).

CONDITIONAL RELEASE

All offenders except those who are executed or committed to prison for "life certain" terms must eventually be released. How well they fare once they are returned to society—whether they are successfully reintegrated or commit further offenses that lead them back into prison—is subject to many complex factors, one of which is the sheer length of time a person has spent in prison. Reid (1981) cites the case of Ralph Lobaugh who was released in 1977 after spending 30 years in prison in Indiana:

> The freedom for which he had fought during 14 years, however, was too much for him. After two months, Lobaugh decided he could not cope with life outside the walls and went back to prison. According to Harold G. Roddy, director of the work-release program in Indiana, Lobaugh "just wanted to live in a cell again and be with his old friends." (p. 282)

The Lobaugh case may be extreme, but the problems of readjustment to a free society for a released prisoner are anything but unusual or atypical.

Parole is the traditional means by which the majority of incarcerated prisoners are released each year from correctional institutions. In this section I examine the parole process and attempt to identify some of the problems and issues that have fueled criticism of parole and have led to moves to abandon parole in favor of determinate sentences. I also discuss some alternative approaches to the conditional release of incarcerated offenders such as work-release, study-release, furloughs, and other kinds of graduated reentry of the prisoner into free society.

PAROLE

Parole is the conditional release, under supervision, of an offender from a correctional institution after he has served a portion of his sentence. The word is taken from the French and is used in the sense of *parole d'honneur*—word of honor. The concept has its roots in military history, referring to the practice of releasing a captured soldier on his parole (i.e., on his word of honor that he would not again take up arms against his captors). Similarly, the inmate is released to free society on his parole, or his word of honor, that he will not again become an enemy of society. Parole differs from probation because it implies that the offender has "served time." Administratively, parole is a function of the executive branch of government, while probation is a judicial act of the court. Selection, supervision, regulations, revocation, and release procedures are similar, and the two kinds of conditional releases often become confusing to the public.

Prisoners have always been released on the arrival of their "mandatory release date"—that is, sentences normally have a termination date. In inmate jargon, this is referred to as serving "flat time" or "day-for-day." Parole is a conditional release. Inmates who appear to be making genuine progress toward rehabilitation are selected to serve a final portion of their sentence, under some form of supervision, in the community.

The Parole Board

Prisoners who are seeking release on parole must follow a procedure of recommendation and review to determine their readiness for this option. In the formative years of parole selection procedures, many states had a single commissioner of parole who was appointed by the governor. This system led to corruption and a great deal of controversy, and it generally was abandoned after World War II. Two models are primarily used today: (1) parole boards that are linked to, or are actually part of, the institutional staff; and (2) parole boards that are independent of correctional institutions and the administrators of the system. A third model, a consolidation of all correctional and parole services, will be discussed later.

The institutional model tends to perceive the parole decision as merely another step in a series of decisions affecting the offender. These institutional staffs maintain that they are best situated to make the parole decision because of their intimate contact with the offender. This argument is countered by the general recognition that the conditions and rules within a prison are seldom related to potential adjustment on the outside. Often the actions of the inmate, which are the basis for the institutional parole board decision, are those that might seriously interfere with the individual's ability to deal with problems on the outside. Complete subordination to institutional rules and regulations, lack of individuality, and the absence of scope for individual decision making are often desired conditions in institutions. These behaviors, which are sought in the interest of smooth institutional operations, are hardly the prerequisite skills for surviving in free society.

On the other hand, parole decisions made by the institutional decision-making agents are likely to be submerged in the invisible activity that takes place behind the walls. Removed from public scrutiny or control, the parole decision becomes just another institutionalized process which treats offenders, who are vitally concerned with the decision, as merely incidental to the outcome.

Independently authorized parole boards became the more widely used model in adult corrections in this century. As a matter of fact, it became so popular that today there is *no* adult parole releasing authority controlled directly by the staff of a penal institution (National Advisory Commission, 1973). The obvious purpose of this type of authority was to eliminate the kinds of problems mentioned earlier from the decision-making procedure. It was felt that, under the institutional board, parole authorities were too easily swayed by subjective impressions, opinions, biases, and attitudes on the part of the institutional staff members. While the purposes of objectivity may be served by an independent board—one that is outside the correctional bureaucracy—this arrangement is susceptible to other sorts of problems. Lack of knowledge of the programs, policies, and conditions within the prisons creates a gap which may cause unnecessary conflict in this kind of system. The problems that are evident in these two models are dealt with in the newest and most popular model, the *consolidated board*.

The consolidated model generally allocates the decision-making authority to the department of corrections, but maintains independent powers in the parole decision. This is consistent with the current move toward consolidation of all correctional services under state departments of corrections. These consolidations include institutional programs, community-based programs and parole, and aftercare programs. The consolidation model views the treatment stages of the offender in the correctional system as a continuum, not as separate unarticulated parts. Proponents of this method claim that the removal of decision-making authority to a level above the institutions, but still within the system, tends to foster objectivity, while maintaining a sensitivity toward the programs and problems of the prison administrators. This kind of model seems to represent the wave of the future for corrections, as over 60 percent of the state parole boards responsible for release of adult offenders now function in common with an administrative structure that includes other agencies for offenders. While this system is preferable to others, it still must struggle to maintain its autonomy. Its autonomy must be protected by thoughtful selection and tenure decisions, along with careful delineation of the parole board tasks and responsibilities.

The Selection Process in Parole

The general practice of most parole boards is to assign cases to individual board members and let them review the cases in detail, after which they make recommendations to the full board when it meets. In most cases, the recommendation of the individual board member is accepted, but sometimes the assembled board will request more details. This is often the case when the prisoner is asked to appear. Some states send individual members of the board to the institutions to interview the inmate and the institutional staff. Others convene the entire board at the individual institutions on a regular schedule. If inmates fail to meet whatever criteria the board uses, their sentences are continued and they "flopped." If parole is granted, the inmate is prepared for turnover to the adult parole authority for a period of supervision determined by the parole board. A major problem in making parole decisions often lies in the boards' disregard of offenders' rights to know the criteria they are expected to achieve and the reasons why they were flopped. Porter (1958) comments on this aspect of the decision-making process:

> It is an essential element of justice that the role and processes for measuring parole readiness be made known to the inmate. This knowledge can greatly facilitate the earnest inmate toward his own rehabilitation. It is just as important for an inmate to know the rules and basis for the judgment upon which he will be granted or denied parole as it was important for him to know the basis of the charge against him and the evidence upon which he was convicted. One can imagine nothing more cruel, inhuman, and frustrating than serving a prison term without knowledge of what will be measured and the rules determining whether one is ready for release. . . . Justice can never be a product of unreasoned judgment. (p. 227)

This problem applies to the correction staff as well, since it must also know the rules of the game in order to guide inmates in the direction desired by the parole board.

Four inmates of the Indiana State Penitentiary have described how parole candidates resent at least three aspects of the parole decision process. First, the tendency of parole boards is to place great emphasis on the candidate's prior record:

What is so frustrating to men who keep getting rejected for parole because of "past record" is that there is obviously nothing that the individual can do about it. It cannot be changed, it cannot be expunged. It therefore generates a feeling of helplessness and frustration, especially in men who take seriously what they are told about rehabilitation and perfect institutional records. These men cannot understand the rationale behind parole denials based on past records if the major goal of the correctional system is rehabilitation and if they have tried to take advantage of every rehabilitation program offered by the institution. The men know that merely serving another two or five years is not going to further the "rehabilitation" process. (Griswold, et al., 1970)

The second source of resentment comes from the attitude of parole boards that their principal responsibility is to protect society and that the rehabilitation of the offender is secondary. With this as their guide, parole boards are reluctant to release offenders who are considered poor risks, preferring to let them serve day-for-day and return to the community without supervision. This practice undoubtedly reduces the recidivism rate for persons on parole and enhances the public image of parole boards. Its impact on the overall recidivism rate, however, should be the paramount consideration. The issue is whether keeping poor parole risks in prison for a longer period of time makes them better parole risks. The answer for some is "yes." The passage of time, more than anything in the dehumanizing prison atmosphere, seems to mature a few inmates. But for most, the longer offenders are subjected to the criminogenic environment of a penitentiary, the more likely they are to absorb the values, techniques, and rationalizations of the criminal subculture.

Third, inmates are convinced that parole boards are more responsive to public opinion and political pressures than to the factual situation and record of the individual applicant. This feeling on the part of prisoners only adds to their cynicism toward the entire parole process.

Another area of the parole decision process that has come under attack is the right to appeal an unfavorable decision. Because of the tenuous nature of the parole decision and the often unarticulated criteria used by the board members, the decisions made are often subject to question, especially when the inmates are denied knowledge as to why they were not granted parole. Future parole selection processes must include self-regulating and internal appeal procedures. Failure to provide these procedures will result in case after case being sent to court, until the Supreme Court steps in and establishes rules and procedures based on the 14th amendment. Some states have seen the handwriting on the wall and have started to establish criteria and to develop appeal procedures, before they are forced to do so by court decisions and class action suits.

Conditions for Parole

Many of the earlier parole procedures imposed restrictions on the released offender which were unreasonable. Too often the rules for parole were simply a convenient pretext for returning the parolee to prison, which was done if the parolee created even the slightest fuss for the parole officer. Today the rules that a parolee is expected to follow are much more reasonable and realistic, as the following model parole contract illustrates:

STATEMENT OF PAROLE AGREEMENT

The Members of the Parole Board have agreed that you have earned the opportunity of parole and eventually a final release from your present conviction. The Parole Board is therefore ordering a Parole Release in your case.

Parole Status has a twofold meaning: One is a trust status in which the Parole Board accepts your word you will do your best to abide by the Conditions of Parole that are set down in your case; the other, by State law, means the Adult Parole Authority has the legal duty to enforce the Conditions of Parole even to the extent of arrest and return to the institution should that become necessary.

The following Conditions of Parole are in effect in your Parole Release:

1. Upon release from the institution, report as instructed to your Parole Officer (or any other person designated) and thereafter report as often as directed.

2. Secure written permission of the Adult Parole Authority before leaving the [said] State.

3. Obey all municipal ordinances, state and federal laws, and at all times conduct yourself as a responsible law-abiding citizen.

4. Never purchase, own, possess, use or have under your control, a deadly weapon or firearm.

5. Follow all instructions given you by your Parole Officer or other officials of the Adult Parole Authority.

6. If you feel any of the Conditions or instructions are causing problems, you may request a meeting with your parole officer's supervisor. The request stating your reasons for the conference should be in writing when possible.

7. Special Conditions: (as determined).

I have read, or have had read to me, the foregoing Conditions of my Parole. I fully understand them and I agree to observe and abide by my Parole Conditions.

Witness .... Parole Candidate ....

Date ....

As recently as 20 years ago, it was common for the conditions of parole to include such rules as one which required the parolee to "only associate with persons of good reputation." Conforming to that sort of requirement would be nearly impossible for an offender whose family members may have included persons with criminal records. Rules of this type gave the parole officer great discretionary power over the parolee. Offenders knew that their parole could be revoked for a technical violation of the conditions at almost any time the parole officer desired. This situation does not create a relationship which is conducive to reform and respect for the law. The parolee's attitude was often one of, "If I'm going to get busted for a technical violation, I might as well do something really wrong." The simpler nonrestrictive rules previously mentioned were aimed at eliminating this kind of rationalization by the parolee.

The Effectiveness of Parole

"No one who works in the field of parole," Keve (1981) observes, "doubts the fact that good work on the part of concerned parole officers has been of real effect in helping some or many ex-prisoners become established successfully on return to the community. At the same time, however, the well-entrenched faith in the necessity of parole supervision is not supported by objective research" (p. 313). Evaluating the success or failure of parole supervision faces many of the same difficulties that are encountered in attempts to gauge the effectiveness of probation. Terms such as "success" and "failure" are extremely difficult to operationalize and measure; comparing the results of various studies, therefore, poses formidable problems.

Keve cites a 1971–1972 Minnesota project which compared two groups of paroled youthful offenders including both boys and girls. One group received routine parole supervision; the second group was not given any attention unless they asked for it. After a trial period of 10 months, the two groups were compared on revocation rate. While there was no discernible difference between unsupervised and supervised girls, the supervised boys showed a significantly higher rate of parole violations than did the unsupervised boys. Says Keve: "It is uncertain what this proves. It easily may be that supervised boys have their paroles revoked more often simply because they are more likely to be caught, whereas the unsupervised boys more easily get by without being caught" (p. 313). Such findings emphasize the dangers involved in the use of recidivism as a success-failure criterion when recidivism is a reflection primarily of technical parole or probation revocations.

A later study (Sacks & Logan, 1979) took advantage of the release of 167 incarcerated felons whose sentences were vacated as the result of a judicial decision by a Connecticut court. A subgroup of these prisoners, whose discharge meant outright release without supervision, was compared with a control group of 57 released prisoners who were given routine parole supervision. The groups were compared after one year on the basis of new arrests and convictions. As the researchers noted, "37% of the control group (parolees) failed while 63% of the experimental group (dischargees) failed" (p. 97). They interpreted these results to indicate that parole had "definite, but modest, effects" on recidivism. This conclusion would seem to be a fair assessment of the effectiveness of parole supervision in general.

Enhancing Parole Prediction: Actuarial Tables

Parole boards are constantly engaged in a type of activity that most people associate with tea leaves and crystal balls—namely, predicting the future. The decision to release or not to release an inmate involves an action based on the appraisal by the parole board members of the individual's likelihood of future behavior—lawful or criminal. In study after study, the main criteria affecting this prediction have been (1) the seriousness of the crime for which the offender was convicted; (2) the individual's criminal record; and (3) the prospects of success on parole for the individual, as viewed by the members of the parole board.

In an effort to increase the objectivity—and consequently the reliability and validity—of prediction, statistical tables have been developed for use by parole boards to augment the subjective aspects of the decision-making process. One of the best known of these approaches is the actuarial table called a Salient Factor Scale which was developed during 1973 and 1974 by the Federal Parole Commission. Use of it was mandated by the Federal Parole Commission and Reorganization Act of 1976. Before describing these federal parole guidelines, we should first try to clarify what is often referred to as the problem of clinical vs. statistical prediction or case-study vs. actuarial prediction.

Given certain kinds of behavior (e.g., dropping out of school), some rather accurate estimates can be made about other kinds of behavior (e.g., being sent to a state training school). To put it another way, given the fact that a young man is in a juvenile correctional facility, one can make some seemingly clairvoyant statements about his background, including the possession of a spotty educational record. These estimates are not guesses in the usual sense: They are derived from *actuarial tables,* with which criminologists are becoming increasingly familiar. Just as life insurance companies build actuarial tables based on life expectancies which determine the premiums that are charged, so also can actuarial tables be built about the expectancy of institutional incarceration for various groups. The actuaries assume that each individual is going to be like others in certain respects. In life span, they assume he will reach a particular age; with a dropout, they assume he will run afoul of the law. In many cases they will be wrong. Some insurees die shortly after affixing their signatures to the policy; some dropouts do well. But insurance companies bank (literally as well as figuratively) on the actuarial approach. Actuaries forecast efficiently with regard to groups. Causation is not their concern; association—what goes with what—is their focus of interest. Predicting individual behavior with the aid of actuarial tables makes the assumption that whatever factors affect the individual will be less influential than those which cause his behavior to conform fairly closely to the pattern exhibited by other individuals who make up the aggregate or group.

Clinical prediction, on the other hand, is based on an intensive and exhaustive study of how many forces and factors have combined to shape the distinctive pattern which reflects the uniqueness of the individual. According to this view, no two people are alike. In fact, no two individuals are more than similar in terms of truly significant bases for comparison. Thus, in order to make an individual prediction, it is necessary to have a deep understanding of whom the person is and how he or she is likely to react to a given situation.

The Salient Factor Scale relates uniform amounts of prison time served to severity of crime and level of risk. Data were obtained from ratings made by parole commissioners, and the base-sentence ranges shown in Table 12.2 were established for each of seven categories of offense by computing the mean amount of time that inmates had served in the past for these crimes.

Four requirements for prediction tables have been identified by Mannheim and Wilkins (1955):

1. *Simplicity*—the tables must be comprehensible to nonspecialists, and their use should involve nothing more complicated than addition, subtraction, or multiplication

2. *Efficiency*—as measured by the extent to which a table achieves its purpose parsimoniously (i.e., with the fewest factors that contribute significantly to the specification of success or failure)

3. *Reliability*—as gauged by the ability of people to achieve comparable results with the table on repeated occasions

4. *Validity*—the most important criterion of all, for validity refers to the extent to which the prediction table enables the user to distinguish between success and failure in the parole decision-making process

No one has suggested that prediction tables, however accurate they may prove to be in field operations, are likely to take the place of parole boards. For one thing, there is little likelihood that parole boards are going to relinquish their authority in the parole decision-making process to any instrument, however well recommended it may be on the basis of scientific research. A more realistic alternative is Glaser's (1964) suggestion that actuarial tables augment and complement the more subjective aspects of parole board deliberations and provide a valuable check on the potential effects of bias or prejudice.

Innovations in Parole

Shock Parole

In 1965, Ohio introduced a program of shock probation, which allowed the courts to impose a sentence consisting of a brief period of incarceration followed by probation. The rationale for this program was to impress offenders with the seriousness of their crimes by giving them "a taste of the bars" (Parisi, 1981), yet releasing them for supervision within the community before they have begun to be "prisonized." Shock probation, as Reid (1981) points out, is a misnomer for this procedure because probation is traditionally and technically an alternative to confinement; whereas conditional release following a period of incarceration constitutes parole.

At any rate, encouraged by their experience with the shock probation program, Ohio passed a shock parole statute that permitted shock parole for a large number of prisoners after serving six months in prison. Criteria for eligibility included the following considerations:

The offense for which sentence was imposed is not aggravated murder or murder.

The prisoner is not a second offender.

The prisoner is not a dangerous offender.

The prisoner does not appear to need future confinement as part of his or her correction or rehabilitation.

The prisoner gives evidence that he or she is not likely to commit another offense. (Ohio House Bill 511, 1974)

TABLE 12.2 The Federal Parole Guidelines

Offense Severity (Some crimes eliminated or summarized)	Salient Factor Score (Parole prognosis)			
	Very Good	Good	Fair	Poor
Low: possession of a small amount of marijuana; simple theft under $1,000	6–10 months	8–12 months	10–14 months	12–18 months
Low/Moderate: income tax evasion less than $10,000; immigration law violations; embezzlement, fraud, forgery under $1,000	8–12 months	12–16 months	16–20 months	28–28 months
Moderate: bribery; possession of 50 lbs. or less of marijuana, with intent to sell; illegal firearms; income tax evasion $10,000 to $50,000; nonviolent property offenses $1,000 to $19,999; auto theft, not for resale	12–16 months	16–20 months	20–24 months	24–32 months
High: counterfeiting; marijuana possession with intent to sell, 50 to 1,999 lbs.; auto theft, for resale; nonviolent property offenses, $20,000 to $100,000	16–20 months	20–26 months	26–34 months	34–44 months
Very High: robbery; breaking and entering bank or post office; extortion; marijuana possession with intent to sell, over 2,000 lbs.; hard drugs possession with intent to sell, not more than $100,000; nonviolent property offenses over $100,000 but not exceeding $500,000	26–36 months	36–48 months	48–60 months	60–72 months
Greatest I: explosive detonation; multiple robbery; aggravated felony (weapon fired—no serious injury); hard drugs, over $100,000; forcible rape	40–55 months	55–70 months	70–85 months	85–110 months
Greatest II: aircraft hijacking; espionage; kidnapping; homicide	Greater than above. No specific ranges because of limited numer and extreme variation in cases.			

Source: Kevin Krajick, "Parole: Discretion Is Out, Guidelies Are In," *Corrections Magazine* 4 (December 1978), p. 46.

The number of inmates released on shock parole in Ohio declined from a high of 691 that was reached in 1974, as a result of factors that included an adverse Ohio Supreme Court decision, negative publicity, and the establishment of newer and more stringent guidelines for parole eligibility. Ironically, as shock parole underwent an eclipse in Ohio, it was discovered by a number of other states, where it was viewed as a possible aid in reducing prison overcrowding. Vito (1984) examined an extensive body of research on shock probation and the policy implications of research findings. He concluded that if shock probation is utilized, it should be used with selected offenders who cannot be considered as good candidates for regular probation.

Contract Parole (Mutual Agreement Programming)

An interesting approach to conditional release involves a three-way formal contract between the inmate, parole board, and correctional authorities. This approach, which has been designated Mutual Agreement Programming (MAP), lays out in a legally binding contractual arrangement a series of specified activities that the inmate agrees to undertake for purposes of self-improvement. The parole board, in turn, agrees to a fixed parole date that is contingent upon the successful completion of this mutually agreed-upon program. It is the responsibility of the correctional authorities—the third party to the contract—to provide the services and resources needed to fulfill the inmate's program objectives and to monitor his progress in meeting the contractual requirements.

There are some substantial advantages to the contractual parole arrangement. As noted by Epstein et al. (1976):

> MAP recognizes two very basic interests of prisoners: (1) it provides specific information about when the prisoner can expect to be released on parole from institutional confinement; and (2) it tells the prisoner what he must do in order to achieve the parole release. In addition, MAP provides greater rationality to the parole board's decision making process, and facilitates long term planning as to services and facilities which must be provided by the correctional authorities. (p. i)

On the other hand, the MAP program is difficult to install in a prison and "requires persistence and determination on the part of administrators" (Keve, 1981, p. 317). Many institutions simply lack the kind of training and counseling services that would permit the inmate to fulfill MAP objectives.

An even more serious handicap in contract parole is the fact that the various parties to the contractual agreement are not co-equals. Since the prisoner knows full well that his agreement to become involved in the program is a crucial factor in determining how long he will have to serve in prison, he can scarcely be considered a free agent in the negotiation (Morris, 1974). Nevertheless, contract parole represents a worthwhile and progressive innovation in parole.

One of the most interesting experiments in parole is currently underway in California. This system, which is described in the following example, was adopted following California's decision in 1977 to adopt determinate sentencing. Parole officials, who were understandably concerned that determinate sentencing all but eliminated parole, maintain that the new model, based on a point system for assessing risks and assigning levels of supervision, will allow researchers to determine whether or not parole supervision has any demonstrable effects on recidivism.

SEPARATING THE COP FROM THE COUNSELOR

Janice M.'s crime was a 10.

"On 3-23-76 the body of the victim was discovered in the orange grove," the presentence report read. "Janice M., along with three others, had been responsible for the torture, beating, stabbing, and strangulation which led to the death of the victim. . . . Janice had been the one who injected the victim with battery acid."

On a form titled "risk assessment," the parole agent wrote "actual torture murder," and then marked down the numeral "10." Leafing through the thick file that the prison sent him when Janice was paroled, he noted that she had several previous convictions for drug offenses and prostitution. He gave her an 8, on a scale of 10, for her past criminal behavior. Her habits of drug and alcohol abuse earned another 10. Janice had previously failed on probation, so that was worth 8 points. He multiplied each score by a fraction that represented its importance, and added up the figures. Overall, on a scale of 10, Janice came out with a risk score of 8.90.

Janice's high score means that she is a potential danger to the community and warrants very close surveillance by a California state parole agent. The point system is part of a "new model" for parole supervision adopted by the California Division of Parole and Community Services in January 1980. The point system is used to determine whether a parolee is a "control" case, a "service" case—meaning that social services are more important than surveillance—or a minimum-supervision case. Parole agents are also divided up into the three categories: minimum-supervision agents, "control" agents, who act as the personal police of parolees, and "service" agents, who arrange for social services. Agents' activities are spelled out in detail and carefully monitored by supervisors; agents complain that most of their discretion has been taken away . . .

This system is a significant change in the way parole is administered in California. The "new model" has several features which make it different from the way that parole has traditionally operated in California and in most other states:

- Numerical assessments of risks and needs. Other states have adopted point systems to determine whether an inmate should be released on parole. But California, where release depends only on the length of the determinate sentence, uses it to determine the type of parole supervision.
- Different styles of supervision. Any parolee with a risk score of 7.5 or above is considered a "control" case . . .
- Minimum supervision. Any case that scores 3.75 on both risks and needs is put into a separate caseload, with few reports required and services provided only upon request.
- Specialization of parole agents by styles of supervision. "Control" agents and "service" agents are forbidden to handle problems outside of their specialties.
- Specific direction by supervisors. They tell a parole agent exactly what actions to take on each case, and how many hours per month they are to devote to it.

Before the system was instituted, administrators predicted that 40 percent of all cases would fall into the control category, 38 percent into service emphasis, and 22 percent would merit minimum supervision. . . . Late last year, 84 percent of the 14,000 parolees in California were classified as control cases; 8 percent were service cases and 8 percent minimum supervision. The assignment of the state's 367 parole agents reflects approximately a six-to-one ratio of control to service.

Gettinger, S. (1981). *Corrections Magazine, 7*, 34–35. Reproduced by permission of the author and publisher.

Legal Issues Affecting Parole

Parole boards have traditionally exercised almost total discretionary powers in both granting and revoking parole. This authority rested on the theory that parole is a privilege, not a right: "The prisoner has no statutory right, even if 'qualified,' to be granted conditional liberty or allowed to remain on parole" (*Morrissey v. Brewer*, 1971). Therefore, since parole is not a right, no reasons need be given for denial of parole. As a federal court stated, elements of due process are not required at the time of the parole decision:

> The Board of Parole is given absolute discretion in matters of parole. The courts are without power to grant a parole or to determine judicially eligibility for parole . . . it is not the function of the courts to review the discretion of the Board in the denial of the application for parole or to review the credibility of reports and information received by the Board in making its determinations. (*Tarlton v. Clark*, 1971)

The reasoning which underlies the federal court ruling is that granting parole is not an adversary proceeding; therefore, due process is not required. In addition, information is often introduced into the deliberations of the parole board which would not be admissible in a trial. This interpretation was shared by the Supreme Court, which refused to review the *Tarlton* case. Seven years later, in the case of *Greenholtz v. Inmates of Nebraska Penal and Correctional Complex* (1979), the Court rejected the contention that a parole hearing requires all of the due process elements involved in a criminal trial.

Parole revocation, on the other hand, does raise due process issues. The matter of due process in parole revocation was expressed in a federal case (*Murray v. Page*, 1970) in the following terms:

> While a prisoner does not have a constitutional right to parole, once paroled he cannot be deprived of his freedom by means inconsistent with due process. The minimal right of the parolee to be informed of the charges and the nature of the evidence against him and to appear to be heard at the revocation hearing is inviolate. Statutory deprivation of this right is manifestly inconsistent with the due process and is unconstitutional; nor can such right be lost by the subjective determination of the executive that the case for revocation is "clear."

A year later, in the landmark case of *Morrissey v. Brewer* (1971), the Supreme Court held that the liberty of a parolee, although indeterminate, includes many of the core values of unqualified liberty and its termination inflicts a "grievous loss" on the parolee and often on others. It is hardly useful any longer to try to deal with this problem in terms of whether the parolee's liberty is a "right" or a "privilege." By whatever name the liberty is valuable and must be seen as within the protection of the Fourteenth Amendment. Its determination calls for some orderly process, however informal.

The Court found it appropriate to state the underlying rationale for its decision in *Morrissey v. Brewer*, which rests on the assumption that parole is a key element in the rehabilitative process:

1. Parole is an integrative part of the correctional system and its primary purpose is to aid in rehabilitation.
2. The parole system implies that an individual may remain on parole until the rules are violated.
3. Revocation of parole "is not part of a criminal prosecution and thus the full panoply of rights due a defendant in such a proceeding do not apply to parole revocation."
4. Whether parole is a right or a privilege is not the crucial question. The issue is the extent to which an individual would be "condemned to suffer grievous loss." The liberty enjoyed by a parolee is important; if terminated, some elements of due process must be involved.
5. The state's interest in protecting society does not preclude or hinder an informal hearing at parole revocation.
6. Society has an interest in not revoking parole unless parole rules have been violated.
7. The requirements of due process fluctuate with particular types of cases.

The elements of due process that the Court identified as required by parole revocation were

1. Written notice of the alleged violation of parole
2. Disclosure to the parolee of the evidence of violation
3. Opportunity to be heard in person and to present evidence as well as witnesses
4. Right to confront and cross-examine adverse witnesses unless good cause can be shown for not allowing this confrontation
5. Right to judgment by a detached and neutral hearing body
6. Written statement of reasons for revoking parole as well as of the evidence used in arriving at that decision

Issues in Parole

One of the most significant issues in parole is the selection of parole authority personnel. It is difficult to choose between those within the system who might be hesitant to challenge a system which brought them up and those outside the system who may represent a danger in that they may be uninformed or politically motivated and may destroy the system by their ignorance or desire for personal gain. Standards have been suggested for the selection of parole authority personnel, but standards do not provide individuals with the required expertise and skills. The only really effective way to develop the kinds of personnel required is to make the standards, whatever they might be, part of the statutes. This would tend to remove the selection of parole authority members from the political arena. Statutory measures must also eliminate barriers that prevent qualified and capable ex-offenders from serving, since they may be effective, especially as hearing examiners. No other person could be more qualified or sensitive to the inmates' problems in presenting a true picture to the parole board.

In addition to careful selection based on statutory criteria, parole authority personnel should undergo extensive training in recent legal decisions, advances in criminal technology, and current correctional practices in the institutions they will serve. It was recommended by the Standards and Goals Commission that such training be provided on a national scale.

Another major issue is the provision of adequate information from which to make a parole decision. Glaser (1964) suggested that a revised reporting system should be used in which staff members having the most contact with the inmate (invariably the custodial personnel) provide data for the board's decision. Currently, the basic sources for data are the reports dealing with the inmate's adjustment to institutional life. The format of such reporting needs to be changed so that it will focus on the inmate's potential for reintegration into the free community. By the time an inmate has adjusted to the institutional life (when he is said to be *institutionalized*), it may be difficult if not impossible for him to reintegrate into the free world. Readiness detection systems also need to be as efficient as possible, so that the offender can be placed on parole as soon as he is determined to be "ready." Studies have shown that once the inmate goes beyond that ready point, his chances for successful readjustment are significantly diminished. Modern informational technology has the capability to provide such data if correctional administrators and parole authorities are willing to develop and use the required procedures.

The last issue concerns the provision of community services. If the California experiment described earlier proves successful and is widely copied, the "service" specialist will become an expert "broker" of community resources and services. The PO will have to become thoroughly acquainted with a wide range of services in such areas as mental health, family counseling, employment, and personal relations. In fact the entire spectrum of human services will undergo some change and expansion in response to the efforts of parole officers. This new role will undoubtedly create demands for broad knowledge on the part of the parole agent of the political and social organization and power base of the community in which the officer operates. Current prejudices against the ex-offender will probably be magnified as more and more parolees are supervised within the community. The parole officer of the future will be required to have an extensive range of skills in order to make the system operate successfully, especially skills in negotiation and administration.

The Beleagured Status of Parole

A bill was introduced in Congress in 1977 to establish a Federal Commission on Sentencing. The objective of this proposal was to reduce the disparity in sentencing practices from judge to judge by providing standard and uniform sentences for various categories of criminal offenses. These sentences would reflect the importance of such factors as the seriousness of the crime, degree of public concern, and the presence of mitigating circumstances. As Keve (1981) observes, "Although the act says nothing about parole, it is the general assumption that it is one firm step in the direction of eventual elimination of parole in the federal system" (p. 305). Thus far have we come since Captain Alexander Maconochie of the Royal Navy said, "When a man keeps the key of his own prison, he is soon persuaded to fit it to the lock."

The attack on parole has come from a variety of diverse sources, ranging from the American Friends Service Committee to U.S. Bureau of Prison Director Normal Carlson. More than a decade ago, the following indictment of parole was delivered by Citizens' Inquiry on Parole and Criminal Justice, Inc. (1975): "Parole is a tragic failure. Conspiring with other elements of the criminal justice system—unnecessary pre-trial detention, over-long sentences, oppressive conditions—it renders American treatment of those who break society's rules irrational and arbitrary" (p. 38).

A couple of years later, California abolished indeterminate sentencing on a broad scale; and along with the abolition of the indeterminate sentence, it also abolished the Adult Authority or parole board. In July 1977, the state that had pioneered the use of indeterminate sentencing made uniform determinate sentencing a fundamental part of its correctional practice and philosophy.

Is the replacement of indeterminate sentencing with mandatory flat-time sentencing an opening or closing of Pandora's box? Not enough time has passed to permit an informed answer to this question. In the meantime, other states have followed California's lead in abolishing indeterminate sentencing. It seems rather unlikely that parole will be abandoned altogether as a form of conditional release from confinement. Even sharp critics of parole such as von Hirsch and Hanrahan (1979) have argued for the retention, at least for some time, of the parole board as a safety net. In addition, as Singer (1979) observes, the movement toward reducing sentence disparities by means of guidelines and sentencing institutes or councils has helped defuse a good deal of the animosity that prisoners have felt toward the parole system. But continuing public clamor for tougher laws and stricter law enforcement makes it abundantly clear that parole will be subjected to close constraints for the foreseeable future.

Other Forms of Conditional Release

Work Release

The pioneering reform efforts of Crofton in Ireland during the nineteenth century were an attempt to provide prisoners with the chance to work within the community for a period of time prior to their release. This idea has been revived in recent years:

The work-release program has become an important adjunct to institutional programs. Under work-release arrangements, offenders are allowed to work at jobs in the community and still receive the benefit of certain programs and services available at an institution.

The origin of work-release legislation is a 1913 Wisconsin statute which allowed misdemeanants to continue to work at their jobs while serving short sentences in jail. North Carolina applied the principles of the Wisconsin statute to felony offenders in 1957, under limited conditions; Michigan and Maryland soon followed suit with similar acts. In 1965, Congress passed the Federal Prisoner Rehabilitation Act, which provided for work-release, furloughs, and community-treatment centers for federal prisoners. Many states followed suit.

Work-release programs are not really alternatives to incarceration in an either/or sense. They provide a chance for the offender to test his work skills and control over his own behavior in the community and allow him to spend the major part of the day away from the institution. Because the inmate is still required to return to the institution, the work-release program is referred to here as only a partial alternative to incarceration.

Work release has benefits other than allowing the inmate to be outside the walls for a period of time each day. The income derived from the work can be used in a number of ways. If he has a family, the earnings can be used to keep them off welfare rolls or to augment the assistance they might be receiving. He may reimburse the victim for his loss, or he may be able to acquire a nest egg for the time when he will be released. One of the major effects, however, is that private citizens will see that an offender can work in the community without creating problems for himself or for others. His association with fellow workers enjoying more stable lives in freedom may also give the offender support and guidance which he cannot gain inside the walls. In the American tradition, the ability to produce a day's work is highly valued and being able to do so tends to instill a feeling of self-worth in many offenders in work-release programs.

Study Release

Study-release programs are a correctional alternative that possesses many of the same features of the work-release concept. Study-release programs are a rather recent innovation in corrections. Prior to 1960, the only state that reported a study-release program in operation was Connecticut. At present, 41 states have study-release programs of some kind—most of them open to both male and female participants (Shichor & Allen, 1977). The range of educational services offered by these programs is extremely broad, from vocational training and basic adult skills training to college-level education. Variables involved in the screening of offenders for study release are comparable to those employed in work-release programs: current offense, length of time served, custody grade, educational needs, attitudes of the offender toward the institution and program, among others. Since educational attainments are a significant employment consideration in our achievement-oriented society, programs that seek to increase the marketability of the offender by raising the level of his job-related skills have a good deal of plausibility as alternatives to imprisonment. We are not in a position, however, to make more than cautious statements about the value of such programs because we are still awaiting reliable and valid information on the evaluation of study-release programs.

Furloughs

Another form of partial incarceration is the furlough. Work- and study-release programs and furloughs extend the limits of confinement by allowing unsupervised absences from the prison. Furloughs and home visits have been used informally for many years. The death of a family member or some other type of crisis have been the most common reasons for granting a furlough. As states have passed legislation making furloughs a legal tool of corrections, furloughs have come to be used for a variety of purposes. Furloughs are usually granted for a home visit during holidays. Furloughs have also been used during the period just prior to release in order to ease the transition from confinement to freedom. It seems probable that furlough practices will gain further exploration and support as correctional administrators acquire experience in their use.

Graduated Release

An offender who has served a long sentence in a total institutional setting may suffer culture shock when suddenly returned to the community from which he came. Just as astronauts must reenter the atmosphere in a series of steps, so too the offender needs to reenter society in gradual stages. This system, referred to as a graduated release program, is intended to ease the pressures of culture shock experienced by institutionalized offenders. Some concepts designed to reduce the adverse effects of reentry are presently being practiced. Others must wait until there is a true correctional continuum in operation. Any preparation for release is better than none, but preparation that includes nonincarcerated periods is even more effective.

The periods immediately preceding and following the release of an offender are especially crucial to his adjustment to society. Despite the bravado of statements to the media, most ex-offenders know that they will have serious problems in trying to reestablish a life for themselves outside the institution. Their fears and apprehensions build as they approach the time for release. Some inmates become "jackrabbits" and run away shortly before they are due to be freed in fear of release. These deliberate offenses allow them to return to the total dependency afforded them in the institution. Recognition of this phenomenon has caused many thoughtful correctional administrators to establish prerelease and postrelease programs aimed at assisting the ex-offender through this critical period. Topics covered in such programs include how to get a driver's license, how to open a savings account, credit buying, how to fill out an employment application, sex and family adjustment, and so on.

The Sam Houston Institute of Contemporary Corrections provides some pointers on the establishment of prerelease and graduated release programs:

1. Prerelease preparation should begin as early as possible in the sentence, and inmates should know in advance the purpose and intention of the program.

2. Reliance must be placed on a sound program and not on the use of special privileges as an enticement to participate.

3. The program should be organized with realistic goals in mind and should be part of the total treatment process.

4. The counseling program should be geared toward dealing with the immediate problems of adjustment rather than with underlying personality problems.

5. Participants should be carefully selected by the staff on an individual basis rather than according to predetermined arbitrary standards.

6. Employee-employer rather than custodian-inmate relationships should exist between the staff and the inmates.

7. Every effort should be made to enlist the support and participation of the community, and family contact should be encouraged.

8. Whenever possible, work release should be included.

The center itself should be minimum security and should encourage personal responsibility. If prerelease programs are to be made a part of the treatment process, there should be some provision for determining their effectiveness (Frank, 1973, pp. 228–229).

Graduated release and prerelease programs are not either/or alternatives to incarceration, but they do recognize the destructive and dependency-producing effects of imprisonment.

CONCLUSIONS

Community-centered correctional programs are regarded as alternatives to confinement: they are situated in local communities; they are usually of smaller size; they include services that have no residential requirements; and they provide more opportunities for interaction between offenders and the community.

The mainstay of community corrections is probation, the assignment of law violators to community supervision as an alternative to confinement in a jail or prison. Supervision is carried out by officers who often combine probation and parole duties. These officers are responsible for securing compliance to the conditions of their probation or parole and for helping them to establish a law-abiding style of life. Probationers who fail to conform to the conditions are subject to revocation. Until the early 1970s, community supervision was considered a privilege that could be withdrawn at any time by the granting authority. In recent years, probation operations—including revocation—have become increasingly subject to due process requirements as a consequence of several U.S. Supreme Court decisions.

Lack of adequate research makes it hazardous to draw conclusions about the effectiveness of probation. Data indicate that direct costs are far lower than those of imprisonment, but findings related to recidivism are inconclusive, due mainly to variations in definition and measurement.

Parole is the administrative process by which incarcerated offenders are released under community supervision prior to the expiration of their maximum sentences. Decision-making by parole boards has been affected by many subjective biases. Attempts to rectify this situation had led to the adoption of parole guidelines in a number of institutions. Research studies using recidivism as the dependent variable have shown that several background characteristics of the offender are related to the probability of parole success; evidence that specific institutional arrangements and treatment modalities can significantly affect success rates is less convincing.

No area in corrections exhibits a greater state of flux than parole and other forms of conditional release. Some correctional practitioners, criminologists, and political figures favor the abolition of parole; others emphasize the crucial importance of conditional release as a safety valve for the nation's overcrowded and volatile prisons. An early end to the debate is not likely, however, because the real issue involved is not parole; it is the conflict between basic philosophies that underlies our societal response to crime and punishment.

REFERENCES

Albanese, J., Fiore, B. A., Powell, J. H., & Storti, J. R. (1981). *Is probation working?* Washington, DC: University Press of America.

Allen, H. E., Carlson, E. W., & Parks, E. C. (1979). *Critical issues in adult probation.* Washington, DC: U.S. Government Printing Office.

Augustus, J. (1852). *A report of the labors of John Augustus, for the last ten years, in aid of the unfortunate.* Boston: Wright and Hasty.

Barkdull, W. L. (1976). Probation: Call it control—and mean it. *Federal Probation, 40,* 3–8.

Barnes, H. E., & Teeters, N. K. (1959). *New horizons in criminology.* Englewood Cliffs, NJ: Prentice-Hall.

Carter, R. M., & Wilkins, L. T. (Eds.) (1976). *Probation and parole: Selected readings.* New York: Wiley.

Citizens' Inquiry on Parole and Criminal Justice, Inc. (1975). *Prison without walls: Report on New York parole.* New York: Praeger.

Cohen, F. (1983). Probation and parole. 2. Procedural protection. In S. Kadish (Ed.), *Encyclopedia of crime and justice.* New York: Free Press.

Conrad, J. P. (1984). The redefinition of probation: Drastic proposals to solve an urgent problem. In P. D. McAnany, D. Thomson, & D. Fogel (Eds.), *Probation and justice: Reconsideration of mission.* Cambridge, MA: Oelgeschlager, Gunn, and Hain.

Conrad, J. P. (1985). The penal dilemma and its emerging solution. *Crime and Delinquency, 31,* 411–423.

Dressler, D. (1969). *Practice and theory of probation and parole.* New York: Columbia University Press.

Epstein, R. et al. (1976). *The legal aspects of contract parole.* Resource Document #8, American Correctional Association.

Frank, B. (1973). Graduated release. In B. Frank (Ed.), *Contemporary corrections.* Reston, VA: Reston Publishing.

Gettinger, S. (1981). Separating the cop from the counselor. *Corrections Magazine, 7,* 34–38.

Gettinger, S. (1985). Intensive supervision: Can it rehabilitate probation? In J. L. Sullivan & J. L. Victor (Eds.), *Criminal justice 85/86.* Guilford, CT: Dushkin Publishing Group.

Glaser, D. (1964). *The effectiveness of a prison and parole system.* Indianapolis: Bobbs-Merrill.

Gottfredson, D. M. (1983). Probation and parole. 3. Release and revocation. In S. Kadish (Ed.), *Encyclopedia of crime and justice.* New York: Free Press.

Gottfredson, D. M., Wilkins, L. T., & Hoffman, P. B. (1978). *Guidelines for probation and sentencing.* Lexington, MA: Lexington Books.

Greenholtz v. Inmates of Nebraska Penal and Correctional Complex, 99 S.Ct.2100 (1979).

Griswold, H. J., Misenheimer, M., Powers, A., & Tromanheiser, E. (1970). *An eye for an eye.* New York: Holt. Rinehart and Winston.

Henningsen, R. J. (1981). *Probation and parole.* New York: Harcourt Brace Jovanovich.

Hoffman, P. B. (1983). "Screening for risk": A revised salient factor score. *Journal of Criminal Justice, 6,* 539–547.

Irwin, B. S. (1985). Evaluation of intensive probation supervision in Georgia. Atlanta: Department of Offender Rehabilitation.

Keve, P. W. (1981). *Corrections.* New York: John Wiley & Sons.

Killinger, G. G., & Cromwell, P. F. (Eds.) (1978). *Corrections in the community: Alternatives to imprisonment.* St. Paul, MN: West.

Killinger, G. G., Kerper, H. B., & Cromwell, P. F. (1976). *Probation and parole in the criminal justice system.* St. Paul, MN: West.

Krajick, K. (1980). Probation: The original community program. *Corrections Magazine, 6,* 7–13.

Mannheim, H., & Wilkins, L. T. (1955). *Prediction methods in relation to borstal training.* London: HM Stationery Office.

McCarthy, B. R., & McCarthy, B. J. (1984). *Community-based corrections.* Monterey, CA: Brooks/Cole.

McCleary, R. (1978). *Dangerous men: The sociology of parole.* Beverly Hills, CA: Sage.

Morris, N. (1974). *The future of imprisonment.* Chicago: University of Chicago Press.

Morrissey v. Brewer, 408 U.S. 471 (1971).

Murchek, P. (1973). Probation without adjudication. *Proceedings of the 18th Annual Southern Conference on Corrections.* Tallahassee, FL.

National Advisory Commission on Criminal Justice Standards and Goals. (1973). *Corrections.* Washington, DC: U.S. Government Printing Office.

National Institute of Justice. (1986). *Electronically monitored home confinement.* Washington, DC: U.S. Government Printing Office.

Norland, S., & Mann, P. J. (1984). Being troublesome: Women on probation. *Criminal Justice and Behavior, 11,* 115–135.

Norris v. State, 383 So.2d 691 (Fla. App. 1980).

Ohio House Bill 511, 1974.

Parisi, N. (1981). A taste of the bars. *Journal of Criminal Law and Criminology, 72,* 1109–1123.

Petersilia, J., Turner, S., Kahan, J., & Patterson, J. (1985). *Granting felons probation: Public risks and alternatives*. Santa Monica, CA: Rand Corporation.

Porter, E. M. (1958). Criteria for parole selection. *Proceedings of the American Correctional Association*. New York.

Reid, S. T. (1981). *The correctional system: An introduction*. New York: Holt, Rinehart and Winston.

Sacks, H. R., & Logan, C. H. (1979). *Does parole make a difference?* Storrs, CT: University of Connecticut School of Law Press.

Schichor, D., & Allen, H.E. (1977). Study release: A correctional alternative. *Offender rehabilitation, 2*, 7–17.

Singer, R. G. (1979). *Just deserts: Sentencing based on equality and desert*. Cambridge, MA: Ballinger.

Smith, A., & Berlin, L. (1979). *Introduction to probation and parole*. St. Paul, MN: West.

Smykla, J. O. (1981). *Community-based corrections: Principles and practices*. New York: Macmillan.

State of Ohio, Department of Rehabilitation and Corrections, Adult Parole Authority. (1973). *Statement of parole agreement (APA-271)*. Columbus, OH: Author.

Sweeney v. United States, 353 F.2d 10 (7th Cir. 1965).

Tarlton v. Clark, 441 F.2d 384, 385 (5th Cir. 1971), cert. denied, 403 U.S. 934 (1971).

Travis, L. F. (1984). Intensive supervision in probation and parole. *Corrections Today, 46*, 34, 36, 38, 40.

U.S. Department of Justice. (1982). *Probationers in the United States*. Washington, DC: U.S. Government Printing Office.

U.S. Department of Justice. (1984). *Report to the nation on crime and justice*. Washington, DC: U.S. Government Printing Office.

Vito, G. F. (1984). Developments in shock probation: A review of research findings and policy implications. *Federal Probation, 48*, 22–27.

von Hirsch, A., & Hanrahan, K. J. (1979). *The question of parole: Retention, reform, or abolition?* Cambridge, MA: Ballinger.

CHAPTER 13

Specific Intent and Diminished Capacity

CHARLES R. CLARK

Considerations of a defendant's actual intent and capacity for intent in regard to an alleged offense have always been at the heart of legal determinations of guilt. Until recently, expert mental health testimony on questions of intent has been confined to cases in which insanity was claimed. Testifying as an expert witness on the more limited questions of criminal intent or diminished capacity presents distinctive difficulties to the forensic psychologist or other specialist. They are problems that are different in kind as well as in degree from those encountered in the insanity defense.

Diminished capacity as a defense is invoked infrequently in comparison with insanity. Its exculpatory rationale and the manner of its application have always differed from insanity, which has a separate history. In common with insanity, however, the diminished capacity defense proceeds from the fundamental Anglo-American legal principle that mental guilt, or mens rea, must in some fashion be involved in the commission of the unlawful act or actus reus for there to be a finding of guilt. If all of the requisite elements of the crime, including the mental elements, are not present, criminal conviction and legal sanctions cannot be sustained. Diminished capacity differs markedly from insanity in its focus on particular mens rea elements, rather than on overall responsibility or blameworthiness.

In the growing case law on diminished capacity, there is virtually no delineation of how evidence, especially mental health expert testimony, can be incorporated operationally into the defense in such a way as to lead to any certain conclusions regarding intent (Dix. 1971). Yet nearly all jurisdictions have come to view mental health testimony on diminished capacity as germane and helpful, if not necessary, and forensic psychologists are regularly called upon to offer their expertise at trials in which the question has been raised. With diminished capacity, the law has created a concept that it assumes has genuine psychological content open to clinical investigation. This assumption begs the question of the extent to which mental health practitioners, as clinicians, can actually conduct such an investigation.

Diminished capacity is at once deceptively simple in theory, and deceptively similar to insanity. Exploring the special problems associated with clinical assessment and opinion testimony on this issue sheds some light on the practical meaning of the central legal concepts of mens rea and intent. It serves moreover to illustrate in an interesting way how law and the mental health disciplines can appear to be speaking the same language while actually occupying very different levels of discourse. The significance of the clinical dilemmas presented by questions of diminished capacity extends beyond the limited scope of this little-used defense. Those dilemmas serve to demonstrate the inevitable limitations in any general project of translating terms of law into meaningful psychological language. The following is an account of how the meanings of central concepts involved in diminished capacity have changed in developing case law, and what the law is looking for in expert testimony on this issue. The merits of alternative ways of responding to questions of diminished capacity will be explored in light of the legal history and logic of the defense.

SPECIFIC INTENT, INSANITY, AND INTOXICATION

The diminished capacity approach is a partial defense which in theory does not lead to the outright acquittal of a criminal defendant but simply reduces the level of the offense for which a conviction is obtained. As a defense strategy, it seeks to establish that a mental state required for the offense charged was absent because of some psychological abnormality—usually short of what would lead to acquittal by reason of insanity. Expert testimony has most commonly been employed to show that the defendant, because of abnormality, was incapable of forming the requisite intent element. As it developed in the United States, the approach has been applicable only to a circumscribed but ill-defined class of crimes requiring what are termed specific intent elements, and not to those incorporating so-called general intent elements. The provision that general intent offenses are not susceptible to a diminished capacity argument is intended to ensure that defendants viewed as abnormal but not legally insane will not evade conviction and punishment entirely. In theory at least, such individuals still may be found guilty of some offense less than and included in the more serious specific-intent crime originally charged.

There are no definitive listings of specific intent offenses or elements, although there has been general agreement that the premeditation and deliberation required for what is usually designated first-degree murder are specific intent elements, while the malice aforethought required for the lesser second-degree murder is a general intent element. With notable exceptions in California, a diminished capacity approach has been capable of reducing a homicide from first- to second-degree murder, but not to manslaughter. Larceny, involving the intention to unlawfully and permanently deprive another of property and convert it to one's own use, has been viewed as a specific intent offense, as have offenses such as robbery or burglary that incorporate larcenous intent elements.

No coherent rationale for designating some crimes as specific intent offenses has been formulated; the doctrine of specific intent developed more as a matter of expediency than as a logical outgrowth of legal theory (Dix, 1971). Basically, however, general intent may be understood to be constituted by a simple aim to commit an act proscribed by law; whereas specific intent involves an intention to do some further act or achieve some additional result (Fingarette & Hasse, 1979). Thus, illegally entering another's premises would constitute only trespass, a general intent offense; doing the same act with larcenous purpose would constitute burglary, a specific intent offense. In the American Law Institute's Model Penal Code (1962), specific intent offenses involve a higher level of criminal liability than do general intent offenses, for which mere recklessness or negligence would suffice to establish guilt; specific intent offenses are done purposefully or knowingly.

Both diminished capacity and insanity are concerned with the mens rea or evil mind requirements of Anglo-American law, but in essentially different ways. Insanity considers mens rea globally, as general moral blameworthiness or culpability, rather than in terms of discrete intent elements of varying degrees of complexity. Diminished capacity approaches mens rea in a piecemeal fashion and is concerned not with the question of whether the defendant should be excused or considered exculpable for whatever illegal act was done, but instead with the question of what particular illegal act was done.

Conceptually and historically, diminished capacity is more closely related to intoxication defense approaches than it is to the insanity defense. It came to be acknowledged in nineteenth-century England and the United States that intoxication might affect or negate the formation of mens rea and that the criminal intent involved in a drunken offense might merit a qualitatively different moral judgment by the law (Fingarette & Hasse, 1979). To prevent the complete acquittal of offenders simply because they were drunk, the specific intent idea developed. By that expedient, the law expressed the view that those who become intoxicated are not thereby absolved from responsibility for the results of their behavior, and it was established in theory that inebriates would be subject to conviction for some criminal offense, though one of lesser severity than might otherwise be the case. The diminished capacity approach to mens rea determinations differs theoretically from the intoxication defense chiefly in that it considers a wider range of mental abnormality as potentially affecting the formation of specific intent.

Diminished capacity has been referred to by the alternative designations of partial responsibility or diminished responsibility. These are confusing misnomers since the approach does not result in a finding that the defendant was less responsible, but rather in a finding of whether a state of mind requisite to an alleged crime was achieved (Bird & Vanderet, 1972). Partial or diminished responsibility is incorporated into the laws of Europe, particularly the United Kingdom (Dix, 1971; Arenella, 1977), but has never been recognized explicitly in the United States. As employed in continental Europe, partial or diminished responsibility does not involve the elements of the offense but is instead an approach which gives the court or jury permission to lower the penalty for a convicted criminal. In England, diminished or partial responsibility similarly does not involve an inquiry into offense elements but provides instead a vehicle for the formal mitigation of guilt. If the trier of fact finds the defendant's mental responsibility for a homicide to have been substantially impaired by mental abnormality, the formal grade of the offense for which the defendant stands convicted is lowered to manslaughter (English Homicide Act of 1957).

In form, the European responsibility models are arguably lesser versions of an insanity defense. In its focus on the formal elements of particular offenses, the American diminished capacity approach is fundamentally different in theory from any form of the insanity offense. Diminished capacity is not in fact doctrinally distinct from any other defense approach which focuses on offense elements; the prosecution always bears the burden of proving all the elements of the offense, including the mental elements (Morse, 1984).

The distinction between the diminished capacity approach on the one hand and the insanity defense and its variants on the other is crucial to an appreciation of the problems diminished capacity presents the potential expert witness. Though such a conclusion must at first appear illogical, under currently operating theory it is entirely possible for an individual to be able to entertain all specific intent elements required for guilt and conviction, yet be found legally insane and not guilty (Arenella, 1977). In most cases of insanity, all of the formal requisite mental intent elements can be expected to be present (Morse, 1979, 1984). It must be apparent that any clinical inquiry into a question of diminished capacity must proceed on a basis different from that used in regard to the insanity defense. A prerequisite for such an inquiry is an understanding of how the law views intent and how much or what type of diminishment of capacity must be present before it can be concluded that intent was not formed.

DEFINING THE SCOPE OF INTENT

Traditional Viewpoints

Expert testimony from the mental health community on mens rea is a relatively recent development. Traditionally, mens rea has simply not been seen by the law to be the business of medicine or psychology. As Dix (1971) points out, mens rea doctrine considerably predates current psychological theory and is fundamentally incompatible with it. While mens rea purports to incorporate mental elements of guilt, the guilt so designated is not identical to commonsense notions, let alone psychological conceptions, of guilt. The clinician called on to discuss mental guilt would probably present a complex picture of cognition, emotion, volition, and developmental history. The great majority of elements incorporated into such a modern conceptualization would be irrelevant to mens rea and criminal intent as traditionally formulated in law. Dix indicates that, historically, evidence does suggest that mens rea originally involved more subjectivity, in the form of bad motivation or evil purpose. The original concept, however, was subjected to reinterpretation in light of policy considerations such as the protection of society. Ultimately, mens rea came to represent a compromise between a subjective viewpoint favoring the assignment of guilt according to the nature of the offender's motives, and an objective viewpoint focusing on the liability of the offender for the consequences of a proscribed act. In the process, mens rea requirements were diluted to little more than simple conscious awareness.

In light of the nature of mens rea in its traditional development, it is not surprising that courts found no need for enlightenment by expert witnesses on questions of whether intent elements had been formed or whether a defendant could have formed them. It could be assumed that virtually any conscious defendant would be capable of entertaining specific intent. Given this purely cognitive view of mens rea as a relatively simple mental state calling for little intelligence or cognitive capability, a defendant would need to suffer from an extremely abnormal mental condition before it could be shown that he lacked the capacity for mens rea—even the premeditation or deliberation needed for murder. As Morse (1979) and Arenella (1977) point out, for this reason, the defendant in such a case would, except in rare instances, meet the criteria for legal insanity itself and thereby erect a complete defense to the charge.

Absent in conventional notions of mens rea is any vestige of real subjective badness or evil. The malice aforethought, for instance, that traditionally differentiates murder from manslaughter has nothing essentially to do with the moral quality of motivation. As already indicated, malice has traditionally been designated as a general intent element outside the ambit of a diminished capacity approach. Malice has become a simple shorthand designation for any of a number of mens rea elements that would sustain a murder conviction (Morse, 1979, 1984). Malice requirements for murder could be met by intent to kill but also by intent to cause great bodily harm, by the willful or wanton disregard for risk to life, or simply by the commission of another felony offense during the course of which the homicide takes place (LaFave & Scott, 1972).

Perhaps most surprising, notions of volition are absent from and irrelevant to mens rea and intent as traditionally developed (Bonnie & Slobogin, 1980). As a crime element defined in an essentially cognitive manner, intent traditionally would not be negated by volitional impairment. Compelled conduct might perhaps be excused in certain instances, but not because intentionality was necessarily lacking (Morse, 1979, 1984). Lack of volition would, in one view, negate not mens rea, but the actus reus itself, which must be a voluntary act (Erlinder, 1983; Dix, 1971).

It is evident that as long as a traditional view of mens rea and criminal intent held sway, there was little opportunity for expert testimony on a defendant's intent or capacity for intent and perhaps seldom much to be gained from a defense point of view in raising the question at all. There the matter would have rested perhaps, except for a remarkable series of legal developments in California in the years following World War II.

A Broadened View of Intent: The California Approach

Most jurisdictions have maintained a distinction between the insanity defense and specific intent approaches to mens rea. In California, as in several other states, this distinction was maintained by means of a bifurcated trial, involving a guilt phase in which evidence pertaining to the elements of the crime would be considered, and an insanity phase, in which evidence of mental abnormality would be received. Bifurcation seeks to avoid prejudice to the defendant, since it would ordinarily be necessary for a defendant to admit to an offense in order to claim insanity. Arguably, an absolute distinction between guilt based on the presence of offense elements—

mens rea and actus reus—and criminal responsibility based on a broader conception of sanity, makes sense only if the mens rea intent elements cannot be negated by evidence of mental abnormality. If guilt as well as criminal responsibility is in some sense genuinely mental, expert testimony on mental abnormality ought to be admissible in the guilt phase as well as in the insanity phase of a trial. Just such a conclusion was reached by the California Supreme Court in 1949 in the historic *Wells* decision (*People v. Wells*).

Wells was a convict serving a sentence in a California penitentiary when he assaulted a prison guard. Charged now with a capital offense, assault with malice aforethought, the defense attempted to introduce evidence on the question of malice at the guilt phase of trial. Defense experts offered that Wells had been laboring under tension resulting from an abnormal fear for his own safety at the time of the offense. Holding that Wells would have lacked malice aforethought if he had acted on the basis of honest though unreasonable fear, the court ruled that the evidence of Wells' claimed abnormality was material to the question of his guilt, and that the refusal by the trial court to admit this evidence during the first phase of the trial had been in error.

It was against the backdrop of *People v. Wells* that the California approach to diminished capacity developed. While *Wells* provided the vehicle for the admission of mental health evidence on mens rea elements, the impetus for doing so across a broad front was provided by the perceived inadequacies of the insanity test in California, which was based on the M'Naghten Rule (Morse, 1979). The M'Naghten insanity test, which allows a finding of culpability if the defendant simply knew the nature and quality of his act and understood that it was wrong, is a strict all-or-none and entirely cognitive approach to responsibility that makes no allowance for other potentially important mental factors such as volition. With any insanity test, but perhaps especially with M'Naghten, it is inevitable that judges and juries in criminal cases would frequently be confronted with defendants who were clearly disordered, but not so disordered as to meet the insanity criteria. As the court admitted in *People v. Henderson* (1963), diminished capacity became the means by which the court could ameliorate the harshness of the M'Naghten Rule. The Court's first real opportunity to implement the ameliorative approach arose in the case of *People v. Gorshen* (1959).

Nicholas Gorshen, a Russian immigrant and longshoreman, came to work one day in an intoxicated condition and was told to go home by his foreman. Gorshen took offense and fought with his supervisor before he went home, obtained a gun, returned to the docks, and shot his foreman dead in front of witnesses, including police. Gorshen was tried for first-degree murder. At the trial, Bernard Diamond, a psychiatrist, testified that Gorshen was a schizophrenic of long standing who had been subject to hallucinations for years. The demand by his foreman to leave work, it was offered, presented a considerable threat to Gorshen's precarious psychological equilibrium because of Gorshen's vulnerability to perceived attacks on his manhood. Consequently, Gorshen was compelled to retaliate against the source of that threat. While Dr. Diamond did not actually dispute Gorshen's own admission that he had formed the conscious intent to shoot his victim, he did testify that Gorshen did not have the mental state required for malice aforethought or anything implying intention, premeditation, or deliberation.

Expert testimony that Gorshen was schizophrenic was not rebutted, yet under the M'Naghten Rule, which does not consider irresistible impulse, he appeared culpable. Gorshen was convicted at a bench trial of second-degree murder. The California Supreme Court ultimately affirmed the conviction but added that the expert testimony that indicated Gorshen to be incapable of the malice needed for a murder conviction—testimony considered but rejected by the trial judge—had been properly admitted at trial. Though the court declined to provide a clear definition of malice, it appeared in effect to approve the redefinition that had been offered by the psychiatric witness—one calling for a clear volitional component (Dix, 1971). The court held that malice aforethought existed when an individual does an act intentionally, and of his own free will, rather than because of an abnormal compulsion. The path leading to a greater consideration of subjective psychological factors in guilt determinations was becoming clear. If traditional mens rea elements did not invite relevant testimony regarding mental abnormality, those intent elements could simply be redefined in such a way as to allow the judge or jury to weigh the defendant's ability to morally assess or control his conduct (Morse, 1979). This process was clearly at work in the next significant case considered by the court, *People v. Wolff* (1964).

Dennis Wolff was a defendant to a murder charge who was perhaps even more obviously disturbed than Gorshen, but who like Gorshen seemed not to qualify for an insanity verdict. Wolff was 15 years old when he developed a peculiar plan to kidnap girls and bring them home for sexual purposes. To implement this plan, he needed to get his mother out of the way, and he did so, after one failed attempt, by beating her to death with an axe handle. As in the case of Gorshen, Wolff was tried for first-degree murder; expert testimony was received that he was a schizophrenic and was legally insane. In spite of this, the jury convicted Wolff of first-degree murder.

On appeal, the California Supreme Court upheld the jury's finding of sanity but held that Wolff had not been capable of the mental processes needed for conviction on first-degree murder—namely, premeditation. It was evident that Wolff had carefully planned the homicide and had applied considerable thought to it. The court held, however, that more was required for premeditation than what Wolff was capable of. The defendant must have been able, it ruled, to "maturely and meaningfully" reflect on the enormity of the offense contemplated. The court accordingly modified Wolff's conviction to second-degree murder. Thus, the court indicated that it was not enough to consider in regard to a defendant whether something resembling, even closely resembling, more common conceptions of premeditation and deliberation had occurred; the "quantum of his moral turpitude and depravity" needed to be appraised. At issue was not the simple apparent fact of intent but rather the quality of whatever intent was in fact formed. The evident fact of mens rea could be negated by a finding that the defendant was morally incapable of the true intent elements.

The expansion of traditional concepts of intent elements continued in California for a decade following *Wolff*. *People v. Conley* (1966) applied the *Wolff* logic of premeditation to the question of malice aforethought. William Conley reportedly had been drinking very heavily for a number of days when he killed his estranged lover and her husband. He later claimed no intention to kill his victims and no memory of having done so. Testimony was received that the amount of alcohol Conley had consumed would have impaired the judgment of an ordinary person. A psychologist testified that Conley was in a dissociative state at the time of the homicides and could not function normally. On an argument that diminished capacity could negate the malice aforethought required for murder, defense requested but was denied jury instructions for voluntary manslaughter. The jury returned a two-count conviction on first-degree murder.

The California Supreme Court reversed the convictions because of the trial court's refusal to give the manslaughter instruction. The de facto redefinition of malice begun in *Wells* and *Gorshen* was elaborated upon. For malice to have been present, the court held, the person must be able "to comprehend his duty to govern his actions in accord with the duty imposed by law." This refinement of malice stands in considerable contrast to the traditional formulations of that element. Though still cast in terms of mens rea, malice under *Conley* had become a mini-insanity test—a cognitive-affective version of the M'Naghten Rule (Morse, 1979). In the process, the way in which diminished capacity "ameliorated" the M'Naghten Rule had become fully apparent.

An expansion of the *Conley* formulation, which added an explicit volitional component analogous to an irresistible impulse insanity test, came in *People v. Poddar* (1974). The California Supreme Court had previously ruled in *People v. Cantrell* (1973) that irresistible impulse, not recognized as grounds for legal insanity in California, could not be a complete defense to a crime. The court in that instance ruled that, for precisely that reason, a defendant claiming diminished capacity must be permitted at the guilt phase of trial to show by competent evidence that the act in question was a result of irresistible impulse in turn due to mental disease. Testimony to that effect was seen to bear specifically on issues of intent to kill and malice aforethought.

Prosenjit Poddar may already be familiar to many as the killer of Tatiana Tarasoff, the subject of the leading case on the question of duty to warn (*Tarasoff v. Regents of University of California*, 1976). Poddar was a naval architecture student from India at the University of California at Berkeley when he was rejected by Tarasoff, a fellow student with whom he had fallen in love. Following a period of despondency and emotional distress, Poddar stabbed Tarasoff to death after shooting at her with a pellet gun. Expert witnesses at trial presented Poddar as a schizophrenic; a prosecution witness disagreed, and the jury refused to find Poddar legally insane, returning a verdict of guilty for second-degree murder. Citing *Conley* and *Cantrell*, the California Supreme Court ruled that at most Poddar could be convicted of voluntary manslaughter unless it could be established that he was both aware of his duty to act within the law and that he was not incapable of so acting.

While the diminished capacity approach is theoretically pertinent only to specific-intent elements and is incapable of negating general intent and thereby providing a complete defense, it remains the case that, in the United States, crimes are not generally graded to include a reasonable lesser offense in cases other than homicide. This was recognized in California in *People v. Wetmore* (1978). Wetmore, charged with burglary, was a chronic psychiatric patient who reportedly broke into an apartment with the delusional belief that the apartment was his. The California Supreme Court held that evidence of mental disorder could be used in the guilt phase of a trial to negate any mens rea element, even if complete acquittal might result. Should an individual accused of burglary—breaking and entering with larcenous intent—be capable of negating the alleged intent to commit larceny, there may be no lesser included felony for which a conviction can be obtained.

Decline and Fall of Diminished Capacity in California

From one point of view, the expanded use of diminished capacity in California could be seen to warrant an enthusiastic welcome from the mental health community. The psychiatrist Bernard Diamond, who had testified for the defense in the Gorshen trial, objected (Diamond, 1961) to the traditional inference of mens rea from mere objective circumstantial evidence without weighing subjective psychological factors. Such an approach, Diamond stated, was "too rigid, mechanical and stereotyped." Rather than leaving the consideration of mental and emotional factors to the all-or-none judgment mandated by the M'Naghten insanity rule, the expanded approach to mens rea approved by the California Supreme Court in *Gorshen* would enable such information to be accorded the attention it deserved and make it possible for a bridge to be built between law and the behavioral sciences. Diamond expressed certainty that, with the new approach, society could no longer evade its obligations to provide the defendant with therapeutic help, since he *"is now officially labeled as sick and the courts have publicly acknowledged his need for treatment"* (emphasis original).

Defense attorneys had obvious and ample reason to welcome the California mens rea model; it opened the door to a qualitatively expanded consideration of mental abnormality of all types and degrees of severity. In California appellate decisions, the concept of diminished capacity had been developed into a "finely honed instrument" for the defense (Bird & Vanderet, 1972). Given the range of psychological and emotional conditions being recognized as applicable to mens rea determinations, it could be hoped that even such traditionally neglected factors as the stress of prison experiences might plausibly be seen as admissible in mitigating guilt (Marx, 1977).

What was in effect such a radical departure from traditional approaches was not without its critics. Dix (1971) cited a number of objections that had been raised to the new diminished capacity defense. Among them were fears that citizens would be endangered by individuals released from prison earlier than would otherwise be the case, and concerns that there would be outright acquittal of some individuals without provision of any protection for society—even the hospitalization mandated for those found legally insane. Fears were cited that the issues involved were simply too complex for juries and that questions of mens rea would be turned over by default to expert witnesses whose testimony would be admitted into evidence despite its unreliability. Morse (1979) pointed out that California's diminished capacity approach provided no clear standards for judges or juries to apply. How should the standard of mature and meaningful reflection for premeditation and deliberation, as set forth in *Wolff,* for example, be used? Such a decision may appear easy enough when applied to clearly normal or clearly abnormal individuals, but diminished capacity is essentially concerned with intermediate cases.

Of particular concern to many was the new emphasis in diminished capacity cases on the role of the mental health expert in guilt determinations, and the manner in which expert testimony would be used. Bernard Diamond himself (1961) warned that the entire business of judging mental capacity to premeditate, entertain malice, or form intent was a kind of sophistry that must not be allowed to remain an end in itself. The end he himself envisioned was the greater recognition of the treatment needs of the mentally ill. His stated preference, despite the nature of his own testimony at Gorshen's trial, was for expert testimony to remain strictly clinical and avoid embracing the legal terms in a conclusory manner. For other commentators, it was the way in which expert testimony had already been and would most likely be used in actuality that proved most objectionable.

Dix (1971) has argued that in *Wells* the court leaped from a finding that evidence of psychological abnormality regarding the question of guilt had logical relevance to a view that such evidence was therefore admissible. A more thorough analysis of the way in which such evidence was employed subsequently, Dix offered, would indicate that psychiatric testimony did not establish the actual absence of some state of mind deemed requisite for criminal liability, but instead simply attributed the defendant's actions as well as his state of mind to unconscious influences. Dix offered the view that the use of psychological abnormality to disprove intent was often a legal fiction allowing the presentation to the trier of fact of a complete dynamic explanation of the defendant's behavior. This practice, he warned, places an unfair burden on the expert witness, who assumes a ritual role in the proceedings, mouthing the magic words that grant the law permission to mitigate guilt.

Arenella (1977) viewed the California developments similarly. The *Wolff* decision, he held, shifted the focus away from whether or not a defendant had actually entertained specific intent to the question of why and how he had entertained it. In this way, diminished capacity had become a disguised version of European diminished responsibility, having nothing intrinsically to do with traditional mens rea. If the supposedly mens rea–based approach were used honestly, Arenella argued, and only evidence that bore on the absence of requisite intent were admitted, the mens rea model would rarely serve any purpose not already served by the insanity defense. Morse (1979, 1984) expands on Arenella's notion that diminished capacity has been treated in American courts as partial responsibility. In his view there is no easy way for testimony confined to questions of mens rea as such to rule out or negate the capacity of the defendant to form those intent elements. Morse (1984) sees no danger in a strictly applied true mens rea approach to diminished capacity, which he along with others holds is constitutionally mandated in any case—strictly applied, it is highly unlikely to benefit the defendant.

If the fundamental rationale of the California diminished capacity approach was the need to ameliorate the harshness of the M'Naghten insanity rule, the continued relevance of the approach was called into doubt (Waddell, 1979) when the California Supreme Court, in *People v. Drew* (1978), adopted for a time the American Law Institute Model Penal Code insanity test. This followed years of reluctance by the court to invade what it had viewed as the province of the legislature to determine the test of insanity as a matter of statute, as well as a remarkable series of appellate decisions seemingly aimed at avoiding the need to do so. The ALI test provides significant differences from M'Naghten. It offers a volitional as well as a cognitive test of culpability, and in its advisedly ambiguous use of the terms "substantial" and "appreciate" grants considerable leeway to the courts in adjudicating insanity. Under an ALI test, Gorshen, Wolff, Poddar, and even Conley might have been found legally insane. The irony of *Drew* did not by itself bring about the demise of diminished capacity in California. In no danger of being viewed as only a historical artifact, it was a defense which had plainly taken on a life of its own. Notoriety, particularly that brought about by the Dan White trial, seemed to be required to produce a serious threat to the position diminished capacity had assumed in California.

Daniel J. White was 32 years old when he shot and killed San Francisco Mayor George Moscone and City Supervisor Harvey Milk on November 27, 1978. As described by a defense expert witness (Blinder, 1981–1982), White was one of eight children of a fireman and was himself a fireman and a former police officer when he decided to run for supervisor in 1977. After a hard-fought campaign, he was elected to represent his working-class district, but he met with considerable frustration and disillusionment from city hall politics and experienced personal financial hardship. White tendered his resignation in early November of 1978 but reconsidered his decision and asked Mayor Moscone to reappoint him to the supervisor post. Reportedly, the mayor first promised White his support and then reneged. On the morning of November 27, White went to City Hall, and a final confrontation took place between himself and the mayor. White had taken a revolver with him, together with 10 extra rounds of ammunition, and avoiding security personnel and metal detectors, entered City Hall through a window. He shot the mayor four times and reloaded his gun. He then encountered fellow supervisor Harvey Milk, a homosexual White apparently believed had been involved in the mayor's decision not to reappoint him. He shot Milk five times, then fled the building before ultimately surrendering to police.

Much has been made of the remarkable way in which the double homicide of two prominent political figures was disposed of at White's 1979 trial, with suggestions of collusion between defense and prosecution motivated by political considerations and antihomosexual prejudice (Szasz, 1981–1982). Whatever factors were brought into play, the ostensible justification for the jury decision to find Dan White guilty of only voluntary manslaughter was provided by expert witness testimony on diminished capacity.

A memorable point in the trial was reached when Martin Blinder, a defense psychiatric witness, testified that White was a manic depressive whose depressive episodes, one of which reportedly led to the homicides, were exacerbated by binging on "junk food—Twinkies, cupcakes, and Cokes" (Szasz, 1981–1982). Diminished capacity was immediately ridiculed by reporters as the Twinkie Defense, though the actual effect on the jury of this aspect of the expert testimony is debatable. The jury did hear conclusory expert opinion by the various defense witnesses to the effect that Dan White had been incapable of forming the intent elements required for first- or even second-degree murder. Dr. Donald Lunde was asked by defense if there had been premeditation in White's act. Lunde responded that not only had White not premeditated or deliberated the killings, but that as a result of his mental condition —a severe depression and compulsive personality—White was not capable of any kind of mature, meaningful reflection (Szasz, 1981–1982). Clearly discernible in this testimony are the terms of the *Wolff* decision of 15 years earlier.

Dr. George Solomon, also testifying for defense, indicated similarly that he had a "reasonable medical certainty" that White had lacked the capacity to maturely and meaningfully premeditate or deliberate (Solomon, 1981–1982). Dr. Blinder related in his report on his examination of White that premeditation and malice all require "reasonably clear thinking," but that at the time of the offenses, White had "no longer had his wits about him" (Blinder, 1981–1982). Echoing the *Conley* decision, Dr. Lunde had addressed the question of malice in his testimony, offering that the last thing White was capable of doing was thinking clearly about his "obligations to society, other people, the law and so on" (Szasz, 1981–1982). White was ultimately sentenced to the maximum prison term allowable for voluntary manslaughter and was released on parole when he became eligible in early 1984. He quietly moved back to San Francisco where he committed suicide in October 1985.

As a result of the Dan White trial and others, pressure mounted to curb the diminished capacity defense in California. What had begun as an effort to justly acknowledge commonsense views of some offenders as mentally abnormal ended, in the view of many, as an offense to both justice and common sense. Closely contemporaneous with the White trial, the California Supreme Court observed in *Wetmore* (1978), as discussed earlier, that diminished capacity could lead to outright acquittal if the crime charged, such as burglary, had no suitable lesser included offense. The court in *Wetmore* had requested legislative clarification of diminished capacity procedure (Morse & Cohen, 1982). What the court received eventually was a legislative repudiation of the entire diminished capacity approach. A measure (California Senate Bill No. 54) in 1981 effectively turned back the hands of time in an effort by the California legislature to abolish diminished capacity and related defenses, including intoxication. Judicial redefinition of intent elements were reversed by the codifying of traditional forms of premeditation and deliberation and of malice. To prove a killing was deliberate and premeditated, the new legislation established that it would not be necessary to prove the defendant maturely and meaningfully reflected on the depravity of the act. An awareness of the obligation to act within the general body of laws regulating society was specifically excluded by the revised code from the definition of malice.

In a related development, California Senate Bill No. 590 (1981) aimed to further restrict the scope of expert testimony on mental disorder by indicating in statute that psychiatrists or psychologists would not be presumed able to determine sanity or insanity. Seeking to drive yet another stake into the heart of diminished capacity, Proposition 8, a ballot measure entitled "The Victims' Bill of Rights" and approved by California voters in 1982, "abolished" diminished capacity as a defense at trial (Krausz, 1983).

Despite events in California, the mens rea or diminished capacity defense did not die. It lives on explicitly in case law if not statute in a number of jurisdictions and is probably constitutionally implicit in the others. But it lives on as it did before *Wells* and *Gorshen* through the use of intent constructs explicitly devoid of subtle, subjective, and deeper meaning. As such, diminished capacity is a potentially far stricter approach toward considering mental abnormality than is insanity. If Gorshen might have been found insane under the ALI insanity test, he would not easily have been found incapable of premeditation and deliberation or malice under a strictly applied mens rea approach. It is significant that three states that recently abolished the insanity defense—Montana (1979), Idaho (1982) and Utah (1983)—substituted, in effect, a diminished capacity standard; their evident aim was to limit the extent to which defendants could escape conviction by using the claim of mental disorder.

No jurisdiction other than California made broadly sweeping and explicit changes in defining intent elements, though others must have had conditions similar to those which spurred the California innovations. Nonetheless, courts in other jurisdictions began considering diminished capacity a fit subject for expert testimony, and use of the defense became more common. In Michigan, for example, where traditional intent elements were never judicially redefined, diminished capacity became significant enough that in 1978 (*People v. Mangiapane*) the Court of Appeals saw fit to establish rules for notice by defendants of intent to claim diminished capacity, together with provisions for mandatory forensic evaluations of those defendants.

This wider interest in diminished capacity may be attributable in part to California's influential legal position but also to conditions in the general social climate favoring consideration of psychological variables in determining guilt and punishment. One particular reason for that interest appears to have been a naive hope on the part of the legal community—a hope shared by some in the mental health community—that clinicians would be capable of fleshing out in terms of science what had come to be mere terms of art. The social climate favoring leniency toward criminals for any reason has clearly changed in later years, and so too has any blind faith in the discerning powers of the mental health disciplines. Specific limitations involved in the application of psychology to questions of criminal intent have not, however, become widely recognized, and they are not as obvious to the lay community as are larger policy objections to a broad and liberal use of diminished capacity.

CLINICAL APPROACHES TO EXPERT TESTIMONY

Redefining Intent

California's experiment with diminished capacity was the only systematic approach that permitted expert testimony to proceed from a qualitative appraisal of the defendant's intent to a conclusory opinion on the defendant's capacity for the requisite intent. As traditionally set forth, intent and capacity for intent ordinarily do not appear to require expert testimony at all. Where definitions of intent or specific intent elements do exist, they tend to be unhelpful to a strictly clinical exploration. In Michigan, for example, (Michigan Criminal Jury Instructions) intent is defined as "a decision of the mind to knowingly do an act with a conscious (fully formed) objective of accomplishing a certain (specific) result." While this definition seems to indicate that consciousness, planning, and judgment of consequences are all required for true intent, it does nothing to indicate at what point, quantitatively or qualitatively, intent could not have been formed. The degree of impairment of judgment, for example, that would render an intent not knowing is not indicated.

The premeditation and deliberation used in some jurisdictions to define first-degree murder are similarly undefined. Simply indicating that premeditation means to think about or contemplate an act beforehand, and that deliberation means to weigh or examine the reasons for or against an act, does little to specify the amount, kind, or quality of thought a defendant must have in order to commit first-degree murder. It is as if the law intended mens rea elements to be understood in their literal commonsense meanings.

One obvious option for the psychologist or psychiatrist called upon to offer an opinion on a defendant's capacity for intent is to follow the route previously taken by some expert witnesses: Offer opinions on capacity for intent based on what, in the expert's view, the intent element ought to require. A clinician may feel, for example, that premeditation and deliberation in murder cannot truly exist if judgment is clouded significantly, as by alcohol or drug intoxication, or that those elements cannot exist unless an individual is of basically average intelligence. A clinician might believe that the intent to kill or to commit some other offense should include an element of volition and that compulsions or drives to do an act compromise volition and thereby negate intent.

From my observations, conclusory expert testimony of this type can often be offered without objection, despite a lack of any support in the law for these idiosyncratic views of mens rea and despite criticism of the approach by scholars. Witnesses, after all, are offering only opinion, and the absence in case law and statute of specific prohibitions against the expert witness offering personal definitions of intent may appear to grant the witness permission to do so. As discussed before, Morse has argued (1979, 1984) that such testimony is accepted and elicited because the courts conflate diminished capacity with partial responsibility. He may be correct, though experience suggests another explanation in the persistent confusion among judges as well as lawyers as to the ability of mental health professionals to define such legal terms as intent, capacity for intent, and a variety of others relevant to different contexts such as insanity. Such constructs are often treated as though their true meaning might indeed lie in the behavioral sciences rather than in the law itself.

Some years ago, a member of the state judiciary involved in drafting an opinion mandating court-ordered evaluations of all defendants raising a defense of diminished capacity was addressing a group of state forensic examiners. Asked by a psychologist to tell the group how these new evaluations of diminished capacity might be done, the judge expressed surprise and indicated that he had thought the clinicians would tell the court. The appropriateness of allowing clinicians to define the parameters of intent may well be questioned by the mental health disciplines themselves if not by the courts.

However sincere the expert is in drawing a conclusion about capacity for intent from an exploration of the quality of intent, such conclusions appear to remain mere value judgments. There is nothing scientific in attempts by experts to redefine legal constructs of intent. There are no definably correct positions for psychologists to take in regard to what is truly required for legal intent elements. As Morse has extensively argued (1978, 1982), there is no reason to believe that a mental health perspective offers any definite answers to legal questions, the resolution of which always involve value judgment based on considerations of law and public policy. If the history of diminished capacity in California demonstrates anything, it is that in the long run, expert testimony that is overly burdened by value considerations, and disconnected from the expert's scientific-clinical base, is counterproductive to any attempt to bridge the gap between law and the behavioral sciences. It is in the province of the judge or the jury to decide when a drunken intent, a compelled intent, or an intent abnormal in any respect is no intent at all under law. It is not apparent on what clinical, psychological basis the expert witness could draw such a conclusion.

The Alternative: A Logical Dilemma

The clinician who avoids redefining intent and who aims instead to base an opinion on capacity for intent on the current legal understanding of mens rea will seldom be able to address the ultimate issue of intent in conclusory language. Regarding mens rea as traditionally construed, facts speak for themselves and do not require an expert witness to articulate them. The expert witness faces an inescapable dilemma with diminished capacity (Clark, 1982). The difficulty in assessing capacity for intent is more logical than clinical. The use of more and better psychological tests, for example, will not yield more information about this capacity. Though some practitioners have courted future embarrassment and have used test data to support a conclusion that an individual is "not the type" of person who could be guilty of a robbery, or is "incapable" of murder, the crucial issue is whether the person did in fact rob or murder. If it appears that something bearing a strong resemblance on its face to the alleged criminal intent was entertained by the defendant, what can be offered on strictly clinical grounds about capacity for intent? Short of declaring on Aesculapian authority that the abnormal intent was no intent at all, it cannot be said that a defendant lacked the capacity for an offense that otherwise appears to have been committed. If the offense was not committed, or if it is unclear that it was, the question of the defendant's capacity to commit it is moot and need not arise. If, for example, a homicide took place in the "heat of passion," and there is no real evidence of premeditation and deliberation, the defendant's capacity for premeditation and deliberation is beside the point, and expert testimony on that capacity would not be necessary to avoid a conviction on first-degree murder.

Because the question of capacity for intent does not arise separately from the questions of fact or actuality of intent, the required capacity cannot be inferred strictly by clinical method any more than can its absence. Examination of a defendant's behavior during the offense itself yields no measure of capacity for intent that is independent of the question of fact. Such behavior would indicate capacity for intent only to the extent that it would, tautologically, indicate the fact of intent. If it is shown that an alleged burglar took property from another's home he had broken into, tried to conceal his actions and avoid apprehension, and later sold the property, his capacity for larcenous intent would also be evident. Capacity to form intent would not have to be clinically inferred in such a case—it would be assumed. No other direct method of inferring capacity presents itself. An inference that capacity for intent must have been present because of a lack of clear indications to the contrary is in a sense insupportable, if as a practical matter such as incapacity cannot be identified anyway. An expert opinion based on such reasoning would only convey the unnecessary information that the defendant might in fact be guilty. Concluding that the defendant had the capacity for the alleged offense from indications that at around the time of the offense the defendant has the capacity for other mental operations such as awareness, logical thought, and decision making would seem to be a more promising methodology. In the final analysis, though, the defendant's capacity for those behaviors collateral to the offense is strictly beside the point; the pertinent capacity is for the criminal intent itself.

Hypothetically, limit cases can be posited which involve individuals whose general cognitive capacities are so meager that it can be fairly concluded, on clinical or other grounds, that they genuinely lacked the capacity for the alleged intent elements. If an individual is charged with shoplifting, for example, but is reliably assessed as moderately mentally retarded with a tested intelligence quotient of 45, it may be that he lacked the ability requisite to larcenous intent to appreciate basic concepts of private property. In my experience, such individuals are not the subjects of actual diminished capacity referrals, or even insanity referrals, though complete exculpation ordinarily would be possible. Such a person walking out of a store with merchandise may be unlikely to be prosecuted at all.

In actual practice, occasional referrals will appear to approximate limit cases, raising genuine questions about capacity for intent. A 39-year-old resident of a nursing home, for example, had been charged with assault with intent to do great bodily harm after he was found in the room of an 83-year-old woman, a fellow resident, holding a belt around her neck. On examination he appeared grossly disoriented and verbally incoherent, and this was reported to be representative of his general condition. He had sustained massive head injuries in a motorcycle accident three years before and had required custodial care since. The defendant demonstrated severe dementia, with greatly impaired judgment and insight, and had a history of volatile moods and repeated violent and impulsive behavior.

It might fairly be asked whether this defendant had been capable of what anyone would take to constitute requisite intent. It might also be asked, however, whether diminished capacity per se would be the appropriate vehicle for introducing evidence of the defendant's disorder. Left unanswered, if he was seen as incapable of the alleged intent, would be the question of exactly what he was doing to the victim. It could not be ruled out, given his behavior alone, that he had formed an intent, however disordered or senseless, to harm the victim. Even in cases like this the dilemma of negating on clinical grounds the intent that is otherwise in evidence would likely reassert itself. A more appropriate, and clinically answerable, question might be insanity itself; in fact, that question was successfully raised by defense in this instance.

Certain cases of intoxication, especially those involving phencyclidine (Siegel, 1978) and other hallucinogens may also occasionally appear to provide limit cases of diminished capacity. A 29-year-old man I examined was charged with assault with intent to commit murder. He reported that, while despondent, he took 10 to 15 "hits" of LSD and that he had no memory for subsequent events. Police were called after he inexplicably began kicking at the door of a neighbor's apartment. Officers reported his highly disorganized speech, which included incoherent references to "Venus, numbers, and other apparently nonsensical things." As two officers led him away, the defendant seized one officer's gun, cocked it, and thrust it in the officer's abdomen. The officer was saved only because his partner jammed his hand between the firing pin and the chamber as the defendant pulled the trigger.

Given his demonstrably disordered state, it may be asked in this case whether the defendant was capable of what anyone would consider to be requisite intent. Again, however, it would need to be asked what, in that event, the defendant had been doing. Even in the absence of a clear motive, it could not be ruled out that he had formed an intent of sorts to kill the officer. Unlike the previous case, given the fact of voluntary intoxication, an insanity defense would not appear to be an option for this defendant.

More commonly encountered diminished capacity referrals do not appear to raise genuine questions of capacity for intent at all, unless the questions strictly involve the quality of the intent formed, rather than the fact or actuality of intent. In my experience, a surprising number of referrals are made on charges of armed robbery. One involved a 28-year-old man who was recorded on video camera during his holdup at gunpoint of a convenience store. He obtained $60 and escaped in a car driven by another man. The defendant was, it was discovered, a narcotics addict who had been drinking and taking a large quantity of a narcotic earlier on the day of the offense. Having run out of drugs and money, he indicated that he became uncomfortable and planned the robbery with his friend; afterward, they purchased drugs with the proceeds.

The defense-retained psychologist offered that the defendant's capacity for intent was "greatly diminished" by his addiction and intoxication. But what does such an opinion contribute to resolving the question of the defendant's intent? If he was not capable of an armed robbery, how may his actions be explained? The question of whether intent was formed is separate from questions of the quality and motivation for whatever intent was formed. Deeming an intent to be abnormal in some way is not tantamount to a conclusion that legally relevant intent was not formed. In such a case, there may be a valid question of whether the defendant's condition would warrant some mitigation of guilt, but it is not a question that can be addressed in a direct way by clinical information or psychological inferences.

In another case similar to *Conley*, a 40-year-old woman was charged with two counts of first-degree murder. She was an alcoholic who had divorced but never quite separated from her similarly alcoholic husband. For almost 24 hours prior to the offenses, she had been drinking with her ex-husband and his girlfriend. A drunken dispute arose over visitation rights for the defendant's daughter. The defendant left, drove home, and returned to the bar with a loaded shotgun. Leaving the gun in her car, she argued further with the girlfriend and was heard to threaten her life. She then left the bar, advising a barmaid in doing so to "hit the floor." She returned with the shotgun, and in rapid succession fatally shot both her ex-husband and his girlfriend.

Once again, it may validly be asked whether such a defendant should be found guilty of first-degree murder. Planning and directed intent of a sort do seem evident, together with a passage of time sufficient for the defendant to consider what she was about to do, but she was by all accounts highly intoxicated. It would be reasonable to ask whether the crime would have even taken place absent the psychological impairments brought about by intoxication, though this question does not bear on intent as such. While the question of the defendant's capacity to genuinely premeditate and deliberate may be asked, it is difficult to see how expert testimony could be brought to bear on the question in any clearly relevant way, unless the expert would indicate on nonclinical grounds, by fiat, that the defendant was simply too drunk to be guilty of first-degree murder. In this sort of instance, it is also unlikely that the court would need to be enlightened by expert testimony about the psychological effects of intoxication.

Another defendant I examined was also facing first-degree murder charges. He had gotten drunk with a friend and, at the urging of that friend's mother, had decided to stay the night, rather than drive home, and sleep with his friend in the only available bed. During the night, the defendant related, his friend woke him by an attempt at anal intercourse. Enraged, the defendant smothered the man with a pillow. Furious at the thought that his friend's mother had created this situation, and believing that she had done so with the knowledge of the consequences, he entered her room and stabbed her to death.

A psychologist retained by defense indicated in effect that the defendant would have been incapable of premeditation and deliberation because of mental retardation (he had a tested IQ of 70), intoxication, and strongly negative feelings about homosexuality. From available information, there would appear to be a question of whether the defendant did commit murder in the first degree of his friend, if not his friend's mother. It would not appear to be the case, however, that any such question could be resolved by clinical inferences about the defendant's mental capacities as such. More to the point would be the ordinary evidence that could be adduced that the defendant had, in fact, been engaged in something resembling ordinary legal conceptions of premeditation and deliberation. If such evidence is found, there is no way for an expert to conclude that it is negated because of incapacity, so long as the degree of mental abnormality, intoxication, or other impairment needed to negate intent is specified in neither law nor clinical science.

TOWARD AN UNDERSTANDING OF CAPACITY FOR INTENT

Generally, it cannot be demonstrated that requisite intent could not have been formed, only that it is not clear that it was in fact formed. In the typical case in which diminished capacity is an issue, the capacity in question is not actually susceptible to clinical investigation but is open only to the subjective moral evaluation of the trier of fact. Capacity for intent, like traditional malice, appears to function as a term of art, not of science; it lacks independent meaning and merely serves to designate whatever state of mind is deemed necessary to prove mens rea as a fact. The question of what state of mind does support a finding that intent was actually formed is an important one but is not inherently scientific or clinical in any real sense. Answering it calls for a moral determination of the extent to which various factors, such as intoxication or mental abnormality, ought to be accorded exculpatory or mitigating significance.

The forensic clinician does not need to endorse the general proposition that conclusory expert opinion on ultimate legal issues is never appropriate in order to acknowledge special problems in regard to diminished capacity. To the extent that statute or case law provide substantive guidance to the forensic examination and resulting testimony, the problems involved in offering opinions on strictly legal questions are lessened. Though all ultimate issues such as guilt, intent, sanity, and competency remain in the final analysis legal and not psychological in nature, all ultimate issues are not created equal. They vary in the extent to which they can be seen to incorporate genuine psychological content open to some sort of relevant clinical assessment. Capacity in the diminished capacity defense appears to be a psychological concept but one that in practical terms eludes psychological evaluation.

The capacity at issue in insanity differs from the capacity in mens rea defenses in both meaning and function. For this reason, conclusory expert testimony on insanity, despite the many problems associated with it, is less problematic than such testimony on diminished capacity. It is virtually impossible to specify any condition which would clearly diminish capacity for intent to such a degree as to preclude the formation of intent. For this reason, the clinical assessment of that capacity is unguided and inconclusive, unless conclusions are essentially grounded in value judgment alone. Regarding insanity, on the other hand, conditions can be identified that could plausibly produce, in terms of the ALI test, for example, a lack of capacity to substantially appreciate an act as criminal or wrong, or even a lack of capacity to conform conduct to the law. It is not unreasonable to conclude that psychotic thought disorder, delusions, and hallucinations can demonstrably impair cognition and reality testing to the extent that an offender fails to apprehend the illegal nature of an act. Compelling command hallucinations and delusions, as well as manic or catatonic excitement, can with similar plausibility provide a powerful drive for some individuals to act illegally, and in that sense at least impair the capacity to conform conduct to the law.

It remains true that any final decision on culpability and insanity cases must rest on a moral judgment that is solely in the province of the judge or jury. The ambiguity of key terms in all insanity tests, and their openness to interpretation, simply underscores the fact that insanity questions cannot be answered definitively by psychologists or other mental health professionals. However, addressing the insanity questions of capacity for appreciation of wrong and conformance of conduct does not place the clinician as expert witness in an untenably illogical position when it also appears that the defendant did indeed do the act alleged. Insanity, unlike diminished capacity, is an affirmative defense; the defendant does not contest the claim that he did the alleged act. With insanity, there is no need for the expert to represent what appears to have been a premeditated murder, for example, as something less because of a posited mental abnormality. In effect, the expert who offers the opinion in a diminished capacity case that a defendant was incapable of the alleged offense is addressing the question of what act was committed in fact, rather than the question of culpability, since the capacity at issue is not separable from the question of fact. Such an opinion implies far more than that the defendant may not have formed intent, or that he was less able than most to form intent, or that the intent he formed was somehow remarkable clinically. To say that a defendant lacked capacity to form intent is to advance an opinion on the black-and-white question of fact. It amounts to an assertion that he did not commit the offense. And the question of the actuality of intent, and not capacity for intent, is clearly the primary question in diminished capacity cases. Though the expert witness is typically asked about capacity for intent, appellate decisions in most jurisdictions that have considered the issue have established that the test for the trier of fact is not whether the defendant could have formed intent, but whether intent was actually formed (Fingarette & Hasse, 1979; Morse, 1984).

EXPLORING THE QUESTION OF FACT: A LIMITED OPPORTUNITY

In practice, a few cases will be encountered in which there may be a legitimate opening for the clinician to consider actuality or fact of intent. In other words, the relevant question strictly involves the actuality or fact of intent rather than the capacity for intent. Those are cases in which the essential meaning of a defendant's behavior is at issue. Expert testimony in such cases would not proceed from a conclusion that intent did not occur because the defendant's mental activity was deficient in some quality deemed necessary for true intent. Consider, for example, expert testimony that a hobo who demonstrates evidence of dementia probably due to alcoholism broke into an abandoned building one winter night not to commit arson as alleged, but that he may have set a fire in a hallway with only the misguided intention to warm himself. In this instance, testimony on the defendant's condition might lend plausibility to an alternative explanation of the fire setting. Such testimony, necessarily tentative and nonconclusory in nature, would not be based on any unwarranted assumptions by the expert as to what constitutes the requisite quality of intent.

As in any case, if the fact of intent cannot be demonstrated, the question of the defendant's capacity to form intent need not arise. Here, the expert does not have to address the clinically unanswerable question of whether the hobo was capable at that time of breaking and entering with intent to commit arson. Morse (1984) points out that one instance in which evidence of mental abnormality might well negate specific intent involves premeditation in murder. If mental abnormality demonstrably led the offender to act instantaneously, on the spur of the moment, premeditation would be negated, but not because it has been shown that the individual was incapable of it as such.

A defendant without prior criminal history, later examined by my colleague, was charged with breaking and entering with intent to commit larceny. The evaluation lent some plausibility to the defendant's unlikely explanation for the incident. He claimed he had entered the department store late at night solely in order to find some anticonvulsant medication he was afraid he had left there the day before. Examination of the defendant and his history revealed him to be a rigidly obsessive, hypochondriacally preoccupied individual with some mild neuropsychological impairment. A persistent, unreasonable worry over the years had been the health of his daughter and of children in general. On this occasion, he claimed, he had dropped a bottle containing his medication on the floor of the cafeteria in the store. He thought he had recovered all the pills but discovered later that night that a number of pills were missing. He reported he was unsuccessful in contacting security guards in the now-closed store. He assumed, no doubt correctly, that if he called the police they would simply tell him to wait until morning. He worried that if he did so, he might be too late to stop some child from finding and ingesting the pills. He claimed that with mounting anxiety he broke into the store to retrieve the pills, but he could not find them. The police reported that when he was apprehended, the defendant had no store merchandise in his possession; an ice machine in the cafeteria had been moved aside. In this case, a question of the defendant's capacity for larcenous intent need not be at issue. What was in question was the meaning of the defendant's behavior—that is, whether he had in fact entered the store with larcenous intent.

Opportunities for relevant psychological contributions to the resolution of questions of fact are, in my experience, highly limited. In the most common cases in which clinical evidence speaks to those questions, the evidence is merely cumulative. Those are instances in which the defendant appears to have met insanity criteria, but also not to have actually entertained the alleged intent. I have had experience with several cases similar to *Wetmore*, involving psychotic defendants who broke into strangers' residences with the reported delusional idea that they owned or lived in them. In one such instance, a young man in a strange city broke into a house he said he believed he had built in the sixth grade. He had bathed and dressed himself in a bizarre assortment of men's and women's clothing. He was confronted by the owners returning home from church. He argued with them at some length over the ownership of the house and, with exasperation, telephoned the police himself. Charged with breaking and entering with intent to commit larceny, the defendant appeared to meet the ALI-based insanity standard used in Michigan. But it also appeared that, given his delusion that he owned the house and its contents, he had not actually formed intent to commit larceny. As in other cases of this type, there would be no relevant question of the defendant's capacity to entertain larcenous intent —that question would be moot. It may be unlikely, on the other hand, that defense would bother with the question of whether a larcenous intent had been formed; defense did not pursue that question in this instance.

In general clinical practice the question of what the "true" intent might be for commonplace behavior is the frequent subject of inquiry. Applied to the question of criminal intent, this inquiry may lead in a few cases to germane testimony. I examined an elderly man who was living with his daughter and her children and who was depressed about his dependency and concerned about the burden he was to his family. He ineffectually robbed a local bank and was immediately apprehended. He had told his grandson just before he left the house that day that he was going away for a long time, but not to worry. If the old man had not in fact intended to steal the bank's money—that is, keep it—and had been seeking imprisonment as he later claimed, had he in actuality formed the larcenous intent required for robbery?

It must be conceded, of course, that in the case of most of the many individuals claiming they committed some crime in order to get locked up, or killed, or get help for themselves, the evidence suggests a different and more ordinary intent. Experience shows that the real intent behind most criminal behavior is exactly what one would expect: Murderers shoot to kill, burglars break in to steal, and robbers steal to get money. In most cases, there is no surprising hidden intent, let along some demonstrable inability to form mens rea.

Nonetheless, the unconscious motive or intent suggests itself as a special case open to expert testimony about the actuality of intent. Generally, this is a mistake. The law does not concern itself with motivation as such when considering intent, much less the unconscious. A strictly applied mens rea approach to intent focuses on what intent was formed, not why it was formed. In the psychodynamic view, unconscious motivations inform all behavior. The simple discerning of the nature of unconscious motivation in a particular act cannot negate the evident conscious intent (see Moore, 1979). A woman I examined reported the history classically associated with kleptomania; she appeared to engage in repeated shoplifting for neurotic reasons. While it might be the case that her conscious intent partook of unconscious motivation, the actuality of her conscious intent seemed to be in no doubt—she repeatedly stole and failed to return a variety of merchandise, with full conscious knowledge of what she was (consciously) doing. Such cases may warrant special considerations, but it cannot be said that the criminal intent charged was simply absent.

The use of hypnosis and other anamnestic procedures such as narcoanalysis, or of psychological testing, to uncover hidden or unconscious intent behind criminal acts is unlikely to lead to relevant conclusions. The law is concerned precisely with conscious intent: what the defendant knew and was aware of. In the many cases in which a defendant claims amnesia and therefore an inability to explain his or her intent, the use of hypnosis and related procedures is still not generally indicated.

Aside from problems of reliability and validity associated with the technique, probability that many if not most such defendants have no genuine memory loss at all, and the evidentiary problems in some jurisdictions in presenting the results of such investigations in court, these techniques would simply not be needed in most cases. In the diminished-capacity case, if not the insanity case, it is infrequent that an offender's own explanation is needed to divine the conscious intent with which an offense was done. The intent as such is likely to be obvious in the nature of the act, in the manner in which it was done, and from circumstantial evidence. If there remain questions of hidden motivation or unconscious intent, they are, again, unlikely to have a real bearing on the strict diminished-capacity issue, which concerns the conscious intent.

THE UNSPOKEN REFERRAL QUESTION

As a practical matter, the actual questions underlying diminished capacity referrals often pertain to issues other than specific intent. The unarticulated reason for referral may be the simple need to understand general psychological factors having to do with the defendant and the defendant's history and with the occurrence of the offense. Experience with routine diminished capacity cases also encourages the suspicion that, occasionally, the attorney may already know all that is needed but cannot introduce that understanding of the defendant and the offense into evidence without claiming diminished capacity and examining an expert witness. However obvious or within the ken of the layman the information may be, for example, the defense may wish the expert to state that the defendant does indeed appear to be an alcoholic and that alcohol intoxication can indeed impair judgment or impulse control. The essential honesty of such an approach may be questioned, as well as the propriety, if not dignity, of participating as an expert witness in proceedings of that type.

Where there is a genuine incomprehension on the part of the trier of fact of the defendant and the offense, good clinical testimony that is descriptive rather than conclusory is more clearly justifiable. It may not be obvious to anyone, certainly, how such a clinical discussion might be directly relevant to the only pertinent question—whether or not the criminal intent was formed. If the expert witness may not be able to address the ultimate issue and conclude that the abnormal intent was no intent at all, there is still no basis for an objection from the behavioral sciences that the trier of fact should not use the expert testimony to reach such a conclusion itself.

SUMMARY AND CONCLUSIONS

Regarding the role the psychologist might play in the adjudication of a mens rea issue, it is perhaps more evident what diminished capacity is not than what it is. Despite past practice, a diminished capacity defense is not properly the occasion for speculation by the expert witness on what the intent elements used by law really mean or how they ought to be defined. Nor is it true that the expert witness has any business seeing that justice is done by framing testimony to effect a result the expert deems desirable.

It is not the case that capacity for intent in the law exists on some type of spectrum or continuum. Capacity for intent is a bright-line, all-or-none test: One either has it or does not, just as one is guilty or is not. It is therefore not the case that *some* diminution of general cognitive or psychological capacity, however it is conceptualized, amounts ipso facto to diminished capacity, in the sense that the actor would be incapable of forming an actual criminal intent element. The primary question is not even one of capacity but of fact, and this is seldom a question for the expert witness: Was mens rea actually formed such that this crime was committed?

It is not the case that the diminished capacity defense is properly viewed in law as a variant or subtype of the insanity test. It is not the case therefore that if a defendant's appreciation of wrongfulness, for example, was diminished by intoxication or some relatively minor psychological disturbance, instead of by the severe mental disease or defect needed for insanity, that the defendant would therefore have diminished capacity.

It is not the case that compulsion, irresistible impulse, or some other volitional impairment yields diminished capacity. Intent in the law is not clearly invested with any volitional component, but appears to be strictly cognitive. Nor is it the case that the discovery of some hidden or unconscious motivation justifies a conclusion of diminished capacity. The law appears concerned with conscious intent, and explanation of that intent does not equate with exculpation.

Diminished capacity is a limited defense strategy which, used strictly, leaves little opportunity for conclusory expert testimony on the ultimate issue of intent. Psychologists called on to address the question of diminished capacity may certainly examine the case at hand to see if there is a foundation in the evaluation for actually concluding that the defendant was incapable of the offense charged. The odds are not great that there will be, even when the defendant appears to have met the insanity criteria. While hypothetically possible, such cases have eluded many a clinician. If psychologists are disposed or obliged to render a conclusory opinion on capacity for intent, honesty and accuracy will generally compel them to state that there is in fact no basis in the results of the evaluation to conclude that the defendant was incapable of intent as such, and that a finding of diminished capacity, whatever its merits might be, goes beyond the data. Occasionally, psychologists will have something of value to offer regarding the actuality or fact of intent. For the most part, though, the clinician can only concentrate on a descriptive exploration of the defendant's state of mind at the time of an offense and psychological makeup in general and leave whatever conclusions might be drawn to the judge or jury.

It is to be expected that a desire by the expert to limit the scope of testimony on diminished capacity to general clinical description, avoiding the ultimate issue, will not meet with much sympathy from attorneys or courts. Lawyers and judges, even if they understand the testimonial problems diminished capacity poses for the expert witness, generally desire the witness simply to be responsive to questions, whatever they are. Controversy about the limits of the expert's role in court, in my experience, tends to be dismissed by working attorneys and judges as a tempest in a teapot—and somebody else's teapot at that. Each party involved in an actual trial may have a stake in the continued practice of eliciting conclusory expert opinion on diminished capacity—the lawyers need to prove their points, and the court needs an established foundation for judgment. It is the expert witness who does not have, or perhaps should not have, a stake in responding to every question asked in the form it is asked. The mental health professions do have a stake in a thoughtful and cautiously limited approach to expert testimony: the preservation of some respect for the psychological perspective in the public forum. The history of diminished capacity and its logic suggest that psychology and other disciplines cannot give relevant responses to every question raised by the law.

REFERENCES

American Law Institute Model Penal Code (1962). Proposed official draft.

Arenella, P. (1977). The diminished capacity and diminished responsibility defenses: Two children of a doomed marriage. *Columbia Law Review, 77,* 827–865.

Bird, R. E., & Vanderet, R. C. (1972). Diminished capacity. In R. M. Cipes (Ed.), *Criminal defense techniques* (chapter 32). New York: M. Binder.

Blinder, M. (1982–1982). My psychiatric examination of Dan White. *American Journal of Forensic Psychiatry, 2,* 12–27.

Bonnie, R., & Slobogin, C. (1979). The role of mental health professionals in the criminal justice process: The case for informed speculation. *Virginia Law Review, 43,* 427–522.

California Senate Bill No. 54 (1981). Amending sections 21, 22, 26, 188 and 189 of the California Penal Code, and adding sections 28 and 29.

California Senate Bill No. 590 (1981). Amending section 1027 of the California Penal Code.

Clark, C. R. (1982). Clinical limits of expert testimony on diminished capacity. *International Journal of Law and Psychiatry, 5,* 155–170.

Diamond, B. (1961). Criminal responsibility of the mentally ill. *Stanford Law Review, 14,* 59–86.

Dix, G. E. (1971). Psychological abnormality as a factor in grading criminal liability: Diminished capacity, diminished responsibility, and the like. *The Journal of Criminal Law, Criminology and Police Science, 62,* 313–334.

English Homicide Act of 1957, 5 & 6 Eliz. 2, ch. II, Sec. 2.

Erlinder, C. P. (1983). Post-traumatic stress disorder, Vietnam veterans and the law: A challenge to effective representation. *Behavioral Sciences and the Law, 1,* 25–50.

Fingarette, H., & Hasse, A. F. (1979). *Mental disabilities and criminal responsibility.* Berkeley: University of California Press.

Idaho Code Annotated, 18–207(a).

Krausz, F. R. (1983). The relevance of innocence: Proposition 8 and the diminished capacity defense. *California Law Review, 71,* 1197–1215.

LaFave, W., & Scott, A., Jr. (1972). *Handbook of criminal law.* St. Paul, MN: West.

Marx, M. L. (1977). Prison conditions and diminished capacity— A proposed defense. *Santa Clara Law Reporter, 17,* 855–883.

Michigan Criminal Jury Instructions. (1977). Section 6–5, 3:1:16.

Montana Code Annotated, 46-14-102.

Moore, M. S. (1979). Responsibility for unconsciously motivated action. *International Journal of Law and Psychiatry, 2,* 323–347.

Morse, S. J. (1978). Crazy behavior, morals, and science: An analysis of mental health law. *Southern California Law Review, 51,* 527–654.

Morse, S. J. (1979). Diminished capacity: A moral and legal conundrum. *International Journal of Law and Psychiatry, 2,* 271–298.

Morse, S. J. (1982). Failed explanations and criminal responsibility: Experts and the unconscious. *Virginia Law Review, 68,* 971–1084.

Morse, S. J. (1984). Undiminished confusion in diminished capacity. *Journal of Criminal Law and Criminology, 75,* 1–55.

Morse, S. J., & Cohen, E. (1982). Diminishing diminished capacity in California. *California Lawyer,* June, 24–26.

People v. Cantrell, 8 Cal. 3d 672, 504 P. 2d 1256, 105 Cal. Rptr. 792 (1973).

People v. Conley, 64 Cal. 2d 310, 411 P. 2d 911, 49 Cal. Rptr. 815 (1966).

People v. Drew, 22 Cal. 3d 333, 583 P. 2d 1318, 149 Cal. Rptr. 275 (1978).

People v. Gorshen, 51 Cal. 2d 716, 336 P. 2d 492 (1959).

People v. Henderson, 60 Cal. 2d 482, 386 P. 2d 677 (1963).

People v. Mangiapane, 85 Mich. App. 379 (1978).

People v. Poddar, 10 Cal. 3d 750, 518 P. 2d 342, 111 Cal. Rptr. 910 (1974).

People v. Wells, 33 Cal. 2d 330, 202 P. 2d 53 (1949).

People v. Wetmore, 22 Cal. 3d 318, 583 P. 2d 1308, 149 Cal. Rptr. 264 (1978).

People v. Wolff, 61 Cal. 2d 795, 394 P. 2d 959, 40 Cal. Rptr. 271 (1964).

Siegel, R. (1978). Phencyclidine, criminal behavior, and the defense of diminished capacity. *Research Monograph,* Series 21, National Institute on Drug Abuse, 272–288.

Solomon, G. F. (1981–1982). Comments on the case of Dan White. *American Journal of Forensic Psychiatry, 2,* 22–26.

Szasz, T. (1981–1982). The political use of psychiatry—The case of Dan White. *American Journal of Forensic Psychiatry, 2,* 1–11.

Tarasoff v. Regents of University of California, 17 Cal. 3d 425, 551 P. 2d 334, 131 Cal. Rptr. 14 (1976).

Utah Code Annotated, 76-2-305.

Waddell, C. W. (1979). Diminished capacity and California's new insanity test. *Pacific Law Journal, 10,* 751–771.

CHAPTER 14

Defining and Assessing Competency to Stand Trial

RONALD ROESCH and STEPHEN L. GOLDING

Competency to stand trial is an important issue for many psychologists. Because competency to stand trial is raised significantly more often than the insanity defense, psychologists involved in forensic assessment and consultation are likely to have frequent experience with it. In this chapter, we will present an overview of the competency laws, research, and methods of assessment with the aim of providing forensic psychologists with the basic information they need to conduct competency evaluations. We do not believe, however, that this chapter will sufficiently prepare a novice forensic psychologist to carry out an evaluation. As we will make clear, the issues surrounding a competency determination are highly complex. An evaluator needs not only a high level of clinical knowledge and skills but also considerable knowledge of the legal system.

We urge the reader interested in pursuing work in the competency area to supplement this chapter with other materials (e.g., Golding, Roesch, & Schreiber, 1984; Petrella & Poythress, 1983; Roesch & Golding, 1985; Williams & Miller, 1981; Winick, 1983) as well as workshops and other forms of continuing education.

DEFINING COMPETENCY

Provisions allowing for a delay of trial because a defendant was not capable of proceeding have long been a part of the legal process. English common law allowed for an arraignment, trial, judgment, or execution of an alleged capital offender to be stayed if he or she "becomes absolutely mad" (Hale, 1736, cited in Silten & Tullis, 1977, p. 1053). Over time, statutes have been created in the United States and Canada that have further defined and extended the common law practice (see Verdun-Jones, 1981, and Webster, Menzies, & Jackson, 1982, for reviews of the Canadian

*This chapter was prepared while the first author was a visiting professor in the Department of Psychology, Arizona State University. Preparation of this chapter was supported in part by a fellowship to the first author from the Social Sciences and Humanities Research Council.

competency law and practice). The modern standard in U.S. law was established in *Dusky v. United States* (1960). Although the exact wording varies, all states use the *Dusky* standard to define competency (Favole, 1983). In *Dusky*, the Supreme Court held that

> It is not enough for the district judge to find that "the defendant is oriented to time and place and has some recollections of events," but that the test must be whether he has sufficient present ability to consult with his lawyer with a reasonable degree of rational understanding—and whether he has a rational as well as factual understanding of the proceedings against him. (p. 402)

Though the concept of competency to stand trial has been established in law, the legal definition, as exemplified by *Dusky*, has never been explicit. What is meant by "sufficient present ability"? How does one determine whether a defendant "has a rational as well as factual understanding"? To be sure, the courts have provided some direction to evaluators. For example, one might plausibly interpret the *Dusky* standard as implying that a defendant with amnesia would be incompetent to stand trial. But a number of legal decisions have held that this is not necessarily the case (e.g., *Ritchie v. Indiana*, 1984; *Wilson v. United States*, 1968). The reasons for this are varied. In *Missouri v. Davis* (1983), the defendant had memory problems due to brain damage. Nevertheless, the Missouri Supreme Court held that amnesia by itself is not a sufficient reason to bar the trial of an otherwise competent defendant. In *Montana v. Austed* (1982), the court held that the bulk of the evidence against the defendant was physical and not affected by amnesia. Finally, in a Maryland decision (*Morrow v. Maryland*, 1982), the court held that, because of the potential for fraud, amnesia does not justify a finding of incompetence. The court also stated that everyone has amnesia to some degree since the passage of time erodes memory. These decisions are of interest because they support the view that evaluators cannot reach a finding of incompetency independent of the facts of the legal case—an issue we will return to later.

The problems in defining and assessing competency should be clear from these few examples. As might be expected, one finds a broad range of interpretations of the *Dusky* standard. Since the courts have given mental health professionals a large share of the responsibility for defining and evaluating competency, it should not be surprising to find that mental status issues such as presence or absence of psychosis have played a dominant role in the findings of evaluators. In fact, evaluators initially involved in assessing competency seemed to be equating psychosis with incompetency (Cooke, 1969; McGarry, 1965; Roesch & Golding, 1980). Furthermore, evaluators in the past rarely took into account the specific demands of a defendant's case.

There is some evidence that this situation is changing. Early evaluators did not usually have any training in legal issues. Most were employed by state mental hospitals—the site of the majority of evaluations of competency. Typically, they had no training in either the assessment of competency or matters of law. As a consequence, the evaluations were based on the same standard mental status examinations that had been used with other patients in the hospital. If psychological tests were used at all, they were used as a diagnostic tool to determine presence or absence of psychosis.

In the past 10 years or so, these entrenched practices have been challenged. Research has provided evidence that the presence of psychosis is not sufficient by itself for a finding of incompetency (Roesch & Golding, 1980). It is also the case that better training programs for professionals in forensic psychology and psychiatry have been developed. Many graduate psychology programs and law schools cooperate to provide instruction in psychology as well as law, and a number of departments of psychology include forensic psychology as an area of expertise (Roesch, Grisso, & Poythress, 1985). Another reason for the changes in existing practices has been the work of McGarry and his colleagues on the assessment of competency (Lipsitt, Lelos, & McGarry, 1971; McGarry, 1965; McGarry et al, 1973). Their work was the starting point for a more sophisticated and systematic approach to the assessment of competency. Before turning to a review of assessment methods, we will provide a brief overview of the legal procedures involved in competency questions.

OVERVIEW OF PROCEDURES

Laws regarding competency vary from state to state, although most jurisdictions follow procedures similar to the overview we will describe in this section. Clinicians should consult their own state statute for the specific law and procedure applicable in each state.

The issue of competency may be raised at any point in the criminal process, and if the court determines that a bona fide doubt exists as to a defendant's competency, it must consider the issue formally and usually will order an evaluation (*Drope v. Missouri*, 1975; *Pate v. Robinson*, 1966). Though many states will allow these evaluations to be conducted on an outpatient basis, most of them are conducted in institutional settings, primarily forensic units within state mental hospitals. We have argued (Roesch & Golding, 1980) that inpatient evaluation is unnecessary in all but perhaps a small percentage of cases. As we will discuss later in this chapter, this is because most determinations of competency are easily made on the basis of a screening interview. This being the case, inpatient evaluations are unnecessarily lengthy and costly.

Efforts in recent years have been aimed at creating community-based evaluation procedures (e.g., Beran & Toomey, 1979; Fitzgerald, Peszke, & Goodwin, 1978; Melton, Weithorn, & Slobogin, 1985). Laben, Kashgarian, Nessa, and Spencer (1977) estimated the cost of the community-based evaluations they conducted in Tennessee was one-third the cost of the typical mental hospital evaluation (see also Fitzgerald, et al., 1978). We expect a major change in the competency procedures in the next 10 years. By then a majority of competency evaluations will take place in outpatient settings or in local jails. The assessment procedures we describe later in this chapter are explicitly designed for use in such settings.

One legal issue that may concern evaluators is whether information obtained in a competency evaluation can be used against a defendant during a trial or other legal proceeding. While some concerns have been raised about possible self-incrimination (Berry, 1973; Pizzi, 1977), it is generally agreed that information obtained in an evaluation will be limited to legal hearings on the issue of competency unless the defendant is informed prior to the evaluation of its potential uses and competently consents (*Estelle v. Smith*, 1981). The defendant may object but still be required to attend an evaluation but may, of course, refuse to cooperate with evaluators. In such a case, any information that was obtained would be limited to a hearing on the competency issue only.

Once a competency evaluation has been completed and the written report submitted (see Petrella & Poythress, 1983, for a discussion of the content of these reports), the court may schedule a hearing. If, however, both the defense and the prosecution accept the findings and recommendations in the report, a hearing does not have to take place. It is likely that in the majority of states, a formal hearing is not held for most cases. If a hearing is held, the evaluators may be asked to testify, but most hearings are quite brief and usually only the written report of an evaluator is used. In fact, the majority of hearings last only a few minutes and are held simply to confirm the findings of evaluators (Steadman, 1979). The ultimate decision about competency rests with the court, which is not bound by the evaluators' recommendations (e.g., *North Dakota v. Heger*, 1982). In most cases, however, the court accepts the recommendations of the evaluators (Steadman, 1979; Williams & Miller, 1981).

At this point defendants found competent proceed with their case. For defendants found incompetent, either trials are postponed until competency is regained or the charges are dismissed. The disposition of incompetent defendants is perhaps the most problematic area of the competency procedures. Until the case of *Jackson v. Indiana* (1972) virtually all states allowed the automatic and indefinite commitment of incompetent defendants. In *Jackson*, the Supreme Court held that defendants committed solely on the basis of incompetency "cannot be held more than the reasonable period of time necessary to determine whether there is a substantial probability that he will attain that capacity in the foreseeable future" (p. 738). The Supreme Court did not specify how long a period of time would be reasonable nor did it indicate how progress toward the goal of regaining competency could be assessed.

The *Jackson* decision did have a substantial effect on commitment laws. Many states revised their statutes to provide for alternatives to commitment as well as limits on the length of commitment (Roesch & Golding, 1979). Twenty-six of the 50 states had, as of 1979, limits ranging from 6 to 18 months. A few states based length of treatment on the length of the sentence which would have been given if the defendant was convicted. It is interesting to note that 24 states continued to allow indefinite commitment, seemingly in contradiction to *Jackson*. It is possible that the laws in some states have changed since our review.

Once defendants are found incompetent, they may have only limited rights to refuse treatment (see Winick, 1983, for a review). Medication is the most common form of treatment, although some jurisdictions have established treatment programs designed to increase understanding of the legal process (e.g., Pendleton, 1980; Webster, Jenson, Stermac, Gardner, & Slomen, 1985) or that confront problems that hinder a defendant's ability to participate in the defense (Davis, 1985).

This brief overview of the competency procedures is intended to provide a basic understanding of the process. For a more complete discussion of the legal issues as well as a review of empirical research on the various aspects of the competency procedures, the reader is referred to Roesch & Golding (1980), Steadman and Hartstone (1983), and Winick (1983).

ASSESSING COMPETENCY

Though there has been some confusion over the definition of competency, there nevertheless appears to be good agreement among evaluators about whether a defendant is competent or not. The few studies of reliability report that pairs of evaluators agree in 80 percent or more of the cases (Golding, et al., 1984; Goldstein & Stone, 1977; Poythress & Stock, 1980; Roesch & Golding, 1980). When base rates of findings of competency are considered, however, these high levels of agreement are less impressive, and they do not suggest that evaluators are necessarily in agreement about the criteria for a determination of competency. A psychologist, without even directly assessing a group of defendants, could achieve high levels of agreement with an examining clinician, simply by calling all defendants competent. Since in most jurisdictions, approximately 80 percent of all referred defendants are competent (for reasons discussed later in this chapter), the psychologist and the examiner would have an excellent percentage of agreement. Though the problem of base rates can be corrected through the use of certain statistics (e.g., kappa), the studies reporting reliability usually have small samples overall and consequently few incompetent defendants. It is the more difficult decisions, involving cases where competency is truly a serious question, that are of concern. How reliable are decisions about these cases? To date, no study has accumulated enough of these cases to answer this question.

High levels of reliability do not, of course, ensure that valid decisions are being made. Two evaluators could agree that the presence of psychosis automatically leads to a finding of incompetency. As long as the evaluators are in agreement about their criteria for determining psychosis, the reliability of their final judgments about competency will be high. As we suggest throughout this chapter, it is possible that the criteria used by too many evaluators inappropriately rely on traditional mental status issues without considering the functional aspects of a particular defendant's case. We know of no studies that have addressed the validity issue except, to a limited degree, the research we will report later in this chapter (Golding, et al., 1984).

Validity is, of course, difficult to assess because of the criterion problem. Criterion-related validity is usually assessed by examining concurrent validity and predictive validity (Messick, 1980). Predictive validity is impossible to assess fully because only defendants who are considered competent are allowed to proceed. It is feasible to look at the predictive validity of decisions about competent defendants, but not possible, of course, to assess the decisions about incompetent defendants, since they are referred for treatment, and judicial proceedings are suspended. Concurrent validity is also difficult to determine because it does not make sense to look simply at correlations with other measures (e.g., diagnosis, intelligence) if one adopts a functional, case-by-case assessment of a defendant's competency. For these reasons, then, there is no "correct" decision against which to compare judgments.

As we have indicated, the courts usually accept mental health judgments about competency. Does this mean that the judgments are valid? Not necessarily, because the court is simply accepting the evaluators' definition of competency. We have argued (Roesch & Golding, 1980) that the only direct way of assessing the validity of decisions about incompetency is to allow defendants who are believed to be incompetent to proceed with a trial anyway. This would be a provisional trial in which assessment of a defendant's performance could continue. If a defendant were unable to participate, then the trial could be stopped. If a verdict had already been reached and the defendant convicted, the verdict could be set aside.

We suspect that in a significant percentage of trials alleged incompetent defendants will be able to participate. In addition to the obvious advantages to both defendants, in terms of briefer periods of confinement, the use of a provisional trial could provide valuable information about what should be expected of a defendant in certain judicial proceedings. Short of a provisional trial, it may be possible to address the validity issue by having independent experts evaluate the information provided by evaluators and other sources. We have used this technique in our research and will discuss this later in the chapter. In the next section, we will review various methods for assessing competency.

We believe the most reasonable approach to the assessment of competency is based on a functional evaluation of a defendant's ability. While an assessment of the mental status of a defendant is important, it is not sufficient as a method of evaluating competency. Rather, the mental status information must be related to the specific demands of the legal case, as has been suggested by legal decisions such as the ones involving amnesia discussed earlier in this chapter. A defendant may be hallucinating and still be found competent to stand trial if those hallucinations do not impair the defendant's ability to consult with his or her attorney and otherwise participate in the legal process.

Some cases are more complex than others and may, as a result, require a higher level of competency. Thus, it may be that the same defendant is competent for one type of legal proceeding but not for others. In certain cases, a defendant may be required to testify. In this instance, a defendant who is likely to withdraw in a catatoniclike state may be incompetent. But the same defendant may be able to proceed if the attorney intends to plea bargain (the way in which the vast majority of all criminal cases are handled).

Florida has passed a statute that requires evaluators to relate a defendant's mental condition to each of 11 legal factors. Each of the following factors must be addressed in the evaluator's report to the court:

1. Defendant's appreciation of the charge
2. Defendant's appreciation of range and nature of possible penalties
3. Defendant's understanding of the adversary nature of the legal process
4. Defendant's capacity to disclose to attorney pertinent facts surrounding the alleged offense
5. Defendant's ability to relate to attorney
6. Defendant's ability to assist attorney in planning defense
7. Defendant's capacity to realistically challenge prosecution witness
8. Defendant's ability to manifest appropriate courtroom behavior
9. Defendant's capacity to testify relevantly
10. Defendant's motivation to help himself in the legal process
11. Defendant's capacity to cope with the stress of incarceration prior to trial (Florida Rule of Criminal Procedure 3.21(a)(1)) (Winick, 1983, p. 7)

A functional approach was adopted in the case of *Wilson v. United States* (1968). In that decision, the Court of Appeals held that six factors should be considered in determining whether a defendant's amnesia impaired the ability to stand trial:

1. The extent to which the amnesia affected the defendant's ability to consult with and assist his lawyer
2. The extent to which the amnesia affected the defendant's ability to testify in his own behalf
3. The extent to which the evidence in suit could be extrinsically reconstructed in view of the defendant's amnesia. Such evidence would include evidence relating to the crime itself as well as any reasonably possible alibi
4. The extent to which the Government assisted the defendant and his counsel in that reconstruction
5. The strength of the prosecutions's case. Most important here will be whether the Government's case is such as to negate all reasonable hypotheses of innocence. If there is any substantial possibility that the accused could, but for his amnesia, establish an alibi or other defense, it should be presumed that he would have been able to do so.
6. Any other facts and circumstances which would indicate whether or not the defendant had a fair trial (*Wilson v. United States*, 1968, pp. 463–464).

One could substitute any symptom for amnesia in the preceding quote. If this were done, the evaluation of competency would certainly be based on a determination of the manner in which a defendant's incapacity may have an effect on the legal proceedings.

Our view of competency has led us to develop a method for assessing competency which would allow consideration of both the mental status questions and the legal issues. Before we review this measure, we will present an overview of the history of competency assessment methods.

MEASURES OF COMPETENCY

Prior to the 1960s, there were no standard methods for assessing competency. One of the first was a checklist developed by Robey (1965), which focuses on court process issues such as understanding of the legal process. Another early procedure used a checklist and a set of interview questions devised by Bukatman, Foy, and DeGrazia (1971). Neither of these early measures was used often (Schreiber, 1978). By far, the greatest impact on competency assessment came first from the work of A. Louis McGarry and his colleagues at the Harvard Medical School's Laboratory of Community Psychiatry. McGarry, a psychiatrist, was involved in the development of two measures: the Competency Screening Test and the Competency Assessment Instrument.

The Competency Screening Test (CST) was created by Lipsitt, et al. (1971) as a screening measure to identify clearly competent defendants and thus minimize the need for lengthy inpatient evaluations. Such a screening process was considered important because the vast majority of defendants referred for evaluations are competent. The reason is that many other factors influence referrals, including the use of the evaluation commitment as a method for denying bail, as a tactical maneuver to delay a trial, as a way of providing a basis for a reduction in charges or sentences, and as a means of getting defendants who are seen to be in need of mental health treatment out of the jails and into the hospitals (Chernoff & Schaffer, 1972; Dickey, 1980; Golten, 1972; Kaufman, 1972; Lewin, 1969; Menzies, Webster, Butler, & Turner, 1980; Roesch & Golding, 1985; Teplin, 1984).

The CST, however, has not often been used as a screening device. Many evaluators have not chosen to use the CST because of the underlying values reflected in its scoring procedures. The CST is a 22-item measure in sentence completion format. Typical items are "Jack felt that the judge_____," or "If the jury finds me guilty_____." Defendants are asked to fill in the blanks to complete the sentence. Each item is given a score of 2 (competent), 1 (questionable), or 0 (incompetent). The CST is designed so that a low total score (Lipsitt et al. used a cutoff score of 20) would identify possibly incompetent defendants.

The scoring method has been criticized (Brakel, 1974; Roesch & Golding, 1980) because of its idealized perception of the criminal justice system. On one item, "Jack felt that the judge_____," responses like "was right" or "was fair" would receive a score of 2, while responses such as "was unjust," "was too harsh," or "was wrong" would get a score of 0. On another item, "When Bob disagreed with his lawyer on his defense, he_____," a score of 0 would be given to "figured there was no sense arguing." We have suggested (Roesch & Golding, 1980) that such responses may actually reflect a sense of powerlessness in controlling one's outcome in the legal system. This may be based on past experiences with the legal system and may well be an accurate interpretation.

The CST has been examined in a number of studies. In their initial study on the CST, Lipsitt, et al. (1971) reported interjudge reliability was .93. Unfortunately, only one other study using the CST has assessed reliability. Randolph, Hicks, and Mason (1981) reported reliability coefficients quite similar to Lipsitt and others in the .90 range. Keeping in mind that these are the only two studies, it would appear that the CST can be scored in a reliable manner. There have been at least four validity studies comparing classification based on CST cutoff scores and hospital evaluation decisions. In general, the CST appears to function reasonably well as a screening device. The errors appear to be in the desired direction—that is, the CST appears to label defendants as incompetent when later evaluations find them competent (false negatives). In the Lipsitt and colleagues study (1971), the false-negative rate was 16 percent (7 of 43 cases) while only three cases were misclassified as competent. Nottingham and Mattson (1981) found that 9 of 50 cases were misclassified as incompetent by the CST, but none was misclassified as competent. In the Randolph et al. study (1981) of the CST, they report an exceedingly high false-positive rate of 47 percent but a false-negative rate of zero. The overall accuracy of the CST, in terms of agreement with a psychiatric evaluation, was 72 percent. Shatin (1979) found that the CST in his study of 21 female defendants misclassified only four cases. Shatin also reported his results on the use of a five-item short form of the CST and found good concordance with the full 22-item CST.

The results of these studies lead one to give a mixed review of the CST. While it appears that the CST is a reliable instrument, serious questions can be raised about its usefulness as a screening device because of the potential for misclassifying possibly incompetent defendants. At this point, it is not possible to recommend that it be used as a sole method of screening defendants.

The other measure developed by McGarry, the Competency Assessment Instrument (CAI), is significantly more useful than the CST. The CAI contains 13 items related to legal issues. The items include "appraisal of available legal defenses," "quality of relating to attorney," and "capacity to disclose pertinent facts." Each item is scored on a 1 to 5 scale, ranging from "total incapacity" to "no incapacity." The CAI manual contains clinical examples of levels of incapacity as well as suggested interview questions.

The CAI has been used in a number of jurisdictions, although perhaps more as an interview structuring device than in the two-stage screening manner (with the CST) as originally intended by McGarry (see Laben et al., 1977; Schreiber, 1978). A revised and extended version has been adopted for use in Canada (Roesch, Webster, & Eaves, 1984). Unfortunately, there are few studies reporting either reliability or validity data. We used the CAI in a North Carolina Study (Roesch & Golding, 1980). Thirty interviews conducted by pairs of interviewers yielded item-percent agreement ranging from 68.8 percent to 96.7 percent, with a median of 81.2 percent. The interviewers were in agreement on the competency status of 29 of the 30 defendants (26 competent, 3 incompetent). The interviewers' decisions were in concordance with the more lengthy hospital evaluation decisions in 27 of 30 cases, or 90 percent. Obviously, more studies are needed, but the CAI appears to hold promise as a brief screening device.

The most recent work on competency assessment is our research on the development of the Interdisciplinary Fitness Interview (IFI). The IFI is designed to assess both the legal and psychopathological aspects of competency. The IFI consists of three major sections: (1) legal issues (5 items); (2) psychopathological issues (11

TABLE 14.1   Interdisciplinary Fitness Interview Items

Section A: Legal Items

1 Capacity to appreciate the nature of the alleged crime, and to disclose pertinent facts, events, and motives
2 Quality of relationship with one's current attorney
3 Quality of relationship with attorneys in general
4 Anticipated courtroom demeanor and trial conduct
5 Appreciating the consequences of various legal options

Section B: Psychopathological Items

6 Primary disturbance of thought
7 Primary disturbance of communication
8 Secondary disturbance of communication
9 Delusional processes
10 Hallucinations
11 Unmanageable or disturbing behavior
12 Affective disturbances
13 Disturbances of consciousness/orientation
14 Disturbances of memory/amnesia
15 Severe mental retardation
16 General impairment of judgment/insight

Section C: Overall Evaluation

1 Overall fitness judgment
2 Rating of confidence in judgment
3 Comment on basis for decision about defendant
4 Other factors rater might wish to take into account in reaching decision

Section D: Consensual Judgment

1 Fitness judgment after conferring with partner
2 Changes in rating of individual items after conferring
3 Reasons for changes

items); and (3) overall evaluation (4 items). The three items in the counsensual judgment section reflect post-assessment resolution of differences between judges. Table 14.1 contains a list of the items.

Each of the general items represents an organizing scheme for more specific subareas that have been seen to influence competency decisions. For example, six subareas are subsumed under the broad "capacity to appreciate" which forms the core of item 1. These are (1) appreciating the nature of the state's criminal allegation; (2) ability to provide a reasonable account of one's behavior prior to, during, and subsequent to the alleged crime; (3) ability to provide an account of relevant others during the same time period; (4) ability to provide relevant information about one's own state of mind at the time of the alleged crime, including intentions, feelings, and cognitions; (5) ability to provide information about the behavior of the police during apprehension, arrest, and interrogation; and (6) projected ability to provide feedback to an attorney about the veracity of witness testimony during trial, if a trial is likely to be involved. Note, however, in line with the open-textured nature of the competency construct, that a complete enumeration is not possible; rather, an attempt is made to summarize the general "lay of the land," allowing for specifics to be a matter of personal judgment.

The IFI was designed so that evaluators would have to consider both legal and mental status issues, but neither in isolation. The format of the IFI requires evaluators to relate their observations to the specific demands of the legal situations. For each item, evaluators are asked to rate the degree of incapacity of the defendant, as well as to give the item a score to indicate the influence that the incapacity might have on the overall decision about competency. Thus, a defendant may receive a score indicating the presence of hallucinations (item 10) but receive a low weight score because the evaluator has determined that the presence of hallucinations would not have much effect on the conduct of the legal case. Another defendant with the same symptom may receive a high weight score because the hallucinations are considered to be more of a potential problem during the legal proceedings.

A lengthy training manual for use of the IFI has been developed as a guide for evaluators. For each item, the manual provides a set of suggested questions and follow-up probes and also gives clinical guidance for the handling of typical interview problems.

The IFI can be used by a single evaluator, and we expect that this would be the manner in which it is most frequently employed. However, in our research on the IFI, we have used two evaluators so that reliability could be assessed. Moreover, we were interested in what the IFI, as a research instrument, could tell us about how competency is being defined. Because we believe that competency is as much a legal construct as it is a mental health one, we were also interested in determining if there were any differences in the way in which legal and mental health professionals would reach decisions about competency. Thus, we departed from the tradition of having only mental health professionals assess competency by inviting lawyers to participate also. In our research, a lawyer and a mental health professional have worked together as co-interviewers of defendants whose competency had been questioned. We believe that this collaboration is an important method that might result in a broader, and it is hoped, more valid assessment of competency. The presence of lawyers forces a different consideration of the legal issues specific to a case, and it also provides a method of training mental health professionals in the law. One of the problems in the past has been that mental health evaluators lacked knowledge about the legal system. While the creation of graduate training programs in law and psychology as well as joint Ph.D./J.D. degree programs may change this situation in the future (see Melton, Chapter 26 in this volume; Roesch, Grisso, & Poythress, 1985), collaborating on forensic assessment could serve as an excellent means of educating existing evaluators about legal issues.

Our first study of the IFI has been published (Golding, et al., 1984), and the results will be summarized here. The subjects were pretrial defendants in the Boston area who were referred by court clinics to a state mental hospital for competency evaluation. They were interviewed by teams composed of a lawyer and either a psychologist or a social worker. The interviews lasted approximately 45 minutes. While the interviews were conducted jointly, each evaluator independently completed the rating form of the IFI. The results demonstrated that judgments about competency can be made in a reliable manner by lawyers and mental health evaluators. They were in agreement on 97 percent of their final determinations of competency. By type of decision, the interviewers found 58 defendants to be competent, 17 incompetent, and disagreed on the remaining 2 cases. While overall agreement was excellent, there were some differences between the professions at the item level.

Interjudge reliability (kappa) ranged from .40 to .91. The interviewers were less in agreement on the legal items (mean kappa = .48) compared to the psychopathology items (.67). This finding reinforces our view that the assessment of competency will be improved as lawyers and mental health professionals come to understand the reasons for their disagreement. These were also significant differences in the strategies used by each profession to arrive at a decision. Principal component analyses (see Golding, et al., 1984) suggested that mental health professionals have a more integrated view of competency because the legal and psychopathology items overlap to a greater degree. For example, the first component for mental health professionals was a combination of legal items (appreciate changes and options) and psychopathology items that might be viewed as clinical correlates of the legal items (insight, absence of thought disturbance, and psychotic belief systems).

Since the defendants in our study were also independently assessed by evaluators at the mental hospital, it was of interest to compare our interviewers' decisions with those of the hospital. The overall agreement was only 76 percent, and there was greater disagreement with respect to decisions that a defendant was incompetent. While the two groups agreed 83 percent of the time on competent decisions, the agreement for incompetency was only 58 percent. It is difficult to interpret these differences because there is no absolute criterion against which to compare them. It is impossible to determine which decision was right and which was wrong. It is conceivable, of course, that both decisions were right because the defendants were seen at different times. A defendant who was incompetent at the first interview could have been competent by the time the second one took place, especially if medication was prescribed.

This discussion illustrates one of the many research problems inherent in studies of competency assessment. Since most defendants are competent (77 percent in our study), it is difficult to obtain a sufficiently large sample of incompetent defendants. Based on our studies in North Carolina and Boston, it has become clear to us that decisions about most defendants referred for competency evaluations are straightforward—that is, they are competent to stand trial, a finding which is evident no matter what the method of assessment. The potential value of the IFI, we believe, is in assessing defendants whose competency is truly questionable. It is here that we also believe that the collaboration of lawyers and mental health professionals will be of greatest value.

We have proposed elsewhere (Roesch & Golding, 1980) that competency can most effectively be evaluated through the use of a screening evaluation that could be conducted on an outpatient basis. The IFI should be a useful guide for these initial evaluations and also for later evaluations by others if competency cannot be determined at the screening evaluation. The initial research on the IFI appears promising. As more evaluators use it, we could begin to assess how effective it is in evaluating incompetency. It would be of particular interest to see how the IFI operates with the more difficult "gray-area" cases in which clear decision about competency is difficult. Furthermore, data on specific decisions will be useful to determine the extent to which the particular demands of a case influence these decisions.

GUIDELINES FOR EVALUATORS

We conclude our chapter with a discussion of several issues to which an examiner must pay special attention when conducting an evaluation of competency. Even before seeing a defendant face to face, it is good clinical practice to speak with both the defense and prosecuting attorneys in order to determine as accurately as possible why the fitness issue was raised, what evidence was offered, and what sort of trial and dispositional alternatives are being considered by both sides. This type of information is most useful if the IFI is used in an interdisciplinary fashion but is also quite helpful to a mental health examiner alone.

All indications of prior mental health contacts should be pursued *before* the interview takes place, so that the examiner has as complete a set of mental health records as possible. Similarly, complete police reports of the alleged crime are necessary and a past criminal history record helpful, particularly if the defendant has cycled through the criminal justice and mental health systems several times. Obviously, if the defendant is an inpatient, observational records should be consulted along with all routine psychological test data. Finally, the examiner should maintain an accurate record of when, where, and how information about the defendant was made available, as well as a date and time record of all contacts with the defendant, attorneys, and other mental health professionals. These records are invaluable at later stages if legal tactics designed to confuse or mislead a witness are attempted.

Having prepared for an examination in this fashion, one can conduct an efficient and comprehensive interview in a short period of time. Most delays in conducting an evaluation and most time spent in an inpatient status can thus be avoided, and a more relevant examination conducted, if these steps are taken. Prior to the interview, the defendant should be fully informed about any limitations on the interview's confidentiality. The possibility of recording the interview should be discussed, although permission should also be obtained from the defendant's attorney.

The examiner should be aware of any aspects of the interview and the resulting report that are covered by statute or accepted practice within the jurisdiction. As an example of the former, some states require *Miranda*-like warnings that inform the defendant of the limitations of confidentiality that may apply. Similarly, other states dictate the form of the report to the court, and an examiner's report may be excluded if it does not comply with the required format.

In *People v. Harris*, for example, a psychiatrist's report (that the defendant was competent) was excluded, and the defendant's subsequent conviction was reversed because the opinion was presented in conclusory terms and failed to give the clinical facts and reasons upon which it was based, thus precluding the trier of fact from independently assessing the weight to be given such an opinion. The current competency statute in Illinois is in many ways a model of this developing trend. It requires the examiner to address the facts upon which the conclusion is based, to explain how the conclusion was reached, to describe the defendant's mental and physical disabilities and how these impair the ability to understand the proceedings and assist in the defense, to discuss the likelihood that the defendant will respond to a specified course of treatment, and to explain procedures that would be employed to compensate for the defendant's disabilities, if any. We applaud this sort of specification and urge examiners to adopt the practice, even if it is not mandated in their own jurisdiction.

The conduct of a competency evaluation and the reports prepared for court should therefore be in complete accord with both the spirit and the letter of contemporary legal standards. The examiner must be thoroughly acquainted with the legal literature and in some sense anticipate developments in one's practice. For example, *Estelle v. Smith* (1981) clearly prohibits the introduction of material obtained under court-ordered competency proceedings at a "critical" (guilt or sentencing) stage of trial. Many states mirror this in their statutes but nevertheless do not regulate the common practice of requesting competency and sanity evaluations at the same time, often resulting in a combined report. We believe this practice is unfortunate and recommend that separate interviews, with distinct reports, be prepared. While a trier of fact is required to separate these issues, it is cognitively almost impossible to do so when the reports are combined. A defendant who is clearly psychotic and "legally insane" at the time of an assault may respond rapidly to treatment upon arrest and be just as nonpsychotic and "legally fit" when actually examined. Caution and fairness dictate keeping the reports separate so that the two issues can be considered independently by the courts.

REFERENCES

Beran, N. J., & Toomey, B. G. (Eds.) (1979). *Mentally ill offenders and the criminal justice system: Issues in forensic services.* New York: Praeger.

Berry, F. D., Jr. (1973). Self-incrimination and the compulsory mental examination: A proposal. *Arizona Law Review, 15,* 919–950.

Brakel, S. J. (1974). Presumption, bias, and incompetency in the criminal process. *Wisconsin Law Review, 1974,* 1105–1130.

Bukatman, B. A., Foy, J. L., & DeGrazia, E. (1971). What is competency to stand trial? *American Journal of Psychiatry, 127,* 1225–1229.

Chernoff, P. A., & Schaffer, W. G. (1972). Defending the mentally ill: Ethical quicksand. *American Criminal Law Review, 10,* 505–531.

Cooke, G. (1969). The court study unit: Patient characteristics and differences between patients judged competent and incompetent. *Journal of Clinical Psychology, 25,* 140-143.

Davis, D. L. (1985). Treatment planning for the patient who is incompetent to stand trial. *Hospital and Community Psychiatry, 36*, 268–271.

Dickey, W. (1980). Incompetency and the non-dangerous mentally ill client. *Criminal Law Bulletin, 16*, 22–40.

Drope v. Missouri, 420 U.S. 162 (1975).

Dusky v. United States, 362 U.S. 402 (1960).

Estelle v. Smith, 49 U.S.L.W. 4490 (1981).

Favole, R. J. (1983). Mental disability in the American criminal process: A four issue survey. In J. Monahan & H. J. Steadman (Eds.), *Mentally disordered offenders: Perspectives from law and social science*. New York: Plenum.

Fitzgerald, J. F., Peszke, M. A., & Goodwin, R. C. (1978). Competency evaluations in Connecticut. *Hospital and Community Psychiatry, 29*, 450–453.

Golding, S. L., Roesch, R., & Schreiber, J. (1984). Assessment and conceptualization of competency to stand trial: Preliminary data on the Interdisciplinary Fitness Interview. *Law and Human Behavior, 8*, 321–334.

Goldstein, R. L., & Stone, M. (1977). When doctors disagree: Differing views on competency. *Bulletin of the American Academy of Psychiatry and the Law, 5*, 90–97.

Golten, R. J. (1972). Role of defense counsel in the criminal commitment process. *American Criminal Law Review, 10*, 385–430.

Jackson v. Indiana, 406 U.S. 715 (1972).

Kaufman, H. (1972). Evaluating competency: Are constitutional deprivations necessary? *American Criminal Law Review, 10*, 465–504.

Laben, J. K., Kashgarian, M., Nessa, D. B., & Spencer, L. D. (1977). Reform from the inside: Mental health center evaluations of competency to stand trial. *Journal of Clinical Psychology, 5*, 52–62.

Lewin, T. H. (1969). Incompetency to stand trial: Legal and ethical aspects of an abused doctrine. *Law and Social Order, 2*, 233–285.

Lipsitt, P. D., Lelos, D., & McGarry, A. L. (1971). Competency for trial: A screening instrument. *American Journal of Psychiatry, 128*, 105–109.

McGarry, A. L. (1965). Competency for trial and due process via the state hospital. *American Journal of Psychiatry, 122*, 623–631.

McGarry, A. L., Curran, W. J., Lipsett, P. D., Lelos, D., Schwitzgebel, R., & Rosenberg, A. H. (1973). *Competency to stand trial and mental illness*. Washington, DC: U.S. Government Printing Office.

Melton, G. B., Wiethorn, L. A., & Slobogin, C. (1985). *Community mental health centers and the courts: An evaluation of community-based forensic services*. Lincoln, NE: University of Nebraska Press.

Menzies, R. J., Webster, C. D., Butler, B. T., & Turner, R. C. (1980). The outcome of forensic psychiatric assessment: A study of remands in six Canadian cities. *Criminal Justice and Behavior, 7*, 471–480.

Messick, S. (1980). Test validity and the ethics of assessment. *American Psychologist, 35*, 1012–1027.

Missouri v. Davis, 653 S.W. 2d. 167 (Mo. Sup. Ct. 1983).

Montana v. Austed, 641 P.2d. 1373 (Mont. Sup. Ct. 1982).

Morrow v. Maryland, 443 A.2d. 108 (MD. Ct. App. 1982).

North Dakota v. Heger, 326 N.W. 2d. 855 (N.Dak. Sup. Ct. 1982).

Nottingham, E. J., & Mattson, R. E. (1981). A validation study of the competency screening test. *Law and Human Behavior, 5*, 329–336.

Pate v. Robinson, 383 U.S. 375 (1966).

Pendleton, L. (1980). Treatment of persons found incompetent to stand trial. *American Journal of Psychiatry, 137*, 1098–1100.

People v. Harris, 133 Ill. App. 3d 633 (1983).

Petrella, R. C., & Poythress, N. G. (1983). The quality of forensic evaluations: An interdisciplinary study. *Journal of Consulting and Clinical Psychology, 51*, 76–85.

Pizzi, W. R. (1977). Competency to stand trial in federal courts: Conceptual and constitutional problems. *University of Chicago Law Review, 45*, 20–71.

Poythress, N. G., & Stock, H. V. (1980). Competency to stand trial: A historical review and some new data. *Psychiatry and Law, 8*, 131–146.

Randolph, J. J., Hicks, T., & Mason, D. (1981). The competency screening test: A replication and extension. *Criminal Justice and Behavior, 8*, 471–482.

Ritchie v. Indiana, 468 N.E. 2d 1369 Ind.Sup.Ct. (1984).

Robey, A. (1965). Criteria for competency to stand trial: A checklist for psychiatrists. *American Journal of Psychiatry, 122*, 616–623.

Roesch, R., & Golding, S. L. (1979). Treatment and disposition of defendants found incompetent to stand trial: A review and proposal. *International Journal of Law and Psychiatry, 2*, 349–370.

Roesch, R., & Golding, S. L. (1980). *Competency to stand trial*. Urbana, IL: University of Illinois Press.

Roesch, R., & Golding. S. L. (1985). The impact of deinstitutionalization. In D. P. Farrington & J. Gunn (Eds.), *Current research in forensic psychiatry and psychology: Aggression and dangerousness*. Chichester, U.K.: Wiley.

Roesch, R., Grisso, T., & Poythress, N. G. (1985). Training programs, courses and workshops in psychology and law. In M. F. Kaplan (Ed.), *The impact of social psychology on procedural justice*. Springfield, IL: Thomas.

Roesch, R., Webster, C. D., & Eaves, D. (1984). *The Fitness Interview Test: A method of examining fitness to stand trial*. Toronto: University of Toronto Centre of Criminology.

Schreiber, J. (1978). Assessing competency to stand trial: A case study of technology diffusion in four states. *Bulletin of the American Academy of Science and the Law, 6*, 439–457.

Shatin, L. (1979). Brief form of the Competency Screening Test for mental competence to stand trial. *Journal of Clinical Psychology, 35*, 464–467.

Silten, P. R., & Tullis, R. (1977). Mental competency in criminal proceedings. *Hastings Law Journal, 28*, 1053–1074.

Steadman, H. J. (1979). *Beating a rap? Defendants found incompetent to stand trial*. Chicago: University of Chicago Press.

Steadman, H. J., & Hartstone, E. (1983). Defendants incompetent to stand trial. In J. Monahan & H. J. Steadman (Eds.), *Mentally disordered offenders*. New York: Plenum.

Teplin, L. (1984). Criminalizing mental disorder: The comparative arrest rate of the mentally ill. *American Psychologist, 39*, 794–803.

Verdun-Jones, S. N. (1981). The doctrine of fitness to stand trial in Canada: The forked tongue of social control. *International Journal of Law and Psychiatry, 4*, 363–389.

Webster, C. D., Jenson, F. A. S., Stermac, L., Gardner, K., & Slomen, D. (1985). Psychoeducational programmes for forensic psychiatric patients. *Canadian Psychology, 26,* 50–53.

Webster, C. D., Menzies, R. J., & Jackson, M. A. (1982). *Clinical assessment before trial.* Toronto: Butterworths.

Wilson v. United States, 391 F. 2d. 460 (1968).

Williams, W., & Miller, K. S. (1981). The processing and disposition of incompetent mentally ill offenders. *Law and Human Behavior, 5*, 245–261.

Winick, B. J. (1983). Incompetency to stand trial: Developments in the law. In J. Monahan & H. J. Steadman (Eds.), *Mentally disordered offenders.* New York: Plenum.

CHAPTER 15

The Assessment of Criminal Responsibity: A Historical Approach to a Current Controversy

STEPHEN L. GOLDING and RONALD ROESCH

The complex of arguments, philosophical debate, opinion, and data on the insanity defense (see particularly Gray, 1972; Hermann, 1983; Pasewark, 1981; Platt & Diamond, 1965, 1966; Smith, 1981; Walker, 1968) cannot be approached without a personal decision to accept or reject a rather simple thesis. Belief in this basic thesis is not subject to scientific argument; rather it is "morally axiomatic"; that is, one either accepts it as a function of one's fundamental moral, religious, and jurisprudential presuppositions or one does not. Given the nonprovable nature of this moral thesis, scientific and logical argument about aspects of the insanity defense and the assessment of mental state are possible, but acceptance or rejection of the argument is not a matter of proof or science.* This fundamental belief may be stated as follows:

> In cognizing and regulating social interactions in terms of fundamental principles of "fairness" and "justice," we assume that all such social interactions, including the societal judgment of criminal or civil responsibility for certain classes of proscribed behavior, are based upon an ethical calculus that assigns individual blame, culpability, liability, punishability, and moral and criminal responsibility as a function of intentionality and mental capacity. The classical formulation of this moral presupposition is the legal maxim, *Actus non facit reum, nisi mens sit rea*, which translates freely into modern English as, "An act is not legally cognizable as evil, and hence criminally punishable, unless it is committed by a person who has the capacity to cognize the act as evil and then freely chooses to do it."**

This fundamental belief goes to the heart of the tension in the public's mind, as well as in the criminal and civil law, between strict or objective liability, on the one hand, and subjective liability, on the other. An examination of the history of the

---

*Thus N. Morris' (1982) reasoned rejection of the essence of this fundamental belief is unassailable on scientific grounds.

**In *Morissette v. United States* (1952) this principle is endorsed as "universal and persistent in mature systems of law" by the Supreme Court. Less freely, it is translated in *Black's Law Dictionary (5th ed.)* (1979) as, "The act does not make [the doer of it] guilty, unless the mind be guilty."

criminal law in Western Judeo-Christian cultures clearly demonstrates the nature of this tension (see especially Crotty, 1924; Gray, 1972; LaFave & Scott, 1972; Platt & Diamond, 1965, 1966; Sayre, 1932). The dilemma is simply this: On the one hand, it is clear that when someone performs a heinous or reprehensible act the person is "guilty" in the commonsense meaning of objective liability. On the other hand, in order to have a theory of action and responsibility that embodies our cultural sense of "fairness" and "justice," and that reflects our increasing knowledge of psychological processes, in general, and psychotic processes, in particular, we have to consider the conjunction of the proscribed behavior (*actus reus*) and an appropriate degree and type of intentionality and mental capacity (*mens rea*) in ascribing guilty or culpable ownership of an act (subjective liability).*

Thus, this chapter does not attempt to address the logically prior moral question about the insanity defense—whether or not it should exist. Our belief, along with most (but not all) scholars who have examined this issue,** is that its existence is integral to the fabric of our social structure, which includes, but is surely not limited to, the structure of our criminal law. Rather, the critical questions for the behavioral sciences are, in a sense, much more difficult ones.† Can one contribute to the understanding of intentionality and responsibility from a legal and scientific perspective? Have we any scientifically verifiable data or acceptable theories that allow us to draw defensible inferences about intentionality and responsibility?

As mental health professionals we are called on to offer expert testimony and scientifically acceptable data on the relationship between behavioral, situational, medical, and psychological characteristics, on the one hand, and a defendant's capacities for intending, cognizing, reasoning, appreciating, and controlling, on the other. Are we able to aid the trier of fact, or are we nothing more than "whores for hire,"‡ as many in the populace and the media seem to believe (Hans & Slater, 1983)?

We hope to demonstrate that forensic psychological data, when properly obtained and presented, have an important role in the adjudication of the insanity defense. The scientific underpinnings are there, and the task is one of both expand-

---

*Just as ordinary social judgments of whether an act was dominant, aggressive, kind, or friendly, for example, cannot be accurately made without some presumption or knowledge of the actor's intentions and capacities, so too in the criminal law the same principle holds, and one finds that blameworthiness or criminal responsibility cannot be "justly ascribed" without the conjunction of an *actus reus* and *mens rea*.

**For extended discussion of this issue, works by Bonnie (1983), Hart (1968), Hermann (1983), Morse (1985), and Sayre (1932) are particularly recommended. Morse's current view, which represents a repudiation of his early objections to the underlying logic of the insanity defense, is especially worthwhile for its directness. Morris' (1982) work remains the best statement of the logic of the abolitionists.

†We do not intend to imply that moral questions are easier. However, such issues do have an affective imperative associated with them, and most individuals who have not confronted personally the problem of justly ascribing responsibility for evil in the context of a criminal trial know what they believe to be morally true without a great deal of internal struggle.

‡The sentiment is certainly not new. Perhaps the most egregious was voiced by crown counsel in his cross-examination of a Dr. Leo who had been previously involved in the famous *Hadfield* trial and who was also a prominent member of the Sephardic Jewish community: "Have you not been here before as a witness and a Jew physician, to give an account of a prisoner as a madman, to get him off upon the ground of insanity?" *Rex. v. Lawrence*, 1801, cited in N. Walker, 1968, p. 82).

ing the empirical and observational data base and bringing modern psychological knowledge to bear on the issue of appropriately and justly ascribing degrees of responsibility. On one end of the responsibility continuum are those mentally disordered individuals who would be inappropriately and unjustly punished for losing control over impulses, cognitions, and the distinction between reality and fantasy as a result of overwhelming internal forces.* The result for this class of individuals** is the loss of the capacity to choose their actions in a manner which society deems accountable. On the other end of the spectrum is what society deems moral weakness or, in the extreme, simple evil. Psychological knowledge plays a critical but nonconclusory role in the moral judgments that distinguish points on this continuum.

In outlining the role that forensic mental health professionals can play in this judgment process, we have chosen to focus on the following major areas: (1) a review of the historical and jurisprudential roots of culpable mens rea; (2) an overview of the major insanity defense tests with special attention to the historically recurring problems and controversies; (3) an examination of the movement to reform the insanity defense, particularly by adopting "guilty but mentally ill" verdict options or abolishing insanity as an affirmative defense; (4) an examination of the particular controversy over the role of the expert witness; (5) a review of more modern approaches to shaping the data base on which such testimony is based; and (6) a sampling of certain current ethical problems and professional issues, such as the limits of confidentiality in insanity evaluations, and the use of videotaped interviews.

THE CONCEPT OF MENS REA

It is well established within the historical and jurisprudential literatures (Gray, 1972; Hermann, 1983; Platt & Diamond, 1966; Pollack & Maitland, 1952; Sayre, 1932; Stroud, 1914) that the fundamental concept of mens rea within Judeo-Christian cultures has been in existence since the earliest recordings of Hebrew law. Platt and Diamond, for example, quote the Babylonian Talmud as observing, "A deaf-mute, an idiot and a minor are awkward to deal with, as he who injures them is liable [to pay], whereas if they injure others they are exempt" (1966, n. 7, p. 1228). This concept may be traced, in a continuous line of development, through Greek and Roman law in which the concept of *culpa* (negligence) is distinguished from *dolus* (intentional fraud). Children under the age of seven, for example, were considered *doli incapax*—that is, "not possessed of sufficient discretion and intelligence to distinguish between right and wrong," hence "incapable of criminal intention or malice" (Black, 1979). Children between the ages of 7 and 12 were presumed *doli*

---

*Morse (1986) prefers to categorize such excusing conditions as "legally and morally sufficient irrationality or compulsion" (p. 77) and leaves open the types of mental condition that may give rise to such states.
**Other classes of individuals have been recognized. The best example are children generally under the age of seven.

incapax unless evidence of capacity to form culpable intention was presented. It is interesting that the pattern of evidence most frequently adduced to infer such intentionality, such as lying about the crime, concealing the body, or other after-the-fact actions, is still used in modern insanity trials as evidence that the person was capable of the prerequisite intentionality at the time of the crime. The culmination of this doctrine in more modern (i.e., since the thirteenth century) jurisprudence is presented in Blackstone's *Commentaries* in its classic form:

> All the several pleas and excuses which protect the committer of a forbidden act from the punishment which is otherwise annexed thereto may be reduced to this single consideration, the want or defect of will. An involuntary act, as it has no claim to merit, so neither can it induce any guilt; the concurrence of the will, when it has its choice either to do or to avoid the fact in question, being the only thing that renders human actions either praiseworthy or culpable. Indeed, to make a complete crime cognizable by human laws, there must be both a will and an act. . . . The rule of law as to . . . (lunatics) . . . is *furiosus furore solum punitur* [The madness of the insane is punishment enough]. In criminal cases, therefore, idiots and lunatics are not chargeable for their own acts, if committed when under these incapacities; no, not even for treason itself. Cited in *State v. Strasburg*, 1910, pp. 1021–1022.

One can show that the entire structure of the criminal law is built upon this principle.* No society seems ever to have been without this means, even if archaic. Sayre (1932) observes that one of the earliest legal texts, *Leges Henrici Primi (The Laws of Henry I)*, alternates between advocating absolute liability, "he who commits evil unknowingly must pay for it knowingly," and advocating the principle of mens rea. It was standard practice for the king to pardon mentally disordered persons found guilty of "absolute liability crimes" or for other financial arrangements to be made. In fact, Sayre's (1932) classic review of mens rea argues that the tradition of criminal law in England since Henry I originates in theological opposition to secular laws of absolute responsibility. This theological opposition was based on a belief that God could not properly hold an infant, idiot, or lunatic justly responsible. It is interesting to note that the age at which children are generally assumed to some degree to be criminally responsible corresponds to the age within all major religions at which they usually pass through a certification ritual and are deemed morally responsible in the eyes of God. Platt and Diamond (1965, 1966) show, in their historical reviews, that the "furiously" insane have been exempted from moral sanction by an extension of the same logic.

Mens rea has been historically interpreted in a broad fashion, making it roughly synonymous with "culpable intentionality" (Stroud, 1914, p. 13) or with the general mental and emotional capacity prerequisite to choose freely to commit proscribed acts. The modern trend in the criminal law has been to construe the mens rea requirement of criminal conduct more narrowly and to equate it with such phrases as

*A comprehensive discussion of the philosophical ambiguities inherent in the concepts of responsibility and liability and examples of strict liability in the criminal and the civil law, both of which are statistical and moral exceptions, may be found in a collection by H. L. A. Hart (1968).

proscribed conduct performed "intentionally," "recklessly," "knowingly," "purposely," and the like. Discomfort with the insanity defense has been associated historically with attempts to either abolish it outright or to change it drastically by restricting the relevance of mental state to such a narrowly defined mens rea (Wales, 1976). In recent times, starting with the first Nixon administration, there have been many attempts in federal and state legislatures to accomplish this shift in the focus of the insanity defense. The typical language has been, "It is a defense . . . that the defendant, as a result of mental illness, lacks the mental state required as an element of the offense charged. Mental illness shall not otherwise constitute a defense" (Utah Code, 1983).

At present this approach is followed in Utah (as noted) and in Montana* and Idaho,** although numerous attempts have been made to introduce similar approaches in other state legislatures and in Congress.† The Montana approach recently survived a constitutional challenge in the Supreme Court of Montana (*State v. Korell*, 1984) when the court held that no constitutional right to an insanity defense existed but that it was necessary for the prosecution to prove each element of the crime charged, including mens rea elements, beyond a reasonable doubt. However, the court also observed that a defendant who acted intentionally but delusionally (e.g., under instructions of God, or believing that he was some special person) *would not have difficulty being acquitted* because he "need only cast a reasonable doubt in the minds of the jurors that he had the requisite mental state" (*State v. Korell*, 1984, p. 1000). Reading between the lines, the court is implying that the concept of narrow mens rea would be expanded to fit an underlying sense of justice in such cases. In the absence of empirical studies it is completely unclear what actual effects such a confusing set of standards would have on the functional adjudication of insanity acquittees. In a curious argument the court also held that Korell's rights were protected because, after having been found guilty, his mental illness could be a mitigating condition, and he would not be subject to imprisonment if, at sentencing, he were found unable to appreciate the criminality of his act by the ALI-like standard found in section 46-14-312(a) of the Montana Code.

From the forensic examiner's point of view it is not clear what effect a narrower interpretation of mens rea will have. In the first place, there are no empirical studies that would allow one to infer how many individuals found not guilty by reason of insanity under a certain standard would also lack the appropriate narrowly construed

---

*A person is not guilty of an offense, other than an offense which involves absolute liability, unless, with respect to each element described by the statute describing the offense, he acts while having one of the mental states described in subsections (33)["knowingly"], (37)["negligently"] and (58)["purposely"] of 45-2-101" (Montana Code, 1982).

**"Mental condition shall not be a defense to any charge of criminal conduct" (Idaho Code, 1982).

†Curiously, the essence of the American Law Institute standard for insanity appears as a mitigating condition at sentencing in both Montana and Idaho: "Evidence of mental condition shall be received, if offered, at the time of sentencing, . . . the court shall consider such factors as . . . the capacity of the defendant to appreciate the wrongfulness of this conduct or to conform his conduct to the requirements of law at the time of the offense charged" (Idaho Code, 1982, section 19-2523(1).

mens rea.* Rogers, Bloom, and Manson (1984) report that 86 percent of all successful insanity acquittees in Oregon between 1978 and 1981 were uncontested by any of the forensic examiners or the prosecution. This implies that changes are likely to affect that subgroup of insanity pleaders whose constellation of crime and mental state have proved, historically, to be most controversial.

Careful reading of the existing (but scant) empirical literature (Fukunaga et al., 1981; Pasewark, 1981; Petrila, 1982; Rogers, Bloom, & Manson, 1984; Steadman et al., 1983) on the degree of agreement between examiners and factors associated with a successful plea, as well as an extensive examination of the major historical trials and controversial cases (Golding, 1984; Roberts & Golding, 1984), leads to a hypothesis that among such controversial cases at least one prototypic case would exist in which the mental state would be difficult to handle under a stricter view of mens rea. When an acutely disturbed defendant acts in an incoherent, bizarre, and "furiously insane" manner, no examiner or trier of fact from the eighteenth century onward would have trouble viewing the person as nonresponsible, whether the test was a strict interpretation of mens rea, Judge Tracy's "wild beast" standard in *R. v. Arnold* (1724) (see Platt & Diamond, 1965), or the modern American Law Institute's (1962) model penal code. However, when a defendant, no matter how disturbed or under the influence of command hallucinations, kills someone in a carefully planned manner, then the strict interpretation of mens rea will clearly not exculpate (unless the *Korell* court's untested "Procrustean" hypothesis is correct).

The most comprehensive scholarly review of this narrowing approach is Wales (1976), who discusses the problem by using the well known metaphor of "squeezing a lemon" (i.e., a defendant, under this narrow view, would not be guilty of killing his wife if, while strangling her, he believes he is merely squeezing a lemon). In other words, the prototypic case envisioned as qualifying for exculpation under the narrow view would be a delusional mistake of fact. In discussing the legislative history of narrowing attempts, Wales makes it clear that the underlying motivation is to eliminate the insanity defense without raising constitutional considerations and to assure that more insanitylike acquittees are dispositionally dealt with as guilty first and in need of treatment for being mentally ill second. Wales agrees that the cases most likely to be acted upon differently are those that involve command hallucinations, affective delusions, and various forms of paranoid processes, when it is clear that the defendant acted knowingly in the narrow sense of the term but the knowingness was conditioned on delusional, hallucinatory, or otherwise psychotic belief systems.

Because no jurisdiction has an extensive history that utilizes the narrow approach without an affirmative insanity defense (with or without a possibility of the death penalty), it is difficult to speculate on the actual consequences.** Roberts, Golding,

---

*However, Keilitz and Fulton (1983, fn. 45) claim that Montana authorities estimate that between 1979 and 1983 eight defendants "would have been found ngri," of which five were found to lack the required mens rea.

**In *Korell* the defendant appears to have had a complex personality disorder rather than being frankly delusional.

and Fincham (1986) have shown that when jury-eligible college subjects are asked to attribute criminal responsibility to defendants under various decisional schemes, evidence of planfulness, in otherwise severely disordered defendants, produces a marked decrease in ngri acquittals even under the ALI standard (the narrow mens rea instructions were not used). Thus, when a severely disturbed paranoid schizophrenic kills someone who is connected thematically to his delusional system in a nonplanful manner, 95 percent of the subjects view the person as not criminally responsible. However, when the same person is described as having purchased the murder weapon the day before the assault, the percentage of ngri acquittals drops to 59 percent. To most experienced forensic professionals, the existence of planfulness in the acts of such patients does not contraindicate irrationality, a lack of substantial capacity to appreciate the wrongfulness of one's actions, or an inability to conform one's behavior to legal requirements, but the average juror seems more troubled by the seeming contradiction. (Indeed, evidence of planfulness of the proscribed action is one of the historical prototypes for overcoming the presumption of *doli incapax* in children between 7 and 12 years of age.)

Although mens rea in the general criminal law has come to be identified with narrower connotations, we believe it would be a historical, jurisprudential, and clinical mistake to substitute such a narrowed definition in cases where the central issue is the impact of a mental disorder on defendants' fundamental ability to appreciate the nature and consequences of their actions and their ability to choose freely to commit a proscribed act. With others (most notably Bonnie, 1983, 1984), we believe that a narrow mens rea, in the absence of an affirmative defense, would produce great distortions in the adjudication of such cases. We are tempted to speculate that such an exclusive narrowing would probably lay the seeds of its own destruction. If our fundamental thesis about the role of the insanity defense in our society is correct, such a narrowing would tend to produce a trend toward expanding the meaning of "knowing," "purposefully," and the like as implied in *Korell*. The final result, with many instances of unjust verdicts, would be a "back-door" insanity defense in the sense that persons who intend knowingly, but delusionally, to commit proscribed acts will be found not guilty on narrowed mens rea grounds. If Judge Bazelon is correct in his reasoning in *United States v. Brawner* (1972) that juries and triers of fact basically use a sense of whether the defendant is justly held to be responsible in light of his or her mental condition (as we believe they are), then such a strict narrowing would force juries and judges alike to "acquit in defiance of the law" and to reconstrue the narrow terms to accord with their sense of fairness and justice.

Thesis: Despite periodic fluctuations, the formulation of the legal test for insanity represents an interaction between Judeo-Christian concepts of culpable intentionality, prevailing knowledge of psychopathology, and pragmatic sociocultural and administrative considerations.

As noted previously, Platt and Diamond (1965, 1966) demonstrate that the moral origins of the insanity defense may be traced at least as far into history as the Tal-

mudic proscription against holding "deaf-mutes, idiots [including the mentally retarded and insane], and minors" responsible for their actions.* Within our own
cultural tradition, the absolute liability that attached to proscribed acts, whether intended or not, was excusable, in principle, by a king's pardon in cases of insanity,
imbecility, or for certain children (Pollock & Maitland, 1952; Sayre, 1932). According to Sayre (1932), the concept of absolute liability was at odds with fundamental Judeo-Christian precepts of the mental and emotional capacities necessary
for moral guilt. Under such theological influence, the judicial system of the twelfth
century began to utilize the concept of mens rea, evolving finally by 1641 into the
well-accepted principle of *actus non facit reum nisi mens sit rea* (see previous discussion of this phrase).

We do not know from the fragmentary case law available how frequently, or in
what manner, these rules were routinely applied. However, from the work of Henry
de Bracton in 1256 onward (summarized in Platt & Diamond, 1965; Sayre, 1932)
there has been clear authority that certain classes of insane defendants were not held
criminally or civilly responsible. Walker (1968) argues, correctly we believe, that
the early cases available to us may lead to a mistaken impression of an overly restrictive view of the insanity defense at the time because they were atypical cases
in generally high profile contexts (as in Hinckley's trial). Thus, Arnold's trial for
the attempted murder of Lord Onslow must be understood in the context that his act
was seen as part of a plot against the king. Nevertheless the metaphoric test of the
period is captured in Judge Tracy's summation to the jury in Arnold's case, "If a
man be deprived of his reason, and consequently of his intention, he cannot be
guilty. . . . it must be a man that is *totally deprived* of his understanding and memory, and doth not know what he is doing, no more than an infant, than a brute, or a
wild beast" (cited in Walker, 1968, p. 56, emphasis added).**

It is difficult to trace the history of how such rules were applied, or how psychopathological testimony influenced the decisions. Because the records of most trials
are incomplete, the available sample is biased in an unknown manner. Also, before
1836 defendants were not provided with counsel unless the charge was treason.
Thus, Arnold and others, required to defend themselves, could appear quite in possession of their rational faculties at the time of trial. Hence the retrospective task of
inferring past mental state was made more difficult and subject to additional bias.
Despite these difficulties, the consistency with which certain themes emerge is sufficient to justify the use of these data when the contextual constraints are made
clear.

Hadfield's trial, however, was distinctly different than Arnold's. Hadfield had
received a serious head wound while in the army and afterward had been incoher-

---

*We are unaware of cross-cultural scholarship attempting to trace such concepts in the history of the
other great religions of the world, but this would be an important study. Oppenheimer's (1909) comparative analysis of lunacy law in the nineteenth century is a start but is limited in its cultural and historical
scope.

**Platt and Diamond (1965) observe that "brute" had a wider meaning in Tracy's day and was hence not
as extreme a term as it is often construed to be today.

ent, with "manifest symptoms of derangement." He was represented by skilled counsel; there were many lay and professional witnesses and the prosecution entered no expert evidence in rebuttal (Walker, 1968, pp. 74–81). Hadfield's psychopathological profile, however, did not fit the "total deprivation" model—his irrationality and madness were periodic, and a physician from Bethlem hospital testified, "When any questions concerning a common matter is made to him, he answers quite correctly; but when any question is put to him which relates to the subject of his lunacy [his delusional belief that he must be destroyed, but not by his own hand], he answers irrationally" (cited in Walker, 1968, p. 76). Hadfield's delusionally inspired attempt at passive suicide did not render him unaware of the nature and consequences of his act. He obviously knew, in the narrow sense, because he intended that, by killing George III, he would be put to death. In fact, he counted on his successful assassination of a monarch to result in his being put to death by the hand of another. This is an exmaple of the moral dilemma, if not frank inconsistency, that faces the narrowed view of mens rea.

In historical context it is important to point out that judges and legislators of Hadfield's time were aware of a conundrum in the adjudication of insanity that modern advocates of abolition of the affirmative defense of insanity (in favor of a narrowed mens rea approach) ignore. If Hadfield were found simply not guilty because he lacked the prerequisite mens rea, he would be set free. Therefore, during Hadfield's trial, Parliament hastily passed the Criminal Lunatics Act (1800) which provided for the special verdict of not guilty by reason of insanity. The result of this special verdict would be that, unlike other acquittals, the defendant would be "kept in strict custody in such place and in such manner as to the court shall seem fit, until His Majesty's pleasure be known." An acquittal on mens rea grounds would simply be an acquittal.*

On clinical grounds it is important to note that Hadfield's delusional system did not render him incapable of "knowingly," "intentionally," and "purposefully" planning the assassination of George III, but it did render his intentionality nonculpable because of the clear influence of underlying mental and organic disorder. Thus, even before M'Naghten's trial (and certainly after), the test that was to be applied by the letter of the law was not necessarily the same that was used, pragmatically, by the trier of fact. At each trial a complex set of factors, which include the social context, the skill of counsel, and the psychopathological profile, interacts with the "deep-lying ethico-psychological concepts" (Sayre, 1932, p. 989).

Although M'Naghten's trial is assumed to be the starting place for the test that

---

*In states that have abolished the affirmative defense and have substituted the narrowed mens rea approach an acquittee whose required mental state is not proven because of mental disorder is treated dispositionally according to the same rules that once governed traditional ngri acquittals. It is doubtful whether this is constitutionally or morally acceptable, but we know of no cases that have challenged the statutes on this ground. Thus, a defendant who lacks the culpable mental state of acting knowingly or purposefully because of extreme emotional distress would not be convicted and would be freed, whereas a defendant who lacked the same state because of mental illness would, in effect, be incarcerated.

to establish a defense on the ground of insanity, it must be clearly proved that, at the time of the committing of the act, the party accused was labouring under such a defect of reason, from disease of the mind, as not to know the nature and quality of the act he was doing; or, if he did know it, that he did not know he was doing what was wrong (M'Naghten's Case, 1843, p. 722).

It is reasonably clear that the knowledge of right and wrong test had already been used implicitly and explicitly in a series of trials in both England and the United States. In fact, there was already considerable discomfort with the perceived narrow scope of the rule. Isaac Ray (1838/1962) had already published his *Treatise on the Medical Jurisprudence of Insanity* in which he had attacked the narrowness of such formulations as not according with modern knowledge of the forms of mental disorder and their influence on behavior, affect, and cognition. The same debates that rage today over the scope of what should be included under "knowledge," "appreciation," and the like were influential in court decisions of the day.

Although the M'Naghten rules were rapidly adopted in the United States, they were almost immediately subjected to challenge on the narrowness ground and were modified significantly by some jurisdictions. In 1844 Chief Justice Shaw of the Massachusetts Supreme Court held that while the right-wrong test was proper, a defendant who acted under the influence of an irresistible impulse was not a free agent, hence was included under the rule because they could not know right from wrong (*Commonwealth v. Rogers*, 1844). In 1866 this logic was made explicit in Justice Somerville's holding in *Parsons v. State* (1866):

If therefore, it be true, as a matter of fact, that the disease of insanity can . . . so affect the mind as to subvert the freedom of the will, and thereby destroy the power of the victim to *choose* between right and wrong, although he perceived it—by which we mean the power of volition to adhere in action to the right and abstain from wrong—is such a one criminally responsible for an act done under the influence of such a controlling disease? We clearly think not (p. 586).

Crotty (1924) documented that the jurisdictions in the United States had fragmented into four sets of rules: (1) relatively "pure" M'Naghten; (2) M'Naghten broadened by interpretation to include irresistible impulse as meeting the test; (3) M'Naghten supplemented by explicit irresistible impulse rules; and (4) the New Hampshire "product" rule, heavily influenced by Isaac Ray and set forth in *State v. Pike* (1869).

Justice Doe, in setting forth New Hampshire's product test, argued that it was a matter of legal fact to be decided by a judge or jury whether a defendant suffered from a disease of the mind and whether the proscribed behavior was a product of that disease. Hence he discarded formal rules of specific states of mind and asserted that it was up to the trier of fact to decide "if [the alleged crime] was the offspring or product of mental disease in the defendant, [then] he was not guilty by reason of insanity" (p. 442). In fact, for a long period of time following M'Naghten there was considerable controversy over insanity rules that surfaced repeatedly.

Charles Guiteau's assassination of President Garfield in 1881 gave rise to a highly controversial trial and execution that took place against the background of a strong concern over "irresistible impulses" and a belief that insanity, especially "moral insanity," was all too easy to feign (Rosenberg, 1968). Rosenberg's scholarly analysis draws out these issues in fine detail, documenting public, legislative, and psychiatric reactions that are strong reminders of current debate. Judge Cox's highly elaborate instructions to the jury in Guiteau's trial left little doubt that the central issue before the jury concerned whether the alleged moral insanity and irresistible impulse fit into a straightforward interpretation of the right-wrong test set out in M'Naghten. Whatever the jury may have thought of the "battle of the experts" and the problems of the insanity defense, however, Guiteau placed himself in fatal jeopardy when he exhibited his uncontested egocentrism and interrupted the prosecutor toward the close of the trial by objecting, "That is not the issue. The issue is, was my free agency destroyed? I was overpowered. That is what the jury is to pass on" (cited in Rosenberg, 1968, p. 201). His rational comments may have allowed the jury to focus on his current mental state—a problem that confronts any defendant who asserts a retrospective insanity defense.

Shortly after Guiteau's trial Dennis Davis—described by his jail physician as "an imbecile acting under a powerful impulse he would not have the power to resist," and by lay witnesses as "weak-minded" and "half-crazy"—was convicted of murder in circumstances in which he intentionally sought out and killed a man who had previously said, after an argument, that he would return and "get" Davis. The idea that insanity was feignable and that all too many individuals were being acquitted on that basis was clearly present in the original trial (see transcript excerpts in petitioner's brief, *Davis v. United States*, 1895). Against this background, the trial judge had instructed the jury to rely on the presumption of sanity unless the defendant proved he was not beyond a reasonable doubt. The Supreme Court of the United States, in one of its rare direct treatments of the insanity defense, touched on an issue that has surfaced repeatedly before and after their decision by focusing on Davis' right to have all elements, including the state of mind of malice, proved against him; that is, to convict, the trier(s) of fact must "say that that evidence before them, by whomsoever adduced, is sufficient to show beyond a reasonable doubt the existence of every fact necessary to constitute the crime charged" (*Davis v. United States*, 1897, p. 493). Because this decision established that mens rea elements must be proved beyond a reasonable doubt (and implied that sanity itself may be one of the elements), legislative attempts to reduce the perceived overuse of the insanity defense by crafting a procedure that places the burden on the defendant to prove his insanity by some standard have become a tricky business.

In a subsequent series of cases the court has steered a reasonably unfathomable course holding that (1) *Davis* applies only to federal jurisdictions (*Leland v. Oregon*, 1952); (2) the state could require the defendant to prove his insanity after the state had proved all elements, including mens rea, beyond a reasonable doubt (*Leland v. Oregon*, 1952; *Rivera v. Delaware*, 1976); (3) Maine could not shift the burden of proof of "heat of passion" to the defendant (*Mullaney v. Wilbur*, 1975); (4) the state must prove all elements of the offense beyond a reasonable doubt (*In re*

Winship, 1970); and (5) New York could place the burden of proving the affirmative defense of extreme emotional disturbance on the defendant (*Patterson v. New York*, 1977). Currently, the burden of proving insanity as an affirmative defense is placed on the defendant in a majority of jurisdictions, and there is an accelerated trend in that direction (Keilitz & Fulton, 1983).

The American Psychiatric Association (1982), acknowledging the potential importance of the burden of proof issue to the nature of expert testimony and admitting the "inherent uncertainties in psychiatric testimony," declined to make a recommendation, deferring to "legislative judgment" but calling (admirably) for "further empirical study." The American Bar Association (1983) was more candid in revealing their internal debate and adopted a resolution calling for assigning the burden to the prosecution in M'Naghten-Rule states and to the defendant in states using the ALI model penal code. Surprisingly, the American Psychological Association simply took no position, "believing that those questions are legal questions, not psychological questions" ("Text of position," 1984).

With respect, we disagree. There is substantial reason to believe that placing the burden on the defendant could have a significant effect on jurors' attributional schemes. Especially when the shift in burden is conjoined with verdict options of guilty but mentally ill, it is too easy for the prosecution to argue that aspects of the defendant's rationality or intentionality show that he was not insane beyond a reasonable doubt. While this aspect of decision making needs detailed study, one could also predict that it will place higher expectations on the expert witness who testifies for the defense, and the style of direct and cross-examination that may be expected, especially if conjoined with the increasing trend to restrict the scope and nature of expert testimony.

Controversy surrounding various definitional and procedural aspects of the insanity defense continued over the first half of this century (e.g., see Ballantine, 1919; Keedy, 1917, 1920, debating a proposal for limiting the insanity defense to the narrower mens rea conception, and the materials on early abolition attempts reviewed in the context of the guilty but mentally ill option, below). In 1954 Judge Bazelon of the District of Columbia Court of Appeals attempted to correct numerous deficiencies in the combined right-wrong/irresistible impulse test in *Durham v. United States* (1954). In *United States v. Brawner* (1972), which ended the District of Columbia Court of Appeals' experiments with the *Durham* product test and adopted the model penal code recommendations of the American Law Institute (1962), Judge Leventhal carefully reviewed the court's logic in adopting *Durham*. First, "the old right-wrong/irresistible impulse rule for insanity was antiquated, no longer reflecting the community's judgement as to who ought to be held criminally liable for socially destructive acts. We considered the *Durham* rule as restated to have more fruitful, accurate and considered reflection of the sensibilities of the community as revised and expanded in the light of continued study of abnormal human behavior" (p. 976).

Second, the older test forced expert witnesses to testify in uncomfortably narrow terms of "right/wrong," making "it impossible to convey to the judge and jury the full range of information material to an assessment of defendant's responsibility"

(p. 976). While it has been asserted (Goldstein, 1967; Livermore & Meehl, 1967) that the test need not be narrowly cognitive and could include a wider range of affective "knowledge" and "appreciation" if interpreted in proper jurisprudential and historical perspective, the concern of the *Durham* court was that this was not typical practice, and therefore needed to be corrected.*

While the *Durham* product test ("an accused is not criminally responsible if his unlawful act was the product of a mental disease or defect") was intended to remedy these problems, it was not perceived as having its intended effect and seemed, rather, to make the problem, of undue dominance by experts testifying in conclusory terms, worse. The majority in *Brawner* therefore adopted the ALI rule and further encouraged judges to adopt instructions which emphasized the importance of nonconclusory testimony and the role of the expert of explaining to the jury the relationship between the defendant's cognitive, behavioral, and affective disturbance and his "substantial capacity to appreciate the criminality of his conduct or to conform his conduct to the requirements of the law" (*United States v. Brawner*, 1972, p. 973, restating the ALI model penal code.

Judge Bazelon, in his partial dissent, agreed that the product test needed to be rejected, but he was more pessimistic, viewing the majority's adoption of the ALI rule as a change which was "primarily one of form rather than of substance" (*United States v. Brawner*, 1972, p. 1010). For Judge Bazelon the purpose of the reformulation should be to "ask the psychiatrist (*sic*) a single question: what is the nature of the impairment of the defendant's mental and emotional processes and behavioral controls?" (p. 1032), leaving "for the jury the question of whether that impairment is sufficient to relieve the defendant of responsibility for the particular act charged" (p. 1032). To emphasize this Judge Bazelon advocated a version of a test first proposed by the British Royal Commission on Capital Punishment in 1953: "A defendant is not responsible *if at the time of his unlawful conduct his mental or emotional processes or behavior controls were impaired to such an extent that he cannot justly be held responsible for his act*" (*United States v. Brawner*, 1972, p. 1032). This "justly responsible" test, Judge Bazelon argued and we agree, has the virtue of making perfectly overt the underlying moral nature of the insanity defense and placing the "hot potato" aspect of such judgments squarely into the hands of the jury as representatives of the community. Nevertheless, the test has not been adopted except in Rhode Island (*State v. Johnson*, 1979).

Although the ALI rule has been widely adopted in federal jurisdictions and many states (Keilitz & Fulton, 1983), the movement to reform the insanity defense, and to limit its perceived abuse, has led to an attempt to eliminate the "volitional prong" of the test ("to conform his conduct to the requirements of law"). Advocates for this al-

---

*Indeed, in Canada, which uses a modification of the M'Naghten standard that employs the term "appreciate" instead of "know," there have been several cycles as to how strictly this should be interpreted. In the current cycle it is recognized that "appreciating" is purposefully broader than "knowing" (*Cooper v. The Queen*, 1980; *Regina v. Barnier*, 1980). However, appreciating "wrongfulness" is construed legally not morally (*Schwartz v. The Queen*, 1981) and is interpreted rather narrowly as appreciating the natural consequences of an act and whether that act is prohibited by law.

teration have included the American Bar Association (1983) and the American Psychiatric Association (1982), following Bonnie (1983). This proposal was adopted into the Federal Code by the United States Congress in the Insanity Defense Reform Act (1984).

The Court of Appeals for the Fifth Circuit has recently agreed with this abolition of the volitional prong, arguing that the position of the American Psychiatric Association (that the profession did not possess sufficiently accurate scientific bases to measure a person's capacity for self-control) was persuasive (*United States v. Lyons*, 1984a). A strongly worded dissent (*United States v. Lyons*, 1984b) argues that the "potential threat to society (supposedly) created by the volitional prong" ignores "empirical data that . . . provide little or no support for these fearsome perceptions and in many respects refute them" (p. 995). The dissent's argument cites various studies undercutting the perceptions of the misuse of the insanity defense. The dissenters also could have included the findings of Rogers, Bloom, & Manson (1984) that personality-disordered defendants, the target of the advocates of abolishing the volitional prong, constituted only 18 percent of the group of successful insanity acquittees. Citing *United States v. Torniero* (1984) where the Second Circuit placed appropriate limits on "creative" uses of the volitional prong for new personality disorders by requiring the defense to show that "respected authorities in the field share the view that the disorder is a disease or defect that could have impaired the defendant's ability to desist from the offense charged" (p. 730), the dissenters argue that the volitional prong was an essential aspect of the concept of guilt, since this concept "presuppose(s) a morally responsible agent to whom guilt can be attributed. By definition, guilt cannot be attributed to an individual unable to refrain from violating the law" (*United States v. Lyons*, 1984b, p. 1000).

We have thus come full circle, and the issue of irresistible impulse is now back in the forefront. Notice, however, that the American Psychiatric Association's disclaimer in this area is not based on empirical evidence but rather is a politically motivated reform. One could say, for example, that modern knowledge of borderline and schizotypal personality disorders is sufficient to argue that there are a class of nonpsychotic defendants whose ability to control their impulses is severely altered by their reasonably reliably diagnosable disorders. The excision of the volitional prong is intended to prevent so-called psychopaths from raising a successful insanity defense, but most data indicate that such persons are rarely acquitted in the first place.

Thesis: Modern attempts to abolish or to reform the insanity defense by instituting the alternative verdict of guilty but mentally ill reflect an ignorance of historical precedent.

Queen Victoria, like many of her fellow citizens then and today, was not pleased with the workings of the insanity defense and was furious at Daniel M'Naghten's acquittal in 1843.

We have seen the trials of Oxford [who attempted to assassinate Victoria in 1840] and MacNaughten (*sic*) [who attempted to assassinate the Prime Minister, Sir Robert Peel, and instead killed his private secretary, Edward Drummond, in 1843] conducted by the ablest lawyers of the day—and they *allow* and *advise* the Jury to pronounce the verdict of not guilty on account of insanity, whilst *everybody* is morally convinced that both malefactors were perfectly conscious and aware of what they did (cited in Walker, 1968, p. 168).

Forty years, and numerous attempted assaults later, Victoria was in no mood for jurisprudential analysis when Roderick MacLean attempted to kill her with a pistol and was acquitted by reason of insanity (like Hadfield, Oxford, and M'Naghten before him). Victoria's response was to fire off a letter to the Prime Minister demanding that the law be changed to reflect her belief that

> Punishment deters not only sane men but also eccentric men, whose supposed involuntary acts are really produced by a diseased brain capable of being acted upon by external influence. A knowledge that they would be protected by an acquittal on the grounds of insanity *will encourage these men to commit desperate acts*, while on the other hand certainty that they will not escape punishment will terrify them into a peaceful attitude towards others (unpublished correspondence of HM Victoria to Prime Minister Gladstone, April 23, 1882, cited in Walker, p. 189; italics added).

Whatever prejudices or biases may have influenced Victoria's jurisprudential sense, she clearly hit the nail on the head in summarizing popular attitudes about the insanity defense. Careful examination of the popular press of our day in and around the time of Hinckley's acquittal for the attempted assassination of President Reagan makes it clear that the popular attitude has changed little if at all; for example, Hans and Slater (1983) sampled public opinion within a month of the Hinckley verdict and found that 87 percent of their respondents viewed the insanity defense as a loophole. Only 14.7 percent would have found Hinckley, based on the information they had, not guilty by reason of insanity.

In the same year as the Hinckley verdict Governor James Thompson of Illinois, co-chairman of the Attorney General's Task Force on Violent Crime, summarized the views of many legislators, governors, and politicians who spoke in favor of adopting the verdict option of guilty but mentally ill when he stated succinctly, "The insanity plea is an example of what the public perceives as a weakness in the criminal justice system. Too many criminals are receiving reduced sentences by pleading insanity and serving sentences for a short time in a mental institution rather than a longer sentence in prison. For reasons like these the insanity as a defense plea has been called 'the scandal of American law'" (Thompson, 1982). Then United States Attorney General William French Smith was more blunt and predicted that adopting the guilty but mentally ill (GBMI) option "would effectively eliminate the insanity defense" ("U.S. Moves," 1982).

Careful examination of the trials of MacLean, M'Naghten, Oxford, and others, however, raises serious questions about whether the scandal lies with these trials or with the political hay made from them. The basic issue addressed by these trials— indeed in most insanity trials, regardless of the potential victim—remains: Is it just to find criminal guilt in a psychotic person whose behavior is apparently a direct and undisputed function of a delusional system, even if acted on in a "planned fashion"? Traditional jurisprudence and most jurors over the centuries have answered this question in the negative, but lay persons, not in a juror role, like Queen Victoria, President Reagan, and many modern legislators, answered the question affirmatively. It is interesting to note that poor Roderick MacLean, whose actions started this historical trend, was just such a fellow. He appears to have been difficult to motivate (anhedonic?) as a child, suffered a head injury in adolescence (of unknown effect), and was involuntarily certified in 1874 and in 1880 for homicidal mania with clear delusions of grandeur, referential thinking, and a delusional conviction that he must kill someone of importance in England to get the English people to stop mocking him by wearing blue. In a letter to his sister, dated May 30, 1880, he says:

> as the English people have continued to annoy me, I thought I would write, as you should not be surprised if anything unpleasant occurred as the people are so antagonistically inclined towards me, make me raving mad. . . . I mean, if they don't cease wearing blue, I will commit murder. I really think I cannot prevent myself having revenge on the English people. I don't mind a bit if they hanged me, as now I see things in a different light [referring to his belief that he was in communication with God through numbers having four in them, and that, to quote from his diary, God had told him, 'Fear not. My help is near and My power will shield you still'] (Trial of MacLean, 1882)

He carefully planned the attempt on Victoria and was found with an explanatory note in his possession. Nevertheless, at his trial all physicians, correctly we believe, argued that he was not guilty by reason of insanity according to the English law of the time.

Similarly, the evidence at M'Naghten's trial was unanimous and even the prosecution "caved in" after this fact was pointed out:

CHIEF JUSTICE TINDAL: Mr. Solicitor-General, are you prepared, on the part of the Crown, with any evidence to combat this testimony of the medical witnesses who now have been examined? Because we think, if you have not, we must be under the necessity of stopping the case. Is there any medical evidence on the other side?

SOLICITOR-GENERAL: No, my Lord.

CHIEF JUSTICE TINDAL: We feel the evidence, especially that of the last two medical gentlemen who have been examined, and who are strangers to both sides, and only observers in the case, to be very strong, and sufficient to induce my learned brothers and myself to stop the case (Townsend, 1850a, p. 400).

Needless to say, Lord Tindal's stopping of the trial was one of the factors that led the House of Lords to "request" that the justices respond to the series of questions and answers, which have come to be known as the M'Naghten rules. Countless authors have speculated as to whether M'Naghten would have been found ngri under the rules that bear his name. Nigel Walker, in describing the proceedings at the

House of Lords, clearly believes that M'Naghten would not have been found ngri, "Nobody [in the House of Lords] was tactless enough to point out that if the judges' answers represented the law M'Naghten should have been convicted" (Walker, 1968, p. 102).

Consistent with our previous arguments, however, the evidence as presented would likely result in an insanity acquittal regardless of letter of the rule or the century in which he was tried. There was undisputed forensic evidence that M'Naghten had long-standing delusions of persecution, that the delusions involved the police forces (Sir R. Peel had created the London Metropolitan Police), and that he had expressed these delusory ideas to many people and had attempted to gain the protection of several individuals including his parish minister, the Glasgow sheriff and chief of police, and the Lord Provost and the member of parliament from his district. All of these individuals were called at his trial, and all testified that he was, in their view, "insane," "daft," or "suffering from strange delusions of persecution." Moreover, M'Naghten had fled England and Scotland to outwit his delusory persecutors. His counsel, Cockburn, argued effectively that

if they [the delusions] had been realities instead of delusions. . . . he acted as a sane man would have done, but manifested beyond all doubt the continued existence of his delusions. He goes to the authorities of his native place, to those who could afford him protection, and with clamours entreats and implores them to defend him from the conspiracy. (Townsend, 1850a, p. 372)

At Oxford's trial the evidence seems to have been less clear-cut, but there was considerable, and relatively uncontradicted, testimony that Oxford had been seen by most as insane (in the lay sense) for a number of years, that many of his family members were viewed the same way, and that he impressed all medical authorities who viewed him at the time of his trial as an imbecile and insane. The jury had no difficulty in adjudging him insane, although they were somewhat confused by Lord Denman's attempt to instruct them that "although he laboured under a delusion, if he fired the loaded pistols at the Queen, knowing the result which might follow from his conduct . . . he would be responsible for his act, and liable to punishment" (Townsend, 1850b, p. 148).

Curiously, Queen Victoria seemed as unaware in her day of existing, highly relevant behavioral science data as do current legislators and other political leaders. In 1869 William Guy, professor of forensic medicine and vice-president of the British Royal Statistical Society, published an analysis of the rates of insanity acquittals before and after salient cases that, with the exception of formal time-series statistics, is a model of careful use of the crude data then (and now) available. Guy attempted to

discover some facts . . . which may go far to set these questions at rest; and perchance the truth, if we can discover it will be found to set us free from the exaggerations which hang about . . . as well as from the panics which are apt to seize on those who make the safety of the State, and the protection of the innocent against violence and fraud, their supreme law (Guy, 1869, p. 159).

Guy presented a time-series from 1836 to 1867 in which the total acquittal rate, as a function of type of crime, was adjusted to a constant population (a minor error) over the period. By careful, albeit nonstatistical analysis, Guy shows that celebrated trials did not result in an increase in insanity pleas and acquittals but, to the contrary, that the entire series is reasonably flat and, that the fluctuations are as observable in minor crimes as in high-profile murderous assaults and in convictions as well as in insanity acquittals.

Professor Guy's conclusions and his appeal to empirically based reason are as appropriate today as they were 118 years ago, but they had little influence then and, it seems, would have little influence today. Thus, at Victoria's request Parliament passed the Trial of Lunatics Act (1883) which provided that when a person is found to have committed a felonious act, but to have been insane at the time, the jury shall return a verdict of guilty but insane. Dispositionally the new statute made little difference, since, from Hadfield's time, this had been under the Criminal Lunatics Act (1800) which provided that, upon such a special verdict, the person should be held under strict custody until His (Her) Majesty's pleasure be known (i.e., held under indefinite criminal commitment). The new verdict was meant to satisfy the Queen's sense that at least there was a finding of guilt, even though, under the law of the time, the person was under government and not judicial control.

As predicted, things soon began to get a little uncomfortable jurisprudentially when Parliament passed the Criminal Appeal Act (1907) providing a mechanism and a court to hear criminal appeals. Soon thereafter, a person found guilty but insane appealed to that court on the basis that he had been found guilty (*R. v. Ireland*, 1910). Several other cases followed in the same vein, with the same argument. Everyone knew, however, that the special verdict was not a conviction, nor was it a straight acquittal (that had been dealt with at Hadfield's trial). Therefore in *Felstead v. Director of Public Prosecutions* (1914) the House of Lords was forced to eat judicial crow and to state that even though the verdict said guilty it really meant acquitted because the person was committed during His Majesty's pleasure and not for a fixed period of time, which would have been the case if convicted! *Felstead* remained the rule until things were again made straightforward in the Criminal Procedure (Insanity) Act (1964), which, in essence, repealed the 1883 Trial of Lunatics Act by changing the wording of the special verdict to, of course, not guilty by reason of insanity.

Thesis: The GBMI alternative is a not-so-hidden attempt to effect a functional abolition of the insanity defense. Although designed to "close a loophole," it may result in untoward consequences.

Twelve states have now enacted GBMI legislation, and it is under consideration in several others (Keilitz & Fulton, 1983). The original GBMI legislation in this century was introduced in Michigan in 1975 in the context of *People v. McQuillan* (1974), a case that had found Michigan's automatic commitment of ngri acquittee's unconstitutional. Subsequent to *McQuillan*, 150 patients were released, and two re-offended most spectacularly, one murdering his wife rather brutally and the other committing two rapes shortly after release. The verdict was also adopted in Indiana in 1979 under similar circumstances. Following Hinckley's assault on President Reagan, the stage was set for the remaining states to pass GBMI legislation in response to the perceived abuses of the insanity plea.* Thus the GBMI verdict of this century was introduced for reasons identical to Queen Victoria's demand in 1882 which resulted in the guilty but insane verdict form adopted in the Trial of Lunatics Act (1883).

Unlike the 1883 verdict, the current GBMI verdict was not intended to replace the verdict of not guilty by reason of insanity. Although both verdicts were introduced to stem the perceived tide of violence committed by offenders who escape justice, the current form was aimed primarily at jurors with the hope that it would allow them a middle ground between guilty and ngri. It was also motivated by knowledge that an elimination of the insanity verdict itself might be considered unconstitutional as it had been in *Strasburg* (1910) and *Underwood v. State* (1873).**

In *Underwood* Judge Campbell of the Michigan Supreme Court expressed his sympathies with the abolitionist argument. He acknowledged outrage at the "absurd lengths to which the defense of insanity has been allowed to go under the fanciful theories of incompetent and dogmatic witnesses," but he believed that the remedy was to be found elsewhere:

> No doubt many criminals have escaped justice by the weight foolishly given by credulous jurors to evidence which their common sense should have disregarded. But the remedy is to be sought by correcting false notions, and not by destroying the safeguards of private liberty (cited in *State v. Strasburg*, 1910, p. 1028).

The Michigan GBMI verdict was intended to assure the detention of the defendant for a significant period of time under the auspices of the department of corrections. Finally, the verdict was intended to make it harder to reach a verdict of ngri (especially in gray areas of severe personality disorder) with the hope that most jurors would respond to the superficial logic of the verdict ("Okay, he's crazy, but he did it, didn't he?") To cover the punitive and abolitionist motivation defenders of the GBMI legislation added a gloss of rehabilitation by arguing that the new verdict provided an explicit means of recognizing that some of those sent to prison were in

---

*Contrary to the public statements of advocates of the GBMI option, there is no support for the contention that the insanity plea is either abused or a loophole. In 1978, for example, there were approximately 2.3 million felony arrests in the United States of which 1,625 (0.07 percent) were adjudicated as not guilty by reason of insanity (Steadman et al., 1983). Furthermore, 80 to 90 percent of these acquittals are by pretrial agreement between the defense and prosecution (e.g., Rogers, Bloom, & Manson, 1984). Finally, postacquittal release procedures are quite strict in most states, and most of the available evidence indicates that ngri acquittees spend as much or more time confined as do those convicted of similar crimes (Braff, Arvanities, & Steadman, 1983; Cooke & Sikorski, 1974; Pantle, Pasewark, & Steadman, 1980; Pogrebin, Regoli, & Perry, 1986).

**As discussed previously, Idaho, Montana, and Utah have eliminated the affirmative defense of not guilty by reason of insanity, and this has not yet been challenged successfully. See *State v. Korell* (1984) for an argument distinguishing Montana's abolition from these prior cases.

need of mental health treatment.* Of course, they did not mention that few, if any, new funds were to be appropriated to the prison system to provide more treatment (Beasley, 1983) and that provisions already existed in every state that passed GBMI to laterally transfer a disturbed prisoner into mental hospital settings for treatment if that was necessary. In commenting on this entire enterprise, Professor Richard Bonnie says, bluntly, "[The guilty but mentally ill verdict] should be rejected as nothing more than moral sleight of hand" (1983, p. 194).

Functionally, the GBMI verdict works as follows in most jurisdictions (using Illinois' 1983 procedure as illustrative): If a defendant asserts the defense of insanity, the judge or jury may return verdicts of not guilty, guilty, not guilty by reason of insanity, or guilty but mentally ill. In order to return the GBMI verdict, the trier of fact (judge or jury) must find "beyond a reasonable doubt that the defendant committed the acts charged and that the defendant was not legally insane at the time of the commission of those acts but that he was mentally ill at such time" (Illinois Revised Statutes, 1983, c. 38, section 115-4). While legally insane is defined (c. 38, section 1005-1-11) as "the lack of a substantial capacity either to appreciate the criminality of one's conduct or to conform one's conduct to the requirements of the law as a result of mental disorder or mental defect," mental illness is defined, for the purpose of GBMI, as a "substantial disorder of thought, mood, or behavior which afflict(s) a person at the time of the commission of the offense, and which impaired that person's judgment, but not to the extent that he is unable to appreciate the wrongfulness of his behavior or is unable to conform his conduct to the requirements of law" (c. 38, section 6-2[d]).

Michigan makes its confusing distinction even fuzzier: Mental illness (not rising to insanity) is a "substantial disorder of thought or mood which significantly impairs judgment, behavior, capacity to recognize reality, or ability to cope with the ordinary demands of life" (Michigan, 1982). While the GBMI plea is supposed to make the juror's job easier, it isn't clear how one could distinguish reliably between such definitions of legal insanity and mental illness. We know of no research that has demonstrated the difficulty in making such distinctions, but in a series of cases defendants have attempted to challenge the statute by claiming that the distinction is irrational and hence violates their equal protection rights. All such appeals have failed.**

There is also reason to believe that such verdict options produce an increase in the threshold of insanity judgments per se. For example, Bruno Montano, who had been previously hospitalized involuntarily, killed his mother and niece while he was in the process of being reinstitutionalized. After having been found incompetent to stand trial and then restored to competency with psychotropic medication, Montano was found guilty but mentally ill of murder and manslaughter in light of conflicting

---

*Constitutional challenges on the basis that the corrections systems did not have the facilities to properly treat the GBMI defendants have failed, but the issues continue to be litigated. See McGraw, Farthing-Capowich, & Keilitz (1985) for a review of recent challenges.
**See *People v. DeWit*, (1984); *People v. McLeod*, (1980); *People v. Rone*, (1981); *Taylor v. State*, (1982).

expert and lay testimony about his mental capacity. The Supreme Court of Indiana (*Montano v. State*, 1984) found that his conviction stood, as the conflicting testimony justified a verdict of GBMI but not a verdict of not guilty by reason of insanity. While such an option may not produce a different result in hands-down cases, it would seem to give the trier of fact an easy out in the hot-potato situation of having to make judgments in difficult cases.

As discussed previously, Roberts et al. (1986) have also presented evidence that such verdict options may result in clearly insane defendants as well as traditionally noninsane personality-disordered defendants being found GBMI, a consequence neither intended nor desirable.*

The forensic examiner's job of accurately detailing a defendant's mental state and emotional, intellectual, and behavior capacities while avoiding the "conclusory whipping boy" trap are difficult enough. (Our sympathies go out to whomever tries to argue the barely perceptible distinction between a substantial disorder that significantly impairs capacity to recognize reality and substantial incapacity to appreciate wrongfulness!) If the courts believe they can make such distinctions, they are more than welcome to it. More cynically, we believe that the addition of the GBMI verdict option serves no useful purpose (increasing the safety of the society; assuring better treatment for the dangerously mentally ill before they are released) and may simply serve as another example of an ill-considered attempt to reform a complex system that is largely misunderstood and relatively unstudied.

Thesis: Although competency to stand trial and legal insanity at the time of the offense are separable issues, they interact in predictable ways that influence the conduct of forensic examinations.

In many fitness evaluations the complementary sanity question arises. Often the defendant is obviously unfit and will be later pleading not guilty by reason of insanity. As we discuss subsequently, the examiner's primary concern in such cases should be to preserve a sufficiently detailed record of the defendant's pretreatment mental state so as to not disadvantage the defendant at trial subsequent to competency restoration. Specifically, the examiner should make a concerted effort, consistent with clinical realities, to assess mental state at the time of the offense, even in an otherwise incompetent defendant. Occasionally, however, the fitness examination concerns the defendant's ability to waive competently an insanity defense and the collateral question whether a court may interpose an insanity defense, *sua sponte*, even over the defendant's objection.

As far as we are able to ascertain an interposed insanity defense has been infrequent in the United States, although it also occurs in Canada and is possible, in re-

---

*McGraw, Farthing, & Keilitz (1985) point out that limited outcome data from Michigan (Smith & Hall, 1982) show no discernible decrease in ngri acquittal rates following implementation of the GBMI verdict option. However, such data primarily reflect the centralized opinions of the Michigan Center for Forensic Psychiatry and the outcome of relatively undisputed plea bargains and bench trials. It remains to be seen whether the Roberts, Golding, and Fincham (1985) data will generalize to actual jury decision making.

stricted form, in England. A leading case in Canada is *Regina v. Simpson* (1977) in which a defendant was found not guilty by reason of insanity on an indictment of two counts of attempted murder, even though he did not place his state of mind at issue during the trial. The *Simpson* court found that Canadian practice allowed the prosecution to introduce evidence of a defendant's insanity, even if the defense had been disclaimed by the defendant. If such evidence were sufficiently substantial and raised a grave doubt that the accused had the capacity to commit the offense, the interest of justice would require the trial judge to submit the defense and the appropriate instructions to the jury as a verdict option. The reader should realize that in Canada the postacquittal commitment of an insanity acquittee is automatic and indeterminant; the defendant is held "until the pleasure of the Lieutenant Governor be known" (similar to the rule in England following *Hadfield*). In reality this means that a provincial review board, not a court, determines release, and this frequently means a period of institutionalization in excess of the time that would be served if convicted (Golding, 1983; Greenland, 1979).

In England the prosecution may enter evidence of insanity only if the defendant introduces his state of mind as an issue at trial. Thus, if a defendant attempts to prove that he suffered a noninsane automatism (which, under English law, results in a simple acquittal with no compulsory hospitalization), the prosecution may attempt to show that the automatism was "insane" (i.e., the product of a disease of the mind, which would result in a mandatory hospitalization (*Bratty v. Attorney-General of Northern Ireland*, 1961). In other cases, however, England does not appear to allow the introduction of such evidence when the defendant does not make his mental state an issue.

In the United States a small group of cases has addressed this issue directly or indirectly. In *Lynch v. Overholser* (1963) the Supreme Court found that a trial judge had not abused his discretion by refusing a defendant's attempt to change his plea to guilty after receiving sufficient evidence to find him not guilty by reason of insanity. However, the Supreme Court did not allow such an interposed insanity defense to result in automatic commitment, as would normally have been the case. In *Whalem v. United States* (1965) the District of Columbia Court of Appeals set forth broad authority for a trial judge to raise the defense of insanity, *sua sponte*, over the objection of the defendant. In *United States v. Robertson* (1974) the same court clarified some of the factors that should be considered in interposing such a defense, including the defendant's behavior at trial, the trial counsel's desire to raise the defense (thwarted by defendant), the bizarreness of the *actus reus*, and the opinions of experts about the defendant's mental state.

Although the *Whalem* rule has never been declared unconstitutional and is followed in several jurisdictions with modifications,* the District of Columbia Court of Appeals was persuaded in *Frendak v. United States* (1979) to modify *Whalem*. Specifically, the court decided, in light of a series of Supreme Court cases stressing a defendant's right to make fundamental decisions about his or her own case *within limits*, that there may be "persuasive reasons why defendants convicted of an of-

---

*See references in *Frendak* (1979, nn. 13–14).

fense may choose to accept the jury's verdict rather than raise a potentially success-ful insanity defense" (p. 376). Among such reasons are (1) a potentially longer pe-riod of confinement than if convicted (especially in light of *Jones v. United States*, 1983), even if commitment is not automatic in *sua sponte* insanity defenses; (2) a desire to receive treatment as a prisoner rather than as a mental patient; (3) a desire to avoid subsequent legal and social stigmatization as "twice cursed" (criminally in-sane); and (4) a desire not to admit the *actus reus* or not to have an act of political or religious protest construed as insane. In light of this, the *Frendak* court held that

> a trial judge may not force an insanity defense in a defendant found competent to stand trial *if* the individual intelligently and voluntarily decides to forgo that defense. In reaching this result, however, we further hold that the court's finding of competency to stand trial is not, in itself, sufficient to show that the defendant is capable of rejecting an insanity defense; the trial judge must make further inquiry into whether the defen-dant has made an intelligent and voluntary decision (p. 367).

In modifying and reinterpreting its rule, the District of Columbia Court of Ap-peals is explicitly adopting the Sieling standard for competency to plead guilty or to waive certain defenses and rights at trial.* In the words of the *Frendak* court:

> The *Dusky* standard is designed to indicate whether the accused knows enough about the facts of the case to relate them coherently to his or her attorney and to understand the nature of the proceedings. It is not intended to measure whether the defendant is also capable of making intelligent decisions on important matters relating to the de-fense . . . because the court is dealing with an individual whose sanity has been ques-tioned, a cursory explanation or a rote interrogation cannot satisfy the court's duty (pp. 379–380, citations and other text omitted).

Thus, when an examiner is confronted with such a defendant, care should be taken to explore the defendant's reasoning in great detail and to avoid injecting one's own feelings about postacquittal hospitalization and stigmatization. This issue usually arises with extremely paranoid defendants, which means that one is fre-quently subjected to various "countertransferential" pulls, eloquently expressed. Thus, few difficulties are posed by a defendant who is unwilling to plead ngri be-cause the person whom he is accused of killing is not capable of dying (on account of magical powers possessed by the victim). However, a defendant who has a great fear of mental hospitals or of involuntary treatment with psychotropic medication that may cause tardive dyskinesia and who believes (against his lawyer's advice) that he can "beat the rap" by telling his (somewhat idiosyncratic) side of the story is an entirely different matter.

Thesis: Attempts to create structured or standardized "mental state at the time of offense" examinations have heuristic value but are premature and deflect attention

---

Sieling v. Eyman (1973); for a review see Roesch and Golding (1980, pp. 10–36) which distinguishes general trial competency by the standard of *Dusky v. United States* (1960).

away from the critical need to develop a better fundamental understanding of the behavioral, perceptual, cognitive, affective, and judgmental correlates of various mental and especially personality disorders.

One response to the general attack on mental health expertise has been to improve the psychometric characteristics of the interview data base on which most forensic examinations are made. It is now reasonably settled that major sources of error and disagreement among mental health examiners can be traced to (1) individual differences among clinicians in their ability to elicit appropriate information, to be sensitive to certain cues, and to place proper weights on the cues; (2) examiner differences in the behavioral referents of psychopathological descriptors (semantic unreliability); and (3) differences in the diagnostic rules used to identify maximally valid diagnostic categories (Blashfield, 1984). Thus, diagnostic agreement for major categories has increased dramatically with the adoption of the explicit "decision-tree model" of DSM-III, especially when such explicit criteria are tied to semistructured elicitation devices like the Diagnostic Interview Schedule (Robins et al., 1981), the Schedule for Affective Disorders and Schizophrenia (Spitzer & Endicott, 1977), and the Present State Examination (Wing, Cooper, & Satorius, 1974). Indeed, semistructured interviews for nearly every psychopathological condition of any salience are beginning to appear (see Helzer, 1983, for a particularly useful overview).

Rogers has attempted to bring the same logic to bear in the evaluation of insanity with a set of scales he entitles the Rogers Criminal Responsibility Assessment Scales (Rogers, Wasyliw, & Cavanaugh, 1984; Rogers & Cavanaugh, 1981). The RCRAS was designed to translate the concept of legal insanity set forth in the ALI rule into quantifiable variables that will meet the standard of reasonable scientific certainty. A clinician is asked to rate a defendant on 25 scales grouped into five areas: reliability of report, organicity, psychopathology, cognitive control, and behavioral control. In addition, the examiner makes ratings of whether disturbance in control (cognitive or behavioral) is attributable to the assessed organic or psychopathological conditions, and a final rating of legal insanity. Rogers, Dolmetsch, Wasyliw, & Cavanaugh (1984) have shown in several samples that the reliabilities for the five area scores are reasonably high and that there is high agreement for the final judgment. Interestingly, the reported reliability for the "product question" (i.e., was the loss of control, if present, attributable to underlying psychopathological disturbance) is quite low (kappa = 0.49).

In another study with the RCRAS Rogers, Cavanaugh, Seman, & Harris (1984) report an overall agreement between examiners and triers of fact of 96 percent with respect to sanity and 70 percent with respect to insanity, corroborating our earlier findings in competency decision making (Golding, Roesch, & Schreiber, 1984) of an asymmetry in decisional agreement. Though the sample on which subsequent analyses were based was small (11 disagreements in 112 cases), Rogers, Cavanaugh, Seman, & Harris (1984) pinpoint two demographic variables (sex [males] and completion of high school [dropouts]) and two psychological variables (schizophrenic diagnosis and prior psychoactive medication history) as accounting for disagreements. With respect to the latter, individuals who had a history of schizophrenia and psychoactive treatment were seen by clinicians as more likely to be insane than by the courts.

It is not clear, however, what the RCRAS contributes, in the long run, to the "reasonable scientific certainty" claimed by Rogers. The RCRAS does force the examiner to be more explicit about the elements of his or her opinion, to be sure, but good forensic testimony has always had that clarity; that is, professionally competent testimony always clarifies exactly what sort of disturbances exists at the behavioral, volitional, and cognitive level and how it seems relevant to the *actus reus*. Forcing the examiner to slap an ordinal number onto the judgment does not increase the judgment's validity, particularly the product judgment. If one wanted to increase the reliability and validity of the underlying interview-assessment-judgment process *with respect to the delineation of psychopathological signs and symptoms*, then one would seem better off using a standardized elicitation and coding procedure (e.g., SADS, or PSE as has been suggested by others including Rogers; Roesch & Golding, 1980; Rogers et al., 1982). The reliability of the final judgment is also quite high in most studies that use no formalized interviews or rating scales (Rogers, Bloom, & Manson, 1984; Fukunaga et al., 1981; Stock & Poythress, 1979).

The critical question remains the association between organic or psychopathological disturbance and control/moral judgment capacities. Putting such a judgment on an ordinal scale is a step forward perhaps, but one that clouds the underlying confusion in gray-area cases (Golding, Roesch, & Schreiber, 1984). Additionally, the construct and incremental validity of the RCRAS is difficult to assess because the published validity data use criterion-contaminated groups—that is, either groups defined as sane or insane on the basis of the RCRAS itself, thus measuring in reality only item-total correlations, or groups based on court decisions where the same examiner's conclusions heavily influence court outcome. In any case, the underlying need to articulate a theory of criminal responsibility and control and to assess the critical elements of such a theory is not advanced a great deal by this method.

Slobogin, Melton, & Showalter (1984) have attempted to pursue a more modest strategy to improve the assessment footing of insanity evaluations. As part of the University of Virginia's Institute of Law, Psychiatry and Public Policy's attempt to create better training materials for forensic clinicians, these authors sought to make mental state at the time of the offense (MSO) evaluations more legally and forensically relevant. The MSO technique they describe is significantly different from standardized psychopathological interviews such as SADS because it is designed as an investigative technique that is influenced strongly by legal criteria and psychopathology in legal context. It was thus developed in a spirit much like our own competency assessment procedure, the Interdisciplinary Fitness Interview (Golding, Roesch, & Schreiber, 1984).

The MSO is a first-generation, loosely structured interview technique that holds great promise for setting a standard as to how such interviews should be conducted. As such, it will be described in some detail here (for greater detail, see Melton et al., 1987). The MSO assumes sophisticated training in legal and psychopathological issues and is tied to a training program at the institute. It relies heavily on an integration of traditional information sources (interviews with the defendant, psychological test data, physical test data, and special tests such as narcoanalysis) and third-party reports within a legal framework. The interview outline depends on obtaining complex third-party information, initially screened for legal admissibility. We applaud this development.

The interviewer is encouraged to consult referral sources; extensive police, prosecutor, and defense files on the *actus reus*; historical, criminological, social, educational, medical, and mental health data and the like *prior* to interviewing the defendant. During the interview, psychopathological state-of-mind data are gathered *and compared to third-party data* with respect to critical psycho-legal issues (i.e., the defendant's response to the offense, and a detailed account of internal (cognitive-emotional) and external (behavioral) events prior to, during, and subsequent to the offense). At this time, the material is not reduced to scores or quantified data, although it could be developed in that direction.

To date, the published data on the MSO technique (Slobogin, Melton, & Showalter, 1984) have concerned its ability to function as a screening device, primarily to screen out defendants for whom an insanity defense is inappropriate. Future work aimed at the agreement of MSO recommendations in uncontaminated samples and the extent to which reports based upon such techniques assist the trier of fact (in line with the work by Petrella & Poythress, 1983) is clearly needed.

Borrowing from Melton et al. (1987) and from our own work, we can conceptualize a comprehensive MSO interview as falling into a series of phases (the Sullivanian terminology is ours): (1) the formal clinical-legal inception; (2) the reconnaissance; (3) the detailed inquiry of present mental state; (4) the detailed inquiry of mental state at the time of the offense; (5) a reconciliation with other data sources (including consultation with other professionals who have evaluated the defendant), and (6) a termination.

INCEPTION.   In addition to rapport building, the inception requires explaining clearly one's role to the defendant, focusing on why he or she is being evaluated, to whom the report will be sent, and what limits are placed on the confidentiality of information. These confidentiality rules vary widely across jurisdictions and are strongly influenced by the context of the case, so the examiner must be fully informed, as a matter of professional competence. In most jurisdictions, once defendants have entered their mental state into the adjudication process by interposing an insanity defense or some other mental state claim, no information revealed to the examiner that can be construed as relevant to that claim is exempted. Jurisdictions differ widely, however, as to whether indirect fruits of such evidence are admissible, so extreme caution is required in the preparation of a report. The broadest coverage is found in the federal courts:

> No statement made by the defendant in the course of any [forensic] examination . . .
> with or without the consent of the defendant, no testimony by the expert based upon
> such statement, and no other fruits of the statement shall be admitted in evidence

against the defendant . . . in any criminal proceeding except on an issue respecting mental condition on which the defendant has introduced testimony. (Federal Rules of Criminal Procedure, 1985)

As indicated, however, jurisdictions vary widely, and the examiner should conform his or her practice to the local rules. It is also good practice to inform a defendant what reports, records, and files have been made available to the examiner, although in cases of suspected malingering, an examiner may choose to do otherwise. This is a matter of judgment, however, since even in nonmalingering situations, it may aid the clinical discovery process to let the defendant tell his or her filtered version first. The examiner may then introduce contradictory evidence at a later point in order to observe the defendant's reaction and to ascertain if the defendant is consciously distorting, having memorial difficulty because of mental state at the time, repressing memories, or suppressing details that are anxiety-arousing, embarrassing, or painful to reveal.

RECONNAISSANCE.   This is a forensically oriented review of the defendant's history. In practice, we use an amended version of Part II of the SADS which focuses on the defendant's lifetime history of disturbance, treatments received, and general variability in mental condition. Of particular importance are prior episodes that have involved criminal charges and/or fitness evaluations, civil commitments, and other such dispositions. The pattern of mental state disturbance and its relationship to psychotherapeutic and psychopharmacological treatment, medical conditions (e.g., hypoglycemia), situational stressors, and alcohol and drug use are particularly important.

DETAILED INQUIRIES: PRESENT MENTAL STATE AND MENTAL STATE AT OFFENSE.   Typically, it is difficult to separate these because a very disturbed defendant will usually be subjected to treatment by rapidly acting psychotropic medications. Nevertheless, it is crucial to bear in mind that these mental states, while related, are separable, albeit with great difficulty. We advise use of sections of structured and semistructured interviews to cover the domain of psychopathology in a relatively standardized fashion to improve inter-examiner reliability in the elicitation and coding of information. In addition to the main standardized interviews, we have found Andreasen's (1979a, 1979b) work on thought disorder, Bellak, Hurvich, and Gediman's (1973) techniques for exploring ego functions, and Pfohl, Stangl, and Zimmerman's coverage of personality disorders (1984) particularly helpful in this regard.

The detailed inquiry with respect to the mental state at the time of the offense must also focus on the relationship of the psychopathological elements to the criminal conduct charged. This part of the interview resembles a psychological autopsy. The defendant must be asked to reconstruct his or her thoughts, perceptions, experiences, attitudes, and behavior and the same reconstructions for those in the "field of action." Retrospective evaluations are difficult for lay persons, jurors, judges, and examiners alike, so great care must be taken to obtain very detailed information and also to avoid, as far as possible, recall-based contamination of the defendant's memories.

In our experience, the retrospective difficulty is frequently translated at trial into fairly grandiose defense and prosecution theories of what implications may be drawn from this or that aspect of the defendant's behavior vis-à-vis the person's mental state. Thus, it may be claimed that an abused wife intended her husband's death because she waited three hours until attempting to dispose of the body. Detailed inquiry may reveal that her husband may have frequently played "possum" following previous abuse situations when he typically passed out after extreme drug intoxication and that the wife, disoriented and substantially impaired in reality contact, may have mistakenly appreciated the situation as one in which he was again playing his favorite game instead of lying dead from a blow to the head. More commonly, a defendant may lie quite rationally about what happened several hours before and in fact be in a dramatically different mental state. Lay persons generally assume a greater degree of stability and cross-situationality of behavior and experience than may be warranted on scientific grounds. The detailed inquiries should enable an examiner, within the limits of current knowledge of psychopathology, to produce a meaningful psychological autopsy of the defendant's *states* of mind during the entire legally significant period.

RECONCILIATION AND TERMINATION.   As emphasized by many advocates and critics of the role of the forensic examiner in the legal process (Bonnie & Slobogin, 1980; Melton et al., 1987; Morse 1978b), and discussed in greater detail later, the role of the expert is not to present legal conclusions or formal psychopathological diagnoses. Rather, the role of examiner, as expert, is to import state-of-the-art scientific knowledge about the existence of various psychopathological conditions and their relationship to various behavioral, perceptual, cognitive, and judgmental capacities into the legal/moral decisional process. Thus, at the reconciliation-termination phase, the examiner should be prepared to integrate the information available at this level and to inform all parties concerned (the defendant, defense counsel, prosecutor, other professionals). One advantage of this openness is that it allows the defendant to produce any additional information wich might explain or clarify discrepancies or other problems, and it helps prevent an uninformed battle of the experts. In certain gray-area cases, there will be legitimate disagreements among experts. It assists the trier of fact if the nature of these disagreements, as well as areas of agreement, are drawn as precisely as possible, with each examiner fully aware and able to comment in advance as to the reasons for disagreement. Such pretestimony consultations also tend to produce higher quality and more informative strategies for direct and cross-examination.

Thesis: The expertise of mental health professionals has a legitimate role, but it is our responsibility to reform that role.

Qualifications of the Expert

Traditionally, expert testimony on insanity issues was restricted to the medical profession. With some exceptions (see Louisell, 1955; Perlin, 1980; Poythress, 1979, for reviews) this remained the case until the landmark case of *Jenkins v. United*

States (1962) where Judge Bazelon found error in the trial court's instructions that, "A psychologist is not competent to give a medical opinion as to mental disease or defect. Therefore, you will not consider any evidence . . . [to that effect] . . . according to the testimony given by the psychologist" (cited in *Jenkins*, p. 643). Judge Bazelon argued that the test for admissibility was not the degree held by the witness, but rather "whether the opinion offered will be likely to aid the trier of fact in the search for truth" (p. 643), and "the actual experience of the witness and the probable probative value of his opinion" (p. 646). Explicitly, Judge Bazelon argued that no expert, regardless of degree or training, should be accepted without a specific "finding in respect to the individual qualifications of each challenged expert" (p. 646).

Predictably, the American Psychiatric Association filed an amicus brief attempting to assert that clinical psychologists were ancillary personnel who were not qualified to testify as to psychopathological disturbances, which, after all, were medical diseases. This type of assertion is clearly a turf battle made not on the grounds of scientific evidence but for protection of the guild (Hogan, 1983; 1979). In fact, Petrella and Poythress (1983) present evidence that psychological and social worker reports are seen as more helpful to triers of fact than those of psychiatrists.

In the spirit of Judge Bazelon's comments, we prefer to focus on the training and expertise of a particular witness qualifying during the voir dire for specific and limited expertise. While many "diplomate," "academy," and "professional examiner" organizations now exist in psychology and psychiatry, we believe that even such certification should not be sufficient or even necessary since there are legitimate professional reasons for not joining such organizations that are independent of one's expertise. For each issue that a proffered expert is to address, the court must examine his or her specific training, experience, and knowledge. Thus, generic psychiatric or clinical psychological training, even with a rotation in forensics, does not an expert make, nor is someone who is qualified in the area of adult responsibility and competency evaluations an automatic expert on dangerousness or child abuse. In our experience, courts have been too liberal in their criteria for demarcating the limits of expertise and have been too willing to accept generic board certification and the like. Since the purpose of expert testimony is to aid the trier of fact by introducing, integrating, and explaining scientific evidence and expert observation, it is not unreasonable to ask a particular witness to demonstrate the depth and boundaries of his or her particular expertise during the voir dire.

A recent case in Champaign, Illinois will illustrate our point. The defendant, accused of murdering her children, pleaded not guilty by reason of insanity, alleging that she was psychotically depressed at the time. The prosecutor attempted to qualify Dr. Thomas Szasz as an expert witness. No one questioned Dr. Szasz's impressive training, experience, scholarship, or membership in a host of respected organizations. However, the public defender astutely cross-examined Dr. Szasz on critical points which he answered straightforwardly. Dr. Szasz stated, in essence, that he did not need to examine the defendant because mental illness was a myth and did not, in any case save perhaps brain disease, prevent a person from freely choosing to know that his or her act was criminal and to refrain from doing it. The defense argued that, despite Dr. Szasz's qualifications, he could not offer expert opinion because his belief was fixed and immutable, hence a dogma that was invariant over the various facts alleged in the case. Dr. Szasz was not permitted to testify.

Difficulties with Expert Testimony

Regrettably, many of the problems of expert testimony are failures of the legal system in interaction with the expert witnesses themselves. Defense attorneys, prosecutors, and judges alike frequently drop the ball and fail to carry out their critical roles in an effective manner. For example, one of the most egregious examples of expert opinion difficulties arose in context of predictions of dangerousness where the prosecution's psychiatrist was subject to perfunctory cross-examination and no defense witnesses were called (*Barefoot v. Estelle*, 1983). In *Barefoot*, no expert witnesses were called to rebut Dr. Grigson's claim that there was a "one hundred percent and absolute chance" that Barefoot would constitute a continuing threat to society, that on a 1 to 10 scale of sociopathy, Barefoot was "above a ten," and that his ability to predict such things was supported by the American Psychiatric Association! While the majority's opinion in upholding Barefoot's conviction has been the subject of scathing criticism, they were clearly correct when they concluded that evidence for the unreliability of such predictions could go to the weight of Dr. Grigson's testimony and that it was the responsibility of the defense counsel to present it. In fact, a great deal of heat, and not much light, has been generated around the issue of the proper limits of expert testimony and whether such expertise exists in the first place. While we will not review this controversy in detail, we wish to make the following conceptual and empirical observations:

1.   While the attack on unfounded, overreaching, and often ethically questionable expert testimony is well founded (see Bonnie & Slobogin, 1980; Melton et al., 1987; Morse, 1978a; Poythress, 1979; Roesch & Golding, 1980), many of the attacks appear to have other targets in mind (the insanity defense itself, judicial liberalism, and the death penalty, to name a few). Well trained and conscientious mental health professionals have always attempted to be punctiliously correct in the testimony they offer to the courts and have been at the forefront of attempts to reform standards of training and practice. Conflating many issues into single rhetorical attacks runs the grave risk of depriving mentally disordered defendants of their right, both moral and constitutional, to have a detailed analysis of their mental state presented to the jury when it is at issue as an element of the offense (for cases, see the preceding discussion of mens rea and *Ake v. Oklahoma*, 1985).

2.   Certain allegations about the misleading role of expert testimony are made in the absence of empirical data, and such scant data as are now available belie many of these allegations. For example, Morse (1978a, 1978b, 1982) has maintained that diagnostic labels and expert conclusory evidence mislead the trier of fact and have (our words not his) an almost mythical, hypnotic, and "totem-like" quality in mesmerizing the judge or jury. Recently, Congress was pursuaded by these arguments, among others, to reform the Federal Rules of Evidence, Rule 704 (Insanity Defense Reform Act, 1984) to bar an "expert witness testifying with respect to the

mental state or condition of a defendant . . . [from] . . . stat(ing) an opinion or inference as to whether the defendant did or did not have the mental state or condition constituting an element of the crime charged or of a defense thereto."

Empirically, however, courts have always jealously guarded "invasions of the province of the trier of fact," and alert judges have always chastised those who presume in their testimony to reach the "ultimate issue" (see especially Roesch & Golding, chapter 4, 1980, and references therein). Moreover, Roberts et al. (1986) have shown that potential jurors reach insanity decisions that accord with normative practice, even when the defendant's mental state is *simply described accurately in common English (as it should be) without diagnostic labels or conclusory testimony.* In a similar vein, Ewing, Levine, and Burns (1984) have shown that even conclusory evidence of future dangerousness only has an impact when it is unrebutted. Is this a problem with expertise or with the trier of fact (for allowing opinion on the ultimate issue for which no federal rule of evidence is necessary) or the defense counsel (for not rebutting it)? Clearly, unrebutted or conclusory testimony may be improper, but considerable fault lies elsewhere.

3.   Careful reading of the trials of notorious cases also makes it unclear whether the juries in such trials are so easily misled, although this is an important empirical question. When a prosecution psychiatrist is not rebutted (as in *Barefoot*) or a defense psychiatrist is not challenged for some outlandish defense (twinkies come to mind), it is not unreasonable to suppose that jurors will either assume that the lack of challenge has probative value, or will exercise their own good judgment in weighing the testimony. Evidence of the latter—in spite of media representation that the jury in the Hinckley case was unduly influenced by the experts—can be found in the testimony of some of the Hinckley jurors before the Senate Subcommittee on Criminal Law (Hearings, 1982). In this highly public context, a group of highly educated Senators, many with law degrees, tried to get the Hinckley jurors to agree that they were confused by the law, were inappropriately persuaded by the defense psychiatrists, and the like. The interchanges are priceless examples of honest citizens struggling to deal with their own implicit sense of morality and justice as opposed to the abstract concepts that are the stuff of Senate jargon:

SENATOR SPECTER: Did you feel that you had a reasonably clear understanding of what the law on insanity was?

MR. LASSITER: Yes, I thought I did.

SPECTER: What did you understand to be the meaning of the terms mental disease or defect?

LASSITER: Well, I understood it to be some kind of problem that he had, not exactly insane but a thing just something that was bothering him that he could not control.

SPECTER: What did you understand by language like lack substantial capacity?

LASSITER: I think that he was able to know what he was doing at the time. I think at that specific time that he didn't.

SPECTER: Able to know what he was doing.

LASSITER: Able not to know.

SPECTER: You say not to know.

LASSITER: Right.

SPECTER: And did you conclude that he was not able to know what he was doing at the time he did it?

LASSITER: At that particular time.

SPECTER: You think he did not know—

LASSITER: Did not.

SPECTER: —what he was doing.

LASSITER: Right.

SENATOR ZORINSKY: Do you think there is any merit of an objective panel of psychiatrists coming into the courtroom and talking to the jury and the judge as to their observations rather than being—well the word has been used—hired guns of the prosecution or the defense? In your mind, would it have more impact if they were as a panel relating neither to the defense or prosecution but being hired by the court to give their comments as to their observations of Mr. Hinckley's well being?

LASSITER: Well, either way, I can't see where there would be any difference. Like I know that the defense had their psychiatrists; so did the prosecution. So, I know that both of them are going to try to influence us that they are right. So, I didn't pay it any mind. I just heard both sides and then took into my own consideration of what—

ZORINSKY: Would you have felt more comfortable if you did not have to continually use the screening process that they are saying that because they are hired by that side and this one is saying that because he is hired by that side?

LASSITER: I do not think so, no.

—with another witness—

ZORINSKY: Ms. Brown, were you offended in any way that there were hired psychiatrists on one side and on the other side debating the issue as opposed to an impartial panel that would just come in and report on their observations?

MS. BROWN: Well, a couple of the psychiatrists, they would start out, OK, you could kind of understand what they were saying. But then they would go into a long lecture or go into all these terms. It really got lost. I did. By the time they get through telling you what it is all about, you have forgotten what the question was. We had a few that really were more pinned up on themselves and you forget the question. So it was kind of hard. Some of them would break it down and stay down, you know. They would not go off into these long journeys or something you don't even understand.

These glimpses into the mind of the jury aren't proof, of course, but they are highly suggestive that one needs to consider seriously whether or not our presumption that lay jurors are so easily fooled doesn't come simply from professional arrogance.

4.   Allegations about the limits of expertise (e.g., Morse, 1978b) are often part truths that distort the value of competent expert testimony. Along with others (Bonnie, 1984; Bonnie & Slobogin, 1980; Melton et al., 1987) we agree most strongly that the ultimate question of moral exculpation inherent in the insanity defense is a social and moral decision to be made by triers of fact who are representatives of the society on the basis of "deep-lying ethico-psychological concepts" (Sayre, 1932, p. 989). "The standard by which sanity is to be tried is the common sense of humanity, and not the opinion of a few scientific men" (Reynolds, 1856, cited in Smith, 1981, p. 77). But when Morse states that "professionals have considerably less to contribute than is commonly supposed" and that "for legal purposes, lay persons are quite competent to make judgments concerning mental disorder" (Morse, 1978b, p. 392), we believe he overstates the case in a most serious, and potentially destructive manner. Obviously, no trier of fact needs expert assistance in cases involving the "furiously insane" or those that are "squeezing lemons." Such cases, however, are rare and are not the basis for good law or forensic practice.

While we are paying the price for decades of exaggerated claims of expertise, it is simply erroneous to view the mental health professions as having made no contributions to the careful delineation, assessment, and conceptualization of the cognitive, affective, and behavioral consequences of various forms of mental disorder. We do not mean to minimize the many methodological and conceptual problems with such a data base, but one needs to inquire as to whether any pragmatically useful scientific data base could survive the type of admissibility threshold implied in Morse's arguments (see, generally, Giannelli, 1980, for a review of the problem of admissibility). A defendant, whose mental state at the time of the offense is at issue, has the right to expect that the best currently available scientific evidence of the nature of the mental state will be adduced at trial. We agree that the limits of expertise in any fact situation are appropriate topics for cross-examination and rebuttal, but global excision of such testimony from the adjudication process is simply atavistic.

5.   The national shift toward reforming the insanity defense is resulting in a concentration of attention to the other end of the problem—namely the question of appropriate modes of sentencing, disposition, treatment, and release for those found either not guilty by reason of insanity or guilty but mentally ill. This shift has begun to raise issues about treatment and the prediction of dangerousness in particular populations that we are ill equipped to address (Golding, 1983). Because treatment, release, and prediction schemes depend heavily on the resources provided and the quality of follow-through and supervision, forensic examiners can be expected to be pulled into yet another societal maelstrom.

Thesis: To protect the rights of a defendant and to improve the quality of the decision making, all forensic interviews and raw test data should be recorded, preferably by videotape.

This is a controversial issue, but we believe the argument for recording the interviews has the upper hand. Approximately 40 percent of all insanity pleaders are found unfit for trial (Criss & Racine, 1980; Golding, 1983; Petrila, 1982) and are treated, primarily with psychotropic medication, until their (predominantly) psychotic symptomatology remits. Conservatively estimated, another 30 percent may receive treatment while in jail awaiting trial. It is therefore extremely likely that a defendant who pleads not guilty by reason of insanity comes to trial disadvantaged in several obvious ways. First, if unfit for trial, an extensive sanity evaluation is unlikely to have taken place, and no relatively neutral record of his or her pretreatment behavioral, perceptual, cognitive, affective, and judgmental capacities at the time of the offense will exist. Second, the defendant may have changed dramatically by the time of the insanity evaluation, especially if medicated. Third, medicated or not, if the defendant was in a disturbed state at the time and in a different state later, he or she will have difficulty recalling or describing the relevant mental state during a subsequent interview. Fourth, the defendant, many months later, has a difficult time convincing a judge or jury of a mental state, especially given the strong societal suspicion of malingering and the defendant's current adequate interpersonal presentation (if fit, the defendant is likely to appear in court looking like anyone else; there will be no overt symptoms of agitation, psychotic anxiety, behaving-as-if-hallucinating, and the like). Finally, in the interest of justice (for both the defense and prosecution), no record would normally exist of the objective data upon which the forensic examiner based his or her inferences. Recording interviews removes the disadvantage of cross-examining an expert who is not only in control of the expertise but also of the data to which that expertise is applied. Thus, in medical forensics a pathologist would testify ordinarily as to the meaning of a certain pattern of blood stains but would not be the only one who saw them!

This latter problem is illustrated forcefully in *United States v. Byers* (1984). Byers was indicted for the murder of his lover. Immediately after his arraignment, he was examined at St. Elizabeth's in Washington, D.C. by a team of psychologists and psychiatrists who found him competent but suffering from paranoid delusions such that "he most likely or probably lacked the substantial capacity to appreciate the wrongfulness of his conduct" (p. 1143, n. 21). The hesitancy stemmed, apparently, from concern over the nature of these delusions (the belief that his lover was "working roots" on him) and the fact that they were situational in nature and in remission at the time of examination.

The prosecutor sought a reexamination at the federal medical facility in Springfield, Missouri. There he was examined primarily by Dr. E. Varhely, a psychologist, and Dr. N. Kunev, a psychiatrist. Varhely conducted numerous interviews and tests and concluded that Byers was sane, although suffering from "magical thinking" not "paranoid delusions" (which did not rise to the prerequisite level of mental illness). Varhely also indicated that while Byers was not malingering, there was evidence in his MMPI profile that Byers was exaggerating but not to a level to invalidate the test (an elevated F-K index?). Kunev, who examined Byers *once*, wrote a report to the trial court which was in substantial agreement with Varhely's opinion. At trial, however, Kunev testified that during his interview Byers had told him, in response to questions about what his reasons were for the shooting, that "Mrs. Byers suggested to him that this could be under the influence of some magic, or spells or some influence of roots" (p. 1143). As might be expected, all hell broke loose at trial since the statement, if true and not distorted out of context, implied that Byer's delusions had been suggested to him by his wife. The trial court characterized the testimony as "devastating" and such that it "perhaps will torpedo the [defendant] out of the water" (p. 1144).

Kunev, unfortunately, had (1) destroyed his notes of the interview; (2) admitted that he did not record the statement in the destroyed notes because he considered it insignificant; (3) did not tell any of his colleagues of the alleged statement; and (4) did not allude to it or any aspect of malingering in his report to the court. Byers was indeed torpedoed by the testimony and was unsuccessful in his attempt on appeal to have his conviction set aside on the grounds that admitting Kunev's testimony violated his fifth amendment privilege against self-incrimination and his sixth amendment right to effective assistance to counsel. A strongly divided court ruled that Byers' statements to Kunev were admissible and did not violate his right to avoid self-incrimination as had been the case in *Estelle v. Smith*, 1981. The court distinguished *Estelle* by arguing that Byers had himself interposed the insanity defense; whereas Smith had not raised either competency or sanity and had been required by the court to submit to an examination to evaluate competency only, and the psychiatrist had later testified at the death-penalty phase of the proceedings based on his competency interview. Quoting *Estelle*:

A criminal defendant, who neither initiates a psychiatric examination nor attempts to introduce any psychiatric evidence, may not be compelled to respond to a psychiatrist if his statements can be used against him at a capital sentencing proceeding. (p. 468)

Nor was the interview of Smith analogous to a sanity evaluation occasioned by defendant's plea of not guilty by reason of insanity at the time of his offense. When a defendant asserts the insanity defense and introduces supporting psychiatric testimony, his silence may deprive the State of the only effective means it has of controverting his proof on an issue that he interjected into the case. Accordingly, several Courts of Appeal have held that, under such circumstances, a defendant can be required to submit to a sanity evaluation conducted by a prosecution's psychiatrist (p. 465).

Similarly, the court rejected Byers' claim that he had been deprived of effective assistance of counsel at the psychiatric interview, relying on the Supreme Court's current test for sixth amendment applicability—namely, that the defendant, to be constitutionally deprived of effective assistance, must be "confronted, just as at trial, by the procedural system or by his expert adversary, or by both" (*United States v. Ash*, 1973, p. 310). Thus, the court argued that there is no constitutional grounding for the requirement of presence of an attorney at forensic examinations: "It is enough that Byers had the opportunity to contest the accuracy of both the details and the conclusion of Kunev's analysis by cross examining him (pointing out, as he did, that the crucial statement on which Kunev based his conclusion was not reflected in the psychiatrist's summary of the interview)" (*Byers*, p. 1121). Interestingly, however, the court, while sticking to its guns, concluded, "Recording psychiatric interviews may be a good idea, but not all good ideas have been embodied in the Constitution in general or in the Sixth Amendment in particular" (*Byers*, p. 1121).

Indeed, it may be folly for the forensic profession to look to the courts for the impetus to reform forensic practice. Whether or not Judge Bazelon, in his strongly worded dissent is right as to the law, he is clearly right as to his review of the social science data on clinical interviews which he uses to conclude the following:

> If defense counsel had an accurate, complete record of the clinical interview he could, with the aid of his own experts, attempt to identify the distortions and interactions that may have affected the substance of the interviewer's reports and testimony. But such a complete, accurate record cannot, by virtue of the very effects I have described, be expected to be forthcoming from the interviewer. The accused, moreover, whatever his mental state, cannot be relied upon to fill in the gaps necessary for a complete and accurate assessment. It is therefore clear that . . . counsel may be unable to detect distortions or to cross-examine meaningfully the government's expert and rebut his conclusions . . . A complete tape recording or videotape of the interview would provide counsel with exactly the sort of objective and precise record that, as I have previously discussed, is often a prerequisite to detection of distortions and to effective cross-examination or rebuttal at trial. As discussed above, such a taped record would facilitate constitutional aims without impairing the interview process itself. (*Byers*, pp. 1171–1172)

Videotaping, however, may produce unforeseen problems. In *State v. Milo* (1982), defendant Milo introduced evidence of his mental state by means of a videotape between himself and a psychiatrist. The prosecution did not seek to have Milo examined but argued that his evidence was not obtained under oath and that he was not subject to cross-examination. Milo was convicted and appealed to the Supreme Court (*Milo v. Ohio*, 1982) on the grounds that he was subject to the prosecutor's adverse comments on his failure to testify.

Although this is an unusual situation (because no one examined Milo for the prosecution), it does highlight the need to exercise caution in anticipating unforeseen consequences. Obviously, there is a distinction between introducing the data on which a forensic examiner bases his or her inferences and "sneaking in" testimony not subject to cross examination. Would the prosecutor have been permitted to make such an argument to the jury if both sides had conducted and presented vieotaped forensic interviews? We think not. Videotaped interviews may also present a problem in those states that would allow indirect evidence obtained as a consequence of information in the interview to be used to develop leads to evidence for use in the guilt phase. In a pretrial examination conducted before a defendant has pleaded not guilty by reason of insanity, it is therefore necessary to use extreme caution and to be well informed of local practice.

CONCLUDING COMMENTS

In this chapter we have attempted to provide a broad overview of the insanity defense and numerous empirical, conceptual, and ethical aspects of this area of forensic practice that professionals are likely to confront. We have been forced to be selective and would therefore advise the reader to pursue many of the excellent empirical and conceptual works cited to gain further depth. Because the underlying logic and history of the insanity defense occupies a central role in our understanding of psychopathology and in our sense of justice, the controversy which surrounds it can be expected to continue as it has for centuries. We hope, however, that a deeper appreciation of the complex issues will allow forensic practitioners, scholars, and researchers alike to continue to build a knowledge base that will increase the quality of the social-moral decision making that is at the heart of the insanity defense.

REFERENCES

Ake v. Oklahoma, 105 S.Ct. 1087 (1985).

American Bar Association. (1983). *Recommendations on the insanity defense*. Washington, DC: Author.

American Law Institute. (1962). *Model penal code*. Philadelphia: Author.

American Psychiatric Association. (1982). *Statement on the insanity defense*. Washington, DC: Author.

Andreasen, N. C. (1979*a*). Thought, language, and communication disorders—I: Clinical assessment, definition of terms and evaluation of their reliability. *Archives of General Psychiatry*, 36, 1315–1321.

Andreasen, N. C. (1979*b*). Thought, language, and communication disorders—II: Diagnostic significance. *Archives of General Psychiatry*, 36, 1325–1330.

Ballantine, H. W. (1919). Criminal responsibility of the insane and feeble-minded. *Journal of the American Institute of Criminal Law and Criminology, 9*, 485–499.

Barefoot v. Estelle, 463 U.S. 880 (1983).

Beasley, W. R. (1983). An overview of Michigan's guilty but mentally ill verdict. *Michigan Bar Journal, 62*, 204–205; 215–217.

Bellak, L., Hurvich, M., & Gediman, H. K. (1973). *Ego functions in schizophrenics, neurotics and normals: A systematic study of conceptual, diagnostic, and therapeutic aspects*. New York: Wiley.

Black, H. C. (1979). *Black's Law Dictionary (5th ed.)*. St. Paul, MN: West.

Blashfield, R. K. (1984). *The classification of psychopathology: Neo-Kraepelian and quantitative approaches*. New York: Plenum.

Bonnie, R. J. (1983). The moral basis of the insanity defense. *American Bar Association Journal, 69*, 194–197.

Bonnie, R. J. (1984). Morality, equality, and expertise: Renegotiating the relationship between psychiatry and the criminal law. *Bulletin of the American Academy of Psychiatry & Law, 12*, 5–20.

Bonnie, R. J., & Slobogin, C. (1980). The role of mental health professionals in the criminal process: The case for informed speculation. *Virginia Law Review, 66*, 427–522.

Braff, J., Arvanities, T., & Steadman, H. (1983). Detention patterns of successful and unsuccessful insanity defendants. *Criminology, 21*, 439–449.

Bratty v. Attorney-General of Northern Ireland, 3 A11 E.R. 523 (1961).

Commonwealth v. Rogers, 7 Metc.(Mass.) 500 (1844).

Cooke, G., & Sikorski, C. (1974). Factors affecting length of hospitalization in prisoners adjudicated not guilty by reason of insanity. *Bulletin of the American Academy of Psychiatry & Law, 2,* 251–261.

Cooper v. The Queen, 1 S.C.R. 1149, (Supreme Court of Canada, 1980).

Criminal Appeal Act, 7 Edw., c. 23 (1907).

Criminal Appeal Act, Great Britain Statutes in Force (1968).

Criminal Lunatics Act, 40 Geo. III, c. 94 (1800).

Criminal Procedure (Insanity) Act, 12 & 13 Eliz. II, c. 84 (1964).

Criss, M. L., & Racine, D. R. (1980). Impact and change in legal standard for those adjudicated not guilty by reason of insanity 1975–1979. *Bulletin of the American Academy of Psychiatry & Law, 8,* 261–271.

Crotty, H. D. (1924). The history of insanity as a defence to crime in English criminal law. *California Law Review, 12,* 105–123.

Durham v. United States, 214 F.2d 862 (D.C. Cir., 1954).

Dusky v. United States, 362 U.S. 402 (1960).

Estelle v. Smith, 451 U.S. 454 (1981).

Federal Rules of Criminal Procedure, 12.2(c) (1985).

Ewing, C.P., Levine, M., & Burns, T.F. (1984). Dangerousness and the adversary process in capital sentencing. Paper presented at the American Psychological Association, Toronto.

Felstead v. Director of Public Prosecutions, 111 L. T. 218 (House of Lords, 1914).

Frendak v. United States, 408 A.2d 364 (D.C. Court of Appeals, 1979).

Fukunaga, K., Pasewark, R., Hawkins, M., & Gudeman, H. (1981). Insanity plea: Interexaminer agreement and concordance of psychiatric opinion and court verdict. *Law & Human Behavior, 5,* 325–328.

Giannelli, P. C. (1980). The admissibility of novel scientific evidence: Frye V. United States, a half-century later. *Columbia Law Review, 80,* 1197–1250.

Golding, S. L. (1983, October). *The assessment, treatment, and community outcome of defendants found not guilty by reason of insanity.* Paper presented at the meeting of the American Psychology-Law Society, Chicago.

Golding, S. L. (1984, August). *The insanity defense in historical, moral, and empirical perspectives.* Paper presented at the Continuing Education Workshop on Criminal Justice–Mental Health Standards and Insanity Defense Issues, American Psychological Association, Toronto.

Golding, S. L., Roesch, R., & Schreiber, J. (1984). Assessment and conceptualization of competency to stand trial: Preliminary data on the Interdisciplinary Fitness Interview. *Law & Human Behavior, 8,* 321–334.

Goldstein, A. S. (1967). *The insanity defense.* New Haven, CT: Yale University Press.

Gray, S. (1972). The insanity defense: Historical development and contemporary relevance. *American Criminal Law Review, 10,* 559–583.

Greenland, C. (1979). Crime and the insanity defense. An international comparison: Ontario and New York State. *Bulletin of the American Academy of Psychiatry and the Law, 7,* 125–138.

Guy, W. A. (1869). On insanity and crime; and on the plea of insanity in criminal cases. *Journal of the Royal Statistical Society, 32(Series A),* 159–191.

Hans, V. P., & Slater, D. (1983). John Hinckley, Jr. and the insanity defense: The public's verdict. *Public Opinion Quarterly, 47*, 202–212.

Hart, H. L. A. (1968). *Punishment and responsibility: Essays in the philosophy of law*. New York: Oxford University Press.

Hearings before the Subcommittee on Criminal Law of the Committee on the Judiciary. (1982). *Limiting the insanity defense*. Washington, DC: Committee on the Judiciary (Serial No. J-97-122, Ninety-Seventh Congress).

Helzer, J. E, (1983). Standardized interviews in psychiatry. *Psychiatric Developments, 2*, 161–178.

Hermann, D. H. J. (1983). *The insanity defense: Philosdphical, historical, and legal perspectives*. Springfield, IL: C. C. Thomas.

Hogan, D. B. (1979). *The regulation of psychotherapists: Vol. 1. A study in the philosophy and practice of professional regulation*. Cambridge, MA: Ballinger.

Hogan, D. B. (1983). The effectiveness of licensing: History, evidence and recommendations. *Law and Human Behavior, 7*, 117–138.

Idaho Code Annotated, section 18-207(a), (1982).

Illinois Revised Statutes, Chapter 38, sections 6-2, 115-1 to 115-4, and 115-6 (1983).

In re Winship, 397 U.S. 358 (1970).

Insanity Defense Reform Act of 1984, Public Law 98-473, sections 401–406 (1984).

Jenkins v. United States, 307 F.2d 637 (D.C. Court of Appeals, 1962).

Jones v. United States, 103 S.Ct. 3043 (1983).

Keedy, E. R. (1917). Insanity and criminal responsibility. *Harvard Law Review, 30*, 535–560, 724–738.

Keedy, E. R. (1920). Criminal responsibility of the insane—A reply to Professor Ballantine. *Journal of American Institute of Criminal Law and Criminology, 10*, 14–34.

Keilitz, I., & Fulton, J. P. (1983). *The insanity defense and its alternatives: A guide for policymakers*. Williamsburg, VA: National Center for State Courts.

LaFave, W., & Scott, A. (1972). *Handbook on criminal law*. St. Paul, MN: West Publishing.

Leland v. Oregon, 343 U.S. 790 (1952).

Livermore, J. M., & Meehl, P. E. (1967). The virtues of M'Naghten. *Minnesota Law Review, 51*, 789–856.

Louisell, D. W. (1955). The psychologist in today's legal world. *Minnesota Law Review, 39*, 235–272.

Lynch v. Overholser, 369 U.S. 705 (1963).

McGraw, B. D., Farthing-Capowich, D., & Keilitz, I. (1985). The "guilty but mentally ill" plea and verdict: Current state of the knowledge. *Villanova Law Review, 30*, 117–191.

Melton, G., Petrila, J., Poythress, N. G., & Slobogin, C. (1987). *Psychological evaluations for the courts: A handbook for mental health professionals and lawyers*. New York: Guilford.

Michigan Compiled Laws Annotated, section 330.1400a, (1982).

Milo v. Ohio, *cert. denied*, 51 U.S.L.W. 3857 (1982).

M'Naghten's Case, 8 Eng. Rep. 718 (1843).

Montana Code Annotated, section 45-2-103, (1983).

Montano v. State, 468 N.E. 2d 1042 (Supreme Court of Indiana, 1984).

Morissette v. United States, 342 U. S. 246 (1952).

Morris, N. (1982). *Madness and the criminal law*. Chicago: University of Chicago Press.

Morse, S. J. (1978a). Crazy behavior, morals, and science: An analysis of mental health law. *Southern California Law Review, 51*, 527–654.

Morse, S. J. (1978b). Law and mental health professionals: The limits of expertise. *Professional Psychology, 9*, 389–399.

Morse, S. J. (1982). Failed explanations and criminal n responsibility: Experts and the unconscious. *Virginia Law Review, 68*, 971–1084.

Morse, S. J. (1985). Excusing the crazy: The insanity defense reconsidered. *Southern California Law Review, 58*, 777–836.

Morse, S. J. (1986). Psychology, determinism and legal responsibility. In G. B. Melton (Ed.), *Nebraska symposium on motivation: Vol. 33. The law as a behavioral instrument* (pp. 35–85). Lincoln, NE: University of Nebraska Press.

Mullaney v. Wilbur, 421 U.S. 684 (1975).

Oppenheimer, H. (1909). *The criminal responsibility of lunatics: A study in comparative law*. London: Sweet and Maxwell.

Pantle, M., Pasewark, R., & Steadman, H. (1980). Comparing institutionalization periods and subsequent arrests of insanity acquittees and convicted felons. *Journal of Psychiatry and Law, 8*, 305–316.

Parsons v. State, 81 Ala. 577, 2 So. 854 (1866).

Pasewark, R. A. (1982). Insanity plea: A review of the research literature. *Journal of Psychiatry and Law, 9*, 357–401.

Patterson v. New York, 432 U.S. 197 (1977).

People v. DeWit, 463 N.E.2d 742 (Illinois Court of Appeals, 1984).

People v. McLeod, 288 N.W.2d 909 (Mich. 1980).

People v. McQuillan, 221 N.W.2d 569 (Mich. 1974).

People v. Rone, 311 N.W.2d 835 (Mich. 1981).

Perlin, M. C. (1980). The legal status of the psychologist in the courtroom. *Mental Disabilities Law Reporter, 4*, 194–200.

Petrella, R. C., & Poythress, N. G. (1983). The quality of forensic evaluations: An interdisciplinary study. *Journal of Consulting and Clinical Psychology, 51*, 76–85.

Petrila, J. (1982). The insanity defense and other mental health dispositions in Missouri. *International Journal of Law and Psychiatry, 5*, 81–101.

Pfohl, B., Stangl, D. & Zimmerman, M. (1984). *Structured interview of the DSM-III personality disorders*. Iowa City, IA: Department of Psychiatry, University of Iowa.

Platt, A. M., & Diamond, B. L. (1965). The origins and development of the "wild beast" concept of mental illness and its relation to theories of criminal responsibility. *Journal of the History of the Behavioral Sciences, 1*, 355–367.

Platt, A. M., & Diamond, B. L. (1966). The origins of the "right and wrong" test of criminal responsibility and its subsequent development in the United States: An historical survey. *California Law Review, 54*, 1227–1259.

Pogrebin, M., Regoli, R., & Perry, K. (1986). Not guilty by reason of insanity: A research note. *International Journal of Law and Psychiatry, 8*, 237–241.

Pollock, F., & Maitland, F. (1952). *History of English law: Vol. I (2nd ed.).* Cambridge: Cambridge University Press.

Poythress, N. G. (1978). Psychiatric expertise in civil commitment: Training attorneys to cope with expert testimony. *Law and Human Behavior, 2,* 1–23.

Poythress, N. G. (1979). A proposal for training in forensic psychology. *American Psychologist, 34,* 612–621.

R. v. Ireland, 1 K.B. 654 (Court of Criminal Appeal, 1910).

Ray, Isaac (1962). *A treatise on the medical jurisprudence on insanity.* Cambridge, MA: Belknap Press (Harvard University). (Originally published 1838)

Regina v. Barnier, 1 S.C.R. 1124 (Supreme Court of Canada, 1980).

Regina v. Duke, 3 All E R 737 (Court of Criminal Appeal, 1961).

Regina v. Simpson, 35 C.C.C. 2d. 337 (1977).

Regina v. Sullivan, 2 All E R 673 (House of Lords, 1983).

Rivera v. Delaware, 429 U.S. 877 (1976).

Roberts, C., & Golding, S. L. (1984, August). *Insanity, responsibility, and the morality of "guilty but mentally ill."* Paper presented at the American Psychological Association, Toronto.

Roberts, C., Golding, S. L., & Fincham F. (1986). *Decision-making and the insanity defense: Implicit theories of responsibility.* Manuscript submitted for publication.

Robins, L. N., Helzer, J. E., Croughan, J., & Ratcliff, K. S. (1981). National Institute of Health interview schedule. *Archives of General Psychiatry, 38,* 381–389.

Rogers, J. L., Bloom, J. D., & Manson, S. M. (1984). Insanity defenses: Contested or conceded? *American Journal of Psychiatry, 141,* 885–888.

Rogers, R., & Cavanaugh, J. L. (1981). Rogers criminal responsibility assessment scales. *Illinois Medical Journal, 160,* 164–169.

Rogers, R., Cavanaugh, J. L., Seman, W., & Harris, M. (1984). Legal outcome and clinical findings: A study of insanity evaluations. *Bulletin of the American Academy of Psychiatry and the Law, 12,* 75–83.

Rogers, R., Dolmetsch, R., Wasyliw, O. E., & Cavanaugh, J. L. (1982). Scientific inquiry in forensic psychiatry. *International Journal of Law and Psychiatry, 5,* 187–203.

Rogers, R., Wasyliw, O. E., & Cavanaugh, J. L. (1984). Evaluating insanity: A study of construct validity. *Law and Human Behavior, 8,* 293–304.

Rosenberg, C. E. (1968). *The trial of the assassin Guiteau: Psychiatry and law in the gilded age.* Chicago: University of Chicago Press.

Sayre, F. B. (1932). Mens rea. *Harvard Law Review, 45,* 974–1026.

Schwartz v. The Queen, 1 S.C.R. 673 (Supreme Court of Canada, 1977).

Sieling v. Eyman, 478 F.2d 211 (9th Cir. 1973).

Slobogin, C., Melton, G. B., & Showalter, C. R. (1984). The feasibility of a brief evaluation of mental state at the time of offense. *Law and Human Behavior, 8,* 305–321.

Smith, R. (1981). *Trial by medicine: Insanity and responsibility in Victorian trials.* Edinburgh: University of Edinburgh Press.

Smith, G.A., & Hall, J.A. (1982). Evaluating Michigan's guilty but mentally ill verdict: An empirical study. *Michigan Journal of Law Reform, 16,* 75–112.

Spitzer, R. L., & Endicott, J. (1977). *Schedule for affective disorders and schizophrenia.* New York: N.Y. State Psychiatric Institute.

State v. Johnson, 399 A. 2d 469 (Supreme Court of Rhode Island, 1979).

State v. Korell, 690 P. 2d 992 (Supreme Court of Montana, 1984).

State v. Milo, 451 N.E. 2d 1253 (Ohio App. 3d, 1982).

State v. Pike, 49 N.H. 399 (1869).

State v. Strasburg, 110 P. 1020 (Supreme Court of Washington, 1910).

Steadman, H. J., Keitner, L., Braff, J., & Arvanities, M. A. (1983). Factors associated with a successful insanity plea. *American Journal of Psychiatry, 140,* 401–405.

Stock, H. V., & Poythress, N. G. (1979, August). *Psychologists' opinions on competency and sanity: How reliable?* Paper presented at the American Psychological Association, New York.

Stroud, D. A. (1914). *Mens rea or imputability under the laws of England.* London: Sweet & Maxwell.

Taylor v. State, 440 N.E.2d 1109 (Mich. 1982).

Text of position on insanity defense. (1984, March). *APA Monitor.* p. 11.

Thompson, J. R. (1982). Introduction. *Toledo University Law Review, 13,* iii–iv.

Townsend, W. C. (1850a). The trial of Daniel M'Naughton for the murder of Mr. Drummond. In *Modern state trials: vol. 1* (pp. 326–411). London: Longman, Brown, Green, and Longmans.

Townsend, W. C. (1850b). The trial of Edward Oxford for high treason. In *Modern state trials: Vol. 1* (pp. 110–150). London: Longman, Brown, Green, and Longmans.

Trial of Lunatics Act, 46 & 47 Vict., c. 38 (1883).

Trial of Maclean. (1882, April 20). *London Times,* p. 11.

Underwood v. State, 32 Mich. 1 (Mich. 1873).

United States v. Ash, 413 U.S. 300 (1973).

United States v. Brawner, 471 F.2d 969 (D.C. Cir. 1972).

United States v. Byers, 740 F.2d 1104 (D.C. Cir. 1984), *cert. denied,* 104 S. Ct. 717.

United States v. Lyons, 731 F.2d 243 (5th Cir. 1984a).

United States v. Lyons, 739 F.2d 994 (5th Cir. 1984b).

United States v. Robertson, 507 F.2d 1148 (D.C. Cir. 1974).

United States v. Torniero, 735 F.2d 725 (2nd Cir. 1984).

U.S.,moves to curb insanity defense. (1982, July, 20). *New York Times,* p. A18, col.3.

Utah Code Annotated, section 76-2-305(1), (1983).

Wales, H. W. (1976). An analysis of the proposal to "abolish" the insanity defense in S. 1: Squeezing a lemon. *University of Pennsylvania Law Review, 124,* 687–712.

Walker, N. (1978). *Crime and insanity in England: Vol. 1. The historical perspective.* Edinburgh: University of Edinburgh Press.

Whalem v. United States, 346 F.2d 812 (D.C. Cir. 1965).

Wing, J. K., Cooper, J. E., & Satorius, N. (1974). *Measurement and classification of psychiatric symptoms.* Cambridge, MA: Cambridge University Press.

CHAPTER 16

Consulting with Police

MARTIN REISER and NELS KLYVER

This chapter provides an overview of some key areas and critical issues in the specialty of police psychology. Our intent is to convey something of the broad scope of police consultation activities and to focus on particular problems and approaches when psychologists work with police. Concise sections on consultation, selection, hostage negotiation, stress, counseling, and training are presented with references to additional material for those wishing a more detailed discussion of particular topics (Reiser, 1971, 1976b, 1979; Brodsky, 1972; Cohen, 1976; Mann, 1973).

In addition to selection, training, therapy and research, the police consultant can be involved in organizational diagnosis and development issues (Levinson, 1972; Cummings, 1980). The consultant may be called on to do survey or questionnaire research to tap the state of the department's health and to make recommendations for problem solving. Generic conflicts between the traditional military-style hierarchy and the current movement toward participative management will likely surface in many symptomatic guises. Notable examples are the street cop versus the brass syndrome, poor upward communications among rank levels, and an emphasis on negative discipline (Reiser, 1979). Communications barriers in bureaucratic organizations are also perennial problems often linked to system-generated stresses (Reiser, 1974a).

When psychologists work with police, some common consultant problems have been identified and need to be considered before effective work can be done. One difficulty has been mutual hostility. Feelings of suspicion and distrust have accompanied the stereotypes on both sides of the police-psychologist interface. Changing these negative percepts requires openness and sensitivity, especially on the part of the psychologist (Reiser, 1970). All too often, potential consultants approach police administrators like professors talking down to college freshmen (Hodges, 1970; Kirkham, 1976). An attitude of humility and the willingness to listen are useful traits at the beginning of the police relationship (Backer, 1983).

What kinds of training and experience are useful for a psychologist to be effective in the police environment? Ideally, training in clinical, organizational, educational, and research psychology would be desirable. Experience in teaching, program development, organizational consultation, counseling and therapy, research design, and implementation would also be helpful. In addition, the ability to work objectively and autonomously in a quasimilitary structure with all of the attendant bureaucratic frustrations is important (Reiser, 1971). A ubiquitous problem the police psychologist faces is the slowness of change in bureaucratic institutions. Police consultants need to be patient and open-minded if they are to hang in for the long run and develop the opportunity to make a meaningful contribution. After all, change is inevitable, and there are indicators in the police milieu, as in other organizations, of movement toward human resources development, participative management, wellness and employee assistance programs, and planning for the future using a systems viewpoint (Nash, 1983; Walsh, 1983).

Another question is whether the psychologist is better off working as a contract consultant or as a staff member of the department. The advantages and limitations of the in-house consultant versus the outside professional have been discussed elsewhere (Elkins & Papanek, 1966; Reiser, 1972). In either case, it is important that the consultant be connected at the highest level possible in the police organization, preferably with the chief of police (Eisenberg, 1975). This can provide the necessary support and power to effect recommendations involving change and innovation. There is a tendency for consultants plugged-in at lower levels to get pigeonholed.

The police consultant may get involved in primary as well as secondary prevention programs (Caplan, 1970). These can range from inoculation talks about the John Wayne Syndrome and the role of the police officer as social scientist (Singer, 1970; Reiser, 1973) to stress management training (Reiser, 1982b). There may also be direct treatment of officers, families, and civilian employees for a wide variety of personal, family, or job-related problems (Reiser, 1972). In this area, privileged communication and the limits of confidentiality are critical considerations (Mann, 1973).

Confidentiality is an especially important issue in police organizations when therapy, assessment, and research are undertaken (Reiser, 1973). At the Los Angeles Police Department (LAPD), a two-track referral system has been operating successfully for over 16 years. Self-referrals are confidential within the same legal constraints for any state-licensed psychologist. Through-channels referrals for job-related questions such as officer dangerousness or victimization (Reiser, 1984) are not confidential, and all parties are so informed up front. Feedback to the referring manager, however, is usually by telephone and is limited to job-related rather than personal issues to avoid misuse and outdating of written reports.

If possible, the consultant should maintain offices outside of a police facility for assessment and therapy work. This would increase the utilization of services by officers who might otherwise fear being seen by supervisors or peers while visiting the "shrink's" office. In this connection it is also useful to have the department include outpatient mental health and inpatient alcohol and drug treatment as part of the officers' health insurance coverage.

The consultant quickly becomes aware of the male fraternal values which exert a powerful influence throughout the organization (Niederhoffer, 1969). Females tend to be denigrated and perceived as interlopers in a male-dominated preserve (Glaser & Saxe, 1982). Because of lawsuits requiring female and minority-male parity, and the movement toward more open systems, the consultant will likely have an opportunity to address the issues of females in police work, minority representation, and the slowly changing nature of the organizational structure (Reiser & Klyver, 1982).

Another somewhat unique area of involvement for psychologists is crime-related consultation (Reiser, 1982a). There may be requests for a profile of a suspect in a bizarre murder case, evaluation of written material threatening harm to a notable person in the community, assessment of the feasibility of a polygraph for a disturbed suspect, or hypnosis with a traumatized rape victim who has repressed important investigative leads.

Psychological profiling is an impresice art consisting of case evidence, probability data from similar cases, psychological information about the victim and possible suspect, possible unconscious as well as conscious motivations, and the meaning of available symbolic communications, including mutilations or ritualistic markings (Geberth, 1981). As in psychodiagnostic assessment, the raw data are combined with inference, and speculative possibilities emerge (Ault & Reese, 1980). The profile does not zero in on a particular person, but merely yields general parameters which may provide an investigative focus and narrow the search populations (Campbell, 1976).

Investigative hypnosis has been used at LAPD since 1975 only in selected major crimes. It has aided in providing additional leads in more than three-fourths of the cases attempted (Reiser, 1980). Of the new data obtained in approximately 700 cases, slightly less than half could be checked independently. This follow-up yielded a corroboration rate around 80 percent in those instances.

Beginning in 1977, controversy has developed over the police use of investigative hypnosis. Critics have attempted to discredit the use of this tool by questioning police motivations and trustworthiness and by arguing that hypnotizing witnesses alters their cognitive functions, interferes with memory, and renders the witness impervious to cross-examination (Diamond, 1980; Orne, 1979). These and related issues have been discussed in detail elsewhere (Reiser, 1984; see Chapter 18 on hypnosis in this volume).

In January 1974 a homicide case led to some interesting results. The only witness acknowledged being extremely intoxicated at the time of her male friend's murder. When interrogated by detectives, she could not remember any useful information. During a later hypnosis interview the witness recalled considerable detail about the suspect, dress, conversation, and a drug transaction, and assisted the police artist in the construction of a composite drawing. As a result, the suspect was identified and prosecuted and the case solved. This incident was important in that it tended to validate the theory of subconscious perception and processing of information (Hilgard, 1977). It also demonstrated that information acquired outside of conscious awareness can sometimes be recovered with special interviewing techniques (Reiser, 1974b).

In addition to crime-specific questions, the psychological consultant may well encounter other more typical problems. One involves the issue of neutrality and objectivity in the face of conflict between union and management, between brass and street cops, between department and politicians, and between department and the media. For example, it would likely exacerbate problems if the police union was dealt with unilaterally in arranging for research or assistance programs without the involvement of the police administration.

For in-house consultants the perennial problem of limited resources for psychological purposes can be ameliorated by developing an internship program with local universities on a quid quo pro basis—supervision and licensing credit in exchange for services to the organization. At LAPD, a pre- and post doctoral internship program in police psychology has been in effect for the past 14 years. Several graduates have earned positions as police psychologists in different departments around the country (Sherven, 1977).

Although documentation is difficult, it is helpful if the services provided by the consultant can be shown to be cost-effective. Each project should have an evaluation process built-in from the beginning before data collection starts. Mental health benefits can be estimated from user surveys and supervisors' ratings (Schwartz, Reiser, Saxe, & Aadland, 1977).

POLICE SELECTION

Over the years, police selection has essentially involved the attempt to screen-out disturbed applicants rather than to select those with a desirable profile (Reiser, 1982c). Some feel that this focus on gross pathology is not sufficient (Stotland & Smith, 1973). However, despite dozens of research projects and considerable federal money, to date attempts to select the ideal officer have not been validated (Reiser, 1971). Although there have been no major breakthroughs in the police selection area (Furcon, 1979), the inclusion of psychological screening is generally recommended as a useful part of the assessment process, and its use has been growing nationally (Spielberger, Spaulding, Jolley, & Ward 1979).

Blum's early review (1964) of police selection approaches concluded that psychological testing can be a valuable part of the initial evaluation process. Across studies, he found a low order of correlation between test measures and job performance. He pointed out a need for local revalidation of measures used to account for variations in environment, policing standards, administrative styles, and desired psychological characteristics of police officers in the community.

Kent and Eisenberg's (1972) later review of the state of the art found that police selection studies often had faulty methodology and used inappropriate statistical analyses. They also pointed out the lack of cross-validation of findings and the need for longitudinal, programmatic research.

One key problem, often overlooked, has been the difficulty in measuring the very powerful shaping influences operating along the officer's career path that interreact and affect the simple personality traits measured at the time of selection (Dunnette & Motowidlo, 1976; Reiser, 1973). Lefkowitz (1977) has concluded that traits like "responsibility" and "self-concept" are not specific enough.

Standard psychological tests frequently used include the Minnesota Multiphasic Personality Inventory (MMPI), the California Psychological Inventory (CPI), and the 16 Personality Factor Questionnaire (16PF) which were not originally designed for use with police populations specifically. Although some police norm groups have since been accumulated, these measures may not provide a net fine enough to capture the relevant variance in an essentially normal group of police recruits (Cattell, Eber, & Tatsuoka, 1970, Gottesman, 1969; Gough, 1957; Saxe & Reiser, 1976).

Henderson (1979) expressed doubts about the predictive validity of the oft-used MMPI. He felt that the CPI was more promising despite the fact that personality measures have not done well overall. This is partly due to applicants answering personality questions differently under test and voluntary conditions. He indicated that intelligence quotient, aptitude, and achievement measures do somewhat better and suggests that validating selection measures is complex, involving problems of sample size, range restriction, test score, and criterion contamination.

In a recent statewide California study Hargrave and Berner (1984) agree that the MMPI has yet to demonstrate its usefulness as a tool in peace officer selection. They feel that it is the best test so far for identifying psychopathological factors in applicants. But like Henderson and Spielberger, they think the CPI is a good instrument for selection purposes.

The majority of police selection studies have used a concurrent validation design of police personnel files—stopping short of testing the predictive validity of the measures selected. This has led to difficulties in replicating the results of seemingly powerful selection measures in diverse police environments (Reiser, 1972; Spielberger, Ward, & Spaulding, 1979). Another problem is the use of academy recruits for testing and the difficulty generalizing the results because there is no correlation between success in training and success in the field (Leiren, 1973). Relatively little information is available about police performance regarding reliability, validity, or sensitivity. There is a need for better job analyses and criterion measures (Dunnette & Motowidlo, 1976). In this connection the use of critical incidents and behaviorally anchored scales have shown some promise (Landy & Farr, 1983).

Also sorely needed are longitudinal studies using predictive validity designs which include cross-validation at different police agencies (Furcon, Froemel, & Baehr, 1973). Longitudinal studies by Snibbe, Azen, Montgomery, & Marsh. (1976) and Dunnette and Motowidlo (1976) confirm that variables related to job performance change. A recent study by Pugh (1984) showed that personality traits in officers also changed over time. During the first two years on the job "capacity for status" was predictive of good performance. After four-and-one-half years on the job the best predictors changed to "well-being," "responsibility," and "socialization," which suggested trait shifts toward stability, social skills, and assumption of responsibility.

Changing values make initial screening difficult. Police occupational influences tend to shape individuals toward cynical and undemocratic attitudes. Sherrid (1979) found that values can be changed by creating dissatisfaction with information about oneself that differs from one's idea of what is considered tolerant or intolerant and becoming aware of the inconsistencies in one's own values and beliefs.

Along with psychological testing and background checks (Cohen & Chaiken, 1972), an interview is often comprised of part of the initial assessment process. This ranges from interview boards who appear to stress conformity (James, Campbell, & Lovegrove, 1984) to individual, structured interviews (Ellison, Marshall, & Fornelius, 1984) to stress interviews designed to evaluate the applicants' responses to personal pressure and challenge (Mills, 1976). The personal interview is an important part of the psychological assessment procedure in that it permits clinical validation or modification of the usually impersonal test results.

The assessment center approach has been used for initial selection as well as for promotion (Filer, 1979). Original enthusiasm about this procedure has been tempered by limitations such as cost, staffing and logistical difficulties, and inadequate predictive validation. One study found that both assessment center and traditional predictors were unrelated to job performance, though assessment center evaluations were predictors of promotability (Turnage & Muchinsky, 1984).

Computer-based testing and reporting have become commercially popular in recent years. It appears to provide the police executive with a quick, economical approach to psychological screening of applicants. Some difficulties have been pointed out, including impersonality and lack of nonverbal inputs (Kiesler, Siegel, & McGuire, 1984). More important is the need to provide validity evidence for the computer programs and procedures used in arriving at the conclusions given in the report. The APA Committee on Professional Standards (1984) has stated that test developers should provide a manual giving the rationale and evidence in support of computer-based interpretations of scores.

Stress factors have become a primary concern in police agencies. There is an interest on the part of managers and employees alike in the sources of stress—personal, organizational, and external—that affect the emotional health and job performance of officers (Reiser, 1974a; 1976b). In addition, there is a current focus on reactions to stress, the development of symptoms of distress, and the search for possible predictors of stress proneness that can be used at the initial selection phase (Haynes, 1978; Reiser, 1982b; Reiser & Geiger, 1984; Territo & Vetter, 1981). Some of the research issues of interest in the interface between stress and selection are hardiness and stress resistance (Kobasa, 1979), life changes and susceptibility to illness (Holmes & Masuda, 1974), and personality styles linked to cardiovascular disease (Friedman & Rosenman, 1974).

The utility of psychological assessment to select personnel for high-risk assignments such as bomb squad and SWAT has been examined (Reiser, Saxe, & Swerling, 1982; Saxe & Reiser, 1982; Sultan, Saxe, & Reiser, 1980; Saxe & Reiser, 1976). Results indicated that past performance, particularly those traits and behaviors related to the role under consideration, was the most reliable indicator of the individual's future performance (Swerling, Saxe, & Reiser, 1982).

Other issues of interest which impact selection criteria are the effects of the quasimilitary structure on training, acculturation factors that shape the officer's attitudes and values over time, and the question of integrity. The need to change from a military model of training, which emphasizes authoritarian behaviors, to a professional model that focuses on communication skills in problem solving has been identified (Reiser & Klyver, 1982). This issue has serious implications for selecting the kind of individual who can successfully adapt to a police environment with a shifting emphasis toward human values and resources (Furcon, 1979).

The problem of police corruption and lack of integrity is a perennial one. Involvement of officers in graft, burglary, narcotics trafficking, and other felony crimes is the bane of every police administrator and the community at large (Beigel & Beigel, 1977; Chevigny, 1969). Attempts have been made to identify predictors of dishonesty that can be used at the time of initial selection. Shealy (1977, 1979) has discussed this issue in detail and recommends that screening test batteries include measures of maturity and moral judgment in order to assess tendencies toward corruption or lack of integrity. Considerable research in this area has been done by Hogan (1973) who developed a model of moral conduct and character which includes five main areas: moral knowledge, socialization, empathy, moral judgment, and autonomy. He found that the internalization of rules relies mainly on personal conscience rather than on the external group.

A recent predictive-validity study found biodata and personality items that descriminated between caucasian male-officer success and failure (Spielberger, Spaulding, Jolley, & Ward, 1979). Four biodata items were predictive of success: participation in high school athletics, fewer family moves, less need for job encouragement, and higher values for achievement and societal contributions. On personality variables successful males scored higher on the CPI scales of capacity for status, intellectual efficiency, sociability, dominance, and achievement via conformance. Hargrave and Berner (1984) made similar personality findings in their study. These results await further cross-validation.

Spielberger, Ward, & Spaulding (1979) have proposed a model for selection which groups research predictor variables into three major categories: (1) physical, biographical, and demographic; (2) psychological assessment procedures; and (3) situational tests. He recommends separate performance criteria for success in training during probation and at journeyman levels. Separate predictors are also needed for women and minorities. Furcon (1979) points to the need to focus on a total assessment of the employment system rather than on its isolated elements, and on effective selection instruments that are job-related and fair.

Currently, at the Los Angeles Police Department, applicant selection includes a psychological assessment component under the jurisdiction of the city personnel department. Traditionally, a personality measure such as the MMPI or the 16 PF test is administered as a screening device, and each applicant is then interviewed individually by a clinical psychologist who has the test results available. In effect, this is using the "successive sieve approach" rather than a true selection model, which awaits further research to find valid and defensible job-related predictors of success for police officers.

Research now in process at the LAPD Academy is concerned with possible predictors of job success, including hardiness, stress resistance, and integrity. If such predictors are found, they will then need to be tested for validity at the applicant stage and again longitudinally to confirm their job relatedness and predictive efficacy.

HOSTAGE NEGOTIATION

Hostage negotiation is a mix of psychological principles, clinical judgment, and street knowledge (Gettinger, 1983). In contradistinction to the typical police incident in which action is demanded, the hostage situation requires buying time, using strategies that defuse, and influencing by verbal and environmental means (Culley. 1974; Miron & Goldstein, 1979).

The role of the psychologist in hostage negotiation is important and multifaceted (Fuselier, 1981). Helping the police department decide on an appropriate model for structuring the crisis team is one aspect. Should the psychologist be in charge and do the negotiating directly with the hostage-taker, or should there be trained police negotiators and a police supervisor in charge of the team?

The Los Angeles Police Department's Crisis Negotiating Team (CNT) uses the trained police negotiator model, which consists primarily of Special Weapons and Tactics Team (SWAT) personnel. Team members include a SWAT supervisor who is liaison between the negotiation effort and the tactical side, primary and secondary officer negotiators, a police psychologist consultant, and one or more detectives assigned to background investigation and contact with other agencies (Reiser, 1982a). In this connection, Powitzky (1979) discusses some of the uses and misuses of psychologists in hostage situations. He feels that the majority of psychologists practicing outside of the criminal justice system would not be helpful, and perhaps even harmful, in a hostage situation because of lack of training and experience in these events.

Another facet of the psychologist's function includes an inferential diagnostic evaluation of the suspect (Hassel, 1975). Three main types of hostage-takers have been classified according to motivation: psychological, criminal, and political. These classifications include (1) the suicidal personality, the vengeance seeker, and the disturbed individual; (2) the cornered perpetrator, the aggrieved inmate, and the felonious extortionist; (3) the social protestor, the ideological zealot, and the terrorist extremist (Goldaber, 1979). Hubbard (1973) has written specifically about skyjackers and their dynamics. There is considerable attention being paid currently to terrorism and this type of hostage possibility (Freedman & Alexander, 1983; Miller, 1978).

Training the members of the negotiating team is a widely accepted part of the psychologist's role (Davidson, 1981). The training typically includes material on normal and abnormal psychology, types of hostage-takers, communication skills, crisis intervention, stress management, suggestibility techniques, a review of prior hostage situations, and role-played scenarios (Training Key 234, 1976; 235, 1976; Kobetz & Cooper, 1979). In addition to persuasion, Ericksonian suggestibility phrases using metaphor and indirect direction are taught (Rossi, 1980), the rationale being that crisis and high-stress situations often are accompanied by an altered state of awareness. This can facilitate the acceptance of suggestions perceived at a subconscious level by the hostage-taker (Reiser & Sloane, 1983).

Hostage situations are stressful, traumatic events for all participants, including the police. There is built-in pressure over time to reduce frustration and anxiety and to end the provocation by taking some kind of action (Reiser, 1982a). Anxious police have been known to behave in a bizarre manner at a negotiation situation when the field commander or others feel compelled to show the psychologist that they are in control (Davidson, 1981). The psychologist member of the team should monitor the fatigue and tension levels of hostage-taker, hostages, and police personnel and may recommend relief replacements, different approaches, topics to avoid, or environmental manipulations such as changes in heat, light, and noise levels. The psychologist's evaluation of the hostage-taker's motives, personality, pathology, control system, and acting-out potential can have important consequences affecting what actions are taken by the tactical team (Boltz & Hershey, 1979). Outlined by Fuselier (1981), negotiation procedures and considerations include what is negotiable, method of contact, exchange of hostages, and selection and training of the psychologist consultant.

The Stockholm Syndrome which involves the development of feelings between hostages and hostake-taker has been discussed in some detail (Hacker, 1976; Strentz, 1979). The syndrome consists of several possible behaviors: The hostages develop positive feelings toward the captor; the hostages develop negative feelings toward the police and authority; the hostage-taker develops positive feelings toward the hostages. Both positive and negative consequences are possible. In addition, the syndrome may also affect the police negotiator, leading to emotional rather than objective reactions (Fuselier, 1981). Close confinement, individual contact, stress of a life-threatening kind, and time are all that are needed for the syndrome to develop.

The hostage negotiation process can be described in four phases. The first is the diagnostic phase which is essentially one of information gathering. Background history of the hostage-taker including criminal, psychological, personal-family, and motivational factors is assembled and evaluated (Poythress, 1980; Reiser, 1982a).

Phase two is negotiation. The diagnostic information is used to construct a tentative profile of the suspect and then decide on the style and content of communications and tactics. The hostage-taker is kept in a decision-making role, and negotiations are on a give-get basis. The assessment of the suspect continues throughout the event as time and transference effects operate and as factors change. Suggestibility phrases may be used when appropriate, and tape recordings from significant others may be played to the suspect as a safe way of injecting desirable personalized affective messages.

The third phase involves termination of the hostage situation, ideally without injury to anyone. There may be a peaceful surrender, an assault by SWAT, or the death of the suspect by suicide or sharpshooter.

The fourth phase focuses on debriefing after the situation has been concluded. The hostages are interviewed individually by using supportive, crisis intervention techniques, and needs are assessed for additional in-house assistance or referral. The crisis negotiation team is also debriefed in a group, and a climate for catharsis and group support is provided (Specter & Claiborn, 1973).

POLICE STRESS

Over the last 15 years more than 100 articles, several books, and numerous manuals have been published on the police stress problem. The general thesis of most of these reports is that police work, because of ever-present danger and frequent emergency response, is a highly stressful occupation which subjects police officers to greater amounts and unique sources of stress than other occupations. Therefore, it has been argued, police officers are at a much higher risk for stress-related disorders than most occupational groups in the population. Although popular, this argument is dubious in our judgment. After a brief discussion of the phenomenon of stress, we will discuss a different analysis of police stress.

Conceptually, stress problems are caused by chronic attempts of the body to prepare for a nonexistent physical attack. According to Selye (1974), this arousal activates a wide range of physiological processes and is suitably named the general adaptation response since it is a nonspecific arousal of the sympathetic branch of the autonomic nervous system (Selye, 1956). While short-term activation of this process in the body is adaptive and useful when a genuine physical attack exists, arousal in response to a symbolic attack serves no functional purpose and depletes needed body resources (Grencik, 1975). Further compounding the problem is that symbolic attacks (such as verbal criticism) tend to persist in the person's environment while physical attacks are most often brief and transient. When the general adaptation response is activated more than necessary for continuing periods, a person may begin to experience dysfunctional symptoms or early warning signs of maladaptive stress (Hinkle, 1973; Reiser, 1976b). The longer this process continues, the greater the likelihood of increasingly serious symptoms. Symptoms experienced often involve physical, emotional, and behavioral domains of functioning (French, 1975; Ellison & Gentz, 1978).

Some of the common maladaptive symptoms believed to be caused by stress are headaches, gastrointestinal distress (gastritis, ulcer, diarrhea), excessive muscle tension (resulting in lower back pain, torn muscles, generalized pain), depression (low self-concept, weight loss or gain, pessimism, fatigue), anxiety, increase in illnesses (due to excessive cortisol levels) acting-out behavior (increased alcohol consumption, yelling, hitting), withdrawal, and general decline in work efficiency and performance (Cobb & Rose, 1973; Cooper & Marshall, 1976; French, 1975). In addition, continued overactivation of the stress response over the years has been blamed for premature deaths from cardiovascular deterioration because the stress response produces an increase in blood pressure and serum cholesterol, both of which have harmful effects on the cardiovascular system (Dohrenwend & Dohrenwend, 1974; Fell, Richard, & Wallace, 1980; Guralnick, 1963).

Evaluation of the police stress evidence does not yield an entirely consistent picture, although many authors treat the subject as if it did. The quality of articles in this area is also a concern. Most of the published reports on police stress appear to be based on the subjective personal opinions of the authors rather than on evaluation of objective empirical findings. It would be possible to conclude from most of these articles that there is no controversy over the police stress issue and general agreement among psychologists that police work itself causes stress. For example, the typical article begins with the pronouncement, "Recent research has shown that the job of policing is an extremely stressful occupation." No further substantiation of this premise was provided by the authors, Cooper and Marshall (1976).

In another representative study the author states that "it is an accepted fact that a police officer is under stress and pressure unequaled in any other profession" and that "psychosomatic illnesses are rampant in police work" (Somodevilla, 1978). Again the only support offered for this contention was personal observations about drinking and divorce based on the author's personal observations. Even Hans Selye, the originator of modern stress research, has made the unsupported observation that "police work ranks as one of the most hazardous occupations, even exceeding the formidable stresses and strain of air traffic control" (Selye, 1978).

In contrast, the comparatively few studies that have evaluated objective data on police stress have produced equivocal results and varied interpretations. One study that compared officers with 22 other occupational groups found that police officers were "higher than average on some stresses, and lower than average on other stresses" and that they were not an extreme group (French, 1975). An examination of all deaths between 1945 and 1969 in a Montreal study revealed that the mortality rate for police officers was lower for them than for other males matched for age. Further, it was found that criminal and accidental death rates were lower for police, and suicide rates did not differ from that of the general population (Arcand, 1976). Similar results were obtained by Gettman (1978).

Within police organizations several anomalous conditions also exist. Rates of applications for stress-related pensions vary considerably across the country. The Los Angeles Police Department granted 175 stress pensions between 1980 and 1984, whereas other large police departments such as New York, Chicago, Kansas City, Dallas, and Houston have granted only a few. It is unlikely that the demands of being a police officer differ radically between Los Angeles and these cities. Within LAPD the greatest number of stress pension applications have come from the areas of the city that are traditionally the slowest and easiest to work (e.g., Valley divisions) and in which the public is affluent and supportive of the police. The fewest applications have come from the busiest areas with the most serious problems on the street and a hostile public (e.g., Southend divisions). However confounding these data, officers in the Valley divisions have an average of more than 10 years on the job, whereas those from the Southend divisions have an average of less than five.

One plausible explanation for stress pension increases is that opportunity and high payoff may encourage exaggeration of symptoms, or at least reinterpretation of symptoms. The Los Angeles pension system is one of the most liberal in the country and officers are granted stress pensions of 55 to 90 percent of their salaries tax-free for the rest of their lives. The attribution process is also significant. An officer may feel discontented for many reasons but may not label the feelings as job stress unless he has learned this interpretation and feels justified in his claim (Klyver, 1983).

Although street police work is often cited as a cause of stress among police officers, in fact most officers appear to enjoy their jobs and the freedom of patroling outdoors (Farmer & Monahan, 1980a). In special cases, such as shooting, trauma reactions may occur (Reiser & Geiger, 1984). Although the question whether police work is a uniquely high-stress occupation may continue to generate controversy, the issue may be mainly academic. Considering the range of power and control that police officers are granted—from temporarily depriving someone of basic rights to using physical force (up to and including shooting)—any stress difficulties an officer experiences may have serious consequences because, as has been noted, stress often interferes with decision making and may contribute to inappropriate acting-out (Blackmore, 1978; Farmer & Monahan, 1980b).

As a result of their concerns, many states now require training in stress management for the basic police certificate. Training of this sort normally entails inoculation preparation, discussion of the dynamics of the stress mechanism, early warning signs of maladaptive stress, awareness of options and problem-solving remedies, resources and referrals, and direct stress-reduction techniques (Davidson & Veno, 1978; Hurrell & Kroes, 1975).

Most often stressors in police work include the same factors that upset other people in their jobs: management style, communication in the organization, supervisory sensitivity, and personal satisfaction (Farmer & Monahan, 1980; French, 1975; Hillgren, 1976; Hillgren & Spradlin, 1975; Kroes, 1976; Reiser, 1972; Schwartz, 1975).

Survey data collected over the last five years at LAPD supports other researchers' findings (Kroes, 1976; Schwartz, 1975) that supervisory and management behavior is the most frequently experienced and most powerful stressor for police officers. Analysis of LAPD concerns with management behavior has yielded a cluster of factors: (1) *Communication*. Frustration caused by the difficulty of getting information up the chain of command and anger over the way in which orders come down the chain (mostly without consultation or involvement of people on the receiving end). (2) *Lack of fit between leadership style and the needs of the officer being led*. Using Hersey and Blanchard's (1982) leadership assessment instrument to assess leadership style, a style most frequently ignored in police work is delegation. Even when people are ready and willing to "run with the ball," it appears that police leaders are unwilling to give up their control. (3) *General lack of consideration and insensitivity*. Sometimes officers appear to get upset over trivial issues such as not getting a desired day off. These problems, however, often center on the way in which the leader's decision is made. Often the officer feels he was not listened to and that he was not part of the problem-solving process.

As a result of these organizational concerns, LAPD's behavioral science unit is now involved in training and consulting with first-line supervisors, lieutenants, captains, and higher level management—each at the appropriate level. We employ a consulting group of five experienced organizational-development Ph.D.'s, each of whom works 15 hours a week. This group is headed by a full-time police psychologist who has the primary responsibility for the program. The program (dubbed ARMS—Assistance and Resources for Managers and Supervisors) is involved in basic training programs for supervisors and managers and has the capability of following up with on-site consultation.

This program attacks the major causes of stress in organizational processes. Personal problems or adjustment concerns are dealt with in personal counseling programs and are discussed in the next section.

COUNSELING WITH POLICE

Most police departments attempt to screen new officers through background checks and psychological testing. The resulting selected police population reflects normal psychological profiles and is overall a stable and responsible group (Reiser, 1972). When police officers experience difficulties in their lives that require counseling, the problems are most often short-duration crisis issues that can often be rapidly resolved with effective, brief counseling (Klyver, 1983). The experience of most in-house police psychologists who have conducted counseling with police officers and their families is that about 80 to 90 percent of the contacts for counseling are centered around relatively common and mundane concerns, such as relationship problems and job difficulties (e.g., promotion and problems with supervisors) (Reiser, 1972).

Although police concerns are often similar to those of most other people, in several areas police officers may experience unique difficulties that are related to the police organization or to the police job (Farmer & Monahan, 1980; Kroes & Hurrell, 1975). Therefore it is desirable for a psychologist counseling with a police officer to be familiar with police terminology and police structure and demands (e.g., discipline system and shift work) (Hillgren & Spradlin, 1975; Reiser, 1972). Police organizations most often operate in a quasimilitary fashion and are legally accountable for the actions of their officers because it may affect the reputation of the department. An officer's off-duty conduct may become the subject of scrutiny. Behavior at an off-duty party, for example, might be classified as conduct unbecoming an officer if it created embarrassment to the department (Blackmore, 1978). Because of the range of implications of police officer behavior, the police therapist needs to be sensitive to the political climate of his department and organizational concerns of the department (Reiser, 1976b).

Another area that may involve unique problems for police is in the use of force. Police officers are one of the few groups in our society that may use physical force over citizens in the course of their work. An officer who is experiencing impulse control problems may inappropriately use force on a citizen. In another vein, an officer who has been involved in a shooting may encounter a number of unanticipated feelings that reflect the conflict of harming another human being and yet carrying out his sworn duty. If these feelings are not managed, they may produce posttraumatic reactions (Reiser & Geiger, 1984).

Several factors in police organizations may make it less likely that officers will seek help even when they need it. Police departments often operate within a legalistic and rigid structure. Officers, so conditioned, may become suspicious of disclosing problems fearing that the information may be used against them later (Stratton, 1984). Further, the male macho mystique maintained in the police culture, which socializes officers to believe that real men should not have personal problems, inhibits help seeking (Blackmore, 1978). Many police psychologists operate a dual-mode intake system reserving one mode for confidential referrals and another mode for through-channels nonconfidential problems. The through-channels mode might be used by commanding officers who are concerned about an officer's ability to function appropriately in the field in regard to issues such as use of force, backing up a partner, and decision making (Reiser, 1976b). Although this two-track system provides information for managers and is also an avenue for confidential use, it may also be misunderstood by officers who are overly suspicious (Stratton, 1984). Hence great care and consideration should be given to ensuring that officers understand the process involved.

An additional consideration for the therapist working with police officers is the need to balance a more extended concept of dangerousness with confidentiality. Because problems surrounding impulse control, decision making under stress, or personality disorders may interfere with appropriate judgment or action, these areas need to be balanced against the need for maintaining confidentiality. Decisions for the therapist may present a number of ethical dilemmas and are often not easy to resolve (Reiser, 1972; Hillgren & Spradlin, 1975).

Given the nature of the police population, short-term counseling (limited to 10 or fewer sessions) is most often the favored choice. The few cases that require long-term therapy are more appropriately referred out to provide the psychologist with time for dealing with a greater number of cases (Reiser, 1972). One option that an in-house psychologist has that has proved to be useful is to conduct training and appear at roll calls in the field. The opportunity to meet the psychologist firsthand provides visibility and helps to break down fears and stereotypes. These opportunities also provide information and knowledge about what the process of counseling is about and make referral less traumatic (Reiser, 1976b; Somodevilla, 1978; Stratton, 1984).

Because officers often feel comfortable talking with a peer about concerns, peer counseling has become another counseling alternative in police organizations (Depue, 1979; Klyver, 1983). Police officers as a group have many personal characteristics that lend themselves to being effective counselors. They tend to be personable, outgoing, and verbal individuals who like helping their colleagues. Without training in counseling, however, they often have difficulty being helpful. Officers' typical attempts at helping more often reflect anxiety to "do something" and quickly "solve the problem." Since police officers are used to quickly resolving situations in the field, it is not surprising that they feel frustrated with the uncertainty and slow-moving quality of counseling. It is also difficult for an officer to see a fellow officer in a crisis. Untrained counseling efforts often involve premature advice giving, rational arguments, smoothing things over, and taking sides.

In our experience, though, motivated officers can learn basic counseling skills in a 24-hour skill development workshop. The workshop training is about 80 percent experiential and teaches reflective listening to establish rapport and clarify the issues and assessment skills to determine the need for a specialized referral as might be the case with marriage, financial, drug, or gambling problems. Finally, peer counselors are taught problem-solving skills. Here, the counselor assists with problem-solving strategies by working through the issues with the officer, by exploring options, reality tests, and making tentative solutions, and by helping to find an approach that will work (Depue, 1979; Klyver, 1983). At LAPD a cadre of 200 trained peer counselors conducted about 5000 hours of counseling in 1985. The majority of contacts involved relationship breaks and job concerns. The remainder of counseling time was spent on concerns such as death and dying situations, post-shooting situations, financial problems, alcohol problems, and other concerns.

Peer counseling is an example of maximizing cost-effectiveness for psychologists. The number of hours of counseling time that is spent by the paraprofessionals far exceeds the amount of time that the psychologist possibly can spend in that mode. Furthermore, peer counselors can serve as an initial assessment screen and refer those cases that genuinely need a psychologist or psychiatrist.

TRAINING WITH POLICE

The job of police officer has become increasingly complex and demanding. In addition to the traditional skills in police work such as use of force (e.g., shooting, control holds), patrol procedures, report taking, and law, the officer is often expected to be knowledgeable in many other areas that have taken on knowledge and skills from the social sciences. Concern is currently reflected in the handling of family disputes, dealing with victims of crime (especially rape victims and battered women), assessing mental illness and drug states, and assessing suicide risk (Klyver & Reiser, 1983; Bard, 1970). Even in traditional areas of police work, increasing demands and accountability for action have become more common as a result of community pressure, political pressure, and law suits. As a result, the officer must not only be able to defend himself or herself and use appropriate force in a situation, but must also be able to justify why they used it (Hartman, 1979).

Similar accountability exists with respect to arrests and reports. In light of the ever-mounting press for accountability of police officers and the growing sophistication of police work, the pressure for effective training is greater than ever (Klyver & Reiser, 1983). Academy curricula are now reflecting the new sophistication of police work (Hartman, 1979). At LAPD, for example, approximately 60 hours of new training has been introduced over the last several years on Spanish, effective dispute management, victimology, mental illness, communications, and human relations (Klyver & Reiser, 1983). Police-officer standards for training in California now require these areas in the basic curriculum. In addition to content changes, greater focus has begun to emerge on the quality and appropriateness of instruction. The traditional large lecture class has been supplanted increasingly by more active learning modes. Teaching techniques now adopted at academies often emphasize interactive workbooks and videotapes, interactive materials, and increased feedback to the recruit on his or her performance. Another major area of improvement is in the use of simulated activities. Simulations allow the recruit to practice skills in a semirealistic fashion and actively integrate the conceptual material and the behaviors required. Simulations are often graduated from simple to complex and may involve a nonevaluative component at first to encourage experimentation and mistakes, and later to move to an evaluative format (Le Doux & McCaslin, 1981; Rodduck, 1974).

Certain areas of police work are difficult to teach without using simulations; for example, in use of force training, particularly shootings, simulations are an ideal mode of training because on-the-job training is too late. One cannot wait until a street situation arises and a shooting takes place to conduct training. Furthermore, the consequences of inappropriate action may be so serious that errors cannot be tolerated. In a simulated situation, however, either through viewing tapes and movies with which the officer can interact or shooting on an interactive range, appropriate responses can be conditioned and mistakes can be useful. Because force situations often require an immediate and reflexive response, lecture-type training would be most inappropriate, for it does not instill immediate response capability.

The academy experience has often been experienced by police officers as a hazing ritual to determine who should be admitted into the fraternity of police officers. In so doing, emphasis has been placed on artificially induced stresses and harsh discipline to separate the "men from the boys" (Earle, 1972; Ruddock, 1974). Evidence has shown that artificially induced stress tends to be ineffective in training and tends to produce recruits who are more aggressive, less flexible, and have greater difficulty making decisions when confronted with problems on the street (Le Doux & McCaslin, 1981; Ruddock, 1974). The field officer today, more than ever, is required to function as an autonomous executive decision maker or as Bard (1970) has said, "A human problem solver" because about 80 percent of modern police work involves helping people rather than handling strictly criminally related issues. However, "If recruits in the academy are taught to see the world as composed of groups hostile to the purpose of the police and police are portrayed as the upholders of moral order who must continuously fight others who are trying to subvert their cause, such a world view creates difficulty for an officer who must deal with gradations of intention and meaning that are found among members of the public" (Baker & Meyer, 1980).

Considering the complexity and difficulty of learning effective police behavior in areas other than use of force, many departments are moving toward improved field training officer programs (Hartman 1979). The field training officer not only needs to be an expert in doing the job but also needs to become effective as a trainer, model, and performance evaluator to the probationer. Field training programs require a clear set of job-related performance objectives to index behavior against operational anchors. Successful programs often require daily performance evaluations to provide timely feedback and opportunity for correction. The training officer must also become sophisticated in how to give feedback without arousing defensiveness and in how to coach for improved behavior without resorting to punishment. The rating phase may be particularly important in a department for those individuals who are ultimately unable to perform up to standards and whom the department may need to dismiss. Insufficient and inappropriate documentation may not stand up to criticism and legal challenges.

Another area of training that is attracting attention is supervisory training. In most departments police supervisors do not receive much training in supervision. At LAPD we are developing new programs that utilize a general leadership approach to supervision with an emphasis on human relations skills. Areas of training include leadership style, motivation of employees, listening skills, counseling skills, stress awareness, management for employees, discipline without punishment, communication skills, teaching and training, team building, ethics, planning and organizing, time management, goal setting, control and audits, conflict resolution, inner-group relations, decision making, and dealing with minority and women. Initial training in these blocks is followed by direct ongoing consultation with a Ph.D.-level organizational psychologist in the supervisor's actual work environment.

Overall, the work of the psychologist consulting with police is endlessly exciting and challenging. The diversity of activities, usually in the mainstream of community interest and concern, precludes boredom and provides the opportunity for meaningful involvement and satisfaction.

REFERENCES

Arcand, S. (1976, August-November). De La Mortalite Policiere, *Crime and/Et Justice, 4*, 147–150.

Ault, R. L., & Reese, J. T. (1980, March). A psychological assessment of crime profiling. *FBI Law Enforcement Bulletin*, pp. 20–25.

Backer, T. E. (1983). Consulting with the Los Angeles Police Department: An interview with police psychologist Martin Reiser. *Consultation, 2*, 48–55.

Baker, R., and Meyer, F. A. (1980). *The criminal justice game*. Boston: PWS Publisher.

Bard, M. (1970). *Training police as specialists in family crisis intervention*. Law Enforcement Assistance Administration.

Beigel, H., & Biegel, A. (1977). *Beneath the badge: A story of police corruption*. New York: Harper & Row.

Blackmore, J. (1978, March). Are police allowed to have problems of their own? *Police Magazine*, pp. 47–55.

Blum, R. H. (1964). *Police selection*. Springfield, IL: C. C. Thomas.

Boltz, F. A., Jr. & Hershey, E. (1979). *Hostage cop*. New York: Rawson, Wade.

Brodsky, S. L. (1972). *Psychologists in the criminal justice system*. Marysville, OH: American Association of Correctional Psychologists.

Campbell, C. (1976, May). Portrait of a mass killer. *Psychology Today*, pp. 110–119.

Caplan, G. (1970). *The theory and practice of mental health consultation*. New York: Basic Books.

Cattell, R. B., Eber, H. W., & Tatsuoka, M. M. (1970). *Handbook for the sixteen personality factor questionnaire*. Champaign, IL: IPAT.

Chevigny, P. (1969). *Police power: Police abuses in New York City.* New York: Pantheon.

Cobb, S., and Rose, R. (1973). Hypertension, peptic ulcer, and diabetes in air traffic controllers. *Journal of the American Medical Association, 224,* 489–492.

Cohen, B., & Chaiken, J. (1972). *Police background characteristic and performance: Summary report (No. R-999-DOJ).* New York: Rand Institute.

Cohen, R., Sprafkin, R. P., Oglesby, S., & Claiborn, W. L. (1976). *Working with police agencies.* New York: Human Sciences Press.

Committee on Professional Standards, APA. (1984). Casebook for providers of psychological services. *American Psychologist, 39,* 663–668.

Cooke, G. (Ed.). (1980). *The role of the forensic psychologist.* Springfield, IL: C. C. Thomas.

Cooper, G. L., and Marshall, J. (1976). Occupational sources of stress: A review of the literature relating to coronary heart disease and mental ill. *Health Journal of Occupational Psychology, 49,* 11–28.

Culley, J. A. (1974, October). Defusing human bombs—hostage negotiations. *FBI Law Enforcement Bulletin,* pp. 10–14.

Cummings, T. G. (1980). *Systems theory for organizational development.* New York: Wiley.

Davidson, G. P. (1981). Anxiety and authority: Psychological aspects for police in hostage negotiation situations. *Journal of Police Science and Administration, 9,* 35–38.

Davidson, M. J., and Veno, A. (1978, July-August). Police stress: A multicultural, interdisciplinary review and perspective. (I), *Abstracts on Police Science 6,* 187–199.

Depue, R. (1979, February). Turning inward: The police counselor. *FBI Law Enforcement Bulletin,* pp. 8-12.

Diamond, B. L. (1980). Inherent problems in the use of pretrial hypnosis on a prospective witness. *California Law Review, 68,* 313–439.

Dohrenwend, B. S., and Dohrenwend, B. P. (Eds.), (1974). *Stressful life events: Their nature and effects.* New York: Wiley.

Dunnette, M. D., & Motowidlo, S. J. (1976, November). *Police selection and career assessment.* Washington, DC: LEAA, U.S. Dept. of Justice.

Earle, H. (1972). *Police recruit training: Stress vs. non-stress - A revolution in law enforcement career programs.* Springfield, IL: Thomas.

Eisenberg, T. (1975, April). *Collaboration between law enforcement executives and social scientists.* Paper presented at the National Conference of Christians and Jews, Berkeley, CA.

Elkins, A. M., & Papanek, G. O. (1966). Consultation with police: An example of community psychiatry. *American Journal of Psychiatry, 123,* 531–535.

Ellison K.W. and Gentz J. L. (1978, March). The police officer as burned-out samaritan. *FBI Law Enforcement Bulletin,* pp. 1–7.

Ellison, K. W., Marshall, W. J., & Fornelius, B. A. (1984, October). A comprehensive selection and training program for a medium-sized police department. *Police Chief,* pp. 32–37.

Farmer, R. and Monahan, L. (1980a). Prevention model for stress reduction - a concept paper. *Journal of Police Science and Administration, 8,* 54–60.

Farmer, R. and Monahan, L. (1980b). *Stress and the police: A manual for prevention.* Pacific Palisades, CA: Palisades Publishers.

Fell, R., Richard, W., and Wallace, W. (1980). Psychological job stress. *Journal of Police Science and Administration, 8*, 139–144.

Filer, R. J. (1979). The assessment center method in the selection of law enforcement officers. In C. D. Spielberger (Ed.), *Police selection and evaluation* (pp. 211–229). New York: Praeger.

Freedman, L. Z., & Alexander, Y. (Eds.). (1983). *Perspectives on terrorism*. Wilmington, DE: Scholarly Resources.

French, J. Jr. Comparative look at stress and strain in policemen. In W. Kroes and J. Hurrell, Jr. (Eds.), (1975). *Job Stress and the Police Officer—Identifying Stress Reduction Techniques*. Washington, DC: Government Printing Office.

Friedman, M., & Rosenman, R. H. (1974). *Type A behavior and your heart*. New York: Knopf.

Furcon, J. (1979). An overview of police selection: Some issues, questions and challenges. In C. D. Spielberger, (Ed.), *Police selection and evaluation* (pp. 3–10). New York: Praeger.

Furcon, J. E., Froemel, E. C., & Baehr, M. E. (1973). Psychological predictors and patterns of patrolmen field performance. In J. R. Snibbe, & H. M. Snibbe (Eds), *The urban policeman in transition* (pp. 53–65). Springfield, IL: C. C. Thomas.

Fuselier, G. W. (1981, June/July). A practical overview of hostage negotiations. Reprinted from the *FBI Law Enforcement Bulletin*.

Geberth, V. J. (1981, September). Psychological profiling. *Law and Order*, pp. 46–52.

Gettinger, S. (1983, January). Hostage negotiations. *Police Magazine*, pp. 10–28.

Gettman, L. R. (1978, Fall). Aerobics and police fitness. *Police Stress, 1*, 22–24.

Glaser, D., & Saxe, S. (1982, January). Psychological preparation of female police recruits. *FBI Law Enforcement Bulletin*, pp. 5–7.

Goldaber, I. (1979). A typology of hostage takers. *Police Chief, 46*, 21–23.

Gottesman, J. (1969). *Personality patterns of urban police applicants as measured by the MMPI*. Hoboken, NJ: Stevens Institute of Technology.

Gouch, H. G. (1957). *Manual for the California Psychological Inventory*. Palo Alto, CA: Consulting Psychologists Press.

Grencik, J. M. (1975). Toward an understanding of stress. In W. H. Kroes and J.J. Hurrell (Eds.), *Job Stress and the Police Officer*. Washington, DC, National Institute for Occupational Safety and Health.

Guralnick, L. (1963). Mortality by occupation and cause of death among men 20-64 years of age, United States, 1950. *Vital Statistics* (Special Report No. 53), Washington, DC, Bureau of Vital Satistics.

Hacker, F. J. (1976). *Crusaders, criminals, crazies*. New York: Norton.

Hargrave, G. E., & Berner, J. G. (1984, December). *Post psychological screening manual*. Sacramento, CA: California Commission on Peace Officer Standards and Training.

Hartman, T. L. (1979, April). Field training officer (FTO): The Fairfax County experience. *FBI Law Enforcement Bulletin*, pp. 22–25.

Hassel, C. V. (1975, September). The hostage situation: Exploring the motivation and the cause. *Police Chief*, pp. 55–58.

Haynes, W. D. (1978). *Stress related disorders in policemen*. San Francisco: R&E Research Associates.

Henderson, N. D. (1979). Criterion-related validity of personality and aptitude scales. In C. D. Spielberger, (Ed.), *Police selection and evaluation* (pp. 179–195). New York: Praeger.

Hersey, P. and Blanchard, K. (1982). *Management of Organizational Behavior: Utilizing Human Resources*. Englewood Cliffs, NJ: Prentice-Hall.

Hilgard, E. R. (1977). *Divided consciousness—Multiple controls in human thought and action*. New York: Wiley Interscience.

Hillgren, J. (1976). Primary stressors in police administration and law enforcement. *Journal of Police Science and Administration, 4* (4), 445–449.

Hillgren, J. and Spradlin, L. (1975, July). Positive disciplinary system for the Dallas Police Department. *The Police Chief*, pp. 65–67.

Hinkle, E. Jr. (1973). The concept of "stress" in the biological and social sciences. *Science, Medicine, and Man, 1*, 31–48.

Hodges, A. (1970, January). How not to be a consultant. *Mental Hygiene*, pp. 147–148.

Hogan, R. (1973). Moral conduct and moral character. A psychological perspective. *Psychological Bulletin, 79*, 217–232.

Holmes, T. H., & Masuda, M. (1974). Life change and illness susceptibility. In B. S. Dohrenwend & B. P. Dohrenwend (Eds.), *Stressful life events: Their nature and effect*. New York: Wiley.

Hubbard, D. (1973). *The skyjacker*. New York: Macmillan.

Hurrell, J. Jr. and Kroes, W. (1975). Stress awareness, In W. Kroes and J. Hurrell, *Job stress and the police officer: Identifying stress reduction techniques.* Washington, DC: U.S. Government Printing Office.

James, S. P., Campbell, I. M., and Lovegrove, S. A. (1984). Personality differentiation in a police-selection interview. *Journal of Applied Psychology, 1*, 129–134.

Kent, D., & Eisenberg, T. (1972). The selection and promotion of police officers and selected review of recent literature. *Police Chief, 39*, 20–29.

Kiesler, S., Siegel, J., & McGuire, T. W. (1984). Social psychological aspects of computer-mediated communications. *American Psychologist, 59*, 1123–1134.

Kirkham, G. (1976). *Signal zero*. New York: Lippincott.

Klyver, N. (1983, November). Peer Counseling for Police Personnel: A Dynamic Program in the Los Angeles Police Department. *The Police Chief*, pp. 66–68.

Klyver, N. and Reiser, M. (1983) Crisis intervention in law enforcement. *The Counseling Psychologist, 11*: 2.

Kobasa, S.C. (1979). Stressful life events, personality and health: An inquiry into hardiness. *Journal of Personality and Social Psychology, 37*, 1–11.

Kobetz, R. W., & Cooper, H. H. A. (1979, June). Hostage rescue operations: Teaching the unteachable. *Police chief*, pp. 24–27.

Kroes, W. (1976). *Society's victim: The policeman*. Springfield, IL: Charles Thomas.

Kroes, W. and Hurrell, J. Jr., (Eds.), (1975). *Job stress and the police officer: Identifying stress reduction techniques*. Washington, DC: U.S. Government Printing Office.

Landy, F. L., & Farr, J. L. (1983). *The measurement of work performance*. New York: Academic Press.

Le Doux, J. C. and McCaslin, H. (1981, October). Designing a training response to stress. *FBI Law Enforcement Bulletin*, pp. 11–15.

Lefkowitz, J. (1977). Industrial-organizational psychology and the police. *American Psychologist, 32*, 346–364.

Leiren, B. D. (1973). Validating the selection of deputy marshals. In J. R. Snibbe and H. M. Snibbe, (Eds.), *The urban policeman in transition* (pp. 83–100). Springfield, IL: C. C. Thomas.

Levinson, H. (1972). *Organization diagnosis*. Cambridge, MA: Harvard University Press.

Mann, P. (1973). *Psychological consultation with a police department*. Springfield, IL: C. C. Thomas.

Miller, A. H. (1978). Negotiations for hostages: Implications from the police experience. *Terrorism, 1*, 125–146.

Mills, R. B. (1976). Simulated stress in police recruit selection. *Journal of Police Science and Administration, 4*, 179–186.

Miron, M. S., & Goldstein, A. P. (1979). *Hostage*. New York: Pergamon.

Nash, M. (1983). *Managing organizational performance*. San Francisco: Jossey-Bass.

Niederhoffer, A. (1969). *Behind the shield: The police in urban society*. New York: Anchor Books.

Orne, M. T. (1979, October). The use and misuse of hypnosis in court. *International Journal of Clinical and Experimental Hypnosis*, pp. 311–339.

Powitzky, R. J. (1979, June). The use and misuse of psychologists in a hostage situation. *Police Chief*, pp. 30–33.

Poythress, N. G., Jr. (1980, August). Assessment and prediction in the hostage situation: Optimizing the use of psychological data. *Police Chief*, pp. 34–36, 88.

Pugh, G. (1984). *The California Psychological Inventory and police selection*. Unpublished manuscript.

Reiser, M. (1970, September). A psychologist's view of the badge. *Police Chief*, pp. 224–226.

Reiser, M. (1971, January-February). The police psychologist as consultant. *Police*, pp. 48–50.

Reiser, M. (1972). *The police department psychologist*. Springfield, IL: C. C. Thomas.

Reiser, M. (1973). *Practical psychology for police officers*. Springfield, IL: C. C. Thomas.

Reiser, M. (1974a, June). Some organizational stresses on policemen. *Journal of Police Science and Administration*, pp. 156–159.

Reiser, M. (1974b, October). Hypnosis as an aid in a homicide investigation. *American Journal of Clinical Hypnosis*, pp. 84–87.

Reiser, M. (1976a). Policemen as mental health agents. In E. J. Lieberman, (Ed.), *Mental health: The public health challenge* (pp. 24–27). Washington, DC: American Public Health Association.

Reiser, M. (1976b, January). Stress, distress and adaptation in police work. *Police Chief*, pp. 24–27.

Reiser, M. (1979). Police consultations. In A. S. Rogawski, (Ed.), *Mental health consultations in community settings* (pp. 73–83). New York: Jossey-Bass.

Reiser, M. (1980). *Handbook of investigative hypnosis*. Los Angeles: LEHI Publishing.

Reiser, M. (1982a, March). Crime specific psychological consultation. *Police Chief*, pp. 53–56.

Reiser, M. (1982b). *Police psychology—Collected papers*. Los Angeles: LEHI Publishing.

Reiser, M. (1982c). Selection and promotion of policemen. In M. Reiser, (Ed.), *Police psychology—Collected papers* (pp. 84–92). Los Angeles: LEHI Publishing.

Reiser, M. (1984). Police use of investigative hypnosis: Scientism, ethics and power games. *American Journal of Forensic Psychology, 2*, 115–143.

Reiser, M., & Geiger, S. (1984). Police officer as victim. *Professional Psychology: Research and Practice, 15*, 315–323.

Reiser, M., & Klyver, N. (1982). *Needed: A modern police training model*. Los Angeles: Los Angeles Police Department.

Reiser, M., Saxe, S. J., & Swerling, J. (1982). Psychological assessment of radio telephone operators in a large urban police department. In M. Reiser, (Ed.), *Police psychology—Collected papers* (pp. 111–115). Los Angeles: LEHI Publishing.

Reiser, M., & Sloane, M. (1983). The use of suggestibility techniques in hostage negotiation. In L. Z. Freedman, & Y. Alexander, (Eds.), *Perspectives on terrorism* (pp. 213–223). Wilmington, DE: Scholarly Resources.

Rieber, R. W. (Ed.). (1984). *Advances in forensic psychology and psychiatry, Vol. 1*. Norwood, NJ: Ablex Publishing.

Rossi, E. L. (Ed.). (1980). *The collected papers of Milton H. Erickson on hypnosis, Four Volumes*. New York: Irvington Publishers.

Ruddock, R. (1974, November). Recruit training—stress vs. non-stress. *The Police Chief*, pp. 47–40.

Saxe, S. J., & Reiser, M. (1976). A comparison of three police applicant groups using the MMPI. *Journal of Police Science and Administration, 4*, 419–425.

Saxe, S. J., & Reiser, M. (1982). A policeman profile on the FIRO-B. In M. Reiser, (Ed.), *Police psychology—Collected papers* (pp. 104–110). Los Angeles: LEHI Publishing.

Schwartz, J. (1975). Special problems of the police officer, In W. Kroes and J. Hurrell, Jr. (Eds.), *Job stress and the police officer: Identifying stress reduction techniques*. Washington, DC: U.S. Government Printing Office.

Schwartz, J. N., Reiser, M., Saxe, S., & Aadland, R. (1977). *An evaluation of police behavioral science services*. Los Angeles: Los Angeles Police Department.

Selye, H. (1956). *The stress of life*. New York: McGraw-Hill.

Selye, H. (1978, December). The stress of police work. *Police Stress*, p. 14.

Selye, H. (1974). *Stress without distress*. Philadelphia: Lippincott.

Shealy, A. E. (1977). *Police integrity: The role of psychological screening of applicants*. Criminal Justice Center Monograph Number 4. New York: John Jay Press.

Shealy, A. E. (1979). Police corruption: Screening and high-risk applicants. In C. D. Spielberger, (Ed.), *Police selection and evaluation* (pp. 197–210). New York: Praeger.

Sherrid, S. D. (1979). Changing police values. In C. D. Spielberger. (Ed.), *Police selection and evaluation* (pp. 167–176). New York: Praeger.

Sherven, J. (1977, July). Division consultation with the Los Angeles Police Department. Los Angeles Police Department.

Singer, H. A. (1970, April). The cop as social scientist. *Police Chief*, pp. 52–58.

Smith, D. H., & Stotland, E. (1973). A new look at police officer selection. In J. R. Snibbe & H. M. Snibbe, (Eds.), *The urban policeman in transition* (pp. 5–24). Springfield, IL: C. C. Thomas.

Snibbe, H. M., Azen, S. P., Montgomery, H. R., & Marsh, S. H. (1973). Predicting job performance of law enforcement officers: A ten and twenty-year study. In J. R. Snibbe, & H. M. Snibbe, (Eds.), *The urban policeman in transition* (pp. 101–116). Springfield, IL: C. C. Thomas.

Somodevilla, S. (1978, April). The psychologist's role in the police department. *The Police Chief*, pp. 21–23.

Specter, G. A., & Claiborn, W. L. (1973). *Crisis intervention*. New York: Behavioral Publications.

Spielberger, C. D., Spaulding, H. C., Jolley, M. T., & Ward, J. C. (1979). Selection of effective law enforcement officers. The Florida police standards research project. In C. D. Spielberger, (Ed.), *Police selection and evaluation* (pp. 231–251). New York: Praeger.

Spielberger, C. D., Ward, J. C., & Spaulding, H. C. (1979). A model for the selection of law enforcement officers. In C. D. Spielberger, (Ed.), *Police selection and evaluation* (pp. 11–29). New York: Praeger.

Stratton, J. G. (1984). *Police passages*. Manhattan Beach, CA: Glennon Publishing.

Strentz, T. (1980). The Stockholm Syndrome: Law enforcement and ego defenses of the hostage. *Annals of the New York Academy of Science, 347*, 137–150.

Sultan, S., Saxe, S., & Reiser, M. (1980). Some stress factors in an airborne law enforcement unit. *Journal of Police Science Administration, 8*, 61–65.

Swerling, J., Saxe, S. J., & Reiser, M. (1982). Psychological assessment of barricaded suspect and hostage negotiators. In M. Reiser, (Ed.), *Police psychology—Collected papers* (pp. 116–123). Los Angeles: LEHI Publishing.

Territo, L., & Vetter, H. J. (1981). *Stress and police personnel*. Boston: Allyn and Bacon.

Training Key 234 (1976). *Hostage incident response*. Gaithersburg, MD.: International Association of Chiefs of Police.

Training Key 235 (1976). *Hostage negotiation*. Gaithersburg, MD.: International Association of Chiefs of Police.

Turnage, J. J., & Muchinsky, P. M. (1984). A comparison of the predictive validity of assessment center evaluations versus traditional measures in forecasting supervisory performance: Interpretive implications of criterion distortion of the assessment paradigm. *Journal of Applied Psychology, 69*, 595–602.

Walsh, W. F. (1983, November). Leadership: A police perspective. *The Police Chief*, pp. 26–29.

CHAPTER 17

What Psychologists Should Know
About Lie Detection

WILLIAM G. IACONO and CHRISTOPHER J. PATRICK

- A five-year-old girl complains to her parents that her 18-year-old babysitter forced her to perform a sexual act. No physical evidence is found to corroborate her story but the suspect agrees to take a polygraph test. He is deemed deceptive and confesses the indecent assault to the police examiner.

- A 28-year-old man, covered with blood when he was arrested at the scene of the crime, confessed to the brutal slaying of a mother and her two infant children. An appeals court overturned his subsequent conviction on a legal technicality. At his retrial five years later he wants the court to consider as evidence his having recently passed a polygraph test.

- When the house of a businessman in financial difficulty burned down a year earlier, his insurance company accused him of arson and refused to honor the claim. He is suing the company, basing his case on the fact that he passed a lie detector test concerning this incident.

- According to a recent divorcée, her four-year-old daughter indicated that the multiple bruises and cuts on her body were inflicted by her father's fiancée. The father and his partner claim the girl fell down the basement stairs and accuse her mother of instructing the little girl to lie. The judge who conducted the child custody hearing in this case is awaiting the results of lie detector examinations administered to all three adults before deciding which parent, if either, is fit to raise the child.

Lie detection is a scientific topic about which almost everyone has strong feelings. It is heralded by some as the court of last resort—a way to establish guilt or innocence in cases that cannot be resolved by other means. To others it is an example of applied technology gone out of control and a threat to basic civil liberties. Whatever one's opinion, the preceding anecdotes illustrate that polygraph tests can have profound effects on the lives of those who agree to take them. It should not be surprising, then, that the psychophysiological detection of lying has been immersed in con-

We should like to express our gratitude to Michael Dawson, David Lykken, and David Raskin for their comments on an earlier draft of this chapter. Some of the work described in it was supported by a grant from the Social Science and Humanities Research Council of Canada.

troversy ever since the technique was first introduced by Harvard psychologist William Marston in 1917. In this chapter we review the most common techniques of lie detection, provide an analysis of their accuracy, and discuss some of the polygraph's typical applications.

THE POLYGRAPH

When a person is asked to take a polygraph test, normally a briefcase-sized instrument like that shown in Figure 17.1 is used to monitor the bodily activity that accompanies responses to test questions. Expandable pneumatic belts positioned around the upper thorax and abdomen provide two separate recordings of the chest movements associated with inspiration and expiration. Changes in skin resistance (the galvanic skin response or GSR) are detected by electrodes attached to the finger tips. A partly inflated blood pressure cuff attached to the cardio channel reflects relative changes in blood pressure and provides an index of pulse. A typical chart that displays the physiological tracings associated with a polygraph test is illustrated in Figure 17.2.

The respiration and cardio channels, both of which are sensitive to changes in air pressure, can be coupled either mechanically or electronically to the polygraph pens. With mechanical coupling, variations in air pressure drive a bellows that is attached directly to the pen. With electronic coupling, these pressure changes are converted to electronic signals which in turn drive motors attached to the pens. The type of coupling that is used depends on the preference of the examiner and does not seem to affect the outcome of a polygraph test. Many polygraphers disdain the electronic systems because they are more complex and are felt to be unnecessary. An electronic cardio, however, has an advantage over the mechanical alternative because the electronic system makes it possible to use less air pressure in the blood pressure cuff. Because the inflated cuff partially occludes blood flow to the arm, reduced pressure in the cuff diminishes the likelihood that the subject will experience discomfort while the cuff is inflated.

As others have pointed out (Kleinmuntz & Szucko, 1982; Lykken, 1981), the polygraph itself is not capable of detecting lies, and there is no pattern of physiological response that is unique to lying. All one can infer by examining polygraph charts is that the subject showed a greater physiological arousal to one question than to another. Although lying may account for this differential arousal, other factors may also cause one question to be more disturbing than another; for example, a question could elicit a large response because it provoked feelings of anger or grief or because it was threatening or embarrassing. The extent to which such factors affect the outcome of polygraph tests is unknown.

THE POLYGRAPHER

The vast majority of polygraphers are not psychologists, but rather graduates of specialized polygraph training institutes staffed with personnel educated in law en-

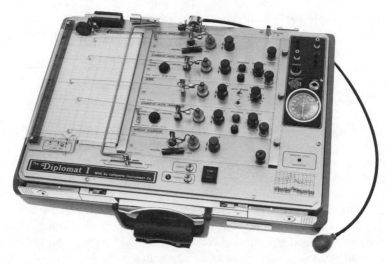

FIGURE 17.1 Modern field polygraph illustrating a typical configuration that employs both mechanical and electronic recording modules. Photo used with permission from the Lafayette Instrument Co., Inc., Lafayette, Indiana.

forcement. In 1985 there were 30 polygraph schools in North America accredited by the profession's main governing body, the American Polygraph Association. One of them, the U.S. Army Military Police School, has been responsible for training almost all U.S. federal government polygraph examiners. In Canada, Royal Canadian Mounted Police examiners and local police polygraphers are trained at the nation's only polygraph school, the Canadian Police College in Ottawa.

Requirements for admission to polygraph schools vary widely. Those with the strictest standards boast American Polygraph Association approval and typically require a bachelor's degree, a personal interview, and a polygraph test. Although approved courses of instruction cover psychology and physiology, instruction on each of these topics may amount to less then 10 hours of an intensive program that, for the vast majority of schools, spans only seven weeks.

Not all practicing polygraph examiners are graduates of APA-approved schools. There is no recognized national agency to regulate polygraph programs. Even in states that have enacted licensing laws there exist polygraph schools that have not been approved for licensing. And in about half of the states and Canada there is nothing to prevent the unscrupulous and untrained entrepreneur from purchasing some cheap recording equipment (sometimes little more than a prop) and hanging out a shingle.

TYPES OF TESTS

Specific Incident Investigations—The Control Question Test

Praised by many, maligned by many, the control question test (CQT) remains the technique of choice among polygraphers who conduct specific incident investiga-

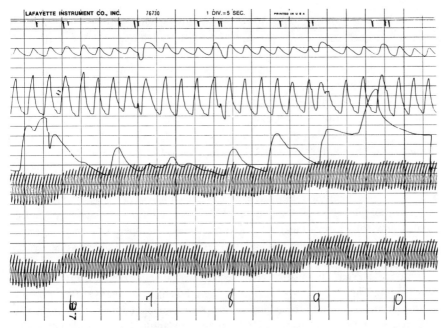

FIGURE 17.2 The physiological tracings produced during a control question polygraph test using the polygraph displayed in Figure 17.1. The five channels recorded are, from top to bottom: (1) mechanical respiration, thorax, (2) electronically enhanced respiration, abdomen, (3) palmar sweating, (4) electronically enhanced cardio, and (5) mechanical cardio. For channels 4 and 5, the blood pressure cuff is attached in parallel to the two cardio channels. The pips along the top edge of the chart, which appear in groups of three, indicate when a question began and ended, and when the subject responded. The number of each question is indicated at the bottom of the chart. Photo used with permission from the Lafayette Instrument Co., Inc., Lafayette, Indiana.

tions like those concerned with criminal acts. The CQT is a complex and subtle procedure with a wide range of administrative and scoring variants. As such, it could easily warrant a chapter of its own or an entire textbook. This section provides an overview of the CQT as we have seen it used by professional examiners. For more detail the reader should consult some of the more comprehensive reference materials available on the subject (e.g., Barland & Raskin, 1973; Lykken, 1981; Reid & Inbau, 1977).

The CQT typically consists of about 10 questions. The two types of question that are important to the determination of guilt or innocence are referred to as relevant and control questions. The relevant questions deal directly with the incident under investigation (e.g., Did you stab John Doe on the night of March 18?). Control items cover past behaviors that one might associate with "the kind of person" who is capable of killing (e.g., Before the age of 24 did you ever try to hurt someone to get revenge?). It is assumed that guilty suspects will be more concerned with the relevant than with the control questions. The reverse pattern is expected with innocent people.

The CQT theory holds that the innocent will be less disturbed by the relevant items because they did not commit the crime and can therefore answer these questions easily and truthfully. Instead, innocent persons will be more troubled by the control items because they are unsure that they can deny them truthfully and thereby avoid incrimination. Put another way, innocent suspects will find the control questions more threatening because they believe they are the only items on which they may be caught in a lie.

The typical control question test consists of a one- to two-hour pretest interview followed by the administration of at least three "charts" (i.e., three separate presentations of the question sequence while the subject's responses are monitored with the polygraph). The positions of control and relevant questions are usually varied from chart to chart to minimize habituation, but in the procedure favored by modern lie detection experts (see, e.g., Barland & Raskin, 1973) each relevant question is always paired with a control item in the question sequence. The latter practice is known as the "zone of comparison" (ZOC) procedure. Developed by Backster (1962), the ZOC format has gained favor because it compensates for variations in subject reactivity during the test and also provides for a more objective analysis of the charts.

Before Backster's innovation chart scoring was always done globally and unsystematically: If the subject's responses to the relevant items seemed larger on each chart than his reaction to the control items, he was declared deceptive; if his reactions to the control items were generally more substantial, he was declared truthful. In Backster's numerical scoring procedure adjacent control/relevant item responses are compared for each separate physiological channel. A score from $+1$ to $+3$ is assigned if the response to the control item is larger, with the magnitude of the score determined by how large a difference is observed. Likewise, a score from -1 to -3 is assigned if the relevant member of the question pair elicited the stronger response. A total score is obtained by summing these values over all channels and charts, with a sufficiently large negative score prompting a deceptive verdict, a sufficiently large positive score a truthful verdict, and scores near zero considered inconclusive. About 10 percent of the control question tests end with inconclusive outcomes.

Having followed the discussion this far, the reader may be unwilling to accept a fundamental tenet of the CQT—that, unlike the guilty suspect, the innocent person will be more disturbed by the possibly trivial issues raised by the control items than by questions that have to do with the matter under investigation. Why aren't the relevant questions just as arousing to innocent suspects, who may view their freedom or livelihood as dependent on their physiological response to these items, as they are to the guilty? Might not many innocent people be telling the truth when they answer the control questions, and if so, why should they give stronger physiological reactions to them? Critics of the CQT argue that skepticism of this kind is only natural, because there really is no reason to believe that innocent suspects will not be threatened or concerned with the relevant items, nor is there any reason to assume they are lying or concerned when they respond to the control questions. Those who use the CQT, on the other hand, believe that such doubts are a product of ignorance. They point out that the theory behind the CQT can be fully appreciated only in the light of what takes place during the interview that precedes the test. A major purpose of this interview is to focus the subject's "psychological set" on the appropriate item category—on the control questions if the examinee is innocent; on the relevant questions if he is guilty.

Two tactics are used. The first is to do everything humanly possible to convince the subject that if he lies, he will be caught. One way to achieve this is to show him that the polygraph can detect a known lie. In a typical scenario the examiner connects the subject to the polygraph and says, "I'm going to ask you to pick a number from 1 to 10, write it down, and then show it to me. Both of us will know which number you've picked. After that, I will say a number and ask you if it is yours. I want you to answer 'no' to each number I say, including the one you picked." The examiner then records the subject's responses to each number and tells him afterward that his largest reaction occurred when he lied; if this were indeed the case, the examiner may point it out to him on the chart. This type of demonstration procedure, often called a "stim test," is used routinely by most polygraphers. Some augment its effect by having the subject pick a card from a stacked deck and then "guessing" which one he or she picked.

A second tactic for establishing the correct psychological set is to continually impress upon the subject during the pretest that he must be truthful *at all times*. No distinction is made between the relevant and the control questions regarding the burden of truthfulness. The examiner reviews the entire question sequence with the subject during the pretest and tells him that it is critical that he be able to answer each and every question truthfully and with complete confidence. The subject is encouraged to make admissions in instances in which he cannot issue a denial with certainty and the corresponding control question is altered to accommodate these admissions. If a subject quickly denies ever having hurt someone, ever having lied, or whatever, the examiner probes his denial: "Are you sure about that? Think hard about your answer, because if you can think of even one thing, you must tell me. It's important that you answer every one of these questions truthfully." Because fully encouraging truthfulness can be seen as weakening the control questions, many polygraphers, including those trained by the federal government, subtly discourage suspects from divulging past transgressions associated with the control questions. Suspects are thus left with the impression that it is important to be truthful, but that too many admissions of wrongdoing will elicit concern from the polygrapher and cast doubts on the suspect's integrity.

Those who believe in the CQT are convinced that these tactics have different consequences for guilty and innocent people and that these consequences are unvarying. Guilty people focus on the relevant questions because they know they must lie to these items and they are afraid they will be caught. Innocent people focus on the control questions because these questions are designed to create doubt in the face of demands for truth and certainty. Whether these contrasting results occur as often as proponents claim they do is an issue that can only be resolved empirically. We try in a later section to evaluate the existing data.

The Employee Screening Test

In many cases polygraph examiners are asked to deal with broader issues than simply, "Did you do it?" One example is the preemployment polygraph test, in which the examiner's task is to verify information provided by a job applicant. Matters of interest will vary according to the nature of the position and the concerns of the employer: Retailers want to know, for example, whether an applicant has been fired from previous jobs, served time in prison, stolen from previous employers, or falsified information about his job qualifications and experience. National security agencies will be concerned as well with the applicant's political leanings, contacts with foreign agents, and involvement in activities that might invite blackmail. A periodic screening of existing employees is another situation in which general information is sought. Here, the polygraph examiner is called on to determine whether current personnel have been pilfering from the company, revealing classified information, or betraying their employer in other ways.

In contrast to specific incident investigations, screening tests contain relevant questions of the form "Have you ever . . . ?" or "During the period in question, did you . . . ?" As such, general controls for these items cannot be constructed; what would be considered control items for a specific incident test are actually the "meat" of the screening test. For this reason most polygraph examiners rely on the relevant/irrelevant (R/I) test format for purposes of pre- and postemployment screening. As its name suggests, the R/I test contains only two types of items: relevant questions concerning matters of interest (e.g., drug use, criminal behavior, and loyalty) and innocuous or irrelevant questions (also called "norms"). The latter include items like "Is your last name_____?" and "Is today Sunday?"

It is important to distinguish between the traditional R/I test and the R/I screening test as it is typically used today (Office of Technology Assessment, 1983). Developed in 1917 by William M. Marston, the father of polygraphic lie detection, and subsequently refined by police officer and medical student John A. Larson, the traditional R/I test was for 30 years the standard question format and was used in all contexts, which include criminal investigations of specific incidents. The test usually contained three relevant questions, each preceded and followed by irrelevant items, with a nonrelevant but evocative item at the end of the list to confirm the subject's ability to respond (Lykken, 1981). Consistently more pronounced reactions to the relevant items were taken as evidence of deception.

Disenchantment with the traditional R/I test grew from the realization that truthful and deceptive persons alike may be more disturbed by the relevant questions. Because of this, the procedure is generally eschewed by modern polygraphers. For employment screening purposes polygraphers are now more likely to rely on a variant of the R/I procedure that might more accurately be designated the Relevant/Relevant (R/R) technique. In this question format irrelevant items appear less frequently and are meant to provide a "rest period or return to baseline," as opposed to a norm for comparison purposes. It is the relative response to the various relevant items that is crucial. The reasoning goes as follows: Because the test covers several separate issues, the examiner can expect a truthful response to at least some of the relevant questions. Deceptive answers should provoke stronger physiological reactions by comparison. The examiner will typically administer three or more question series by covering the same topics but varying the form of the questions and their order. If the subject shows persistently strong reaction to one or more content areas in relation to the rest, the examiner will conclude that the subject has lied or that he is particularly sensitive about these issues for some hidden reason. In this case the examiner will usually ask the subject to explain what might have provoked these responses and may conduct additional tests that focus on these issues.

Although the R/R test format seems preferable to the traditional R/I test in terms of protecting the innocent, Lykken (1981) points out some of its limitations. In the first place it is extremely difficult to guarantee that all relevant items will be equally disturbing for a truthful subject; more threatening questions may provoke stronger reactions even when answered truthfully. A second issue concerns the practice of altering questions in response to admissions by the subject. It is customary for the examiner to review the questions with the subject before the test and also to ask for clarification between charts about items that provoked a response. If the subject makes a confession in a certain area, the related question is modified to read, "Apart from what you have told me . . ." The assumption is that if the subject has admitted everything of importance in regard to that item he will be able to respond to it with a clear conscience and minimal chart reaction thereafter. That this result is obtained in all cases is doubtful. In fact, the control question test relies on the contrary assumption that truthful subjects should still be concerned with control items even after they have been modified to accommodate their admissions.

As a final comment, we should note that much of this criticism becomes moot when the screening test is considered from a utility standpoint as opposed to a validity standpoint (cf. Office of Technology Assessment, 1983). Proponents of the employment screening polygraph test point out that its usefulness stems largely from its power to elicit damaging confessions. For this reason, Lykken (1981) has described the test as a "bloodless third degree." The implication is that in actual practice employment screening examiners may not hold to any rigidly standardized approaches to test administration and evaluation; therefore, the distinction between traditional R/I and R/R test procedures may become blurred. As Ferguson (1966) states in one of the few published works on employment-related polygraph procedures, "The cardinal rule in chart interpretation is, 'Any change from normal requires an explanation'" (p. 161). Probably much more so than in specific incident investigations, screening examiners rely on the polygraph as an interrogational tool. In this sense the employment screening polygraph test is very much a "clinical lie test" (Lykken, 1981)—an essentially subjective assessment of the subject's truthfulness—with all its attendant biases. In many instances, however, the final outcome, rather than being based on the subjective or "objective" assessments of the charts or the subject, is based on the admissions made by the subject.

Guilty Knowledge Test

An alternative to the CQT for specific incident investigations is the Guilty Knowledge Test (GKT) (Lykken, 1959, 1960). Rather than asking the subject point blank,

"Did you do it?" the GKT probes for guilty knowledge—items of information about a crime or incident that only the culprit would be aware of. A GKT would include a series of questions about the crime posed in multiple-choice format. Each question would concern one detail of the crime, with multiple-choice alternatives that include the correct answer as well as other plausible but incorrect choices. An example of a GKT question concerning a bank holdup might be as follows: "If you robbed the bank, then you wrote a note to the teller you held up giving her instructions. Was that note written on (a) a piece of yellow paper? (b) a one dollar bill? (c) the back of a photograph? (d) part of a brown paper bag? (e) a candy bar wrapper?" When confronted with this kind of crime question, the real perpetrator would be expected to give his largest physiological response to the correct answer, whereas an innocent person, knowing nothing about the incident, would tend to respond at random.

Proponents (Iacono, 1985; Kleinmuntz & Szucko, 1982; Lykken, 1981) believe that the GKT should be used in place of the CQT whenever possible because of its inherent capacity to protect the innocent. An innocent suspect who knows nothing about the crime would have only one chance in five of responding most dramatically to the relevant alternative. With a GKT comprised of 10 such questions, the odds are astronomically small (less than one chance in 10 million) that an innocent person would react most strongly to the relevant item in each and every test question.

In addition to protecting the innocent, the GKT offers a built-in safeguard against deliberate efforts to defeat the test. As Lykken (1960) demonstrated, any response pattern that deviates significantly from random suggests the use of countermeasures to cover guilt; for example, even if subjects were to augment their responses artificially to one irrelevant alternative on each test question they might still give themselves away by consistently showing their second largest response to the relevant alternative. Similarly, a response pattern in which reactions to relevant items were consistently the smallest would be statistically aberrant and suggestive of distortion.

VALIDITY

Criteria for an Acceptable Validity Study

As any psychologist knows, there is no such thing as a perfect study, and the lie detection literature offers no exception to this rule. The conclusions that are drawn about the accuracy of the polygraph test are determined in part by the range and quality of evidence that a reviewer is willing to consider. Because there are so many studies that touch on the accuracy issue, we should preface our evaluation of the literature with a summary of the more important methodological issues that a serious investigation of polygraph validity must address.

Field versus Laboratory Investigations

Polygraph studies can be divided into two broad categories, depending on the circumstances under which the polygraph test is administered. Field studies involve real-life cases and circumstances. The subjects are actual criminal suspects. Laboratory studies require naive volunteers to simulate criminal behavior by enacting a mock crime. The latter approach provides unambiguous criteria for establishing ground truth but cannot be used to establish the accuracy of the procedure because the motivational and emotional concerns of the suspects are too dissimilar from those involved in real-life examinations. Unlike those faced with an actual criminal investigation, guilty subjects in the laboratory have little incentive to try and "beat" the test, and both guilty and innocent subjects have little to fear if they are diagnosed deceptive. Administering the CQT to laboratory subjects is especially likely to lead to overestimates of accuracy for the innocent. Innocent subjects can reasonably be expected to respond more strongly to the potentially embarrassing control questions concerning their personal integrity and honesty than to the relevant questions dealing with a simulated crime they carried out only to satisfy experimental requirements. On the other hand, laboratory research does permit more efficient investigation of the influence of "extra-guilt" variables and the relative merits of different testing procedures. In general, although laboratory and field studies should be used hand in hand, the results of laboratory studies should not be used to estimate the accuracy of polygraph tests. A possible exception to this rule, the analogue field study (Ekman, 1985), is discussed shortly.

Establishing Guilt and Innocence

The advantage of field investigations, that they are based on actual crimes, is also a significant drawback because prima facie evidence of innocence or guilt is often lacking. One unsatisfactory procedure to deal with this problem relies solely on judicial outcomes. The potential for establishing the truth is limited with this approach because some people are falsely convicted of crimes, and for practical reasons some innocent individuals will plead guilty to crimes they did not commit. Also, because of legal technicalities that prevent the admission of evidence and the notion that one must be proved guilty beyond a reasonable doubt, many guilty defendants will escape conviction. Finally, the judicial decision may not be independent of the polygraph test results.

An improvement over the use of judicial verdicts involves the use of a panel of jurists experienced in criminal law. These experts can be asked to review all the case facts (minus the polygraph findings), ignore legal technicalities, and render a judgment based on the available evidence. The possibility of errors can be minimized by accepting only those cases that the judges can decide with a high degree of confidence.

A third method for operationalizing ground truth is to rely on confessions to identify the culpable and clear the innocent. Although occasionally confessions are false, and those who confess may differ in important ways from those who do not, the major problem with this strategy concerns the likelihood that the confession, even if obtained after the psychophysiological recording is completed, is not independent of the original polygraph examiner's assessment. For reasons that are unrelated to test accuracy confessions may be associated almost exclusively with charts that indicate a deceptive outcome. When this occurs, the verified cases included in the validity study will be biased in favor of demonstrating high accuracy for the technique.

To make this point clear consider the following example. Ten women are suspects in a criminal investigation. A polygrapher tests them one by one until a deceptive outcome is obtained, say on the sixth suspect tested. (In these circumstances the remaining four women would not be tested unless the crime was believed to involve more than one perpetrator.) According to usual practice, the examiner then attempts to extract a confession. If the examinee fails to confess, her guilt or innocence cannot be confirmed. It is possible that the polygrapher committed two errors in testing these six cases: The person with the deceptive chart may have been innocent, and one of those tested before her could have been guilty. In the absence of verification, however, the polygraph records from these six cases will never be included as part of a sample in a validity study. On the other hand, if the sixth suspect does confess, these six charts, all of which confirm the original examiner's assessment, will be included. The resulting sample of cases would consist entirely of charts the original examiner judged correctly and would never include cases in which an error was made.

Although not quite stated in these terms, a number of authorities have questioned the utility of some or all of the validity studies that depend on confessions (Horvath, 1976; Lykken, 1981; Raskin, 1978). They claim that when the confession confirms the original polygrapher's diagnosis, having other examiners rescore the same charts provides more an index of interscorer reliability than a measure of validity.

Evaluation of Polygraph Charts

As indicated previously, polygraphers reach conclusions using either a global approach to chart interpretation or semiobjective numerical scoring. Because both approaches are still currently taught and used, studies of polygraph accuracy should examine both practices. Investigations comparing the two approaches are especially needed; the only two studies to do so to date have obtained quite different conclusions (Ginton, Daie, Elaad, & Ben-Shakhar, 1982; Raskin, Barland, & Podlesny, 1978).

Regardless of the procedure used to score the charts, the field examiner normally has been exposed to extra-polygraphic cues such as the case facts, the behavior of the suspect during the examination, and sometimes a confession from the examinee. But the critical issue in determining validity is the accuracy of the psychophysiological test, not the ability of a human being to use the available evidence to reach a correct judgment. For an investigation to provide a useful estimate of polygraph accuracy the original examiner's charts must be reinterpreted by "blind" evaluators who have no knowledge of the suspect or case facts.

Control Question Test

Field Studies

There are nine field studies designed to assess the accuracy of the CQT (see also Office of Technology Assessment, 1983; Saxe, Dougherty, & Cross, 1985). The characteristics of all but one of these studies are summarized in Table 17.1. The one in-

TABLE 17.1 Characteristics of Control Question Test Field Studies

Study	Number of Cases		% Correctly Classified[a]			Guilt/ Innocence Criterion	Used Blind Scoring?	Reproducible Case Sample?	Used Numerical Scoring?	Number of	
	Innocent	Guilty	Innocent	Guilty	Overall[b]					Original Examiners	Chart Evaluators
Bersh (1969)	87	70	92	93	92	Panel	No	Yes	No	Unknown	—
Horvath & Reid (1971)	20	20	91	85	88	Confession	Yes	No	No	1	10
Hunter & Ash (1973)	10	10	86	88	87[c]	Unknown	Yes	No	No	1	10
Slowick & Buckley (1975)	15	15	93	85	89	Unknown	Yes	Yes	No	Unknown	7
Wicklander & Hunter (1975)	10	10	95	92	93	Unknown	Yes	No	No	2	6
Barland & Raskin (1976)	11	40	45	98	71	Panel	Yes	Yes	Yes	1	1
Horvath (1977)	28	28	51	77	64	Confession	Yes	Yes	No	Unknown	10
Kleinmuntz & Szucko (1984a)	50	50	63	75	69	Confession	Yes	Yes	No	Unknown	6

[a]Inconclusive cases were eliminated when these figures were computed.

[b]Based on the mean of the accuracies computed for the innocent and guilty cases.

[c]Accuracy figures based on the average of two blind chart analyses performed by each chart evaluator.

vestigation not included (Davidson, 1979) is not comparable to those listed because a panel of examiners was used to interpret the polygraph charts. Hence the accuracy figures reported by the author are based on a panel consensus rather than on the independent scoring of blind chart evaluators. Comparing this study to the others is further complicated by the use of a type of physiological recording not commonly employed in field tests. Finally, although the panel performed well, confidence in this report is undermined by the exclusion of 30 percent of the randomly selected charts from the data analysis.

The remaining eight investigations can be divided into three sets. The first consists solely of the Bersh (1969) report. In this study the accuracy of the original examiner's decision was compared to the judgment of a panel of attorneys. Because the examiner's assessment did not depend solely on the polygraph record, as Bersh (1969) noted, it is impossible to determine the relative contribution of the polygraph charts to the polygrapher's diagnosis. This study, therefore, was not designed to estimate the accuracy of the test itself and will not be considered further.

The second set of investigations was published in a police science journal by polygraphers associated with Reid College for the Detection of Deception in Chicago (Horvath & Reid, 1971; Hunter & Ash, 1973; Slowick & Buckley, 1975; Wicklander & Hunter, 1975). As Table 17.1 indicates, the percentages of correct classification obtained in these four studies were 85 or better, with generally higher hit rates reported for innocent than for guilty suspects.

Unfortunately, these reports are lacking in important details the reader must have to place confidence in the findings. Three of the four investigations (Hunter & Ash, 1973; Slowick & Buckley, 1975; Wicklander & Hunter, 1975) did not specify the criteria used to establish ground truth. In addition, three of the four (Horvath & Reid, 1971; Hunter & Ash, 1973; Wicklander & Hunter, 1975) failed to describe in sufficient detail how the polygraph records were chosen. As a result, the representative nature of the charts remains unknown and it is impossible to reproduce the case samples. In addition, in one of these studies (Horvath & Reid, 1971), cases were deleted from the original sample based on subjective decisions made by the authors. Thirty-five of seventy-five initially identified cases were eliminated "because they did not require any exceptional skill to interpret" (p. 277). The resulting sample is characterized as containing neither these "obvious" cases nor those that would "be uninterpretable by even the most skilled examiner" (p. 278). None of these studies, including that of Horvath and Reid (1971), specified the criteria used to identify the initial sample of cases; the reader is told only that the polygraph charts came from suspects tested by the authors.

In the absence of adequate information Raskin (1982) and Lykken (1981) have offered quite different interpretations of these studies. Raskin (1982) asserts that in all four studies the charts "were selected so as not to represent extremely clear examples of polygraph chart outcomes" (p. 345), thereby implying that these studies provide a conservative test of polygraph accuracy. Lykken (1981), on the other hand, argues that in all of these studies the deck was probably stacked to obtain inflated accuracy estimates. Lykken suggests that the intitial case samples were selected such that only charts scored correctly by the original examiner were chosen. Under such circumstances, the charts would contain the expected physiological response patterns associated with deceptive and truthful outcomes, and it should be no surprise that blind interpreters trained to look for these patterns reached the same conclusion as did the original examiner. As already noted, this line of argument can be used to classify these investigations as reliability rather than validity studies.

The final three investigations (Barland & Raskin, 1976; Horvath, 1977; Kleinmuntz & Szucko, 1984a) were conducted by social scientists, three of whom (Barland, Horvath, and Raskin) are also trained polygraphers. The Barland and Raskin (1976) and Horvath (1977) reports were based on the dissertations of first authors; the Kleinmuntz and Szucko (1984a) study was conducted with cases and chart evaluators that also came from Reid College. It can be seen in Table 17.1 that the results of these three studies are markedly different from those obtained in the earlier investigations. Hit rates for both the guilty and innocent are lower and the blind-chart evaluators performed at about chance level with innocent suspects.

These reports are also subject to various criticisms, some of which are subtle and cannot be derived from the information contained in the published reports. In the Barland and Raskin (1976) study, the majority decision of a panel of two defense attorneys, two criminal prosecutors, and a judge was used to establish ground truth. According to Barland and Raskin (1976), the investigative data presented to the panel were compiled by inexperienced university students who had difficulty collecting case facts from the police, defense counsel, and prosecuting attorney. The resulting incompleteness of many of the dossiers may have resulted in criterion errors. Barland and Raskin (1976; Barland, 1982; Raskin & Podlesny, 1979) have argued that the panel decision was probably biased toward incorrect conclusions of innocence because evidence against a suspect was more likely to be absent from case files than was supportive information and because lawyers tend to interpret a poorly substantiated charge as an indication of innocence. According to Barland (1982), even though panelists were instructed to conclude "no decision" rather than "probably innocent" under such circumstances, conversations with two of the panelists at the end of the study indicated that they did not follow this rule. To the extent these assertions about the direction of bias are true, the poor performance of the polygraph with criterion innocent suspects could stem from criterion decisions, rather than from polygraph tests that were fallible.

Because of this criticism, attention has been directed toward another aspect of this study that involves 16 suspects whose charts were verified by confessions (Raskin et al., 1978). The polygraph records from these subjects were scored blindly by 25 polygraphers, seven of whom scored the charts numerically. Excluding inconclusive judgments, 90 percent of the decisions of the blind evaluators were correct, and those using numerical scoring performed better than those using the global approach. Unfortunately, only four of the subjects were innocent, accuracies were not presented separately for guilty and innocent groups, and the percentage of correct decisions is not comparable to the overall percentages listed in Table 17.1. Rather, it is derived from the number of subjects correctly classified without regard to the unequal size of the two subject groups. Because 75 percent of the subjects were guilty and the panel study indicated that guilty subjects were accurately classified, this report adds little to the accuracy estimate provided by the panel study.

Cases selected for the Horvath (1977) study were drawn from the files of a police agency. Although the polygraph records were chosen at random, only confession-verified charts that agreed with the original examiner's decision were used. No information is given to show how confessions were obtained, but it is likely that they were obtained by the polygrapher from suspects who failed the test. As mentioned previously, a field study derived from this type of confession-verified sample is probably biased toward confirming the original examiners' decisions, and, as a result, Horvath (1976) and Raskin (1978) have suggested that this report is concerned primarily with reliability. However, this study had the lowest hit rate of any listed in Table 17.1.

Raskin (1978; Raskin & Podlesny, 1979) has attributed these low accuracy figures to the fact that the blind reviewers were not trained in numerical scoring. In the absence of the extra-polygraphic data they have become accustomed to they may have been unable to make adequate assessments using only the physiological recordings. This explanation seems unlikely, however, because the interrater reliability coefficient for the group of 10 evaluators was .89. In addition, only 1 percent of the examiners' judgments fell in the inconclusive category, indicating that they were confident in their ability to render meaningful decisions.

A more serious criticism has been raised by Barland (1982) who asserted that Horvath's low hit rate for criterion innocent subjects could be attributable to special characteristics of the suspects in the innocent group. Although the subjects of Horvath's study were all described as "criminal suspects" who committed "crimes against a person" or "property crimes," 13 were "victims" who were tested because they were suspected of falsifying their reports to the police (Horvath, personal communication, September 18, 1984). Information regarding the nature of these alleged false reports has not been made available. However, to give one example, it is not uncommon for rape victims to undergo polygraph tests to substantiate their claims. Such confirmatory polygraph tests, because they are conducted with someone involved with the crime, often elicit strong emotional feelings and are believed by many polygraphers to be prone to false-positive errors, especially when they are conducted by inexperienced examiners. The fact that 50 percent of the innocent suspects were victims could therefore account for the 51 percent accuracy obtained for this group. According to Horvath, however, (personal communication, September 18, 1984), the inclusion of victims had little effect on the blind interpreters' judgments. With the victims excluded from the data analysis, the overall accuracy rises from 64 to 67 percent. Moreover, the "false positive rate of the 10 evaluators was similar whether or not the decisions on the 'victims' were included or excluded."

In the Kleinmuntz and Szucko (1984a) study no information was presented concerning how the original examiner scored the charts or how confessions were obtained. As with the other studies that used confession-verified cases, it is likely that the original examiner obtained a confession based on a chart indicative of deception. Nonetheless, the accuracy rates are rather low.

One explanation for this outcome derives from Kleinmuntz and Szucko's (1984a) selecting only cases involving crimes of theft (Office of Technology Assessment, 1983). Horvath (1977) found that suspects involved with crimes against property were harder to detect than those charged with crimes against persons, perhaps because the latter are more emotion laden. All the other field studies presumably included both types of crime (crime type is not discussed by Bersh, 1969), although the exact proportion of the different types contained in the study samples is seldom specified.

Other aspects of the Kleinmuntz and Szucko (1984a) investigation may have served to deflate accuracy rates. In a subsequent paper that presented information pertinent to this study Kleinmuntz and Szucko (1984b) revealed that the polygraphers based their decisions on a single chart (a minimum of three is standard) and that they were not allowed to categorize the outcome as inconclusive. In addition, the six judges, who used the global scoring approach, were described as "polygraph trainees at the end of their internship training period" (p. 772). All of these factors provide for a less-than-optimal test of polygraph validity—a conclusion that is reinforced by the fact that in these circumstances the interjudge reliability coefficient averaged only .43.

Comment

The field studies of CQT validity can be divided into two groups—each converging on conclusions that are markedly different. The four Reid College studies suggest that the CQT is highly accurate and that it works equally well with guilty and innocent persons. More recent investigations describe a technique that is quite fallible and strongly biased against the innocent. All of these studies are subject to various criticisms. How damaging the shortcomings of a study are to its internal validity seems to depend more on where one is willing to extend the benefit of the doubt than on the nature of the defect. Can the reports of professional polygraphers, which did not undergo the scrutiny of scientific review prior to publication and are lacking in crucial detail, be trusted? Do the three most recent studies, each of which is imperfect, provide a fair test of polygraph accuracy?

From our analysis we conclude that based on the field studies presently available, the validity of the CQT has not been established. There remains a critical need for more field investigations. All of the studies indicate that the CQT works at well above chance levels with guilty individuals. The important issue to be addressed in subsequent studies concerns its effectiveness with innocent suspects.

A number of recommendations for future research on polygraph accuracy can be made. The validity of the CQT should be assessed for different types of crime. Horvath's (1977) data suggest that property crimes are more difficult to detect than those against people, but it is also possible that more serious crimes and those associated with harsher penalties will elicit stronger emotional reactions and a greater incidence of false-positive outcomes (as may be the case with victims). A detail that has been ignored in all the field studies concerns how confessions were obtained. The source of the confession must be reported, and cases should be analyzed separately, depending on whether the confession was associated with or independent of the polygraph test.

Another critical factor that has been overlooked concerns the experience of the original examiners. It is generally felt that the skills of the examiner are paramount to the success of the CQT, especially with respect to establishing the proper psychological set, wording the relevant questions, and selecting contol questions that are not so trivial that the innocent will be unconcerned with them nor so "hot" that the guilty will be more threatened by them than by the relevant questions. The correctness of blind chart interpretations will always be limited by the expertise of the original examiner. Without information on the characteristics of both the blind and original examiners, the extent to which the results of a study can be generalized to the field at large will remain unknown. The method used to analyze charts merits additional attention. Only one of the eight studies listed in Table 17.1 used numerical scoring. This systematic approach to chart analysis may hold more promise than the global approach (see Raskin et al., 1978) and clearly deserves more attention in studies of polygraph validity.

Finally, it should be noted that there are two dimensions along which the validity of the CQT can be assessed. One involves determining how accurate the technique is as it is practiced by the thousands of polygraphers who earn their livelihood conducting polygraph tests. These individuals vary in their levels of education, training, interviewing skills, and how they apply the technique. It is important to know how the typical polygrapher performs because after all it is this individual who gives a polygraph test to the average suspect.

Another approach to the accuracy question that provides for more efficient and productive use of research time is to determine how well the test works with the most competent polygraphers. While it is debatable how best to identify such examiners, a good place to start might be with those employed and trained by government agencies (such as the U.S. military, FBI, or Secret Service and, in Canada, the Royal Canadian Mounted Police). Admission to the training programs is competitive; only those with appropriate educational, professional, and personal characteristics are accepted. The nature and quality of training is well documented, and graduates typically have opportunities to review and update their skills in continuing education programs. Most important, perhaps, is the fact that examiners administer tests in a carefully prescribed, relatively standardized fashion. If such examiners cannot achieve acceptable accuracy with the test, it is unlikely that the average professional polygrapher could perform any better. On the other hand, should high accuracy be demonstrated, it should be possible to pinpoint the essential features of both a good polygraph test and a competent examiner and, in turn, to develop and refine standards for training and the administration of tests.

Analogue Field Studies

As already discussed, both laboratory and field investigations of polygraph test validity are problematic: In laboratory studies real-life motivational conditions are usually lacking. In field studies it is difficult to gather a representative sample of criterion-verified cases. A useful alternative approach is what Ekman (1985) has termed the analogue field study. This refers to a situation in which polygraph test subjects are genuinely concerned about the outcome of the test, and a certain criterion of guilt or innocence is available for the entire sample. To our knowledge only two studies meet these criteria. Ginton et al. (1982) created an opportunity for police trainees suspected of cheating on a course exam to exonerate themselves by taking a polygraph test. Circumstances were arranged so the cheaters could be identified without a doubt, and polygraph test subjects were led to believe that the outcome of the test could affect their future as policemen. Under these conditions 15 of the 21 trainees, two of whom were guilty, agreed to take a control question polygraph test administered by an experienced examiner. Based on independent blind chart evaluations, one of the two guilty subjects and five of the 15 innocent subjects were classified correctly. There was one false-positive decision and eight inconclusive decisions. Although suggestive, these results are clouded by the highly select nature of the sample (i.e., police trainees), the small number of guilty subjects tested, and the fact that less than half of the decisions were conclusive.

More recently we conducted an analogue field study with incarcerated criminals. This study employed a group contingency threat to simulate real-life motivational conditions. Forty-eight inmate volunteers, half of whom had committed a mock theft, were tested on this issue by experienced professional polygraphers using contemporary field equipment and CQT procedures. The examiners did not know which inmates committed the theft and were unaware of the base rate for guilt. Subjects were informed before being tested that consequences for the entire group were dependent on individual performance: If no more than 10 of the 48 volunteers failed the polygraph test, everyone would receive a bonus of $20 at the end of the study. If more than 10 were judged to be deceptive, then no one would receive the bonus. Further, an agreement was made that if more than 10 failed and the bonuses were not distributed, a list would be posted in the prison at the end of the study naming those individuals who had failed the test and who were thus responsible for the payments being withheld. (In actual fact the bonuses were ultimately awarded without regard to group performance.)

Because of the strong peer pressure that exists in the prison, the inmates were concerned about the outcome of their polygraph tests and the possibility that their poor performance could lead to their peers being deprived of what, by prison standards, is a substantial sum of money. Under these conditions blind, independent chart evaluations based on numerical scoring resulted in correct classifications for 20 of 24 guilty subjects and 10 of 24 innocent subjects. Excluding inconclusives, 87 percent of the guilty and 56 percent of the innocent were accurately identified. These results support the findings of the recent field studies of the CQT (e.g., Barland & Raskin, 1976; Horvath, 1977; Kleinmuntz & Szucko, 1984a), which suggest that innocent persons may be particularly susceptible to misclassification.

The Employee Screening Test

Before reviewing evidence concerning the accuracy of employee screening tests we should remind the reader that there are important differences between the traditional

R/I procedure and the version of the test that is typically used for screening purposes (the R/R test). Although these differences may become blurred in practice, one should still exercise caution in generalizing accuracy figures for one procedure to the other. Unfortunately, few studies have shed light on the accuracy of either technique. All of the relevant field studies were conducted before the CQT was invented (in 1946) and dealt with specific incident crimes, not employee screening.

The only existing validity studies of the traditional R/I test using blind chart evaluations are incompletely described and methodologically flawed. In a study reported by Larson (1938), nine judges evaluated the charts of 62 criminal suspects and declared from 8 to 52 percent of the suspects deceptive. Although Larson does not specify how many of these individuals were, in fact, guilty, in most studies conducted before 1950 only one suspect was expected to be guilty. Thus Lykken (1981) has argued that the Larson findings support the contention that truthful as well as deceptive persons are likely be more disturbed by the relevant material in the R/I test. In any event, Larson's results indicate poor reliability. Another study of blind chart evaluations (Heckel, Brokaw, Salzberg, & Wiggins, 1962) has been cited as a validity study of R/I techniques (Department of Defense, 1984), but the question sequence used in that study was a cross between the R/I and CQT formats. This study is also difficult to interpret because it involved an experiment in which subjects, all of whom were innocent, were led to believe they were suspected of a crime that they all knew had not been committed. This situation is dissimilar from the circumstances encountered by suspects implicated in real-life crimes.

All other field studies involving R/I techniques (Bitterman & Marcuse, 1947; Larson, 1921; Lyon, 1936; MacNitt, 1942; Marston, 1921; Winter, 1936) suffer serious methodological deficiencies. None of these investigations used blind chart analysis, and in only two (Larson, 1921; Winter, 1936) was ground truth established without doubt. In several of these reports (Bitterman & Marcuse, 1947; Larson, 1921; Winter, 1936), residents of college dormitories were tested to determine if one student had been robbing the others. In two of these studies (Larson, 1921; Winter, 1936) the untruthful individual confessed and in the other (Bitterman & Marcuse, 1947) all suspects were eventually deemed to be innocent. These seemingly impressive results must be considered in light of the fact that the examiner had the luxury of knowing that only one suspect was likely to be guilty and the chart decisions were not made independently of one another. These efforts represent little more than case reports. One wonders how many similar investigations were not published because the experimenters failed to prove the utility of the polygraph.

Although no field validity investigation of the R/R test has been conducted, a recent study by Thurber (1981) raises important questions. Subjects were 34 police officer candidates who were asked to take a polygraph screening test to gain entrance into a training program. They also completed the California Psychological Inventory (CPI). Of the total sample 19 candidates were denied admission to the program because of elevated physiological responses to relevant questions concerning drug abuse and criminal activity. Subsequent analyses revealed candidates who passed the polygraph test and those that failed could be classified as such with 97 percent accuracy using just their CPI scores. The main discriminating variable was found to be the Good Impression (GI) subscale—a measure of the tendency to "fake good" or behave in a socially desirable fashion. The author's interpretation of this finding was that those able to create a favorable impression on the polygrapher were less likely to be autonomically reactive to relevant questions. An alternative and not necessarily competing interpretation stems from the view of screening tests as "clinical lie tests" (Lykken, 1981). If subjective assessment plays an important role in employment polygraph testing, and guilt and innocence here involve shades of gray as opposed to black and white, then test verdicts may depend more on the subject's ability to gloss over his gray areas than on the examiner's ability to ferret out important truths.

Finally, Sackett and Decker (1979) provide a logical argument as to why the screening test is probably much less accurate than any specific-incident test. Even if the accuracy of the polygraph test approximated 90 percent, the cumulative error rate associated with multiple judgments would cut the overall accuracy rate considerably: the more material covered, the more potential for error. Sackett and Decker also point out that the limited time devoted to each issue in the screening test might decrease single-item accuracy as well; estimates of the validity of specific-incident tests are usually based on criminal investigative work, in which the time devoted to a single issue is usually two to three hours, as opposed to a few minutes.

In summary, the validity data available on the traditional R/I test procedures are inadequate, and a thoughtful analysis of the technique suggests that it is transparent and biased against the innocent. With regard to the R/I test variant commonly used for employment screening (the R/R test), we must concur with the authors of the OTA report, who concluded: "There appears, as yet, to be no scientific field evidence that polygraph examinations . . . represent a valid test to prescreen or periodically screen . . . employees" (Office of Technology Assessment, 1983, p. 58). Perhaps it is inappropriate even to consider the screening test in terms of conventional criterion validity. Unless, as in specific-incident investigations, we can expect that examinees will either be completely truthful or completely deceptive in their responses, how are we to verify examiner judgments of veracity? What is the appropriate criterion? Although there is no clear answer to these questions, Thurber's (1981) study suggests that in situations where guilt and innocence are not clear-cut, examiners may be inordinately influenced by factors that have nothing to do with the polygraph charts.

The Guilty Knowledge Test

There are no field studies that deal with the GKT. Indeed, there is no evidence that the GKT is used to any significant extent by field polygraphers. This is an unfortunate state of affairs because, unlike the situation with the other polygraph procedures, the assumptions on which the GKT is based are not controversial. From a theoretical point of view the GKT can be constructed so that it is virtually impossible for an innocent person to fail, and a positive outcome indicates almost certain guilt (Lykken, 1981, p. 300).

Laboratory demonstrations of simulated crimes have shown the GKT to be accurate. In a recent review of mock-crime investigations conducted between 1959 and 1984 (Iacono, 1984) the GKT was 100 percent accurate in classifying innocent subjects in five of seven studies. Correct classification rates for guilty subjects ranged from 59 percent to 92 percent, with four of seven studies reporting 88 percent or better hit rates. All the laboratory experiments found that false-negative errors were considerably more common than false-positives, indicating that the GKT may be biased in favor of guilty suspects.

The extent to which this bias poses a real problem for the GKT can only be assessed by conducting field studies. Good laboratory experiments arrange the situation so that subjects must attend to details of the "crime" that the examiner is also aware of and can use to construct the GKT. In real life, a criminal may not attend to the aspects of a crime that an investigator views as salient, and many details may be forgotten. On the other hand, if a person does remember the details of a real-life crime, they should elicit greater autonomic reactions, thereby making it easier to detect the guilty.

Countermeasures

Those who criticize the polygraph usually stress the false-positive issue because our legal system is designed to protect the innocent. No less important from a law enforcement and a scientific standpoint, however, are the factors that may allow people to beat a polygraph test. Of the wide variety of potential countermeasures that exist (e.g., Barland & Raskin list nine separate categories in their 1973 chapter), three have attracted particular attention in the last few years; that is, personality, drugs, and physical maneuvers.

A number of authorities (e.g., Barland & Raskin, 1973; Ferguson & Miller, 1974; Floch, 1950; Lykken, 1981) have postulated that psychopathic individuals may be able to foil the lie detector. As described by Cleckley (1976), the typical psychopath is an experienced liar who breaks the law without remorse and without fear of the consequences. Further, there is evidence that persons low in socialization, a personality construct related to psychopathy, can defeat a polygraph test (Waid, Orne, & Wilson, 1979). In the one study to date that has examined the hypothesis directly Raskin and Hare (1978) tested diagnosed criminal psychopaths using CQT procedures and found that they were just as easily detected as nonpsychopathic prisoners. The validity of this finding has been challenged because (1) the polygraph charts in the Raskin and Hare study were not scored blindly and (2) the examinees were motivated by monetary gain and had nothing to lose by failing the test (Lykken, 1978, 1981). The latter may be a significant problem because psychopaths have been shown to be just as physiologically responsive in a monetary reward context as nonpsychopaths (Schmauk, 1970).

To determine whether psychopaths would have an advantage in a more threatening polygraph test situation the authors arranged for equal groups of psychopathic and nonpsychopathic prison inmates to be tested in a group contingency situation. As outlined in the earlier section on analogue studies, subjects were led to believe that monetary rewards for the entire group were dependent on individual test results, with an underlying threat of public disclosure if the rewards were not obtained. In contrast to the Raskin and Hare study, there were no individual monetary incentives involved. Assessments of psychopathy were performed with Hare's diagnostic criteria (Hare, 1980), and equal groups of psychopaths and nonpsychopaths were assigned randomly to guilty and innocent conditions. Subjects were tested regarding their involvement in a mock crime by experienced examiners blind to guilt and psychopathy status, using standard field equipment and control question procedures.

Blind independent chart evaluations using numerical scoring produced a high rate of correct classifications of guilty subjects. Excluding inconclusives, 83 percent of the guilty psychopaths and 90 percent of the guilty nonpsychopaths were identified as deceptive. Consistent with the findings of Raskin and Hare, psychopaths were no more successful at beating the tests than nonpsychopaths. This finding remains controversial in light of popular conceptions of the psychopath as lacking guilt and anticipatory fear. It may be the case that in situations involving an imminent and meaningful personal threat, psychopaths do experience "normal" fear reactions even though their behavior belies this.

Another controversial issue is whether drug or alcohol ingestion is an effective countermeasure. Waid, Orne, Cook, and Orne (1981) reported that 73 percent of the guilty subjects who took the polygraph test while under the influence of a tranquilizing drug (400 mg of meprobamate) escaped detection. The drug was successful on two fronts. It selectively reduced responsiveness to the critical (i.e., crime-related) test items while affecting behavior so subtly that the examiner could not discriminate between tranquilized and nontranquilized subjects. Iacono et al. (1984), on the other hand, found that 100 percent of the guilty subjects who took diazepam (another tranquilizer) or methylphenidate (a stimulant) were classified as guilty when charts were scored blindly and the examiner could identify those who had taken a tranquilizer.

Because the two studies differed in a number of ways aside from the choice of drugs, we recently carried out a study using both types of tranquilizers and the same procedures employed by Iacono, Boisvenu, and Fleming (1984). We found that 83 percent of guilty subjects taking diazepam and 100 percent of those receiving meprobamate produced guilty outcomes. Also of interest was our finding that propranolol, a commonly prescribed cardiac medicine that blocks certain aspects of sympathetic nervous system activity, was equally ineffective as a countermeasure drug. Hence, within the constraints of these studies, it appears that antianxiety drugs and propranolol cannot be used to defeat a polygraph test.

Evidence has emerged for the effectiveness of another kind of drug effect. Bradley and Ainsworth (1984) found that mild alcohol intoxication at the time a crime is committed decreased detectability in a subsequent polygraph test. This is an important finding because many crimes are committed by persons who are inebriated at the time. The possibility exists that other widely used street drugs, such as marijuana, barbiturates, and amphetamines, may have similar effects.

Physical countermeasures also have been the subject of recent debate. Honts, Hodes, and Raskin (1985) and Honts, Raskin, and Kircher (1983) found that up to 78 percent of highly motivated subjects trained in the use of two physical countermeasures could effectively conceal their guilt from a polygraph examiner. This result was obtained by having subjects bite their tongues or press their toes on the floor when they responded to control questions. Counter-countermeasures may provide at least a partial solution to this problem: Honts et al. (1983) were able to identify 80 percent of their countermeasure subjects from a blind analysis of electromyographic (EMG) recordings taken during the polygraph test. Unfortunately field polygraphs are not designed to monitor EMG activity and polygraphers cannot easily take advantage of this safeguard in routine field tests.

APPLICATIONS

Polygraph tests are administered for a wide variety of purposes, including the testing of suspects, complainants, and witnesses in police investigations; defense counsel checks on the veracity of their clients; the identifications of prison inmates suspected of violating institutional rules; employer screening of prospective and future employees; insurance claim investigations; paternity and child custody cases; and family court hearings. The only factor limiting the application of the polygraph is the imagination of those who work with the tests; for example, in addition to the conventional uses just cited, a lie detector test might also be used to determine an individual's sexual orientation or to resolve marital discord by confirming the faithfulness of a spouse. In the following sections we discuss a few of the more common applications of polygraph tests.

Criminal

The Polygraph in Court

As Lykken (1981) has noted, the results of polygraph tests often find their way into criminal court through one of two routes. One involves the stipulated test in which polygraph examinations are administered with the prior agreement of prosecuting and defense attorneys. Often the prosecution will agree to a stipulated test when the case against the defendant is weak. In these circumstances, if the suspect passes the test, the charges are dropped. If the test is failed, the prosecution reserves the right to submit the polygraph findings to the court. Twenty-four U.S. states endorse the use of stipulated tests, but so far Canadian courts have refused them.

Another way that polygraph results may enter a courtroom is over the objection of the prosecution in cases where it can "advance the cause of the defense." This practice is common in Massachusetts and New Mexico, and occasionally judges in other states and provinces and in military courts are asked to consider this argument. As recently as 1984 the Quebec Court of Appeal overturned a conviction because a lower court judge refused to consider polygraph evidence submitted by the defense. Here, in contrast to the stipulated test situation, the prosecution may have rather compelling evidence against the defendant.

In the absence of examiner bias (see the end of this section) the accuracy of a lie detector test is independent of whether the test is stipulated or introduced by the defense over objection. However, the accuracy of those tests *presented to the court* will depend not only on their overall validity but on the base rate of guilt in these circumstances (Kleinmuntz & Szucko, 1984b; Lykken, 1981; Meehl & Rosen, 1955). The base rate refers to the proportion of individuals in a given population who possess the characteristic (in this case, guilt) that a test is designed to identify. As the base rate of guilt shifts to values less than 50 percent, it becomes more difficult to identify guilty people without misclassifying many innocent persons as guilty. A shift in the opposite direction will make it harder to identify the innocent without misdiagnosing guilty individuals as truthful.

To illustrate this point consider the following example. Assume that the CQT is 75 percent correct with innocent suspects, 85 percent accurate with guilty people, and has an overall hit rate of 80 percent. These estimates closely approximate those obtained when accuracy figures for field studies that have used blind scoring (see Table 17.1) are averaged. We should like to stress that we do not consider that these figures reflect the actual accuracy of the CQT. We do not feel that sound estimates can be derived with the studies conducted so far. However, these figures are not completely arbitrary and are convenient for this discussion.

Let us assume further that among 1000 individuals who agree to take stipulated tests only 250 are guilty. The base rate of guilt in this situation, although unknown, is probably less that 50 percent and greater than zero; 25 percent is not an unreasonable figure. Among the 250 guilty persons 85 percent or 212 will be correctly labeled guilty and presented before the court. Among the 750 innocent suspects, 25 percent or 188 will be misclassified as guilty and also presented before the court. Hence among the 400 polygraph cases presented before the court 188 or 47 percent will be in error even though the test is 80 percent accurate!

Presumably, when the prosecution has enough evidence to proceed to trial, it is more often right than wrong. Among those criminal suspects brought to trial how many are actually guilty is not known; the figure is certainly less that 100 percent and probably well over 50 percent. For the purposes of our continued discussion let us assume that prosecutors are right 75 percent of the time, that is, the base rate of guilt is 75 percent when a case proceeds to trial. In these circumstances 750 of the 1000 defendants who undergo polygraph tests will be guilty but 15 percent or 113 will be erroneously labeled innocent; 187 or 75 percent of the 250 innocent suspects will also be diagnosed truthful. Again, even though the test is 80 percent accurate, 38 percent of the 100 cases defense attorneys take before the court, will be in error.

As others have pointed out (Kleinmuntz & Szucko, 1984b; Lykken, 1981; Orne, 1975), a more subtle factor may bias the outcome of stipulated tests and those requested by defense attorneys. In both cases it is in the interest of the polygrapher to produce a desired outcome. The prosecution, which often arranges stipulated tests, anticipates a verdict of "deception indicated." Likewise, a defense lawyer whose client is proceeding to trial is hopeful that a truthful verdict will be obtained. It is in the interest of the examiner, whose livelihood is partly derived from testing such cases, to provide the expected result. Although it is our impression that many experienced polygraphers are sensitive to this issue and would not deliberately manipulate a test to produce a desired outcome, the potential for bias and a resulting test with compromised validity always exists.

The Polygraph as an Investigative Tool

Lykken (1974) has argued that the polygraph could be used as a relatively cost-effective means of increasing the efficiency of police work, provided the results of a test are regarded as tentative. In cases of multiple suspects the polygraph could be used to eliminate unlikely candidates from consideration and direct the attention of investigators to those most likely to be culpable. If the results of the test were not admissible in court, false-positive errors would be unfortunate but not damning because corroborative evidence would still have to be gathered to secure a conviction.

Police agencies (and private examiners), however, seldom use the polygraph in routine cases. Polygraph tests are usually administered only when all other lines of investigation have reached a dead end in the hope that the polygraph will bring resolution to the case. The results of the test are often accepted as conclusive; they afford the police an opportunity to elicit confessions from those generating deceptive outcomes. According to the Office of Technology Assessment (1983) report, it is not uncommon for government police examiners (e.g., the FBI, Secret Service) to report that they obtain confessions from well over 50 percent of the suspects who fail polygraph tests. To the extent that such confession rates generally prevail proponents argue that the polygraph test has great utility when employed in these situations.

Employment and Screening

Estimates of annual private sector usage in the U.S. range from 300,000 (OTA, 1983) to as many as 2 million tests (Samuels, 1983). Among the 143 companies that responded to a survey of 400 firms drawn from *Fortune's* list of the largest U.S. companies 20 percent had made use of the polygraph and most of them had been using it for at least five years (Belt & Holden, 1978). The largest consumers were retail firms and commercial banks. Fifty percent of respondents in each of these categories admitted to using the polygraph. Many U.S. state and municipal police departments, as well as federal security agencies like the National Security Agency and the Central Intelligence Agency, also use polygraph screening tests regularly (Lykken, 1981). According to Samuels (1983), 23,000 government employees underwent polygraph tests in 1982—more than ever before.

Employment-related uses of the polygraph include three main practices: preemployment screening, periodic or aperiodic checks on existing employees (also referred to as employee screening), and specific-incident investigations of theft, sabotage, unauthorized disclosures, and other job-related offenses. We will forgo any detailed discussion of the last of these practices because procedures and issues discussed earlier in regard to criminal investigations apply here as well. Two caveats are in order, however. First, employment-related, specific-incident examinations are typically conducted by private examiners without benefit of prior investigative work. As a consequence, the number of potential suspects is usually not narrowed to a select few, as is typical in criminal cases, thereby making it likely that far more innocent than guilty people will be tested. As already indicated, when the base rate of guilt in a population of suspects is very low, even a highly accurate lie test will produce a large proportion of false-positive errors. A second point is that the consequence for an employee of failing a specific-incident polygraph test is usually that he is fired, period. Criminal suspects who fail a polygraph test are usually given the benefit of further police investigation, or at least due process of law, to establish their guilt or innocence.

The preemployment polygraph test is used to find out whether a job candidate is the kind of person who is likely to be a bad employment risk. Information is usually sought regarding the individual's employment background, history of job-related misconduct, health problems (especially a history of workers' compensation claims), commitment to the job, and problems with drugs or alcohol (Sackett & Decker, 1979). Preemployment screening tests are particularly common for jobs involving access to money, valuable merchandise, or drugs, and for jobs involving access to confidential information, especially where blackmail is a problem (Barland & Raskin, 1973). Aperiodic screening checks are usually done to find out whether existing employees have been honest in their work and whether they remain loyal to the company. In security-related positions questions regarding continued propriety and confidentiality may be paramount.

As we discussed earlier, scientific data on the validity of the polygraph screening test are scarce, and as yet there is no basis for claims that the test can separate liars and truthtellers with a high degree of accuracy. Even if the test were highly accurate, the base rate issue would once again apply. The vast majority of those undergoing screening tests are innocent, and most of the classification errors would result in these people being denied employment or being fired.

Another objection to the employee screening test stems from the relatively small proportion of people—about 25 percent, according to Lykken (1981)—who don't admit to anything during the screening test. According to Lykken, this statistically atypical population may include a substantial number of "habitual liars and deliberate villains" who are not sufficiently moved by guilt to confess. Contrary to its intended purpose, the polygraph test may screen out honest and highly conscientious persons in favor of "undersocialized types who easily pass polygraph tests" (Lykken, 1984)

Those who advocate employee screening tests argue that the value of the polygraph as a screening tool has little to do with its validity per se, and that the base rate issue is not pertinent to most employment applications. For purposes of preemployment screening the test's main utility stems from its power to elicit admissions. Horvath (1985), a proponent of the practice, states that "the information obtained during the examination process, and not the test result, is the salient and distinguishing feature of preemployment polygraph testing" (p. 45). He and many others argue that there is just no other feasible means of collecting the kind of information that polygraph examiners regularly obtain from job applicants. The screening test also provides a cheaper and more efficient way to verify information that could be obtained by other methods such as background investigations and reference checks.

In addition to its use as a "bloodless third degree" to detect dishonest employees, the aperiodic screening test serves another function. The knowledge that they may be asked to submit to a polygraph test at any time is thought to deter existing employees from engaging in theft and other forms of misconduct. In effect, the polygraph establishes a climate of fear in which employees are less inclined to be dishonest because they fear detection (Samuels, 1983).

CONCLUSION

After decades of contentious debate surrounding the validity and appropriate uses of polygraph tests no consensus has emerged on their accuracy or how they should and should not be used. It is our feeling that it will be impossible to reach a consensus with the existing (almost nonexistent) data base. The 65 years that have elapsed since the first polygraph test was administered have given rise to far more questions than answers. Because psychologists have ignored this area of applied psychology, there remains a great and pressing need for additional research.

REFERENCES

Backster, C. (1962). Methods of strengthening our polygraph technique. *Police, 6*, 61–68.

Barland, G. H. (1982). On the accuracy of the polygraph: An evaluative review of Lykken's *Tremor in the blood: Polygraph, 11*, 258–272.

Barland, G. H., & Raskin, D. C. (1973). Detection of deception. In W. F. Prokasy & D. C. Raskin (Eds.), *Electrodermal activity in psychological research* (pp. 418–471). New York: Academic Press.

Barland, G. H., & Raskin, D. C. (1976). *Validity and reliability of polygraph examinations of criminal suspects.* (Report No. 76-1, Contract No. N1-99-0001). Washington, DC: National Institute of Justice, Department of Justice.

Belt, J. A., & Holden, P. B. (1978). Polygraph usage among major U.S. corporations. *Personnel Journal, 57*, 80–86.

Bersh, P. J. (1969). A validation study of polygraph examiner judgements. *Journal of Applied Psychology, 53*, 393–403.

Bitterman, M. E., & Marcuse, F. L. (1947). Cardiovascular responses of innocent persons to criminal interrogation. *American Journal of Psychology, 60*, 407–412.

Bradley, M. T., & Ainsworth, D. (1964). Alcohol and the psychophysiological detection of deception. *Psychophysiology, 21*, 63–71.

Cleckley, H. (1976). *The mask of sanity* (5th ed.). St. Louis, MO: Mosby.

Davidson, W. A. (1979). Validity and reliability of the cardio activity monitor. *Polygraph, 8*, 104–111.

Department of Defense. (1984). *The accuracy and utility of polygraph testing.* Washington, DC: Author.

Ekman, P. (1985) *Telling lies: Clues to deceit in the marketplace, politics, and marriage.* New York: Norton.

Ferguson, R. J. (1966). *The polygraph in private industry*. Springfield, IL: C. C. Thomas.

Ferguson, R. J., & Miller, A. L. (1974). *Polygraph for the defense*. Springfield, IL: C. C. Thomas.

Floch, M. (1950). Limitations of the lie detector. *Journal of Criminal Law, Criminology, and Police Science, 40*, 651–653.

Ginton, A., Daie, N., Elaad, E., & Ben-Shakhar, G. (1982) A method for evaluating the use of the polygraph in a real life situation. *Journal of Applied Psychology, 67*, 13–137.

Hare, R. D. (1980). A research scale for the assessment of psychopathy in criminal populations. *Personality and Individual Differences, 1*, 111–119.

Heckel, R. V., Brokaw, J. R., Salzberg, H. C., & Wiggins, S. L. (1962). Polygraphic variations in reactivity between delusional, nondelusional and control groups in a crime situation in a crime situation. *Journal of Criminal Law, Criminology, and Police Science, 53*, 380–383.

Honts, C. R., Hodes, R. L., & Raskin, D. C. (1985). Effects of physical countermeasures on the physiological detection of deception. *Journal of Applied Psychology, 70*, 177–187.

Honts, C. R., Raskin, D. C., & Kircher, J. C. (1983). Detection of deception: Effectiveness of physical countermeasures under high motivation conditions. *Psychophysiology, 20*, 446 (abstract).

Horvath, F. S. (1976). Detection of deception: A review of field and laboratory research. *Polygraph, 5*, 107–145.

Horvath F. S. (1977). The effect of selected variables on interpretation of polygraph records. *Journal of Applied Psychology, 62*, 127–136.

Horvath, F. S. (1985). Job screening, *Society, 22*, 43–46.

Horvath, G. S., & Reid, J. E. (1971). The reliability of polygraph examiner diagnosis of truth and deception. *Journal of Criminal Law, Criminology, and Police Science, 62*, 276–281.

Hunter, F. L., & Ash, P. (1973). The accuracy and consistency of polygraph examiners' diagnoses. *Journal of Police Science and Administration, 1*, 370–375.

Iacono, W. G. (1984, May). Research on the guilty knowledge test. In D. T. Lykken (Chair.), *The detection of deception in 1984*. Symposium conducted at the meeting of the American Association for the Advancement of Science, New York.

Iacono, W. G. (1985). Guilty knowledge. *Society, 22*, 52–54.

Iacono, W. G., Boisvenu, G. A., & Fleming, J. A. (1984). The effects of diazepam and methylphenidate on the electrodermal detection of guilty knowledge. *Journal of Applied Psychology, 69*, 289–299.

Kleinmuntz, B., & Szucko, B. (1982). On the fallibility of lie detection. *Law and Society Review, 17*, 84–104.

Kleinmuntz, B., & Szucko, J. (1984a). A field study of the fallibility of polygraphic lie detection. *Nature, 308*, 449–450.

Kleinmuntz, B., & Szucko, J. (1984b). Lie detection in ancient and modern times: A call for contemporary scientific study. *American Psychologist, 39*, 766–776.

Larson, J. A. (1921). Modification of the Marston deception test. *Journal of the American Institute of Criminal Law and Criminology, 12*, 391–399.

Larson, J. A. (1938). The lie detector: Its history and development. *Journal of the Michigan State Medical Society, 37*, 893–897.

Lykken, D. T. (1959). The GSR in the detection of guilt. *Journal of Applied Psychology, 43*, 385–388.

Lykken, D. T. (1960). The validity of the guilty knowledge technique: The effects of faking. *Journal of Applied Psychology, 44*, 258–262.

Lykken, D. T. (1974). Psychology and the lie detector industry. *American Psychologist, 29*, 725–739.

Lykken, D. T. (1978). The psychopath and the lie detector. *Psychophysiology, 15*, 137–142.

Lykken, D. T. (1979). The detection of deception. *Psychological Bulletin, 86*, 47–53.

Lykken, D. T. (1981). *A tremor in the blood: Uses and abuses of the lie detector*. New York: McGraw-Hill.

Lykken, D. T. (1984). Polygraphic interrogation. *Nature, 307*, 681–684.

Lyon, V. W. (1936). Deception tests with juvenile delinquents. *Journal of Genetic Psychology, 48*, 494–497.

MacNitt, R. A. (1942). In defense of the electrodermal response and cardiac amplitude as measures of deception. *Journal of Criminal Law and Criminology, 33*, 266–275.

Marston, W. M. (1917). Systolic blood pressure symptoms of deception. *Journal of Experimental Psychology, 2*, 117–163.

Marston, W. M. (1921). Psychological possibilities in the deception test. *Journal of the American Institute of Criminal Law and Criminology, 11*, 551–570.

Meehl, P. E., & Rosen, A. (1955). Antecedant probability and the efficiency of psychometric signs, patterns, or cutting scores. *Psychological Bulletin, 52*, 194–216.

Office of Technology Assessment. (1983). *Scientific validity of polygraph testing: A research review and evaluation*. Washington, DC: Author.

Orne, M. T. (1975). Implications of laboratory research for the detection of deception. In N. Ansley (Ed.), *Legal admissibility of the polygraph* (pp. 94–119). Springfield, IL: C. C. Thomas.

Raskin, D. C. (1978). Scientific assessment of the accuracy of detection of deception: A reply to Lykken. *Psychophysiology, 15*, 143–147.

Raskin, D. C. (1982). The scientific basis of polygraph techniques and their uses in the judicial process. In A. Trankell (Ed.), *Reconstructing the past* (pp. 317–371). Netherlands: Kluwer.

Raskin, D. C., Barland, G. H., & Podlesny, J. A. (1978). Validity and reliability of detection of deception. (LEAA Report 027-000-00892-2).

Raskin, D. C., & Hare, R. D. (1978). Psychopathy and detection of deception in a prison population. *Psychophysiology, 15*, 126–136.

Raskin, D. C., & Podlesney, J. A. (1979). Truth and deception: A reply to Lykken. *Psychological Bulletin, 86*, 54–58.

Reid, J. E., & Inbau, F. E. (1977). *Truth and deception—The polygraph technique* (3rd ed.). Baltimore: Williams & Wilkins.

Sackett, P. R., & Decker, P. J. (1979). Detection of deception in the employment context: A review and critical analysis. *Personnel Psychology, 32*, 487–507.

Samuels, D. J. (1983). What if the lie detector lies? *Nation, 237*, 566–567.

Saxe. L., Dougherty, D., & Cross, T. (1985). The validity of polygraph testing: Scientific analysis and public controversy. *American Psychologist, 40*, 355–366.

Schmauk, F. J. (1970). Punishment, arousal, and avoidance learning in sociopaths. *Journal of Abnormal Psychology, 76,* 325–335.

Slowick, S. M., & Buckley, J. P. (1975). Relative accuracy of polygraph examiner diagnosis of respiration, blood pressure, and GSR recordings. *Journal of Police Science and Administration, 3,* 305–309.

Thurber, S. (1981). CPI variables in relation to the polygraph performance of police officer candidates. *Journal of Social Psychology, 113,* 145–146.

Waid, W. M., Orne, E. C., Cook, M. R., & Orne, M. T. (1981). Meprobamate reduces accuracy of physiological detection of deception. *Science, 212,* 71–73.

Waid, W. M., Orne, M. T., & Wilson, S. K. (1979). Effects of level of socialization on electrodermal detection of deception. *Psychophysiology, 16,* 15–22.

Wicklander, D. E., & Hunter, F. L. (1975). The influence of auxilary sources of information in polygraph diagnoses. *Journal of Police Science and Administration, 3,* 405–409.

Winter, J. E. (1936). A comparison of the cardio-pneumopsychograph and association methods in the detection of lying in cases of theft among college students. *Journal of Applied Psychology, 20,* 243–248.

CHAPTER 18

Forensic Uses of Hypnosis

DAVID SPIEGEL and HERBERT SPIEGEL

Forensic uses and abuses of hypnosis will be reviewed in this chapter in the context of modern definitions of hypnosis as a shift in concentration characterized by parallel awareness and a relative suspension of critical judgment, rather than as a passive form of sleep. Uses and abuses of hypnosis with defendants, witnesses, and victims involved in criminal proceedings will be reviewed as will studies of the effects of hypnosis in memory enhancement procedures. We then present guidelines for appropriate forensic use of hypnosis and explain the underrecognized problem of spontaneous hypnotic states and their influence on the legal process.

HISTORY

Hypnosis has been in the courtroom for more than 100 years. In the latter half of the nineteenth century, there was considerable debate between the rival French schools of Nancy and Salpêtrière over the possibility that a hypnotized person could be induced to commit a crime (Ellenberger, 1970, p. 164). Even Bernheim (1889), who stood out by viewing hypnosis as a normal, rather than a pathological, phenomenon argued that while most people could not be induced with hypnosis to commit crime, those who suffered from amorality or a weakness of the will might be susceptible to such influence. He went so far as to state that autosuggestion played an important role in many criminal cases.

Although the main forensic interest in hypnosis has shifted toward its use in eliciting information from witnesses and victims, Bernheim's theme remains of interest in that only recently a major debate took place in the courtroon over the well-known Hillside strangler case in which one group of hypnosis experts argued that the defendant was, in fact, a multiple personality and underwent spontaneous dissociations and therefore was not responsible for his actions. In this case experts for the prosecution argued that the defendant was feigning the multiple-personality syndrome and cited evidence of earlier psychopathic behavior and a large store of books on psychology in the suspect's basement. The judge ruled that he intended to take the personality that committed the crime, put him in jail, and throw away the key, and what the other personalities did was up to them.

Controversy and intense disagreement has thus been an important part of the history of forensic applications of hypnosis because hypnosis has often been mystified and because it deals with issues of crucial importance to the law (i.e., will, choice, responsibility, and awareness). Hypnosis remains an area of theoretical, if not frequently practical, importance in relation to the more common and thorny issues of criminal and civil responsibility related to psychiatric illness.

In this century the primary forensic uses of hypnosis have been for the purpose of assisting victims, witnesses, and occasionally defendants in enhancing memory of a crime. This use of hypnosis has likewise been subject to continued debate and considerable controversy, culminating in a flurry of appellate decisions affecting legal as well as clinical practice.

HYPNOSIS: A DEFINITION

Hypnosis is a complex alteration in consciousness which can be understood as attentive, receptive concentration characterized by parallel, or dissociated, awareness. This shift in concentration may result in intense absorbing perceptual experiences but is always controllable and reversible. It may involve sensitivity to internal cues in self-hypnosis. The interaction between focal attention and peripheral awareness is a constant theme in human consciousness, but with hypnosis there appears to be a relative diminution of peripheral awareness to facilitate the enhancement of focal concentration. Although at no time does peripheral awareness disappear entirely, its suspension allows for the relative suspension of critical judgment, or suggestibility, often observed in particular in highly hypnotizable individuals. People in a trance tend to focus on what to do rather than why they are doing it. They are capable of experiencing profound sensory alterations such as tingling, lightness, or heaviness in extremities, alterations in motor control (e.g., letting an arm float up in the air with a feeling that they cannot control it, although, in fact, they can). They also experience changes in temporal orientation, such as reliving the past as though it were the present and dissociation (e.g., feeling a part of the body or a part of their awareness as being separate from the rest).

The everyday experience most analogous to the hypnotic experience is that of becoming so absorbed in a good novel, movie, or play that one enters the imaginary world and temporarily suspends awareness of the real one. Laboratory research has, in fact, shown that highly hypnotizable individuals are more likely to have these hypnoticlike (Shor, Orne, & O'Connell, 1962) or absorbing (Tellegen & Atkinson, 1974) experiences. Research in the laboratory and the clinic over the past several decades has demonstrated that hypnotizability is a stable and measurable trait (Hilgard, 1965; Spiegel & Spiegel, 1978), as stable during the adult life span as intelligence (Morgan, Johnson, & Hilgard, 1974). It is at its peak during the human life cycle in late childhood (Morgan & Hilgard, 1973) and declines gradually throughout adolescence and the adult life span into senescence (Stern, Spiegel, & Nee, 1978–1979). Approximately one-fourth of a psychiatric outpatient population was found not to be hypnotizable, and only 5 to 10 percent can be considered highly hypnotizable (Spiegel & Spiegel, 1978). Thus, some people are not at all hypnotizable, a few are extremely hypnotizable, and the majority of the population has some moderate capacity to experience hypnosis. Hypnotizability tests provide a series of instructions after hypnotic induction and then assess the number of items that the subjects are capable of experiencing, such as sensory and motor alternations, temporal reorientation, and vividness of imagery.

Hypnosis is a field that has lent itself to mystification, of which there has been no small amount in the forensic setting. The dramatic and compelling examples of previously amnesic material unearthed with hypnosis, especially in a traumatized witness or victim, led to hopes that hypnosis could be used as a kind of truth serum, and that the material elicited with it had some higher order of veracity than ordinary memories. The limitations of this approach have been documented at least as far back as Freud's famous and still controversial recantation of his original theory of the etiology of neuroses. Along with Breuer, he used hypnosis to help patients with hysterical symptoms relive early events which had led to the formation of the symptoms. He initially uncovered material suggesting that their parents had sexually abused these patients. He later revised his theory, reinterpreting these memories as fantasies produced by the patient. It is clear that at the very least the sensitivity of the hypnotized person's relatedness to his or her environment makes it critically important to take into account any pressure being placed upon him to provide certain kinds of information. Even in the best of cases it is possible for a subject to come up with material that is responsive to internal needs or external factors rather than the truth. Recently a number of reports have emerged illustrating either self-serving and feigned stories elicited under hypnosis (Orne, 1979; Spiegel & Spiegel, 1984), or an artificially induced experimental confabulation in a highly hypnotizable subject instructed to stick by an invented story (Spiegel, 1980). Thus, it is clear from the clinical literature that it is possible for hypnotized individuals to come up with compelling stories that are not necessarily true.

FORENSIC EXPERIENCE WITH HYPNOSIS

Abuses with Defendants

In several cases hypnosis has been abused in an effort to obtain information from a defendant about a crime. In *Leyra v. Denno* (1954), hypnosis was used in an attempt to coerce a confession from Leyra, who was accused of killing his parents. After hours of intense interrogation shortly after the murders, a doctor offered to treat Leyra for a headache. The doctor hypnotized Leyra and told him that he might as well confess to the murders and assured his patient that he would see to it that the police would "go easy" on him. Leyra confessed to the doctor. Shortly after this, he was taken to the front of the police station and in the presence of his business partner repeated the confession. He was found guilty and sentenced to the electric chair, but this conviction was reversed on appeal with the reasoning that the confession had been coerced using hypnosis. At the next trial he was found guilty, this time on the basis of his second confession made in front of his business partner. This conviction went all the way to the U.S. Supreme Court and, on a split decision, a new trial was ordered. The majority opinion, written by Justice Black, held that the second confession should be considered part of a continuum clearly related to the first confession and thereby similarly coerced. By the time a third trial was undertaken, the remaining evidence was largely circumstantial and inadequate. Despite this, he was again found guilty but, because of the sparse evidence, the case was reversed on appeal. Leyra was eventually freed of all charges because of a coercive misuse of hypnosis to elicit a confession, and no one else has ever been convicted of the crime.

Orne reports the opposite kind of problem in the case of *State v. Papp* (Orne, 1979). A defendant who claimed amnesia for parts of the crime underwent hypnosis. His performance during hypnotic age regression suggested his own exoneration. Expert witnesses for the prosecution testified, however, that his behavior was typical of someone simulating, rather than experiencing, hypnosis. On the strength of this testimony, the hypnosis session was interpreted as self-serving and was not introduced in court. In another case, *People v. Ritchie* (1977), Orne reports that a defendant undergoing hypnosis implicated his wife rather than himself, but the court eventually decided to exclude the hypnotic evidence.

Hypnosis with Witnesses and Victims

There is widespread agreement in the courts that the content of hypnotically induced testimony is inadmissible under the Frye Rule (*Frye v. U.S.*, 1923) in that there is insufficient consensus in the scientific community that the product elicited is reliable. This, however, does not eliminate all use of hypnosis, since it is more commonly used to elicit information which can then be subjected to further corroboration. The importance of corroboration cannot be overestimated, since there is no evidence that information elicited with hypnosis is any more credible than information elicited using any other memory enhancement technique.

The greatest interest in the use of hypnosis with victims and witnesses of crime remains in those cases in which the person was emotionally or physically traumatized by the criminal activity and adopts a defensive repression or denial in response. Such individuals claim no memory for some or all of the events, and this amnesia cannot be accounted for on the basis of head injury or intoxication. Traumatic amnesias may be reversible using hypnosis, usually accompanied by the experience of strong emotion. Indeed, the greater accessibility of these memories when the emotion can be experienced and, it is hoped, controlled by hypnosis is explained by recent theories of state-dependent memory (Bower, 1981). This research demonstrates that people are better able to remember the content of material learned when they are in the same emotional state while trying to recall it that they were in when the material was learned. Often, traumatized individuals avoid thinking about the content of the trauma because it naturally elicits the painful emotions of helplessness, fear, and rage that they experienced during the event. There is some agreement in the field that such spontaneously elicited memories, coming as a complete reversal of a previous amnesia and without suggestion regarding the details, deserve serious attention (Orne, 1979). Nonetheless, such memories cannot be presumed automatically free of either internal or external contamination.

In *People v. Hurd* (1981) a woman awoke to find herself being stabbed repeatedly in the neck. She had no memory of any perceptions prior to the knife approaching her neck. She was hypnotized in the presence of the police, and the conventional screen technique (Spiegel & Spiegel, 1978) was used in an effort to elicit clues regarding her assailant. During this trance experience she spontaneously abreacted with a great deal of emotion, crying, and shouting while reliving the assault. She gave descriptive information about the assailant but initially refused to identify him. When asked whether it was, in fact, her ex-husband, she tearfully assented that it was. After the trance she expressed some dismay at this new information and said that she had somehow known who it was but had not wanted to admit it to herself. Unfortunately the police case ended rather than began at this point, and no additional corroborative information was obtained. The victim's previous posttraumatic stress disorder, which included insomnia, nightmares, irritability, and reduced ability to function, was reversed after the hypnotic abreaction. The court ruled, however, that in the absence of additional corroboration it was possible that the information she produced under hypnosis was the result of suggestion or some self-serving memory. Therefore the victim's testimony was ruled inadmissible and eventually the charges were dropped. Although clinical improvement can be seen as lending credence to the accuracy of the events recalled under hypnosis (Orne, 1979; Breuer & Freud, 1893–1895), the legal standard of "beyond a reasonable doubt" requires substantial corroboration of hypnotically elicited memories.

In recent years it has become more common to use hypnosis to refresh recollection not subject to traumatic repression. The most widely cited of these approaches (Reiser, 1980) has been adopted by police departments around the country to refresh or improve previously existing recall in situations in which no trauma may be involved. Hypnotized subjects are told that their memories are analogous to a videotape recorder and that the use of hypnosis can help them provide additional details of which they are unaware. This approach may have the unfortunate effect of encouraging them to come up with fantasies that are reported as memories (confabulation) or developing an artificial sense of certainty about the veracity of their memory because they survived a hypnotic interrogation (concreting).

For example, in *U.S. v. Miller* (1969) Miller was found guilty of transporting a large amount of heroin and sentenced to 12 years in prison. He was convicted almost entirely on the basis of the testimony of a man named Caron who was initially vague and then somewhat more certain in his identification of the defendant. Yet, after Caron returned from an interrogation in Texas that dealt with another aspect of the same case, he became quite certain that Miller was the man he had seen. The defense and prosecution agreed to allow this witness to be hypnotized, and it was then discovered that he had already been hypnotized by a psychologist in Texas who was working with the prosecution. It became clear that Caron's own pending sentence as an illegal alien would be influenced by his degree of cooperation with his prosecutor. During the initial hypnosis, undertaken presumably to see if Caron could recall a license number, the prosecutor repeatedly referred to the defendant, Miller, as the guilty man. This amounted to a suggestion to Caron during hypnosis that indeed Miller was guilty, and Caron's subsequent testimony became considerably stronger. Thus, the hypnosis had the effect of concreting his testimony and making it more credible than it otherwise would have been. Miller was acquitted on appeal on the grounds that the prosecutor had not revealed to the jury that hypnosis had been used. Of particular interest in this case is the fact that neither the prosecutor nor the psychologist who used hypnosis in Texas was consciously attempting to influence the witness. Nonetheless, their apparently casual allusion to Miller as the guilty party, together with Caron's hypnotizability and his eagerness to please them, produced an artificially confident witness.

In *State v. White* Orne (1979) reports that a witness who was initially reluctant to testify against the defendant in a trial produced new and incriminating information about him after a hypnotic session in which she was strongly encouraged to tell the truth—the implication being that the truth would be incriminating evidence about the defendant. She did shortly thereafter, but the court ruled that the hypnotic session may have amounted to a suggestive experience that created rather than uncovered the witness's story. In another widely cited case *State v. Mack* (1979), the witness's memory about how a wound had been acquired was reorganized after suggestion during hypnosis. Although it is clear that memory may be influenced and, indeed, distorted in a variety of ways [e.g., by leading questions (Loftus, 1979)], a hypnotized and especially a high hypnotizable person is vulnerable to subtle or overt suggestion regarding the content of memory.

One case that epitomized the extreme in terms of the abuse of hypnosis and a legal overreaction to such abuse is the case of *People v. Shirley* in California (1982). Donald Lee Shirley was indicted for rape and convicted largely by the testimony of his victim. The two had met earlier that evening in a local bar and returned to the victim's home. Both had been drinking a good deal and subsequently engaged in sexual activities. The defendant then left her to get some beer from his own apartment. She sat at home and made no effort to contact the police. He returned with the beer, a friend came to visit, and shortly thereafter the defendant left. After talking for some time with her friend the victim decided that she had been raped and called the police.

Because of her intoxication, her memory of the facts of the case was poor and a number of inconsistencies in her repeated descriptions of the events were evident. The night before she was to testify at the trial she was hypnotized by one of the prosecutors and her testimony conveniently became more consistent. This led to the defendant's conviction and to a reversal by the Supreme Court of California. In its lengthy opinion the court relied heavily on Diamond's (1980) argument that whenever a witness is subjected to hypnosis the dangers of confabulation—making up new information reported as memory, or concreting, a false sense of confidence on the part of the witness—are so serious that the witness should be precluded from testifying. This, in fact, was the way the court ruled. This opinion held that any witness or victim who had been hypnotized for forensic purposes would not be allowed to testify at all regarding the facts of the case. Thus this ruling went far beyond the prevailing belief that the product of hypnotic interrogation should not be admitted and excluded witnesses themselves.

The Supreme Court of California modified its *Shirley* ruling to indicate that retroactivity would be decided case by case, and also that the ruling does not apply to defendants. This interesting modification was necessitated by several appeals by defendants who had been hypnotized and who argued that because they had been hypnotized they could not testify, and because they could not testify they could not mount a defense in their own behalf, thus violating their constitutional protection of due process. The court was understandably reluctant to dismiss cases on such technical grounds. It does, however, leave the California law in a rather strange state, for if both victim and defendant have been hypnotized the defendant may testify, whereas the victim may not. In a related decision, *People v. Guerra* (1984), the California Supreme Court reasserted the retroactivity of the *Shirley* ruling but allowed for the possibility that witnesses who had been hypnotized might be allowed to testify about their prehypnosis recall, especially in situations in which little or no new information was elicited during hypnosis.

One other state, Maryland (*Polk v. State*, 1981), has a ruling similar to *Shirley*. Arizona, which also had a ruling, has since retreated from it (*Collins v. Sup.Ct.*, 1982). The law currently in Arizona and in New York (*People v. Hughes*, 1983) is that witnesses who have been hypnotized may testify in regard to their prehypnosis recollection of events.

In the Brinks case (*People v. Boudin*, 1983) the defense argued at a pretrial hearing to prevent admission of testimony of several police officers and witnesses because they had been hypnotized to determine whether they could remember further relevant details. The state argued that according to transcribed records no new significant information had been elicited under hypnosis. Therefore their prehypnosis testimony was ruled to be admissible. At trial their testimony was crucial and the defendants were found guilty. This trial occurred before the *Hughes* decision but the state's strategy anticipated it. The same issue emerged in *People v. Smith* (1983). The memory recall of the witnesses pre- and posthypnosis was essentially the same. The court allowed the testimony and the defendant was found guilty of murder.

This approach may solve certain problems but it does not help in the case in which a traumatized witness uncovers an amnesia under hypnosis. This new information may not be testified to under the *Hughes* guidelines. Clearly, *Shirley*-type rulings mean that contemplated use of hypnosis with a victim or witness must be weighed carefully against the risks to the legal prosecution of the case. It is clear that a witness who has been hypnotized will be subject at least to challenge by opposing counsel. At the same time there are a number of problems with this kind of ruling, one of which is that a nonhypnotizable person subjected to a hypnotic ceremony will not experience hypnosis, yet may be vulnerable to challenge on the basis of presumably having been hypnotized. This is a situation in which the measurement of hypnotizability is extremely important. Because it is clear that hypnotizability is a stable and measurable trait and because people vary in their hypnotic capacity from no responsivity to very high, it is important to take into account hypnotic responsivity and the nature of the attempt at a hypnotic ceremony to determine whether hypnosis has indeed occurred.

The Supreme Court of Alaska (*Alaska v. Contreras*, 1983) ruled that presumably hypnotized witnesses could be allowed to testify and the use of hypnosis should affect the weight given the testimony rather than the admissibility of the testimony. In New Jersey, the *Hurd* decision (*People v. Hurd*, 1981) held that a hypnotized witness may testify, presuming that certain guidelines are followed. These guidelines, promulgated by Orne (1979), include complete electronic recording of all contact before, during, and after hypnosis and thorough documentation of prior knowledge of the facts in the case by both the witness and the professional using hypnosis. However, these guidelines have been criticized as impractical by the California Supreme Court (*People v. Shirley*, 1982), but similar ones have been employed by the California legislature (1984) in protecting the testimony of hypnotized witnesses.

STUDIES OF HYPNOTIC MEMORY ENHANCEMENT

The experimental literature has attempted to answer some of the questions of the effectiveness of hypnosis on improving recall but has been limited by the strained analogy between the laboratory and the forensic setting. The literature has shown convincingly that there is no enhancement of recall of nonsense material by hypnosis (Barber and Calverley, 1966; Dhanens & Lundy, 1975; Rosenhan & London, 1963) and that there is no enhancement of the recognition of meaningful material, analogous to a photo lineup (Timm, 1981). The more interesting area has been the study of enhancement of recall of meaningful material. A number of studies indicate greater recall of meaningful material under hypnosis, but the price paid is an increase in incorrect recall and an increased sense of confidence not justified by the ratio of incorrect to correct new material. It should be noted that very few of these studies have attempted to control response bias. This is important because it is clear that repeated trials, even without hypnosis, can result in an increase in the reporting of new correct and incorrect information (Erdelyi, 1970). Indeed, the proportion of correct-incorrect responses is similar in hypnosis and nonhypnosis recall conditions; there is simply more productivity in the hypnosis condition (Dywan & Bowers, 1983).

In the study which most carefully controlled for response bias by Sheehan and Tilden (1983), no increase was noted either in correct or incorrect material produced by hypnosis, only an increase in confidence about the material. Thus, many of the studies that show an increase in productivity for hypnosis may merely be reflecting an increase in the willingness of the subject to report marginal information as a memory—a lowering of the response criterion. Several studies show a relationship between hypnotizability and increased responsiveness, whether or not formal hypnosis is introduced (e.g., Zelig & Beidleman, 1981). Some, like Dywan and Bowers (1983), show an interaction between the two. This study is particularly interesting because it demonstrates that low hypnotizables in the hypnotic condition perform no differently from high or low hypnotizables who are not hypnotized. It was only the high hypnotizables in the hypnosis condition who showed an increase in productivity and confidence.

Several studies have shown that high hypnotizables are especially vulnerable to leading questions (Putnam, 1979; Zelig & Beidleman, 1981). In these studies, however, the hypnotized subjects were made aware that more was expected of them, and, again, response bias may account for the differences. They are also plagued by methodological problems in that all subjects in both studies gave a higher percentage of correct answers in the leading-question condition compared with the nonleading-question condition and produced a reverse Loftus effect that makes the other results hard to comprehend. Loftus (1979) demonstrated that leading questions contaminate answers and the fact that the subjects in these studies gave more correct answers when they were being deliberately misled is quite puzzling. This kind of methodological problem afflicts other analog studies (e.g., Timm, 1981), which in general show some enhanced sensitivity to leading questions and no great increase in productivity of correct information for the hypnosis condition.

One interesting study, Laurence and Perry (1983), shows that hypnotized individuals, told that they heard something while they were sleeping, which in fact they did not hear, tended to report as real memories this hypnotically induced memory seven days later. This is reminiscent of the "honest liar" experiment reported by Spiegel (1980). It is important to remember that the concept of confabulation is originally derived from the description of Korsakov's psychosis, in which a severe vitamin deficiency results in obliteration of the ability to record and retrieve short-term memory. When such patients are asked a simple memory question, they will tend to confabulate or make up an answer, so that it *appears* that they have a memory when they do not. This use of the term *confabulation* is instructive because it reminds one that confabulation consists of both the construction of a pseudomemory and the deficiency or absence of an original memory. It is easier to confabulate in a situation in which there is no real memory to be pushed aside, as occurred in the *Shirley* case, where real memories were obliterated by an alcoholic blackout.

A number of other limitations exist in the possible analogy between laboratory and forensic settings. The usual problem in the court is deciding the effect of hypnosis on a witness months or years after the event occurs. All but one of the analog studies that demonstrated hypnotic effects on content or confidence did so during a hypnotic session or immediately after it. These effects, although statistically significant, are usually not large. Given the general difficulty in maintaining actively sought behavioral change caused by hypnosis over a follow-up period of months or years, it is at best speculative to assume that a hypnotic effect demonstrated in the laboratory within the first few hours of hypnotic interrogation will last months or years afterward. Even in the Laurence and Perry (1983) study only a minority of highly hypnotizable subjects was affected seven days later, although the effect was significant. Thus there is little empirical evidence to demonstrate that the effects of hypnosis on hypnotizable individuals last for months or years required by the legal process.

Second, even in experiments that attempt to replicate the kind of emotional arousal that may occur in rape or assault, in a staged mock assassination (Timm, 1981) or in a gory film (Putnam, 1979), such artificial settings cannot reproduce the sense of fear, pain, and helplessness that real victims and witnesses may experience during a crime. Thus the intertwined roles of emotion and content in memory retrieval cannot be adequately replicated in a laboratory. Third, motivational issues are clearly important in testimony. It is very different for a college student to attempt to recall information to perform in an experiment than for a witness to provide information that may lead to someone's incarceration. These motivational factors are crucial, especially when they affect the response criterion (i.e., the willingness of the subject to report something as a memory), and it cannot be assumed that factors that influence the response criterion in a laboratory experiment are the same as those that affect a witness's willingness to testify. Finally, none of these laboratory studies deals with the kind of global amnesia for an event and its spontaneous recovery by hypnosis that may occur in the clinical forensic setting.

Recently the Council on Scientific Affairs of the American Medical Association convened a panel to prepare a report on the scientific status of refreshing recollection by the use of hypnosis. This report was approved by the House of Delegates for publication in the *Journal of the American Medical Association* (Orne et al., 1985). The panel concluded that there is no evidence that hypnosis enhances recall of meaningless material or any kind of recognition memory, such as a photo identification lineup. When hypnosis has been used to facilitate recall of meaningful past events, it has elicited a mixture of accurate and inaccurate information which cannot be disentangled without external corroboration. Furthermore, the hypnotic ceremony may enhance confidence in memory without enhancing accuracy. However, hypnosis may be especially useful in situations in which witnesses or victims have been traumatized and suffer from amnesia. Guidelines recommended for such use included careful efforts to elicit the best memory prior to hypnosis, precautions against suggesting specific responses or the need to produce new information, tape recording of all contact between the hypnotist and the witness, and an assessment of the witness's hypnotic responsiveness.

There have been reports of successful uses of hypnosis to reverse amnesia or enhance information provided. Perhaps the most widely known occurred in the Chowchilla kidnapping (Kroger & Douce, 1979), in which an entire school bus of children was hijacked and kidnapped: the bus driver was able to recall the numbers of the license plate of the assailants. Although they were given in the wrong order, this information led to the arrest and conviction of the perpetrators. It has been our combined experience that significant new information about a case is supplied by hypnosis in only one out of five investigative procedures. When there is no undue pressure on witnesses to produce new information, they usually respond with no new information. However, even a small detail or a rare uncovering of new information may be important from the investigative point of view because it can lead to new clues and/or corroborative evidence.

GUIDELINES

Clearly, given the appropriate concerns about potential abuse of hypnosis, certain guidelines for its use are indicated:

Qualifications of the Professional Using Hypnosis

The ideal is to have a professional using hypnosis in a forensic setting who is both well trained and skilled in clinical diagnostic assessment and management and in appropriate techniques of nonleading interrogation. In fact, in the past, forensic uses of hypnosis have been conducted either by psychiatrists and psychologists who are well trained clinically but inexperienced in investigative procedures, or by policemen who are experienced in investigation but inexperienced in clinical assessment and the use of hypnosis. As a result, mistakes have been made by both groups, either by suggestively contaminating interrogations or by naively or abusively coercing statements from hypnotized witnesses.

The Society for Clinical and Experimental Hypnosis has taken the position that only a trained and licensed psychologist or psychiatrist who is independent of the police department should conduct a forensic hypnosis interrogation. The Federal Bureau of Investigation has a model in which an agent who is not otherwise involved in the investigation may be present and conduct an interrogation with the hypnotized witness. The hypnosis is supervised by a licensed psychologist or psychiatrist. There is understandable concern that inexperienced police may use hypnosis to produce convenient testimony or to cut short necessary investigative procedures.

Clearly, there is a need for increased sophistication in the psychological management of forensic investigation, both with and without hypnosis. As it is properly understood in the clinical setting, forensic hypnosis should also be viewed as one additional tool which has its indications and contraindications. One resolution of this dilemma may be the development of a new profession of forensic psychology and psychiatry which would require training and competence in both investigative procedures and clinical assessment and management.

Prehypnosis Records

It is important that a record be kept of what the person inducing the hypnosis knew about the case; for example, who the suspect was, whether there was a suspect in mind at the time of the interrogation, and what the witness recalled before the induction of hypnosis. Witnesses or victims should be questioned carefully about the case before hypnosis is used in order to document their best recollection.

Electronic Recording of Hypnosis Session

All prehypnosis, hypnosis, and posthypnosis interaction between the person inducing hypnosis and the subject should be recorded electronically, preferably on videotape. The recording should provide a view not only of the hypnotized subject but of the hypnotist to enable others to evaluate any subtle or overt influences on the hypnotized person. However, it must be borne in mind that even a good video recording of a hypnotic session cannot document all possible influences on a hypnotized person.

Measurement of Hypnotizability

The hypnotizability of the subject should be tested using one of the standardized hypnotizability scales such as the Hypnotic Induction Profile (HIP) (Spiegel & Spiegel, 1978), the Stanford Hypnotic Susceptibility Scales (SHSS) (Weitzenhoffer & Hilgard, 1959), the Stanford Hypnotic Clinical Scale (SHCS) (Hilgard & Hilgard, 1975), or the Barber Creative Imagination Scale (BCIS) (Barber & Wilson, 1978–1979) to document the subject's degree of hypnotic responsivity, if any. Indeed, if a subject fails to demonstrate any hypnotic responsivity on formal testing, the person conducting the session would be well advised to forgo any further hypnotic ceremonies since the subject is unlikely to respond, and the problems inherent with the appearance of having induced hypnosis can be avoided.

On the other hand, if the subject proves to be highly hypnotizable, caution should be taken during the hypnosis and in all subsequent interrogation proceedings regarding influence on the subject, with or without the formal use of hypnosis. Furthermore, the subject's opinion of the hypnotic experience should be obtained immediately after the hypnosis and should include recall of how much time has elapsed and a sense of the effect of the hypnotic ceremony on his or her recollection.

Prehypnosis Briefing

It is important that the person conducting the investigation neither press for answers nor instruct the subject that new information will be recalled or that the memory of the experience will be clearer. This is intended to provide protection against confabulation and concreting, although either can occur even if the person conducting hypnosis is attempting to avoid it.

Management of the Hypnotic Session

Once hypnosis has been induced, any of a variety of techniques can be used to help enhance memory. For highly hypnotizable people age regression, in which they relive the event in question as though it were occurring in the present may be appropriate. The majority of individuals will not be capable of such regression or may avoid it because of the intensity of emotion aroused by the event. In this case some metaphorical state in which the person reviews the event as though it were occurring on a movie or TV screen may be more useful. In any event, the person conducting the interrogation should provide a setting in which the subject can remember new facts if there are any, but in which none is introduced in the questioning. Initially, the person should simply be allowed to review the events as they occurred, with little prompting or, at most, questions like, "And then what happens?" rather than questions that can have the effect of being suggestions, such as, "Did you see the stop sign?"

Selective Use

Hypnosis in the forensic setting should never be used as a substitute for routine investigative measures. The main indications would be a witness who was emotionally or physically traumatized by the crime and who has an amnesia for part or all of the events that cannot be accounted for on the basis of head injury or intoxication, or the need for even a few additional details to allow further investigation.

SPONTANEOUS HYPNOSIS AND FALSE CONFESSIONS

Although some individuals cannot experience hypnosis, the other side of the coin is the extreme hypnotizability of approximately 5 percent of the population. The previously cited literature (Shor, Orne, & O'Connell, 1962; Tellegen & Atkinson, 1974) demonstrates that spontaneous hypnoticlike experiences do indeed occur more frequently in people who on formal testing are highly hypnotizable. This theme has been further amplified clinically. Highly hypnotizable psychiatric patients have been described as having a number of hypnoticlike attributes, including a naive posture of trust, a proneness to affiliate with new ideas without adequate critical appraisal, a sense of inferiority that reinforces their own willingness to suspend their critical judgment, a vulnerability to exploitation, and a tendency to rationalize or confabulate (Spiegel, 1974). These individuals may experience many interpersonal contacts in their life as hypnotic events, even though no one is attempting to induce hypnosis. Their lifestyle is replete with intense, dramatic, absorbing experiences and a desire to please. Many of the attributes of the formal hypnotic experience occur spontaneously. Under duress these patients often experience spontaneous hypnoticlike symptoms, including amnesia and fugue episodes in which they seem to function normally but lose awareness of their customary identity (Spiegel and Fink, 1979). These extreme dissociative phenomena may also occur under highly motivated circumstances such as a desire to comply with police authority.

The dangers of confabulation and an artificial sense of confidence noted by Diamond (1980) and the California Supreme Court (*People v. Shirley*, 1982) are especially applicable to this small subgroup of the population, whether or not hypnosis has formally been used. An intense, structured, and leading police interrogation or preparation for testimony by an attorney could theoretically have the same effect that a formal hypnotic ceremony could have. Factors that can influence eyewitness testimony and the vulnerability of witnesses to being led by examiners using hypnosis should be viewed as part of the same continuum. Indeed, one issue often overlooked in the forensic setting is that of individual differences. On the basis of experience with hypnosis, some individuals are clearly more malleable and vulnerable to exploitation of this kind than others, whether or not a formal trance is induced. This is especially important in the area of coerced confessions (Spiegel & Spiegel, 1984).

The courts have been cautious about the circumstances under which a confession is elicited in order to protect the constitutional privilege against self-incrimination. In our experience the subgroup of individuals who are extremely hypnotizable may be especially vulnerable to even subtle as well as overt coercion regarding confession. Their ability to suspend critical judgment, which becomes a proneness to do so in a coercive setting, may enable them to accept an imposed premise of guilt, even when they are not guilty. This is a serious problem, since the law assumes, as its fundamental understanding of behavior, the concept of the reasonably prudent man, who is not likely to act in a manner contrary to his own best interests. However, some individuals are vulnerable to acting in a way contrary to their own best interests even though they are psychiatrically competent.

As an example, a 26-year-old Vietnam veteran who was attending college wrote to the Veterans Administration to complain that he had not received the last two checks for his veteran's benefits toward his tuition, totaling approximately $5000. He was visited by Secret Service agents who showed him the two checks, presumably signed by himself, and who then arrested him for attempting to defraud the government. He claimed to have no memory of receiving or endorsing the checks. He agreed to undergo a polygraph examination and was told that it was a scientific measure of truthfulness that was "100% accurate." After the examination he was informed that the test showed that he was lying. He then signed a confession on the premise that he must have had amnesia for the crime although, right after signing it, he stated that he still did not have the money or any memory of having received it and was then surprised when he was prosecuted for fraud.

At a pretrial hearing handwriting experts disagreed predictably over whether the signature was his, and no fingerprints of his were found on the checks in question. The defense revealed that his older brother had been convicted two years before on charges of forging checks. On psychiatric examination the defendant was found to be highly hypnotizable and indeed had gone into such a profound hypnotic trance during an earlier demonstration in a psychology class that the professor had had some difficulty bringing him out of the hypnotic state. The psychiatric expert testified that the defendant had entered a spontaneous trance during and after the polygraph examination and that his signature on the confession represented spontaneous hypnotic compulsive compliance evoked by the stressful situation rather than a freely elicited confession of guilt. On the basis of this testimony, the prosecution offered to dismiss charges after a six-month prosecutor's probation period.

In *People v. Lewis* (1980) a woman was pushed onto the subway tracks and lost her hand as a result. A man was arrested and confessed to the assault. On review of a videotape of the defendant's confession, an expert witness testified that he thought the defendant was in a spontaneous trance state. As a result of this testimony, the jury discounted the initial confession, which the defendant had later recanted and the defendant was acquitted.

In another case in California, *People v. Reilly* (1978), a young man was put on trial for the murder of his girlfriend's stepparents. When he was arrested, he was informed that his girlfriend had already told the police that he had murdered her parents. After hearing this report from the arresting officer he confessed to both murders. However, hypnosis was used later on this young man, and he changed his story to state that he had arrived at the home of his girlfriend only to find that she had murdered her mother with a hammer. He had brought a gun with him as she had instructed him to do and was then confronted by the girl's father. When the father lunged at him, he fired the gun, killing him instantly. He maintained this story throughout his trial. When examined, he was found to be extremely hypnotizable, and although the content of his hypnotic recall of the events was appropriately not admitted his high hypnotizability was used as grounds for challenging the meaningfulness of his initial confession, which was viewed as a response to the police having informed him that his girlfriend had turned against him. Despite this, he was convicted by a jury outraged over the crime itself and the fact that the girlfriend, who was a minor, had received a rather short sentence for the killing. Although he was convicted, he persists in his claim of innocence of the murder of the mother, despite the fact that at this point a confession might have resulted in earlier parole. Other facts also failed to support the initial confession, including his expert marksmanship and the unlikely use of a hammer to murder the mother when he could more easily have shot her with the gun he had brought with him (Levine, 1982).

The main point is that a highly hypnotizable individual in a coercive setting is excessively vulnerable to manipulation, even without the formal use of hypnotic techniques. Furthermore, some of the experimental literature bears this out, indicating that high hypnotizability may be an equal or more important factor to the formal use of the hypnotic ceremony (Zelig & Beidleman, 1981), although not all studies indicate this. Some, for example, Dywan and Bowers (1983), show that both high hypnotizability and a formal induction of hypnosis is necessary to produce an alteration in the recall of information. In any event, it is clear from clinical experience that hypnoticlike events may occur even when a formal hypnotic induction ceremony has not occurred. For that reason, hypnosis cannot ever be excluded from the legal setting—even if everyone agreed that it was a good idea. Thus, there is value in measuring hypnotic responsivity in the forensic setting and in sensitivity to the possibility that hypnoticlike events may occur in coercive settings. Highly hypnotizable people are especially vulnerable to their environments, even to the extent of abandoning their own enlightened self-interests. They are not always reasonably prudent individuals.

CONCLUSION

In summary, hypnosis is a naturally occurring phenomenon, an extreme of concentration with intensity of focus and relative suspension of peripheral awareness. It may be formally applied in certain limited circumstances to reverse amnesias, especially those related to traumatic events. It may also occur spontaneously under duress. Hypnosis can be a useful tool in the forensic setting but may also create difficulties. The measurement of hypnotic responsivity can be useful in determining to what degree such problems are likely to have occurred. Hypnosis is no shortcut or replacement for standard forensic investigative procedures, but it may be of help in special circumstances, especially when trauma has occurred and there is accompanying functional amnesia or when the possible uncovering of even a small amount of new information would lead to the discovery of important additional evidence.

REFERENCES

Alaska v. Contreras, File No. 6266, 1983 (also see Grumbles v. Alaska).

Barber, T. X., & Calverley, D. S. (1966). Effects of recall of hypnotic induction, motivational suggestions, and suggested regression: A methodological and experimental analysis. *Journal of Abnormal Psychology, 71*, 169–180.

Barber, T. X., & Wilson, S. C. (1978–1979). The Barber Suggestibility Scale and the Creative Imagination Scale: Experimental and clinical applications. *American Journal of Clinical Hypnosis, 21*, 84–96.

Bernheim, H. (1964). *Hypnosis and suggestion in psychotherapy: A treatise on the nature of hypnotism*. C. A. Herter (Trans.). New Hyde Park, NY: University Books. (Original work published 1889)

Bower, G. H. (1981). Mood and memory. *American Psychologist, 36*, 129–148.

Breuer, J., & Freud, S. (1955). *Studies on hysteria* (Vol. 2, Stand. ed.). J. Strachey & A. Freud (Trans.). London: Hogarth Press. (Original work published 1893–1895)

California Legislature A. B. 2669, Approved by Governor July 17, 1984.

Collins v. Sup.Ct. of Arizona, decided en banc on May 4, 1982, 31 Cr. L. 2156.

Dhanens, T. P., & Lundy, R. M. (1975). Hypnotic and waking suggestions and recall. *International Journal of Clinical and Experimental Hypnosis, 23*, 68–79.

Diamond, B. L. (1980). Inherent problems in the use of pretrial hypnosis on a prospective witness. *California Law Review, 68*, 313–349.

Dywan, J., & Bowers, K. S. (1983). The use of hypnosis to enhance recall. *Science, 222*, 184–185.

Ellenberger, H. F. (1970). *Discovery of the unconscious: The history and evolution of dynamic psychiatry*. New York: Basic Books.

Erdelyi, N. H. (1970). Recovery of unavailable perceptual input. *Cognitive Psychology, 1*, 99–113.

Frye v. United States, 293 F. 1013, 34 A.L.R. 145 (D.C. Cir. 1923).

Grumbles v. Alaska, File No. 6408, Ct. of App.Opin.No.318, December 16, 1983.

Hilgard, E. R. (1965). *Hypnotic susceptibility*. New York: Harcourt, Brace and World.

Hilgard, E. R., & Hilgard, J. R. (1975). *Hypnosis in the relief of pain*. Los Altos, CA: Kaufmann.

Kroger, W. S., & Douce, R. G. (1979). Hypnosis in criminal investigation. *International Journal of Clinical and Experimental Hypnosis, 27*, 358–374.

Laurence, J. R., & Perry, C. (1983). Hypnotically created memory among highly hypnotizable subjects. *Science, 222*, 523–524.

Levine, R. M. (1982). *Bad blood: A family murder in Marin County*. New York: Random House.

Leyra v. Denno, 347, U.S. 556 (1954).

Loftus, E. F. (1979). *Eyewitness testimony*. Cambridge, MA: Harvard University Press.

Morgan, A. H., & Hilgard, E. R. (1973). Age differences in susceptibility to hypnosis. *International Journal of Clinical and Experimental Hypnosis, 21*, 78–85.

Morgan, A. H., Johnson, D. L., & Hilgard, E. R. (1974). The stability of hypnotic susceptibility: A longitudinal study. *International Journal of Clinical and Experimental Hypnosis, 22*, 249–257.

Orne, M. T. (1979). The use and misuse of hypnosis in court. *International Journal of Clinical and Experimental Hypnosis, 27*, 311–341.

Orne, M. t., Axelrad, A. D., Diamond, B. L., Gravitz, M. A., Heller, A., Mutter, C. B., Spiegel, D., Spiegel, H., & Smith, R. J. (1985). Scientific status of refreshing recollection by the use of hypnosis. *Journal of the American Medical Association, 253*, 1918–1923.

People v. Boudin et al., Rockland Co., N.Y. 81 285, 1983.

People v. Guerra, C-41916 Super.Ct. Orange Co., CA, 1984.

People v. Hughes (1983) *New York Law Journal 190:4*, 4.

People v. Hurd, 173 N.J. Super. 333, 414 A.2d 291, *aff'd*, 86 N.J. 525, 432 A.2d 86 (1981).

People v. Lewis, 3511/79N Super. Ct. N.Y., January 1980.

People v. Reilly, Conn. 5825 (1978).

People v. Ritchie, No.C-36932 Super. Ct. Orange Co., Calif., April 7, 1977, unrep.

People v. Shirley, 31 Cal. 3d 18. 641 P.2d 775 (1982).

People v. Smith, 63 N.Y.2d 41, 1983.

Polk v. State, 48 Md.App. 382, 427 A.2d 1041 (1981).

Putnam, W. H. (1979). Hypnosis and distortions in eyewitness memory. *International Journal of Clinical and Experimental Hypnosis, 27*, 437–448.

Reiser, M. (1980). *Handbook of investigative hypnosis.* Los Angeles: LEHI Publishing Co.

Rosenhan, D., & London, P. (1963). Hypnosis in the unhypnotizable: A study in rote learning. *Journal of Experimental Psychology, 65*, 30–34.

Sheehan, P. W., & Tilden, J. (1983). Effects of suggestibility and hypnosis on accurate and distorted retrieval from memory. *Journal of Experimental Psychology: Learning, Memory, Cognition, 9*, 283–293.

Shor, R. E., Orne, M. T., & O'Connell, D. B. (1962). Validation and cross-validation of a scale of self-reported personal experiences which predicts hypnotizability. *Journal of Psychology, 53*, 55–75.

Spiegel, D., & Fink, R. (1979). Hysterical psychosis and hypnotizability. *American Journal of Psychiatry, 136*, 777–781.

Spiegel, D., & Spiegel, H. (1984). Hypnosis: *The psychosocial therapies.* American Psychiatric Assn. Comm. on Psychotic Therapies, Part II, pp. 701–737.

Spiegel, D., & Spiegel, H. (1984). Uses of hypnosis in evaluating malingering and deception. *Behavioral Sciences and the Law, 2*, 51–65.

Spiegel, H. (1974). The Grade 5 Syndrome: The highly hypnotizable person. *International Journal of Clinical and Experimental Hypnosis, 22*, 303–319.

Spiegel, H. (1980). Hypnosis and evidence: Help or hindrance? *Annals of New York Academy of Science, 347*, 73–85.

Spiegel, H., & Spiegel, D. (1978). *Trance and treatment: Clinical uses of hypnosis.* New York: Basic Books.

State v. Mack, 292 N.W. 2d 764 (Minn. 1980).

State v. Papp, No.78-02-00229, C.P. Summit Co., Ohio; Lorain Co. No. 16862, Mar. 23, 1978; unrep; app'd U.S. Sup. Ct. No. 79-5091, *cert. den.* 10/1/79.

State v. White, No. J-3665, Cir.Ct. Br. 10, Milwaukee Co., Wisc. 3/27/79, unrep.

Stern, D. B., Spiegel, H., & Nee, J. C. (1978–1979). The Hypnotic Induction Profile: Normative observations, reliability and validity. *American Journal of Clinical Hypnosis, 31*, 109–132.

Tellegen A., & Atkinson, G. (1974). Openness to absorbing and self-altering experiences ("absorption"), a trait related to hypnotic susceptibility. *Journal of Abnormal Psychology, 83*, 268–277.

Timm, H. W. (1981). The effect of forensic hypnosis techniques on eyewitness recall and recognition. *Journal of Police Science and Administration, 9*, 188–194.

United States v. Miller, 411F.2d, 825, (2d Cir. 1969).

Weitzenhoffer, A. M., & Hilgard, E. R. (1959). *Stanford Hypnotic Susceptibility Scale: Forms A and B*. Palo Alto, CA: Consulting Psychologists Press.

Zelig, M., & Beidleman, W. B. (1981). The investigative use of hypnosis: a word of caution. *International Journal of Clinical and Experimental Hypnosis, 24*, 401–412.

PART FOUR

Communicating Expert Opinions

CHAPTER 19

Writing Forensic Reports

IRVING B. WEINER

Effective consultation flows from effective communication. Applied psychologists have usually learned this lesson well from their training and professional experience; they know that their opinions and recommendations are valuable only to the extent that they can be meaningfully conveyed to others.

No matter how sharply they have honed their communication skills as consultants in other contexts, however, most psychologists must learn some new ground rules when they enter the forensic arena. As helping professionals they have been accustomed to working toward the betterment of everyone connected with a case in which they are involved, and not knowingly to the detriment of anyone. The administration of civil and criminal justice marches to a very different drummer, however, known as the *adversarial system*. As exemplified by typical courtroom proceedings, the adversarial system pits verbal combatants against each other to produce a winner and a loser. Contrary views are debated, and the arguments that hold sway result in a judgment that gratifies some parties to the case and dismays others.

In conformance with the adversarial system, attorneys strive to further their own client's interests while knowingly trying to prevent the opposing attorney's client from keeping or getting something he or she wants badly to have. The judge's concern is not with who gets what or which party feels better or worse, but rather with safeguarding due process and strict adherence to the rules of evidence. In this way every litigant is ensured a full and equal hearing before the bench—his or her "day in court"—whatever the outcome. The familiar statue of the blindfolded goddess of justice, allowing the scales to balance where they will, vividly portrays this feature of the judicial process.

Given the nature of the adversarial system, psychologists beginning in forensic work are likely to be what Brodsky and Robey (1972) have called "courtroom-unfamiliar." As one step in becoming effective consultants, they need to familiarize themselves with the adversarial system and become comfortable with offering opinions that may contribute to severe penalties and crushing disappointments on the losing side of a case.

In addition, psychologists undertaking forensic consulting must learn to deal with impersonal clients. Forensic clients are not individuals seeking service directly on their own behalf. In some cases they are an entity, such as a court seeking advice, a prosecuting agency seeking a conviction, or a company seeking to defend it-self against charges of negligence or malfeasance. In other cases they are attorneys acting on behalf of persons they are representing in litigation. Although forensic psychologists will typically have some direct contact with a plaintiff or defendant, this will not be the person with whom they are likely to discuss such professional ar-rangements as the purpose of the evaluation, when it will be conducted, how the re-sults will be used, and what the fee will be. Such matters will be discussed through the intermediary of the entity or attorney who constitutes the psychologist's client (see Monahan, 1980).

Working within the adversarial system and with impersonal clients has numerous implications for the writing of forensic reports. Especially important in this regard is deciding whether a report should be written at all and, if so, how it should be fo-cused. This chapter discusses how these decisions should be made and then con-cludes with some specific suggestions for writing forensic reports in a clear, rele-vant, and informative manner.

DECIDING WHETHER A REPORT SHOULD BE WRITTEN

Deciding whether to write a report may seem to be a frivolous consideration; psy-chologists are accustomed to writing reports as a necessary and expected culmina-tion of providing consultative services. In forensic work, however, the inevitability of a written report is tempered by rules concerning the nature of evidence. Expert opinions become evidence not when they are formulated in a consultant's mind, but only when they are stated orally under oath or written down—either in formal re-ports that are voluntarily submitted in evidence or informal notes that are subpoe-naed. It is for this reason that attorneys advise persons involved in any kind of litiga-tion to think whatever they like but write down only what they are prepared to testify to in a court of law. With this consideration in mind, the decision to write a report is influenced by the preferences of the client and by certain ethical principles and professional realities that govern the practice of law and psychology.

Respecting the Preferences of the Client

Forensic clients differ in the kinds of information they want to have. Judges seeking help in reaching a decision usually want as much information as possible and are in-terested in any opinion, whatever its implications, that can guide their actions. Hence in consultation to a court a written report will typically be expected, and the fullest possible elaboration of the nature and significance of the psychologist's find-ings will be welcome.

By contrast, an attorney trying a case is seeking to enter in evidence only opin-ions that will strengthen the plea being made on behalf of the attorney's client or agency. If the consultant's conclusions would be damaging to the case, the attorney may prefer not to have a report written. The following three cases, each of a type common in the practice of forensic psychology, illustrate circumstances in which the attorney expressed such a preference.

CASE 1.

Mr. A was a 33-year-old systems analyst who had undergone surgery in connection with an accurately diagnosed medical condition. As an apparent consequence of some careless surgical procedures, he had suffered some unanticipated postoperative complications. Although not permanently disabling, these complications had prolonged Mr. A's recovery, delayed his return to work, and required him to undergo a physical rehabilitation program. His attorney believed that medical malpractice could be demonstrated and that Mr. A would receive personal injury compensation. He believed further that his client must have suffered undue psychological as well as physical distress, which would entitle him to a larger award than if his iatrogenic problems were only physical.

The psychologist's evaluation suggested that Mr. A was an emotionally resourceful individual who was coping effectively with his unfortunate medical situation. Compared to most people with his illness who had required surgery, he seemed to be adjusting very well psychologically. He was in fact the kind of patient one hopes to see on a rehabilitation service, for whom an optimistic prognosis for full recovery without emotional setbacks seems indicated. As a compassionate individual, the attorney was pleased to receive an oral report to this effect. As Mr. A's representative in a personal injury suit, however, he recognized that the psychologist's opinion, if introduced as evidence, would be more likely to reduce than increase the amount of the compensation that would be awarded. Hence he did not ask for a detailed written report.

CASE 2.

An attorney sought a psychologist's opinion while preparing to defend Mr. B, a 37-year-old elementary school teacher accused of sexually molesting several girls in his fifth-grade class. Mr. B had allegedly fondled these girls during class sessions by reaching into their underclothes while he was sitting at his desk and they approached him to ask a question or hand in an assignment. Aside from doubting that his client would have committed such acts so publicly, the attorney was puzzled by the manner in which the complaints had emerged. The initial allegation of molestation was made by just one girl, who spoke to her parents about it. Later, after this girl's parents had talked with the school principal and the police had been called to investigate, several other girls in Mr. B's class told their parents that they too had been fondled by him. Interestingly, reports from the school indicated that the girl who had complained first was very popular and a leader among her peers. Also of note was the impression of several interviewers that none of the girls seemed particularly upset while talking about being molested; instead, they told their stories as if pleased and proud about them. As for Mr. B, he had for many years been a highly admired teacher in this school, known especially for a warm and caring attitude toward his students.

The attorney wondered whether there was any reason to think that a group of girls who had not been molested would say that they had. Some possibilities will come quickly to the minds of psychologists familiar with the romantic fantasies and peer-group interactions that commonly characterize prepubescent development in 10- and 11-year-old girls.

Consider the possibility of a young girl first fantasizing about an appealing, perhaps paternal male teacher making a sexual overture toward her and then fabricating such a story as a way of feeling attractive and grown-up and impressing her parents and peers in certain ways. Consider further the possibility of other girls in the class, having heard this story from a popular trend-setter, claiming, "He did it to me too." This is the well-known stuff of which mass hysteria is made, as described in such classical papers as "The Phantom Anesthetist of Matoon" (Johnson, 1945) and in the recounting of the Salem witch trials (Starkey, 1949).

In mentioning these possibilities to the attorney, the psychologist indicated that they constituted clinical formulations and could not be substantiated with solid empirical evidence. Having a possible explanation that child specialists would find plausible is one thing; having a line of defense that will stand up in a court of law may be quite something else. The psychologist advised the attorney that many of the compelling speculations in this case, if offered in testimony, could be made to look foolish under skillful cross-examination and might thereby detract from other aspects of the defense he was building. Hence a report was not written.

CASE 3.

This third illustration, because of publicity surrounding it, must be presented in bare outline only. An attorney representing a young man charged with a serious crime was planning to file a plea of incompetency to stand trial. He had been struck by his client's strange and disturbed behavior and expected that a formal psychological examination would provide corroborating evidence of incompetency. On the basis of his examination the psychologist concluded with considerable certainty that the young man was indeed "acting" strangely but was in fact malingering. When he conveyed his opinion to the attorney in a telephone conversation, the attorney's response was to indicate that the psychologist should bill him for his time and that a report would not be required.

Ethical Principles and Professional Realities

For psychologists unfamiliar with forensic consulting, situations of the kind illustrated by Case 3—being in effect dismissed from the case before a written report has been prepared—can raise some disturbing questions concerning proper practice. The psychologist in this case provided an expert opinion that an accused felon was attempting to fake psychological disturbance. How could the attorney ignore these findings and continue building a case for incompetency and should the psychologist allow this to happen? The answers to these questions touch on some ethical and realistic considerations in the practice of law and psychology.

The Quality of Expert Opinions

To prepare themselves for sometimes unenthusiastic responses to their opinions, forensic consultants need to remain sufficiently humble to allow that they may be mistaken, or at least not possessed of all the answers. Clinicians must recognize in particular that their skill and judgment do not transcend all of the imperfections in their assessment tools. As Shapiro (1984, chap. 4) reminds forensic consultants, expert psychological opinions are not statements of fact but only reasonable conclusions based on the information that is available. The psychologist in Case 3 who was "reasonably certain" that the defendant was malingering would not have been prepared to testify that he was absolutely, 100 percent certain. From the attorney's point of view, then, the opinion concerning malingering could be taken as a possibility but not necessarily as the only one. The attorney might also have had in hand information unknown to the psychologist—perhaps even another expert opinion—that in his view argued against malingering (see Maloney, 1985, chap. 12).

Like the imperfections of assessment methods, the existence of multiple, contradictory expert opinions brings a sobering measure of reality into forensic consulting. One expert's opinion is neither the only nor the last word. There are no obligations that would have prevented the attorney in Case 3 from listening to the psychologist's opinion concerning malingering and then turning to a new consultant, or perhaps a string of experts, until a duly-licensed psychologist was found in whose opinion the defendant was truly incapable of understanding the charges against him and participating in his own defense.

Learning of such an outcome, the first consultant could feel strongly that this last expert lacked sufficient experience or diagnostic acumen to recognize a clear case of malingering. However, assuming this last expert was properly credentialed, the court would not be passing judgment on his or her professional skills. To be sure, issues of competency and criminal responsibility frequently feature professional testimony on both sides of the case, and arguments may ensue concerning which of several duly-credentialed experts are best qualified to give reliable testimony. With respect to the present discussion, however, the point is that it is entirely appropriate and consistent with prevailing practice for attorneys to question or reject the opinions of a consultant they have retained and to seek other consultants whose opinions will support more effectively the case they are trying to build.

Considerations in Practicing Law

Instead of questioning the quality of expert opinions that fail to meet their needs, attorneys may decide on the basis of a consultant's opinion to change their approach to a case or even not continue with it at all. Becoming convinced that a client has been faking emotional disturbance, or is lying about his or her guilt, or has in other ways behaved in a reprehensible manner may lead an attorney to decline to represent that person further.

Yet our system of criminal justice entitles everyone to a defense, no matter how despicable the alleged offense, how guilty the accused appears of having committed it, or how unsavory the person's way of life has been in other respects. No matter how many attorneys elect not to represent certain kinds of clients, every defendant in a criminal action will end up being represented by a member of the bar. Furthermore, this eventual attorney will be ethically responsible for presenting the strongest possible case on behalf of the defendant. A weak or half-hearted defense of a defendant whom an attorney regards as being guilty or having few redeemable qualities can result in the attorney's appearing inept or unethical in the eyes of the legal community. An ineffective or unprepared trial lawyer may even risk being publicly chastened by the bench for having done a poor job in his or her client's behalf.

In addition to preventing such negative consequence, a strong case presented on behalf of a difficult client can enhance an attorney's professional reputation. Hence attorneys may enjoy and even seek opportunities to take on a challenging case and construct a convincing brief, especially in trials that capture media attention.

The forensic psychologist needs to appreciate these realistic motivations for an attorney's properly continuing to build a case that an expert consultant thinks is flawed. Moreover, there are instances in which attorneys have no choice but to continue with a case, no matter how strong their reservations about the worthiness of the client or the weight of the evidence. For example, attorneys appointed by the court to represent a defendant rarely have an option to withdraw from the case and can expect the court to be especially intolerant of a lackluster effort. Likewise, prosecuting attorneys may be assigned cases by the office for which they work, without being given much latitude to choose which ones they would prefer to try. These various considerations provide ample basis for conscientious and ethical attorneys to decline to have their consultants furnish evidence that would be damaging to their case.

Considerations in Practicing Psychology

What about the second troublesome question raised by Case 3: How can the psychologist let this happen? Keep in mind that the psychologist in this case was firmly convinced that an accused felon, whose attorney was preparing an incompetency plea, was in fact faking incompetency. How could he sit silently while a competency hearing was taking place? To make matters worse, suppose daily newspaper accounts of the hearing were predicting that the defendant would be found emotionally disturbed and sent for treatment.

Psychologists struggling with this kind of question need to recognize that it derives from their professional experience with the case-conference model. In the case-conference model all relevant information is sought, and a wide range of opinions is considered in arriving at a diagnostic formulation and treatment plan. This model is seldom approximated in forensic consulting, except when the client is the court. Then, as noted earlier, any testimony will be welcome that helps the court decide on a disposition.

For attorneys, however, who in conformance with the adversarial system are pleading just one side of a case, the only welcome testimony will consist of evidence that supports their arguments. If expert opinions exist that would support the other side of the case, it is up to the opposing attorney to find and produce them. How does the psychologist feel when confronted with this slice of reality? A sense of disappointment, perhaps, or anger, or maybe even outrage? Possibly a belief in situations such as Case 3 that his or her findings should be brought to light, to prevent a malingering criminal from escaping justice? Maybe even a strong urge to call the prosecuting attorney or the judge and volunteer his or her opinion, or perhaps even a temptation to inform the local newspapers that critical information concerning the case is being suppressed?

Except in unusual circumstances, the responsible psychologist must assiduously check any such urges and temptations. To do otherwise would abuse the defendant's right to confidentiality and violate the Ethical Principles of Psychologists adopted by the American Psychological Association (1981, pp. 635–636):

> Psychologists have a primary obligation to respect the confidentiality of information obtained from persons in the course of their work as psychologists. They reveal such information to others only with the consent of the person or the person's legal representative, except in those unusual circumstances in which not to do so would result in clear danger to the person or to others.

Issues of respecting confidentiality and assessing dangerousness are complex topics in their own right, as discussed in chapters 4 and 9 of this book. For consulting psychologists distressed by the fact that their findings are not being introduced as evidence in a hearing or trial, the main point in the context of the present chapter is this: The unwritten report should remain unwritten and the psychologist's voice stilled, if that is what the client wants, except when the psychologist feels convinced of a clear and present danger.

The forensic consultant's decisions in such instances seldom come easily. With respect to the danger of violence, for example, widely publicized case law identifies seemingly comparable situations in which ethically minded and well-meaning professionals have sometimes been found culpable for not reporting dangerousness (as in the *Tarasoff* case mentioned in Chapter 4) and at other times, having made such a report, been considered to have inappropriately breached their client's confidentiality. Faced with imperfect knowledge concerning potential dangerousness, the best psychologists can do is to rely on cumulative clinical wisdom and what little confirmatory research evidence has been reported (see Maloney, 1985, chap. 6; Monahan, 1982; Mulvey & Lidz, 1984). Thus persons who have a previous history of violent behavior and display low frustration tolerance, limited self-control, poor judgment, and preoccupation with aggression should be considered at risk for doing harm to themselves or others. The more marked these characteristics, the greater the risk and the more initiative the psychologist should take in making sure that appropriate persons in authority are informed about it.

Even this guideline is not the last word, however, at least in the minds of some psychologists. Siegel (1977) has argued for a more conservative posture than the one taken in the Ethical Principles, in which no circumstances of any kind should be regarded as justifying a breach of confidentiality. The American Psychological Association's Task Force on the Role of Psychology in the Criminal Justice System (1978, p. 1101), on the other hand, has questioned whether dangerousness is too restrictive a criterion for breaking confidentiality and should be liberalized: "Might there not be some limited number of severe cases where, all else failing, a 'whistle-blowing' breach of confidentiality is the *only* appropriate ethical response, even though a 'clear and imminent danger' of physical violence is not present?"

DETERMINING THE FOCUS OF FORENSIC REPORTS

Once it has been decided that a report will be written, the forensic psychologist's next step is deciding what to write. At this point it is especially helpful to keep in mind that whatever is written down may become entered in evidence. Furthermore, when psychologists are called to testify in a legal proceeding, their testimony on direct examination will ordinarily be based largely on their previously written reports, and everything that appears on these reports will be subject to question on cross-examination. As a basic principle, then, forensic psychologists should limit their written reports to conclusions that they feel prepared to express with confidence in the courtroom and defend against reasonable challenge.

Beyond this preliminary consideration, the appropriate focus of forensic reports varies from one case to the next in relation to the needs of the client. As in providing other kinds of psychological services, the forensic consultant should be guided by the familiar principle of giving clients what they want, within the limits of professional ethics and propriety. This does not imply that psychologists should provide attorneys whatever opinions or conclusions they would like to have in order to strengthen their case. Meeting the clients' needs refers to providing the desired *services*, not the desired *findings*. The implication for reports is that they should focus on the topics of concern to the client without necessarily including all of the psychological observations that could be made about a person or situation being evaluated.

Hence a distinction must be made between acts of commission and acts of omission. Regarding commission, the forensic psychologist should under no circumstances compromise his or her integrity by knowingly including in a written report a misleading or inaccurate statement. Regarding omission, on the other hand, there is rarely any compelling need to answer questions that the client has not asked. Beyond this consideration, a forensic evaluation focused to meet the client's needs will vary in breadth in relation to the nature of the case and the line of attack or defense the attorney is intending to pursue.

Providing Narrowly Focused Consultations

In some forensic cases the questions being asked by the client call for fairly limited data collection and a rather narrowly focused written report. The following two cases illustrate such circumstances.

CASE 4.

A young man accused of burglarizing some homes in his neighborhood had signed a confession. His attorney felt that he had been frightened into signing a confession that he was incapable of understanding. The psychologist asked to assess this possibility administered a Wechsler Adult Intelligence Scale (WAIS) and the Shipley-Hartford. The accused appeared unfamiliar with many of the vocabulary items on these two tests, including several that are listed in the Thorndike-Lorge index as being more frequently used than some of the key words in the confession he had signed. The psychologist's report consisted of stating this finding and indicating its implications for a reasonably certain conclusion that the young man did not fully understand the text of his confession.

CASE 5.

An attorney preparing to plead diminished capacity in defending a man charged with attempted murder had received some discrepant reports from several consultants concerning his client's mental status. As one step in trying to resolve this discrepancy, he asked a psychologist experienced in the Rorschach assessment of schizophrenia to review the defendant's Rorschach protocol and answer two questions: Does the record appear to have been administered properly and is it consistent with a DSM-III (Diagnostic and Statistical Manual of Mental Disorders, 3rd ed.) diagnosis of schizophrenia? In the consultant's opinion the answers to these two questions were "yes" and "no" respectively, and this is what was communicated to the attorney in a relatively brief and narrowly focused report.

These examples of narrowly focused forensic consultation may appear to incorporate some clinical practices that are generally frowned upon. For one thing, the psychologist in both cases based his opinion on just one or two specialized tests. This is contrary to widely stated and well-founded convictions that psychodiagnostic assessment should involve a multifaceted test battery and provide sufficiently extensive data to identify broad aspects of a person's cognitive and affective capacities, preferred coping styles, level of adaptation, and amenability to alternative modes of intervention (Holt, 1968; Korchin, 1976, chap. 9; Weiner, 1966).

Second, in Case 5 the psychologist conducted a blind analysis of the test protocol, without seeing the subject or knowing anything about him except his age and sex. Most clinicians regard such blind analyses as appropriate only for didactic or research purposes. In actual psychodiagnostic practice the clinician, not the test, should make the diagnosis, and clinicians' judgments should derive from a thoughtful integration of test findings with relevant information about the subject's history and circumstances. This kind of contextual approach helps psychologists avoid being cast in the role of "testers." By immersing themselves knowledgeably in all relevant aspects of a case, psychological examiners establish themselves as expert diagnostic consultants who use tests as just one source of information in formulating a broadly based set of impressions and recommendations (Bersoff, 1982; Korchin & Schuldberg, 1981; Smith & Allen, 1984; Weiner, 1972).

Third, the psychologist in Case 5 commented on the protocol solely in terms of DSM-III criteria for schizophrenia, as the attorney had asked. This may appear to constitute implicit acceptance of DSM-III as the ultimate diagnostic guideline against which Rorschach and other clinical test data should be compared. Yet in fact, DMS-III represents just one of several contemporary approaches to classifying psychopathology, possessing both strengths and weaknesses, and is neither the only nor the last word in assessing schizophrenia (Eysenck, Wakefield, & Friedman, 1983; Millon, 1984; Sprock & Blashfield, 1983). Moreover, there is much to be gained from a conceptual approach to psychodiagnostic assessment in which test behavior is used first to identify patterns of adaptive and maladaptive personality functioning and only secondarily to select diagnostic categories that may capture the essence of these patterns (Holt, 1968; Maloney & Ward, 1976; Weiner, 1977).

With these considerations in mind, a psychologist might understandably have declined to provide the narrow kind of consultation requested in Cases 4 and 5. On the other hand, when psychologists feel sufficiently self-assured concerning their role as expert diagnostic consultants, even Case 5 can be seen as involving a reasonable request. The psychologist in the case was confident that he could examine a Rorschach protocol, decide whether it was validly interpretable, and determine its consistency with a DSM-III diagnosis of schizophrenia (reported as "yes," "no," or "can't say"). This did not prevent him from also assuming an appropriate educative function with the attorney and pointing out that (1) use of a test battery and contextual information increases the reliability of a diagnostic formulation, and (2) that there is more to understanding the nature and implications of schizophrenic disorder than is contained in DSM-III criteria for it. However, having already worked with several consultants, the attorney was fully aware of these facts. His immediate problem was deciding which way to turn in attempting to resolve the divergent opinions he had received. Without intending any professional disrespect or being unaware of broader issues involved, he wanted just one piece of information from this particular consultant, which he received.

Broadening the Focus of Forensic Consultations

Although instances of narrowly focused forensic consultations are important to identify and put in perspective, they do not arise very often. Much more commonly when a forensic psychologist's opinion is sought, multiple sources of information will be required to provide a useful report. Even when the psychologist is being consulted primarily as an expert in psychological test evaluation, he or she, as already noted, should approach the case as a broadly knowledgeable mental health professional who will integrate interview data, background information, and test findings into a far-reaching set of opinions and conclusions. Psychologists testifying on the basis of a written report that deals solely with test findings, and who must plead ignorance when asked to comment about other key elements of the case, are poorly prepared to acquit themselves effectively. Their client's arguments are weakened by the testimony of an expert who, it is revealed, does not really know very much about the case, and their own professional status is demeaned by their failure to conduct themselves as anything but testers.

Adequate attention to the context of a forensic report does not always entail extensive data collection, however. Sometimes just a few bits of background information suffice for providing an effectively focused report, as in the following case:

CASE 6.

Mr. C was a 34-year-old man who had suffered a closed head injury in an accident for which there was alleged liability. He had been rehabilitated on a neurological service to the point where he was considered to have achieved his maximum recovery. His attorney wanted to establish how much permanent loss of function remained as a consequence of the accident. A WAIS, administered as part of an extensive test battery, yielded a Full Scale Intelligence Quotient (IQ) of 103. No preaccident WAIS IQ was on record to provide a baseline. However, Mr. C's history revealed that he had received a Ph.D. in chemical engineering from a major university and enjoyed a successful career in this field up to the time of his accident. This fact alone, given the considerable unlikelihood of such prior accomplishment by a person with an IQ of 103, established a solid basis for arguing that at least some loss of mental capacity—probably too much to allow him to resume his career—could be attributed to the accident. The written report was accordingly focused on these particular findings.

Turning to more general guidelines in determining the scope of a report, the previously noted difference between the typical expectations of attorneys and judges influences the amount of information a forensic consultant gathers and reports. To recap this difference, attorneys are operating as adversaries on their clients' behalf and are interested in expert opinions that support the case they are making, whereas judges hold no brief for either side of a case and are interested in as many relevant opinions as they can obtain. Hence reports prepared for attorneys will ordinarily be more limited in scope and more narrowly focused on conclusions pointing in one particular direction than reports prepared for the court. As another factor, the breadth of the psychologist's focus will be influenced by the *time frame* of the inquiry, with specific respect to whether attention must be paid primarily to present, past, or future circumstances.

Addressing Present Circumstances

When the forensic psychologist's opinions must address primarily the present status of a plaintiff or defendant, the data that need to be collected are relatively limited and the task of interpreting them relatively uncomplicated. In competency evaluations, for example, the main question concerns a defendant's current capacity to understand the charges and participate in the defense. Consultants may struggle with translating this legal definition of competency into psychological terms (see Chapter 14 in this book), and they may encounter cases of marginal competency that are difficult to call one way or the other. Nevertheless, the critical data in the evaluation will come from currently available sources, and currently obtained interview, test, and observational findings will provide a reasonably reliable index of the defendant's present functioning capacity.

Assessment of personal injury also focuses mainly on current mental state or functioning capacity. This evaluation is a bit more complicated than determining competency, because current capacity must ordinarily be compared against some baseline of previous functioning, prior to an allegedly harmful incident. However, verifiable records of past events often provide a readily available baseline for such comparisons. These include previously obtained intelligence test scores, a particular history of educational or occupational accomplishment (as in Case 6), and testimony from relatives and long-time acquaintances concerning earlier patterns of behavior and adjustment.

Addressing Past Circumstances

Opinions that must address the past status of an individual ordinarily require more extensive data collection than present-status evaluations and a more broadly focused report in which the conclusions are less certain. The most commonly encountered cases of this kind involve questions of criminal responsibility: What was the defendant's mental state at the time of an offense, and did this mental state contribute to the commission of the offense? To attempt answers to these questions, the psychologist must look to information and confront uncertainties that go well beyond the relatively comfortable confines of a present-status evaluation.

For example, suppose a defendant, whose attorney is pleading him or her not guilty by virtue of insanity or diminished capacity during a crime committed three months earlier, shows substantial evidence on psychological examination of a long-standing schizophrenic disorder. This may constitute good reason to believe that the accused was in all likelihood suffering from significant psychological disturbance three months earlier. To put it another way, this person was unlikely to have been free from diagnosable disturbance three months earlier. Even if uncontested, however, neither conclusion demonstrates that the disorder was responsible for the offense having been committed.

CASE 7.

Just prior to the 1984 Summer Olympics, a man named Daniel Lee Young drove his car recklessly onto a crowded sidewalk in Los Angeles, killing one pedestrian and injuring 54 others. In his subsequent trial he was identified as having a chronic paranoid schizophrenic disorder. It was nevertheless found that his schizophrenia was not a contributing factor in his homicidal acts. He was considered to have been legally sane at the time of the crime and was sentenced to a prison term of 106 years and four months to life on one count of first-degree murder and 48 counts of attempted murder.

Suppose as a contrasting example that a criminal offender presently appears so well-adjusted and psychologically capable as to make it extremely unlikely that he or she was seriously disturbed or impaired just a few months earlier, when the crime was committed. Couldn't it nevertheless be argued that any person, no matter how well he or she is currently functioning, could have suffered an acute psychotic episode or a brief period of "temporary insanity" during a previous period of great duress? Or suppose a psychologist concludes from currently obtained interview and test data that a defendant is not the kind of person who is likely to fall prey to such conditions as a fugue state or an "irresistible impulse." In both of these hypothetical instances the conclusions would be unimpressive from a legal point of view unless they could be convincingly amplified with respect to the nature and amount of stress the defendant was probably experiencing just prior to the criminal act and how he or she actually behaved while committing it.

With this in mind, the forensic psychologist addressing questions of criminal responsibility needs to investigate carefully the events leading up to and occurring during the crime. The defendant's own recollections, the official police report, and statements given by eyewitnesses and other informants should be integrated with current personality evaluations to yield informed opinions concerning whether the defendant's behavior while committing the crime and the stresses impinging on him or her at that time seem consistent with a judgment of reduced criminal responsibility (see Blau, 1984, chap. 7; Shapiro, 1984, chap. 3).

Addressing Future Circumstances

Three other frequent forensic questions challenge the psychologist not to reconstruct the past, but to predict the future. Two of these involve sentencing: Should a convicted offender be sent to prison or placed on probation, and should an offender currently in prison be paroled? As noted in Chapter 12, the answer to these questions depends on how some other questions are answered: How likely is the offender to commit further crimes, especially violent ones? How responsive will the person be to counseling, psychotherapy, job training, or other interventions attempted outside of prison? How adequate will the available services be in providing the kinds of nonprison interventions that offer promise of a successful outcome?

These are difficult matters to determine from currently available research findings, and forensic reports concerned with them will almost always be more complicated, detailed, and tentative than reports concerned with current functioning alone. To extrapolate effectively from current assessment data to future expectations bearing on the advisability of probation or parole, the forensic consultant will have to muster whatever clinical and empirical knowledge can be obtained concerning recidivism, violence, treatment response, and available service resources and relate that knowledge to the case at hand.

The third common forensic question involving future circumstances concerns child custody and visitation rights in divorcing families. Which parent will provide the better home for the children, and how much contact should the noncustodial parent have with them? These too are difficult questions to answer from data obtained in the present. Typically, the psychologist is faced with evaluating not just one person, but all members of the family who will be affected by a custody decision, including both parents and all dependent children. If a remarried parent is seeking a contested custody, the potential stepparent may also need to be evaluated. In addition, relevant research findings and clinical wisdom concerning developmental aspects of child-parent relationships, together with the accumulating body of knowledge concerning the impact of divorce on children and their parents (see Hetherington, Cox, & Cox, 1982; Wallerstein & Kelly, 1980), need to be utilized in presenting opinions in custody cases, in order to lend some reasonable certainty to such efforts to predict the future (see Maloney, 1985, chap. 11; and Chapter 5 of this volume.)

The distinction drawn in this section between evaluations focused on present circumstances and those involving past or future circumstances reflects one of the basic lessons that has been learned in the study of personality and behavior. As Kurt Lewin first elaborated many years ago and as sophisticated personologists keep rediscovering, behavior is a complex function of people and their environments (Endler, 1984; Eron & Peterson, 1982). This is why it is easier to describe personality (which is usually sufficient for present-status evaluations) than it is to predict behavior (which is usually required in the assessment of possible past or likely future circumstances). By keeping this lesson in mind the forensic consultant can avoid expressing more certainty than is warranted in commenting on how a subject did respond or will respond in situations that can be only vaguely surmised.

ON BEING CLEAR, RELEVANT, AND INFORMATIVE

As the chapter has indicated thus far, being able to write a useful forensic report requires (1) gaining a good grasp of the legal and behavioral issues surrounding a case, (2) determining what kinds of information will help to resolve these issues, and (3) gathering and evaluating such information. With these tasks accomplished, what remains in providing an effective consultation is for the psychologist to express his or her impressions and conclusions in a clear, relevant, and informative manner.

Clarity

Forensic reports should ordinarily begin by indicating the sources of information the consultant has used. When, where, and in what fashion was the plaintiff or defendant directly evaluated? What other records were examined, such as depositions, police reports, medical charts, and school or military files? Which other individuals were interviewed or assessed to provide additional data? To what extent were other discussions, reviews of psychological literature, or examinations of case law undertaken to further the consultant's knowledge and understanding of the case. Explicit answers to such questions as an introductory feature of a forensic report promote clarity by eliminating any uncertainty concerning the bases on which the consultant has formed the opinions to be stated in the report.

In proceeding to state these opinions, the psychologists should strive to write in ordinary English with a minimum of technical jargon. As mentioned earlier, a written report may be read in its entirety in the courtroom. Attorneys may in fact prefer to have a consultant's report entered verbatim on direct examination, to avoid having imprecise or poorly worded statements slip into an extemporaneous presentation. Hence consultants should not plan on writing a formal, somewhat technical report for the record and then giving their courtroom testimony in an informal, conversational manner that is easy to follow and understand. Instead, the written report itself should be as clear and conversational as the psychologist can make it. This means using unstilted and uncomplicated language that will be comfortable for the consultant to repeat on the witness stand and comprehensible to the audience.

Along with using ordinary language in reports, the forensic psychologist should concentrate on writing about the *person* who has been evaluated, rather than about psychological processes. A statement such as "Coping capacities are good" does not communicate as clearly as "Ms. D has good capacities to cope with stressful experiences without becoming unduly upset." When psychologists fail to guard against being murky, impersonal descriptions of psychological processes often go hand in hand with jargon. Compare, for example, "Much castration anxiety is present," with "This man appears to be more fearful than most people of being harmed physically." Sometimes consultants may not realize that certain expressions commonly used by professionals are not generally understood by the public. For example, "Reality testing is poor" reads better as "Mr. E's reality testing is poor" but even better as "Mr. E often fails to see things the way most people do and consequently tends to show what most people would regard as poor judgment."

Relevance

As in responding to consultation requests in other areas of practice, psychologists achieve relevance in forensic reports by addressing themselves primarily and explicitly to answering the referral question. Being relevant almost always means *not* including everything that could be said about an individual's personality characteristics and probable ways of responding in various kinds of past, present, and future circumstances. Instead, what is required for relevance is a distillation of those features of the individual that bear directly on the issues in the case and on the client's questions about them.

But what are these questions? To conduct an adequate evaluation and write a relevant report, the forensic psychologist needs to be pursuing some specific question, such as whether an accused is competent to stand trial or an allegedly injured person has suffered demonstrable loss of function. If no such question has been framed, one must be elicited from the client by asking, "Why do you want to have this person evaluated?" or "What is it that you would like to learn from me?"

In addition to indicating what information is critical to obtain and how it might best be organized to provide a relevant report, a clear referral question allows the psychologist to anticipate how well it can be answered. Sometimes what a prospective client would like to know cannot be answered at all from a psychological evaluation, in which case the psychologist may decline to accept the consultation. Declining to consult in such circumstances reflects good clinical judgment and is also consistent with one of the recommendations of the Task Force on the Role of Psychology in the Criminal Justice System: "Psychological assessments of offenders should be performed only when the psychologist has a reasonable expectation that such assessments will serve a useful therapeutic or dispositional function" (American Psychological Association, 1978, p. 1104).

In other circumstances, the psychologist with an answerable referral question in hand may nevertheless have some expectations that can be shared with the client concerning how powerful the psychological data will be. For example, alerting an attorney that evaluations of possible future behavior generate less certain results than those concerned with a person's present status can enhance the effectiveness of the eventual report by minimizing any unwarranted expectations on the attorney's part.

Forensic psychologists can increase the relevance of their consultations further by acquainting themselves with the statutory and case law applicable to a case in the particular jurisdiction in which it is being tried. Being cognizant of applicable laws is one of the chief characteristics that differentiate forensic assessments from more traditional kinds of clinical assessments (Rosenhan, 1982).

As an illustration of this need for legal knowledge, there is no single accepted definition of criminal responsibility. Various state and federal jurisdictions employ differing criteria for what constitutes a mitigating mental circumstance in criminal behavior (see Chapter 13 this volume; see also Shapiro, 1984, chap. 2). To express a relevant opinion concerning criminal responsibility, then, forensic psychologists must have some sense of how their findings fit with the applicable ways of defining it. In a jurisdiction in which the M'Naghten Rule applies, for example, the utility of the consultant's report is enhanced by the following kind of statement: "Mr. F frequently has difficulty perceiving events in his life realistically, and he often misjudges how his behavior affects other people. The severity of this problem and strong indications that he has had it for a long time make it reasonable to think that he was less capable than most people of appreciating the wrongfulness of his actions at the time of the crime."

Informativeness

Like clinical reports, forensic reports should be writen in an informative manner that educates the nonpsychologist reader. As also stressed by Dillon and Wildman (1979), the expert should help such inexperienced persons as jurors to reach a decision by teaching them about psychological issues relevant to the particular case.

This informational objective is usually achieved by relating psychological data and impressions to benchmarks that the audience will recognize. For example, a report stating that a subject has earned a WAIS-R Full Scale IQ of 100 says everything that another psychologist needs to know about the person's overall IQ level. To make this finding intelligible to most people, however, certain educational information should be added: that the WAIS-R is the currently most widely used measure of adult intelligence and is composed of several subtests sampling different kinds of abilities; that, although there is some error of measurement associated with a WAIS IQ, an obtained score of 100 means that there is a 95 percent probability that the subject's true IQ is between 95 and 105; and that about half of all people will earn a higher IQ score on this test and half a lower score. Similarly with respect to impressions of psychological disorder, the consultant should indicate as in Case 5 how the findings compare will well-known standard nomenclatures; for example, "The way this person is thinking and feeling, as reflected in the interview and test data, is consistent with a DSM-III diagnosis of Major Depressive Episode."

In other circumstances the consultant may summarize in textbook fashion a set of circumstances pointing to a particular conclusion. In a criminal case involving consideration of a suspended sentence, for example, the psychologist wrote the following informative opinion: "I am concerned about having this man return without supervision to his previous place of residence. Being a white male in his late 50s, who would be living alone in a run-down section of town, and who has previously attempted to take his own life, he is in a very high risk group for suicidal behavior."

An informative educational approach of this kind, in a report that is easy to understand and speaks explicitly to the issues at hand, promotes effective communication. Combined with good judgment concerning when reports should be written and how narrowly or broadly they should be focused, these communication skills— being clear, relevant, and informative—contribute substantially to the psychologist's providing effective forensic consultation.

REFERENCES

American Psychological Association. (1978). Report of the Task Force on the Role of Psychology in the Criminal Justice System. *American Psychologist, 33,* 1099–1113.

American Psychological Association. (1981). Ethical principles of psychologists. *American Psychologist, 36,* 633–638.

Bersoff, D. N. (1982). Regarding psychologists testily: The legal regulation of psychological assessment. In C. J. Scheirer & B. L. Hammonds (Eds.), *Psychology and the law* (pp. 41–68). Washington, DC: American Psychological Association.

Blau, T. H. (1984). *The psychologist as expert witness.* New York: Wiley.

Brodsky, S. L., & Robey, A. (1972). On becoming an expert witness: Issues of orientation and effectiveness. *Professional Psychology, 3,* 173–176.

Dillon, C. A., & Wildman, R. W. (1979). The psychologist in criminal court. *Clinical Psychologist, 32,* 16–18.

Endler, N. S. (1984). Interactionism. In N. S. Endler & J. McV. Hunt (Eds.), *Personality and the behavior disorders* (2nd ed., pp. 183–217). New York: Wiley.

Eron, L. D., & Peterson, R. A. (1982). Abnormal behavior: Social approaches. *Annual Review of Psychology, 33,* 231–264.

Eysenck, H. J., Wakefield, J. A., & Friedman, A. F. (1983). Diagnosis and clinical assessment: The DSM-III. *Annual Review of Psychology, 34,* 167–193.

Hetherington, E. M., Cox, M., & Cox, R. (1982). Effects of divorce on parents and children. In M. E. Lamb (Ed.), *Nontraditional families: Parenting and child development* (pp. 233–288). Hillsdale, NJ: Erlbaum.

Holt, R. R. (1968). Editor's foreword. In R. R. Holt (Ed.), rev. ed. of D. Rapaport, M. N. Gill, & R. Schafer, *Diagnostic psychological testing*. New York: International Universities Press.

Johnson, D. M. (1945). The "phantom anesthetist" of Matoon: A field study of mass hysteria. *Journal of Abnormal and Social Psychology, 40*, 175–186.

Korchin, S. J. (1976). *Modern clinical psychology*. New York: Basic Books.

Korchin, S. J., & Schuldberg, D. (1981). The future of clinical assessment. *American Psychologist, 36*, 1147–1158.

Maloney, M. P. (1985). *A clinician's guide to forensic psychological assessment*. New York: Free Press.

Maloney, M. P., & Ward, M. P. (1976). *Psychological assessment: A conceptual approach*. New York: Oxford University Press.

Millon, T. (1984). The DSM-III: Some historical and substantive reflections. In N. S. Endler & J. McV. Hunt (Eds.), *Personality and the behavior disorders* (2nd ed., pp. 675–710). New York: Wiley.

Monahan, J. (Ed.). (1980). *Who is the client?* Washington, DC: American Psychological Association.

Monahan, J. (1982). The prediction of violent behavior: Developments in psychology and the law. In C. J. Sheirer & B. L. Hammonds (Eds.), *Psychology and the law* (pp. 151–176). Washington, DC: American Psychological Association.

Mulvey, E. P., & Lidz, C. W. (1984). Clinical considerations in the prediction of dangerousness. *Clinical Psychology Review, 4*, 370–401.

Rosenhan, D. L. (1982). Psychological abnormality and the law. In C. J. Sheirer & B. L. Hammonds (Eds.), *Psychology and the law* (pp. 93–118). Washington, DC: American Psychological Association.

Shapiro, D. L. (1984). *Psychological evaluation and expert testimony*. New York: Van Nostrand-Reinhold.

Siegel, M. (1977, February). Editorial. *APA Monitor*, p. 5.

Smith, W. H., & Allen, J. G. (1984). Identity conflicts and the decline of psychological testing. *Professional Psychology, 15*, 49–55.

Sprock, J., & Blashfield, R. K. (1983). Classification and nosology. In M. Hersen, A. E. Kazdin, & A. S. Bellack (Eds.), *The clinical psychology handbook* (pp. 289–307). New York: Pergamon.

Starkey, M. L. (1949). *The devil in Massachusetts*. New York: Knopf.

Wallerstein, J. S., & Kelly, J. B. (1980). *Surviving the breakup: How children and parents cope with divorce*. New York: Basic Books.

Weiner, I. B. (1966). Psychodiagnosis in schizophrenia. New York: Wiley.

Weiner, I. B. (1972). Does psychodiagnosis have a future? *Journal of Personality Assessment, 36*, 534–546.

Weiner, I.B. (1977). Approaches to Rorschach validation. In M. A. Rickers-Ovsiankina (Ed.), *Rorschach psychology* (2nd ed., pp. 575–606). Huntington, NY: Krieger.

CHAPTER 20

Consulting and Testifying in Court

MARGARET THALER SINGER and ABRAHAM NIEVOD

Entrance into the legal system places the evaluative psychologist before the bench of common law or conscience (equity) and asks that he use his professional training, experience, and judgment to help the court to resolve an issue in controversy. The psychologist's sojourn in this "other" world tests the ability to inform an average, reasonable person (the jury member) as to the psychological status of another who has put his cause before the court. This journey offers fascinating and provocative challenges as the psychologist becomes the representative of the profession outside the usual confines of academia, the clinic-office setting, or the public forum.

At an initial stage of consultation the psychologist both works to understand the legal issues at trial and the attorney's purpose in seeking an expert opinion and also organizes the tools and methods of psychology to solve the problems encountered. Should this opinion provide valuable information in clarifying a party's cause, the psychologist enters a second stage of participation: preparing to offer his opinion as testimony at trial and anticipating being cross-examined by the opposing counsel. Some experts are asked to participate in a third stage: preparing the attorney for the challenges posed by the opposing side's experts. Each stage along the path offers an opportunity to blend psychological and forensic perspectives. Each stage along this path is filled with land mines, pitfalls, and booby traps for the uninitiated.

A consultation model is offered as an organizing schema for forensic consultation. The model consists of three parts, reflecting the three stages: (1) orientation-delineation; (2) preparation for direct testimony and cross-examination; and (3) evaluation of opposing expert viewpoints.

This consultation model is designed to meet the needs of both psychologist and attorney. It differs significantly from the nonforensic model of psychological consultation. In the latter situation, a client is referred to a psychologist to be interviewed and tested, with a written evaluation and diagnostic opinion given to the referring agency or individual practitioner. Contact between professionals is brief and formulaic. The agency or individual psychologist is primarily seeking diagnostic or treatment assistance with difficult therapeutic dilemmas. By contrast, we are advocating a collaborative, continuing consultation model that starts at the point of contact between attorney and psychologist and moves through predictable stages—the stages being dictated by the legal needs in each case.

STAGE ONE: ORIENTATION-DELINEATION

During the orientation and delineation stage, the psychologist and attorney progress toward the selection of a legal focus for the psychological evaluation and subsequent testimony. The following procedures should occur at the outset of the case preparation. The attorney should carefully outline the central issues on which psychological testimony will be needed, highlighting what must be proved by the evidence in the particular case. The role of the attorney is to inform, focus, and outline the relevant legal issues to which the psychologist's investigation must be directed. Often legal cases focus on topics rarely included in a standard clinical evaluation (e.g., outlining the cultural mores of an immigrant group or call for activities that differ vastly from those normally carried out (i.e., interviewing a number of other persons about the behavior of the client, reading depositions given by other witnesses, the police, or the litigant).

A shared and agreed upon evaluative perspective must be adopted. At the start of the interaction, the needs of the attorney and the typical attitudinal set of the psychologist come into conflict. The often frustrating and disappointing confrontation between attorney and psychologist results from a failure at this stage of the consultation process. Some attorneys stereotypically view psychologists as soft thinkers, lacking in discipline, while psychologists often regard attorneys as narrowly focused, rigid, and inflexible. These stereotypes result from a failure to understand the other's professional needs at the outset of the consultation.

Attorneys are bound by well-honed standards of proof which must be established in each case. They have organized their case in terms of the prima facie elements required to either establish or defend against a legal cause of action. They approach psychologists looking for evidence to support perhaps one or two circumscribed and narrowly defined elements of their case. All too often the attorney does not make clear the narrowness of the focus, and, as a result, the inexperienced forensic psychologist wastes much time on irrelevant issues.

To sharpen this discussion and provide an illustrative example an extreme situation is described. In utilizing an expert opinion, the attorney may be seeking the answer to only one question: "Did Mr. Smith suffer emotional harm as a result of the acts of Mr. Jones?" By necessity, the attorney must ask two other questions: first, "On what basis or by what methods did you form your opinion?" and, second, "Please state your education, training, and work history (so that the court, first, and jury, second, may judge if you are qualified to offer your opinion at trial)." These questions form the only necessary basis for expert opinion. Subtlety and theoretical underpinnings are obviously secondary to such an approach. Yet this approach is fundamental to legal training and method.

For example, a man working for a retail store allegedly was unjustly accused of theft, then interrogated, humiliated, and later fired by the store's security manager. The ordinary psychological evaluation would focus on this man's history, diagnosis, and intrapsychic life. The referring attorney had a case in which he had to prove the intentional infliction of emotional distress. This attorney was seeking an assessment of the impact of a series of traumatic events on the client and the resultant degree of incapacity. The legal standard requires proof that the conduct of the manager was so outrageous and egregious that a reasonable person would have foreseen that such conduct would have been substantially certain to produce emotional distress in the average person. The outrageous conduct must do the harm. Therefore the psychologist must determine (1) whether the manager's conduct exceeded reasonable limits and could be characterized as outrageous; (2) the impact of the manager's conduct; and (3) the causal relation between the manager's behavior and the victim's emotional distress.

A traditional evaluation by a psychologist who does not understand the legal requirements in the case might focus more on intrapsychic processes rather than on the transaction system implied in the legal standard. As Prosser and Keeton (1984, p. 61) state: "The extreme and outrageous nature of the conduct may arise not so much from what is done, as from abuse by the defendant of some relation or position which gives the defendant actual or apparent power to damage the plaintiff's interests." Were an attorney to receive a report that focuses on the plaintiff's responses to esoteric psychological tests, his language style, or his intrapsychic conflicts, the attorney might be puzzled as to how this material could be used. The psychologist must organize the broad range of information available in any case to bear directly on the circumscribed elements of the attorney's case (Allen, 1975; Bromberg, 1979; Gutheil, 1982; Halleck, 1980; Morris & Tonry, 1983; Scheirer & Hammonds, 1983; Slovenko, 1985).

Dealing with the Extraordinary

The circumstances and conditions under which forensic clients are seen present special problems. The forensic psychologist often evaluates persons whose behavior has breached the boundaries of civilized conduct. Alternately, the psychologist may assess persons who have been exposed to outrageous, grievous, exploitative, and unusual acts at the hands of others. Both perpetrators and victims present difficult diagnostic problems.

Many persons fit easily into the standard categories of the *Diagnostic and Statistical Manual of Mental Disorders* (3rd ed.) (DSM-III), while others present conditions infrequently encountered in typical clinic or office practices (Lehman, 1980). In describing the breadth of the domain the forensic psychologist must consider when consulted, we wish to call attention to a few of these extraordinary conditions as well as to the surrounding circumstances involved in forensic examinations.

In ordinary clinical evaluations, a psychologist would accept a client's history and behavior and, perhaps, be alerted to an unusual situation by obvious inconsistencies. In a forensic setting, the psychologist must consider that the client may desire to create a certain picture of the self, so that memory and behavior are being altered, hidden, distorted, or created for self-serving reasons. From the initial moment of meeting with a client the forensic psychologist must consider the possible presence of malingering (Albert, 1980; Weiss & David, 1974; Yudofsky, 1985; Ziskin, 1981); factitious disorders (Sussman & Hyler, 1985); impostors (Grinker, 1961); Ganser syndromes (Weiner & Braiman, 1955); Munchausen's syndrome

(Asher, 1951; Black, 1981; Phillips, Ward, & Ries, 1983), and direct lying (Arieti & Meth, 1959; Cleckley, 1982).

As Orne, Dinges, and Orne (1984, p. 121) wrote, "The defendant's symptom reports simply cannot be taken at face value without independent verification, nor can it be assumed that the defendant's primary interest is necessarily to obtain relief from private suffering caused by the disorder. . . . Only after malingering has been successfully excluded can we begin to apply usual diagnostic criteria." From the beginning moments of meeting clients in a forensic setting, competing and contradictory hypotheses must be taken into consideration and carefully evaluated. The forensic psychologist must weigh additional factors into the clinical evaluation: specifically, that the legal setting and the adversarial system itself may contribute to client's motivation and/or symptomatology.

Beyond these extraordinary circumstances, issues of selecting the most appropriate diagnosis and terms for labeling what is discovered are especially important in legal cases. It behooves the practitioner to become familiar with the history of psychological terminology and psychiatric diagnoses in order to select the most appropriate labels; for example, terms like monomania, inadequate personality, exhaustion states, prison psychosis, psychopathic personality, catathymic crisis, and travel syndrome (Menninger, Mayman, & Pruyser, 1963), found in older diagnostic systems often present clinical descriptions and case histories of value for dealing with the unusual behavior found in a number of legal cases. A study of these syndromes and their role in earlier legal cases is invaluable in learning to conceptualize behavior for courtroom work.

Need for Current Knowledge

Most attorneys, unless specialists, only occasionally try cases with psychological components—as infrequently as every few years. Consequently, the average attorney has only general and often outdated psychological knowledge. Even the attorney who is a specialist acquires knowledge in areas immediately pertinent (e.g., prosecutors or criminal defense attorneys may repeatedly encounter insanity defense cases but have no reason to investigate issues of undue influence). Thus when unusual psychological features appear, expert consultation is needed early in case preparation to plan an appropriate strategy. The attorney who is provided with the current and broad informational resources that psychology has to offer possesses the requisite basis to determine the client's most effective case; for example, prosecutors occasionally have cases in which victims were kidnapped, held hostage, or otherwise detained and brutalized during confinement by their captors. On release, captives have often voiced approval and positive regard for their captors and reveal periods during which escape seemingly could have occurred and yet did not. In fact, the person may show more shock and anxiety about freedom than about captivity (Ginsberg, 1984; Reza, 1980; *United States v. Hearst*). The prosecutor in such a situation may doubt the victim's suffering or even victimization and question the client's effectiveness in testifying. The experienced forensic psychologist would recognize this behavior as fitting the criteria for the Stockholm syndrome and other phenomena seen in victims emerging from enforced dependency situations (Ochberg, 1978; Strentz, 1980; Symonds, 1975, 1980a, 1980b). By providing this critical information, the psychologist truly functions as an expert, informing the attorney and the court of knowledge beyond that possessed by the average person. An added benefit may be derived from helping the victim explain his or her own apparently inconsistent behavior.

Expert evaluation is essential in assisting the nonpsychologically sophisticated attorney assess the true nature and extent of emotional harm suffered by a client. Often emotionally harmed or damaged persons appear in an attorney's office, displaying the outward signs and symptoms of an acute or severe mental disorder. They may appear looking disheveled, emotionally disordered, and communicating in an odd language style. The individual may have a psychosis, a severe depression, or other major reaction from which they have not recovered. The psychological consequences of having been injured or defrauded at the hands of others may produce outward behavior that causes attorneys to dismiss them summarily or not fully consider their complaint.

For example, a young man was bilked out of his inheritance by a professional investment adviser in whom the man had placed his trust and confidence. When he sought legal counsel, he appeared dressed like a "mountain man," speaking in a fragmented manner, and giving the general impression of having just wandered in from the back ward of a mental hospital. The attorney referred the man for a psychological evaluation, while still being unsure to what extent he had been harmed by the investment adviser or to what extent he was simply a bizarre person with a made-up tale. Later the attorney confided that the man's appearance and behavior seemed so withdrawn from all social and occupational ties that the attorney barely believed the story. It seemed inconceivable that a man with this appearance had once functioned at the high level reported. His present state reflected none of his former abilities. The psychological examination and retrospective history, verified by relatives and friends, revealed that the trauma, of having lost his entire financial assets and the subsequent guilt at being duped, had driven the man into isolation. The ancillary persons interviewed revealed the man had been extremely bright, socially skillful, and on the road to a successful career prior to the trauma of losing his life savings.

Such an individual is merely one example of a large group in which psychological damage at the hands of others produces a level of demoralization, depression, and decompensated behavior that causes them to be ignored and neglected when they seek aid. It is the wise and humane attorney who refers such a person for evaluation.

A parallel problem to the attorney who possesses little psychological sophistication is the psychologist who is uninitiated into the ways of the legal system. The combination of an inexperienced psychologist and an uninformed attorney generally leaves both feeling frustrated and wondering what went wrong. Such a psychologist may simply obey an attorney's request for an evaluation, being guilty of focusing concretely on the single-opening probe rather than exploring the problem domain. Recently, an attorney called a psychologist requesting testing to determine whether a client was mentally competent. After dutifully testing, interviewing, and evaluating the client; the psychologist submitted a report indicating the man had average intelligence and no signs of psychotic thought processes or organic brain damage. The attorney was annoyed and dissatisfied. He turned to another psychologist who developed the consultation along the lines suggested here by engaging in a prolonged conversation designed to elicit the needed legal guidelines. The case hinged on potential undue influence, not competency; more relevant interviewing and testing strategies were developed and later properly advanced.

A significant difference between the general clinical case and the forensic referral is the availability to each side of extensive documentary materials. Each attorney assembles a voluminous case record in preparation for trial. The psychologist must learn the range of materials available, as well as request any further documentation needed to form an opinion. Such materials may be significant at four distinct levels. First, many past documents are relevant to the psychologist interested in reconstructing a life history to further his understanding of a person's current behavior. Materials may range from school records, prior psychological evaluations and hospital admissions, depositions of family members or social relations, or police records and reports. Psychologists must ask to read police reports, depositions, affidavits, and the formal complaint and to see certain physical evidence in addition to having access to important characters in the person's life. A good diagnosis and evaluation is made on the basis of considering all important information.

Second, in order to apply the diagnostic criteria of the DSM-III (1980) specific time-dependent criteria must be fulfilled, often from information to be found in other sources. For example, the diagnosis of schizophrenia is made only on the basis of continuous signs of illness for at least six months at some time during the person's life with some current signs of the illness. To substantiate this diagnosis during direct testimony or cross-examination, the psychologist generally requires outside verification of duration. Third, as previously indicated, attorneys may not realize the significance of psychological materials until pointed out by the expert. Fourth, the psychologist should never allow himself to be placed in a position where an important fact or piece of evidence is revealed to him for the first time during cross-examination.

Preparation Time

Proper preparation is, of course, essential to an effective presentation. The expert must be familiar with all aspects of the case to demonstrate that an opinion is well grounded in actual fact and can be sustained through the expected challenges of opposing counsel. The expert's information should be current, documented, fully studied, and relevant to the particular legal issues of the case. Therefore adequate preparation translates into a time-consuming enterprise. Brodsky (1977, p. 271), among others, has pointed to the need for adequate preparation and lead time, advising, "make an appointment at least a few days in advance of your testimony with the attorney who actually will be conducting the direct examination." Our experience endorses even earlier meetings between attorney and psychologist, sharing of information, and strategic planning of preparation time. The fee for such preparation time must be accurately estimated and fully discussed at the start of the consultation.

As outlandish as it may seem, we have had numerous attorneys call to say: "We are in trial at the moment in this case that needs expert testimony. Can you come in tomorrow afternoon and testify about child abuse (undue influence, standards of practice, etc.)?" The same attorneys seem baffled and annoyed when an expert declines to appear on such short notice. A few mental health professionals appear in court without having sufficiently studied the case issues and become embarrassments to the field (McQueen, 1979). Some are discredited when an alert opposing counsel is able to exploit their lack of specific, specialized knowledge and unfamiliarity with trial evidence.

Delineation and Focus

Learning the legal issues is the first step in the psychological investigation, preceding sifting through documentation, interviewing, or testing. The attorney should frame his expectations for the results of the consultation in the form of a question. That question becomes the organizing principle of the psychologist's investigation; for example, a district attorney's case involved a major figure who was kidnapped by the accused (Ginsberg, 1984; Reza, 1980). This attorney asked, "How can the behavior of this alleged victim be explained so that the jury understands why this young man did not run away from his captor, even though he had the opportunity to do so on many occasions?" Another attorney in a civil case asked, "Is there a direct, causal connection between the sexual relations this woman's therapist had with her during her therapy and her current mental condition?" The psychologist in both cases would develop an investigative strategy to answer such specific questions. In the second case, the psychologist studies the women's past and present behavior; examines any relevant documentation such as treatment notes, prior reports, and work records; interviews persons who have known her across time; or reads their depositions and affidavits. The psychologist organizes his method to ascertain if the therapist's conduct was the actual and proximate cause of the woman's emotional distress.

The investigative focus is on the central legal issue. This focus reflects both the case's prima facie elements, to be proved at trial, and the bases of the expert's subsequent testimony. The psychologist cannot afford to lose the perspective that testimony is made meaningful by the legal requirements of the case. The psychologist does not begin by administering a Rorschach, an MMPI, a Wechsler, and a TAT and dutifully writing a report discussing test response characteristics or other standard therapist-diagnostician interests. As in the case of the captive man, it would be of secondary or remote importance to diagnose him as a man of bright-average intelligence with good verbal skills. The danger in such an approach is of obscuring the most important point: that is, the man's enforced dependency and all that may be entailed in his captivity.

Once the legal framework of the psychological study is established, the attorney and expert plan the tentative sequence of the work. The psychologist must accurately estimate the amount of time needed and the costs involved. The investigative plan and fees are settled on by the two professionals before proceeding. The psychologist proceeds with the study, eventually organizing the findings in terms of their relevancy.

In this section our emphasis has been on how the psychologist and attorney can beneficially interact in the first or initial stages of consultation. Stage two outlines the presentation of such findings at a deposition and the offering of testimony at trial.

STAGE TWO: DEPOSITION, TESTIMONY, AND CROSS-EXAMINATION

Using modern rules of civil procedure for joinder of claims, attorneys may join together alternative causes of action to redress the same situation, with only one of these claims having a psychological component. Thus, in the case of the young man defrauded by his investment adviser, his attorney may join together causes of action for fraud, conversion, and negligent infliction of emotional distress. Each cause of action seeks compensation for the invasion of a separate right (i.e., ownership of property and peace of mind). To substantiate each claim, the plaintiff must prove separately the particular prima facie elements of each alleged wrong. Proof is established by the submission of factual evidence. The psychologist's findings and opinion would be admitted as evidence for the purpose of proving a required element. (When opposing sides submit contradictory facts, a trial results in which a jury must decide whose facts are to be believed.)

After interviewing and evaluating the client, the psychologist meets with the attorney to discuss the psychological findings. At this stage, the psychologist should be able to outline the findings, documenting and supporting every opinion, and group these findings according to legal points. The psychologist provides an invaluable service by being prepared to discuss the strong and the weak points of his opinion and the most advantageous means of informing the jury of these points.

Expert opinion must be independently derived from a careful study of case materials. This guideline does not stand in the way of the expert and the attorney consulting and preparing the questions used in direct testimony to elicit and permit an opinion to be expressed in the best light. An attorney, inexperienced in using expert testimony, facing an equally inexperienced or inept psychological expert is a nightmarish combination that needlessly prevents the presentation of material in the form and manner needed to clarify the controversy.

After receiving the psychologist's evaluative investigation, the attorney must decide whether the information adds to his case. If the material is relevant and adds evidentiary weight to the argument, and the expert would prove to be a good witness at trial, the attorney and psychologist would begin a second stage of consultation.

Discovery and Deposition

After an attorney had made a decision to use a psychological component and to work with a particular expert, the attorney must reveal the general substance of the expert's findings and the identity of the expert. Modern trial practice has moved away from sanctioning surprises during the trial phase. A policy has been enacted in the form of procedural rules endorsing full disclosure of the factual bases of claims, in the hope that full disclosure will significantly narrow the scope of triable issues, promote pretrial settlements, and quicken the pace of proceedings. The most important means given attorneys to ensure full disclosure are the methods subsumed under the broad category of discovery. The purpose of discovery is to provide both parties with the best and most complete evidence possible to prove their contentions *and* to provide each counsel with a good knowledge of their adversary's claims and the factual bases of the claims.

The treatment of experts is in some measure a recognition of the special role of such testimony, being indispensable to certain types of trials. Expert testimony, in general, involves technical intricacies to which an opposing party needs to be prepared in order to meet its challenge at trial.

When an expert witness is expected to testify in a civil proceeding, the opposing counsel has the privilege of discovering the expert's identity and the substance of the facts and opinions to which the expert will testify at trial. As part of the pretrial discovery process an expert witness may be deposed by opposing counsel to learn the substance of later testimony.

A deposition is an examination of a witness under oath and in the presence of a court reporter. Depositions are governed by specific rules of procedure. Deponents have the right to be represented by counsel. A deposition may take place at any point in a pending case. Each party has the right to take the deposition of any witness who may provide relevant information bearing on the cause of action. A witness is generally subpoenaed to appear at a deposition and give testimony. The standard practice is for deponents to be examined orally, with the opposing party examining first. Alternatively, the examining party may choose to conduct the examination in the form of written questions, which are submitted and reviewed in advance, but answered orally in the presence of a court reporter.

An attorney may object to a question and instruct the witness not to answer; however, a record is made of the objection and the refusal. If later the objection is determined to be unwarranted, the witness may be required to answer. Often the attorney objects, allows the witness to answer, and later the trial judge determines if the question and answer are to be struck from the deposition record. A deponent is given the privilege of reviewing a transcript of the testimony to correct any mistakes, but any changes are subject to being questioned during trial. Generally, statements made in depositions are hearsay and therefore inadmissible at trial. However, a deposition that contradicts testimony given at trial may be admitted for the purpose of impeaching the witness.

The Expert's Work Product

Under the rules of discovery, the opposing side is granted extreme latitude to discover the factual materials relied on to form an opinion. Where the expert is expected to testify at trial, the adversary is entitled to discover the factual bases and substance the expert will rely on at trial. Only when an expert has been retained to develop information or opinions for use in preparing for trial but is not expected to testify is that report deemed not discoverable except under exceptional circumstances.

Therefore the psychologist should realize that opposing counsel will have access to all interview notes, correspondence, tape recordings, transcribed recordings, full copies of testing notes, transcriptions of tests if recorded, test forms, videotapes, and preliminary and final reports. In other words, almost any case documentation done by the expert is discoverable. Only wisdom and personal preference can dictate how extensively to maintain case records. There is no one way. If the psychologist takes few notes, an opposing attorney may attempt to characterize these notes as skimpy, careless, or the work of a cursory effort.

During the trial expert witnesses may take any material to the stand for reference. Such material, however, becomes instantly available to opposing counsel. Attorney and psychologist decide what notes or materials are brought to the witness stand, in order to avoid disclosing materials that are privileged to nondisclosure.

Planning the Testimony

Pretrial preparation must aim toward carefully and honestly analyzing both the strong points and the weak point of the psychologist's testimony. This type of analysis prepares the witness for both direct testimony and cross-examination attacks. Strong and weak points can be presented in the most favorable light by careful preparation of the direct testimony to bring out the strongest points of the expert's opinion. Careful preparation can also avoid situations in which the psychologist is surprised by an unexpected question or the attorney is surprised by an unexpected answer. Immediately prior to testifying, the witness should have a clear idea of the questions to be asked, the flow of one question or topic area into another, and each question's purpose in the evidenciary argument.

An example of an attorney-psychologist relationship gone astray occurred as follows. Both individuals had met several times and agreed on the testimony's broad contours. Two days before the trial the attorney called with a final set of questions he intended to pose and asked the expert to plan on this basis. The expert spent the intervening time assiduously preparing. At a prearranged meeting one half hour before court opened, the attorney seemed to have forgotten their plan and listed a totally new set of questions. The expert internally adjusted his thinking, only to appear on the witness stand moments later and be asked a third and totally different set of questions that the attorney had "a feeling" were the "right" questions to be asked then and there. During the lunch recess, the attorney and expert prepared the remaining questions only for the expert to find later on the stand that the attorney replaced half of the questions with new material. Needless to say, the expert did best on cross-examination when opposing counsel asked questions the expert had expected to be cross-examined on.

Outlining the Direct Examination

The attorney and psychologist must organize and plan the sequence and content of the material to be covered during direct examination. If a general criticism can be leveled at attorneys, it would be directed toward those attorneys who frequently fail to make clear the amount of explanatory material desired from the expert, especially from the less experienced and somewhat taciturn expert witnesses.

In observing expert witnesses, it has been our impression that a number of cautious, conservative experts "underexplain" their answers, thus making the attorney's task more difficult during direct examination. The expert may be unsure of his presentation because of inexperience or working with an attorney who has not instructed the witness in what is proper and desired. The net effect is a witness who fails to reach the jury because of a flat, ungiving recitation. We also have seen the other extreme—experts prattle, ramble, and find themselves cornered into defending impulsive and half-thought-out ideas.

It is essential that a general outline of the direct testimony be developed and gone over prior to trial. For example, in one case in which a polygraph examination was a central issue, the psychologist prepared an outline of the sequence of stresses the complainant had undergone using three time frames: first, the stressors that preceded the polygraph examination; second, those that occurred during the actual examination; and third, those that immediately followed and the longer term sequela. The time-frame outline structured and focused the direct examination, allowing the testimony to appear spontaneous, while still permitting the jury to hear the material in clear segments. Thus, the jurors could visualize, remember, and empathize with the plaintiff in each of the three segments. This method enabled the jury to understand psychologically the growing impact of damaging events that, if discussed separately, might appear only moderately disquieting.

The Expert's Role

The expert's role is to inform the judge and jury of relevant psychological issues. The expert is to supply knowledge that the average person, taking his or her seat as a juror, does not possess. "If scientific, technical, or specialized knowledge will assist the trier of fact to understand the evidence or to determine a fact in issue, a witness qualified as an expert by knowledge, skill, experience, training, or education, may testify thereto in the form of an opinion or otherwise" (*Federal Rules of Evidence*, Rule 702). The emphasis is placed on *assist*—assisting the jury member in obtaining sufficient knowledge to decide facts in dispute.

In one type of example, the psychologist can assist the court in understanding the individual who has acted under duress or social pressure. Several cases have recently reported the accounts of youths and adults, having been kidnapped or held hostage, whose behavior of not running away or seeking help is contrary to ordinary expectations. Steven Staynor, (Reza, 1980; *People v. Parnell*) kidnapped at age 10, did not run away from his captor until age 17, when he saw a seven-year-old being abducted. In another instance, a woman allegedly was held seven years, much of the time in a box, before leaving her captor (Ginsberg, 1984; *People v. Hooker*).

In another type of example, an individual's behavior may be consistent with the values of an ethnic subgroup, but the same acts may subject them to legal consequences when considered by the standards of society as a whole (e.g., Southeast Asian refugees trapping ducks and squirrels in municipal parks). In these cases, a psychologist may be called on to explain the subgroup's cultural values and mores as a means of mitigation (Diamond, 1978).

The Art of Being an Expert Witness

Being a useful consultant and effective expert witness is a complex art. While extensive knowledge of both psychology and the law are essential, other skills are necessary for forensic consultation and testimony. To function well in the courtroom, the expert must be an articulate, interesting, and believable teacher. Most clinicians and professors live a protected life in which they talk of personality, behavior, and social interactions in abstractions and jargon that others (mostly students) are forced to adapt to by learning to decipher sphinxlike riddles. The forensic psychologist, on the other hand, must be able to explain technical and theoretical concepts in a manner that interests the juror in what is being said, in a style of language free from jargon, and with a demeanor that gives no hint of condescension. The elegance of well-reasoned, jargon-free explanations of behavior can be appreciated by judge and jury. The effective giving of expert testimony demands the expert maintain a quiet warmth and poised dignity, while keeping his or her emotions under control. The expert's attitude should imply knowledge and a willingness to be informative.

It is the jury who literally decide how believable the testimony appears; the jury will base their decision on the total content, conduct, and person of the witness. The skills that enable one to be a credible and persuasive witness—speaking clearly in ordinary language, being adept at explaining ideas, having conviction in the knowledge one has and flexibility in admitting what one doesn't know—combined with an ability to relate in a warm, professional way are the same skills needed for effective consultation with attorneys. Truly forensic work is for psychologists well beyond their first years in the field for it appears to take some time to know one's field well enough to explain its workings in simple yet elegant terms.

In a recent case, a psychologist deficient in all these areas was observed. He trembled and perspired on the witness stand, while appearing ill-prepared as he fumbled through poorly organized papers. He gave lengthy, jargon-filled responses on the MMPI in a case in which the test was clearly inappropriate. Cross-examination made him appear even less believable as he lost track of lines of thought and points of reference. The latest arriving spectators became quickly convinced that he never should have entered the case. An opposing psychologist was more at ease, organized, and responded to both opposing attorneys with equal warmth. He appeared to become neither defensive nor brittle during cross-examination, maintaining an air of genuine enthusiasm for the concepts he explained.

Helpful general overviews of expert testimony are to be found in Allen, Ferster, and Rubin (1975); Berger (1979); Blinder (1973); Bromberg (1979); Gutheil (1982); Halleck (1980); Morris and Tonry (1983); Perlin (1977); Perr (1977); Pollack (1977); Scheirer and Hammonds (1983); Schlensky (1977); Shubow and Berkstresser (1977); Slovenko (1985); Stone (1976); Watson (1978); and Ziskin (1981). Specific suggestions for the psychologist as expert witness have been presented by Blau (1984); Brodsky and Robey (1972); Brodsky (1977); Nash (1974);

and Poythress (1980). Table 20.1 devised by Brodsky and Robey summarizes pretrial, witness stand, and posttrial behavior by comparing the conduct and attitudes of the "courtroom-oriented" versus the "courtroom-unfamiliar" expert witness. The table is filled with practical wisdom.

Demeanor of the Expert

As the psychologist stands before the court and the jury, he is projecting the content of his training and experience and his own personality. The expert's attitude toward the jury and the attorneys who question him or her, is often as important and, occasionally, more important than the content of the expert's knowledge. Jury members and expert witnesses are strangers to the courtroom, while attorneys and judges are both familiar with and practiced in the art of the courtroom arena.

The expert who allows himself or herself to become angry, defensive, and rigid in open court has been maneuvered into a most damaging position. Opposing counsel usually has had years of experience in eliciting anger from witnesses. Such attorneys know that the coping and reasoning ability of an angry person is more primitive, that an angry witness is often less skillful in controlling language, and that an angry witness will communicate in rigid or regressed ways or even reveal damaging information unintentionally.

Another problematic response of the expert occurs when the expert "freezes" during the direct examination. The lawyer and the expert have done their pretrial work as outlined, and the attorney expects the expert to be as articulate in the courtroom as he or she was during informal work sessions. In freezing, the expert fails to respond fully to direct examination questions, appears withholding and reluctant, and acts as if the attorney is an adversary. Some experts are highly successful at the consultation stage, often lecturing and instructing in a demeanor more familiar to an academic setting. In the courtroom, however, some freeze into competitive and withholding stances and simply do not "give." They quickly become known as great consultants but treacherous witnesses.

Experts should take into consideration a trial's setting and locale, including the social-class status of the community and the representative jurors: How the expert dresses may have a decided impact; for example, attorneys in small, rural towns may ask experts to respect the social-class expectations of their community. In many regional areas most of the citizenry, regardless of their own financial status, wear clothing like that found in large national chain stores. Overdressing and flamboyant clothing is not standard. In other areas adult women do not appear in churches, courthouses, and offices dressed in slacks or pant suits, being regarded according to custom as leisure wear.

Attorneys are well aware of the customs and prejudices of their community and may ask "imported" experts to respect the mores and expectations of the area. Failure to observe such decorum might substitute a superficial bias or diversion in place of having full attention directed to the content of an expert opinion. An attorney reported that in one situation a knowledgeable male expert wearing heavy, clanking gold jewelry was not well received by a jury of working-class men and women. The

TABLE 20.1 Comparison of the Courtroom-Oriented and the Courtroom-Unfamiliar Expert Witness

Stage	Courtroom-Oriented	Courtroom-Unfamiliar
	Pretrial	
Training	Legal-medical institutes, court clinics, or other training centers with legal background; sometimes self-taught, by bitter experience	No relevant training
Point of entry of witness into proceeding	Early in legal procedure; extensive pretrial conference with emphasis on appropriate questions to elicit evaluation-related content	Late entry; minimal or no pretrial conference with attorney; minimal or no preparation with attorney on technique for eliciting opinion
Knowledge of law, evidence, and constitutional privilege	Usually aware; occasionally more so than the particular lawyer in the trial	Usually unaware of minimally informed
Record keeping	Thorough; tends to anticipate cross-examination; exact as to dates, times, places, detail, prior hospital records	Often tends to be variable or average; omits or uncertain of dates, time, etc.
Reaction to subpoena	Minimal emotional reaction; reviews record, calls lawyer, determines basis of subpoena and information desired by lawyer; sets up conferences with lawyer	Distress and anxiety; usually does not call lawyer; no conference unless requested by lawyer—even then minimal; unaware of legal position
	On the Witness Stand	
Written report	Clear, concise, equivocal where necessary; avoids legal problems but answers legal questions raised	Technical language, poorly understood by lay readers; often does not answer legal questions raised
Target of testimony	Jury or judge	Lawyer or mental health colleagues
Language	Spoken English	Professional terminology
Purpose of testimony	Persuasion; teaching; mild advocacy of his findings	"Objective" presentation of clinical information
Courtroom activity	Active; may sit and advise lawyer	Passive; sits in back of courtroom; does not communicate with lawyer
Testimony process	Steady; consistent; aware of "traps"; concedes to minor points easily	May be badly manipulated; gets stubborn; backs into corner
Reaction to cross-examination	Normal acceptance as routine procedure	Resentment, anger, professional confusion

TABLE 20.1   *(Continued)*

Stage	Courtroom-Oriented	Courtroom-Unfamiliar
Setting up rebuttal on redirect examination	Active involvement; awareness of techniques	No activity; unaware of techniques
	Posttrial	
Reaction after court findings, especially to distortion of opinion and loss of case by client	Acceptance; learns; reappears in court	Nonacceptance; alienation; reacts by future avoidance
Results of court ad-judication	More consistent with expressed view of witness whether oppos-ing testimony is present or not	Less consistent with expressed view, particularly in border-line or contested cases with op-posing testimony
Fees	Higher, based on actual time spent in evaluation, reporting, and courtroom time; based on reg-ular private practice fees	Variable; generally low or occa-sionally unrealistically high compared with regular private practice fee for service time

appropriate and traditional practice for members of the bar is dressing conserva-tively—a standard others should adopt if there are doubts.

Cross-Examination

In preparation for cross-examination, attorney and expert must face squarely the weakest points of the expert's testimony. In doing so, each must predict and prepare for the challenges certain to be advanced by opposing counsel. Cross-examination exposes the psychologist's testimony to intense scrutiny.

Cross-examination is one method of impeaching (discrediting) the testimony of an opposing witness. Cross-examination is generally designed to elicit facts from the witness which discredit the witness's own testimony. A witness may be im-peached by demonstrating (1) *bias or interest* in the outcome; (2) having a "charac-ter" marred by a history and pattern of *dishonesty* and *misconduct*; (3) proof of *prior inconsistent statements*; (4) *contradictions*; and (5) a *lack of knowledge*.

On the last point, the credibility of an expert witness may be attacked by cross-examination as to both his general knowledge of the field in which a claim is made of expertise and specific knowledge of the facts upon which an expert opinion is based. During cross-examination, the attorney's intention is to impugn the general and specific methods and conclusions of the opposing expert and/or the entire field of psychology, as not adding significantly to the juror's knowledge. Failing to be successful at the latter approaches, the attorney may turn toward the former by fo-cusing on the character and reputation of the witness in order to discredit an unfa-vorable and successful substantive opinion.

The major work used by attorneys who are confronted by potential psychological evidence is that of Ziskin (1981). Although many others have criticized the role of psychology in the courts, Ziskin's work presents a thorough and useful compilation of commonly used cross-examination strategies. The psychologist who expects to give courtroom opinions and impressions in the same manner as done in the average clinic or case conference is in for a nasty surprise when confronted by an attorney well-versed in every argument cited by Ziskin. Even the most cursory glance through approximately 1000 pages of strategy and trial techniques reveals that no aspect of psychology goes unchallenged. Doctoral oral examinations pale by comparison in their narrow topic coverage and the almost helpful academic atmosphere. The chary expert should expect to discuss anything Ziskin's books have taught attorneys. In preparing for this type of cross-examination, the expert should work with the counsel, whom he is representing, to create variants of some of Ziskin's challenges which apply to the case at hand. It is important to listen to an experienced trial attorney's suggestions of how to field cross-examination questions.

For example, underlying some of Ziskin's strategies is a technique of positing questions that force psychologists to offer *legal* opinions when their role is to offer professional opinions and provide scientific, technical, or specialized knowledge not possessed by the ordinary person. The question that asks the expert to state a legal opinion or voice an opinion on the ultimate issue of the trial is beyond the scope of the psychologist's expertise: that is, a defendant's culpability in a criminal proceeding. The culpability of a defendant who may or may not have a mental disorder is a question of fact to be decided by the trier of fact. Strictly speaking, the domain of the expert is to offer an opinion based on his or her education, training, and experience that comments on the past, present, or future psychological status of the plaintiff or defendant. Being drawn out of their base of expertise and voicing an opinion on issues of fact, first, may divert attention from the substantive elements of the testimony and, second, discredit that substantive testimony by demonstrating a weakness in offering a legal opinion. Another tactic, with the same effect in mind, is to try to expand the area of cross-examination testimony outside the domain of expertise. Such a tactic is seen when an expert on alcoholism treatment is lured into making statements concerning statutes, labor management, or other topics only collaterally related to the expert's special knowledge.

Many strategies and tactics for attorneys to use are offered by Ziskin. We offer here a condensed sampling of his interrogatories that should indicate the tenor and direction of his challenges:

> "There is no expertise shown by psychologists or psychiatrists in most legal testimony that is better than the judgment of the ordinary man or woman."

> "The expert has not demonstrated a clear relationship between the diagnosis and its alleged consequences."

> "Isn't there considerable controversy about the usefulness of psychological evidence in regard to legal matters?"

> "Can you offer any scientific evidence that the psychiatric theories upon which you base your conclusions have some basis in fact?"

> "How do you determine if your professional opinions are correct?"

"Has there ever been a scientific study of the accuracy of your professional judgment?"

"You have never gathered evidence which indicates that the conclusions you offer in the courtroom are usually correct?"

"So you haven't any idea if the diagnostic opinions you have been offering year after year are really correct?"

"Are you aware of the great number of studies which show that more experienced psychiatrists are no more accurate in their assessments than inexperienced ones, or even lay people?"

Some of the attacks are made on the personal skills of the expert; others are aimed at the entire field of psychology or psychiatry; still others concern issues on which the expert should have current knowledge.

A number of articles and books present excerpts from trials and detailed discussions of possible responses to these challenges: Blinder (1973); Brodsky (1977); Bromberg (1979); Eysenck (1983); Morey (1980); Poythress (1980); Spitzer (1975, 1976); Webb, Gold, Johnstone, and Diclemente (1981).

STAGE THREE: DEPOSITIONS AND CROSS-EXAMINATIONS OF OPPOSING EXPERTS

Attorneys often seek collaboration in preparing to depose or cross-examine the other side's experts. In reality the process is the mirror-image of the process undertaken during preparation for the expert's own cross-examination. At this stage the expert provides assistance in matching the strong points of one's own arguments with the weak points and inconsistencies of the opposition. The first steps are to read the other expert's documentation obtained through discovery (i.e., interview notes, test data, written reports, and prior depositions). Further research may be done by ascertaining what the expert has said or written on the case subject in the past and anticipating similar results in the current case.

Often attorneys seek help not only with the substantive issues but also in developing a method of dealing psychologically with an expert. What psychological and rhetorical ploys will the expert handle least well? Can the expert be led into areas beyond his or her domain of competence? How easy or hard to follow are the expert's remarks? What vanities, rigidities, and response sets are apparent? The expert must decide whether to become involved in this area and what are the ethical limitations of the consultation.

Trends in Consultation and Testimony

Attorneys are becoming aware of the need to work with the demeanor and communication skills of potential important witnesses. Often an attorney must use a taciturn, verbally withholding, and emotionally unresponsive client, whose demeanor may pose a major stumbling block to properly presenting a case to the jury. Jurors may be put off by the ungiving, flat style of the witness and mistake unresponsiveness for hostility and rancor. In many cases the jury must be able to like and feel sympathy for the witness or at least understand that the person is trying to respond under adversarial conditions; for example, in a personal injury case in which a man allegedly had had poor dental surgery the man had become depressed and morose and tended to bow his head to keep his now disfigured jaw from prominent view. This mannerism, combined with a natural shyness and an elliptical style of speech, projected the image of a reluctant, angry man, indifferent to the outcome of the trial or other events in his life. A psychologist used video replay to teach the man how to be warm, spontaneous, and more direct in a conversation, so that the attorney-client interaction would be more productive and natural in court.

Psychologists are appearing more as members of the trial team seated at the counsel table, not only during the jury selection stage, but also during the cross-examination phase of opposing expert witnesses. Such consultation experiences can go well or poorly. A recent disastrous example occurred in a trial in which a plaintiff's attorney used a courtroom-inexperienced sociologist to pass questions to him as he cross-examined an experienced clinical psychologist. Though they were academically related, some questions were without foundation in the direct testimony and irrelevant to the cause of action. Thus these questions were not allowed. The questions that were allowed permitted the expert to add further persuasive information in subject areas in which the expert was well versed.

In contrast, two other cases were observed in which the results of using a psychologist as part of the trial team were excellent. In the first the psychologist was retained before trial and asked to critique the written reports of the opposing psychiatrists thoroughly. Sentence by sentence the reasoning was dissected, questions were developed that challenged the conclusions, and the attorney was thoroughly briefed prior to the trial on the material and in that domain of psychology. During the ensuing cross-examination, the psychologist sat at the counsel table providing further written questions. The results demonstrated to the jury that in one case the expert could not translate his professional jargon into readily understood terms, and in the other case the expert was not current on the diagnostic criteria and research on the condition ascribed to the defendant.

In still another instance a prosecutor elected not to block the testimony of a defense sociologist; rather he chose to have his own experts present to provide questions during the cross-examination. He was able to discredit the expert's testimony by showing that the expert's training in sociology did not qualify him as an expert for the subject matter of the case at bar. These examples highlight an expanding area of forensic consultation—the team approach to proper points in a trial.

In the past psychologists were called on primarily to consult in three situations: competency evaluations, assessment of emotional harm or distress in civil proceedings, and the study of exculpating factors in criminal proceedings. Now, however, there are multiple situations and topics on which attorneys seek psychological information. These expanding areas run parallel to the legal profession's broadening conception of what constitute appropriate circumstances for legal redress of conflictual events. Many new causes of action are now being permitted to reach a trial stage which in the past were not considered the proper subject for litigation and/or not compensable, such as the tort of the intentional infliction of emotional distress.

Consultation and testimony are sought on issues ranging from jury selection (Harrington & Dempsey, 1969; Rothblatt, 1966; Sanitto, 1979; Shepherd, 1964; Suggs & Sales, 1978; Tate, Hawrish, & Clark, 1974), child development (Conger, 1973; Mussen, Conger, & Kagan, 1979; Rosen, 1983; Weiner, 1982), child abuse and beaten women (American Psychological Association, 1983; Baumann, 1983; Gelles, 1980; Huston, 1984; Kempe & Kempe, 1984; Walker, 1984; Walter, 1982), the impact of brain damage on behavior (Lezak, 1983), learning disabilities (Johnson & Myklebust, 1967), brainwashing (Delgado, 1977, 1984; Lunde & Wilson, 1977; Ofshe & Singer, 1985; Singer, 1979, 1985; West & Singer, 1980), custody issues (Karras & Berry, 1985), social and peer pressure, dangerousness (Hinton, 1983; Monahan, 1978, 1981, 1983; Monahan & Steadman, 1983), cultural and ethnic identity issues (deRueck & Porter, 1968; Diamond, 1978; Hsu, 1961), family dynamics (Wynne, Weber, & McDaniels, 1985), the standards of practice in the mental health field (Berman & Cohen-Sandler, 1983; Berger, 1979; Blau, 1984; Corey, Corey, & Callanan, 1984; Ethical Principles of Psychologists, 1981; Haas & Fennimore, 1983), sexual conduct of therapists (Bouhoutsos, Holroyd, Lerman, Forer, & Greenberg, 1983; Kardener, Fuller, & Mensh, 1973; Slovenko, 1975; A. Stone, 1976; M. Stone, 1976); to hypnosis and multiple personality (Cleckley, 1982; Deyoub, 1984; Orne, Dinges, & Orne, 1984; Reiter, 1958; Thigpen & Cleckley, 1984).

This range of requests demands that psychologists have a general knowledge of the legal system, specific knowledge of the legal issues in controversy, and expertise in their own special areas of knowledge. It behooves the ethical psychologist to refer attorneys to other experts when the needs of the consultation and later trial testimony exceed the clinician's personal and professional skills. Experts are ethically obligated to remain within their area of expertise. Certainly their qualifications to offer an expert opinion will be severely scrutinized during the legal process. Moreover, professional psychologists have a responsibility to refer prospective clients to more appropriate fellow professionals when indicated (Corey, Corey, & Callanan, 1984; Ethical Principles of Psychologists, 1981).

Forensic consultants are being asked to have knowledge of and assist in ever-broadening and complex social and cultural phenomena. It is no longer possible for the psychologist to take an exclusively intrapsychic view of individual behavior. The expert witness is increasingly being called on to inform the court of the multiple social and psychological contexts impinging on an individual (Andreasen, 1985; deRueck & Porter, 1968; Diamond, 1978; Hsu, 1961; Ofshe & Singer, 1985; Singer, 1985; West & Singer, 1980). The psychologist who lacks the requisite skills to place an individual's behavior in multiple social, ethnic, and cultural contexts is becoming antiquated.

Developing Areas

As society changes, new forces come to have dominant effects on individual lives. Invariably these new forces become the subject of litigation. Both contemporary society's emphasis on psychological well-being and, paradoxically, the psychological manipulation of behavior have been the subject matter of controversies in which the psychological expert is called on to assist the judicial process. Courts are trying cases in which plaintiffs have been subjected to various forms of what we term the systematic manipulation of social and psychological influences or the practice of coercive influence and behavior control (Ofshe & Singer, 1985). These situations include such techniques as undue influence, brainwashing, and systematic thought-reform programs. Social and psychological pressures have been inflicted on individuals in significant proportions to produce triable causes of emotional harm, with a number of cases adjudicated in favor of the plaintiff/victim (Deyoub, 1984; *George v. ISKON; Bingham v. Lifespring; Christofferson v. Scientology; Bjorquez v. Erhard Seminars Training (est), Werner Erhard, et al.; Susskind v. Lifespring, Inc. et al.; Jones and Jones v. Lifespring, Inc., et al.; Roe and Doe v. Lifespring, Inc., et al.*).

The case of Patricia Hearst (*United States v. Hearst*, (1978) is the best known example of a situation in which the kidnap victim was subjected to intense thought-reform techniques to produce behavior inconsistent with her history (e.g., while still a prisoner of her captors she participated in a bank robbery). In *George v. ISKON* a young woman was awarded damages because of the intense thought-reform and brainwashing regime she underwent at age 14. In the course of attempting to locate his daughter, a legal minor, the father was allegedly subjected to a number of stressors by the defendants which culminated in the father's death from a heart attack. A number of other cases have been tried or settled in which the plaintiff's alleged emotional harm grew out of attendance at large group awareness training sessions.

Psychologists have been helpful in explaining behavior in other situations: released hostages often displaying the Stockholm syndrome (Ochberg, 1978; Strentz, 1980; Symonds, 1975, 1980a, 1980b); the enforced dependency of abused captives (Finkelhor, Gelles, Hotaling, & Strauss, 1983; Gelles, 1980; Ofshe & Singer, 1985; Walker, 1984; West & Singer, 1980). In such situations the psychologist must supplement traditional diagnostic techniques with analysis of individual and group behavior done by sociologists, anthropologists, and police intelligence units—to mention only the more obvious.

SUMMARY

This chapter has recommended that the consultation between psychologist and attorney rest on proper preparation, continuing collaborative effort over time, and evolve according to a three-stage model. The procedure moves from a period of orientation and delineation of the legal issues for which expert testimony is sought, through preparing for direct testimony and cross-examination at the trial stage, to coping with opposing expert testimony.

Emphasis has been placed on the expanding role of psychological testimony in litigation, paralleling society's shifting forces, and the realization that these new forces are the impetus for new types of litigation. As a result, psychologists and other mental health experts must expand their competence base to include perspectives and analytic techniques drawn from multiple ethnic, social, and cultural contexts. An increasing professionalism is needed in the area of forensic consultation to meet the alliance between psychology and the law.

REFERENCES

Albert, S., Fox, H. M., & Kahn, M. (1980). Faking psychosis on the Rorschach: Can expert judges detect malingering? *Journal of Personality Assessment, 44*, 115–119.

Allen, R. C., Ferster, E. Z., & Rubin, J. G. (1975). *Readings in law and psychiatry*. Baltimore: Johns Hopkins University Press.

American Psychological Association. (1983). *Brief of amicus curiae: Hawthorne v. State of Florida*. District Court of Appeal, N.AN-435.

Andreasen, N. C. (1985). Posttraumatic stress disorder. In H. I. Kaplan & B. J. Sadock (Eds.), *Comprehensive textbook of psychiatry* (4th ed.) (pp. 918–924). Baltimore: Williams and Wilkins.

Arieti, S., & Meth, J. M. (1959). Rare, unclassifiable, collective, and exotic psychotic syndromes. In S. Arieti (Ed.), *American handbook of psychiatry*. New York: Basic Books.

Asher, R. (1951). Munchausen's syndrome. *Lancet, 1*, 339–341.

Baumann, M. A. (1983). Expert testimony on the battered wife syndrome. *Saint Louis University Law Journal, 27*, 407–435.

Berger, L. S. (1979). Expert clinical testimony and professional ethics. *Journal of Psychiatry and Law, 7*, 347–357.

Berman, A. L., & Cohen-Sandler, R. (1983) Suicide and malpractice: Expert testimony and the standard of care. *Professional Psychology, 14*, 6–19.

Bingham v. Lifespring, Inc., United States District Court, 82-5128 (E.D. Pa. 1982).

Bjorquez v. Erhard Seminars Training, Werner Erhard et al., Santa Clara (California) Superior Court. Case 449177 (April, 1980).

Black, D. (1981). The extended Munchausen's syndrome: A family case. *British Journal of Psychiatry, 138*, 466–469.

Blau, T. H. (1984). Psychological tests in the courtroom. *Professional Psychology, 15*, 176–186.

Blinder, M. (1973). *Psychiatry in the everyday practice of law*. Rochester, NY: Lawyer's Cooperative.

Bouhoutsos, J., Holroyd, J., Lerman, H., Forer, B., & Greenberg, M. (1983). Sexual intimacy between psychotherapists and patients. *Professional Psychology, 14*, 185–196.

Brodsky, S. L. (1977). The mental health professional on the witness stand: A survival guide. In B. D. Sales (Ed.), *Psychology in the legal process* (pp. 269–276). New York: Spectrum.

Brodsky, S. L., & Robey, A. (1972). On becoming an expert witness: Issues of orientation and effectiveness. *Professional Psychology*, pp. 173–176.

Bromberg, W. (1979). *The uses of psychiatry in the law*. Westport, CT: Quorum Books.

Christofferson v. Scientology. Multnomah County (Oregon) Supreme Court. Case A-7704 05184 (1982).

Cleckley, H. (1982). *The mask of sanity*. New York: New American Library.

Conger, J. J. (1973). *Adolescence and youth: Psychological development in a changing world*. New York: Harper and Row.

Corey, G., Corey, M. S. & Callanan, P. (1984). *Issues and ethics in the helping professions* (2nd ed.). Monterrey, CA: Brooks/Cole.

Delgado, R. (1977). Religious totalism: Gentle and ungentle persuasion under the first amendment. *Southern California Law Review, 51*, 1–98.

Delgado, R. (1984). When religious exercise is not free: Deprogramming and the constitutional status of coercively induced belief. *Vanderbilt Law Review, 37*, 1071–1115.

de Reuck, A. V. S., & Porter, R. (1968). *The mentally abnormal offender*. Boston: Little, Brown.

Deyoub, P. L. (1984). Hypnotic stimulation of antisocial behavior: A case report. *International Journal of Clinical and Experimental Hypnosis, 32*, 301–306.

Diagnostic and statistical manual of mental disorders (3rd ed.). (1980). Washington, DC: American Psychiatric Association.

Diamond, B. L. (1978). Social and cultural factors as a diminished capacity defense in criminal law. *Bulletin of the American Academy of Psychiatry and Law, 6*, 195.

Ethical principles of psychologists (rev. ed.). (1981). Washington, DC: American Psychological Association.

Eysenck, H., Wakefield, J. A., & Friedman, A. F. (1983). Diagnosis and clinical assessment: The DSM III. *Annual review of psychology, 34*, 167–193.

Finkelhor, D., Gelles, R., Hotaling, G., & Strauss, M. (1983). *The dark side of families*. Beverly Hills, CA: Sage Publications.

Gelles, R. (1980). Violence in the family: A review of the research in the 70's. *Journal of Marriage and the Family, 42*, 873–885.

George v. ISKON, Orange County (California) Superior Court.

Ginsberg, M. (1984, November 21). Kidnap victim tells bondage ordeal. *San Francisco Examiner*, p. A-10.

Grinker, R. R. (1961). Imposture as a form of mastery. *Archives of General Psychiatry, 5*, 449–452.

Guthiel, T. G. & Appelbaum, P. S. (1982). *Clinical handbook of psychiatry and the law*. New York: McGraw-Hill.

Haas, L. J. & Fennimore, D. (1983). Ethical and legal issues in professional psychology: Selected works, 1970–1981. *Professional Psychology, 14*, 540–548.

Halleck, S. L. (1980). *Law and the practice of psychiatry: A handbook for clinicians*. New York: Plenum Medical.

Harrington, D. C., & Dempsey, J. (1969). Psychological factors in jury selection. *Tennessee Law Review, 37*, 173–184.

Hinton, J. W. (1983). *Dangerousness: Problems of assessment and prediction*. London: George Allen & Unwin.

Hsu, F. L. K. (1961). *Psychological anthropology: Approaches to culture and personality*. Homewood, IL: Dorsey.

Huston, K. E. (1984). Ethical decisions in treating battered women. *Professional Psychology, 15*, 822–832.

Johnson, D. J., & Myklebust, H. R. (1967). *Learning disabilities: Educational principles and practices*. New York: Grune & Stratton.

Jones and Jones v. Lifespring, Inc., United States District Court, District of Columbia. No. 82-881 (1982).

Kardener, S. H., Fuller, M., & Mensh, I. N. (1973). A survey of physicians' attitudes and practices regarding erotic and nonerotic contact with patients. *American Journal of Psychiatry, 130*, 1077–1081.

Karras, D., & Berry, K. K. (1985). Custody evaluations: A critical review. *Professional Psychology, 16*, 76–85.

Keeton, W. P., Dobbs, D. B., Keeton, R. E., & Owen, D. G. (1984). *Prosser and Keeton on the law of torts*. St. Paul, MN: West.

Kempe, R. S., & Kempe, C. H. (1984). *The common secret: Sexual abuse of children and adolescents*. New York: W. H. Freeman.

Lehman, H. E. (1980). Unusual psychiatric disorders, atypical psychoses, and brief reactive psychoses. In H. I. Kaplan, A. M. Freedman, & B. J. Sadock (Eds.), *Comprehensive textbook of psychiatry*, (3rd ed.) (pp. 1986–2002). Baltimore: Williams and Wilkins.

Lezak, M. D. (1983). *Neuropsychological assessment* (2nd ed.). New York: Oxford University Press.

Lunde, D. C., & Wilson, T. E. (1977). Brainwashing as a defense to criminal liability. *Criminal Law Bulletin, 13*, 341–382.

McQueen, R. (1979). The psychologist to the witness stand. *Clinical Psychologist, 32*, 4–6.

Menninger, K., Mayman, M., & Pruyser, P. (1963). *The vital balance*. New York: Viking.

Monahan, J. (1978). The prediction of violent criminal behavior: A methodological critique and prospectus. In A. Blumstein, J. Cohen, & D. Nagin (Eds.), *Deterrence and incapacitation: Estimating the effects of criminal sanctions on crime rates*. Washington, DC: National Academy of Science.

Monahan, J. (1981). *The clinical prediction of violent behavior*. Washington, DC: U.S. Government Printing Office.

Monahan, J. (1983). The prediction of violent behavior: Developments in psychology and law. In C. J. Scheirer & B. L. Hammonds, (Eds.), *The master lecture series volume II: Psychology and the law*. Washington, DC: American Psychological Association.

Monahan, J., & Steadman, H. (1983). Crime and mental disorder: An epidemiological approach. In N. Morris & M. Tonry (Eds.), *Crime and justice: An annual review of research*. Chicago: University of Chicago Press.

Morey, L. C. (1980). Differences between psychologists and psychiatrists in the use of DSM III. *American Journal of Psychiatry, 137*, 1123–1124.

Morris, N., & Tonry, M. (1983). *Crime and justice: An annual review of research*. Chicago: University of Chicago Press.

Mussen, P. H., Conger, J. J., & Kagan, J. (1979). *The psychological development of the child* (5th ed.). New York: Harper and Row.

Nash, M. M. (1974). Parameters and distinctiveness of psychological testimony. *Professional Psychology, 5*, 239–243.

Ochberg, F. (1978). The victims of terrorism: Psychiatric considerations. *Terrorism, 1*, 147–168.

Ofshe, R., & Singer, M. T. (in press). Attacks on peripheral versus central elements of self and the impact of thought reforming techniques: Review and analysis. *Journal of the Theory of Social Behavior*.

Orne, M. T., Dinges, D. F., & Orne, E. C. (1984). On the differential diagnosis of multiple personality in the forensic context. *International Journal of Clinical and Experimental Hypnosis, 32*, 118–169.

People v. Hooker, San Mateo County (California) Superior Court, No.C 14661 (Judge Smith, August, 1985).

People v. Parnell, 119 C.A. 3d 392 (1981).

Perlin, M. S. (1977). The legal status of the psychologist in the courtroom. *Journal of Psychiatry and Law, 5*, 41–54.

Perr, I. N. (1977). Cross-examination of the psychiatrist, using publications. *Bulletin of the American Academy of Psychiatry and Law, 5*, 237–331.

Phillips, M. R., Ward, N. G., & Ries, R. K. (1983). Factitious mourning: Painless parenthood. *American Journal of Psychiatry, 140*, 420–425.

Pollack, S. (1977). Cross-examination of the psychiatrist using publications: Point counterpoint. *Bulletin of the American Academy of Psychiatry and Law, 5*, 332–335.

Poythress, N. G. (1980). Coping on the witness stand: Learned responses to "learned treatises." *Professional Psychology, 11*, 139–149.

Reiter, P. J. (1958). *Antisocial or criminal acts and hypnosis: A case study.* Copenhagen: Munksgaard.

Reza, H. G. (1980, March 4). Kidnap victim's story of seven-year odyssey. *San Francisco Chronicle*, p. 1.

Roe and Doe v. Lifespring, Inc., United States District Court, District of Columbia, No. 81-3215 (1981).

Rosen, R. H. (1983). The need for training in forensic child psychology. *Professional Psychology, 14*, 481–489.

Rosenhan, D. L. (1973). On being sane in insane places. *Science, 179*, 250–258.

Rothblatt, H. B. (1966). Techniques for jury selection. *Criminal Law Bulletin, 2*, 14–29.

Sannito, T. (1979). *A psychologist's voir dire.* Dubuque, IA: Forensic Psychologists.

Scheirer, J. C., & Hammonds, B. (1983). *The master lecture series volume II: Psychology and the law.* Washington, DC: American Psychological Association.

Schulman, J., Shaver, P., Colman, R., Emrich, B., & Christie, R. (1973). Recipe for a jury. *Psychology Today, 6*, 37–84.

Shepard, J. C. (1964–1965). Techniques of jury selection from the defendant's point of view. *Proceedings of the American Bar Association Section of Insurance, Negligence, and Compensation Law* (pp. 359–362). Chicago: American Bar Association.

Shlensky, R. (1977). Psychiatric expert testimony and consultation. *Medical Trial Techniques Quarterly, 24*, 38–44.

Shubow, L. D., & Berkstresser, C. D. (1977, July). Handling the psychiatric witness. *Trial Magazine*, pp. 320–335.

Singer, M. T. (1979). Coming out of the cults. *Psychology Today, 12*, 72–82.

Singer, M. T. (1985). Consultation with families of cultists. In L. C. Wynne, T. Weber, & S. McDaniel (Eds.), *The family therapist as consultant.* New York: Guilford Press.

Slovenko, R. (1965). *Sexual behavior and the law.* Springfield, IL: C. C. Thomas.

Slovenko, R. (1985) Forensic psychiatry. In H. I. Kaplan & B. J. Sadock (Eds.), *Comprehensive textbook of psychiatry* (4th ed.) (pp. 1960–1990). Baltimore: Williams and Wilkins.

Spitzer, R. L. (1975). On pseudoscience in science, logic in remission and psychiatric diagnosis: A critique of Rosenhan's "On being sane in insane places." *Journal of Abnormal Psychology, 84*, 442–452.

Spitzer, R. L. (1976). More on pseudoscience in science and the case for psychiatric diagnosis: A critique of D. L. Rosenhan's "On being sane in insane places." *Archives of General Psychiatry, 33*, 459–470.

Spitzer, R. L., Forman, J. B. W. (1979) DSM III Field trials: II. Initial experience with the multiaxial system. *American Journal of Psychiatry, 136*, 818–820.

Spitzer, R. L., Forman, J. B. W., & Nee, J. (1979). DSM III Field trials. I. Initial interrater diagnostic reliability. *American Journal of Psychiatry, 136*, 815–817.

Spitzer, R. L., Williams, J. B. W., & Skodol, A. E. (1983). DSM-III: The major achievements and an overview. *American Journal of Psychiatry, 137*, 151–164.

Stone, A. A. (1976a). *Mental health and law: A system in transition.* New York: Jason Aronson.

Stone, A. A. (1976b). The legal implications of sexual activity between psychiatrist and patient. *American Journal of Psychiatry, 133*, 1138–1141.

Stone, M. H. (1976). Boundary violations between therapist and patient. *Psychiatry Annals, 8*, 8–21.

Strentz, T. (1980). The Stockholm syndrome: Law enforcement policy and ego defenses of the hostage. *Annals of the New York Academy of Sciences, 437*, 137–150.

Suggs, D., & Sales, B. D. (1978). Using communication cues to evaluate prospective jurors during the voir dire. *Arizona Law Review, 20*, 629–642.

Susskind v. Lifespring, Inc., et al., United States District Court, Eastern District of Pennsylvania, No. 83-4370 (1983).

Sussman, N., & Hyler, S. E. (1985). Factitious disorders. In H. I. Kaplan & B. J. Sadock, (Eds.), *Comprehensive textbook of psychiatry* (4th ed.) (pp. 1241–1247). Baltimore: Williams and Wilkins.

Symonds, M. (1975). Victims of violence: Psychological effects and after effects. *American Journal of Psychoanalysis, 35*, 19–26.

Symonds, M. (1980a). Victim responses to terror. *Annals of the New York Academy of Sciences, 347*, 129–136.

Symonds, M. (1980b). The "second injury" to victims [Special edition]. *Evaluation and Change*, pp. 36–38.

Tate, E., Hawrish, E., & Clark, S. (1974). Communication variables in jury selection. *Journal of Communication, 24*, 130–139.

Thigpen, C. H., & Cleckley, H. M. (1984). On the incidence of multiple personality disorder: A brief communication. *International Journal of Clinical and Experimental Hypnosis, 32*, 63–66.

United States v. Hearst, 563 F.2d 1331 (9th Cir., 1977), *cert. denied*, 435 U.S. 100 (1978).

Walker, L. E. (1984) *The battered woman syndrome.* New York: Springer.

Walter, P. D. (1982). Expert testimony and battered women. *Journal of Legal Medicine, 3*, 267–294.

Watson, A. S. (1978). On the preparation and use of psychiatric expert testimony: Some suggestions in an ongoing controversy. *Bulletin of the American Academy of Psychiatry and Law, 6*, 226–246.

Webb, L. J., Gold, R. S., Johnstone, E. E., & Diclemente, C. C. (1981). Accuracy of DSM-III diagnoses following a training program. *American Journal of Psychiatry, 138,* 376–378.

Weiner, H., & Braiman, A. (1955). The Ganser syndrome. *American Journal of Psychiatry, 3,* 767–773.

Weiner, I. B. (1982). *Child and adolescent psychopathology.* New York: Wiley.

Weiss, J. M. A. & David, D. (1974). Malingering and associated syndromes. In S. Arieti & G. Caplan (Eds.), *American handbook of psychiatry* (2nd ed., pp. 270–287). New York: Basic Books.

West, L. J., & Singer, M. T. (1980). Cults, quacks, and the nonprofessional psychotherapies. In H. I. Kaplan, A. M. Freedman, & B. J. Sadock (Eds.), *Comprehensive textbook of psychiatry* (3rd ed., pp. 3245–3258). Baltimore: Williams and Wilkins.

Winer, J. A., & Pollock, G. H. (1980). Disorders of impulse control. In H. I. Kaplan, A. M. Freedman, & B. J. Sadock (Eds.), *Comprehensive textbook of psychiatry* (3rd ed., pp. 1817–1829). Baltimore: Williams and Wilkins.

Wynne, L. C., Weber, T., & McDaniels, S. (1985). *The family therapist as consultant.* New York: Guilford Press.

Yudofsky, S. C. (1985). Conditions not attributable to a mental disorder. In H. I. Kaplan & B. J. Sadock (Eds.), *Comprehensive textbook of psychiatry* (4th ed., pp. 1862–1865). Baltimore: Williams and Wilkins.

Ziskin, J. (1981). *Coping with psychiatric and psychological testimony* (3rd ed.). Venice, CA: Law and Psychology.

PART FIVE

Treatment

CHAPTER 21

Intervention with Incarcerated Offenders

MICHAEL A. MILAN and JOSEPH H. EVANS

This chapter describes the delivery of psychological services in closed institutions for convicted adult felons. To appreciate the problems that the mental health professional confronts in these institutions this chapter first discusses clinical impressions of the harmful effects of imprisonment on inmates. This is followed by a review of a representative cross section of empirical studies documenting the incidence of mental disorders in prison populations and exploring whether inmates are actually harmed by the prison experience. Guidelines for the operation of mental health programs in correctional settings are then outlined. This is followed by an elaboration of the application of a community psychology model to the practice of correctional psychology. This model prescribes certain primary, secondary, and tertiary prevention practices that may be deployed to prevent, reduce the severity of, and treat mental health problems in correctional settings. The chapter concludes with a critical assessment of the roles of the correctional mental health professional and a discussion of nontraditional roles psychologists may assume in correctional settings.

THE EFFECTS OF IMPRISONMENT: CLINICAL OBSERVATIONS

Until recently little attention has been directed to the psychological needs of incarcerated offenders or to the effects of imprisonment on the mental health of inmates. Evidence that has become available now indicates that the psychological needs of offenders are pronounced. At a time when more and more citizens and political leaders are calling for the incapacitation of greater numbers of offenders for longer periods of time as the solution to the problem of crime it is important that the public have a complete understanding of the conditions of confinement to which these offenders will be subjected, the expected effects of these conditions on the offenders, and the released offenders' readjustment in the community after experiencing those conditions.

Zusman (1973) reviews several clinical descriptions of the effects of institution-

The authors express their appreciation to Elaine Beal of Georgia State University and Carol Frazier of the University of South Florida for their assistance in preparing this manuscript.

alization on psychiatric patients. Professionals familiar with correctional institutions would undoubtedly add that the conditions of confinement in prisons are in many ways similar to or more regressive than those described by Zusman, and that the resulting changes in affect, behavior, and cognition, termed the *social breakdown syndrome*, would be expected to occur as a function of those conditions in prison inmates as well as in psychiatric patients. More specifically, the general deterioration said to occur as a result of institutionalization has been attributed to being crowded into locked, barred, unstimulating rooms, to staff attitudes that give little hope for rehabilitation, and to an unchanging daily routine.

Barton (1959) first used the term *institutional neurosis* to characterize a syndrome of difficulties that he observed developing in response to institutionalization. The common signs of this syndrome include apathy, lack of initiative, loss of interest in things and events not of immediate relevance, deterioration of personal habits, lack of interest in the future, and a loss of individuality. The factors that Barton identified as the cause of the syndrome are as characteristic of correctional institutions as of psychiatric hospitals. These include a loss of contact with the outside world because of the placement of institutions in remote areas and the restrictions often placed on the time and nature of visits. A second cause is enforced idleness which results from a lack of programs and restrictions on permissible activities. In addition, staff take a superior attitude with respect to the inmates, make decisions for them, withhold information, and the like. Inmates also lose touch with personal friends and are denied or required to relinquish many of their personal possessions, thereby relinquishing much of their personal identity. The general atmosphere of deprivation, sterility, and disrepair characteristic of many institutions also contributes to the institutionalization process. Finally, the prospects for success in finding a satisfying and productive life outside the institution that will allow inmates to obtain the goods and activities that society values are bleak and unpromising.

As true as these conditions are of both correctional institutions and psychiatric hospitals, prison life subjects inmates to additional, perhaps even more regressive, conditions (Toch, 1975). Inmates must be ever-vigilant lest they offend a powerful fellow inmate or a member of the correctional staff and, as a consequence, be subject to physical abuse or subtle discrimination in treatment within the institution. Inmates must also be constantly on guard against predatory inmates who will take advantage of any sign of weakness to subjugate them personally, financially, and sexually (Bowker, 1980). Finally, the high potential for violence in institutions in conjunction with the indifferent brutality to which inmates are subjected by their peers creates an environment for the desensitization of feelings of empathy toward others and the development of insulation, suspicion, and hostility for survival.

THE EFFECTS OF IMPRISONMENT: EMPIRICAL FINDINGS

In recent years research questioning whether the experiences of imprisonment do in fact have a regressive effect on the mental health of all or at least a significant portion of the inmate population has been reported. This research has looked at signs of mental disorders in both jail and prison populations and has compared the incidence and severity of disorders of inmates incarcerated for short and long periods of time.

Porporino and Zamble (1984) provide one of the more comprehensive reviews of the research on the effects of imprisonment on the mental health of inmates. They make clear that indices of mental illness are higher in prison populations than in the general population. For the years 1970 through 1983, there were three times as many suicides in Canadian prisons than for males of comparable age. Similarly, higher-than-expected suicide rates occur in American (Austin & Urkovic, 1977) and British (Topp, 1979) prisons, as well as in jail populations (Hayes, 1983). These suicidal acts appear most problematic during the early stages of imprisonment (Sloan, 1983), as do acute psychotic episodes (Paskind & Brown, 1940) that are triggered by incarceration. Serious self-injury is also more common in the incarcerated than in the general population (Gibbs, 1982; Toch, 1975), as are stress-related disorders and acute physical ailments (Heather, 1977; Jones, 1976). Depression (Cooper, 1974) and anxiety (Lipton, 1960) appear to develop as imprisonment continues.

Although most would agree that these data reveal a higher incidence of mental health difficulties in prison than in the community, there is disagreement as to whether the difficulties are due to imprisonment. Indeed, Monahan and Steadman (1984) argue that the incidence of mental disorders in criminals, while higher than in the general population, is no more than the incidence of mental disorders in the specific subpopulations from which they come: the poor, the undereducated, and the socially and culturally deprived. As Wormith (1984) points out, the methodological difficulties involved in resolving this disagreement are considerable, and the research conducted to date suffers in general from inadequate experimental designs, unsystematic sampling procedures, poor control comparisons, and the like. It is difficult, then, to determine whether inmates as a group bring their problems with them through the prison gates, the pathological conditions within the prison create these problems, or inmates are predisposed to react to the conditions within prisons in different, and sometimes pathological, ways.

In an attempt to understand the impact of incarceration on individuals Bukstel and Kilman (1980) reviewed 90 studies that examined the psychological effects of imprisonment on performance, personality, and attitudinal variables. They considered only experimental studies that specifically addressed the effects of imprisonment on confined individuals. They excluded from their data base descriptive case studies, simulation studies, laboratory studies, simple comparisons of inmate and noninmate populations, prisoner perception studies, studies that described inmate characteristics, studies that examined the relationship between length of imprisonment and postrelease adjustment, programmatic outcome studies, and epidemiological studies. Bukstel and Kilman conclude that imprisonment is not harmful to all individuals, and while some persons deteriorate in response to confinement, others show no appreciable change, and still others improve their functioning. They also point out that an individual's response to confinement seems to be influenced by individual difference variables, institutional orientation, degree of crowding, phase of sentence, and peer group affiliation.

Some of Bukstel and Kilman's (1980) specific findings deserve elaboration, for they present as clear a picture as is currently available of both the effects of imprisonment and the time course of those effects. Based on 31 studies of the manner in which incarceration affects an array of personality variables, they confirm the often-heard, anecdotal observation that inmates manifest a curvilinear adjustment pattern. Upon admission to an institution, inmates may be predicted to show an increase in distress stemming from the shock of the conditions of confinement and of having to adjust to life under those conditions. As inmates adapt to confinement and develop adjustment strategies, there is a return to their more usual personality profile and behavioral functioning. Then, as time of release approaches, an increase in anxiety and distress, characterized as "short-timer's syndrome" may be predicted to develop.

A similar curvilinear pattern of "prisonization" was identified in a review of 12 studies of inmates' adoption of the values of the inmate counterculture in contrast to prosocial values. In general, inmates tend to endorse prosocial values when they are first incarcerated. As the period of incarceration lengthens, there occurs a shift to the endorsement of the values of the counterculture which appears greatest during the middle portion of imprisonment. As release approaches, there is a second shift in attitudes as inmates return to an endorsement of prosocial values. A closer analysis reveals that differences in this prisonization process exist as a function of the orientation of the institution in which the inmates are confined. The previously described curvilinear relationship between phase of imprisonment appears to hold for rehabilitation-oriented institutions but not for those that are punitively oriented, where there appears to be a steady movement toward the endorsement of the values of the counterculture throughout the imprisonment period. Moreover, individual differences in age, race, and type of offense also play an important part in determining each inmate's endorsement of counterculture or prosocial values throughout imprisonment.

Although Bukstel and Kilman (1980) review additional studies bearing upon an array of other important topics, they conclude that few other findings can be viewed as anything more than suggestive or ambiguous. It appears that no broad-spectrum, systematic, longitudinal program of study has been conducted to yield the answers to the many questions about the affective, behavioral, and cognitive impact of imprisonment on the diversity of inmates incarcerated in the variety of correctional institutions now operative. In addition, much of the research that has been conducted is flawed seriously by the failure to use standardized assessment instruments and control for selection biases, by attrition and other threats to internal validity, and by not considering other variables such as personality characteristics and prison milieu.

Consequently, while much can be said about the characteristics of inmates, little can be concluded about the contribution of the prison experience to those characteristics or the predictable response of inmates to imprisonment and the opportunities and requirements that it entails. In the absence of this data base, it is therefore difficult for the corrections professional to prescribe intelligently the programs required to redesign the prison milieu, to assist inmates in adjusting to prison life and overcoming deficits they bring with them to the prison, and to prepare them for their eventual return to the community. Nonetheless, it is the correctional psychologist's responsibility to deal with these issues.

This chapter now looks at guidelines for the operation of correctional mental health programs. The remainder of this chapter then draws on current community psychology knowledge and theory that suggest practices, procedures, and programs that may be implemented in correctional settings. We elaborate on what we call "the practice of correctional community psychology," which extends into the prison the concepts of primary, secondary, and tertiary prevention that are the substance of community psychology. We conclude with a discussion of the role conflict and opportunities these efforts will involve.

GUIDELINES FOR THE DELIVERY OF CORRECTIONAL MENTAL HEALTH SERVICES

Dvoskin and Powitzky (1984) propose a model of mental health service delivery based on the input of a number of correctional psychologists who participated in a mental health seminar sponsored by the National Academy of Corrections. In designing a program of psychological services within the correctional system, one must first establish the mission and goals of such services. Dvoskin and Powitzky viewed the mission of prison mental health as providing programs and services that are designed to evaluate, prevent, and treat inmate mental health problems and that contribute to safe, humane prison environments.

The mental health services in the correctional setting that they suggest include (1) psychiatric and psychological evaluation and treatment of acute and chronic mental disorders to aid inmates in adjusting to and profiting from normal prison activities and programs; (2) programs to facilitate short-term and long-term behavior changes in inmates in order to foster improved adaptation and functioning in the community on release; (3) specialized services and/or programs that address the needs of special populations within the prisons such as the mentally retarded, brain damaged, or substance-abusing inmates; (4) training that can foster growth in life skills and personal development; (5) ongoing assessment of the needs of the prison, its inmate population and staff, as well as individual inmates themselves; and (6) consultation and training to other prison personnel (especially line staff) to aid in accomplishing these goals.

Correctional psychologists can provide valuable services to the overall functioning of the institution by providing services not only to the inmate population but also to correctional officers and administrators. Some of the service areas in this category include assistance in personnel selection and training of staff in personal development skills such as stress management, motivation, professionalism, and positively oriented management. The correctional psychologist is also, at times, called on by correctional staff with whom they have developed a personal relationship to discuss personal or family difficulties. The psychologist may, at these times, provide short-term counseling for staff or may make referrals to external counseling or therapy resources such as employee assistance programs, community mental health programs, or private therapists.

The American Association of Correctional Psychologists (AACP) (1980) has adopted standards for the delivery of psychological services in adult prisons and jails. The AACP standards are based on the premise that government has the obligation to provide (among many other things) a humane, decent living environment to its citizens—including those in jails and prisons. Therefore, there should be available in every correctional facility adequate services to meet the mental health needs of its inmate population. The AACP goes on to posit that the very fact of incarceration may induce psychological distress, severe depression, psychosis, or suicidal behavior and, thereby, intensify the need for mental health services beyond what is required in the general population. The standards adopted to meet these needs establish the *minimum* acceptable limits for psychological services in jails and prisons.

The AACP has established a total of 57 standards covering the areas of administration, staffing and professional development, programs, access to psychological services, screening and evaluation, inmate treatment and management, consultation, in-service training, use of volunteers, planning, and research and record keeping. Consequently it is not possible to describe adequately the full range of issues addressed in the standards. A general overview of the standards will therefore be provided and the readers encouraged to consult the original source for a thorough examination of the material reviewed.

The AACP standards make it clear that the quality of services provided within correctional facilities must be no less than that of services provided in the general population. Just as is expected of their colleagues in other settings, psychologists working in prisons and jails are expected to conform to the professional guidelines established by the American Psychological Association. The practice of psychology in correctional settings is also expected to conform to all appropriate state or federal laws and regulations. Specifically, AACP recognizes that the practice of psychology is regulated by statute. It mandates that psychologists employed by correctional facilities be licensed or certified in that jurisdiction and that at each facility there is at least one person responsible for psychological services who has an appropriate doctoral degree and relevant training and experience.

Psychological services should be a separate entity in the table of organization of the facility, and the psychological staff should have professional autonomy for psychological services within the constraints of appropriate security regulations applicable to all institutional personnel. Adequate space, equipment, supplies, secretarial support, and funds as determined by the psychologist in charge of services should be provided. The AACP standards require that all psychological staff receive orientation training and regular continuing education appropriate to their activities. There should also be an internal quality assurance program to provide timely information concerning the level of performance of psychological services and the existence of any barriers which prevent more effective functioning.

The AACP standards also make it clear that the principles of consent that affect psychological examination and treatment of the general population apply to inmates as well, and the provisions that govern involuntary treatment in the general population also apply to inmates of jails and prisons. In order to establish and continue an effective working relationship and to satisfy professional obligations, psychologists should not be required (except in life-threatening circumstances) to disclose their records without the informed consent of their clients. Inmates should be informed of the procedures for gaining access to psychological services, and the nonpsychological staff should receive training concerning potential psychological emergency situations, signs and symptoms of mental disturbances, and the procedures for making referrals for psychological service. Each system should have adequate resources for handling severely disturbed inmates and for providing chronic and convalescent care.

The AACP's screening and evaluation standards require that all inmates be screened for past and present mental disturbances and for their current mental state, including behavioral observations immediately upon admission to the facility and prior to being placed in the general housing area. The screening is necessary to prevent newly arrived inmates from harming themselves or others and to provide those in need rapid appropriate care. Crisis evaluations should be conducted as soon as possible, but not later than 24 hours after referral. All newly committed prison inmates with sentences over one year should also be given a routine psychological evaluation within one month of admission. This should consist, at a minimum, of behavioral observations, records review, group testing to identify emotional and intellectual abnormalities, and a written report of findings. Referrals for more intensive, individualized assessment should be made when indicated by this routine evaluation. Individual assessments of all inmates referred for comprehensive evaluations should be completed within 14 days. All inmates requiring psychological services should have a written treatment plan. It should include a description of the course of therapy and of the roles of psychological and nonpsychological personnel in carrying out the plan. The plan should be goal oriented and include provisions for interim progress notes, a termination summary, and planning for the management of the problem(s) experienced by the inmate. All evaluation, treatment planning, and treatment activities are done by or under the supervision of a qualified psychologist.

The AACP standards require that the inmate in a therapeutic relationship be made aware of what is reported to any decision-making authority and have the opportunity to refute information contained in such reports. Psychological test protocols and other "raw" data should be maintained separately from the prison records and should not be made available to inmates or untrained laymen. The psychological record, excluding test protocols, is part of the prison record and contains all screening forms, diagnoses, records of treatment, treatment summaries, and dispositions. Written authorization by the inmate is necessary for transfer of psychological record information to any third party unless provided for by law or administrative regulation having the force of law. Finally, AACP encourages psychological services personnel to conduct basic and/or applied research that will improve the delivery of psychological services and contribute to the development of theory and practice as it relates to correctional psychology. This research should conform to the ethical standards proposed by the National Commissions for the Protection of Human Subjects.

THE PRACTICE OF CORRECTIONAL COMMUNITY PSYCHOLOGY

The community psychology movement has sensitized mental health workers to the importance of prevention in the profession's attempts to reduce the incidence and prevalence of dysfunctional behavior in the populations with which they work (e.g., Zax & Spector, 1974). Prevention efforts in community psychology and psychiatry in general are characterized traditionally as involving three distinct areas of endeavor that have been termed primary, secondary, and tertiary prevention (e.g., Caplan, 1964). This conceptualization of the functions of psychology and psychiatry has also been applied to prevention and rehabilitation efforts within the criminal justice system (Milan & Long, 1980). Tertiary prevention is the area of community psychology with which mental health and corrections professionals are most familiar, but one that they do not typically view as a preventative endeavor and instead as a traditional treatment or correctional effort. As Cowan (1983) has made clear, the goals of limiting a disability, remediating disordered behavior, or correcting criminal conduct are necessary and worthy, but they should not be termed prevention if that term is to have discriminative meaning. Nonetheless, it has been traditional to describe such activities as the treatment of diagnosed schizophrenics and the rehabilitation of convicted felons as tertiary prevention.

Secondary prevention is more properly viewed as true prevention, for its goals involve the early diagnosis and prompt treatment of disorders. The emphasis here is on preventing less severe disorders from becoming more severe and chronic, and on identifying early signs of dysfunction in order to provide treatment that will reverse the progress or development of the disorder. Secondary prevention is similar to tertiary prevention in that its goals involve serving individuals who manifest disorders. Secondary prevention differs from tertiary prevention, however, in that it deals with less severe disorders in order to prevent the more severe disorders that are treated in tertiary prevention.

Primary prevention differs in important ways from secondary and tertiary prevention and is more similar to the popular meaning of prevention than are the other two forms of prevention. Primary prevention operates in the absence of any signs of disorder and has the goals of truly preventing the onset of disorder and of promoting health and positive adjustment as barriers to the development of disorders. This wellness orientation has led to target populations, goals, and precedures that set primary prevention apart from the other two forms of prevention and has set community psychology apart from more traditional approaches within psychology as well.

Another aspect of community psychology that distinguishes it from more traditional approaches within psychology is the locus of treatment intervention (Reiff, 1975). The traditional model of psychotherapy and offender rehabilitation identifies the individual as the focus of treatment and works to accomplish such individualized goals as controlling hallucinations or correcting criminal behavior (tertiary prevention); providing social skills training to adults showing early signs of interpersonal problems or devising strategies to encourage improved school attendance and performance of students with marginal records (secondary prevention); and providing the as-yet unsymptomatic children of schizophrenics or abusive parents preventative services and counseling (primary prevention).

Recently traditional psychology has expanded to emphasize interventions at the group level. This can be seen most clearly in the new emphasis on family therapy in many tertiary prevention efforts. However, the inclusion of significant others in prevention efforts can be extended to other naturally occurring groups, such as in the classroom, work setting, or recreational center. Moreover, the potential of the natural change agents in these groups can be directed to the achievement of primary and secondary prevention goals as well as the tertiary prevention goals of most family therapy efforts.

Preventative interventions are also possible at the organizational, community, and societal levels. Here, existing organizations can be reorganized and redirected, or new organizations can be created to better achieve prevention goals of all types; communities can mobilize to better serve its members through such programs as self-help groups and the creation of support systems; and societal-level changes in the form of new laws, programs, the assurance of rights, and the like to influence communities and organizations can be accomplished.

Tertiary Prevention

Not surprisingly, most practitioners have concerned themselves with tertiary and, to a lesser degree, secondary prevention at the individual and group levels as exemplified by their emphasis in Dvoskin and Powitzky's (1984) traditional model of prison mental health services. This has been as true of mental health professionals working within correctional institutions as it has been of their colleagues working in hospital and community settings. Indeed, the model followed in corrections has often been adopted from those other settings, and practitioners consequently devote much of their effort to inmates who have either been self-referred or referred by staff for treatment of particular difficulties. In addition, the forms and formats of mental health treatment provided in corrections have been similarly adapted from those practiced in other settings, often consisting of client-centered, dynamic, or eclectic psychotherapy with individuals or small groups that is conducted over a number of weekly sessions in the therapist's office.

This tertiary prevention approach to working with inmates experiencing psychological disorders or other difficulties stemming from the multitude of stressors that accompany imprisonment is and will continue to be a central ingredient in efforts to deal with the mental health problems of inmates. However, practitioners in hospital and community settings are identifying limitations of this traditional model of service delivery and are developing supplementary strategies that may also prove to have a role in correctional settings. Perhaps the most influential innovation in mental health treatment has been the development of the so-called briefer approaches to psychotherapy. As Budman and Gurman (1983) point out, characterizing this approach as brief or short-term may be misleading, for brief therapy is not defined by the number of therapy sessions involved or by the number of days, weeks, or months over which they are distributed. Instead brief therapy consists of therapeutic relationships in which the number of sessions or amount of time that will be allocated to treatment is rationed or specified before treatment is begun. By so doing, the therapist structures the relationship in a manner in which the client may experience maximum change or improvement with minimum therapist time or client expense.

The factors that have contributed to the development of brief therapy are as common or more common in correctional settings than they are in the hospital and community settings in which the movement first appeared. These include low-cost or free services, large numbers of potential clients, small numbers of service providers, and long waiting times for treatment. Moreover, these conditions affect therapists apart from their theoretical orientation, so it is not surprising that the brief therapy movement is not identified with any one particular form of psychotherapy but instead cuts across a variety of schools of therapy. Budman and Gurman (1983) provide a thought-provoking analysis of brief therapy. They point out that it involves the most direct attack on the problem possible, with the therapist trying first the least invasive treatment appropriate for that problem. Consequently, the brief therapist respects the client's wish to remediate the presenting problem and works with the client to accomplish this. However, brief therapists are also aware that clients can err in their definitions of problems, and in such cases therapists must work with the client to better formulate the problems being experienced before treatment may begin.

The brief therapist recognizes that the approach is problem-directed, and the goal of therapy is to better enable clients to meet the challenges of the tasks confronting them and to cope with the stress that those tasks induce. The goal of brief therapy is not to induce major changes in clients' personality or to inoculate clients against all future emotional or behavioral difficulties. Indeed, the utility and effect of long-term therapy in achieving this goal may be questioned, for it may be that the nature of life is that it constantly challenges individuals and as a consequence engenders, to a greater or lesser degree and for longer or shorter periods of time, quite "natural" feelings of anxiety, depression, self-doubt, frustration, and the like as well as their behavioral counterparts. Instead, brief therapy recognizes that people are influenced by the situations and roles in which they find themselves, that people are constantly changing, and that therapeutic assistance at various stages of life experience is often called for.

Budman and Gurman (1983) point out that the practice of brief therapy requires a high degree of therapist activity rather than the more reflective or passive stance of some longer-term therapists. This active involvement in the solutions of the problems confronting the client includes setting achievable short-term goals and structuring or focusing the treatment sessions so that those goals are achieved. The brief therapist also structures therapy to include, or perhaps more correctly emphasize, what transpires between therapy sessions. This reflects brief therapy's recognition that it is what goes on in the real world, rather than what transpires in the therapy session, that is the root of the clients' problems and where changes must be made.

Consequently the brief therapist makes use of problem-solving strategies with clients, assigns clients therapeutic "tasks" that are to be carried out between sessions, involves clients in other structured protherapeutic activities available in the real world—such as participation in Narcotics Anonymous—and to the degree possible, involves significant others in clients' lives in the therapeutic process. Although at first glance these strategies may appear more appropriate for some therapeutic models than for others, they represent more a way of thinking about and conducting therapy than an attempt to encourage one form of therapy at the expense of another. As in our society in general, the realities of providing services in the criminal justice system will lead to increased reliance on brief therapy as the treatment of choice for clients seeking or referred for psychotherapeutic treatment in correctional settings.

Secondary Prevention

Secondary prevention—the early identification of developing problems—will undoubtedly prove in the long run to be a more cost-effective approach to treatment than treating serious problems after they have become sufficiently debilitating or dangerous to self or others that they demand attention. Indeed it may be argued that the predictability of some problems in some populations, such as suicide in the early days of incarceration, dictate that formal procedures be implemented to detect and provide preventative services to those who show early signs of those problems. Moreover, it may also be argued that the organization that fails to take such reasonable precautions should be held legally and financially responsible when undetected difficulties result in undue distress, injury, or death. In correctional institutions, the secondary preventation effort naturally begins with reception, assessment, and classification.

The correctional officers having initial and then continuing contact with inmates should be especially sensitive to manifestations of early signs of disorders and report these promptly to their supervisors and mental health professionals. A case in point is the American Jail Association's (undated) guidelines for the management of the suicidal inmate which emphasize the role of the correctional officer in preventing suicides. The guidelines describe the behavioral symptoms of potential suicide that line officers can and should detect. These include (1) the presence of suicidal thoughts or plans, (2) voicing feelings of hopelessness or despair, (3) emotional withdrawal or isolation, (4) providing self-damaging information, and (5) unusual reactions to being confined, as well as a history of previous suicidal gestures and psychiatric care. Predisposing factors are also outlined for correctional officers so that they can assess risk more efficiently. These include (1) recent excessive drinking or drug intoxication; (2) recent loss of stabilizing resources, such as spouse; (3) poor appetite, sleeplessness, or agitation; (4) chronic aggressive behavior; and (5) being more than 45 years of age with progressive health problems.

The American Jail Association guidelines also recommend actions that line correctional officers can take to prevent suicides in at-risk inmates. These include taking all threats of suicide seriously, arranging for a meeting between the inmate and a mental health professional in a reasonably short time, and securing prompt medical treatment for any actual or claimed injury, no matter how implausible the threat of suicide or bizarre the claim of injury. In addition, it is recommended that the correctional officers take special care to show interest in inmates expressing suicidal symptoms and suggest ways of coping with feelings and urges in the here and now. When the problem involves loss of contact with important others, the correctional officers are urged to arrange a quick phone call or visit between involved parties.

Correctional officers are also urged to pay careful attention to suicide-prone inmates during searches for concealed weapons or drugs in order to detect self-injurious drugs or weapons and to ensure that inmates receive and consume prescribed medication rather than roll it back under their tongues and either spitting it out later or accumulating it for a suicide attempt. Finally, correctional officers are warned never to keep suicide-prone inmates in isolation. Instead, placement in a small group dormitory of not more than 10 others is recommended on the grounds that this will decrease feelings of isolation and alienation as well as create a situation in which other inmates can help to keep watch on the suicidal inmate while offering other assurances.

The preceding guidelines are in the best tradition of secondary prevention efforts, because they stress the early detection of the problem, emphasize the roles of correctional officers and other inmates as natural care givers, and include organizational practices, such as quick contact with significant others and a reversal of the older practice of single-celling suicidal inmates, in the prevention effort. Similar practices are appropriate to other forms of emotional or behavioral disorders. The early detection aspects of these prevention efforts should be supplemented by a review of records accompanying inmates or maintained within the correctional system. Such a check helps to identify inmates with a past history of psychological difficulties in the community, detained in jail, and during any previous periods of imprisonment so that appropriate observation, prevention, assessment, and mental health referral procedures may be implemented.

The early identification and treatment effort should continue through the reception, assessment, and classification process as mental health professionals participate in the interviewing and then psychological testing of inmates identified as being in need of more in-depth examination. Finally, the secondary prevention effort should follow all inmates throughout their involvement in the correctional system. Correctional officers, work supervisors, and instructors who have regular contact with them can be trained and alert to the detection of the early signs and symptoms of emotional and behavioral disorders so that appropriate referrals may be made.

Primary Prevention

Much has been written about the role of stress as a precursor or precipitant of new emotional and behavioral disorders (e.g., Dohrenwend & Dohrenwend, 1974), and as an "irritant" that exacerbates existing disorders (e.g., Neufeld & Mothersill, 1980). Stress has been conceptualized in two ways: as a label for situations that tax a person's psychological or physical systems, and as the person's emotional or behavioral response to those situations. Primary prevention of psychological disorders can focus on either or both of these domains. Perhaps one of the most discussed stressing condition in correctional settings is prison overcrowding.

Early research suggested that situational variables that taxed psychological or physical systems involved (1) the number of people per unit of space within a room, cell block, or residence (inside density); (2) the number of people per unit of space outside the room, cell block, or residence (outside density); (3) the duration of exposure to the situation; and (4) the characteristics of the setting, such as the arrangement of furniture or presence of partitions (e.g., Zlutnick & Altman, 1972). More recent research, however, has indicated that it is not these factors alone that have debilitating effects, but their interaction with other variables, such as perception of personal control (Langer & Saegert, 1977), the types of activities performed (Desor, 1982), and the social structure of the group (Freedman, 1975).

The consensus now appears to be that it is not density per se that is stressful but density in combination with other characteristics of the environment such as those just mentioned that produce the harmful effects of overcrowding that have been attributed to stress (Anderson & Pettigrew, 1985). Nonetheless, overcrowding itself has generally (e.g., D'Atri, 1975; Megargee, 1976; Paulus, Cox, McCain, & Chandler, 1975), but not universally (e.g., Jan, 1980; Nacci, Teitelbaum, & Prather, 1977), been found to be associated with higher levels of emotional, behavioral, and physical difficulties.

Several primary prevention strategies to modulate the commonly reported stresses associated with imprisonment are suggested by the previously cited literature. The most obvious are community-level and organizational-level attacks on overcrowding. Although community-level interventions—such as the decriminalization of some offenses, greater use of alternatives to imprisonment for other offenses, and the like, as well as the more costly construction of newer and larger institutions if the former interventions are rejected—are beyond the professional responsibilities of the institution-based mental health worker. They are not, however, beyond their responsibility as members of our society. Indeed, the correctional mental health professionals' involvement as citizens and as members of professional organizations in the advocacy of increased use of such practices would probably give increased weight to their consideration in deliberations of city, county, and state decision makers. There are additional actions that mental health professionals may take within the correctional system to reduce overcrowding. Perhaps the most significant of these actions involves the classification process.

Clements (1982) has argued that when prisons become overcrowded, classification decisions become more haphazard and more restrictive. As a consequence, many inmates are overclassified, placed in maximum security settings, and overtax those settings. Clements posits that this is the beginning of a vicious circle wherein the overtaxing of resources slows inmate progress through the system, slowed progress produces slow exit, slow exit perpetuates or increases overcrowding, and the increased overcrowding further distorts the classification process resulting in even more overclassification. Thus the vicious circle is closed. The circle may be broken at several points. Paroling inmates at the earliest possible opportunity would be a step in this direction, but one that mental health professionals can initiate only indirectly. Improving the classification process to minimize or eliminate initial overclassification is a more obvious place for mental health professionals to begin. This combined with the reclassification and movement of inmates to less restrictive, more open settings in which there are opportunities for more normal social and personal relationships most probably reduce the harm of overcrowding if not reducing the overcrowding itself.

Of course, other interventions and interventions at other levels may also be developed to reduce the effects of stress and to deal with other problems as well; for example, Palmer (1984) describes a group-level program called *Life Servers* for long-term inmates. The program is similar to a community service club in terms of the group's organization and purpose in that it provides a framework within which members can find assistance and support goals that they establish for themselves. These goals consist of such things as personal growth, service to others in the prison, and service to the group membership. Moreover, the group has achieved a fairly sophisticated view of the emotional pressures and changes experienced by inmates serving long sentences. An important function of the group is the communication of understanding and coping strategies to others in what approximates peer counseling and big-brother relationships. Finally, the inmates add that their participation in the program gives them a sense of individuality, dignity, worth, hope, and peace of mind that aids the adjustment to the stresses of longer-term imprisonment. It is likely that similar programs designed for other characteristics of other inmate groups would serve similar purposes.

Many individual-level tertiary prevention procedures that have been employed in the community are also appropriate for the institutional setting. These efforts can range in focus from those at risk for certain difficulties, such as inmates most likely to be exploited sexually, to interventions appropriate for all members of the inmate population, such as strategies to promote general physical health through nutrition and exercise. The individual-level strategies that may be used in these programs range from individual counseling, skill building, and competency enhancement (e.g., Danish, Galambos, & Laquatra, 1983) to progressive muscle relaxation, self-control training, and contingency contracting (e.g., Rachman & Philips, 1980). Clearly, the types of problem attacked in primary, secondary, and tertiary prevention programs are limited only by foresight of the correctional mental health professionals, and the individual, group, and organizational interventions that they develop is limited only by their creativity.

THE CONFLICTING ROLES OF CORRECTIONAL MENTAL HEALTH PROFESSIONALS

In the delivery of both traditional and nontraditional mental health services in correctional settings, psychologists may encounter a number of conflicts between the institution's needs for security and control in contrast to the mental health professional's desire to rehabilitate through environmental change or improvements in the conditions of the inmate's treatment. At other times, conflict is created by differences in role expectations between corrections administration, direct line correctional staff, and mental health professionals.

In its handbook for psychology services in prisons, the U.S. Department of Justice (1978) describes the professional duties of correctional psychologists to include evaluation and assessment, screening, test administration, filling out and filing reports, group and individual therapy, crisis intervention and administration. Morgan

(1982) adds follow-up referral and prevention. Brodsky (1982), in a discussion regarding models of mental health service delivery in jails, includes components related to emergency services, counseling and psychotherapy, therapeutic communities within the jails, a "one stop" social service center, life-skills enhancement programs, suicide prevention programs, and mental health services by and for custodial staff. The roles required to provide services of the magnitude and variety proposed are, at best, in conflict and not clearly defined (Kaslow, 1980). The remainder of this chapter discusses the role conflicts that the traditional mental health professional in the field of corrections faces and concludes with an elaboration of the nontraditional correctional community psychology model of service delivery within the correctional system.

Although correctional psychologists strive to meet therapeutic and rehabilitative goals in their roles within the institutional setting, there are also external, day-to-day pressures on psychologists to meet other goals of the institution that involve issues of security, safety, and management of inmates. Psychologists frequently find themselves in roles that are imposed on them by the management requirements of the institutional setting. Much of the conflict that arises between correctional psychologist and the institution occurs as a result of the institutional demands placed on the psychologist's services versus the amount of control and/or power that the psychologist possesses to alter the environment that may, in fact, be contributing to inmate problems. Conflict is created, in other words, not only by incompatible roles but also by competition of requirements within roles because of the assignment of a large amount of responsibility to someone who has a relatively small amount of prescribed and perceived authority (Duddy, 1976). Some examples of role conflict for practitioners within the correctional system follow.

Crisis Interventionist

Correctional psychologists are frequently called on to provide crisis intervention services to inmates. The types of crises that arise may be either intrapersonal, such as in cases of a suicide or depression, or interpersonal, as in an attack made on another inmate or a correctional officer. In both cases the psychologist is expected to "cure the problem" by dealing with the inmates, calming them down, assisting inmates see the "error" of their ways, and helping them to adjust to and accept the demands of the institution.

Conflict arises for the correctional psychologist in the common belief that the inmates are solely responsible for their problems and that it is the inmates who must adjust and alter their behavior, beliefs, and perceptions in order for the problems to be resolved. Elements such as the inmate's treatment by other inmates or security personnel within the institution are often downplayed, if not entirely overlooked, in the expectation that the psychologist will "solve" its crises. Further conflict is created in the psychologist's role in that the change in the environment or behavior of other inmates or correctional officers could alleviate problems that lead to crises but over which the psychologist has little, if any, influence or control.

An example of this situation might be an instance where an inmate has become agitated and has attacked a cell mate, seemingly without provocation. During the interview session, however, it becomes clear that the inmate has been "preyed upon" by several stronger inmates within the cell block and has become more agitated and depressed over time to the point that he has finally retaliated. The inmate is now extremely anxious for fear of retaliation by a predatory inmate group. The inmate sees the only method of defense against these inmates as a request to be placed in administrative confinement—a condition that will result in a loss of educational programming, preferred job situation, and access to close friends. A psychologist in th·s situation is frequently expected by the correctional staff to help the inmate adjust to this situation and to discontinue being a management problem when, in fact, the institutional environment has actually created a mental health problem for the inmate, and the psychologist has little control over altering this situation.

Classification Agent

Classification of inmates for both placement and management purposes is a role in which correctional mental health practitioners often find themselves. Upon entrance into the correctional system, inmates usually undergo some form of psychological screening and testing. This classification function may be conducted at a centralized reception center, at a regional site, or at the institution to which the inmate is assigned. Due to the large numbers of inmates entering the system, psychological testing is generally conducted in a large group using paper and pencil testing procedures occasionally accompanied by a brief interview. Should potential problems emerge from the screening process, further testing, interviews, and observations are generally recommended.

While the classification function is an extremely important part of the inmate assignment process and has direct impact upon how inmates will be treated during their stay in the correctional system, the enormity of the screening and classification task can provide a source of role conflict for the correctional psychologist. A single psychologist may be required to review literally hundreds of profiles and test results each month. He or she must then take the responsibility to either recommend further follow-up or conduct additional testing to decide whether to diagnose inmates as having possible mental illness or to allow the inmates to enter the "general population" in which case they might be victimized and/or commit some type of violent behavior. Errors in judgment can produce serious repercussions within the correctional system for both other inmates and staff. As discussed previously, psychologists may therefore find themselves erring in the direction of being overly conservative, and may provide diagnoses which will lead to greater levels of security than may actually be required. Additionally, since the actual classification assignment is performed by an Institutional Classification Officer, conflict is further established for psychologists in that their input and recommendations may or may not be followed.

Finally, conflict can arise for the correctional psychologist as a classification agent in that mental health, counseling, educational, and/or special treatment programs recommended through the assessment process may not be available. There are, for example, few programs for the treatment of mentally retarded offenders (Cohen, 1985). In most states mentally retarded offenders are mixed into the general population with convicted felons who may take advantage of their handicap. Other specialized populations, such as the mentally disordered sex offender, also create a source of conflict for the correctional mental health practitioner acting as a classification agent. Specialized treatment may be required but may not be available anywhere in the prison system.

Predictor of Dangerousness

Psychologists and other correctional mental health professionals are repeatedly called on to assist administrators, correctional officers, classification officers, and parole boards regarding the assessment of dangerousness of individual inmates and the degree of risk involved in inmate placement decisions. Decisions such as whether an inmate is an escape risk for road-crew work outside of the prison compound, whether an inmate is a risk to the community if placed in a work-release program, and even decisions related to visitation by child family members to a convicted sex offender are often referred to the correctional psychologist for consideration. An even more difficult decision that is often referred to the prison psychologist is the determination of readiness for parole for inmates who become eligible for a reduction in their sentence.

Conflict for the correctional psychologist in the role of predictor of dangerousness and risk comes from several areas. First, the prediction of dangerousness is, at best, an imprecise science (Megargee, 1976). Inmates who adjust well to the institutional setting and do not create management problems are not necessarily "good bets" for adjustment in the less structured setting of the work-release center or under the weekly monitoring system provided in the community under the parole system. On the other hand, it is a questionable practice to keep persons imprisoned if they have the possibility of being able to make it in the community.

Questions regarding dangerousness and risk to the institution and community may be inappropriate for consideration by the correctional psychologist. Nossi (1975) has gone so far as to suggest that psychiatrists and psychologists should not sit on disciplinary boards or screening committees and that therapy should cease to be a prerequisite for parole and should not be linked, in any way, to an inmate's term of confinement. In Nossi's view, such decision making on the part of a mental health professional damages the therapeutic relationship between practitioner and inmate and, therefore, should be avoided.

As can be seen from these examples, conflict is created for the correctional psychologist in the form of demands by the administration that psychologists assist in risk assessment and inmate parole decisions versus mental health practitioners' desire to form and maintain therapeutic relationships with the inmate population. Additionally, as a consequence of being turned down by the parole board, inmates may blame psychologists who participated in the parole screening interview for their failure to be paroled. Indeed, we know of several instances in which inmates were advised that their parole was denied because they had "failed" their interview with a mental health professional.

The conflict in this particular role for psychologists comes from the correctional system, the community, and the inmate population itself. From the institution and community are pressures to be conservative and minimize any possible risks to the safety of the institution and the community. From the inmate population comes an opposite pressure to create positive, reinforcing relationships between the correctional mental health staff and the inmates through giving the benefit of the doubt to inmates and allowing them a chance to function in the community.

Therapist

In a survey of mental health services in adult correctional systems, Otero, McNally, and Powitzky (1981) found that the provision of clinical services was the predominant activity of correctional psychologists. Correctional mental health practitioners spend a majority of their time providing either individual or group therapy to inmates. Referrals for therapy may come from correctional officers, staff of reception centers, inmate self-referrals, and the prison administration. Reasons for referral may vary from concerns over institutional management and security to manipulative attempts by inmates to influence parole decisions to genuine requests for help and therapeutic intervention.

Conflict is created for the correctional psychologist as a therapist in a variety of ways. First, the psychologist is often placed in the role of assisting the administration in managing the behavior of its inmates. The goal of therapy often becomes assisting an inmate to live in the "abnormal society" of the institution with little attention paid to the problems of the individual. At other times, psychologists become frustrated because the individual goal of therapy for inmates may be to simply gain documentation that they have participated in a therapeutic activity that will be positively viewed by a classification officer or parole board. In such cases inmates may use therapeutic intervention as a method of manipulating the correctional system into sentence reduction or transfer to a less restrictive environment. A third source of conflict for the psychologist as therapist arises from situations in which inmates are sentenced by the court with the requirement that they receive therapy for a particular problem. In these cases, inmates are coerced into a therapeutic relationship because they will not become eligible for early release unless such conditions are met.

As can be seen, the majority of therapeutic and other role activities ascribed to psychologists in correctional settings involve tertiary prevention services. Inmates are most often referred because of recognized mental health difficulties in adjustment to the prison setting or for being labeled as having a mental disorder prior to conviction. Pure numbers of referrals for these tertiary prevention services can create further conflict for the correctional psychologist in forcing choices of who is to receive services, placement of inmates in group therapy when the psychologist feels that individual sessions would be favorable, or detraction of available time from other specified duties.

NONTRADITIONAL ROLES FOR CORRECTIONAL PSYCHOLOGISTS

While it may sound contradictory, the addition of certain activities and responsibilities to the role of the correctional psychologist may, in actuality, reduce conflict and increase productivity. The proferred roles are derived from the previously described community psychology prevention model and emphasize more primary and secondary prevention activities, rather than the individual-level tertiary practices just discussed. In essence, it is suggested that involvement in activities such as training, consultation, program development, and program evaluation expand the influence of correctional psychologists within the institutional setting, clarify the role of the psychologist to inmates, staff, and administrators, and involve the paraprofessional input of correctional officers as care givers, referral agents, data collectors, and evaluators. By utilizing this preventive strategy psychologists would apply principles of community psychology and may, in the long run, make their jobs easier but give them paradoxically, more impact. The following are suggested roles for correctional psychologists to consider for addition to their more traditional mental health responsibilities in the institutional setting.

The Correctional Psychologist as Trainer

The role of the correctional psychologist in primary and secondary prevention may best be expressed by identification of the psychologist as a trainer. Training activities not only meet the secondary and primary preventive roles of community psychology but also expand the network of care givers such that treatment becomes a community enterprise of correctional staff, mental health staff, and administrators. As already discussed, training can be considered a primary prevention role in that correctional officers within the system can in many cases be taught to recognize and refer for treatment those problems that may go undetected within the overall management of a prison setting. Training by correctional psychologists in recognition of such symptoms and appropriate methods of referral for treatment or observation can lead to intervention at the secondary level.

Correctional officers having the greatest amount of contact with disturbed inmates (and, in many cases, the most meaningful contact) can be taught basic intervention skills as well as the early recognition of problem behaviors. At the tertiary level correctional staff can be taught to "defuse" crisis situations through training in conflict and crisis management. Correctional psychologists can contribute to this effort by engaging in training activities at both a preservice or training academy level as well as by offering in-service training and support to staff development efforts.

Several benefits accompany the correctional psychologist's efforts in providing training for the correctional staff. First, the staff become familiar with the psychologist on a personal as well as "student" basis which tends to build a relationship between the staff and the mental health providers. Second, serving as a trainer adds to the credibility of psychologist's role within the institution and legitimizes the role of the psychologist as a resource for the officers in their day-to-day activities. Finally, training creates an extension of the psychologist's role in the cell blocks such that a ready source of referral becomes available from the staff.

As mentioned earlier, correctional officers are, in many cases, the most meaningful contact for inmates throughout the day. Whether or not they are cognizant of the fact, correctional officers often may be involved in counseling activities on an ongoing basis. Training in basic counseling skills (such as a problem solving orientation) are possible for implementation by correctional staff in their daily interactions with inmates. Given such skills, correctional officers may be able to take care of many of the problems which are inappropriately referred to psychological staff for resolution as well as giving officers a better understanding of when to refer problems of a significant nature.

Training can also be placed in a primary prevention framework when "training" of inmates is identified as a role for psychological staff. In this case the word training equates with treatment, but treatment that is designed for a multitude of inmates, not necessarily those presenting psychological problems. Training of inmates may include instruction in stress management techniques, "adaptive strategies" for prison living, mental health education, anger management, communicative skills, assertiveness training, conflict resolution, and so forth. By offering such "courses," correctional psychologists functions at the level of primary prevention in that they may prevent psychological disorders from developing as a result of incarceration within the correctional institution setting.

A second area of training for inmates involves activities that will lead to an increase in inmate's social skills designed to facilitate successful living in prison as well as increased functioning when the inmate returns to society. Some specific topics to be covered in this primary prevention activity are communication skills, anger control, assertiveness training, conflict resolution skills, and appropriate social skills for heterosexual, vocational, and educational settings. A final area of training for inmates involves the preparation of the inmate to return to the community. Training in community living skills to include money management, utilization of community resources, proper ways to find a job, leisure skills, and how to find an apartment are all important skills for inmates to learn. The correctional psychologist, in consort with the prison educational program, can have a major role in the preparation of inmates for prison release.

The Correctional Psychologist as Consultant

An additional role in tertiary prevention for the correctional psychologist is that of "consultant" to the institution. In recognition of the fact that the environment influences the behavior of inmates, the correctional psychologist can apply treatment strategies on the cell block for individual inmates by taking on the role of consultant. A consultant, in this context, is defined as a treatment provider who consults with correctional officer staff regarding problems of both a psychological and "management" nature. Taking the perspective of community psychology, the correctional psychologist as consultant (1) gathers information regarding an inmate's behavior from correctional officer staff, classification officers, work supervisors and so forth, (2) gathers information regarding the perceptions of the problem from the inmate him/herself, (3) if necessary, takes observational data regarding the problem as it occurs in the "natural" setting of the cell block, (4) devises treatment strategies that can be administered by the correctional staff, (5) designs measures to indicate whether or not treatment strategies are being effective, and (6) reviews information gathered by correctional officers and the inmate and makes treatment strategy changes when necessary.

The correctional psychologist as a consultant provides a service both to the inmate in terms of treatment as well as to the institution by assisting in behavioral management. Dvoskin and Powitzky (1984) have addressed this apparent mixing of "treatment" and "security" activities. In their analysis, security is a synonym for safety, and increasing the safety of an institution for staff and inmates is perhaps the most psychologically helpful activity imaginable. In fact, there are very few situations in which it is not to the mutual advantage of the prison, its staff, and the inmates to assist them in ceasing disruptive activities. Problems that may be addressed by the correctional psychologist as a consultant include behavior management of disruptive inmates, programs designed to decrease suicidal attempts by identified at-risk inmates, cleanliness programs to increase the hygiene of individual prisoners, and individual incentive programs for inmates to participate in required prison activities.

Before inmates become so severely disturbed that they need to be removed from the prison setting, there are many interventions that can be supplied by the correctional staff with minimal guidance and program review by the psychologist who is serving as a consultant to cell-block staff. An example of a consultative interaction to the correctional psychologist and prison staff would be the treatment of a withdrawn, depressed inmate. The referral for evaluation of such an inmate might come from a correctional officer who, following an evaluation of the situation by the psychologist, might be asked to simply count the number of social interactions observed between the inmate and others in the cell block.

Following the gathering of this baseline information, a strategy of having the correctional officer stop by the inmate's cell a minimum of four times per shift with the goal of engaging the inmate in conversation might be an appropriate treatment strategy that could be applied by the correctional staff on the cell block. In this case, the correctional psychologist would serve as a consultant to the cell-block staff, would help design measures of improvement, would assist in coming up with a strategy for intervention, and would review data from the staff regarding progress of the inmate. Other consultative services might involve review of crisis intervention procedures used by correctional staff in a particular instance, review of program components used in inmate management, and provision of quality control for services offered to inmates in confinement status.

The Correctional Psychologist as Program Designer

One role, within correctional systems, in which psychologists may choose to become involved is that of program designer. By virtue of their training in human behavior and in research methods, many psychologists are invited to participate in correctional· program-planning task forces and committees. The psychologist may end up playing the role of adviser, writer, evaluator, or even program director. Psychologists may either initiate or participate in the program design process. The specialized training and expertise of psychologists makes their role as program designer an important one within the overall correctional system. The correctional psychologist can provide a major service to the institution by becoming involved in prisonwide program design services. The design of vocational, educational, and recreational activities for inmates can have an important impact on the management and safety of the institution as well as create a humane environment for inmates. These programs may involve the educational, vocational, treatment, recreational, or social aspects of inmate life within the prison setting. Programs in this context represent procedures and/or experiences conducted by correctional staff, to which inmates are exposed in order to meet a set of outcome goals.

Some examples of programs that have been successfully implemented in institutional settings include cell-block token economies, psychosocial treatment programs, and psychoeducational programming. In these three examples, inmates' entire days are structured into treatment activities. Inmates can earn points or tokens which can, in turn, be exchanged for desirable items within the prison setting, or they can attend classes in which skills such as communication, assertion, and conflict resolution are taught in group-related activities conducted throughout the day. In other programs inmates meet regularly to work on the problems of an individual group member as such problems arise throughout the day. In these cases psychologists have been allowed significant input in the design of programs and have sometimes actually administered them.

In other cases correctional psychologists may be called on to review relevant literature that might relate to current program needs. It is paramount for correctional psychologists to be aware of relevant journals, books, or written reports, as well as other sources of information regarding successful correctional programs in other settings. For this reason it is of great importance for the credibility of psychologists within the correctional system that they maintain a good grasp of the current programming literature within the field of corrections. Many problems in program implementation can be avoided if the mistakes made in other correctional settings can be avoided through review of successful and unsuccessful program designs used in other settings.

Finally, the correctional psychologist can serve the needs of special inmates and of the correctional system itself in designing and implementing programs for inmates with special problems. Some examples of special-needs programs that can be established within the correctional institution are designed for retarded inmates, learning disabled individuals, sex offenders, posttraumatic stress disordered inmates, and depressive or suicidal inmates. Although the institution has an obligation to meet the specialized needs of such subpopulations within the overall correctional system, it is the correctional psychologist who many times is called on to design and assist in the implementation of these treatment strategies.

The Correctional Psychologist as Program Evaluator

A relatively new role for the correctional psychologist is that of evaluator of both individual and group programs within the correctional setting. From their training as researchers during their academic preparation to become psychologists, the correctional psychologists have skills in measurement and assessment that aid in this endeavor. To a significant degree the correctional psychologist as program evaluator takes on the role of quality control for the correctional institution.

A function of paramount importance within the role of program evaluator is the design and selection of measures that will reflect accurately the outcomes of both individual and group programs. In creating such measurements, the correctional psychologist becomes a reviewer of relevant research with the unique assignment of selecting measures that are compatible with the overall correctional setting. Examples of measurement that might occur in an individual case include assessments of the number of days that an inmate shows up on time for work as an indication of the successful implementation of a program in reinforcing this behavior with a prisoner getting ready for work release. Another example might be measurement of numbers of educational objectives completed toward a specialized reading program for learning disabled inmates.

Correctional psychologists also become involved in evaluation of larger group programs for inmates which attempt to alter more global variables of inmate functioning. In such cases, attitudinal measures might be indicated for assessment of overall program effectiveness in, for example, a sex-offender treatment program strategy. Conversely, other growth measures of behavior such as overall adjustment might be taken to assess the effectiveness of a coping program for inmates during their first three months in confinement. Finally, behavioral indicators such as numbers of violations of rules and regulations following the introduction of a behavior management program might be valuable in evaluating overall program effectiveness.

Another important goal for the correctional psychologist as a program evaluator is that of reviewing data and providing relevant feedback to decision makers. As an evaluator of program effectiveness, the psychologist performs both formative and summative evaluations. In formative evaluations, the correctional psychologist reviews information regarding the program and makes relevant suggestions for changes in the program that "form" the program into its final shape. In summative evaluation, the psychologist assesses the overall effectiveness of a program on a prepost basis such that it can be determined whether the program, as a whole, has been effective.

Finally, the psychologist as a program evaluator must also service as a trainer and disseminator in the transfer of knowledge gained through program evalution to other parts of the correctional institution, the correctional system, or the existing professional literature. To a large degree, it is the responsibility of the correctional psychologist to write up successful results, publish reports regarding program outcomes (whether they be successes or failures), and assist in the creation of training manuals and/or procedures designed to disseminate successful programs to other institutional components.

CONCLUSIONS

We have discussed the traditional tasks performed by correctional psychologists, proposed the adoption of a community psychology model, outlined several role conflicts that correctional psychologists now experience, and proposed additional roles that they may create for themselves to increase their contributions to the treatment and rehabilitation activities of correctional institutions. There are many services to be performed by correctional psychologists, and no one task is more worthy or important than another. There are demonstrated needs for clinical services, education and training activities, and basic and applied research programs in correctional settings if we are to understand and overcome the many problems experienced by inmates and the institutions in which they reside. We have chosen to characterize many of these roles as "non-traditional." The psychologist as trainer, as consultant, as program designer, and as program evaluator are not, of course, non-traditional roles in many, or most, noncorrectional settings where psychologists have for many years contributed their expertise to these and other activities. Moreover, some psychologists in some correctional settings have broken out of the assessment and treatment stereotype and created other roles and other programs for themselves, their clients and their institutions (e.g., Ayllon, Milan, Roberts, & Mckee, 1979). Nonetheless, most bureaus or departments of corrections, most institutional administrators, and perhaps even most correctional psychologists continue to view psychology's role in the criminal justice system as little more than diagnostician and psychotherapist.

Until the knowledge and skills of psychology and correctional psychologists are recognized and brought to bear in the criminal justice system to the degree that they have in other areas of endeavor, inmates, staff, and citizens will be denied the specific and general benefits of the psychological perspective in the prevention, management, and rehabilitation missions of contemporary correctional programs. Many of these contributions lie in the community, where the psychological perspective has contributed to prevention efforts within the juvenile justice system (Milan & Long, 1980). There is every reason to believe that the psychological perspective can contribute equally to the preventive efforts of adult probation and parole programs as other chapters within this volume suggest.

We have focused on institutional programs where the potential benefits of the psychological perspective have been less readily accepted and, for that reason, less adequately studied. The correctional community psychology model proposed in this chapter represents our attempt to systematize the various important ways that the psychological perspective can contribute to the design and operation of institutions and institutional programs that will better-serve inmates, staff who work with them, and the communities to which they will eventually return. The full range of primary, secondary, and tertiary programs at the individual, group, and organizational levels has only been hinted at in this chapter. Much exciting and beneficial research and practice remains for the professionals who choose to meet the challenges of contemporary correctional psychology.

REFERENCES

American Association of Correctional Psychologists. (1980). Standards for psychological services in adult prisons and jails. *Criminal Justice and Behavior, 7*, 81–127.

American Jail Association. (Undated). *Management of the suicidal inmate.* Arlington, VA.

Anderson, P. R., & Pettigrew, C. G. (1985). Indices of stress associated with overcrowding. *Corrective and Social Psychiatry and Journal of Behavior Technology Methods and Therapy, 31*, 27–32.

Austin, W., & Unkovic, C. (1977). Prison suicide. *Criminal Justice Review, 2*, 103–106.

Ayllon, T., Milan, M. A., Roberts, M. D., & McKee, J. M. (1979). *Correctional rehabilitation and management: A psychological approach.* New York: Wiley.

Barton, R. (1959). *Institutional neurosis.* Bristol, England: John Wright & Sons.

Bowker, L. H. (1980). *Prison victimization.* New York: Elsevier.

Brodsky, S. L. (1982). Intervention models for mental health services in jails. *Crime and Delinquency Issues, 82-1181*, 126–148.

Budman, S. H., & Gurman, A. S. (1983). The practice of brief therapy. *Professional Psychology: Research and Practice, 14*, 277–292.

Bukstel, L. H., & Kilman, P. R. (1980). Psychological effects of imprisonment on confined individuals. *Psychological Bulletin, 88*, 469–493.

Caplan, G. (1964). *Principles of preventative psychiatry.* New York: Basic Books.

Clements, C. B. (1982). The relationship of offender classification to the problems of prison overcrowding. *Crime and Delinquency, 28*, 72–81.

Cohen, F. (1985) Legal issues and the mentally disordered inmate. In *Sourcebook on the mentally disordered prisoner.* Washington, DC: U.S. Department of Justice.

Cooper, H. H. (1974). The all-pervading depression and violence of prison life. *International Journal of Offender Therapy and Comparative Criminology, 18*, 217–226.

Cowan, E. L. (1983). Primary prevention in mental health: Past, present, and future. In R. D. Felner, L. A. Jason, J. N. Moritsugu, & S. S. Farber (Eds.), *Preventative psychology: Theory, research, and practice* (pp. 11–25). New York: Pergamon.

Danish, S. J., Galambos, N. L., & Laquatra, I. (1983). Life development intervention: Skill training for personal competence. In R. D. Felmer, L. A. Jason, J. N. Moritsugu, & S. S. Farber (Eds.), *Preventative psychology: Theory, research, and practice* (pp. 119–215). New York: Pergamon Press.

D'Atri, D. A. (1975). Psychophysiological responses to overcrowding. *Environment and Behavior, 7*, 237–257.

Desor, J. A. (1972). Toward a psychological theory of crowding. *Journal of Personality and Social Psychology, 21*, 79–83.

Dohrenwend, B. S., & Dohrenwend, B. P. (Eds.). (1974). *Stressful life events.* New York: Wiley.

Duddy, A. (1976). *Prison psychologists—A prisoner's view*. Perth, Australia: Western Australia Department of Corrections.

Dvoskin, J. A., & Powitzky, R. (1984). *A paradigm for the delivery of mental health services in prisons*. Boulder, CO: National Academy of Corrections.

Freedman, J. L. (1975). *Crowding and behavior*. San Francisco: Freeman.

Gibbs, J. (1982). Stress and self-injury in jail: Going from the street to jail. In N. Parizi (Ed.), *Coping with imprisonment*. Beverly Hills, CA: Sage.

Hayes, L. M. (1983). And darkness closes in . . . A national study of jail suicides. *Criminal Justice and Behavior, 10*, 461–484.

Heather, N. (1977). Personal illness in "lifers" and the effects of long-term indeterminate sentences. *British Journal of Criminology, 17*, 378–386.

Jan, L. (1980). Overcrowding and inmate behavior. *Criminal Justice and Behavior, 7*, 293–301.

Jones, D. A. (1976). *The health risks of imprisonment*. Lexington, MA: Lexington Books.

Kaslow, F. W. (1980). Ethical problems in prison psychology. *Criminal Justice and Behavior, 7*, 3–9.

Langer, E. J., & Saegert, S. (1977). Crowding and social control. *Journal of Personality and Social Psychology, 35*, 175–182.

Lipton, H. R. (1960). Stress in correctional institutions. *Journal of Social Therapy, 6*, 216–223.

Megargee, E. I. (1976). The prediction of dangerous behavior. *Criminal Justice and Behavior, 3*, 3–22.

Milan, M. H., & Long, C. R. (1980). Crime and delinquency: The last frontier? In D. Glenwick & L. Jason (Eds.), *Behavioral community psychology: Progress and prospects* (pp. 194–230). New York: Praeger.

Monahan, J., & Steadman, H. J. (1984). *Crime and mental disorder*. Washington, DC: National Institute of Justice.

Morgan, C. H. (1982). Service delivery models: A summary of examples. *Crime and Delinquency Issues, 82-1181*, 34–68.

Nacci, P. L., Teitelbaum, H. E., & Prather, J. (1977). Population density and inmate misconduct rates in the federal prison system. *Federal Probation, 6*, 26–31.

Neufeld, R. W., & Mothersill, K. J. (1980). Stress as an irritant of psychopathology. In I. G. Sarason & C. D. Speilberger (Eds.), *Stress and anxiety, Vol. 7* (pp. 31–56). Washington, DC: Hemisphere.

Nossi, A. J. (1975). Therapy of the absurd—A study of punishment and treatment in California prisons and the roles of psychiatrists and psychologists. *Corrective and Social Psychology and Journal of Behavior Technology Methods and Therapy, 21*, 21–27.

Otero, R. F., McNally, D., & Powitzky, R. (1981). Mental health services in adult correctional systems. *Corrections Today, 43*, 8–18.

Palmer, W. R. T. (1984). Programming for long-term inmates: A new perspective. *Canadian Journal of Criminology, 26*, 439–457.

Paskind, H. A., & Brown, M. (1940). Psychoses resembling schizophrenia occurring with emotional stress and ending in recovery. *American Journal of Psychiatry, 96*, 1379–1388.

Paules, P., Cox, V., McCain, G., & Chandler, J. (1975). Some effects of crowding in a prison environment. *Journal of Applied Social Psychology, 5*, 86–91.

Porporino, F. J., & Zamble, E. (1984). Coping with imprisonment. *Canadian Journal of Criminology*, 26, 403–421.

Rachman, S. J., & Philips, C. (1980). *Psychology and behavioral medicine*. New York: Cambridge University Press.

Reiff, R. (1975). Of cabbages and kings. *American Journal of Community Psychology*, 5, 42–50.

Sloan, B. C. (1973). Suicide attempts in the D. C. prison system. *Omega: Journal of Death and Dying 4*, 37–50.

Toch, H. (Ed.). (1975). *Men in crisis: Human breakdowns in prison*. Chicago: Aldine.

Topp, D. (1979). Suicide in prison. *British Journal of Psychiatry*, *134*, 24–27.

U. S. Department of Justice. (1978). *Overview of psychology services—A training orientation and reference handbook*. Washington, DC: U.S. Bureau of Prisons.

Wormith, J. S. (1984). The controversy over the effects of long-term incarceration. *Canadian Journal of Criminology*, *26*, 423–437.

Zax, M., & Spector, G. A. (1974). *An introduction to community psychology*. New York: Wiley.

Zlutnick, S., & Altman, I. (1972). Crowding and human behavior. In J. F. Wohlwill & D. H. Carson (Eds.), *Environment and the social sciences: Perspectives and applications*. Washington, DC: American Psychological Association.

Zusman, J. (1973). Some explanations of the changing appearance of psychotic patients: Antecedents of the social breakdown syndrome concept. In R. H. Price & B. Denner (Eds.), *The making of a mental patient* (pp. 280–313). New York: Holt, Reinhart and Winston.

CHAPTER 22

Intervention as Prevention

JOAN McCORD

Folk wisdom has long maintained that misbehaving children become adolescent delinquents and adolescent delinquents become adult criminals. Recent studies in several cultures support this wisdom.

In London, among a group of working-class males, those who had been troublesome between the ages of 8 and 10 were most likely to be convicted for serious delinquent acts between the ages of 10 and 13, and an early conviction was an efficient predictor of later convictions (Farrington, 1986).

In Sweden, among males studied first in the third grade and traced to the age of 26, those who were more aggressive at ages 10 and 13 committed more crimes and were more likely to commit serious crimes both as adolescents and as adults (Magnusson, Stattin, & Duner, 1983).

In Finland, boys identified as bullying classmates at the age of 8 were most likely to have police records by the age of 20 (Pulkkinen, 1983).

In St. Louis, men who reported symptoms of conduct disorders in childhood were most likely to exhibit adult antisocial behavior and alcoholism (Robins & Ratcliff, 1979).

In Massachusetts, early convictions for juvenile crimes predicted subsequent convictions (McCord, 1981).

In an urban ghetto on the South Side of Chicago, aggressiveness in the first grade predicted delinquent behavior 10 years later (Ensminger, Kellam, & Rubin, 1983).

The evidence seems to support conflicting intervention strategies. On the one hand, if the evidence vindicates the common belief that crime is a result of personality deficiencies or faulty socialization, reformative practices would be justified. On the other hand, if that common belief promotes the link between early aggressiveness and criminality, the best strategy for prevention would avoid setting in motion self-fulfilling prophecies.

Intervention strategies of the first type include attempts to correct personality problems, change socialization practices, educate, or deter through fear. Intervention strategies of the second type include diversion programs designed to avoid hav-

584

ing youngsters perceived by themselves or others as "bad." Intervention strategies of both types can focus on correcting personality problems, changing socialization practices, and education. The differences between the two strategies are brought most sharply into focus by contrasting the effects of punitive approaches with those of diversion.

This review first considers evidence about the effectiveness of punishment as a deterrent to further crimes. It then considers evidence about diversion as a deterrent. After showing that neither increases in punishments nor diversion programs show much promise for decreasing crime, the review considers evidence about effects of counseling. Again the evidence is not encouraging. Finally, the review turns to evidence about effects of environmental manipulations. Preschool programs, educational programs, guided peer groups, and at least one postincarceration program seem to offer promising strategies for breaking the path from early misbehavior to crime.

PUNISHMENT AS PREVENTION

The view that fear of punishment reduces crime is as old as Western thought. Plato attributed to Protagoras the argument: "He who desires to inflict rational punishment does not retaliate for a past wrong which cannot be undone; he has regard to the future, and is desirous that the man who is punished and he who sees him punished may be deterred from doing wrong again" (Plato, 324). During the eighteenth century Beccaria (1764/1963) and Bentham (1789/1939) placed this view at the foundation of criminology.

So obvious had the link between pain and motivation appeared that its scientific scrutiny awaited the second half of the twentieth century. If fear of punishment deters crime, increasing sanctions should reduce criminality. Measures of the relationship between criminal activities and indices of the certainty and severity of punishment therefore offered promise for testing the role of hedonic calculations in motivations for crime.

Criminologists have bifurcated expected effects of punishment. Those that influence the punished are considered to be specific deterrents. Those that influence others who might commit crimes are considered to be general deterrents. As a specific deterrent punishment is expected to prevent repetitions. When repetition occurs, theory suggests that punishment has been too lenient. This view has a deceptively obvious appearance. Yet several studies show that severity of sanction is not monotonically related to rates of recidivism (e.g., Crowther, 1969; McCord, 1985; Wolfgang, Figlio, & Sellin, 1972).

Possibly, criminals who receive long sentences learn to accept the procriminal values expressed by convicts (Glaser, 1969). Possibly, longer sentences increase resentment or decrease the socializing values that could control aggressive desires. Possibly, as the opponent process theory suggests, punishments acquire positive incentive value (Solomon, 1980).

Although severe punishments seem no more effective as crime deterrents than mild ones, the fear of pain continues to be thought of as an essential motivator. This belief may account for the widespread acceptance of a program in New Jersey which received publicity under the title "Scared Straight" (Heeren & Shichor, 1984; Miller & Hoelter, 1979). In that program lifers dramatically showed young delinquents about life in prison. Despite its popularity, however, the Scared Straight approach has not been shown to be effective (Finckenauer, 1979; Lewis, 1983).

If street crimes are committed by youngsters to prove their courage, perhaps confirming the risks they are taking should not be expected to deter them. Perhaps, too, when people consider whether to commit a crime, they ignore potential sanctions. Although the latter hypothesis cannot be tested directly, Carroll (1982) tested it indirectly. He asked both offenders and nonoffenders to evaluate crime opportunities that varied in relation to amount of potential gain, severity of possible punishment, probability of gain, and probability of punishment. The results suggest that most people consider only one of the four features when evaluating opportunities. The amount and probability of gain had more than twice as much influence on their evaluations as the amount and probability of punishment.

Effective punishments would seem to require that the individual at risk for punishment knows what would be punished. Studies of young children suggest that the timing of punishment as well as its regularity influence this knowledge (Bandura & Walters, 1963; Parke, 1969). The criminal justice system does not lend itself to administering clear and consistent signals for learning what society considers wrong. In an interesting discussion of this issue Moffitt (1983) suggests that court delays, rewards for successfully executing crimes, and the sporadic nature of apprehension reduce the likelihood that legal sanctions can influence recidivism.

Fear of punishment could be ineffective in deterring further crime among criminals and nevertheless effectively reduce the probability that others would commit crimes. The *Uniform Crime Reports* seemed to provide a means for testing this general deterrence effect. In 1969 Tittle reported the results of an analysis of the *Uniform Crime Reports* for the years 1959 to 1963. He showed strong negative correlations between crime rates and his measure of the certainty of punishment, the ratio of convictions to crime rates. Using average length of sentence to measure severity, Tittle found a weak but positive correlation between severity of sanction and crime rate. Chiricos and Waldo (1970), however, reanalyzed the data and contested the conclusion that anything other than chance relationships between crime rates and certainty or severity had been discovered.

A rash of studies followed. Many, like the one by Antunes and Hunt (1973), used data from the *Uniform Crime Reports*. Antunes and Hunt defined the ratio of prison admissions to crimes known to the police in the preceding year as their measure of certainty. Median length of prison sentence provided their measures of severity. Using data for 1959 to 1960 as evidence of homicide, sex crimes, robbery, assault, burglary, larceny, and auto theft, they tested five linear models. Models predicting crime rates from certainty supported hypotheses that the threat of punishment reduces crime. Models based on severity, however, suggested that increases in severity of punishment increased crime rates. As possible explanations for these increases, Antunes and Hunt suggested stigmatization, alienation, and a heightened sense of injustice.

Uses of official records of crime to study the effects of punishment have three major problems. First, official crime rates may not accurately measure crime. At a minimum, the records reflect behavior of victims, police, and judges as well as behavior of criminals (Ebbesen & Konecni, 1982; Goldkamp & Gottfredson, 1985; Greenberg, Wilson, & Mills, 1982). Second, correlational approaches to causality cannot uncover essential linkages between events. The direction and size of correlations between crime rates and other social factors depend on the statistical conditions under which the correlations are assessed (Greenberg & Kessler, 1982b). Third, motivation may have no relation to the reality being measured through official statistics. Motivation depends, at least in part, on how individuals perceive their opportunities. These problems and research generated in attempts to deal with them are discussed below.

Crime and clearance rates are used to assess police and prosecutor efficiency. Not surprisingly, they are subject to manipulation for political purposes. Nagin (1978) illustrated this by comparing recorded crimes, clearances, and clearance rates before and after a change of administration in New York City. His computations show that although the number of robberies cleared increased 9 percent between 1965 and 1966, the clearance rate declined 58 percent over that period of time. Police discretion and plea bargaining add further "noise" to what might appear to be objective measures of deterrence.

Researchers have used records of fatal automobile crashes as indirect measures of drunken driving. Ross (1982) used interrupted time series analyses to detect effects of changes in laws related to driving under the influence of alcohol. He reviewed effects of such changes in Norway, Sweden, Great Britain, Canada, Holland, France, New Zealand, Australia, Finland, and the United States. That review failed to show a reduction in accidents attributable to increasing the severity of punishment. Increasing the perceived certainty of punishment (e.g., in campaigns to enforce laws against driving while intoxicated) appeared, however, to reduce fatal accidents at least temporarily.

Changes in the social climate lead to changes in the law. These social changes may, of course, account for either presence or absence of apparent effects of changes in the law. To avoid contamination among measures, one would like to manipulate threats of punishment experimentally, using random assignment or matched controls. Then, if crime could be measured accurately before and after the manipulation, it might be possible to discern effects of changes in celerity, certainty, or severity of punishment. Sadly, few studies have succeeded in providing adequate control groups and appropriate measures of crime (Zimring, 1978).

Among the problems encountered in attempting to learn how to prevent crime is that of convincing relevant authorities that they do not already know how best to handle crime. Sherman and Berk (1984), for example, planned a study of misdemeanor domestic violence in which police were expected to arrest, provide advice, or separate couples according to a random assignment. Only a few officers were willing to participate in the study, and even those few sometimes failed to follow the random assignments.

Critical of correlational studies for their failure to produce reliable evidence, Cook (1977) cited natural experiments that tended to support a view that increasing the probability of punishment would decrease crime. Crimes decreased on New York subways during 1965 when police increased their presence. Crime rates remained constant in a precinct that increased police patrols by 40 percent, while crime rates rose in the rest of the city. A 25 percent reduction in accidents followed closely upon advertisement of new rules regarding arrests for drunken driving embodied in the British Road Safety Act of 1967.

After Chaiken (1978) discovered that police records inflated evidence of effectiveness of the patrolling policies on New York subways Cook (1980) reviewed 11 studies based on natural experiments and concluded that they justify only modest claims. Acknowledging that identifying causal conditions in a nonexperimental setting can be extremely difficult, Cook suggested that police presence may increase the likelihood for people to report crimes.

Greenberg and Kessler (1982a) attempted the task of detecting a causal relationship between crime rates and clearance rates as a measure of certainty among 98 U.S. cities with populations of more than 25,000. As in other studies, simple correlations based on cross-sectional rates produced evidence that could be interpreted as support for a deterrence hypothesis. Zero-order analyses showed negative correlations between clearance rates and murder, assault, robbery, and larceny. The data also indicated that crime rates were influenced by population density, unemployment and poverty.

Greenberg and Kessler reasoned that crime rates must have some influence on arrest rates. To include this assumption in the models, they calculated two- and three-year lags between crime rates and arrest rates. Consistent effects from certainty of punishment disappeared when population, population density, unemployment, income, skewness of income, and proportion of households headed by women were taken into account.

Some of those who argue that fear of punishment will deter crime justifiably criticize the use of clearance rates to measure certainty and the use of changes in sentencing practices to measure severity. Fear depends on perceptions, and these measures of certainty and severity may be unrelated to perceived certainty or perceived severity of punishment.

Studies based on perceptions have typically asked people to estimate their likelihood for being caught and the severity of anticipated punishments. In one study, for example, students estimated penalties for two crimes: theft and smoking marijuana (Waldo & Chiricos, 1972). They also estimated the probability of arrest for these crimes. They then reported on their own thefts of less than $100 and their own use of marijuana. The students who reported smoking pot gave lower estimates of the likelihood of being caught and lower estimates of the likelihood for receiving a maximum penalty should they be caught. Students who reported having stolen also gave lower estimates of the likelihood for being arrested, but their estimates for penalties were not lower than those made by students who reported no thefts. The authors suggested that severity and certainty of punishment have a greater influence on crimes considered mala prohibita than on those considered *mala in se*.

Doubts that perceived penalties influenced use of marijuana were raised, however, when Meier and Johnson (1977) reported results from a national probability sample of adults over 18. In the national sample those most likely to use marijuana were also likely to perceive punishments for its use as most severe. The data showed no relationship between perceived certainty of punishment and marijuana use.

Attempting to account for some of the inconsistencies and to specify more clearly how fear of punishment should influence crime, Grasmick and Bryjak (1980) explained the interactions that an adequate test would involve: Only if apprehension is viewed as a cost should one expect certainty of arrest to influence behavior, and only if arrest is perceived as reasonably likely should one expect estimates of severity to influence behavior. To test their refined propositions Grasmick and Bryjak asked 400 randomly selected people to report whether they had participated in eight types of illegal activity. These activities included petty theft, theft of something worth at least $20, illegal gambling, intentional physical injury of another, income tax evasion, littering, illegal use of fireworks, and driving under the influence of alcohol. For each of these crimes respondents estimated the probability that they would be arrested if they participated, estimated the chance they would be put in jail if arrested, and reported on the severity of problems that would be created by whatever punishment they considered a plausible consequence for participation.

As in the Meier and Johnson study, some of the evidence adduced by Grasmick and Bryjak seemed to show that more severe punishments increased criminal behavior. Those who gave larger estimates of the likelihood of being put in jail if arrested reported participating in more crimes. Analyses taking into account the severity of problems that would be encountered by probable punishments yielded a different picture. Among those whose scores for perceived certainty of punishment were in the highest quartile, subjective estimates of severity were significantly negatively correlated with participation; that is, the data supported the authors' interpretation that those who believed they were likely to be arrested if they committed crimes were influenced by their estimates of the effects of probable punishments. And, except for those who reported little anticipated inconvenience from the plausible outcome of arrest, criminal behavior appeared to be influenced by estimates of the certainty of punishment.

Estimates of the likelihood for punishment have been based on hypothetical situations in which respondents are asked to assume that they have broken the law. Jensen and Stitt (1982) added a dimension to understanding such estimates by asking respondents to report the likelihood that they would commit certain types of crime. High school students reported their past misbehavior, their probable future misbehavior, and the probabilities of punitive responses under hypothetical conditions of misbehavior. With prior misbehavior controlled statistically, perceived risk of punitive response was related to the students' hypothetical choice to use marijuana, to become drunk, to use more serious drugs, to be truant, to participate in shoplifting, to commit vandalism, and to participate in burglary.

These studies of deterrence based on perceived penalties had shared a bias that attributed reported behavior to expressed beliefs. Yet none of them could show whether the respondents' behavior had influenced their beliefs about punishment or whether their beliefs about punishment had influenced their behavior. Longitudinal studies could shed light on the direction of impact.

Reasoning that prior experience would affect estimates of punishment, Paternoster et al. (1982a,b) collected data from 300 college students at two interviews. During each interview the students reported whether they had stolen something worth less than $10 and whether they had used marijuana or hashish during the prior year. Also during each interview the students estimated the likelihood of being caught, being arrested, and being convicted for these acts. The investigators considered correlations between time-one reports of behavior and time-two perceptions of punishment to be experiential effects; they considered correlations between time-one perceptions of punishment and time-two reports of behavior to be deterrent effects. Correlations of the first type were stronger than those of the second. The authors concluded that experience influences judgments about punishment and that perceptions of punishment do not influence theft or drug use.

Bishop (1984), too, used a longitudinal design to study effects of perceived sanctions. More than 2000 high school students responded to two questionnaires asking about participation in 13 types of crime and about three types of constraint. As measures of the three types of constraint, students were asked to estimate the risk of legal sanctions, the risk of losing their friends if they got into trouble with the law, and the degree to which they believed in the rightness of the law. Bishop analyzed responses to the constraint questions from the first questionnaire as predictors of responses to the delinquent-involvement questions in the second questionnaire. Using multivariable linear regression, she found that all three types of constraint appeared to reduce criminality. Bishop interpreted the data as showing deterrent effects, but because she did not control for prior delinquency the evidence does not distinguish experiential from deterrent effects.

Although not without problems, the studies based on subjective evaluations of penalties vindicated some of the assumptions of those utilitarians who believe that behavior is a consequence of attempts to maximize self-interest. These studies showed that a rational model of the relationship between perceived pain and intentional choice could give an account of some forms of criminal behavior. Yet these studies failed to link actual punishments with motivations for crime. Unless subjective estimates of severity and certainty could be shown to be systematically related to objectively defined severity and certainty, a deterrent model of intervention would have no practical value.

In one of the few experimental studies of effects of punishment Buikhuisen (1974) included measures of perception and an objective measure of illegal activity. Buikhuisen arranged to have an enforcement campaign against driving dangerous vehicles in one town. As a control, he arranged not to have an enforcement campaign in a similar town. Using before-and-after measures based on random selection of automobiles, Buikhuisen discovered increased compliance with the law only in the town that had introduced the campaign of enforcement. There, a majority of those who did and those who did not comply with the law were aware of the police campaign and knew of potential penalties. Those who disregarded the law were among the group most likely to appear in court for other offenses. They were younger, poorer, and less educated.

DIVERSION AS PREVENTION

During the twentieth century sociologists began to notice how frequently behavior could be conceived as the playing of roles assigned by one's associates (Cooley, 1902/1956; Mead, 1934; Tannenbaum, 1938; Thomas, 1923). The set of observations involved in this way of portraying behavior became known as interaction theory or labeling theory. To many it seemed reasonable that actions of the criminal justice system provided a role which could lead to further criminal behavior (Ageton & Elliott, 1974; Becker, 1963; Erikson, 1962; Garfinkel, 1956; Kitsuse, 1962; Lemert, 1951; Payne, 1973; Schur, 1971). To avoid increasing crime through expectations imposed when a youngster was adjucated delinquent, courts were urged to avoid using a stigmatizing label.

Until recently the belief that the probability of further delinquency was reduced by diverting youngsters away from the courts seemed too obvious to require evaluation. Indirectly, however, some of the studies that evaluated the deterrence model had also tested the theory that the criminal justice system increases crime by imposing expectations for misbehavior. Positive correlation between severity of sanction and crime rates could be interpreted as evidence of such a labeling process. Klein (1974) tested the theory more directly by looking at recidivism rates as a function of diversion from the criminal justice system.

In 1969 the proportions of arrested youths released by the police in Los Angeles County ranged from 2 to 82 percent in different departments. Klein selected the eight departments with the highest and the five departments with the lowest diversion rates. These 13 departments had roughly comparable recording procedures. Overall comparisons failed to show a pattern related to differences in diversion rates. When the delinquents were divided into first offenders and multiple offenders, however, a pattern emerged. Among first offenders, those arrested in districts with high diversion rates were less likely to commit additional crimes during the two-year follow-up period. Among multiple offenders, those arrested in districts with low diversion rates were less likely to commit additional crimes during the two-year follow-up period. On this evidence it would be reasonable to conclude that a labeling effect is more likely to influence first-time offenders.

To test the generality of such a conclusion McCord (1985) examined the criminal careers of 197 men who, as juveniles, had committed minor crimes that brought them to the attention of the police. In 1938 the police established a Crime Prevention Bureau to deflect juveniles from the courts. The Crime Prevention Bureau had processed and then released 163 of the juveniles at the time of their first encounter with the police; only 34 had been sent to court for a misdemeanor first offense. Comparison of those sent to court with those diverted through the Crime Prevention Bureau indicated neither racial nor social-class bias. About half of both groups came from broken homes. Although both groups ranged in age from 7 to 17, those sent to court tended to be the older boys.

More than 30 years later, in 1975, McCord gathered criminal records for the men. These records did not support the hypothesis that a court appearance would increase crime. More than half of the boys who had been "given a break" by the Crime Prevention Bureau (51 percent) were subsequently convicted for at least one serious (i.e., Index) crime. Fewer than a quarter (23 percent) of the 26 boys who had been convicted and fined, released, or placed on probation subsequently were convicted for any serious crimes. Of the eight sent to reform school, three (38 percent) were later convicted for serious crimes. The diversion project had failed to decrease criminality. But the data also offered no support for a deterrence model.

A movement to avoid labeling by diverting youths from the juvenile courts became popular in the United States after World War II. Studies of these projects show that many of their clients would never have appeared on court dockets. Typically, these studies report that the diversion programs tend to bring new groups of people into the criminal justice system without effectively reducing crime (Elliott, Dunford, & Knowles, 1978; Gibbons & Blake, 1976; Klein, 1979; Severy & Whitaker, 1982; Van Dusen, 1981).

The Children and Young Person's Act of 1969 reflected concern over possible effects from court processing in Great Britain. This act introduced "cautioning," a formal warning procedure believed to be less serious and less stigmatizing than court processing. Farrington and Bennett (1981) studied effects of the new law by examining files of juveniles who had been younger than 15 when first arrested. Their sample included 202 who had been sent to court and 705 who had been issued a police caution. Disposition appeared to have been strongly influenced by age and seriousness of the offense. Even after statistically controlling effects of sex, age, race, social class, area, and seriousness of crime, those who received police cautions were less likely than those sent to court to have been rearrested during a 34-month follow-up period. Farrington and Bennett scrutinized the records of 47 cases in order to learn more about the delinquents. These records included information about family size, attitudes of the parents and the juvenile, academic performance, and school behavior. Analyses indicated that the juvenile's attitude predicted both disposition and rearrest. After statistically controlling effects of these attitudes, rearrest rates following cautions appeared to be greater than those following court appearance.

Probably the most coherent study of how labeling affects juveniles has come from the West and Farrington (1977) study of 411 youths reared in London. These youngsters had been interviewed about delinquent acts at ages 14–15, 16–17, and 18–19. When the youths turned 21, West and Farrington reviewed their court records. Farrington (1977) coordinated the court records with the self-reports of delinquency for the 383 youths who had been interviewed all three times. As measured through their own reports of crime, in agreement with the hypothesis of negative labeling effects, the convicted boys had actually committed more crimes.

To discover how the label as delinquent affected self-reported delinquency Farrington matched 27 boys who had been first convicted between the ages of 14 and 16 to 27 boys who reported similar crimes at the age of 14 but had not been convicted. At age 16 the convicted group admitted to committing 84 more crimes. Their reports at age 16 included 251 crimes to which they had confessed at age 14 and an additional 65 crimes committed before age 14. At age 16 the unconvicted group confessed to 232 crimes they had previously acknowledged and added 43 to the earlier confessions. Because 41 of the 84 crimes that differentiated their self-reports at the age of 16 could be attributed to reporting errors, Farrington concluded that about half the effects of convictions were due to reduced concealment and half to increased criminal behavior.

The longitudinal study of London youths shows that effects of encounters with the court depend on the nature of these encounters. Delinquency reports of those first convicted between the ages of 18 and 21 showed almost no increase among those who had been fined as a penalty; among those who had been discharged without penalty, however, the self-reports showed marked increases (Farrington, Osborn, & West, 1978).

Data from several perspectives suggest that neither increasing the severity of punishment nor avoiding labeling youngsters has much influence on criminal behavior. In sum, the evidence has failed to support either punitive or diversionary strategies.

COUNSELING AS PREVENTION

Intervention programs have been designed with knowledge that delinquents typically have rejecting, aggressive parents (Dinitz, Scarpitti, & Reckless, 1962; Farrington, 1978; Glueck & Glueck, 1950; Lewis, Sharok, Pincus, & Glaser, 1979; McCord, 1979; Pulkkinen, 1983; Rutter, 1978). Not unreasonably, therefore, some programs have tried to provide substitutes for parental care.

One such project, the Cambridge-Somerville Youth Study, randomly assigned boys to a treatment or a control group. The program included both difficult and average youngsters between the ages of 5 and 13. Between 1939 and 1945 social workers tutored and counseled 253 boys from 232 families, assisting the boys and their families in a variety of ways (Powers & Witmer, 1951). In 1975, when the boys had become middle-aged men, their names and pseudonyms were checked through vital statics, court and mental hospital records, and centers for treatment of alcoholism. When interviewed, many of the men in the treatment program recalled their counselors with affection, and a majority believed the program had helped them lead better lives. Yet, when compared with their matched controls who had not received help through the program, those in the treatment group fared badly: they were more likely to have serious criminal records, to have been diagnosed manic-depressive, schizophrenic, or alcoholic, and were more likely to have died at a young age (McCord, 1978, 1982).

Other counseling programs, too, have seemed to have detrimental effects. Adults who had received clinic treatment as children in St. Louis (Cass & Thomas, 1979) and in Hawaii (Werner & Smith, 1977) were less well adjusted than their untreated peers. Discouragingly, Gersten, Langner, & Simcha-Fagan, (1979) discovered that delinquents in New York were more likely to sustain delinquent activities if they had been referred for treatment. Aware that labeling might be thought to account for this, Gersten and her colleagues noted an absence of enhanced risk among those referred during latency. Because those referred for treatment had not been randomly selected, results of most of the negative evaluations have been treated as anomalies.

Attempts to teach parents of aggressive children techniques for modifying behavior may be more promising, though attrition and absence of appropriate comparison groups pose problems in evaluating these attempts (Arnold, Levine, & Patterson, 1975; Fleischman, 1981; Johnson & Christensen, 1975; Patterson, 1974; Patterson & Fleischman, 1979). Unfortunately some evidence suggests that improvement in parenting is temporary when the parent has primarily aversive contacts in the community (Wahler, 1980).

A spate of therapies have been devised in the attempt to reduce antisocial behavior. Reality therapy (Glasser, 1965) seems to be best known among them. Kaltenback and Gazda (1975) claimed success for the approach in group practice; Yochelson and Samenow (1977) claimed success with hard-core criminals. Unfortunately, because the approach has not yet been used in a well-controlled study, conclusions about its effectiveness appear premature.

ENVIRONMENTAL MANIPULATIONS AS PREVENTION

Use of random assignment has permitted evaluation of several programs designed to affect criminality through manipulating the environment of people at high risk for crime. In one program (Reckless & Dinitz, 1972) educational environments were manipulated to provide vulnerable boys with programs designed to improve their self-esteem. Sixth-grade teachers in Columbus, Ohio, nominated good and bad boys. The latter were randomly assigned to experimental or control classes in the seventh grade. The program lasted for three years. The experimental group received special help in reading; their discipline was based on mutual respect, and special lessons with role model techniques were introduced to teach them how to act. Ratings made by their teachers at the end of ninth grade suggested that the experimental boys were more cooperative, comfortable, honest, and less delinquent. However, no differences were found in the proportions who had police contacts or in the proportions whose crimes were part-one index offenses. Nor were there differences in school performance, dropout rates, or school attendance.

Boys in the Ohio experiment designed by Reckless and Dinitz had been assigned to homogeneous groups of bad boys for their experimental treatment. Perhaps this feature of their experiment accounted for the failure to show benefits — at least by objective measures. Klein (1971) discovered that programs designed to alter the lives of gang members through group activities tended to be particularly damaging for 12- to 15-year-olds. Program activities increased cohesiveness of the gangs but also increased delinquency of the members. So clear was the evidence that Klein concluded that "there is good reason to doubt the desirability of continuing such programs or mounting new ones" (1971, p. 119).

The impact of peers on delinquents has been more recently evaluated in an experimental study in St. Louis. Feldman and his coworkers (Feldman, Caplinger, & Wodarski, 1983) studied the impact of using nondelinquent peers to alter behavior of delinquents. They employed a random procedure to assign antisocial boys either to groups of antisocial boys or to groups that were composed primarily of nondelinquents at the Jewish Community Center. The mixed groups contained regular participants in the community center's activities. Some regular participants were members of groups without antisocial boys. Nonparticipant observers attended all group meetings and reported the boys' behavior for 10-second intervals, in rotation. The records showed that boys assigned to experienced leaders in mixed groups improved in behavior while in the group. The nondelinquent boys in mixed groups did no worse than those assigned to unmixed groups. It is disappointing that the investigators report little about behavior outside the groups or after termination of the program. Yet the evidence suggests that placing delinquents among nondelinquents may change the behavior of delinquents without affecting that of nondelinquents.

The Department of Labor sponsored a program testing effects of altering the social environment (Lenihan, 1977). A randomly selected group of men were given $60 a week for 13 weeks after release from prison. The men eligible for this program had committed property crimes, were under 45 years in age, had spent less than three months on work release, had less than $400 in savings, and were not first-time offenders. After release those who received money were more likely to help pay for household expenses and help support their families. The money appeared to delay return to theft. In the two years of the study fewer men who received the $60 had been arrested for theft. The beneficial effects increased with increasing age and were most dramatic among the poorest risks: those discharged without parole and poorly educated. Reports by participants suggest that the money enabled them to buy clothes, helped them feel better, and allowed them time to find a decent job. Timing of the help may have been important to its effectiveness. Evidence from a pilot project conducted by Miller and Ohlin (1985) suggests that experiences after release have a greater impact on recidivism than either background or program experiences.

Perhaps the most promising approach to intervention has been through education. In 1962, a project known as High Scope began random assignment of children from low-income neighborhoods to either a preschool or a no-preschool group (Berrueta-Clement, Schweinhart, Barnett, Epstein, & Weikart, 1984). These two groups have been traced both in school and as young adults. The preschool program appeared to have increased commitment to school. Those who had attended preschool were both more satisfied with their experiences and more likely to have graduated from high school. Preschool also appeared to have an effect on employment. A higher proportion of those who attended preschool were employed, and a higher proportion reported that they were self-supporting at age 19. The long-term effects of preschool seem also to have included reduction in crime: The preschool group were less likely to have been arrested and were arrested for fewer crimes than the control group.

Of course, until the project has been replicated, it would be foolish to assume that we know that early education will help prevent crime. Meanwhile evidence to suggest that education is a key to reducing crime can be found in studies that have included educational components; for example, the Opportunities for Youth Project included a program in which teenagers were randomly selected to evaluate teaching machines for use with younger children (and incidentally received tutoring themselves) or to perform Saturday work on projects like gardening. Hackler and Hagan (1975) assessed the project four years later. Relative to the control group, those assigned to work projects had increased their delinquencies, but those assigned to work with the teaching machines had reduced their rates of delinquency. Experiments have shown that academic tutoring can change the behavior of young children (Coie & Krehbiel, 1984). Whether such changes are permanent and whether they lead to reduction of crime remains to be seen. Yet targeting education as an appropriate form of intervention has few inherent dangers.

SUMMARY

The evidence suggests that when a delinquent fails to receive penalties supporting the law, delinquency is likely to continue. Yet the evidence does not show that serious penalties have more potent effects than mild penalties. It seems reasonable to interpret the receipt of penalties as a type of information from which youths can learn how society expects them to act.

Although a labeling effect seems to account for some criminal behavior, diversion programs have had only minor impact. Obviously, too little is known about how to produce socialized behavior. Counseling programs have typically been ineffective. Family training may be helpful, though judgments about the effectiveness of this approach are premature. Some, but not all, educational programs have had beneficial results. Those that seem effective should be replicated. New programs, designed for appropriate evaluation, should be started. Perhaps as a consequence, it will become possible to regard intervention as prevention.

REFERENCES

Ageton, S., & Elliott, D. S. (1974). The effects of legal processing on delinquent orientations. *Social Problems, 22*, 87–100.

Antunes, G., & Hunt, A. L. (1973). The impact of certainty and severity of punishment on levels of crime in American states: An extended analysis. *Journal of Criminal Law and Criminology, 64*, 489–493.

Arnold, J. E., Levine, A. G.; & Patterson, G. R. (1975). Changes in sibling behavior following family intervention. *Journal of Consulting and Clinical Psychology, 43*, 683–688.

Bandura, A., & Walters, R. H. (1963). *Social learning and personality development*. New York: Holt, Rinehart & Winston.

Beccaria, C. B. (1963). *On crimes and punishments*. Indianapolis, IN: Bobbs-Merrill. (Original work published in 1764.)

Becker, H. S. (1963). *Outsiders*. Glencoe, IL: Free Press.

Bentham, J. (1939). An introduction to the principles of morals and legislation. In E. Burtt

(Ed.), *The English philosophers from Bacon to Mill*. New York: Random House. (Original work published in 1789.)

Berrueta-Clement, J. R.; Schweinhart, L. J.; Barnett, W. S.; Epstein, A. S., & Weikart, D. P. (1984). *Changed lives: The effects of the Perry preschool program on youths through age 19*, Ypsilanti, MI: High Scope.

Bishop, D. M. (1984). Legal and extralegal barriers to delinquency. *Criminology, 22*, 403–419.

Buikhuisen, W. (1974). General deterrence: Research and theory. *Abstracts on Criminology and Penology, 14*, 285–298.

Carroll, J. S. (1982). The decision to commit the crime. In J. Konecni & E. B. Ebbesen (Eds.), *The criminal justice system*, (pp. 49–67). San Francisco: Freeman.

Cass, L. K., & Thomas, C. B. (1979). *Childhood pathology and later adjustment*. New York: Wiley.

Chaiken, J. M. (1978). What is known about deterrent effects of police activities. In J. A. Cramer (Ed.), *Preventing crime*, Beverly Hills, CA: Sage.

Chiricos, T. G., & Waldo, G. P. (1970). Punishment and crime: An examination of some empirical evidence. *Social Problems, 18*, 200–217.

Coie, J. D., & Krehbiel, G. (1984). Effects of academic tutoring on the social status of low-achieving, socially rejected children. *Child Development, 55*, 1465–1478.

Cook, P. J. (1977). Punishment and crime: A critique of current findings concerning the preventive effects of punishment. *Law and Contemporary Problems, 41*, 164–204.

Cook, P. J. (1980). Research in criminal deterrence: Laying the groundwork for the second decade. In N. Morris & M. Tonry (Eds.), *Crime and justice: Vol. 2*. Chicago: University of Chicago Press.

Cooley, C. H. (1956). *Human nature and the social order*. New York: Schocken. (Original work published in 1902).

Crowther, C. (1969). Crimes, penalties, and legislatures. *Annals of the American Academy of Political and Social Science, 381*, 147–158.

Dinitz, S.; Scarpitti, F. R.; & Reckless, W. C. (1962). Delinquency vulnerability: A cross group and longitudinal analysis. *American Sociological Review, 37*, 515–517.

Ebbesen, E. B., & Konecni, V. J. (1982). Social psychology and the law: A decision-making approach to the criminal justice system. In J. Konecni & E. B. Ebbesen (Eds.), *The criminal justice system* (pp. 3–23). San Francisco: Freeman.

Elliott, D. S.; Dunford, F. W., & Knowles, B. A. (1978). *Diversion—A study of alternative processing practices: An overview of initial study findings*. Boulder, CO: Behavioral Research Institute.

Ensminger, M. E.; Kellam, S. G.; Rubin, B. R. (1983). School and family origins of delinquency: Comparisons by sex. In K. T. Van Dusen & S. A. Mednick (Eds.), *Prospective studies of crime and delinquency*. Boston: Kluwer-Nijhoff.

Erikson, K. T. (1962). Notes on the sociology of deviance. *Social Problems, 9*, 307–314.

Farrington, D. P. (1977). The effects of public labelling. *British Journal of Criminology, 17*, 112–125.

Farrington, D. P. (1978). The family backgrounds of aggressive youths. In L. A. Hersov & Berger (Eds.), *Aggression and antisocial behaviour in childhood and adolescence* (pp. 73–93). Oxford: Pergamon.

Farrington, D. P. (1986). Stepping stones to adult criminal careers. In J. Block, D. Olweus, & M. R. Yarrow (Eds.), *Development of antisocial and prosocial behavior*. New York: Academic Press.

Farrington, D. P., & Bennett, T. (1981). Police cautioning of juveniles in London. *British Journal of Criminology, 21*, 123–135.

Farrington, D. P.; Osborn, S. G., & West, D. J. (1978). The persistence of labeling effects. *British Journal of Criminology, 18*, 277–284.

Feldman, R. A.; Caplinger, T. E.; & Wodarski, J. S. (1983). *The St. Louis conundrum*. Englewood Cliffs, NJ: Prentice-Hall.

Finckenauer, J. O. (1979). *Prepared statement: Oversight on Scared Straight*. Washington, DC: U.S. Government Printing Office.

Fleischman, M. J. (1981). A replication of Patterson's "Intervention for boys with conduct problems." *Journal of Consulting and Clinical Psychology, 49*, 342–351.

Garfinkel, H. (1956). Conditions of successful degradation ceremonies. *American Journal of Sociology, 61*, 420–424.

Gersten, J. C.; Langner, T. S., & Simcha-Fagan, O. (1979). Developmental patterns of types of behavioral disturbance and secondary prevention *International Journal of Mental Health, 7*, 132–149.

Gibbons, D. C., & Blake, G. F. (1976). Evaluating the impact of juvenile diversion programs. *Crime and Delinquency, 22*, 411–420.

Glaser, D. (1969). *The effectiveness of a prison and parole system*. New York: Bobbs-Merrill.

Glasser, W. (1965). *Reality therapy*, New York: Harper & Row.

Glueck, S., & Glueck, E. T. (1950). *Unraveling juvenile delinquency*. New York: Commonwealth Fund.

Goldkamp, J., & Gottfredson, M. R. (1985). *Policy guidelines for bail*. Philadelphia: Temple University Press.

Grasmick, H. G., & Bryjak, G. J. (1980). The deterrent effect of perceived severity of punishment. *Social Forces, 59*, 471–491.

Greenberg, D., & Kessler, R. C. (1982a). The effect of arrests on crime: A multivariate panel analysis. *Social Forces, 60*, 771–790.

Greenberg, D. F., & Kessler, R. C. (1982b). Model specification in dynamic analyses of crime deterrence. In J. Hagan (Ed.), *Deterrence reconsidered* (pp. 15–32). Beverly Hills, CA: Sage.

Greenberg, M. S.; Wilson, C. E.; & Mills, M. K. (1982) Victim decision-making: An experimental approach. In J. Konecni & E. B. Ebbesen (Eds.), *The criminal justice system* (pp. 73–94). San Francisco: Freeman.

Hackler, J. C., & Hagan, J. L. (1975). Work and teaching machines as delinquency prevention tools: A four-year follow-up. *Social Service Review, 49*, 92–106.

Heeren, J., & Shichor, D. (1984). Mass media and delinquency prevention: the case of "Scared straight." *Deviant Behavior, 5*, 375–386.

Jensen, G. F., & Stitt, B. G. (1982). Words and misdeeds. In J. Hagan (Ed.), *Deterrence reconsidered* (pp. 33–54). Beverly Hills, CA: Sage.

Johnson, S. M., & Christensen, A. (1975). Multiple criteria follow-up of behavior modification with families. *Journal of Abnormal Child Psychology, 3*, 135–154.

Kaltenbach, R. F., & Gazda, G. M. (1975). Reality therapy in groups. In G. M. Gazda,

(Ed.), *Basic approaches to group psychotherapy and group counseling* (pp. 196–233). Springfield, IL: C. C. Thomas.

Kitsuse, J. I. (1962). Societal reaction to deviant behavior. *Social Problems, 9,* 247–256.

Klein, M. W. (1971). *Street gangs and street workers.* Englewood Cliffs, NJ: Prentice-Hall.

Klein, M. W. (1974). Labeling, deterrence and recidivism: A study of police dispositions of juvenile offenders. *Social Problems, 22,* 292–303.

Klein, M. W. (1979). Deinstitutionalization and diversion of juvenile offenders: A litany of impediments. In S. E. Martin, L. B. Sechrest, & R. Redner (Eds.), *New directions in the rehabilitation of criminal offenders.* Washington, DC: National Academy Press.

Lemert, E. (1951). *Social pathology,* New York: McGraw-Hill.

Lenihan, K. J. (1977). *Unlocking the second gate: The role of financial assistance in reducing recidivism among ex-prisoners.* Washington, DC: U.S. Department of Labor (R & D Monograph 45).

Lewis, D. O., Shanok, S. S., Pincus, J., & Glaser, G. H. (1979). Violent juvenile delinquents. *Journal of the American Academy of Child Psychiatry, 18,* 307–319.

Lewis, R. V. (1983). Scared straight—California style. *Criminal Justice and Behavior, 10,* 284–289.

Magnusson, D.; Stattin, J.; & Duner, A. (1983). Aggression and criminality in longitudinal perspective. In K. T. Van Dusen & S. A. Mednick (Eds.), *Prospective studies of crime and delinquency.* Boston: Kluwer-Nijhoff.

McCord, J. (1978). A thirty-year follow-up of treatment effects. *American Psychologist, 33,* 284–289.

McCord, J. (1979). Some child-rearing antecedents of criminal behavior in adult men. *Journal of Personality and Social Psychology, 37,* 1477–1486.

McCord, J. (1981). A longitudinal perspective on patterns of crime. *Criminology, 19,* 211–218.

McCord, J. (1982). The Cambridge-Somerville Youth Study: A sobering lesson on treatment, prevention, and evaluation. In A. J. McSweeny, W. J. Femouw, & R. P. Hawkins (Eds.), *Practical program evaluation for youth treatment.* Springfield, IL: C. C. Thomas.

McCord, J. (1985). Deterrence and the light touch of the law. In D. P. Farrington & J. Gunn (Eds.), *Reactions to crime, The public, the police, courts, and prisons.* London: Wiley.

Mead, G. H. (1934). *Mind, self, and society from the standpoint of a social behaviorist.* Chicago: University of Chicago Press.

Meier, R. F., & Johnson, W. T. (1977). Deterrence as social control: The legal and extralegal production of conformity. *American Sociological Review, 42,* 292–304.

Miller, A. D., & Ohlin, L. E. (1985). *Delinquency and community: Creating opportunities and controls.* Beverly Hills, CA: Sage.

Miller, J. G., & Hoelter, H. H. (1979). *Prepared testimony: Oversight on Scared Straight.* Washington, DC: U.S. Goverment Printing Office.

Moffitt, T. E. (1983). The learning theory model of punishment: Implications for delinquency deterrence. *Criminal Justice and Behavior, 10,* 131–158.

Nagin, D. (1978). General deterrence: A review of the empirical evidence. In A. Blumstein, J. Cohen, & D. Nagin (Eds.), *Deterrence and incapacitation: Estimating the effects of criminal sanctions on crime rates.* Washington, DC: National Academy of Sciences.

Parke, R. E. (1969). Effectiveness of punishment as an interaction of intensity, timing, agent nurturance, and cognitive structuring. *Child Development, 40*, 213–235.

Paternoster, R.; Saltzman, L. E.; Chiricos, T. G., & Waldo, G. P. (1982a). Perceived risk and deterrence: Methodological artifacts in perceptual deterrence research. *Journal of Criminal Law and Criminology, 73*, 1238–1258.

Paternoster, R.; Saltzman, L. E.; Waldo, G. P.; & Chricos, T. G. (1982b). Causal ordering in deterrence research. In J. Hagan (Ed.), *Deterrence reconsidered* (pp. 55–70). Beverly Hills, CA: Sage.

Patterson, G. R. (1974). Interventions for boys with conduct problems: Multiple settings, treatments, and criteria. *Journal of Consulting and Clinical Psychology, 42*, 471–481.

Patterson, G. R., & Fleischman, M. J. (1979). Maintenance of treatment effects: Some considerations concerning family systems and follow-up data. *Behavior Therapy, 10*, 168–185.

Payne, W. D. (1973). Negative labels: Passageways and prisons. *Crime and Delinquency, 19*, 33–40.

Plato. *Protagoras* (translated by B. Jowett).

Powers, E., & Witmer, H. (1951). *An experiment in the prevention of delinquency: The Cambridge-Somerville youth study*. New York: Columbia University Press.

Pulkkinen, L. (1983). Search for alternatives to aggression in Finland. In A. P. Goldstein & M. Segall (Eds.), *Aggression in global perspective*. Elmsford, NY: Pergamon.

Reckless, W. C., & Dinitz, S. (1972). *The prevention of juvenile delinquency: An experiment*. Columbus: Ohio State University Press.

Robins, L. N., & Ratcliff, K. S. (1979). Risk factors in the continuation of childhood antisocial behavior into adulthood. *International Journal of Mental Health, 7*, 96–116.

Ross H. L. (1982). Interrupted time series studies of deterrence of drinking and driving. In J. Hagan (Ed.), *Deterrence reconsidered* (pp. 71–97). Beverly Hills, CA: Sage.

Rutter, M. (1978). Family, area and school influences in the genesis of conduct disorders. In L. A. Hersov & M. Berger (Eds.), *Aggression and anti-social behaviour in childhood and adolescence*. Oxford: Pergamon.

Schur, E. M. (1971). *Labelling deviant behavior: Its sociological implications*. New York: Harper and Row.

Severy, L., & Whitaker, J. M. (1982). Juvenile diversion: An experimental analysis of effectiveness. *Evaluation Review, 6*, 753–774.

Sherman, L. W., & Berk, R. A. (1984). The specific deterrent effects of arrest for domestic assault. *American Sociological Review, 49*, 261–272.

Solomon, R. L. (1980). The opponent-process theory of acquired motivation: The costs of pleasure and the benefits of pain. *American Psychologist, 35*, 691–712.

Tannenbaum, F. (1938). *Crime and the community*. Boston: Ginn.

Thomas, W. I. (1923). *The unadjusted girl*. Boston: Little, Brown.

Tittle, C. R. (1969). Crime rates and legal sanctions. *Social Problems, 14*, 409–422.

Van Dusen, K. T. (1981). Net widening and relabelling: Some consequences of deinstitutionalization. *American Behavioral Scientist, 24*, 801–810.

Wahler, R. G. (1980). The insular mother: Her problems in parent-child treatment. *Journal of Applied Behavior Analysis, 13*, 207–219.

Waldo, G. P., & Chiricos, T. G. (1972). Perceived penal sanction and self-reported criminality: A neglected approach to deterrence research. *Social Problems, 19,* 522–540.

Werner, E. E., & Smith, R. W. (1977). *Kauai's children come of age.* Honolulu: University Press of Hawaii.

West, D. J., & Farrington, D. P. (1977). *The delinquent way of life.* London: Heinemann.

Wolfgang, M. E.; Figlio, R. M., & Sellin, T. (1972). *Delinquency in a birth cohort.* Chicago: University of Chicago Press.

Yochelson, S., & Samenow, S. E. (1977). *The criminal personality, Vol. 2: The change process.* New York: Jason Aronson.

Zimring, F. E. (1978). Policy experiments in general deterrence: 1970–1975. In A. Blumstein, J. Cohen, & D. Nagin (Eds.), *Deterrence and incapacitation: Estimating the effects of criminal sanctions on crime rates.* Washington, DC: National Academy of Sciences.

CHAPTER 23

Psychotherapy with Criminal Offenders

MAX J. MOBLEY

This chapter is intended to provide the trained therapist with some insights into treatment of offenders. I begin with a discussion of estimates of treatment needs and then break down the tasks of the therapist into crisis intervention, long- term management, short-term therapy, and therapeutic programs. Each task is presented in terms of the characteristics of the clients, therapist, and system that have a bearing on its success or failure.

There is no such thing as a "how to" book for therapists working with offenders. There is too much variability among therapists, offenders, and systems. Working with offenders is like sailing against the wind. Forward progress may take a lot of tacking back and forth. I hope this chapter provides some marker buoys to help sailors keep from running aground while learning the waters.

MENTAL DISORDER IN OFFENDER POPULATIONS

How serious a problem is mental disorder in the offender population? I recently asked administrators of mental health programs in several states to estimate the percentage of inmates in their systems who were "mentally disordered, to the point of needing to be housed in special facilities." Their estimates showed considerable variation, ranging from less than 1 percent to 25 percent of the inmate population. Previously published estimates of psychiatric disorder have ranged from less than 5 percent (Petrich, 1976) to over 60 percent (Kal, 1977). Gibbs (1982) has pointed out the problems related to sampling and inconsistent definitions which have contributed to the confusion.

Studies that have used standardized criteria, reviewed by Coid (1984), suggest that "major psychosis was no more common" among offenders than in the general population. Similarly, Denkowski and Denkowski (1985) found much lower rates of mental retardation (about 2 percent) in state prison systems when more reliable psychometrics were used.

This brings into question the opinion of many mental health professionals cited as early as 1972 by Abramson, and recently reviewed by Teplin (1983). These opinions have speculated that mentally ill behavior has been "criminalized" and that many individuals who would formerly have been in mental hospitals are curently being dumped on "the system that cannot say no" (Levinson, 1984).

Teplin (1984) cites National Institute of Mental Health Statistics which show that between 1969 and 1980 the inpatient census declined by 66 percent, and the average length of stay decreased by about 45 percent between 1969 and 1978. During an overlapping period, 1970 to 1980, the number of prisoners increased by about 61 percent (Travisono, 1984). The symmetry of these figures has suggested to some that the burden of caring for the chronically mentally ill may have shifted from mental health to the criminal justice system. A study conducted in Ontario (Allodi, Kedward, & Robertson, 1977) did find an increased number and proportion of psychiatrically disordered individuals in jails during the period of reduction in hospital beds, although the jail census did not increase disproportionately.

Many law enforcement officials will admit, usually off the record, that the needs of their communities are often better served by pressing criminal charges against individuals whom the community would prefer to do without than by taking them to a mental health facility. The individual may not be any more "cured" on release, but, at least, the sheriff and the community get a little longer breathing space.

An example from my experience is an individual who was received after several hospitalizations—usually short term because of his hypersexuality often involved other patients. There was no problem arresting him because he tended to walk into other people's houses, undeterred by closed doors, helping himself to clothes and food.

He had no income in prison but traded sexual favors for cookies, cigarettes, or pieces of paper on which he drew cryptic designs, biblical quotes, and words which had five letters. At times he would get overloaded by the sexual demands of other inmates and become blatantly psychotic. This was usually easy to detect because he would not enter the office unless all electrical devices and my briefcase had been removed. However, once stabilized, he adamantly refused medication.

He did improve enough to make parole but was back at the prison gate two days later saying that he could not make it "out there." His mother called after about a week asking that he be let back in because she could not work and keep him from sexually abusing her other children at the same time. She was informed that we could not take him back unless he committed a crime or violated probation. He was back a short time later for stealing a pair of pants off a clothes line.

He flattened his time (completed his sentence without parole) and was discharged. He was not welcome back in his home town and drifted until he was struck and killed by a car while panhandling quarters by flagging down cars on a bridge.

This case is not intended to illustrate what happens to all the mentally ill, nor is it an isolated instance.

Studies of arrest seem to suggest that mentally disordered individuals are likely to find their way into the criminal justice system. Sosowsky's (1980) data suggest that mental status is causally related to the increased arrest rate. Teplin (1984) looked at individuals at the point of arrest and concluded that the mentally disordered had a significantly greater chance of being arrested than nonmentally disordered persons for similar offenses.

Given an apparently higher arrest rate of mentally disordered individuals, it is reasonable to hypothesize that the number of them in jails has probably also increased. The hypothesis is difficult to test because information is not collected uniformly on representative samples nor analyzed to give proper epidemiological estimates (Gibbs, 1982).

Steadman and Ribner (1980) found that the percentage of inmates in a county jail who had prior inpatient hospitalization increased from 9 percent in 1968 to 12 percent in 1975. While a prevalence increase of 3 percent sounds like only a bit more of a nuisance, the number of individuals in the county jail also increased by 225 percent from 1968 to 1975. Thus the 3 percent increase in prevalence represented a 300 percent increase in the actual number of offenders with a history of prior inpatient hospitalization in the study.

The percentage or number of offenders with prior inpatient hospitalization does not provide a clear picture of the treatment needs of incarcerated offenders. Often hospitalization may be a legal maneuver rather than the treatment modality chosen by a mental health professional. Lawyers who have not had time to prepare their cases may request a court-ordered evaluation to get their clients out of the jail and give themselves more time. Psychiatric assessment may be mandated by state law for certain felonies. Lacking a solid defense for other felonies, a lawyer has little to lose by sending a client to the state hospital for a 30-day evaluation and hoping that the doctors can come up with something that the defense can use. Thus offenders with prior histories of hospitalization may never have been hospitalized for treatment of a mental disorder.

A clearer picture is provided in a study by Collins and Schlenger (1983) comparing lifetime prevalence rates of DSM-III psychiatric disorders among male inmates of the North Carolina Department of Correction with rates for nonoffender samples from the Epidemiological Catchment Area program sponsored by the National Institute of Mental Health.

It is not surprising that the rate of antisocial personality diagnoses (28.9 percent) was 6 to 14 times higher than in the other samples. Alcohol abuse/dependence (49.5 percent) was two to three times higher. Substance abuse/dependence (18.8 percent) was 2 to 23 times higher. Schizophrenia (1.0 percent) and schizophreniform disorders (0.2 percent) were only marginally higher than the rates found in the other samples. Although manic episodes (1.1 percent) were only slightly higher among the offenders, major depressive episodes (5.3 percent) were more than twice as prevalent as among a nonincarcerated sample from the same state. Only anorexia nervosa, panic disorders, and somatization disorders were reported to affect a smaller percentage of incarcerated individuals. Overall, 70 percent of the incarcerated sample qualified for any diagnosis—approximately twice the rate for the nonincarcerated sample.*

---

*The 0.0% prevalence of somatization disorder may be misleading. There tends to be a high rate of expression of symptoms by offenders. Medical personnel, in institutions that require hard manual labor, learn to accurately predict the length of sick call lines by the weather and the type of task. Physical com-

These percentages are important because they provide one type of needs assessment for treatment services. The percentages themselves can be argued. As Collins and Schlenger (1983) note, the prevalence of antisocial personality diagnosed by DSM-III rules in their study is lower than that found by James, et al. (1980) using DSM-II criteria and lower than that diagnosed by judges in the Hare (1983) study. In addition there are great differences in the treatability of various disorders and the impact they have on the operations of correctional systems and vice versa.

Asking how large a problem the mentally ill offender is to the correctional system is much like asking how big a problem a toothache is to an individual. If viewed as a percentage of the mass of a human body, a toothache is insignificant. However, a severe toothache can significantly reduce the functioning of the whole individual. The fact that hundreds of individuals are confined together greatly increases the impact of the problems of any one person on the others. At the same time, this effect also extends the effects of treatment, success or failure, both more broadly and more intensely than would be the case outside a correctional setting.

The seriousness of an individual's problem is also likely to be exacerbated by incarceration. The individual is separated from previously established support systems. Methods of escaping from or dealing with problems that worked previously may not be feasible in prison. The new stresses of adapting to the prison environment are added. The individual's self-confidence and ego strength are further undermined by concrete evidence of once again being a loser.

In brief, treatment of emotional disorders is needed by a greater percentage of the population and is needed more intensely in a correctional setting than anywhere else, outside a psychiatric hospital.

TYPES OF TREATMENT

The variety of diagnoses seems to interact with the characteristics of the setting to produce four types of treatment for offenders: management, maintenance, psychotherapy, and programs. These types are outlined in Table 23.1 and are much more vague and interdependent than described. The typology is intended primarily to conceptualize the three-way interaction of therapist, client, and system. Brodsky (1982) provides a similar description of program models for local jails.

Management

Management usually means crisis management. Crisis may occur concurrently with or independent of the other three treatment tasks. In prison settings it most commonly occurs in conjunction with marital or child custody problems, failure to gain parole, or setback in appeals or other legal action, disciplinary action that the indi-

plaints that are dismissed as malingering or seen as real but not limiting duty may become the focus of the offenders attention and brought to the therapist as an example of institutional neglect. Therapists new to the system tend to be taken aback when an inmate presents hemorrhoids for view. This is usually an invitation to become the offender's champion and leads to conflict rather than problem solving.

TABLE 23.1 Therapy Tasks in a Correctional Setting

	Management	Maintenance	Psychotherapy	Programs
Problem type	Situational reaction Manipulation Severe depression	Psychosis Mental retardation Aftermath of trauma	Poor controls Anxiety/depression Fear/weak/passive Family problems	Antisocial personality Alcohol/drug dependence Sex offenses
Referral source	Emergency request Staff referral Peer referral	Psych. history Intake evaluation Staff referral	Self-referral Judge/lawyer/family Recommends	Self-referral Judge/lawyer/family recommends
Precipitated by	Increase in stress Lost support system Situational crisis	Observed regression Bizarre behavior Suicide attempt	Depressive episode Existential crisis Family pressure	Repeated arrests Acknowledges problem Improve parole chance
Treatment goal	Crisis resolution Symptom reduction Prevent self-harm	Prevent deterioration Social/coping skill Cure/remission Stabilization	Insight/options Appropriate behavior Belief/attitude change	Control of behavior Acceptable alternatives Social skills
Treatment duration	1 to 5 sessions within 1 to 3 days	30 days to 5 months to Duration of sentence	6 to 12 individual 12 group sessions Ongoing	12 to 24 months 30-day intensive
Setting	Housing area Infirmary Observation cells	Specialized unit Restricted housing State hospital	Office Group room	Separate unit Restricted housing

vidual considers unfair, threats by fellow inmates, sexual abuse or homosexual panic, or inability to tolerate conditions of incarceration, particularly punitive isolation.

An offender is made more vulnerable to crisis by the feeling of being alone. The family may be unable to visit, may have given up on the offender, or may never have been any support. Inmates do not have "friends" in prison, they have "associates." These associates are usually viewed with only slightly more trust than the correctional officers. Certain crimes, particularly rape and child molestation, make some inmates outcasts even among other offenders.

The very fact that a person is known as an offender suggests poor coping mechanisms. Experiences of having gone through several agencies, therapists, and programs which never "worked" only served to prove (in the offender's perspective) the impossibility of getting helped. Many offenders view admission of problems, expression of feelings (other than anger), and compromise as signs of weakness that invite victimization and abuse. These beliefs and experiences further shut down options for dealing with the crisis.

Mental health workers employed by the correctional facility are likely to be thought of as part of the system. This may mean that the professional is seen by offenders as being on the wrong side of the we/they dichotomy and either not caring or likely to snitch them off to the cops. Mental health workers may also be viewed as being there for the crazies and contact with them to be stigmatizing. Such views shut the inmate off from resources for dealing with the problem.*

Management of Self-Destructive Behavior

Crises are intensified by the multitude of pressures inherent in the environment, the limits on options, the lack of perceived resources, and fear of dealing with representatives of the system. Scarred wrists are a common sight in prison. There were 117 suicides in American prisons in 1984. This rate (26.3 per 100,000) is more than twice the U. S. rate (12.4 per 100,000) (Camp & Camp, 1985).

Suicide is an even bigger problem in jails than in prisons with 293 suicides in 1983 (U.S. Dept. of Justice, 1984). The National Institute of Corrections has produced a document entitled *Suicide in Jails* (1983) which provides information, training materials, and forms. The National Sheriffs Association (1984) has produced a videotape training aid entitled "Suicide: The silent signals." A paper by Huggins (1985) for sheriffs is also available through NIC.

The techniques of crisis intervention taught to most psychologists and counselors (e.g. Cohen, Claiborn, & Specter, 1983) are usable in correctional settings if the therapist takes some of the following aspects of the environment into account.

1. Ensure that as little as possible positive reinforcement is given for self-destructive behavior. Inmates who feel that they have nothing else to bargain with

---

*This is one reason that close ties with the chaplains are important. While it may not be acceptable to have psychological problems, it may be OK to have religious problems. Thus chaplains are an important referral source and can also be most helpful in maintaining psychological stability within the inmate population.

may, in effect, hold themselves hostage. If their demands are acceded to, their threats against themselves are likely to increase. On the other hand, if their bluff is called, a gruesome demonstration of their determination may follow.

Several years ago adolescents at one unit began swallowing razor blades. Embedded in cheese or wrapped carefully in toilet paper, the blades could be swallowed without harm but still show up clearly on x-rays. The consulting physician, seeing a life- threatening situation, performed immediate surgery. However, when one of the inmates was presented for the fourth time for this surgery, the physician determined that he was at greater risk from repeated incisions through the adominal wall than from the razor blade. The inmate was locked up, given a bed pan, and told to present evidence when he passed the razor blade. Vital signs were monitored regularly, but no trip to the hospital or other extra attention was provided.

Subsequent cases have been treated in much the same fashion without incident. However the frequency of razor blade swallowing and, with it, the risk of death or serious injury declined drastically. In the boredom and perceived oppressiveness of incarceration, some individuals will go to great, and potentially fatal, lengths to produce a change in their circumstances.

Offenders correctly perceive that the correctional system, all too often, operates on management by crisis. And they do not hesitate to manufacture a crisis when their needs are felt strongly enough. This is not to say that all or, for that matter, any suicide attempts by offenders are solely for secondary gain. There is often an element of excitement in gambling with death that can turn a manipulative gesture into a lethal action. There is often a test question involved: "Does anybody care?" An answer in the negative can lead to genuine despair. Finally, problems clearly need to be addressed whenever an individual chooses suicide, threats, or gestures as the coping method of choice in dealing with any stressful situation.

2.   A usual precaution for individuals prone to suicide is to keep them around other people. This keeps the individual from obsessing about problems and does not allow the privacy needed to carry out the suicidal act. However, in a correctional setting, other inmates may provide motivation, encouragement, and actual help in carrying out a suicide attempt. Fellow inmates have been known to provide pieces of glass, sharp metal, hoarded medications, insecticides, syringes, and other potentially lethal objects to inmates who requested them for attempting suicide. They have even been known to cover for other inmates during a suicide attempt. Many have watched with interest and called other inmates to watch a suicide attempt, making no effort to notify anyone in authority.

An individual, with no record of prior suicide attempts and no suicide threats, committed suicide by hanging himself. It was later found that other new inmates had discovered that he was very fearful of being abused or used sexually by other inmates. Although the inmate was in a single cell, the others played on his fears to the point that, apparently, death seemed preferable.

He was a middle-aged white male with a history of depression and alcoholism, sentenced on a drug-related crime. His suicide generally fit the pattern described in an article by Hayes (1983) on jail suicides.

As in the case just described, most jail and prison suicides occur in one-man cells. Therefore it is essential to ensure continuous observation and appropriate interpersonal support.

3. Offenders with more antisocial characteristics tend to place greater emphasis on giving their word. Usually a "No Suicide Contract" is reliable if the individual is not psychotic and the therapist can get the offender's "convict word." (The word these individuals usually give to "free-world" people may carry no real obligation for them.) The other side of this is that anything the therapist states a willingness to try to do is likely to be seen as a promise. Nothing destroys a therapist's credibility quicker than not doing what was "promised." It is therefore imperative that the therapist have a clear understanding of the available options within the system.

4. There is a tendency for the type of suicidal gesture, particularly if it is novel, to be copied by other inmates. It is helpful to have an action plan ready for a repitition after a novel suicidal gesture. This plan needs to have been developed jointly with medical, security, and administrative staff to avoid confusion and missed signals.

5. The individuals who are most likely to have first awareness of a crisis are the jailers or correctional officers. An important function of a psychologist or counselor in a correctional setting is preservice and inservice training of officers in recognition of and proper response to crises. Proper anticipation and early intervention can keep most problems from growing to crisis proportions. Officers' responses may otherwise range from ignoring what they consider to be manipulation, to trying to make jokes and get the individual to see how ridiculous it is, to actually offering advice about how to "do it right."

An officer who was busy unpacking some cleaning supplies was asked by an inmate if he could use a piece of baling twine from one of the boxes to hang himself. The officer, thinking that the inmate was joking, said he thought it would do. A few minutes later the officer was holding up the inmate waiting for someone to untie the twine from the stair railing.

Not all management cases involve suicidal ideation. Offenders tend to have an external locus of control that may be exaggerated by the authoritarian and restrictive atmosphere of correctional facilities. Deprivation heightens the importance of the commonplace. This results in professionals being besieged with pleas for help, many of which are manifestations of learned helplessness and the manipulative tendencies of offenders. This can easily become a trap for the professional who may find it easier and more gratifying to "fix" problems with mail, classification, the parole department, or the like, than to confront dependency, teach problem solving, and risk being confronted for being "uncaring" and "just like the rest of them."

Management of Violent Behavior

Mental health workers may also be called on to manage the violent, disruptive acting-out individual. There are several subtypes of what Toch (1982) calls the DDI's (disturbed disruptive inmates). Some are clearly mentally disordered individuals in a manic or schizophrenic episode. Some tend to be limited intellectually or, at least, in their repertoire of responses, and see no option other than to fight back against any limits. Some do "crazy" things to earn admiration, be left alone, mess with the guards, or for any of a variety of objectives which they can usually clearly articulate.

1. The mentally disordered individuals can usually be handled well by clinically trained staff. There is usually an element of fear in their agitation which is exacerbated and converted to anger by orders and threats and allayed by calm reassurance that the situation is under control and the therapist is neither anxious nor afraid. Once they have been given a chance to talk over whatever precipitated the outburst and given a clear idea of what will happen next, they usually cooperate.

> I was called to a city jail where a manic individual was housed following arrest for alleged parole violation. The individual had seriously damaged the steel fixtures of his cell and was so loud and convincing in his threats that six parole officers, the city police, and transport officers from the department of correction had chosen discretion as the better part of valor.
> The parolee was known to have fears about being beaten and was quite good at standing off authority figures with his ferocity and tremendous strength. After being told twice about the sequence of events he could expect and being given assurance that I would stay with him until he was returned to prison, he submitted to handcuffing and transport.

2. A limited number of individuals who showed little or no social control and few verbal skills have required physical intervention to keep them from hurting themselves or someone else. In my experience some have regressed to infantile tactics such as holding their breath, biting themselves, banging their arms, and lying on the floor kicking and screaming. They tended to recycle an anger-producing event for hours, keeping others upset with their temper tantrums. The technique of ignoring these outbursts may not work in a setting where their behavior can produce severe agitation in others who share their confinement. Rapid tranquilization is often the most practical method of managing these individuals but becomes questionable on ethical grounds when it is done more for the benefit of the staff and other inmates than for the individual himself.

Where do developmentally disabled persons get sent when their sexual, aggressive, and destructive behaviors are so extreme that they endanger staff and other clients in a residential treatment setting? Usually back to their families who have had no success in controlling them either. After a brief stay they tend to get arrested and wind up again in the department of correction.

One such individual developed a pattern of spitting at, throwing urine on, and physically attacking the officers assigned to meet his needs. In addition he would scream and kick the door of his cell for much of the night, falling asleep out of exhaustion in the early morning. At some point, his screaming began to affect the mental stability of the other inmates. The officers were so angered by his abuse that they feared losing control and hurting him.

At that point, "danger to self and others" takes on a new dimension. The ethical question of using medication, in the absence of a treatable illness, wanes in importance. The inmate slept for some hours after an injection of Thorazine and awoke calm and puzzled over why everybody had been so upset.

3.   Inmates who intentionally do "crazy" things tax the resources and skills of the entire system. The inmate who forgoes personal hygiene and engages in bizarre behavior to make himself unattractive as a sexual object may be indistinguishable to most officers from the chronic schizophrenic. While correctional officers tend to be highly skilled at spotting mentally disordered behavior, effective management of instrumental "crazy" behavior may take considerable explanation and inservice training.

An inmate who injected saliva* into his foot, knowing that one of his peers lost a leg with the same technique, is definitely viewed as abnormal by officers and administration. Yet when mental health staff talked to him, he stated that he did it because he did not want to work. Asked why he did not simply refuse to turn out to work, he replied that he did not want to get sent to punitive isolation. His past experience showed that the disciplinary report usually got lost in the urgency of responding to his medical needs. Thus instead of going to punitive isolation, he spent a week in the hospital and two or three more weeks in the department's aftercare facility.

Security staff are justifiably nervous in dealing with inmates who are willing to use their own bodies as weapons. Mental health staff are justifiably reluctant to reinforce such behavior by removing inmates from the circumstances that they were trying to escape. Correctional officers tend to see behavior that differs from their norms as "crazy." Psychologists may see the same behavior as being manipulative

---

*Syringes usually bring a high premium in a correctional setting. Many medications which have little abuse potential on the street, such as diphenhydramine and propoxyphene, may be "cooked down" and injected in prison. Virtually any medication that will affect the individual's state of consciousness, even though the effect is not particularly pleasing, is subject to abuse in prison.

When syringes are not available, any piece of metal can be sharpened and used to puncture a vein. Liquid can then be injected by using a strip of cellophane from a cigarette pack rolled into a cone shape, inserted into the wound, and squeezed.

and kick it back to security as a management problem, in an effort not to reinforce the "crazy" behavior with attention. This creates a dilema for security personnel, who are liable for charges of neglect if they ignore the "crazy" behavior. The therapist may be seen as sidestepping obligations to the system to avoid dealing with a frightening or undesirable client. Management problems must be handled cooperatively; neither security nor treatment staff have the skills and resources to handle them alone.

Maintenance

As discussed earlier, psychosis and mental retardation appear to be only slightly more prevalent among offender populations than in the general population. As in the general population, many of these individuals are able to integrate themselves into the prison community. They may require medication, treatment programs, and additional supervision and structure. Others cannot reach a level of adaptive behavior which allows them to be on their own either in the community or the correctional facility.

Correctional administrators have long recognized the presence of such individuals in their facilities and stated that they did not belong in prison. As a group they do not function well, having a significantly higher rate of disciplinary infractions (Adams, 1983). At the same time, state hospitals have gone to open wards, have eliminated many facilities for long-term care, and are adhering to accreditation standards that are inconsistent with jail-type operations. The responsibility for making sure that these inmates' needs are provided for has been thrust upon corrections.

All departments of correction now have either mental health areas within correctional facilities, designated health service facilities, or access to forensic facilities within state hospitals. The majority view among correctional administrators, though with notable reluctance, appears to be that these problems are best handled within the secure confines of correctional facilities. McCarthy (1985) reported results of a nationwide survey of mentally ill and mentally retarded offenders in corrections. Combined statistics of reporting departments classified 6 percent of the total inmate population as mentally ill. However the prevalence rates varied widely from less than 1 percent to 12.5 percent (see Brodsky, 1972).

Although mentally disordered offenders represent only 6 percent or so of the offender population, they typically receive the bulk of the available mental health resources. Even if their level of adaptive behavior can be raised to a level that allows reintegration into the broader population, they often require extensive long-term aftercare. And some offenders will spend most, if not all, of their incarceration in mental health housing.

One individual with a history of schizophrenia was being taken to the county courthouse for involuntary commitment proceedings by his family. While walking down the hall in the courthouse, he broke free. He then grabbed a woman who worked in the courthouse and dragged her into an elevator. He stopped the elevator between floors and attempted to rape his captive.

The man was found competent to stand trial, sentenced to 40 years and sent to prison. Soon after his arrival, while apparently trying to flee from the voices he commonly hears, he ran from his assigned area and refused all orders to return. He backed into a corner and held several correctional officers at bay for some time. (This individual's height is about 6 feet 9 inches and weight unknown because the scales available calibrate only to 350 pounds.)

After that and for the past five years, this man has been in a mental health management area of the department. At no time has he been completely clear of psychosis, despite massive doses of psychotropic drugs. He has a work assignment, attends group therapy, and is generally involved in the activities of the mental health unit. He has a behavioral contract that, when the voices get to be overpowering, he will put on a headset radio turned to the maximum volume he can stand. The other inmates tend to be very reliable about reminding him to do this, and, if they doubt its efficacy, retire quickly to their rooms.

He frequently incorporates staff into delusions which have to do with them trying to hurt him or make him perform sexual acts against his will. He may suddenly become loud and agitated in response to delusions confronting staff with the fact that he is going to stop them from doing "it" to him. Once the episode is over, he is usually docile and tearful, begging for help not to be that way again.

The techniques that would be used in a Veterans Administration or state hospital inpatient setting are, by and large, applicable to a mental health unit within a correctional setting. However, there are some differences related to the setting and others related to the fact that the patients are also offenders.

Characteristics of the Setting

1. Any individual in a setting that is, by definition, punishing can be expected to try to escape that setting. Many inmates request placement in a mental health unit, though most do not get there. Once placed in a mental health unit, nobody in their "right mind" would want to leave the relative safety, quiet, and sanity of a mental health unit to be with normal inmates in a more oppressive setting. Thus patients must seem to work on their problems to stay in the unit but must not show rapid improvement (also to stay in the unit). The perceived desirability of being on a mental health unit also creates problems for staff in screening out malingerers.

One individual had been told in county jail that being "crazy" or "queer" would cause him to be placed in housing apart from the other inmates. He was well coached by another offender who had spent much of his time in mental health units and had firsthand knowledge of what symptoms impressed the shrinks. This particular inmate took no chances and claimed to be both queer and crazy.

However he overplayed the crazy and was put on a sizable dose of a neuroleptic which had effects that made him think that he was really going crazy. In a panic, he admitted the whole scheme.

Malingering is usually detectable either because the individual gets carried away with his act and overplays the role, or because the individual gets tired of maintaining the role. However some inmates are highly skilled in playing mentally ill (Yochelson & Samenow, 1976). Cavanaugh and Rogers (1984) provide some techniques for identifying these inmates. The most difficult manipulation to detect is that presented by inmates who have a real psychological disorder and have learned to continue or exaggerate their symptoms for secondary gain.

2.   The second problem has to do with the fact that mentally disordered individuals are confined with offenders who model antisocial behaviors. Most mentally disordered offenders already have some degree of personality disorder, which may be minimal during an acute episode of psychopathology but emerge as the individual is stabilized. Those who have not previously shown antisocial personality characteristics see those behaviors apparently reinforced with possessions and good times. It does not take long for them to model and adopt the manipulative, sexual, and aggressive behaviors.

3.   The treatment unit is usually located within the confines of a larger unit or system and, to a degree, regulated by it. Necessarily, the needs of the larger unit dictate schedules such as meals, movie availability, pill calls, counts, doctor and dental call, and so on. Shared facilities such as infirmaries, gyms, mess halls, and the like may not be available at desirable times. Movement may be limited by other activities going on in the larger unit. Security concerns may become acute when inmates of different security levels are mixed, or when a particularly high security risk inmate is seen as being in need of inpatient treatment. These problems can usually be resolved, or other options developed, with the cooperation of the warden but must be considered in setting up any programming.

4.   Correctional settings often require the management of an individual for years with no clear stopping point or transition to another support system. It is usually not feasible or at least not responsible to drop inmates from treatment or urge them to find another therapist. Failures and dropouts remain around to haunt the therapist on a daily basis. The long-term presence of many of these clients raises issues of transference and countertransference to breadths and intensities that are seldom otherwise encountered outside of psychoanalysis proper. This raises a burnout danger for the therapist who takes on a task that almost amounts to reparenting or, at least, involves long-term services to a highly demanding and sometimes psychologically primitive population. There is also a potential for physical danger as the therapist becomes incorporated into delusional systems of individuals with records of hurting others.

One female inmate with a history of chronic schizophrenia became aware of feeling "different." She hypothesized that these strange feelings were drug induced and searched her body for needle marks. When she found what she interpreted to be needle marks and was unaware of having been given an injection, she concluded that she was being injected while she slept. She began staying awake several days at a stretch, but would inevitably succumb to sleep. Upon awakening she always found more "needle marks." She concluded that I, the therapist, was living in a nearby closet and sneaking out to inject her whenever she fell asleep.

She filed a very cogent writ which was accepted for trial by the federal court.

5. Like most institutions, correctional facilities operate on rules and expectations and principles of consistent treatment. It becomes problematic, at best, to deal with offenders who do not fit the mold. Should inmates in a mental health unit be required to work, if the policy of the department is that all inmates, who are able to work, do so? If a mentally disordered inmate runs for the fence, does the officer in the tower shoot? If a "crazy" breaks a rule in the hall, should the correctional officer write a disciplinary? Correctional officers, unless they have had specialized training and experience, have difficulty responding normally to the abnormal. Similarly psychologists have difficulty helping their clients adapt to a system that challenges their ethics and expectations about how people should be treated. (For a discussion of ethical issues, see Brodsky, 1980; for a discussion of the legal issues, see Cohen, 1985; for a discussion of applicable standards, see Cohen and Griset, 1985.)

> When the mental health unit was moved to a new parent unit, a number of the officers, long assigned to the parent unit, avoided the area unless ordered to enter it. Officers who worked for mental health were asked, "How can you work with *them*?" Inmates who had moved out of a mentally disordered state and had begun limit testing were "cut extra slack" by sympathetic officers. Generally the mental health inmates were seen, in turn, as unpredictable and dangerous, or as incompetent and not to be held responsible.

This set of issues is one of the more difficult to resolve because the cognitive impairment of the inmate fluctuates, thus altering what can reasonably be expected from them. Even professional staff have problems determining levels of control and responsibility as inmates learn to use their symptoms to relieve themselves of responsibility for their actions.

The issue of expectations and rules is further complicated by the interactions of the custody and treatment environments. The prison environment may be seen by the psychologist as not only failing to correct but, in many cases, doing harm. The harshness and oppressiveness may be seen as meeting the needs of the staff and having in reality, little to do with managing inmates. On the other hand, the treatment environment may be seen by security staff as overly permissive, covering inmates with pity instead of making them stand up and get on with life, or irrelevant to the real problems of convicts. Some members of security staff may even see treatment as undermining the authority of officers and the order of the institution.

The conflict here is powerful and attractive to cynics. It is easy to say, "Therapy is impossible in such a punitive environment." This makes it easy to form an unhelpful psychological alliance with prisoners around their perceived mistreatment. Therapists, being human, inevitably get hooked by this conflict, from time to time. At such times, it may help the therapist to recall the levels of brutality and destruction that have occurred when the system has broken down (Attica, New Mexico Penitentiary) and look for ways to improve rather than undermine it.

The inequities and negative aspects of the system, both real and imagined, can and should be brought into treatment. It is possible to use misperceptions to teach reality-based thinking, and real unfairness to teach frustration tolerance and empathy for victims. Some therapists in private practice seek "creative anxiety" to move their patients. Therapists in corrections may find this task already done for them.

The System as the Client

This is not to say that the correctional environment or current techniques are as humane and effective as possible. They are not. But several factors should be considered before taking on the system as a client.

1.   Efforts to change the system should be kept separate from therapy. Otherwise, the prisoner-client may wind up a pawn. The process may give permission for rebellious and self-defeating behaviors. And the therapist may find himself alienated and isolated from the resources necessary to do the job.

2.   Efforts to change the system should not be undertaken unless both the aspect needing change and the direction of the change are clear. The therapist may need to spend a good deal of time in diagnosing the problems before undertaking to "fix" them. Situations are usually much more ambiguous than they first appear. If easy fixes were available, there would be no problem to solve. Affixing blame fixes nothing.

3.   Efforts to change the system should follow good psychological techniques. In a setting where the dominant feeling is anger, it is easy to give rein to righteous indignation and condemnation. This is useful with the system about as often as it is with an individual client.

4.   Offenders and corrections staff tend to see themselves as highly dissimilar. Their differences often get so highly polarized that no resolution seems possible. The therapist who chooses sides only serves to heighten the conflict. All parties in corrections—inmates, officers, and even treatment staff—tend to wear gray hats. It is possible to empathize with all of them and work with the system as one would with a troubled family.

The therapist who tries to punish the system for punishing the offender will seldom find the method to be corrective. The therapist who is willing to participate fully in an imperfect system and model positive methods of dealing with people and problems can have a therapeutic impact considerably greater than the caseload alone. An effective therapist is quickly recognized by guards and staff as a powerful resource and can exercise considerable leverage in changing the system.

Outpatient Psychotherapy

Outpatient therapy is an elective rather than a requirement in many correctional settings. As long as crisis management keeps incidents from happening that would produce liability or bad press for the system, as long as the staff do not have to deal with the mentally ill and retarded inmates, and as long as there are some programs that signify rehabilitation opportunities, there may be little or no administrative emphasis placed on treatment services for the bulk of the offender population (Lombardo, 1985). This leaves the field fairly clear to offer elective treatment and to be eclectic in approach—the limits being imposed by a lack of staff resources.

There is no point in listing all of the approaches. Suffice it to say that they have run the gamut from Assertiveness Training to Zen. Each of the approaches has claimed some measure of success. Usually this success has been in terms of improvement on some psychometric device or adaptation to incarceration rather than lasting changes in behavior. Most approaches have been attacked: the more humanistic for coddling criminals, the more behavior oriented for brainwashing or depriving inmates of constitutional rights. Attempts have been made to stamp them all "null and void" under the "nothing works" blanket, (Martinson, Lipton, & Wilks, 1975).

It is, in fact, easy to come to believe that nothing works when the therapist daily encounters inmates who have not benefited from treatment. In mental health centers and private practice, a therapist can, at least, fantasize that the client who dropped out or was terminated has undergone a healthy transformation. In a correctional setting, the failures tend to stay on while the successes leave and get on with their lives.

Nor does the therapist in a correctional setting have the selection opportunities available elsewhere. Mental health centers and private practitioners can transfer responsibility for nontreatment, premature terminations, and failures with a mere wave of the "not motivated for treatment" wand, and the miscreant disappears. The therapist in a correctional setting may refuse or terminate treatment because of the client's behavior, but still be held responsible for the treatment of all those whom the court has seen fit to send.

Nowhere else does the client have so much time to put into treatment. Nowhere else can so many environmental factors be known and maintained at so nearly a stable level. Nowhere else is so much external observation and reporting possible, or the potential for follow-up so high.

In brief, correctional facilities offer the possibility of greatly expanding the frontiers of psychotherapy, only provided that the frontiersmen are a hardy enough breed to survive some very severe trials. Therapy in a correctional setting encounters much the same problems that therapy encounters in any setting. Some problems are more prevalent; most problems are intensified as they echo off the walls. Even so, therapy seems to work as well and fail as badly in prison as it does anywhere else. The mistakes are just more difficult to keep buried.

This is not the same as saying that all therapists can succeed in psychotherapy with offenders. There are characteristics of therapists, offenders, the correctional environment, and success that must be taken into account.

Therapists

I have told all applicants for therapist positions in my department that they would have to work at least six months before they could expect to become effective, but if they stayed in the system for three years, they would find themselves "getting crazy." This was based on my own experience and was usually laughed off by new staff. However, those staff members who have stayed, and many who have left, indicated that what they had taken as a joke turned out to be a fairly accurate prediction. Therapists who have remained and become effective seemed to share some common characteristics.

Therapists most likely to succeed in therapy with offenders are those who can empathize without sympathy, confront without demeaning, care without carrying, direct without controlling, see manipulation as a poor coping strategy rather than a personal assault, find satisfaction in erratic progress toward limited goals, tolerate the ambiguities and conflicts of the setting, and accept their own limits so that they do not burn out.

Therapists who sympathize will find no shortage of offenders who love them and need a great deal of their time. Nor will they find any shortage of life events among the offender population deserving of their sympathy. They will receive much flattery and many demands for their services. However they will ultimately find themselves being used up, working "instead of" rather than "with" the offender, feeling used, being disappointed and becoming angry with their clients.

Therapists who have difficulty confronting will be seen as sympathetic and receive much the same payoffs as just described. Therapists who confront in anger or with put downs may effectively shape the way that the offender interacts with the therapist and the group. However the change that occurs may not be generalizable progress. For some offenders, confrontive therapy may simply represent a new external locus of control. Unless it is followed by techniques for developing internal controls and learning and practicing prosocial behaviors, what it does accomplish may be lost. Angry, demeaning confrontation may have its place, like the proverbial two-by-four to get the mule's attention. But it is a poor mule trainer who does not know when to put down the two-by-four.

Caring is likely to be seen by the offender as a weakness that makes a person a good mark for a con. The natural response of most offenders to caring is, "Do me something, and show that you really care." A demonstration of good faith is likely to lead to demands for further demonstrations. Rescue is a severe temptation in a correctional setting as relatively solvable problems take on epic proportions and offer the therapist an easy route to heroic stature. The therapist who sees rescue as necessary should remember to throw a line rather than a lifeboat and avoid crushing the drowning victim.

The therapist who refuses to be directive with offender clients may never progress beyond the level of small talk or silence. The average education level of the clients is likely to be around sixth grade. Verbal interaction may have been mostly used in asking for things and rarely in problem solving or conflict resolution. The offender is likely to see the purpose of talking about problems as an effort to find out who is to blame. On the other hand, direction must take the shape of coaching, not controlling. Many offenders have never taken responsibility for their lives and would be only too happy to give apparent control to the therapist. The best outcome of giving control over to the therapist is likely to be that the offender has someone new to blame for how screwed up things are.

In a setting in which an individual has no power, one is going to look for the nearest outlet and attempt to plug into it. Offenders can be counted on to attempt to manipulate the therapist to do the things they lack the energy or perceived power to do for themselves. This is not only normative behavior for a correctional setting, it is necessary for survival. The therapist can monitor this by checking what feelings are being hooked, what beliefs are being played to, and what obligations generate resentments. It may be appropriate to pull the plug. However, if the therapist is close to being as effective a manipulator as the offender, it may be feasible to bill for the power. It usually only wastes energy to get angry over manipulation (although, at times, it may work well to *act* angry).

Offenders

There are characteristics likely to be found in any offender group that can lend themselves to the therapy process. Therapy may proceed efficiently and effectively if the therapist understands these characteristics and how to make them work for the therapeutic process.

The majority of offenders have written off school fairly early in their academic careers. Although the average claimed education level of inmates entering the Arkansas Department of Correction in 1985 was likely to be eighth to eleventh grade, depending on local pressure to stay in school, academic attainment as measured by achievement tests was more likely to be sixth or seventh grade. Over a third of the inmates coming into many departments of correction are functionally illiterate (Wilson & Herrnstein, 1985). Thus didactic techniques are likely to be written off as "just words," unless activities, participation, role playing, and the like are built into the lessons. Pretraining can also be helpful in teaching these individuals to use therapy services effectively (Hilkey, Wilhelm, & Horne, 1982).

Many offenders have high needs for excitement and drama in their lives. These individuals can often be "hooked" by psychodrama (Schramski & Harvey, 1983) and confrontive therapies (Dies and Hess, 1971). Much energy can be directed into and appropriately released through role play. But unless these are properly planned and directed toward clear goals, they tend to become entertaining pastimes with little therapeutic gain.

Many offenders lack self-discipline and frustration tolerance. They want to see immediate results and may quickly lose interest in programs that require them to practice on their own. Thus relaxation techniques, self-hypnosis, and meditation may produce dramatic effects initially but be dropped as the newness wears off. Therefore if is usually necessary to build in a support group, strengthening or feedback sessions, or some other method of sustaining interest.

Many offenders are astute observers who are quick to see the games, faults, and weaknesses of others. They may be much quicker to identify some negative behavior patterns than a trained therapist. Thus group therapy tends to be the modality of choice. Carefully supervised peer counselors may develop better therapy skills, in dealing with offender-type clients, than the supervising therapist.

These skills as astute social observers can also become liabilities. Most offenders have long histories of finding fault with others which they use to justify their own behavior or to shift attention from their own misdeeds. These skills can also be used to find the range of therapists and become their ego support and reality check. It is crucial that therapists check their relationships and perspectives frequently to ensure that they are still seeing through their own eyes.

Usually, when confronted about a particular action, offenders do not know why they did it, or indicate that it was the fault of the victim, a third party, or a psychoactive drug. Wherever the causes of criminal behavior are to be found, they are usually not in the explanations offered by offenders. Similarly the past history of offenders, while often moving enough to be the basis of a soap opera, may provide little more than an opportunity for the offender to control the session.

Many offenders, despite some highly romanticized and largely fictional tales, usually have a history of poor relationships. The interaction usually starts off intense and crashes when the other person finally recognizes that his or her role is more that of a victim than a partner in a relationship. The offender is then entitled to feel betrayed and to conclude that other people are "no damn good." This pattern usually transfers to therapy but can be modulated somewhat by damping the intensity of the highs and lows. This is difficult when the therapist is alternately invited to be the hero, a punisher, and a righteously angered victim.

Other characteristics tend to act as land mines in the treatment field. A good general source for exploring these is the two-volume set of books by Yochelson and Samenow (1976). A more detailed picture can often be developed from reviewing facility records such as disciplinary reports and seeking information from the staff who work with the offender on a daily basis.

Correctional Environment

The correctional environment is, in some ways, a reflection of the offender. Planning occurs at times but the system is mostly reactive, management by crisis. It has a strong tendency to victimize all who come into contact with it, staff and inmate alike, with an almost total lack of empathy. Its goals, other than security, are usually unclear and often conflicting. Its means can be self-defeating. It sometimes creats high drama and excitement as the staff play "cops" to the offender's "robbers." And, like the offenders, it usually gets public notice only by "messing up."

It is as alien, frightening, and often hostile an environment to newly arrived treatment staff as it is to first offenders. On the other hand, the injection of mental health workers by the courts has probably been no less traumatic for some correctional systems. The dialectic process should benefit both systems.

Corrections departments usually operate on paramilitary models with sergeants, lieutenants, chain-of-command, and the assumption of absolute loyalty and blind obedience. Monahan (1980) states the question astutely in the title of the volume he edited, *Who is the client?* Correctional officers tend to assume that psychologists are typically unaware of the nature of offenders, likely to believe any allegation against them that an offender makes, and likely to take the offender's side in we/they controversies. The offender, on the other hand, knows who pays the psychologist's salary and may see the therapist as just another part of the system that must be avoided or manipulated. There seems to be no permanent resolution to this problem. The best approach may be for the psychologist to take an ethical position on the various issues, proclaim that stand to staff and inmates, and stick to it.

Zimbardo's classic experiment in setting up a mock prison (Zimbardo, Haney, Banks, & Jaffe, 1975) gives some insight into the effects that such pronounced differences in power have on people in a prison environment. The only analogues of such discrepancies in power seem to be found in the parent-child and master-slave relationships. These levels of paternalism and authoritarianism may not be desirable, but they are real and must be taken into consideration. This may require that the offender be taught discrimination skills, along with any other new skills. The inmate who tries out assertiveness training with an officer in the hall, or problem-solving skills with the classification committee, may be in for a difficult time.

The powerlessness of the inmates exists only in a formal, position power sense. The psychological power of the inmate culture must be reckoned with by any therapist who hopes to facilitate changes for individuals. Security staff manage behavior largely by focusing on rule violations and removing reinforcers, usually for a set period of time during which positive behavior on the part of the inmate cannot earn them back. The items and behaviors that are positive reinforcers, and not guaranteed by law, are more likely to be dispensed by inmates than staff. Thus for many inmates, the influence of the inmate culture may outweigh that wielded by the staff. The therapist may need to inoculate the client to resist the temptations of the inmate culture and persist in the face of ridicule, scorn, or negative attitudes of peers.

Corrections departments generally remove an offender's right to privacy along with clothing, at the point of intake. Most psychologists believe that therapy requires a modicum of privacy. Privacy may be more desirable than necessary, at times. However, ethics require that an offender be told the limits of confidentiality that can be maintained in a correctional environment. Usually these include the duty to warn of planned or threatened actions that could harm self or others. In a group setting there is usually one member who will put other members' "business on the street." Most offenders, who have been around, know this already, and frank discussion of the problems of confidentiality may support rather than limit openess. For some offenders, confidentiality may most clearly be conceptualized in terms of respect and their feelings about snitching.

A more important issue in confidentiality is the degree to which the actions of the therapist affect the liberty interests of the inmates. Often inmates want the fact that they have been in treatment to go into their records, hoping that the parole board will be duly impressed by their seeking rehabilitation. Other inmates may feel stigmatized by the same treatment. Even more crucial are the psychological assessments that are done at various times during incarceration. Ethics require that the inmates be informed of the purpose and intended distribution of such assesments and their right to refuse.

Defining Success

Those who indicate that therapy with personality disorders usually fails, often neglect to indicate the critrion for success. If failure is defined as failure to restructure an individual's personality then certainly therapy, as it is legally and ethically practiced, fails. Anyone who has ever tried to lose weight can attest to failures to restructure even this well-defined, circumscribed behavior. Eating and drinking behaviors, with their built-in reinforcers, may be appropriate models for many of the behaviors that characterize the antisocial personality. It is patently absurd to say, "A house can't be built. I know because I tried all day and didn't build one." Success in any task requires understanding what the task is, selecting proper tools, and using them correctly.

A free-world person seeks therapy to alleviate emotional distress, to learn to control a troublesome behavior, to deal with conflicts in a relationship, to straighten out confusion and misperceptions, and for a variety of other problems.

This is not good enough for most correctional administrators (and many therapists). Mental health is seen as an expensive service. And, if all it can do is help offenders lead better lives and do their time better, it is likely to be seen as nice, but a luxury. The benchmark in corrections is the recidivism statistic. It may seem rather perverse that a system that deals with the problem of an individual by removing that person from society produces only token community-based and reentry programs and uses successful adaptation to that same society on release as its criterion for success. However, it is no less perverse for a discipline that claims a basis in empirical methods to say, "It can't be done" instead of, "Where do we go from here?" (Shamsie, 1982).

Programs

Programs vary considerably in focus, ranging from a specific behavior of most offenders, to antisocial personality, to offenders in specific offense categories. Regardless of the focus, programs have a number of advantages that would seem to raise the chances of success over those seen in outpatient therapy.

1. Most programs provide opportunities for many more contact hours than would be feasible in outpatient treatment. Alcohol and drug programs usually operate intensively, with 30 days dedicated strictly to treatment, and/or extensively throughout the individual's incarceration. Programs for sex offenders commonly take 18 months to two or three years. Therapeutic communities, treating persoanlity disorder, usually involve the individual for more than six months up to several years.

2. Most treatment programs provide some degree of separation from the general population. This simultaneously limits the impact of the inmate culture and sets up an environment that offers some psychological protection and permission along with positive role models.

3. Few programs have sufficient free-world staff, and many rely to varying degrees on inmate peer counselors. These individuals do not generate the automatic resistance that authority figures do. They are usually also adept at translating pyschobabble into a language which speaks to the needs of offenders. They often have the zeal and energy of new converts and can greatly extend the effectiveness of a therapist. At the same time, they are no more immune from corruption or abuse of power than anyone else and require careful supervision.

4. Programs are costly, both in terms of dollars and in terms of wear and tear on the correctional system. That, together with the amount of staff time invested in

programs, has usually led to clear mission statements and task definition. This makes it likely that the therapist and the clients, having plans and blueprints, can build a better house together than by going where the mood takes them.

5.   Therapy programs tend to process a group of people through emotionally loaded shared experiences toward a common goal. This may produce a powerful conversionlike experience and a vehement renunciation of old deviant or self de-structive behaviors. However, the types of behaviors—drug use, deviant sex, and the constellation of antisocial personality behaviors—have such habit strength and such powerful reinforcers tied to them that short-term treatment can be expected to have only short-term effects. Treatment effects are likely to be sustained only if the individual participates in ongoing support groups. Support groups may be prohib-ited by the department of correction's rules limiting contacts among parolees.

The difficulties attendant in operating programs in a correctional setting are in proportion to their potential for producing real and relevant change. A program usu-ally has the irritant effect in a correctional system that a foreign substance has in the human body. The fact that a program is good does not guarantee its success or even its survival. The following are some considerations that need to be taken into ac-count for a program to continue to function.

1.   It helps if the program is mandated by the federal court, state law, or strongly felt administrative needs. Programs are costly in terms of space, staff re-sources, and inmate time. In a period of prison overcrowding, limited budgets, and doubt and cynicism about the efficacy of treatment, it is much easier to close a pro-gram down than to start or expand one.

2.   Access to inmates needs to be built into the classification system of the facil-ity. Good convicts are much in demand for institutional needs. "Screwups" (jargon modified somewhat) are seen as needing straightening out (punishment and hard work), not some soft assignment to a treatment unit. Many of the other inmates do not have sentences long enough to allow them to complete treatment. Others have sentences so long that the opportunity for them to apply some types of treatment will be years in coming.

3.   The program needs to be monitored frequently from the outside. There is a tendency for prison-based programs to get "dirty." Individuals in programs are usu-ally involved in them over a substantial period of time. It is to be expected that, once inmates learn the program, they will try to manipulate it to their own ends and inject their value system into it. Periodic house cleanings are required to ensure that the program stays on track and that the participants stay on task. As the changes that lead to a program getting dirty tend to be insidious, it usually requires a therapist not connected with the day-to-day operations to see them.

4.   Programs tend to have two major effects on staff. One is that programs pro-vide excellent training in therapy. The other is that they produce the fastest burnout. Wherever possible, programs should provide for staff rotation or relief. Staff rota-tion can provide quality therapists for the other treatment areas. Staff relief can be built in either by having other therapists who can cover or by closing down the pro-gram to allow brief sabbaticals periodically. These shutdown periods can be used to

provide staff training and rejuvenation and allow time for program evaluation and changes.

5.   The program needs to be carefully explained to correctional staff. While nobody questions the number of years it takes to earn a high school diploma or learn a professional skill, immediate results are expected of treatment programs. Officers become suspicious of the length of time inmates are expected to stay in the program. In addition, the type of open trusting relationship considered by therapists to form the basis for treatment is antithetical to what officers have been taught about handling convicts. The therapist who fails to address these and similar concerns is likely to spend more time trying to overcome obstacles than doing treatment.

6.   Public relations is essential. The political entity whose resources enable the programs to exist needs to be told frequently about the good being done by the program. It is much easier politically to allocate resources for education and the elderly, the recipients of both having clearly defined political constituencies. Other agents of the criminal justice system need accurate information about the program. These are the individuals who "refer" the clients, explain to offenders and their families what is going to happen in prison, and make decisions about sentencing, revocation of parole, probation, and the handling of offenders in general.

Program Types

Three types of programs have seen fairly wide use with offenders. These are sex offender treatment, substance abuse treatment, and therapeutic communities for treating personality disorders.

Sex offender programs are well described for adolescents (Knopp, 1982) and for adult offenders (Knopp, 1984; Brecher, 1978). Dynamics are discussed by Groth & Birnbaum (1979). Assessment and treatment strategies are presented in a book edited by Greer and Stuart (1983). Therapists who are not involved in treating paraphilias may gain considerable insight into the needs of offenders, the impact of various types of programming, the necessary duration of treatment, and reasonable expectations for effects from examining the sources cited here.

Alcohol and drug treatment has been brought to offender populations by Alcoholics Anonymous before much other treatment was available. This has been in response to a recognized need of a disproportionate number of the chemically dependent within correctional settings (U.S. Dept. of Justice, 1983a, 1983b). A recent outcome study (Wexler & Lipton, 1985) suggests that treatment for chemical dependence in a therapeutic community format can have a significant effect on parole outcome.

Resources are available in terms of materials (Kelly Foundation, 1980) and volunteers from local AA groups. Programs for releasees can be located through the *National Directory of Drug Abuse and Alcoholism Treatment and Prevention Programs* (U.S. Dept. of Health and Human Services, 1984) as well as through local AA groups within the community. Brown (1985) provides excellent information for psychotherapists working with alcoholics.

Harry Wexler and his associates have information on about 160 programs and are collecting data on 70 of these. Information and contact people may be reached at

Narcotic and Drug Research Inc.; 2 World Trade Center, Room 6755; New York, NY 10047.

Therapeutic communities of various sorts have been tried in prison settings. Some have grown out of the work of Maxwell Jones which has been evolving since 1947 (Jones, 1976). Asklepion communities have combined techniques evolved in Synanon drug treatment with transactional analysis, behavior modification, and other techniques. Except for Maxwell Jones's own community, some therapeutic communities have had a life of about five years (e.g., Groder's Asklepion Community at Marion, The Chino experiment (Briggs, 1980)) or have become integrated with the larger correctional systems and gone on for some years.

A therapist wishing to utilize the therapeutic community format will find few written materials to help. Most documentation has been provided by Maxwell Jones (1976, 1979) and does not portray work with offenders in correctional settings. The other body of literature (DeLeon & Beschner, 1976) relates largely to drug rehabilitation programs. This should not be viewed as minimizing the potential effectiveness of therapeutic communities. There are a sizable number of success stories from among antisocial personalities. The therapeutic community is probably the most effective modality for treating personality disorders. It is also one of the most difficult types of programs to sustain (Levinson, 1980).

A (PERSONAL) SUMMARY

Through nine years of practice I have periodically despaired. Some offenders appeared to make no changes or trivial changes. Others made changes which I suspected were superficial and as enduring as their time to parole. I have also seen offenders leave after a year or two in treatment and lead lives whose quality surpassed that of the average citizen. A number have become counselors, the quality of whose interventions I often envy.

I have resigned once and seriously considered it so many times that I have lost count. This has always been related to the behavior of the bureacracy rather than of the inmates. I have had to face much harsher and harder realities than I often had the guts to deal with.

However, I have gained my personal and professional growth precisely by solving these problems and moving on. I would encourage the therapist who has an interest in this area to try it. The staff I have seen leave the system through the years have almost universally expressed that they learned more working with offenders than in any of their other professional experiences.

Permit me to reiterate briefly some of the points I have tried to make.

1. Motivation need not be a problem for most offenders. The wreckage of their lives and past endeavors can be called up to provide that. The problem is a mixture of healthy and unhealthy skepticism that anything can really change.

2. The situation need not be a problem. One of my former professors angered me at the time by denying my request to provide a better site for an experiment. He said, "If you can demonstrate the effect only under perfect conditions, the effect is probably too trivial to be worth fooling with."

3. Therapists, or rather the lack of them, is a problem. There are too few universities training therapists to work with offenders. There is still the stigma of correctional psychology being for those who can not handle real jobs. And it takes an astute therapist six months or more to learn that some of the techniques learned in graduate school do not work, or worse.

4. Success criteria need to be explained to therapists, judges, offenders, families, and all who have an interest in the criminal justice system. Antisocial personality characteristics cannot be cured. The offender can learn controls but not quickly, easily, or cheaply. The offender, having learned these controls, still has the option of choosing to use them or not.

5. Since it is a control not a cure situation for the personality disorder aspect, the ongoing availability of a support group is essential for offenders to continue to exercise their controls in the face of so much temptation.

Psychotherapy has not been tried and failed. We simply thought we could run a steeple chase while we were still in our toddler stage. We must clarify our goals, refine our techniques, and accept and publicly acknowledge realistic limits.

REFERENCES

Abramson, M. F. (1972). The criminalization of mentally disordered behavior: Possible side-effect of a new mental health law. *Hospital and Community Psychiatry, 23*, 101–105.

Adams, K. (1983). Former mental patients in a prison and parole system: A study of socially disruptive behavior. *Criminal Justice and Behavior, 10*, 358–384.

Allodi, F. A., Kedward, H. B., & Robertson, M. (1977). "Insane but guilty": Psychiatric patients in jail. *Canada's Mental Health, 25*, 3–7.

Braginsky, B. M., Braginsky, D. D., & Ring, K. (1969). *Methods of madness: The mental hospital as a last resort.* New York: Holt, Rinehart & Winston.

Brecher, E. M. (1978). *Treatment programs for sex offenders.* Washington DC: National Institute of Law Enforcement and Criminal Justice, U.S. Department of Justice.

Briggs, D. (1980). An enclave of freedom: Starting a community at Chino. In H. Toch (Ed.), *Therapeutic communities in corrections.* New York: Praeger.

Brodsky, S. L. (1972). *Psychologists in the criminal justice system.* Urbana, IL: University of Illinois Press.

Brodsky, S. L. (1980). Ethical issues for psychologists in corrections. In J. Monahan (Ed.), *Who is the client?* Washington, DC: American Psychological Association.

Brodsky, S. L. (1982). Intervention models for mental health services in jails. *Crime and Delinquency Issues,* National Institute of Mental Health, No. 82-1181, 126–148.

Brown, S. (1985). *Treating the alcoholic: A developmental model of recovery.* New York: Wiley.

Camp, G., & Camp, C. (1985) *The corrections yearbook*. South Salem, NY: Criminal Justice Institute.

Cavanaugh, J. L., & Rogers, R. (Eds.). (1984). Malingering and deception. *Behavioral Sciences & the Law, 2*, 3–168.

Cohen, F. (1985). Legal issues and the mentally disordered inmate. In *Source book on the mentally disordered prisoner*. Washington, DC: National Institute of Corrections.

Cohen, F., & Griset, P. (1985). Standards by legal topic. In *Source book on the mentally disordered prisoner*. Washington, DC: National Institute of Corrections.

Cohen, L. H., Claiborn, W. L., & Specter, G. A. (1983). *Crisis intervention* (2nd ed.). New York: Human Sciences Press.

Coid, J. (1984). How many psychiatric patients in prison? *British Journal of Psychiatry, 145*, 78–86.

Collins, J. J., & Schlenger, W. E. (1983). *The prevalence of psychiatric disorder among admissions to prison*. Paper presented at the American Society of Criminology, Denver.

DeLeon, G., & Beschner, G. M. (Eds.). (1976). *The therapeutic community: Proceedings of Therapeutic Communities of America*. Washington, DC: National Institute of Drug Abuse.

Denkowski, G. C., & Denkowski, K. M. (1985). The mentally retarded offender in the state prison system: Identification, prevalence, adjustment, and rehabilitation. *Criminal Justice and Behavior, 12*, 55–70.

Dies, R., & Hess, A. K. (1971). An experimental investigation of cohesiveness in marathon and conventional group psychotherapy. *Journal of Abnormal Behavior, 77*, 258–262.

Gibbs, J. J. (1982). On "demons" and "Gaols": A summary and review of investigations concerning the psychological problems of jail prisoners. In C. S. Dunn & H. J. Steadman (Eds.), *Mental health services in local jails: Report of a special national workshop* (pp. 14–33). Rockville, MD: National Institute of Mental Health.

Greer, J. G. (1983). *The sexual aggressor: Current perspectives on treatment*. New York: Van Nostrand-Reinhold.

Groth, A. N., & Birnbaum, H. J. (1979). *Men who rape: The psychology of the offender*. New York: Plenum.

Hare, R. D. (1983). Diagnosis of antisocial personality disorder in two prison populations. *Americal Journal of Psychiatry, 140*, 887–890.

Hayes, L. M. (1983). And darkness closes in . . . A national study of jail suicides. *Criminal Justice and Behavior, 10*, 461–484.

Hilkey, J. H., Wilhelm, C. L., & Horne, A. M. (1982). Comparative effectiveness of videotape pretraining versus no pretraining on selected process and outcome variables in group therapy. *Psychological Reports, 50*(3, pt. 2), 1151–1159.

Huggins, M. W. (1985). *Special issues in jail management for urban county sheriffs*. Paper presented to urban county sheriff's group, Dallas & Fort Worth, Texas. (Available through National Institute of Corrections)

James, J. F., Gregory, D., Jones, R. K., & Rundell, O. H. (1980). Psychiatric morbidity in prisons. *Hospital and Community Psychiatry, 31*, 674–677.

Jones, M. (1976). *Maturation of the therapeutic community*. New York: Human Sciences Press.

Jones, M. (1979). Learning as treatment. In H. Toch (Ed.), *Psychology of crime and criminal justice*. New York: Holt, Rinehart & Winston.

Kal, E. (1977). Mental health in jail. *American Journal of Psychiatry, 134,* 463.

Kelly Foundation. (1980). *Recovery dynamics.* Little Rock, AR: author.

Knopp, F. H. (1984). *Retraining adult sex offenders: Methods and models.* Syracuse, NY: Safer Society Press.

Knopp, F. H. (1985). *Remedial intervention in adolescent sex offenses: Nine program descriptions* (rev. ed.). Syracuse, NY: Safer Society Press.

Levinson, R. (1980). TC or not TC? That is the question. In H. Toch (Ed.), *Therapeutic communities in corrections.* New York: Praeger.

Levenson, R. (1984). The system that cannot say no. *American Psychologist, 39,* 811–812.

Lombardo, L. X. (1985). Mental health work in prisons and jails: Inmate adjustment and indigenous correctional personnel. *Criminal Justice and Behavior, 12,* 17–28.

Martinson, R., Lipton, D., & Wilks, J. (1975). *The effectiveness of correctional treatment: A survey of treatment evaluation studies.* New York: Praeger.

McCarthy, B. (1985). Mentally ill and mentally retarded offenders in corrections. In *Source book on the mentally disordered prisoner.* Washington, DC: National Institute of Corrections.

Monahan, J. (Ed.). (1980). *Who is the client?* Washington, DC: American Psychological Association.

National Institute of Corrections. (1983). *Suicide in jails.* Boulder, CO: Library Information Specialists.

National Sheriffs Associations (1984). Suicide: The Silent Signals. [videotape] Alexandria, VA.

Pattison, E. M., & Kaufman, E. (1982). *Encyclopedic handbook of alcoholism.* New York: Gardner Press.

Petrich, J. (1976). Rate of psychiatric morbidity in a metropolitan county jail population. *American Journal of Psychiatry, 133,* 1439–1444.

Schramski, T. G., & Harvey, D. R. (1983). The impact of psychodrama and role playing in the correctional environment. *International Journal of Offender Therapy and Comparative Criminology, 27,* 243–254.

Shamsie, S. J. (1982). Antisocial adolescents: Our treatments do not work—Where do we go from here? *Annual Progress in Child Psychiatry and Child Development,* pp. 631–647.

Sosowsky, L. (1980). Explaining increased arrest rate among mental patients. *American Journal of Psychiatry, 137,* 1602–1605.

Steadman, H. J., & Ribner, S. A. (1980). Changing perceptions of the mental health needs of inmates in local jails. *American Journal of Psychiatry, 137,* 1115–1116.

Teplin, L. (1983). The criminalization of the mentally ill: Speculation in search of data. *Psychological Bulletin, 94,* 54–67.

Teplin, L. (1984). Criminalizing mental disorder: The comparative arrest rate of the mentally ill. *American Psychologist, 39,* 794–803.

Toch, H. (1983). The disturbed disruptive inmate: Where does the bus stop? *Journal of Psychiatry & Law, 10,* 327–349.

Travisono, D. N. (1984). *Directory of juvenile and adult correctional departments, institutions, agencies and paroling authorities.* College Park, MD: American Correctional Association.

U.S. Department of Health and Human Services. (1984). *National directory of drug abuse and alcoholism treatment and prevention programs*. Rockville, MD: author.

U.S. Department of Justice. (1983a). *Prisoners and alcohol*. Washington, DC: author.

U.S. Department of Justice. (1983b). *Prisoners and drugs*. Washington, DC: author.

U.S. Department of Justice. (1984). *The 1983 jail census*. Washington, DC: Bureau of Justice Statistics.

Wexler, H. K., & Lipton, D. S. (1985, September). *Outcome: Evaluation of a prison therapeutic community for substance abuse treatment: Preliminary results*. Paper presented at the Ninth World Conference of Therapeutic Communities, San Franciso.

Wilson, J. Q., & Herrnstein, R. J. (1985). *Crime and human nature*. New York: Simon & Schuster.

Yochelson, S. & Samenow, S. (1976) *The Criminal Personality, Volume I: A profile for change*. New York: Jason Aronson.

Yochelson, S. & Samenow, S. (1977). *The criminal personality, volume II: The change process*. New York: Jason Aronson.

Zimbardo, P. G., Haney, C., Banks, W. C., & Jaffe, D. (1975). The psychology of imprisonment: Privation, power, and pathology. In D. Rosenhan & P. London (Eds.), *Theory and research in abnormal psychology* (2nd ed.) (pp. 270–287). New York: Holt, Rinehart & Winston.

CHAPTER 24

Intervention with Victim/Survivors

LENORE E. AUERBACH WALKER

The concept of *victim* dates back to ancient times when the practice of sacrifice was a common religious ritual. Then, as now, a victim was commonly harmed by others without respect for the individual's own rights. Only since the 1960s have the victim and the victim's rights been considered as an integral part of the criminal justice system.

Several areas have been pursued in trying to compensate a crime victim. First, there has been the rise of monetary compensation programs designed to reduce the added financial burden often incurred by victims. These compensation programs are in addition to the standard civil tort remedies. Second, direct psychological services for crisis intervention have increased such as those provided by rape crisis workers or victim/witness programs within the prosecutors' offices. Third, a new grassroots movement provides self-help support groups for victims of crime. Fourth, victims have been given a greater degree of control in the criminal justice process. This includes completing mandatory victim impact statements prior to sentencing the offender and consulting with prosecutors when plea arrangements are negotiated. And fifth, there has been a recent trend for mental health practitioners—with or without specialized training—to provide services to victims.

Victim compensation programs have originated in other countries. In this country the first state to adopt such a compensation program was California. Numerous states have followed suit, and in 1984 the Congress passed a national victim compensation law which allows states to collect additional court costs from convicted criminals to be used to assist all victims. With the establishment of these programs, it became formally recognized that victims of criminal acts have had something important taken from them and that financial compensation could help to restore this loss. Since then, a considerable body of literature on the victim has been developed (see, e.g., Viano, 1976).

The idea that victims of crime could benefit from psychological service is new. The American Psychological Association's Task Force on the Victims of Crime and Violence reports psychology's awakening to this potential new group of clients (APA, 1984). Since the criminal justice system is based on an adversarial process between the accused defendant and the state, typically, victims of crime are likely to be ignored or forgotten. The crime is prosecuted as being against the state and not against the individual victim. Victims, then, are seen as relevant only so far as they provide relevent evidence; their testimony is needed for a conviction. Intervention to address victims' psychological needs simply has not been a priority. In fact, many believe the victim gets in the way of the defendant's rights to a fair trial.

Within the last decade concern for victims' rights has spurred the development of a new, interdisciplinary field of study called *victimology*, representing the academic disciplines of psychology, sociology, medicine, social work, psychiatry, political science, law, and criminology. Many victims, today, prefer to be identified as *survivors* rather than imply they are permanently scarred by their relationship to the violence. Because sometimes they are victims, and other times survivors, both terms are used individually and together in this chapter.

Currently in this country the focus of attention has turned to the impact of crime on the victim since, by law, presentence reports must include a victim impact statement. Victims' psychological injuries are beginning to be documented. Victims of bank robberies (Weisaeth, 1984), rape (Burt & Katz, 1985), child sexual abuse (Finkelhor, 1985; Russell, 1984), burglary (Burt & Katz, 1985), and industrial disaster (Weisaert, 1984b) have been studied. National crime surveys in the United States (Skogan, 1981) as well as in other countries (for example, The Netherlands (Steinmetz, 1985) and England (Hough, 1985)) have indicated that victims of violent crimes are most likely to need immediate support following their victimization. The APA Task Force on the Victims of Crime and Violence also identifies families of violent crime victims as needing special services (APA, 1984). Now that family violence has been criminalized, the psychological impact on the victim/survivors of incest (Conte, 1985; Finkelhor, 1986), battered women (Walker, 1979, 1984a), elder abuse (Kosberg, 1984), and marital rape (Russell, 1982) has indicated the urgency of the problem. Victimologists believe that the tip of the iceberg has just been uncovered.

WHO ARE THE VICTIMS?

Victims of crime, particularly of interpersonal violence have been the most commonly defined victims needing assistance, although the strict definition includes any person who is overpowered by another and harmed without regard for his or her rights or feelings. In the 1970s the Law Enforcement Assistance Agency (LEAA) provided monies to state and district attorneys' offices around the country to establish victim/witness programs. Often lay people were hired to fill these positions. A major part of their job was to support victims who were going to be used as witnesses in order to prosecute cases. Although some victim/witness advocates had training in mental health skills, most did not. They provided good support and advocacy, but they quickly found themselves in over their heads when faced with serious psychological reactions. The sheer numbers of victim/witnesses who emerged once they learned of the assistance were unpredicted. In fact, the President's Commission on Victims of Crimes (1982) found that crime victims rated the services provided by these often minimally trained, overworked, but caring people to be most important in carrying forth a successful prosecution.

Rarely could the various victim/witness programs provide more than a minimal amount of money to cover some medical treatment in addition to the supportive information sharing they provided. Many had limits of $1000 or less, and all had restrictions of one kind or another. The American judicial system encourages the filing of a tort action in civil court to recover damages or receive compensation for pain and suffering inflicted by the offender. This assumes the offender has property that can be claimed. In Europe compensation programs have been adopted into the criminal court deliberations allowing for restitution and other financial schemes to be an alternative to prison. Because victims in both systems have little influence over the outcome of criminal proceedings, it is not known which, if any, has a more beneficial effect on the victim's mental health.

Some victimology scholars want the definition of the victim to go beyond the criminal justice system and be linked with the international human rights declarations. Elias (1985), for example, suggests that victimologists ignore much worldwide misery and political suffering when they only study victims of legally defined crimes. He restates much of the debate within the field about whether or not to include social injustices such as those relating to consumers, pollution, poverty, malnutrition, displacement, persecution, colonialization, and political crimes. There are those who favor including the victims' families and bystanders into the victim category while more liberally minded believe that the offender surely is a victim too.

Focusing on a narrower definition of victim permits relative ease of assessing needs while also diverting social pressure from calling for attention to other heinous abrogations of human rights. Recognizing the lively debate within this young social science (much of which can be read in *Victimology: An International Journal*), this chapter will concentrate on one type of victim who is extremely prevalent in our society: victims of interpersonal violence.

Defining Victims of Interpersonal Violence

Victims of interpersonal violence generally include women, children, and other less powerful members of our society. The national crime surveys in various countries suggest that poor, young, racial and ethnic, dark-skinned men are most likely to be both victims and perpetrators of violent crimes (Skogan, 1981; Steinmetz, 1985; Hough, 1985). Certainly the courts and prisons in this country are filled with these offenders. If, however, the violence that occurs behind the closed doors of families is included, then men are most likely the perpetrators and women and children, not other men, are the victims.

Epidemiological studies show that there is some physical abuse reported in at least 28 percent of American homes (Straus, Gelles, & Steinmetz, 1980). This is considered a serious underestimate by most researchers in the field who are more likely to agree with a 50 percent estimate (see, for example, Finkelhor, Gelles, Hotaling, & Straus, 1983). Within that family there are often multiple victims. One man may be abusing his wife and children. Victims may also become abusers; most commonly, boys who have been abused begin abusing their sisters, mothers, or grandparents (Kelly, 1983; Patterson, 1982; Walker, 1984a). In one homicide case in which I testified, the father shot and killed his 21-year-old son who had recently broken the father's arm and was terrorizing other family members. Psychological and physical abuse had existed earlier in this family where both parents admitted having a problem with controlling their alcohol drinking.

Patterson (1982), Reid, Taplin, and Lorber (1981), and their colleagues at the Oregon Social Learning Institute have been observing aggressive boys for over 15 years. They found that children from abusive families have a higher rate of aggressive behavior particularly when the abuse crosses gender lines. It is expected that more rapists and batterers will have come from that pool of aggressive boys upon follow-up, and they are making current efforts to find and study that population (John Reid, personal communication). Kalmuss (1984) has found that children who witness their parents' domestic violence are more likely to use physical abuse in their own family homes.

My own research on 400 battered women, reported in detail elsewhere (Walker, 1984a), shed some light on the interaction between family violence and other victims of crime. The women reported that over 75 percent of the batterers with whom they lived had also been arrested for other crimes, and approximately half of them had been convicted of whatever behavior for which they had been arrested. In 44 cases which ended in homicide, 90 percent of the batterers had previously been arrested (Browne, 1983). Half of the women interviewed at some time had had a relationship with a man who did not batter her. Only one-third of those nonabusive men had ever been arrested, and less than one-fifth had been convicted.

Family violence has been found to escalate to the point of homicide. It is more likely that the man will kill the woman or child even though more data are available on the battered woman who kills in self-defense (Browne, 1983; 1985; Jones, 1981; Walker, 1984b). New data from women in prison suggest that at least 80 percent of the inmates report physical or sexual abuse by men who loved them. Vulnerability of women to further abuse has been demonstrated in various studies, including Herman's (1981) study of incest victims, Hilberman's (1980) and Walker's (1984a) studies of battered women, and Carmen, Rieker, and Mills' (1984) study of a psychiatric inpatient population.

The interrelatedness between family violence and sexual assault has also been demonstrated, particularly with the work of Diana Russell. Her survey of over 900 women in San Francisco indicated that many woman were multiple rape victims. Often, they were first sexually assaulted at home by a family member (usually father or stepfather) or by a close family friend (Russell, 1984), then raped again by an acquaintance (sometimes a man whom they dated) and again by their husbands (Russell, 1982). Unlike stranger rapes, these sexual assaults are rarely brought to the attention of the criminal justice system.

Redefining family violence as part of the criminal justice system has been slow and has met with considerable resistance. Martin (1976) traces the long history of legal support for men to discipline their wives and children. The patriarchal nature of society stemming from early religious dogma has been determined by feminist social scientists to be a major cause of violence (see, for example, Dobash & Dobash, 1981). Although the laws in America have made wife beating a crime in every state for at least 50 years now, police have been reluctant to make arrests. Poorly kept records often combine bar and street fights with those occurring in the family in the domestic disturbance category. This gives rise to the prevalent, though often erroneous (Jones, 1981), police perception that they are in grave danger when responding to such a call. An inappropriate intervention, however, might refocus the violent offender or even the female victim's anger toward the police. Reports of the man being calm while the victim appears out of control or, even more frustrating, both insisting everything is fine by the time the police arrive have added to the difficulty in persuading law enforcement to take spouse abuse seriously.

The President's Commission on Victims of Crime chose to eliminate family violence from the crime victims to be studied in 1982. Grassroots groups protested during the testimony taken in most cities. In San Francisco, Mayor Diane Feinstein used her allotted time before the commission to discuss domestic violence. At the next hearing in Denver, a community coalition concerned with the needs of battered women simultaneously conducted additional hearings in the State Capitol, one floor above where the commission met. This was done to combat the commission's excuse that such testimony from battered women was too complicated to arrange.

By then Assistant U.S. Attorney General Lois Herrington, the commission chair, understood the point: Family violence created crime victims, and they couldn't be ignored. She allowed some testimony at the Denver, Houston, and St. Louis hearings, and the commissioners were fully convinced another round of hearings was needed to focus the seriousness of family violence as a national problem. They persuaded President Reagan to create the Attorney General's Task Force on Family Violence following the conclusion of the earlier commission. Its final report, released in the fall 1984, calls for the partnership between the criminal justice system and the mental health system in decreasing the severity and frequency of violence against family members. Herrington heads a new division within the Department of Justice to administer the funds created by the laws which resulted from her work.

THE VICTIMS' RIGHTS MOVEMENT

The President's Commission on Victims of Crime was formed at the height of the victims' rights movement. Fear of crime paralyzed large segments of the urban population (Burt & Katz, 1985). Many elderly persons refused to leave their homes, frightened of being attacked, while others lived with rows of deadbolts on their front doors and bars on their windows. News reports were filled with serial murders and other senseless killings. Moving to the suburbs or even to a part of rural middle America was not an effective escape. Children grew up, drank too much alcohol or abused drugs, and hurt themselves or others while driving.

While prosecutors blamed the liberalization of the rules of evidence for not convicting defendants at trials, it sometimes seemed that this was an excuse for inadequate investigations. Law and order factions vied for control, claiming the crime problem was due to too many defendants' rights. A broader perspective—that perhaps the widening economic gulf between the privileged class and others who coveted their material possessions and lifestyle coupled with less flexible social mobility—seemed too theoretical and not practical enough to be translated into social policy statements. Amid this societal unrest were born numerous citizen groups lobbying for victims' rights.

Supporting victims' rights is relatively safe for politicians as it catches both conservative and liberal sympathizers for different reasons. Recently, some victims' rights groups have become more formally organized into political action groups; for example, Mothers Against Drunk Driving (MADD) came about when victims and their families coalesced to encourage legislators to pass tougher drunk driving laws. Society's League Against Molesters (SLAM) helped enact numerous new laws to facilitate prosecution of child molesters while protecting the child. Particularly, they have urged that the courts admit into evidence statements by the child victim to others about the molestation, and substitution of a videotaped deposition of the child, conducted by a child psychologist, in lieu of the child's open court testimony. Other groups like Alabama's Victims of Crime and Leniency (VOCAL) have won victims the right to be present and heard at trials and sentencing. Some are demanding that persons considered dangerous to the community be denied bail, and others advocate longer prison sentences and abolition of parole (cf., Smith, 1985).

These groups can be found in a directory prepared by another relatively new organization, the National Organization for Victim Assistance (NOVA). They seem to provide victims a successful outlet through which to become reempowered. Energy that could be dissipated in anger or sadness which goes nowhere is channeled into building an organization to prevent further tragedy. At the same time the nation's prisons are so overcrowded, underfunded, and understaffed that inmates have won class-action lawsuits requiring more humane conditions. Although most states sentence offenders to prison for punishment and deterence, victims know that the persons who hurt them will be released soon enough to remember their prey. Rehabilitation—the only chance our society has to avoid revictimization—seems a larger task than can be done, given our limited financial resources.

Voluntary Organizations, Support Groups, and Self-Help Programs

The victims' rights movement has spawned the development of voluntary support groups in addition to the political action groups previously mentioned. These groups are better organized in European countries such as England and The Netherlands, probably because they do not have a psychotherapy industry as does the United States. The supporters of the British system suggest that the victim movement in Europe is less anti-offender and more oriented to the needs of the victims (Reeves, 1984). It is not expected to provide services for battered women, as that is done by the British National Women's Aid Federation.

Britain's National Association of Victim Support Services at the end of 1984 had 222 operational support schemes, as they call them, which are run by volunteers, who are not trained social workers or other mental health professionals, to avoid the view that victims are somehow damaged. Their philosophical statement acknowledges the sense of shared community responsibility for victims of crime because it is a problem that could cause unexpected emotional reactions. The volunteers are trained to make a home visit, offer practical help such as changing locks and repairing windows after a burglary, and to provide emotional support. It is expected that the victim's own resiliency and competence will quickly return, given this small amount of neighborly caring (Reeves, 1984). Similar support programs are operating in Holland; often they continue to meet in a group for some time after the crime.

Proponents agree that they are seen as helpful to victims of nonviolent crimes like burglary but question the effectiveness for rape victims and other crimes of interpersonal violence. Steinmetz's (personal communication) preliminary data analysis of the Dutch groups suggests that when it comes to physical and sexual assault, victims' emotional distress may even increase when they are in a group of mixed crime victims. Measurement problems, as discussed later, and the need for more highly skilled leaders or counselors trained to work with rape victims and battered women may explain his results.

The American experience with trained rape crisis volunteers indicates that immediate support and help with cognitively reframing of the sexual assault can speed up the victim's healing process. Battered-women task forces, safe homes, and shelters have provided training for many volunteers who report their successes in providing support for women victim/survivors (Schechter, 1982). Child-abuse self-help groups, such as Parents Anonymous and Parents United, for sexually abused children also provide emotional support in a group setting for victims and offenders.

All of these efforts depend on the unpaid volunteer to be there when a victim is in need. The sense of compassion that is shared between the volunteer advocate and the victim/survivor promotes healing. In fact, many victims become volunteers once they begin to regain their own emotional equilibrium. To be able to regain sufficient self-mastery and strength so as to give to another person in pain may complete the cycle from victim to survivor.

Sometimes, the healing process is facilitated when crime victims strive to regain their own sense of control and predictability. Weisaeth (1984) has studied posttraumatic stress reactions in victims of bank robberies. He found that bank tellers' emotional distress was dramatically reduced if a small piece of tape was put on a doorway in their view so they could better estimate the height of any future bank robbers. Their access to an alarm system also facilitated healing from the past trauma. Those working with victims find that personal competence, ability to interact with others, cognitive control, ability to direct one's attention, control of impulses and arousal level, and resistance to overwhelming terror are the qualities seen in those victims who quickly become survivors. But what about the others?

PSYCHOLOGICAL INTERVENTION

There has been little training of mental health professionals to provide services to victims of crime and violence. The American Psychological Association's Task

Force on the Victims of Crime and Violence (1984) does not adequately discuss the lack of knowledge about measurement or remediation of the resultant psychological impact. It is typical for therapists to avoid dealing with the disorganizing features of an attack, rationalizing their concentration on the victim's past history by reciting a maxim taught in graduate school about recovery being influenced by premorbid personality. Clients who have been victims discuss the questionable value of this process, but therapists say it helps, perhaps because it matches the skills they have to offer.

There are two specific and definable periods in a victim's recovery. The first is the acute crisis period which generally lasts for six to eight weeks and is characterized by feelings of dysphoria, disorganization, and disequilibrium. Various coping techniques can be employed to help victims attain stability. Crisis intervention strategies are most useful here and will be discussed later. Sometimes grassroots counselors are better at providing services during this period because they do not "clinicalize" the reactions of the victims. Victims need to believe they are not "going crazy," as they may fear, but rather are simply doing the best they can with a "crazy-making" situation. Mental health professionals may reinforce an illness model, either openly or inadvertently. The extreme nature of their feelings may scare both victims and their therapists. Thus appropriate training is mandatory.

The second period in recovery for violence victims is the long-term reorganization period where the assault is finally understood, accepted, and integrated within the rest of their lives. Vulnerability issues are raised as well as those the crisis brought forth which had not previously been resolved. Victims can use the crisis as an opportunity to promote their further psychological growth. Perhaps the desire to change certain areas in their lives came about because of a crisis precipitated by the violence. These areas can include life-cycle issues such as marital transition, career patterns, educational decisions, child raising, aging, or a whole set of existential issues concerning the meaning of life. Although therapeutic intervention may seem to progress in a manner similar to that of a nonvictim, the vulnerabilities and psychogenic coping strategies must be dealt with in an ongoing way, which then creates a different type of therapy.

One basic issue in providing therapeutic services for crime victims concerns the measurement of their psychological distress. Another issue is how therapeutic intervention facilitates or interferes with successful prosecution goals. A certain amount of nurturance has been demonstrated to assist in victim/witness testimony crucial to favorable prosecution (President's Commission on Victims of Crime, 1982). But it raises competing issues for legal and mental health professionals. On one hand, it is important to facilitate the victim's recovery. On the other hand, such recovery might make the witness less credible and therefore making it less possible to obtain an appropriate conviction, which in itself has been found to help victims recover.

Victims are usually able to accurately recount the details of what happened if their memory is not tampered with. The work of Loftus (1979) on adult memory and Goodman (1984) on children's memory suggest ways of preserving such evidence. Many therapeutic interventions encourage denial, repression, or simply forgetting of those details. Some even use hypnosis or other guided imagery techniques to help victims experience regaining control. Obviously, such interventions could be seen as witness tampering. Supportive therapy for victims, however, could also preserve their accurate testimony and reduce anxiety so that courtroom performance is enhanced. The continuous balance between preservation of the evidence for trial and restoration of the victims' mental health is a constant theme throughout the field of victimology. It becomes even more problematic in civil cases where speedy trial rules do not apply and trial dates can be set for two to four years after the traumatic incident.

Assessment and Measurement Issues

Assessment of the impact of psychological injuries from the violence has been a neglected area in psychology until recently. Much of what we know comes from victims' self-reports, which have the same difficulties as self-reports in any standard clinical evaluation. Numerous psychological symptoms are reported. These generally make up the diagnostic category of the Post-Traumatic Stress Disorders (PTSD)—acute, chronic, and delayed types. Complete descriptions can be found in the American Psychiatric Association's *Diagnostic and Statistical Manual of Mental Disorders* (3rd ed.) (DMS-III), (American Psychiatric Association, 1980, pp. 236–238). It describes an expected, albeit dysfunctional, reaction to an abnormal and trauma-producing situation. This is different from adjustment reactions which also classify similar psychological symptoms occurring from reactions to external situations. In the adjustment reactions, however, the symptomatology is stronger than deemed appropriate; in PTSD, the victims react in an expected way to a trauma which is seen as outside the usual human expectations.

PTSD victims usually demonstrate symptoms of anxiety and depression. Their interpersonal relationships are disrupted. They have sleep and eating disorders, a numbing of emotional responses, and a hypervigilance to cues of impending violence. They commonly experience flashbacks of the traumatic event when exposed to stimuli associated with its original occurrence. Panic reactions may occur as well as other phobic responses that originate from the trauma. It is not unusual for victims to report an avoidance of the general area where the violence occurred, or, if impossible, an increase in symptomatology when approaching the site or some other associated stimuli. Common physiological reactions include hyperventilation, skin rashes, gastrointestinal disorders, and skeletal muscle tension. If sexual assault has occurred, gynecological and urinary disturbances are frequent sequela.

Cognitive disturbances are also reported by crime victims. If the victimization has been repeated, such as occurs with battered women and incest victims, then confusion, concentration disorders, and difficulties in expressing one's thoughts are usual outcomes. Ruminating about possible ways to have avoided the attack is common; perhaps it is a way of regaining mastery over an unpredictable environment. Sometimes there are large gaps in the memory of the violence usually associated with life-threatening situations. The need to tell and retell the story may weary friends and therapists. But it does provide cognitive clarity and facilitates healing from the experience.

Assessment of the impact on affective functioning has been hampered by the lack of precise objective measurement tools. Standard anxiety and depression measures have so few items at the upper end of the scales that little discrimination has been possible although it is known that violence victims experience significant amounts of each. The Modified Fear Survey has been used by researchers measuring rape reactions (Kilpatrick, Veronen, & Resick, 1979; Kilpatrick, Resick, & Veronen, 1981), but no comparable measures have been used for other victims. Standardized tests, such as the Minnesota Multiphasic Personality Inventory (MMPI), have been misinterpreted, and violence victims erroneously have been diagnosed as schizophrenic or borderline because their distress level is so high on that test. From her research, Rosewater (1985) has isolated a battered woman's profile on the MMPI, which she warns must be differentiated from a more serious mental health diagnosis using subscale analysis and a good psychosocial history from the woman.

Although less structured personality tests such as the Rorschach, Thematic Apperception Test, and Sentence Completion test may reveal themes associated with vulnerability, violence, and specifics to the individual's trauma, victims who are unable to cope without repression and denial of violence may not be detected. In fact, it is not unusual for incest victims and others who were abused as children to totally repress the memories of details of the abuse. Burt and Katz (1985) have been trying to adapt other objective measures to the experience of rape victims.

Much more research is needed to develop appropriate objective measures of the psychological impact of violence. Corroboration of victim's self-reports, particularly in battering cases, has been done in homicide cases where battered women and children have killed their abusers. Witnesses who have seen bruises, heard verbal abuse, and perhaps observed some violence are more likely to testify if the batterer is dead. Their fear of repercussions and injury to themselves and their families often causes them to be reluctant to come forward in assault cases or civil actions. Children often corroborate family violence reports, too, though in child sexual abuse it is common for no one to know besides the offender and victim. Hospital records, doctors' notes, mental health reports, and police statements all are useful in corroborating victims' stories, especially in legal actions. From these records we have seen that offenders and victims typically minimize and underreport the severity of the abuse. A rule to guide therapists would be to remember that if there are different stories about what happened, the truth does not lie in the middle but is always worse than what is reported.

Dissociation or a splitting of the mind and body during repeated abusive incidents can cause a blunting of the affect from the experience. It is similar to a mild hypnotic trancelike state which protects victims from feeling the full impact of pain from their injuries. This may partly explain why so few battered women and child abuse victims seek medical assistance for their injuries unless they are very serious. But they do seek psychological assistance when the tension is lessened for a variety of other reasons; rarely is the violence a presenting problem unless therapy has been recommended by a volunteer advocate—or someone else who knows.

The difficulties with individual measurement of impact of violence continue into the large-scale surveys designed to assess incidence levels. The Bureau of Justice Statistics administers the National Crime Survey. The data are gathered by the U.S. Census Bureau. There have been numerous criticisms of the methodological limitations to collecting accurate data; most suggest that there is a serious underreport (see, for example, Skogan, 1981). The most recent concern was raised at a National Institute of Justice meeting of family violence and criminal justice researchers in October 1984. There it was revealed that family violence questions would be added to the next National Crime Survey, but no precautions were planned to be sure family members were interviewed separately from each other and from the abusive member. Such insensitivity to the added jeopardy of those who continue to live with their abusers places them in greater danger and compromises the survey results.

INTERVENTION WITH BATTERED WOMEN

A separate discussion of intervention techniques with victims of repeated violence who may still be living with their abusers is necessary when describing interventions with victim/survivors. Although my own research and clinical interventions have specialized in the area of battered women and child sexual assault victims, most of the focus is on the continued risk of further harm and the profound impact of betrayal when a loved and trusted person does the exploitation and violation.

Specific intervention techniques have been developed for battered women who have been repeatedly physically, sexually, and psychologically abused by men who love them. Support groups of other battered women represent one of the most useful therapy modalities, although sensitive individual therapy is also beneficial. Systems approaches and intrapsychic dynamic therapies are less useful than therapy based on feminist, supportive, and social learning theory principles. Elsewhere, it is suggested that any therapy that omits a feminist political approach will simply leave a woman vulnerable to becoming a victim of future violence while therapy that encourages a reempowerment of the victim may help change the underlying societal causes of violence against women (Walker, 1984a, 1984b, 1985).

Family systems therapy is often seen as a way to retrain women and men in conflict resolution, anger management, and stress reduction skills. Battered women are less able to heal their own wounds in this type of treatment as they must participate in assisting the batterer to control his violence. Research on male aggression suggests that social skills training in gender-specific groups may be more important in reversing the learned violence patterns (Sonkin, Martin, & Walker, 1985; Burgess, 1985). One therapist cannot meet both the woman's and the man's dissimilar needs because neither will trust neutrality. Despite some professionals' entrancement with this therapy approach, there are no long-term follow-up studies to demonstrate that it can stop the violence (see Bograd, 1984, for a complete discussion).

Termination of the relationship may be helpful in stopping the violence although the point of separation is often the most dangerous time. Forced sharing of children through joint custody or visitation arrangements perpetuates harassment and abuse, often leaving the children to cope with memories of severe violence both witnessed and experienced without a protective parent. Studies show that children who are so exposed are at greater risk to repeat the abusive cycle as adults (Kalmuss, 1984).

Adolescent children are especially sensitive to the pain of both parents and may switch loyalties back and forth when they perceive that neither parent can allow them to maintain a simultaneous relationship with the other. Appointment of a *guardian ad litem* or lawyer for the children and subsequent court-ordered psychological evaluations are viewed as intrusive and an impossible task because battered women (and the batterers at times) believe that they are being spied on and judged. Children old enough to take advantage of the situation often do so, manipulating both parents against each other. These long, costly, bitter battles continue the abuse and prevent the victim from being able to heal.

The repetition of the cycle of abuse encountered in battering relationships makes future violence fairly certain. Teaching the battered woman and the batterer to chart their own cycle, using data obtained during the gathering of an abuse history, is the best way to change the cycle. Details from the first significant battering incident remembered, the second one, the most typical, one of the worst, and the last one prior to this report gives a good analysis of the frequency and severity of the violence. Presence of weapons in the home, threats or use of them or other life-threatening actions, like choking, add to the lethality potential. Browne (1983) found that the most significant factors that differentiated between battered women who killed and those who did not were related to the men's perceived control of their violent behavior. Women who kill reported greater levels of violence both in frequency and severity, more concurrent child abuse, and a feeling of desperation—their terror was overwhelming.

Identifying a battered woman is sometimes problematic in a clinic or private practice if she does not seek treatment in a crisis period following an acute battering incident. Because it is characteristic for battered women to minimize or deny the violence, she may not start out by describing the abuse. Battered women may give other reasons for seeking assistance such as depression, anxiety disorders like panic attacks, or other PTSD symptoms. It is essential to routinely ask about previous assault experiences, sexual exploitation or abuse, and current risk for abuse. The women expect clinicians to discover the battering behavior and can accept that they do not fool a therapist easily. Carmen, Riecker, and Mills (1984) found that about half of the psychiatric inpatient population in a large teaching hospital reported abuse in their background or current situation. Such an abusive history was particularly common in those who were self-destructive and seemed unforgivably angry with themselves.

Many battered women need to progress slowly along their own timetable regardless of the pressures of urgency not to continue being hurt. Creating a "fire drill" safety plan is one way to make sure that her reactions will work should an acute battering incident occur. To create a safety plan, the woman must become aware of the clues that she may perceive when she is about to be battered. Often it is described as a certain look in his eyes; his face may turn a reddish color; he may begin mispronouncing words; perhaps he has a favorite expression or theme he harps on; maybe his fingers twitch and the like. Most women can describe such cues if they think about it in the context of a previous battering incident. The goal is to help her identify the clues earlier than she previously has done so she can escape before she is hurt.

The details of how she can escape need to be carefully thought through. If there is anything of value that she cannot leave without, care of the item must be arranged. A second set of car keys, some cash to tide her over temporarily, change for a telephone call, a list of important telephone numbers like the nearest battered woman shelter, a previously arranged signal with a neighbor, and a change of clothes for her and the children are all necessary to organize, whenever possible. A review of the exits in the house and ways to get the children to safety all must be rehearsed mentally, then verbally, and then in vivo. Encourage her to do a walk through like a "fire drill" at a low-risk time, perhaps when the batterer is not at home.

Such careful planning may not seem as appropriate as other issues for a therapy session, but it is for several reasons. First, it conveys the therapist's concern and sense of danger which challenges the woman's minimization and denial. Second, it prepares the woman to take action when needed to protect herself. Third, it allows the therapist to avoid making successful therapy dependent on a battered woman terminating her relationship. Fourth, it allows the therapist to let the woman have the control she needs with the knowledge she may be able to escape if a crisis develops.

The battered woman shelter is the key to successful intervention even if the woman never has to use it. The knowledge that there is a safe place which will protect women and children from further abuse gives women and therapists strength and courage. Most communities today have a system of safe homes or shelters organized by a battered woman task force which usually has communication with other state, regional, and national groups. They can be located through the National Coalition against Domestic Violence in Washington, D.C., and sometimes they are listed in the yellow pages under *battered women*. It is possible to get women and children hidden from one end of the country to another with this latest version of an "underground railroad." In rural areas many task force volunteers have divided their area into 25-mile checkpoints where drivers meet, exchange the woman, and go on to the next point.

Lawyers and mental health professionals, sympathetic and trained to work with victims of family violence, donate untold hours to organize community support systems or to directly intervene with individuals. Although there is always fear of retaliation by an angry batterer, abusive men who threaten and verbally abuse professionals rarely follow through. Still, precautions are suggested because batterers are unable to understand that helping a woman to stay safe is not synonymous with antagonism to him. In fact, most battered women advocates do not concern themselves with the men who are the batterers. They concentrate on keeping the woman safe. The issue of safety cannot be emphasized enough. Even otherwise good therapy without such precautions can place victims at further risk for harm.

Once the crisis period has passed and the woman is still in treatment it is possible to help her begin to look at the residual impact from her victimization. Supportive and noninterpretative therapy is important initially, focusing on adaptive behaviors which helped her survive the violence yet may be unnecessary at this time. To date, no data support the development of a particular personality pattern in victims (Walker & Browne, 1985). There are five specific areas where problematic behavior can be expected. They are issues with manipulation, expression of anger, dissociation, denial and minimization of the violence, and excessive compliance with an exaggerated willingness to please others. Understanding the survival benefit of these behaviors and validating the woman's perceptions without expecting her to do anything are important therapeutic strategies.

Battered women learn to manipulate as a necessary survival skill to maintain control in an unstable world. Some view them as excessively suspicious and even paranoid, but the hypervigilance serves to keep her safe and gives her warning clues of impending violence early enough so she can try to minimize the damage. Therapy can validate the woman's skill at recognizing danger cues and teach her when it is appropriate to manipulate people or the environment and when it is unnecessary. Assisting women in analyzing for evidence of their "superwomen" behavior can relieve some of the pressure. A battered woman expects to be able to do everything perfectly, just as her lover wants, and she feels guilty when she falls short of such impossible expectations. Sharing information openly, setting therapy goals together, and not struggling for control over traditional tension points, like appointment-setting hassles, can avoid major manipulations of the therapy. Nonetheless, battered women will test a therapist for ability to be manipulated, and those who do not meet the test will often not be given important information.

Dealing with the feelings which come from experiencing anger, whether it is one's own anger or that of someone else's directed toward oneself, is an area that causes problems for battered women. They associate confrontation with pain and harm from previous experience. So they withdraw from conflict. Often they bottle up their feelings of anger until it is expressed in one big outburst. Some battered women will not allow themselves to express anger for fear they will experience an uncontrollable rage. Indirect expression of anger such as sarcasm, passive-aggressive techniques, talking behind someone's back, and the like is more common. Therapy needs to concentrate on validating the woman's feelings of anger and separating feeling from expressing anger. Slowly she must deal with her reservoir of rage and legitimate feelings of injustice. She may get punished for expressing anger as most people do not like or accept an angry woman. Helping her deal with safe interpersonal issues and anger is especially appropriate in group treatment. Therapists must deal with their own tolerance of women's anger which makes men especially uncomfortable so that they react by trying to close off the anger too soon.

Dissociation or a splitting of mind and body frequently occurs in repeated abuse victims as a way to dull the immediate pain from the beating. It is possible to ascertain severity level from descriptions of the dissociative state. As the abuse gets worse, the dissociative state lasts longer and occurs more frequently. Life-threatening events often cause partial psychogenic amnesia and intermittent memory loss. Of course, the most dramatic is the multiple personality who has generally suffered great physical, sexual, and psychological abuse when a young child. But battered women also use the same hypnotic trancelike states to protect their psyche without the fragmentation of personality. They also telescope events by reporting things that have happened out of time sequence. This can cause great difficulties when trying to recreate a homicide scene.

It is important that therapy strategies are designed to help battered women understand PTSD and reassure them that their out-of-body experiences are not indications that they are really crazy. Self-control over the mild hypnoticlike trances can be taught by using hypnosis or relaxation training. Guided imagery can facilitate healing some of the split. Imaging different, more empowering conclusions to battering incidents can also promote changing a victim into a survivor. Use of body awareness techniques and body therapy can also heal the split. Jogging, aerobics, or even learning to use bubble baths or lotions can help a battered woman get back in touch with her body. This area can be an initial point for therapy, even with women still living with their batterers, as it helps them regain some control.

Denial and minimization has been discussed earlier. Battered women cannot acknowledge the pain and danger or they would have to give up hope the men will change. For many battered women, a state of confusion may result from the denial and minimization of the abuse. Therapeutic strategies to reduce these effects include validation of her experience of the abuse directly following the second phase of the acute battering incident when minimization is least likely to occur; keeping a journal of her thoughts, feelings, and reactions to the abuse; pictures of injuries; honest feedback from child witnesses; and documentation of continued harassment. The latter can be easily done by using a telephone-answering machine to record angry confrontations. The therapist can listen to the tape later.

The final area that can help identify therapy issues for a battered woman is her excessive compliance and exaggerated willingness to please, particularly those in an authority position. This behavior is widely reported in other victims of trauma such as prisoners of war, hostages, and concentration camp survivors. Its purpose is to calm the abuser to lessen the probability of an attack. Battered women may return to live with the batterer, forgive him, or respond pleasantly as one way of trying to minimize further harm. These responses are misinterpreted as being inconsistent with fear, although they are strategies to reduce the anxiety. Women will engage in rescuing behavior like bailing the batterer out of jail, covering up for him, or continuing to take care of him in other ways. Their trust level of others is very low as they explore their feelings of betrayal, of being hurt and rejected by the person who loved them.

Therapy must help battered women to recognize the clues they get when they are in danger and to develop an adequate response and self-protection. There must also be a differentiation between sexual seduction and pleasant cross-gender friendships. It is not unusual for battered women to try to please men by using seductive behavior. They say they do not want sex, but rather they want to be nice to the men with whom they flirt. This behavior is obvious with male therapists.

In addition to the previously mentioned behaviors displayed by battered women, some show symptoms of more severe emotional dysfunction. Multiple victimization may have damaged the woman's self-esteem so that she is unable to function adequately. Carmen et al. (1984) found that battered women who were hospitalized in a psychiatric inpatient unit were likely to have a wide range of diagnoses. Perhaps one category is all that is needed to capture the trauma of domestic violence victims.

BATTERED WOMEN AND THE CRIMINAL JUSTICE SYSTEM

Battered women's reactions to the new criminal justice policies have been interesting to watch. Following the publication of research findings that arrest and a night in jail is the most successful police strategy for deterrence (Sherman & Berk, 1984), many law enforcement agencies have changed their policies to reflect an aggressive pro-arrest stance. The Denver project is similar to most other cities with good community cooperation. The police chief changed the rules to a pro-arrest policy upon probable cause from a previous pro-mediation, avoid arrest policy. The county court judges removed domestic violence assault from the bonding schedule requiring a stay in jail until the next regularly scheduled arraignment hearing. A no-contact order is entered at the time bond is granted. Such a policy change is permissible under Colorado law for crimes of violence.

Domestic violence calls have increased to 200 per week. There are at least two times as many arrests, which have gone from 50 to 100 per week, and the jails are full. Less than 10 percent of the arrests were women. Almost all of the women arrested were in a battering relationship. Their batterers accused them of physical abuse, too, and the police found probable cause to take them in. Evidence is carefully documented including photographs. Paramedics are called to the scene to document injuries even if the woman refuses treatment. The officer signs the complaint, not the female victim, and only the city attorney can decide if charges are to be dropped.

The batterers are permitted to plead guilty (more than 50 percent now do so) and, if found eligible, have their sentences probated to 24 or 48 weeks in a special group therapy program for abusive men (AMEND). The battered women are more likely to cooperate and testify if it goes to trial because they want the men to get into treatment. But there is enough evidence to go to trial even if the woman is uncooperative. Experts can explain why she does not testify. An advocate makes contact with the victim as soon as possible, usually before the arraignment hearing, and gives her information about the new program and explains her options. Referrals to qualified and trained counselors/therapists or shelters are made, if appropriate. The advocates monitor the project to see that cases do not fall through the cracks in the system. Probation is revoked when men reoffend, and they are sent to jail for the rest of their terms.

Therapy for batterers is different from what is typically practiced. Confidentiality is not possible given the mandatory nature of treatment. Battered women are called on, usually monthly, to see if there has been contact and if any violence has reoccurred. A behavioral and practical approach is more useful than insight-oriented treatment. The primary goal is to stop the violence. Improved social skills, stress and anger management, and conflict resolution tactics are built into the therapy as is some consciousness raising about male-female sex role stereotypes (see Sonkin,

Martin, & Walker, 1985, and Sonkin & Durphy, 1981, for a more complete discussion).

One of the important features of this program is the sense of relief felt by the victim. She is better able to take care of herself since she knows she has a compassionate justice system to support her. Many of the advocates are formerly battered women who choose to volunteer to assist another woman. As mentioned earlier, such advocacy helps more victims progress to a survivor role. Only time will tell if such a new policy will reduce the escalation of domestic violence.

Sometimes battered women become involved with the criminal justice system themselves. Recent work with women in prison suggests that over three-fourths of inmates have been victims of abuse. Some were physically abused as children, others sexually abused, and even more were battered women. Many were in prison for crimes committed under duress—trying to avoid another beating or protect a batterer. But few used their duress as part of their defenses.

The case of Francine Hughes, who was found not guilty of killing her abusive husband by reason of insanity, was highly publicized by the 1984 television movie, *The Burning Bed*, adapted from the book by the same title (McNulty, 1980). A more detailed account of the psychological examination has been provided by the examining psychologist (Berkman, 1980). However, insanity defenses are very difficult and often unsuccessful (Jones, 1981). The battered woman's self-defense assertion has provided greater relief when symptoms of the battered woman syndrome are observed, and the theory can be applied to explain what might otherwise not appear to be traditional self-defense (Thyfault, Browne, & Walker, 1987).

Most women who kill abusive partners do so in self-defense. Expert witness testimony at their trials can reduce murder charges or find that the women were justified in killing to save their own lives (Walker, 1984c). These women need psychological help with their grieving, as they are in the peculiar position of having become widows by their own acts. New programs for battered women in prisons are beginning, especially as the states are resolving class-action lawsuits seeking to improve prison conditions. Statewide coalitions of battered women are making efforts to provide such services whenever possible (Bauschard, 1986).

SOCIAL POLICY CHANGES

Victims of interpersonal violence recently have received much more attention and validation. They are seen as having been psychologically injured in addition to their suffering from other trauma. Much of the change occurred around sexual assault and spouse abuse cases. The intersection between the legal and mental health systems has occurred with issues in which the victim is often a woman. It is interesting to speculate why this policy change happened in this fashion.

In the early and middle 1970s the women's movement mounted a strong campaign to change the way rape prosecutions were handled. Too often the female victim was injured a second time by the legal process (APA, 1984). Grassroots rape crisis centers sprang up; volunteers went to the hospitals, police stations, and wherever there was a rape victim; and police became more sensitive to victims who did not behave in stereotypical ways. As more women reported their experiences, it became obvious that rape trauma produces long-lasting psychological injury. Sexual assault became defined in more inclusive terms so that date, acquaintance, and even marital rape were found to be traumatic. We began to understand it as a crime of violence and power and recognized that men in power relationships can and do sexually exploit women.

Women who have suffered damage began to sue those who harmed them in civil court. Men in positions of trust, such as educators, therapists, lawyers, and the like, were found to be sexually abusing women. Now they are more likely to lose their licenses to practice and have to pay large damage awards, although the process is long and complicated and usually traumatic for the victim. Although many women so exploited do not consider themselves victims initially, after a time the effects begin to emerge (Bouhoustos, 1984). Often sexual assault victims go after third parties for negligence or malpractice so that they can get monetary relief when the offender has no assets. It is hoped that the economic consequences of violating a woman will serve as a deterrent to men.

National policy toward victims of violence certainly has changed within the past decade. Most of the victims have been battered and sexually abused women. The courts are beginning to listen to women's stories, taking into account the different way women and all violence victims experience the world (Walker, 1984c). It is possible to expect full recovery from most violent attacks. Perhaps, we may even approach the eradication of violence in our lifetimes.

REFERENCES

American Psychiatric Association. (1981). *Diagnostic and statistical manual of mental disorders* (3rd ed.). Washington, DC: Author.

American Psychological Association. (1984). *Task force on the victims of crime and violence: Final report*. Washington, DC: Author.

Attorney General's Task Force on Family Violence. (1984). Washington, DC: U.S. Attorney General.

Bauschard, L. (1986). *Voices set free: Battered women*. St. Louis: Women's Self-Help Center.

Berkman, (1980). The State of Michigan versus a battered wife. *Bulletin of the Menninger Clinic, 44*, 603–616.

Bograd, M. (1984). Family systems approaches to wife battering: A feminist critique. *American Journal of Orthopsychiatry, 54*, 558–568.

Bouhoustos, J. (1984). Sexual intimacy between psychotherapists and clients. In L. E. A. Walker (Ed.), Women and mental health policy (207–227). Beverly Hills: Sage.

Browne, A. (1983). *Battered women who kill*. Unpublished dissertation, The Union of Experimental Colleges and Universities.

Browne, A. (1985). Assault and homicide at home: When battered women kill. In L. Saxe & M. L. Saks (Eds.), *Advances in applied social psychology: Vol. 3*. Hillsdale, NY: Lawrence Erlbaum.

Burgess, R. (1985). Social incompetence as a precipitant to and consequence of child maltreatment. *Victimology, 10*, 72–86.

Burt, M. R., & Katz, B. L. (1985). Rape, robbery, and burglary: Responses to actual and feared criminal victimization with a special focus on women and the elderly. *Victimology, 10*, 325–358.

Carmen, E. (Hilberman), Rieker, P. P., & Mills, T. (1984). Victims of violence and psychiatric illness. *American Journal of Psychiatry, 141*, 378–383.

Conte, J. R. (1985). The effects of sexual abuse on children: A critique and suggestions for future research. *Victimology, 10*, 110–130.

Dobash, R. E., & Dobash, R. P. (1981). *Violence against wives.* New York: Free Press.

Elias, R. (1985). Transcending our social reality of victimization: Toward a new victimology of human rights. *Victimology, 10*, 6–25.

Finkelhor, D. (1986). *A source book on child sexual abuse.* Beverly Hills: Sage.

Finkelhor, D., & Browne, A. (1983). *The traumatogenic impact of child sexual abuse.* Paper presented at the Second Family Violence Researcher's Conference, Durham, NH.

Finkelhor, D., Gelles, R., Hotaling, G., & Straus, M. (1983). *The dark side of families.* Beverly Hills, CA: Sage.

Goodman, G. (1984). Children's testimony in historical perspective. *Journal of Social Issues, 40*, 9–32.

Herman, J. L. (1981). *Father-daughter incest.* Cambridge, MA: Harvard University Press.

Hilberman, E. (1980). Overview: The wife beater's wife reconsidered. *American Journal of Psychiatry, 137*, 1336–1347.

Hough, M. (1985). The impact of victimization: Findings from the British Crime Survey. *Victimology, 10*, 488–497

Jones, A. (1981). *Women who kill.* New York: Holt, Rinehart & Winston.

Kalmuss, D. (1984). The intergenerational transmission of marital aggression. *Journal of Marriage and the Family, 51*, 11–19.

Kelly, J. (1983). *Treating child abusive families.* New York: Plenum.

Kilpatrick, D. G., Resick, P. A., & Veronen, L. J. (1981). Effects of a rape experience: A longitudinal study. *Journal of Social Issues, 37*, 105–122.

Kilpatrick, D. G., Veronen, L. J., & Resick, P. A. (1979). Assessment of the aftermath of rape: Changing patterns of fear. *Journal of Behavioral Assessment, 1*, 133–148.

Kosberg, J. I. (1983). The special vulnerability of elderly parents. In J. I. Kosberg (Ed.), *The abuse and maltreatment of the elderly: Causes and preventions.* Littleton, MA: John Wright—PSG, Inc.

Kosberg, J. I. (1985). Victimization of the elderly: Causation and prevention. *Victimology, 10*, 379–396.

Loftus, E. (1979). *Eyewitness testimony.* Cambridge: Harvard University Press.

Martin, D. (1976). *Battered wives.* San Francisco: Glide.

McNulty, F. (1980). *The burning bed.* New York: Harcourt, Brace, Jovanovich.

Patterson, G. (1982). *Coercive family processes.* Eugene, OR: Castaglia.

President's Commission on Victims of Crime. (1982). Washington, DC: U.S. Government Printing Office.

Reeves, H. (1984). *Victim support schemes: The United Kingdom model.* Paper presented at the NATO Conference on Victimology, Lisbon, Portugal.

Reid, J., Taplin, P., & Lorber, R. (1981). A social interactional approach to the treatment of abusive families. In R. B. Stuart (Ed.), *Violent behavior: Social learning approaches to prediction, management, and treatment*. New York: Bruner/Mazel.

Rosewater, L. B. (1985). Feminist interpretation of traditional testing. In L. B. Rosewater & L. E. A. Walker (Eds.), *Handbook of feminist therapy: Psychotherapy issues for women* (pp. 266–273). New York: Springer.

Russell, D. E. (1982). *Rape in marriage*. New York: Macmillan.

Russell, D. E. H. (1984). *Sexual exploitation: Rape, child sexual abuse, and workplace harassment*. Beverly Hills, CA: Sage.

Schechter, S. (1982). *Women and male violence: The visions and struggles of the battered woman's movement*. Boston: SouthEnd.

Sherman, L. W., & Berk, R. A. (1984). *The Minneapolis domestic violence experiment*. Washington, DC: Police Foundation Reports.

Skogan, W. G. (1981). *Issues in the measurement of victimization*. Washington, DC: U.S. Department of Justice, Bureau of Statistics, NCJ74682.

Smith, B. L. (1985). Trends in the victim's rights movement and implications for future research. *Victimology, 10*, 34–43.

Sonkin, D., & Durphy, M. (1981). *Learning to live without violence: A workbook for men*. San Francisco: Glide.

Sonkin, D., Martin, D., & Walker, L. E. A. (1985). *The male batterer*. New York: Springer.

Steinmetz, C. (1985). Bystanders of crime: Some results from a national survey. *Victimology, 10*, 441–460.

Straus, M. A., Gelles, R. A., & Steinmetz, S. K. (1980). *Behind closed doors: Violence in the American family*. Garden City, NY: Anchor/Doubleday.

Thyfault, R. K., Browne, A., & Walker, L. E. A. (1987). When battered women kill. In D. Sonkin (Ed.), *Domestic violence on trial*. New York: Springer.

Viano, E. (Ed.). (1976). *Victims and society*. Washington, DC: Visage.

Walker, L. E. A. (1979). *The battered woman*. New York: Harper & Row.

Walker, L. E. A. (1983). Victimology and psychological perspectives of battered women. *Victimology: An International Journal, 8*, 82–104.

Walker, L. E. A. (1984a). *The battered woman syndrome*. New York: Springer.

Walker, L. E. A. (1984b). Battered women, psychology, and public policy. *American Psychologist, 39*, 1178–1182.

Walker, L. E. A. (1984c). *Women and mental health policy*. Beverly Hills, CA: Sage.

Walker, L. E. A. (1985). Feminist therapy with victims/survivors. In L. B. Rosewater & L. E. A. Walker (Eds.), *Handbook of feminist therapy: Psychotherapy issues with women*. New York: Springer.

Weisaeth, L. (1985). Psychiatric studies in victimology in Norway: Main findings and recent developments. *Victimology, 10*, 478–487.

Weisaeth, L. (1984b). *Stress reactions to an industrial disaster*. Oslo, Norway: The University of Oslo Psychiatric Institute.

PART SIX

Professional Issues

CHAPTER 25

The Ethics of Forensic Psychology

ALLEN K. HESS

Man is the only animal that blushes, or needs to.

MARK TWAIN

Trenchant as always, Twain addresses the idea that people have reflective capacities. This seemingly simple observation leads to the notion that behaviors or actions are manifestations of values, recognized or unrecognized, predisposing the person toward actions. Philosophically, the study of values, termed axiology, includes aesthetics and ethics—the study of the relationship between actions and values.

This chapter will describe the nature of ethical conflicts arising in forensic psychology. Ethical dilemmas from actual cases will illustrate dilemmas in ethical judgment, and references will be provided for issues requiring more attention than can be given here. Finally, fundamental value systems characterizing Western thought will be presented in helping the reader to understand his or her own values and to negotiate ethical shoals.

VALUE CONFLICT AND CHOICE

One night one of my children had a nightmare. The next morning I asked her what her nightmare, which had awoken us, was about. She smiled and declined to tell me. I teased her and said that of course she could tell me, I am a psychologist. She grinned and said, "You are my daddy," recognizing both a role conflict and the priority of filial values over professional values for both of us.

Intrapersonal Role Conflicts

In daily life, we occupy various roles. Each of the roles entails our assuming complex matrices of values from which our decisions and actions flow, often without our awareness of their connections. Sometimes we are aware of our role conflicts as when a psychotherapy supervisee of mine let me know that his wife's judgment was mistaken on a real estate venture. Her company managed my pension plan, and she

653

had urged me to invest in the real estate purchase. The dilemma of how to make a financial decision, knowing the information was gained in the confidential relationship of supervision, was an anguishing one. Obviously, I could not "forget" this datum which could affect my family's well-being, nor would I want to be in the position of using the information obtained from the confidential supervisory relationship.

Twain captures in his insight on the moral reflectiveness of people that ethical dilemmas are not easily solved, mental calculus problems, as Bentham and the social utilitarians would have us believe in their dictum: "the greatest good for the greatest number." Rather, the weighing of values, their planes [i.e., "Never help a killer" may not apply if I consider it a higher plane or greater good to help train police officers in firearms proficiency, or if I offer postshooting, trauma-reducing counseling sessions to police officers (Loo, 1986)], the process or means, and the ends, all impinge to create the type of moral angst or "fear and trembling" that Kierkegaard felt (1968).

Kierkegaard posed the problem of the suspension of the ethical using the story of Abraham's willingness to sacrifice Isaac. The father bound his son and raised his knife preparing to kill Isaac, according to the Lord's demand for supreme faith. Kierkegaard describes that moment as Abraham's stepping beyond the ethical realm. The tragic hero remains within ethical boundaries, reaching for higher expressions of the ethical as Kohlberg (1976) claims levels five and six describe. In contrast, Kierkegaard says the "tragic hero is great by reason of his moral virtue, Abraham is great by reason of his personal virtue." Abraham's is a personal virtue, not a universal one (involving a complete personal commitment rather than an adherence to some code of professional conduct such as the "welfare of the client" or the "social good"). This is a dilemma we will face again when we consider the "whistleblower" and exposure of agency wrongdoing. For now, we note that professional ethics codes call for standards of conduct, at the least implying some universality to the imperatives. Also, note that to rely on personal virtue only belies what we know of human nature and undermines professional and societal regulation, leading to moral nihilism. It may be instructive to consider some particular ethical conflicts and see if we can further define this ethical dialectic.

Interpersonal Role Conflict

Ethical dilemmas can arise from the different value bases of actors in the criminal justice drama. The battle between the guards' mission of security and the correctional psychologists' of rehabilitation can lead to conflict. Consider one chief psychologist who solved the dilemma by leaking selected confidences gathered by his staff to the warden. He justified his actions by the "good rapport" his psychology service had with the warden. However, prisoner tensions ran high in this modern, clean facility, and psychology staff turnover was unseemingly high considering the good salaries, benefits, and physical state of the facility.

An illustration of interrole conflict creating ethical tensions concerns the expert witness. The lawyer is concerned with winning; whereas, the expert witness, occupying that role by virtue of the scientific status accorded that role (Blau, 1984), is concerned with a balanced, objective view of truth. Anyone with experience in the expert witness role, and the pretrial or prehearing rehearsal with the attorneys, is familiar with both subtle and heavy-handed pressure to present evidence in a certain light. The expert witnesses can help themselves by (1) clarifying on the initial telephone contact that findings will be presented in accord with objectivity, the harmful with the beneficial (the attorney has the option of not retaining the expert, although once witness lists are given to the court, the other side can access the witness), and (2) noting when the pronoun *we* is used by the expert when referring to the attorney and expert witness as a team, as in "we can win this case." At that point one must question one's own objectivity.

Another illustration of interrole conflict can be seen in the community mental health psychologist who opens a storefront outreach center for youth who are prone to drug abuse, in an effort to divert the youth from addiction. Suppose, too, that the resistance which was arising among store owners and neighboring residents quickly and inexplicably died down. After six weeks the psychologist finds that police are keeping the storefront under surveillance, quieting neighborhood fears but raising critical issues of credibility for the storefront center. The police tell the psychologist that they know some of the friends of the center's clients are drug dealers, and while the police will not touch those they know to be center clients, they are duty bound to follow leads and to arrest drug dealers. In fact, the police ask the psychologist what assurance they have that if they, in effect, provide a sanctuary, the psychologist can assure them the center is not a "dealing pad." This places the psychologist in the position of being a potential law enforcement officer, on one hand, or having the center jeopardized by neighborhood resistance and the threat of continual police raids if he or she does not cooperate.

These dilemmas are derived from structural conflicts between roles. Administrative restructuring of roles needs to occur, for example, to get the police, the psychologist, or both to be able to suspend an enforcement part of their role so the preventative-rehabilitative center can function as such and not as an ethical snare.

Abusive Exercise of Power

The person in an authority position can act within the bounds of his or her authority but exercise it to an abusive extent. For example, a prison administrator can assign a social worker with a heart condition the task of interviewing newly admitted convicts residing in a multitier cell block, entailing the continual climbing of stairways. In another case, a head of a community treatment center assigned a single, attractive female therapist to evening group therapy sessions with male drug addicts in a slum-based locale. A female receptionist was the only other staff person on duty at the time, thus setting up a rape situation. These actual examples are neither merely contemporary nor, regrettably, unique. Melville's *Billy Budd* depicts Claggart's villainy in abusing Billy Budd within the rules, and Captain Veres, in trying to emulate Lord Nelson, hangs Billy Budd from the yardarm for Claggart's murder. Few will want to emulate Billy Budd's fate. In a later section we shall consider ethical options in dealing with abusers of power.

AREAS OF ETHICAL VULNERABILITY

This section will address some of the ethical dilemmas confronting the psychologist involved in forensic areas. The dilemmas will be illustrated by case material.

Expert Witness

There seem to be three key elements involved in performing as a competent expert witness: preparation, preparation, and preparation. First, the client needs to be identified. Is the client an attorney or another party (prosecutor, defendant, plaintiff, or social agency or court)? Second, after getting a thumbnail sketch of the issues from the client, the psychologist must determine what service he or she can offer the client and what are the client's expectations of the expert? This phase is integral because if the client cannot articulate a compelling role for the witness or if the expert witness cannot clarify the skills he or she can bring to bear on the problem, as well as the limitations to those skills, during this early, reconnaissance phase, it may be best for all parties for the client to seek another expert. Third, the terms (fees, expenses), who will pay (attorney, client), when payment will be rendered, times the expert will be needed, times the expert will be unavailable, and the scope of the project must be clear to all parties. Blau (1984) sagely suggests these terms be reduced to contractual forms, which he presents in his book. Even if one party hires the expert, there will be several constituencies one needs to determine, much like in a family therapy case. Who yields what kind of power, and what are the "real" questions that need answering? The issues may not be known to the various parties.

Fourth, the psychologist needs the latitude to operate (access to key figures in a case) and then to educate the client as to the findings. It is perfectly permissible for the attorney to rehearse the questions the witness will be asked in deposition and in court as well as questions the other side's attorney may raise. The attorney may caution the witness when the witness is unwittingly using language that has particular meaning in a courtroom or hearing room, such as a Social Security or worker disability hearing. However, psychologists must be true to their findings. The prepared psychologist will be familiar with two literatures: the content area and the expert witness (Blau, 1984; Singer & Nievod, Chapter 20 of this volume).

The content area, because of the nature of science, will have contesting theories, differing methodologies, and ongoing debates. The strengths and weaknesses of the various positions should be well known to the expert. The expert should be able to render a clear opinion with a fair degree of confidence, should be able to articulate and support this opinion with extant literature, and should be able to defend it against opposing theories. A good rehearsal strategy is to anticipate that the other side will present the leading proponent of the opposing school of thought to argue (the root of the term *forensics*) against the witness. That would be the worst that can happen. Most likely what does happen will be within the preparation of the witness. The best source of hostile questions to use in preparing for the pitfalls in one's literature is Ziskin's (1970) book in which his express purpose is to show that psychiatric and psychological evidence "does not meet reasonable criteria of admissibility, and should not be admitted in a court of law and if admitted should be given little or no weight" (p. 1). Moreover, the plan of his book is

> to supply the attorney with a systematic and methodical basis for objecting to the admission of psychiatric and psychological evidence by utilizing the scientific literature of their own fields. In the event the objection fails, and the testimony is admitted the same information can be utilized to educate judge and jury and to systematically and methodically reduce the credibility of psychiatrists and clinical psychologists to the point where it is difficult to that a judge or jury attach any weight whatsoever to their testimony. (p. 6)

Robinson (1980) provides trenchant critique about the growing role of psychologists in the courtroom. Karl Menninger (1966) concludes, "What all courts should do, what society should do, is exclude all psychiatrists from the courtroom!" (p. 138). However psychology has become established with a scientific corpus of knowledge in many areas, and courts need access to this information. As Diamond (1983) argues, the roles, functions, and capacities in which the expert witnesses testify may need adjustment, but the courts have long recognized the need for experts.

Freud was less intrepid in forensic arenas than he was in other areas. Though he mentioned the gathering of evidence via psychoanalysis, he refused lavish offers from the *Chicago Tribune*, including $25,000 (in 1927 dollars) and sole use of a chartered ocean liner, to observe and comment on the Leopold and Loeb trial (Jones, 1957). For the more intrepid, Silverman (1969) presents a useful essay on clarifying one's concept of the role of determinism in psychological theory since it may present problems concerning testifying about choice and responsibility. Louisell (1955) suggested the psychologist be a witness, not an advocate, candid in one's degree of certainty, clear in language, frank in admitting limitations of one's specialty, not scornful of the judicial process regardless of his or her opinion of particular judges, juries, or attorneys, confident though not cocksure, and proud of his or her profession while humble about one's human limitations. With these admonitions in mind, let us see how particular problems can arise.

Courtroom Preparation and Two Capital Murder Cases

An attorney contacted the psychologist and said he needed an assessment regarding the client's abilities. Despite assurances that they would have ample time to discuss the results and the attorney's theory of defense, only a hurried conference took place just before the psychologist's appearance in court. On the stand, the attorney questioned the psychologist in detail about the defendant's ability to understand the four components of the Miranda warning issue upon arrest, given the defendant's low measured intelligence quotient. The jury found the defendant not guilty since critical information had been obtained by the police from the defendant, who could not comprehend the Miranda warning.

A colleague told the psychologist that the attorney's behavior had been unusual and that the attorney was usually scrupulously prepared. Several months later the attorney called again on another murder case. The attorney told the psychologist that this time they would schedule a pretrial conference to prepare the strategy of the psychologist's involvement. The attorney asked for a personality assessment but said he could not specify a defense until they discussed the defendant. After assessment, the attorney did not schedule a conference nor could he be reached by the psychologist for such a conference because of his court calendar. This time the defendant was not as lucky as the first one. The psychologist was asked on the stand about the defendant's paranoid propensities, given the death of his brother and subsequent death threats against himself from the deceased whom he then killed in presumed self-defense. Given no hint of the defense theory, the psychologist had not tested specifically for threat sensitivity and had to examine on the stand his test data on this issue. The psychologist subsequently informed the attorney of his unavailability in the future.

The reader may wish to go over their profession's ethics code as an exercise to see which principles would be violated if subsequent cases were accepted from this attorney given his modus operandi. The American Psychological Association's (1981) ethical principles which may be breached include No. 1 (The psychologist is responsible for the appropriate use of his or her services, and these are rendered at the highest professional standards), No. 6 (welfare of the consumer—in this case, the defendant), and No. 8 (misuse of assessment techniques).

Preparation and an Expert with No Role

The psychologist received a phone call from a woman pleading that the psychologist help her brother. He was fighting to keep his four children from his murderous wife's custody in an impending divorce trial. The psychologist suggested a meeting be arranged by the brother between the brother, the brother's attorneys, and the psychologist. At the meeting one attorney was skeptical of psychologists, while the other sought the psychologist's expertise. The brother thought the psychologist was desperately needed to go through a 4-inch-thick pile of the wife's psychiatric hospital records and unravel the technical jargon and then help determine her dangerousness to the children. In agreement with the other parties, the psychologist consented to serve as a consultant, not examining her so he would not be called as an expert witness.

The psychologist proceeded to explain the records regarding how they related to the wife's stability and her ability to care for herself and the children. Also, the psychologist, attorneys, the husband, and his sister discussed the possible strategies of the wife's attorneys and the flaws of the strategies, and ways to bring this out from her expert witnesses. The psychologist researched the types of children that resulted from mothering by a person with the wife's disorder. This included 10-point intelligence quotient deficits compared with children of schizophrenic mothers, and elevated suicide risks in the children of such mothers.

At court the skeptical attorney tried most of the case. He consulted the psychologist twice in the week-long trial, not using the information either time. The psychologist kept the husband and his family (sisters, parents, and relatives) informed as to the proceedings when they had questions. Otherwise, he was not used at all. Later the psychologist learned the skeptical attorney had a serious, adverse experience with a psychologist to whom he attributed the loss of a family life due to undetected suicidal intention.

Was the psychologist in violation of any ethical principles? Probably not, but the waters of forensic practice are spotted with dangerous shoals. The advent of new roles and the complex relationships between sets of clients require the forensic psychologist to travel carefully. Fersch (1979) and Shapiro (1984) can provide helpful guides.

Juries for a Just Cause

When a scientific enterprise is used in the service of social ends (Zimring & Hawkins 1971), many ethical questions are raised. Regarding jury selection, the first question is can psychologists predict juror decision making any better than seasoned attorneys? If not, then claims to the effect that social scientists can provide an advantage would be unethical and possibly illegal. If such services can be shown to be effective, then other issues arise. For example, to what degree can such involvement unfairly tip the scales of justice? If a psychologist is highly adept at helping the attorneys with juror selection and, to further his or her particular philosophy, elects to help certain causes, is the psychologist subordinating justice and fairness to further his or her own sociopolitical agenda in a way that compromises professional ethics? Probably not, but proceeding a step further, what if the psychologist takes such cases knowing the party engaging the psychologist is guilty of the charge? Again, particular circumstances beg a definitive conclusion, since the legality and morality of charges themselves may be at issue as in the case of Jim Crow laws supporting racial segregation. Then the higher cause of trying the justness of such laws in a court of law is served.

Finally, such a psychologist might be aware that after serving in a dozen such trials, should they serve as an expert witness or in offering congressional testimony, their position as an unbiased expert would be severely compromised. Such a situation happened to a noteworthy psychologist who was asked, "Sir, do you testify *only* for plaintiffs in prisoners' rights cases? Have you *ever* testified for the state, or only against it?"

THE POLICE

Psychologists work with police in a number of ways (cf. Reiser & Klyver, Chapter 16). Some of the same issues concerning the police may arise for the psychologist working with corrections and parole and probation officers and their agencies.

Selection

Personnel selection is an activity fraught with general ethical issues (London & Bray, 1980). Yet there is a surprisingly sparse literature in this area. Practitioners must rely on the American Psychological Association's *Standards for Educational and Psychological Tests* (1985), their professional ethics code, and little else. In addition, psychologists selecting officers need to be aware of particular problems in forensic areas. Consider the limitations of selection strategies and instruments given the complex, shifting, and partially defined criteria for a "successful" officer. For example, Van Maanen (1975) and Niederhoffer (1967) describe changes in a police officer's role and personality factors on the job. Our selection procedure may be aimed at a moving target, depending on the measure of the successful officer (consider diverse criteria such as does paperwork, good collegial relations, good public rapport, cultivates informants, does not damage departmental vehicles) and when the measure is taken. For example, we may select a good patrol officer who is promoted on his patrol proficiency record to a position which severely taxes skills less relevant for patrol functions but vital for management or supervisory roles such as accounting skills or anticipating manpower needs.

The psychologist must negotiate beforehand as to what kind of information (a "yes–no" decision, a composite score, or qualitative data) is to be passed on to which persons in the department. Once the information is out of the psychologist's hands, control over its access may be lost, but the ethical responsibilities for the use of the information may continue. Research is necessary particularly in developing local norms. Did the psychologist negotiate for this expensive activity? Will a complete group actually be passed through with no people weeded out so an adequate validation study of the procedure can be conducted? This is the *Arrowsmith* dilemma (Sinclair Lewis, 1952) whereby a medical researcher must decide whether to give a placebo and risk people's health, or give the drug which Arrowsmith feels will work and save lives. Does the psychologist allow for a true field test of the selection procedures involving allowing candidates to become officers despite poor predictor scores, and, if so, how can potential harm by these candidates be diminished?

Training

Many of the same issues articulated for selection are relevant for training. In addition, questions may be raised as to whether certain training procedures such as human relations training may be contraindicated for some situations the officer may encounter, while being highly adaptive for others (domestic violence) (Stotland & Berberich, 1979). Given the paramilitary nature of police organizations, some social scientists must determine beforehand whether training goals are compatible with their own philosophies. As mentioned earlier, some will find it difficult to support a goal such as refining psychomotor functioning in firearms proficiency, even if the greater goal is the public's safety. Engaging in training activities contrary to one's own values, in the hope of changing the system from within, courts being unethical.

Counseling

The question, "Who is the client?" (Monahan, 1980) is most appropriate here. If one is helping victims, is one's priority to victims' well-being or to evidence gathering? Should these conflict? At what point do strictures of confidentiality precede a psychologist's revealing a victim's secrets? Is the psychologist an extension of the police and therefore someone who needs to deliver Miranda warnings? In a related case, (*Oregon v. Miller*, 1985), a psychiatrist on a hospital emergency room hotline kept a murderer talking while the phone call was traced. The courts held the ulterior motive of the psychiatrist did not prevent the patient's claim of privilege in that a usual clinical procedure was used in response to a legitimate request for professional assistance by the murderer.

Police and correctional officer positions typically rank among the five most stressful jobs in various studies. Provision of mental health support service is essential. However, what kind of guarantees of confidentiality does the officer have? Was the counseling ordered by a superior officer? Is the client's attendance monitored? Is the client's progress to be reported? Is an outside or an in-house psychologist arrangement better regarding various facts of the counseling? More general issues of confidentiality are discussed later, but these questions are critical, particularly since there is a quite violent aspect to police work which may render an officer the subject of violent impulses. When are these unusual and close to being acted upon?

One more aspect of police work concerning us is that of officer integrity. The psychologist needs to be trusted to function effectively. Can the psychologist hear of officer misconduct and not reveal it, probably becoming an accomplice? Or does the psychologist reveal dishonesty and risk losing particular, informal "in group" statuses that may be important to acceptance by the close-knit police brotherhood? As a rule, the psychologist who is a "little" compromised, is compromised. As a practicality, the decision is tougher, much as in the officer's decision as to when a free cup of coffee is merely neighborly or when it is a merchant's small payment or bribe for an anticipated favor or to ensure good response time on the officer's part to a call by the merchant.

CORRECTIONS: CLASSIFICATION AND TREATMENT

This section concerns treatment in correctional settings. Some issues such as confidentiality will be the concern of this section as they relate to corrections, and the concern of a later section as they have to do with the practice of psychotherapy generically.

Classification

In one of the largest prisons in the United States, I observed the subtest and total scores of the Beta I.Q. test with interest. These prisoners scored about 10 points higher than other such samples, particularly on two subtests. I asked the psychologist in charge of the diagnostic and reception center for the state system why the scores on two particular subtests were elevated. He was proud to explain that prisoners usually scored 10 to 15 points below normal persons which he felt was a bias built into the test. So he decided to let the prisoners have as much time on the timed subtests as they needed to finish the tasks to help the prisoners overcome what he saw as a societal prejudice.

Test are used heavily in corrections (as well as in other forensic applications such as custody, competency, and sanity hearings). It seems almost sophomoric to advise readers who have doctorates and who have taken and even taught psychological assessment courses to be familiar, if not intimate, with the Buro's *Mental Measurement Yearbooks*, the *Technical Recommendations on Tests and Measurements* (Mitchell, 1985), the test manuals, and the research literature germane to the instruments and the procedures (such as Rorschach scoring systems or group versus individual testing) being used or being considered. Yet when faced with processing hundreds of prisoners a month and using inmate help or baccalaureate-trained psychometricians, one can forget to monitor such activities as test administration procedures. Since virtually all prison testing is conducted by psychological assistants, the responsible psychologist must be vigilant that a gross mistake as in the previous example does not occur. Training of new testers is the direct responsibility of the supervising psychologist.

More subtle problems can arise. Consider a well-known, highly competent psychologist who searched the literature and selected an excellent screening procedure. He used it but failed to notice that over time the population changed, and hence the base rate of the condition he was predicting—violence potential—shifted. What had been an exemplary effort, eroded over time and began to accumulate more errors, which, to his credit, he noticed and corrected. The psychologist needs to consider the population (e.g., literacy level), conditions of testing, local norms, and suitability of the particular instrument for the task at hand in developing assessment procedures.

Access to the files is critical. As mentioned, understaffed prisons all too often use inmates as psychological assistants. When prisoners have access to critical information concerning other prisoners' fates, such as the classification information, which determines to which facility an inmate will be sent to serve his sentence, abusive situations can result.

The consumption of test information is critical. Who will present the data to whom? Is the presenter and the audience (e.g., parole board) sufficiently knowledgeable about test data or do they need a workshop concerning test scores? Even more profound is the fact that many dollars are spent on classification but to what avail? If meaningful differential treatment is not forthcoming, is the psychologist participating in a cosmetic exercise which serves only to give a patina of legitimacy to imprisonization? More searching questions need to be raised by ethical forensic and correctional psychologists as to the functions of classification and the development of better programs to serve the prisoners' needs. This information should be forthcoming from well-designed assessment systems.

Confidentiality, Privilege, and Tarasoff

An inpatient drug addict in the beginning stage of psychotherapy told the student therapist that he had "50 cc's of liquid cocaine on the block." The student pondered with his therapy supervisor whether to reveal this information to the security officers. The supervisor advised him to reveal it. The student kept the confidence, suspecting it was a test and concluding that imminent danger was not involved. Subsequently the patient revealed intimate information, and therapy progressed well.

In this case moral conclusions are hard to draw. Complicating this case was the inclusion of a supervisor who abided by the therapist's wishes despite the "respondant superior" and "captain of the ship" doctrines which make the supervisor ultimately responsible for the conduct of treatment. What constitutes imminent danger which triggers a duty to warn and the breaking of confidentiality? Imminent danger is a nice phrase to introduce at the beginning of psychotherapy, but when the particular instance arises, the decision can be blurred by the dynamics of the case, including but not limited to the type of harm, the identifiability of the victim, the nature and urgency of the threat, the stage of treatment, and the available supporting milieus. Some of these dynamics can be seen in the next case.

Halfway through a 6-month federal drug addiction treatment program, a therapy patient revealed that she was a Canadian citizen, thus ineligible for the program and that she therefore was guilty of falsely claiming citizenship on a number of legal forms. When she found out that the therapist did not reveal this information, she revealed it to others and, storming angrily into his office, proclaimed that somehow he violated her expectations that like every male she knew (pimps and "johns") he was supposed to have "turned" (betrayed) her. The therapy focused on her inability to relate to men on any but a prostitute addict level, precipitated by the therapist's unexpected (by her) adherence to ethical principles. She terminated this individual therapy and began therapy with a group therapist from whose group her confidences become known. She accomplished her apparent goal of being betrayed by the group, confirming her low self worth.

Here the moral conclusion includes the costs of ethicality in that the therapist "lost" the client by maintaining confidentiality and by disconfirming her view of both men's lack of trustworthiness and her own lack of being worthy of their trust. What happens when Tarasoff warnings, the warning to a third party who is specifiably at physical risk by a therapist's patient, are exercised? The following case shows a bit of the costs of Tarasoff.

The client trusted the therapist based in part on a previous family therapy treatment when the client was a teenager and the therapist had helped the family resolve conflicts several years earlier. The therapist had told the client and his family how the client manipulated them and fooled himself, thus helping the client behave more authentically. Several years later the client asked to be seen regarding his post-drug addiction depression. In the course of treatment the client revealed fantasies of dropping his plugged-in electric razor into his wife's filled bathtub during their morning ablutions and dumping cooking vessels filled with hot soup on his wife's head.

Should the spouse be warned? If so, to what end, since the client was intellectually facile enough to devise other lethal methods of dispatching his wife, to claim the therapist took a fantasy too seriously, or not to inform the therapist of any further such impulses. Clinical and legal bases for civil commitment were shaky at best, and not justified. Besides, the client would be released quickly, even if civilly committed, in the absence of further threat.

The client was informed that the therapist would inform the spouse about the client's anger toward himself and his spouse. The client responded as predicted and said he could just laugh off the information in the joint session with the spouse and say that the therapist took it more seriously than he should have. The client said that if "I cannot tell my therapist these feelings with a guarantee of confidence, what sense is there to psychotherapy?" In addition to the manipulative aspects to the client's questions, he raised some real issues, too.

Again, while the particular operationalization of confidentiality principles is a difficult decision, the reader can be better prepared by consulting some of the following sources. First, one's state law provides for privilege, which typically refers to the client's right to have certain information excluded from court. Originally confined to husband–wife and attorney–client relationships, privilege now includes the patient–physician, client–psychologist, and worshipper–clergy relationships. The right is a derivative of judicial interpretation of the 1st, 4th, 5th, 9th, and 14th amendments. The right belongs to the client (Van Hoose & Kottler, 1977).

Confidentiality, a more general term, is based on a profession's assumed duty to a client usually expressed in its code of ethics. Thus, the second source of information for the reader are professional ethics codes. The codes of the American Psychological Association, the American Personnel and Guidance Association, the American Association for Marriage and Family Therapy, the National Association of Social Workers, the American Psychiatric Association, and the National Academy of Certified Clinical Mental Health Counselors are available from the respective organizations and are reprinted in Corey, Corey, and Callanan (1984). Grossman (1978) provides historical and conceptual developments of confidentiality while Donnelly (1978) grapples with some of a therapist's real-world concerns. Beis

(1984) extends the discussion of confidentiality to include various situations including the making of the controversial documentary *Titticut Follies* (which involved the filming of patients in a mental hospital), the publishing of verbatim psychotherapy material, and the interviewing of a therapist who was sued by two patients with whom he had sexual intercourse. In the last case, the therapist was questioned about other clients with whom he may have had sexual intimacies, and he, in a display of irony, refused to discuss this based on the confidentiality shield *to protect his patients.*

Smith (1980) develops the constitutional basis for privacy in psychotherapy, while Ryan and Bagby (1985) review research concerning the Wigmore rules (1940), which justify privilege: (1) the original relationship is borne in confidence; (2) privilege is essential to the relationship; (3) the community supports the privilege because the relationship is important; and (4) resultant damage of disclosure exceeds the benefits of disclosure. They find some empirical support for item 1, mixed results for rule 2, and little or no research on rules 3 and 4. They note the paradox that the science of psychology produced no empirical data to help the courts determine psychologists' fate at the very time when courts are depending on psychology's empiricism in ever-increasing degrees. Swoboda, Elwork, Sales, and Levine (1978) and Switzer (1986) discuss child abuse reporting laws.

Finally, Knapp and Vandencreek (1985) discuss privilege and custody cases, while Slawson (1979) raises the issue of patient–litigant exception to privilege—a particular hazard in third-party cases such as when a parent's fitness for child custody is challenged on the basis of the parent's being in psychotherapy. Boyer (1983), Corey et al. (1984), Donnelly (1978), Grossman (1978), Halleck (1980), Mappes, Robb, and Engels (1985), Slovenko (1973), Van Hoose and Kottler (1977), and Wexler (1981) provide discussion on the nature of confidentiality, privilege and their limits, particularly with emphasis on the ongoing Tarasoff debate. Brodsky (1980) and Kaslow (1980) address the more specific application of these principles to correctional clients, and Kaslow and Mountz (1985) describe ethical and legal concerns in treating alcohol and substance abusers. Scott (1985) reviews ethical issues in counseling prisoners, and Ritchie (1985) describes handling resistance in the involuntary client.

Right to Treatment and to Refuse Treatment

A number of excellent reviews are devoted to the right of prisoners and other involuntarily confined people to receive treatment and to decline treatment: Barton and Sanborn, (1978), Beis (1984), Halleck (1978), Monahan (1980), Shah (1981), Stone (1975), Tancredi, Lieb, and Slaby (1975), and Wexler (1981). Practitioners need to be aware of the legal issues involved, yet one issue has been unrecognized and another has been understated. The former is the right of the therapist to refuse cases either for fear of personal safety as well as for therapeutic considerations. Tryon (1986) surveyed clinicians and found 81 percent experienced at least one incident of physical, verbal, or other (e.g., telephone calls) abuse. Bernstein (1981) found 76 percent of patients who threatened or physically attacked their therapists had violent histories—precisely those with whom the forensic specialist works. Does the therapist have a right to work in a secure fashion? Secondly, therapy concerns need to be considered. Kavaler (1986) describes the poignant situation where a severely disturbed, manipulative adolescent, Linda C., and her Legal Aid attorney prematurely terminated residential treatment. It describes the therapist's views and the subsequent (mal)adjustment of Linda C. Certainly the patient's rights issues have been long denied and are necessary, yet we may be ready now to include the therapist and therapy considerations in the ethics of treatment issues.

Informed Consent

Again, the reader is referred to sources such as Beis (1984), Corey et al. (1984), Halleck (1978), Slovenko (1973), Van Hoose and Kottler (1977), and Wexler (1981) for basic principles underlying the concept of consent. Bray, Shepherd, and Hays (1985) enunciate the viewpoints, elements, standards of disclosure, definition of the responsible party who may give consent, and liabilities in failing to meet consent standards. Lawyers and mental health professionals view patient decision making from different perspectives (Kaufman, Roth, Lidz, & Meisel, 1981). Lawyers tend to want patients to make decisions rather than delegate treatment decisions to others such as relatives or the treating psychiatrist (one psychiatrist, anticipating a patient refusal of treatment, opined, "I would not want to condemn the patient to the misery of his disease"). The lawyer would have the patient decide his own tolerance for misery. For the psychologist, informed consent can be perplexing.

It may be the very purpose of an assessment to determine competency to render consent, or such a determination may be incidental to an assessment for other purposes. Yet, in either case, the consent a psychologist obtained from the client, now determined to be incompetent, leaves the psychologist with no consent.

Such a case occurred when a surgeon testified that his surgery was necessary since vascular occlusion debilitated his patient. An attorney was using his testimony to show why relatives should have custody over the patient's properties. The patient's attorney asked the surgeon whether the consent for his surgery, given by the patient, was therefore invalid, and had he in fact not obtained legally valid consent? Of course, if consent is routinely obtained from relatives, then a patient's rights to privacy and self-determination may be compromised. Two further complications arising for forensic workers are the questions some theorists raise about whether incarcerated persons can freely give consent since they are in a compromised, captive situation. Second, outpatients' abilities to self-govern may be quite variable. Consider treatment of impulse-disordered people such as a compulsive sexual offender, a drug addict, a gambler, or a suicidally depressed person. They may be capable of fully informed consent on Monday but, in the throes of the impulse disorder, be incapable of such rationality on Wednesday.

Finally, can fully informed consent be given when a treatment program is experimental? An encounter group for drug addicts may involve interactions more potent than the professional expected, or since the encounter is not focused on the professional, he or she may not realize its potency even as the professional witnesses the encounter. Again, the competent professional will consider these issues beforehand in the ethical practice of forensic psychology and, at the least, consult respected peers in search of solutions. In the latter case periodic review by an independent professional to "take the emotional temperature" of the group may serve as, at least, one check on an otherwise unfettered group process.

Malpractice

Since prisoners are a litigious lot, it would seem that forensic psychologists would be likely targets of lawsuits. However, sparse data exist on this issue. Butler and Williams (1985) showed that a predominant number of the 13 violations heard by the Ohio State Board of Psychology concerned sexual improprieties. Some seven concerned dual relations with female clients, followed by improper supervision of trainees, and fraudulent misrepresentation of credentials. Slawson (1979) reported California psychiatrists who were defendants were sued for suicide (25 percent), misdiagnosis or mistreatment (19 percent), drug reactions (16 percent), unlawful detention (13 percent), sexual impropriety (3 percent), and breach of confidentiality (2 percent). Areas of vulnerability for those with forensic interests focus on incorrectly assessing a person, mistreating clients, abusing staff members or clients, and misrepresentation.

If a psychologist misclassifies a callow prisoner and the prisoner is raped by chronic and predatory offenders, the psychologist must take care to have used classification procedures conforming to the standards of the profession. Such a case occurred when a person known to some inmates as an informer was placed in a prison which housed his enemies. Within a month he was killed. The psychologist was sued for not considering the decedent's reputation among inmates when sending him to that prison. In a similar situation, the individual convicted of the infamous bombing of a Birmingham, Alabama, black church during the civil rights confrontations of the 1960s in which four girls died was placed in an isolation cell in part so he would be separated from the prison population which was 60 percent black and highly likely to kill him if the opportunity arose.

Assessment of violence potential to one's self and others is one task the psychologist undertakes. Litwack and Schlesinger (Chapter 9) discuss pragmatics of these issues. The ethics of such activities are dependent on the claims the psychologist makes and the degree to which his or her practice conforms to the best available methods (also see Monahan, 1984, and Warren, 1979). Essentially, whenever a right is granted, a duty is imposed. When a surgeon gains the right to cut another's body, a duty is imposed on the surgeon to conform to standards of care in that area of performance that exceed the obligations all other citizens bear. When an officer is given the right to carry firearms, duties are imposed on the officer and his or her superiors that he or she exercises this right in a highly disciplined fashion.

Szasz (1986) says that mental health professionals, either explicitly or implicitly, contracted to prevent suicide and now are mired in a situation where they assumed responsibilities for people that are rightfully the individual's responsibilities. Szasz argues for the relinquishing of this erroneously claimed duty. Whether this occurs or not, such a duty will endure for those who have charge over prisoners and patients for a longer time than it will last for other professionals because the free-will capability of those in custody is limited. Just as a jail must provide dental services because an inmate is not free to contract for those services, so too must those in charge care for the life of the inmate, including suicide prevention.

One other liability of forensic psychologists concerns false imprisonment. While lawsuits have arisen concerning a psychologist releasing an inmate who then kills someone, psychologists can be vulnerable to falsely detaining a person, or false imprisonment. A review of the literature revealed no papers on this subject; however, those who use marathon therapy or a treatment milieu such as Synanon or cult activities, such as Jim Jones' People's Church that involves detaining individuals when they wish to leave, may be vulnerable to false imprisonment, kidnapping, and custodial interference charges while professionals would be additionally subject to malpractice charges.

The best way to face the malpractice issue is by prevention. Again, using the best available procedures according to the literature, awareness of ethical codes and of the literature on professional practice, and collegial consultation are prophylactic. Sued physicians report experiencing significant physical and emotional distress, are likely to limit the types of patients they see, consider earlier retirement, and even discourage their children from medical practice as a career (Charles, Wilbert, & Franke, 1985). Yet before one joins the panic toward tort reform, consider that 54 percent of those in Slawson's 1979 survey never heard anything beyond an initial notification of a potential claim, 21 percent stopped short of a settlement, and the four that were tried resulted in no paid judgments. The 20 guilty judgments resulted in a total of $440,000 over 5 years or $4400 per year per case. Considering the chance of a significant claim is 0.4 for 100 psychiatrists, the estimate of $50,000 for legal costs and $500 for investigative costs, the actual annual cost of insuring a psychiatrist in California in the mid-1970s was $108, exclusive of a reserve pool, insurance company expenses, and profit. The percentage of jury-tried cases resulting in paid awards by insurance companies in tort cases is 2 percent (National Insurance Consumer Organization, 1986).

Treisman (1986) chronicles the difficult path of the plaintiff in "The Pizza Hut Papers." Clearly more scrutiny is needed of the insurance industry as well as more study concerning protecting professionals from liability costs and claims. Rather than limiting an individual's right to seek tort relief by putting ceilings and other restrictions on claims, and rather than boosting premiums, some clear analysis of actual costs is needed (psychologist liability premiums quadrupled between 1983 to 1985 absent any information justifying this increase). Whatever the results of these analyses, sound and informed practice remains the best prophylactic.

RELATIONSHIPS

Forensic work involves relationships with colleagues, with one's profession through credentialing and regulation of practice, (e.g., advertising), and with organizational wrongdoing.

Colleagues

The United States House Subcommittee on Health and Long Term Care heard testimony that 1 in 50 physicians is an imposter and that 500,000 Americans have counterfeit diplomas or credentials [*Harper's*, 1986 Index). Estimates have been made that 5 to 15 percent of practicing physicians are inadequately skilled and educated, or addicted to drugs or alcohol, and are incompetent to practice [*Time*, 1986 (May 26), pp. 57–58].

To date no such data have been published regarding psychologists. But we, too, face the situation where colleagues may be falsely credentialed, or where their competence is surely suspect. This raises grave questions. Some cases may be clear as in the case of the social psychologist at a federal drug addiction treatment facility who smoked a variety of illegal substances with small groups of addicts with whom he claimed to be doing research. He had not filed any research protocols nor obtained permission to use the controlled substances, both viable alternatives at the facility. Rumors circulated that one of the "young psychologists was doing dope with the patients," and several of his colleagues labored under suspicion until his appointment at the facility was terminated.

Perhaps the first step one can take in hearing of collegial wrongdoing is to assess the veridicality of the information about misconduct. If a patient tells of a previous therapist's sexual advances or one hears of a colleague doing drugs with the patients, some corroboration is needed. This may be gained from other patients, from colleagues, or by direct contact with the offending individual. Of course, gaining information from patients is tricky since if such information arises in a therapy setting, confidentiality and betrayal of trust are critical issues. But watching the conduct and comments of patients emerging from the social psychologist's office was revealing, as were the emanating odors. Our ethics code suggests we discuss information with colleagues directly; this can lead to correction if our colleague was unaware of the misconduct or its impact on others. This unawareness is not common since most misconduct is clearly such. A bit more common is a misperception by observers. For example, if the social psychologist had an approved research protocol, was supplied the drugs by the authorities, and was operating under auspices, even though his conduct may have been flamboyant and portray a lack of judgment in the way it was carried out, it would be ethical (one can debate the ethics of the research, but that is a separate issue). The best way to confront the seemingly unethical person is to have one of the respected, "Dutch uncle" professionals gather the information and talk with the person. Consider the following case.

A graduate student had been so offensive on numerous occasions to about 25 different students and to 3 faculty to the extent that several had threatened her well-being. She had telephoned several students who failed their doctoral exams, inviting them to a party to celebrate with the rest of the students who passed. She told a faculty member that a smart, good-looking person like that faculty member surely could get a better-looking, more virtuous wife than he had. She was insensitive to her impact on them and of the potential threat to her person. A senior clinical faculty member discussed with her a variety of her encounters and their impacts. She seemed genuinely surprised at her effect on others. Further discussion revealed how she operated out of tremendous insecurity feelings, yet she could not see how these seemingly powerful and self-assured colleagues and faculty could react to her so strongly. She agreed to enter psychotherapy, to severely restrict her comments, and to check with the "Dutch uncle" to assess her progress. Surprisingly, the combination of confrontation and the reassurance that she would not be dismissed from the program if she followed through with the agreement produced dramatic results. Follow-up almost a decade later reveals a person who has matured and who is gifted in treating highly disturbed clients (perhaps deep, source traits were rechanneled, but can we ask more of human beings?).

We do have some reluctance to confront others who are thought to be unethical. Levenson (1986) details some of the reasons and suggests guidelines for intervention. Toch (1981) describes the difficulty in sorting out where the line is drawn regarding ethicality. The partisan nature of ethics charges (often research ethics charges are raised by opponents of the science-industrial complex, while scientists circle the wagons to protect their colleague) and the nature of ethics codes, in contrast to legal charges or loss of third-party payments, make pursuit of ethics charges somewhat perilous. Derbyshire (1983) examines medical self-regulation and concurs that self-interests confound pursuit of principled professional self-regulation. Rose (1983) explores the current controversies and the underlying forces fueling debates on professional regulation.

Organizations

As difficult to handle as collegial transgressions are, organizational transgressions are monumental and sometimes fatal. Glazer and Glazer (1986) describe whistleblowers as people who have prepotent beliefs in individual responsibility, in the concept of good, and in their duty to the community of humans transcending organizational well-being. They persist in their ethicality despite the punishment of demotions, transfers, firing, personal harassment and intimidation, and possibly death. Ernest Fitzgerald (Pentagon cost overruns) saw his career reach a dead end, Serpico (police payoffs) and Ragghianti (Tennessee Board of Pardons and Paroles payoffs) faced death threats, and Silkwood (unsafe nuclear facility) died under mysterious circumstances.

The Glazers offer advice that includes (1) gather the facts; (2) go through channels; (3) do not expect the boss to solve the problem; (4) expect job insecurity and threats; (5) prepare to persist and endure; and (6) consult your loved ones (whistleblowing will either strengthen or break your marriage). Soeken (1986) a whistleblower and a therapist to other whistleblowers, describes a seven-stage process whistleblowers experience. He describes the psychological toll of revealing organizational wrongdoing. There has developed a support group to buffer whistleblowers from the extreme stresses they face and to provide information and advice.

One tactic and one strategy not mentioned in the sparse literature on uncovering organizational wrongdoing is, (1) be sure true copies of records are made and kept in physically secure and undisclosed places because if one gives the sole copy of evidence to those in the chain of command, it is literally out of one's own hand; and (2) enlist resources of those with an interest in uncovering the wrongdoing. Consider staff members who are transporting drugs to prisoners and, naturally, not declaring their proceeds on their tax returns. Various governmental agencies would have an abiding interest in those tax evaders whose ill-gotten gains would become public upon audits and legal charges.

One cannot end this section without reflecting on Ibsen's (1928) wisdom in describing Dr. Stockmann in *Enemy of the People*. Dr. Stockmann experiences the pressures described by Glazer and Glazer when he reveals that the baths at the town's spa may be contaminated and should be closed. This would ruin the town's source of income from tourism. The experiences of Dr. Stockmann and his family captivated a century of readers and remain as vivid and riveting as the controversy and blame shifting regarding the *o* rings on the ill-fated space shuttle *Challenger*.

EDUCATION

The necessity of educating students in ethical issues seems to be accepted, as seen in its inclusion in the model core curriculum of the APA accreditation manual (APA, 1983). Yet, some feel "teaching ethics" is almost an oxymoron since few faculty can be intimate with the ethics of such diverse fields as animal care, psychiatric use of physical restraints on inpatients, handling media contacts, treatment of drug addicts, and requiring undergraduates to participate in research for extra credit. Others feel ethics can best be learned in supervised field placements (Veatch & Sollito, 1976). Handelsman (1986) discusses problems of ethics training by osmosis. His arguments are compelling: Ethics should be taught and should include active learning through discussion, values clarification (Abeles, 1980), guest lecturers, and even field trips. Certainly, the content of such courses should be broadened to include forensic issues. While clinical psychology has been defined traditionally as focusing on abnormal people who are schizophrenic and neurotic, recent developments —(Hess, 1985) including the development of the DSM-III Axis 2 which concerns personality disorders, the treating of borderline and narcissistic disorders, the epidemic of drug abuse, and the entry of psychologists in the courtroom arena— have exposed psychologists to many ethical risk areas in forensic psychology that need to be included in ethics courses.

Ethics courses including forensic topics might include materials such as Korchin and Cowan (1982) and Schmidt and Meara (1984) while anyone teaching the ethics of conducting research should include the report on research involving prisoners from the National Commission for the Protection of Human Subjects of Biomedical and Behavioral Research (1976). The particular typesm7f research (pharmacology, chemical castration, diet restriction, sensory deprivation, addiction-cure-readdiction, psychosurgery, new product testing, aversive conditioning), which had been done on prisoner subjects, who some argue are incapable of voluntary, informed consent, provide a fertile area for classroom debate on research ethics. The advantages of prisoner subjects (controlled diet and environment and ease of accessing subjects for follow-up sessions) can be contrasted with ethical costs. Prison psychologists and administrators can host a visit by the class, and prisoners can be involved in dialogue on research ethics and their experiences and opinions.

This is but one example of forensic ethics education. Topics such as lie detection, child abuse reporting, whether to credential expert witnesses, and the ethical use of hypnosis in forensic applications provide ample material for ethics courses. Of course, if ethics is taught, and psychologists must make ethically sound decisions, some exposure to value theory is called for. This is the focus of the next section.

ETHICAL THEORIES

Wheelwright's (1959) critical review of ethical theory forms the basis for this section. A review of values theories should help any reader clarify his or her own values.

Pleasure

Hedonism has a lengthy history. Aristippus, Epicurus, Bentham, and J. S. Mill number among noteworthy hedonist theorists. The calculus of gaining the greatest pleasure and least pain characterize Bentham's view and leads to a marketplace or capitalistic moral perspective. One works to gain pleasures and avoids the illegal to avoid punishment. The essence of the insanity defense rests on the hedonic principles in that the insane has an inability to properly weigh or "appreciate the nature of his action" in contrast to the consequences. His rational capacities to seek pleasure are defective. The intensity, duration, probability, promptness, fecundity, purity, and social extent of sensation are components in the pleasure–pain regression equation. For Bentham, the regression equation of pleasure–pain governs whether an executive embezzles, whether a husband cheats on his wife, or whether a psychologist accepts a fee-paying client with a problem beyond the psychologist's competencies, given the consequences of discovery.

Criticism of hedonism includes (1) the limits of the assumption that pleasure–pain serves as the sole motivation of humans; (2) the idea that even if hedonism governs motivation, it does not follow that it *should* do so if our ethics are to be more than merely appetitive; and (3) the notion that quantification of hedonic units, if not impossible, certainly is far from being a reality. While hedonism gives us an opportunity to examine motivation, the next theory carries this a quantum step further.

Power

Wheelwright (1959) observes that Chief Justice O. W. Holmes whimsically defined Truth as the majority vote of the nation possessing the most battleships. Von

Clausewitz defined war as "violence pushed to its utmost . . . to compel our opponent to fulfill our will" (Wheelwright, 1959, p. 71). Darwin and Spencer's evolutionary theory softens the exterior of the philosophy of power, but the struggle for survival of the fittest describes Nature's warfare in which reproduction, nourishment, education, and any potentiating function becomes a moral obligation. This thrust for power is not merely for selfish reasons but for one's society. James' Pragmatism employs "successful working" as one of its criteria for truth (Pepper, 1942), in effect saying, "what works is true."

Nietzsche's "will to power" idealizes the person able to engage in creative pursuits or "transvaluate," much as Abraham's intent to sacrifice Isaac, ordinarily seen as barbarous, led to monotheism.

Critique of the philosophy of power includes the following questions: (1) whether the origin of our species, a historical pursuit, is being confused with the moral pursuit—namely, what *should* be our goals; (2) is evolution necessarily progress, or might certain species be on a terminal course; (3) Nietzsche's conception omits motives such as benevolence, justice, and love; and (4) Nietzsche's aristocrat, Knight, or superman calls for others to be seen as resentful slaves and jealous inferiors.

We find that justification for the use of punishment for allocations of resources in our country, and for the courtroom combats based on the adversarial process theory, to be based on the assumption that what is right or good will survive and what is being punished deserves it. Philosophies of power and, to some extent, of pleasure exclude a moral dimension—that of duty.

Duty

Essentially when considering ethics, we consider that actions have moral dimensions—that is, they include the concept "ought" or "should." When Spencer considers that the oyster survives a long time, he also considers the texture of breadth of the oyster's experience in contrast to a human's experience. A human can decide to forgo a current pleasure for a later, greater one or decide what is "the greatest good for the greatest number" of people. A conscience or regard for other values concerns us here, one that places the valuing process inside the person rather than being a matter of pleasure or dominance. The following value theory focuses on the forms that duty takes.

Rationalism

When conscience calls us, in what voice does it speak? Stoics claim that consistent and true universal laws, of which human conduct was a small part, govern the universe. Habit, practicality, and personal inclination were not bases for such laws. The assumption of a rational, good world in which the actor discerns what is in his or her power to do and what is beyond it allows for the legendary Stoic choice. Posidonius, suffering a disease, can say, "Do your worst, pain, do your worst: you will never compel me to acknowledge that you are an evil", illustrating the with-holding of moral opprobrium, the following of a logical consistency regardless of consequences. Yet this obeisance to one's sense of duty, while giving absolute free-dom to follow the right course, begs the question of the nature of right except as that duty is defined by the individual. In a practical sense, we see whistleblowers re-sponding to a strong sense of duty and abiding the pain as a real but irrelevant con-sequence of doing what is right. Kant addresses the nature of that right.

Kant sees the locus of moral worth in the unconditional expression of our will. We do what is right because it is right, not for a consequence. If we do successful therapy on a drug addict, but he becomes an equally successful and prolific contract killer because of his newly found sobriety, the moral good of the therapy remains. But what are the benchmarks for the goodness of our will? First, consistency would impel each act as if it were a universal law. I would not do better court testimony or psychotherapy for one client than I would for another for any conditional considera-tions (pro bono versus paying client). If this maxim, and its underlying rationality, is accepted, then the human is seen as having intrinsic worth, not merely instrumen-tal value, and being an end in himself. So one should treat humans as an end, says Kant in his second maxim, not as a means.

Kant can be criticized for the ambiguity of his first maxim since we have seen that one should not kill, but an officer faced with a terrorist about to ignite a bomb will do well to fire a fatal shot into the terrorist. Perhaps one can argue that the word *kill* is used in two different senses, but such ambiguity would start the slide from Kant's imperative to some other value theory. Despite the ambiguities, Kant still provides a basis for decisions — two interlocking maxims which call for consistency and human worth.

Humanism

We have seen that ethical judgment is many-sided: Neither pleasure, nor power, nor duty can be exclusive bases of morality. Also, while transcendent fragments such as Society, Nature, and God can be a basis for ethics, humanism would locate morality in the nature of the human and in the latent possibilities of that entire nature includ-ing pleasure, creativity, self-control, and so forth. Socrates searches for Good and finds that it is specific to the nature of the entity. The human being's entity is three-fold: (1) desires and aversions which have self-control as their virtue; (2) active im-pulses such as anger and enthusiasm, the virtue of which is courage; and (3) deliber-ation and choice, with wisdom as its epitome. These combine to form the just soul. Plato objectifies this by declaring social functions corresponding to these virtues, exemplified in his "philosopher-King." Aristotle, preceded by Confucious and fol-lowed by Maimonides, sees the political nature of human life in that one person may be a good automobile mechanic while another is a good attorney. Each needs the other and contributes to the other. Thus his "Golden mean," often a catchword to describe his view of the life lived well, does not refer to a person who is excellent at auto repair and law and cooking and sewing, but to a person who has a "vital well-being," a reflective consciousness integrating the threefold nature of the human with society and who does well at whatever he or she is able to, with self-control, courage, and wisdom.

Principles in self-development common to some contemporary, growth-oriented personality theorists, also termed humanists, are clear. The problems with humanism surface when we persist in asking the question of the substance of Good, and when we examine "vital well-being" in the context of stressful environments. Consider a person facing a situation where capitulation to a dishonest practice, for example, fee splitting, would serve appetitive and active impulse needs. That is, he or she would earn money, be fulfillingly engaged in helping patients, and upon reflection, see that a well-oiled system serving the professional community and the patients would be disrupted by protestations of fee splitting. What becomes of the concept of the well-regulated life when we apply it to tough situations? Maybe the venerable, strongly entrenched Chinese and Greek cultures made Good clearer for Confucious and Aristotle than for us, the dwellers of a microchip-dependent, global village where values seem ephemeral, or perhaps they addressed this question by calling for a wiser political system nourished by an enriched education. The next and last value theory described here addresses this question by having the nature of Good revealed to people transcendentally.

Religious Ethics

The revealed Truth is illusory in religion. As St. Ignatius said, "Words have a power, a terrible power, of intruding between man and God." Taoists claim, "The *Tao* that can be known and followed is not the real TAO." Where humanism seeks self-development, religion, as seen in the Tao example, has us surrender to a greater good as a spoke surrenders individuality to a wheel and thus attains its possibilities. The ethical, charitable person feeds the poor for God's sake, not for the return of gratitude. The principles of attunement to all people and to benevolence emerge for all developed religious theories. The first principle is stated well in the Hebraic sense of justice while the second principle Westerners realize is in the Christian ethic of love.

Problems with religious ethics are immediate. First, the demands of justice and love are uncompromising: Those who are truly religious are rare. Second, religion has been suffused with false prophets, or rather false prophets flock to religion to cloud the simple person's vision. We need go no further than the television evangelism or the Jonestown horror for examples. Third, the dual demands of justice and love can lead a person to withdraw from the world in efforts at self-perfection and relief from the world's imperfection, as in the case of some monastic orders. Fourth, love and justice are easily said but as hard to define as the critical terms in other value theories: "maximize pleasure," "pursue power," "heed the conscience," "seek consistency," "seek harmony," and "develop self."

ABRAHAM AND ISAAC

Returning to where we left Abraham, knife poised above Isaac, prepared to suspend the ethical, how can we understand Abraham? Buber (1952/1975) tries to help by telling us not to confuse the voice of the Absolute with those imitation voices of Moloch's apes. Ethics usually is not a matter of knowing right from wrong, unless one is demented. Consultation with colleagues and recent literature can reveal when one practices outside one's own bounds of competence. Is the sexually exploitive therapist really able to delude himself or herself into thinking it was for the "patient's good"? Probably not. Because others are "low balling" (making unreasonably low bids to drive out competitors, with the idea of later raising prices when an agency is committed to one's services) may be a handy justification for selling a testing service to a prison, but the person knows he or she has transgressed.

The story of Abraham tells us that ethicality resides in the act of faith when all else has been contemplated. The theories described here contribute to one's understanding of morality; colleagues help one see the consequences of our decisions; and ethics codes illuminate organizational concerns; but fortification of one's volition or spirit to do what is right is transcendent. The Abraham in each of us cannot escape the absolutes we know, and it is the Abraham in each of us that must find the integrity to sacrifice penultimates such as gain, security, affability, and status to simply do what is right and in so doing to have a share in the world.

REFERENCES

Abeles, N. (1980). Teaching ethical principles by means of value confrontations. *Psychotherapy: Theory, Research and Practice, 17*, 384–391.

American Psychological Association. (1981). Ethical principles of psychologists (revised). *American Psychologist, 36*, 633–638.

American Psychological Association. (1983). *Accreditation handbook* (rev. ed.) Washington, DC: APA Committee on Accreditation.

American Psychological Association. (1985). *Standards for educational and psychological tests*. Washington, DC: Author.

Barton, W. E., & Sanborn, C. J. (Eds.). (1978). *Law and the mental health professions: Friction at the interface*. New York: International Universities Press.

Beis, E. B. (1984). *Mental health and the law*. Rockville, MD: Aspen Systems Corporation.

Bernstein, H. A. (1981). Survey of threats and assaults directed toward psychotherapists. *American Journal of Psychotherapy, 35*, 542–549.

Blau, T. H. (1984). *The psychologist as expert witness*. New York: John Wiley & Sons.

Boyer, J. (1983). Law and the practice of clinical psychology. In C. E. Walker (Ed.), *The handbook of clinical psychology* (Vol. 2, pp. 1389–1419). Homewood, IL: Dorsey.

Bray, J. H., Shepherd, J. N., & Hays, J. R. (1985). Legal and ethical issues in informed consent to psychotherapy. *American Journal of Family Therapy, 13*, 50–60.

Brodsky, S. L. (1980). Ethical issues for psychologists in corrections. In J. Monahan (ed.), *Who is the client?* (pp. 63–92) Washington, D. C.: American Psychological Association.

Buber, M. (1975). On the suspension of the ethical. In W. R. Durland & W. H. Bruening (Eds.), *Ethical issues: A search for the contemporary conscience* (pp. 87–90). Palo Alto, CA: Mayfield Press. (Reprinted from *Eclipse of God*, 1952. New York: Harper & Row).

Butler, R. W., & Williams, D. A. (1985). Description of Ohio State Board of Psychology hearings on ethical violations: From 1972 to present. *Professional Psychology, 16*, 502–511.

Charles, S. C., Wilbert, J. R., & Franke, K. J. (1985). Sued and nonsued physicians' self-reported reactions to malpractice litigation. *American Journal of Psychiatry, 142*, 437–440.

Corey, G., Corey, M. S., & Callanan, P. (1984). *Issues and ethics in the helping professions* (2nd ed.). Monterey, CA: Brooks/Cole.

Derbyshire, R. C. (1983). How effective is medical self-regulation? *Law and Human Behavior, 7*, 193–202.

Diamond, B. L. (1983). The psychiatrist as expert witness. *Psychiatric Clinics of North America, 6*, 597–609.

Donnelly, J. (1978). Confidentiality. The myth and the reality. In W. E. Barton & C. J. Sanborn (Eds.), *Law and the mental health professions* (pp. 185–205). New York: International Universities Press.

Fersch, E. A. (1979). *Law, psychology, and the courts*. Springfield, IL: C. C. Thomas.

Glazer, M. P., & Glazer, P. M. (1986). Whistleblowing. *Psychology Today, 20*, 36–43.

Grossman, M. (1978). Confidentiality: The right to privacy versus the right to know. In W. E. Barton & C. J. Sanborn (Eds.), *Law and the mental health professions* (pp. 137–184). New York: International Universities Press.

Halleck, S. L. (1980). *Law in the practice of psychiatry*. New York: Plenum.

Handelsman, M. M. (1986) Problems with ethics training by "osmosis". *Professional Psychology, 17*, 371–372.

Harper's Index (June, 1986), *Harper's Magazine*, p. 13.

Hess, A. K. (1985). The coming of age of character disorders (book review). *Contemporary Psychology, 30*, 458–459.

Ibsen, H. (1928). *The works of Henrik Ibsen*. Roslyn, NY: Black's Reader Service.

Jones, E. (1957). *The life and work of Sigmund Freud: Vol. 3*. New York: Basic Books.

Kaslow, F. W. (1980). Ethical problems in prison psychology. *Criminal Justice and Behavior, 7*, 3–9.

Kaslow, F. W., & Mountz, T. (1985). Ethical and legal issues in the treatment of alcoholics and substance abusers. In T. Bratter & G. Forest (Eds.), *Current treatment of substance abuse and alcoholism*. New York: Free Press.

Kavaler, S. A. (1986). Law versus clinical treatment: The case of Linda C. *American Journal of Psychotherapy, 40*, 135–143.

Kaufman, C. L., Roth, L. H., Lidz, C. W. & Meisel, A. (1981). Informed consent and patient decisionmaking: The reasoning of law and psychiatry. *International Journal of Law and Psychiatry, 4*, 345–361.

Kierkegaard, S. (1968). *Fear and trembling and the sickness unto death* (W. Lowrie, Trans.). Princeton, NJ: Princeton University Press.

Knapp, S. J. & Van de Creek, L. (1985). Psychotherapy and privileged communications in child custody cases. *Professional Psychology, 16,* 398–407.

Kohlberg, L. (1976). Moral stages and moralization: The cognitive developmental approach. In T. Lickona (Ed.), *Moral development and behavior: Theory, research, and social issues.* New York: Holt, Rinehart & Winston.

Korchin, S. J., & Cowan, P. A. (1982). Ethical perspectives in clinical research. In P. C. Kendall & J. N. Butcher (Eds.), *Handbook of research methods in clinical psychology* (pp. 59–94). New York: John Wiley & Sons.

Levenson, J. L. (1986). When a colleague practices unethically: Guidelines for intervention. *Journal of Counseling and Development, 64,* 315–317.

Lewis, S. (1952). *Arrowsmith.* New York: Harcourt, Brace.

London, M., & Bray, D. W. (1980). Ethical issues in testing and evaluation for personnel decisions. *American Psychologist, 35,* 890–901.

Loo, R. (1986). Post-shooting stress reactions among police officers. *Journal of Human Stress, 12,* 27–31.

Louisell, D. W. (1955). The psychologist in today's legal world. *Minnesota Law Review, 39,* 235–272.

Mappes, D. C., Robb, G. P., & Engels, D. W. (1985). Conflicts between ethics and law in counseling and psychotherapy. *Journal of Counseling and Development. 67,* 246–252.

Menninger, K. (1966). *The crime of punishment.* New York: Viking.

Mitchell, J. V. (1985). *The ninth mental measurements yearbook* (Vols. 1 & 2). Lincoln, NE: University of Nebraska Press.

Monahan, J. (Ed.). (1980). *Who is the client?* Washington, DC: American Psychological Association.

Monahan, J. (1984). The prediction of violent behavior: Toward a second generation of theory and policy. *American Journal of Psychiatry, 141,* 10–15.

National Commission for the Protection of Human Subjects of Biomedical and Behavioral Research. (1976). *Research involving prisoners: Report and recommendations.* Bethesda, MD: Author DHEW Publication No. (05)76–131.

National Insurance Consumer Organization. (1986). Cited in *Harper's Magazine, 272* (no. 1633), p. 13.

Neiderhoffer, A. (1967). *Behind the shield: The police in urban society.* New York: Anchor.

Oregon v. Miller, No. 530798, Oregon Supreme Court, November 5, 1985.

Rennie v. Klein, 462 F. Supp. 1131 (1978).

Ritchie, M. H. (1985). Counseling the involuntary client. *Journal of Counseling and Development, 64,* 516–518.

Robinson, D. (1980). *Psychology and law.* New York: Oxford University Press.

Rogers v. Okin, 478 F. Supp. 1342 (1979).

Rose, J. (1983). Professional regulation: The current controversy. *Law and Human Behavior, 7,* 103–116.

Ryan, D. P., & Bagby, R. M. (1985). Psychologists and privileged communication. *Canadian Psychology, 26,* 207–213.

Schmidt, L. D., & Meara, N. M. (1984). Ethical, professional and legal issues in counseling psychology. In S. D. Brown & R. W. Lent (Eds.), *Handbook of counseling psychology* (pp. 56–96). New York: John Wiley & Sons.

Scott, N. A. (1985). Counseling prisoners: Ethical issues, dilemmas, and cautions. *Journal of Counseling and Development, 64*, 272–273.

Shah, S. A. (1981). Legal and mental health system interactions: Major developments and research needs. *International Journal of Law and Psychiatry, 4*, 219–270.

Shapiro, D. L. (1984). *Psychological evaluation and expert testimony: A practical guide to forensic work.* New York: Van Nostrand Reinhold.

Silverman, H. (1969). Determinism, choice, responsibility and the psychologist's role as expert witness. *American Psychologist, 24*, 5–9.

Slawson, P. F. (1979). Psychiatric malpractice: The California experience. *American Journal of Psychiatry, 136*, 650–654.

Slovenko, R. (1973). *Psychiatry and law.* Boston: Little, Brown.

Soeken, D. R. (1986). J'accuse. *Psychology Today, 20*, 44–46.

Smith, S. R. (1980). Constitutional privacy in psychotherapy. *George Washington Law Review, 49*, 1–60.

Stone, A. A. (1975). *Mental health and the law: A system in transition.* Rockville, MD: N.I.M.H. DHEW Publication No. (ADM) 75-176.

Stotland, E., & Berberich, J. (1979). The psychology of the police. In H. Toch (Ed.), *Psychology of crime and criminal justice* (pp. 24–67). New York: Holt Rinehart & Winston.

Switzer, J. V. (1986). Reporting child abuse. *American Journal of Nursing, 86*, 663–664, 667.

Swoboda, J. S., Elwork, A., Sales, B. D., & Levine, D. (1978). Knowledge and compliance with privileged communication and child abuse laws. *Professional Psychology, 9*, 448–458.

Szasz, T. (1986). The case against suicide prevention. *American Psychologist, 41*, 806–812.

Tancredi, L. R., Lieb, J., & Slaby, A. E. (1975). *Legal issues in psychiatric care.* Hagerstown, MD: Harper & Row.

Toch, H. (1981). Cast the first stone? Ethics as a weapon. *Criminology, 19*, 185–194.

Treisman, E. (1986). The pizza hut papers. *Harpers Magazine, 273*, 54–60.

Tryon, G. S. (1986). Abuse of therapists by patients: A national survey. *Professional Psychology, 17*, 357–363.

Van Hoose, W. H., & Kottler, J. A. (1977). *Ethical and legal issues in counseling and psychotherapy.* San Francisco, CA: Jossey-Bass.

Van Maahen, J. (1975). Police socialization: A longitudinal examination of job attitudes in an urban police department. *Administrative Science Quarterly, 20*, 207–228.

Veatch, R. M. & Sollito, S. (1976) Medical ethics teaching: Report of a national medical school survey. *Journal of the American Medical Association, 235*, 1030–1033.

Warren, C. A. B. (1979). The social construction of dangerousness. *Urban Life, 8*, 359–384.

Wexler, D. B. (1981). *Mental health law.* New York: Plenum.

Wheelright, P. (1959). *A critical introduction to ethics* (3rd ed.). Indianapolis, IN: Odyssey Press.

Wigmore, J. (1940). *Evidence* (3rd ed., vol. 8). Boston: Little, Brown.

Zimring, F., & Hawkins, G. (1971). The legal threat as an instrument of social change. *Journal of Social Issues, 27,* 33–48.

Ziskin, J. (1970). *Coping with psychiatric and psychological testimony.* Beverly Hills, CA: Law and Psychology Press.

CHAPTER 26

Training in Psychology and Law

GARY B. MELTON

Psycholegal studies may be fairly termed as psychology's new growth industry. Besides the development of new professional organizations (e.g., the American Psychology–Law Society of the American Psychological Association), there has been a mushrooming of scholarship on psychology and law, albeit still predominantly in relatively narrow areas of criminal and family law (Monahan & Loftus, 1982).

To give just one example of the recent growth in interdisciplinary research and commentary, most of the research cited by a study group of the Society for Research in Child Development in *Children's competence to consent* (Melton, Koocher, & Saks, 1983) had been conducted since 1980. Even in traditional areas (e.g., child custody consultation), the development of a clearly relevant scientific body of knowledge has happened largely in this decade (see Melton, 1984, for a review of developments in developmental psychology and law).

It would not be surprising to find these organizational and scholarly developments accompanied by striking changes in opportunities for training in psychology and law. First, the rise in scholarly interest might be expected to create additional coverage in course work, at least at the graduate level. Second, the increase in sophistication of psycholegal studies has unmasked the poor quality of much interdisciplinary work and, therefore, the need for more intensive training in psychology and law.

Critics (e.g., Loh, 1981; Melton, 1985; Monahan & Loftus, 1982) have attacked the field for ignoring whole areas of law and often failing to make even the most basic accommodations to external validity in psycholegal research. By the same token, commentators have criticized forensic clinicians for often making conclusory judgments based on insufficient knowledge of legal standards and inadequate—perhaps an inherently inadequate—scientific foundation (see, e.g., Bonnie & Slobogin, 1980; Melton, Petrila, Poythress, & Slobogin, in press; Morse, 1978, 1982a; Roesch & Golding, 1980). Legal decision makers themselves have been analogously criticized for cajoling such judgments from clinicians (e.g., see Morse, 1982b; Poythress, 1978, 1982). One logical response to all of these criticisms is to increase training in interdisciplinary matters. Third, as will be discussed later in this chapter, both constitutional and fiscal constraints have led to a trend toward decentralization of forensic services and, therefore, a demand for more forensic clinicians or, perhaps more precisely, general clinicians with forensic training (see, e.g., American Bar Association, 1984; Melton, Weithorn, & Slobogin, 1985). A logical corollary to this demand for more forensic clinicians is a need for more forensic training.

The expected increase in training in psychology and law has in fact materialized, although there are still relatively few universities with organized training programs in psycholegal studies. In a study conducted in 1978–1979, Grisso, Sales, and Bayless (1982) found five joint-degree programs and a few predoctoral specialty programs. By the time a similar survey was conducted by Melton (1983), not only was the list far from complete but most of the programs extant in 1979 had changed their emphases and format. Grisso et al. (1982) found that almost one-fourth of graduate psychology departments offered courses in legal topics in 1978, with another 11 percent reporting that they were planning to develop such a course. Of special interest was the fact that three-fourths of the psycholegal courses offered in 1978 had been offered for the first time since 1973. Moreover, the first integrated joint-degree program (University of Nebraska–Lincoln) has celebrated only its tenth anniversary.

Analogous growth has taken place in applied forensic training. In a survey conducted in 1975 (Levine, Wilson, & Sales, 1980), 55 percent of APA-approved internship sites reported the availability of some opportunities for forensic experience. Within four years, this figure grew to 77 percent (Lawlor, Siskind, & Brooks, 1981), although only one-third included didactic forensic instruction, and just 10 percent reported that they involved attorneys in the training.

In view of both the number of programs and the speed with which any list of programs will be outdated, no attempt will be made in this chapter to provide detailed descriptions of available programs. Rather, the focus will be on the merits of the various models of psycholegal training and directions for training in psychology and law. (For a list of opportunities for psycholegal training, see Melton, 1983.)

PRINCIPLES OF TRAINING

In evaluating training in psychology and law, the starting point must be an analysis of the proper goals of such training. There has been much discussion of the need for lawyers and behavioral scientists to talk to one another, to understand each other's terminology, and to reconcile differences in libertarianism-paternalism attitudes. According to such an analysis, all that is needed to integrate psychology and law is to cure a problem in communication. Just as one can facilitate communication between people of different nationalities by teaching at least one partner the language of the other, one should be able to enhance interdisciplinary work by educating at least one partner in the jargon of the other. Therefore, specific goals might be to ensure that psychologists know the legal meaning of *insanity* and that lawyers know the technical meaning of *schizophrenia*.

At most, many argue, the problem is one of a rapprochement of attitudes and values. Often this value gap is itself thought to be a product of the language barrier. Thus, some mental health professionals believe that if lawyers knew what schizophrenics were really like, then there would be no interdisciplinary conflict. If lawyers were educated about the stress that comes with adversariness, then procedures more consonant with those familiar to mental health professionals would be adopted in the legal system.

Such a view is clearly naive. First, it overlooks the differing purposes of the two disciplines. Thus, for example, rejection of adversary procedures might increase the objectivity and comprehensiveness of mental health professionals' testimony. However, abandonment of the adversary system in mental health cases would defeat the legal system's principal purpose of the pursuit of justice, of the provision of an opportunity for each party to put its best case forward (cf. Thibaut & Walker, 1978). Moreover, a requirement of a report for the court alone in criminal cases would frustrate a defendant's ability to explore defenses and interfere with his or her fifth amendment rights (American Bar Association, 1984; Slobogin, 1982).

Second, learning the core concepts in the other discipline will not eliminate the fundamental disciplinary differences in philosophical assumptions (see Haney, 1980; Melton et al., in press, chap. 1) or style of thinking and analysis. Indeed, increased fluency of communication will illuminate such differences, not reduce them.

I do not wish to underemphasize the significance of differences in knowledge and attitudes. A mental health professional cannot give assistance to the fact finder in a legal proceeding if the clinician misunderstands the standard to be applied. Similarly, in order to be of significant help to legal policymakers, psychological researchers need to be aware of specific empirical questions and assumptions in the law. Nonetheless, beyond certain core knowledge, it seems that a primary need is for familiarity with the methods and philosophy of the two disciplines.

In short, behavioral scientists need enough training in relevant areas of the law to formulate relevant questions and to be able to "think like a lawyer" well enough to communicate effectively with attorneys and to analyze the policy implications (and limitations) of behavioral science research. On the other hand, attorneys need enough behavioral science training to be acquainted with and, most important, able to evaluate the empirical literature relevant to legal issues and to be able to collaborate in the design and implementation of policy-relevant research projects. Behavioral scientists in the area require a knowledge of basic law, particularly legal analysis; lawyers need basic research training.

This analysis of primary psycholegal training needs has two major implications for development of training models. First, it seems that inclusion of attorneys as trainers is essential to an effective training program in law and psychology. Both disciplinary paradigmatic differences (cf. Rappaport, 1977) and core knowledge in the law are more likely to be communicated effectively by a lawyer than by a psychologist, particularly in training settings where there are opportunities for interaction only with other behavioral scientists or mental health professionals. In making such an assertion, I do not mean to imply that psychologists sophisticated in law cannot do such training. Rather, my point is that something important is lost by not including lawyers. Indeed, it is perhaps in informal conversations with lawyers that paradigmatic differences are most likely to become evident. As a general matter, lawyers are also obviously more likely to have knowledge of the relevant law, even though some psychologists may have acquired more expertise than most lawyers in particular legal specialties.

My analysis is applicable to training of clinical practitioners in forensic psychology, as well as to training of policy researchers. Forensic clinicians need to be sensitive to differences in philosophical assumptions (e.g., the nature of voluntariness; the nature of a fact; the utility of application of group probability data to individual cases) which may make translation of their findings to the legal system difficult. Moreover, although there are undoubtedly some special clinical problems inherent in forensic assessment (e.g., evaluation of claims of dissociative states; expertise in particular forms of criminal conduct, such as sexual deviations), much of the special forensic knowledge that a generally competent clinician needs to perform forensic evaluations is purely legal (e.g., implications of the fifth amendment for forensic evaluation; clinical issues in provocation and self-defense; relevance of amnesia to competency to stand trial). Therefore, training in forensic clinical practice is best done at least partially by lawyers. In my view, their inclusion as teachers in forensic training programs is in fact more important than the inclusion of forensic clinicians, although there obviously is some expertise that senior forensic clinicians and researchers can add. Not only is sophistication in relevant legal issues important as a matter of competence of forensic clinicians (cf. American Psychological Association, 1981, Principles 1f and 2), it is also ethically required to avoid invasion of clients' civil rights (cf. APA, 1981, Principle 3c).

In addition to the implication that interaction with, and direct training by, lawyers is essential to psycholegal training, there is a second major implication of the argument that the key to such training is an appreciation of the second discipline's methodology and core knowledge. The second implication is that having both degrees is unnecessary for making a contribution to psycholegal studies. Indeed, expertise in one discipline with a *basic* knowledge in the other is probably sufficient. Whether pre- or postdegree, a concentrated program specifically on law-psychology interaction and paradigmatic differences is likely to be generally as effective and certainly less costly than joint-degree programs in training scholars in psychology and law, although there may still be special benefits accruing from joint-degree opportunities for some students. We turn now to looking at each training model with respect to its special merits and liabilities.

MODELS OF TRAINING

Joint-Degree Programs

Not only are two degrees unnecessary for making a contribution to psycholegal studies, they are also insufficient. Simply having earned two degrees does not necessarily imply having integrated them. One can be a psychologist and a lawyer without being a psychologist-lawyer. Some persons earn a second degree as part of a career change. Others perhaps intend to integrate the disciplines but instead lead dual careers. In reviewing J.D.-Ph.D. resumes as part of a faculty search, I was struck by how many are psychologists by day and lawyers by night (or vice versa); they did not succeed in developing even an interdisciplinary approach to their dissertations and other scholarly work. Still other J.D.-Ph.D.s achieve some minimal integration, but in a narrow, self-serving way. There are the psychologists (and lawyers) who collect degrees to pad their advertisements in the yellow pages. Then there was the physician-lawyer who wrote a letter to the editor of the *Wall Street Journal* to encourage his medical colleagues to attend law school so that they might learn tax loopholes useful in managing their practice!

Of course, some of the most distinguished contributors to psycholegal studies have been J.D.-Ph.D.s who achieved an integration of their dual training on their own. Nonetheless, it is intuitively clear that the likelihood of joint-degree students' becoming psychologist-lawyers (instead of psychologists *and* lawyers) is increased by their participation in interdisciplinary programs of training. Although some of the joint-degree programs have been programs only in the sense of rules permitting dual enrollment in the law school and the graduate school, most of the current joint-degree programs do in fact have a distinctive curriculum apart from the standard requirements for the J.D. and the Ph.D. degrees.

The Nebraska curriculum is representative in form, although the specific content of each of the joint-degree programs is unique.* Joint-degree students at Nebraska typically begin their graduate studies by taking the standard first-year curriculum in the College of Law. Nebraska, like most law schools, requires all students to be full-time during their first year, because of the crucial importance first-year courses are presumed to have in teaching students to think like lawyers. Therefore, first-year law/psychology students differ little from regular first-year law students. Indeed, the only deviation in their studies is attendance at colloquia sponsored by the law/psychology program.

It is unclear whether the first-year law curriculum should come in the first or the second year of the joint-degree curriculum. Students frequently report some difficulty in going from the first year of training in one discipline to the first year of training in the other. To a certain extent, this difficulty in transition is the inherent result of doubling the stresses and low status of the first year in any graduate or professional curriculum. However, there are special problems in the transition between the first year of law and the first year of psychology. Students describe their first year in law as being uncomfortable (with distant, sometimes adversary relationships with professors), but with clear boundaries between professors and students, and a high degree of anonymity, which offers a certain degree of protection.

On the other hand, the first year in graduate school is typified by collegiality inside and outside the classroom, blurring of role boundaries, and a feeling of living in a fishbowl. Thus, beyond whatever conflict is engendered by the disciplinary differences themselves, students often experience some confusion as to how they should behave as students. Given that such role disparity is apt to occur, there is some reason to support beginning the program with the first-year psychology curric-

---

*The director of the Arizona program, Bruce Sales, was the first director of the Nebraska program. The director of the Hahnemann/Villanova program, Amiram Elwork, was also formerly associated with the Nebraska program. Both Arizona and Hahnemann/Villanova follow the general format of the Nebraska program, but the interdisciplinary courses and emphases differ substantially. For example, Hahnemann/Villanova offers the J.D.-Ph.D. only in clinical psychology; therefore, the interdisciplinary courses emphasize mental health issues and legal problems of clinical practice.

ulum. Some students have speculated that they might have been more active in their first-year law classes if they had begun their graduate career in psychology, where the tradition is for students to be highly involved in class discussions—indeed, leading class discussions—from the beginning.

Another reason to place the first year of law school in the second year of a joint-degree curriculum is to provide some opportunities for interdisciplinary work and identification as joint-degree students from the beginning. Because all first-year law students take precisely the same courses, there is insufficient flexibility in the first-year law curriculum to permit any interdisciplinary studies.

On the other hand, it may be unrealistic to expect students to begin to integrate their studies without a basic knowledge of legal doctrines and problems. Therefore, placing the first year of law school at the beginning of the program may maximize the early integration of studies by enabling students to look at psychology, from the beginning, in terms of potential relevance to legal issues. The initiation of study with the first year of law also avoids interruption of the first stages of the student's research program by intense, full-time course work.

In short, there are sound arguments in support of either potential ordering of first years. It is probably worth noting that there is a likely paradoxical effect of whatever choice is made. Beginning the program with the first year of law may actually lead students to identify themselves more as psychology students. The law curriculum is sufficiently structured that if students move from the first year of law to a second year consisting largely of psychology courses, they "lose" their law class. Students are thus likely to find that their social and intellectual relationships with peers are likely to be with psychology students, not law students. Taking the first year of law in the second year may diminish this effect, because students would then be in several upper-division courses with their law classmates.

As already noted, at Nebraska joint-degree students typically begin their studies in the College of Law. In the second year, the integration begins. Second-year students enroll in basic psychology courses (e.g., quantitative methods; proseminars in selected subdisciplines of psychology) and begin an interdisciplinary research program under faculty supervision. Also, they have their first exposure to interdisciplinary courses, and they participate in a law/psychology research group and attend interdisciplinary colloquia. In succeeding years, students take a mix of law, psychology, and law/psychology courses, and they collaborate with faculty members in both disciplines on research. They also typically obtain some teaching experience, and they participate in practica in which they can use their dual-disciplinary skills (e.g., state legislative aide, planner in state agency, law clerk for public defender of respondents in civil commitment proceedings).

Most of the interdisciplinary courses are cross-listed, and students can take them for credit toward both degrees. At Nebraska, J.D.-Ph.D. students are able to apply 12 credit hours of coursework and 6 credit hours of research to both of their degree programs. The courses include law and behavioral science (an overview of the law's use, misuse, and nonuse of the behavioral sciences), mental health law, and topics in law and psychology. The topics course is repeatable, and its theme changes. Among the topics considered have been issues in mental health policy, legal policy and child development research, and psychological issues in employment discrimination. The interdisciplinary courses are taught by core faculty in the law/psychology program or team taught by a law professor and a psychology professor.

As compared with other models of psycholegal training, there are three possible major advantages of joint-degree programs. First, because of their broader exposure to the law than students who obtain only a Ph.D., J.D.-Ph.D.s may be better able to identify important issues in areas of law which psychologists have seldom explored (e.g., contracts, tax, trusts and estates). Because psychological assumptions are not limited to criminal, juvenile, family, and mental health law, students with broad legal training should be better equipped to explore and expand the field of psycholegal research. Similarly, legal problems in the organization and delivery of mental health services are not limited to mental health law. Such topics as land use planning, corporation law, and public employment law may all have important places in the psycholegal study of the mental health system. It may not be reasonable to expect even highly specialized Ph.D.s to acquire such broad legal expertise.

Second, there may be something special about being exposed in concentrated form to both disciplines at the same time. The process of moving back and forth between thinking like a lawyer and thinking like a psychologist—discussing topics with oneself using different epistemologies—may be particularly helpful in creating interdisciplinary scholarship.

Third, the possession of basic credentials in both disciplines may assist in achieving entry into diverse settings. To a certain extent, this argument is so obvious as to require no verification. Psychologists are not going to be hired to work in law firms, no matter how well they know mental health law and how skilled they are in advocating patients' interests. Both guild definitions and licensing restrictions bar such employment for psychologists. Analogously, no matter how knowledgeable attorneys without Ph.D.s are about social psychological processes and how experienced they are in inducing organizational and societal change, they are very unlikely to be hired to teach courses in social and community psychology. It may also be reasonable to expect that because of their diverse training and credentials, J.D.-Ph.D.s would have entry into settings traditionally the province of either psychology or law and that they would have an advantage over other applicants.

The employment advantage of J.D.-Ph.D.s, however, may not be as great as one might expect intuitively. For example, one reason sometimes asserted for J.D.-Ph.D. programs is the need to train psychologically sophisticated lawyers who can "infiltrate" law schools and shape the law's responsiveness to psychological evidence. The underlying assumption that J.D.-Ph.D.s will be able easily to obtain positions on law faculties is naive. The track into teaching law in the United States is clear. Most law professors are drawn from a few select national law schools. Law schools look for J.D.s who were members of Order of the Coif, signifying rank in the top 10 percent of one's graduating class, and law review, usually signifying high class rank at the end of the first year of law school. Immediately after graduation, prospective teachers will maximize their chances of eventually joining the faculty of a good law school by accepting a high-status job which will provide substantial experience in legal research and writing (clerk for a respected judge, attorney in the justice department honors program or a federal regulatory agency, or associate in a large firm). Even when a law school has an interest in interdisciplinary studies, it is likely to choose an applicant who has the traditional credentials over a J.D.-Ph.D. who has solid, but not stellar, law school grades. Indeed, a Ph.D. with a record of outstanding scholarship in legally relevant areas will often have easier entree. Exacerbating the situation is the fact that most of the joint-degree programs are located in law schools which are not usually regarded as being in the track for producing law teachers.

As a general matter J.D.-Ph.D.s may find that they are often placed in the position of proving that they are real lawyers (or psychologists). Merely having completed the requirements for two terminal degrees and having diverse skills may not be enough. To establish credibility with their colleagues in both disciplines, joint-degree students need to establish conspicuous credentials as both lawyers and psychologists. Because of the clear tracking based on law-school performance, this point is especially clear in terms of building credibility as a lawyer. At Nebraska, we seek to ensure that students do not just complete both the J.D. and the Ph.D. and integrate them satisfactorily, but that they also develop strong records in each discipline according to traditional criteria. Thus, students are encouraged to pay special attention to law grades, to join law review, and to seek judicial clerkships. They are expected to do both substantive, lengthy legal analyses and empirical research. They are also encouraged to obtain teaching experience in psychology. Even having completed such a rigorous program, J.D.-Ph.D.s may often have to educate potential employers as to what they can do.

Lest this analysis sound too negative, it should be pointed out that J.D.-Ph.D.s are special. When they perform well in both disciplines and their integration, they are in demand, even within traditional status hierarchies. For example, despite the fact that Nebraska is not a school that typically leads law students into judicial clerkships and law teaching, three advanced joint-degree students in the past two years have been successful in obtaining federal clerkships (out of three who have applied). Nonetheless, the point is that some of the special access to positions often presumed to accompany joint degrees is contingent upon special effort and outstanding achievement.

Even if these practical problems are potentially overcome, students may not be sufficiently motivated to seek positions that are truly interdisciplinary. Stanford University has deemphasized its J.D.-Ph.D. option for such a reason. Graduates were finding the opportunity costs of eschewing large-firm law practice (the usual career goal of Stanford lawyers) were too great. Therefore they were not really using their Ph.D. degrees. Consequently, Stanford now emphasizes the master of legal studies (MLS) degree, a one-year law degree, as the complement to the Ph.D. for students in psycholegal studies to ensure that they do not head to law practice. Analogously, Nebraska has dropped the J.D.-Ph.D. option for students majoring in clinical psychology. All of the clinical J.D.-Ph.D.s were finding it very easy to move straight from their internship into practice as clinical psychologists.

Although interdisciplinary background may be useful in law (and psychology) practice, it is hard to imagine a situation in which lawyers in practice would use the level of behavioral science training required for a Ph.D. Analogously, some legal background is useful—indeed, essential—for forensic clinicians, but much of law-school education would be superfluous to a practicing clinical psychologist. Thus, J.D.-Ph.D. programs are inefficient means of training psychologically sophisticated legal practitioners and legally sophisticated clinical psychologists.

Beyond the questionable costs of J.D.-Ph.D. programs as a means of training interdisciplinary practitioners, it is important to note that there are special ethical problems of dual practice. Is the counselor giving the divorcing spouse legal advice or performing psychotherapy? Can an expert have any credibility when he or she is also an attorney in the firm representing the party calling for an opinion?

In summary, there may well be some special pedagogical benefits of joint-degree programs. However, careful analysis needs to be undertaken of the particular kinds of psycholegal careers for which a program leading to both J.D. and Ph.D. degrees is optimal. This analysis is ultimately empirical. There is still a limited data base from which to draw inferences. Logic does dictate, though, that joint-degree programs probably are not the most cost-efficient means of training interdisciplinary practitioners.

Ph.D. Specialty Programs

The major difference between the joint-degree and Ph.D. specialty programs is one of breadth. In the latter programs, students take interdisciplinary courses, do supervised research on psycholegal topics, and participate in practica requiring interdisciplinary skills and knowledge. Indeed, at Nebraska, students in the Ph.D. specialty program take the same interdisciplinary courses as the joint-degree students, identify themselves as law/psychology students, participate in law/psychology colloquia and other activities, and work with the same faculty research sponsors as the joint-degree students. They also take some law courses, although well short of the requirements for the law degree. Rather, specific courses are selected to match the specialty. At Nebraska, the Ph.D. specialty program is for students in clinical psychology who are specializing in forensic psychology. In keeping with this focus, students might take criminal law, family law, juvenile law, and evidence, as well as the cross-registered courses in law and behavioral science, mental health law, and so forth. In addition, they complete a special core course in forensic assessment, and their research, practica, and internship are expected to be compatible with the specialty.

The most common type of Ph.D. specialty program is, like the Nebraska program, intended to produce forensic clinicians. As noted in the preceding section, there are special problems in applying the joint-degree model for such a purpose. (Programs offering a Ph.D. specialty program need not, of course, also offer a joint-degree track. For model curricula for such a program in forensic psychology alone, see Fenster, Litwack, & Symonds, 1975, and Poythress, 1979.) Potentially, though, a specialty program could be developed in any area of law/psychology interaction. Virginia and SUNY-Buffalo offer a major in children, psychology, and the law. Similarly, a specialty program might be developed in environmental policy, psychology, and the law. Students in such a specialty program would complete course work in relevant areas of psychology (e.g., environmental psychology, behavioral toxicology) and law (e.g., environmental law, natural resources law), and they would concentrate research and practica on related topics. Whatever the specialty, the commonality is instruction in interdisciplinary methods and philosophy.

The major disadvantages of the Ph.D. specialty mirror the advantages of the joint-degree model. Students might miss key issues in areas of law which do not appear germane at first glance. For example, the area of law which has the most effect on family structure may be wills and trusts, not family law. Similarly, legal definitions of a family are likely to appear in zoning law, not family law. A student in a specialty on children, psychology, and the law may be less likely than a joint-degree student to be aware of such connections. It is also possible that graduates of specialty programs will have less access to policymaking positions and law school faculties than their peers who completed joint degrees.

On the other hand, students in specialty programs will have achieved mastery of a particular area of psycholegal studies and key problems in interdisciplinary scholarship and practice generally, and they will have done so with significantly less expenditure of time and money for law courses. Moreover, specialty programs provide in-depth study of a specific area. If well designed, they are structured to give all of the students' graduate work an integrated purpose. In some sense the joint-degree student may have to be more active in finding an integrated focus of study.

The advantages and disadvantages of the Ph.D. specialty model apply as well to similar J.D. programs. In such programs, law students acquire basic knowledge of psychological methods and research and theory in particular areas of psychology, and they participate in interdisciplinary seminars and research. Usually they will complete the requirements for a master's degree or its equivalent in the process. J.D. specialty students seek to obtain enough psychological expertise to be collaborators in scholarship (e.g., on problems of family policy) or practitioners in areas of law in which psychology plays a major role (e.g., mental health law).

Ph.D. Minor

Minors in psychology and law differ from joint-degree and specialty programs in breadth, depth, and intensity. Typically, students pursuing a minor in psychology and law will not identify themselves primarily as law/psychology students. Rather they will be working with a major professor interested in a particular aspect of psycholegal studies or taking a few interdisciplinary or law courses because of their relevance to the students' major studies or simply their interest to the student. Students completing a minor will generally not become expert in psycholegal studies, but they may develop sufficient competence to use their work in psychology and law fruitfully.

An analogy can be made to developmental social psychology. Such a psychologist is likely to identify himself or herself primarily as a developmentalist, but he or she will need more than incidental knowledge of social psychology, albeit less than a psychologist whose primary identification is as a social psychologist. Similarly, a social psychologist with a minor in psychology and law may see relevance of his or her work to legal problems and feel a need for background in interdisciplinary studies, even though he or she does not need or wish to become a psycholegal scholar per se. A general clinical psychologist may reasonably seek familiarity with legal issues in practice and basic skills in forensic assessment, even though he or she has no desire to be a forensic specialist.

There is no generally accepted format for a minor in psychology and law, and the depth of training is likely to vary substantially. At Nebraska, the minimum requirements for the psycholegal minor include successful completion of any three interdisciplinary courses and a comprehensive examination. An enterprising student can expand the minor, though, to resemble an individualized psycholegal specialty program.

Postdoctoral Programs

Postdoctoral programs differ from Ph.D. specialty programs primarily in terms of when they occur (i.e., after, rather than during, doctoral training in psychology). (Analogous post-J.D. programs may also be offered.) Consequently, their advantages and disadvantages relative to joint-degree programs are essentially the same as those of specialty programs. Relative to specialty programs, the major disadvantage of postdoctoral study is that it delays identification as a psycholegal scholar; in so doing, there may be missed opportunities for integration of studies from the beginning. Probably the major advantage is that, because competence as a psychologist has already been achieved, there can be a year or two of immersion in attaining competence as a psycholegal scholar. The experience may, therefore, resemble joint-degree programs in the intensity of cognitive conflicts presented (and the need to resolve them).

The professional maturity of postdoctoral trainees may also enable them to use their interdisciplinary studies expeditiously. Because they will have a stronger foundation than predoctoral students in the core discipline, they should be more efficient in identifying psycholegal questions. At Nebraska, there is an attempt to capitalize on these experiences by stimulating postdoctoral fellows to learn interdisciplinary work through their collaboration with each other. Thus, postdoctoral fellows take essentially the same specialized course work as their predoctoral counterparts (i.e., Ph.D. specialty students or J.D.-M.A. students). However, the most powerful education experience often comes from working with other fellows who are not of the same discipline. We pair psychologists with lawyers for experience in collaborative research. They co-teach and even share an office. This pairing usually results in experiential learning itself. Moreover, there is often a mutual tutorial relationship. The lawyer assists the psychologist with the vagaries of first-year law courses, and the psychologist helps the lawyer in the fine points of behavioral science methods.

Conclusions

Perhaps the clearest statement that can be made on the basis of this review of models of psycholegal training is that no model is clearly superior for all purposes. For example, it seems unlikely that joint-degree programs are optimal for training in a particular area of psycholegal study, but it may be that there are some advantages, substantive or practical, of joint-degree programs in training scholars who identify their primary area of concentration as psychology and law, rather than in a traditional subdiscipline.

Two important points follow from this general conclusion. First, before a program is established, there needs to be careful analysis of whether there is a logical relation between the goals and the methods of training. A joint-degree model should not be adopted merely because it sounds intriguing, nor should it be rejected simply because the administrative arrangements sound cumbersome or there is uncritical espousal of pure disciplinary training, even on interdisciplinary topics. Probably the more specific that hypotheses are about the crucial processes involved in achieving particular kinds of interdisciplinary training, the more likely that a program will be designed to foster the desired integration.

Second, most of the purported pros and cons of the various models are in fact hypotheses. Now that programs are reaching sufficient maturity that they can follow graduates, there is an opportunity for evaluation research. The need for such research is particularly profound because of the diversity of extant programs. Research on the process of training would also be useful. What is it like to begin thinking like a psychologist-lawyer or a legally sophisticated psychologist? What sorts of training activities are most likely to provide such "aha" experiences?

Finally, whatever the actual merits of the various models, their popularity will be contingent to a large extent on structural and ideological factors within the professions. For example, current federal policies favoring postdoctoral training will affect universities' willingness to enter into postdoctoral training in psycholegal studies.

Similarly, the conventional wisdom as to the desirability of specialization and subspecialization in predoctoral psychological training generally (e.g., whether students should be permitted or encouraged to major in clinical child psychology instead of general clinical psychology) is likely to shape departments' attitudes toward forensic specialty programs, especially if prevailing attitudes of the profession as a whole are translated into accreditation standards.

CONTINUING EDUCATION

Continuing Education of Specialists

It is a cliché that professionals have a duty to stay abreast of developments in their field. For most professionals, this obligation represents a task that they would likely fulfill anyway, simply because of interest in their work. Nonetheless, because changes in the law are often abrupt rather than gradual, forensic specialists bear a special duty to maintain a systematic continuing education program for themselves. The significance of this duty is heightened because of the potential consequences of forensic assessments. Consider the following example. A clinician is asked to perform an evaluation pursuant to a capital sentencing proceeding. Unbeknownst to the clinician, though, the legislature has enacted a change in the standard for imposition of the death sentence, or the state supreme court has issued an opinion which clarifies the meaning of the standard. The specter of a clinician performing such an evaluation with literally life-and-death consequences without accurate knowledge of the controlling law is chilling.

Although the consequences of a psycholegal researcher's not keeping up with changes in the law relevant to his or her interests are less grave, at least in the short term, researchers also need to keep an up-to-date knowledge of changes in the law, if their work is to retain usefulness to the law. Unless researchers systematically follow appellate opinions in their area of interest, they also may miss those golden opportunities when a court invites empirical research by suggesting in dicta that it might reach a different result if particular empirical evidence were available.

There are several ways in which forensic specialists can stay abreast of changes in the law. Probably the most efficient, although sometimes rather costly, means of keeping up is to subscribe to *United States Law Week* and specialized reporters in one's area of interest (e.g., *Family Law Reporter*; *Mental and Physical Disability Law Reporter*). Such materials will be available in any good law library. It is also worthwhile to make a periodic trip to the law library to scan the advance sheets of appellate courts in one's jurisdiction and the session laws of the state legislature for developments relevant to one's practice.

In addition to perusing the relevant law reporters and specialized journals (e.g., *Law and Human Behavior*; *Criminal Justice and Behavior*; *Bulletin of the American Academy of Psychiatry and Law*; *Law and Behavioral Science*), forensic specialists can often obtain needed information quickly by reading newsletters (e.g., *American Psychology–Law Society Newsletter*; "Judicial Notebook" in the *APA Monitor*) which contain nutshells of at least some important developments. The *AP–LS Newsletter* also lists relevant articles in recent issues of major law reviews, a type of source that even major researchers in psychology and law often underutilize (Morris, 1985).

Advanced workshops and symposia at professional meetings are, of course, other sources of information about current developments. One problem, though, with this source of continuing education is that, in a given jurisdiction, there may not be enough forensic specialists to warrant such formal opportunities. At least in terms of forensic clinical practice, the state department of mental health or the attorney general's office can do a real service by systematically disseminating changes in the law to the relevant practitioners. A model of such a program is at the Institute of Law, Psychiatry, and Public Policy at the University of Virginia. Under contract with the Virginia Department of Mental Health and Mental Retardation, the Institute publishes a newsletter, *Developments in Mental Health Law*, and also conducts periodic workshops and consultation for clinicians who have passed a basic training course and examination in forensic assessment, as described in the following section.

Basic Training through Continuing Education

It is unlikely that the university training programs will meet the demand for forensic psychologists in the foreseeable future. Besides the fact that there are still few joint-degree, Ph.D. specialty, and postdoctoral programs, the trend is toward making forensic services a routine part of community mental health practice. There has been a recognition that most forensic evaluations can be done validly and reliably in brief outpatient assessments (Melton et al., 1985; Roesch & Golding, 1980; Slobogin, Melton, & Showalter, 1984). Given that lengthy inpatient evaluations in forensic hospitals intrude on a defendant's liberty and his or her rights to bail, a speedy trial, and effective assistance of counsel, such unnecessary hospitalization is probably unconstitutional (ABA, 1984; Melton et al., 1985). Moreover, the cost to the state of forensic mental health services for indigent defendants is much higher than necessary when the state relies on a central forensic hospital. If these points are followed to their logical conclusion, then states should move their forensic services into the community. Such a service model requires training of teams in community clinics to perform the necessary evaluations.

It is inevitable that general clinicians who do not perceive themselves as having forensic services as part of their workload will also be drawn into forensic practice on occasion, whether willfully or not, whether prepared or not. When a client becomes involved in a custody dispute or possibly subject to civil commitment or guardianship or enters treatment as a condition of probation, the mental health professional is likely to be called on to give expert opinions to the court.

In view of such involvement of clinicians in the legal system, even though they were not trained as forensic psychologists in graduate school or postdoctoral study, there is a need for development of forensic knowledge and skills among general clinicians through continuing education. There is evidence that such basic training through continuing education is possible, but only under certain conditions. In an experiment mandated by the Virginia General Assembly, Melton et al. (1985) provided an eight-day training program for teams of community mental health professionals in selected centers across the state. Integral to the success of the program was that it involved institution of a community-based *system* with the support of the commissioner of mental health, the attorney general's office, and the state supreme court. Rather than just training clinicians, the program staff worked with state and local authorities to ensure that evaluations in the experimental communities were performed in the community clinics. The training itself involved a sophisticated mix of law, research, and clinical technique taught by an interdisciplinary faculty at the UVa Institute of Law, Psychiatry, and Public Policy. The materials served as the basis for a large handbook of forensic assessment (Melton et al., in press).

The Virginia program in fact resulted in a substantial decrease in inpatient evaluations and a corresponding large decrease in costs, without an undue net-widening effect (Melton et al., 1985). Of particular interest in the present context, though, is that the training program resulted in trainees' obtaining a level of forensic knowledge commensurate with diplomates in forensic psychology. The trainees were found to have knowledge of relevant law, research, and clinical technique greater than several groups of general clinicians and a sample of trial judges. Their reports were also judged as superior by trial judges, prosecutors, and defense attorneys who rated the reports blind to the identity of the authors.

Within the comparison groups, level of forensic training made no difference in knowledge of forensic issues. Having taken relevant courses in graduate school, previous training programs at the UVa Institute, or continuing education workshops did not affect level of knowledge. It is thus suggested that, while training as a forensic specialist can be accomplished through a continuing-education course, it will have substantial effect only if there are structures in place for actually using the new knowledge. Otherwise, there are insufficient incentives for adequately acquiring, maintaining, and expanding knowledge of forensic psychology. An occasional workshop is unlikely to provide the depth of knowledge necessary for someone to function competently as a forensic psychologist.

CONCLUSIONS

Whatever the means psychologists have of obtaining training in psychology and law, the potential utility of such training seems beyond dispute at this point. The law is filled with behavioral assumptions—at its most basic, the assumption that the law in fact affects behavior (Melton, 1985). There is a need for psychologists, lawyers, and psychologist-lawyers to determine and evaluate these assumptions so that public policy can be made and implemented rationally. Similarly, insofar as a knowledge of psychology will inform adjudication of individual cases, justice demands the careful application of this knowledge. Before entering the legal system psychologists should be educated in the nature of the inquiry and the specialized psychological knowledge (and its limits) relevant to the particular legal issues.

As indicated throughout this chapter, there are multiple models of acquiring the necessary training, but the optimum form and content of training is still undecided even for particular purposes. The questions about training in psychology and law will be answered only with empirical study. In the meantime, however, several considerations might guide prospective students in deciding upon a training program.

First, and most obviously, the prospective student should be certain that the goals of the program match his or her own. Does it seek to train researchers or practitioners? What areas of psychology and law does it purport to cover? Second, the curriculum should be examined to ensure that it really offers an integration of psychology and law and that it gives due attention to the philosophical problems in applying psychology to the law. Third, is there a strong core faculty with a track record of psycholegal scholarship, and are both psychology and law faculty integrated into the program, even if they do not identify themselves primarily as psycholegal scholars? Fourth, is there a core group of students in the program? Given that learning often occurs through interaction with peers inside and outside the classroom, the availability of students with similar interests is an important consideration which is often overlooked. It is particularly important in an interdisciplinary program because of the especially acute issues in establishing a professional identity. Fifth, the prospective student should examine the reputation of the program and the departments or colleges of which it is a part; for example, if a student's ultimate goal is law teaching, he or she should give special attention to programs located in law schools with a national reputation.

No doubt, other considerations may be important in individual cases, including personal preferences (e.g., geographic preference). Whatever the calculus, the student who is successful in achieving admission to, and ultimately graduating from, a top-notch program in psycholegal studies can be assured of an exciting career. The field of psycholegal studies is still sufficiently novel that an outstanding psychologist can quickly achieve visibility. There is the possibility of substantial contribution, whether professional or scientific or both, to social welfare.

REFERENCES

American Bar Association. (1984). *Criminal justice mental health standards.* Washington, DC: Author.

American Psychological Association. (1981). Ethical principles of psychologists. *American Psychologist, 36,* 633–638.

Bonnie, R. J., & Slobogin, C. (1980). The role of mental health professionals in the criminal process: The case for informed speculation. *Virginia Law Review, 66,* 427–522.

Fenster, C. A., Litwack, T. R., & Symonds, M. (1975). The making of a forensic psychologist: Needs and goals for doctoral training. *Professional Psychology, 4,* 457–467.

Grisso, T., Sales, B. D., & Bayless, S. (1982). Law-related courses and programs in graduate psychology departments. *American Psychologist, 37,* 267–278.

Haney, C. (1980). Psychology and legal change: On the limits of a factual jurisprudence. *Law and Human Behavior, 4,* 147–199.

Lawlor, R. J., Siskind, G., & Brooks, J. (1981). Forensic training at internships: Update and criticism of current unspecified training models. *Professional Psychology, 12,* 400–405.

Levine, D., Wilson, K., & Sales, B. D. (1980). An exploratory assessment of APA internships with legal/forensic experiences. *Professional Psychology, 11,* 64–71.

Loh, W. (1981). Psycholegal research: Past and present. *Michigan Law Review, 79,* 659–707.

Melton, G. B. (1983). Training in psychology and law: A directory. *Division of Psychology and Law Newsletter, 3,* 1–5.

Melton, G. B. (1984). Developmental psychology and the law: The state of the art. *Journal of Family Law, 22,* 445–482.

Melton, G. B. (1985). Introduction: The law and motivation. In G. B. Melton (Ed.), *Nebraska Symposium on Motivation: The law as a behavioral instrument* (Vol. 33, pp. xiii-xxvii). Lincoln, NE: University of Nebraska Press.

Melton, G. B., Koocher, G. P., & Saks, M. J. (Eds.). (1983). *Children's competence to consent.* New York: Plenum.

Melton, G. B., Petrila, J., Poythress, N. G., Jr., & Slobogin, C. (in press). *Psychological evaluations for the courts: A handbook for mental health professionals and lawyers.* New York: Guilford.

Melton, G. B., Weithorn, L. A., & Slobogin, C. (1985). *Community mental health centers and the courts: An evaluation of community-based forensic services*. Lincoln, NE: University of Nebraska Press.

Monahan, J., & Loftus, E. F. (1982). The psychology of law. *Annual Review of Psychology, 33*, 441–475.

Morris, R. A. (1986). *Law in applied social research*. Unpublished doctoral dissertation, University of Nebraska-Lincoln.

Morse, S. J. (1978). Crazy behavior, morals and science: An analysis of mental health law. *Southern California Law Review, 51*, 527–563.

Morse, S. J. (1982a). Failed explanations and criminal responsibility: Experts and the unconscious. *Virginia Law Review, 68*, 971–1084.

Morse, S. J. (1982b). Reforming expert testimony: An open response from the tower (and the trenches). *Law and Human Behavior, 6*, 45–47.

Poythress, N. G., Jr. (1978). Psychiatric expertise in civil commitment: Training attorneys to cope with expert testimony. *Law and Human Behavior, 2*, 1–23.

Poythress, N. G., Jr. (1979). A proposal for training in forensic psychology. *American Psychologist, 34*, 612–621.

Poythress, N. G., Jr. (1982). Concerning reform in expert testimony: An open letter from a practicing psychologist. *Law and Human Behavior, 6*, 39–43.

Rappaport, J. (1977). *Community psychology: Values, research, and action*. New York: Holt, Rinehart & Winston.

Roesch, R., & Golding, S. (1980). *Competency to stand trial*. Urbana, IL: University of Illinois Press.

Slobogin, C. (1982). *Estelle v. Smith:* The constitutional contours of the forensic evaluation. *Emory Law Journal, 31*, 71–138.

Slobogin, C., Melton, G. B., & Showalter, C. (1984). Feasibility of a brief screening evaluation of mental state at the time of the offense. *Law and Human Behavior, 8*, 305–320.

Thibaut, J., & Walker, L. (1978). A theory of procedure. *California Law Review, 66*, 541–566.

Author Index

Aadland, R., 440
Abeles, N., 671
Abramson, M.F., 602
Adams, W., 612
Adorno, T., 298
Adserballe, H., 219
Ageton, S., 591
Ainsworth, D., 481
Ajzen, I., 300
Akeson, W.H., 136, 140
Alba, J.W., 259, 268
Albanese, J., 330
Albert, S., 531
Alessi, G., 158, 178
Alexander, C.P., 188
Alexander, J.F., 260
Alexander, Y., 440
Alfini, J.J., 303
Alford, J.M., 120
Algozzine, B., 158, 172, 174, 181–182
Allen, H.E., 326, 346
Allen, J.G., 520
Allen, R.C., 531, 540
Allodi, F.A., 603
Alper, A., 276
Altman, I., 569
Aman, C., 264
Anastasi, A., 158
Anderson, P.R., 569
Andreasen, N.C., 421, 547
Andriks, J.L., 275
Anthony, N., 141
Antunes, G., 586
Applebaum, P., 227
Arcand, S., 447
Arenella, P., 354–356, 361
Arieti, S., 532
Arnold, J.E., 594
Arnold, T., 31

Arvanities, T., 413
Ash, P., 472
Asher, R., 532
Askinazi, C., 215, 218
Atkeson, B.M., 112
Atkinson, G., 491, 502
Attig. M.S., 268
Augustus, J., 322
Ault, R.L., 439
Austin, W., 559
Avery, M.C., 279
Ayer, J., 144
Ayllon, T., 580
Azen, S.P., 441

Bach-y-Rita, G., 224, 234
Backer, T.E., 437
Backster, C., 464
Baddeley, A.D., 260, 263, 274, 276
Badger, L.W., 133
Baehr, M.E., 441
Bagby, R.M., 665
Bahrick, H.P., 265
Bahrick, P.O., 265
Bailis, K. L., 276
Baker, E., 297, 303
Baker, R., 452
Baker, T.B., 182
Ballantine, H.W., 406
Bandura, A., 17, 586
Banks, W.C., 621
Barber, T.X., 497, 501
Bard, N., 451
Barkdull, W.L., 330
Barland, G.H., 463–464, 470, 473–474, 477, 480
Barnes, H.E., 322
Barnett, W.S., 595
Baron, R.A., 17

Baron, R.S., 267
Baron, S.L., 311
Barr, J.S., 136
Barry, H., Jr., 136
Barth, R.P., 119–120
Bartlett, F., 259, 262
Bartol, C.R., 29, 39–40
Barton, W.E., 665
Barton, W.E., 662
Bassett, H.T., 145
Batsche, G., 174
Bauman, M.A., 547
Baumann, R.C., 120
Bauschard, L., 646
Bayless, S., 682
Bazelon, D., 189
Beals, R.K., 133–134, 144
Beasley, W.R., 414
Beccaria, C.B., 585
Beck, E.L., 311
Beck, J., 219, 226
Becker, E., 196
Becker, H.S., 591
Becker, L., 174
Beidleman, W.B., 497–498, 504
Beidleman, W., 217
Beigel, A., 443
Beigel, H., 443
Beis, F.B., 664–666
Bekerian, D.A., 269
Bell, D.J., 117–118
Bellak, L., 421
Belohlavek, N., 120
Belt, J.A., 484
Bender, L.A., 175, 177
Bennett, R., 182
Bennett, T., 592
Ben-Shakhar, G., 470
Bentham, J., 585
Beran, N.J., 380
Berberich, J., 29, 660
Berdie, R., 14
Beres, D., 247
Berg, B., 113
Berg, K., 298
Bergan, J., 178
Berger, L.S., 540, 547
Berk, R.A., 297, 587, 645
Berkman, 646
Berkowitz, L., 17
Berkstresser, C.D., 540
Berlin, L., 323
Berman, A.L., 547
Berman, J., 294, 296

Berner, J.G., 441, 443
Bernheim, H., 490
Bernstein, B.E., 111, 116
Bernstein, H.A., 665
Berrueta-Clement, J.R., 595
Berry, F.D., 381
Berry, K.K., 547
Bersh, P.J., 472, 475
Bersoff, D., 160, 169, 174, 520
Beschner, G.M., 625
Billig, M., 276
Binet, A., 5, 10
Birch, J.W., 181
Bird, R.E., 354, 360
Birnbaum, H.J., 624
Bishop, D.M., 590
Bitterman, M.E., 478
Black, D., 532
Black, H.C., 395, 397
Blackman, N., 234, 239
Blackmore, J., 448–450
Blake, G.F., 592
Blanchard, K.H., 448
Blashfield, R.K., 418, 520
Blau, T.H., 90, 145, 523, 540, 547
Bleechmore, J., 16
Blinder, M., 362–363, 540, 545
Blisk, D., 113
Bloom, J.D., 400, 413, 419
Blum, R.H., 440
Blumberg, A.S., 29, 31
Boehm, V., 298–299
Bograd, M., 118, 640
Bohn, M.J., 234
Boice, R., 275
Boisvenu, G., 481
Bolton, F.G., 5
Boltz, F.A., Jr., 445
Bonnie, R.J., 356, 396, 401, 414, 422, 424, 681
Bordens, K.S., 308
Borgida, E., 118
Bothwell, R.K., 310
Bottoms, A., 206
Boucher, R., 207–208, 210, 212, 231
Bouhoustos, J., 547, 647
Bower, B., 25
Bower, G.H., 260, 493
Bowers, J.M., 269
Bowers, K.S., 497, 504
Bowker, L.H., 558
Bowlby, J., 110
Boyer, J., 665
Bradley, M.T., 481
Bradshaw, J.M., 268

Braff, J., 413
Braiman, A., 531
Brakel, S.J., 385
Brancale, R., 234
Bray, D.W., 660
Bray, J.H., 666
Bray, R.M., 293
Brecher, E.M., 624
Bregman, N.J., 268–269
Breuer, J., 494
Briggs, D., 625
Brigham, J.C., 272, 273, 275, 282, 310
Britt, S.H., 13
Broderick, J.J., 29
Brodsky, S.L., 437, 511, 534, 540–541, 571, 605, 612, 615, 665
Brokaw, J.R., 478
Bromberg, W., 531, 540, 545
Bronner, A.F., 8
Bronson, E.J., 303
Brooks, J., 682
Brown, A.C., 38
Brown, E.L., 274–275
Brown, F.G., 158
Brown, M., 13, 559
Brown, R., 280
Brown, S., 624
Brown, S.E., 118
Brown, T., 136
Browne, A., 633, 641, 643, 646
Brownsword, R., 206
Bruce, D., 268
Bruner, J.A., 262
Bryjak, G.J., 589
Buber, M., 676
Buchanan, R.W., 304
Buckhout, R., 260–261, 270–271, 274, 276
Buckley, J.P., 472
Budman, S.H., 565–566
Bugden, W., 210
Buikhuisen, W., 590
Bukatman, B.A., 385
Bukstel, L.H., 39, 559–560
Bulkley, J., 278
Bull, R., 275
Burgess, A.W., 119
Burgess, R., 640
Buri, J., 275
Burke, R., 274
Burkowitz, P., 275
Burnam, M.A., 135
Burns, H.J., 267
Burns, T.E., 263
Burns, T.F., 425

Burquest, B., 234
Bursten, B., 193
Burt, M.R., 631, 634, 639
Burtt, H.G., 13
Butler, A., 144
Butler, B., 220
Butler, B.T., 385
Butler, R.W., 667
Butters, M.J., 270

Cady, H.M., 13, 270
Cahn, E., 15
Caillet, R., 133
Cairns, D., 144
Cairns, H., 13
Callanan, P., 547, 664, 666
Calverley, D.S., 497
Camara, K.A., 113
Camp, C., 607
Camp, G., 607
Campbell, C., 439
Campbell, I.M., 442
Cantrill, H., 262
Caplan, G., 438, 564
Caplan, L., 25
Caplinger, T.E., 594
Carlson, E.W., 326
Carmen, E.H., 633, 644
Carroll, J.S., 586
Carter, R.M., 323
Cass, L.K., 593
Cattell, J.M., 4, 6
Cattell, R.B., 441
Cavanaugh, J.L., 418, 614
Ceci, S., 268, 277
Chaiken, J.M., 442, 588
Chamelin, N.C., 9
Chance, J., 141, 273–275
Chandler, J., 569
Charles, S.C., 668
Charrow, P., 304
Chelune, G.J., 144
Chern, S., 276
Chernoff, P.A., 385
Chevigny, P., 443
Chiang, B., 179
Chiricos, T.G., 586, 588
Christensen, A., 594
Christiaansen, R.E., 268–269
Christie, R., 294
Claiborn, W.L., 446, 607
Clark, C.R., 366
Clark, K., 15

Clark, R., 234
Clark, S., 547
Clarparede, E., 5
Cleckley, H., 480, 532, 547
Clements, C.B., 569
Clemmer, D., 39
Clifford, B.R., 260–261, 274–276
Climenshaw, H.K., 113
Climent, C., 224
Cobb, S., 446
Cocozza, J., 206, 211, 213–214, 224, 231
Cofer, C.N., 141
Cohen, B., 442
Cohen, E., 363
Cohen, F., 40, 324, 573, 615
Cohen, J., 297
Cohen, J.S., 31
Cohen, L.H., 607
Cohen, M., 210
Cohen, R., 437
Cohen, R.C., 277
Cohen, S., 244
Cohen-Sandler, R., 547
Cohn, A., 31
Coid, J., 602
Coles, G.F., 181
Collins, J.J., 604–605
Collins, R., 308
Colman, R., 294
Comfort, J.C., 299, 301–302
Conger, J.J., 547
Conrad, J.P., 330
Constantini, E., 304, 311
Conte, J.R., 631
Cook, M.R., 481
Cook, P.J., 587–588
Cooke, G., 379, 413, 439
Cooley, C.H., 591
Cooper, D.S., 271, 279, 281
Cooper, G.L., 446–447
Cooper, H.H., 444, 559
Cooper, J.E., 418
Cooper, R., 140–141
Corey, G., 547, 664, 666
Corey, M.S., 547, 664, 666
Cornell, C.P., 117
Corsini, R., 14
Courtois, M.R., 275
Cowan, C.L., 302
Cowan, P.A., 671
Cowen, E.L., 564
Cox, M., 113, 224, 242–243, 524
Cox, R., 524, 113
Cox, V., 569

Crane, P., 144
Craswell, R., 35
Criss, M.L., 427
Cromwell, P.F., 322
Cronbach, L., 158
Cross, T., 470
Crotty, H.D., 396, 404
Crouch, B.M., 40
Crowther, C., 585
Crump, D., 303
Culley, J.A., 444
Cummings, T.G., 437
Cutler, B.L., 293, 304, 306–307, 310–311

Daie, N., 470
Dale, P.S., 278
Damarin, F., 275
Daniels, M., 34
Danish, S.J., 570
Danzig, E.R., 13
Darley, J.G., 14
David, D., 531
Davidson, G.P., 444–445, 448
Davidson, H.A., 119–120
Davidson, M.J., 448
Davidson, T., 117
Davidson, W.A., 472
Davies, G., 260, 274
Davis, D.L., 382
Dawson, J.G., 141
DeBobes, L., 38
Decker, P.J., 479, 485
Deffenbacher, K., 263, 272–275, 310
DeGrazia, E., 385
DeLeon, G., 625
Delgado, R., 547
Delugach, F., 155
Dembitz, N., 223
Dempsey, J., 547
Denkowski, G.C., 602
Denkowski, K.M., 602
Deno, S.L., 158, 179
Dent, H.R., 270–271, 278
Depue, R., 450–451
Derbyshire, R.C., 670
deReuck, A.V.S., 547
Desor, J.A., 569
Devine, P.G., 271, 282
Deyoub, P.L., 547–548
Dhanens, T.P., 497
Diamond, B.L., 220, 360–361, 395–398, 400–402, 439, 495, 502, 540, 547, 657
Dickey, W., 385
Diclemente, C.C., 545

Dies, R., 619
Dillon, C.A., 526
DiMona, J., 294
Dinges, D.F., 532, 547
Dinitz, S., 593–594
Distad, L.J., 120
Dix, G.E., 352–356, 358, 360–361
Dix, G., 205, 214, 224, 226, 244
Dobash, R.E., 117, 633
Dobash, R.P., 633
Dodd, D.H., 268
Dodge, R.E., 280–281
Dodson, J.D., 263
Doerfler, L.A., 140
Dohrenwend, B.P., 446, 568
Dohrenwend, B.S., 446, 568
Donnelly, J., 664–665
Doob, A.N., 273
Douce, R.G., 499
Dougherty, D., 470
Doxey, N.C., 144
Drasgow, J., 144
Dreher, R., 144
Dressler, D., 323
Dritsas, W.J., 268
Drobny, J., 36
Droemueller, W., 118
Duddy, A., 571
Duncan, E.M., 277
Dunford, F.W., 592
Dunner, A., 584
Dunnette, M.D., 440–441
Durphy, M., 646
Dutton, D.C., 118
Dvoskin, J.A., 561, 565
Dyk, R., 275
Dywan, J., 497, 504
Dzioba, R.B., 144

Eagly, A.H., 268
Earle, H., 452
Easterbrook, J.A., 263
Eaves, D., 386
Ebbesen, E.B., 25, 30–31, 293, 587
Ebbinghaus, H.E., 5, 260, 265, 266
Eber, H.W., 441
Edgerton, R., 181
Egan, D., 266, 272
Egeth, H.E., 259, 263–264, 272, 283
Eisenberg, T., 438, 440
Ekman, P., 476
Elaad, E., 470
Elias, R., 632
Elkins, A.M., 438

Ellenberger, H.F., 490
Ellenson, G.S., 120
Ellinwood, E., 246
Elliot, E.S., 276
Elliot, R., 41
Elliott, D.S., 591–592
Elliott, R., 169
Ellis, H.D., 260, 265–266, 274, 276
Ellison, K.W., 442, 446
Ellsworth, P.C., 271, 302
Elwork, A., 303–304, 313, 665
Emory, R., 206
Emrich, B., 294
Emrich, R., 210
Endicott, J., 418
Endler, N.S., 524
Engels, D.W., 665
English, H.B., 15
Ennis, B., 206, 208, 212, 221, 225–226, 229, 231, 233
Ennis, P., 29
Ensminger, M.E., 584
Entwisle, D.R., 273–274
Epstein, A.S., 595
Epstein, R., 340
Erdelyi, N.H., 497
Erhard, W., 548
Erikson, K.T., 591
Erlinder, C.P., 356
Eron, L.D., 524
Ervin, F., 224, 234, 245
Estrich, S., 222
Etzioni, A., 294
Evans, R., 217
Everett, C.A., 111
Ewing, C.P., 425
Eysenck, H.J., 10, 17, 38, 276, 520, 545

Fagan, T.K., 155
Fant, E., 215, 218
Faria, G., 120
Farmer, R., 448–449
Farr, J.L., 441
Farrington, D.P., 584, 592–593
Farthing-Capowich, D., 414–415
Faterson, H., 275
Favole, R.J., 379
Feinman, S., 273–274
Feldman, M.S., 308
Feldman, R.A., 594
Fell, R., 446
Fennimore, D., 547
Fenster, A., 110
Fenster, C., 213, 689

Ferguson, R.J., 480
Ferguson, T.J., 304, 310
Fernald, G.M., 7–8
Fersch, E.A., 659
Ferster, E.Z., 540
Figlio, R.M., 585
Figueroa, D., 274
Filer, R.J., 442
Fincham, F., 401, 415
Finckenauer, J.O., 586
Fingarette, H., 35, 353–354, 371
Fink, R., 502
Finkelhor, D., 119, 548, 631–632
Fiore, B.A., 330
Fishbein, M., 300
Fitzgerald, J.F., 380
Fitzgerald, R., 302
Fivush, R., 261, 266
Fleischman, M.J., 594
Fleming, J.A., 481
Floch, M., 480
Flor, H., 133
Flynn, M.B., 268
Flynn, R., 144
Ford, D., 33
Fordyce, W.E., 133–134
Forehand, R.L., 112
Forer, B., 547
Fornelius, B.A., 442
Foster, H.H., 107–108, 112
Foster, K.R., 37
Foster, M.W., Jr., 134, 136
Fowler, R., 217
Foy, J.L., 385
Frank, B., 348
Franke, K.J., 668
Frankel, M.E., 31
Frazier, P., 118
Freed, D.J., 107–108, 112
Freedman, J.L., 569
Freedman, L.Z., 444
French, J., Jr., 446–447
Frenkel-Brunswik, E., 298
Freud, A., 116
Freud, S., 10
Friedman, A., 262
Friedman, A.F., 520
Friedman, M., 442
Froemel, E.C., 441
Fukunaga, K., 400, 419
Fuller, M., 547
Fulton, J.P., 406–407, 412
Furcon, J.E., 440–441, 443
Fuselier, G.W., 444–445

Galambos, N.L., 570
Gallucci, N.T., 142
Galper, R.E., 273–275
Gansler, D., 275
Gardner, K., 382
Garfinkel, H., 591
Garofalo, R., 207–209, 214, 218, 231
Gayral, L., 235
Gazda, G.M., 594
Geberth, V.J., 439
Gediman, H.K., 421
Geiger, S., 442, 448–449
Gelles, R.A., 632
Gelles, R.J., 117, 234, 547–548
Gentz, J.L., 446
Gerard, H.B., 262
Gerbasi, K.C., 298
Gerber, G.L., 110, 213
Gerber, M.M., 162, 181
Gerken, K.C., 162
Gersten, J.C., 593
Gerver, I., 31
Gettinger, S., 328, 342, 444
Gettman, L.R., 447
Giannelli, P.C., 427
Gibbons, D.C., 592
Gibbs, J.J., 602, 604
Gibbs, J., 559
Gibson, J.G., 133
Gilbert, D.G., 144
Gilbert, M.A., 25
Gilbert, R., 311
Gill, M., 175
Gilliland, A., 274
Gilliland, M., 307
Ginsberg, M., 532, 535, 539
Ginton, A., 470, 477
Girdner, L.K., 108
Glaser, D., 338, 344, 438, 585
Glaser, G.H., 593
Glasser, W., 594
Glazer, M.P., 670
Glazer, P.M., 670
Glickman, S.E., 263
Glueck, E.T., 593
Glueck, S., 593
Goble, G.W., 25
Goddard, H.H., 10–11
Goebel, J., 87
Goetze, H., 274
Gold, R.S., 545
Goldaber, I., 444
Goldberg, R.W., 129
Golden, C.J., 144

Golding, J.M., 278
Golding, S.L., 34, 378–383, 385–386, 388–389, 400, 415–419, 424–425, 681, 694
Goldkamp, J., 587
Goldstein, A.G., 266, 273–274, 273–276
Goldstein, A.P., 444
Goldstein, A.S., 407
Goldstein, J., 116
Goldstein, R.L., 382
Goldzband, M.G., 89, 106, 108, 116
Goleman, D., 192
Golten, R.J., 385
Goode, S., 38
Goodenough, D., 275
Goodman, G.S., 193, 258, 264, 277–279, 637
Goodman, S.A., 10
Goodwin, J., 117
Goodwin, R.C., 380
Gorenstein, G.Y., 271
Gottesman, J., 14, 16, 441
Gottfredson, D.M., 321
Gottfredson, M.R., 587
Gough, H.G., 441
Graden, J., 158, 172, 174, 181–182
Graesser, A., 262
Grainey, T.F., 136, 140
Grasmick, H.G., 589
Gray, S., 395–397
Greenberg, D.F., 587–588
Greenberg, J., 14–15
Greenberg, M., 547
Greenberg, M.S., 31, 295, 587
Greene, E., 267–268, 304, 308–309
Greenland, C., 416
Greer, J.G., 624
Gregory, D., 605
Grencik, J.M., 446
Gresham, F., 168
Grimes, J., 174
Grinker, R.R., 531
Griset, P., 615
Grisso, T., 380, 388, 682
Griswold, H.J., 334
Gross, H., 17
Gross, M.L., 41
Grossman, H., 172
Grossman, M., 664–665
Grote, D.F., 111
Groth, A.N., 119, 210, 624
Gruendel, J., 261
Gudeman, H., 419
Guidubaldi, J., 113
Gunn, J., 224
Guralnick, L., 446

Gurman, A.S., 565–566
Guth, M., 191, 275
Guthiel, T.G., 531, 540
Guttmacher, M., 240
Guy, W.A., 411

Haas, L.J., 547
Haber, H.G., 196
Haberman, B.G., 116
Hacker, F.J., 445
Haith, M.M., 278
Hale, M., 5–6
Hall, H., 208
Hall, J.A., 415
Hallahan, D., 156
Halleck, S.L., 234, 237, 531, 540, 665–666
Hamilton, V.L., 268
Hammonds, B.B., 531, 540
Handelsman, M.M., 671
Haney, C., 39–40, 302, 312, 621, 683
Hanley, C.P., 275
Hanrahan, K.J., 345
Hans, V.P., 35, 396, 409
Hans, V.T., 293–294, 298
Harding, T., 219
Hare, R.D., 17, 480–481, 685
Hargrave, G.E., 441, 443
Harlow, C.W., 31
Harnick, M.A., 277
Harper, D.C., 135
Harring, S., 297
Harrington, D.C., 547
Hart, H.L.A., 396, 398
Hartman, T.L., 451–452
Hartshorne, T.S., 166
Hartstone, E., 382
Harvey, D.R., 619
Hasher, L., 259, 268
Hasse, A.F., 353–354, 371
Hassel, C.V., 444
Hastie, R., 31, 297, 300–301, 305
Hastorf, A.H., 262
Hawkins, G., 659
Hawkins, M., 400, 419
Hawrish, E., 547
Hayes, L.M., 559, 609
Haynes, W.D., 442
Hays, J.R., 666
Healy, W., 7–8
Heather, N., 559
Heaton, R.K., 144
Heckel, R.V., 478
Heeren, J., 586
Heider, F., 36

Helfer, R.E., 118
Heller, K., 180
Helzer, J.E., 418
Henderson, N.D., 441
Hennessy, M., 297
Henningsen, R.J., 322
Henson, R.D., 24
Henze, F., 304
Hepps, R.B., 246
Herbsleb, J.D., 294
Herman, J.L., 633
Hermann, D.H.J., 395–397
Hernstein, R.J., 619
Herron, J.L., 40
Hersey, P., 448
Hershey, E., 445
Hess, A.K., 25, 38, 41, 90, 619, 671
Hess, R., 40, 113
Hesse, K.A., 113
Hetherington, E.M., 113, 524
Heuer, L.B., 304–305
Hewett, J.E., 140
Hickman, N., 133–134, 144
Hicks, T., 385
Hilberman, E., 633
Hilgard, E.R., 439, 491, 501
Hilgard, J.R., 501
Hilgren, J., 448–450
Hilkey, J.H., 619
Hilliard, A., 175, 178
Hillman, D., 234
Hinkle, E., Jr., 446
Hinton, J.W., 547
Hirschfeld, A.H., 140
Hirschfeld, M.L., 140
Hirschman, J., 264
Hobbs, N., 156, 181
Hodes, R.L., 481
Hodges, A., 437
Hoelter, H.H., 586
Hoff, E., 274
Hoffman, C., 275
Hoffman, P.B., 330
Hogan, D.B., 423
Hogan, R., 443
Holden, P.B., 484
Holmes, D., 191
Holmes, D.L., 275
Holmes, O.W., 24, 28
Holmes, T.H., 442
Holmstrom, L.L., 119
Holroyd, J., 547
Holt, R.R., 519–520
Holtzman, W., 180

Honts, C.R., 481–482
Hooper, F., 217
Horne, A.M., 619
Horney, J., 273
Horowitz, A., 293, 308
Horowitz, I.A., 14
Horvath, F.S., 470, 472–475, 477, 485
Hosch, H.M., 271, 275, 279, 281, 311
Hotaling, G., 548, 632
Hough, M., 631–632
Houts, M., 274
Howe, B., 24, 41–42
Howells, T.H., 274
Hoyt, E.B., 166
Hubbard, D., 444
Hudson, J., 261
Huggins, M.W., 607
Hull, R., 188
Hult, L., 135
Hunt, A.L., 586
Hunt, J.F., 141
Hunt, T., 275
Hunter, F.L., 472
Hurrell, J., Jr., 448–449
Hurvich, M., 421
Huston, K.E., 547
Hutchins, R.M., 4, 13
Hyde, L.M., 108, 111
Hyler, S.E., 531

Iacono, W.G., 468, 480–481
Ibsen, H., 671
Inamdor, S., 244
Inbau, F.E., 463
Irving, H.H., 107
Irwin, B.S., 328

Jackson, M., 220
Jackson, M.A., 378
Jacobson, D.S., 113
Jacoby, J., 211
Jaffee, D., 621
James, J.F., 605
James, S.P., 442
James, W., 6
Jan, L., 569
Janis, I.L., 37
Jastrow, J., 4
Jensen, A.R., 180
Jensen, F., 216
Jensen, G.F., 589
Jenson, F.A.S., 382
Jesness, C.P., 38
Jess, P.H., 312

Johnson, C., 260, 264, 267, 276
Johnson, D.J., 547
Johnson, D.L., 491
Johnson, D.M., 514
Johnson, J.T., 36
Johnson, S.M., 594
Johnson, W.T., 588
Johnston, I.D., 40
Johnstone, E.E., 545
Jolley, M.T., 440, 443
Jones, A., 633–634, 646
Jones, D.A., 34, 559
Jones, E., 657
Jones, H.P.T., 275, 278–279
Jones, L.R., 131, 145
Jones, M., 625
Jones, T., 217
Judson, A.J., 141
Jurow, G., 299
Justice, B., 118–119
Justice, R., 118-119

Kaess, W.A., 274
Kagan, J., 547
Kagan, S., 275
Kagehiro, D.K., 39
Kahan, J., 330
Kairys, D., 297
Kal, E., 602
Kalmuss, D., 640
Kaltenbach, R.F., 594
Kaplan, L.V., 34
Kaplan, S., 270
Kardiner, A., 137
Kardiner, S.H., 547
Karlin, M.B., 260
Karp, S., 275
Karras, D., 547
Kashgarian, M., 380
Kaslow, F.W., 108, 571, 665
Kasper, C.J., 120
Kassin, S.M., 299
Katz, B.L., 631, 634, 639
Kauffman, J., 156
Kauffman, R.A., 299
Kaufman, C.L., 666
Kaufman, H., 385
Kavaler, S.A., 666
Kaye, J., 158, 178
Kedword, H.B., 603
Keedy, E.R., 406
Keeley, S., 39
Keenan, J.M., 280
Keeton, R.E., 531

Keilitz, I., 406–407, 412, 414–415
Kellam, S.G., 584
Keller, E.I., 8
Keller, R.A., 143
Kelly, J., 633
Kelly, J.B., 113, 524
Kempe, C.H., 118–119, 547
Kempe, R.E., 119
Kempe, R.S., 547
Kennedy, F., 248
Kent, D., 440
Kent, J., 279
Keogh, B., 174
Kerper, H.B., 322
Kerr, N.L., 31, 293
Kessler, R.C., 587–588
Ketchum, K.E., 267
Keve, P.W., 336, 345
Kicklighter, R., 155
Kierkegaard, S., 654
Kiesler, S., 442
Killinger, G.G., 322–323
Kilman, P.R., 39, 559–560
Kilmann, R.H., 37
Kilpatrick, D., 639
King, J., 304, 311
King, M.A., 275, 277
Kircher, J.C., 481
Kirkham, G., 437
Kirschenbaum, H., 273
Kitsuse, J.I., 591
Klatsky, R., 260
Klein, M.W., 591–592, 594
Kleinmuntz, B., 38, 461, 468, 473–475, 477, 483
Kleinsmith, L.J., 270
Kline, F.G., 312
Kluger, R., 15
Klyver, N., 439, 443, 448–451, 659
Knapp, S.J., 665
Knight, R., 110
Knopp, F.H., 624
Knowles, B.A., 592
Kobasa, S.C., 442
Kobetz, R.W., 444
Koestler, A., 31
Kohlberg, L., 654
Konechi, V.J., 25, 30–31, 293, 587
Koocher, G.P., 681
Koppitz, E., 177
Korchin, S.J., 519–520, 671
Korgeski, G.P., 141
Kosberg, J.I., 631
Kottler, J.A., 664–666
Kovac, P., 191, 275

Kozol, H., 207–210, 212, 218, 231, 236
Krafka, C., 271
Krajick, K., 320–321, 339
Kramer, D.A., 112
Kratochwill, T.R., 178
Krause, H.D., 104
Krausz, F.R., 364
Kravitz, J., 273
Kroeger, R.O., 141
Kroes, W., 448–449
Kroger, W.S., 499
Kubiszyn, T., 144
Kuchler, F.W., 96
Kuehn, J.K., 145
Kuehn, L.L., 280–281
Kuhn, T.S., 42
Kukic, M., 174
Kukic, S., 174
Kulik, J., 280
Kuna, D.P., 7
Kunen, S., 277
Kuperman, S.K., 144
Kurdek, L.A., 113
Kutash, I., 234, 240
Kutzer, D., 247

Laben, J.K., 380, 386
LaFave, W., 356, 396
Lamb, M.E., 113
Landy, F.L., 441
Lane, A.B., 260
Langer, E.J., 569
Langner, T.S., 593
Lanzkron, J., 244
Laquatra, I., 570
Lasky, H., 131–133
Laughery, K.R., 260–261, 274
Lavigueur, H., 273
Lavrakas, P., 275–276
Lawlor, R.J., 682
Lazarus, R.S., 37
LeDoux, J.C., 452
Leeper, J.D., 133
Lefkowitz, J., 440
Lefkowitz, M., 234
Lehman, H.E., 531
Lehman, R.A.W., 144
Leippe, M.R., 261, 264, 271, 273
Leiren, B.D., 441
Lelos, D., 380
Lemert, E., 591
Lenihan, K.J., 595
Leon, G.R., 141
Lerman, H., 547

Lerner, B., 169
Lerner, M.J., 40
Lester, J.T., 144
Leu, J.R., 275
Levenson, J.L., 670
Levester, J., 245
Levine, A.G., 594
Levine, D., 665, 682
Levine, M., 24, 41–42, 425
Levine, R.M., 504
Levinson, D., 298
Levinson, H., 437
Levinson, R., 218, 602, 625
Levy, M.R., 110, 120
Lewin, K., 25
Lewin, T.H., 385
Lewis, D.O., 593
Lewis, J., 245
Lewis, R.V., 586
Lewis, S., 660
Lezak, M.D., 547
Lickona, T., 192
Lidz, C., 205, 213, 221, 234
Lidz, C.W., 517, 666
Lieb, J., 23, 665
Lindberg, F.H., 120
Lindner, H., 8
Lindsay, R.C.L., 273, 304, 310–311
Lindsey, D., 98
Linton, M., 261
Linz, D., 303
Lion, J., 224, 247
Lipinski, R.M., 39
Lipsitt, P.D., 380, 385
Lipton, D.S., 617
Lipton, H.R., 559
Lipton, J., 266, 270
Liszt, F.V., 5
Little, J.M., 140
Litwack, T., 110, 206, 208, 213, 221, 225–226, 229, 233, 667, 689
Livermore, J.M., 34, 222
Lloyd-Bostock, S.M., 258
Loftus, E.F., 4, 24, 41, 258–260, 262–263, 267–269, 275–278, 282–283, 303–304, 308–311, 498, 637, 681
Loftus, G.R., 260, 262, 274
Logan, C.H., 336
Loh. W.D., 4, 13–14, 17, 294, 681
Lombardo, L.X., 617
London, M., 660
London, P., 497
Long, C.R., 564
Loo, R., 654

Looney, J., 234
Lorber, R., 633
Lothstein, L., 217
Louisell, D.W., 4, 11–12, 15, 422, 657
Lovegrove, S.A., 442
Loving, N., 118
Lower, J.S., 16
Luce, T.S., 273
Lunde, D.C., 547
Lundell, F.W., 143
Lundy, R.M., 497
Lush, D.E., 13, 270
Lykken, D.J., 38
Lykken, D.T., 461, 463, 468, 470, 472, 478–480, 482–485
Lyon, V.W., 478

Maass, A., 272, 273
McAllister, H.A., 268–269
McArdle, P.A., 195
McBride, L., 273
McCain, G., 569
McCarthy, B.J., 319
McCarthy, B.R., 319
McCarthy, B., 612
McCarty, D.G., 13
McCary, J.L., 13
McCaslin, H., 452
McCleary, R., 330
McCloskey, M., 259, 263–264, 268, 272, 283
McCord, J., 584–585, 591, 593
McDaniel, S., 547
MacDonald, J., 218, 246–247
McGarry, A.L., 379–380, 385–386
McGill, C.M., 135
McGillis, D., 222, 224
McGinley, H., 34
McGraw, B.D., 414–415
McGuire, J., 217
McGuire, T.W., 442
McIntyre, P., 311
Mack, J., 95
McKee, J.M., 580
Mackworth, N.H., 262
McLaughlin, R., 174
McNally, D., 574
MacNitt, R.A., 478
McNulty, F., 646
McQueen, R., 535
MacWhinney, B., 280
Magnusson, D., 584
Magrab, P.R., 113
Maitland, F., 397, 402
Malmquist, C.P., 34, 222

Maloney, M.P., 515, 517, 520, 524
Malpass, R.S., 271, 273, 276, 282
Mandler, G., 276
Mann, P., 437–438
Mann, P.J., 326, 328
Mannheim, H., 337
Manocherian, J., 108
Manson, S.M., 400, 413, 419
Mappes, D.C., 665
Marbe, K., 11
Marburger, W., 260
Marchioni, P.M., 271
Marcus, E.H., 131, 138, 147
Marcuse, F.L., 478
Margolick, D., 192
Marin, B., 191
Marin, B.V., 275, 277
Mariner, W.K., 195
Mark, V., 234, 245
Marquis, K.H., 261, 268, 270–271
Marsh, S.H., 441
Marshall, J., 260–261, 266, 268, 446–447
Marshall, W.J., 442
Marston, W.M., 12, 478
Martens, T.K., 311
Martin, D., 117–118, 633, 640, 646
Martin, R.A., 129, 131
Martinson, R., 617
Marx, M.L., 360
Mason, D., 385
Masuda, M., 442
Matarazzo, J.D., 42
Mattson, R.E., 386
Mayfield, D., 245
Mayhew, D., 280
Mayman, M., 235, 532
Mayzner, M., 275
Mead, G.H., 591
Meara, N.M., 671
Medlicott, R., 239
Meehl, P.E., 34, 222, 407, 483
Megargee, E.I., 17, 206, 208, 213, 217, 222–223, 234, 569, 573
Meier, R.F., 588
Meisel, A., 666
Melton, G.B., 89, 192, 380, 388, 419–420, 422, 424, 681–683, 694
Menninger, K., 235, 532, 657
Mensh, I.N., 547
Menzies, R.J., 219–220, 378, 385
Mercer, J., 156–157
Mermin, S., 87
Merrill, M.A., 9
Messick, S., 180, 275, 382

Meth, J.M., 532
Meyer, F.A., 452
Michelli, J.A., 193
Mihajlovic, S., 307
Milan, M.A., 564, 580
Millard, B.A., 276
Miller, A.D., 595
Miller, A.H., 444
Miller, A.L., 480
Miller, D., 234
Miller, D.G., 267
Miller, D.J., 111
Miller, H.L., 16
Miller, J.G., 586
Miller, K.S., 378, 381
Millon, T., 520
Mills, M.K., 587
Mills, R.B., 442
Mills, T., 633
Milner, D., 276
Milo, T., 133
Mirkin, P.K., 179
Miron, M.S., 444
Misenheimer, M., 334
Mitchell, J.V., 662
Mitroff, I.I., 37
Moffitt, T.E., 586
Monahan, J., 4, 24, 41, 205, 208–212, 219, 221,
    224–226, 233, 512, 517, 547, 559, 620, 661,
    665, 667, 681
Monahan, L., 448–449
Monroe, R., 234
Montandon, C., 219
Mooney, V., 144
Moore, D.M., 117
Moore, M., 222, 224
Moore, M.S., 373
Moran, G., 299, 301–302
Morey, L.C., 545
Morgan, A.H., 491
Morgan, C.H., 570
Morgan, J., 297
Morgenbesser, M., 111
Morris, N., 340, 395, 531, 540
Morris, R.A., 693
Morse, S.J., 145, 355–359, 361, 363, 365–366,
    371–372, 396–397, 422, 424, 681
Moskowitz, M.J., 6–7
Mothersill, K.J., 568
Motowidlo, S.J., 440–441
Mountz, T., 665
Mrazek, D.A., 119
Mrazek, P.B., 119
Muchinsky, P.M., 442

Mueller, J.H., 275–276
Muench, J.H., 110, 120
Mullen, J., 217–218
Mulvey, E., 205, 213, 221, 234, 244, 517
Munsterberg, H., 6–7, 12, 24, 293
Murchek, P., 323
Murphy, R.W., 136
Murphy, T., 210
Murray, D.M., 272, 282, 310
Musetto, A.P., 110
Mussen, P.H., 547
Myklebust, H.R., 547

Nacci, P.L., 569
Nagin, D., 587
Napoli, D.S., 8
Nash, M., 438
Nash, M.M., 145, 540
Nasr, S.J., 244
Novaco, R., 217
Nee, J.C., 491
Neff, R.L., 119
Nehls, N., 111
Neidig, P.H., 118
Neisser, U., 280
Nemiah, J.C., 136
Nessa, D.B., 380
Neufeld, R.W., 568
Newnan, O.S., 144
Ney, P.G., 40
Neiderhoffer, A., 29, 438, 660
Noble, D.N., 110
Norland, S., 326, 328
Nossi, A.J., 573
Nottingham, E.J., 386
Nowicki, S., 276
Nussbaum, K., 140

Ochalek, K., 268–269
Ochberg, F., 533, 548
Offerman, J.T., 276
Ofshe, R., 547–548
Oglesby, S., 437
Oglesby, T.W., 14, 16
Ohlin, L.E., 595
Okun, J., 294
Oppenheimer, H., 402
Orne, E.C., 481, 532, 547
Orne, M.T., 439, 480–481, 491, 493–495, 497,
    499, 502, 532, 547
Osborn, S.G., 593
Oskamp, S., 261, 268
Ostrom, T., 264, 273
Otero, R.F., 574
Owen, D.R., 34

Pacht, A.R., 145
Packard, N., 41
Padawer-Singer, A.M., 311–312
Palmer, W.R.T., 570
Papanek, G.O., 438
Paradis, A.A., 129
Parisi, N., 338
Parke, R.E., 586
Parker, J.C., 140
Parks, E.C., 326
Parlour, R.R., 131, 145
Pasewark, R.A., 34, 395, 400, 413
Paskind, H.A., 559
Paternoster, R., 590
Paterson, D.G., 9
Patrick, J., 173
Patterson, G.R., 594, 633
Patterson, J., 330
Patterson, K.E., 274
Paulsen, M.G., 87
Paulsen, N., 118
Paulus, P., 569
Payne, W.D., 591
Pear, T.H., 261
Pearson, J., 110
Pedroza, G., 311
Pendleton, L., 382
Pennington, N., 297
Pennybaker, J.W., 135
Penrod, S.D., 271, 297, 301, 303–306, 308–311
Pepper, S., 670
Perlin, M.C., 422
Perlin, M.L., 16
Perlin, M.S., 540
Perlman, M., 303
Perr, I.N., 540
Perry, B., 39
Perry, C., 498
Perry, J.D., 113
Perry, K., 413
Peszke, M.A., 380
Peter, L.J., 188
Petersilia, J., 330
Peterson, D.R., 524
Peterson, J.L., 307
Peterson, P.J., 140
Peterson, R., 245
Petrella, R.C., 378, 381, 423
Petrich, J., 602
Petrila, J., 400, 427, 681
Pettigrew, C.G., 569
Pfeffer, C., 234
Pfohl, B., 421
Pfohl, S., 219–221

Philips, C., 569
Phillips, E.L., 133
Phillips, M.R., 532
Phillips, P., 244
Pierce, L., 120
Pierce, R., 120
Pilpel, H., 199
Pilpel, M.E., 13
Pincus, J., 593
Pittner, M., 266
Pizzi, W.R., 381
Plate, T., 28
Platt, A.M., 395–398, 400–402
Platz, S.J., 275
Podlesny, J.A., 470, 473–474
Progrebin, M., 413
Pollack, D.R., 136, 140
Pollack, S., 540
Pollock, F., 397, 402
Porporino, F.J., 559
Porter, E.M., 333
Porter, R., 547
Postman, L., 262
Poulton, E., 276
Powell, J.H., 330
Powers, A., 334
Powers, E., 593
Powers, P.A., 275
Powers, R. 234
Powitzky, R., 444, 561, 565, 574
Poythress, N.G., 378, 380–382, 388, 419–420,
    422–424, 445, 541, 545, 681, 689
Prasse, D., 160, 169
Prather, J., 569
Press, A., 192
Price, D.N., 128–129
Price, D.W., 278
Prosser, W.L., 129, 531
Pruyser, P., 532
Pryor, B., 304
Pugh, G., 441
Pulkkinen, L., 584, 593
Putnam, W.H., 498

Quay, H.C., 17, 38
Quinsey, V., 219, 222

Rachman, S.J., 570
Racine, D.R., 427
Rader, C.M., 133
Ramos, S., 199
Ramsey, G., 218
Randolph, J.J., 385
Rankin, J.H., 16

Rapaport, D., 175
Rappaport, J., 683
Rashid, S., 279
Raskin, D.C., 463–464, 470, 472–474, 476–477, 480–481
Ratcliff, K.S., 584
Rathburn, L., 278
Ray, I., 404
Rayback, I., 396
Read, J.D., 268
Reckless, W.C., 593–594
Redmount, R.S., 33
Reed, R.S., 277
Reese, J.T., 439
Reeves, H., 635
Regoli, R., 413
Reich, P., 246
Reid, J.E., 463, 472, 633
Reid, S.T., 331, 338
Reiff, R., 564
Reinehr, R., 217–218
Reinhardt, H., 222
Reinhardt, L., 144
Reinke, P., 280)
Reis, H.T., 298
Reiser, M., 437–446, 448–451, 494, 659
Reiter, P.J., 547
Renshaw, D.C., 192
Repko, G.R., 140–141
Reschly, D., 160, 163, 169, 173–175, 178, 180–181
Resick, P., 639
Revitch, E., 234, 236, 239–240, 242
Reynolds, C., 181
Reza, H.G., 532, 535, 539
Ribner, S.A., 604
Richard, K.M., 112
Richard, W., 446
Richards, V.J., 260, 276
Rieber, R.W., 439
Rieker, P.P., 633
Ries, R.K., 532
Riger, S., 40
Ritchie, M.H., 665
Robb, G.P., 665
Roberts, A.H., 134, 144–145
Roberts, C., 400, 415, 425
Roberts, M.D., 580
Robertson, L.S., 130, 133, 135
Robertson, M., 603
Robey, A., 385, 511, 540–541
Robins, L.N., 418, 584
Robinson, D., 657
Robinson, E.S., 14

Robinson, H.L., 111
Robison, J., 209–210
Rocchio, P.H., 144
Roesch, R., 378–383, 385–386, 388–389, 417–419, 424–425, 681, 694
Roff, M., 13
Rofman, E., 215, 218
Rogers, J.L., 400, 413
Rogers, O., 11
Rogers, R., 418–419, 614
Rose, J., 670
Rose, R., 446
Rose, T., 215
Rosen, A., 483
Rosen, R., 547
Rosenberg, C.E., 405
Rosenhan, D.L., 497, 526
Rosenman, R.H., 442
Rosenthal, R., 302
Rosewater, L.B., 639
Rosnow, R.L., 302
Ross, D., 268
Ross, H.L., 587
Rossi, E.L., 444
Ross-Reynolds, J., 166
Roth, L.H., 666
Rowe, M.L., 135
Roy, M., 117
Ruback, R.B., 31, 295
Rubin, B.R., 584
Rubin, J.G., 540
Ruddock, R., 452
Rudy, L., 279
Ruotolo, A., 239
Russell, D.E.H., 631, 633
Rutter, M., 112, 593
Ryan, D.P., 665
Ryckman, R.M., 299

Sackett, P.R., 479, 485
Sacks, H.R., 336
Saegert, S., 569
Sage, N., 294
Sainsbury, P., 133
Saks, M.J., 31, 294, 298, 681
Sales, B.D., 294, 296, 303, 547, 665, 682
Salomone, P.R., 140, 144
Salvia, J., 158, 174
Salzberg, H.C., 478
Samenow, S.E., 594, 614
Samuels, D.J., 484, 486
Sanborn, C.J., 665
Sanders, G.S., 261
Sanford, N., 298

Sannito, T., 547
Santrock, J.W., 114
Sass, R., 37
Satorius, N., 418
Satten, H., 239
Satten, J., 235
Saxe, L., 470
Saxe, S.J., 438, 440–442
Sayre, F.B., 396–398, 402–403
Scarpitti, S.R., 593
Schaeffer, M.A., 135
Schafer, R., 175
Schaffer, J.W., 140
Schaffer, W.G., 385
Schecter, S., 636
Scheirer, J.C., 531, 540
Schichor, D., 346
Schill, T., 275
Schlenger, W.E., 604–605
Schlensky, R., 540
Schlesinger, L.B., 234–236, 239–240, 242, 248
Schlesinger, L., 667
Schlesinger, S., 219
Schleske, D., 120
Schmauk, F.J., 480
Schmidt, A.K., 33
Schmidt, L.D., 671
Schmolesky, J.M., 304–306
Schneider, S., 143
Schneller, F.S., 45
Schooler, J.W., 268
Schramski, T.G., 619
Schreiber, J., 378, 385–386, 418–419
Schrenck-Notzing, A., 5–6
Schuldberg, D., 520
Schulman, J., 294–295, 297
Schumann, E.L., 308
Schur, E.M., 591
Schwartz, J.N., 440, 448
Schweinhart, L.J., 595
Scott, A., 356, 396
Scott, B., 260–261, 264, 276
Scott, J., 276
Scott, N.A., 665
Scott, P., 222, 238
Sedman, G.A., 235
Seeleman, V., 262
Selby, M., 217
Selleck, H.B., 129
Sellin, T., 585
Selye, H., 446–447
Sepejak, D., 216, 219
Severance, L.J., 303–304
Severy, L., 592

Sgroi, S.M., 119
Shah, S., 205, 222, 225, 665
Shamsie, S.J., 622
Shapiro, D.L., 90, 515, 523, 526, 659
Shapiro, L., 210
Shapiro, P., 310–311
Sharok, S.S., 593
Shatin, L., 386
Shaughnessy, P., 275
Shaver, K.G., 25, 30
Shaver, P., 294
Shaw, C., 28
Shealy, A.E., 443
Sheehan, P.W., 497
Sheehy, N.P., 41
Shepard, J.C., 547
Shepard, L.A., 159, 175, 182
Shepard, M.J., 182
Sheperd, J.W., 260, 265–266, 273–275
Shepherd, J.N., 666
Sherman, L.W., 587, 645
Sherrid, S.D., 441
Sherven, J., 440
Shichor, D., 586
Shor, R.E., 491, 502
Showalter, C.R., 419–420, 694
Shubow, L.D., 540
Siegel, J., 442
Siegel, J.M., 276
Siegel, M., 517
Siegel, R., 368
Siesky, A.G., 113
Sikorski, C., 413
Silberman, L.J., 108
Silten, P.R., 378
Silver, D., 297
Silverberg, G., 276
Silverman, F., 118
Silverman, H., 118, 657
Simcha-Fagan, O., 593
Simmonds, D.C.V., 276
Simon, R.J., 298
Singer, A.N., 311
Singer, H.A., 438
Singer, M.T., 547–548
Singer, R.G., 345
Siskind, G., 682
Skelton, J.A., 135
Skillings, L.S., 182
Skogan, V.G., 631–632, 640
Slaby, A.E., 23, 665
Slaikeu, K.A., 138
Slater, D., 35, 396, 409
Slawson, P.F., 667–668

Slesinger, D., 4, 13
Sloan, B.C., 559
Sloane, M., 445
Slobogin, C., 356, 380, 419–420, 422, 424, 681
Slomen, D., 382
Slomovitz, M., 276
Slovenko, R., 34–35, 194, 531, 540, 547, 665–666
Slowick, S.M., 472
Smith, A., 323
Smith, B.L., 635
Smith, D.H., 440
Smith, G.A., 415
Smith, G., 209
Smith, R., 395
Smith, R.E., 311
Smith, R.S., 593
Smith, S.R., 665
Smith, W.H., 520
Smykla, J.O., 321
Snee, T.J., 13, 270
Snibbe, H.M., 441
Snibbe, J.R., 140
Snodgrass, J., 8
Snyder, L.D., 273
Soeken, D.R., 670
Sollito, S., 671
Solnit, A.J., 116
Solomon, G.F., 363
Solomon, R.L., 585
Sommer, R., 262
Somodevilla, S., 447, 450
Sonkin, D.J., 118, 640, 645–646
Sonquist, J.A., 297
Sosis, R., 299
Sosner, B., 140
Sosowsky, L., 603
Spaulding, H.C., 440–441, 443
Spaulding, K., 273
Spaulding, W.J., 33
Specter, G.A., 446, 564, 607
Spencer, L.D., 380
Spiegel, D., 491–492, 494, 501–502
Spiegel, H., 491–492, 494. 498, 501–502
Spiegel, R., 303
Spielberger, C.D., 440–441, 443
Spitzer, R.L., 418, 545
Spradlin, L., 448–450
Sprafkin, R.P., 437
Sprenkle, D.H., 107–108
Sprock, J., 520
Stangl, D., 421
Stanton, A.M., 102
Stanton, W.C., 39

Starkey, M.L., 514
Starr, R., 118
Staten, M., 132–133
Stattin, J., 584
Staynor, S., 539
Steadman, H.J., 206, 211, 225–226, 234, 381–382, 400, 413, 547, 559, 604
Steele, B., 118
Steinhauser, P.D., 110
Steinmetz, C., 631–632
Steinmetz, S.K., 117, 632, 636
Stephenson, G.M., 270, 272
Stermac, L., 382
Stern, D.B., 491
Stern, L.W., 5, 10
Sternbach, R.A., 134, 136, 140
Sternberg, R.J., 42
Stillman, R., 245
Stitt, B.G., 589
Stock, H.V., 382, 419
Stone, A.A., 540, 547, 665
Stone, M., 382
Stone, M.H., 547
Storm, C.L., 107–108
Storti, J.R., 330
Stotland, E., 29, 440, 660
Stratton, J.G., 450
Straus, M.A., 117, 632
Strauss, M., 548
Strawn, D.V., 304
Strentz, T., 445, 533, 548
Strickman, L.P., 96, 104
Strodbeck, F.L., 39
Stroud, D.A., 397–398
Sturgill, W., 274
Sue, S., 311–312
Suggs, D., 547
Sullivan, R., 119
Sultan, S., 442
Sussman, N., 531
Sutherland, E.H., 28
Swan, J., 297
Swanson, C.R., 9
Swanson, D., 244
Sweeney, J.D., 268
Swerling, J., 442
Swift, W.J., 112
Swoboda, J.S., 665
Symonds, M., 533, 548, 689
Szasz, T., 362–363, 667

Tanay, E., 233–234
Tancredi, L.R., 23, 665
Tanford, S., 304, 308–309

Tannenbaum, F., 591
Taplin, P., 633
Tapp, J.L., 4
Tate, E., 547
Tatsuoka, M.M., 441
Tatten, H.A., 140
Taylor, A.G., 129
Taylor, K.P., 304
Taylor, R.L., 158
Taylor, S., 25
Teeters, N.K., 322
Teitelbaum, H.E., 569
Tellegen, A., 491, 502
Telzrow, C., 181
Teplin, L., 385, 602–603
Terman, L.M., 9, 12
Terr, L., 281
Terrio, L., 9
Territo, L., 442
Theonnes, S.N., 110
Thibault, J., 683
Thigpen, C.H., 547
Thomas, A., 174
Thomas, C.B., 593
Thomas, W.I., 591
Thompson, J.R., 409
Thompson, W.C., 302, 304, 307–308
Thoreson, R., 144
Thornberry, T., 211
Thurber, S., 478
Thurlow, M., 158, 172, 174, 181–182
Thurstone, L.L., 9
Thyfault, R.K., 646
Tickner, A., 276
Tilden, J., 497
Timm, H.W., 497–498
Tindall, R., 155
Tinklenberg, J.R., 246
Tinsley, L.C., 129
Toch, H., 17, 24, 558–559, 610, 670
Toglia, M., 268
Tombari, M., 178
Tonry, M., 531, 540
Toomey, R.C., 380
Topp, D., 559
Torney, J.V., 40
Tousignant, J.P., 311
Townsend, W.C., 411
Travis, L.F., 329
Travisono, D.N., 603
Treisman, G., 668
Trimble, M.R., 137
Tromanheiser, E., 334
Tryon, G.S., 665

Tucker, J., 174
Tullis, R., 378
Tulving, E., 271
Turk, D.C., 133
Turnage, J.J., 442
Turnbull, W., 141
Turner, R.C., 385

Udolf, R., 31
Uelman, G.F., 195
Umbeck, J., 132–133
Ungar, S.J., 294
Unkovic, C., 559

VandenCreek, L., 665
Vanderet, R.C., 354, 360
Vander Mey, B.J., 119
Vanderplas, J.H., 222
Vanderplas, J.M., 222
Van Dusen, K.T., 592
Van Hoose, W.H., 664–667
Van Maanen, J., 660
Varendonck, J., 10–11
Veatch, R.M., 671
Vega, S., 131, 140
Veno, A., 234, 448
Verdun-Jones, S.N., 378
Verinis, J.S., 276
Veronen, L.J., 639
Vetter, H.J., 442
Viano, E., 630
Vidmar, N., 293–294, 298
Vito, G.F., 339
Volgy, S.S., 111
von Hirsch, A., 345

Waakland, P., 39
Waddle, C.W., 362
Wade, T.C., 177, 182
Wadlington, W., 87
Wadsworth, J., 267
Wagenaar, W.A., 268
Wahler, R.G., 594
Waid, W.M., 480–481
Wakefield, J.A., 520
Waldo, G.P., 586, 588
Wales, H.W., 399–400
Walker, L.E., 117–118, 547–548, 631, 633, 640, 643, 646, 683
Walker, N., 395–396, 402–403, 409, 411
Walker, V., 276
Wallerstein, J.S., 113, 524
Walsh, W.F., 438
Walter, P.D., 547

Walters, R.H., 17, 586
Wang, M., 181
Ward, J.C., 440–441, 443
Ward, M.P., 520
Ward, N.G., 532
Warnick, D., 261
Warren, C.A.B., 667
Warren, L.W., 139
Warrington, E.K., 263
Warshank, R.A., 114
Wasyliw, O.E., 418
Watson, A.S., 540
Webb, L.J., 545
Weber, T., 547
Webster, C., 219–220
Webster, C.D., 378, 385–386
Weeks, D.P., 30
Weihofen, H., 194
Weikart, D., 595
Weinberg, H.I., 267, 311
Weiner, B.A., 112
Weiner, H., 531
Weiner, I.B., 90, 519–520, 547
Weiner, T.S., 45
Weinstein, J.P., 111
Weisaert, L., 631, 636
Weiskrantz, L., 263
Weiss, D.J., 139
Weiss, J., 239
Weiss, J.M., 531
Weithorn, L.A., 97–98, 380, 682
Weitzenhoffer, A.M., 501
Weld, H.P., 13
Weldon, D.E., 273
Wells, G., 258, 261, 264, 272–273, 282–283
Wells, G.L., 304, 310–311
Wenk, E., 209–210, 231
Werner, E.E., 593
Werner, P., 214–215, 219, 226
Wertham, F., 235, 246
Wesson, C., 158, 174, 181–182
West, D.J., 592–593
West, L.J., 547–548
Westman, J.C., 112
Wettstein, R.M., 205, 217, 220, 226
Wexler, D.B., 665–666
Wexler, H.K., 624
Wexler, O., 224
Wheelwright, P., 672
Whipple, G.M., 4, 277
Whitaker, J.M., 592
Whitcomb, D., 119
White, L., 129–131
Whitney, P., 277

Whittaker, A.H., 129
Wicklander, D.E., 472
Wiener, D.N., 139
Wigdor, B.T., 143
Wiggins, S.L., 478
Wigmore, J.H., 6, 13, 24, 191, 665
Wilbert, J.R., 668
Wilcox, P., 141
Wildman, R.W., 526
Wilkins, L.T., 323, 337
Wilks, J., 617
Willging, T.E., 14, 293
Williams, D., 245
Williams, D.A., 667
Williams, M.C., 25
Williams, W., 378, 381
Wills, E.J., 276
Wilson, C.E., 587
Wilson, J.Q., 619
Wilson, K., 682
Wilson, S.C., 501
Wilson, S.K., 480
Wilson, T.E., 547
Wiltse, L.L., 144
Wing, J.K., 418
Winick, B.J., 378, 381–382, 384
Winick, C., 12, 31
Winkler, J.D., 310
Winograd, E., 260, 276
Winter, J.E., 478
Wishnic, H., 238, 243
Witkin, H., 275
Witmer, H., 593
Witryol, S.L., 274
Wittlinger, R.P., 265
Wodarski, J.S., 594
Wolf, S.R., 136
Wolff, H.G., 134
Wolfgang, M., 237, 585
Woodhead, M.M., 276
Wormith, J.S., 559
Wrightsman, L.S., 299
Wyatt, S., 261
Wynne, L.C., 547

Yarmey, A.D., 192, 258, 275, 278–279, 310
Yerkes, R.M., 263
Yesavage, J., 215, 226
Yllo, K., 117
Yochelson, S., 594, 614
Ysseldyke, J., 156–158, 172, 174, 181–182
Yudofsky, S.C., 531
Yuille, J.C., 268

Zadny, J., 262
Zamble, E., 559
Zanni, G.R., 268, 276
Zaragosa, M., 268
Zarski, J.J., 110
Zarski, L.P., 110
Zax, M., 564
Zeisel, H., 294
Zelig, M., 497–498, 504

Zimbardo, P.G., 621
Zimmerman, M., 421
Zimring, F.E., 587
Zimring, F., 659
Ziskin, J., 90, 138, 145, 147, 178, 531, 540, 544, 656
Zlutnick, S., 569
Zuckerman, M., 298
Zusman, J., 557–558

Subject Index

Actus reus, 25, 352, 396
Amnesia, 379
Annulment, 104
Army Alpha, 8–9
Army Beta, 8–9

Back injury, 135–136
Battered women, 117, 640–645
Baxtrom studies, 211–213
Behavioral assessment, 178
Bender Motor Gestalt Test, 175–178
Best interests of the child doctrine, 97–98
Blended families:
    bonding in, 116
    treatment of children in, 115–116
    working with, 116

Cambridge-Sommerville Youth Study, 593
Capacity, 33–35. *See also* Diminished capacity,
    as a defense
Catathymic violence, 235–236, 239
Child abuse, 118–119
Children, as witnesses, 277–279
Classification, ethical issues in, 662–663
Code of Hammurabi, 23
Competency:
    of child witnesses, 191–192
    and family law, 97–98
    and informed consent, 66–69, 76–79
    to contract, 194–195
    of jurors, 304–312
    and medical care, 195–196
    of minors to consent to treatment, 196–199
    of professionals, 189–190
    to make a will, 193–194
    of witnesses, 190–193
    see also Competency to stand trial
Competency Assessment Instrument, 386

Competency Screening Test, 385–386
Competency to stand trial:
    and amnesia, 379
    assessment of, 382–384
    definition of, 378–380
    guidelines in evaluation of, 390–391
    and insanity, 415–417
    measures of, 385–390
    procedures for establishing, 380–382
Conditional release:
    as furloughs, 347
    as graduated release, 347–348
    as study release, 346–347
    as work release, 345–346
    see also Parole
Confidentiality:
    and informed consent, 69–71
    ethical issues in, 663–665
    in police consulting, 438
Contract parole, 340–342
Control Question Test, 462–466
    field studies of, 470–476
    validity of, 476–477
Correctional community psychology, 563–570
    primary prevention in, 568–570
    secondary prevention in, 567–568
    tertiary prevention in, 565–567
Correctional mental health services, 561–563
Correctional psychologists:
    as classifiers, 572–573
    conflicting roles of, 570–574
    as consultants, 576–577
    as crisis interveners, 571–572
    nontraditional roles for, 575–580
    as predictors of dangerousness, 573–574
    as program designers, 577–578
    as program evaluators, 579–580
    as therapists, 574
    as trainers, 575–576

Correctional psychology, ethical issues in, 661–668

Counseling:
  effectiveness of, 593–594
  with police, 449–451
  of victim/survivors, 636–645
  see also Psychotherapy; Treatment for offenders

Court reports, 55–59

CPI, in police selection, 441–443

Crime, development of, 584–585

Crime prevention:
  by counseling, 593–594
  by diversion, 591–593
  by environmental manipulation, 594–596
  by punishment, 585–590
  see also Delinquency prevention

Crime rates, and punishment, 586–588

Criminal justice, early psychology of, 7–10

Criminal responsibility:
  assessment of, 417–422
  and insanity defense, 406–409
  and *mens rea* concept, 397–399
  see also Insanity defense

Crisis intervention, 571–572, 605–612

Crisis management:
  of self-destructive behaviors, 607–610
  of violent behavior, 610–612
  see also Correctional community psychology

Cross-examination, 543–545

Cross-racial identification, 273

Custody disputes, 109–112

Dangerousness, *see* Violence prediction

Death-qualified juries, 302–303

Delinquency prevention, 591–596. *See also* Crime prevention

Deposition, 536–537

Diminished capacity, as a defense, 352–355
  California approach to, 360–364

Direct examination, 538–539

Discovery, 536–537

Diversion, effectiveness of, 591–593

Divorce, 104–106, 112, 114

Domestic court:
  dispositions by, 93–94
  jurisdiction of, 91–92
  position of, 86–88
  procedures in, 92–93
  psychologist's role in, 88–90
  responsibility of, 90–91
  see also Family law

Domestic violence, 117–120
  and child abuse, 118–119
  and sexual abuse, incest, 119–120
  and spouse abuse, 117
  treatment of, 117–118

Educational assessment, *see* Psychoeducational assessment

Education of All Handicapped Children Act, 162–166

Educational rights cases, 167–168

Electronic monitoring, of probationers, 329

Employee Screening Test, 466–468, 477–479

Environmental issues, legal aspects of, 35–38

Environmental manipulation, effectiveness of, 594–596

Ethical issues:
  and confidentiality, 663–665
  in classification, 662–663
  in collegial relationships, 668–670
  in correctional psychology, 661–668
  in education, 671–672
  in expert testimony, 656–659
  and informed consent, 666
  in jury selection, 659
  in malpractice, 667–668
  in organizational relationships, 670–671
  in police consulting, 659–662
  in report writing, 514–518
  in right to treatment, 665–666
  see also Value conflicts

Ethical theories, 672–675

Expert testimony:
  difficulties in providing, 424–430
  ethical issues in, 656–659
  on eyewitness testimony, 282–283
  on intent, 364–370
  qualifications for offering, 422–424
  see also Testifying

Expert witness:
  art of being an, 540–541
  demeanor of, 541–543
  role of, 539–540

Eyewitness testimony:
  by children, 10–11, 277–279
  by crime victims, 279–281
  by the elderly, 279
  and jury decision-making, 510–511
  and memory, 258–276
  early research on, 4–5
  expert testimony on, 282–283

Face recognition, 273–274

False confessions, 502–504

Family court, *see* Domestic court

Family law, and best interests of the child doctrine, 97–98
Family law:
    and competency, 97–98
    and custody disputes, 109–112
    and effects of divorce, 112–114
    and domestic violence, 117–120
    and marriage contract, 96–97, 99–101
    and parent-child obligations, 98–109
    and *parents patriae* doctrine, 95
    and privacy, 101–102
    and privileged communication, 102–103
    and stepfamilies, 114–116
    themes in, 94–98
Family violence, 632–634
Forgetting, *see* Memory
Furloughs, 347

Graduated releases, 347–348
Guilty but mentally ill (GBMI) verdict, 408–415
Guilty Knowledge Test, 467–468, 479–480

Handicapped classification, 156–159
    and diagnostic constructs, 171–175
    federal definitions for, 172
    medical model for, 156–157
    and placement decisions, 158–159
    and planning-intervention decisions, 159
    social system model for, 157–158
    state definitions for, 172–174
High Scope project, 595
Hostage negotiation, 444–446
Hypnosis:
    definition of, 491–492
    electronic recording of, 500
    forensic abuses of, 492–493
    forensic history of, 490–491
    guidelines for use of, 499–502
    management of hypnotic sessions in, 501
    in memory enhancement, 497–499
    in police consulting, 439
    prehypnosis briefing in, 501
    prehypnosis records in, 500
    professional qualifications for using, 500
    selective use of, 501–502
    spontaneous, 502–504
    susceptibility to, 491–492, 501–502
    with witnesses and victims, 493–497
Hypnotizability, 491–492, 501–502
Hypnotized witnesses, 495–497

Imprisonment, effects of, 557–561
Incompetency, *see* Competency; Competency to stand trial

Individual differences, legal implications of, 38–39
Informed consent:
    and competency, 76–79
    and comprehension of information, 72–74
    and confidentiality, 69–72
    elements of, 65–69
    ethical issues in, 663
    historical perspectives on, 63–65
    and patient decision-making, 75–76
    patient reactions in, 74–75
    in research, 64–65
    research on, 73–79
    and treatment, 63–64
Insanity defense, 353–355, 406–409, 415–417. *See also* Guilty but mentally ill (GBMI) verdict; *Mens rea*
Institutional neurosis, 558
Intent:
    California approach to, 356–360
    defining scope of, 355–364
    fact of *vs.* capacity for, 371–374
    offering opinions on, 364–370
    understanding capacity for, 370–371
Interdisciplinary Fitness Interview, 386–389
Interpersonal role conflict, 654–655
Intoxication, as a defense, 354
Intrapersonal role conflicts, 653–654

Joined trials, 308–310
Joint degree programs, 684–689
Juror Bias Scale, 299–300
Juror competence:
    and application of presumption instructions, 306–307
    and comprehension of legal instructions, 304–306
    and decision-making in joined trials, 308–310
    and pretrial publicity, 311–312
    and response to eyewitness testimony, 310–311
    and statistical information, 307–308
Jury selection:
    and attitude-verdict relationships, 297–302
    and death penalty attitudes, 302–303
    ethical issues in, 659
    evaluation of methods for, 297–302
    questionnaires in, 296–297
    representativeness in, 296
    social scientific methods for, 293–303
    survey method for, 296–297
Juvenile justice system, *see* Domestic court

Law, types of, 50–52
Learning disability, *see* Psycoeducational assessment

Least restrictive environment, 162
Legal Attitudes Questionnaire, 298–299
Legal literature:
  in court reports, 55–59
  general reference sources for, 53–55
  in law libraries, 52–53
  in statutes, 59–60
Legal system:
  corrections in, 31–33
  judge and jury in, 30–31
  offender in, 28
  police in, 29
  prosecutor in, 29–30
  psychological aspects of, 25–33
  victim in, 28–29
Lie detection:
  drug effects in, 481
  effects of psychopathy on, 480–481
  establishing guilt and innocence in, 469–470
  evaluation of polygraph charts in, 470
  field *vs.* laboratory investigations of, 468–469
  types of tests in, 462–468
  validity of, 468–482
  see also Polygraph test
Lineup fairness, 273

Maintenance therapy, 612–616
Malingering, 136–138, 531–532
Malpractice, 667–668
Marriage contract, 96–97, 99–101, 103–109
Memory:
  acquisition stage of, 260–263
  effects of anxiety on, 276
  confidence and accuracy in, 272
  effects of context reinstatement on, 271–272
  effects of expectation on, 262–263
  and eyewitness testimony, 258–276
  and face recognition, 273–274
  hypnotic enhancement of, 497–499
  individual differences in, 274–276
  effects of intelligence on, 274–275
  effects of interviewing techniques on, 270–271
  malleability of, 266–268
  effects of misinformation on, 268–269
  effects of personal style on, 275
  reconstructive view of, 259
  retention stage of, 265–269
  retrieval stage of, 269–274
  selective attention in, 261–262
  sex differences in, 275–276
  effects of stress on, 263–265
  temporal factors in, 260–261, 265–266
  effects of training on, 276
Mens rea, 23, 352, 354, 355–364, 396

  case law on, 402–406
  historical concepts of, 397–399
  present approaches to, 399–402
Mental disorders, in prison populations, 558–561, 602–605
Mental health services, in correctional settings, 561–563
Mental state, assessment of, 417–422
Mental state at the time of the offense (MBO) interview technique, 419–422
MMPI, a prognostic indicator in personal injury cases, 143–145
  in evaluating personal injury cases, 138–145
  in individuals receiving workers' compensation, 140–141
  in police selection, 441–443
  in psychiatric disability claimants, 141–143
Mutual agreement programming, 340–342

Nebraska psycholegal program, 685–687
Nuremberg Code, 6–43

Opportunities for Youth project, 595–596
Overcrowding, in correctional settings, 568–569

Parens patriae, 91–95, 196
Parole:
  beleaguered status of, 345
  conditions for, 334–335
  contract, 340–342
  effectiveness of, 336–338
  issues in, 343–344
  legal issues affecting, 342–343
  role of parole board in, 332–333
  prediction in, 336–339
  selection process in, 333–334
  shock, 338–340
Parole agreement, 335
Parole board, 332–333
Personal injury:
  evidence of, 143–145
  forensic evaluation in, 145–147
  see also Physical disability
Physical disability:
  and back pain, 135–136
  claims in, 136
  malingering of, 136–138
  MMPI evaluation in, 138–145
  psychological factors in, 133–147
  see also Personal injury
Physical disease, psychological factors in, 134–135
Placement bias cases, 161–162, 168–170

Police:
  counseling with, 449–451
  selection of, 9, 14, 16–17, 440–444
  stress among, 446–449
  training of, 451–453
Police consulting:
  confidentiality in, 438
  ethical issues in, 659–661
  hypnosis in, 439
  issues in, 437–440
  psychological profiling in, 439
  training in, 437–438
Police selection, 440–444
Polygrapher, 461–462
Polygraph test:
  applications of, 482–486
  countermeasures in, 480–482
  in criminal court, 482–484
  in employment screening, 484–486
  as an investigative tool, 484
  relevant/irrelevant format in, 466
  relevant/relevant format in, 467
  see also Lie detection
Post-traumatic stress disorder, 638
Presumption instructions, 306–307
Primary prevention, 568–570
Privacy, in family law, 101–102
Privileged communication, in family law, 102–103
Probation:
  conditions of, 324
  electronic monitoring of, 329
  history of, 322
  methods of implementing, 322–323
  nature of, 320–321
  revocation of, 324–325
  and role conflict of probation officer, 325–326
  selection for, 323–324
  sex differences in, 326–328
  success rates in, 326–327
  supervision in, 328–329
  vs. suspended sentence, 321–322
Probation officer, 325
Psychoeducational assessment:
  administrative proceedings in, 170–171
  alternative evidence in, 179–180
  and adequacy of instruments, 182–183
  behavioral, 178
  Bender Motor Gestalt Test in, 175–178
  and classification system reform, 181–182
  and Education of All Handicapped Children Act, 162–166
  and educational rights cases, 167–168
  handicap classification in, 156–159

legal influences on, 160–171
  levels of inference in, 175–178
  multiple normative comparisons in, 178–179
  outline for, 174–176
  overidentification of handicaps in, 181
  and placement bias cases, 161–162, 168–170
  professional competence in, 182
  and right to education cases, 160–161
  test bias in, 180–181
Psycholegal training:
  degree programs for, 44–45
  early history of, 12–13
  in joint degree programs, 684–689
  models of, 684–692
  Nebraska program of, 685–687
  need for, 681–682
  in Ph.D. minor programs, 690–691
  in Ph.D. specialty programs, 689–690
  in postdoctoral programs, 691
  principles of, 682–684
  through continuing education, 692–695
Psychological criminology, emergence of, 16–17
Psychological profiling, 439
Psychologist as expert witness, early history of, 10–12, 14–16
Psychology-law interactions, 39–44. See also Psycholegal training
Psychotherapy, 565–567, 574–575
  with battered women, 640–645
  confidentiality in, 69–71
  effects of correctional environment on, 620–621
  defining success in, 621–622
  offenders' characteristics in, 619–620
  outpatient, 616–622
  therapists' problems in, 617–619
  with victim/survivors, 636–645
  see also Counseling; Treatment for offenders
Public Law, 94–142, 162–166
Punishment:
  and crime rates, 586–588
  effectiveness of, 585–590

Remembering, see Memory
Reports:
  addressing circumstances in:
    present, 521–522
    past, 522–523
    future, 523–524
  broadly focused, 520–524
  clarity in, 524–525
  deciding whether to write, 512–518
  determining the focus of, 518–524
  ethical principles in, 514–518

Reports (*Continued*)
  narrowly focused, 518–520
  professional realities in, 514–518
  respecting client preferences in, 512–514
  see also Testifying
Right to education cases, 160–161
Right of sanctuary, 321
Rogers Criminal Responsibility Assessment
    Scales, 418–419

Secondary prevention, 567–568
Sex offender programs, 624
Shock parole, 338–340
Sixteen Personality Factor Questionnaire, in po-
    lice selection, 440–444
Social breakdown syndrome, 558
Spontaneous hypnosis, 502–504
Spouse abuse, 117, 640–645
Stanford-Binet, 9
Stare desisis, 51
Statute books, 59–60
Stepfamilies, 114–116
Stepparents, 114–116
Stockholm Syndrome, 445, 532
Study release, 346–347
Substance abuse programs, 624–625
Suicide prevention, 567–568, 607–610
Survivors, *see* Victim/survivors
Suspended sentence, 321–322. *See also* Probation

TARP system, in legal research 53
Tertiary prevention, 565–567
Test bias, in psychoeducational assessment, 180–
    181
Testifying:
  consultation model of, 529
  cross-examination in, 543–545
  deposition in, 536–537
  direct examination in, 538–539
  discovery in, 536–537
  on expert testimony, 545–548
  dealing with the extraordinary in, 531–532
  investigative focus in, 535–536
  need for current knowledge in, 532–534
  orientation and delineation in, 530–536
  preparation time in, 534–535
  see also Expert testimony; Reports
Testimony:
  early psychology of, 4–7, 10–12
  planning of, 538–539
  preparation for, 534–535
  see also Eyewitness testimony; Testifying
Therapeutic communities, 625

Treatment, right to refuse, 625–626
Treatment for offenders:
  crisis management in, 605–612
  maintenance therapy in, 612–616
  programs of, 622–625
  psychotherapy in, 616–622
  types of, 605–625
  see also Counseling; Psychotherapy
Twinkie defense, 363

Value conflicts:
  and abusive exercise of power, 655
  and interpersonal roles, 654–655
  and intrapersonal roles, 653–654
Victimology, 635
Victims' rights movement, 634–636
Victim/survivors:
  assessment of, 638–640
  compensation of, 630–631
  definition of, 631–634
  hypnosis with, 493–497
  of interpersonal violence, 632–634
  psychological intervention for, 636–645
  as witnesses, 279–281
Violence prediction:
  base rate problem in, 222–223
  in the community, 207–213
  evidentiary considerations in, 225–226
  in institutions, 213–217, 573–574
  by mental health professionals, 226
  by paraprofessionals, 218
  reliability of, 219–220
  research on, 207–226
  sources of error in, 220–221
  Supreme Court opinions on, 226–233
  and threats of violence, 218–219
  validity of, 226–233
  see also Dangerousness; Violent behavior
Violent behavior:
  assessment of impact of, 638–640
  catathymic, 235–236, 239
  clinical prediction of, 233–249
  compulsive, 236, 240–241
  environmentally motivated, 235, 237
  impulsive, 235, 238–239
  in intoxicated persons, 245–246
  management of, 610–612
  motivational spectrum for, 234–236
  non-violence predictors of, 241–244, 246–249
  in organic persons, 245
  in paranoid persons, 244–245
  situationally motivated, 237–238
  and threats of violence, 246–247

without specific intentions, 247–249
see also Violence prediction

Wigmore rules, 665
Witnesses, hypnotized, 493–497
Work release, 345–346

Workers' compensation:
  forensic evaluation in, 145–147
  historical landmarks in, 129–130
  present status of, 130–133

Zone of Comparison procedure, 464

(*continued from front*)

Women in the Middle Years: Current Knowledge and Directions for Research and Policy *edited by Janet Zollinger Giele*

Loneliness: A Sourcebook of Current Theory, Research and Therapy *edited by Letitia Anne Peplau and Daniel Perlman*

Hyperactivity: Current Issues, Research, and Theory (Second Edition) *by Dorothea M. Ross and Sheila A. Ross*

Review of Human Development *edited by Tiffany M. Field, Aletha Huston, Herbert C. Quay, Lillian Troll, and Gordon E. Finley*

Agoraphobia: Multiple Perspectives on Theory and Treatment *edited by Dianne L. Chambless and Alan J. Goldstein*

The Rorschach: A Comprehensive System, Volume III: Assessment of Children and Adolescents *by John E. Exner, Jr. and Irving B. Weiner*

Handbook of Play Therapy *edited by Charles E. Schaefer and Kevin J. O'Connor*

Adolescent Sexuality in a Changing American Society: Social and Psychological Perspectives for the Human Service Professions (Second Edition) *by Catherine S. Chilman*

Failures in Behavior Therapy *edited by Edna B. Foa and Paul M.G. Emmelkamp*

The Psychological Assessment of Children (Second Edition) *by James O. Palmer*

Imagery: Current Theory, Research, and Application *edited by Aneés A. Sheikh*

Handbook of Clinical Child Psychology *edited by C. Eugene Walker and Michael C. Roberts*

The Measurement of Psychotherapy Outcome *edited by Michael J. Lambert, Edwin R. Christensen, and Steven S. DeJulio*

Clinical Methods in Psychology (Second Edition) *edited by Irving B. Weiner*

Excuses: Masquerades in Search of Grace *by C.R. Snyder, Raymond L. Higgins, and Rita J. Stucky*

Diagnostic Understanding and Treatment Planning: The Elusive Connection *edited by Fred Shectman and William B. Smith*

Bender Gestalt Screening for Brain Dysfunction *by Patricia Lacks*

Adult Psychopathology and Diagnosis *edited by Samuel M. Turner and Michel Hersen*

Personality and the Behavioral Disorders (Second Edition) *edited by Norman S. Endler and J. McVicker Hunt*

Ecological Approaches to Clinical and Community Psychology *edited by William A. O'Connor and Bernard Lubin*

Rational-Emotive Therapy with Children and Adolescents: Theory, Treatment Strategies, Preventative Methods *by Michael E. Bernard and Marie R. Joyce*

The Unconscious Reconsidered *edited by Kenneth S. Bowers and Donald Meichenbaum*

Prevention of Problems in Childhood: Psychological Research and Application *edited by Michael C. Roberts and Lizette Peterson*

Resolving Resistances in Psychotherapy *by Herbert S. Strean*

Handbook of Social Skills Training and Research *edited by Luciano L'Abate and Michael A. Milan*

Institutional Settings in Children's Lives *by Leanne G. Rivlin and Maxine Wolfe*

Treating the Alcoholic: A Developmental Model of Recovery *by Stephanie Brown*

Resolving Marital Conflicts: A Psychodynamic Perspective *by Herbert S. Strean*

Paradoxical Strategies in Psychotherapy: A Comprehensive Overview and Guidebook *by Leon F. Seltzer*

Pharmacological and Behavioral Treatment: An Integrative Approach *edited by Michel Hersen*

The Rorschach: A Comprehensive System, Volume I: Basic Foundations (Second Edition) *by John E. Exner, Jr.*

The Induction of Hypnosis *by William E. Edmonston, Jr.*